THE CAMBRIDGE HISTORY OF
RENAISSANCE PHILOSOPHY

The Cambridge History of Renaissance Philosophy

GENERAL EDITOR
CHARLES B. SCHMITT

EDITORS
QUENTIN SKINNER   ECKHARD KESSLER

ASSOCIATE EDITOR
JILL KRAYE

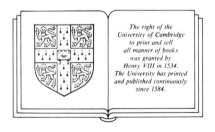

The right of the
University of Cambridge
to print and sell
all manner of books
was granted by
Henry VIII in 1534.
The University has printed
and published continuously
since 1584.

CAMBRIDGE UNIVERSITY PRESS

CAMBRIDGE

NEW YORK   PORT CHESTER

MELBOURNE   SYDNEY

Published by the Press Syndicate of the University of Cambridge
The Pitt Building, Trumpington Street, Cambridge CB2 1RP
40 West 20th Street, New York, NY 10011, USA
10 Stamford Road, Oakleigh, Melbourne 3166, Australia

First published 1988
Reprinted 1990

Printed in Great Britain at The Bath Press, Avon

British Library cataloguing in publication data

The Cambridge history of Renaissance
philosophy.
1. Philosophy, Renaissance
I. Schmitt, Charles B.
190'.9'031   B775

Library of Congress cataloguing in publication data

The Cambridge history of Renaissance philosophy.

Bibliography: p.
Includes indexes.
1. Philosophy, Renaissance.   I. Schmitt, Charles B.,
1933–86.   II. Skinner, Quentin.   III. Kessler,
Eckhard.   IV. Kraye, Jill.
B775.C25   1987   190'.9'024   87-5212

ISBN 0 521 25104 4

CONTENTS

CONTRIBUTORS

PROFESSOR E. J. ASHWORTH
Department of Philosophy, University of Waterloo

PROFESSOR BRIAN P. COPENHAVER
Department of History, Oakland University

PROFESSOR JOHN F. D'AMICO
Department of History, George Mason University

PROFESSOR ANTHONY GRAFTON
Department of History, Princeton University

PROFESSOR PAUL F. GRENDLER
Department of History, University of Toronto

PROFESSOR ALFONSO INGEGNO
Facoltà di lettre e filosofia, Università di Urbino

DR LISA JARDINE
Jesus College, University of Cambridge

DR NICHOLAS JARDINE
Darwin College, University of Cambridge

PROFESSOR DONALD R. KELLEY
Department of History, University of Rochester

PROFESSOR ECKHARD KESSLER
Institut für Geistesgeschichte und Philosophie der Renaissance, Universität München

JILL KRAYE
The Warburg Institute, University of London

PROFESSOR EMERITUS PAUL OSKAR KRISTELLER
Department of Philosophy, Columbia University

PROFESSOR CHARLES H. LOHR, S. J.
Raimundus-Lullus-Institut, Albert-Ludwigs-Universität, Freiburg i. Br.

PROFESSOR KATHARINE PARK
Department of History, Wellesley College

PROFESSOR EMERITUS RICHARD H. POPKIN
Department of Philosophy, Washington University

PROFESSOR ANTONINO POPPI
Facoltà di lettere e filosofia, Università di Padova

DR CHARLES B. SCHMITT
Late of The Warburg Institute, University of London

PROFESSOR QUENTIN SKINNER
Christ's College, University of Cambridge

PROFESSOR CESARE VASOLI
Facoltà di lettere e filosofia, Università di Firenze

PROFESSOR BRIAN VICKERS
Centre for Renaissance Studies, Eidgenössische Technische Hochschule Zürich

PROFESSOR WILLIAM A. WALLACE, O. P.
Department of Philosophy, Catholic University of America

DR MICHAEL J. WILMOTT
Formerly Research Student at The Warburg Institute, University of London

PREFACE

The present History had a complex genesis, so it may be best to begin by explaining how the project took shape. During the summer of 1980, Dr Jeremy Mynott of the Cambridge University Press invited me to submit a proposal for a volume to follow *The Cambridge History of Later Medieval Philosophy*. The scheme I originally drew up, which sought to cover much of the seventeenth century as well as the Renaissance, was then sent out to a number of experts for their comments. One of the referees chosen by the Press was, naturally, Charles Schmitt. He responded with such a robust set of criticisms, and such a persuasive commitment to the idea of a volume entirely devoted to Renaissance philosophy, that Dr Mynott invited him to collaborate in producing an alternative proposal along the lines he had sketched. This he duly did, and after further consultations and revisions the Press Syndicate of the University of Cambridge finally accepted the scheme in December 1981. Charles was thereupon appointed general editor of the History, I agreed to serve as one of its two editors, and at Charles' suggestion Professor Eckhard Kessler was called in to complete our team.

Charles proved a superb editor, moving swiftly to commission the individual chapters and persuading virtually all our contributors to deliver their manuscripts by the beginning of 1984. These were then submitted to a panel of experts agreed by the Press in addition to being read and discussed by Charles, Eckhard Kessler and me. We are deeply grateful to all those who helped us with their many and searching criticisms at that crucial stage: Professors Ashworth, Copenhaver, Grafton, Grendler, Kelley, Kristeller, Park, Rubinstein and Wallace.

Although most of the History was ready in draft by the beginning of 1984, the stringent refereeing procedures on which Charles had rightly insisted meant that we were unable to deliver our typescript to the Press as soon as we had originally hoped. By the end of 1985, however, practically all the revisions and additions we had asked our contributors to make had been cheerfully completed. When Charles left in April 1986 to deliver some lectures in Padua, he took with him the notes for our introduction, intending to complete that one remaining section of the book before returning at the end of the month.

From Padua came the appalling news of Charles' sudden death on 15 April 1986. It is no consolation, but it is at least some relief, to be able to record that – as I learnt from a letter which arrived after his death – Charles had finally satisfied himself that our History had reached the standard he had set for it. It is now our earnest hope that it may serve as something of a memorial to him: to his astonishing erudition and the unassuming air with which he wore it, to his exemplary (if daunting) standards of scholarship, to his invariable helpfulness to fellow-workers in the field.

We were left with several problems to surmount before our volume could be printed. The introduction still had to be put into final form, a task I finished on the basis of Charles' almost completed drafts. But our main problem was of course posed by the sheer amount of work involved in seeing such a large book through the press. The division of labour within our editorial team had been such that this was to have been Charles' task. His death came at an exceptionally busy time for both Eckhard Kessler and me, with the result that neither of us was in a position to undertake this further obligation except at the cost of seriously delaying the appeareance of the book. We were therefore very fortunate that Jill Kraye of the Warburg Institute, whom Charles had already involved informally in our project, agreed at that point to join us as associate editor with the job of putting the History into final shape. She read the revised versions of all the contributions, as well as checking the bibliographies and biobibliographies. She worked closely with Ms P. R. Marsh, the subeditor appointed by the Press, to whom we are also very grateful for the patience, care and technical expertise she brought to bear on our vast and unwieldy typescript.

Jill Kraye would never have been in a position to shoulder these heavy burdens if she had not been granted special leave from her position as assistant librarian at the Warburg Institute. We accordingly owe a special debt of gratitude to the Director of the Warburg, Professor J. B. Trapp, who has been a kind and enthusiastic friend to this History from its inception, and who generously arranged to reorganise Jill's library duties in such a way as to leave her free to work on the volume throughout the whole of July 1986.

The list of other scholars and institutions to whom we are beholden is a long one. I should like first of all to offer our warm thanks to the officers of the Cambridge University Press, particularly to Dr Jeremy Mynott. He not only initiated this History, but steered it to completion with an unfailingly sure and tactful hand. The other Press officers to whom we feel especially indebted are Jonathan Sinclair-Wilson, who played a large part in planning the volume, and Joanna Rainbow, who worked in close and effective cooperation with Jill Kraye and Ms Marsh in the final stages.

At the time when contributions were arriving, Charles called upon the help of a number of scholars, most of them connected with the Warburg Institute, to whom I should also like to extend our grateful thanks. Constance Blackwell read and commented on several chapters. Dr Angus Clarke translated the three chapters originally written in Italian; David Membrey typed a great deal of material into Charles' computer and Richard Simpson printed it out on the Warburg's laser printer (for access to which we are also very grateful); Dr Michael Wilmott helped to compile the two consolidated bibliographies, in addition to writing most of the biobibliographical section in collaboration with Charles himself. For supplying some of the funds needed to secure this assistance, I should also like to express my appreciation to the managers of the Political Science Fund of the University of Cambridge.

Above all, however, it would have been Charles Schmitt himself, I am sure, to whom everyone connected with the production of this History would have wished to offer their most heartfelt thanks. The design of the History was very much an expression of his mind; I hope it may stand, not unworthily, as a monument to his work.

Cambridge   Quentin Skinner
                                                                        1987

INTRODUCTION

As the scale of this volume attests, the period of the Renaissance was one of intense philosophical activity. It is only recently, however, that the extent of this activity has come to be recognised fully. Although eighteenth-century historians of philosophy such as Jakob Brucker saw in the Renaissance an important period of reorientation, their awareness did not in general carry over into nineteenth-century attempts at historical synthesis. Burckhardt's celebrated essay remained virtually silent about the contributions of philosophy to the civilisation of the Renaissance, while Anglo-Saxon traditions of scholarship generally treated the two centuries after the death of William of Ockham, if at all, merely as a backdrop to the heroic age of Francis Bacon and the 'new philosophy'. A few Renaissance thinkers – Ficino, Bruno, Campanella – occasionally found a place in nineteenth-century histories, but even then the interpretation of their work tended to remain deficient in several respects. One problem was that the kind of historical research needed to make possible a comprehensive evaluation of Renaissance philosophy largely remained to be carried out. A further weakness derived from the fact that most nineteenth-century historians were more interested in tracing the roots of 'modern' thought than in considering the ebb and flow of philosophical teaching and speculation at different times. Even when Renaissance writers were discussed, they were generally treated as pawns in the philosophical battles of later centuries, not as thinkers of their own age and in their own right.

It was during the latter part of the nineteenth century, however, that this situation first began to improve. Pioneering work by Renan, Mabilleau, Fiorentino, Tocco, Amabile and a few others brought to light a great deal of new information, and began to establish a body of monographic literature on which future historians could build. A further important step was taken in the first quarter of the present century, when the efforts of two scholars in particular gave a much clearer definition to the physiognomy of Renaissance philosophy. One was Giovanni Gentile, who wrote pioneering studies on Bruno, Telesio and other philosophers of the Italian Renaissance.

The other was Ernst Cassirer, the first volume of whose massive *Das Erkenntnisproblem* tried for the first time to trace the rise of modern philosophical concerns to the period of the Renaissance. Cassirer's contribution, extended in many subsequent works, was of special significance. Paying little or no heed to modern linguistic or national boundaries, he began to do justice to one of the most essential factors separating Renaissance from later philosophy – its fully international character, based on the use of Latin as an almost universal language of scholarship.

Out of these and other early initiatives, an increasingly scholarly and sophisticated approach to the study of Renaissance philosophy has gradually developed over the past fifty years. For the most part, however, the fruits of these researches have yet to find their proper place within the broad outlines of the history of the subject. This applies above all to English-language histories, most of which remain defective in a number of obvious ways. They still tend to be written by scholars who are not specialists in the Renaissance, and accordingly lack an adequate grasp of both the primary and secondary literatures. They tend to focus on an eccentric group of thinkers, frequently devoting more space to such figures as Leonardo da Vinci, Columbus or Paracelsus than to writers whose professional interests lay within philosophy. Above all, they tend to characterise the boundaries of the discipline in an anachronistic fashion, omitting much that was vital as well as concentrating on much that was inessential to philosophy as it was then understood.

We feel, therefore, that there remains an especially pressing need for a readable and reliable outline in English of the varied and intense activities of the philosophers of the Renaissance period. As a glance at the bibliography in the present volume will reveal, an immense amount of detailed research continues to go forward in the field of Renaissance thought. What has hitherto been lacking is an attempt to distil these findings into a series of synthetic and comprehensive accounts. It is this task that the present volume aspires so far as possible to discharge.

The main ambition we hold out for this History is that it should offer its readers as balanced an account of as many facets of its subject as possible. One imbalance we have sought to counter is the tendency, evident in a number of recent histories, to equate the most important with the most novel features of Renaissance philosophy. Although we have of course included surveys of Neoplatonism, and of the astonishing developments in the philosophy of nature, we have tried not to imply that their distinctiveness makes them alone worthy of sustained attention. We have also made a conscious effort not to over-emphasise Aristotelianism. Recent scholarship has stressed the extent to which the Aristotelian synthesis remained the most widely known in the Renaissance, in addition to being the approach most generally favoured in the institutional dispensation of philosophical knowledge. While taking note of these re-evaluations, we have striven to avoid extreme claims about the influence and originality of this school of thought.

The balance we have sought to strike is one that seeks above all to avoid anachronistic views about what should count as philosophy. The teaching of logic, so central to current Anglo-Saxon conceptions of the subject, was an important but by no means a dominant concern in the Renaissance, and we have tried to treat it accordingly. By contrast, we have sought to underline the fact that certain topics – such as rhetoric, poetics and history – enjoyed an important place in the schemata of philosophy which they have since largely forfeited. Lastly, we have tried to acknowledge (but not be carried away by) the thought that magic and astrology not only occupied an accredited position in the hinterland of philosophy during the Renaissance, but also entered from time to time into 'purely philosophical' contexts from which they have since been indignantly removed.

An earlier plan for this History included an even broader range of topics, including the relations of philosophy to music, literature, law and several other subjects. Although we decided at an early stage that such an outline ran the obvious risk of becoming too unwieldy, we still hope that the plan we eventually adopted will be sufficient to illustrate our fundamental historiographical point. This is, of course, that there can be no hope of writing satisfactory histories of philosophy so long as we find ourselves tempted to assume that the discipline is constituted by a certain determinate range of themes. To work with this assumption leads all too naturally to the unhistorical conclusion that the most satisfactory histories will be those which concentrate on the parts of the subject most readily recognisable as philosophical to twentieth-century students. We have attempted, by contrast, to follow out the implications of the fact that the term 'philosophy' in the Renaissance comprehended a rather different and above all a much broader range of topics than the same term comprehends in present-day universities of the English-speaking world. We see the resulting volume not just as a history of what might nowadays be considered the more 'philosophically interesting' aspects of the subject, but as a more broadly based introduction to the intellectual world of the Renaissance as a whole.

The outcome of this approach should not be thought of, however, as an inter-disciplinary or a cross-disciplinary work. Rather we have sought to identify the ramifications of one particular discipline at a particular period of time. Later ages split up this unity into a large number of different areas of knowledge. The aim of the present History is to join the pieces together again, seeking to furnish a guide to the subject as far as possible in its own terms.

To this end, we have divided the volume into three component parts. Part 1 considers the intellectual background of Renaissance philosophy, as well as indicating the type of framework within which the various branches of the subject functioned in the Renaissance. The institutional setting, the restrictions philosophers faced, the techniques and sources available to them are all surveyed.

Part 2 constitutes the core of the volume, focusing on the different branches of philosophy in themselves. Within the Renaissance textbook tradition, the subject was in general divided into four main fields: logic, natural philosophy, metaphysics and moral philosophy. As our contents list indicates, we have tried so far as possible to articulate the various parts of our treatment in the same way. We have felt free, however, to break down some of these headings into smaller and more manageable units – for example, by marking a division (as some Renaissance philosophers did) between moral and political philosophy. And at one point we have felt compelled to resort to more modern categories, in particular to accommodate questions about knowledge and belief and about the epistemology of the sciences. Part 2 ends with a survey of the general character of Renaissance philosophical knowledge and its position in relation to a number of humanistic disciplines closely affiliated with philosophy throughout our period.

Part 3 consists of various supplementary materials. The appendices add to the information contained in Part 1 by describing available philosophical authorities and the means by which their doctrines were usually imparted to students. The biobibliographies offer brief accounts of approximately 140 of the more prominent figures discussed in the volume, and are meant at the same time to form a basis for further study. The bibliography is mainly confined to authorities cited by individual contributors, although a number of other items of particular importance have been added.

The system of references employed throughout the volume is as follows. References in footnotes are given in the most abbreviated form possible; these are then keyed, as appropriate, to the bibliography of primary and secondary sources. References to classical or medieval authors are normally given in the generally accepted style – for example, Cicero, *Academica* II.38.119. To make the best use of the volume, it is also important to bear in mind that information supplied in the biobibliographies is not usually repeated elsewhere.

As the above account indicates, we have basically chosen to organise the History around the different fields of philosophy. While this approach has the effect of breaking up the work of individual thinkers into several fragments, it embodies what we take to be the major virtue of presenting the internal development of individual aspects of the subject -- such as metaphysics or ethics – as coherent and evolving structures of thought. For us it is no great demerit of this approach that it tends in consequence to play down the role of dominant individuals. We are more interested in long-term developments and a continuing preoccupation with certain central problems; we are in any case unhappy with the assumption that even the most influential thinkers can be said to embody anything like the spirit of the age. We hope, moreover, to do justice to the fact that – with some very significant exceptions – the philosophers of the Renaissance saw their enterprise very much as a corporate and cooperative search after truth. For any reader who may regret the lack of specific sections on particular figures, however, we hope that the biobibliographies may do something to reinstate a more traditionally individualist perspective.

We must end by emphasising that, although we invoke the word 'Renaissance' in our title, we are not committed – nor have we sought to commit our contributors – to upholding any particular ideological position with respect to the employment of that much-discussed term. Despite the vast literature on the meaning, the chronological scope and the geographical boundaries of the Renaissance, we have decided to avoid discussing such issues as much as possible. The most we feel inclined to say is that the volume seeks to cover philosophical activity within the area in which Latin was used as a cultural language from the age of Ockham to the revisionary work of Bacon, Descartes and their contemporaries. But even this suggests too precise a characterisation of what we have attempted. Some contributors have necessarily ranged more widely, taking in earlier developments indispensable to the understanding of our period; others have focused more narrowly, treating the concept of the Renaissance as the name of a category or style of thought within our period as a whole. This has of course resulted in some inconsistencies and even disagreements. But we believe that this also reflects the current state of scholarly opinion in the subject. It is certainly clear that there is no standard or unified view among specialists about the relative importance of the various strands of thought which, as the rest of this volume will seek to demonstrate, went to make up the rich and often strange fabric of Renaissance philosophy.

PART 1

THE INTELLECTUAL CONTEXT

I

THE CONDITIONS OF ENQUIRY

I

MANUSCRIPTS

Manuscripts proved to be an effective vehicle for the expression and dissemination of ideas throughout the later Middle Ages and the Renaissance. Even though the invention and advance of printing narrowed their scope, printing never rendered manuscripts completely irrelevant. Numerous treatises either did not require to be or could not be printed or were published only long after their composition. Such texts had to be read in manuscript. Philosophical manuscripts in particular retained their value, both for the continuation of traditional philosophical schools and procedures and for the exposition and communication of new ideas. The manuscript culture which had developed in the Middle Ages continued to serve a variety of readers throughout the sixteenth century.

A comprehensive history of the role played by manuscripts in Renaissance thought is yet to be written. Renaissance philosophical manuscripts as a topic of scholarly investigation have been ignored for a variety of reasons. On the one hand, they have fallen victim to the medievalists' concentration on the various scholastic traditions in the Middle Ages to the exclusion of their (and other philosophical schools') later manifestations, while on the other hand the Renaissance humanists' hostility towards scholasticism and Aristotelian logic and metaphysics have caused historians to slight many branches of Renaissance philosophy. We lack large-scale studies delineating the diffusion of philosophical manuscripts and their use in the Renaissance on which to base large-scale generalisations, even for such fundamental writers as Aristotle and Thomas Aquinas. Here only a brief sketch can be offered by way of providing certain general organising themes and proposing a coherent explanation for the continued importance of manuscripts as a philosophical medium throughout the Renaissance.

In discussing the place of manuscripts in Renaissance philosophical thought two traditions must be carefully distinguished. The first was the continued circulation and recopying of medieval and some ancient philosophical authors (who had been available in medieval Latin translations) in the Renaissance. Partly this was the expression of the vitality of certain medieval philosophical schools in early modern intellectual history. School texts – those philosophical works which the universities and the schools conducted by the religious orders had accepted as standard for teaching – also account for this continuity. The second consisted of the production and dissemination of new texts written by Renaissance philosophers and scientists and used to express their own ideas. These works could take a variety of forms such as commentaries on other thinkers or original discussions of problems. Included in this tradition were the writings of philosophers who had been ignored in the Middle Ages and were rediscovered in the Renaissance; among these were Greek philosophical texts available during the Middle Ages but reintroduced into the western philosophical tradition in new humanistic Latin translations.

MANUSCRIPT PRODUCTION

Manuscript production in the Latin West can be broadly divided into two periods, representing the special needs of a changing reading public. The first was the era of monastic scriptoria which had supplied a monastery's liturgical, theological and spiritual needs from the Carolingian age. Monastic reading was part of a meditative process; a monk read a text as a spur to meditating on its spiritual significance. While interested in classical and early Christian learning, a monk did not consider a manuscript as part of an encyclopaedic scholarly enterprise, and the monastic manuscripts generally reflected this orientation. This functional attitude accounts for the monastic tendency to collect and bind together texts having little relationship to each other. Some monasteries remained attached to the handwritten text well after the advent of printing. In 1492 the monk scholar Abbot Johannes Trithemius of Sponheim urged monks to continue to practise their writing skills for a variety of reasons, some spiritual in nature but others related to guaranteeing the availability of a variety of texts and to avoiding errors which, he argued, occurred in printed books.[1] Monastic manuscripts, however, were not primary disseminators of philosophical ideas.

The second period, dating from the thirteenth century, differed from the monastic period in organisation, personnel and aims. Secular interests and university needs greatly determined which types of manuscripts were produced. This second period witnessed the increase in the number of

---

1. See Trithemius 1973, 1977.

manuscripts available to a reading public who, while lacking the time or inclination to copy their own manuscripts, displayed a growing appetite for various forms of the written word. The growth of literacy in the later Middle Ages expanded the need for written works outside the relatively narrow confines of monasteries and of government offices.

Increased manuscript production paralleled the development of the means both of achieving augmented output through the spread and the use of paper and of distributing the greater volume of material through the concentration of production in workshops. Paper allowed large quantities of books to be produced relatively cheaply; this both responded to and furthered increased literacy and education. Vellum and parchment were usually limited to the production of specific varieties of books, especially those intended for wealthy clients and permanent government records. Centralisation in workshops made possible the acquisition of manuscripts by a larger number of individuals in cities, just as bookfairs permitted the growth of an international market. Entrepreneurs who either produced the finished product itself or acted as middle men in selling or reselling manuscripts appeared to service an expanding clientele. In time manuscript merchandising became a specialised business with individuals devoting themselves and their shops solely to manuscripts (earlier in the Middle Ages, merchants sold manuscripts together with spices, armour, clothing and so on, just as later in the Renaissance bookdealers sold both manuscripts and printed texts). The famous Florentine bookseller Vespasiano da Bisticci (1421–98) represents the high point of Italian Renaissance manuscript bookselling; he employed scribes able to write in Greek and Hebrew and engaged in the international book trade. Vespasiano supplied the greatest book collectors of his day with a steady volume of books usually written in his own workshop.[2] While the most successful of the Florentine book-dealers of his day, Vespasiano was only one of the fourteen bookdealers active in that city.

A significant element in the commercialisation of manuscript production and sale was the substitution of stocks of ready-to-sell manuscripts for the production-on-demand system, a change evident by the end of the twelfth century. Scribes produced large quantities of those texts which dealers felt would attract an audience, rather than responding only to the particular requests of wealthy clients. Shops employed their own lay and clerical scribes, illustrators and other specialists to provide all they needed for

2. See De la Mare 1965.

producing standard types of books. Such shops could offer a customer a variety of books in any format, at a wide range of prices, immediately or in a relatively short period of time. Mass production, of course, did damage the quality of the final product. Not surprisingly, during the early years of printing these manuscript dealers became the major producers and distributors of printed books. As in many other respects, such as format and subject-matter, so in personnel, gradualism marked the transition from manuscript to printed book.

LIBRARIES

The increased demand for manuscripts as well as established means of obtaining desiderata through professional bookdealers accompanied the development of the 'public' library in the Renaissance, places where books could be read and consulted and not simply conserved.[3] Monasteries usually had libraries reflecting their particular interests, and the books therein were not meant for regular outside use. This did not mean that monastic books never circulated; there was a brisk lending activity in the Middle Ages. Monks even copied books for individuals outside their houses (although in the later Middle Ages monasteries often employed outside scribes to fill their needs), and the humanists felt free to borrow texts from monasteries and often did not bother to return them. But the monastic libraries were not meant to be general research centres. A different form of library arose in the houses of the mendicant orders, especially the Dominicans and the Franciscans; their libraries were often connected with *studia generalia*, the theological schools maintained by the religious orders to train their members.[4] The Dominicans from their beginnings in the early thirteenth century stressed learning and required their houses to maintain libraries where often appreciable holdings of philosophical texts were housed and read. Unlike the monasteries, the mendicant houses usually did not produce the manuscripts themselves but purchased them from professional scribes. The use of chains to conserve the manuscripts attests to their use by a wide range of readers. One order, the Brethren of the Common Life in the Netherlands and Germany, produced manuscripts specially for laymen.

The medieval university libraries housed significant collections of philosophical manuscripts. However, the universities developed libraries only gradually, as adjuncts to their teaching function; nevertheless, in time

---

3. On the medieval library, see Thompson 1939 and Christ 1984.   4. See Humphrey 1964.

special collections appeared for the use of both masters and students, although most university libraries contained relatively small holdings meant to supplement classroom teaching. In due course they became depositories for a large volume of philosophical manuscripts and maintained their manuscript character even after the advance of the printed book as the primary pedagogical instrument.

The library of the Sorbonne of the University of Paris, for example, was founded in 1257. Its collection grew as a result both of the donation of books and their purchase from professional booksellers. It had two sections: one containing books for reference where the more valuable books were chained, and the other functioning as a lending library which included duplicates and relatively unused works; masters were permitted to hold books on loan for long periods of time. A deposit was required when borrowing books. The Sorbonne also maintained a list of works available at the monastic libraries in Paris which students could consult; there was even a rudimentary interlibrary loan system. By the middle of the fourteenth century the collection had reached approximately two thousand texts, and it remained a major source of philosophical works throughout the Renaissance. Petrarch and Coluccio Salutati both owned Latin translations of Platonic treatises which had been copied from manuscripts in the Sorbonne.[5]

While public libraries existed in the Middle Ages, the Renaissance occasioned the development of large collections open to the public, usually independent of monasteries, universities and *studia generalia*. Italy led the way in providing libraries for a broad spectrum of scholars. The first such public library was that of San Marco in Florence, endowed by Cosimo de' Medici and functioning by 1444. It incorporated manuscripts from the large and valuable collection of the Florentine bibliophile Niccolò Niccoli (1364–1437) as well as special books purchased from Vespasiano da Bisticci. It provided the inspiration for subsequent public libraries. Individuals of noble birth, such as the Este princes of Ferrara, also assembled large manuscript collections, but such libraries certainly did not specialise in philosophy. Yet the library of the Duke of Milan in 1459 contained 950 items with a substantial minority devoted to philosophical and scientific texts. This collection's lack of interest in recent scholastic philosophical and scientific works reflected humanistic distaste for scholasticism.

The most important of these libraries was the Vatican. Originally

5. See Ullman 1973, pp. 41–53.

planned by Nicholas V, who had worked on the establishment of the San
Marco library, it received its official form under Sixtus IV in 1475, at which
time it contained 2,527 manuscript volumes. Scholars and ecclesiastics in
Rome could read and borrow manuscripts from the collection. One
element which distinguished the Vatican from other contemporary
libraries was its relatively large number of Greek manuscripts and recent
translations of philosophical and patristic works from Greek into Latin.
Valuable also for Greek works was the library of Cardinal Bessarion, which
was housed in Rome during his lifetime and then bequeathed to Venice,
where it formed, after decades of neglect, the basis of the Marciana Library.
Outside Italy there were collections such as those of the King of Hungary,
Matthias Corvinus (1440–90), which was built on the Italian model, of
the Englishman Humfrey, Duke of Gloucester, which included a wide
variety of manuscripts, and of the Duke of Burgundy, whose large library
reflected his medieval tastes. These libraries remained manuscript collections well after the invention of printing. In fact, Federigo da Montefeltro,
Duke of Urbino (1444–82), specifically eschewed printed books when
founding his large personal library. Many libraries housed more manuscripts than printed books well into the sixteenth century.

   A different type of library, but one which had some importance in the
diffusion of philosophical texts in the Renaissance, was that of individual
scholars. University students and professors often formed collections of
texts for their own specialised use, often maintaining catalogues with
apposite comments on the whole collection. Individuals also made their
own collections of excerpts, called *florilegia*, from philosophical authorities, thereby bringing together from many manuscripts the material they
felt important to their research. These libraries are especially difficult to
judge since they were often dispersed after the death of their owners and the
extant catalogues are often incomplete. Further, we have no way of
knowing how many scholars would have had access to these collections.
The library of Giovanni Pico della Mirandola, which included a large
number of philosophical texts, ancient and medieval, was sold to his
nephew, Gianfrancesco Pico, but was dispersed after his death. Later there
were the exceptionally large and varied collections of Fulvio Orsini (1529–
1600) in Rome and Gian Vincenzo Pinelli (1535–1601) in Padua. These
manuscripts subsequently entered other collections. The library of Giorgio
Valla in Venice was especially rich in Greek scientific treatises and during its
owner's lifetime was open to scholars interested in mathematics. After
Valla's death the books were dispersed. Whatever the limits of our

knowledge of such libraries, they provided large depositories of manuscripts which could be consulted by others.

MANUSCRIPTS FROM THE THIRTEENTH TO THE FIFTEENTH CENTURY

The selection of manuscripts to be written, sold and collected reflected readers' scholarly and popular tastes. The church, including the monasteries, continued to produce a limited quantity of manuscripts for liturgical purposes (there simply was no need for more than one or two copies of service books for each monastery or church); the universities, as will be seen, specialised in large, regular production; readers generally searched for works which appealed to their religious and literary tastes. Romances, spiritual readings and vernacular treatises appeared in abundance for a large and growing public. The broader social origins of Renaissance readers also accounts for the variety of manuscripts produced – from unadorned, paper manuscripts to the expensive, illuminated texts on vellum which have received the bulk of scholarly attention.

In the fourteenth and fifteenth centuries the balance of manuscripts was altered. This was especially a function of the deep commitment to ancient writers, first Latin and then Greek, whose works had previously had a limited circulation, or had existed in unique exemplars, or were unknown because of the general ignorance of Greek among academic philosophers. The humanists in their search for ancient writings made available the writings of both popular and obscure ancient authors and those Fathers of the church whose ideas had been uncongenial to the dominant scholastic syntheses. Of these ancient texts certainly the most important for philosophy were the Platonic and Neoplatonic writings which appealed to philosophers, poets and theologians. The sceptical writings of Sextus Empiricus are another example of Greek philosophical texts which were rediscovered and popularised.

In the post-monastic period there were basically three types of professional book producers. The first were the large, commercial bookdealers who were independent entrepreneurs and produced a great variety of manuscripts. The second were the individual scribes who copied manuscripts to fulfil particular commissions; they generally worked alone. While a scribe might specialise in philosophical manuscripts, generally these two groups were not devoted specifically to producing philosophical books. The third group was connected with the universities either directly or indirectly. The development of the curriculum and teaching procedure required the creation of a new type of book production which was closely connected to the university administration.

The introduction of systematic philosophy into the universities in the thirteenth century significantly affected both the type of manuscripts available and the way they were produced and circulated. Manuscripts clearly reflected educational practice. In content they included both original texts, especially Aristotle, and the means of explaining them, above all the commentaries by university teachers. Indeed, the commentary became the distinctive teaching tool of the universities, and a variety of forms were devised to integrate commentary and text. Scholars have identified no less than ten arrangements of commentary with text used in philosophical, theological and legal manuscripts.[6] The standardisation of university teaching around certain authorities required the lecturers to invent a means of providing students with large numbers of required texts. This need occasioned a major break with the normal medieval conception of the manuscript, which viewed it as a unique entity and which ignored the problem of ensuring accuracy for a large number of copies of the same book.

In order to solve this problem, the universities sponsored the *stationarii*, or stationers, who swore an oath to the university and were empowered to produce, sell and/or loan the texts needed by the students and written according to specifications laid down by a committee of masters elected annually. The *stationarii* pledged to produce, to keep in stock, to advertise and to sell at a fixed price the required textbooks. The university *stationarii* were also a major supplier of books to the libraries of the mendicant orders. As professional bookdealers, the *stationarii* employed their own scribes to copy manuscripts. The means used to produce many of the texts was the *pecia* or piece system. While there is some scholarly disagreement concerning the full operation of the system, we can summarise its basic elements and relate them to the availability of philosophical material in the Renaissance.[7]

In the *pecia* system the university committee deposited a text of an approved author with the *stationarius*. This text, called the *exemplar*, was divided into pieces or *peciae* of approximately four leaves which the *stationarius* distributed to his scribes to be copied out section by section. The *exemplar* was essentially a university publication and had been approved for

6. See Powitz 1979.   7. See Destrez 1935; Fink-Errera 1957, 1962; Pollard 1978.

accuracy by the masters' committee, which also inspected the texts to guarantee fidelity. Since there was only one *exemplar* or original base text for subsequent versions, the number of errors resulting from the copying of several texts was limited. The designated committee each year approved the text used; if it was found deficient in some way, the *stationarius* was required to correct the faults. If it was acceptable, then the *stationarius* could rent sections of entire treatises to students for recopying, or could sell copies of the entire text which he had had made. The university established the prices for such texts, and to prevent tampering with the price, Italian universities detailed the number of letters to a line, of lines to a column and columns to a *pecia*. Students and masters, in turn, would lend their own copies to others to be copied. Second-hand trade in manuscripts also flourished. The *stationarius* acted as a middle man in second-hand transactions while the university regulated the prices charged. The *stationarii* of the major universities, such as Paris and Bologna, also exported manuscripts to other areas of Europe. As a consequence, a substantial percentage of surviving philosophical manuscripts can be traced to an original *pecia* text.

A clear indication of how important and extensive the *pecia* system was can be seen in the survival of copies of Thomas Aquinas' commentary on Aristotle's *Metaphysics*, the *In duodecim libros Metaphysicorum Aristotelis expositio*.[8] This long commentary exists in eighty-seven manuscripts of which seventy-two are essentially complete and are scattered throughout Europe. The original version of the *Expositio* deposited with the *stationarius* at the University of Paris in the fourteenth century consisted of fifty-three *peciae*. Seventeen of the extant manuscripts can be traced directly to this *exemplar*. While several other independent versions of the *Expositio* exist, the largest percentage of the manuscripts can be traced back to the Paris edition. Similarly, Thomas' commentary on Aristotle's *Ethics* originally consisted of thirty-eight *peciae*, and the surviving manuscripts depend greatly on descendants of this version.[9]

There were limits to the *pecia* system as a means of producing manuscripts. Only eleven universities used the system, and it functioned primarily in the faculties of theology and canon law. Further, the *pecia* system lasted only through the thirteenth century in Paris, although it seems to have had a longer life in other universities. Students in the arts faculty did not depend on the *pecia* system. They copied out the texts read by the masters, a procedure called *reportatio*. Such a system could not be controlled

8. See Reilly 1972.   9. See Brounts 1970.

for errors; but it remained an important element in university education well into the Renaissance, and a large number of philosophical texts exist today in *reportatio* copies, such as those of Pietro Pomponazzi.[10] Whether through the *pecia* or the *reportatio* system, the university teaching procedures formed a vital element in the production and dissemination of philosophical and scientific texts. Not surprisingly, after the invention of printing the university-sanctioned texts which had occasioned the creation of the *pecia* system were printed early and often.

While the university system guaranteed a ready supply of texts for students, it also limited the type of material available. There existed little in the way of overt, organised manuscript censorship in the Middle Ages and early Renaissance. An ecclesiastical body might condemn the writings of a modern author and order them to be destroyed, but this was not very common. Further, the various medieval inquisitions lacked any mechanism for the systematic scrutiny of manuscripts. Pre-publication censorship simply did not exist; what control there was occurred after a text was published or when a writer voluntarily submitted his work to church authorities for approval before publishing it.[11] In general, manuscripts circulated freely. Nonetheless, real constraints on the type of texts copied and circulated did exist. While individuals could copy any manuscript for their own personal use, a bookdealer would not invest his limited capital in material which did not enjoy an assured audience or the blessings of the university curriculum. The university system guaranteed abundant copies and wide circulation of some authors but also helped to limit the diffusion of others. All this helps to explain the existence of certain works in numerous manuscripts in the Renaissance but the precarious survival of many others.

PHILOSOPHICAL MANUSCRIPTS IN THE RENAISSANCE

In addition to the availability of standard philosophical works from the later Middle Ages, above all Aristotle and his interpreters Averroes and Thomas Aquinas, the Renaissance marked the introduction of Greek texts, especially of the ancient Greek commentators on Aristotle and of new translations of his writings. This is different from the humanists' search for ancient writers discussed above. Aristotle had been extensively, if not always accurately, studied in the West since the twelfth century, but the scholastics had not felt compelled to read him in the original. Indeed, humanists condemned the

10. See Kristeller 1955.   11. See Flahiff 1942.

scholastics for their indifference, and occasional hostility, to Greek scholar-ship. While there were certain exceptions to the humanists' rejection of scholastic procedures and authorities – Coluccio Salutati knew a variety of scholastic writers and some humanists favoured Thomas Aquinas for his clarity – in general humanists did not copy scholastic texts and translations but preferred instead to study ancient philosophers in the original or in new translations.

A new type of manuscript which printing occasioned was the texts transcribed from printed editions. Since small runs limited the circulation of texts, copying from printed books was one solution to this problem. Two sixteenth-century copies of Bruni's translation of the pseudo-Aristotelian *Oeconomics* produced in Poland were probably copied from printed editions. This phenomenon continued through the sixteenth century and beyond. It was especially common among students who could not afford a printed book, or could not find a copy of a desired work, or who wished to have only a particular section for reference. Platina's *De honesta voluptate* was copied in the sixteenth century from two different incunabula. Machiavelli's *Il principe* circulated in manuscript in Italy after its condemna-tions in 1559 and 1564 even though it had been published in 1527 and thereafter and also continued to be available from non-Italian sources.[12]

The form of philosophical manuscripts underwent some change in the Renaissance. The medieval philosophical manuscript had by no means maintained a fixed, unchanging format. It altered to fit the needs of expanding knowledge. Scholars had to devise ways of cross-referencing other works, not an easy task since there existed no standard reference system before printing, and even then it evolved slowly. The text of an *auctor* or commentary or a compilation of texts often incorporated scholarly apparatuses, such as indexes, chapter headings and paragraph divisions, devised by manuscript readers which the printed book took over and improved. All such *scholia* were meant to render the text more accessible and usable for reading and study. Philosophical manuscripts were unpaginated and usually written in Gothic script. Those produced through the *pecia* system used different scripts for a text and its commentary. They were usually of a large format, written in double columns with wide margins for notes. During the Renaissance smaller manuscripts became more common, and slowly the new humanist handwriting displaced Gothic among philosophers and educated men generally, first in Italy and

12. See Milham 1972; Nebbiai 1978; Reeve 1983.

then throughout Europe. As the format changed, so did other elements. Abbreviations, an especially important element in scholastic philosophical and professional texts, allowing for speed of copying and for economy, declined in use. When these manuscripts were recopied by scribes who had been humanistically trained, they often could not read the abbreviations since the new education rejected their abundant use, and they had not been taught to read them. As a consequence, Renaissance copies of medieval texts introduced new sources of error in transcription.

Despite this innovation in form, many medieval themes, authors and procedures continued to be found in Renaissance philosophical manuscripts. This can be seen in the continuity of the commentary as the major means of discussing a text. However, the humanists did make some changes in form and added their own methods of discussing texts, such as the *oratio* and the *praefatio*. Commentaries on Aristotle from university centres remained a consistent element in philosophical training and thought. They were to be found throughout Europe and a large percentage of them remain and were read in manuscript.[13]

The entire problem of the diffusion of philosophical manuscripts is only partially understood. The opportunities for diffusion were many. Medieval and Renaissance academics moved around freely and usually took their manuscripts with them. Students seem to have brought their textbooks with them when they returned home from university. We find a relatively broad spread of manuscripts of works not often printed in the Renaissance. This is especially true of works belonging to members of religious orders with international connections. A clear example of this type of diffusion, and the anomalies which could result from it, is the fate of the logical and natural philosophical manuscripts from England.[14] English logical studies in the fourteenth century were centred in Oxford, which boasted of a large body of international students made up to a great extent of Italians and members of the mendicant orders. Italian mendicants usually returned home after their studies, taking their manuscripts with them and placing them in their orders' libraries. So through a normal academic procedure, English manuscripts (or Parisian copies of them) spread through Italy. A further source of such manuscripts was the presence of English churchmen in Italy, usually at the papal court, who died there and bequeathed their libraries to religious establishments. Scholars have found some of the best manuscripts of these logicians in Italy rather than their original academic

---

13. See Lohr 1974b, pp. 228–30.   14. See *English Logic* 1982, pp. 13–32 (Courtenay).

home. Further, the clergy played an important role in spreading Italian manuscript writings outside Italy. Italian manuscripts of Bruni's translation of the pseudo-Aristotelian *Oeconomics*, for example, were carried to Northern Europe by Italian clerics.[15]

One aspect of the medieval manuscript tradition the Renaissance inherited was cosmopolitanism. This is evident in the case of Walter Burley's *De vita et moribus philosophorum* (pre-1346), which appealed particularly to laymen.[16] Burley, an Englishman, wrote his treatise in Avignon while visiting the papal court; it became especially popular in Italy and Central Europe, even serving as a school text in Bohemia, and was translated into several vernaculars. Over 100 manuscripts exist spread throughout Central Europe and Italy, and it continued to be copied into the age of printing. Indeed, the manuscripts are the best indication of what Burley had written, since when the text was printed its editors regularly altered its Latin to make it conform to humanist stylistic ideals.

When philosophical texts were printed, the editors usually did not collate manuscripts. The *editio princeps* of a text tended to be based on only one manuscript; and subsequent editions usually just reproduced the previously printed text with variants resulting from an occasional consultation of manuscripts. Aldus Manutius' great Greek Aristotle (1495–8) was based on a limited number of manuscripts and did not utilise the several copies which were to be found in Venice as part of the Bessarion library. Isaac Casaubon in his 1590 edition of Aristotle's *Opera* relied on previously printed editions for the base text and only sporadically investigated manuscripts for more acceptable readings.[17]

A major example of the interaction between manuscript and printed text and the continued viability of manuscripts is the case of the intellectual influences on the young Galileo. Recent studies of the manuscript sources of Galileo's thought have provided important findings which illustrate the dangers of underestimating the manuscript culture of the Renaissance.[18] In seeking philosophical and scientific stimulation Galileo made use of the writings of the Jesuits of the Collegio Romano. He personally read and copied material still in manuscript. The philosophy lectures at the Collegio were usually arranged for publication after being delivered and were carefully copied by a professional scribe. While publication was anticipated, there was often a long period, ranging from a few years to several decades,

15. See Soudek 1958, 1968. 16. See Stigall 1957; Prelog 1983.
17. On the Aldine edition, see Sicherl 1976; on Casaubon, see Glucker 1964.
18. See Wallace 1981a, 1984.

between the lectures, copying by the professional scribe, deposition in the university archives, and publication. During the intervening years, lecturers and students could consult them. Hence, citation from such writings may derive from the manuscript rather than the printed versions, while the manuscripts of one set of lectures might incorporate material which came from a printed text but which was passed on to a reader through a manuscript transcription. Galileo acquired his knowledge of certain philosophical and scientific ideas through this complex relationship between manuscript and printed text. It is unwise to make hard and fast divisions between manuscripts and printed texts; they were too interdependent.

Scientific texts in manuscript remained important for yet another, technical reason. The exact reproduction of complicated designs of the heavens required a technological advance which was not available in the first century of printing. Printed designs and drawing could not reproduce details as clearly and as accurately as needed, so scholars had to rely on handmade copies in order to secure the fidelity and accuracy demanded by more complicated scientific study.

While the most significant body of philosophical material circulating in the Renaissance was in printed form, manuscripts remained an important means for the dissemination of ideas throughout Europe. Well into the eighteenth century manuscripts could be found which were meant for a small body of readers, especially those interested in philosophical and scientific questions. A scholar could also use a manuscript to collect a variety of writings in one place. Certainly such manuscripts were closely related in form and intellectual audience to the printed book, and may be seen as supplementary to it. Whether personal collections, school texts or lecture notes, manuscripts remained part of the philosophical culture of the Renaissance.

2

PRINTING AND CENSORSHIP

THE IMPACT OF PRINTING

Printing had an enormous effect on all learning, but its impact was neither revolutionary nor sudden. Instead, over a period of fifty to one hundred years it so greatly facilitated the dissemination of the results of enquiry as to propel philosophy and all other branches of learning into a new era. This brief survey attempts to explain how printing affected the conditions of learning in the Renaissance, and especially how the press communicated the results of scholarly enquiry. The perspective is that of author and reader, with the printer as usually helpful but occasionally as an obstructionist intermediary.*

The development of printing

An earlier innovation helped make printing possible: paper came from China through the Near East into the West about 1100. It spread quickly throughout Europe until the majority of manuscript books were written on paper in the early fifteenth century. Paper suited printing far better than vellum (prepared animal skin): it was more pliable, absorbed ink better than vellum, and was considerably cheaper.

Johann Gutenberg at Strasburg and Mainz experimented for years before he and his associates were able to solve the technical problems necessary for printing. Their first major achievement was the beautiful forty-two-line Bible, probably begun in 1452 and certainly completed by 1455. But printing did not make a significant impact on learning until presses had multiplied, their production had diversified, and the reading public had become aroused. This led gradually to a broad system of distribution and marketing. This process began about 1470 and came to full fruition about 1500. By the end of the year 1470, some nineteen towns had printing presses;

---

* I wish to thank those who read and criticised a draft of this chapter: Peter Bietenholz, Audrey and Patrick Douglas, Rudolf Hirsch, Robert Kingdon, Martin Lowry and Gerald Strauss.

by 1500, about 255 towns did. By the end of the incunabular period,[1]
European presses had produced over 30,000 editions, a large majority of
them in the 1480s and 1490s. Moreover, any count omits those books which
disappeared without trace; that is, not a single copy of the press run survives
to document its existence. Possibly 10 to 25 per cent of fifteenth-century
editions may have been lost, and the figure may be higher in the sixteenth
century. Printing expanded severalfold in the sixteenth century, but
counting the editions is not yet possible because insufficient bibliographies
of countries, places and individual printers have been compiled. A great
number of towns of 2,000 or more inhabitants, and many smaller ones, had
a press at one time or another between 1455 and 1600, some of them
continuously. Compared with the production of manuscripts, printing
multiplied the available stock of books by a factor that is difficult to
estimate. But it never completely eliminated the scribe, partly because some
readers and book collectors preferred manuscripts for their beauty and
historicity.

The first printed books imitated manuscripts, and like them, lacked title
pages in the modern sense. Instead, following the custom of manuscripts,
the recto (front or righthand) side of the first leaf presented very brief
information about the contents, perhaps with the author's name. It then
launched into the text. Much of the information about the book frequently
appeared at the end of the text in a colophon, which consisted of a few lines
giving several or all of the following: title, author, name of printer, the
person who commissioned the printing (i.e., paid the expenses), place of
publication, and perhaps the day, month, and year of the completion of
printing.

Gradually printers departed from the model of the handwritten book.
Since books were usually shipped as unbound sheets, the recto of the first
leaf became easily soiled; so printers in the 1460s and 1470s often kept it
blank. Between 1470 and 1480 they began to create the title page by placing
a word or two that indicated the contents on the otherwise blank page.
Only after 1520 did almost all printed books provide title pages that listed
most or all of the following: title, author, printer's mark, sometimes a
comprehensive description of the contents, name of dedicatee, name of
publisher, and year of publication. Indeed, the printer's emblem became a

---

1. The use of the term 'incunable' (*incunabula* (plural) in Latin, meaning 'swaddling clothes' and, more
figuratively, 'cradle' or 'origin') for books printed before 1501 began in the middle of the
seventeenth century and has been used ever since. Although convenient, it arbitrarily divides the
books of one century from another, and has led scholars and collectors to concentrate their energies
on incunabular publishing to the neglect of sixteenth-century printing. Fortunately, this attitude is
changing. On *incunabula*, see Geldner 1978; Bühler 1960.

famous and striking feature of title pages. Few symbols anywhere match the beauty and simplicity of the Aldine dolphin and anchor. Title pages of the second half of the sixteenth century became cluttered with too much of everything for modern tastes: information, decoration, several sizes and kinds of type. They reflected the growing variety of the tools at the printer's command and an almost baroque artistic standard.

Printed books evolved into better-designed packages of information. Since they cost less per copy than manuscripts, they could include certain 'extravagances', such as better spacing, clearer type, fewer abbreviations, illustrations, contents lists and indexes, if the publisher was confident of sufficient sales. Successful and clever printers adjusted their typography to meet the taste and requirements of the readership that they hoped to attract for given kinds of books. Humanists liked to read the classics on clear and readable well-spaced pages; the Italians especially preferred the Roman type resembling the letters in the humanist book hand. Transalpine printers who made sparse use of Roman type during the fifteenth century frequently employed a rounded Gothic type (*rotunda*) as a compromise solution. Lawyers, even in Italy, preferred Gothic type and seem not to have objected to a cramped setting and abbreviations. There was no type preference for philosophical works, possibly because of the wide range of texts used by philosophers. These distinctions slowly, but not quite completely, disappeared.

Most manuscripts had limited foliation and rarely pagination; contents lists and indexes were uncommon. Printers developed such aids to readers gradually and adopted them selectively. Gaining experience as producers and sellers, printers adjusted their output to meet the requirements of different readers, ranging from the schoolboy to the learned humanist, lawyer or university professor teaching Aristotle. In the sixteenth century especially, large comprehensive volumes such as the Bible, theological *summae*, and compilations like Erasmus' *Adagia* became festooned with indexes, contents lists, marginalia, lists of authorities and Greek terms.

Diffusion and distribution

Once well established, the printing press had the great advantage over the scriptorium of the ability to produce numerous identical copies in a comparatively short time.[2] There is a tendency to contrast the error-filled

2. On the history of printing and the book trade in the Renaissance, see in general Scholderer 1966; Febvre, Martin *et al.* 1971; Hirsch 1974; see also Lenhart 1935; Goldschmidt 1943; Kingdon 1964. For Germany, see Kapp 1886; for Frankfurt, Thompson 1911, R. J. W. Evans 1975; for Strasburg, Chrisman 1982a, 1982b; for Basle, Bietenholz 1959, 1971; for Geneva, Chaix 1954, Chaix, Dufour and Moeckli 1966, Bremme 1969; for Paris, Pallier 1976; for Antwerp, Voet 1969–72; for Venice, Lowry 1979.

single manuscript, each the unique product of a scribe's labours, with the hundreds and thousands of exact copies that streamed from the press. The contrast is overdrawn. At least some manuscript copying had developed safeguards against error, guaranteeing that copies were identical in essentials. Printed books, on the other hand, added printers' errors and editorial mistakes; if these were caught during the press run, ad hoc corrections were made in some copies. Errors and variants stemmed from lack of experience, poor craftsmanship and economic pressure. The preparation of copy (which might be a slovenly manuscript, a heavily annotated one or even an emended printed book), composition (setting of type in the forme),[3] correction (running off a sample, reading it for errors, then correcting the type), presswork (the mechanical part of pressing the images on paper) and dispersing the type (taking it out of one forme in order to prepare the next sheet) went on more or less simultaneously. Renaissance printers generally lacked the equipment to set up the type for an entire book, to proofread and correct, then print from corrected type, in separate stages. Because paper was expensive, printers tried to use everything that was printed, making corrections as they went along. Printers might hire cheap labour; if so, numerous people might participate, helping to get the job done but increasing the possibility of error and variation. Given the far from ideal working conditions, it is remarkable that Renaissance printers produced relatively accurate copies.

How many copies? The number of copies in a press run (i.e., a single edition or printing) was modest at first but then rose. The estimates of the press run for the Gutenberg Bible range from 54 copies on paper and 16 on vellum to 240 on paper and 30 on vellum. Between 1465 and 1471, Sweynheym and Pannartz, the pioneer printing firm of Rome, apparently printed press runs of 275 copies of a varied group of Latin works, the majority classical and patristic titles, in different formats. Press runs of 400 copies were also common at this time, and ones of 1,000 had already appeared in the early 1470s. Press runs of about 1,000 became common perhaps as early as the 1480s and definitely by the close of the incunabular period. The figure of 1,000 remained the norm for Venetian imprints of titles of ordinary sales potential throughout the sixteenth century.

The Antwerp Press of Christophe Plantin (active 1555–89) printed average press runs of 1,250 or 1,500 copies because a single press in Plantin's shop could print 1,250 sheets of a normal edition in one day. But individual

---

3. The forme is the frame holding the composed type ready to be impressed on the paper.

press runs in the sixteenth century varied a great deal, from as few as 100 copies for commissioned works intended for limited distribution to as many as 5,000 copies for books of great interest and anticipated high sales. Luther's *An den Christlichen Adel deutscher Nation* (Wittenberg 1520) had an initial press run of 4,000 copies plus numerous reprints. But the high number of copies and the circumstances were unusual. Books intended for a scholarly audience (legal, philosophical and scientific titles, for example) were likely to have press runs of up to 1,000 copies, and often considerably fewer. Works demanded by a wide audience or intended for an assured readership (bibles, liturgical manuals, school texts like Latin grammars, vernacular classics, such as Ariosto's chivalric epic poem *Orlando Furioso*, and works of controversy on contemporary issues) had larger press runs.

The number of reprints, if any, presents a truer measure of a book's diffusion. Publishers did not risk a large first edition, unless they had evidence of a considerable demand, because of the high cost of printing and the lack of legal protection (see below). But when a title sold well, a publisher or his competitor issued reprints. A popular title might go through numerous editions within a few years, both those issued by the first publisher and those issued by others. The press runs of reprints were probably the same size as first editions.

Practically all major publishers printed books in Latin and the regional vernacular language. Specialised publishers in important commercial centres also published in other European vernaculars and/or Greek, Hebrew, Arabic and so on. For example, Spanish titles were printed in Venice, and Italian titles in Elizabethan London.

Book distribution was remarkably international. Latin titles, which included most works in humanistic studies, and works on philosophy (although moral philosophy was a limited exception), theology, law, medicine and physical sciences were printed widely and sold across Europe. Although the majority of vernacular books were sold in one linguistic area, a few were distributed internationally. Regular and extensive commercial networks developed so that, for example, Venetian publishers shipped their books as far away as London, Madrid, Cracow and the Near East. Publishers stocked not only their own imprints but, acting as booksellers, those of other presses. Regional and international trade fairs played a key role in the international distribution of books. Frankfurt hosted the best-known fair; it met semi-annually for two to three weeks in the second half of Lent and from late August to early September, with the exact dates varying a little from year to year. Publishers, booksellers, and scholars from all over Europe attended the Frankfurt fairs. A catalogue of the books available at the fair, plus individual publishers' catalogues, helped advertise the titles.

The price of books

A great advantage of printing was that the total cost of manufacture was applied to the entire edition, while in the case of a commercially produced manuscript the outlay was for each separate, single codex. From the origins of printing through the Renaissance, the cost of paper comprised the major expense of printing, once capital costs (chiefly those of type and the machinery of the press) had been financed. For an individual book, the paper usually cost as much as or more than the expense of labour and ink combined. This is the chief reason why the prices of individual volumes depended on the format (folio, quarto, octavo and the rest) and the number of pages: the more paper used, the higher the selling price. Books became cheaper in the two centuries following the invention of printing, despite the inflationary times, because the cost of paper declined. Furthermore, printers used poor-quality paper for certain types of books, and crowded more words on a page by using smaller type and reducing the width of margins. This often happened in the late sixteenth and the seventeenth centuries. Readers responded with a chorus of complaints about the deteriorating appearance and physical quality of books.

Printing greatly reduced the cost of acquiring the fruits of learning – but not immediately. While most printed books were less expensive than manuscripts from the start, it took some time before printed books became sufficiently cheap for various classes of society to benefit from them. In the first two decades of printing, the retail prices of books were high, as much as 2 to 8 ducats per volume. But then prices dropped. Aldus Manutius published the first Greek edition of Aristotle's *Opera* in five volumes between 1495 and 1498, offering them for sale for 1.5 to 3 ducats per volume and 11 ducats for the complete set. Since a humanist schoolmaster or university teacher of modest reputation earned 50 to 100 ducats annually, he might be able to afford the Greek Aristotle, although the outlay took a significant fraction of his annual income.[4] Famous university professors in

4. The Renaissance used two monetary systems: a money of account based on gold, and a silver system of small coins in which payment was usually made. The famous monetary units used internationally, above all the Venetian gold ducat and the Florentine florin, were both actual coins and, more importantly, moneys of account. In 1455 the Venetian government pegged the gold ducat at 124 *soldi* (6 *lire* 4 *soldi*), and this value held through the sixteenth century. The florin had about the same value. The incomes for various occupations given here are approximate rather than absolute, because perquisites often raised or lowered the real worth of earnings.

the faculty of arts, and the majority of professors of law and medicine, who earned salaries of 200 ducats and more, could more easily afford it. Lawyers and ducal secretaries who earned similar and higher incomes, and princes, nobles and wealthy merchants who enjoyed annual incomes of thousands of ducats, could purchase it with ease.

But some books sold for as little as 12 to 20 *soldi* even in the incunabular era, and low prices were common in the sixteenth century. A Latin folio volume of a classical, legal, medical or philosophical text might be purchased for a ducat (124 *soldi*) or less. Books in smaller formats, especially vernacular titles in 8°, 12°, or 16° comprising 150 to 400 pages, sold for as little as 40, 30, 20, 10, 8, 6 or even 4 *soldi*. Simple vernacular books, containing a comedy, a volume of poetry, a devotional treatise, a work of history, or one of the ubiquitous vernacular translations of classical texts sold for these prices. Such books were well within the means of artisans. In the second half of the sixteenth century, a Venetian master mason earned 30 to 50 *soldi* per day (producing an annual income of 50 to 100 ducats, depending on how many days he worked), and his assistant 20 to 37 *soldi* daily. Hence, a literate artisan could afford to own a few books, a schoolteacher more volumes, a well-paid university teacher a hundred or more, and a patrician collector several thousand.

Relations between author and printer

The Renaissance scholar had a new means of communicating with his public: the printing press. When an author finished his book, he took his text to a publisher, and the two joined forces. If the printer was willing, they entered into some kind of verbal or, rarely, written agreement to publish. Instead of a standard contract, authors and printers made a variety of ad hoc agreements. Renaissance men boasted that printing conferred immortality on authors, but few received direct financial reward for their books. The following arrangements are typical for both scholarly and popular books.

First, the printer might ask the author to bear all the printing costs. A wealthy author could pay them from his own pocket; if he had a patron, such as a prince, ecclesiastical lord or religious institution, the patron bore the cost. Author or patron subsidised publication either with an outright payment or by agreeing to purchase a large number of copies. Since printing might involve several hundred ducats or more, a substantial amount of money changed hands.

When the author partially subsidised publication – a more common accord – author and printer shared printing costs and finished volumes. The author might agree to purchase a substantial part of the press run (perhaps

300 of a press run of 600 copies), leaving the rest for the printer to sell. Third, the printer frequently published at his own risk and retained the entire press run except for a few – twenty-five or fifty – author's copies. The printer paid the author nothing; he bore the risk and earned a profit if his judgement was good.

The fourth arrangement, probably least common and a later development, was that the publisher paid the author a small sum for his manuscript. Obviously he would do that only when he felt certain that the book would be a commercial success. But payment did not depend on a fixed standard, such as royalties calculated as a percentage of sales: the publisher would give the author a lump sum and/or payment in kind depending on his eagerness to publish. Even Erasmus could not change the system. Between 1517 and 1520, he tried to persuade Johann Froben of Basle, his major publisher and good friend, to pay him on a regular fixed basis, but Froben remained evasive. Froben gave Erasmus occasional gifts and sums of money, and named his son Johannes Erasmius, but offered no contract. However, Froben did publish Erasmus' first editions of the Church Fathers, paraphrases of the New Testament, and Greek New Testament.

The author might gain indirect rewards by selling the copies he received. Indeed, printers sometimes promised to delay offering the book for sale for a short period, such as a month, in order to give the author a better opportunity to dispose of his copies.

The author also sent copies of his book, accompanied by flattering letters, to potential patrons. This was a variation on the common practice of prefacing a book with a dedicatory letter to a prince, noble or prelate. Indeed, some authors dedicated each section of a book to a new patron. Although these sycophantic letters make uncomfortable reading and might suggest that the author had sold his integrity, this was not necessarily the case. Authors viewed such letters as commercial ventures: they expected to receive favours for their praise. Patrons, in turn, liked to be 'honoured' and accepted it as an obligation to support learning. Moreover, flattering dedicatory letters burnished a prince's or cardinal's reputation. And if the patron did not sent a gift, the author might hint at the patron's miserliness in his next book.

While authors received little or nothing for their books, the printer bore responsibilities and expenses that went beyond press work. The publisher might have to arrange and pay for the preparation of indexes and tables and for proofreading in the author's absence. If the author was present, he might live in the publisher's house and work closely with the printer and his staff.

These happy circumstances produced the warm collaboration of author, editor, publisher and workmen seen in the house of Aldus Manutius in Venice and Johann Froben in Basle. Then publishing truly became an enterprise of common purpose and close bonds. More often, proofreading and indexing were done by an employee or a local collaborator, such as a schoolteacher, who worked for a small fee. Author and readers then complained bitterly about the numerous errors.

Lack of copyright protection

Behind the publisher's parsimony toward authors lay the lack of copyright protection. Publishers were loath to risk much of their own money on a new book because they would almost always see it quickly pirated. That is, another publisher would obtain a copy of the first edition and reprint it without compensating the original publisher. Since the original publisher had no effective means of stopping his rival, his own edition would have to compete with the pirated reprint, and he might be left with hundreds of unsold copies on his hands. So publishers demanded that authors should bear most of the financial risk of initial publication.

Printing began without any legal restrictions on the right of publication, and the concept won only limited acceptance in the sixteenth century. As early as the 1480s and 1490s, and with increasing frequency later, an author or more often the publisher might obtain a copyright (called a 'privilege') giving him exclusive publication rights for a limited period of time (typically ten years) to be enforced through threat of fines and confiscation of illegal editions. But the privilege was valid only within the political jurisdiction (city, princedom or similar) which granted it, and sometimes had limited efficacy there. International copyright did not exist, even though a volume might carry pompous and threatening privileges of king and pope. These were intended more for advertising purposes than copyright protection; printers hoped that the approval of authority would help to sell copies.

So, despite the privilege, a printer in another political jurisdiction, which might be a city only fifty miles away, could obtain a copy of the book and reprint it under his own name. For example, from 1509 to 1520, Erasmus' *Moriae encomium* appeared in at least thirty-five editions in nine different cities, printed by fourteen or more publishers. The places of publication were Antwerp, Basle (two publishers), Cologne, Florence, Mainz, Paris (four publishers), Sélestat, Strasburg and Venice (two publishers), plus editions lacking typographical information. Reprinting was almost routine at a time when the concept of literary property or binding commercial restrictions hardly existed. Only large and complicated books, such as those with technical illustrations, escaped unauthorised reprinting because they were too much trouble and expense to pirate.

Authors and printers complained about the lack of protection, but hastened to take advantage of the situation. A famous author like Erasmus could even turn the publishers' piracy to his advantage. After the first edition of a work of his appeared, rival publishers offered Erasmus money for a revised version. Erasmus obligingly made a few changes, wrote a new prefatory letter, and the publisher issued the work as a 'new edition revised by the author'. Readers then bought the new edition, leaving the original publisher and booksellers with unsold copies on their hands. The Paris publisher Josse Bade had been victimised by Erasmus in this way and complained to him in 1516:

Such is your reputation among your fellow-men, that if you announce a revised edition of any of your works, even if you have added nothing new, they will think the old edition worthless; and losses of this kind have been forced on me in respect of the *Copia*, the *Panegyricus*, the *Moria*, the *Enchiridion* (I had undertaken for 500 copies), and the *Adagia*, of which I had bought 110. It would thus be greatly to our advantage if you would assign each individual work to a single printer, and not revise it until he has sold off all the copies.[5]

But Erasmus never did follow this advice, nor did publishers refrain from undercutting their rivals.

The lack of copyright protection had serious financial disadvantages for author and publisher, and encouraged the sharp practices characteristic of the printing industry. But it aided the dissemination of ideas. Luther's views could not have spread so astonishingly quickly without the unrestricted reprinting of his tracts.

Books of less inflammatory subject-matter also enjoyed the same freedom of wide diffusion. A good edition of Cicero's *Epistulae ad familiares*, a text used in schools across Europe, could be reprinted at will. It meant that teachers and students everywhere could use the text at small cost, because unrestricted reprinting probably drove down the price.

Printing the classics

One area of printing deserves special mention: the press produced millions of copies of classical texts formerly available only in a limited number of

---

5. Erasmus 1974–, IV, p. 88. On Erasmus' relations with printers, see P. S. Allen 1934, pp. 109–37; Bietenholz 1975.

manuscripts. Editions of the vast majority of Latin authors were printed by the end of the incunabular era, and of Greek authors by 1520; nearly all other ancient texts known to the Renaissance followed by the end of the sixteenth century. Scholars and printers across Europe participated in this phase of the classical revival, but there is space only to list the high points of successive waves of publication. Italy pioneered in the printing of classical texts. Between 1468 and 1475, Sweynheym and Pannartz published in Rome the *editiones principes*[6] of Apuleius, the *Commentarii* of Caesar, the *Epistulae ad Brutum*, *Epistulae ad familiares*, *Opera philosophica* and *Orationes* of Cicero, the letters of Jerome, the *Decades* of Livy, the *Pharsalia* of Lucan, the *Opera omnia* of Ovid, the *Punica* of Silius Italicus, the *Geographia* of Strabo and the *Opera omnia* of Vergil. Giovanni Andrea Bussi (1417–75), bishop and librarian to Pope Sixtus IV, edited them quickly but with numerous errors. Aldus Manutius and a fluctuating group of associates of whom Marcus Musurus (1470–1517) was the most important produced a second wave of *editiones principes*, especially of Greek texts, between 1495 and 1515: Aristophanes, Aristotle, Demosthenes, Euripides, Herodian's *History*, Herodotus, Philostratus' *Life of Apollonius*, Pollux, Theophrastus, Thucydides and other works. Erasmus and other northern scholars who published mostly with Basle presses between 1515 and 1536 issued *editiones principes*, or amplified and improved editions, of patristic authors (Ambrose, Augustine, Cyprian, Hilary, Jerome, and Tertullian), some pagan classics and, above all, the Greek New Testament of 1516. The printing of the basic works of pagan and Christian antiquity was an enormous achievement. Indeed, printing guaranteed the survival of some texts which might otherwise have been lost. For example, a few letters of Cicero and Pliny, and some Greek texts, survive only in printed versions.

At first, printing contributed more to diffusion and preservation than to accuracy. Aldus and others were teachers first and editors second; they felt a mission to teach men how to live good lives according to the examples of the ancients and to write well according to the rules of antiquity. They were fascinated with the content of the books that they edited, but had only rudimentary notions of textual criticism, stemmatics, and how to collate manuscripts. They often based the printed text on a single manuscript or a handful of manuscripts chosen for availability rather than antiquity, authenticity or reliability.

Worse, once a text was printed, the manuscript on which it was based was

---

6. The *editio princeps* was the first printed edition. However, it was sometimes not the first edition but the first comprehensive or significant printed edition which earned this title of honour.

sometimes discarded. A Venetian patrician expressed the layman's attitude towards manuscripts in the 1490s. Reacting to the efforts of a few senators determined to build a library to house the manuscripts given to Venice by Cardinal Bessarion, he dismissed the whole matter in his diary: 'They [the manuscripts] were not worth much, since you could buy printed copies.'[7]

But editing improved. Erasmus' editing, especially his Greek New Testament of 1516, illustrates the failures and achievements of humanist textual criticism and printing. At one point Erasmus lacked manuscript authority for a passage; so he translated the Latin Vulgate into Greek and inserted a reading not found in any manuscript! Nevertheless, his triumphs outnumbered his failures. He consulted a large number of manuscripts, collecting numerous variant readings which found their way into subsequent revisions. He delighted in exposing scribal corruptions, especially those introduced for apologetic or theological purposes. He recognised the importance of patristic writings as sources for scriptural readings. By his intense concentration on textual problems, he began to intuit solutions that later scholars formulated into critical principles. Above all, he demonstrated that the Scriptures were documents transmitted by fallible human beings. Once Erasmus had examined critically a work that had been more revered than studied as a text, others could more easily do the same.[8]

Certainly the desire to spread knowledge and to sell books sometimes led to hasty editing and an error-ridden printed text. And this text might become the *lectio recepta*[9] to be reprinted again and again without serious attempts at improvement. Yet, the good effects of editing and printing far outweighed the bad. Scholars of the late Renaissance vastly improved on the textual work of the pioneers. For example, Justus Lipsius' editions of Tacitus (published 1574 with subsequent revisions) and Seneca (1605) were notable achievements. And building on the efforts of Renaissance editors, eighteenth- and nineteenth-century scholars ushered in the great age of textual criticism.

Size of libraries

More people owned more books as a result of printing. A few individual libraries in the manuscript era were large: Petrarch after a lifetime of collecting had about 200 volumes, a magnificent collection by fourteenth-

---

7. *Annali veneti* 1843–4, p. 655: '. . . se ben dapuo' i val poco, per trovarse in stampa'; noted and translated by Lowry 1979, p. 230.
8. Metzger 1968, pp. 98–103; Reynolds and Wilson 1974, pp. 142–6; Bentley 1983, pp. 112–93.
9. The *lectio recepta* is the base text, on which all subsequent editions are based. On the printing of classical texts, see Kenney 1974; Reynolds and Wilson 1974; *ad indicem* s.v. printing.

century standards. Coluccio Salutati may have had 800 manuscripts; Niccolò Niccoli of Florence (1364–1437) certainly did. But the average library was very small. A fifteenth-century scholar or professional, such as a physician, had only a handful of books, and the merchant, shopkeeper or elementary school teacher would be lucky to own a book of hours, a devotional work and/or a book of tables for money exchange, before large quantities of printed books became available at reasonable cost.

Printing changed this dramatically. Famous collectors now owned truly magnificent libraries: Ferdinandus Columbus of Seville (d. 1539), the natural son of the explorer, had 15,000 titles. Gian Vincenzo Pinelli (1535–1601), a Neapolitan noble who lived in Padua, had about 6,400 printed books and close to 900 manuscripts (338 in Greek).[10] Collections of several hundred to a thousand or more were not uncommon in the sixteenth century. The university arts professor or lawyer of average income for his profession could own good working collections of up to 100. Even the vernacular poet could own the works of a half-dozen or so major authors, and some of the minor ones, in his language. Many more shopkeepers and merchants now owned perhaps a dozen vernacular books: chivalric romances, devotional treatises, saints' lives, a chronicle or history, a commercial arithmetic and the Bible in some form. Printing made possible riches in books for men of all levels of society beyond the dreams of their ancestors in the manuscript era.

The wide range of subject-matter was as important as the number of books in major libraries. Pinelli owned all the major Greek and Roman authors (the important titles in numerous editions), most medieval authors, contemporary works of scholarship in many fields, a large number of works of Italian, French and German literature, many volumes of current history and politics, a few titles in Hebrew, Syriac and Arabic and an Ethiopian psalter. For a short period of history – roughly the boundaries of the sixteenth century – the dedicated collector could shelve all of learning in his home. The moment passed; although private libraries grew precipitously in the seventeenth and eighteenth centuries, learning multiplied and fragmented beyond the powers of a single man to collect its fruits in his library.

The contribution of the printing press

Printing quickened the pace of intellectual discovery, communication, discourse, and learning. The Renaissance did not depend on the press for its

---

10. M. T. Grendler 1980.

birth or survival. The intellectual, civic, economic and political circumstances that nurtured the 'revival of learning' in Italy long preceded the date
at which printing began to make an impact (not before *c.* 1470). Petrarch,
Leonardo Bruni and other key figures lived and died before the advent of
printing. Major discoveries of classical texts were made before printing.
Above all, the *studia humanitatis* and the scholars and schools who
perpetuated them were well established in Italy before printing. In like
manner, the intellectual stirrings that produced the Renaissance in Northern
Europe were under way by the time that printing came of age. Printing did
facilitate the diffusion of ideas from Italy to the North, and their circulation
there, thus compressing into a generation or two developments that had
taken three to four generations in Italy.

   Printing enhanced or altered the conditions of enquiry in great and small
ways, most of which contemporaries judged to be beneficial. Some changes
are self-evident, others are more subtle. A significant but sometimes
overlooked contribution of early printing was to make quickly and widely
available the corpus of medieval philosophy. Incunabular publishers
printed the works of Albertus Magnus, Duns Scotus, William of Ockham
and others in great number. For example, over 200 printings of the works of
Thomas Aquinas appeared before 1501. Thereafter, the printing of
medieval philosophical texts slowed considerably with the exception of
those that retained their position in the curriculum. Peter of Spain's
Summule logicales (1246) was printed over 150 times before 1600 because it
continued to serve as a university text for logic. The massive printing of
medieval philosophy during the first fifty years of printing ensured its
survival and continuity; philosophers then accepted, modified or rejected
the medieval traditions.

   While printing perpetuated the old, it also ensured quick and wide
diffusion of the new. Lorenzo Valla died in 1457, just at the appearance of
the printing press. It spread his new views in *De voluptate, De libero arbitrio*
and other works, in Italy and beyond long before 1500. The *Elegantiae
linguae Latinae libri sex*, his linguistic and cultural manifesto that so
influenced the humanistic perception of language and history, had
numerous incunabular editions, and was printed again and again through
the sixteenth century, either in its original form or in abridged versions.
Printing also helped give birth to new philosophical doctrines by making
available ancient sources. The emergence of a sceptical tradition was
primarily the consequence of the recovery and printing of ancient
collections of sceptical ideas, above all the publication in 1562 and 1569 of

Latin editions of the works of Sextus Empiricus. While his works remained in manuscript, they were barely known; in print they had considerable influence.

The astonishing multiplicity of books produced by the printing press greatly facilitated the mastery of basic skills that were the prerequisites for learning. Incunabular presses printed more Latin grammars than any other kind of book; sixteenth-century presses probably followed suit, although the low survival rate of copies, even of whole printings of these books, makes the statement tentative. School-children and adult learners could own printed copies of Latin grammars, glossaries and elementary reading texts. The same was true for other kinds of textbooks: the classics studied in school, the books used in the university curriculum, arithmetics, technical manuals, vernacular self-help books and letter-writing manuals. Even writing could be taught more easily through printed texts. It is likely that printing helped broaden intellectual participation, because anyone with facility in Latin and a rudimentary knowledge of the pagan and Christian classics could join in the major scholarly, political and religious discussions of the age. This state of affairs lasted so long as the unity of knowledge persisted. After the sixteenth century, the centrifugal forces unleashed by the destruction of Christian unity, the growth of the vernaculars (which the press also encouraged) and the addition of new subjects of study fragmented the republic of letters.

For the scholar, the sheer quantity of available books broadened and deepened his scholarship. If the meaning of a passage in Aristotle baffled him, he could examine his own copies of other works of Aristotle, plus the commentaries, and the texts of other classical and medieval authors for clarification. He could also refer to the original Greek, if he read it. In similar fashion, scholarship became more cumulative and wide-ranging, because the Renaissance scholar could use a greater variety of authors and texts to make his point than could his medieval predecessor. Printing facilitated the eclecticism so typical of Renaissance philosophy; philosophers gloried in being able to use the numerous philosophical works now printed. And printing largely freed readers from geographical constraints: the London scholar could own books printed in Basle. Indeed, a sign of the geographical freedom conferred by the press is that few university towns became large publishing centres, while commercial and population centres did.

In science, the printed book offered the great technical advantage of the means of duplicating the graphic arts (woodcuts and engravings) for scientific illustration. A manuscript drawing was unique; it required an artist of equal skill to copy it, and his copy would not necessarily be identical. Now printing could reproduce thousands of identical illustrations. The anatomical drawings in medical works, geometrical and trigonometrical diagrams in mathematical works, pictures of plants in botanical books, illustrations of animals in works of zoology, maps in geographies, and diagrams of mechanical contrivances in books of technology contributed greatly to these fields. Even inaccurate illustrations, such as the fanciful animals to be found in early zoological books, were useful, because they could be improved or rejected after the real thing had been seen.

Printing made possible the diffusion of knowledge through translation and popularisation to a degree unimaginable earlier. The press produced an immeasurable number of translations, especially in the sixteenth century. Practically all ancient Greek works were translated into Latin. There were also many translations from those languages into one or another vernacular, a smaller number from one vernacular to another, and relatively few from the vernacular into Latin. Translations of ancient works of history, literature and moral philosophy into vernacular languages were especially numerous. This suggests that those who lacked the opportunity to learn Latin and Greek had a great desire to acquire the wisdom of the ancients, and they succeeded. Popularisations of learned material achieved the same results. One example among many is the theory of love articulated by Marsilio Ficino from Plato and the later Neoplatonists. Ficino first synthesised his doctrine of 'Platonic love' in a learned Latin commentary on Plato's *Symposium*; Platonic love later had remarkable diffusion among writers of prose and poetry in many vernacular languages.

Printing certainly broadened and probably intensified controversy in an already contentious age. Before printing, two men engaged in a public disputation in an academic setting, or exchanged letters, and only a small audience heard or read their words initially; it took time for their views to spread. Not so after printing, for the press offered the opportunity to respond quickly and repeatedly to an ever-widening audience. Anyone with access to a press could join in as quickly as the author could write and the printer print. In extreme cases, this was a matter of days. Controversy carried on by means of inflammatory printed matter began in the early years of printing, but Savonarola's tracts printed in Florence in 1494–8 against those who opposed his reforms demonstrated the great polemical power of the press. Subsequent debates attracted European-wide participation and audiences: the controversy over Reuchlin and the value of Hebrew literature, 1511–18; Erasmus' numerous battles with his critics from 1516 until his death in 1536; Luther versus his Catholic and Protestant opponents, especially in 1517–21 but continuing until his death in 1546; the political pamphlet warfare that accompanied the French Wars of Religion, 1560–98; the argument over the rights of church and state engaged in by theologians, political theorists and jurists across Europe during the Venetian Interdict of 1606–7 and for years after; and the struggle over the heliocentric thesis of Copernicus and Galileo that lasted over a century. These are just the better-known disputes. Renaissance men may not have been more argumentative than their predecessors of the age of script, but the press amplified their words enormously.

CENSORSHIP AND FREEDOM OF EXPRESSION

Censorship and freedom of expression coexisted uneasily in the Renaissance.[11] On the surface, it appears that the machinery of censorship and the prevailing attitudes of authoritarian governments and paternalistic churches severely restricted free expression in politics, religion and philosophy. Church and state imposed precise limits on expression, and the penalty for transgression could be severe, up to death. In practice, the machinery of censorship often broke down, and the fragmentation of political and ecclesiastical authority left many loopholes: if an author might not publish in one jurisdiction, he could in the next. Finally, intellectuals relied on a counter-tradition encouraging openness to novelty. The end result was so mixed and inconsistent as to defy summary statement: one can view the Renaissance as a period of severely limited freedom of expression that was occasionally circumvented, or as an epoch of openness punctuated by crackdowns.

Neither state nor church in the Renaissance – or at any other time in history – believed in complete freedom of expression, but tried to suppress the ideas considered dangerous and promote those judged to be beneficial. Before the Reformation, most authors acknowledged an unspoken political censorship enforced by the threat of punishment. A subject did not criticise his ruler or his policies openly unless he could avoid the consequences. For example, in 1428 a friend who had participated in the just concluded war between Venice and Milan (1426–7) encouraged Guarino da Verona to

11. On censorship in the Renaissance, see Hirsch 1955, 1973; Lopez 1972; Rotondò 1982; for Italy, Firpo 1950–1, Patrizi [da Cherso] 1970, M. T. and P. F. Grendler 1976; for Venice, P. F. Grendler 1977, 1978; for Geneva, Santschi 1978; for England, Loades 1974; for Germany, Eisenhardt 1970.

write a history of the conflict. The humanist, a Venetian subject, declined. Guarino referred approvingly to Cicero's famous dictum that history is the 'light of truth' (*De oratore* II.9.36). But, he went on, following Cicero's precept was perilous today. The historian would have to lay bare the causes of the war, the honesty and valour (or their opposites) of the contestants, and much else. Telling the truth would cost the historian his head![12]

Guarino had reason to be concerned: governments tended to view criticism as sedition. They were even sensitive to attacks on other rulers coming from their subjects speaking in a private capacity, because they feared that such private attacks would invite retaliation on the state as a whole. Nevertheless, political dissent flourished. Critics wrote a great number of extremely vitriolic political pamphlets – but anonymously. The anonymous printed pamphlet lacked the name(s) of author, publisher and/or place of publication, or gave pseudonyms, and was very difficult to trace. In times of conflict, such as the French Wars of Religion, hundreds and thousands of printed pamphlets appeared, and they sometimes articulated new and controversial political, religious and philosophical views, as well as criticism. The division of Europe into many political jurisdictions and the existence of innumerable exiles greatly facilitated freedom of expression. The dissenter could almost always find a publisher just across the border who was willing to print a polemic for reasons of money or sympathy.

Political dissent was one thing, heresy another. Neither prince, prelate nor scholar believed that heresy had the right to be heard. Heresy threatened the souls of believer and unbeliever alike as well as the fabric of society itself. The Renaissance drew upon a centuries-old tradition whose roots went back to Plato's *Laws* and *Republic*, as well as Christian antiquity, to justify censorship of religious, moral and philosophical views: the three were not easily separated in the period. But another tradition favouring a more open attitude countered it. Humanists successfully argued in favour of reading ancient literature that praised paganism and portrayed vice attractively, even though such literature might produce harmful effects on readers.

Taking their inspiration from the *Exhortation to Youths as to How They Shall Best Profit by the Writings of Pagan Authors* of St Basil the Great (*c.* 330–79), scholars argued that the pagan classics ultimately encouraged virtuous behaviour. Readers should focus on the underlying truths found in classical authors and refuse to be disturbed by surface impieties. Most humanists held

---

12. Guarino da Verona 1915–19, I, p. 617.

that both pagan and Christian learning led to virtue. They also liked to cite St Paul: 'To all who are pure themselves, everything is pure; but to those who have been corrupted and lack faith, nothing can be pure' (Titus 1:15). Hence, many thinkers celebrated an optimistic view of human potentiality and left it to the individual reader, rather than church and state, to select the good and to reject the evil. They did not challenge the right of authority to censor, but quietly ignored the rules of church and state. This optimistic vision of man's power of judgement encouraged an openness to discordant ideas that was especially relevant for contemporary philosophy, which was both eclectic and heavily dependent on ancient texts.

The beginning of press censorship

The two attitudes – authority's responsibility to protect society against error, and a general confidence that the mind should be free to explore the books of Christian, pagan and infidel in search of truth – coexisted with remarkably few conflicts until the Reformation. Before Luther, church and state occasionally intervened to prohibit the diffusion of philosophical ideas. In 1487, the papacy condemned a handful of Giovanni Pico's nine hundred theses as heretical, rash and/or likely to give scandal to the faithful. Pico altered the theses, and Alexander VI in 1493 granted him absolution. In 1512, Emperor Maximilian I condemned the polemical tracts of Johannes Reuchlin, who was defending Hebrew studies against attack. The papal Bull *Apostolici regiminis* of 19 December 1513 condemned the opinion that the soul is mortal and other propositions of secular Aristotelianism. Pomponazzi and others continued to teach that the immortality of the soul was knowable by faith, not by reason. A handful of additional civil and ecclesiastical decrees issued between 1475 and 1517 condemned a few books and proclaimed the principle of press censorship, but their effect was very limited.

Almost immediately after the beginning of the Reformation, Catholic states sought to prevent the spread of Protestantism through press censorship. The papal brief *Exsurge Domine* of 15 June 1520 condemned Luther's writings and threatened him with excommunication unless he repented; on 3 January 1521 the papacy carried out its threat. Emperor Charles V in the Edict of Worms of 26 May 1521 included a 'Law of Printing' (*Gesetz der Druckerei*) which prohibited the printing, sale, possession, reading or copying of Luther's books anywhere in imperial and Habsburg possessions. Other Catholic governments followed suit. The Spanish crown began inspecting bookshops for Lutheran works as early as

1536. Milan in 1523, then other Italian states in the next thirty years, promulgated censorship decrees against the increasing number of Protestant books. So did the English crown. In France, the king, the Parlement of Paris and the faculty of theology of the University of Paris, but not always in concert, condemned as heretical works of Luther, Erasmus and other authors in the 1520s and 1530s.

Protestant princes and theologians moved just as quickly to suppress the books of Catholics and other Protestants with whom they differed. As the city of Strasburg joined the Reformation, it confiscated in 1522 the entire press run of a polemic against Luther issued by a Strasburg publisher. The city then established press censorship and forbade printed attacks on others in 1524. But this decree was not meant to halt Strasburg imprints that assaulted the papacy and, later, the Jesuits. In 1523, the City Council of Zurich under the religious leadership of Zwingli appointed a committee of laymen and ministers to exercise prepublication censorship. No book could be printed without their permission. In 1525, Luther urged his civil lord, the Elector of Saxony, to prohibit the writings of Andreas Bodenstein von Karlstadt, an early follower who had become more radical than Luther in the break from Catholicism. On the urging of Luther and Melanchthon, Elector John of Saxony in 1528 forbade the purchase and reading of the books of 'Sacramentarians' (i.e., Zwingli and his disciples) and Anabaptists.[13] When Leipzig turned Protestant in 1539, its Lutheran government ordered prepublication censorship, inspection of the bookshops and the imprisonment of a publisher, all in that year. Such measures tended to accompany a change in religion.

The authorities made sporadic efforts to halt the diffusion of the doctrines of religious opponents, skirmishes in the religious struggle rather than systematic censorship. These efforts had slight consequences for intellectuals and printers unless they were directly involved in the doctrinal struggle. France was an exception: numerous arrests and some executions followed in the aftermath of 'l'affaire des placards', the printing of Protestant broadsheets and their posting in public places in Paris in October 1534. Later, Étienne Dolet, Latin scholar, poet and printer, was arrested – not for

---

13. 'Anabaptist' is a generic term used in the sixteenth century for a wide variety of Protestant sects (Mennonites, Hutterites and others) who stood outside the territorial Lutheran and Calvinist churches. Many did reject infant baptism, but their other views and actions differed greatly. A group of religious radicals took control of the city of Münster in Westphalia in 1533, and practised community of goods, polygamy and murder, until overthrown in June 1535. As a result, all so-called Anabaptists were persecuted. One might use the terms 'Protestant sectarians' or 'religious radicals' but because censorship decrees often referred to Anabaptists without clarification, it is preferred here.

the first time in his stormy career – on the dual charges of denying the immortality of the soul and distributing Calvinist titles. He was executed as a relapsed heretic in Paris in 1546.

Press censorship after 1550

By mid-century, Catholic and Protestant authorities realised that only coordinated press censorship could prevent the spread of heresy and that effective press censorship had to include three components. First, the censors needed a catalogue identifying offending books, authors, and/or ideas. Such a catalogue might list specific authors and titles, or it could ban in general terms entire classes of books; many did both. Second, prepublication censorship to halt the new printing of heretical books within one's own state had to be instituted. Church and state usually did this in collaboration by appointing readers to examine a manuscript before granting permission to print. The readers perused the manuscript to ensure that it was neither heretical, seditious, nor offensive to good morals. Third, governments tried to control book commerce by inspecting books entering the state (usually at the customs house) and by periodically visiting bookshops to make sure that booksellers obeyed the laws. Both Catholic and Protestant authorities used these same techniques of censorship.

A harsher, less tolerant attitude became evident at mid-century in Rome. A sign of the changing times was the burning of the Talmud and other Hebrew books across Italy in 1553 for their alleged anti-Christian sentiments. Hebrew printing revived, but the Talmud was not published again in Renaissance Italy. The turning-point for the freedom of enquiry in the Catholic world came with the promulgation by Pope Paul IV of an *Index librorum prohibitorum* (*Index of Prohibited Books*) in early 1559.[14] For the first time, the supreme spiritual authority of Catholicism defined for Catholics which books and authors could not be printed or read. The so-called Pauline Index was very restrictive: it prohibited the *opera omnia* of about 550 authors as well as additional individual titles. It went beyond heresy to ban anti-clerical and lascivious works: it condemned the *opera omnia* of Pietro Aretino, Erasmus, Machiavelli and Rabelais. It reached back in time to ban two dialogues of the ancient Greek satirist Lucian of Samosata and selected titles of the medieval philosopher William of Ockham. Most important for learning, it banned the *opera omnia* of a long list of northern Protestant scholars, the bulk of whose writing dealt with non-religious

14. On the Index, see Reusch 1883–5, 1886; Hilgers 1904; *Index de l'Inquisition espagnole* 1984; *Index de l'Université de Paris* 1985.

topics even though they had usually written one or more anti-Catholic titles. The Pauline Index felt that the religious convictions of an author contaminated all his writing. Such banned authors included the botanist and polymath Konrad Gesner, another botanist Otto Brunfels, the medical scholar Janus Cornarius, the legists Christoph Hegendorff and Johann Oldendorp, the geographer and natural philosopher Jacob Ziegler, the cosmographer Sebastian Münster and Philipp Melanchthon, known as much for his titles in grammar, rhetoric and dialectic as for his religious treatises. It also promulgated sweeping rules designed to control book distribution. The Index even banned all the publications of about sixty Northern European publishers including some prominent ones who published non-religious titles. The Pauline Index was widely criticised within Catholic circles and met with much opposition. After a tenacious struggle between Italian printers, governments and the papacy, during which thousands of books were destroyed but compliance was very grudging, Paul IV died on 18 August 1559. Enforcement stopped, and Pius IV announced in March 1560 his intention to moderate the Pauline Index. It had lasted less than a year. The common practice of twentieth-century scholars of viewing the Index of 1559 as the definitive, enduring statement of Catholic censorship is inaccurate. Nevertheless, the Pauline Index signalled a decisive turn in papal policy which could be modified but not repudiated.

Pius IV promulgated the Tridentine Index (so-called because it had been authorised by the Council of Trent although prepared by the papacy) in the spring of 1564. Unlike its predecessor, it won immediate and widespread, but not total, acceptance in Catholic lands, because the Council of Trent had sanctioned it. The Tridentine Index repeated ninety-nine per cent of the condemnations of authors and titles of the Pauline Index. It also promulgated numerous and complex guidelines for prepublication censorship, the enforcement of the Index and the regulation of the printing industry. But the changes from 1559 were significant; they moderated some of the most criticised features of the previous Index. For example, the Tridentine Index banned only six titles of Erasmus (*Colloquia, Moriae encomium, Lingua, Institutio Christiani matrimonii, Epistola . . . de interdicto esu carnium* and an Italian translation of the *Paraphrasis in Evangelium Matthaei*), leaving the enormous bulk of Erasmus' original works and his numerous editions of classical and patristic authors and the New Testament to be expurgated. The list of proscribed publishers was dropped.

The Tridentine Index reflected the conflict between total hostility against anything tainted, however slightly, by heresy, and the lingering but weakened humanistic belief that man could find truth amidst error. The prohibitions and rules were generally sweeping and harsh, but a few offered concessions; books containing some error but whose 'chief matter' was 'good' might be held in expurgated form. Texts accompanied by concordances, indexes and other scholarly apparatus prepared by heretics might be held after expurgation. These moderations signified a grudging awareness that Catholics and Protestants inhabited a common scholarly world based on Christian and pagan antiquity. Expurgation was the compromise decreed by the Tridentine Index for those who wished to read non-religious books written by Protestants. Numerous surviving copies of sixteenth-century volumes with passages inked out by hand, or pages cut out, or glued together, document the practice of expurgation. By the end of the sixteenth century, printed expurgated texts were also common.

The Index condemned heretical religious works and attacks on the papacy. It banned or ordered expurgated only a few philosophical works judged to be heretical, atheistic, materialistic, or objectionable in some other way. (It is not always easy to determine the precise reasoning behind a condemnation, although the general cause is usually clear.) The Tridentine Index banned three titles of Lorenzo Valla: *De libero arbitrio*, *De voluptate* and *De falsa credita et ementita Constantini donatione declamatio*. The last was not a philosophical text but a historical, philological and legal attack on the origins of papal temporal power. The Clementine Index (a revision promulgated by Pope Clement VIII in 1596) ordered three works of the natural philosopher Bernardino Telesio to be expurgated: his major work *De rerum natura iuxta propria principia*, and two minor ones, *Quod animal universum ab unica animae substantia gubernatur* and *De somno*. The Roman Congregation of the Index ordered Francesco Patrizi da Cherso to make changes in his *Nova de universis philosophia* (1591), another work of natural philosophy favouring Plato and attacking Aristotle. It later banned the works of Giordano Bruno. Part of the papal hostility towards innovative natural philosophy in the last decade of the sixteenth century came from the general climate of tension, as Catholic and Protestant powers moved toward the Thirty Years War (begun 1618). The papacy and some academic circles tended to see attacks on Aristotelian metaphysics and physics as challenges to Catholic doctrine.

The Indexes also enunciated general rules that forbade a few works of philosophical interest, although not in traditional philosophical fields. The Tridentine Index banned in general terms works of magic and other occult arts – a prohibition widely ignored. The Clementine Index refined this prohibition: it banned books or passages arguing that fate or fortune determined man's actions and limited free will. Presumably this is why Pomponazzi's *De naturalium effectuum admirandorum causis seu de incantationibus* was banned at that time. The Clementine Index also ordered the expurgation of three titles of Jean Bodin: *Daemonomania*, *De republica*, and *Methodus ad facilem historiarum cognitionem*. The latter two were works of politics and history, and may have fallen victim to another general rule, the one prohibiting arguments in favour of *raison d'état* and tyranny.

The Tridentine Index with its prohibitions and rules for enforcement provided the approach and structure for Catholic censorship. Governments implemented prepublication censorship and regulation of the book trade on the local level usually by means of an enforcement body of civil and ecclesiastical representatives supported by the police power of the state. The French and Spanish monarchies asserted their traditional claims of jurisdictional autonomy from Rome by assuming power over censorship without reference to papal authority. Spain, for example, issued its own *Index librorum prohibitorum*. But it was modelled on the Tridentine Index, and the prohibitions were much the same. Other papal indexes followed through the next three and a half centuries, while individual decrees banning new titles appeared between official revisions. The Index was formally abolished in 1966.

Protestant censorship also became sterner after mid-century; it followed the same pattern as Catholic censorship with a few differences in emphasis and organisation. First, because most Protestant religious leaders invested the state with substantial authority over the church, the state naturally assumed the leading role in censorship. The Peace of Augsburg of 1555, which had the effect of creating a series of state Protestant churches presided over by prince or city council, heightened civil pre-eminence. Second, the religious divisions within Protestant ranks meant that other Protestant titles as well as Catholic works were often prohibited. A Lutheran state might not permit the publication of Calvinist books within its borders and vice versa; both Lutheran and Calvinist states prohibited the books of Anabaptists and Catholics. Finally, because of the fragmentation of Protestant Europe, its censorship failed to achieve the comprehensiveness of Catholic censorship: Protestant states did not issue indexes and could not censor beyond local political boundaries. Perhaps Protestants censored the press less effectively than did Catholics. This is only a surmise, because Protestant censorship has been little studied.

A few examples will illustrate the nature of Protestant censorship. In 1543, the City Council of Nuremberg ordered the expurgation of a Catholic philosophical work where it differed from Lutheran doctrine. Even tolerant Basle passed censorship decrees in the 1540s and 1550s, and occasionally took punitive action. In 1559 it exhumed and burnt the body of the Anabaptist David Joris along with his books. After the chartering of the Stationers' Company (the printers' guild) in 1557, the English crown had an effective tool with which to regulate the press. The Stationers' Company not only licensed publications, but searched out and destroyed works of sedition, whose definition included religious dissent. Under Elizabeth I, the crown suppressed Catholic and, to a lesser extent, Puritan publications. In the 1580s, the Estates General of the Netherlands forbade the publication of 'papist superstition'; it confiscated and burnt Socinian[15] books in 1598. Protestant states did not promulgate indexes of prohibited books but did issue decrees banning categories of books. For example, the Lutheran Duke Friedrich I (Beutelsbach) of Württemberg in 1601 banned the books of Calvinists, papists, Anabaptists and Schwenkfeldians.[16]

Calvinist Geneva probably controlled its press more tightly than any other Protestant state. Or perhaps it only appears that way because the Genevan records have been studied more intensively. From 1550 on, the Council (the civil government) with the support of the Venerable Company of Pastors (the supreme authority of the Genevan Church) oversaw the press. The Pastors and faculty members of the Genevan Academy read manuscripts before they might be printed. Periodic visits to the printing houses ensured compliance with regulations. The authorities primarily sought to prevent the publication and diffusion of Catholic and Anabaptist religious works. But the definition of 'papist' included works of canon law and the books of Thomas Aquinas, which could not be printed in Geneva. Nor were many Latin and Greek patristic authors published in the second half of the sixteenth century. The Genevan authorities exercised moral censorship which meant prohibiting the printing, and/or demanding the destruction of existing copies, of the works of Rabelais, chivalric romances, the *Facetiae* (humorous and lascivious tales) of Poggio Bracciolini and even the comedies of Terence and love poetry of Ovid at one time or another. Finally, the Genevan pastors tried to censor Calvinist intellectuals outside Geneva.

15. They were followers of Fausto Sozzini or Socinus (1539–1604), who denied the divinity of Christ.
16. Followers of Caspar Schwenkfeld (1490–1561), a Protestant mystic who first accepted, then rejected Luther.

As a result of censorship and the division of Europe along religious lines, the press also fractured. Presses in Catholic areas such as Italy and Spain and such German cities as Cologne and Ingolstadt did not publish the works of Protestant writers even when the subject-matter was not religious. Presses located in Lutheran cities like Leipzig, Nuremberg and Wittenberg did not publish the works of Catholics or Calvinists. And few printers anywhere published the books of Anabaptist authors. The warring parties extended the religious divisions back into the past as well. Presses in strongly Lutheran or Calvinist cities did not often print authors and books identified with the Catholic tradition that they had rejected, notably some patristic authors, medieval scholastics, and fifteenth-century Italian humanists.

But some presses transcended religious boundaries. The Plantin press of Antwerp, a Catholic city, published numerous scholarly titles of Protestant authors and the occasional Protestant religious work. The Basle press was the most open in the Protestant world, thanks to a cosmopolitan tradition and distinguished printers. Long after the religious differences had split Europe, Basle presses published the *opera omnia* of such major fifteenth-century Italian humanists as Giovanni and Gianfrancesco Pico (printed in 1557 and again in 1572–3 and 1601), Giovanni Pontano (1566) and Lorenzo Valla (1540), as well as a limited number of the works of sixteenth-century Italian Catholic scholars. Basle also published in 1554 the condemnation of Servetus' execution and plea for religious tolerance written by the Savoyard Protestant biblical scholar Sébastien Chateillon (Castellio). It was a milestone in the history of toleration. Frankfurt and Strasburg presses printed a few scholarly works written by contemporary Catholic scholars. For example, some of the medical works of Girolamo Mercuriale (1530–1606), who held the chair of medicine at the University of Padua, were printed in Frankfurt, and the historical works of Carlo Sigonio (*c.* 1520–84), who taught at Bologna, were printed in Strasburg. Moreover, the works on natural philosophy and logic by Italian Catholic scholars such as Andrea Cesalpino and Jacopo Zabarella enjoyed a substantial *fortuna* in the editions printed in Protestant Germany.

Frankfurt in particular continued to be an open printing and distribution centre. Andreas Wechel, a French Calvinist refugee of humanistic tastes, and his successors presided over the major Frankfurt press which published learned works by authors of varying religious backgrounds including Giordano Bruno. Above all, Frankfurt continued to host the major bookfair where printers, authors and individual buyers from all over Europe gathered every six months. An imperial book commission attempted to bar the entry of Protestant books to the fair, but with indifferent results. Only in the seventeenth century, through a combination of political, religious and economic pressures, did the fair decline.

'libertas philosophandi'

The political and religious divisions seldom touched philosophy directly but had significant indirect effect on learning. Professors and university students were expected to conform outwardly to the local religion. Pope Pius IV in 1564 issued a Bull requiring all university teachers and students in Catholic lands to profess Catholicism as a condition for teaching and receiving degrees. The Bull was not always enforced; Protestant students from England, Germany and elsewhere continued to study at Italian universities and found ways to circumvent the Bull. But professors had to conform. Universities in Protestant Europe might also demand that a scholar adhere to a credal statement; as a result they barred Catholics and scholars from other Protestant communions. Overall, the free movement of professors and students characteristic of earlier education was circumscribed.

Intellectuals might hold any heterodox conclusions they wished privately, but could not articulate them in lecture hall or in print without risk of dismissal or worse. When philosophical views contradicted religious orthodoxy, the consequences for the speaker could be tragic. Geneva burnt Michael Servetus at the stake in 1553 for his anti-Trinitarian views, and Rome burnt Giordano Bruno in 1600 as an unrepentant materialist and heretic. But such notorious examples of repression were not the norm. A great deal of freedom of enquiry existed so long as speculation did not touch essential religious doctrine, or the scholar did not publish his views.

Religious differences affected the reception of ideas as well. Before the Reformation, new scholarship sooner or later spread across Europe winning adherents if others found it convincing and useful. Now the scholar's religious commitment became a factor, although not the only one, in determining the acceptance of his learning. Petrus Ramus was a somewhat unorthodox French Huguenot (i.e., Calvinist) with a combative personality. His religious views, especially after his murder in the St Bartholomew's Day Massacre of 1572, probably helped spread his logic and rhetoric in some lands and check it elsewhere. But the pattern was not uniform. His works had great influence in Germany and the Protestant Netherlands, especially in circles touched by Calvinism. His method prevailed in Puritan England, Scotland and New England, and attracted some other English followers. As might be expected, Ramus had less influence in France after 1572, and hardly any in such Catholic countries as Italy and Spain. But Calvinist Geneva also ignored Ramism, because Calvin and Theodore Beza had detested him.

To cite another example, Catholic scholars edited a significant number of Christian patristic authors and medieval theologians in the second half of the sixteenth century. Rome encouraged them, no doubt hoping that their scholarship would provide support for Catholic doctrines. And, indeed, the Thomist revival became an essential part of Spanish philosophy at this time. But the religious factor should not be over-emphasised: Protestant intellectuals also participated in patristic and medieval studies by the end of the sixteenth century. And other learning, such as Aristotelian studies, transcended confessional lines.

Despite religious and political differences, men of learning maintained scholarly contact. The notion that an iron curtain of religious differences separated them is simply not true. Communication was not always easy and might require discretion, but it went on. The Catholic Mercuriale and the Protestant Theodore Zwinger corresponded and exchanged books in the 1570s and 1580s.[17] Pinelli, a Catholic bibliophile and amateur scholar of wide interests, maintained an extensive and friendly scholarly correspondence with several Protestants.[18] They included Charles De L'Écluse (Clusius, 1526–1609), a distinguished botanist whose most important works were published by the Plantin Press, Andreas Dudith (Duditius, 1533–89), a Hungarian astronomer and mathematician who also wrote anti-papal tracts, and Justus Lipsius, who even visited Pinelli in Padua.

In similar fashion, traffic in prohibited books between Catholic and Protestant lands flourished despite elaborate censorship machinery designed to prevent it. Book smuggling was so widespread that it might more accurately be termed 'the clandestine trade', i.e. a kind of adjunct to the lawful commerce. Members of the book trade bought prohibited books in Frankfurt and then shipped them, along with innocent volumes, through the normal channels. The carrier, the man who accompanied shipments of books over long distances, hid a few contraband volumes among hundreds of permissible books. Then he found ways to circumvent the inspection of his merchandise when he reached his destination: a lackadaisical inspector, a bribed official or a false title page eased their passage. International contacts and local influence also helped. In 1574, Pinelli wrote a revealing letter to a

17. Rotondò 1973, pp. 1449–50.   18. Rivolta 1933, pp. xxii–xxiii, xl, xiv–xix.

friend in Paris, asking him to obtain some books for him, and then to arrange to ship them via Frankfurt into Italy through Venetian territory, rather than by another route – 'because here in Venice I have the father inquisitor who is my friend. And he will give me immediately everything that is not truly pernicious in its total substance, which might not happen with other inquisitors.'[19] Thanks to such friends, Pinelli acquired prohibited books and made them available to scholars who needed them.

The concept of freedom of enquiry did not exist in the Renaissance. There was no historical precedent, and it was too much to expect from men who went through the bitter upheaval of Reformation and Counter-Reformation. Certainly the religious and, to a lesser extent, the political divisions seriously impaired free expression. The philosopher was freer to express heterodox views before the Reformation than after; a few intellectuals suffered grievously from the religious split, and an indeterminate number were inhibited. Nevertheless, men found ways to circumvent censorship. The philosophical heritage of an optimistic view of man's potentiality favoured an open search for learning; it continued to live throughout the Renaissance era. Eventually, in the late seventeenth and the eighteenth centuries, scholars developed a full principle of freedom of enquiry.

19. Pinelli 1574: '. . . perche qui in Vinegia ho il padre inquisitore, ch'è mio amico. et mi rendera subito ogni cosa, quando non sia veramente perniciosa in tota substantia, che non m'avverrebbe con altri Inquisitori'. The letter is dated 5 August 1574. I am indebted to William McCuaig, who discovered it and provided me with a transcript.

II

THE RENAISSANCE CONCEPT OF PHILOSOPHY

3

THE RENAISSANCE CONCEPT OF PHILOSOPHY

THE ORIGINS OF RENAISSANCE PHILOSOPHY: SCHOLASTIC THOUGHT AND THE NEEDS OF A NEW CULTURE

Any approach to the meaning of philosophy in the Renaissance requires some preliminary qualification and explanation. How far, for instance, is it permissible to speak of a specifically Renaissance philosophy – a philosophy that might be said to reflect the growing complexity of intellectual activity in this particular historical situation? May the term be applied to ways of thinking which, though current in the fifteenth and sixteenth centuries, perpetuate typically medieval thinking? Do the speculative currents which emerged in the mid thirteenth century, above all in Italy, represent continuity or a break with the past? How closely are scholastic natural philosophy and logic connected with the scientific revolution? Was 'humanist rhetoric' an obstacle to what might otherwise have been a swift and linear development? The historical significance of many of the issues discussed in this volume cannot be assessed without considering those social factors, which shattered the ideological unanimity of western *Christianitas* in the thirteenth century, emphasising the difference rather than the similarities between intellectual centres and ushering in new ways of thought. There is little point in trying to define the Renaissance concept of philosophy if no heed is paid to the cultural institutions emerging outside the universities, the social class and status of their members, their aims, their rivalries and their audiences. From the early fourteenth century there was a complex interaction between scholasticism and humanism with the former profiting from the methodological and linguistic advances made by the latter. The universities of Western and Central Europe shared a similar organisation and the great Italian centres – Padua, Bologna, Pavia, Florence, Sienna, Perugia and Naples – still flourished, despite falling to a greater or lesser extent under political control. There were three main faculties: theology, law and medicine, as well as those devoted to

57

preliminary instruction in philosophy, the arts, astronomy and astrology. Those who mastered this learning were destined to become senior clergy, lawyers, notaries, physicians and those natural scientists who typically eschewed practical research in favour of pure theory. The social, political and economic ferment of late thirteenth- and early fourteenth-century Italy was generating new forms of government and public institutions, and traditional professional training was becoming increasingly inadequate. The mercantile culture posed moral and theological problems which could no longer be handled by theologians trained in biblical exegesis and by students of Peter Lombard's *Sententiae* and of the various *summae*. The traditional legal education was insufficient for princely secretaries and the chancellors of the new communes, particularly those of more than local ambition. They needed training in history and some literary and rhetorical polish. Medical training was also moving towards a more critical analysis of the ancient authorities, increasingly demanding empirical evidence. The more radical tendencies in scholastic thought – Ockhamism and the like – were undermining the unified notion of *sapientia* which had so far resisted the thirteenth century's cultural transformations. Analysis of the language of logic and its semantic structures had abolished the distinction between *res* and *verba*, between the individual's concrete and intuitive awareness and the concepts or signs generated by the intellect. The papacy and the empire – the two fundamental authorities in the medieval world – were in disarray. Authority was passing from the theoretically indivisible monolith of *Christianitas* to a medley of particular institutions operative at all levels of civic life.

THE *DISPUTA DELLE ARTI* AND THE PRIMACY OF THE MORAL DISCIPLINES

University teaching, founded invariably on the analysis and exegesis of *auctoritates* and canonical texts (in the case of philosophy, for instance, the *corpus Aristotelicum* and its commentaries), was encountering growing criticism. Irked by the narrow curricula of traditional scholasticism, its opponents refused to believe, for example, that there was no more to philosophy than metaphysics and discussions of the premises of Aristotle's *Physics*. Even at the beginning of the thirteenth century university professors and students, at Padua for example, were going directly to certain classical texts for linguistic and stylistic models as well as rich sources of moral *exempla*.

The activity of these pre-humanists is instructive, revealing that it was generally thinkers with a legal training who were most critical of the traditional approach and techniques of the Glossators. The most advanced levels of scholastic thought, so important to the prehistory of modern formal logic, did far more than merely exacerbate the polemics against scholastic jargon and sophistry: the *cavillationes* of the 'barbarous Scots and Britons' whom Petrarch and others had already accused of polluting the 'holy' Latin language. As far as the early humanists were concerned, the incipient formalisation of logical techniques and scholastic language confirmed the unbridgeable gulf between the language of the professional scholastics, which was comprehensible only to themselves, and the need for a straightforward and effective language of civic administration suitable for political and ethical discourse. The contrast between curricula was becoming increasingly evident. The traditional type, tied to *lectio*, commentary and *quaestiones*, differed markedly from that of the new schools. Invariably developing outside official academic institutions, these schools cultivated grammar, rhetoric and such linguistic models as were appropriate to political office, moral discourse and the deeper understanding of classical language and literature. Behind the early criticisms of the scholastic mentality and method, it is not difficult to detect the first signs of a new notion of philosophy, its meaning, its purpose and its place in the new learning. This is confirmed by the interminable disputes about the relative importance of the faculties; whether or not jurisprudence was superior to medicine, natural science to letters or history.[1] However, the contrast between the philosophy of man championed by the early humanists and the 'futile curiosity' of physicians and natural philosophers should not be regarded as a schematic dichotomy like that between ideas and letters, between natural science and rhetoric, or between the philosophising of the traditional teachers and the philological expertise of the new ones. The assault on scholasticism's barbarous jargon and the argument that its dialectic was irrelevant to genuine human concerns were also assertions of a different way of thinking: one that promoted the *artes* useful to civic life and made them central to education and the basis for training new intellectual classes outside traditional academic hierarchies. The protagonists of this new thinking were concerned with the ethical, religious and political issues of their time – issues aggravated by the institutional crises of fourteenth-century Europe. For these individuals the only way out of centuries of

---

1. See *La disputa delle arti* 1947.

darkness, decadence and corruption was by returning to the ancient *sapientia* and recovering its exemplary ways of living and thinking as well as the language which was its vehicle. Thus the myth of *renascentia* and the kindred notion of historical cyclicity lie at the heart of the return to the ancients and the repudiation of what was seen as a moribund and barbarous way of thinking with its impenetrable thickets of comments and *quaestiones*, its language and formalising logic so far removed from the models of antiquity, its theology and jurisprudence shrunken to a handful of obscure and sophistical contentions.

THE RETURN TO ANCIENT SOURCES AND TO THE UNIFYING CONCEPT OF *SAPIENTIA*

It would be wrong, however, to interpret the humanist aversion to scholastic methods and language as a radical rejection of philosophy. Even less was it an attempt to contain culture within a literary and rhetorical formalism, indifferent to the great problems of western thought. Since it fails to explain the deeper and more complex motives for this intellectual reform, the view of humanism as merely an educational system based on rarefied oratorical techniques, pedantic grammatical analysis and nascent philology must be regarded as unhelpfully unilateral. Admittedly, the first generations of humanists ignored the arduous problems of metaphysics, logic and theology on which the scholastics continued to work. Nor did they pay any attention to the increasingly problematic exegesis of the natural philosophy texts of Aristotle and the major texts of the Greco-Arabic medical and scientific traditions. But even the most obsessive advocates of a return to the pure springs of classical learning and the *studia humanitatis* could not be unaware of the texts generated by Buridan and Swineshead which had spread as far as the Italian universities. Nor were they unaware of the disputations on logic and physics which, under the influence of the *calculatores* or other teachers like Oresme, had come to be the principal activity in many scholastic circles.[2] Nor were they ignorant, unless for purposes of argument – as has been shown to be the case with Petrarch – of the work of contemporary physicians, logicians and natural philosophers, whose relations with humanist circles were by no means always strife-torn, as the examples of Peter of Mantua and Blasius of Parma show.[3] Rather, the typical humanist approach to the philosophical tradition

---

2. For sources, see in particular *Medioevo e Rinascimento* 1955, I, pp. 217–53 (Dionisotti).
3. See in particular the letter from Coluccio Salutati to Peter of Mantua in Salutati 1891–1911, III, pp. 318–22; for the relationship between Salutati's circle and Blasius of Parma, see Gherardi 1975, *ad indicem*.

was to seek out the most ancient sources unmuddied by centuries of dubious exegesis and to shift the chief focus of attention away from metaphysics towards ethics and politics in search of virtues with good classical credentials and yet relevant to the needs of their changing society.

No wonder then that philological analysis and literary exegesis become an apologia for both an ancient and a modern model of wisdom. No wonder also at the resurrection of the classical ideal, neatly caught in a famous dictum of Cicero's, of a single *sapientia* which holds within itself 'the knowledge of all things human and divine' and knows how to express them with all the persuasive powers of *eloquentia*. The same ambition motivated even the repeated appeals to Augustine as the corner-stone of a true Christian philosophy uncluttered with dusty theological formulae and intricate dialectical sophistries. The humanists wished religiosity to rely principally on the individual's inner assurance of faith and to be experienced as a continuing meditation on man's transcendent destiny. So, though scholastic distinctions and divisions were rejected, the very conception of philosophy was changing because its chief object was now man – man was at the centre of every enquiry – and because the direct appeal to classical models demanded the rejection of traditional epistemological methods. Even the humanist insistence on rhetoric and its techniques implicitly emphasised a profound questioning of values. In this process philosophy was stripped of its ahistorical character and swept up in the transience and mutability of human existence. For reasons such as this it is impossible to find a single definition of philosophy which holds for the 250 years under consideration. Probably the most typical characteristic of Renaissance thought was its constantly changing notion of philosophy, its scope, its purpose, its objects and its methods. Almost every generation of thinkers produced new solutions, different both in content and approach, to the great problems which have exercised the western philosophical tradition. Contributions to these new solutions came from ethical and political deliberations, from discussions about the worth of scientific knowledge and from attempts to find a theology in harmony with personal religious experiences, from debates about the meaning of art, from the honing of dialectical and rhetorical skills and the advances in philological technique which meant that new light could always be shed on even the most well-worn problems. The rediscovery of the great philosophical schools of antiquity – the revival of Epicureanism and Pyrrhonism, for instance – had a pronounced theoretical influence over many thinkers. The critique of traditional disciplines was no less influential: the birth of humanist jurisprudence, the critique of Galenism, the emergence of a medical theory still heavily indebted to esoteric beliefs, the dissolution of the ancient Ptolemaic-Aristotelian *imago mundi*, the new importance of the *artes* and the growing prestige of mathematical methods – all these made their contribution. Finally there were all the repercussions of the crisis in Christianity which ran throughout the entire Renaissance period. So in the Renaissance there was a disconcertingly complex variety of factors which prevented rigid boundaries between such disciplines as theology, the sciences and political theory. This complexity was the fundamental characteristic of a philosophy which was having to cope with rapidly changing mentalities and ways of life, new political, religious and educational institutions and the particular problems associated with emergent nationalism. Throughout this period, however, the dominant philosophical theme was the centrality of man, which was reinforced by the preference given to techniques favouring communication and persuasive methods, such as the dialogue, the epistle and the oration.

THE PHILOSOPHY OF MAN FROM PETRARCH TO VALLA

This return to a conception of philosophy rooted in the Greco-Roman tradition can be understood by looking at the notion of *sapientia* propounded by Petrarch, whom humanists regarded as their first master.[4] His researches into classical culture were inspired by the conviction that the time had come 'to reveal man to himself once more'. He believed that neither human frailty nor time could diminish the perennial worth of a philosophy which recognised man's destiny: a wearisome struggle against *accidia* in order to achieve supreme nobility as a creation of God. Only in the solitude and *silentium* of a mind turned inward upon itself away from worldly distractions could man find that divine link which united all men and committed them to the service of their kind.[5] For this reason the new and ancient *sapientia*, which Petrarch contrasted with the haughty doctrines of the *recentiores*, entailed the exercise of both *caritas* and the *sermo* through shared human experience. Beyond earthly horizons there was a destiny far greater than human virtue and glory, but the fervent readers of Augustine

---

4. Some of Petrarch's philosophical writings are still only to be found in early editions (Venice 1501 and 1503; Basle 1554 and 1581). I have used Petrarch 1554. For his letters, which are often mini-treatises, see Petrarch 1933–42; for the *Rerum senilium libri*, see Petrarch 1554, but see also the Italian translation with commentary in Petrarch 1869–70; his *Epistolae sine nomine* (very important in the confrontation between Petrarch and the Avignon papacy) are edited in Piur 1925; good, but not definitive, texts of the *Secretum*, the *De vita solitaria* and the *De sui ipsius et multorum ignorantia* are in Petrarch 1955, which also contains some of the *Seniles*.
5. Petrarch 1955, pp. 568–70 (*De vita solitaria*).

never gave up hope of reconciling Christ and literature, of achieving in the survival of their writings the immortality promised by the gospels.[6] In this way even the awareness of death transmuted itself into an unceasing quest for the simplicity and purity of a moral commitment whose ground rules were formulated in pagan classical antiquity. In his *De sui ipsius et multorum ignorantia*[7] and *Invectiva contra medicum*[8] Petrarch contrasted the knowledge of the secrets of nature, which he saw as futile and misleading, with the wisdom of the philosophers and poets, which could heal the maladies of the soul. Thus he found in Plato and Cicero the essentials of a doctrine which would restore to philosophy its moral dimension.

From Petrarch the early humanists learnt their conviction that the revival of *humanae literae* was only the first step in a greater intellectual renewal which would coincide with the highest achievement of man's civic and cultural destiny. Consequently their philosophy tended to dwell not on the personal virtues of the solitary ascetic but on those virtues which equip men jointly to defend their freedom from the looming menace of fate. Typically the humanists directed their knowledge of classical learning towards the problems of civic life, the arts by which men may live well and the *sapientia* which teaches how man may achieve perfection while still in this life. Coluccio Salutati, Chancellor of the Florentine Republic during one of the most dramatic periods of its history, saw philosophy as 'the empress and mother of all arts and sciences', guiding man's earthly journey. Leonardo Bruni, also Chancellor of Florence and deeply involved in the events of his day, theorised similarly in the introduction to his new Latin translations of the *Politics*[9] and the *Nicomachean Ethics*.[10] He assigned primacy to the practical virtues that work for the common good, and considered an education grounded on the *studia humanitatis* as the best way to inculcate such virtues. In his *De studiis et litteris*,[11] however, he stressed that literary studies were barren if they did not lead to *cognitiones reales*, that is, the study of philosophy and the sciences. Poggio Bracciolini, particularly in his *Contra hypocritas*[12] and *De avaritia*,[13] rejected the more extreme forms of monastic asceticism, celebrating instead man's energetic and hard-working commitment to humanise his world. He also acknowledged that all men

6. *Ibid.*, pp. 72ff. (*Secretum*).   7. *Ibid.*, pp. 710–67.   8. Petrarch 1950; see also Petrarch 1949.

9. Bruni 1928, pp. 70–3 (*Epistola super translatione Politicorum Aristotelis ad dominum Eugenium Papam IV*) and pp. 73–4 (*Praemissio quaedam ad evidentiam novae translationis Politicorum Aristotelis*).

10. *Ibid.*, pp. 75–6 (*Praefatio in libros Ethicorum Aristotelis ad dominum Martinum Papam V*) and pp. 76–81 (*Praemissio quaedam ad evidentiam novae translationis Ethicorum Aristotelis*).

11. *Ibid.*, pp. 5–19, especially 18–19.

12. Poggio Bracciolini 1964–9, II, pp. 39–80 (*Dialogus adversus hypocrisim*).

13. *Ibid.*, I, pp. 1–31 (*Historia convivalis disceptativa de avaricia et luxuria*).

might legitimately aspire to some moderate happiness in this life even though some might be destined never to achieve it.

Poggio, whose rediscovery of Lucretius' *De rerum natura* played a crucial part in the fifteenth-century revival of Epicureanism, was not the only humanist to adopt such a secular view. Lorenzo Valla's *De vero falsoque bono*[14] is a carefully weighed critique of the contamination of Christianity by Stoicism, which had transformed the promise of eternal life into a denial of the most natural desires. In Epicureanism Valla found a harmony between the Christian's pursuit of heavenly joy and the enjoyment of those healthy earthly pleasures which the *natura divina* itself had instilled into us. In his view, philosophy taught morality and an insight into man's desires, needs and hopes. Though this ethical concern never attracted the greatest humanists to metaphysics, it did not exclude an often deeply pessimistic awareness of the tragic face of human destiny at both the personal and historical levels. In his *De varietate fortunae*[15] and *De miseria humanae conditionis*[16] Poggio argued that men were frail, inevitably and invariably destined to live a life of pain and misfortune, endlessly repeating the same mistakes and crimes.

The *Intercoenales*[17] of the youthful Leon Battista Alberti have an even greater cogency and dramatic tension, especially when they insist on the futility of existence and the absurdity of an irresistible destiny in a world without providence, ruled only by an arbitrary fortune. Later, in his *Teogenio*[18] and *Momus*,[19] he calls man the most ferocious of creatures, 'lethal to others and to himself', and proclaims the inherent fragility of his every achievement and the transience of earthly life where princes, philosophers and ordinary men alike delude themselves into thinking they can comprehend an ever-changing reality.

THE RELATION OF PHILOSOPHY TO A NEW APPRAISAL OF THE ARTS AND TO PHILOLOGICAL CRITICISM

Renaissance philosophy had therefore assimilated the classical and medieval ethical traditions and did not restrict itself merely to the rhetorical celebration of man's dignity. It also clearly reflected the bitter conflicts of

---

14. L. Valla 1970a.
15. Poggio Bracciolini 1964–9, I, pp. 131–7 (*De fortunae varietate urbis Romae, et de ruina eiusdem descriptio*) and II, pp. 497–654 (*Historiae de varietate fortunae libri quatuor*).
16. *Ibid.*, I, pp. 88–131.
17. For the texts of the *Intercoenales*, which have a complex history, see Alberti 1890, pp. 122–235, and 1964.   18. Alberti 1960–73, II, pp. 53–104.   19. Alberti 1942.

the age. Humanist philosophy was concerned as well with the arts and instruments which make it possible for man to exercise his precarious dominion over things and events. There was frequent praise for jurisprudence and laws, which in Salutati's opinion constituted the 'mystic body' of the human community,[20] and for poetry as the special medium of truth. Even more frequent were the reappraisals of the arts and the techniques which permitted man some insight into the inner workings of nature itself.

Alberti, architect, mathematician and philosopher, is the key figure here. In his specialised treatises, particularly the *De re aedificatoria*,[21] the artisan – constructor of buildings, machines and tools to extend man's powers – becomes an artist-savant who strives unceasingly to give form to matter. Around the middle of the fifteenth century Giannozzo Manetti in his *De dignitate et excellentia hominis*[22] embroidered his rehearsal of the Hermetic doctrine of the *theosanthropos*, the focus of all reality, with an eloquent celebration of the arts and sciences from painting to sculpture, from architecture to history, from astronomy to law, from poetry to *sapientia*, in which the 'great miracle of man' was revealed.

The early fifteenth-century conception of philosophy, while closely tied to the development of philology, the linguistic disciplines and a new historical consciousness, was capable of re-evaluating both past and present. This changing idea of the object of philosophy was profoundly influenced by the labours of the philologists. By discovering and editing partially or indeed completely unknown scientific and philosophical texts they began to separate antiquity and its traditions from myth and fable. Valla's works[23] show how the attempt to apply linguistic analysis to logical procedures developed into an increasingly radical critique of metaphysical principles and concepts, trespassing even into the sacred province of the *scientia de divinis*. The philology at the heart of Valla's discussions of the most heterogenous aspects of his culture was more than a reagent for dissolving spurious and corrupt philosophical traditions. It was the principal instrument for evaluating the testimony of the past, be it legal exegesis or scriptural commentary. The subordination of theology to the essential *auctoritas* of God's word and the pruning out of centuries of maundering exegesis and dialectical logic-chopping were entirely consistent with the main thrust of humanism.[24]

20. Salutati 1947, p. 255.   21. Alberti 1966b.   22. Manetti 1975.
23. See especially L. Valla 1471, 1982, 1984.   24. See L. Valla 1970b.

SACRED AND PROFANE PHILOSOPHY IN THE THOUGHT
OF NICHOLAS OF CUSA

Contemporary with Valla but active in very different circles and still close
to certain typically medieval traditions (the Albertist School at Cologne,
Ockhamism, German mysticism), Nicholas of Cusa contributed decisively
to the new metaphysico-religious conception of *sapientia*. His service to the
church in the dramatic years between 1435 and 1460[25] brought him into
close contact with many of the greatest Italian humanists and gave him a
singularly acute insight into the emerging intellectual and religious crisis.
Unlike many humanist thinkers of his time, Nicholas concentrated on
theological issues: the oneness of God, the Trinity, the nature of Christ and
his role as the supreme mediator. However, an admixture of classical and
medieval Neoplatonism and mathematical ideas transmuted these essentially theological concerns into an unconventional cosmology and into a
new way of conceiving the relationship between divine unity and the
world's multiplicity. Knowledge, according to Nicholas, consisted in
recognising the incommensurability between the ultimate object of human
enquiry and the conceptual and linguistic tools used in that enquiry, that is
to say, recognising that absolute reality could not be enclosed within the
limitations of logical language.[26] Since the mind was finite and could only
deal with finite things, a given *res* was to be thought of both as a negation of
the infinite and as a sign of total being, initiating the *via negationis* which led
to the eternal and immutable bedrock of being. In this way Nicholas could
move from considering the mathematical laws of motion to contemplating
the divine wisdom which pervaded the universe and constituted the perfect
harmony which was always expressed in musical and geometrical terms.
Just as by increasing the number of its sides a polygon could approach, but
never become, a circle, so human knowledge could approach its objects by a
process of approximation. It remained, however, uncertain and infinitely
distant from its object and could never span the gap between infinity and the
finite.[27] Nevertheless, *docta ignorantia* – the Socratic 'learned ignorance' –
demonstrated the infinite wealth and potential of any positive knowledge,
showing how procedures of a geometrical type permitted reason to move
unconstrainedly towards ever more complete truths. Consequently, since

25. For the proceedings of the Council of Basle, see Santacroce 1955, and *Acta Graeca Concilii Florentini* 1953.
26. Nicholas of Cusa 1932–, I, pp. 11–12 (*De docta ignorantia*, lib. I, cap. 5).
27. *Ibid.*, pp. 54–6 (lib. I, cap. 26).

material reality in its multiplicity reflected absolute being, it too must be infinite, without centre or boundaries, and not contained within the finite enclosure of the heavenly spheres.[28] Therefore Nicholas entrusted philosophy with the responsibility for establishing a new relationship between the infinite points which resulted from the dissolution of the finite classical cosmos. While affirming that all truths, relative and particular, should be regarded as approximations of the unique Truth, he emphasised the affinity between this and arithmetical progressions, each of which potentially contained infinity in itself. Just as mathematicians passed from straight to curved lines by a series of ever closer approximations, so metaphysical knowledge could come to comprehend the Absolute and the One by an infinite process which unfolded in the finite multiplicity of the created earth. It is not surprising, therefore, that Nicholas perceived beneath the most diverse religious rites and beliefs a common if limited attempt to approach the unattainable and ineffable divine truth of being.[29] Thus, faith and science, theology and philosophy, were different but ultimately convergent paths leading through civic and religious peace to a single common destination.

FICINO AND PICO: *PIA PHILOSOPHIA* AND THE PHILOSOPHY OF CONCORD

Nicholas of Cusa has often been seen as the instigator of the late fifteenth-century Platonic revival, and Cassirer has argued, not entirely convincingly, for his influence over Marsilio Ficino. In reality, the roots of Ficino's thought lie closer to the debates between the Byzantine émigrés like George of Trebizond and Cardinal Bessarion about the relative superiority of Aristotle and Plato, and to the idiosyncratic religious metaphysics of Pletho.[30] Also, some doubt must now surround the hypothesis that there was a radical discontinuity between the humanist philosophy of man in the first half of the fifteenth century and Ficino's revival of a primarily speculative doctrine owing much to classical metaphysics. First, Ficino's philosophical development reveals specific elements of continuity: the interest in Plato shared by many Florentine humanists (Salutati, Bruni, Manetti and Palmieri) and a number of ideas which were widespread in the fourteenth century: for example, Ficino's version of Dante's *Monarchia*.[31] Second, Ficino was writing for a lay public without scholastic training, and

28. *Ibid.*, pp. 61–75 (lib. II, cap. 1–4). 29. *Ibid.*, VII (*De pace fidei*).
30. See Pletho 1858. 31. P. Shaw 1978.

he used rhetorical methods and myths in a Platonic fashion. Finally, he was defending a unified notion of *sapientia*. He put forward his Platonism as a new theology and metaphysics (the two terms are interchangeable here) which, unlike that of the scholastics, was explicitly opposed to Averroist secularism. His *sapientia* was linked to the notion of a revelation transmitted from the ancients by a chain of inspired thinkers until it achieved a final synthesis in Christian dogma.[32] In his view philosophy should first and foremost include and explain the essence of every *sapientia*, of every true theology and every moral doctrine, that is, the absolute and divine unity which generated the hierarchical and providential order of a universe whose multiplicity reflected the supreme creator.[33] Ficino imagined the world as a perfectly harmonious heavenly melody or as a mirror reflecting the myriad faces of God. The intention of the *pia philosophia*, which Ficino expounded mainly in his *Theologia platonica* and *De Christiana religione*, was to illuminate the profound convergence of philosophical truth and religious certainty. In this convergence the *prisci theologi*, such as Hermes Trismegistus, Zoroaster and Orpheus, had already detected the germs of a perennial wisdom which was now endangered by impious pseudo-philosophers and incompetent theologians.

There has been some exaggeration of the importance of astrology and antique magical elements in Ficino's philosophy. Nevertheless, he did regard the entire universe – the heavens, the elements, plants, animals and man himself – as subject to cosmic influences acting through sympathies and antipathies. In his *De vita coelitus comparanda*[34] he analysed the relationship between the powers of the heavenly souls and man's *spiritus* and found sufficient justification for placing man at the centre of the universe as the microcosm which recapitulated the order of the macrocosm. The great success of Ficino's *pia philosophia* occurred partly because it elevated to the level of literary metaphor a number of ideas which were congenial to the fin-de-siècle mood, troubled by millenarian and spiritual anxieties.

Just as successful were the ideas of Giovanni Pico, who combined an orthodox training in scholastic philosophy with youthful humanist influences and – a typical feature of sixteenth-century esotericism – cabala. Firmly opposed to any rhetorical reductionism in philosophy, Pico saw himself as searching for the deepest common truth, where *sapientia* and its

32. Especially in *Della religione cristiana*, 1st edn, Florence 1474.
33. Especially in *Theologia platonica de immortalitate animorum*, 1st edn, Florence 1482; see Ficino 1576, I, pp. 78–424, and 1964–70.
34. 1st edn Florence 1489; see Ficino 1576, I, pp. 493–572, and 1978.

various temporal manifestations might reside, untroubled by doctrinal squabbles. His missionary zeal and enthusiasm for a philosophy of concord and a great spiritual renewal leading to the universal brotherhood of man did not square with Ficino's idea of *docta pietas*. Pico proposed the absolute value and centrality of man, his cosmic responsibility, his freedom and dignity. This idea lies at the heart of his celebrated *Oratio*,[35] offered as a manifesto for the great conference of learned men which Pico wished to be held in Rome at Epiphany in 1487.[36] The desire to defend human liberty also inspired Pico's *Disputationes adversus astrologiam divinatricem*,[37] a harsh and radical assault on astrology and the absolute determinism which a belief in it ultimately entailed. In his *Heptaplus* and *De ente et uno*,[38] inspired by both cabala and pseudo-Dionysian theology, Pico discovered in the Scriptures a perfectly harmonious philosophical interpretation of the universe and recognised in the inscrutable reality of God that radiant darkness with which man identified utter perfection. Pico praised magic and man's ability to control the most occult powers of nature because he regarded them as 'the practical part of the natural sciences', able to increase our freedom in a world over which God had given us dominion.

THE PLATONIC TRADITION AND SIXTEENTH-CENTURY ARISTOTELIANISM

The new ideas of the fifteenth century foreshadow the main themes of sixteenth-century philosophy. Valla's philology and theology, Ficino's *pia philosophia* and Pico's philosophy of *concordia* were necessary antecedents for the *philosophia Christi* and the uncompromising pacifism of Erasmus. Ficino, Pico and Nicholas of Cusa stand behind Jacques Lefèvre d'Étaples and his school; and there is a specifically fifteenth-century tone in the speculations of Juan Luis Vives and Thomas More as well as Erasmus. Of course, to account fully for such influences it is necessary to follow other developments of sixteenth-century philosophy, such as Agostino Steuco's *philosophia perennis*. This synthesis of Ficino's *pia philosophia* and Pico's *concordia* had passed to Francesco Giorgi, Henricus Cornelius Agrippa and Paracelsus and then to the magical and occult traditions.

The circulation of Platonic, magical, Hermetic and cabalistic ideas should not obscure what is one of the sixteenth century's most important

[handwritten marginalia: not so much direct linkage as implied here]

---

35. G. Pico 1942, pp. 101–65.
36. For the *Conclusiones* intended for the conference in Rome, see G. Pico 1572, pp. 63–113.
37. G. Pico 1946–52.   38. G. Pico 1942, pp. 167–383, 385–441.

philosophical characteristics: the development of a revivified Aristotelianism. Already in the fifteenth century individuals like Paul of Venice, Paul of Pergula and Gaetano da Thiene – all educated at Padua – were taking their cue from the Oxford and Paris logicians, who were themselves following such teachers as Alessandro da Sermoneta, Jacopo Ricci and Apollinare Offredi. In the decades around the turn of the fifteenth century the powerhouses of the Aristotelian revival were the two greatest northern Italian universities, Bologna and Padua, where such luminaries as Nicoletto Vernia, Alessandro Achillini, Pietro Pomponazzi, Marcantonio Zimara and Agostino Nifo were active. Unlike their late medieval predecessors these scholastics adopted a number of typically humanist procedures, especially in their approach to texts. There is no doubt that the Thomist and Scotist schools at Padua continued to evolve, alongside and rivalling the Averroist and Alexandrist professors. But the influence of such surviving terminist tendencies was considerably outweighed by that of the Greek commentators whose diffusion owed much to the labour of such humanist philologists as Ermolao Barbaro and Girolamo Donato. At Padua in 1497 Niccolò Leonico Tomeo began to teach Aristotle from the Greek texts, and the Aldine *editio princeps* of Aristotle was published at Venice between 1495 and 1498.[39] Instead of dwelling on the various interpretative or syncretist currents within Aristotelianism, it is more useful here to concentrate on the difference between Aristotelianism in general and the humanist philosophy of man, its notion of a unified *sapientia* and the religious character of the ideas of Ficino, Pico and Nicholas of Cusa.

Aristotelians drew a sharp distinction betwen philosophy and theology and jealously resisted any attempt to submit Aristotle's ideas to the higher truths of religion. Critical of beliefs which obstructed the exercise of reason, they defended the independence of philosophy and espoused a number of Peripatetic doctrines (for instance, the Averroist account of the intellect and the eternity of the world) which had long been rejected by theologians. Aristotelians retained the various canonical sub-divisions of philosophy, affirming – in contrast to the humanists – the superiority of speculative over poetical philosophy; and, in accordance with the university curricula, they established a well-defined syllabus for the study of philosophy.

It would, however, be wrong to see sixteenth-century Aristotelianism as a rational philosophy anticipating *libertinisme* and to regard it as anti-theological and even anti-religious in contrast with the *docta pietas* of Ficino

---

39. Aristotle 1495–8; on this edition, see Sicherl 1976.

and Steuco. Admittedly, the *De immortalitate animae*, the *De fato* and the *De incantationibus*[40] of Pietro Pomponazzi, the most original and influential sixteenth-century university philosopher, are emphatically opposed to rhetorical or consolatory doctrines. He emphasised the rigorous order of natural laws and the natural and temporal dimension of human existence, which was demonstrated by the indivisible unity of the body-soul compound that constituted our reality and by the substantial connection between all its functions. In his *De incantationibus* Pomponazzi turned an unusually open mind on several features of religion, which he reduced to their natural causes. He also subscribed to the belief that the origins and courses of the great religions were caused by astral influences. However, the majority of Aristotelians were considerably more cautious, accepting some elements of Platonic theology and admitting that Aristotelianism could have a propaedeutic value in grasping some of its mysteries. In any case, the procedures of the *Seconda Scolastica* were much indebted to the Aristotelian tradition and to sixteenth-century Italian Aristotelian studies. Also noteworthy is the success of Paduan authors in the Protestant universities of Germany which had been reformed by Philipp Melanchthon, a self-proclaimed follower of Aristotle.

PHILOSOPHY AS METHOD: THE SIGNIFICANCE OF THE SIXTEENTH-CENTURY PHILOSOPHY OF NATURE AND THE ANTI-ARISTOTELIAN POLEMIC

Though sharply disagreeing about the relative worth of their logical and linguistic tools, humanists and Aristotelians were both concerned to evolve a general methodology, a theory of how knowledge should be acquired and organised. Much of sixteenth-century thinking about philosophy is obscure unless attention is paid to those debates about important issues such as the role of philosophy in the sciences, the rhetorical or logical character of knowledge and the relationship between teaching and research. Lorenzo Valla, for instance, in the context of teaching the *artes sermonales*, clearly favoured rhetorical and dialectical procedures. This preference was assimilated by George of Trebizond in his insistent criticisms of the sophistic logic of the schools;[41] and between the late fifteenth century and the middle of the sixteenth century, it influenced first Rudolph Agricola[42] and then a

---

40. Pomponazzi 1954, 1957, 1556.
41. George of Trebizond *c*. 1470, frequently reprinted in the late fifteenth and early sixteenth centuries.
42. Agricola 1523.

number of important European humanists, including Philipp Melanch-thon,[43] Johannes Sturm[44] and Juan Luis Vives.[45] With differences of emphasis each of these thinkers assigned a fundamental importance to *methodus* as essential in any organisation of knowledge and to procedures either of the topic type or connected with the rhetorical doctrine of *dispositio*. Particularly favoured by Protestants, this tendency culminated in Petrus Ramus' concept of the *methodus unica*, the basic instrument in the creation of a systematic, encyclopaedic and organic knowledge.[46] At the heart of Ramus' polemic was a comparison between his unified philosophi-cal method and the multiplicity of methods and techniques suggested, in particular, by the Aristotelians.

The problem of method was particularly important at Padua, where Jacopo Zabarella in his *De methodis* discussed the various instruments of knowledge and analysed their relationship to the different forms of knowledge and to the structure of the sciences.[47] Zabarella's logical and methodological ideas had a considerable influence in late sixteenth- and early seventeenth-century Europe, reaching even Theodor Zwinger and Bartholomaeus Keckermann, both of whom had had a Ramist training. Revealingly, it was philosophers trained at Padua who most strongly challenged the primacy and predominance of Aristotelian philosophy, as well as proposing radical ideas about the nature of speculative philosophy. Bernardino Telesio, for instance, criticised traditional philosophers for over-confidence, for 'arbitrarily creating their pretend world', and proposed instead a new philosophy of nature based on the senses and therefore suited to understanding the innermost structures of nature. Another thinker trained at Padua was Francesco Patrizi, whose *Discussiones peripateticae*[48] offer the most radical critique of the contradictions, whether genuine or supposed, in the Aristotelian system. In his *Nova de universis philosophia*[49] he condemned the impiety of Aristotle's thought, questioned the notion of a closed and finite universe and proposed a renewed Christian philosophy founded on a strongly hermeticising Platonism and a pantheis-tic conception of reality.

43. See Melanchthon 1537 chiefly; the first edition was 1528 and subsequent editions were drastically reworked; for the *Erotemata dialectices* of 1547, see Melanchthon 1834–60, XIII, cols. 513–752.
44. See especially Sturm 1539, expanded to three books in the Strasburg 1543 edition and to four in the Strasburg 1560 edition.
45. For *In pseudodialecticos*, see Vives 1555, ff. 272–86, 1979a, 1979b; for *Libri de causis corruptarum artium, De tradendis disciplinis* and *Libri de artibus*, see Vives 1555, ff. 288ff.
46. See, e.g., Ramus 1543a, 1543b, and Ramus and Talon 1556, reprinted with several changes in Paris in 1566 and 1572.
47. See J. Zabarella 1578.   48. Patrizi [da Cherso] 1581.   49. Patrizi [da Cherso] 1591.

The critique of Aristotle and Aristotelianism, nourished by Pythagorean and Democritean ideas, culminated at the end of the sixteenth century with Giordano Bruno's call for radical renewal in ethics and his notion of an infinite universe coincident with its divine foundation. The humanist rebellion against traditional codifications of knowledge found other forms of expression which were no less influential in the long evolution of modern thought. The recovery of the classical scepticism of Pyrrho and Sextus Empiricus (which united the dissimilar activities of Gianfrancesco Pico and Michel de Montaigne) encouraged the view of philosophy as systematic doubt, methodically revealing the contingency and uncertainty of all pre-established truths.

THE LEGACY OF RENAISSANCE PHILOSOPHY

Thus it can be seen that in coming to terms with the scientific revolution and a variety of new moral, political and religious problems, late Renaissance philosophy anticipated some of the themes which would characterise seventeenth-century philosophy. The reaction against traditional scholastic authorities had grown into a questioning of all authorities, even the classics. The myths which had nourished Neoplatonic metaphysics (Hermeticism and cabala) came under the ever closer scrutiny of philologists. The new philosophy of nature, often more welcoming to scientific and technical developments, was beginning to dissolve the *imago mundi* which had enclosed theology and philosophy for so long. The context of these changes was a religious crisis of unprecedented gravity whose political and social consequences deeply affected philosophy in all its aspects. Bruno's thought, with its doctrinal problems and complexities, stands at the end of this cycle. It demonstrates in an extreme fashion how the process of criticism initiated by the early humanists grew to envelop even the most ancient and respected authorities. Apart from the new awareness of methods and procedures, one great legacy of Renaissance philosophy was the seventeenth century's grand attempt to re-establish the unity and completeness of knowledge, to recreate – with a new and fuller awareness of the difficulties and dangers involved in such a project – the *ordo scientiarum*. From Campanella to Bacon, from Descartes to Leibniz, the same themes lie at the heart of a continuous dialectic between tradition and innovation, at the heart both of grandiose utopian projects for social renewal and of thoughtful reminders of the concrete reality of the critical exercise of knowledge. Above all, the principal lesson from the various Renaissance conceptions of philosophy – a lesson whose force was to be felt over the next two centuries – was the need to jettison pre-established truths, to re-evaluate constantly all doctrinal and methodological choices and to respect the perpetual newness of the problems with which philosophy and scientific research have to deal.

III

TRANSLATION, TERMINOLOGY AND
STYLE IN PHILOSOPHICAL DISCOURSE

4

TRANSLATION, TERMINOLOGY AND STYLE IN PHILOSOPHICAL DISCOURSE

THE SCOPE OF PHILOSOPHICAL TRANSLATION

Between Roberto Rossi's translation of the *Posterior Analytics* in 1406 and Niccolò Leonico Tomeo's rendering of the *Parva naturalia* in 1522–5, eighteen Italian and Byzantine scholars produced nearly fifty different Latin versions of half as many of Aristotle's works – including spurious works and counting the *Parva naturalia* as one work. In the sixteenth century more than fifty scholars from various parts of Europe produced nearly 200 Latin translations of over forty texts ascribed to Aristotle. The most productive of the fifteenth-century translators were the Byzantines George of Trebizond and Johannes Argyropulos, who each completed ten texts, but in the sixteenth century the Frenchman Joachim Périon challenged even the prolific William of Moerbeke by turning more than twenty works into Ciceronian Latin.[1] These three scholars took very different approaches to philosophical translation. George of Trebizond stayed as close to the verbal structure of the text as comprehensible Latin would permit, while Argyropulos translated so loosely that he was often condemned as a paraphraser. George believed that transliteration was sometimes justified by an untranslatable word or phrase in Greek, but Périon wanted to find a Ciceronian equivalent for everything the Stagirite had said – unlike Argyropulos, who was content with some of the unclassical Latin that medieval translators had introduced.[2] Variations in translation served varieties of audience, and the audience changed with time as it was educated by new accomplishments in translation. Before the 1520s, most works of Aristotle that were printed were medieval Latin translations; only after that time did readers of Aristotle see more humanist Latin in print or much Greek at all.[3]

---

1. Garin 1951; Cranz and Schmitt 1984, pp. 225–41; Schmitt 1983a, p. 73; George of Trebizond 1984, pp. 698–709, 758.
2. Monfasani 1976, pp. 76–7; George of Trebizond 1984, p. 299; Hankins 1983, p. 151; *Platon et Aristote* 1976, pp. 362–3 (Cranz); Schmitt 1983a, pp. 72–7. I am particularly indebted to Dr Hankins for permission to cite his thesis.   3. Cranz and Schmitt 1984, pp. xii–xiv.

The *Nicomachean Ethics*, which Leonardo Bruni translated early in the 1400s, continued to attract humanist translators through the sixteenth century, but no one published its Greek text outside the collected editions until 1523. After this date, at least twenty-five editions containing the Greek appeared by the end of the century, many of them motivated by the philological interests of the humanists. During the same period, the Greek *De anima*, which was less interesting to humanists, was separately edited only four times, and none of these editions was philological. Yet Latin translations of *De anima* appeared frequently because it was a crucial philosophical text.[4] Evidently, the readership for translations of Aristotle was not unitary. Its division into humanist and philosophical segments – though these were not well defined or always separated – is also borne out by the lapse of a century between the Aldine *Opera omnia* (1495–8) of the Greek Aristotle and Isaac Casaubon's Greek–Latin edition (1590) of the complete works. The whole *corpus* as it was known before the nineteenth century had appeared in humanist Latin by the early sixteenth century. Benedictus Fontana attempted a humanist collected works as early as 1496, but he had to fill many gaps with medieval translations. The Basle *Opera omnia* in translation prepared by Simon Grynaeus in 1538, however, was solidly humanist. New translating and the polemic stimulated by it continued through the century, and bilingual editions multiplied after 1550, but the late date of the Casaubon edition suggests that there was no single, large group of scholars pressing to read all of Aristotle in a translation that also referred systematically to the original.[5]

Differences of audience were reflected in the commentary literature as well. The publication of choice for philosophers was, at first, a Latin translation explicated by a Latin commentary; later in the sixteenth century, a Greek original might join the two Latin texts. The selection of commentaries also widened. In the late fifteenth century, Ermolao Barbaro began the process of translating those Hellenistic commentaries on Aristotle that were unknown to the Middle Ages, while Jewish scholars encouraged by Giovanni Pico della Mirandola and others revised familiar commentaries of Averroes and presented new ones in Latin versions based on Hebrew intermediaries. Some humanists, like Bruni, saw Aristotle not simply as a philosopher but also as one of the *summi auctores*, the admired giants of antiquity. Interested as much in eloquence as in philosophy, they produced their own, independent commentaries in the form of philological

---

4. *Platon et Aristote* 1976, pp. 359–61 (Cranz).
5. *Philosophy and Humanism* 1976, pp. 117, 124 (Cranz).

adnotationes that concentrated on grammar, literature and history.[6] But philological erudition failed to interest many philosophers, who continued, like Pietro Pomponazzi, to write commentaries in the older, philosophical style and also to consult medieval commentaries, especially those of Thomas Aquinas, which naturally depended on medieval translations. Because the versions of Bruni and his colleagues threatened a breach of terminological continuity with scholastic philosophy, Alonso de Cartagena and other critics of humanist translation recommended using the Vulgate versions, partially in order to sustain a commentary tradition whose unawareness of the Greek texts or indifference to them appalled the humanists. Some were content, however, to read Thomas as if he had read Bruni. 'Even if Thomas explained the old version', wrote Ludovicus de Valentia, 'he seems to interpret the new', and Ludovicus arranged an alliance between saint and chancellor by expunging offensive transliterations from Thomas' commentary. Lefèvre d'Étaples devised another, very popular solution by printing the Argyropulos 'paraphrase' of the *Nicomachean Ethics* along with Bruni's translation and the rival medieval version defended by Alonso. The strongest marriage between the accomplishments of humanist translation and the needs of the philosophical community came in 1562 with the second of the great Giunta editions of Aristotle–Averroes, originally published in 1550–2.[7]

Aristotle was fundamental to the university curriculum, but Plato was not. Only four of his dialogues had been translated, partially or completely, in antiquity or the Middle Ages. Not surprisingly, early modern translation of Plato was smaller in scope than the Latinising of Aristotle; it involved fewer scholars and depended far more on the work of one great translator, Marsilio Ficino, who published his Latin *Opera omnia* in 1484. Not counting Ficino, there were thirteen fifteenth-century translators – attracted by Plato's eloquence, his compatibility with Christianity, his justification of a tyrannical politics – who produced two dozen different versions of eighteen genuine and spurious dialogues and letters. In the whole period between Manuel Chrysoloras' initial attempt at the *Republic* around 1400 and the

6. *Platon et Aristote* 1976, p. 364 (Cranz); *Philosophy and Humanism* 1976, pp. 119, 125 (Cranz); *Dictionary of Scientific Biography* 1970–80, I, p. 274 ('Aristotle'); Schmitt 1983a, pp. 16, 49 and 1984, §VIII, pp. 129, 132–3, 137; Soudek 1968, p. 67; Kristeller 1965b, pp. 166–7; in George of Trebizond 1984, p. 640, see his *scholium* on Aristotle, *Problems* I.1 (859ᵃ2) for a fifteenth-century example of the form of an *adnotatio* to a philosophical text.
7. Ludovicus to Francesco Piccolomini in the Rome 1492 edition of the *Politics*, cited in Cranz 1978, p. 172: 'Nam etsi Divus Thomas veterem exposuerit, novam tamen interpretari videtur'; *ibid.*, pp. 158–62, 172–6; Cranz and Schmitt 1984, p. xiii; 1976a, pp. 125–7; Schmitt 1983a, pp. 16, 20, 47; Soudek 1968, pp. 85–90, 95–6; Lefèvre d'Étaples 1972, pp. 41–5, 548.

1602 reissue of the revised Ficino *Opera*, more than forty scholars turned more than forty Platonic texts into Latin in nearly ninety different versions. However, about half of these were translated only in the *Opera omnia* of Ficino or by his two lone competitors, Janus Cornarius and Jean de Serres, whose collections saw only a single printing each. Next to Ficino, the most active of the fifteenth-century translators was Bruni, who rendered seven works early in the century. A notable habit of these early Renaissance Platonists was a readiness to bowdlerise their translations and adapt the meaning of the Greek to various ideological ends. Even Ficino, a fastidiously faithful translator, once or twice tried to improve on Plato. Sixteenth-century translators concentrated largely on spurious works – the *Axiochus* was remarkably popular – or on revising older translations to match them with commentaries or making literal translations for pedagogical use.[8]

Plato and Aristotle dominated philosophical translation as they dominated philosophy, but Renaissance scholars also made other important thinkers more familiar to the West. Ficino's versions of Plotinus, Iamblichus, Proclus, Porphyry, Synesius, Hermes Trismegistus, Pseudo-Dionysius and lesser figures are well known. It is likely that Ambrogio Traversari also translated parts of the *Platonic Theology* of Proclus, but he made his most important contribution to philosophy between 1424 and 1433 by Latinising Diogenes Laertius, whose *Lives* became the basis of early modern knowledge of the Presocratics and the Hellenistic schools, especially Epicureanism. In 1479 Angelo Poliziano translated the *Problems* then ascribed to Alexander of Aphrodisias and the *Enchiridion* of Epictetus, apparently without realising that Niccolò Perotti had already translated the latter in 1450. The *Enchiridion* was important as one of the few non-fragmentary Greek sources on Stoicism. Another was the *Meditations* of Marcus Aurelius, which despite the fame of its author remained little more than an empty title until William Xylander brought out his *De seipso seu vita sua* in 1559 along with the Greek *editio princeps*. For the sceptics, Traversari's Diogenes was also indispensable, especially since useful translations of Sextus Empiricus came only in 1562 (Henri Estienne's *Outlines of Pyrrhonism*) and 1569 (Gentian Hervet's *Adversus mathematicos*). Another significant doxographic collection was the *Placita* of Aetius, attributed to Plutarch when Guillaume Budé translated it in 1503–5.[9]

---

8. Hankins 1983, pp. 2, 8–13, 16, 38, 88, 98, 152, 157–65, 180, 208, 211–12, 224, 204*–215*; *Medioevo e Rinascimento* 1955, I, pp. 314–72 (Garin); Festugière 1941, pp. 146–9; Ficino 1981, pp. 40–2; *Platon et Aristote* 1976, p. 66 (Kristeller).
9. Stinger 1977, pp. 44, 70–7; Garin 1961, pp. 75, 78; I. Maïer 1966, pp. 374–86; Epictetus 1954, pp. 17–19, 28–9, 32; Schmitt 1983c; McNeil 1975, pp. 10, 14; Cammelli 1941–54, I, pp. 85–8; Aurelius 1968, pp. xx–xxix.

Guarino da Verona, Poggio Bracciolini, Rinuccio d'Arezzo, Giovanni Aurispa and other fifteenth-century translators contributed Latin versions of Lucian's *Dialogues*, which prepared the way for Nicolò da Lonigo's *volgare* treatments and Leon Battista Alberti's Lucianic imitations in the *Intercoenales* and related works. These earlier humanists read the newly accessible Latin Lucian as if his parodies were serious descriptions of the Hellenistic schools of philosophy. But Lucian's motivations were literary, not historical. When he depicted Socrates as (in Christopher Robinson's words) 'a bald, snub-nosed, hypocritical, pederastic lecher, who swore by dogs and plane-trees [and] held a dotty theory of ideas', he gave scant attention to Socratic doctrine, depending instead on the sure-fire comic contrast between the pretensions of the φιλόσοφος (philosopher) and the peccadilloes of the ἀλαζών (charlatan). In their passion for the antique – and perhaps because the compulsive moralising of the Hellenistic schools, even when caricatured, rang true to their kindred sensibilities – the humanists sometimes mistook Lucian's comedy for a history of ideas. Introducing his translation of *Philosophers for Sale*, Rinuccio d'Arezzo recognised that Lucian wrote 'playfully', but Luca d'Antonio Bernardi da San Gimignano treated the same work as a textbook survey of the schools. On it he based a school play, *De venditione et emptione philosophorum*, for his grammar students, at least one of whom, Marsilio Ficino, was eventually to acquire a more refined understanding of the philosophies of late antiquity.[10] In the next century, Erasmus and Thomas More could read, translate and imitate Lucian with greater sensitivity to his fundamentally comic impulse, yet for his own campaign against philosophical theology Erasmus picked blunt weapons from Lucian's anti-philosophical armory. 'He is especially hostile to philosophers', wrote Erasmus on Lucian's *Cock*, 'Pythagoreans and Platonists because of their magical tricks, and . . . Stoics on account of their . . . arrogance. And quite right too.' Erasmus, whose pedagogic authority was paramount, recommended Lucian as an ideal author for beginners in Greek, and after 1506 he gave Greekless readers an extraordinarily popular selection of translations of Lucian. Despite the thin, sporadic and repetitive philosophical content of the *Dialogues*, it is hard to underestimate the influence of the Latin Lucian (printed in a complete edition along with the Greek by 1538) on the reputation of philosophy in the early modern period.[11]

Petrarch and Boccaccio tried to learn Lucian's language from the Italian Greeks Barlaam and Leonzio Pilato, while Coluccio Salutati and his friends

---

10. C. Robinson 1979, pp. 14–15, 27–31, 40, 50–1, 81–95, 99–100; Marcel 1958, pp. 171–2.
11. The introduction by Erasmus to Lucian's *Somnium sive gallus* is translated in C. Robinson 1979, pp. 166–7, 195.

revised medieval translations of Greek authors without knowing their language at all. But Salutati also helped bring to Florence the Byzantine scholar who effectively inaugurated the age of humanist translation, Manuel Chrysoloras. Chrysoloras, who arrived in 1397, doubtless subordinated translation to his more fundamental obligations as a teacher. Nonetheless, he soon prepared a rough, literal version of the *Republic* which rather contradicted in practice his famous theoretical declaration against *ad verbum* translation. It was revised by Uberto Decembrio and revised again after four decades by Uberto's son, Pier Candido, in 1440.[12] Meanwhile, another Byzantine scholar, George of Trebizond, had come from Crete to Venice in 1416. His thirteen translations of Aristotle and Plato were rigorous and literal, but the latter quality won him the scorn of Theodore Gaza and others. Cardinal Bessarion, originally attracted like other Greek émigrés to the Council of Ferrara and Florence in 1438–9, contributed a version of Aristotle's *Metaphysics* that closely followed the Vulgate, which is perhaps why it was Lefèvre d'Étaples who chose to publish its first edition in 1515. Of all the Byzantines, however, the most influential translator was Argyropulos, whose freer renderings of Aristotle ruled the arena of new translation in the fifteenth century and remained well known in the next.[13]

The most productive student of the Byzantines was Leonardo Bruni. His first round of Plato translations between 1400 and 1415 grew out of literary and religious motives, which were later dampened by his dislike of Socratic scepticism and of Plato's teachings on community of women and goods.[14] Turning to Aristotle, he next decided in 1416 to revise Robert Grosseteste's widely used version of the *Nicomachean Ethics*. He was not aware of Grosseteste's authorship, but his intentions toward the medieval version were consciously hostile, as his introduction makes clear. The tone of these prefatory remarks as much as the unaccustomed style of his translation provoked reactions from Ugo Benzi, Alonso de Cartagena and others which involved him in a long exchange of polemics. One of his apologies, *De interpretatione recta* (c. 1424–6), was the first substantial theoretical statement on translation since St Jerome's letter to Pammachius.[15] It lit the

---

12. Voigt 1893, II, pp. 101–12; Geanakoplos 1962, pp. 20–2; Seigel 1968, pp. 116–18; Cammelli 1941–54, I, pp. 85–8, 91, 123; Hankins 1983, pp. 67–9, 96–7.
13. Minio-Paluello 1972, p. 265; Monfasani 1976, pp. 8, 54–77; George of Trebizond 1984, pp. 698–709, 744–8, 758; Garin 1951, pp. 59, 75–83, 86; Hankins 1983, pp. 150–1; Schmitt 1983a, pp. 70–2.
14. Hankins 1983, pp. 33–7.
15. Birkenmajer 1922, pp. 130, 144–6, 164–6; *Medioevo e Rinascimento* 1955, I, pp. 301–5, 310–11; Grabmann 1926–56, I, pp. 440–8; Lockwood 1951, p. 185; Bruni 1928, pp. 81–3; Baron 1966, p. 554; Garin 1951, p. 72; Hankins 1983, p. 28; Schmitt 1983a, p. 67; Steiner 1975, pp. 236–69; Bartelink 1980, pp. 1–7, 46–7.

way for many other controversialists and theoreticians over the next two centuries; the most important were Périon, speaking for Ciceronian translation in *De optimo genere interpretandi* (1540), and Étienne Dolet, setting guidelines for vernacular translators in *La Maniere de bien traduire* (1540).[16] In 1419–20 Bruni set out to replace another piece of the medieval Aristotle, the *Recensio Durandi* of the *Oeconomics*. Judging by the number of manuscripts, this was a very successful work, but his most fortunate effort was his last in philosophical translation, the *Politics* (1438). 'My reason for translating it', he wrote, 'was the same that led me to do the *Ethics* . . . the very refined style of the Greek . . . reduced by the sins of a bad translator to . . . laughable stupidity.' Bruni had compared his fate in his battles over translation to that of St Stephen stoned by the Judaisers, but in more than twenty years not much had changed. Recovering from his martyrdom, he had even returned to Plato, in 1423–7 and 1437; the influence of Bruni's Platonic translations was enormous until Ficino published his in 1484.[17]

Italians and Byzantines nearly monopolised philosophical translation in the 1400s and also left their mark on progress made in the next century, when the French established a healthy tradition in Latin and the vernacular. The first texts translated from Greek by a Frenchman were the works of Plutarch Latinised in 1503–5 by Budé, who also rendered the pseudo-Aristotelian *De mundo* in 1526 and served other translators invaluably with his philological work.[18] Lefèvre had begun to edit translations of other scholars earlier, with the popular *Tres conversiones* (1497) of the *Nicomachean Ethics*. His editing generally included the sort of revising he described in his *Metaphysics* of 1515: 'I have compared Bessarion's translation . . . with the Greek and have called it back to its senses wherever it strayed . . . To his version I have added the Argyropulos, which smacks more of paraphrase, while Bessarion better plays the part of a translator.' He revised medieval versions of the *Topics* and *Sophistici elenchi* more thoroughly and encouraged his students to translate as well.[19] François Vatable, for example, published the first Renaissance Latin version of the *Parva naturalia* in 1518

16. *Platon et Aristote* 1976, p. 377 (Stegmann); Schmitt 1983a, p. 74; *Critical Prefaces* 1950, pp. 77–83; Kalwies 1978, pp. 599–600.
17. Bruni 1928, pp. 73–4: 'Convertendi autem interpretandique mihi causa fuit eadem illa, quae . . . ad conversionem *Ethicorum* induxit. Nam cum viderem hos Aristotelis libros, qui apud Graecos elegantissimo stilo perscripti sunt, vitio mali interpretis ad ridiculam quamdam ineptitudinem esse redactos . . .'; Birkenmajer 1922, p. 180; Goldbrunner 1968, p. 224; Garin 1951, pp. 62, 67; Soudek 1968, p. 65; Hankins 1983, pp. 38, 45–7.
18. McNeil 1975, pp. 10, 14, 86; Wilamowitz-Moellendorf 1982, pp. 47–8; R. Pfeiffer 1976, pp. 101–2.
19. Lefèvre d'Étaples 1972, p. 356: '. . . Bessarionis interpretationem . . . cum Graeco contuli et ad intelligentiam sicubi in devium flectebatur iter revocavi . . . Cui adieci Argyropylum, qui magis sapit paraphrasten; Bessario vero potius partes interpretis agit . . .'; *ibid.*, pp. 41–5, 49, 86–9, 150–4, 442, 548, 552–4, 560; *Humanism in France* 1970, pp. 133–5 (Rice).

along with *De generatione* and the *Meteorology*. Other important French scholars who followed in the tradition of Budé and Lefèvre were Gerard Roussel, Adrien Turnebus, Denys Lambin, Jacques Charpentier, Henri Estienne, Gentian Hervet and Isaac Casaubon, but the grand champion was Périon. His many translations of Aristotle succeeded in the sense that they were frequently reprinted, but they also provoked severe criticism. Even after Nicolas Grouchy revised them, they were not deemed fit to appear in Casaubon's bilingual *Opera* of 1590, and they were of little use in university teaching.[20] Périon's loyal readers must have had enough humanist education to parse his Ciceronian periods but not enough philosophical sophistication to worry over his abandonment of standard terminology.

Likewise, although Latin was still the universal and very nearly the sole language of learned communication, there was a special and growing audience for vernacular translation of philosophy and for original philosophising in the vulgar tongues. In judging the depth of this activity, one should recall that while Montaigne (who used vernacular translations) said he knew no Greek, he surely understood enough natural theology to write the *Apologie de Raymond Sebond*. His exceptional erudition and Machiavelli's troubling originality occupied one extreme of a spectrum of vernacular philosophical discourse at whose other end one finds the more predictable and superficial motives of the courtiers and princes who often patronised translators. Under Francis I, enrichment of the French language became national policy. Francis became as energetic a patron of vernacular translations of Cicero, Plutarch and Plato as Pope Nicholas V had been of Latin. Moreover, he had the advantage of precedent in the similar patronage of his predecessor, Charles V, and in a history of French translation of philosophy reaching back to Jean de Meung's Boethius (*c.* 1300) and Nicole Oresme's Aristotle (1370–7).[21] French translators became quite active after 1530; some of the finest talents in the country, including Étienne Dolet, François Hotman and Philipe Le Plessis, were enlisted in the cause. The most important were Jacques Amyot for his Plutarch (1559, 1572) and Louis Le Roy for his Plato (1551–63). Even in Aristotle translations, which were less popular in the vernacular, France outstripped England and Spain, though it fell far short of what such figures as Antonio Brucioli accomplished in Italy.[22] One theoretical problem that was more

---

20. Lefèvre d'Étaples 1972, p. 406; R. Pfeiffer 1976, pp. 111–12, 120–2; Wilamowitz-Moellendorf 1982, pp. 55–6; *Platon et Aristote* 1976, p. 378 (Stegmann); Cranz and Schmitt 1984, p. xiv; *Platon et Aristote* 1976, p. 364 (Cranz); Cranz 1978, p. 178; Schmitt 1983a, pp. 77–9.

21. Pouilloux 1969, p. 60; Kalwies 1978, p. 597; Larwill 1934, pp. 7–13, 20, 57; Oresme 1968a, pp. 3–7, 10–15; Vespasiano da Bisticci 1963, p. 50; Voigt 1893, II, pp. 71–3, 156–60, 180–1; Garin 1951, p. 73.

22. Larwill 1934, p. 36; R. Pfeiffer 1976, p. 107; Pouilloux 1969, pp. 48, 60–3; Gundersheimer 1966, pp. 31–48; Cranz and Schmitt 1984, *ad indicem*.

pressing for vernacular than for Latin translators was that of propriety and security. Was it a good idea, for example, to make the political or religious ideas of the *Republic* available to a lay audience? Some vulgarisers feared being blamed for profaning philosophy's secrets and for doing so in an indecorous tongue. John Florio had a good answer, which was not entirely in keeping with the spirit of his age: 'Learning cannot be too common, and the commoner the better . . . Why but the vulgar should not knowe all?'[23]

François Sauvaige expressed the more typical attitude in the prologue to his *De l'ami et du flatteur* (1520), the first French vernacular rendering of any of Plutarch's *Moralia* to appear in print:

> this effort . . . is not thought so worthy that those who understand Greek or Latin should lower themselves to look at this work . . . [which] I have endeavoured to translate for the instruction of the common people; thus, if among my readers anyone has ears more delicate, let him please be tolerant of the ignorance and crudity of my style, waiting upon some other effort more carefully wrought than this.[24]

The ground for the vernacularisation of Plutarch's philosophically rich and eclectic treatises had been cultivated since the early fifteenth century, when the Italian humanists – Guarino, Francesco Filelfo, Antonio Cassarino and many others – first began to Latinise them, thus creating demand for the Greek *editio princeps* issued by Aldus in 1509 and the complete Latin translation by William Xylander in 1570. The greatest spur to the diffusion of the Latin *Moralia* in the sixteenth century was the widely read selection first published by Erasmus in 1514. There followed not only Froben's revision of the Greek text in 1542 and Henri Estienne's in 1572 but also many collections of selected Latin treatises by a number of translators – sixty of them from Italy, France, Spain, Germany, England, Holland and Hungary who rendered sixty-five of Plutarch's essays by the time Xylander had finished his complete Latin *Moralia*. Vernacular alternatives to the Latin had entered the market before 1500, but even after the Greek text had been printed almost all were based on earlier Latin or vernacular versions, the notable exceptions being Willibald Pirckheimer's German, Thomas Elyot's English and Diego Gracian's Spanish. It was the French more than any others to whom the broader, Latinless readership of the sixteenth century owed its philosophical (as well as its historical) Plutarch. By 1571, twenty

---

23. Ebel 1969, pp. 595–8; Fubini 1966, p. 347; cf. Hankins 1983, p. 44.
24. Sauvaige's 'Prologue', cited in Aulotte 1965, p. 87: 'ce labeur . . . n'est tenu tel ne si vallable que ceulx qui ont intelligence de grec ou latin se humilient à veoir ceste lecture . . . Mon estude a esté translater ce livre pour l'enseignement du commun peuple; ainsi, si aulcun ayant les oreilles plus delicates se mesle parmy, supporte, s'il luy plaist, l'ignorance et rudesse de mon stile, attendant quelque aultre labeur, plus curieusement compilé que cestuy.'

translators, including Estienne Pasquier, Geoffroy Tory and Estienne de la Boétie, completed twenty-three French *Moralia*, but only five of these consulted the original. Scrupulous attention to the Greek, specifically that of Aldus and of Froben, was the hallmark of Amyot's complete *Oeuvres morales et melées* of 1572, though he also used Xylander and other Latin and French versions, especially those of Louis Le Roy. Amyot aimed for clear, faithful and stylistically varied language, but his notion of fidelity permitted him compressions, expansions and variations in the interest of lucidity and symmetry. His wish to avoid a Latinised or neologised French led sometimes to oddly contemporary (*gentilshommes* for οἱ καλοὶ κἀγαθοί) or Christian (*péchés* for ἀδικήματα) representations of Greek ideas and at other times (*attenter aucune nouvelleté* for νεωτερίζειν) to careful periphrasis. The success of Amyot's efforts was such that his century saw only two other French translations of any of the *Moralia*. Montaigne made use of Amyot's masterpiece, which along with the Greek also underlay Philemon Holland's English *Morals* of 1603.[25]

BASES OF PHILOSOPHICAL TRANSLATION

Before printing was invented, before a large vernacular readership for philosophy was thinkable, the worries that Manuel Chrysoloras had to face were confined to a smaller group of people. The Byzantine scholar, according to his Florentine students, taught that 'conversion into Latin *ad verbum* was worthless . . . a complete perversion of the meaning of the Greek. He said it was necessary to translate *ad sententiam* . . . without changing the character of the Greek in any way.' Manuel's proclamation that the appropriate locus of correspondence between translation and original was meaning (*sententia*, which can also mean 'sentence') rather than word (*verbum*), though it had been anticipated in practice by Salutati's circle and in programmatic statements of Jerome, Jean de Meung and Oresme, has been taken as the charter of Renaissance translation theory.[26] And in fact, the philosophical translations of Leonardo Bruni and others who were influenced by Chrysoloras and Salutati differed from the medieval versions of James of Venice, Robert Grosseteste and William of Moerbeke on just this question of fidelity to the word. By inventing Latin equivalents for

25. Aulotte 1965, pp. 12–16, 21–128, 141–6, 150–3, 167–9, 187, 191, 197–9, 225, 253, 259–60, 280–9.
26. Bertalot 1975, II, p. 133: 'ferebat Manuel . . . conversionem in latinum ad verbum minime valere. Nam non modo absurdum esse asseverebat, verum etiam interdum grecam sententiam omnino pervertere. Sed ad sententiam transferre opus esse aiebat . . . ut nullo modo proprietas greca immutaretur . . .'; Seigel 1968, p. 120; Larwill 1934, pp. 8, 29.

Greek lexical and syntactic forms (particles, word order, certain participles, various negative constructions) not present in classical Latin, medieval translators developed codes which enabled them to map Greek originals on to Latin versions with such precision that modern scholars can sometimes reconstruct the Greek from the Latin.[27] What such versions can have meant to contemporary readers who knew neither the translator's code nor the Greek that it represented remains a puzzle, though the inclination of most medieval commentators to treat the Latin text as primary, not intermediary, betrays the philological poverty of their philosophy. But it was tradition, not ignorance of Greek, that shaped the decisions of the best medieval translators. Jerome, who agreed with Cicero and Horace that *sensus* was the criterion for secular translation, had as a student of the early rabbis and a reader of the Septuagint insisted on rendering the Bible *verbum e verbo* since even its word order was an act of God. Given the celebrity of the Vulgate and its centrality for Christian philosophy, it was natural that Boethius and John Scotus Eriugena should imitate Jerome in their philosophical translations and that later scholars should follow them.[28] While the choice of meaning over word begins to distinguish Renaissance philosophical translation from that of this earlier age, it does not complete the distinction nor do justice to the complexity of translation theory in the fifteenth and sixteenth centuries. Besides meaning and word, four other choices for the locus of correspondence in translation emerged in the early modern period: language (*lingua*), structure (*ratio*), content (*res*) and style (*eloquentia, elegantia, venustas* etc.).

Faced directly or indirectly with questions about the need for new versions of texts already available in medieval translation, Renaissance scholars routinely replied by echoing Chrysoloras' denunciation of the verbal method. Yet the response of the most famous of the Renaissance theorists, Leonardo Bruni, was more modulated: 'First I preserve all the meanings (*sententias*) . . .; then, if it can be rendered word for word without any awkwardness or absurdity, I do so gladly; if not, . . . I depart a bit from the words to avoid absurdity.'[29] He and other Renaissance translators also

27. Troilo 1931–2, pp. 276–7; Pelzer 1964, pp. 159–60; Minio-Paluello 1972, pp. 203–4, 251–2, 259–60; *Dictionary of Scientific Biography* 1970–80, IX, p. 436 ('William of Moerbeke'); Goldbrunner 1968, p. 208.
28. Troilo 1931–2; Bruni 1928, p. 96; Schwarz 1944; Kloepfer 1967, p. 19; Stinger 1977, pp. 19–20, 101–2, 107.
29. Bruni 1741, I, p. 17: 'Primo igitur sententias omnes ita conservo ut ne vel minimum quidem ab illis discedam. Deinde si verbum verbo sine ulla inconcinnitate aut absurditate reddi potest, libentissime omnium id ago; sin autem non potest, . . . paulisper a verbis recedo ut declinem absurditatem'; *Medioevo e Rinascimento* 1955, I, p. 363 (Garin).

explained why a consistent *ad verbum* method was unworkable. One great obstacle was idiom: because a phrase like *gero tibi morem* ('I humour you') was not the sum of its lexical parts ('I do' + 'to you' + 'conduct'), making each word a unit of translation was literally senseless. Another was the necessity for translating a given Greek word, such as λόγος, by a variety of Latin words (*verbum, sententia, dispositio, ratio*) in the same text, or the desire to render a single Greek word, such as αἰσθητά, periphrastically in Latin (*ea quae sensibus percipiuntur*).[30] Such technical considerations, reinforced by the Ciceronian conviction that the aesthetic and semantic properties of language were inseparable and, perhaps, by the ambiguity of the word *sententia* ('meaning'/'sentence'), convinced most of Bruni's successors to opt for meaning over word. But in the sixteenth century, some translators who specialised in philosophy, like Simone Simoni, praised the verbal method for its precision and for its terminological continuity with the medieval textual tradition. Even in Bruni's century, George of Trebizond, whose work as a translator was broader than Simoni's, explicitly preferred to render philosophical texts 'word for word as far as Latinity permits', a decision which seems to have governed Ficino's translating as well.[31]

Although early modern scholars rejected the word as a unit of translation in their ideological statements, in practice important translators like Ficino, George of Trebizond and Bruni continued to strive for some measure of verbal correspondence when rendering philosophical texts. They had two practical reasons for doing so. First, since the whole terminological structure of western philosophy after Cicero rested on direct or indirect Latinisation of Greek texts, there was a premium on preserving an intellectual edifice erected at such cost. Lorenzo Valla was apparently willing to dispense with terminological continuity in order to advance his own powerful but idiosyncratic philosophy of language, as Périon and others were ready to sacrifice it on the altar of Ciceronianism. But not all Renaissance translators were so radical; their caution is evident in the fact that much of their work lies along a continuum between original translation and simple revision.[32] Here was a second motive for modifying rather than discarding the verbal method: revising, which for an acquired language is

---

30. *Medioevo e Rinascimento* 1955, I, p. 344 (Garin); Bruni 1928, p. 84; *Platon et Aristote* 1976, p. 384 (Stegmann); Schmitt 1983a, p. 75.
31. George of Trebizond 1984, p. 191: 'conatus sum, ut in Physico etiam feci auditu, verbum verbo prout Latinitas patitur reddere'; Minio-Paluello 1972, p. 265; Harth 1968, p. 56; Schmitt 1983a, p. 81; Hankins 1983, pp. 150–1.
32. Garin 1951, pp. 61, 66–7, 70, 74, 78; Seigel 1968, pp. 116–19; Schmitt 1983a, pp. 65–6; Hankins 1983, pp. 154, 209–10.

quicker and safer than translating *de novo*, inclines one to consider and often to preserve a predecessor's choice of words.

The evolution of texts through translation by revision is visible in the following Latin versions – two medieval, six early modern – of the first sentence of the *Nicomachean Ethics*, a favourite of humanist translators; changes in successive versions are italicised:

1. Πᾶσα τέχνη καὶ πᾶσα μέθοδος, ὁμοίως δὲ πρᾶξίς τε καὶ προαίρεσις, ἀγαθοῦ τινὸς ἐφίεσθαι δοκεῖ· διὸ καλῶς ἀπεφήναντο τἀγαθόν, οὗ πάντ' ἐφίεται. (Ι.Ι (1094ᵃ1-3), ed. I. Bywater; 22 words)

2. Every art and every mode of enquiry – likewise, moral action and choice – is thought to aim at some good; thus they have rightly defined the good as that at which all things aim. (B. P. Copenhaver; 33 words)

3. Omnis ars et omnis doctrina, similiter autem et operatio et proheresis boni alicuius operatrix esse videtur; ideoque optime enuntiant bonum, quod omnia optant. (*Ethica nova*; *c.* 1200; 23 words)³³

4. Omnis ars et omnis doctrina, similiter autem et *actus et eleccio bonum quoddam appetere* videtur; *ideo bene enunciaverunt* bonum, quod omnia *appetunt*. (Robert Grosseteste; 1246–7; 22 words)³⁴

5. Omnis ars *omnisque* doctrina, similiter autem et actus et electio bonum quoddam appetere videtur; *quapropter* bene *ostenderunt summum bonum*, quod omnia appetunt. (Leonardo Bruni; 1416–17; 22 words)³⁵

6. Omnis ars omnisque doctrina, similiter autem et actu et electio bonum quodam appetere videtur; *quo circa* bene enunciaverunt *ipsum bonum*, quod omnia appetunt. (Giannozzo Manetti; before 1457; 23 words)³⁶

7. Omnis ars omnisque doctrina, *atque* actus *itidem et* electio bonum quoddam appetere videtur; quapropter bene *veteres* bonum ipsum *id esse dixerunt*, quod omnia appetunt. (Johannes Argyropulos; *c.* 1460; 24 words)³⁷

8. Omnis ars omnisque *discendi via, actio item atque* electio bonum quoddam *expetere* videtur; quapropter bene id esse bonum ipsum *asseruerunt*, quod omnia *expetunt*. (Giovanni Bernardo Feliciano; 1541; 23 words)³⁸

9. Ars omnis et omnis doctrina, *itemque* actio et *propositum* bonum aliquod expetere videtur; *itaque probe* bonum *definierunt*, id quod expetunt omnia. (Adrien Turnebus; 1555; 21 words)³⁹

10. Omnis ars omnisque *docendi via*, atque *institutio* itemque actio et *consilium* bonum aliquod appetere videtur; *iccirco pulchre* veteres id esse bonum *pronunciaverunt*, quod omnia appetunt. (Denys Lambin; 1558; 25 words)⁴⁰

The translators render Aristotle's twenty-two Greek words with a maximum of twenty-five Latin words, and although these vary considerably across the eight versions – especially for problematic terms like

33. Pelzer 1964, p. 133.   34. Aristotle 1972, p. 1.
35. Aristotle 1479, sig. biʳ.   36. Garin 1951, p. 72.
37. Aristotle 1549a, p. 603.   38. Aristotle and Averroes 1562–74, III, p. 1.
39. Aristotle 1567, p. 1.   40. Aristotle 1566, p. 1.

μέθοδος, προαίρεσις, τἀγαθὸν and ἀπεφήναντο – the continuity from
revision to revision is clear. On average, about three-quarters of the text
remains stable, reckoning stability as the tendency to preserve features of
earlier versions and counting even stylistic and minor changes; in fact,
though this single case cannot necessarily be taken as representative, it
suggests greater distance between Grosseteste and the older medieval
version than between Grosseteste and Bruni or Lambin. Medieval
translations *ad verbum* influenced even the humanist productions meant to
replace them.

The humanists' desire to make language (*lingua*) an additional locus of
correspondence for translation is a stronger clue to their philological
intentions than criticism of the verbal method. Bruni formulated this point
most clearly and repeated it several times: 'A translation is entirely correct if
it corresponds to the Greek; if not, it is corrupt. Thus, all argument about
translation moves from one language (*lingua*) to another.'[41] His conception
of translation as the transference of an author's text from *lingua Graeca* to
lingua Latina meant that both version and original, along with their
linguistic contexts, were human objects, ephemeral but philologically
accessible, conditioned by time but knowable through history. The very
different ideas of Bruni's most forceful critic, Alonso de Cartegena,
highlight the diachronic character of Bruni's philological scheme of
translation. Where Bruni insisted on fidelity to the historically contingent
language of the original, Alonso required fidelity to a privileged
metachronic structure (*ratio*) discoverable in the text but unconstrained by
history and expressible in any language. 'Reason (*ratio*) is common to every
people', he argued, 'though it is expressed in various idioms. So let us discuss
whether the Latin language supports [a translation], . . . whether it agrees
with reality (*res ipsae*), not whether it accords with the Greek.' Alonso's
views were compatible with the philosophical grammar of the later Middle
Ages which, despite its unconscious commitments to Latin as the learned
lingua franca, attempted to expose timeless structures belonging to
language-in-general and deriving somehow from reality. His thoughts also
foreshadowed the witty question that Giovanni Pico della Mirandola asked
later in the century in his debate with Ermolao Barbaro: 'Can people live
without hearts if they are all tongue (*lingua*), are they not then . . . simply
dead dictionaries (*glosaria*)?' Pico meant that a language, whose phonetic

---

41. Birkenmajer 1922, p. 189: 'interpretatio autem omnis recta, si Graeco respondet, vitiosa si non
respondet. Itaque omnis interpretationis contentio unius linguae ad alteram est'; *ibid.*, pp. 194, 204;
Bruni 1928, p. 83; Troilo 1931–2, p. 383; Harth 1968, p. 46.

properties make it a material entity, can fall short of the deeper, immaterial thoughts it tries to express, which, so he argued, is why Pythagoras would have preferred to explain his philosophy through silence rather than speech.[42]

Pico also wrote that Cicero advised 'settling the thought (*mens*) rather than the expression (*dictio*), taking care to guide the reason (*ratio*), not the speech (*oratio*)', but Bruni and most other humanists took the opposite lesson from Cicero and Quintilian – the primacy of *oratio* over *ratio* as the distinctly human activity. Bruni consequently saw translation as a *transformatio orationis*, where *oratio* represented an indissoluble amalgam of semantic and aesthetic values.[43] This implied that style (*eloquentia, elegantia*) was also a locus of correspondence between text and version, and it stimulated the translator's own artistic ambitions. Bruni knew that Cicero in his translations had rejected the duties of a mere go-between (*interpres*), insisting on the orator's creative role. Likewise, Poggio Bracciolini claimed the rights of an author (*scriptor*) for himself as translator. Valla and Dolet urged the translator not to reproduce but to improve upon the formal qualities of the original, and Bruni compared his work to that of the poet, sculptor or painter, thus attributing to the translator the artist's autonomy. Introducing a revision of his *Physics* translation, Argyropulos advised 'transferring the author's *sententiae* but using a greater number of words to extend their meaning', and in his *De anima* Périon called himself 'an interpreter and evaluator of words . . . not of content (*res*)'.[44] The Ciceronian Périon carried the oratorical ideal in translation to its extreme by confining himself to the philological dimension of the text and ignoring its philosophical content, but most Renaissance translators regarded content (*res*) as another locus of correspondence. Even Argyropulos, often dismissed as a paraphraser, admitted that 'both issues are rightly of concern to us . . .

42. Birkenmajer 1922, p. 166: 'Ratio enim omni nationi communis est, licet diversis idiomatibus exprimatur. An ergo Latina lingua toleret proprieque scriptum sit et rebus ipsis concordet, on an Graeco consonet, discutiemus'; *Prosatori latini* 1952, p. 820: 'qui, excordes, toti sunt lingua, nonne sunt mera, ut Cato ait, mortua glosaria? Vivere . . . sine corde nullo modo possumus'; *ibid.*, pp. 810, 813–14; Harth 1968, pp. 44–8; Ashworth 1974a, pp. 26–7; Apel 1963, p. 162.

43. *Prosatori latini* 1952, p. 814: 'Tullius . . . sciebat tam prudens quam eruditus homo, nostrum esse componere mentem potius quam dictionem, curare ne quid aberret ratio, non oratio'; Chomarat 1981, I, pp. 62–7; Seigel 1968, p. 159; Apel 1963, p. 171; Kelley 1970a, pp. 28–9; Harth 1968, pp. 43, 53.

44. Garin 1951, p. 84: 'recte quidem sententias referentes auctoris, latius autem eas explicandas pluribusque verbis'; Aristotle 1553a, p. 100: 'Verborum enim in iis sum, non rerum, explanator atque aestimator'; *Platon et Aristote* 1976, p. 363 (Cranz); Minio-Paluello 1972, p. 268; Schwarz 1944, p. 74; Cuendet 1933, p. 382; De Petris 1975, p. 18; Gravelle 1972, p. 281; Bruni 1928, pp. 83–6, 127; Apel 1963, pp. 181–2; *Critical Prefaces* 1950, p. 81.

understanding of content . . . and elegance of language'. However, the
distinction between *res* and *ratio* as bases of translation remains unclear in
Renaissance theorists, and the meaning of terms as broad as these was
predictably slippery. To Alonso de Cartagena *res* could mean 'the reality
represented' by a text, while for Salutati it seems to have meant something
like 'style' as well as 'content'.[45]

ORATORY AND STYLE IN PHILOSOPHICAL DISCOURSE

Salutati's student Roberto Rossi prefaced his version of the *Posterior
Analytics* with an apologetic defence of style: 'How would it harm the
work', he asked, 'if it were more pleasant?' By the end of the century,
eloquence was better established as a value in philosophical translation. It
was the chief motivation, for example, of Ermolao Barbaro's unfulfilled
plan for a complete Latin Aristotle, in which he would 'render all the works
and enhance them with as much clarity, taste and elegance as possible'.[46]
Despite elements of continuity between their work and that of their
medieval predecessors, Renaissance translators constructed their sense of
style in terms of historical polemic, against the backdrop of the regretted
decline of antiquity into barbarity and the contemporary campaign to
recover ancient culture. The obligation to translate philosophy was given in
the humanist programme, yet it was important that duty should not be
drudgery, that it should be an ennobling service to high culture. This is what
made Bruni's slogan of *transformatio orationis* so meaningful in its time. If
translation was akin to oratory, then it was fit work for the intellectual hero,
the *orator*, as Cicero and Quintilian had described him. But oratorical
translation also implied commitment to classical rhetoric, an approach to
language which since the age of the sophists had possessed its own technical
baggage as well as certain anti-philosophical impulses. Thus, when Bruni
obliged the translator of Plato or Aristotle to render figures of speech
(*figurae dicendi*) and embellishments (*exornationes*) as well as meaning, he had
in mind something that was profounder than prettification but also unlike
poetry.[47]

45. Argyropulos to Cardinal Della Rovere in his second version of the *De anima*, cited by Minio-
    Paluello 1972, p. 268: 'Utrumque curae non iniuria nobis est . . . rerum inquam notitia . . . et
    elegantia linguae . . .'; Seigel 1968, pp. 116–17.
46. Roberto Rossi's dedication of his version of the *Posterior Analytics, c.* 1406, cited in Garin 1951, p. 60:
    'Quod si suavior etiam illa fuisset, quid tamen in hoc opere detrimenti?'; *ibid.*, p. 88: 'omnes
    Aristotelis libros converto, et quanta possum luce, proprietate, cultu exorno'; *ibid.*, pp. 89–90.
47. Seigel 1968, pp. 6–19, 31–62, 103; Bruni 1928, pp. 86–90, 133–4; Harth 1968, pp. 53, 56, 58; De
    Petris 1975, pp. 24–5.

But since Boethius had set out to make a Latin Aristotle, there existed another, anti-rhetorical strain of philosophical translation which feared a view like Bruni's as a threat to meaning. Alonso represented this other tradition when he complained that one 'who think[s] to subjugate moral meaning to eloquence, . . . to subordinate the most involved arguments of the sciences to the rules of eloquence, does not understand that the rigour of science abhors the adding and subtracting of words that belongs to charming persuasion'. Giovanni Pico, George of Trebizond, Johannes Dullaert and others also represented it when they said that eloquence was unnecessary or indeed undesirable in philosophical discourse.[48] There were concomitant objections to pleasure as a goal of philosophical translation, even though in making their work enjoyable and easy to read the basic motive of the humanist translators was pedagogic. In general, since oratory was meant to result in action, the persuasion that Alonso distrusted was the primary object of eloquence: translation must charm if it hopes to teach. Moreover, translation as *transformatio orationis* required an oratorical education in language, letters and history. Bruni considered this humanist curriculum an antidote to the barbarism of the schools, but a university philosopher like Agostino Nifo worried that it would disqualify the young for the study of philosophy. Bruni called the orator 'the agent of truth', but Pico wished to exclude his rhetorical arts from philosophy because they were deceptive and beguiling.[49] These anxieties were justified. Valla, who spoke of 'the great sacrament of Latin speech' and referred to 'the eloquent . . . [as] pillars of the church', taught that 'petty reasonings of dialecticians . . . metaphysical obscurities and . . . modes of signification should not be mixed up in sacred enquiries . . . since [the Fathers] did not lay the foundations of their arguments on philosophy'. He and Erasmus and Juan Luis Vives gave authoritative voice to the anti-philosophical impulse in oratorical humanism, which was muted by an older conviction, present

48. Birkenmajer 1922, p. 175: 'errorem illorum . . . qui putant sententiam moralem eloquentiae subiugandam . . . qui scientiarum districtissimas conclusiones eloquentiae regulis subdere vult, non sapit, cum verba addere ac detrahere ad persuasionis dulcedinem pertinet, quod scientiae rigor abhorret'; Grabmann 1926–56, I, pp. 443–4; Fubini 1966, p. 339; Schwarz 1944, p. 76; Gravelle 1972, p. 276; Schmitt 1984, § VIII, p. 133; Vives 1979a, pp. 20–1; Hubert 1949, p. 229; George of Trebizond 1984, p. 303. It should be noted (cf. Gray 1963, pp. 507–10) that in Pico's debate on eloquence with Barbaro, elements of irony, satire and rhetorical convention make a consistently literal interpretation of his remarks problematic.

49. Bruni 1928, pp. 133–4: 'poetae quidem multa conceduntur, quo in re ficta delectet . . .; oratori autem, qui est veritatis actor, haec superflua verborum adjunctio . . . fidem rebus . . . minueret . . .'; *Prosatori latini* 1952, p. 808; *Medioevo e Rinascimento* 1955, I, p. 362 (Garin); Hubert 1949, p. 216; De Petris 1975, pp. 16–17; W. F. Edwards 1969, p. 850; Harth 1968, p. 43; Heath 1971, pp. 31, 40, 63–4; Ashworth 1974a, p. 22, 1976, p. 358; Vives 1979a, pp. 20–1.

from Petrarch to Bruni and beyond, that rhetoric could join with philosophy in a practical, persuasive wisdom.[50]

The source of this belief, of course, was Cicero, whose philosophical authority seemed as compelling to the humanists as that of Plato or Aristotle. They were aware of Cicero's achievements in translating Greek philosophy and in creating a Latin philosophical terminology; his success proved to them that his Latin was an adequate vehicle for philosophy. Eventually, however, the doctrinaire Ciceronianism that Erasmus ridiculed and the dissatisfaction of professional philosophers with Ciceronian versions more elegant than clear (Périon's *De anima* required a glossary in more familiar Latin) betrayed the shortcomings of the oratorical style.[51] Censuring Cicero for confusing Aristotle's ἐντελέχεια ('actuality') with ἐνδελέχεια ('continuity'), Argyropulos went so far as to challenge the competence of the master himself. Yet it was Cicero's professed admiration for Aristotle's eloquence that stimulated humanist translation of his works. Unaware that Cicero had found his 'golden stream of eloquence' in Aristotle's lost exoteric writings, Bruni and many others concluded from his approval of Aristotle that the Stagirite's works had been ruined by the barbarians and that his eloquence must be restored. Petrarch and George of Trebizond, however, were ambivalent about the excellence of Aristotle's style or the best way to translate it, and others simply denied that he was eloquent. Valla found his terminology in need of reform. Vives accused him of obscurantism. On the beauty of Plato's language consensus was stronger, though George of Trebizond, warning that 'too much . . . verbal embellishment and ostentatious writing destroy all solemnity', noted that the *Parmenides* was denser and more concise than other dialogues.[52]

50. *Prosatori latini* 1952, p. 596: 'Magnum ergo latini sermonis sacramentum . . . magnum profecto numen . . . sancte ac religiose per tot saecula custoditur . . .'; p. 620: 'qui ignarus eloquentiae est, hunc indignum prorsus qui de theologia loquatur existimo. Et certe soli eloquentes . . . columnae ecclesiae sunt . . .'; *Renaissance Philosophy: New Translations*, pp. 23–4 (L. Valla, 'In praise of St Thomas Aquinas'); Erasmus 1965, p. 190; Gray 1965, pp. 39–40, 45; Apel 1963, pp. 184–5; Chomarat 1981, I, pp. 166, 188, 446–9, 602, 680–1, II, pp. 799, 1123–8; Harth 1968, p. 63; Seigel 1968, pp. 6–19, 31–62, 103.

51. Bruni 1928, p. 116; *Medioevo e Rinascimento* 1955, I, pp. 343, 355 (Garin); Seigel 1968, pp. 4, 101–3; L. Jardine 1977, p. 149; Schmitt 1983a, p. 74; Birkenmajer 1922, p. 174; *Platon et Aristote* 1976, pp. 364–5 (Cranz) and pp. 383–4 (Stegmann); Erasmus 1965, pp. xxxii–xlix; Ebel 1969, p. 599.

52. George of Trebizond 1984, p. 303: 'Verborum enim ornatus et compositionis pompa, si latius confluat . . . omnem gravitatem suam infringit'; *Medioevo e Rinascimento* 1955, I, pp. 349, 353, 363, 373 (Garin); Bruni 1741, I, pp. 15–17; Cicero, *Tusculan Disputations* I.10.22 and *Academica* II.38.119; Bruni 1928, pp. 45–8, 74; Cammelli 1941–54, II, pp. 176–80; Birkenmajer 1922, p. 158; Garin 1951, pp. 57–8; *Prosatori latini* 1952, p. 58; Minio-Paluello 1972, p. 265; Breen 1968, pp. 30–1; Seigel 1968, pp. 31–62, 110, 121–2, 135; Gravelle 1972, pp. 275, 283–5; Vives 1979a, pp. 37–9; Camporeale 1972, p. 229; Chomarat 1981, I, p. 233; *Platon et Aristote* 1976, pp. 378, 388 (Stegmann); Schmitt 1983a, p. 80; Hankins 1983, p. 102.

In general, the effect of the recovery and publication of Greek philosophical texts was to encourage translations of them that were more sensitive to classical Latin style than the efforts of medieval scholars. This new emphasis on style was as much a result of attitudes towards the Greek language as of progress in Latin philology. Like the ancient Romans they admired, even those humanists who considered Latin the equal of Greek or its superior described the rival tongue in terms that hinted admiration for its powers. If Greek was prolix, it was also rich in words; if it was abstract, it was also a good tool for formal analysis. All this loose comparison, however misguided or narrowly motivated, focused the translator's attention on the formal properties of Greek and on means for achieving comparable or compensating stylistic effects in Latin translation. Valla, who passionately preferred Latin to Greek, maintained that it was a better medium for philosophy because it was concrete and that many perplexities in logic could be traced to the absence of this quality in Greek. The Byzantine George of Trebizond was equally ardent for the pre-eminence of his native tongue, and even Pier Candido Decembrio, an Italian, conceded that Aristotle 'explains weighty issues with words of such brevity that Latin words can scarcely do justice to his Greek terms, which carry more meaning'. Greek became inevitable in the humanist curriculum, and some claimed that it was indispensable for philosophy. Writing in 1520, by which time humanists had Latinised the whole Aristotelian corpus, Thomas More told Martin Dorp that 'Aristotle himself . . . could not be completely known to you without a command of Greek letters . . . for nothing of his has been so aptly translated that it would not better penetrate the mind if it were heard in his own words.'[53] More's ideal was not realised. While a university philosopher like Jacopo Zabarella might have a good command of Greek, among his colleagues it was not a universal attainment. In Oxford John Case found Hellenists to consult, but he apologised for his own Greek in trying to find stylistic grounds for calling the second book of the *Oeconomics* spurious. Philosophers commonly taught from Greek texts by the middle of the sixteenth century, but they also continued to buy Greekless Thomistic commentaries. Some reasons for the slow penetration

---

53. Hankins 1983, p. 130, n. 84: 'Ceterum res ponderosas adeo brevissimis verbis explicat Philosophus ut vix verba latina satisfaciant graeca quae significantiora sunt'; *ibid.*, pp. 96, 103; Vives 1979a, p. 192: 'Ad Aristotelem ipsum venio . . . Hic ergo ipse non poterit totus tibi sine Graecarum peritia litterarum innotescere . . . quod nihil eius tam commode versum est ut non idem ipsum suis ipsius verbis acceptum in pectus influat potentius'; Bruni 1928, pp. 102–4; Baron 1966, pp. 284–5; Garin 1951, p. 70; Camporeale 1972, pp. 173, 176–7; Gravelle 1972, pp. 269–74, 281–4; Breen 1968, p. 10; George of Trebizond 1984, pp. 143, 160, 191–2.

of Greek into the general world of philosophical discourse are evident. The
first group of Byzantines who brought Greek to the Italians might have
been regarded as incompetent Latinists even if they had succeeded in
mastering the language. Such prejudice reinforced a facile distrust of Greek
that went back to Petrarch and to Cato and was sustained by the absence of
adequate lexical and grammatical material through the fifteenth century.
Substitutes as poor as the *Graecismus* of Eberhard de Béthune or the
Derivationes of Uguccione da Pisa could only deepen the unease of Italian
scholars whose Latinity began to grow refined in the fourteenth
century.[54]

TERMINOLOGY, TRANSLITERATION AND NEOLOGISM

When preparing Chrysoloras' trip to Florence, Salutati had urged a protégé
studying with Manuel in Constantinople to 'bring as many lexical writers
(*vocabulorum auctores*) as can be obtained', but systematic help came slowly.
Working without the reference tools that modern scholars take for granted,
Traversari nearly despaired of his translation of Diogenes Laertius: 'One
stumbles into such a forest of terminology, . . . that I am almost without
hope of finding Latin words that translate the Greek and are fit for the ears of
a learned reader.'[55] George of Trebizond encountered similar difficulties
with Aristotle, but Bruni, whose experience as a translator was certainly
extensive, struck a different pose:

> I do not see how Latin letters are surpassed by Greek . . . Even if the Greek are richer
> than ours, how does this prevent us from saying elegantly in Latin just what was said
> in Greek if, instead of chasing words like boys in a game, we follow the meanings of
> what is said (*sententiae dictorum*)? If they can express anything in more ways than we
> can, this is actually a kind of superfluity and profusion, but our Latinity . . .
> certainly has its tools and equipment, not profuse, to be sure, but powerful and
> abundantly sufficient to every need.

Bruni's dispute with Alonso de Cartagena, wherein he spent pages on the
proper rendering of τἀγαθόν (see above, pp. 89–90), testifies to his sensitivity
to philosophical diction, but his use above of the game metaphor, which
implies that words are secondary tokens in the *Sprachspiel*, reveals a contrary
and eirenic inclination to forget mere verbal differences as philosophically

---

54. W. F. Edwards 1969, p. 844; Schmitt 1983b, p. 178; Stinger 1977, p. 103; B. Bischoff 1961, pp. 215–
    16; Chomarat 1981, pp. 209–11; see below, p. 107.
55. Salutati to Jacopo d'Angelo della Scarperia, cited in Cammelli 1941–54, I, p. 33: 'Platonica velim
    cuncta tecum portes et vocabulorum auctores quot haberi possunt . . .'; Traversari 1759, p. 310:
    'Tanta illic offenditur vocabulorum silva, ac praecipue in explicandis disciplinis, ut fere desperem
    Latina reperiri posse, quae Graecis reddita erudito lectori aures impleant'; Ullman 1963, pp. 118–24;
    De Petris 1975, p. 20; Stinger 1977, p. 72.

unimportant.[56] One side of the coin that Bruni struck purchased the conciliatory response of those sixteenth-century editions which, like Giulio Pace's *Organon*, provided philological notes offering a choice of readings and versions for difficult words. The obverse, polemical mood issued in Périon's Ciceronianism, which was impoverished philosophically. Though Périon's work was philologically fruitful, leading to the Ciceronian lexica of Henri Estienne and Alexander Scot, it forced philosophical translators to choose either responsivity to the literary fashions of one century or responsibility to an intellectual tradition of seventeen centuries.[57]

Since so many readers of Latin philosophical translations were practitioners or students of philosophy, Périon's fate was settled on practical, professional grounds, but the context for his wish to produce a Ciceronian Aristotle was polemic. The relevant debates were not only the famous controversies involving Gianfrancesco Pico, Pietro Bembo and Erasmus but also the smaller struggles, private and public, spontaneously provoked by the role of revision in philosophical translation. The decision to revise or replace a translation often moved the reviser to belittle it. Opportunities to conceive of one's revision as the latest and crucial improvement in a series of translations increased as the new printing technology permitted the multiplication and wide diffusion of editions, but the growth of polemic did not wait on these changes. At mid-century, Theodore Gaza dedicated to Nicholas V his version of the same books of Aristotle that George of Trebizond had already presented to the pope. His justification was that previous translators had 'either said in Greek what Latin people want to hear in Latin or wrongly applied the word for one thing to something else or clumsily invented new words on their own, and they distorted the meaning of the author throughout . . .'. It was clear to contemporaries that Gaza was thinking as much of his countryman George of Trebizond as of the scorned barbarians. Gaza's charges of transliteration and neologism, faults bitterly criticised in medieval versions, rubbed salt in his rival's wounds.[58]

56. Bruni 1928, pp. 103–4: 'non video qua in re Latinae litterae a Graecis superentur . . . etsi uberiores sunt Graecae quam nostrae, quid tamen vetat, si non verba ut pueri in ludo sed sententias dictorum sequamur, posse cum elegantia id ipsum Latine dicere quod dictum sit Graece? Nam si pluribus modis illi quam nos quidlibet exprimere possunt, est illa quidem superabundantia quaedam atque luxuries, Latinitas vero nostra . . . mundum certe habet et supellectilem suam, non luxuriosam quidem, sed tamen opulentam et quae ad omnem usum abunde sufficiat'; cf. *ibid.*, pp. 27–8; Garin 1951, p. 77; Seigel 1968, pp. 104–5; George of Trebizond 1984, p. 142.

57. Schmitt 1983a, pp. 43, 48, 76; *Platon et Aristote* 1976, pp. 387–9 (Stegmann).

58. Garin 1951, pp. 76–81: 'Aut enim graece illi dixere quae latine audire homines Latini desiderant, aut rerum aliarum nomina aliis improprie tribuerunt, aut nova ipsi inepte finxerunt. Sententiam vero auctoris passim . . . depravarunt . . .'; Erasmus 1965, pp. xxxii–xlix; Seigel 1968, p. 119; Schmitt 1983a, pp. 65–6; Eisenstein 1979, pp. 107–11; George of Trebizond 1984, pp. 107, 132–4, 163, 165, 411, 707–9.

Actually, as George was aware, it was no barbarian but Cicero himself
who had set the guidelines for creating philosophical terminology through
neologisms and transliterations of Greek into Latin. In the dialogue of the
Academica, he represented the learned lexicographer Varro as promising to

> speak Latin except where custom already prescribes words like *philosophia* or . . .
> *dialectica* . . . Thus, what the Greeks call ποιότητες, which is a philosophical rather
> than an ordinary word in Greek, I have named 'qualities' . . . None of the logicians'
> terms is common. They use their own – nearly a universal practice in the arts. For
> new names must be given to new things or else they must be transferred from
> elsewhere . . . If this is what the Greeks do in [philosophy,] at which they have
> laboured for ages, how much more should be allowed to us, who are only now
> beginning to try to deal with it? . . . Therefore, . . . with your approval we will
> venture to use new words if it is necessary.

Cicero wrote that Varro 'would earn the thanks of [his] countrymen if [he]
were to enlarge their supply (*copia*) not only of facts but also of words'.[59]
Though the Latin resources of the translator of the *Ethica nova* were not
Varro's or Cicero's, his rendering (see above, pp. 89–90) of Aristotle's
προαίρεσις ('purposeful, morally significant choice') as *proheresis* was
similarly motivated. Such transliteration, whose necessity to the growth of
Latin terminology Cicero had conceded, was a hallmark of medieval
translation from Greek. Medieval writers also extended the philosophical
reference of classical Latin terms, as when translators of the *De anima* used
forma and *species* to distinguish real from intentional aspects of εἶδος, a
difference expressed in neither of the ancient tongues. Thus, transliteration
was not the only way of neologising, but it was the most conspicuous, and
so it attracted comment from the humanists. Vives objected that words
newly devised or newly applied were private language: 'No one but the
person who invented them can understand many of these expressions.' But
George of Trebizond, who believed that much philosophical Greek was
untranslatable, called transliteration an index of good translation. Valla,
arguing that language was conventional and mutable, echoed Cicero's

---

59. *Academica* I.7.25: 'enitar ut Latine loquar nisi in huiuscemodi verbis, ut philosophiam aut . . .
dialecticam . . . quibus ut aliis multis consuetudo iam utitur pro Latinis. Qualitates igitur appellavi
quas ποιότητας Graeci vocant, quod ipsum apud Graecos non est vulgi verbum sed philosophorum
. . . Dialectorum vero verba nulla sunt publica; suis utuntur. Et id quidem commune omnium fere
est artium. Aut enim nova sunt rerum novarum facienda nomina aut ex aliis transferenda. Quod si
Graeci faciunt qui in his rebus tot iam saecula versantur, quanto id magis nobis concedendum est qui
haec nunc primum tractare conamur? Tu vero, inquam, Varro, bene etiam meriturus mihi videris
de tuis civibus si eos non modo copia rerum auxeris . . . sed etiam verborum. Audebimus ergo,
inquit, novis verbis uti, te auctore, si necesse erit'; cf. *Academica* II.6.17; *De optimo genere oratorum*
VII.23; *De finibus* III.1.3–2.5; Quintilian, II.14.1–4; Eucken 1879, pp. 52–4; Gravelle 1972, p. 274;
George of Trebizond 1984, p. 143.

point that 'a new object requires a new term'. Even Erasmus condoned coining in moderation, and the practice is evident in several non-Byzantine translators of the fifteenth century: P. C. Decembrio, Antonio Cassarino and Ficino, for example. Vernacular translators in particular were keenly aware of the benefits of neologism, although Dolet preferred non-Latinate coinages. Dolet would have been pleased with Ralph Lever's extraordinary *Witcraft*, an English logic manual in which 'proposition' became 'saying', 'predicate' became 'backset' and 'category' became 'storehouse'.[60]

In his debate with Bruni, Alonso de Cartagena made the strongest case for neologising: 'Latin would be impoverished and altogether destitute if it were closed within set limits. But its potential is enormous and nearly infinite; it can take whatever it wants not just from the Greeks but from . . . every people of the world.' Alonso knew that a philologically rigid Latin was philosophically dead, a point whose wider application came to be generally appreciated through the Ciceronian controversy. This lesson of the *Ciceronianus* will not have been lost on the sixteenth-century translators and editors who, like Michael Sophianus, wished to preserve their terminological access to the medieval tradition. Preparing his *De anima* for the Giunta Aristotle–Averroes of 1552, Sophianus wrote that he had translated 'moderately . . . so as not to move far from the structure of the old translation and the accustomed terminology of the schools'.[61] Bruni's very different reaction to Alonso's brief for verbal invention came in an earlier time, before argument and experience had soiled the toga of the heroic Ciceronian orator. Bruni applauded Cicero's neologising but condemned it in medieval translators; they invented out of ignorance, he out of a perfect command of his mother tongue and of Greek. In *De interpretatione recta*, Bruni scolded the barbarians for

leaving words in Greek . . ., so many that a . . . translation seems semi-Greek. Yet nothing has been said in Greek which cannot be said in Latin! I will, nevertheless, permit some few strange and recondite terms if they cannot be readily translated into Latin, but where we have perfectly good words it is the height of ignorance to

60. Vives 1979a, p. 52: 'Sunt enim pleraque, quae nosse nemo potest nisi is qui confinxit . . .'; L. Valla 1962, I, p. 504: 'nova res novum vocabulum flagitat'; Pouilloux 1969, pp. 50–1; Ebel 1969, p. 596; *Platon et Aristote* 1976, pp. 360, 369–71 (Cranz); Dunbabin 1972, p. 466; Minio-Paluello 1972, p. 189; Hubert 1949, p. 220; Dewan 1982, pp. 37–96; Gravelle 1972, p. 278; Stinger 1977, p. 72; Percival 1975, p. 255; Waswo 1979, p. 260; Chomarat 1981, II, pp. 722–3; Erasmus 1965, p. 148; Hankins 1983, pp. 95–6, 103, 150–1, 208; Howell 1956, pp. 57–63.
61. Birkenmajer 1922, p. 168: 'inops namque esset et prorsus egena si certis finibus clauderetur. Sed ingens et paene infinita est potentia eius, et nedum a Graecis sed a barbaris et universis mundi nationibus quicquid ei libet licet accipere'; Aristotle 1562–74, III, p. 2: 'ita me temperavi ut non ita longe me a ratione veteris interpretationis et usitatis scholarum vocabulis removerim'; *Platon et Aristote* 1976, p. 363 (Cranz).

leave them in Greek. For why would you leave me with *politia* in Greek when you can and should say it with the Latin word *res publica*? Why force *oligarchia*, *democratia* and *aristocratia* upon me in a thousand places. . . .? Our Latin authors have said *paucorum potentia* and *popularis status* and *optimorum gubernatio.*

The very durability of the words Bruni wished to replace by clumsy periphrasis proves Alonso's point and shows how little Bruni yielded to what Philipp Melanchthon was to call 'new and prodigious fancies and monstrous expressions'.[62]

ORDINARY LANGUAGE, JARGON AND BARBARISM

Part of Alonso's defence of medieval transliteration was the claim that there was 'common and public use (*usus*) . . . of many Greek words' not just in learned discourse but also in the 'language of the uneducated' and 'vulgar idiom', but his examples – *grammatica, logica, rhetorica, philosophia* and *theologia* – show that Alonso was thinking of the common talk of scholars, not of ordinary language.[63] He and Sophianus found the jargon of the schools useful and indispensable, yet it was precisely to a criterion of *usus* that Bruni also appealed, for it sharply distinguished his philological approach to translation from Alonso's formalism. In the preface to his version of the *Nicomachean Ethics*, Bruni asked why the medieval translator had

departed from the customary speech (*usus loquendi*) of Cicero, Seneca, Boethius, Lactantius, Jerome and other writers of our language . . . I believe . . . that he has never read them, that he has taken the words *delectatio* [instead of *voluptas* for ἡδονή] and *tristitia* [instead of *dolor* for ἄλγος] from the common people (*vulgus*), but he ought to have read those most uncommon authors for the common people have by no means proved expert in speaking.[64]

62. Bruni 1928, p. 95: 'Quid de verbis in Graeco relictis dicam, quae tam multa sunt ut semigraeca quaedam eius interpretatio videatur? Atqui nihil Graece dictum est quod Latine dici non possit! Et tamen dabo veniam in quibusdam paucis admodum peregrinis et reconditis si nequeant commode in Latinum traduci. Enim vero quorum optima habemus vocabula, ea in Graeco relinquere ignorantissimum est. Quid enim tu mihi "politiam" relinquis in Graeco cum possis et debeas Latino verbo "rem publicam" dicere? Cur tu mihi "oligarchiam" et "democratiam" et "aristocratiam" mille locis inculcas? . . . Latini enim nostri "paucorum potentiam" et "popularem statum" et "optimorum gubernationem" dixerunt'; Gravelle 1972, p. 275; Schmitt 1983a, p. 68; Breen 1968, p. 39.
63. Birkenmajer 1922, pp. 167–8: 'nedum in omnibus fere scientiis et artibus sed in communi ac forensi usu loquendi non paucis verbis utamur Graecis . . . iam tam doctorum quam indoctorum linguis contrita sub vulgari idiomate comprehendi credantur'; Garin 1951, p. 64.
64. Birkenmajer 1922, 160–1: 'Primum quaero quae causa fuerit ab usu loquendi Ciceronis, Senecae, Boëthii, Lactantii, Hieronymi et aliorum nostrorum recedendi. Respondebit credo, si vera fateri volet, numquam se istos legisse, "delectationis" autem et "tristitiae" verba e vulgo sumpsisse. At

His claim that *usus* was the right criterion for philosophical diction became a fundamental humanist position: Valla spoke of *usus, consuetudo* and *sermo communis*, Vives of *usus loquendi communis, loquentium consensus* and *sensus communis*. Although notions of custom, mutuality and intelligibility were implied generally in this terminology, the humanists differed among themselves on the kind of language that had these properties – perhaps because the classical authorities were themselves unclear. Bruni had precedent in Cicero for excluding ordinary talk from a linguistic *usus* that would be of use to philosophical translators, but Cicero had also criticised philosophers for writing abstrusely, and this oratorical zeal for a genuinely communicative language lay behind Valla's contempt for 'the philosopher who disregards use and custom in speaking'. For Bruni the only valid *usus* was that of 'the best authors' – a norm also found in medieval writers like John of Salisbury – but Valla, who believed that all oratory must have the power of public address, was willing to take his evidence of linguistic custom from a wider, public sphere of discourse. 'People speak better than philosophers', he wrote, 'and the greatest authors agree with them . . .'[65]

This quarrel over the domain of *usus* was related to a larger debate about the uses of philosophy and to one of its most prominent episodes, the Pico–Barbaro–Melanchthon correspondence. Was the philosopher a teacher whose ideas might lead to public action, as Melanchthon proposed, or was Pico correct in making philosophy esoteric, exclusive, contemplative? If the latter, then either Alonso's technical formalism or Bruni's élitist classicising would seem appropriate, for both their audiences were composed of specialists. But if the ambitions of philosophy were public, as those of oratory were supposed to be, then Vives would be right in demanding that the 'dialectician . . . use those words, those phrases which anyone will understand who knows the language that he speaks' and that 'the philosopher as much as he can . . . should express what he says in language and words taken from the people'. Railing against professional logicians, Vives called it 'lucky for these men that they still dispute . . . in some semblance of Latin speech, for if such madness were understood by the common people, the whole mob of workmen would hoot them out of

enim hos praestantissimos viros legisse oportuit; nam vulgus quidem haudquaquam probatus est loquendi magister.'
65. L. Valla 1962, I, p. 658: 'Quis enim dixerit . . . nisi philosophus, usum consuetudinemque loquendi pro nihilo habens?'; *ibid.*, p. 685: 'Melius igitur populus quam philosophus loquitur, cum quo summi quique autores consentiunt . . .'; Vives 1979a, p. 57; Vasoli 1957, p. 430; Percival 1975, pp. 254–5; Seigel 1968, pp. 24–7, 163; Kelley 1970a, pp. 28–9; Camporeale 1972, pp. 150–1, 190; Waswo 1980, pp. 601, 605; Trentman 1968, p. 288.

town . . . with hisses, shouts and banging of their tools'.[66] His bitter joke unwittingly reveals why any clear conception of ordinary language as the domain of *usus* was impossible in the early modern period – for the humanists or for their opponents. At some level Vives understood that incomprehension must be the response of an untutored public not only to the jargon of the 'pseudodialecticians' but to any learned Latin, his own included. The range of scholastic Latin was confined by the philosophical requirement for a specialist terminology and a formal notation (*formaliter loqui*), though the attempt of philosophical grammarians to make medieval Latin its own metalanguage actually impaired effective formalisation. The range of humanist Latin, even if emancipated from Ciceronianism, was defined and made finite by a classical authority that resisted terminological growth. A philosophy expressed in either kind of Latin was lost on those who knew only the younger vernaculars. Thus, while oratorical humanism strongly wished to be communicative, it did not actually speak to many people, and even those who insisted most zealously on an enlarged domain for *usus* had second thoughts. Vives confessed that

> the uneducated common people sometimes misuse [the meanings of words and] in ordinary speech people with more education make what allowances they can for the common folk, though among themselves they think and speak differently . . . mainly about obscure, philosophical matters which the people do not grasp as precisely as they are understood by philosophers.

Though it was scarcely democratic, the oratorical view of language that Vives preached was humanising inasmuch as it sought to regulate speech through the study of human artifacts, the classical texts, not through rules abstractly derived. Man makes his words, but he formulates his linguistic conventions in historical circumstances whose contingency constrains all who become party to the language contract.[67]

Bruni maintained that the meaning (*significatio*) of a word could be learnt from its denotation (*vis*) or from its use (*usus*): understanding *vis* required

---

66. Vives 1979a, pp. 52–4: 'Dialecticus enim iis uti debet verbis, iis enuntiationibus quas nemo non intelligat qui sciat linguam illam qua is loquitur . . . praeclare agitur cum istis hominibus quod disputant . . . aliqua . . . specie sermonis latini, nam si a vulgo tales dementiae intelligerentur, tota opificum turba illos e civitate supploderet sibilis, clamoribus strepituque suorum instrumentorum eiiceret'; Vives 1782–90, III, p. 193: 'philosophus . . . quae dicat ea, quoad eius facere poterit, lingua et verbis de vulgo sumtis eloquatur . . .'; Waswo 1980, p. 605; Breen 1968, pp. 15–68 *passim*.
67. Vives 1979a, p. 68: 'sunt et vocibus sua significata, suae vires, quibus nonnunquam indoctior ipsa multitudo abutitur. Doctiores indulgent utcunque plebi in sermonis usu, ipsi inter se et aliter sentiunt et loquuntur . . et fere in philosophicis abditisque sint rebus, quas ipse populus non ita exacte callet ut a philosophis intelliguntur'; *ibid.*, pp. 55, 67, 169, 175; Waswo 1979, p. 256; Ashworth 1974a, pp. 8–9, 26–7; Bursill-Hall 1975, pp. 209–12; Hubert 1949, pp. 212–15.

etymological analysis of the word, while *usus* was investigated by discovering instances (*testimonia*) of its occurrence in texts. The latter procedure, synthetic and inductive, became the favourite of the humanists in grammar and lexicography. On the other hand, the modist philosophical grammars of the later Middle Ages, which were not written for literary use, treated language analytically, and they assumed a set of correspondences between metaphysical structures (substance/accident), universal linguistic structures (noun/adjective) and particular linguistic structures (*homo/ philosophicus*). Once the timeless structures of the universal language were uncovered, language rules could in theory be formulated to represent them; in practice, however, since there was only one tongue available to the modists, the actual features of Latin tended to blur into the ideal features of language-in-general. This confusion impeded the search of the modists for a rational grammar and made their approach to language a scandal to the humanists, who rejected philosophical grammars with rules designed by logicians and metaphysicians and replaced them with philological grammars based on the literary and historical study of Greek and Latin texts. Valla, in a 'rhetorical nominalism' that resembled earlier nominalist attacks on the modists, ventured a radical reversal of the traditional assumption that reality governed language. And in a dispute with Poggio, who was offended by his remark that St Jerome 'preferred to speak Latin rather than grammar', Valla gave impetus to the humanist revival of the non-philosophical and literary functions of the grammarian. Alexander Hegius, the teacher of Erasmus, proclaimed that the grammarian was a teacher who understood how to speak and write correctly, not a contemplative who perverted normal usage in a quest for esoteric, philosophical truth. The first step in finding correct usage was to go back to the grammarians of late antiquity, Donatus and Priscian; the next was to develop new grammars synthetically by reading the *auctores*. Logic and metaphysics continued to influence humanist grammars, but their role was much diminished until J. C. Scaliger revived an Aristotelian philosophy of language in his *De causis linguae latinae*.[68]

By the time Scaliger published in 1540, the humanist polemic against philosophical grammar had driven from the market not only relatively specialised works like that of Michel de Marbais on the *modi significandi* but

68. Birkenmajer 1922, p. 202; Heath 1971, pp. 18, 45–7; Bursill-Hall 1975, pp. 198–214; Percival 1975, pp. 240–7; Camporeale 1972, p. 149; Kelley 1970a, pp. 32–3; Padley 1976, pp. 58–62; IJsewijn 1971, p. 301; Chomarat 1981, I, pp. 22, 153, 165, 215–24, 232, 259–62, 275–6, 446–9, 602, 608, 680–1, II, pp. 799, 842, 1123–8.

even the very popular *Doctrinale* of Alexandre de Villedieu. The *Doctrinale*, written around 1200, long remained so basic a university text for first-year grammar that it saw more than two hundred editions by 1525. Before this decade, grammar was effectively a prerequisite to the dialectic of Peter of Spain's *Summule*, which was itself presented as a study of language. Afterwards, the fashionable humanist manuals eroded this curricular link between grammar and philosophy, though in the meantime Valla and Rudolph Agricola had begun to forge a new bond between rhetoric and dialectic which envisioned a pragmatic role for the latter discipline much more to the taste of oratorical humanism than traditional, technical logic. This new marriage of the ancient members of the *trivium* would lead eventually to the *Dialectique* of Petrus Ramus, a minimalist logic entirely at the service of clear and simple pedagogy.[69]

The success of the scholastics, limited as it was, in constructing a philosophical language capable of formalism, abstraction and fine analysis was to many humanists an anathema. They denounced as barbarous and obscurantist formal devices such as using alphabetical variables to replace terms or writing the romance article 'ly' to mark words used as terms. They believed that the scholastic method of analysis by distinction was an invitation to sophistry and rancour. Valla, in particular, found the very idea of abstraction inimical to sound thinking about language, which he required to be empirical and synthetic. Assailing what he took to be a false distinction between abstract *forma* and concrete *figura* in the familiar hylemorphic statue of the Aristotelians, Valla railed against 'the Peripatetic breed . . . perverter of natural meanings'.[70] The refinements of later medieval logic seemed a special affront to the 'natural' Latin diction and syntax of the *summi auctores*. The exaggeration and artificiality of Vives' mockery of *sophismata* extracted from context does not much dilute his point; he caricatured sentences in his *Adversus pseudodialecticos* that are hard to take in any language; this one, for example:

Only any non-donkey *c* of any man except Sortes and another *c* belonging to this same man begins contingently to be black.[71]

69. Heath 1971, pp. 11–19; Percival 1975, pp. 240–5; Ashworth 1974a, pp. 10–17, 22; Chomarat 1981, 1, pp. 204–9; L. Jardine 1974a, pp. 19–25.
70. L. Valla 1962, 1, p. 673: 'O depravatrix naturalium significationum peripatetica natio'; Kelley 1970a, p. 29; Vives 1979a, pp. 10, 13–16, 21–2, 61, 65, 93; Hubert 1949, p. 222; Camporeale 1972, p. 176; N. W. Gilbert 1971, pp. 216–17; L. Jardine 1974a, p. 23.
71. Vives 1979a, p. 52: 'Tantum cuiuslibet hominis praeter Sortem quilibet non asinus *c* et alterum *c* ipsiusmet hominis nigrum contingenter incipit esse'; cf. *ibid.*, p. 53; Vives 1979b, p. 32; Ashworth 1974a, pp. 8–9.

Although some humanists were less hostile than others to scholasticism and its Latin – of which the above is by no means typical – a tradition well established since Petrarch's time inclined many to find the speech of medieval philosophers bizarre and ugly. Some of what seemed absurd or frivolous in scholastic language, like the strange *sophismata* concocted to teach the doctrine of fallacies, grew out of specific technical requirements in logic, but the humanists found the price of such progress too high. Since the fourteenth century, when Petrarch had warned of 'a new kind of monster armed with double-edged enthymemes', humanists had associated the logic that repelled them with aliens, Britons and Teutons, who excelled at it. Even the names of the foreigners came to stand for their grotesque way of talking – *quisquiliae suicetiae* ('suicetial garbage').[72]

When Vives made fun of 'that monstrous terminology [of] *tantum, alter, alius, uterque, incipit, desinit* [and] *immediate*', he was chipping away at the linguistic foundations of one of the major components of the *logica moderna*, the analysis of syncategorematic terms. Doing away with clumsy language meant either abandoning the philosophy it expressed or rebuilding the terminological base. Humanists, in fact, attempted such reconstruction in various ways, none of them altogether enduring. Some were superficial. Titles of familiar works, for example, could become more stylish, as when *De generatione et corruptione* begat *De ortu et interitu*. Others were more systematic but still not philosophically motivated. As part of his larger Ciceronian campaign, Périon tried to beautify commonplace logical expressions, making the syllogism a *ratiocinatio* and a circular argument a *mutua probatio*.[73] But the boldest venture in terminological reform was Valla's, a philological *coup d'état* which sought to ban from philosophical discourse any expressions that violated grammar – not the rules of a philosophical grammar constructed *a priori* but the experience of a humanist grammar derived from reading classical Latin texts. The terminology that Valla proscribed or revised was not trivial. It included the categories, the transcendentals, syncategorematic terms, modal propositions and the whole class of abstractions ending in *-itas*. A successful critique of these long-accustomed words, resulting in their simplification and replacement, would have endangered not only philosophical doctrines as central as

72. Seigel 1968, pp. 65–7, 80–1, 232, 237–9; N. W. Gilbert 1971, pp. 204, 210, 216–17, 219, 224; Vives 1979a, pp. 3–7, 11–12; *Prosatori latini* 1952, pp. 56–8; Harth 1968, p. 43; *Platon et Aristote* 1976, p. 360 (Cranz); Breen 1968, pp. 11f.; *Renaissance Philosophy of Man* 1948, p. 135.
73. Vives 1979a, pp. 5–8, 48, 214; *Platon et Aristote* 1976, p. 378 (Stegmann); Schmitt 1983a, pp. 75–6, 86–7.

hylemorphism and four-term causality but also theological dogmas as important as Providence and the Trinity. In effect, Valla's insistence that philosophy should not be done without philology meant that scholastic philosophy was not to be done at all. Two centuries before Descartes, Europe was not ready for Valla's revolution. His scrapping of the categories provoked heresy charges, and his greatest work of philosophy, the important and difficult *Disputationes dialecticae*, went unprinted for seven decades after its composition.[74]

HUMANISM AND THE PHILOSOPHICAL LEXICON

Unlike Valla's project to govern philosophy with philology, the more effective changes in philosophical terminology during the early modern period were evolutionary. They were aided by the accomplishments of humanism in translation, grammar and lexicography, but most were not the effects of a partisan ideology like Valla's or a public movement like Ciceronianism. It was the more diffuse humanist conviction that the good fight was against barbarism that had a direct and lasting influence on the development of a post-medieval language for philosophy, and it was Bruni who best explained what philosophy had at stake in this struggle:

In this great shipwreck of all learning, in this great dearth of learned men, how could it be that these know-nothing [philosophers] . . ., who know no Latin literature, much less Greek, would not be ignorant of . . . [Aristotle]? It is impossible . . . that they understand anything well, especially since these books which they say are Aristotle's have suffered such a transformation that if anyone brought them to Aristotle himself he would no more recognize them for his own than Actaeon's dogs knew him after he was changed into a deer.[75]

When the barbarians emasculated letters they had also unmanned philosophy, whose hope therefore lay in a reinvigoration of learning. Valla's historical vision of the calamity was well defined. The last learned Romans were Donatus, Servius and Priscian. Isidore and Boethius announced the

74. Camporeale 1972, pp. 8, 38–42, 60–2, 105–6, 151–66, 175–6; Vasoli 1957, pp. 425–31; Kelley 1970a, pp. 30–1; Gravelle 1972, pp. 283–5; L. Jardine 1977, p. 158; cf. Ashworth 1974a, p. 10; Stinger 1977, p. 112.
75. *Prosatori latini* 1952, p. 58: 'Quem igitur philosophum ipsi philosophi . . . eo tempore ignorabant . . . cum in hoc tanto doctrinarum omnium naufragio, in hac tanta doctorum hominum penuria, isti nihil sapientes homines, quibus nedum graecae, sed ne latinae quidem litterae satis cognitae sunt, non ignorabunt? Fieri non potest . . . ut illi quicquam recte teneant, praesertim cum hi libri, quos Aristotelis esse dicunt, tam magnam transformationem passi sunt, ut si quis eos ad Aristotelem ipsum deferat, non magis ille suos esse cognoscat quam Actaeonem illum, qui ex homine in cervum conversus est, canes suae cognoverint.'

age of ignorance. 'After this', wrote Valla, 'Papias and others more unlearned, Eberhard de Béthune, Uguccione da Pisa, *Catholicon*, Aymo and others not worth naming taught ignorance at great cost and sent away the student stupider then when he came.'[76] These primitive word-lists that Valla denounced, products of the eleventh to the thirteenth centuries, continued to be used in the age of printing, but the humanists badly wanted to replace them, first by recovering Varro, Festus, Nonius Marcellus and the other classical lexicographers and then by compiling their own dictionaries. The two most important humanist lexicons of the fifteenth century, the *De orthographia* (1449) of Giovanni Tortelli and the *Cornucopiae* (1478) of Niccolò Perotti, were primarily of literary interest, but they did advance Europe's general command of Latin, which progressed even further with the work of the Estiennes in the next century. Tortelli's work, devoted to the spelling of Greek words in Latin and equipped with long historical articles on Greek philosophers, schools and divisions of philosophy, was the more significant for philosophical terminology and the new consciousness of its Greek origins. The Greek in the medieval lexicons, disfigured by far-fetched etymological speculations, was a joke to the humanists, who, like Traversari or Ficino, sometimes compiled their own word-lists out of the Septuagint or Julius Pollux or other sources. They lacked a really useful Greek dictionary until the work of Varinus Favorinus in 1523. Five decades later, Henri Estienne completed his *Thesaurus linguae Graecae*, which is still consulted. Specialised dictionaries of philosophy also first appeared in print in the late sixteenth century, inspired, perhaps, by the *tabulae* keyed to Aristotle editions by Marcantonio Zimara. The first of these new compendia was the *Seminarium totius philosophiae* (1582–5) of Giovanni Battista Bernardi, followed by a dozen other major Latin dictionaries of philosophy published in the early eighteenth century.[77]

One of the most influential was the *Lexicon philosophicum* (1613–15) of Rudolphus Goclenius the Elder. The first part of the *Lexicon* devoted 1,143 pages to articles on Latin words, parts of words and phrases significant in

---

76. *Prosatori latini* 1952, p. 602: 'Post hunc Papias aliique indoctiores, Hebrardus, Hugutio, *Catholicon*, Aymo, et ceteri indigni qui nominentur, magna mercede docentes nihil scire, aut stultiorem reddentes discipulum quam acceperunt'; Percival 1976, pp. 79–81; Chomarat 1981, I, pp. 184–8.
77. Tortelli 1501, ff. 24^r, 28^v, 34, 40, 57, 64, 67^r, 86^v, 126^r–7^v; Perotti 1517; IJsewijn 1971, pp. 302–3, 310, 314; P. S. Allen 1914, pp. 36–55; Grubmüller 1967, pp. 13–33; Birkenmajer 1922, p. 168; Percival 1975, pp. 233, 238; Chomarat 1981, I, pp. 192–201, 212–14; Korshin 1974, pp. 306–7; Wilamowitz-Moellendorf 1982, p. 54; Oliver 1953, pp. 1257–71; Epictetus 1954, pp. 6, 11–15, 146; Rinaldi 1973, pp. 227–31, 259–60; Cortesi 1979, p. 464; B. Bischoff 1961, pp. 215–16; Stinger 1977, p. 19; Pintaudi 1977, pp. 9–14, 23–9; Geanakoplos 1962, pp. 121, 154, 220, 286; Schmitt 1983a, pp. 56–9, 101–2; Gerber 1967, pp. 174–7.

logic, metaphysics, ethics and psychology and also in subjects (music, astronomy, biology, pharmacy) now divorced from philosophy. Entries, arranged in two separate alphabetical series for vowels and consonants, varied in length from a paragraph to twenty pages or more. Longer articles were accompanied by the bifurcating charts made popular by the Ramists. Goclenius wrote historical sketches of movements, schools and ideas but dealt only incidentally with biography.[78] The second part of his work, a *Lexicon philosophicum graecum*, gave most of its 362 pages to an alphabetical Greek glossary, but in the last eighty pages – very much in the spirit of humanism – Goclenius surveyed neologisms, barbarisms and other words identified as obsolete or not well received.[79] Valla would have admired his identifying *acceptibilitas* as 'scholastic' and his recommending a five-word periphrasis for the unclassical *possibilitas*, but not his comment on the equally dubious *activitas*: 'I tolerate these things in philosophical disputations because the philosophers have their own diction ($\lambda \acute{\epsilon} \xi \iota s$).' Such pragmatic concessions to specialist jargon compromised the philological ideal, but they also sustained terminological growth without surrendering all claims to normative and prescriptive judgement. When Goclenius recommended a list of alternatives for the neologism $\dot{a}\mu\epsilon\vartheta\acute{o}\delta\iota\kappa os$, he noted that 'all these are Ciceronian'.[80]

'Amethodic' has not survived, but its cousin, 'method', made a brilliant if erratic career in early modern philosophy. Plato and Aristotle used $\mu\acute{\epsilon}\vartheta o\delta os$ in technical applications, which Cicero understood but preferred to render with a Latin periphrasis, *via et ratio*. Medieval Latin versions of Aristotle sometimes transliterated $\mu\acute{\epsilon}\vartheta o\delta os$, sometimes (see above, pp. 89–90) avoided it, but medieval instances of the transliteration did not carry the technical weight of the Greek word, which continued to be expressed by Latin phrases like *via doctrinae*. Thus, when humanist translators shunned the transliteration (above, pp. 89–90), their respect for Ciceronian precedent had been reinforced by the technical poverty of medieval occurrences of the term. In passages of the *Politics* where William of Moerbeke wrote *methodus* in Latin, Bruni resorted to six unrelated words – *doctrina, labor, disciplina, praecedens, materia* and *tractatus* – and Lambin rang the changes on *institutio, disputatio* and *docendi ratio*. Ironically, the very success of the humanists in making Greek familiar to European philosophy broke down this resistance,

78. Goclenius 1613, pp. 87–9, 106–8, 124, 132–3, 144–6, 170–89, 283, 334–8, 344–5, 386–9.
79. Goclenius 1615, pp. 282–362.
80. Goclenius 1615, p. 285: 'ego ista tolero in disputationibus philosophicis cum sua sit $\lambda \acute{\epsilon} \xi \iota s$ philosophi'; *ibid.*, pp. 287–8, 325.

even as it continued to be expressed by recalcitrants like Mario Nizolio. Perotti, who defined *methodus* more in the manner of John of Salisbury than of Plato, at least recognised the word, and Guillaume Budé's fuller description found its way into Henri Estienne's *Thesaurus*. After mid-century it entered the English vernacular in technical philosophical senses. Goclenius defined it as 'any system of teaching . . . or the order of a whole art . . . whereby the parts of the art are explained'.[81]

Goclenius codified other, lesser known terms of philosophical interest – 'theory', 'criterion', 'phenomenon' – which emerged from the fuller humanist consciousness of Greek and managed eventually to overcome the absence or weakness of precedent in classical and medieval Latin.[82] Victorious neologisms named the divisions of philosophy. Tortelli recognised *metaphysica*, a common medieval word unknown to the Latin *auctores*, while Quintilian had used *dialectice*, which gained ground over *logica* in the fifteenth century because Valla liked it. *Cosmologia, ontologia, psychologia* and their vernacular derivatives first appeared in the early modern period, while 'aesthetics' and 'epistemology' were more distant echoes of humanism in the eighteenth and nineteenth centuries.[83] Philosophical schools and controversial positions were also named in the Renaissance or because of it. We owe 'scepticism' to Traversari's translation of Diogenes Laertius. Classical Latin referred only indirectly to atheism with the transliterations *atheos* or *atheus*, epithets of the poet Diagoras and of Theodorus of Cyrene; *atheos* was still the lemma for the article in which Goclenius discussed *atheismus* although vernacular analogues of problematic reference were known in the sixteenth century. *Atheus* appeared rarely in Renaissance Latin and almost always as a personal designation for a notorious unbeliever in God's existence. *Impius, impietas* and various paraphrases normally rendered other uses of ἄθεος and its cognates, as when they referred pejoratively to polytheism from a monotheist point of view – or the reverse.[84] Some terms seem to have grown out of a more complex interaction of Greek with Latin. There is no *speculatio* or *speculativus* in ancient Latin, where a *speculator* is a spy or lookout, but Perotti associated the adjective with *theorice* as the part of

---

81. Goclenius 1613, p. 683: 'omnis docendi ratio . . . sive ordo totius artis . . . quo partes artis explicantur'; Perotti 1517, p. 691; N. W. Gilbert 1960, pp. xxii–xxiii, 6, 39–66; L. Jardine 1974a, pp. 26–47, 51, 54–5.
82. Goclenius 1613, pp. 491–2; Goclenius 1615, pp. 101–2, 255–6; Micraelius 1662, sigs. T2ᵛ–3, Qqq4ʳ; Eucken 1879, pp. 16–17, 27, 105.
83. Quintilian, II.17.42; Tortelli 1501, ff. 63ʳ, 68ᵛ, 126ᵛ; Perotti 1517, p. 200; Goclenius 1613, p. 707; Ashworth 1974a, p. 22; Michaud-Quantin 1969; Lapointe 1973, pp. 138–47; Eucken 1879, pp. 75, 133–4, 188; MacIntyre 1967.
84. Tortelli 1501, f. 42ᵛ; Goclenius 1615, p. 3; Bianca 1980b; Febvre 1947, pp. 124–42, 440.

an *ars* not involving action, and the *Lexicon philosophicum* of Johannes Micraelius likewise defined the noun by reference to θεωρία.[85] In natural philosophy, the weightiest known result of such cross-breeding involved the Latin *momentum* and the Greek ῥοπή, both terms of wide reference. Classical usage of *momentum* might have helped medieval translators of ῥοπή ('weight', 'critical increment of weight') in Aristotle's *Physics* because part of that usage was physical, referring to weight and the exertion of weight or force. But during the Middle Ages temporal meanings of *momentum* ('moment of time') had crowded out reference to weight as a cause of movement (*moveo*), so medieval versions made little use of the word. After Renaissance lexicographers (Perotti, Nizolio) had recovered the full range of *momentum* from the Latin of the Romans, Argyropulos and other translators of the *Physics* had a new term for rendering ῥοπή, and its future in natural philosophy was to be great. The full effects of *momentum* freshly understood would be felt first in the vernacular *momento* of Galileo, as the *stato* of Machiavelli helped fix the new meaning of 'state' – an abstract political entity unlike the more concrete and personal *status principis* or *status regni* of the Middle Ages.[86] In the Latin *De motu*, Galileo also distinguished *experientia* as a general and epistemologically limited source of information from a *periculum*, a specific and purposeful testing of a particular claim about the world. Jacopo Zabarella once used the term *experimentum* to mean a sort of thought experiment – something between Galileo's *periculum* and the *experientia* which had often connoted exceptional or occult experience in medieval texts. Neither Galileo nor Zabarella, however, succeeded in making a clear and strong distinction between 'experience' and 'experiment' or in connecting either term with a fully developed sense of 'empirical' method. Fuller expression of these ideas, as of many other concepts of philosophical importance, awaited linguistic and intellectual-historical developments begun but not completed in the Renaissance.[87]

---

85. Perotti 1517, p. 619; Micraelius 1662, pp. 1277–8.
86. Perotti 1517, p. 936; Goclenius 1613, pp. 707, 1081; Galluzzi 1979, pp. 3–21, 89–98, 106–12; Hexter 1973, pp. 154–5, 167; Skinner 1978, II, pp. 352–8.
87. Tortelli 1501, f. 76ᵛ; Perotti 1517, p. 916; Eucken 1879, pp. 25, 32; Schmitt 1981, § VIII.

IV

HUMANISM

5
HUMANISM

THE MEANING OF HUMANISM

Humanism was one of the most pervasive traits of the Renaissance, and it affected more or less deeply all aspects of the culture of the time including its thought and philosophy.

Humanism has been described and interpreted in many different ways, and its meaning has been the subject of much controversy, just as has been the concept of the Renaissance itself.[1] Whereas the term 'humanism' in current discourse often denotes an emphasis on human values unrelated to any intellectual or cultural traditions, Renaissance humanism was understood and studied by most historians of the nineteenth and early twentieth centuries as that broad concern with the study and imitation of classical antiquity which was characteristic of the period and found its expression in scholarship and education and in many other areas, including the arts and sciences. The modern term 'humanism' has been used in this sense since the early nineteenth century and was derived from the term 'humanist' coined in the late fifteenth century[2] to designate a teacher and student of the 'humanities' or *studia humanitatis*.[3] The word 'humanity' and its derivatives were associated with a 'liberal' education by several Roman writers, especially Cicero and Gellius.[4] The term was revived by Petrarch, Salutati and others in the fourteenth century, and by the middle of the fifteenth century it came to stand for a well-defined cycle of studies, called *studia humanitatis*, which included *grammatica*, *rhetorica*, *poetica*, *historia* and *philosophia moralis*, as these terms were then understood. Unlike the liberal arts of the earlier Middle Ages, the humanities did not include logic or the *quadrivium* (*arithmetica*, *geometria*, *astronomia* and *musica*), and unlike the fine arts of the eighteenth century, they did not include the visual arts, music, dancing or gardening.[5] The humanities also failed to include the disciplines

---

1. Kristeller 1979, chs. 1 and 5; *The Renaissance: Essays in Interpretation* 1982.
2. Rüegg 1946.   3. Kristeller 1979, ch. 5; Campana 1946.
4. Cicero, *Pro Archia* I.1-III.4; Aulus Gellius, *Noctes Atticae* XIII.17.1.   5. Kristeller 1980, ch. 9.

that were the chief subjects of instruction at the universities during the later Middle Ages and throughout the Renaissance, such as theology, jurisprudence and medicine, and the philosophical disciplines other than ethics, such as logic, natural philosophy and metaphysics. In other words, humanism does not represent, as often believed, the sum total of Renaissance thought and learning, but only a well-defined sector of it. Humanism has its proper domain or home territory in the humanities, whereas all other areas of learning, including philosophy (apart from ethics), followed their own course, largely determined by their medieval tradition and by their steady transformation through new observations, problems or theories. These disciplines were affected by humanism mainly from the outside and in an indirect way, though often quite strongly.

PROFESSIONAL ACTIVITIES

If we want to understand the role of the humanists and of humanism during the Renaissance and their impact on learning and philosophy, we must consider not only the place of their subject-matter, the humanities, in the classifications of the arts and sciences and among the subjects taught in the schools and universities, but also their professional activities and their literary production. The humanists are best known for their role as educators, and they actually played an important part as theorists, teachers and tutors in reforming secondary education, first in Italy and then in the rest of Europe.[6] The core of their instruction was the careful study of classical Latin, its vocabulary and grammar, metrics and prose style, and to a lesser extent of classical Greek, and the attentive reading and interpretation of the major ancient writers, both Latin and Greek, in prose and in verse. The schools of Guarino da Verona in Ferrara and of Vittorino da Feltre in Mantua attracted students from all over Europe, and their curriculum and methods were followed everywhere, serving as a model for the Protestant Reformers as well as for the Jesuits. The humanistic school, animated by the idea that the study of classical languages and literature provided valuable information and intellectual discipline as well as moral standards and a civilised taste for the future rulers, leaders and professionals of its society, flourished without interruption, though with some significant changes, until our own century, surviving many religious, political and social revolutions. It has but recently been replaced, though not yet completely, by other more practical and less demanding forms of education.

6. Woodward 1897, 1906; Garin 1957; *Pensiero pedagogico* 1958; G. Müller 1969, 1984.

The role of the humanists in Renaissance universities was not as powerful as in the secondary schools which they came to dominate completely, but it was not as insignificant as is often believed.[7] The view expressed quite recently by authoritative scholars that humanism played no role in the universities of the Renaissance is certainly wrong.[8] In the curriculum of the universities, grammar played a minor but persistent role as an elementary and preliminary subject, but rhetoric and poetry, which involved the reading of major classical Latin poets and prose writers, including the historians and the moralists, was a regular subject of teaching at the Italian universities from the early fourteenth century on, and the teaching of Greek language and literature was added with increasing frequency during the fifteenth century. By the late fifteenth and early sixteenth century, the chairs of Latin and Greek oratory and poetry had greatly increased in number and prestige and even in salary, and sometimes were given the more ambitious and fashionable title of 'the humanities'. Moreover, if we study the career of individual humanists, we find that many of them, great and small, were professors at various universities, including the Florentine *Studio*, or provided advanced instruction with a public salary in cities which had no regular or complete university, such as Lucca, Venice or Milan.

Another professional activity frequently practised by the humanists was that of acting as chancellors or secretaries.[9] Popes, cardinals and bishops, emperors, kings, princes and republics as well as many prominent patricians and businessmen needed and employed a large staff of trained people capable of composing and copying the numerous documents and papers, letters and speeches that constituted an essential part of the daily routine of politics and administration. As masters of Latin prose composition, the humanists were eminently equipped to perform these functions, and it is well known that numerous humanists, famous and obscure, had their careers, not as teachers or professors, but as chancellors and secretaries. Even Petrarch occasionally served the princes of Milan and Padua who were his patrons as an informal secretary or orator, and a long line of distinguished humanists served the papal Curia, the Florentine Republic, the kings of Naples, the dukes of Milan and other princes and republics.[10] Humanist chancellors appear also at the courts of foreign kings and princes, and it was

---

7. Kristeller 1953b, 1956b.
8. R. Pfeiffer 1976, p. 56. Contrary to Pfeiffer's statement, the *Studio* of Florence was of course a university.   9. Martines 1963; Garin 1961, part 1, ch. 1.
10. The list includes Coluccio Salutati, Leonardo Bruni, Poggio Bracciolini, Antonio Beccadelli (Panormita), Giovanni Pontano, P. C. Decembrio and many others.

often the Italian humanists who pursued a career abroad.[11] Many of the
humanist chancellors both in Italy and elsewhere were also commissioned
to write an official history of the kingdom or republic, for history was a part
of their training, and they also had easy access to the archives that contained
the source material for their undertaking. Machiavelli received a stipend
from the University of Pisa for his history of Florence, and the Venetian
Republic employed a whole series of official historiographers.[12]

Although the chanceries were important centres of humanist activities,
they were not the only ones, as is often assumed. Apart from the humanist
teachers mentioned above, we must also keep in mind that many of the
students trained in humanist schools were princes or patricians who in later
life were not obliged to earn a living on the basis of their humanist training,
as were the teachers and secretaries, but were active as churchmen or
statesmen, bankers or merchants. Many of them were patrons of humanist
scholarship and literature, but some were distinguished and productive
scholars and writers themselves in their leisure time. Pius II continued to
write when he was a cardinal and pope, and many humanists happened to be
bishops, clerics or monks, or members of the ruling circles in Florence or
Venice.[13] Moreover, after the middle of the fifteenth century, we
encounter many professionals, lawyers and physicians, as well as
theologians, who had received a more or less thorough humanist education
in school or at university and who became humanist scholars or writers in
their spare time, or even applied the standards of humanist scholarship to
their professional work and thus helped to transform traditional and
medieval subjects. Finally, we should not forget another more modest
activity which provided a living for a large number of humanist scholars,
that is, the book trade. The manuscript book had traditionally served the
needs of monastic and cathedral libraries, or of ecclesiastical, princely and
noble collectors, and later of university professors and students. During the
fourteenth and fifteenth centuries, there was a new demand for classical
Latin texts and for the writings of contemporary scholars. We find many
humanists who in their youth or in periods of unemployment worked as
copyists or calligraphers and were employed by princely or patrician
patrons who started or expanded their own private libraries, by successful

11. Enea Silvio Piccolomini, later Pope Pius II, served as secretary at the imperial court; Philippus
    Callimachus in Poland; and Polydore Vergil in England.
12. Among them we find M. A. Sabellico and Pietro Bembo; on humanism and historiography, see
    Cochrane 1981; Kelley 1970a.
13. The last group includes Donato Acciaiuoli, Alamanno Rinuccini and Giannozzo Manetti in
    Florence; Francesco and Ermolao Barbaro, Leonardo and Bernardo Giustiniani in Venice.

scholars such as Petrarch who could afford to have their own secretaries, or by professional booksellers such as Vespasiano da Bisticci who sold their manuscripts to princes and scholars alike. The products of these humanist scribes were written in one of two new styles of handwriting that were both different from the earlier 'Gothic' script and were invented and propagated by the humanists: the so-called Roman script invented by Poggio Bracciolini after the model of the Carolingian minuscule which he mistook for an ancient Roman script; and the humanist cursive, presumably invented by Niccolò Niccoli, which was a favoured book hand during the second half of the fifteenth century and became the model for italic type. These two scripts, and especially the first, are the kind of writing we are accustomed to employ both in our longhand and our printed characters, and our use of the humanist rather than the Gothic script is the direct consequence of the reform brought about by the Italian humanists of the fifteenth century. It is perhaps the most lasting effect of Renaissance humanism on our modern world. The palaeographical analysis of Renaissance hands and of humanist script has only recently become a subject of serious study, and the identification of individual humanist hands is often an important instrument when it comes to establishing the date and authorship as well as the diffusion of Renaissance texts.[14]

The technique of printing with movable type was invented by Gutenberg in Mainz about 1450, but it took some time for it to reach other countries, and even after that time the manuscript book continued for many decades to compete and to coexist with the printed one. The contribution of the humanists to the production and diffusion of printed books was no less important than their role during the period of the manuscript book. The printing press was introduced to Italy in 1465, and from that time on an ever-increasing amount of printed books were published, first in Subiaco and Rome, and soon afterwards in many other cities, including Florence, Milan and Venice. Many of the early printed books contained classical Latin texts and the writings of contemporary humanists, and they were usually printed in the same roman and italic characters that had been used in the humanist manuscript books of the same or immediately preceding period, whereas many of the university textbooks and religious or popular writings were printed in Gothic characters. The humanists soon became involved with the printing presses in several ways. They saw their own writings through the press, as we know in a number of cases, and they acted from the

14. Ullman 1960; De la Mare 1973–.

very beginning as advisers for some of the texts to be printed, and as responsible editors for the classical Latin texts published by the presses. Giovanni Andrea de'Bussi, Bishop of Aleria, performed this service for the first classical editions printed in Subiaco and in Rome, and many of the first editions printed in Paris were selected and edited by Guillaume Fichet. The same is true of the first editions of Greek classical authors, which appeared rather sparingly during the first decades of printing and became more frequent only during the sixteenth century. Among the early printers we encounter a few humanist scholars of distinction, although they probably acted as publishers rather than as typesetters: Aldus Manutius in Venice and later several members of the Estienne and Morel families in Paris were all renowned for their scholarly editions of both Latin and Greek classical authors. By the sixteenth century countless printing presses were active all over Europe and in numerous towns, but the leading international centres of publishing and of the book trade were Venice, Lyons and Basle, especially for books of classical or humanist content. Humanist scholars continued to be active as editors of classical texts and of their own writings, and often also as proofreaders working for their publishers.[15] Erasmus worked for years as an editor and proofreader for Aldus in Venice and for Froben in Basle, and he also maintained close relations with other publishing houses in Paris and Antwerp. Without these relations, his enormous scholarly production would not have been possible. We know that he travelled a good deal to supervise the printing of his works and of the texts edited by him, and we have reason to believe that a part of his income derived from the work he did for his printers and publishers.[16]

SCHOLARLY ACHIEVEMENTS AND LITERARY PRODUCTION

Having discussed the intellectual interests and the professional activities of the humanists, we must now briefly describe their scholarly and other achievements, and above all the form and content of their literary production, as well as some of the basic attitudes that underlie and pervade it.[17] Needless to say, much of their production was closely related to their

15. Scholderer 1935; Bühler 1960, 1973; Hirsch 1974, 1978; Eisenstein 1979; *Prefaces* 1861; Bussi 1978; Kristeller 1964b; Renouard 1834; *Annales . . . des Estiennes* 1837–8; Lowry 1979; Baudrier 1895–1963; Luchsinger 1953; Bietenholz 1959, 1971; Welti 1964.
16. P. Smith 1923; Mann Phillips 1959.   17. Voigt 1893; V. Rossi 1956.

professional activities, although the tastes and preferences of individual humanists also played an important role.

The deep interest in classical literature and history which was common to all humanists was not only expressed in their activity as copyists and editors. Before a text could be copied or edited, it had to be located or discovered, and it was essential to find old and correct manuscripts that deserved to be copied or edited rather than late and inaccurate manuscripts which offered a corrupt text. The search for old manuscripts of the Latin classics all over Europe was a favourite concern of many leading humanists; Petrarch, Boccaccio, Salutati and Poggio were especially persistent and successful in this enterprise. They and their companions and successors found not only older, better or more complete manuscripts of known classical writers, but also discovered additional authors or writings that had not been well known or read during the preceding medieval centuries.[18] It has been argued that we should not speak of real humanist discoveries since the manuscripts they found were copied in Carolingian times and hence not unknown to the copyists or to their contemporaries. Yet the fact remains that these texts survived in only one or two copies and that they had not been known or read for centuries, whereas the humanists introduced them into the mainstream of western scholarship and helped to bring about their wide diffusion in manuscripts and in printed editions. The newly discovered texts included Manilius and Celsus, a complete Quintilian, many works of Cicero, and above all, Tacitus and Lucretius. As for the Greek classics, prior to 1350 the number of Greek and especially of classical Greek manuscripts in western libraries was very small. It was during the period from 1350 to 1600 that most of the classical Greek manuscripts that are now in the West and that have been the basis of all modern editions were brought over from the Greek East, both before and after the Turkish conquest of Constantinople, by western scholars visiting the East and by Byzantine scholars who fled to the West.[19]

Once the Latin (and Greek) classical texts were available in manuscript and later in print, the humanists carefully annotated their texts, recording variant readings from other manuscripts and their own emendations, and adding explanatory notes and glosses. We have many manuscripts annotated by Petrarch, Salutati, Bruni, Valla and Leto, and many early printed editions annotated by Poliziano and numerous later scholars. We

18. Sabbadini 1967.
19. Bolgar 1954, pp. 455–505 ('Greek manuscripts in Italy during the fifteenth century').

also have a large body of fully-fledged commentaries by humanist scholars on practically all ancient Latin texts then available, some in manuscript and some in print, which were usually the result of class lectures given on these authors at various schools or universities and copied by a student or sometimes by the teacher himself. Classical Greek authors were also copied and edited by the humanists, Byzantine or western, and frequently annotated and glossed in Latin. From the sixteenth century we have a number of Latin commentaries on Greek classical texts.

However, the knowledge of Greek, even among humanist scholars, was never as thorough or as widespread as was their knowledge of Latin, because the study of Greek was a new and purely scholarly pursuit that lacked the indigenous tradition and the practical usefulness which the study of Latin had inherited from the Middle Ages. As a result, a large amount of effort was dedicated by the humanists to the task of translating ancient Greek texts into Latin in order to make them available to a larger number of their contemporaries, even among the humanists. This effort was encouraged and rewarded by many important patrons, among them Pope Nicholas V and his successors, many princes and the early Medici. During the fifteenth and sixteenth centuries, the humanists translated into Latin practically all classical Greek authors then available, some of them more than once, and many for the first time, as well as making new translations of those texts that had been available in medieval Latin translations.[20] These translations introduced for the first time practically all of Greek poetry, oratory and historiography as well as a sizeable proportion of Greek writings on mathematics, geography, medicine and botany, and also Greek patristic literature. The philosophical texts translated for the first time included many works of Plato and Proclus, all of Plotinus and of other Neoplatonic authors, Epictetus and Marcus Aurelius, Sextus Empiricus, Diogenes Laertius (who contains several texts of Epicurus), Lucian and Plutarch, and most of the Greek commentaries on Aristotle. In other words, most of the sources of ancient Platonism, Stoicism, Epicureanism, scepticism and popular philosophy were made available for the first time, while the writings of Aristotle came to be studied not only from the medieval Latin translations and commentaries but also from the Greek text, from new humanist translations and from the Greek commentators. The scholarly study of Hebrew and Arabic also made progress among western scholars, some of them humanists, and benefited the study of the Old Testament and

---

20. See *Catalogus translationum* 1960–.

rabbinical and cabalistic literature, as well as the Koran and Arabic philosophy.[21]

The reading public of the Renaissance consisted not only of people who had received a humanist or university education and hence were able to read Latin, but also of many intelligent and curious people, especially merchants, craftsmen and women, who knew no Latin but were eager to read not only poems and narratives but also works of varied instruction in their native vernacular. Many humanists catered to this audience, which also included many princes and noblemen, and made vernacular translations of both classical and humanist writings, or even composed some of their own works in the vernacular. This happened in Italy, especially in Tuscany, as early as the fifteenth century; and during the sixteenth century, if not before, a large body of classical and humanist literature was translated into French, Spanish, German and English.[22] Also an increasing number of writings that were humanist in form and content came to be composed in those languages, the most illustrious example being the *Essais* of Michel de Montaigne.

In order to facilitate the reading and understanding of classical authors, the humanists wrote commentaries on Donatus, Priscian and other ancient grammarians, and also produced a number of textbooks of Latin grammar and a few of Greek. Niccolò Perotti added to his bulky *Cornucopiae*, a detailed commentary on parts of Martial, an extensive word index and thus provided for the first time a detailed vocabulary of classical Latin.[23] In the sixteenth century the big *Thesauri* of Greek and Latin produced by the Estienne family were more than adequate and remained in use until the eighteenth and nineteenth centuries.

Whereas the study of Greek was mainly aimed at the reading of the classics, that of Latin served the additional purpose of mastering it as a written and even as a spoken language. The humanists were keenly aware of the great difference that separated medieval and especially scholastic Latin from that of the ancient Roman writers, above all Cicero. They made it their avowed goal to imitate in their own writings the Latin of classical writers and to avoid all those 'barbarous' features that separated medieval from classical Latin. They attempted with some success to imitate and restore classical Latin as a living language and to bring about a kind of

---

21. The list of these orientalists includes Giannozzo Manetti, Giovanni Pico, Johannes Reuchlin and Guillaume Postel.
22. Bolgar 1954, pp. 506–41 ('The translations of the Greek and Roman classical authors before 1600'); Beardsley 1970; Worstbrock 1976–.   23. Kristeller 1981.

linguistic and literary revolution that discredited and gradually abolished many, if not all, features of medieval Latin. This reform affected spelling, prosody and punctuation, vocabulary and phraseology, inflection and syntax, and the whole structure and rhythm of sentences. While some scholars allowed new words for objects and concepts unknown to the ancient Romans, others would ban any words not sanctioned by the usage of ancient Roman writers, especially Cicero. Lorenzo Valla's *Elegantiae* were composed as a handbook that would help students and scholars to write fluent Latin, to use the proper classical terms and phrases and to avoid barbarisms. It served this function for several centuries. The result was a neo-Latin language and literature that were much closer to those of the ancient Romans than anything written in Latin after the end of antiquity.[24] In the learned disciplines, including philosophy, this humanist reform tended to abandon the technical terminology that had become refined and precise through usage and discussion over several centuries and had often served to render in Latin some philosophical terms of ancient Greek origin that had not been adopted or rendered by Cicero or other ancient Roman writers. This humanist habit led in some instances to an emphasis on a smooth literary style and vague phraseology at the expense of the conceptual precision needed for an adequate philosophical discourse.

All the activities and writings described so far might be roughly subsumed under *grammatica*, as this term was understood at the time. It now remains to mention briefly the literary contribution of the humanists to the other *studia humanitatis*. Rhetoric, which was the second of the humanities and in many ways the core of them all, consisted primarily in the theory and practice of prose composition, but also in the theory of plausible or probable arguments and in the theory of persuasion. The humanists produced a large number of commentaries on the rhetorical works of Cicero and Quintilian and later of Aristotle, and they also analysed Cicero's orations for their rhetorical qualities. They wrote a number of rhetorical textbooks that tended to multiply during the sixteenth century, as well as many treatises on more specific subjects, such as the figures of speech or imitation. Like their medieval predecessors, they used some of their own compositions as models of style to be imitated by their students, or composed formularies of fictitious letters or just parts of them, such as *exordia* or *salutationes*.[25]

More important was the claim advanced by most humanists that the

24. Norden 1923.
25. G. A. Kennedy 1980; *Renaissance Eloquence* 1983; Monfasani 1976, ch. 9; for Fichet, see Kristeller 1964b.

pursuit of eloquence (*eloquentia*) was a major task for the educated scholar and writer and that it was inseparable from the pursuit of wisdom (*sapientia*). This meant that philosophy should always be combined with rhetoric, an ideal for which Cicero served as a teacher and an example. In the name of this ideal, many humanists beginning with Petrarch criticised scholastic philosophy. Many of them tended to subordinate philosophy to rhetoric, and at least one leading humanist, Lorenzo Valla, came close to replacing philosophy with rhetoric, or at least with a kind of philosophy which he chose to call rhetoric.[26]

The rhetorical practice of the humanists was much more extensive than their theoretical literature. The genres most frequently cultivated by them were the oration and the letter, both of them closely connected with their professional activity as chancellors and secretaries. The speeches composed by them and often delivered by others were seldom of the judiciary or deliberative type prevalent in classical theory and practice, but usually epideictic and linked to the social and institutional practice of their time: funeral and wedding speeches, speeches by ambassadors in the name of their government, speeches of congratulation to newly elected popes or prelates, princes or magistrates, speeches of welcome to distinguished visitors, speeches at the beginning of a school year or of a particular university course, speeches given at the graduation of students, at the opening of lay or religious gatherings or of a disputation, or in praise of saints or other illustrious people, and many more.[27] In fifteenth-century Italy the sermons preached on holidays or on special occasions were often delivered by priests or friars who had received a humanist education, and these sermons were influenced in their form and content, if not in their religious doctrine, by the secular oratory of the humanists. The extensive literature of humanist speeches was widely copied and printed, but it has not been frequently read or studied by modern scholars, although it contains a large amount of biographical, historical and scholarly information, and although some of it expresses the author's thought and touches on problems and themes often discussed in other writings of the same period.[28]

Even larger and probably more interesting is the literature of humanist letters.[29] The ancient models for the letter were less numerous than for the speech or other genres, and ancient rhetorical theory provided but scanty guidance for its composition. Yet the state letter was the most important

26. Breen 1968, ch. 1; Gerl 1974.
27. Galletti 1904–38; Kristeller 1980, pp. 9–10.
28. J. W. O'Malley 1979. 29. Kristeller 1980, pp. 8–9.

assignment for humanist chancellors and secretaries, and although they were bound to follow the example of their predecessors, the medieval notaries and *dictatores*, for the content and legal terminology, they did their best to improve upon the script, vocabulary and style of their official letters and documents. For their private letters, the humanists were not limited by any constraints, except their own taste and the example of such ancient writers as Seneca, Pliny the Younger and above all Cicero. They maintained an extensive correspondence with their patrons, friends and colleagues; and they often preserved, collected and edited their own letters, considering and treating them as an important part of their literary production. Actually, the letters of the humanists have enjoyed more favour with modern scholars and readers than most of their other writings. This is due to their elegant style and to their interesting content, which often reflects the life of the author and of his friends, the events of his day, and his thoughts and opinions on a variety of subjects. For reconstructing the thought of a humanist, his letters are as important witnesses as any of his other writings.

Although the skill of the humanists as orators and practising rhetoricians found its most direct expression in their speeches and letters, it also shaped the form and style, if not the content, of all their other prose compositions, including their historical and philosophical writings. As authors of histories and biographies dealing with ancient, medieval and contemporary subjects, and of antiquarian works dealing with ancient topography and mythology, the humanists cultivated a fluent and elegant style, and the fictitious speeches which they inserted in their histories after the example of their ancient and medieval predecessors gave them a special opportunity for showing their rhetorical expertise. On the other hand, and for this they have not always received due credit, they used their critical judgement and their knowledge of older sources and documents to expose forgeries and conventional errors and to reconstruct the events of the past in a rational and plausible fashion, and thus they often attained a high degree of accuracy and credibility.[30] The humanists' concern with history led them to reflections on the method, sources and theory of history which first appeared in the prologues to their courses and commentaries on ancient historians and later found expression in special treatises on the art of history.[31]

Among the many prose works composed by the humanists on a great variety of topics, we find a considerable number of treatises dedicated to

---

30. Cochrane 1981.   31. E. Maffei 1897; B. Reynolds 1953; Cotroneo 1971.

moral and other philosophical problems. They all show the same concern for style and elegance that characterises their other prose works, and also pay their tribute to ancient authors by frequent quotations, examples and allusions. Aside from the plain treatise, the humanists had a marked preference for the invective and the dialogue. The invective, often used by Petrarch and other humanists, had its models in some of Cicero's speeches and in the apocryphal invectives attributed to Cicero and Sallust, which enjoyed a wide circulation and popularity. It enabled the authors to give a more personal tone to their discourse and to exaggerate their points beyond the limits of plausibility, something they evidently enjoyed.[32] The dialogue, usually patterned after the model of Cicero rather than of Plato, offered the advantage of presenting more than one opinion or viewpoint on the same subject without seeming to take a definitive stand (although the author's true opinion may often be inferred from his preface, from the composition of the dialogue itself or from his other writings). The dialogue also gave a personal and almost dramatic vivacity to the problems discussed. On the other hand, it provided a literary excuse for avoiding the tight argument and precise terminology that had characterised the philosophical literature of the ancient Greeks and of the medieval scholastics.[33]

The narrative prose of the humanists, apart from their historical works, is limited to a few short stories in Latin, some of them translations from Boccaccio's *Decameron*, and a few descriptions and eulogies of cities and countries.[34] Much more extensive is their contribution to Latin poetry.[35] It has with few exceptions not received much applause from modern critics, but has been more widely studied in recent decades. Apart from isolated pieces, there are many collections of epigrams and elegies composed on the model of the ancient Roman poets. Poliziano, Pontano and a few others have had a fairly continuous reputation, and several more have been rescued from oblivion by recent scholars. Odes and other Horatian strophes are much rarer because of their greater metrical difficulty and the limited knowledge of ancient prosody. There are quite a few long poems in epic hexameters which are historical or mythological, religious or didactic in content. Some of the didactic poems deal with philosophical or scientific topics and hence are interesting for their doctrinal content as well as for their literary form. There are some hymns and pastoral poetry patterned after Vergil's *Eclogues*, which had enjoyed great popularity ever since the early

32. Vismara 1900.   33. Tateo 1967, pp. 221–421; Marsh 1980.
34. Kristeller 1956a, ch. 19, 1984.
35. V. Rossi 1956 *passim*; Bottiglioni 1913; Ellinger 1929–33; Bradner 1940; W. L. Grant 1965.

fourteenth century. More limited, though not without interest, is the humanist contribution to dramatic literature.[36] They composed few Latin tragedies but a somewhat larger number of Latin comedies, most of which were written and performed at the universities of northern Italy. In the sixteenth and seventeenth centuries, the genres of Latin comedy and tragedy were much cultivated by the Jesuits, who in this sector, as in some others, followed the humanist tradition. Humanist influences came to be felt also in the vernacular literatures. Many of the genres of classical and humanist poetry came to be imitated and adopted in the vernacular literatures, and leading vernacular poets, including Ariosto, Ronsard and Spenser, received a humanist education.

The humanists also played an important role in the development of poetical theory and literary criticism. The defence of poetry against the theologians led to the formulation of some interesting principles. The commentaries on the ancient poets, especially their introductions, contained some pertinent reflections. Horace's *Ars poetica* was commented upon and occasionally imitated in separate treatises on poetics; and in the sixteenth century Aristotle's *Poetics*, which had been practically unknown during the preceding centuries, was extensively discussed in commentaries. There were also some treatises on poetics, culminating in the work of Julius Caesar Scaliger.[37]

In concluding this survey of the literary production of the humanists, I should like to emphasise that it was characterised throughout by a desire to imitate ancient authors and to emulate them in the elegance of their style, vocabulary and literary composition, but that the humanists added a dimension that is not typical of ancient literature and that is largely new: the tendency to take seriously their own personal feelings and experiences, opinions and preferences. An air of subjectivity pervades all humanist literature from Petrarch to Erasmus and Montaigne that is absent from most classical literature and also from much modern literature prior to Romanticism. It accounts for the often uninhibited gossip, flattery and polemics present in much humanist literature, and it also helps to explain the Renaissance preference for such literary genres as the invective, the dialogue, the speech, the letter and the essay. I should like to think that this is what Jacob Burckhardt meant when he spoke of the individualism of the Renaissance, a concept that has been more often criticised than understood.[38] In the sense in which I understand it, it is perfectly valid, if not for

36. Stäuble 1968.   37. Greenfield 1981; Trinkaus 1966; Weinberg 1961.
38. Burckhardt 1860, part II ('Die Entwicklung des Individuums').

the Renaissance in all of its aspects, then at least for that large sector of its thought, learning and literature that is dominated by the humanists.

THE ORIGINS OF HUMANISM

Since most of the contributions of the humanists to the philosophy of the Renaissance will be treated in other chapters of this volume, I shall limit myself in the remainder of this chapter to a brief history of Renaissance humanism and shall conclude my remarks with a short description of its impact on the philosophy and general thought of the period.

The origins of Renaissance humanism have traditionally been traced to the work and writings of Petrarch, but more recently to a group of scholars active in northern and central Italy during the late thirteenth and early fourteenth century.[39] Among these pre-humanists or proto-humanists, Albertino Mussato of Padua stands out as the author of some Latin poems, a Latin tragedy and several historical works in the classical style, and as a defender of poetry. Giovanni del Virgilio of Bologna is notable as an early professor of rhetoric and poetry at his university, as a commentator on Ovid, and as the author of Vergilian eclogues that were addressed to, and answered by, no less a person than Dante Alighieri.[40] For the appearance of classical studies and classicist literature at this particular place and time various explanations may be offered, including the first stirring of a national feeling that looked to the ancient Romans as the true ancestors of the Italians, and the economic and political rise of the city republics which in their institutions as well as in their intellectual interests felt more akin to classical antiquity than to the imperial, ecclesiastical and feudal culture of the rest of Europe and of their own immediate past. This early humanism was due to the merger of two previous traditions that had been quite distinct from each other and that in their combination brought forth something new and different. On the one hand, there was in Italy and especially in Bologna a strong tradition of rhetoric, called the *ars dictaminis*, which flourished from the late eleventh to the early fourteenth century and which with the help of textbooks and formularies provided instruction and training for future notaries and secretaries – a large, influential and literate class of lay citizens – helping them to compose documents and letters, both public and private, and later also speeches, usually in Latin but sometimes also in the vernacular.[41] The link with humanist epistolography and

39. Roberto Weiss 1947, 1949; G. Billanovich 1953.   40. Kristeller 1961b.
41. Galletti 1904–38; *Medieval Eloquence* 1978; Murphy 1974, who fails to mention secular eloquence and to recognise the continuation of the *ars dictaminis* after 1300.

oratory is obvious, both in professional and in literary terms, and it is confirmed by the fact that Giovanni del Virgilio himself composed a treatise on *dictamen*. On the other hand, the *dictamen* tradition was purely practical, and it had in its patterns, style and content few if any classical features. The study and imitation of ancient writers was the job of the grammarians, not the rhetoricians, and the tradition of reading and interpreting ancient Roman writers in school was very much alive in France and other northern countries from the ninth to the early fourteenth century, whereas the Italian share in this tradition was very slight up to the late thirteenth and early fourteenth century. It is significant that the study of Roman writers began to emerge in Italy at a time when it had declined in France and the North, and we have at least some evidence that the French grammarians and commentators of the Middle Ages influenced their Italian successors.[42] The fact that the medieval *dictamen* had some influence on the epistolography and oratory of the Italian humanists does not mean that the *dictamen*, even in conjunction with the grammatical tradition, should be credited with the activities and achievements of Renaissance humanism as a whole.

In the middle of the fourteenth century Italian humanism had its first culmination, if not its beginning, in Petrarch, whose work and personality attained international fame during his own lifetime and who was thus able to raise the prestige and to promote the diffusion of humanistic studies all over Italy and elsewhere. Petrarch's fame rested not only on his Italian poems, which have been rightly admired and imitated until modern times, but also on his voluminous Latin writings, which make him one of the leading humanist scholars and authors and which have been the subject of much recent study. They include a number of Latin poems, especially epigrams, eclogues and an epic poem of historical content, the *Africa*, a few speeches, several historical works, above all a series of treatises, some of them in the form of invectives or dialogues, and a very large number of private letters, which he carefully collected, edited and published. His invectives include his writings against the physicians and his treatise *De sui ipsius et multorum ignorantia*, in which he offers a defence of poetry, eloquence and ethics, that is, of the humanities against the claims of scholastic philosophy and science. These invectives document not the victory of humanism over scholasticism, as is often claimed, but the

42. Kristeller 1964a (appendix); F. Ghisalberti 1933; Wertis 1979. I recently found a humanist miscellany written in Italy during the fifteenth century which contains, among other humanist and classical texts, the twelfth-century commentary of Arnulf of Orléans on Lucan (Lisbon, Biblioteca nacional, fundo geral 3307, ff. 65–191^v).

affirmative praise of the humanities as against the sciences, and they represent an interesting episode in that continuing battle of the arts and of various 'cultures' that is still with us. The *De otio religioso* and the *De vita solitaria* offer a defence of the contemplative life, and the latter work at least illustrates the secularisation of this ideal, transferring it from the monk to the lay scholar (although Petrarch himself was a cleric). The *De remediis utriusque fortunae* offers a detailed discussion of the virtues and vices, based on Stoic doctrines and patterned on a shorter treatise attributed to Seneca. The *Secretum*, a dialogue between the author and St Augustine (who was one of his favourite writers), offers a highly personal and moving account of his moral conflicts and includes some memorable reflections on fame and on melancholy. Petrarch's letters, the most extensive and probably the most impressive part of his work, are important for the wealth and variety of their biographical, historical and scholarly content and for their subtle and vivid style which echoes Seneca, and also for their thoroughly personal and subjective approach, obviously influenced by the letters of Cicero recently discovered in Verona. Petrarch was understood by himself and by his contemporaries as a poet and orator, historian and moral philosopher, and was crowned with the laurel as a poet and historian. He was not a grammarian in the ordinary sense of the word, for he was not a teacher and he left no commentaries, but his work as a classical scholar allows us to consider him as a grammarian as this term was understood in his time. His library included most ancient Roman authors and many Latin Church Fathers, two Greek manuscripts containing Homer and Plato, and almost no works of the medieval scholastics. Many manuscripts owned and annotated by him have been identified and studied. His glosses show his rich knowledge of Roman and patristic literature and of ancient history, as well as his exceptional skill as a careful reader and textual critic. His knowledge of ancient philosophy was limited to Latin writers, such as Cicero, Seneca and Boethius, Augustine and Jerome, and to some of the available Latin translations of Greek philosophers, such as Plato's *Timaeus* and *Phaedo* and Aristotle's *Nicomachean Ethics*. Some of his attitudes anticipated and influenced later developments: he encouraged Leonzio Pilato to translate Homer into Latin; he praised Plato as superior to Aristotle; and he opposed the original Aristotle to his medieval Latin translators and commentators.[43]

During Petrarch's later years and after his death, humanistic studies were carried on in various centres by his friends, correspondents and admirers,

43. Nolhac 1907; Sapegno 1948, ch. 5; G. Billanovich 1951; Wilkins 1961; Petrucci 1967; U. Bosco 1968; Kristeller 1983b.

such as Giovanni da Ravenna, and above all Boccaccio and Salutati in
Florence. Boccaccio was the author not only of the *Decameron* and of many
Italian poems but also of important antiquarian works in Latin that deal
with ancient mythology and topography. He also discovered manuscripts
of Tacitus and other ancient authors, and he sponsored Leonzio Pilato in
his translation of Homer and in the teaching of Greek, which he offered in
private and, as we now know, also in public.[44] Salutati, for many years
Chancellor of the Florentine Republic, played a major political role when in
his state letters he defended Florentine liberty against its enemies. His
extensive private correspondence is notable for his defence of poetry and for
his frequent praise of the active life of the statesman and businessman.
His prose treatises, many of which have been published only recently,
deal with such topics as the secular and religious life, fate and fortune,
the relative superiority of medicine and law, and an allegorical interpretation of the labours of Hercules. Like Petrarch, he was an ardent book
collector, and we know a number of manuscripts that he owned, some
of them copied by or for him or annotated in his own hand. He was
responsible for bringing Manuel Chrysoloras, a distinguished Byzantine
scholar, to the University of Florence as a teacher of Greek.[45] It was not due
to Leonzio but rather to Chrysoloras, who taught for a number of years at
Florence and then at Pavia and who attracted many promising students
from all over Italy, that the study of Greek language and literature came to
acquire a firm and lasting place in the academic and intellectual life of Italy
and later of Europe.[46]

THE FIFTEENTH AND SIXTEENTH CENTURIES

The fifteenth century has been rightly considered as the high point of Italian
humanism, and Italian and other historians have often called it the age of
humanism.[47] It was that century which witnessed a wide and unprecedented diffusion of classical Latin literature in manuscripts and later in
printed editions, including some newly discovered authors, the beginnings
and spread of humanist script and of humanist education, and a steady
progress in the textual criticism and interpretation of ancient writers, and in

44. Branca 1975.   45. Ullman 1963; Witt 1976, 1983; Langkabel 1981.
46. Geanakoplos 1962, 1966; Roberto Weiss 1977.
47. The age produced Bruni and Poggio Bracciolini, Vergerio and Traversari, Niccoli and Marsuppini,
    Filelfo and Guarino, Valla and Biondo, Leto and Calderini, Alberti and Manetti, Panormita and
    Pontano, Francesco and Ermolao Barbaro, Landino and Poliziano, and many other scholars and
    writers who were less famous but quite respectable.

the study of classical Latin grammar and vocabulary, spelling and prosody. It also witnessed the steady rise of Greek scholarship, and the arrival in the West of many prominent Byzantine scholars, who were able to transmit the methods and traditions of Byzantine scholarship to their western students and colleagues.[48] A few western scholars were able to write in classical Greek,[49] and later in the century Poliziano and Ermolao Barbaro attained a level of Greek scholarship that was still recognised during the following centuries. A large part of the humanist literature – letters and speeches, histories and biographies, moral and other treatises and dialogues – was produced in fifteenth-century Italy, as were numerous commentaries on the classics and countless Latin translations from the Greek. The antiquarian interests of the humanists also led to the beginnings of such related studies as epigraphy and archaeology.[50]

One aspect of Italian humanism that has attracted much scholarly attention in recent decades is the civic humanism of Bruni and other Florentine writers of the early fifteenth century. They used their classical scholarship for the defence of the Florentine Republic and of its free institutions in its struggle against the Visconti princes, and also advocated a classical education for the leading citizens of the republic.[51] This is an important and attractive facet of Italian humanism, but it is limited to Florence during the early fifteenth century and characterises only one aspect in the work of Bruni and his friends. Within the comprehensive picture of Renaissance humanism, let alone of Renaissance thought, the civic humanism of Bruni and his circle represents only one out of many aspects and phases of a much more complex and varied movement.

When we reach the latter half of the fifteenth and the sixteenth century, a new phenomenon must be taken into consideration. Many scholars who had received a humanist secondary education proceeded to study other subjects at the universities or on their own, and many humanist scholars extended their interests and activities to fields other than the humanities in the strict sense of the term. Thus we find many humanists who were also philosophers, scientists, physicians and medical scholars, jurists or even theologians.[52] It is this combination of interests that has often led to a vague or confused interpretation of Renaissance humanism and Renaissance

---

48. They included Cardinal Bessarion and Theodore Gaza, George of Trebizond and Argyropulos, Demetrius Chalcondylas and Marcus Musurus, Constantine and Janus Lascaris and many others; see Geanakoplos 1962, 1966.
49. Especially Bruni, Filelfo and Poliziano. 50. Roberto Weiss 1969. 51. Baron 1966.
52. E.g., Marsilio Ficino and Giovanni Pico; Leon Battista Alberti and Giorgio Valla; Niccolò Leoniceno; Andrea Alciato; Giles of Viterbo and many others.

thought and learning in general. We must distinguish between the
contributions the humanists made to the humanities, which constituted
their proper domain, and those they made to other branches of knowledge
on account of their subsidiary scholarly interests or their amateur curiosity.

As the sixteenth century progressed, humanism in Italy changed its
physiognomy and also lost some ground. It did not, however, disappear, as
is often believed, but rather continued to flourish. The scholarly tradition of
the humanities persisted, producing important philologists and historians.[53] Vernacular literature increased in volume and importance and came
to deal more and more with scholarly and philosophical topics, although
often in a popular fashion, a development that had begun in the fifteenth
century. Aristotelian philosophy and the other academic traditions actually
gained new strength, although they did not remain untouched by
humanism.[54] The theological controversies of the Reformation also had
repercussions in Italy, and there were many new developments in the
sciences and in philosophy proper that did not derive either from humanism
or from scholastic Aristotelianism.

Outside Italy, the sixteenth century was the great age of humanism, and it
is at that time that northern humanism actually surpassed Italian humanism.
Italian humanism had spread its influence to the rest of Europe during the
fifteenth century, mainly through Italian humanists travelling or teaching
abroad or dedicating their works to foreign patrons, and through foreign
students and scholars who visited Italy and her universities and returned
home with new books, new knowledge and new ideas.[55] Thanks to
Petrarch and others, Italian humanism reached other countries, especially
Bohemia and France, as early as the fourteenth century; and during the
fifteenth century the court of Matthias Corvinus in Hungary was for a
while a leading centre of Italian humanism.[56] Yet it was the sixteenth
century when scholars of other countries, well read in ancient and Italian
sources but trained at home or outside Italy, attained an international
reputation and influence comparable to that of Petrarch and the leading
Italian humanists of the fifteenth century and surpassing that of their own
Italian contemporaries. It is sufficient to mention Johannes Reuchlin and
Erasmus, Guillaume Budé, Thomas More and Juan Luis Vives, who made
outstanding contributions to humanistic scholarship, including Greek,
biblical, patristic and legal studies, to Latin literature and to moral thought.
With reference to Erasmus and his circle, scholars have often spoken of

53. E.g., Pier Vettori and Carlo Sigonio.   54. Schmitt 1983a.
55. Roberto Weiss 1967; Parks 1954; Kristeller 1980, ch. 3.   56. Csapodi 1978.

Christian humanism and have contrasted it with the paganism of the Italians. The term has some validity if we denote by it those humanists who applied their classical scholarship to biblical and patristic studies and who adopted and defended in their writings some tenets of Christian religion or theology. Taken in this sense, Christian humanism is only one of many currents within the broader humanist movement. Moreover, many northern humanists were not Christian humanists in this sense, while many Italian humanists were.[57] On the other hand, we should remember that most, if not all, humanists were Christian believers, although they may not have touched on religious subjects in their work as scholars or writers.

By the late sixteenth and early seventeenth century, humanist Latin poetry and prose were as widespread in the North, West and East of Europe as in Italy, and flourished in Scotland, Portugal and Poland no less than in England, Spain, France and Germany. During the same period, France and the Low Countries became the leading centres of classical scholarship, both Latin and Greek.[58] Earlier in the sixteenth century, Vives made the attempt to replace the scholastic tradition in all fields of learning with ancient and humanist scholarship, and this attempt had considerable influence on later educational theory and practice.[59] In the seventeenth century pure classical scholarship tended more and more to loosen its ties with the rhetorical and literary endeavours which it had inherited from Renaissance humanism.

HUMANISM AND PHILOSOPHY

Renaissance humanism was thus rich, varied and pervasive. It was essentially a scholarly, educational and literary movement, and among its many concerns, philosophical thought was not the only or even the dominating one. On the other hand, Renaissance philosophy as a whole owed no less to the traditions of medieval scholasticism and to the original ideas of contemporary thinkers than it did to humanism and to the ancient ideas transmitted by the humanists. Much of the work of leading humanists and all of the work of many minor humanists has no significance whatsoever for philosophy in any sense of the term, but only for scholarship or literature. Vice versa, much of the philosophical literature of the Renaissance was not due to the humanists, but to Aristotelian philosophers

57. E.g., Petrarch, Lorenzo Valla, Giannozzo Manetti, and Ambrogio Traversari (on whom, see Stinger 1977).
58. It is sufficient to mention Adrien Turnèbe, Justus Lipsius, J. J. Scaliger and their numerous colleagues and successors. See Sandys 1908; R. Pfeiffer 1976, part III; Grafton 1983–.
59. Vives, *De tradendis disciplinis* (first published in 1531).

with a scholastic training, to Platonist metaphysicians influenced by both humanism and scholasticism and above all by Plato and the Neoplatonists, such as Ficino and his followers, or to original thinkers marginally influenced by humanism, from Nicholas of Cusa down to Telesio, Bruno and Francis Bacon.

The influence of humanism on philosophy was very great indeed, but its precise importance depends on our conception and definition of philosophy. If 'philosophy' is limited to the systematic and technical discussion of the subjects and problems defined by ancient, medieval and modern traditions, the humanist contribution is still significant, especially in ethics and politics and to a lesser extent in logic. It is much greater if philosophy is taken in a broader sense to include the wide areas of less systematic and more popular thought and discussion and the philosophical implications of other disciplines such as theology and jurisprudence, the arts and the humanities, and especially rhetoric and poetics, which occupied a place even in the Aristotelian corpus.

To assess this contribution, as will become apparent in other chapters of this volume, one must distinguish between the direct and the indirect contributions of Renaissance humanism to philosophy and between the contributions due to the movement as a whole and those due to individual humanists whose ideas and intellectual interests were not necessarily shared by other humanists.

The direct contribution of humanism to philosophy was concentrated in the area of moral philosophy and its ramifications, including political thought. Moral philosophy was the only branch of philosophy which was recognised as a part of the humanities and was hence of professional concern to the humanists. Even the university chairs of moral philosophy were at times, though not consistently, assigned to humanists, and it is the only area of philosophy where the humanists found themselves in direct conflict and competition with their scholastic contemporaries. The humanists actually produced a large body of moral treatises and dialogues, as we have seen, which expressed their ideas on a variety of traditional or new problems. It is this part of their work which has always and understandably attracted and even monopolised the attention of historians of philosophy. The moral thought of the humanists has been extensively studied,[60] and it will be duly treated elsewhere in this volume. The humanists not only offered traditional or new thoughts on conventional problems, but also formulated

---

60. Garin 1958b, 1961, 1966; Rice 1958; Tateo 1967; Trinkaus 1940, 1970, 1983.

or emphasised problems that were either new or had not occupied the centre of attention in earlier thought. They wrote extensively on such themes as fate and free will, the highest good, the various virtues and vices, the active and contemplative life, will and intellect, the immortality of the soul and the dignity of man.[61] Moreover, the ideas of the humanists on a variety of moral and other philosophical questions were not only expressed in the treatises they dedicated to the respective themes but also often hidden away in their letters, orations or other writings.

Important contributions to other areas of philosophy are not due to humanism as a general current but to individual humanists. Most significant, and recently much discussed, is the form of logic attempted by a group of humanists from Valla and Agricola to Ramus and Nizolio.[62] They were concerned with didactic clarity rather than with conceptual precision and replaced the syllogism with the invention of topics and arguments, a method evidently borrowed from rhetoric. Individual humanists made contributions to the arts and their theory (for instance, Alberti) or to mathematics (for instance, Giorgio Valla) whereas many of the leading philosophers and scientists of the late fifteenth and of the sixteenth century had a strong humanist background in addition to their specialised training, as was the case with Ficino and Pico, Copernicus and Vesalius, Patrizi and even Galileo.[63]

Of equal and perhaps of even greater importance was the indirect contribution of humanism to Renaissance thought. The humanists were actively involved in making the sources of ancient philosophy and science available to their contemporaries by discovering, copying and editing classical Latin texts, by translating Greek texts into Latin (and later into the vernaculars), and by discussing and interpreting them in their commentaries. Many important works of ancient and especially of Greek philosophy and science were made available for the first time, while others that had been previously known were more widely discussed and better understood. Many of the new texts contributed to the advance of mathematics, medicine, botany and other sciences. The direct knowledge of the Greek commentators on Aristotle influenced the interpretation of the philosopher by Renaissance Aristotelians, and the new knowledge of ancient philosophers who were outside the Aristotelian tradition led to increasing doubts about the exclusive validity and authority of that tradition, to a widespread eclecticism and to a renewed interest in, and

61. Di Napoli 1963; Kristeller 1979, chs. 9–11.
62. Ong 1958a; N. W. Gilbert 1960; Vasoli 1968a.   63. Rose 1975.

adherence to, other ancient schools of philosophy, especially Neoplatonism, Stoicism, Epicureanism and scepticism (Academic and Pyrrhonian).[64] The libraries and the minds of Renaissance readers and thinkers were stocked with many texts and ideas unknown to their predecessors, and even if we were to deny any lasting validity to the doctrines of most Renaissance philosophers, the intellectual ferment brought about by the addition of new sources and of new ideas to the medieval heritage was an important factor in preparing the intellectual climate for the new science and the new philosophy of the seventeenth century. The great role played during the Renaissance by astrology, alchemy, magic and other occult sciences has few links with humanism or for that matter with Aristotelianism, but came to be associated with Platonism. But this area of thought was cultivated by at least some humanists and was influenced by some ancient sources made available by the humanists.[65]

The indirect influence of the humanists on thought and philosophy was not limited to the diffusion of ancient texts or of ancient and new ideas. It also affected, and perhaps in a more pervasive and lasting way, the style and pattern of philosophical literature. The philosophical dialogue continued to flourish to the early nineteenth century although it has since practically disappeared. However, if most philosophical literature in recent centuries, even the most technical, follows the form of the short essay or of the neatly composed treatise rather than that of the commentary or the *quaestio*, this fact is clearly due to humanism rather than to scholasticism, as is the practice of arguing precisely and also plausibly instead of accumulating arguments regardless of their relative strength, as had been the medieval scholastic practice. Philosophical literature has also followed the rules of Latin vocabulary, syntax and composition as defined by the humanists, rules that were later transferred to the modern vernacular languages after Latin ceased to be used for academic and scholarly discourse (which happened much later and much more gradually than is usually believed). In view of the fact that terminology has always played a vital part in philosophical discourse, the impact of humanism on the development of philosophical terminology seems to be in need of much further exploration. The subjective and individualistic attitude that characterises and pervades humanist discourse from Petrarch to Montaigne and that to some extent explains the humanist preference for the letter, the dialogue and the essay also tends to penetrate

64. For Stoicism, see Zanta 1914; Saunders 1955; Abel 1978; Oestreich 1982; for Academic scepticism, Schmitt 1972; for Pyrrhonian scepticism, Popkin 1979.
65. Yates 1964; Walker 1958, 1972.

much philosophical and scientific literature during the fifteenth and sixteenth centuries and appears even in authors where we might least expect it, such as Pomponazzi.[66] This tendency seems to recede in later philosophical literature, but it is not entirely absent in Descartes, Spinoza or Leibniz.

Finally, if we view Renaissance philosophy and Renaissance thought in the broader context of the history of western philosophy, we may assert that philosophy for a long time was linked, though not identified, with religion and theology, as in the Middle Ages, and with the mathematical and natural sciences, as during much of the last four centuries. We should not be surprised if philosophy during the Renaissance was to some extent allied with the humanities, that is, with rhetoric, poetry, and historical and classical scholarship. We might even wonder whether this may provide a lesson for the present and for the future. If philosophers were to pay greater attention to the humanities, as a few of them have done in our century, this might be beneficial not only for the humanities and humanist scholarship but also for philosophy and for a more complete and more balanced understanding of our world and experience.

66. Kristeller 1966a, p. 47.

PART 2

PHILOSOPHY AND ITS PARTS

V

LOGIC AND LANGUAGE

6

TRADITIONAL LOGIC

LOGIC 1350–1600

The study of Aristotle

The *Organon* of Aristotle played a central role throughout the period, at least in principle. During the medieval period, the *Organon* was divided into two parts. The *Categories* and the *De interpretatione* along with Porphyry's *Isagoge* formed the *Logica vetus*, which was already known in the twelfth century. The *Prior* and *Posterior Analytics*, the *Topics* and the *Sophistici elenchi* formed the *Logica nova*, which became known only during the twelfth century. Both the *Logica vetus* and the *Logica nova* were firmly embedded in the university curriculum, with the single exception of the *Topics*. It was not included in the list of books prescribed by the Vienna statutes of 1389 or in the list of books read at Erfurt in 1420, and at Greifswald in 1456 it was to be lectured on only for the master's degree, although at all these places the other books of the *Organon* were specifically mentioned as part of the undergraduate course.[1] In many places, including Paris, only four books of the *Topics* were to be read;[2] and it was sometimes specified that these books were to be I, II, VI and VIII.[3] An obvious result of humanist influence in the sixteenth century was the renewed attention paid to the *Topics*, though this interest was not to last.

There were several waves of commentaries during the period after 1350. Some of these were on individual books from the *Organon*, such as the commentary on the *Prior Analytics* by Marsilius of Inghen, which was published in Venice in 1516, and the commentary on the *Posterior Analytics* by Paul of Venice, which had been published seven times by 1518, nearly

---

1. For Vienna, see Lhotsky 1965, p. 236; for Erfurt, see *University Records* 1944, p. 297; for Greifswald, see *Cambridge History* 1982, pp. 18–19 (Kenny and Pinborg).
2. See, e.g., the Paris statutes of 1366: *University Records* 1944, p. 246; and a 1419 decree of St Andrews: *Acta Facultatis Artium Sancti Andree* 1964, p. 15.
3. Freiburg im Breisgau 1463: Ott and Fletcher 1964, p. 40; Glasgow: Durkan and Kirk 1977, pp. 87–8. In 1405 Bologna specified books I, II, IV and VI: *Statuti* 1888, p. 251. Only books I, II, III and IV were commented on by George of Brussels, 1504, ff. ccxvii^{ra}–xlvi^{ra}; Johannes de Magistris 1487, sigs. T 6ra–x 7ra; Tartaretus 1503a, ff. ciii ^{va}–xvii^{ra}.

always in Venice.[4] In the fifteenth century we find important commentaries on both the *Logica vetus* and the *Logica nova* being produced by the Thomists at the Bursa Montis in Cologne[5] and by Johannes Versor in Paris. However, such commentaries were soon to disappear. Bartholomaeus Arnoldi de Usingen, who taught at Erfurt, seems to be one of the last to write specifically on the *Logica vetus* (1514) and the *Logica nova* (1507, 1516) as such. Of the earlier medieval commentaries the most popular was that on the *Logica vetus* by Walter Burley, which had thirteen printed editions, the last in Venice in 1541. The most prevalent form of commentary from the late fifteenth century on dealt with the entire *Organon* in one book. The first commentaries of this sort, such as those by George of Brussels and Petrus Tartaretus (both first published at Paris in 1493) were in a traditional style, but almost at once the influence of humanism became apparent. In Paris Jacques Lefèvre d'Étaples produced his *Paraphrases et annotationes in libros logicorum* (eleven editions up to 1588) and in Germany in 1516–17 Johannes Eck published a complete commentary based on the new translations of Johannes Argyropulos but using the work of logicians in the medieval tradition.[6] Eck's work was produced for the University of Ingolstadt, and was prescribed by the statutes of 1519–20; but it is not clear how much it was actually used.[7]

There followed a period of rapid change which by the end of the sixteenth century had produced a totally new style of writing on Aristotle. There were several reasons for these changes. First, there was the influence of new translations of Aristotle and new attitudes to the Greek text. In his preface to a new translation by Johannes Franciscus Burana, Hieronymus Bagolinus wrote scathingly of the medieval translators who had 'presented all the thoughts of Aristotle as if they were enveloped in a perverted, corrupt and noisome fog'.[8] An excellent example of the new Greek-based texts is

---

4. For general information on both manuscripts and printed editions of Aristotle commentaries, see Lohr 1967 to 1974a and 1974b to 1982.
5. For some information about the Cologne commentators, see Lohr 1971, pp. 310–12. A 'bursa' was a kind of college in which students lived and were taught.
6. The full title of Aristotle 1516–17 is instructive: *Dialectica: cum quinque vocibus Porphyrii Phenicis: Argyropilo traductore: a Joanne Eckio Theologo facili explanatione declarata: adnotationibus compendiariis illustrata: ac scholastico exercitatio explicata: videbis o Lector priscam Dialecticam restitutam: ac Neotericorum subtilitati feliciter copulatam.* For discussion of Eck, see Seifert 1978.
7. See Heath 1971, p. 59.
8. Preface to Burana 1539, sig. A ii[r]. Bagolinus begins: 'Quum superioribus annis, viri clarissimi, ac omni scientiarum genere eminentissimi, in academia philosophantium Patavina, ad contextus Logicae Aristotelis cum expositoribus Graecis publicè interpretandos, scholasticis annuentibus, fuissem constitutus, ob id scilicet quòd anteà non nisi per neotericos quosdam interpretes, qui omnia Aristotelis sensa depravata, corrupta, ac teterrima quadam caligine involuta legebant,

found in the *Organon* edition of Giulio Pace, which was first published in 1584 and appeared in 1597 with an analytic commentary. In it we find the Greek text side-by-side with a new translation designed not only to read well (as was the humanist goal) but also to capture the philosophical significance of Aristotle's words. In the margins we find a commentary dealing with difficult points both of theory and translation.[9] A second reason for change was the publication of the Greek commentators on Aristotle's logic: Alexander of Aphrodisias, Themistius, Ammonius, Philoponus and Simplicius. Ample evidence of their influence can be found in the commentaries of Agostino Nifo. A third reason was the new emphasis on Averroes, both brought about by and reflected in the great Aristotle–Averroes edition of 1550–2.[10] These changes were also taken note of by Bagolinus, who praised Burana for his use of both Greek and Arabic commentators, including new translations of the Arabic from the Hebrew.[11] A fourth, but more minor, reason for change was the new popularity of Thomas Aquinas. Even though there was a rapid decline in the publication of Thomas' Aristotle commentaries after 1570,[12] the Coimbra commentators in particular were to make numerous references to 'Divus Thomas'.

At the end of the sixteenth century we find both new texts and new emphases in the curricula of various institutions. There are three kinds of text which are particularly noteworthy. First, there are commentaries on specific works by Aristotle, such as Jacopo Zabarella's commentary on the *Posterior Analytics* which, along with his other works, was to be extremely popular in the first part of the seventeenth century, especially in Germany. Second, there is the extensive commentary on selected parts of the whole *Organon*, most notably the *Commentarii in universam dialecticam Aristotelis* by the Coimbra Jesuit Sebastian Couto, which first appeared in 1606. It has been described as presenting a fusion of two late sixteenth-century approaches to Aristotle, the philosophical one of Zabarella and the philological one of Pace.[13] Third, there are numerous shorter works which

exponerentur: nec Posteriores Resolutorios ultra primi dimidium scholares degustarent: qui verò Priores Resolutorii nuncupantur, prorsus omitterentur: eo anno, non sine maximis laboribus ad id continuata lectione perveni, ut et Priores et Posteriores Resolutorios cum Alexandri, Simplicii, Philoponi, et aliorum quorundam expositionibus integros enucleaverim: nec non diebus festis libros Elenchorum: quos sanè à nullos penitus sine Graecorum expositione rectè intelligi posse existimaverim. Hi enim certè sunt qui ab ipso Aristotele, Theophrasto, atque Eudemo, summis Peripateticis, ad novissimos usque quasi haereditario quodam iure doctrinam Peripateticam integram atque illabefactatam conservarunt.'
9. For discussion, see Schmitt 1983a, pp. 83–5.   10. See Schmitt 1984, § VIII, pp. 131–140.
11. Burana 1539, sig. A ii[r].   12. Cranz 1978, p. 179.   13. Schmitt 1981, § VI, p. 170.

offer a complete introduction to the logic of Aristotle, such as those by Toletus and Fonseca (see below, p. 163).

So far as the curriculum is concerned, the most important influence was that of the Jesuits, whose constitution committed them to follow Aristotle in logic. The *Ratio studiorum* of 1586 refers to this commitment, but also notes that material more properly belonging to metaphysics should be passed over, as should the *Topics* (except for books I and II) and the *Sophistici elenchi*, though the material of the topics and fallacies should be presented in some more orderly way.[14] These exhortations are shown to be effective by the brief treatment given to the *Topics* and the *Sophistici elenchi* in the Coimbra commentary.[15] Other examples of the place of Aristotle in the curriculum can be found in the philosophy course given by the *collèges de plein exercise* in France, which was 'not so much a commentary as an ordered or simplified exposition of Aristotle's logical works'.[16] At Oxford, the new Laudian statutes of 1636 followed the practice of the previous century in requiring Aristotle to be followed in logic.[17] As we shall see, this emphasis on Aristotle and Aristotle alone was a sixteenth-century phenomenon. On the other hand, neither in France nor in Oxford is there much evidence that Aristotle himself was read. The main teaching emphasis seems to have been on introductory textbooks, and indeed the Jesuit *Ratio studiorum* of 1586 and again in 1599 recommended such texts (see below, p. 163).

Developments in medieval logic 1350–1530

In order to understand the full scope of the changes which took place in logic during the sixteenth century, it is necessary to consider the range of non-Aristotelian topics treated by medieval logicians.[18] The most important developments in medieval logic were presented in the form of treatises on individual subjects. These were normally regarded as complete in themselves and needing no justification in terms of Aristotelian logic. Only

14. *Monumenta Germaniae paedagogica* 1887, pp. 129–30: 'In Logica . . ., et Philosophia naturali et morali, et Methaphysica doctrina Aristotelis sequenda est'; p. 138: 'Topicorum quoque, praeter primum forte et secundum librum, et Elenchorum textus praetereundus est: Loci tamen et fallaciae in commodiorem quendam ordinem redigantur, nec a Logicis ignorentur.'
15. *Collegium Conimbricense* 1607, cols. 733–66.
16. Brockliss 1981a, p. 135. Philosophy teaching in seventeenth-century France took place at these colleges rather than at the universities, though there were occasional exceptions: *ibid.*, p. 131.
17. McConica 1979, pp. 291–2, noted that Aristotle's texts had been placed at the heart of the statutory curriculum under Henry VIII and Edward VI.
18. For analysis of various doctrines which will be referred to below, see *Cambridge History* 1982 for the period up to 1350 and Ashworth 1974a for the period from the late fifteenth to the seventeenth century. For a bibliography of printed primary sources, see Risse 1965.

occasionally did authors such as the Thomists of Cologne feel the need to relate the new developments to the *Organon*, and their attempt was somewhat perfunctory.[19] For instance, they related the new treatises on obligations to Aristotle's remark in *Metaphysics* IX.4 (1047^{b}15–25) that a possible proposition could not imply an impossible proposition, and they completely ignored the seemingly much more obvious relationship between obligational disputations and Aristotle's discussion of disputations in the *Topics*.[20]

There are three distinct groups of these new treatises, and each will be discussed in turn. The first group consists of the *parva logicalia*, or treatises dealing with the properties of terms. The core of the *parva logicalia* is formed by the treatises which (in the printed editions at least) are found in tract VII of Peter of Spain's *Summule logicales*, i.e., the treatises on supposition, relative terms, ampliation, appellation, restriction and distribution.[21] To these were later added a tract on exponibles and a tract on syncategorematic terms.[22] The Cologne Thomists noted that many people refused to ascribe the tract on exponibles to Peter of Spain himself, and it is obviously much too late to have been written by him.[23] Peter of Spain was neither the originator nor the sole author of the *parva logicalia*. Two other important authors of such tracts were Thomas Maulvelt (or Manlevelt), probably a mid-fourteenth-century Englishman, whose works were very popular in Germany in the fifteenth century; and Marsilius of Inghen, who probably wrote his logical treatises between 1362 and 1367.[24] He too was very popular in Germany, and in Eastern Europe.

The second group of treatises consists of the 'three tracts of the moderns', as the Cologne Thomists called them, i.e., tracts on consequences,

---

19. [Cologne] 1493, f. i^{r-v}. They remarked (f. i^v): 'Secundo dicendum quod quamvis Arestoteles non invenit istam logicam quae hic traditur in se et in propria forma istorum tractatuum, tamen invenit istos tractatus in suis principiis, quia posuit quaedam principia ex quibus isti tractatus ulterius eliciuntur et fiunt.'

20. *Ibid.*, f. i^v. Although various medieval authors used the phrase *disputatio temptativa* (that used to translate the Greek phrase for Aristotle's examination argument) in this context, so far as I know only Boethius of Dacia related obligational disputations to Aristotle's discussion in the *Topics*: see Boethius of Dacia 1969–, VI, 1, pp. 329–31 (*Quaestiones super librum Topicorum*). The links were once more noticed in the sixteenth century: see Nifo 1521b, f. 151 $^{ra-rb}$.

21. Peter of Spain 1972, p. xcix. For an explanation of the terminology, see Maierù 1972.

22. Both tracts are found, e.g., in [Cologne] 1493 and 1494 and also in Versor 1572. However, the *Syncategoremata* is not found, e.g., in [Cologne] 1496.

23. [Cologne] 1493, f. i^r. Cf. Peter of Spain 1972, p. xcix, where de Rijk says that the tracts on the properties of terms were supplemented from about 1350 onwards by the tract on exponibles, 'which seven tracts were taken together as *Part Seven* of the *Tractatus* or *Summule*'.

24. Marsilius of Inghen 1980, p. 9.

obligations and insolubles.[25] A great many such tracts survive, and I shall mention only a few of the most important for our purposes. Of those writing shortly after 1350, three names are particularly prominent. First, there is the Englishman Ralph Strode. His insolubles made little impression, but there are forty or more manuscripts containing his consequences, eleven with the obligations as well. There are also ten printed editions of the consequences and four of the obligations.[26] He was particularly popular in Italy. Second, there is Marsilius of Inghen, who wrote on all three topics and whose consequences were printed in an abbreviated form along with his tracts on supposition in Vienna in 1512 and 1516. Third, there is John of Holland, who may have studied at Oxford before he went to Prague, and whose obligations and insolubles were popular in the fifteenth century, though they were printed only once in an abbreviated form (Vienna 1509). It is not known who wrote the three tracts which were commented on by the Cologne Thomists, but Henry of Gorkum (d. 1431), the founder of what came to be called the *Bursa Montis*, is known to have written on obligations and insolubles,[27] and there may be some relation.

The third group of treatises has two sub-groups. First, there are treatises on sophisms. Here William Heytesbury, from the first part of the fourteenth century, is the most outstanding figure; but later treatises by Albert of Saxony (mid fourteenth century) and Paul of Venice were also to prove popular, both being printed several times. Heytesbury also wrote a tract on the composite and the divided sense which was to have considerable influence, though the only noteworthy later writer on this topic was Paul of Pergula.[28] The material dealt with was very closely related to that discussed in the second sub-group of treatises, those dealing with the proof of terms. These treatises in turn overlapped with treatises on exponibles and syncategoremata because they included a discussion of exponible terms, such as 'only', 'except', and 'in so far as', whose presence caused a proposition to need further analysis. They also discussed 'official' (or 'functionalisable') terms, i.e., modal terms and such terms as 'knows' and 'believes' which govern a *dictum*, that is, an infinitive and accusative

---

25. For an interesting discussion of the way in which the phrase *logica modernorum* has been extended in recent times to refer to all the new developments of medieval logic, see *Antiqui und Moderni* 1974, especially pp. 111–15 (N. W. Gilbert). Agostino Nifo is a good example of a sixteenth-century author who used a variety of names to classify his predecessors. *Iuniores* seem to be opposed to writers of the classical period; *neoterici* are more recent writers (cf. the use of the term by Eck, n. 6 above, and by Bagolinus, n. 8 above); *Sorticolae* (probably logicians who used *Sortes* in their examples) explicitly included Marsilius of Inghen and Paul of Venice.

26. For details, see *English Logic* 1982, pp. 87–8 (Maierù).

27. Weiler 1962, p. 85.   28. Paul of Pergula 1961.

construction. The third type of term discussed was the so-called resoluble term, whose presence in a proposition indicates that it should be shown to be true by appeal to an expository syllogism involving a move from general terms (such as 'human being') to such indicator terms as 'this'. The most famous author of a treatise on the proof of terms was Richard Billingham. His *Speculum puerorum*, also known as *Terminus est in quem*, was written in the mid fourteenth century and it became extremely popular, especially in Southern and Central European universities.[29]

As well as treatises on individual topics, medieval logicians wrote *summulae*, or general textbooks. The most famous example is the thirteenth-century work by Peter of Spain which gives a complete outline of Aristotelian logic, including categories, syllogisms, topics and fallacies. More than 300 manuscripts of this work survive, and about 200 printed editions, mostly with a commentary.[30] However, it would be a mistake to think that Peter of Spain had no rivals. Two other general textbooks were to be of great importance in the fifteenth century. The first is the *summulae* by Jean Buridan, which was printed several times with a commentary by Johannes Dorp.[31] Buridan's treatise is a reworking of Peter of Spain, but supposition is discussed in tract IV, and tract VIII, on division, definition and demonstration, was completely new. The second is Paul of Venice's *Logica parva*, probably written in 1395–6.[32] Its contents list is worth considering in some detail. Tract I presents the material of the *summulae* and deals with terms, nouns, verbs, propositions, equipollence, conversion, hypothetical propositions, predicables, categories and syllogisms – that is, everything that Peter of Spain had covered except for topics and fallacies. Tract II deals with the material of the *parva logicalia*, i.e., supposition, relative terms, ampliation and appellation. Tracts III, V and VI are versions of the so-called 'tracts of the moderns', i.e., consequences, obligations and insolubles. Tract IV is on the proof of terms, including exponibles. The last two tracts contain objections to the *summulae* and to the consequences. The *Logica parva* was very popular. Over seventy manuscripts survive, and it was printed many times.[33] There were sixteen editions in Venice alone, six between 1525 and 1580; and the last that I know of was as late as 1614. An important feature of

29. De Rijk's introduction to *Some Fourteenth-Century Tracts* 1982, p. *3*. See *ibid.* for an edition of some alternative texts, by Billingham and others. See Maierù 1969 for an edition of Billingham.
30. Peter of Spain 1972, p. c.
31. Dorp was active in the German nation at the University of Paris from about 1393 to 1404, and was last heard of at Cologne in 1418: see *Antiqui und Moderni* 1974, pp. 446, 455 (Gabriel). For Dorp's commentary, see Buridan 1499.
32. For the dating of this work see *Scienza e filosofia* 1983, pp. 90–1 (Bottin).
33. For a list of the manuscripts see Bottin 1981, pp. 59–60.

the *Logica parva* is its close relationship to the so-called *Logica Oxoniensis*, a loose collection of treatises which was popular in the fifteenth century, especially in Italy,[34] and which was printed a number of times in England up to 1530.[35] This collection began with a brief *summulae* and among others included tracts on all the topics covered by Paul.

A glance at the curricula of fifteenth-century universities will give some idea of the part played in logic teaching by the different types of medieval texts. In Italy, Paul of Venice's *Logica parva* was a prescribed text at Padua in 1496, along with works by Strode, Heytesbury and Paul of Pergula.[36] The Vienna statutes of 1389 refer to supposition, ampliation, appellation, obligations, insolubles and consequences;[37] and the acts of the faculty of arts at Vienna show that John of Holland, Marsilius of Inghen, Billingham and Heytesbury were read.[38] At Erfurt in 1420, Billingham, John of Holland and Thomas Maulvelt were read;[39] and the Erfurt statutes of 1412 together with the additions of 1449 also mention Heytesbury, Albert of Saxony, Buridan and Marsilius of Inghen.[40] The Freiburg im Breisgau statutes of 1463 required the first five tracts of Peter of Spain, the *Parva logicalia* of Marsilius, and his consequences.[41] There was a cult of Marsilius at Heidelberg at the end of the fifteenth century.[42] Heytesbury was read at Leipzig up to 1496, when he was withdrawn from the curriculum on the grounds that his logic was of little value.[43] At Greifswald in 1456 there were lectures on the *parva logicalia* with exercises in Peter of Spain and *sophismata* or *sophistria*.[44] Peter of Spain's *Summule* was read at Ingolstadt in 1478, and it was still mentioned by the statutes of Ingolstadt in 1526.[45] In Poland

34. See Rijk 1977 for the *Logica Oxoniensis* and Rijk 1975 for the similar *Logica Cantabrigiensis*. For a study of the origins and *fortuna* of some of the obligations treatises in the collection, see Ashworth 1985.
35. See Ashworth 1979a, 1979b, and (for a similar printed collection associated with Oxford) 1978a.
36. Paul of Pergula 1961, p. vii.
37. Lhotsky 1965, p. 236. The same list of required tracts was mentioned by [Cologne] 1493 f. i^r.
38. *Acta Facultatis Artium Universitatis Vindobonensis* 1968 *passim*. Billingham and Heytesbury were mentioned once; John of Holland's insolubles was mentioned twice and his obligations once; Marsilius of Inghen's insolubles was mentioned once, his supposition twice, his consequences four times and his obligations nine times.
39. *University Records* 1944, pp. 296–7.   40. *Antiqui und Moderni* 1974, pp. 467–8 (Gabriel).
41. Ott and Fletcher 1964, p. 40.   42. *Antiqui und Moderni* 1974, pp. 463–4 (Gabriel).
43. Fletcher 1981, p. 30. The text is ordered to be withdrawn 'quia parum fructus in se habeat'. On p. 35, n. 109, it is identified through the phrase 'lectio loicae Hesbri'.
44. *Cambridge History* 1982, p. 18 (Kenny and Pinborg). Heath 1971, p. 45, noted that works on *sophismata* were more popular than tract vi of Peter of Spain (on fallacies). The latter was left to the second year at Freiburg, Ingolstadt and Tübingen.
45. Heath 1971, p. 49. In 1478 the masters of Ingolstadt decided that tracts i, iv, v and vii of the *Summule logicales* should be read. That is, they omitted the material on predicables, categories and fallacies. See *ibid.*, p. 59 for the statutes of 1526, which mention the first five tracts of Peter of Spain.

Buridan was popular.[46] In Paris the nominalist faction, in a document of *c*. 1474, showed that it prided itself on the attention it paid to the properties of terms, including exponibles, to obligations and to insolubles, unlike the realists, who were said to neglect and despise these matters.[47] In Scotland the year 1438 saw some interesting developments at St Andrews University.[48] On 13 October the Congregation ruled that Buridan should be read in place of the logical doctrines of Albertus Magnus and the *Summule* of Peter of Spain. There was such an outcry that on 14 November it was ruled that the masters could follow the *via* of Albertus, or whomever else they wished, provided he was free from errors in logic and philosophy. Finally, in Oxford the *Logica Oxoniensis* was read well into the sixteenth century, if publishing history is anything to go by. These scattered remarks do not, of course, enable one to appreciate the detail of any particular university's curriculum, but they should be enough to indicate that a considerable variety of authors were read across Europe and that there was no tendency to read just Aristotle, or just Peter of Spain.

Considerable changes took place in the first thirty years of the sixteenth century. Some of these changes were internal to the medieval tradition, and I shall examine these first. Some medieval topics simply disappeared. Although old *sophismata* texts were published, new ones were not written. An exception is the modest treatise *De sophismatibus* which followed the treatise on exponibles in George of Brussels' commentary on Peter of Spain.[49] Treatises on the composition and division of terms also vanished, though several Italians, including Alessandro Sermoneta and Benedetto Vettori (d. 1561) did write a commentary on Heytesbury's treatise.[50] Treatises on *syncategoremata* were no longer written, no doubt partly because much of the material was common to other treatises, including those on exponibles. Billingham's work on the proof of terms seems never to have been printed, and the topic appears only occasionally. For instance, both Johannes Gebwiler and Gregorius Breytkopf wrote short sections on the proof of terms in longer works, and Nifo has a chapter on the topic in his *Dialectica ludicra*.[51] By contrast, separate treatises began to be written on traditional topics which had usually been discussed in some wider context. The most notable example is that of treatises on the various divisions of

46. See Markowski 1971.
47. *Antiqui und Moderni* 1974, p. 95, n. 25 (N. W. Gilbert). See also *University Records* 1944, pp. 355–60.
48. *Acta Facultatis Artium Sancti Andree* 1964, pp. 48–9.
49. George of Brussels 1491a, sigs. G 3rb–H 6rb.
50. See Maierù 1972, pp. 35–8, for a discussion of these commentaries and their authors.
51. Breytkopf 1507, sigs. C v^r ff.; Gebwiler 1511, (tract III) sigs. K 4^v–M 3^v; Nifo 1521b, ff. 119ra ff.

terms, e.g., categorematic and syncategorematic, complex and incomplex, first and second imposition or intention, univocal and equivocal. This material had always been included to some extent in various *summulae* and commentaries, but now at least twenty distinct treatises were published by such authors as Antonio Coronel, Johannes Dullaert, John Mair and Fernando de Enzinas, all of whom taught at the University of Paris.[52] Separate treatises were also written on *oppositiones*, the logical relations between different kinds of categorical propositions, and on syllogisms.

At the same time, separate treatises and commentaries in the old style continued to be written. Insolubles, consequences and obligations continued to be the subject of discussion, as did the *parva logicalia*, including exponibles. Moreover, various new commentaries on Peter of Spain were produced in Germany as well as in France and Spain. The Paris commentary by George of Brussels has already been mentioned, and other Parisian authors include Petrus Tartaretus and John Mair. Nicholas Tinctor's *dicta* on Peter of Spain were published by the Tübingen masters in 1486,[53] and Johannes Eck's commentary was published in 1516. Spanish commentators included Domingo de Soto (Burgos 1529) and Augustinus Sbarroya (Seville 1533). While it is true that little of the material in these works was novel, there were occasional flashes of originality. For instance, Thomas Bricot put forward a solution to the problem of semantic paradoxes which was new in detail if not in principle;[54] and in their writings on supposition theory the Parisian masters introduced 'a' and 'b' as special signs of supposition to help them in the analysis of propositions containing relational terms such as 'Every man has a head' and 'Of every man, some donkey is running.'[55]

By about 1530 most of this activity had come to an abrupt end. New commentaries on medieval authors disappeared except in Spain, where Thomas de Mercado's commentary on Peter of Spain was first published as late as 1571. Treatises on individual topics ceased to be written, with an occasional exception such as Antonius Kesler's treatise on consequences of 1623.[56] The publication both of the newer works in the medieval tradition and of the older ones virtually ceased.[57] At the same time the university curricula changed. Authors such as Rudolph Agricola and Johannes

---

52. A good bibliography of works by Spanish authors can be found in Muñoz Delgado 1972.
53. *Antiqui und Moderni* 1974, p. 483 (Gabriel). Tinctor went to Ingolstadt from Paris.
54. See Ashworth 1977 for a discussion.
55. See Ashworth 1978b for a discussion. See also Broadie 1983, pp. 50–4.
56. See Ashworth 1973a for a discussion.
57. For more details see *Cambridge History* 1982, p. 790 (Ashworth).

Caesarius were required in place of the medieval texts,[58] and Philipp Melanchthon's simplified summary of Aristotelian logic swept Germany. Later, Petrus Ramus was to enjoy a runaway success. Yet the most important and influential texts of the last years of the sixteenth century were by no means simplified humanist manuals, and they contained not only considerably more syllogistic logic than Lorenzo Valla, Agricola or Ramus had thought appropriate, but also treatments of such medieval doctrines as supposition theory.

PHILOSOPHY OF LANGUAGE 1350–1600

Speculative grammar

By 1350 the doctrines of speculative grammar had already lost their importance for philosophers of language. No original contributions had been made after 1300, and the theoretical framework had been subjected to strong attacks.[59] For the period we are concerned with, there is only one brief work in support of speculative grammar which needs to be mentioned, the *Generalis doctrina de modis significandi grammaticalibus* by the Polish author John of Stobnica (1470–1518).[60] Otherwise, the two important pieces of writing were vicious attacks on the doctrine: the *Destructiones modorum significandi* written by Pierre d'Ailly in the last quarter of the fourteenth century,[61] and the *Invectiva in modos significandi* written by the Westphalian humanist Alexander Hegius (*c.* 1433–98) in about 1480.[62] There was some publication of the earlier writings. The *Expositiones modorum significandi* of Johannes Josse was published in France (undated).[63] The *Quaestiones Alberti de modis significandi* was published twice in England (1496?, *c.* 1515), and Thomas of Erfurt's *Grammatica speculativa* was published in a variety of places including Deventer (1489), London (1515), Venice (1499, 1512, 1519), Pavia (1520) and Paris (1604, 1605).[64] It was

---

58. For details see *Cambridge History* 1982, pp. 800–1 (L. Jardine).
59. *Cambridge History* 1982, p. 256 (Pinborg).
60. See Gansiniec 1960, pp. 149–54, for the text. See also Pinborg 1967, p. 211.
61. See Pinborg 1967, pp. 202–10.
62. For an edition see IJsewijn 1971. For discussion see *Cambridge History* 1982, p. 814 (Percival).
63. Johannes Josse *c.* 1495 [Bodleian Library, Oxford]. The edition is not listed by Pinborg 1967.
64. To the list of editions given by Pinborg 1967, p. 318, one can add: London 1515 [STC 272]; Venice 1519 (edited by Maurice O'Fiheley) [Bodleian Library]; Pavia 1520 (edited by O'Fiheley) [British Library]; Paris 1605 (in *Gymnasium speculativum*, edited by A. Gothutius) [British Library]. For a modern edition, see Thomas of Erfurt 1972. The *Quaestiones Alberti* is a separate work by an otherwise unknown author: see Pinborg 1967, pp. 93, 309. It has recently been edited: see Albertus Magnus, Pseudo- 1977.

variously attributed to 'Albertus' and to Johannes Duns Scotus; and it is
probably because of its inclusion in the works of Scotus that it had some
influence on the work of the new universal grammarians of the seventeenth
century.[65] As can be inferred from the publication record, at the beginning
of the sixteenth century speculative grammar enjoyed its greatest popularity in England, and this is born out by contemporary references. Thomas
More, in his *Epistola ad Martinum Dorpium*, denounced the extravagant
delight some people took in the 'exceedingly trifling trifles' put forward by
'a certain Albert'.[66] However, this delight was short-lived, for in 1521 John
Skelton wrote in his poem 'Speke Parott':

> Albertus *De modo significandi*
> And Donatus be dryven out of scole.

While it is true that the characteristic doctrine of the speculative
grammarians, that there is a correspondence between the *modi significandi* of
words, the *modi intelligendi* in the mind and the *modi essendi* in the world, is of
little importance for understanding the philosophy of language put forward
by late medieval and Renaissance logicians, it is also true that the
grammatical classifications of the speculative grammarians were often used.
Modi significandi were sometimes appealed to in order to explain the
difference between a word's lexical meaning and its accidental signification,
i.e., the meaning it acquired by virtue of grammatical case;[67] and the notion
of *congruitas* or grammatical correctness appears in logic texts.[68] Albert of
Saxony explained that a grammatically correct utterance is subordinated to
a grammatically correct mental construction;[69] and the *Logica Oxoniensis*
defined a proposition as a grammatically correct, perfect, indicative
sentence which signified the true or the false.[70] Interestingly, this definition
reappeared in several later authors.[71] Other notions, such as that of a *vox*

65. See *Cambridge History* 1982, pp. 815–16 (Percival); Padley 1976, pp. 179ff.
66. In Vives 1979a, p. 171; for a discussion see Kinney 1981, pp. 182–3.
67. See Ashworth 1982, p. 75, for some references.
68. See Thomas of Erfurt 1972, pp. 306ff.
69. Albert of Saxony 1522, f. 2rb: 'causa originalis quare una constructio ex constructionibus ad
    placitum institutis composita est congrua, et alia incongrua, non alia est nisi quod ista quam dicimus
    congruam subordinatur uni constructioni mentali congrue, et illa quam dicimus incongruam
    subordinatur uni constructioni incongrue: unde sicut terminus subordinatur termino, et ita oratio
    orationi'.
70. 'Propositio est oratio indicativa, congrua et perfecta, verum vel falsum significans': see Ashworth
    1979a, p. 150.
71. See Case 1584, p. 17; Sanderson 1618, p. 71; Brerewood 1619, p. 1. These authors all added the
    phrase *sine ambiguitate*, which is found in Melanchthon's definition of a proposition: Melanchthon
    1834–60, XIII, col. 577. Trentman 1976, p. 187, discusses Brerewood but seems to interpret his use
    of *congrua* as showing the influence of Thomas of Erfurt or Roger Bacon.

articulata, which appear in sixteenth- and seventeenth-century texts,[72] and which have been attributed to the influence of speculative grammarians,[73] are more likely to show the influence of Roman grammarians mediated through such humanists as Aldus Manutius.[74] In general, there seems to be a tendency in the secondary literature to over-emphasise the direct influence of speculative grammar on sixteenth- and seventeenth-century writers. Heath, for instance, says of Eck's *Elementarius dialecticae* (1518) that 'the theories of the *modistae* are neatly dovetailed with the reinterpreted Ockham'.[75] He cites Eck's use of such commonplace notions as *congruitas* and *constructio*; and he makes much of Eck's concentration on mental terms – an approach which is found in the anti-modist Pierre d'Ailly, to mention but one possible source for Eck's doctrines.[76]

Language and the logicians

Medieval and Renaissance philosophy of language is characterised by two central doctrines, which can only be fully understood in conjunction: the doctrine that spoken language is purely conventional and the doctrine that spoken language corresponds to a mental language, which has natural signification. I shall begin by considering the doctrine that spoken language is conventional, which has its origin in the works of Aristotle, e.g., *De interpretatione* IV (17^a1–2). The purely conventional nature of utterances, other than 'the groans of the sick or the barking of dogs',[77] was insisted on by all logicians from Peter of Spain onwards, and there was very little discussion of alternative views. Thomas Aquinas in his commentary on *De interpretatione* mentions the view that names are the natural similitudes of things.[78] Another of these rare references to an alternative view is found in Henry of Ghent, who explored Augustine's claim that the Stoics believed

72. See, e.g., Seton 1545, sig. A v^r. For some further references, see Ashworth 1981a, p. 306.

73. Trentman 1976, p. 184, cites Seton's definitions of such terms as 'vox, vox articulata, inarticulata vox, vox significativa, consignificativa, vox significans ad placitum, naturalis vox' (see Seton 1545, sig. A v^{r-v}) and says 'it is an interesting and worthy representation of the medieval tradition of speculative grammar'. Incidentally, Trentman in *Cambridge History* 1982, p. 821, is wrong when he says that Seton's work was not published until 1572: editions had already appeared in 1545, 1563, 1568 and 1570.

74. See Padley 1976, p. 34. See also Ashworth 1981a, pp. 305–6. Even during the medieval period the notion was not uncommon.   75. Heath 1971, p. 57.

76. See Ailly 1980, especially pp. 18–27. He also used the notions of *congruitas* and *constructio*: see Pinborg 1967, p. 204: 'Congruitas, regimen et constructio competant orationi mentali per se et proprie.'

77. Peter of Spain 1972, p. 2 :'Vocum significativarum alia significativa ad placitum, alia naturaliter. Vox significativa naturaliter est illa que apud omnes idem representat, ut gemitus infirmorum, latratus canum. Vox significativa ad placitum est illa que ad voluntatem instituentis aliquid representat, ut *homo*.'   78. Thomas Aquinas 1964, p. 21, §47.

words to have a natural origin because the sound of a word could have a natural similarity to a thing.[79] Both Thomas Aquinas and Henry of Ghent concluded that Aristotle's view was correct.

Serious discussion of the possibility of a naturally significant spoken language seems to have been purely a sixteenth- and seventeenth-century phenomenon. It was due in part to the rediscovery of Plato's *Cratylus* and other classical sources, in part to the strong Renaissance interest in magic and the cabala, with the concomitant hope that a knowledge of natural language would enable one to exercise some control over the objects signified, and in part to renewed biblical studies.[80] Genesis 2:19 says 'Whatsoever Adam called every living creature, that *was* the name thereof', and this suggested to commentators that the language of Adam, the original *lingua humana*, was a natural language, reflecting the nature of things. There were numerous attempts to rediscover Adam's language, which was often thought to be a form of primitive Hebrew.[81] All these issues were reflected in the works of later logicians. For instance, in his Coimbra commentary Sebastian Couto took up the matter at some length.[82] After a consideration of Plato and various other sources he concluded that although language as such is a natural phenomenon, its meaning is conventional; and that when Moses wrote Genesis 2:19 he meant to convey only that Adam had used the Hebrew words still current when Moses was writing.[83] Couto did hold that the original giver of language was God;[84] but this was not allowed to detract from the conventionalist thesis. It is important to emphasise these points, because it is often erroneously suggested that the conventionalist

---

79. Henry of Ghent 1520, ff. cclxiiii[r]–vii[v]. See Augustine 1975, pp. 91–9.
80. For references and discussion, see Aarsleff 1982, pp. 59–60, 281–2; Cornelius 1965, p. 5; Grazia 1980, p. 324; Padley 1976, pp. 139–41. It is interesting to note that the influential grammarian Francisco Sanchez discussed the issue of naturally significative language in the introduction to his *Minerva*: see Sanchez 1587, ff. 5[r]–7[v]. He wrote (f. 6[r]): 'Nomina certe et verba rerum naturam significare cum Platone assererem libentissime, si hoc ille tantum de primaeva omnium linguarum asseverasset.'
81. See Cornelius 1965, p. 10; Knowlson 1975, pp. 12–13.
82. *Collegium Conimbricense* 1607 (part II), cols. 48–59. For other references, see Ashworth 1981a, pp. 307–8.
83. *Ibid.*, cols. 58–9: 'Ad illud, quod subditur de impositione nominum animalium facta ab Adamo, variae sunt doctorum interpretationes, inter quas duae praecipuae. Una, dici ea nomina propria animalium, quia in modo proferendi cohaerebant cum animalium natura et proprietatibus, ut quae significabat leonem, maiestatem prae se ferret atque terrorem; quae Philomelam, suavitatem. Secunda verior, significasse Moysem illis verbis, ijsdem nominibus appellasse Adamum animalia in orbis conditione, quibus ea suo tempore Hebraeis nuncupabant.'
84. *Ibid.*, col. 58. Couto's reasons for suggesting God as the original impositor had to do with the difficulties involved in supposing that either Adam alone or both Adam and Eve together created a language: see col. 55. So far as I know, the problem of how the original imposition took place, or who was responsible, was not often raised, at least by logicians.

view was a seventeenth-century phenomenon. Both Hobbes and Locke have been praised for their innovation and insight,[85] whereas at least in the case of Locke, very close correlations can be found between parts of his discussion of language and the discussion found in the scholastic logicians who were read at Oxford.[86] In taking the conventionalist position and rejecting Adamitic language, Locke was aligning himself with a continuous tradition stretching back through the Middle Ages to Aristotle, whereas Leibniz's interest in Adamitic language was a relative novelty.

The second crucial doctrine was that spoken (and hence written) language corresponds to an inner mental language which is naturally meaningful, and without which no utterance could be significant. This doctrine had its origin in *De interpretatione* I (16^a3-8) and was reinforced both by St Augustine's discussion in *De trinitate* XV.10–11 and by Boethius' two commentaries on *De interpretatione*. The doctrine is common to logicians throughout the Middle Ages, and it continued well into the seventeenth century, being found in both Locke and Leibniz. In order to understand the doctrine several issues have to be considered: the nature of signification, the relation of words to both things and concepts, and the supposed structure of mental language.

First, an account must be given of signification. The word *significatio* is all too easily translated as 'meaning', but as Spade has noted, 'signification is a psychologico-causal property of terms'.[87] One early account of significa-tion was drawn from Boethius' translation of *De interpretatione* III (16^b19), which suggested that to signify something was 'to establish an understand-ing' of it.[88] This definition leaves one in doubt both about the status of syncategorematic terms (such as logical connectives) and about the status of mental terms themselves, since no mental term can be said to signify in the sense that it causes or brings about a concept. For this reason, the early sixteenth-century author Raulin (*c.* 1443–1514) explicitly stated that the Boethian definition applied only to a sub-class of signs.[89] Another early account of signification was drawn from St Augustine: 'A sign is something which is itself sensed and which indicates to the mind something beyond the sign itself.'[90] Although St Augustine's definition was frequently quoted, it

85. See Aarsleff 1982, pp. 63, 284. Grazia 1980, p. 326, specifically mentions Hobbes' view that language was conventional, although created by God, as if this were a novel doctrine. Cf. Martinich 1981, pp. 351–2.

86. For a study of Locke's scholastic sources, see Ashworth 1981a and 1984. I do not, of course, wish to suggest that all Locke had to say about language was traditional in nature.

87. *Cambridge History* 1982, p. 188 (Spade).   88. *Ibid.*   89. Raulin 1500, sig. g v^{ra-rb}.

90. Augustine 1975, p. 87. The most common source for the definition is Augustine, *De doctrina Christiana* II.1.

gave rise to the same difficulties as the Boethian definition. Accordingly in the fifteenth and early sixteenth century, we find two developments. First, there is a widespread use of Pierre d'Ailly's definition of *significare*: 'Now to "signify" is to represent (a) something, or (b) some things or (c) somehow, to a cognitive power by vitally changing it.'[91] The presence of the term 'somehow' (*aliqualiter*) was expressly intended to extend the definition to syncategorematic terms. Second, there is a close attention paid to different kinds of sign. Pierre d'Ailly himself had noted that some signs, namely mental terms or concepts, affect the cognitive power by virtue of their nature,[92] and in some early sixteenth-century authors such as Soto we find a careful classification of both signs and types of signification. Spoken words were said to be instrumental signs, because of their causal properties, and mental terms were said to be formal signs because they represented by their very nature.[93] These classifications were elaborated in later sources, such as the Coimbra commentary;[94] and in the seventeenth century John of St Thomas took up the topic in considerable detail.[95]

Unless one realises that to signify is to represent or to make known,[96] it is impossible to understand the debate whether spoken words signify concepts or things. This question first became popular in the late thirteenth century, and it appears in commentaries on the *De interpretatione* through the Middle Ages and into the seventeenth century.[97] It is discussed by Toletus,[98] by Sebastian Couto in the Coimbra commentary,[99] by the Polish Jesuit Martinus Smiglecius, whose *Logica* was first published in 1618,[100] and in John of St Thomas.[101] Echoes of the debate reappear in ordinary logical textbooks such as Burgersdijk's *Institutionum logicarum libri duo*[102] and in John Locke's *Essay*, when he writes 'Words in their primary or immediate Signification stand for nothing, but *the ideas* in the Mind of him that uses them . . .' (III.2.2). All the participants in the debate agreed on certain issues. They agreed that concepts play an essential role in the significative process, for we cannot refer to objects we do not know; nor can we speak

---

91. Ailly 1980, p. 16, §2.   92. *Ibid.*, p. 16, §1; p. 17, §8.   93. Soto 1529, ff. v^{ra}–vi^{ra}.
94. *Collegium Conimbricense* 1607 (part II), cols. 7–33.
95. John of St Thomas 1930, pp. 9–10, 646–722.
96. Pratus 1530, f. ii^{va}, said that *significare* could be taken as equivalent to *manifestare, facere formare* or *facere cognoscere*.
97. For full discussion and references see Ashworth 1981a and forthcoming.
98. Toletus 1596, pp. 208–9.   99. *Collegium Conimbricense* 1607 (part II), cols. 34–45.
100. Smiglecius 1658, pp. 436–8.   101. John of St Thomas 1930, pp. 104–8.
102. Burgersdijk 1637, p. 110, wrote: 'Voces articulatae significant animi conceptus, primò scilicet, atque immediatè: nam res etiam significant, sed mediantibus conceptibus.'

meaningfully when we have nothing in mind.[103] Equally, everyone agreed that words, at least some of the time, are used to pick out things in the world. If I say 'Some human beings are running', what I say is true (if at all) of individual things and not of my concepts. The debate concerned the way in which the role of concepts in the significative process was to be described. Some authors held that words primarily signified or made known concepts and only secondarily signified things.[104] Others, such as Eck, held that words signified things alone while being subordinated to concepts.[105] Yet others, including Couto, preferred to say that while the signification of things had a certain primacy, both concepts and things were made known by words, which thus enjoy a double signification.[106]

The debate just described concerned categorematic words, or lexical items. The role of syncategorematic terms, such as quantifiers and logical connectives, is also of considerable interest, but only a handful of early sixteenth-century logicians at the University of Paris seem to have discussed the matter in any detail. One important writer is Fernando de Enzinas, who in his *Tractatus de compositione propositionis mentalis* discussed not only the role of syncategorematic terms in mental language but also the way in which the relationship between lexical items and grammatical features should be accounted for at the mental level.[107] He noted that different languages dealt with case and number in different ways, and suggested that these features should be represented at the mental level by syncategorematic acts, analogous to those representing the force of quantifiers and logical connectives, rather than by postulating different concepts for each grammatical case of a lexical item.

The question of the structure of mental language also arose in relation to the definition of a standard categorical proposition as having a subject and predicate, both in the nominative case, and a copula formed from the verb 'to be'. The main problems arose from sentences with so-called adjectival verbs such as 'runs', or indeed any ordinary verb other than the verb 'to be',

103. For a discussion of the role of speaker intentions, see *Collegium Conimbricense* 1607 (part II), cols. 34–5 and 42–4. Contrary to Martinich 1981, pp. 127–8, Hobbes was not the first to notice the imporance of speaker intentions.

104. This seems to have been a Thomist position: for some references see Ashworth forthcoming, n. 55. John of St Thomas 1930 holds both that concepts are more immediately signified and that things are more principally signified: see pp. 106–7.   105. Aristotle 1516–17, I, f. lxxii^ra.

106. *Collegium Conimbricense* 1607 (part II), cols. 39–40. The notion of double signification was attacked by John of St Thomas 1930, pp. 105–6.

107. Enzinas 1528. It was also printed in Paris in 1521, 1526 and 1528. For discussion see Ashworth 1982.

sentences with impersonal verbs such as 'pluit' ('It is raining')[108] and sentences containing deictic words such as 'this' or 'I'.[109] There were two levels of discussion. At the practical level, the problem concerned how to rewrite these sentences so that they could be converted for use in syllogistic. Medieval logicians discussed conversion at great length. One good example is found in Marsilius of Inghen's commentary on the *Prior Analytics*, in which he considers such examples as 'I am Socrates', whose conversion will have to be 'Socrates is I.'[110] Many of Marsilius' examples were taken up by Nifo over a century later in his commentary on the *Prior Analytics*.[111] However, this is one of the topics that dropped from view during the sixteenth century. Later authors content themselves with the occasional remark about problems of conversion,[112] and tend to present their syllogisms already in standard form.

At the theoretical level, the problem concerned the structure that such sentences would have in mental language. Some debate took place during the fourteenth and fifteenth centuries, but once more the most interesting discussions are found in Fernando de Enzinas and other early sixteenth-century writers at the University of Paris.[113] One of the important features of the debate is that although they thought that mental sentences did have a structure, they also thought that logically equivalent sentences could have different structures. There was little indication of a belief that any of these structures mirrored reality.[114]

These remarks have by no means dealt with all the problems in the philosophy of language that were discussed between 1350 and 1600. I shall conclude by mentioning two other issues, both of which were treated at length in Gregory of Rimini's influential commentary on the *Sententiae* of Peter Lombard, which was written in the 1340s. One of the questions he discussed was how it was that a mental proposition functions as a united whole, with a force that its apparent parts taken separately do not possess. Gregory argued that there were no parts to be joined together at the mental

---

108. *Natura pluit* or some such locution is a standard expansion of *pluit*: see Marsilius of Inghen 1516, f. 11[ra]; Dorp in Buridan 1499, sig. a 5[rb]. These expansions were later taken up by humanist grammarians: see Padley 1976, p. 54.
109. For a discussion and references, see Ashworth 1982.
110. Marsilius of Inghen 1516, f. 11[ra]. His discussion of conversion is found in ff. 5[va]–11[ra].
111. Nifo 1553a, ff. 7[va]–21[va]. He did not like Marsilius' treatment of 'Ego sum Sortes': see f. 18[ra–rb].
112. Du Trieu 1662, first published 1614, notes on p. 3 that 'Deus est', 'Johannes studet', 'Petrus orat Deum' are implicitly equivalent to 'Deus est existens', 'Johannes est studens', 'Petrus est orans Deum.'   113. See Ashworth 1982.
114. This is important because there is a tendency in the literature to suggest that the very notion of a mental language carries with it a belief that mental language mirrors the world and hence offers a special insight into phenomena: cf. Padley 1976, pp. 63–5; Slaughter 1982, pp. 87–8.

level; and his opponents, who included Fernando de Enzinas nearly two centuries later, argued that there were parts, which were bound together by syncategorematic acts, the mental correlates of syncategorematic terms.[115] This topic did not altogether disappear during the sixteenth century, for it is discussed by Martinus Smiglecius in his *Logica*;[116] and in Robert Pinke's list of questions on logic, metaphysics and ethics published in 1680 for the use of Oxford students, one of the logic questions was 'Is a mental proposition a simple quality?'[117]

The other question popularised by Gregory of Rimini had to do with *complexe significabilia*, i.e., 'propositions' in the sense adopted by some modern philosophers.[118] According to medieval and post-medieval logicians, a proposition was an indicative sentence capable of being true or false which was the object of an act of assertion. As such it was firmly tied to a particular occasion of utterance or thought. The question then arose whether there was something which propositions signified, or something which was named by the *dictum* in an accusative and infinitive construction, such as 'Petrum legere' in 'Verum est Petrum legere.' Gregory of Rimini (following Adam Wodeham) postulated *complexe significabilia* to fulfil this function. He described them as eternal beings, neither mental nor physical nor yet identical with God, which were at once the significates of indicative sentences, the bearers of truth and falsity and the objects of knowledge or belief. One opponent of Gregory's view was Jean Buridan, and many subsequent authors including Paul of Venice followed Buridan in arguing that propositions could only have significates in so far as their subject terms picked out some objects in the world. Such a view has many difficulties, particularly because many propositions will turn out to have no adequate significate. Another view opposed to that of Gregory is found in some Parisian authors, including Enzinas. He argued that propositions have no significates in the sense of things named or referred to. Instead they signify *aliqualiter*; they function as syncategorematic rather than categorematic terms.[119] In accordance with this interpretation Enzinas recommended replacing accusative and infinitive constructions with a 'that' clause. Thus ' "Human beings are animals" signifies human beings to be animals' should be rewritten as ' "Human beings are animals" signifies that human beings are animals', which removes the temptation to interpret the *dictum* as a

115. For details of the discussion, see Ashworth 1981b. See also Nuchelmans 1980, pp. 27–44, 94–101.
116. Smiglecius 1658, pp. 453–6. See also John of St Thomas 1930, pp. 150–7.
117. Pinke 1680, p. 12.
118. For details of the discussion see Ashworth 1978c. See also Nuchelmans 1980, pp. 45–73.
119. Enzinas 1528, f. xxxv[rb–va].

name.[120] After Enzinas, the question of what a proposition signifies seems virtually to have disappeared from philosophical discussion.

THE PERIOD 1530–1600

A useful insight into the changes in logic which took place during the sixteenth century can be obtained from a consideration of two groups of textbooks – four transitional texts and two texts which appeared in the Jesuit *Ratio studiorum* at the end of the century. One interesting transitional text is Nifo's *Dialectica ludicra*, which was first published in Florence in 1520. It is an introduction to logic by a skilled humanist and commentator on Aristotle who was also well acquainted with late medieval logic. All the typically medieval doctrines are discussed, but some, such as insolubles, are presented in a classical light; others, notably supposition theory, are truncated in order to serve the purposes of syllogistic.[121] A more influential text is the *Logicae compendium* of Javelli, which is also called *Commentarii in logicam Aristotelis*.[122] Its purpose was to introduce the student to Aristotle, but in order to do this Javelli retained certain medieval doctrines, such as supposition theory, proofs of terms and, to a lesser extent, the theory of consequences. His work, first published posthumously in 1551, received a number of editions in Italy, France and Germany.[123] A third transitional text is the *Dialectica* of John Seton, published in London in 1545, and later to become popular with the annotations of Peter Carter. In his preface Seton refers to Agricola and Melanchthon, and he says that his purpose is to make Aristotle easier for adolescents.[124] He discusses supposition theory and he mentions insolubles. It is interesting to note that book IV, which dealt with the topics, was not included in the 1545 edition. The fourth text, the *Summulae* by the Spaniard Domingo de Soto, is transitional in the fullest sense, for its editions themselves exhibit an internal change which mirrors the general changes taking place in the sixteenth century. The first edition, in 1529, was a loose but lengthy collection of treatises. It opened with *Introductiones dialecticae*, which began with the three *modi sciendi*, definition, division and argumentation, and then gave a full treatment of terms and supposition theory. There followed a commentary on Peter of Spain's first tract, on nouns, verbs and propositions; a work on exponibles; a

---

120. *Ibid.*, ff. xxxv^{vb}–vi^{ra}. 121. For discussion, see Ashworth 1976.
122. I have inspected the 1560 Venice edition of the *Commentarii*. I assume the other editions do not differ.
123. For a list of editions see Lohr 1977, pp. 731–2.
124. Seton 1545, sig. A ii^v: 'ut Aristotelem meo studio redderem faciliorem, et adolescentibus magis familiarem'. Insolubles are discussed under 'Dilemma', sigs. K vi^v–viii^r, and supposition on sigs. E iiii^r–v^v.

commentary on Peter of Spain's fourth tract, on syllogisms; a work on insolubles, and a work on obligations. The second edition (Salamanca 1539) is much briefer.[125] The material is organised into five books. The first is on terms; the second, which includes remarks on definition, division and argumentation, is on propositions and supposition theory; the third is on oppositions, i.e., the relations between propositions; the fourth is on exponibles; and the fifth on syllogisms. There follow the rewritten works on insolubles and obligations. In his preface Soto explained that while the sophistic excesses of late medieval logic had made it horrifying and inaccessible to boys, there was still a need for a fairly detailed introductory text. It was not enough to take a few examples from Cicero and think that one had given sufficient treatment to logic. Aristotle himself was hard to read, making some preparation necessary. Moreover, preliminary exercises were essential, and to that end Soto had retained 'some quibbles and a few sophisms'.[126]

The point that Aristotle, while paramount, needed an introduction was implicit in the Jesuit *Ratio studiorum* of 1586, which recommended the *Summula* of Fonseca for its breadth, clarity, relevance to Aristotle and lack of sophistry.[127] In the *Ratio studiorum* of 1599 the name of Toletus was added to that of Fonseca.[128] Both authors were extremely popular throughout Europe. The *Introductio in dialecticam* of Franciscus Toletus was first published in 1561 in Rome, and the last of its eighteen editions appeared in Milan in 1621.[129] The *Institutiones dialecticae* of Pedro Fonseca was first published in Lisbon in 1564, and the last of its fifty-three editions appeared in Lyons in 1625.[130] Both works included material on supposition theory and consequences, but in tone and approach they are much closer to the textbooks of the first half of the seventeenth century than to those of the early sixteenth century. Whether medieval material was included in the seventeenth-century texts, as it was in Du Trieu[131] and Sanderson,[132] or

125. The subsequent editions do not differ significantly from the second edition. I have inspected the fourth edition of 1571 and the last edition of 1582, both published in Salamanca. See Soto 1554: the title page says that it is the second edition and gives the date 1554; f.16ʳ has the heading 'Editionis Tertiae Summularum . . . Liber Secundus'; the end page, f.159ᵛ, gives the date 1555.
126. The introduction to the 1539 edition is reproduced in Soto 1554, sig. A 2ʳ⁻ᵛ.
127. *Monumenta Germaniae paedagogica* 1887, p. 131: 'Logicae Summula praemittatur, et Summula quidem P. Fonsecae esset forte magis ad rem: quia latior, clarior, accommodatior Aristoteli, et sine tricis, quae et inutiles sunt, et deterrent tirones.'
128. *Ibid.*, p. 332.   129. For details see Lohr 1982, p. 200.
130. For full details see Fonseca 1964, I, pp. xxxv–xlvi.
131. Philip Du Trieu taught at Louvain before becoming a Jesuit. His *Manuductio ad logicam* first appeared in 1614, and was frequently reprinted up to 1748: see Risse 1965.
132. Robert Sanderson's *Logicae artis compendium* was first printed in Oxford in 1615, and was very popular in England.

excluded as in Burgersdijk[133] and Jungius,[134] it was made clear that the main business of logic was to discuss categories, propositions, syllogisms, demonstration, topics and fallacies. The humanist and Ramist attempts to exclude some of this material had failed,[135] and the medieval material which remained had been integrated in a way which changed its significance.

There are three features of the late sixteenth-century textbook which particularly distinguish it from the early sixteenth-century and late medieval texts. First, the syllogism is presented as the focal point of the study of valid inference. It is not just one type of consequence among others, as it had been in Albert of Saxony's *Perutilis logica*,[136] or to be passed over rapidly as it had been in Paul of Venice's *Logica parva*. Second, there is a complete absence of the sophisms which had formed so prominent a feature of earlier texts, whatever the topic. For instance, in early sixteenth-century Parisian treatises on syllogisms, the standard procedure was to test each syllogistic mode by examining elaborate counter-examples. To quote just one case, in his treatment of *Barbara*, Dolz discussed the apparent counter-example: 'Only what begins to be every man's begins to be a man's donkey, and every braying thing except Brownie is beginning to be a man's or will be immediately after this; therefore every braying thing except Brownie begins to be a man's donkey.'[137] Third, there is a completely new attitude to language, which is signalled both by the general disappearance of sophisms and by the disappearance of special problem cases from the discussion of such matters as exponibles[138] and conversion.[139] Logicians in the medieval tradition had been particularly concerned with the effects of

---

133. Franco Burgersdijk's *Institutionum logicarum libri duo* first appeared in 1626. In 1635 the Estates ordered that it should be used by all schools in the Netherlands.

134. Joachim Jungius' *Logica Hamburgensis* was published in 1638. Risse 1965 also lists a 1635 edition, which contained the first three books.

135. See Ashworth 1974a, pp. 16–17 for a brief account of the Philippo-Ramist school of the 1590s, which aimed at a reconciliation of Melanchthon's Aristotelianism with the doctrines of Ramus, and which reintroduced first the categories, then the equivalence, conversion and opposition of propositions, together with the standard syllogism.

136. Albert of Saxony 1522, f. 28[vb]: 'Postquam visum est de consequentiis simplicibus formalibus, nunc videndum est de consequentiis formalibus syllogisticis.'

137. Dolz 1511, sig. c i[vb]: 'tantum cuiuslibet hominis incipiens esse incipit esse hominis asinus et omne rudibile preter brunellum hominis incipiens esse est vel immediate post hoc erit ergo omne rudibile preter brunellum incipit esse hominis asinus'. Another good example is found in Antonio Coronel 1517, f. xvi[vb], where he gives this counter-example to Ferio: 'Cuiuslibet hominis b. asinus et asinus non sunt asini alicuius angeli, omnes asini hominis quilibet asinus et quilibet asinus sunt: ergo alicuius angeli omnes asini non sunt asini.' (Note the use of the special quantifier 'b'.) This is the kind of thing that made humanists froth at the mouth. Cf. Vives 1979a p. 53.

138. For a succinct account of the treatment of exponibles in the sixteenth century, *see Cambridge History* 1982, p. 792 (Ashworth). See also Ashworth 1973b.

139. For references to the discussion of conversion, see nn. 110–11 above.

word order and of various syncategorematic terms, including exponible terms themselves as well as quantifiers of one sort and another, on sentence-meaning. They had tried to express semantic differences through different syntactic structures. For instance, 'Papam vidi' ('The pope I saw') was said to differ in meaning from 'Vidi Papam' ('I saw the pope').[140] Partly as a result of humanist attacks,[141] these attempts ceased completely, and the only examples admitted to logic texts were already couched in a standardised form.

I shall now turn to consider the process of integration as it affected both specifically medieval doctrines and Aristotelian syllogistic itself. Some doctrines were never integrated. For instance, insolubles were not seen to have any role in syllogistic, or the treatment of topics and fallacies; and most authors did not mention them. Those who did tended to use a classical vocabulary, speaking of *inexplicabiles* rather than of *insolubilia*, and citing such classical puzzles as the crocodile or the story of Protagoras and Euathlus.[142] Soto had given a fairly full account, but had remarked that there was little utility in the material.[143] At the end of the century the only interesting discussion is found in Thomas Oliver who, perhaps out of an antiquarian rather than a philosophical interest, gave a survey of the literature including Heytesbury, Buridan and Marsilius of Inghen.[144] One reason for the general disappearance of insolubles may well be that medieval logicians themselves had tended to see them only as interesting puzzles, rather than as paradoxes which strike at the very heart of our semantic assumptions.[145] They were thus thrown out together with the other sophisms.

Obligations are another doctrine which failed to be integrated in the late

---

140. For this example, drawn from appellation-theory, see Ashworth 1974a, p. 95. For Vives' reaction, see Vives 1979a, p. 137. For More's reaction, see *ibid.*, p. 173. Soto did admit the case, even in later editions: see Soto 1554, f. 51vb: 'Nec sequitur, Papam vidi, ergò vidi Papam.'

141. For instance, Nifo 1553a, f. 17^{ra-va}, attacked the rules of the *Sorticolae* for dealing with negative propositions in which the predicate was said to be undistributed, because it preceded the negative term, e.g., 'Quidam homo animal non est' (f. 17ra). He denied that the syntactic order affected the semantic structure: 'In hac autem, quidam homo animal non est, licet negatio situ sequatur illum terminum animal, intellectu praecedit: quia, si ille terminus animal est praedicatum, oportet ut intellectu sequatur' (f. 17va). Cf. Vives on word order, in Vives 1979a, p. 123.

142. For a full account and references see Ashworth 1972, pp. 35–7. See also Nifo 1521b, ff. 156^r–63^r, 'De dilematibus sive insolubilibus'.

143. Soto 1554, f. 151rb: 'Sed Moderni, praeter rei dignitatem, dilataverunt istam materiam: in qua tamen revera, parum est utilitatis, et ideo nos eam breviter transcurremus.'

144. Oliver 1604, pp. 8–14. Oliver is famous for his illustration of the written liar on p. 9: see Ashworth 1974a, p. 114 for a reproduction. For discussion, see I. Thomas 1965.

145. *Cambridge History* 1982, p. 253 (Spade): 'the medievals did not seem to have had any "crisis mentality" about these paradoxes. Although they wrote a great deal about them there is no hint that they thought the paradoxes were crucial test cases against which their whole logic and semantics might fail . . . [they] did not draw great theoretical lessons from the insolubles.'

sixteenth-century textbook. The traditional theory had been presented by various authors in the first decades of the century, some of whom were notable for their adherence to Marsilius of Inghen.[146] The latest exponents were Sbarroya and Soto.[147] In the first editions of his *Summulae*, Soto had already omitted a number of standard sophisms, especially those to do with the imposition of terms, i.e., the introduction of arbitrary new meanings,[148] and at the end of the treatise he described the topics discussed as trifling.[149] In the third edition he was considerably more forthright. At the beginning of the much shortened treatise he described obligations as 'a game for boys';[150] and at the end he said 'It is shameful to pursue this kind of filth and these dregs of nursery songs, which can produce only nausea.'[151]

In order to understand what replaced the theory of obligations in at least some textbooks, we must go back to the works of Josse Clichtove, who described two quite different kinds of disputation.[152] In his commentary on the *obligationes* of Jacques Lefèvre d'Étaples, he presented the standard doctrines, albeit completely shorn of their sophisms, and with no reference to the imposition of terms.[153] He made it quite clear that the purpose of obligational disputations was to test the ability of boys to handle logical inferences. At the same time, in his own two works *In terminorum cognitionem introductio* and *De artium scientiarumque divisione introductio* he described what might be called a doctrinal disputation.[154] The difference between the two kinds of disputation can be briefly summarised. In an obligational disputation the opponent begins by putting forward a false proposition. In the most usual kind of obligational disputation (*positio*) the respondent had to grant this initial *positum*.[155] The opponent then put

146. E.g., Thomas Bricot, John Mair and Domingo de Soto himself. The hallmark of Marsilius' doctrine was his division into three types of obligational disputation, *positio*, *depositio* and *dubiepositio*, in accordance with the three possible ways in which a proposition could be presented. Marsilius' *Tractatus de arte obligandi* was printed in Paris in 1489 under the name of Pierre d'Ailly.

147. Sbarroya 1533, ff. lxviii^{rb}–ix^{rb}.

148. Soto 1529, f. cl^{ra}, wrote 'Nempe quamvis doctrina haec non nihil possit summulistae conducere (nam de praedestinatione, caeterisque id genus disputanti vix scias nisi obligatorie respondere), impositiones tamen et casus qui hic plurimi multiplicari solent, indigni revera sunt, in quibus extricandis et tempus et operam perdas.'

149. *Ibid.*, f. cliii^{vb}. His closing words are 'Sed satis nobis sit, huiusmodi naeniis hactenus lusisse.'

150. Soto 1554, f. 156rb: 'Est enim ars haec velut puerorum ludus.'

151. *Ibid.*, f. 159vb. His closing words are: 'At verò, pudet id genus sordes ac naeniarum faeces persequi: quae non nisi nauseam movere possunt.'

152. For a full discussion and references, see Ashworth 1986.

153. See Clichtove's *Ars obligationum* in Lefèvre d'Étaples 1520, ff. 101^v–34^r.

154. *Ibid.*, ff. 2^r–19^v.

155. Strictly speaking, the respondent had to rule on the admissibility of the *positum* before he accepted it. Clichtove omitted this step of *admissio*. In other forms of obligational disputation, the respondent could require that the initial proposition be denied (*depositio*) or doubted (*dubiepositio*).

forward a series of new propositions, and the respondent had to reply to each by saying 'I grant it', 'I deny it' or 'I doubt it.'[156] In each case his reply was supposed to depend on the logical relationship the new proposition had to the set of propositions already granted. If it followed he had to grant it, and if it was inconsistent he had to deny it – hence the testing function of an obligational disputation. In the doctrinal disputation the respondent had to uphold a *thesis* or *quaestio*, which was supposed to be true. The opponent attacked the thesis by offering arguments against it, and the respondent had to reply to each attack by analysing the argument and by saying 'I grant it', 'I deny it' or 'I distinguish it' to each part of the argument, as well as to the argument as a whole. Obviously the doctrinal disputation also had a testing function, for both the respondent and the opponent had to be aware of all the relevant logical relations, but both the atmosphere and the procedures were different. The substance of the initial thesis is now a genuine issue; truth is paramount; and 'I distinguish' has replaced 'I doubt.' In later authors, including Seton, Toletus, Fonseca and Augustinus Hunnaeus, the type of disputation described is the doctrinal disputation.[157]

The most notable part of medieval logical writings to be incorporated in the late sixteenth-century textbook was the *parva logicalia*. This included a simplified discussion of some exponibles,[158] but I am most concerned here with supposition theory, together with the related doctrines of ampliation and appellation. Even some humanists were willing to allow a place to these doctrines, and Thomas More wrote 'All the same, that book of the *Little Logicals* (so named, I think, because it contains but little logic) is worth the trouble to look into for suppositions, as they call them, ampliations, restrictions, appellations.'[159] Javelli argued that the *parva logicalia* were

156. Clichtove in Lefèvre d'Étaples 1520, f. 129^v, also allowed the response 'distinguo'. This was not usual, though it occasionally appeared in fifteenth-century sources, e.g., Paul of Pergula 1961, p. 102; [Cologne] 1493, f. lxxxiii^r. The latter argued that 'distinguo' was already covered by the allowed responses 'affirmo' and 'nego'.

157. Seton 1545, sigs. H iiii^v–vii^v; Toletus 1587, ff. 6vb–7rb; Fonseca 1964, II, pp. 612–22 (his discussion is somewhat unlike the other sources); Hunnaeus 1584, pp. 87–116. There is a discussion of the doctrinal disputation in Angelelli 1970, with references to Hunnaeus and Toletus. Angelelli says that obligational disputations exhibit the *question* method and what I have called doctrinal disputations, the *argument* method. It should be noted that the doctrinal disputation has its roots in medieval writings (not to mention practices): see Albertus Magnus, Pseudo- 1498. This treatise has been edited with other material in *Die mittelalterlichen Traktate* 1980.

158. Toletus 1587 devoted book III (ff. 20va–7rb) to modal and exponible propositions. Cf. Fonseca 1964, I, pp. 230–48. See n. 138 above for further references. Toletus should be compared with Du Trieu 1662, sig. A 3^r: 'Cùm enim, ut antea dixi, disponendis ad logicam adolescentibus omnia tradi non possint, delectus habendus est, eaque potius tradenda, quae et minus spinosa sunt, et magis necessaria. Hinc nihil dico de enuntiationibus modalibus, exponibilibus, de inventione medii, et nonnullis aliis generis ejusdem.'

159. More's *Epistola ad Dorpium*, in Vives 1979a, p. 171.

essential to the understanding of syllogistic and disputation;[160] and Fonseca
suggested that the doctrines were needed to deal with fallacies.[161] He
warned that they were 'unrefined, uncouth and remote from use', and that
to dwell on them at length was dangerous to good language. However, he
said, some loss would come about from ignoring the doctrines altogether;
and he proceeded to give a full account of supposition, appellation and
ampliation.[162] Remnants of the theory are still to be found in the
seventeenth century, even in such resolutely non-scholastic writers as
Franco Burgersdijk.[163] It seems that Nifo's arguments to the effect that
supposition theory was not Peripatetic, and both should and could be
replaced by genuinely Peripatetic principles, had had little effect.[164]

The theory of consequences was also incorporated into some of the new
textbooks, but in a severely truncated form. Javelli prided himself on
omitting the various views of modern logicians which obscured more than
they clarified,[165] and neither Toletus nor Fonseca dwelt on the matter at
great length.[166] Gone are the lengthy definitions of a consequence, and the
lengthy analyses of the criteria for a valid formal consequence; gone too are
most of the examples of different kinds of consequences.[167] Instead we find
just a few consequences to do with truth and modality. The most interesting
feature is that the so-called paradoxes of strict implication, 'From the
impossible anything follows', and 'The necessary follows from anything',

160. Javelli 1580, p. 83B: 'quaedam opuscula, quae parva Logicalia nuncupantur, sine quibus penè
     impossibile est assequi veram et perfectam syllogizandi ac disputandi scientiam'.
161. Fonseca 1964, II, pp. 676–8: 'Sunt autem adeo inculta, horrida, et ab usu remota, quae superioris
     aetatis homines in hisce, ac similibus rebus commenti sunt, ut, nisi plurima reiiciantur, satius sit ea
     prorsus not attingere. Verum ut in his multum, ad diis immorari inutile est, ac bonis literis
     perniciosum, sic ea omnino contemnere (quod multi hoc tempore faciunt) non sine mediocri
     iactura contingit.'
162. Fonseca 1964, II, pp. 687–752. Cf. Toletus 1587 (lib. II), ff. 13ra–18ra. In cap. 12 (f. 18ra) he moves on
     to opposition, followed by aequipollence (cap. 15, f. 19rb) and conversion (cap. 16, ff. 19vb–20rb).
163. Burgersdijk 1637, p. 124: 'Concreta acceptio scholasticis dicitur *personalis*, qui admodum prolixè
     disputant de vocabulorum acceptionibus, sive, ut illi loquuntur, de suppositionibus.' Cf. Du Trieu
     1662, pp. 90–9, for a discussion of supposition theory, but not of ampliation and appellation. Like
     Javelli he thought that a knowledge of supposition theory was necessary for syllogistic:
     'Praemittimus autem hunc tractatum tractatui de argumentatione et syllogismo, quia ad
     cognoscendas regulas et vitia argumentationis, ac praecipue syllogismi, ejus notitia est necessaria'
     (p. 90). For a longer seventeenth-century discussion of supposition theory, see John of St Thomas
     1930, pp. 29–42, 166–182.
164. For Nifo's discussion of supposition theory see Nifo 1521b, ff. 86^r–103^r. See also Nifo 1553a, f.
     16^{va-vb}.
165. Javelli 1580, p. 97B: 'In hoc nostro tractatu de consequentiis non est intentio nostra immorari in
     recitandis modernorum logicorum variis et captiosis sententiis, quae magis involvunt quàm
     illuminent addiscentis intellectum.'
166. Toletus 1587, cap. 1–2, ff. 27va–8va; Fonseca 1964, I, pp. 328–50. Fonseca's account is the fullest. Cf.
     John of St Thomas 1930, pp. 59, 196–200. Such authors as Du Trieu ignore consequences.
167. For details of the material that had disappeared see Ashworth 1974a, pp. 120–42.

appear only in a reinterpreted form, whereby the impossible can lead to necessary, contingent or impossible propositions, and the necessary can follow from such propositions, provided that they stand in a meaning relation to the antecedent.[168] In adopting this view Fonseca and Toletus were rejecting the tradition of Buridan and Marsilius of Inghen, in which the paradoxes of strict implication had been accepted as formally valid consequences[169] and were apparently aligning themselves with the fourteenth-century English tradition of Richard Billingham, the *Logica Oxoniensis* and Ralph Strode, as well as with Paul of Venice and the fifteenth-century Thomists of Cologne. In the English tradition, valid inferences had been defined as involving some kind of meaning relationship;[170] and the paradoxes of strict implication accepted only as materially valid.[171]

The relation of the theory of consequences to syllogistic is of some interest. There are three issues: the status of conversion, the status of consequences in syllogistic reduction and the status of the syllogism itself. In each case the problem arises from the Aristotelian characterisation of argumentation as embracing the syllogism, enthymeme, induction and example. Whether the rules of conversion could be fitted into this scheme or not had been a topic of much debate for logicians from Kilwardby and Albertus Magnus in the thirteenth century to Nifo in the sixteenth century.[172] The problem arose because an enthymeme should be expanded into a syllogism, yet syllogisms in the second and third figures could only be reduced or proved by the use of conversion, and this led to circularity. This problem in turn affected the status of the other rules used in syllogistic reduction. On the whole the later authors solved these problems by maintaining silence on the issues, and by dropping explicit references to the consequences used in syllogistic reduction, except for the rule: 'Whatever

---

168. Fonseca 1964, I, pp. 342–4; Toletus 1587, f. 28rb. Neither makes an explicit reference to a meaning relation, but their examples make it clear that they are presupposing this.
169. See Buridan 1976, p. 31; for Marsilius, see Pschlacher 1512, f. 203^{v}. This tradition was followed by various early sixteenth-century Parisians and by Nifo: see Ashworth 1974a, p. 134.
170. *Logica Oxoniensis* s. XV, f. 4vb (*Consequentiae*): 'Consequentia est bona et formalis quando consequens formaliter intelligitur in antecedente, ut homo currit ergo animal currit.' See also Strode 1973, p. 2: 'Consequentia bona de forma dicitur cuius si sicut adequate significatur per antecedens intelligatur sicut etiam adequate significatur per consequens intelligitur; ut si quis intelligit te esse hominem, intelliget etiam te esse animal.'
171. *Logica Oxoniensis* s. XV, f. 5rb: '13a regula quod consequentia bona et materialis est quando antecedens est impossibile vel consequens necessarium'; Billingham s. XV, f. 56^{r} (*Consequentiae*); Strode 1973, p. 2. See also [Cologne] 1493, ff. ciii^{v}–ciiii^{r}; Paul of Venice 1472, pp. 65–6. For some discussion see Ashworth 1974a, p. 135.
172. See *Cambridge History* 1982, pp. 292–3 (Stump); Nifo 1553a, ff. 9va–10ra. He quotes Kilwardby, whom he calls Culverbinus, a number of times, here and elsewhere.

follows from the conclusion of a valid consequence follows from the premise.'[173] However, so far as the syllogism itself was concerned, Fonseca and Couto both appealed to the notion of a consequence. They explained that the notion of consequence was wider than that of argumentation. An argument was a special kind of consequence in which a term could appear in the premises which did not appear in the conclusion.[174] Hence a syllogism was a formal consequence. A supplementary issue was the definition of a syllogism as an *oratio*, a sentence or piece of discourse. Earlier authors had often explained that the *oratio* in question was a hypothetical proposition of the form: 'If A and B then C.'[175] Javelli took up the question, and summarised the positions which could be taken, without settling the issue.[176] By the seventeenth century, authors tended to ask neither about the relation of a syllogistic argument to consequences nor about the sense in which a syllogism could be called an *oratio*.

The most burning issue with respect to the syllogism had to do with the status of the fourth figure.[177] The issue revolved around the three different definitions of major and minor terms. Peter of Spain had defined the major term as that which appears in the major, i.e., the first, premise, and the minor as that which appears in the minor, i.e., the second, premise.[178] As Buridan recognised, this definition clearly allows for a fourth figure.[179] It also warrants indirect modes in which the minor term is the predicate of the conclusion. Some late medieval logicians followed Buridan in recognising a fourth figure;[180] others were more hesitant.[181] In the sixteenth century there were three developments. First, the renewed Aristotelianism led to the reappearance of Aristotle's definition of the major and minor terms with reference to their comprehension.[182] On this definition, there are only three figures but indirect modes are possible. Second, the renewed

173. This rule is found in Toletus 1587, f. 31rb; Fonseca 1964, I, p. 404. For a discussion of syllogistic reduction and the way in which consequences were used in the early sixteenth century, see Ashworth 1974a, pp. 239–46.
174. Fonseca 1964, I, pp. 328–9, 358; *Collegium Conimbricense* 1607 (part II), cols. 265–6. If a non-syllogistic consequence is defined as one in which all terms in the premise must appear in the conclusion, there is another reason for rejecting the paradoxes of strict implication, in which the premise and conclusion can exhibit completely different terms.
175. E.g., Marsilius of Inghen 1516, ff. 2va–3rb. His final definition (f. 3ra) is: 'Syllogismus vocalis est oratio hypothetica in qua quibusdam positis aliud in voce et in significatione a premissis et qualibet earum sequitur in consequentia necessaria virtute propria premissarum.'
176. Javelli 1580, p. 76A. Nifo 1553a, f. 5rb mentioned the view of Averroes that an *oratio* was a rational hypothetical proposition but (f. 4va) seems to have taken it for granted that one could call a sequence of distinct propositions an *oratio*.
177. For a full discussion see Ashworth 1974a, pp. 224–9.
178. Peter of Spain 1972, pp. 43–4. Cf. Toletus 1587, f. 28vb.   179. Hubien 1975.
180. Tartaretus 1503a, f. lxv$^{rb–va}$; Eck in Aristotle 1516–17, II, f. xii^{rb}.
181. Marsilius of Inghen 1516, f. 26$^{ra–vb}$.
182. Fonseca 1964, I, p. 364; *Collegium Conimbricense* 1607 (part II), col. 357.

importance of Averroes led to the popularisation of his arguments against the fourth figure, culminating in Jacopo Zabarella's treatise on this issue.[183] These arguments had mainly to do with an informal distinction between natural and unnatural argumentation, and the fourth figure was rejected as unnatural. Third, yet another definition of the major and minor terms appeared, whereby the major term was said to be the predicate of the conclusion and the minor term to be its subject.[184] On this definition there is a fourth figure and there can be no indirect modes. The definition is found in Philoponus,[185] but he does not seem to have been cited by those using the definition. Another possible source for the definition is the frequent remark made in texts which followed Peter of Spain, that the major term is, as a matter of fact, normally the predicate of the conclusion.[186] This second source may help to explain the fact that many writers, especially in the early seventeenth century, tended to define the major and minor terms in accordance with their position in the conclusion while at the same time denying the fourth figure and recognising the indirect modes.[187] If these writers were really following Philoponus, they were committing a logical crime; but if they merely believed that in most cases the major term would be the predicate of the conclusion, they were on safer ground. The only writer I know of who explicitly defended such a position was Laurentius Maiolus, at the end of the fifteenth century. He argued that although the major term should be defined as the predicate of the conclusion, the relation of the middle term to the other terms in the first figure was such that the major term could be recognised in the absence of the conclusion. It was then possible for the natural order of the terms to be reversed in the conclusion, and for indirect modes to be formed.[188] He also explored at some length the issue of three possible definitions of the major and minor terms, and the effect that each would have on Galen's claim that there was a fourth figure.[189] A century later Pace remarked that the popular definition of the major term as the predicate of the conclusion must be wrong because it ruled out the possibility of indirect modes.[190]

---

183. J. Zabarella 1597, ff. 101–32 (*Liber de quarta syllogismorum figura*).
184. Nifo 1553a, f. 27[rb]; Keckermann 1600, p. 407; Sanderson 1618, p. 123; Burgersdijk 1637, p. 170.
185. Philoponus 1544c, f. 17[va].
186. Seton 1545, sigs. H iii[r], H iiii[v]. Cf. Melanchthon 1834–60, XIII, col. 596 (*Erotemata dialectices*). In his first logic text, *Compendiaria dialectices ratio*, he had made no reference to the order of the terms in the conclusion and gave Peter of Spain's definition: *ibid.*, XX, col. 732.
187. See I. Thomas 1964 for an analysis of the flaws in various Oxford logicians, including Robert Sanderson. Earlier Nifo had accepted the fourth figure as a consequence of his definition: Nifo 1553a, f. 27[vb]. Unfortunately he did not attract followers.
188. Maiolus 1497, sigs. C i[r–v], e i[r–v]. 189. *Ibid.*, sigs. d vi[v]–e iiii[r], especially e i[v]–ii[r].
190. Pace in Aristotle 1597, p. 139[a–b].

With these two exceptions, sixteenth-century discussions of indirect modes and the fourth figure seem to have ignored the fundamental question of how the initial definition of syllogistic terms affected the issue of what modes and figures were logically possible. Moreover, many textbooks simply adopted a position without enquiring whether it could be given a logical justification. Syllogistic may have been regarded as central to logic, but it was not always handled well.

7
HUMANISTIC LOGIC

LOGIC: CRITICISMS BY HUMANISTS

Introduction

Humanism encountered Aristotelian logic as a central component in the scholastic curriculum, a curriculum which it was humanists' ambition to replace with one more appropriate to a 'classical' education.[1] Because it was from their position as teachers of the liberal arts that humanists challenged traditional treatments of logic, their interventions in the field have tended to be characterised as crucially disruptive and destructive, and they have been blamed for producing a hiatus in the development of formal logic from which the discipline has barely recovered.[2] Although recent scholarly work has established humanist dialectic as an area of energetic intellectual activity, the secondary literature continues to give credence to the view that the activity was fragmented and eclectic, and continues to assume a fundamental lack of relevance of developments associated with humanist dialectic to the development of logic proper.[3]

This is, however, to underestimate the importance of Renaissance developments in logic, both in the context of specifically humanist interventions and, perhaps even more importantly, in the light of cross-influence and interaction between humanist and scholastic scholarly contributions. In spite of scholastic logicians' insistence on the formal nature of their concern with ratiocination (as opposed to the more 'linguistic' interest of terminists and *moderni*), technical exploration of argument forms was inevitably conducted with at least sidelong glances at other available approaches.[4] Furthermore, separate specialist discussions do not remain

---

1. See, e.g., the account of Petrarch's knowledge of, and attitude towards, traditional logic in Garin 1969, pp. 137–77. For an example of the way in which this combination of technical knowledge and intellectual hostility towards scholastic logic persisted as a feature of humanist involvement with the subject, see the account of Juan Luis Vives' attack on traditional logic in Vives 1979a.
2. See, for example, Kneale 1962, p. 300.
3. See Risse 1964, Ashworth 1974a, Prantl 1855–70.
4. See Ashworth in this volume on the relation between logic and philosophy of language.

neatly cut off from one another in the context of the curriculum and the textbook. Thus (to take a single example) the Aristotelian Agostino Nifo chooses to react to the humanist Lorenzo Valla's reformulated dialectic in his *Dialectica ludicra* ('Schoolroom dialectic/Playful dialectic'), rather than to dismiss it out of hand.[5] By the end of the period, logic textbooks tend to be more readily characterisable as 'hybrid' than as 'scholastic' or as 'humanist', because of the cross-fertilisation which has gone on between schools. And whatever their avowed affiliation, they have tacitly discarded the more technical aspects of medieval logic (especially those, like *suppositio* theory, which had grown up independently of the material contained in Aristotle's texts on logic). In evaluating humanist contributions to dialectic, it should be borne in mind that by the end of the sixteenth century, the sources on which a professed *Aristotelian* might draw were markedly more varied and unhomogeneous than during the Middle Ages.[6]

To assess a peculiarly humanist approach to logic and the contribution it made to Renaissance logic as a whole it is desirable to begin by abandoning the now customary approach of tracing modifications in dialectic teaching from chronologically prior to chronologically subsequent humanist pedagogue, and from textbook to textbook.[7] Such an approach concedes a linear notion of 'development', as of 'influence', and inevitably charac- terises individual authors as representatives of artificially constructed 'schools'.[8] Whilst the present treatment is bound to proceed chrono- logically, it will concentrate on individual humanists' contributions to dialectic as part of their overall perspective on the liberal arts and as part of their commitment to a revised programme of university education suited to their liberal arts goal. And it will emphasise the closely similar development in Aristotelian treatment of the appropriate areas of *their* logic teaching, suggesting considerable communication amongst authorities in different schools, and testifying to an inevitable convergence, historically, in their aims and attitudes. By avoiding the cataloguing and classificatory approach to Renaissance logic I hope to give an account which will prevent the reader

---

5. See Ashworth 1976, L. Jardine 1981.
6. See, for instance, Schmitt 1983b, chs. 1 and 4, and McConica 1979 for discussion of the varied nature of Aristotelianism in the English universities in this period.
7. This approach was firmly established, for obvious reasons of convenience and expository clarity, by pioneering authors in the field like Risse 1964, Vasoli 1968a, N. W. Gilbert 1960 and Howell 1956. It enabled them to describe the contours of the field and to catalogue and describe economically hitherto neglected treatises and textbooks.
8. Although his work is compendious, and does proceed largely in chronological sweeps for convenience of exposition, Vasoli 1968a manages to avoid such simple notions of 'influence' – remarkably, considering the pioneering nature of the work. My own debt to Professor Vasoli and to this work is immense.

being tempted into dismissively discarding the whole run of texts which will concern us here, as muddled and derivative. For a rounded view, I suggest that this account of specifically *humanist* criticism of, and innovation in, logic should be read in close conjunction with chapter 6, 'Traditional logic', which maps out the developments with which humanist treatments interacted.[9]

The history of medieval and Renaissance logic has traditionally been the history of the great medieval syllogistic logicians and the *fortuna* of their innovatory treatments down through the fifteenth and sixteenth centuries.[10] When historians of logic characterise humanist dialectic as a misguided and non-rigorous intervention which disrupted the smooth development of medieval syllogistic logic, they confirm their own commitment to the interests and techniques pioneered by logicians like William of Sherwood.[11] It is not surprising, then, if these scholars find the very different approach of the humanists trying. They hold up against the 'non-rigorous' humanist treatment of ratiocination, the 'rigour' of a commitment to formal validity as the central focus for the study of logic – a commitment, that is to say, to those fixed patterns of argumentation which guarantee that from any true premises whatsoever one can only infer a true conclusion.[12] Humanist treatments of logic, on the other hand, have a good deal in common with the interests of some recent, modern logicians, who have chosen to give a good deal of attention to non-deductive inference, and to 'good' arguments (arguments which can be counted on to win in debate), and the problematic nature of their validity.[13] Like modern logicians they are interested, above all, in 'good' arguments.

A humanist treatment of logic is characterised by the fundamental assumption that *oratio* may be persuasive, even compelling, without its being formally valid (or without the formal validity of the argument being ascertainable). It takes the view, therefore, that any significant study of argument (the subject-matter of logic/dialectic) must concern itself equally with argument (strictly, argumentation) which is compelling but not amenable to analysis within traditional formal logic.[14] It is this fundamental difference of opinion over what is meant by 'compelling' argument which accounts for the dogmatic insistence (on ideological grounds) of the scholastic (and of the historian of scholasticism) that the humanist is a

---

9. See Ashworth in this volume. Risse's account (Risse 1964) may also usefully be set alongside the present discussion. See also Risse 1965.
10. See, for example, *Cambridge History* 1982.   11. See, for example, Kneale 1962.
12. Formal validity is defined at the outset of any reputable modern logic textbook.
13. See, for example, Hamblin 1970.   14. See Nuchelmans 1980.

'grammarian' or a 'rhetorician'. Either term announces that what the humanist is concerned with is not 'rigorous' in the restricted scholastic sense: all discourse not amenable to such 'rigorous' analysis is, for the scholastic, a matter for the grammarian (to parse and construe) or the rhetorician (to catalogue its persuasive devices). It is in the same spirit that humanists always refer to their study of ratiocination as 'dialectic' (reasoning conducted between two interlocutors), rather than as 'logic', to emphasise the active, pragmatic nature of the argumentation which captures their interest.[15]

Early humanists

Petrarch had ostentatiously little time for formal logic.[16] In a list of his most loved books, jotted on the flyleaf of one of his manuscripts, he includes a single standard medieval treatment of logic and stresses 'nothing beyond that' (as a gesture towards the prominence of such study in the traditional curriculum).[17] In the face of the strictly formal interests of high scholasticism, Petrarch's inclination is to disparage logic teaching altogether, rather than to replace it. It is, in his view, an unnecessarily time-consuming and distracting pedantry, not to be confused with real understanding and intellectual maturity, which issue from genuine intimacy and familiarity with antiquity:

Consider those who spend their entire life in dialectical altercations and cavillings; this is what I predict for all those things: the repute of those matters, and certainly of themselves, will evaporate, and a single grave will suffice for their bones and their name. For since death freezes the tongue, not only are they compelled to remain silent, but those matters also are silenced.[18]

Petrarch readily concedes that dialectic is a necessary propaedeutic to knowledge; what he deplores is the tendency of logicians to treat their subject as a goal in itself, rather than as a means to a larger end: 'Dialectic can be a part, but it is certainly not an end; and it can be a part for early in the morning, but not far into the evening.' In his disparagement of unnecessarily technical and 'quibbling' logic Petrarch specifically singles out the

---

15. See, for instance, Nifo 1540 on this choice of label for a logic which centres on topics.
16. On Petrarch's attitude to logic, see Garin 1969, pp. 139–77; Vasoli 1968a, pp. 9–15.
17. See Ullman 1973, pp. 127–8: 'Tractatus et nil ultra'. Ullman suggests that the work intended is Peter of Spain's *Summule logicales*, which is plausible. See also Reynolds and Wilson 1974, p. 117.
18. Petrarch 1933–42, I, p. 18 (1.2): 'Respice et hos qui in altercationibus et cavillationibus dyalecticis totum vite tempus expendunt seque inanibus semper questiunculis exagitant; et presagium meum de omnibus habeto: omnium nempe cum ipsis fama corruet unumque sepulchrum ossibus sufficiet ac nomini. Cum enim mors frigidam linguam stare coegerit, non modo ut sileant necesse est, sed ut de his etiam sileatur.' See Vasoli 1968a, p. 9.

English logicians and their technically refined formal logic for opprobrium, establishing them as the main butt of humanist ribaldry and vituperation down to the seventeenth century.[19]

Humanist criticism of logic, then, begins with criticism of the professional logician, and the structuring of the university curriculum around the terminology and the technical problems of the logic course. Early humanist educators are unanimous in their insistence on the comparatively modest role logic ought to play within a student's total training. Associated with this disparagement of traditional logic instruction is a general commitment on the part of humanist educators to initiating language study with a study of grammar which attends to the subtleties of the Latin language rather than to the terminology and technical niceties which would be required at a later stage if the student were to pursue logical studies into their higher specialist reaches. Thus early humanist treatises on education, like Vergerio's *De ingenuis moribus*,[20] make passing reference to the need for competence in the trivial arts of grammar, logic and rhetoric, but insist upon eloquence and in-depth familiarity with the literary works of antiquity as the basis for true learning.[21] The same kind of emphasis is to be found less programmatically in a work like Bruni's *Ad Petrum Paulum Histrum dialogus* ('Dialogue for Pier Paolo Vergerio'). Celebrating Salutati's formative influence, Bruni writes of his approach to Latinity:

Neither are you one of those, in my view, who takes pleasure in vain loquacity. Nor do you incite us in that direction, but rather to speak gravely, steadily, and so that we seem to understand and feel what we speak. To which end, your desire is that we should have a sound grasp on that about which we dispute, not simply in itself, but so that we have an understanding of its consequences, its antecedents, its causes, its effects, and everything in short which relates to the matter in hand. For no debater who is ignorant of these things will be able to dispute without appearing inept.[22]

This sensitivity to language is not, in Bruni's view, to be confused with the preoccupations of contemporary dialecticians. They, on the contrary, distort that subject, as all scholastic study distorts and deforms true learning:

But what about dialectic, which is a most essential art for conducting disputations? Does dialectic maintain a flourishing reign, subjected to no calamitous defeat in this

19. *Ibid.*, p. 38 (1.7): 'Dyalectica pars esse potest, utique terminus non est; et potest pars esse matutina, non serotina.' For Petrarch's hostility to English logic and logicians, see *ibid.*, pp. 35–38 (1.7) *passim*.
20. On Vergerio see, in this context, Robey 1980.   21. See, for instance, Robey 1980, p. 47.
22. *Prosatori latini* 1952, p. 52: 'Neque enim tu es, ut opinor, quem garrulitas vana delectet, neque ad eam rem nos cohortaris; sed ut graviter, ut constanter, ut denique ita verba faciamus, ut ea quae dicimus sapere atque sentire videamur. Itaque tenenda probe res est, de qua disputare velis; nec ea solum, sed consequentium, antecedentium, causarum, effectuum, omnium denique quae ad eam rem pertinent habenda cognitio. His enim ignoratis nemo disputator poterit non ineptus videri.'

war of ignorance? Not at all. For that barbarity which resides across the ocean has launched an attack on dialectic also. But what people, for God's sake? Those whose very names make me shudder: Ferebrich, Heytesbury, Ockham and others of this kind, who all seem to have dragged their names from the cohort of Rhadamanthus. And what is there, Salutati, leaving aside this pleasantry, what is there, I say, in dialectic which has not been thrown into confusion by British sophisms? What which has not been diverted from that ancient and true way of disputing and transformed into absurdities and trivialities?[23]

These humanist educators stress the fact that Roman approaches to ratiocination (such as Cicero's) are more appropriate guides to this study than the technical disciplines developed from Aristotle's *Organon* by the *moderni*. If we bear in mind the fact that the study of Roman dialectic and rhetoric had been continuous down through the Middle Ages, whereas that of Aristotelian logic had been hampered by poor texts, a need to rely on secondary accounts and on Roman 'versions' of Greek sources, this amounts to a criticism of relatively 'new' specialisms as against old practical preparations for public office. Humanist pedagogues couple this preference for 'general' education with the view that if one *is* going to study Aristotelian logic, it must be from the Greek texts and with the help of a Greek tradition in commentary. In other words, if logic is to exist as a specialist discipline it must be a 'humanised' specialism. It is not, however, until we come to Lorenzo Valla that we find a humanist whose criticism of contemporary logic and its teaching extends to a replacement discipline, as opposed to a vague general preference for Roman accounts of argument practice over Greek theory (as propounded by traditional Aristotelians).

Lorenzo Valla

Two of Valla's major works are concerned with the crucial position of the study of language for learning: the *Dialecticae disputationes* and the *Elegantiae*. The latter is a detailed, subtle and justly celebrated account of nuances of Latin meaning and usage. The former is increasingly widely acknowledged as a seminal work in humanist dialectic.[24] The two make up

23. *Ibid.*, pp. 58–60: 'Quid autem de dialectica, quae una ars ad disputandum pernecessaria est? An ea florens regnum obtinet, neque hoc ignorantiae bello calamitatem ullam perpessa est? Minime vero. Nam etiam illa barbaria, quae trans oceanum habitat, in illam impetum fecit. At quae gentes, dii boni? Quorum etiam nomina perhorresco: Farabrich, Buser, Occam, aliique eiusmodi, qui omnes mihi videntur a Rhadamantis cohorte traxisse cognomina. Et quid est, Coluci, ut haec ioca omittam, quid est, inquam, in dialectica quod non britannicis sophismatibus conturbatum sit? Quid quod non ab illa vetere et vera disputandi via separatum et ad ineptias livitatesque traductum?' On 'Buser', see *English Logic* 1982.
24. On the importance of Valla's *Dialecticae disputationes*, see Kristeller 1964a, pp. 33–5; Vasoli 1970, p. 256; L. Jardine 1977, 1983.

what one might call a tripartite critique of the tactics and technical achievements of scholastic logic. In the *Elegantiae* Valla contends that many of the 'problems' which preoccupy philosophers and logicians admit of ready solution by careful consideration of grammar and syntax.[25] Whilst the traditional logician (and historian of logic) is bound to throw up his hands in despair at such wilful misunderstanding of the fundamental assumptions of formal logic, Valla's challenge is a real one. He maintains that a genuine desire to extend the range of problems on which formal logic can gain a purchase has produced a spuriously difficult series of subsidiary branches of logic, for instance, those dealing with *suppositio*. To fit a discussion of problems raised by the slipperiness of ordinary language usage to a discussion of formal validity whose focus is the syllogism does indeed require something like *suppositio* theory to deal with problems of meaning and reference of terms. But, Valla suggests, one might prefer to concede formal logic's limited sphere, and tackle ordinary language problems from the point of view of the linguistic specialist (a preference shared by modern linguists).

The second and third parts of Valla's attack on the logic curriculum are launched in his *Dialecticae disputationes*, and both contribute towards dislodging validity from its central position in discussion of ratiocination.[26] In the first place, Valla privileges Quintilian's version of a programme of instruction in ratiocination suitable for the 'orator' (that is, effectively, for the average non-specialist user of ratiocinative skills). The account of *loci* – seats of argumentation or topics – which Valla takes verbatim from the *Institutio oratoria* in the *Dialecticae disputationes* makes 'apt' arguments (ratiocinative strategies which do the job in hand, regardless of their formal validity) the focus of the dialectician's attention. Formal validity is here only one amongst a number of possible guides to choice of argument in support of a given position.[27] Informal validity (as Jonathan Barnes has engagingly called it)[28] and soundness are locally acceptable guides to the appropriateness of a particular chain of reasoning. This shift in emphasis is already hinted at in Bruni's remark quoted earlier that Salutati was not simply content to grasp what might 'fittingly' (*probe*) be said on a given subject, but

25. See Vasoli 1968a; *Cambridge History* 1982, pp. 808–17 (Percival); Grafton and L. Jardine 1986.
26. The *Dialecticae disputationes* survive in a number of redactions, of which the published text is in fact (probably for political reasons) least explicit about its shifted focus of attention. For the various texts, see Zippel's introduction in L. Valla 1982.
27. On topics-logic and its influence (largely through the impact of Boethius' *De differentiis topicis*), see Stump in Boethius 1978 and in *Cambridge History* 1982, pp. 273–99; Bird 1960, 1962.
28. *Boethius* 1981, p. 82 (Barnes).

required knowledge of its antecedents, its consequences, its causes, its effects, and whatever pertained to it – in other words, was interested in rules of inference tailored to the orator's needs.

Several things happen (from the historian of logic's point of view) when the focus of attention is switched from Aristotle's classic discussions of syllogistic and their associated *scholia* to topics-theory. In the first place, demonstrative inference ceases to be privileged over non-demonstrative inference. The fact that one kind of reasoning holds universally, whilst the other is strictly 'occasional', is irrelevant to the issue of whether, in context, one or the other is tactically more suitable to persuade an audience. Secondly, formal validity as such ceases to preoccupy the dialectician/ logician, as opposed to how 'good' the argument in hand is for the purpose – whether *on the whole* arguments of a certain form command assent. An inference like 'Socrates is married. Therefore Socrates is not a bachelor' takes its place with an inference like 'If it is day, it is light. But it is day, therefore it is light', even though the former is not formally valid, whereas the latter is.[29] One of Valla's contributions to this latter discussion is to challenge the view that the list of expressions generally agreed to be logical constants is self-evidently complete and exclusive, thus opening the possibility that arguments traditionally judged to be ad hoc might have a claim to be considered as generalisable argument forms.[30]

It is unfortunately difficult to allude to such a 'shift of emphasis' on Valla's part without inviting the kind of disparaging comment from historians of logic which has steadily accompanied any reference to topics-theory as a source of inspiration for humanist dialecticians.[31] But it will become apparent when we consider the important textbook of Rudolph Agricola that this shift is the key to humanist redefinition of dialectic as a curriculum subject. Linked to this shift, however, and less easily dismissed by logicians as mere 'soft' thinking is the interest Valla displays, in the final book of his *Dialecticae disputationes*, in a number of argument strategies discussed by Greek and Roman logicians and judged on occasion to be compelling, but whose logical nature is problematic. These include *sorites* – the heap – and *antistrephon* – dilemma, or the horned argument – as well as more familiar forms like induction.[32] The extensive treatment of these argument

29. On the importance of the notion of commanding the audience's assent as a vital part of choice of argument, see Burnyeat 1982b and unpublished.
30. For further discussion, see L. Jardine 1983.
31. See, for example, Ashworth 1974a, Stump in Boethius 1978 and in *Cambridge History* 1982, pp. 273–99.
32. For recent discussion of such argument forms, particularly in the context of ancient treatments (some of which were sources for humanist dialecticians), see Barnes 1982, Burnyeat 1982b.

strategies in Valla's work succeeds in bringing into ratiocinative prominence techniques of dubious or problematic validity, which historically had
fascinated Roman orators by their ability to prove irresistible in debate.
Valla's careful discussion of 'good' (compelling) and 'foolish' (overtly
sophistical) uses of *sorites* and *dilemma* is a natural development out of his
determination to extend the range of strategies covered in dialectic, so as to
include open discussion of 'convincing' argumentation. However, the
significance of the argument strategies considered in Valla's third book was
apparently lost on a number of later authors of treatises on dialectic whose
treatment was otherwise indebted to Valla's *Dialecticae disputationes*. It is a
mark of the wide influence of Valla's *repastinatio* of dialectic that virtually
every post-fifteenth-century humanist dialectic manual includes some
minimal treatment of classic *sorites*, in spite of its not finding a place in any
medieval manuals.[33] But it is equally the case that textbook treatments
betray little understanding of the significantly different outlook which is
implied in that inclusion. For the 'heap' argument is irresistible when used
astutely in debate, in spite of the fact that its formal validity remains
problematic.[34]

Rudolph Agricola

Rudolph Agricola's *De inventione dialectica* marks the turning-point in the
fortunes of a humanistically inspired dialectic. Not only was this work
fundamentally innovative as a teaching text, but its *fortuna* was directly
linked with the emergence within the European universities of humanistic
courses of study, separate from the traditional faculties, which included
their own versions of the key *trivium* subjects, and specifically of dialectic.[35]
Completed around 1480 and published in 1515, the *De inventione dialectica*
enjoyed a modest reputation until the 1530s, when it 'took off' as a teaching
text, reprinted in numerous editions, paraphrased, epitomised and adapted
for the use of particular faculties in particular universities across Europe. At
the same time, it is not a textbook, in the sense of eclectically assembling *all*
current material as more or less part of an introductory logic course.
Agricola's treatise runs a strong sceptical philosophical line, and the material
it covers is insistently partial in accordance with its promotion of a
recognisably partisan view of ratiocination.[36]

33. As it is in modern textbooks. For discussion of the 'heap' argument, see Wright 1976.
34. For a fuller discussion of Valla's treatment of *sorites*, see L. Jardine 1983, pp. 272–5.
35. On the pervasive influence of the *De inventione dialectica*, see Prantl 1855–70, IV, ch. 21; Vasoli 1968a;
    Heath 1971; L. Jardine 1974b, 1975. For a checklist of the numerous editions of Agricola's treatise,
    see Ong 1958b.
36. On Agricola's scepticism, and its relation to his treatment of dialectic, see L. Jardine 1983. On
    scepticism in the Renaissance, see Popkin in this volume.

Agricola's title is suitably propagandist and controversial. It advertises the work as a *topics-logic* treatise ('De *inventione*'), whilst at the same time insisting that topics–logic is the core of dialectic (rather than a subsidiary part of it, or even a part of rhetoric: the art of ad hoc persuasion in traditional terms) – 'De inventione *dialectica*'. As a polemical gesture Agricola's choice of title has been as effective a deterrent of serious modern scholarly interest as it was provocative around 1500 – an extraordinary amount of scholarly energy (past and present) had been expended on trying to decide whether Agricola's work is a contribution to rhetoric, or an intervention in the history of logic. The answer one gives, of course, relates directly to one's view of the traditional logicians' claim that topics–theory was essentially a debased branch of the study of argumentation, best treated with 'rhetorical' topics as a division of rhetoric. If one accepts this view (as propounded in, say, Peter of Spain's *Summule logicales*),[37] then Agricola 'rhetoricises' and debases dialectic. If, however, one regards topics–logic as providing an account of a less restrictive and non-demonstrative logic, and as a possible contender in this respect with Aristotelian demonstration, where the discourse to be analysed deliberately defies syllogistic rigour (the Socratic dialogue, for instance), then Agricola's move has to be treated seriously.[38] It marks a conscious move towards an account of systematic reasoning which includes reasoning which falls short of the deductively rigorous, and towards the development of a logic of language use. Such a study, amongst other things, reveals limitations in traditional notions of certainty and absolute truth in relation to ratiocination, and opens the way forward to modern empirical notions of truth.[39]

The three books of Agricola's work consolidate Valla's innovatory emphases into something like textbook form. The first book catalogues and surveys the Aristotelian/Ciceronian topics, in a treatment which clearly owes much to Boethius' *De differentiis topicis*.[40] The second book deals with argument forms, and allocates a significantly subsidiary role to formal validity (and specifically to the syllogism). Here, as in book I, the emphasis is on the informal validity of practical arguing, rather than on the absolutely guaranteed forms. Characteristic of Agricola's outlook is the view (which

37. For the text of the *Summule*, see Peter of Spain 1972. On the content of the *Summule*, see Mullally 1945.
38. For the view that Aristotle himself took a less rigid stance than traditional readings allow, see Owen 1968, *Aristotle on Dialectic* 1968, Burnyeat 1982a. In this case humanist dialecticians may have been more astute readers of the ancient logical texts than their detractors are prepared to admit.
39. See L. Jardine 1983, Dear 1984, Burnyeat 1982a.
40. See Stump in Boethius 1978 on Boethius' topics.

might be philosophically supported by a modern logician) that syllogisms are of limited use in arguing a case, because it is necessarily the case that any reasonable person who accepts the premises of a syllogism as true already accepts the conclusion. More usually, he argues, the debater is concerned to shift the audience's beliefs sufficiently to persuade them to accept a hitherto unacceptable conclusion. The third book of the *De inventione dialectica* pursues this theme by discussing in detail the 'art of influencing',[41] including persuasive strategies, delivery and a variety of subterfuges designed to command assent. If one wanted to characterise this closing discussion, one might say that Agricola's view of disputation is Socratic, involving the interplay of participants' discourse in dialogue, rather than Aristotelian. The work ends with an elegantly worked example of an argument between opponents who hold fundamentally incompatible beliefs, which shows the necessity for 'commanding assent' by logically unconventional means. An Academic sceptic proposes to convince an Epicurean that 'quisquis sine uirtute sit, eum esse infelicem' (whoever lacks virtue is unhappy):

He will not assume at the start that virtue is the greatest good, for that is in no respect more probable than that which was aimed at: nor again that whence is derived this proposition, that man's greatest natural concern is for virtue. Therefore he commences further back. He asks whether it is admitted that the soul is better than the body? But this also must be built from a Socratic induction. It must be asked whether the driver is superior to his chariot, the helmsman to his ship, the master to his house, and the ruler to his people, or in general whether he thinks that that which commands is superior to that which serves, and whether he thinks the body is ruled by the soul. Which if he concedes it, it will be necessary for him to concede that the soul is superior to the body. Which when it has begun to be agreed, it follows necessarily from this that the actions and whatever pertains to the soul are superior to things of the body. Whence if we have taught that virtue is peculiar to the soul, pleasure peculiar to the body, it will be established that virtue is better than pleasure. Which itself will perhaps be required to be shown . . .[42]

41. Ashworth 1974a, p. 11.
42. Agricola 1539, p. 447: 'Non sumet ille co(n)tinuo uirtutem esse summum bonum: id enim nihilo probabilius est, quam id quod intendebatur: nec id etiam unde istud deducitur, uirtutis curam maxime naturalem esse homini. Altius igitur ordietur. Quaeret ecquid fateatur animam corpore meliorem esse? Sed et hoc quoq(ue) muniendu(m) est Socratica inductione. Qu(a)erendum est, an aurigam curru, & naue gubernatorem, & dominum domo, & principem popularibus, & in uniuersum quod imperet praestantius esse putet eo quod paret, an & animi imperio putet corpus regi. Quae si concedat, necesse erit concedat, animum corpore potiorem esse. Quod ubi constare coepit, sequatur hinc necesse est, actiones & quaecunq(ue) animi corporis rebus esse potiora. Quod si docuerimus hinc, propriam animi uirtutem, propriam corporis uoluptatem esse: constabit uirtutem esse meliorem uoluptate. Quod ipsum erit fortasse quaerendum . . .'

And so on. The choice of an Academic sceptic as adversary in this model debate is a self-conscious one. For it is the Academic who claims to hold nothing as certain (no premises as true), but to argue reasonably towards the most plausible possible case – in this instance a case which will convince an Epicurean, although the Epicurean's key beliefs are not shared by the Academic.[43] What is striking here, once again, is the shift of emphasis. Although scholastic exercises like the disputation and the obligation hinge crucially on the 'pro-syllogisms', or manoeuvring strategies prior to a clinching formal inference, instruction is focused on the latter.[44] Agricola shows himself primarily concerned with training the would-be debater in the skirmishes for position which accompany any attempt to drive an argument home ('we must start further back'). And this is undoubtedly the stage in actual debating which requires most ingenuity and mental agility, both in written texts which argue a case and in familiar oratorical contexts – most notoriously in the law-courts.[45]

It should perhaps be added that, in my view, Agricola's approach to dialectic *teaching* is essentially a return to a position prior to the strenuous professionalisation of the study and teaching of logic during the high Middle Ages. In the intervening period logic as a science had overshadowed logic as an art, a fact that humanist dialecticians were fond of stressing.[46] Agricola's *De inventione dialectica* is therefore influential in two differing, but equally important, ways. On the one hand he challenges the Aristotelian view of logic at a philosophical level, and identifies humanist dialectic with the 'art of persuasion' as part of an intellectual case for 'likelihood' over 'certainty'. On the other he heralds in the applied dialectic handbook, exclusively concerned with practical argument strategies at the expense of the study of formal inference, which brought humanist dialectic into ill-repute. In this latter respect he prepared the way for the most notorious of the advocates of 'loose' reasoning, Petrus Ramus.

Petrus Ramus

Petrus Ramus was the dialectician who succeeded in popularising the new humanist dialectic as an alternative focus for the arts curriculum. Although

---

43. Agricola's interest in Academic scepticism is emphasised by Alardus throughout his commentary in the 1539 edition of the *De inventione dialectica*; see L. Jardine 1983, pp. 268–9.
44. On scholastic debating procedures, see Schüling 1969, ch. 6. See also Hamblin 1970, pp. 89–134 ('The Aristotelian tradition').
45. On the dialogue and the dialectical (in our modern sense) argument as key humanistic genres see C. J. R. Armstrong 1976.
46. See, for example, Vives' attack on traditional logicians in his *In pseudodialecticos*: Vives 1979a.

modern scholars are undoubtedly correct in their opinion that intellectually he was neither a major innovator nor the most outstanding dialectician of his generation, his open commitment to the revised dialectic programme (centred on topics-logic) of Valla and Agricola as *controversial* and *progressive*, and his own position as a Protestant martyr (he was murdered in the St Bartholomew's Day Massacre in Paris in 1572), brought that programme to prominence throughout Northern Europe.[47] Ramus took the original and conceptually somewhat obscure developments of Agricola, made their consequences for the teaching of dialectic explicit and packaged them for mass consumption. His importance is thus as much a matter of the *number* of popularising versions of this new approach he made available as a question of his own originality (contemporary adversaries like Antonio de Gouveia were quick to point out how much Ramus owed to earlier innovators like Agricola).[48] In his pioneering work on Ramus, W. J. Ong established a quite remarkable publishing history for Ramus' rather modest works on dialectic.[49] Ramus' contribution to humanist dialectic is thus represented in the literature primarily as a cornering of the market in textbooks – a reasonably accurate version of the story in my view.[50]

However, it would not do to understate Ramus' actual influence on developments in humanist logic. As I said when discussing Agricola, one version of the change in outlook on logic/dialectic effected by humanists is that they drew Socratic dialogue within the consideration of the logician. Following on from this position, Ramus advertised himself as a Platonist (although he was driven to moderate his claims for his dialectic in the face of more sophisticated Academics' objections to the inconsistency of his 'Platonic' position). In the spirit of Plato, he continued to stress the importance for logic of 'dialectical' (in our modern sense of the word) argument and of dialogue techniques. He asserted the equivalence of the rules of dialectical argumentation (as derived from Agricola via his own teacher Johannes Sturm) with the rules of operation of natural reason.[51] He maintained that given certain technical constraints on the 'axioms' from which argumentation started, dialectical reasoning would yield absolute truth.[52] And he privileged dichotomous 'method' (display of material) as

---

47. For a scathing assessment of Ramus' contributions to logic see Ashworth 1974a.
48. Gouveia 1543, e.g., f. 2^v, f. 14^v, ff. 17^v–18^r. See Vasoli 1968a, p. 412.
49. Ong 1958a, 1958b.
50. For a detailed study of the various modifications and revisions of Ramus' dialectic in successive versions of his textbook, however, which argues for a significant intellectual influence on sixteenth-century thought, see Bruyère 1984.   51. See Vasoli 1968a, pp. 333–404.
52. On Ramus' three rules, see L. Jardine 1974a, N. W. Gilbert 1960, Bruyère 1984.

the ideal method of presentation on the grounds that this was the procedure favoured by Plato himself.[53]

Ramus' dichotomous method is a procedure for displaying material (for instance, the material proper to a particular teaching discipline like geometry or grammar) in the most clear and most easily grasped fashion for comprehension by the student. The teacher commences with the most general definition of the subject ('dialectic is the art of discoursing well'), followed by the division of that subject into two parts ('dialectic consists of invention and judgement'), with explanations and examples displayed under the two heads. He then proceeds to key down each arm of the array in turn, conveniently displaying the material under each head in tabular form. In this way, theoretically, no material is omitted, and the process always moves from the more to the less general concepts of the subject under discussion.[54]

Dichotomous keying became an extremely voguish way of proceeding in organising teaching, and in textbook and manual presentation. But it would not do to be too dismissive of the original incentive to modify traditional methods, simply because the 'school' came to abuse it. It must be said, however, that once we move to consideration of the impact of Ramist method, we have moved away from developments *within* logic into the emergent discipline of textual exegesis. It is, however, desirable to do so, in order to anticipate and avoid the confusion which tends to be caused by attempts to assess humanist attention to method (which strives in the direction of textual and literary problems) alongside scholastic incursions into deceptively similar areas associated with their particular professional interest in mathematical and scientific reasoning. Whilst the histories of the two are inevitably somewhat intertwined, peculiarly humanist contributions tend to be to their own field of expertise – that is, to text criticism.[55] Almost all critics who have dealt with 'method' as a general term have run scientific and literary discussions of method together. It probably was the case that the humanists fudged the issue by deliberately employing the technical term 'method' for more or less systematic sequences of reasoning analysed out of texts.

53. On Ramus and method, see in particular Bruyère 1984; see also Crescini 1965, L. Jardine 1974a, N. W. Gilbert 1960.
54. For a full discussion of Ramist method in relation to other ancient and Renaissance treatments of methodical presentation, see Bruyère 1984.
55. See N. W. Gilbert 1960, Vasoli 1968a, Crescini 1965.

HUMANIST LOGIC AND DEVELOPMENTS IN TEXTUAL EXEGESIS

Introduction

In pointing out that the context for humanist dialectical innovations was their preoccupation with oratory and with textual exegesis, I do not mean to imply that the significance of contributions of major humanist dialecticians like Valla and Agricola was confined to the study of the non-rigorous and descriptive use of language. A distinction does, however, need to be drawn between the original and influential work of Valla, Agricola and distinguished specialists in the Greek of the ancient logical texts and the humanist textbook writers of the latter half of the sixteenth century.[56] There is little doubt that the humble manual writers serving the immediate needs of universities and schools failed to understand the significance of the trail-blazing dialecticians' major breaks with traditional logic, or if they did, failed to transmit it in their textbooks. In part this is the fate of textbook writers. Even today, logic textbooks include material which a standard notion of curriculum suggests 'ought' to figure, because it is 'part of the baggage which has been dragged through the centuries with the label "Aristotle" on one side and "logic" on the other', whether or not it is any longer pertinent to contemporary views on the nature of logic.[57] Because of their avowed interest in problems of textual exegesis and oratory, humanist textbook writers did give prominence to those topics likely to prove useful to the intending lawyer, courtier or other practitioner of oratorical and exegetical skills. Inevitably this meant giving increased space to discussion of 'informal' sequences of arguments which at its worst amounts to an almost metaphorical notion of 'logic' as a discipline appropriate to the art of discourse.

Furthermore, humanist dialecticians were concerned with ratiocination in types of discourse whose structure they correctly considered opaque to syllogistic analysis, notably the increasingly fashionable dialogue form (arguing equally plausible alternative points of view to a balanced probabilistic conclusion).[58] Where for scholastic logicians their study was a

---

56. For details of the textbook tradition, see *Cambridge History* 1982, pp. 797–807 (L. Jardine). See also Risse 1964, Vasoli 1968a.
57. See, for instance, Burnyeat's remarks about the way in which enthymeme continues to figure in textbooks in Burnyeat unpublished.
58. See L. Jardine 1977, 1983; C. J. R. Armstrong 1976, Dear 1984.

stage along the road to the higher disciplines of natural science, theology and metaphysics, for humanists it was a means to the analysis and understanding of canonical texts (literary and legal), and orations (ancient and modern; forensic and epideictic), and an aid to composition of discursive writings emulative of 'golden' Latin. All those humanists whose names are now catalogued as authors of reforming texts on logic/dialectic regarded those works as merely one item in a revised arts curriculum, whose focus was the study of the great textual relics of antiquity – what down to the early decades of the present century were called the 'classics'.

Valla's *Elegantiae* was the mainstay of humanist discussions of the lexical and syntactical subtleties of the Latin language. Agricola's Latin version of the fourth-century Greek manual of oratorical practice, Aphthonius' *Progymnasmata*, was probably as influential within the revised curriculum as his *De inventione dialectica*. The *Progymnasmata* are a graded series of exercises in eloquence starting with the invented fable, passing through the first-person imaginary speech of a famous hero or heroine of antiquity on some occasion celebrated in literature, and concluding with a law-court declamation.[59] The prominence in educational terms of both these works is shown by the fact that Erasmus, who dedicated himself to the production of suitable texts for liberal arts teaching in the mid sixteenth century, published a condensed edition of the former, and emulated the latter in his *De copia*, his *De conscribendis epistolis* and his *De ratione studii*.[60] Set alongside the two authors' dialectic texts, these major works in *eloquentia* do indeed provide a liberal arts context for the reorientation of dialectic studies. Specifically, they pin the study of dialectic to occasion, pragmatic requirements and the one-off argument.[61]

As a whole, the pedagogic works of Valla and Agricola provide a characteristically 'grammatical' approach to language (both Valla and his detractors refer to his *Dialecticae disputationes* as the work of a 'grammarian'). Concentrating as they do on 'usage' (the Latin of the best authorities of antiquity), they feel obliged, in their treatment of argumentation, to try to account for extended persuasive discourse (of the kind found in Cicero's orations, say), as well as isolated valid sequences of propositions. The absence of such discussion in the traditional logic syllabus has consequences beyond the study of logic itself. A glance at a late medieval commentary, or

---

59. On the *Progymnasmata*, see Marrou 1958; Bonner 1977, p. 251.
60. On Erasmus and the humanist dialectical/rhetorical tradition, see Chomarat 1981.
61. On humanist education and its liberal arts focus, see Grafton and L. Jardine 1986, Bolgar 1954.

indeed a commentary by an early humanist textual exegete like Guarino da Verona, on any ancient text makes it clear that, packed as these commentaries are with significant textual detail, they offer no analysis of the discursive framework into which this material is fitted, making it difficult for the student to follow the narrative thread or *sense* of the work. Battista Guarino's version of his father Guarino's lecture notes on Pseudo-Cicero's *Ad Herennium* is vividly anecdotal, cumulatively overwhelming, but discursively unhelpful after this fashion.[62] When Agricola maintains, at the outset of his treatment, that one of dialectic's duties is to 'teach', in Cicero's extended sense (communicating some knowledge to someone), he paves the way for the enthusiastic use of topical analysis and dichotomous method as procedures for clarifying the structure of a piece of writing (or speech) so that the student can grasp its discursive organisation, or as one might loosely say, its 'argument', and is thereby taught how to employ a similar procedure for his own compositions.[63]

Ramus' dichotomous keying was embraced enthusiastically by arts teachers in the middle and later decades of the sixteenth century for its ability to make vivid to the student in a clearly tabulated version the complex running threads in any sophisticated piece of writing.[64] William Temple's *A Logical Analysis of Twenty Select Psalms* (1605), Johannes Piscator's *Analysis logica epistolarum Horatii omnium* (1596) and his *analysis logica* of the gospels and St Paul and Abraham Fraunce's logical analysis of one of Horace's *Odes* are typical products of this tradition.[65] Whilst a far cry from formal logic, they do provide a method of reading which identifies and groups thoughts and illustrations so that the argument or arguments of the work are accessible to the reader. In essence, these are the early tools of text criticism in our modern sense.[66] It is significant as proof of the hold that methodical analysis as promoted by the Ramists took on the popular academic imagination that while dialecticians like Charpentier and Digby challenged the uniqueness of Ramist dichotomous method, they nevertheless felt called upon to give prominence to alternative methodical procedures for textual analysis and composition of their own.[67]

---

62. See Grafton and L. Jardine 1982.   63. Agricola 1539, p. 1 (prooemium).
64. See Ong 1958a; L. Jardine 1974a, pp. 41–7.
65. On Temple, see L. Jardine 1974a, Howell 1956. On Piscator and Fraunce, see Howell 1956, Ong 1958a.
66. See Ong 1958a, Grafton and L. Jardine 1986.
67. On the Digby/Temple dispute over method see L. Jardine 1974a. On Digby, see N. W. Gilbert 1960, pp. 200–8. On Charpentier, see N. W. Gilbert 1960, pp. 145–52.

Abraham Fraunce

In this context we may take as a single example of the text-exegetical wing
of humanist dialectical development Abraham Fraunce's *The Lawiers Logike*
(1588).[68] This little manual is a typical compromise between an urge to
demonstrate the practical usefulness of humanist topics-logic and a desire to
'cover' the standard teaching material.[69] It is also typically Ramist in its
conflation of rudimentary humanist dialectic and practical 'reading'
techniques suitable for literature and for the analysis of existing law-court
speeches and the preparation of fresh ones. It formed a pair with its
companion volume *The Arcadian Rhetorike* (thus, incidentally, making clear
the deliberate distinction sustained by humanist educators between so-
called 'rhetoricised' dialectic and rhetoric itself) to provide the English
gentleman with a practical, vernacular treatment of all he needed to know
about use of language in the two major areas in which he was likely to need
such knowledge – namely, applied forensic debate (in his capacity as lawyer,
statesman or civic functionary) and the reading and appreciation of 'high'
works of literature (a suitable pastime for those of gentle birth). Fraunce's
manual is included here as a characteristic example of humanist-influenced
dialectical practice, the typical successor to the theoretically stringent and
innovative works of Valla, Agricola, Caesarius, Melanchthon and other
major figures.[70]

Practical considerations have apparently utterly overwhelmed abstract
and theoretical considerations in Fraunce's work. Indeed, the most
appropriate term to use, in my view, for the function of dialectic in
Fraunce's, and any number of other similarly motivated manuals of the last
decades of the sixteenth century, is 'occasional'. Suiting the occasion,
concentrating on locally generalised or generalisable rules binding form and
content of an argument, is the object of the instruction offered. One might
add that the difference between the 'occasional' focus of such a manual and
the abstract and theoretical emphasis of the late scholastic manual is in many
ways the difference between the educational aspirations of the two systems
– the goal of the latter being 'expertise', that of the former being
'urbanity'.[71] Furthermore, crucial assumptions of the new dialectic, such as
the assumption that inference forms other than those handled by medieval
logicians might be entitled to serious and systematic consideration (a main

---

68. On Fraunce, see Howell 1956; Hamblin 1970, pp. 139–42.   69. Hamblin 1970, p. 140.
70. See Risse 1965, Vasoli 1968a.   71. See Grafton and L. Jardine 1986.

plank in Valla's and Agricola's argument), and that something like Boethius' topical maxims might offer further locally valid rules guaranteeing argumentation, have been lost from view. Fraunce refocuses his treatment of a dialectic embracing a relaxed notion of 'reasoning' around the contention that all argumentation, however superficially loose, is ultimately to be checked for validity by reducing it to syllogistic form, because only the syllogism is 'certain' (it is not to be *used* in such form, but it should be thus tested):

Now if these propositions bee doubtful, then therof be made questions, which are to bee prooued by third arguments, fet from the affections of the other two which were ioyned in the axiome, and lastly are to be concluded by syllogisme, the onely iudge of all coherence or consequence: as finally, Methode has only to deale with the ordering and setling of many axioms, thereby to giue sentence of methodicall proceeding or vnorderly confusion. And therefore I see no reason why I should with the common Logicians, chop in Canons, Maximaes, and rules of consequence, as they call them, applying them to euery argument of inuention, seeing that syllogismes, and onely syllogismes are the true and onely rules of consequence and inconsequence, as I said before.[72]

Fraunce does go on to make it plain that he countenances an almost unlimited range of ad hoc argument strategies as 'pro-syllogisms', in actual discourse, thus aligning himself with the 'any good argument is admissible' school, but the flexibility of the notion of alternative types of inference has been sacrificed in the interests of textbook neatness.

Fraunce himself makes it clear that by 'new' logic he means a new type of practical handbook (preferably tailored to the needs of particular individuals – logic for lawyers, logic for preachers and so forth), facilitating clear-thinking and persuasive argument. Neither he nor any of the other English manual writers of the second half of the sixteenth century (Seton and Carter, Wilson, Fenner and so on) make claims for the originality of their work for formal logic as a specialist discipline.[73] They do insist that some mastery of their discipline (such as it is) is a prerequisite for a career based on an arts education.

Humanist dialectic and scientific method

Agricola's *De inventione dialectica* is exclusively concerned with the analysis of the kind of texts, or the kind of discourse, which will be encountered by

72. Fraunce 1588, f. 7^{r-v}.
73. For details of these authors' manuals, see Risse 1964, pp. 25–31, 82–105; L. Jardine 1974a; Howell 1956.

students of the liberal arts. But some post-Agricolan dialectic manuals do attempt to deal with scientific reasoning or 'demonstration'. By the very nature of the humanist dialectic manual, discussion of demonstration, or reasoning leading to scientifically certain conclusions, tends to be included out of an urge for completeness rather than out of any real interest in or specialist understanding of this topic.[74] This is the case in 'hybrid' manuals like those of Caesarius and Melanchthon. Both these authors associate their discussion of demonstrative procedures with *a priori* and *a posteriori* methods of proof used by geometers.[75] In the light of the present account, it is not surprising that humanist dialecticians are derivative and muddled in their discussion of demonstration, since it harks back to a kind of logical analysis which the whole drift of their own version inclines against.

It was, however, the inadequacy (and sometimes incompetence) of this part of the 'new' dialectic manual which attracted the scorn of sixteenth-century Aristotelian logicians and has since attracted similar scorn on the part of historians of formal logic, not to mention historians of science absorbed with the origins of scientific method.[76] It would, of course, have been better had humanist dialecticians decided not to tackle scientific reasoning at all, rather than dealing with it in an inadequate or confused fashion. Here we come up against the inevitable interaction between history and individual achievement in intellectual history. As long as distinguished thinkers like Valla proposed a radically different approach to reasoning, namely a sceptical acknowledgement that an argument must always fall short of certainty, and that greater or lesser degrees of likelihood were the object of the logician's attention, they could hold their own against their scholastic adversaries. But once schoolteacher dialecticians had expanded their textbook treatment from Agricola's framework of plausible reasoning to include schoolroom subjects which needed to be 'covered', they proved vulnerable to charges of woolly thinking and absence of logical rigour. By the end of the sixteenth century the diffusing of focus in the humanist dialectic manual had paved the way for the reintroduction of the systematic Aristotelian manual, uncontroversially covering the material of Aristotle's *Organon* for the student in need of a clear introduction to traditional logic.

74. See N. Jardine in this volume for a full treatment of scientific demonstration.
75. On demonstration in the humanist manual, see L. Jardine 1974a, pp. 47–58. See also N. Jardine 1976 and 1979; N. W. Gilbert 1960, pp. 86–92. N. Jardine 1984, p. 240, points out the comparatively greater sophistication of Melanchthon in discussing scientific method. On Melanchthon, see also Boisset 1967.   76. See Risse 1964.

THE IMPACT OF HUMANIST GREEK STUDIES ON LOGIC

Introduction

Apart from individual humanists' explicit technical interest in dialectic, their influence is to be felt on logic studies as a result of activities more conventionally associated with their linguistic specialism: the retrieval of uncorrupted texts in the ancient languages, the establishing of *editiones principes* of the *opera* of major and minor authors, and the translation of Greek into classical Latin. A striking example of the unobtrusive but powerful effect of such activities is provided by the *editio princeps* of the Greek works of Aristotle, published at Venice by Aldus Manutius between 1495 and 1498.[77] The Aldine Greek Aristotle printed the logical works as a body of texts which thenceforth became codified as the 'Organon' (the *Categories, De interpretatione, Prior* and *Posterior Analytics, Topics* and *Sophistici elenchi*). But it appears that the supposed chronological order of the works and the title (*Organon*), which gives unity and fixity to Aristotle's logic, are established for the first time with the Aldine printed text.[78]

The Latin Aristotle of the Middle Ages had meant, where the logical works were concerned, Boethius' translations (or translations attributed to Boethius), together with supporting works fortuitously grouped with Aristotle's works in the curriculum (such as the pseudonymous *Liber sex principiorum*).[79] With the establishing of a standard Greek text came emended Latin translations, which in turn prompted revised commentaries from specialist logicians. Because of his commitment to the texts of a 'pure' Latin Aristotle, established by Lefèvre d'Étaples, the commentator Johannes Eck, despite his overt commitment to conventional scholastic logic, found himself led in the direction of revised readings and reconsidered interpretations of Aristotle's texts, even though he was not in general in sympathy with the 'grammatical' dialectic of the humanists. Discussing Aristotelian demonstration, for example, he comments as follows:

Demonstration [apodeixis] is syllogism conferring knowledge. This the ancient texts read corruptly as 'apotiticon' or 'apodytecon', and [Jodocus Trutfetter]

---

77. Minio-Paluello 1972, pp. 483–500 at 491 ('Attivita filosofico-editoriale aristotelica dell'umanesimo').
78. *Ibid.*, pp. 492–3. See p. 144 above for the 1493 date for the first commentary on the complete *Organon* (by George of Brussels and Petrus Tartaretus).
79. See Minio-Paluello 1972; Lohr 1967 to 1974a; *Cambridge History* 1982, pp. 45–79 (Dod).

Isennachensis derived 'apotiticon' from 'apos', that is 'concerning', and 'titicon', that is 'discipline'. But Lefèvre d'Étaples has eruditely and assiduously expunged this mistake.[80]

Even before the establishing of standard 'pure' Greek printed texts and Latin translations, partial translations into elegant Latin of individual logical works by distinguished humanists like the Byzantine Argyropulos encouraged noted humanists like George of Trebizond and Poliziano to offer their own contributions in areas conventionally left to the specialist logician's attention.[81]

The Greek commentaries

It was not only the new humanistic translations of the texts of the logic corpus themselves which led to modified readings, and hence a revised view of dialectic itself (for instance, Argyropulos' translations of Aristotle's logical works, and Lefèvre's paraphrases).[82] Humanist-inspired Greek expertise also made it possible for commentators to appeal to the authentic tradition of the early Greek commentators on the Aristotelian corpus. These Greek commentators were already familiar as sources of Boethius' commentaries.[83]

In their own explorations of the texts of Aristotle's works on dialectic, specialists in Greek language texts like Argyropulos and Poliziano stressed the vital importance of the works of Alexander of Aphrodisias, Ammonius, Simplicius and Philoponus for a 'true' (i.e., Greek) understanding of Aristotle.[84] In his *Praelectio de dialectica*, Poliziano expresses the hope that the 'barbarous moderns' 'Burley, Herveus, Ockham, Heytesbury and Strode' have been superseded. 'If, therefore, you were to ask me', he writes, 'who were my instructors in the Peripatetic School, I would be able to show you piles of books in which you might enumerate Theophrastus, Alexander, Themistius, Ammonius, Simplicius, Philoponus, and others besides, from

80. Aristotle 1516–17, II, f. 63ᵛ: 'Demonstratio est syllogismus faciens scire. Hic antiqua litera corrupte legit apotiticon seu apodytecon, et d(ominus) Isennachensis flexit apotiticon ab apos, id est de, et titicon, disciplina. At d(ominus) Stapulensis erudite et diligenter hanc mendam expunxit.' On Eck, see Seifert 1978. On Jodocus Trutfetter Isennachensis, see Lohr 1970, pp. 151–2.
81. On Poliziano and dialectic, see *Il Poliziano* 1957, pp. 161–72 (Vasoli) and Vasoli 1968a, pp. 116–31.
82. Minio-Paluello 1972, Cranz and Schmitt 1984.
83. See Stump in Boethius 1978 for the influence of the Greek commentators on Boethius' reading of Aristotle's *Topics*.
84. The impact of these commentators is on Aristotelianism as a whole, taking in the scientific and metaphysical works as well as logic. For the relation between new translations and commentaries, see Schmitt 1983a.

Aristotle's household.' These it is who give access to the 'purity' of Aristotle ('Aristotelis puritatem').[85] For Poliziano, the soundness of a reading will depend upon the commentator's knowledge of the Greek original of the text and the attention he pays to Greek commentators' interpretations and explanations. A fine example of a commentator who lived up to Poliziano's expectations in this respect is Agostino Nifo. Calling himself a 'Peripatetic' rather than an Aristotelian, in order to indicate his allegiance to the 'real' Aristotle of the Greek texts, Nifo produced a sequence of intelligent and sensitive commentaries during the early decades of the sixteenth century.[86]

Agostino Nifo

I have already described the mature humanist response to the 'new' Aristotle in the work of Valla and Agricola, both of whom insist that their approach is not inconsistent with a humanised *Organon*. Nifo's commentaries on Aristotle's logical works, and in particular his commentary on the *Topics*, are a crucial part of the 'grammatical' developments in logic of the late fifteenth and early sixteenth centuries. He is also an appropriate case to take in the context of the present discussion, since his sensitivity to the new texts of Aristotle, coupled with his persisting loyalty to the Aristotelian logic camp, has resulted in his being chastised by traditional historians of logic for diluting or muddling the treatment of logic, whilst he is largely ignored by historians of humanist logic. I shall concentrate here on Nifo's treatment of the *Topics*, since I have argued that this is the focus of humanist logical interest and curriculum reform.

For the *Topics* Nifo, like other commentators, uses a substantially Boethian translation of the text, although he adds marginal remarks on the Greek of the text wherever appropriate. One of the incidental (and perhaps not accidental) consequences of this is that Boethius' own commentaries on Aristotle's and Cicero's *Topics* remain pertinent to discussion (the *De differentiis topicis* and the *In Topica Ciceronis*). Nifo begins his own commentary with a definition of dialectic in relation to topics-theory, which is entirely characteristic of his urge to defer to the Greek commentators:

By dialectic Alexander understands not all of logic, but topical method, which Aristotle teaches in these books. Averroes, in the proemium to his paraphrase of the *Topics*, infers this from the fact that dialectic means speech between two [people],

85. In Poliziano 1553, pp. 528–30 at 529. On the Greek translator's views on the Greek commentators, see Vasoli 1968a, pp. 106–31.   86. See Risse 1964, p. 218.

one of whom struggles to vanquish the other, and since Aristotle assigns the 'places' by means of which this can be achieved to these books, he rightly adopts the term dialectic for this topical method.[87]

And he closes his commentary with a firm statement about the vital importance of the Greek tradition:

These are the things we have written on the *Topics*, expounded both from Alexander and from Ammonius. For in Aristotle's words we find many obscurities, and many differences in the written texts. For in the Greek codices which were at hand, we read several fragmented texts. We collated in turn many Greek exemplars and interpreted from them in such a way as seemed better to us. We looked at the expositions of many Latin authors . . . In addition we looked at certain new translations of Averroes, or rather his more blathering confusions, which since the translator did not understand, no one can understand them. In addition we looked at Albertus whose surname was Magnus, who expounded this book most obscurely, yet much better than he expounded the books of natural philosophy. For in those latter he said nothing of any value. For he followed translations from Arabic into Latin, in which there are as many errors as words. Indeed, because in logic he followed translations from Greek into Latin, therefore he made fewer errors. We looked also at several running commentaries by foreigners, which are not reasonably called running commentaries, because nothing concerning what Aristotle wrote is interpreted. From these, therefore, we received no assistance, but only inextricable questions which are directed towards what they themselves say, not to those things on which Aristotle pronounced . . . Therefore, if we had not read the expositions of Alexander and Ammonius, scarcely one word would have been well interpreted by us. For it is a disgrace that those who wish to interpret Aristotle's works dare to interpret them without knowledge of the language in which Aristotle wrote and without any expositors of Greek to show them the way.[88]

87. Nifo 1540, f. 2ᵛ: 'Et per dialecticam no(n) omnem logicae partem Alexand(er) intellexit, sed methodum topicam, quam in his libris edocebit Aristoteles, cuius causam Auerroes in proemio paraphrasum librorum topicoru(m) assignat ex eo, quia dialectica significat sermonem inter duos, quoru(m) alterum alter vincere enititur. & cum Aristoteles his libris assignet loca, ex quibus hoc fieri potest, iure dialectice nomen huic topice methodo Aristoteles appropriauit.'
88. *Ibid.*, f. 139ᵛ: 'Haec sunt, qu(a)e scripsimus in libros topicoru(m), tu(m) ex Alexa(n)dri, tu(m) ex Herminii [Ammonii] expositio(n)ibus. habuimus aut(em) in verbis Arist(otelis) no(n) paruas obscuritates, & in scripturis differe(n)tias. na(m) in codicibus graecis, qui p(rae) manibus habe(n)tur, co(m)plures text(us) fragme(n)tos legimus. co(n)tulimus ad inuice(m) multa graeca exe(m)plaria, & sic ex ipsis interpretati sumus, vt melius nobis visum est. vidimus multoru(m) Latinoru(m) expositio(n)es, vt Hedenalphi, vt Angeli camerinatis, vt Roberti Culuerbini, vt Britannici, vt cuiusda(m), que(m) o(mn)es co(m)mentatore(m) voca(n)t. Insuper vidimus Auerrois nouas quasdam translatio(n)es, imo potius blacteritias confusiones, quas cum translator non intellexerit, nemo potest eas intelligere. Insuper vidimus Albertu(m) cognome(n)to magnu(m), qui obscurissime hu(n)c libru(m) exposuit, longe tamen melius, qua(m) exposuerit libros philosophiae naturalis. In illis enim nihil boni dixit. nam sequutus est translationes ex arabico in latinum versas, in quibus sunt tot errata, quot verba. quia vero in logica sequutus est translationes ex graeco in latinum

Nifo's running comments throughout the *Topics* insist on the lack of competence of the logician without good Greek.

Not surprisingly, in view of Boethius' own indebtedness to Alexander, Nifo's reading of the *Topics* takes him in the direction of the *De differentiis topicis*, which in turn takes him towards humanist dialecticians like Valla. Unlike traditional scholastic logicians, Nifo regarded topics-logic – or 'dialectic' – as an independent and independently interesting exploration of ratiocination, which concerns itself with 'good' arguments in the practical context of debating. And the detail of his commentary offers a view of Aristotle's exploration of argument forms which allows for the possibility of systematic study of non-demonstrative inference. On this view, the *Topics* presents a wide range of arguments the acceptability of whose conclusions will depend upon the ability of the disputant to convince his audience of the acceptability of the premises. As far as the argument forms are concerned, their validity is assured if and only if they can be recast in one of the formally valid syllogistic moods. This is certainly the view of the relation between syllogistic and topical dialectic which Nifo offers in his textbook, the *Dialectica ludicra*.[89] It is a fitting tribute to Nifo that his kind of reading of Aristotle's text of the *Topica* is currently enjoying the approval of ancient philosophers.[90]

Humanist programmes for a revised dialectic curriculum reflected a desire for a flexible *organon* reorientated to include the kinds of ad hoc and occasional arguments appropriate to oratory and the law-courts. Together with humanistic influence on the establishing of a 'pure' Aristotle and humanist contributions to the retrieval and appreciation of the substantial body of early commentary on Aristotle's scientific and logical works, it ensured that the study of logic or dialectic – whether explicitly 'reformed' or avowedly Aristotelian – was permanently altered by the impact of humanism. In the end, the value of this humanist influence probably lies in

factas, ideo minus errauit. vidimus etia(m) co(m)plures externoru(m) cursus, quos non ab ratione cursus voca(n)t, quia nihil de verbis Arist(otelis) interpreta(n)tur. ex his igitur omnibus nihil iuuamenti accepimus, sed solum inextricabiles quaestiones quae mouentur ad ea quae ipsi dicunt, non autem ad ea quae Arist(oteles) tradit. In his abundant, & in his maiorem partem expositionis faciunt. Nisi igitur legeremus Alex(andri) & Herminii expositio(n)es, vix unum verbu(m) bene esset a nobis interpretatum. turpe enim est vole(n)tibus exponere Aristo(telis) libros, vt illos audeant interpretari ignorata lingua, in qua Aristoteles scripsit: nullisque graecis expositoribus iter demonstrantibus.'

89. See Ashworth 1976; L. Jardine 1981.
90. Nifo is here taken simply as one representative and competent example of a trend in reading the *Topics* (of a kind which we have argued was inspired by humanism). For similar representative interest to be found in Nifo's discussion of demonstration, see N. Jardine in this volume.

its variety, as well as in its impressive linguistic and exegetical competence. And it may well be that when humanist contributions are evaluated as part of a serious debate about classical treatments of inference and the *ars disserendi*, it will transpire that modern reappraisals of Aristotelian logic were already anticipated by humanist-influenced commentators.

VI

NATURAL PHILOSOPHY

8

TRADITIONAL NATURAL PHILOSOPHY

The natural philosophy of the Renaissance was far from being a homogeneous body of knowledge uniformly accepted and taught in the universities. As one might expect during a rebirth of learning, new views of nature and of man's place in nature took their place alongside those of classical antiquity then being rediscovered and explored for a wisdom long lost. Yet a surprising amount of energy was focused on what might be termed 'traditional natural philosophy', i.e., a philosophy of nature hallowed by tradition in the Latin West from the twelfth century onwards and constituting a major part of university studies. In essence this was an Aristotelian philosophy, for the texts that were commented on were those of the Lyceum, but it also contained a considerable accretion of Neoplatonic elements as well as the developments of Islamic, Jewish and Christian commentators. The diversity of sources from which it sprang and the variety of situations in which its teachings took root argue against its ever having been a monolithic system of thought.[1] Indeed, the tradition it embodied was complex, hardly capable of being characterised in simple terms. More, its written expression was prolix, and few scholars have had the inclination or the stamina to read and analyse the many printed works and manuscripts in which its teachings are preserved. Yet it was a particularly fruitful tradition, for it provided the seed-bed from which many disciplines now respected as parts of 'modern science' emerged. The difficulty of studying it is matched only by its importance, which until recent years has not been fully appreciated by intellectual historians.

The following account makes no claim to completeness: it proposes only to sketch the main outlines of this natural philosophy and to supply a sampling of illustrations that may enable the reader to capture its spirit, its values and its limitations. It begins with a brief description of the transition from the Middle Ages to the Renaissance and of how disciplines concerned

---

1. For a survey of the diversification within Renaissance Aristotelianism, see Schmitt 1981, § VI and 1983a; on the similar situation within the Middle Ages, see *Dictionary of the Middle Ages* 1982–, I, pp. 456–69 (Wallace).

with nature fared over the years roughly between 1200 and 1650. The main exposition is concerned with methodological and stylistic innovations within the period, with the way in which natural philosophy fitted into the overall structure of knowledge, how as a philosophy it stood in relation to the more specialised sciences, what its empirical content was in particular and the various ways in which it was systematised by writers interested in philosophical synthesis. Concluding sections focus on the relationship between natural philosophy and medicine, and on critiques of the former that led to its downfall and the rise of the modern era.

THE MEDIEVAL–RENAISSANCE TRANSITION

At one time it was fashionable to propose a sharp dichotomy between the philosophy of the Middle Ages and that of the Renaissance, as though their subjects of interest and methods of investigation were markedly different. In the study of nature it has been found difficult to identify and to maintain such a distinction. The development of thought in this area from the onset of the thirteenth century to the mid seventeenth may be likened more to a continuum than to a series of discrete jumps. Beginning with Albertus Magnus at Paris and with Robert Grosseteste and Roger Bacon at Oxford, and continuing to the textbook syntheses of four centuries later, natural philosophy was concerned with much the same questions and yielded answers that were intelligible within a fairly constant framework. By and large the setting was that provided by Aristotle's *libri naturales*, i.e., the *Physics*, *De caelo*, *De generatione et corruptione*, *Meteorology*, *De anima*, *Parva naturalia*, and so on, with accretions from other sources. Sensible matter, that is, material things as they appear to the senses, provided the generic subject of consideration. This served to distinguish natural philosophy or natural science (*philosophia naturalis* and *scientia naturalis* were used inter-changeably throughout the period) from mathematics, which was concerned with quantitative being, and from metaphysics, which was concerned with being in general, abstracting from its material and im-material instantiations.[2] Within this generic subject, various disciplines were identified as concerned with the different kinds of things that incorporated sensible matter in their make-up. The eight books of the *Physics* supplied the basic principles behind these disciplines, whereas the remaining treatises examined the causes and properties of the heavens,

---

2. The distinction of the sciences on this basis is explained by Thomas Aquinas 1963a, pp. 3–18, 50–65 (qq. 5 and 6 of his commentary on the *De trinitate* of Boethius).

elements and compounds, the atmospheric region and different organisms (including man) that inhabit the universe.

A number of features may be noted as characteristic of natural philosophy throughout this time span. For one, it was usually part of a systematic world view, expressed in a technical language that, if not barbarous from the viewpoint of Latinity, approached jargon in its actual employ. Again, it was characterised by divisions into schools, many arising from the traditions of geographically diverse universities, others associated with religious orders such as the Augustinians, Dominicans and Franciscans. In the context of Thomist, Scotist and Ockhamist thought natural philosophy was invariably oriented towards metaphysics and ultimately theology, whereas in Averroist circles it was more commonly ordered towards medicine. In both cases it was pursued for its instructional value – providing general (and later, classical) knowledge of the world of nature that would be open to either speculative or practical development. And by and large its problems were approached speculatively, with little reliance on experimentation or refined methods of observation, and with a general mistrust of mathematics as an effective instrument of philosophical reasoning.

Against this common background, however, it is possible to identify changing emphases that became more noticeable as the centuries progressed and led ultimately to the 'new science' of the seventeenth century. The major innovation was the return to classical sources, with the increase this brought in knowledge of the Greek text of Aristotle and of the many Greek commentaries on his works. The *Aristoteles Latinus* of earlier centuries showed little critical awareness of texts and was based on translations of varying, often inferior, quality; this limitation, coupled with the pervasive desire for systematisation, led to benign interpretations of the Stagirite that could seriously depart from his thought. Fifteenth- and sixteenth-century commentaries on the *libri naturales* were more faithful to the text and more intent on discerning, and usually defending, its original meaning. But the resulting linguistic and philological expertise was not an unmixed blessing; it encouraged an inherent conservatism among Renaissance Aristotelians that was hardly characteristic of their medieval counterparts, who would freely depart from the pagan Aristotle if they saw this to be in the service of truth.[3]

---

3. Such conservatism was caricatured by Galileo in his portrayal of Simplicio in his 1632 and 1638 dialogues; the extent to which Cesare Cremonini may have been the model for Simplicio is discussed in Schmitt 1984, § XI.

A counterbalancing feature of the Renaissance study of sources was the knowledge it provided of alternative approaches to nature. The complete works of Plato became available and along with them Neoplatonic interpretations of Aristotle that conciliated him with the teachings of his mentor.[4] A fuller knowledge of Neopythagorean doctrines also resulted, as did that of the Hermetic tradition. Stoic and atomist texts were similarly made available, and these provided new insights into physical problems, carrying over into the seventeenth century. But even at the beginning of the sixteenth century a fairly tolerant attitude towards opposing schools began to manifest itself.[5] Within scholastic Aristotelianism, for example, nominalist positions insinuated themselves within both the Thomist and the Scotist traditions, and when the Jesuits attained prominence a studied eclecticism characterised their works. The fierce partisan loyalties of the Middle Ages were somewhat relaxed; to a remarkable degree the physical works of Aristotle supplied common ground on which followers of Alexander of Aphrodisias and Simplicius, Avicennians and Averroists, Neoplatonists and scholastics of various affiliations could argue out their differences.

Another contrast between the earlier and the later ambiences was the emergence, especially in sixteenth-century Italy, of strong technological and artisan traditions.[6] Extensive work in architecture and military engineering fostered interest in the applied branches of mathematics, notably in the mechanics of Archimedes. The recovery of the *Mechanics* attributed to Aristotle and his school induced natural philosophers to reconsider the mechanical doctrines of the ancients and to locate these within the larger corpus of physical science.[7] Similar developments in painting and the fine arts led to renewed interest in optics or *perspectiva*, and Copernicus' proposal of a Pythgorean, as opposed to a Ptolemaic, universe gave new life to astronomy.[8] In the Middle Ages these *scientiae mediae* pertained to the *quadrivium*, to preparatory studies, but in the Renaissance they entered directly into the university curriculum. The fact that disciplinary domains were jealously guarded did not prevent some crossing over from

4. Jacopo Mazzoni, for example, attempted a complete reconciliation of the philosophies of Plato and Aristotle: see Mazzoni 1576 and 1597; for details see Purnell 1971 and 1972. On the introduction of Platonic philosophy into the universities of the Renaissance, see Schmitt 1981, § III.
5. This is particularly manifest in the work of John Mair and his disciples at Paris, to be discussed below; see García Villoslada 1938 and Élie 1950–1.
6. Excerpts from treatises in the technological tradition are given in English translation in *Mechanics* 1969; see also the review of this by Schmitt 1981, § XII.
7. For the place of the *Mechanics* in Renaissance culture, see Rose and Drake 1971.
8. The *perspectiva* tradition is surveyed in Lindberg 1976; on Copernicanism see n. 17 below.

mathematics to natural philosophy, with consequent debate over the strengths and weaknesses of a physical mathematics, that is, a mathematics concerned essentially with physical problems.[9] Court patronage subsidised studies in this field for their practical value, and provided a setting wherein new instruments and even experiments could be devised to study the motion of weights and similar subjects.[10]

A related infusion into natural philosophy came from the close alliance that was promoted between the practical science of medicine and its speculative underpinnings as found in the study of nature. Just as Galileo claimed for himself the title of philosopher as well as that of mathematician, so physicians in the late Middle Ages and the Renaissance saw themselves as both *philosophi* and *medici*, with their university degrees qualifying them in this way.[11] Such an orientation did more than advance the study of herbs and *materia medica*. It led to refined observation in analysing symptoms, to contrasting methods used by Aristotle and Galen when identifying the principal organs of the human body and to the study of such organs through the practice of surgery and accurate pictorial representation.

Somewhat connected with the medical development came a shift of interest within logic as an academic discipline. The late Middle Ages saw an extensive development of the *summulae* tradition and a nominalist concern with formal logic and *sophismata*, both of which served well the instructional needs of the young.[12] The Renaissance reacted against the hair-splitting such *logica docens* involved and directed attention to a *logica utens* instead. Not only did Aristotle's *Rhetoric* and *Poetics* now come in for their share of attention, but the *Topics* and the *Posterior Analytics* became fields of concentration also. The thirteenth century had pioneered in studies of scientific methodology; with the recovery of Greek commentaries on the *Analytics* and a deeper understanding of the methods employed in medicine

9. The area of investigation where this first occurred was astronomy, because of the fact that physical astronomy, as contained in Aristotle's *De caelo*, was taught by philosophers, whereas mathematical astronomy, as presented in Ptolemy's *Almagest* or Sacrobosco's *Sphaera*, was taught by mathematicians; inevitably mathematicians began to speculate about the physical reality of their constructs (e.g., eccentrics and epicycles), and philosophers had to be concerned whether their spheres fitted the mathematical theories being taught. See Westman 1980. The same merging of interests began to manifest itself in the study of motion. Girolamo Borro wrote a treatise *De motu gravium et levium* (1575) while teaching natural philosophy at Pisa; some years later the professor of mathematics there, Filippo Fantoni, composed a similar *De motu*, and so did Galileo when he replaced Fantoni in that post. For details, see Galilei 1960, pp. 13–131; Schmitt 1981, §§IX, X, XI; and Wallace 1984, pp. 230–48.
10. Most of the treatises mentioned in n.6 above were composed under the patronage of, for instance, the Duke of Urbino, the Duke of Savoy and the Grand Duke of Tuscany; see also Westfall 1985.
11. See Galilei, 1890–1909, X, p. 353. On the education of physicians at that time, see Bylebyl 1979.
12. *Cambridge History* 1982, pp. 159–381.

by Hippocrates and Galen, in pure mathematics by Euclid and Pappus and in applied mathematics by Archimedes and Hero, these studies proliferated. Significant advances were made, particularly in the logic of discovery associated with the demonstrative *regressus* and related methods of resolution and composition.[13]

METHODOLOGICAL AND STYLISTIC INNOVATIONS

From the foregoing it is apparent that methodology was one of the areas wherein pronounced changes began to become manifest with the advent of the Renaissance. At the risk of oversimplifying, in what follows these changes, some of which were also stylistic, will be grouped in four categories, namely mathematical, observational, technological and disputational, so as to provide a framework in which major contributions may be discussed. The division is proposed not as exhaustive but as illustrative of the types of innovation discernible within the period.

By mathematical changes are meant developments in applied mathematics that ultimately were to have significant impact on the study of nature, as exemplified, say, in the works of Oresme and Copernicus. Both Grosseteste and Roger Bacon had introduced a form of mathematicism at Oxford with their 'metaphysics of light', but it remained for Bradwardine and others at Merton College in the fourteenth century (especially Heytesbury and Swineshead) to offer detailed quantitative solutions to problems respecting local motion and qualitative change.[14] The findings of these *calculatores*, as they were called, were quickly assimilated at Paris by Buridan and his students, among whom Oresme is particularly noteworthy.[15] Apart from working out techniques for calculating ratios and graphing changes geometrically, Oresme proposed a clockwork model of the motions of the

13. A comprehensive survey of this development is *Aristotelismo veneto* 1983, I, pp. 221–77 (Papuli); see also *ibid.*, pp. 435–57 (Berti); N. W. Gilbert 1960; Randall 1961; Wallace 1972–, I, pp. 117–49.

14. On Grosseteste, see Crombie 1953 and McEvoy 1982; for Bacon, see R. Bacon 1983; on the Merton School or the Oxford Calculators, as they were called, see *Reinterpreting Galileo* 1986, pp. 53–108 (Sylla); *Cambridge History* 1982, pp. 540–63 (Sylla); Clagett 1959; Wallace 1972–, I, pp. 53–62; among its members are usually included Thomas Bradwardine, John Dumbleton, William Heytesbury and Richard Swineshead. See also *Dictionary of Scientific Biography* 1970–80, V, pp. 548–54 ('Grosseteste'); I, pp. 377–85 ('Bacon'); II, pp. 390–7 ('Bradwardine'); VII, pp. 116–17 ('Dumbleton'); VI, pp. 376–80 ('Heytesbury'); XIII, pp. 184–213 ('Swineshead').

15. Sometimes referred to as the *Doctores Parisienses*, following Duhem 1906–13 *passim*. On the more important of these writers, see *Dictionary of Scientific Biography* 1970–80, II, pp. 603–8 ('Jean Buridan'); I, pp. 93–5 ('Albert of Saxony'); IX, pp. 136–8 ('Marsilius of Inghen'); X, pp. 223–30 ('Nicole Oresme'); for a summary of their contributions and their influence on Galileo, see Wallace 1972–, I, pp. 103–14 and 1981a, pp. 192–252, 303–19.

heavens and speculated that the earth might be in motion also, undergoing slight translational shifts as it adjusted its centre of gravity to be in the centre of the universe. He recognised that astronomical phenomena could be saved equally well by having the earth rotate daily on its axis as by having the heavens do likewise, but regarded this as insufficient basis for rejecting scriptural teaching on the stability of the earth. Oresme further adopted Buridan's notion of impetus to explain the acceleration of heavy bodies during fall, and possibly saw that velocity of fall would increase directly with time of fall, without offering any distance calculations to substantiate this result. Oresme's influence on subsequent investigators is difficult to ascertain, since his writings remained largely in manuscript, but they illustrate the degree of mathematical sophistication already reached in the mid fourteenth century.[16] Copernicus, on the other hand, writing almost two centuries later, was to have a profound effect on the development of astronomical science. A calendar-maker who had studied in Italy, this Polish canon worked out a complete heliocentric alternative to the Ptolemaic system of the world, publishing it in his *De revolutionibus orbium caelestium* of 1543. Although Osiander in an unsigned preface to the volume proposed it as a pure mathematical hypothesis, Copernicus regarded his system as physically true, and inspired others, such as Kepler and Galileo, to become advocates of the 'new astronomy' and achieve its general acceptance by the end of the seventeenth century.[17]

The observational component of methodological change was enhanced from a variety of directions, ranging from humanist critiques of the natural history of Pliny, through studies in medicine and surgery aimed at improving (and correcting) the teachings of Hippocrates and Galen, to a renewed emphasis on the empirical base for the Aristotelian corpus. This inevitably augmented the observational content of natural philosophy and even led to the use of experimental procedures, to be treated more fully below. Behind this development was a general conviction that the human mind can safely reason from effects or *symptomata* to their hidden causes, and then use such causes, newly discovered, to structure scientific explanations of the phenomena that had been observed. Although generally endorsed and explained previously by figures such as Albertus Magnus and Thomas

16. Recent editions of Oresme's writings make his thought accessible to scholars; see particularly those of 1966, 1968a, 1968b and 1971.

17. The fifth centenary of the birth of Copernicus (*Dictionary of Scientific Biography* 1970–80, III, pp. 401–11) in 1973 made a wealth of information available concerning him; see the collections of essays in *Nature of Scientific Discovery* 1975; *Science and Society* 1975; *Copernican Achievement* 1975; also Gingerich 1973, 1983.

Aquinas, this type of *a posteriori* reasoning reached perfection at the University of Padua towards the end of the sixteenth century. The groundwork was laid there earlier by Pietro d'Abano in medical contexts and then, in the fifteenth century, by Paul of Venice and Gaetano da Thiene. The latter, together with Ugo Benzi da Siena and Jacopo da Forlì, combined an interest in 'calculatory' techniques with a search for causes by resolving effects to them, and then composing causes with these effects to achieve *propter quid* explanations. The culmination of this movement is found in the writings of Agostino Nifo and Jacopo Zabarella. Zabarella worked extensively in logic and natural philosophy, and is particularly noteworthy for his insistence on observation and empirical grounding when studying nature, not only in practice but in the logical justification of his investigative procedures.[18]

Technological improvements, together with the perfecting of the printing press and its contribution to graphical representation and wide distribution of results, also enhanced natural philosophy, though in a less direct way. Experimentation would not have been possible without skill in instrument making, and artisans and craftsmen could only work with the materials industry made available to them. Architects and engineers rediscovered the works of Vitruvius, and in the building of domes and elaborate edifices had to make use of, and so perfect, their knowledge of mechanical principles. Leonardo da Vinci is usually singled out as an important innovator in this regard.[19] His *Notebooks*, it is true, contain ingenious sketches and mechanical designs in advance of his time, but they were never circulated and so exerted little influence on his contemporaries. More significant were Francesco di Giorgio (Martini), some of whose engineering designs were appropriated by Leonardo; Georg Bauer (Agricola), whose *De re metallica* gave an excellent view of advanced mining techniques; and Vanoccio Biringuccio, whose *De la pirotechnia* did the same for metallurgical processes.[20] Mention should also be made of Andreas Vesalius' *De fabrica corporis humani* of 1543, whose graphic illustrations of the organs of the human body did more to promote medical knowledge in the mid sixteenth century than any other work of the time.[21]

18. There is an extensive literature on these Paduan Aristotelians; see *Aristotelismo veneto* 1983 for a recent collection of essays, as well as the earlier studies of Cassirer 1911; Randall 1940, 1961; N. W. Gilbert 1960, 1963; W. F. Edwards 1960, 1967; Poppi 1970a, 1972a; and Wallace 1972–, I, pp. 117–55.
19. *Dictionary of Scientific Biography* 1970–80, VIII, pp. 192–245 ('Leonardo da Vinci').
20. *Ibid.*, IX, pp. 146–8 ('Martini'); I, 77–9 ('Agricola'); II, pp. 142–3 ('Biringuccio').
21. *Ibid.*, XIV, pp. 3–12 ('Vesalius'); the illustrations of the *De fabrica* have been reissued in facsimile, with descriptions of each plate, in Vesalius 1950.

As the Middle Ages gave way to the Renaissance there were finally changes in dialectical and disputational modes that are reflected in the ways natural philosophy and medicine were treated. The medieval *disputatio*, with its presentation of arguments *pro* and *con*, proof of these and replies to objections, continued to influence the way the *scientiae naturales* were taught over a considerable period. Since Aristotle was the main authority, commentaries on his writings were an important vehicle, but these were supplemented by 'questionaries' that treated disputed points and school positions in exhaustive detail.[22] This scholastic mode influenced medical writing as well as that on nature throughout the fourteenth and fifteenth centuries.[23] Under humanist influences, however, the later Renaissance saw a reaction against scholastic method and the arid treatises it tended to produce. Particularly in Italian universities a more discursive and literary style was adopted, with classical allusions and more attention to philology and the Greek text. The works of Nifo and Zabarella, to say nothing of Boccadifero, Buonamici, Cremonini, Mazzoni, Pendasio and Porzio, are very different from those of Paul of Venice or Blasius of Parma, and that simply on the basis of style of argument and presentation of results.[24]

NATURAL PHILOSOPHY IN THE STRUCTURE OF KNOWLEDGE

Notwithstanding these different emphases, the content of natural philosophy remained much the same throughout the centuries under discussion, when it had a much broader meaning than it has in the present day. Philosophy itself then extended to all that is knowable by human reason, and a major part of its concern was with the world of nature. To give some idea of the extent of both disciplines in the Renaissance curriculum, a representative division of their respective structures is given here. Some authors departed considerably from the following, which is based on

22. Representative works are the textbooks on natural philosophy produced at Paris in the early sixteenth century, especially those of George of Brussels, Petrus Crockaert, Juan de Celaya and Luis Coronel; see García Villoslada 1938 and Élie 1950–1 for listings and surveys of their works. These had a pronounced influence in Spain, particularly at Salamanca, where the commentary and 'questionary' on the *Physics* by Domingo de Soto enjoyed great popularity. One of the most synthetic treatments of the materials in the *Physics*, juxtaposing the teachings of the various schools, is the *Physica* published at Valencia by Diego Mas in 1599, to be discussed below. See also Schmitt in this volume, pp. 792–804 below.

23. Bylebyl 1979 and forthcoming.

24. Most of these works are listed in Lohr: Boccadifero (Buccaferrea), 1974b, pp. 281–6; Buonamici, 1974b, p. 272; Cremonini, 1975, pp. 728–39; Nifo, 1979, pp. 532–9; Pendasio, 1979, pp. 556–62; Porzio, 1980, pp. 667–70; and J. Zabarella, 1982, pp. 233–42.

Franciscus Toletus, but his classification has the merit of epitomising the Greek and Latin textual traditions as well as the scholastic revivals in Italy and the Iberian peninsula.[25]

The function of philosophy, for Toletus, is to dispel man's ignorance in three areas: in his contemplation of the truth, in his learning how to live reasonably and in his knowing how to provide the material necessities of life. These goals give rise to philosophy's three principal parts: *speculativa*, *practica* and *factiva*.[26] The first, speculative philosophy, is made up of metaphysics, mathematics and physics. Metaphysics treats the most common principles and properties of all being, whereas physics treats of everything that falls under the senses. Mathematics is two-fold: pure, which studies entities that do not depend on motion and are abstracted from it, namely numbers and figures; and middle (*mathematica media*), which studies them as abstracted but as still found in motion, as do *perspectiva* and music.[27] Active philosophy has the practical task of directing man's activities precisely as human; its parts are ethics, which directs one's personal life, oeconomics, which governs home and family, and politics, which orders the city and the republic.[28] Factive or constructive philosophy, otherwise known as *mechanica*, is then divided into arts that are necessary for human living (e.g., agriculture), those that are useful (e.g., navigation) and those that provide pleasure (e.g., singing). An alternative division would be based on matter: those preparing it (e.g., mining or metallurgy); those employing

25. *Commentaria una cum quaestionibus in VIII libros De physica auscultatione*, first published at Cologne in 1574 and often thereafter. Citations in what follows are taken from the Venice edition of 1600.
26. Toletus 1600, f. 2ra: 'Philosophia vero in hunc finem investigata, ut ignorantia, quam miser homo propter peccatum incurrit, quo ad fieri posset, expelleretur, homo autem per peccatum haec tria praeter alia sibi comparavit, rerum veritatis ignorantiam; eorum, quae secundum rationem agere oportebat, similiter ignorantiam, et rursus eorum, quibus ad vitae sustentationem, et conservationem, propter peccatum indigebat, ignorantiam: unde omni ex parte ignarus factus est in speculabilibus, agilibus, et factibilibus, indiguit igitur scientia, qua ens verum cognosceret, qua agenda, et facienda consideraret: et ista est philosophia, in tres praecipuas partes divisa secundum ignorantiarum numerum, in speculativam nempe, qua veritates rerum tantum contemplaretur, in activam, qua ea quae secundum rationem agere oportet, doceretur, et in factivam, qua ea, quibus exterius indigeret, facere sciret.'
27. *Ibid.*, f. 2rb: 'Speculativa subdivitur in metaphysicam, quae omnium communissima principia, et passiones generales speculatur, in mathematicam puram, quae ea, quae secundum se a motu non dependent, secundum rationem abstrahendo a motu tractat, ut figuras, numeros, et his accidentia, et in mathematicam mediam, quae ea, quae secundum naturam suam abstracta sunt, in motu tamen considerat, ut perspectiva, et musica, et similes, et in physicam, quae res sensibiles speculatur.'
28. *Ibid.*, f. 2rb: 'Rursus activa dividitur in ethicam, qua homo ea, secundum quae se rationabiliter ordinare debet cognoscit: et in oeconomicam, qua familiam, et domum regat: et politicam, qua usus reipublicae, et civitatis, cuius pars est, rectos cognoscat, et exequatur.'

it in construction (e.g., building); and those using the things constructed (e.g., military operations).[29]

Physics, or natural philosophy, had a similarly broad scope. Basing himself on Simplicius and Themistius, Toletus first gives a division based on the principles of natural things, treated in the eight books of Aristotle's *Physics*, and on the entities into whose composition they enter, discussed in the remaining natural treatises.[30] Natural entities are either simple or composed. If simple, they are incorruptible, as the heavens, or corruptible, as the elements. The former are treated in the first two books of *De caelo*, the latter in the last two: elements are also discussed in *De generatione et corruptione* under the aspect of their coming to be and passing away, a feature they share with composites or compounds.[31] Composed entities are inanimate or animate. The inanimate again are of two types: those found in the upper regions, imperfect composites such as rain and things seen in the atmosphere, explained in the *Meteorology*, and the more perfect type found in the earth, such as stones and metals, explained in *De mineralibus*.[32] Animate entities then have a fuller treatment: their general features are discussed in the three books of *De anima*, after which come particular aspects in books devoted to sleep and waking, youth and old age, life and death and so on. Finally there are the more specialised treatises devoted to specific types of living things: plants, studied in *De plantis*; and animals, studied in

29. *Ibid.*, f. 2rb: 'Factiva rursus, quae mechanica dicitur, bifariam subdividi potest: primo in artes necessarias, quae nempe usum vitae necessarium ministrant, ut lanificium, agricultura, aratura, et in utiles, quae usum faciliorem vitae faciunt: ut in navigatoria, militaris, equestris, et in delectabiles, quae usum vitae iocundiorem reddunt, ut saltandi ars, venandi, cantandi, et similes. Rursus dividi potest in eas, quae materiam praeparant, ut ars fodiendi metalla, conficiendi ferrum, coquendi lateres, et in eas, quae materiam disponunt, et componunt, ut domificatoria, fabrilis, sutoria, et in eas, quae materia composita utuntur, ut militaris, equestris, navigatoria.'
30. *Ibid.*, f. 6ra: 'Circa tertium de divisione philosophiae naturalis, videtur mihi satis commoda illa, quam assignant Simplicius, et Themistius: nempe, haec quae in philosophia naturali continentur, aut sunt de principiis, aut de his, quae ex principiis componuntur, de principiis omnium rerum naturalium, et de communibus est liber physicorum, de compositis sunt reliqui.'
31. *Ibid.*, f. 6^{ra-b}: 'Quae autem componuntur ex primis, aut sunt simplicia corpora ex aliis corporibus, non constituta, aut sunt composita, et mixta. Si simplicia sunt, aut incorruptibilia, et sic sunt coeli, de quibus traditur in libris duobus prioribus de caelo, aut corruptibilia, ut elementa, et de his agitur in duobus posterioribus libris de caelo, de his enim omnibus primo traditur, tanquam de simplicibus corporibus. De compositis vero, quia hoc omnibus est commune, nempe generatio, et corruptio, et non solum his, sed etiam ipsis simplicibus elementis, ob id primo de generatione et corruptione disseritur, postea de ipsis seorsum.'
32. *Ibid.*, f. 6rb: 'Haec autem composita, quaedam inanimata, quaedam animata sunt. Primo de inanimatis agitur: deinde de animatis. Atque inter illa quaedam sublimia sunt, quae meteora dicuntur, quae supra nos fiunt, venti, pluviae, irides, halones, et similia, de quibus in libris meteororum: quaedam subtus in intrinsecis terrae partibus, ut metalla, lapides, de quibus in libro de mineralibus.'

the various books *De animalibus* relating their history, modes of generation and various parts.[33]

From this overview one may gain an idea of the extent of natural philosophy in the Renaissance mind. The *Physics* laid out the fundamental concepts of all the natural sciences and dealt with the type of question now discussed in courses on the philosophy of science. The *De caelo* was the equivalent of physical astronomy, the *De generatione et corruptione* of physics and chemistry and the *Meteorology* and *De mineralibus* of atmospheric science and geology respectively. Moreover, the *De anima* explained the general principles of biology and of comparative psychology, while *De plantis* and *De animalibus* covered the entire content of botany and zoology. All of these disciplines were linked together in a common conceptual structure, so that a change in one, particularly in the *Physics* or the *De anima*, would cause radical revisions in most of the others. There were also areas of ambiguity: for example, astronomy, where the heavenly bodies were treated as physical entities in the *De caelo*, and as objects whose motions could be calculated in middle or applied mathematics; or dynamics, where motion was analysed in terms of its causes and properties in the *Physics*, and in terms of the forces and times required to move heavy objects in mechanics. It was precisely in these areas that conflicts and problems arose, not to be solved until the seventeenth century with the rise of modern science.

Also worthy of note is the emphasis accorded various parts of philosophy in the curriculum, for not all were given equal treatment. In the 1580s at Pisa, for example, both *ordinarii* and *extraordinarii* (ordinary and extraordinary professors) seem to have lectured on a three-year cycle, focusing in detail on particular books without regard for pedagogical order in the development of the doctrine.[34] In 1581 the *ordinarii* taught the *De anima* and the *extraordinarii* the *De sensu*; in 1582 the *ordinarii* covered the first book of the *Physics* and the *extraordinarii* the *De generatione et corruptione*; and in 1583 the *ordinarii* lectured on the *De caelo* and the *extraordinarii* on the *Meteorology*. The year 1584 saw the resumption of *De anima*, and so on. Each year, however, the logic professor at Pisa taught the *Posterior Analytics* and

---

33. *Ibid.*, f. 6rb: 'Animata autem, quia animam habent communiter, prius de anima agitur in libris tribus de anima, et de quibusdam ex anima procedentibus, videlicet de somno, vigilia, iuventute, senectute, vita, morte, et similibus, in libro qui parva naturalia dicitur, tractantur. Post haec de ipsis animatis, atque horum, quaedam animalia, quaedam plantae: de animalibus in libro de historia, et in libris de partibus animalium, et generatione ipsorum late disseritur: tandem de plantis.'

34. On philosophy instruction at Pisa, see Fabroni 1791–5 *passim*; Schmitt 1981, § IX, 1983d; and Wallace 1984, pp. 92–4.

the *Isagoge* of Porphyry, so the student was always assured of beginning logic at any point in the philosophy cycle.[35] At Padua, on the other hand, there was an even greater degree of specialisation. In 1593, for instance, the *ordinarii* in philosophy taught the first and second books of *De anima*, while the *extraordinarii* covered the third book; in logic the first and second books of the *Posterior Analytics* were taught concurrently; and two commentaries on the first book of the *Metaphysics* were offered, one *in via Scoti* and the other *in via Sancti Thomae*. In 1594 the concentration was on the first and eighth books of the *Physics* and on the seventh book of the *Metaphysics*, following a similar schema, with logic remaining the same. The subsequent year saw the *ordinarii* covering the *De generatione et corruptione* and the *extraordinarii* the *De caelo*, with the metaphysicians concentrating on the twelfth book of the *Metaphysics*, and the logicians continuing to give the *Posterior Analytics*.[36] In Rome, at the Collegio Romano, philosophy was taught more systematically during the same period, so that a student at any time could progress through his three years in the following order: first year, the whole of logic, from the *Categories* to the *Posterior Analytics*; second year, *Physics*, *De caelo*, first book of *De generatione et corruptione* and *Meteorology*; and third year, second book of *De generatione et corruptione*, *De anima*, and selected books of the *Metaphysics*.[37]

Even from this brief survey it may be seen that natural philosophy received a major share of attention in the university curriculum. Little or no attention seems to have been given at any of these institutions to the 'active' or 'factive' branches of philosophy listed by Toletus, or to detailed studies of minerals, plants, and animals as contained in the full *corpus Aristotelicum*.

PHILOSOPHY AND THE SCIENCES

It should be clear by now that the natural philosophy of the Renaissance included much material that would later pertain to the sciences, in the recent understanding of that term. In one way of looking at it, natural philosophy may be regarded as the parent of modern scientific disciplines, for considerable overlap may be discerned in the subjects of both. Yet in another respect the Renaissance study of nature was deficient in its use of observation and experiment, and generally in the role it assigned to

---

35. Pisa, Archivio di Stato, Università G.77, ff. 164^v–94^v.
36. Padua, Archivio antico, Università di Padova, Rotuli Artistarum, Pars prima 1520–1739, cod. 242, ff. 25^r–49^v.
37. García Villoslada 1954, pp. 84–115; Wallace 1984, pp. 6–7, 58–70.

mathematics in its reasoning processes. The latter deficiency was gradually remedied by the importation of materials from the *scientiae mediae* into natural philosophy, even though this was regarded by many as an illicit crossing of disciplinary lines.[38] To furnish some idea of the materials appropriated by modern science from natural philosophy, and also of those taken from the mixed science tradition, a few examples will now be discussed. These are drawn mainly from studies of the structure of matter and the continuum and those relating to alteration and local motion, but they are representative of changes taking place in other areas of investigation as well.

Aristotle's *Physics* contained a number of teachings that proved fruitful for an understanding of matter and its structure. The hylemorphic doctrine of the first book required an exposition of the basic substrate or protomatter underlying substantial change, *materia prima*, concerning which a number of questions were raised in the sixteenth century.[39] One series had to do with the homogeneous or continuous character of the elemental bodies, obviously related to the problem of atomism and the structure of the continuum, another to the presence of matter in the heavenly bodies and what kinds of changes the heavens might undergo.

With regard to the first, in the thirteenth century Albertus Magnus had suggested that *minima naturalia* might be identified with the atoms of Democritus, but otherwise did not develop the suggestion.[40] In the fourteenth, under nominalist influences the question was broached anew and assimilated to quantitative teachings on *maxima* and *minima*. Thus Buridan focused attention on the quantitative requirements for the existence of natural substances, arguing that a substance becomes unstable when its quantity falls below the *minimum naturale*; Albert of Saxony went

---

38. On the *scientiae mediae*, see Laird 1983; *Reinterpreting Galileo* 1986, pp. 29–51 (Lennox); the difficulty posed by *metabasis*, or the use of principles outside a genus subject to demonstrate properties of the subject, is examined in detail by Livesey 1982.

39. *Physics* 1.7–9 (189^{b}30–192^{b}4); philosophical questions relating to this teaching are listed by Mas 1599, pp. 368–449, as follows: 'Quaest. 1. An detur materia prima, 368; Quaest. 2. An materia prima fuerit in tempore producta a Deo, 372; Quaest. 3. An materia prima sit ens, 375; Quaest. 4. An materia prima sit substantia, 377; Quaest. 5. An materia sit distincta a forma, 379; Quaest. 6. An materia sit pura potentia, 382; Quaest. 7. An potentia sit de essentia materiae primae, 398; Quaest. 8. An materia sit in potentia ad omnes formas, 408; Quaest. 9. An materia habeat potestatem ad formam, quam amisit, 411; Quaest. 10. An materia appetat formam, 413; Quaest. 11. An appetitus materiae reipsa differat a materia, 415; Quaest. 12. An materia prima sit ortui, et interitui obnoxia, 418; Quaest. 13. An sit materia prima una numero in his quae oriuntur et intereunt, 421; Quaest. 14. An materia habeat ideam, 426; Quaest. 15. An materia ex se, suapteque natura sit intelligibilis, 428; Quaest. 16. An materia prima sit bona, nec ne, 432; Quaest. 17. An materia sit entium omnium infima, et ignobilior, 434; Quaest. 18. An materia fuerit aliquando sine forma, 439; Quaest. 19. An materia possit esse sine forma, 439; Quaest. 20. Quid sit materia proxima, et quibus discriminibus separetur a prima, 448.'   40. Albertus Magnus 1890–9, IV, p. 354^b.

further to maintain that under normal conditions it could not exist below that minimum.[41] In the sixteenth century, Nifo cited approvingly Averroes' doctrine that every increase or decrease in a substance consists in the addition or subtraction of a certain number of *minima naturalia*, thus emphasising the discontinuity involved in such processes. He also pointed out that, when elements react upon each other, they are divided into *minima*.[42] His contemporary, Julius Caesar Scaliger, theorised that the *minima* of different substances vary in size, and attempted on this basis to explain their coarseness and density.[43] He also argued that chemical composition (*mistio*) is the motion of such *minima* toward mutual contact, with the result that union is effected. Toletus took up the same teaching: reacting substances are divided into *minima naturalia*; in combination the *minima* of one substance come alongside those of the other, and they act on each other until a third substance, having the substantial form of the compound, is generated.[44] Finally, in the early seventeenth century, Sennert undertook a complete reconciliation of Aristotelian *minima* theory with Democritean atomism and went on to explain all known chemical phenomena, involving both elements and compounds, in terms of their ultimate material constituents.[45]

An analogous development took place with respect to Aristotle's analysis of the continuum in the sixth book of his *Physics*. There he had argued that the continuum could not be composed of indivisibles.[46] Nominalists of the fourteenth century reopened the question, asserting that points are actually present in extended magnitudes and using an example drawn from mathematics to support this, namely that a sphere touches a plane at a point, which must therefore exist in the plane.[47] The sixteenth century saw extensive discussion of the mode of presence of indivisibles in the continuum, for example, whether they are present actually or only potentially, are infinite or finite in number and so on.[48] It was generally conceded that indivisibles exercise a terminating or continuing function

41. Van Melsen 1960, pp. 62–3.   42. *Ibid.*, pp. 64–9.
43. Lohr 1980, pp. 714–16; Van Melsen 1960, pp. 73–7.   44. Van Melsen 1960, pp. 69–70.
45. Lohr 1980, pp. 725–6; Van Melsen 1960, pp. 81–9; Molland 1982.
46. *Physics* VI.1 (231^a21–233^b32); Mas 1599, pp. 1181–1214, lists the following as typical questions: 'Quaest. 1. An in continuo dentur actu aliqua indivisibilia, 1181; Quaest. 2. An punctum, et alia indivisibilia sint entia privativa, 1190; Quaest. 3. An indivisibilia reipsa, et a substantia, et a magnitudine distinguantur, 1193; Quaest. 4. An continuum componatur ex indivisibilibus, 1197; Quaest. 5. An continuum sit divisibile in semper divisibilia, 1205; Quaest. 6. An in continuo dentur actu partes infinitae, 1208; Quaest. 7. An magnitudo, motus, et tempus habeant eandem rationem divisionis, 1212.'
47. *Cambridge History* 1982, pp. 573–84 (Murdoch); *Source Book* 1974, pp. 312–24; Wallace 1984, pp. 165–6, 313.
48. *Cambridge History* 1982, pp. 567–73; Mair 1938; Soto 1555, f. 42^v–52^v.

with respect to the divisibles of which the continuum is clearly composed, but only the divisibles were regarded as its parts. Some authors, however, began to speak of *partes divisibiles* and *partes indivisibiles* as components of the whole, thus conferring on indivisibles the status of parts also.[49] Galileo appropriated this terminology and spoke of *parti quante* and *parti non quante* in the sensible continuum, conceiving them respectively after the fashion of minute atoms and intervening vacua.[50] The latter could be infinite in number, in his estimation, and he used them to explain the cohesion of material substances on the basis that nature abhors a vacuum.

With regard to the heavenly bodies, the question of their constitution was argued extensively during the sixteenth century. The stimulus in this area came from the mixed science of astronomy, where accurate measurements of the positions of *novae* and comets provided evidence that alterative changes, and not merely changes of position, were taking place in the superlunary regions of the heavens.[51] The question whether the heavens are simple or composed bodies had long been argued; Averroists thought of them as completely simple, whereas most scholastics regarded them as simple only in the sense of not being composed of the four sublunary elements.[52] The latter position still allowed for the matter-form composition of superlunary bodies, but raised questions concerning whether their forms are 'informing forms' or merely 'assisting forms' (i.e., intelligences that assist their motion), and whether their matter is the same as that of sublunary bodies or not.[53] For Thomists, who regarded *materia prima* as pure potency and thus incapable of being intrinsically differentiated into kinds, the admission of a second type of matter in the heavens presented great difficulty. Capreolus and Cajetan offered ingenious suggestions to explain this possibility, but none was completely satisfying.[54] After he himself had measured the parallax of the *nova* of 1572, Clavius concluded that superlunary bodies do undergo alteration (if not substantial change), and in this sense are similar to the sublunary.[55] His researches stimulated his

49. E.g., Ruggiero 1590–1, f. 348ʳ (lecturing on the *Physics* at the Collegio Romano in 1591): 'Quarto animadvertendum quod totum hoc nihil aliud significat quam quod hoc ipso quod assignamus in motu aliquod mutatum esse, i.e., aliquam partem indivisibilem motus, necessario supponere debemus quod illam partem praecesserit aliqua pars divisibilis eiusdem motus'; see also Wallace 1984, p. 167.   50. Galilei 1890–1909, VII, p. 746.
51. Tycho Brahe (*Dictionary of Scientific Biography* 1970–80, II, pp. 401–16) pioneered in the development of these measuring techniques.   52. Galilei 1977, pp. 81–92.
53. *Ibid.*, pp. 103–58.   54. *Ibid.*, pp. 139–47; Wallace 1981a, pp. 160–90.
55. Clavius 1581, pp. 193–4: 'Quae cum ita sint, ita mihi persuadeo, stellam illam vel tunc a Deo Opt. Max. procreatam esse in caelo octavo, ut magnum aliquid portenderet (quod cuiusmodi sit, adhuc ignoratur), vel certe in ipso caelo gigni posse cometas, sicut in aere, licet rarius id contingat . . . Hoc

colleagues in philosophy at the Collegio Romano to investigate the topic more thoroughly.[56] Thus, well before Galileo's observations in 1609 of mountains on the moon, the ground had been prepared for a revision of medieval views on the material composition of the heavens.[57]

Such discussions were not without their impact on theses relating to the four terrestrial elements and the qualities that characterise them. Medieval teaching had accounted for accidental changes in nature through Aristotle's four alterative qualities (hot, cold, wet and dry) and his two motive qualities (*gravitas* and *levitas*), explained in his *De generatione et corruptione* and *De caelo* respectively. Attempts to account for fevers and other medical phenomena led Renaissance physicians to make adaptations in this doctrine, suggesting, for example, that coldness might be the mere absence of heat, or that there might be two types of coldness, one real, as found in the elements, the other privative, as in other bodies.[58] Cardano proposed that neither coldness nor dryness exist as such, but are merely the privation of heat and wetness respectively.[59] Telesio thought of all four as real, but maintained that wetness and dryness are not qualities at all – rather they are substances whose presence in a body make it either fluid or solid.[60] Scaliger, on the other hand, defended Aristotle's original teaching, arguing that all four are true qualities, real and positive in the order of nature.[61]

si verum est, videant Peripatetici, quomodo Aristotelis opinionem de materia caeli defendere possint. Dicendum enim fortasse erit, caelum non esse quintam quandam essentiam, sed mutabile corpus, licet minus corruptibile sit, quam corpora haec inferiora.'

56. Menu, Vitelleschi, and Ruggiero all discuss the matter. The last presents his conclusions in three propositions; see Ruggiero 1591, f. 65^r: 'Prima propositio. Non esset usque adeo improbabile asserere coelum generabile et corruptibile per mutuam transmutationem cum inferioribus . . . Secunda propositio. Multo probabilius est asserere coelum generabile et corruptibile, sed per solam transmutationem substantialem inter ipsas coeli partes'; f. 65^v: 'Tertia propositio. Probabilissimum tamen est, et probabilius quam superiora, coelum esse ingenerabile et incorruptibile, quamquam id positive demonstrari non potest.' In support of the last proposition, since it cannot be demonstrated, Ruggiero simply argues from the authority of Peripatetics and scholastics in this matter. See also Benedetti 1585, p. 197.   57. Dales 1980; E. Grant 1983, 1984b.

58. Galileo discusses this question in his early notebooks: see Galilei 1977, pp. 230–4, dating from around 1590. Excerpts from the Latin text are given in the following notes.

59. Galilei 1890–1909, I, p. 160: 'Prima sententia fuit quorumdam antiquorum, apud Plutarchum lib. De primo frigido, qui dixerunt frigiditatem esse privationem caloris. Horum sententiam secutus est Cardanus, lib. 2° De subtilitate, qui idem affirmat etiam de siccitate, quam vult esse privationem humoris.'

60. *Ibid.*, p. 161: 'Tertia sententia est aliorum dicentium, omnes has qualitates reales esse et positivas: sed humorem et siccitatem non esse qualitates, sed substantias; idest humorem esse substantiam fluentem; siccitatem vero, substantiam consistentem.' Vitelleschi, in his exposition of this subject-matter, attributes this *sententia* to Telesio.

61. *Ibid.*: 'Quarta sententia, vera, est Aristotelis et omnium Peripateticorum, in t. 8 secundi De generatione et in 4 Meteororum et alibi, dicentium omnes quatuor qualitates esse veras, reales, et positivas: quam sententiam optime tuetur contra Cardanum Scaliger, Exercitationum 18, 19, 22, et Plutarchus.'

An analogous discussion took place with regard to the existence of *gravitas* and *levitas* in the elements. The development of Archimedean teaching on specific gravity and on the role of the medium in hydrostatic phenomena led Benedetti, for example, to question whether *levitas* is necessary to account for upward motion, i.e., motion away from the centre of the earth, or whether degrees of heaviness (equating the light with the less heavy) are adequate for this purpose.[62] Galileo wavered on this decision in his early writings, then opted for *gravitas* as offering sufficient explanation, while admitting but meagre understanding of its true nature.[63]

It was in the speculative discussion of local motion, moreover, that the ground was laid for Renaissance advances in the study of dynamics. With regard to motion, Ockhamists of the fourteenth century had questioned its reality and its mode of distinction from the object in motion and the terminus it attains.[64] Related problems concerned the nature of place and the requirement of a medium for local motion; of particular significance were discussions of the possibility of motion in a void or vacuum, and if possible, whether motion there would be instantaneous or not.[65] The contrariety and specification of local motions also attracted attention. Would the upward and then downward motion of a projected stone constitute two motions or one? The answer could depend on the difference between a violent motion and a natural motion (in the stone's case, upward and downward respectively), or alternatively, on whether or not a moment of rest occurs at the summit or point of reflection. And then there was the recurrent task of tracing moving agents in natural motions so as to safeguard the principle 'whatever is moved, is moved by another'.[66] All of these questions were argued with increasing intensity in the sixteenth century, as treatises began to be written on the motion of heavy and light bodies (*De motu gravium et levium*) and experimental evidence began to be introduced for their solution, to be described below.[67]

Apart from such contributions from the mixed science of mechanics, others should be mentioned from the sciences of optics and music. Aristotle's speculative discussion of light and colour pertained to his *De anima* and *De sensu*, but it was the Renaissance revival of *perspectiva*, coupled

62. Benedetti 1585; *Mechanics* 1969, p. 218.   63. Wallace 1984, pp. 245–8.
64. *Cambridge History* 1982, pp. 530–6 (Weisheipl); Wallace 1981a, pp. 341–8.
65. *Source Book* 1974, pp. 324–60, 554–68; E. Grant 1981a *passim*.
66. Wallace 1984, pp. 162–5, 173–8, 191–202.
67. Treatises of this kind were composed by Zimara (Lohr 1982, p. 251); Borro (*Dictionary of Scientific Biography* 1970–80, XV, pp. 44–6; Schmitt 1981, §IX, pp. 267–71); J. Zabarella (Schmitt 1981 § VIII, pp. 92–106); Fantoni (Schmitt 1981, § X); and Galileo (Wallace 1984, pp. 230–48), among others.

with studies of the anatomy of the eye, that led to significant advances in the understanding of human vision. The medieval contribution had consisted essentially of the work of Alhazen and in Avicenna's emendations to Galenic doctrine, supplemented by contributions from Roger Bacon, Pecham and Witelo. Renaissance artists such as Brunelleschi, Alberti, Ghiberti and Leonardo worked out theories of linear perspective that enabled one to trace the geometrical paths of light rays with considerable accuracy.[68] Ocular anatomists, and among these Achillini, Vesalius, Colombo and Platter should be mentioned, investigated the eye's structure and the respective roles of lens and retina in vision. The findings of both groups were synthesised by Maurolyco, Della Porta, Risner and finally Kepler, the last developing a full-blown theory of the retinal image that put visual theory on its modern footing.[69]

Theory of music also underwent substantial development during the sixteenth century.[70] Previous to that, Boethius' transmission of Greek harmonic theory had constituted the main source for a theoretical understanding of music as a quadrivial science. The invention of new instruments and polyphonic scales, together with increasing skill in the performing arts, led to further studies of harmony by Tartaglia and Stevin. These finally culminated, in the latter part of the century, in a thorough reworking of Pythagorean mathematical harmony by Zarlino.[71] Zarlino's proposals, however, were questioned by Benedetti and by Galileo's father, Vincenzo, both using physical considerations to correct the purely mathematical reasoning of the musical theorist. Vincenzo, probably with the help of his son, then about twenty-four years of age, even performed experiments with tuned strings of varied diameter, length and tension to disprove Zarlino's polyphonal theory.[72]

THE EMPIRICAL CONTENT OF NATURAL PHILOSOPHY

The empirical sciences are usually thought to differ from natural philosophy not only because of their mathematical techniques but also because of their use of experimentation or controlled observation to establish their results. As can be seen in the cases of visual and musical theory just mentioned, a number of questions discussed in sixteenth-century philosophy

---

68. Lindberg 1976, pp. 122–68. 69. *Ibid.*, pp. 172–208.
70. Palisca 1961; Walker 1978, pp. 14–33; Cohen 1984.
71. Palisca 1956 and his edition of Mei 1960; Drake 1970, pp. 43–52.
72. Drake 1970, pp. 52–62.

lent themselves to empirical tests of one kind or another, and it seems only natural that experimental methods would have evolved out of the contexts in which they were raised. Some questions, of course, such as those respecting the nature of matter or the definition of motion, were too general to have testable consequences, but others were more specific and capable of verification in sense experience.

The study of local motion under the two aspects later known as kinematics and dynamics turned out to be of pivotal importance for the development of the science of mechanics.[73] Aristotle's teachings in the fourth and seventh books of his *Physics* were the point of departure for much of this investigation. In the fourth book, arguing against the atomists' belief in a void, Aristotle had proposed a series of ratios linking together the weight of a body, the resistance of the medium through which it moves and its velocity of motion, while in the seventh book he had invoked similar ratios to show how one might formulate rules for comparing motions one with another.[74] Commentators were divided over whether Aristotle himself thought these ratios and rules were actually verified in nature or whether he employed them dialectically to refute the proposals of his atomist adversaries.[75] From the fourteenth century onwards, however, the consensus seemed to be that the Stagirite had been serious in entertaining them, and thus Aristotelians turned to their defence and subsequent revision.

Much of the work of Bradwardine and the Oxford *calculatores* had been directed at reformulating the mathematical ratios that might lie behind such rules so as to remove the contradictions that appeared to be latent within them. This and related studies by Heytesbury were carried out in a theoretical vein in England, that is, *secundum imaginationem* and not with reference to the works of nature.[76] When taken up by Albert of Saxony and Oresme on the Continent they took on a more practical orientation.[77] At Paris, for example, the revised ratios were understood as applying not to imaginary cases but to the actual motions of the heavens and of heavy and light bodies.

73. Clagett 1959, p. 163, justifies the use of the modern division into kinematics and dynamics in his study of mechanics in the Middle Ages.
74. Medieval attempts to justify and improve upon these rules are discussed in Crosby 1955, Clagett 1959 and Oresme 1966. Representative excerpts in English translation are given in *Source Book* 1974, pp. 292–312.
75. Thomas Aquinas, for one, saw their use as merely dialectical; see Thomas Aquinas 1963b, p. 240; also Weisheipl 1974, pp. 476, 487.
76. *Cambridge History* 1982, pp. 555–63 (Sylla); Wilson 1960, p. 25.
77. Duhem 1906–13 *passim*; A. Maier 1949, pp. 81–154 and 1958, pp. 59–144.

In a context such as this an expression used by Heytesbury, 'uniformly difform' (*uniformiter difformis*), took on particular interest.[78] As said of an increase in local motion, the expression meant that the velocity of the motion varied, i.e., that it was non-uniform or difform and so accelerated, but that the velocity variation took place in a uniform way – another way of saying that it was uniformly accelerated. Throughout the fourteenth and fifteenth centuries there was prolonged discussion of how expressions such as this might be applied to different motions, with Gaetano da Thiene playing a key role. It was only in the mid sixteenth century, however, that Domingo de Soto, teaching at Salamanca and building on the earlier work at Paris of John Mair, Johannes Dullaert of Ghent and Juan de Celaya (Soto had studied under Juan de Celaya), proposed that heavy bodies accelerate uniformly in their fall and decelerate uniformly when thrown upward.[79] Soto even supplied numerical examples that show he understood such statements in the modern sense, though he supplied no empirical evidence to substantiate them.[80]

It is difficult to ascertain when assertions of this type were first subjected to actual test. The main problem, it would appear, was that of securing an accurate way of measuring short periods of time, of the order of magnitude of a human's pulse beat.[81] Bodies close to the earth's surface can be seen to fall quickly, but variations in their velocity are not easy to detect, and for many it appeared that they fall at a uniform rate.[82] If one took Aristotle's ratios at face value, however, not only would the velocity of fall be uniform,

78. Heytesbury 1494, ff. 37ʳ–40ʳ; the edited text is in Clagett 1959, pp. 238–42.
79. Wallace 1981a, pp. 105–7. See Soto 1555, f. 92ᵛᵇ, for the text in which he makes this application of the expression *uniformiter difformis*: 'Hec motus species proprie accidit naturaliter motis et proiectis. Ubi enim moles ab alto cadit per medium uniforme, velocius movetur in fine quam in principio. Proiectorum vero motus remissior est in fine quam in principio; atque adeo primus uniformiter difformiter intenditur, secundus vero uniformiter difformiter remittitur.'
80. Thus, in comparing the motion of two bodies, *A* and *B*, the first in uniformly accelerated motion and the second in uniform motion, he states, *ibid.*, f. 94ʳᵃ: 'Exempli gratia, si *A* mobile una hora moveatur intendendo semper motum a non gradu usque ad 8 tantumdem spatii transmittet quantum *B*, quod per simile spatium eodem tempore uniformiter moveretur ut 4.'
81. Other problems were associated with the difficulty of comparing the velocities of objects over a long distance of fall. See Vitelleschi 1589–90, f. 365ᵛ, in his 1590 commentary on *De caelo*: 'Equidem in hac re experientiam nullam omnino certam habeo, et quas habeo, illae potius obstant sententiae Aristotelis. Verum multa sunt qui suspectas mihi faciant omnes experientias de hac re, in qua tamen maxime standum esset experientiae. Primum enim vix videtur posse fieri ut figura corporum qui moventur, resistentia medii, et cetera omnia qui ad motum concurrunt sint omnino paria. Secundo, non potest percipi huiusmodi differentia in velocitate motus nisi motus fiat per magnam distantiam, ut constat etiam experientia. In magna autem distantia multa accidere possunt quae experientiae detrahant aliquid certitudinis. Quare cum haec ita se habeant nihil de hac re statuo, neque enim ad rei materiam necesse est in praesentia.'
82. Even Galileo, in his *De motu antiquiora*, thought that acceleration was an initial and temporary phenomenon, following which a body would fall at uniform speed; see Galilei 1960, pp. 6–9.

but for a given medium it would be directly proportional to the weight of the falling body. As early as 1544 tests were performed to show that the latter statement cannot be true. Details of these are lacking, but their results were reported by the Florentine historian Benedetto Varchi and attributed by him to a Dominican philosopher at Pisa, Francesco Beato, and to a Bolognese physician and botanist, Luca Ghini.[83] Benedetti, in a work written at Venice in February 1554, gave a rational disproof of the velocity-proportional-to-weight assertion. In its introduction and conclusion he acknowledges the approval of the Dominican philosopher and theologian Petrus Arches, then visiting him in Venice, who had discussed the proof with Aristotelians in Rome the previous summer and had convinced them of its validity.[84] Since Soto, also a Dominican, was in northern Italy around the time of his writing of falling motion as uniformly accelerated, his analysis could thus have had some empirical support.[85]

Later, in 1576, the Paduan mathematician Giuseppe Moletti brought additional evidence to bear. He reported a test (*prova*) in which a lead ball and a wooden ball, both of the same size, were released from a height and seen to reach the ground at exactly the same time.[86] A year previously, one of Galileo's teachers at Pisa, Girolamo Borro, had discussed an experiment (*experimentum*) he had performed repeatedly with pieces of wood and lead of the same weight projected from a high window. Borro found that the wood invariably reached the ground *before* the lead, even though the wood's density was much less than that of the lead.[87] It was this experiment

83. Varchi, *Questioni sull'alchimia*, p. 54, cited by Caverni 1891–1900, IV, p. 270: 'e Aristotile e tutti li altri Filosofi, senza mai dubitarne, hanno creduto e affermato che, quanto una cosa sia più grave, tanto più tosto discende, il che la prova dimostra non esser vero. E se io non temessi d'allontanarmi troppo dalla proposta materia mi distenderei più lungamente in provare questa opinione, della quale ho trovato alcuni altri, e massimamente il reverendo padre (non men detto Filosofo che buon Teologo) fra Francesco Beato, metafisico di Pisa, e messer Luca Ghini, medico e semplicista singolarissimo.' On Beato, see Lohr 1974b, p. 263; on Ghini, *Dictionary of Scientific Biography* 1970–80, V, pp. 383–4.   84. *Mechanics* 1969, pp. 31–41, 154–65.

85. Soto was present at the Council of Trent between 1545 and 1551, the second date being that of the first complete edition of his questions on the *Physics*, which includes the statements cited in nn. 80 and 81 above. For details, see Beltrán de Heredia 1960, pp. 117–205.

86. Caverni 1891–1900, IV, p. 272, quoting a dialogue composed by Moletti: 'anzi vengono tutti in uno stesso tempo, e di ciò se n'é fatta la prova, non una volte, ma molte. E v'é di più che una palla di legno, o più o men grande d'una di piombo, lasciata venir giù d'una stessa altezza, nello stesso tempo con quella di piombo, discendono e trovano la terra o il suolo nello stesso momento di tempo.'

87. Borro 1575, p. 215, describes the experiment in the following words: 'eadem ergo duo adinventa aequalis ponderis frustula, ex altiore nostrarum aedium fenestra pari impulsu, eodemque tempore proiiciemus: plumbum segnius descenderet, super lignum enim, quod prius in terram ceciderat, omnes quotquot ibi, rei exitum expectabamus, illud praeceps ruere vidimus: idque non semel, sed saepenumero eodem successu tentavimus. Cuius rei experimento ducti omnes in eamdem nobiscum pedibus iuêre sententiam.'

that stimulated Galileo to perform his first tests (*pericula*) with falling bodies, possibly from the Leaning Tower of Pisa, which he reported in his *De motu* of about 1590.[88] When Galileo actually secured definitive proof of uniform acceleration in free fall is disputed among scholars. It is unlikely that he did so much before 1609, and when he did he did not employ time measurements directly, but seems to have argued from distances of travel which he could measure with considerable accuracy in an apparatus he had constructed.[89] The particular chronology of discovery is not too important here; what is important is that such factual questions were being asked by the turn of the seventeenth century, and it was only a matter of time before experimental techniques would be devised to secure answers to them.[90]

Another example, not unrelated to the velocity of fall, is that of the experimental evidence adduced in the sixteenth century for and against the existence of a void in nature.[91] Aristotelians differed from anti-Aristotelians in the conclusion they were attempting to establish in this matter, with the Aristotelians against the natural existence of any void space, maintaining that the rarefaction and condensation of continuous matter could explain all phenomena for which interstitial vacua were being invoked. They did allow, to be sure, for the possibility of a vacuum being produced by supernatural power, and continued the late medieval discussion of various thought experiments relating to motion and its velocity through a void. Those reacting against Aristotle, on the other hand, recovered the ancient writings of Lucretius and Hero and used their ideas to develop pro-vacuum arguments.[92]

What is remarkable about this dispute is that both sets of protagonists invoked empirical evidence to support their respective conclusions, analysing phenomena associated with the operation of bellows, with water

88. After mentioning Borro's result, Galileo states that his test from a high tower shows the opposite: even though the wood moves faster than the lead at the beginning of the fall, the lead quickly catches up and reaches the ground long before the wood does. See Galilei 1890–1909, I, p. 334: 'Experientia tamen contrarium ostendit: verum enim est, lignum in principio sui motus ocius ferri plumbo; attamen paulo post adeo acceleratur motus plumbi, ut lignum post se relinquat et, si ex alta turri demittantur, per magnum spatium praecedat: et de hoc saepe periculum feci.' The English is given in Galilei 1960, p. 107.

89. Apart from the inclined plane and pendulum experiments described in the *Due nuove scienze*, it is known that Galileo performed other experiments he never reported but whose vestiges are preserved in manuscript fragments. These have been analysed and discussed in Drake 1973, Drake and MacLachlan 1975, and Naylor 1976, 1980a and 1980b. For a reconstruction of the way in which their findings may be seen to confirm the principle of uniform acceleration in free fall, see Wallace 1981a, pp. 150–6, and 1984, pp. 265–8, 323–7, and 343–7.

90. See Schmitt 1981, § VIII for a balanced account of attitudes toward experimentation in the study of motion at the end of the sixteenth century.

91. Schmitt 1981, § VII.   92. For a full discussion, see E. Grant 1981a.

freezing in a closed container, with water clocks and with air withdrawn or evacuated from a container.[93] In the case of the bellows, Toletus argued that they could not be opened if their orifice were tightly shut, whereas Patrizi maintained that they could be opened and that a vacuum would be produced by opening them. Both parties believed that water contracted when frozen, but Soto and Toletus held that a closed container, no matter how strong, would break rather than permit a vacuum to be formed, whereas Patrizi and Telesio thought just the opposite.[94] Similar arguments _pro_ and _con_ the production of a vacuum were developed by the same pairs of thinkers from their understanding of water clocks and the evacuation of vessels.[95] Unlike the study of falling bodies, however, in these instances no experiments are known to have been performed and the debate took place generally at an _a priori_ level. The most one can detect here is that an empiricist mentality was gradually being formed throughout the sixteenth century that would lead, more or less directly, to the work of Torricelli, von Guericke and others in the century to follow.

Somewhat surprisingly, those with Aristotelian sympathies were generally more empirically minded than the proponents of new philosophies of nature.[96] This can be seen especially in the life sciences, with the growth of botany as a university discipline and the resulting interest in botanical gardens.[97] Ghini pioneered in this field, first at Bologna and later at Pisa, and numbered among his students Aldrovandi, Anguillara, Cesalpino and Maranta. University gardens were established at Padua and Pisa around 1544, and Aldrovandi built up an impressive natural history museum at Bologna in 1570, during which time he had expanded his interest in plants to include animals and fossils. The anatomical theatre dates from this period also.[98] The importance of accurate observation and realistic portrayal of human organs led to an emphasis on ocular demonstration that produced exceptional results, for example, in studying the motion of the heart and the blood. Vesalius and Fabricius of Aquapendente laid the foundations on which Harvey would later base his justly famous, but thoroughly Aristotelian, analysis of the blood's circulation.[99]

The less traditional philosophies, however, were not entirely bereft of

93. All of these cases are analysed in Schmitt 1981, § VII.
94. _Ibid._, pp. 355–9.   95. _Ibid._, pp. 359–62.
96. This is Schmitt's judgement when comparing Zabarella with the young Galileo in their studies of motion: _ibid._, § VIII, p. 124.
97. This development is discussed in Schmitt 1984, § XIV, pp. 39–44.
98. Schmitt 1981, § V, pp. 502–4.
99. See William Harvey 1628. Harvey's experimental techniques and his use of ocular demonstration are analysed in Wallace 1974, pp. 253–67.

empirical content. The programmes on which Paracelsus and his followers embarked in iatrochemistry, and Della Porta in natural magic and optics, led to important experimental work being done in those fields. The occult works of nature, mainly the influences exerted by magnets and the ebb and flow of the tides, seemed to encourage speculation along more mystical lines than were entertained within the peripatetic tradition. William Gilbert's *De magnete* of 1600 is an experimental treatise as good as any in the century it inaugurated, and even if it was basically Aristotelian in its search for the proper causes of magnetic phenomena, it invoked principles that were also at variance with those of the Stagirite.[100]

THE EVOLUTION OF SYNTHESES

The penchant for systematisation in scholastic circles resulted in a number of syntheses of natural philosophy being produced in the Renaissance, some of which were read widely and thus had a pronounced influence at the beginning of the modern period. The earlier of these grew out of commentaries on Aristotle's *libri naturales*, to which it became customary to add *quaestiones* on the more difficult points and to list the various positions that had been taken on them, after the fashion of a disputation. As they evolved they gradually took the form of a manual useful for teaching, wherein the author would work out his preferred theses and refute the teachings of opposed schools.[101] In their fully developed form they became part of a *cursus philosophicus*, such as that of Coimbra at the end of the sixteenth century, which became a standard text in Jesuit universities. The syntheses differed from the extensive commentaries on Aristotle produced by Pomponazzi, Cremonini and others in that they were not directed exclusively at understanding the classical text (though such exegesis was part of their aim), but incorporated materials from medieval and Renaissance authors, including those with anti-Aristotelian sympathies, so as to arrive at a fuller understanding of truths about nature.

Before describing these synthetic treatises, it may be well to survey the commentary tradition that preceded them, much of which was strongly influenced by Averroes, the *Commentator* par excellence, in his extensive expositions of Aristotle's texts. Two of the foremost Aristotelians of the early sixteenth century, both of whom taught partly at Padua, were

100. See Wallace 1974, pp. 241–53.
101. Some details of this development are given in Reif 1969; see also *Cambridge History* 1982, pp. 13–33, 91–8, and 787–96.

Pomponazzi and Nifo. Most of the former's lecture notes survive in manuscript, and these show that he lectured repeatedly on the first four books of the *Physics*, especially on the first and second books, but also concentrated on the eighth book. In addition Pomponazzi wrote cursorily on the *De caelo*, *De generatione et corruptione*, *Meteorology*, and *De anima*, the last consistently claiming his attention. Nifo left excellent published commentaries on all of Aristotle's *libri naturales*, explaining not only the text of the master but also the exposition of Averroes on the same, and noting as well the emendations of other commentators from the Greeks to his contemporaries. At Bologna, Achillini lectured on the first two books of the *Physics* and the first book of *De anima*, also following the Averroist tradition; his notes are conserved in the Ambrosiana library in Milan. A student of his, Boccadifero, published more extensively, leaving commentaries on the first book of the *Physics* and on most of the remaining natural treatises in printed form.[102] At Ferrara, Antonio Montecatini published an exhaustive 519-page exposition of the eighth book of the *Physics*, where the eternity of the universe is in question, and another detailed analysis of the first part of the third book of *De anima*, dealing with the human mind – both of which posed serious problems for Averroist Aristotelians from the viewpoint of Christian doctrine.[103] But the most indefatigable commentator, again at Padua, was Jacopo Zabarella, who complemented his many works on logic with detailed expositions of the first, second and eighth books of the *Physics*, the entire *De generatione et corruptione* and *Meteorology* and the three books of *De anima*.

These commentaries were so prolix that many professors thought it incumbent on them to write briefer treatises summarising the essential content of their teaching. Zabarella himself did this in the thirty books of his *De rebus naturalibus*, published posthumously in 1590, which encapsulated the whole of his natural philosophy. Earlier, Pomponazzi had issued a series of Peripatetic treatises defending Averroist positions, to which his student Gasparo Contarini replied with an orthodox discourse on the immortality of the soul. Another Averroist, Zimara, prepared a series of tables and compendia comparing and summarising the teachings of Aristotle and Averroes to make them more accessible to students.

At Paris, in the first two decades of the sixteenth century, more substantial textbooks combining commentaries with 'questionnaires' began to appear under the influence of Mair and his associates.[104] These are

102. Lohr 1984.   103. Lohr 1978, p. 595.
104. García Villoslada 1938, pp. 371–421; Élie 1950–1.

generally viewed as eclectic because of the diversity of teachings they embraced, but their authors invariably worked in one or other school tradition and were consistent in assimilating divergent views within it. Though all were acquainted with nominalist thought, most had some realist affiliation in which they were also interested. Thus Mair inclined towards Scotism, Dullaert towards the Augustinianism of Giles of Rome and Paul of Venice, and Petrus Crockaert towards Thomism. Their views on natural philosophy were incorporated mainly into expositions of the *Physics*; in some instances they extended their summaries to the *De caelo* and *De generatione et corruptione*, and even to the *De anima*, but these were less frequent.

A distinctive feature of such Parisian texts was the amount of space they devoted to the study of motion and the ways in which they integrated English calculatory techniques into their presentation. As already noted, Aristotle's ratios and rules were presented in the fourth and seventh books of the *Physics*, and not in the third book, whose chief subjects were change in general and the infinite. Dullaert's *Questions* on the *Physics* transfers all of this material to the third book, whose exposition covers 62 of the 151 folios that make up the entire work.[105] Luis Coronel and Juan de Celaya, both Spaniards who taught at Paris, show a similar emphasis, the latter offering especially good analyses of problems relating to kinematics and dynamics from three different perspectives, namely those of the nominalists, the realists and the Thomists, the last of whom he saw as intermediate between the other two. Mathematicians from the Iberian peninsula who also taught at Paris, notably Gaspar Lax and Alvaro Thomaz, influenced these Spanish natural philosophers to favour the use of mathematics in physics more than commentators who worked from Aristotle's text alone.[106]

In the 1530s and 1540s there was a diminution of this activity, though Simon Brossier produced a brief epitome of natural philosophy in twelve books (totalling but fifty-nine pages) at Paris,[107] and Frans Titelmans a somewhat longer compendium from the Franciscan viewpoint, like Brossier's extending to the *De anima*, at Antwerp. Melanchthon wrote a *Physicae seu naturalis philosophiae compendium* at Wittenberg in 1543 that survives only in manuscript form, but he also published introductions to physical doctrine (*Initia doctrinae physicae*) that went through many editions.

105. Wallace 1981a, pp. 64–90.
106. See *Dictionary of Scientific Biography* 1970–80, III, pp. 420–1 ('Coronel'); III, pp. 171–2 ('Celaya'); VIII, p. 100 ('Lax'); XIII, pp. 349–50 ('Thomaz'); Lohr 1975, pp. 723–4 on Coronel and pp. 708–9 on Celaya. See also Rey Pastor 1926; Muñoz Delgado 1964a and 1967a.
107. On Brossier, see Lohr 1974b, p. 278.

More extensive summaries of the *Physics* and of all the *libri naturales*, paying close attention to the Greek commentaries, were produced by Jacob Schegk at Basle in 1546 and 1550. At around the same time, the Dominican Crisostomo Javelli composed a voluminous *Epitome* of all of Aristotle's physical works, furnishing a Thomist interpretation of their doctrine and combatting alternative Averroist views then being entertained in Italy. More progressive were Soto's *Commentaria* and *Quaestiones* on the *Physics*, partially published at Salamanca around 1545 and in complete editions in 1551, but based on his teaching at Alcalá after returning from Paris in the 1520s. These were companion volumes containing Latin summaries of the Greek text and questions argued from a position intermediate between those of the *nominales* and the *realissimi*. The 'questionary', in particular, made available to Spanish students the wealth of teachings developed by Mair and his Parisian associates in the first decades of the century.

Soto's synthesis of physical doctrine found an appreciative disciple in Toletus, who had studied under him at Salamanca before entering the Jesuit Order and being sent to Rome to teach at the newly founded Collegio Romano. Toletus' expositions of the *Physics* and the *De generatione et corruptione* are similar to Soto's, except that they combine summaries of Aristotelian teachings with related *quaestiones* in single volumes. A quite different type of textbook was produced by Toletus' colleague at the Collegio, Benito Pereira. This was printed at Rome in 1576 with the title *De communibus omnium rerum naturalium principiis et affectionibus*, though an earlier version had appeared there in 1562. In 512 pages, divided into fifteen books, the *De communibus* presents a systematic exposition of Aristotle's *Physics*, taking full account of the Greek and Latin commentary traditions, and among the Latins favouring Thomist positions, though not to the exclusion of Scotist and nominalist views.[108] Pereira was also more open to Averroist interpretations than other Jesuits at Rome and disparaged mathematics both as a science and as a usable tool in the development of physical doctrine.[109] The latter tactic alienated him from Clavius, the senior mathematician at the Collegio, who urged a more positive attitude

108. The titles of the books in Pereira 1576 are as follows: 'Primus liber est de philosophia. II. De philosophia naturali. III. De via et ordine doctrinae physicae. IIII. De antiquis philosophis, et variis eorum, circa principia rerum naturalium, opinionibus. V. De materia et privatione. VI. De forma. VII. De natura. VIII. De caussis. IX. De fortuna, casu, et contingentia. X. De quantitate. XI. De loco. XII. De tempore, aeternitate, et aevo. XIII. De natura motus. XIIII. De varietate et praecipuis divisionibus motus. XV. De motus et mundi aeternitate.'
109. Wallace 1984, pp. 136–7; Giacobbe 1977; Lohr 1976b; Scaduto 1964, part 4, pp. 283–6. Scaduto writes, p. 284, that Pereira had conceded too much to the philosophy of Averroes: 'dato troppo alla filosofia d'Averroe'.

towards his discipline and had a specific endorsement of mathematics written into the *Ratio studiorum* of the Society.[110]

After Pereira a succession of young Jesuits taught natural philosophy in the Roman college; more respectful of Clavius, they developed new teaching materials for their courses.[111] *Reportationes* of the lectures of Antonio Menu, Paolo Valla, Muzio Vitelleschi and Ludovico Ruggiero are still extant, and show a remarkable command of current literature and of problems arising from empirical investigations.[112] None of their notes were published, but Galileo based his expositions of the *De caelo* and the *De generatione et corruptione* on them, later used ideas derived from them in composing his *De motu antiquiora* and earlier appropriated Paolo Valla's lectures on the *Posterior Analytics* for his notes on the same.[113] Ruggiero's synthesis is noteworthy, for a manuscript copy of his entire philosophy course has been preserved, with all lectures numbered and the dates on which he began and ended various tracts indicated.[114] This shows that, over the three-year period from 1590 to 1592, Ruggiero gave 1,090 lectures in all; of his entire course, 63 per cent of the time was given over to natural philosophy, 28 per cent to logic and only 9 per cent to metaphysics – which indicates how importantly the study of nature then figured in the curriculum of the Collegio Romano.

Around this time the Portuguese Jesuits began to publish a complete course of studies in philosophy as it was being taught in their college at Coimbra, the famous *Conimbricensis Collegii Societatis Iesu commentarii*. The work of several authors, the course covers much the same matter as was taught in Rome, but somewhat more conservatively, with greater attention paid to speculative issues important for theology and less to empirical detail. Reprinted repeatedly, it became a standard reference work throughout Europe for the scholastic Aristotelianism being taught by the Jesuits in the late Renaissance. A similar work was the extensive commentary on Aristotle, four of whose volumes were devoted to natural philosophy, by a Spanish Jesuit who had taught for many years in Mexico, Antonio Rubio.[115] A more compendious treatment of the whole of philosophy from the

110. Cosentino 1970, 1971; Crombie 1977.
111. Galilei 1977 and Wallace 1981a and 1984 *passim*.
112. Wallace 1981a, pp. 110–26, 243–52 and 320–40, and 1984, pp. 99–216.
113. Galilei 1977 *passim*; Wallace 1984, pp. 16–23, 33–53, 230–48; *Reinterpreting Galileo* 1986, pp. 3–28 (Wallace).
114. Bamberg, Staatsbibliothek, Msc. Class. Cod. 62–1 (anno 1589) through Cod. 62–7 (anno 1592).
115. On Rubio, see Lohr 1980, pp. 702–3. Earlier the Augustinian Alonso Gutierrez de la Vera Cruz (Lohr 1977, pp. 711–12), also working in Mexico, had composed textbooks of logic and natural philosophy, drawing heavily on the works of Domingo de Soto.

Augustinian viewpoint, which included a substantial section on natural philosophy, was published by Diego de Zúñiga at Toledo in 1597; its author wrote also a commentary on Job wherein he allowed that Scripture could be interpreted in ways not opposed to the Copernican system, and later achieved notoriety on that account.[116] Also noteworthy is a two-volume summary of the *Physics* by the Valencian Dominican Diego Mas, published in 1599.[117] This is especially valuable for the attention it pays to sixteenth-century natural philosophers, mainly those writing in Spain, Italy and France, as its author works out a Thomist *via media* between the extremes of nominalism and the varieties of realism proposed by Scotists and textual Aristotelians. Somewhat later, the Carmelites of Alcalá produced their *cursus artium*; the three volumes of the *cursus* devoted to natural philosophy, written by Antonius a Matre Dei, are more general, briefer and even less empirical than the corresponding treatises in the *cursus philosophicus* of the Coimbran Jesuits.[118]

Three synthetic treatises written by non-scholastic philosophers are particularly worthy of mention. The first of these is the *De motu libri decem* of Francesco Buonamici, published at Florence in 1591, important if only for the fact that Buonamici was Galileo's teacher at the University of Pisa in the early 1580s.[119] Its ten books treat successively the nature of natural philosophy, matter, form, the elements, local motion, generation and corruption, growth, alteration, mutation and the movers of the heavens. Buonamici's method consists in providing a causal analysis of each of these subjects. His style is eclectic and prolix (the volume contains over a thousand folio-size pages), with extensive citation of the Greeks and Arabs, less sympathetic treatment of the Latins and intermittent interpolations of Greek and Latin poetry. More compact and systematic is the *Physiologia peripatetica* of Johannes Magirus, first published at Frankfurt in 1597 and often thereafter, including a Cambridge 1642 edition that was used by Sir Isaac Newton in his early studies.[120] In six books it explains the principles of natural things, the universe in general, the elements and their properties, meteorology, composite substances (metals, plants and animals) and the soul and its powers. Finally there are the *Ancilla philosophiae* and the *Lapis*

---

116. Lohr 1982, pp. 178–9.   117. Lohr 1978, pp. 569–70.   118. Lohr 1975, pp. 716–17.
119. The full title of Buonamici's work is *De motu libri X, quibus generalia naturalis philosophiae principia summo studio collecta continentur, necnon universae quaestiones ad libros de physico auditu, de caelo, de ortu et interitu pertinentes explicantur; multa item Aristotelis loca explanantur, et Graecorum, Averrois, aliorumque doctorum sententiae ad theses peripateticas diriguntur.* Apart from citations of individual authors, Buonamici cites the *Graeci* as a group 249 times, the *Latini* 153 times and the *Arabes* 24 times. See also Helbing 1976, 1982.   120. See Newton 1983 for his excerpts from Magirus.

philosophicus of John Case, both printed at Oxford in 1599, which are expositions of Aristotle's *Physics*. Case's aim, like Magirus', is primarily pedagogical, but for one writing in Elizabethan England he manifests a surprising knowledge of scholastic authors, including Thomas Aquinas, Toletus, Pereira, the *Collegium Conimbricense*, Mas and most of the syntheses already mentioned.

PHILOSOPHICAL MEDICINE

Traditional natural philosophy, as detailed thus far, proved useful for general education and for formation in theology; it was also seen as an essential preparation for medicine, particularly in Italian universities, then the leaders in medical education.[121] In the period under discussion medicine was viewed not only as an art but also as a science with both speculative and practical branches, which required an underpinning in the study of nature. One consequence of this requirement was that courses in philosophy came to be taught mainly by physicians, and even *physica*, the classical term for natural philosophy, took on the connotation of 'physic' as used in medical practice. The training of medical doctors was based heavily on Galen and Avicenna, both of whom were in turn indebted to Aristotle, but differences of emphasis and orientation altered the content of their philosophical syntheses to a considerable degree.[122]

In this area Pietro d'Abano, working at Padua, exerted an influence somewhat analogous to that of the *calculatores* in the study of motion. Early in the fourteenth century Pietro produced his *Conciliator differentiarum philosophorum et praecipue medicorum* (from whose title he came to be known as 'the Conciliator') to explain and reconcile differences that had developed between philosophers and physicians.[123] With the invention of printing this work received wide circulation and thus set the pattern for later discussions. Structured into 210 'differences' (*differentiae*), it outlined the main medical teachings of the Greeks and the Arabs and proposed ways in which they might be reconciled with more general teachings on nature. The first ten queries (*quaesita*, a term used with the same connotation as *differentia* by Pietro) are concerned with problems common to theoretical and practical medicine; following this the next hundred queries are concerned with theory, and then the last hundred with practice.[124] Among

121. Siraisi 1973, 1981.   122. Bylebyl 1979 and forthcoming.
123. *Dictionary of Scientific Biography* 1970–80, I, pp. 4–5; Siraisi 1973 *passim*.
124. Abano 1472, f. 1^r: 'In quarum utique prima quesita statuentur communia et velut forinseca modi reique utriusque partis medicine: theorice videlicet et practice . . . Secunda vero theorice continebit dubitata. In tertia quidem que practice subdentur finalia . . .'

the theoretical questions are those relating to elements, complexions and humours; the concepts of *membrum, virtus* and *spiritus*; the naturals, non-naturals and preternaturals; signs and their various uses; and finally the notions of crisis and critical days. Of the practical queries few have philosophical import: twenty are devoted to procedures conservative of health and the remaining eighty to restorative or curative measures.

Much the same approach as Pietro's is reflected in the *Controversiarum medicarum et philosophicarum . . . editio secundo* published at Alcalá in 1564 by Francisco Vallés, professor of medicine there. A contemporary of Soto but critical of the latter's teachings, Vallés takes the 'doctors and philosophers' of his title to refer primarily to Greek and Arab authors, and his work is replete with references to Aristotle, Hippocrates, Galen, Avicenna and Averroes, with occasional mentions of Plato, the Epicureans and the Stoics. He identifies no contemporaries by name, only citing their opinions as those of *hodierni philosophi* or *neoterici*. Of the ten books making up the *Controversiae*, he characterises the first two as concerned with matters common to philosophy and medicine; the third, he says, is devoted to questions on the pulse and on urine, the fourth and fifth to questions of pathology, the sixth to preserving health, the next three to curative measures and the last to prognostics.[125]

As Vallés conceives it, the last part of philosophy deals with physiology, and this is itself the beginning of medicine. Not only must the physician know the body's members, its humours and temperaments, but he must understand all of these in terms of the elements that compose them with their distinctive qualities and virtues. To this end he discourses on how elements are present in compounds, the ways in which their qualities act on, or interact with, each other, their relation to temperament and how medicines of different types can be effective in the treatment of disorders.[126]

---

125. Vallés 1564, f. 1va: 'Quoniam vero in quovis opere nihil contingere potest legentibus, aut iocundius, aut utilius ordine delectationi, et memoriae eorum, qui in hunc librum inciderunt, consulentes, in decem libros totum opus censuimus distribuendum, quorum priores duo, controversias, quas philosophi habent cum medicis communes, contineant: tertius quaestiones de pulsu et urina habeat: (Debetur enim signorum dignitati propria disputatio) nam 4 et 5 pathologicas dabimus questiones: sexto eas, quae ad artem tuendae valetudinis spectant. Tres sequentes habebunt curativas: ultimus prognosticas, quinque enim his, tanquam praecipuis partibus, tota medicina constat.'

126. *Ibid.*, ff. 1va–7rb: 'Ergo eas, quae ad physiologicam spectant partem, primum pertractabimus. Nam haec, ut philosophiae finis, ita medicinae principium est. Sternit enim philosophia medicinae viam: potissimum qua parte temperamenti, et compositionis humani corporis notitiae sese accommodat. Componitur vero humanum corpus, compositiori quadam ac propria constitutione, ex membris organicis: capite (inquam), thorace, ventre, cruribus, brachiis, et reliquis. Sed ante hanc singula

It is interesting to observe that Galileo, in his early notebooks, is critical of Vallés' analysis of elemental reaction and resistance in chapter 5 of book 1 of the *Controversiae*, just as he is critical of the teaching of a Pisan physician, Flaminio Nobili, on the same subject.[127] Vallés, he writes, regards resistance as being formally the same as action, which it is not, whereas Nobili distinguishes two kinds of resistance, one an action and the other an impotency, which is also not correct.[128] This example, plus the differences already mentioned between Cardano, Telesio and Scaliger on active qualities, gives some idea of the content of philosophical medicine in the Renaissance. Obviously it was a considerable advantage for medical doctors to be able to organise their entire discipline in a way that put it into continuity with the *scientia naturalis* of their day. Still, their reasoning remained largely at a speculative and qualitative level, and it was only with the new observational and experimental methods developed towards the end of the sixteenth century that progress began to be made in the direction of modern science.

CRITICISM AND DECLINE

From the foregoing survey it is a simple matter to discern flaws in Aristotelian natural philosophy as it developed in the Renaissance. Its very pluralism worked against it, and its inability to integrate materials coming from mathematical and empirical investigations led to its decline and ultimate rejection by the end of the seventeenth century.

To oversimplify, the conservative and textual strain within the discipline proved too attached to the authority of Aristotle and too insistent on

illorum ex hoiomeris, ut carne, nervo, arteria, et vena: haec rursus elementis quibusdam, qua ab Hippocrate et Galeno dicuntur secunda, humoribus, inquam componuntur. Hanc compositionem habet homo cum omnibus sanguine praeditis, communem: ante quam rursus habet illa omnium primam, ex primis elementis, quae illi cum omnibus mixtis natura constantibus communis est. Merito igitur compositiva doctrina nobis instituentibus, primum habet in disputatione locum ea quaestio, quae de modo quo elementa in mixto sunt inter philosophos et medicos intercedit.
Caput primum. De modo quo elementa prima sunt in corporibus substantiis . . . Caput secundum. Sit ne aqua humidior aere? . . . Caput tertium. Sit ne aer calidus, an frigidus? . . . Caput quartum. De qualitatibus contrariis in eadem substantia . . . Caput quintum. De actione reciproca, quae vulgo reactio dicitur, et de antiperistasi.'
127. Galilei 1977, pp. 243–5; on Renaissance teachings relating to action and reaction, see Russell 1976.
128. Galilei 1890–1909, I, p. 170: 'Prima dubitatio sit, quid sit resistentia. Vallesius, primo Controversiarum capite 5, et alii, dixerunt, resistentiam esse actionem, et resistere esse quoddam agere . . . Dico, primo: resistentia non est formaliter actio . . .'; p. 172: 'Ex quo apparet error Nobilii qui, primo De generatione dubio 11 in capite 7, distinxit duplicem resistentiam: aliam animalium, quae consisteret in nixu quodam, qui est quaedam actio; aliam in caeteris rebus, quam reduxit ad impotentiam ad patiendum; ubi, ut videtis, accepit causam extrinsecam resistentiae pro resistentia formaliter, cum tamen distinguantur.'

apodictic proof before making adjustments in the entire system. Admittedly such proof was hard to come by, for empirical data were difficult to collect and evaluate, and many of the claims of those proposing them were certainly arguable. On the other hand, the basic Aristotelian theses concerning the heavens and the elements were themselves disputable, and their proponents seemed largely unaware of the vast amount of dialectical construction, as opposed to demonstrative reasoning, on which their own system was based.

The progressive strain, as seen in the work of the Jesuits, for example, ran into obstacles of another sort. Most natural philosophy was then geared to an educational system that was pragmatically oriented to the professions, with theology more often than not occupying the key position. As the reforms of the Council of Trent were implemented, the more specialised areas of natural philosophy, that is, those making contact with empirical disciplines, were sacrificed to make greater room for metaphysics and moral philosophy. This meant that professors who taught such subjects, and these were the principal natural philosophers of the day, could devote little time to precisely the issues that required attention. Then there was the problem of censorship, pervasive throughout the church and especially troublesome among the Jesuits.[129] As mathematicians and scientists of the Society became more specialised they drifted further apart from its metaphysicians, and any of their teachings that seemed to compromise the *praeambula fidei* were quickly censured.[130] To be on the safe side, as it were, there was need for caution, and this had an inhibiting effect on practically all innovation.

In such an atmosphere, the tradition itself was easily criticised and even parodied by proponents of the new philosophies. Francis Bacon could offer a new style of investigation, with the accent on inductive reasoning and extensive experimentation. Galileo similarly could inveigh against scholastic logic; even more effectively he could exploit the Peripatetics' reliance on the master's text and ridicule the many details of Aristotle's system that were not easily reconcilable with the new data. Both he and Descartes, though in different ways, could exalt the power of mathematics to lay bare the secrets of nature. Gassendi and others could revive the atomism of the Greeks and propose it as a viable alternative to the substantial forms and occult qualities of the Aristotelians. And Molière could give the *coup de grace* to the speculations of medical theorists who had situated their entire practice within a Peripatetic framework.

Under such attacks, what is remarkable about Aristotelian natural

129. Redondi 1983 *passim*.   130. Wallace 1984, pp. 17–18, 137, 139, 147, 283–4.

philosophy is not so much that it declined and passed out of favour but rather that it endured as long as it did. A good part of its success no doubt came from the social institutions that tended to preserve its teachings, notably the universities and church authorities, Protestant and Catholic alike. But it also had its own intellectual appeal, and this too serves to explain why it remained the dominant view of nature throughout the Renaissance.

9

THE NEW PHILOSOPHY OF NATURE

The intellectual ferment of the early sixteenth century profoundly influenced the education and training of a group of thinkers who by the middle of the century were beginning to elaborate a new vision of nature. Its principal features were first, a new cosmology, showing in some cases the influence of Copernicus and always critical of the dominant categories of Aristotelian physics (space, place and motion), and second, the view that nature might be usefully transformed in the interests of mankind. This latter view oscillated between speculations about operative magic linked with astrology and ideas of direct intervention in nature armed with an empirical understanding of the specific causes of particular phenomena.

Despite their differences – and the speculations of some, like Cardano, Bruno and Campanella, often took on a religious significance of prophetic inspiration – a common theme was the demise of the belief that the study of nature consisted solely in the study of Aristotle, who had reduced its whole structure to a handful of categories capable of explaining its universal processes. The natural philosopher could no longer rest content with glosses and commentaries that clarified textual rather than concretely physical problems. Indeed, it began to seem as if nature consisted of an almost infinite number of processes awaiting discovery, and any general account of causality required this unveiling of nature's 'secrets' to be linked to empirically acquired knowledge.

A number of factors influenced this broad line of development. Florentine Neoplatonism in particular provided a new impetus and conceptual framework for magical and astrological ideas. There was also the internal revision of Aristotelianism worked out by Pomponazzi and the influence of humanism, which spread to fields beyond those moral and practical areas where it had initially flourished. Finally, there was the revolution in astronomy, which polarised these thinkers' anti-Aristotelian inclinations, lending a new edge to their critiques of the principles of

236

Aristotelian physics and establishing a complex relationship between them and the scientific revolution. Thanks to Copernican cosmology, such criticism focused on the connection between Aristotelian physics and metaphysics, and led, via Bruno's notion of an infinite universe, to a thorough reappraisal of philosophical problems.

MARSILIO FICINO

While Ficino's concerns were primarily philosophico-religious, his *Theologia platonica* (1482) and his commentaries on Hermes Trismegistus, Plato and Plotinus had a considerable influence on developments in the philosophy of nature. He had intended to erect a Christian apologetic against heterodox tendencies like Alexandrism, Averroism and Epicureanism. His first step was to reconstruct a traditional philosophy which, from remotest antiquity down to Plotinus, had demonstrated the concord of pagan thought with the truth of Christian revelation, whose highest mysteries it had prefigured. Ficino chose to demonstrate the homogeneity of that particular brand of philosophy and Christianity because he recognised both the difficulty of reconciling Christian beliefs with Aristotelianism and the failure of previous attempts to deal with those areas where Aristotelianism and Christianity differed. Such areas included the question of the eternity of the world, the mortality of the soul, the unicity of the intellect and an astrological determinism that regarded the individual person, and indeed religion itself, as transient phenomena bound by astrological cycles.

At the heart of Ficino's cosmological attempt to reconcile cyclical and eschatological notions lay his desire to ensure that the cosmic location of the rational soul – a category which included the human soul – guaranteed both its origin and its imperishable destiny. The location of the rational soul at the centre of the hierarchy of being, between the perceptible and the intelligible, was a recognition of its privileged position in the created universe, where it gave life and awareness to the perceptible world. The rational soul thus sanctioned the ontological difference between the two realms while also establishing a constant relationship between them. According to the Neoplatonic tradition, this ensured a reading of the cosmos, of its forces and of the correspondences between levels in the hierarchy of being in which Ficino could find an ever-changing and different reflection of God's actions.

Ficino followed the main lines of Aristotelian cosmology, with its hierarchy of celestial and elemental spheres centred on an immobile earth. He concentrated, however, on reducing the gulf between the supralunary and sublunary realms. The weight of magic in his work shows that the metaphysical structure of the real, with its secret web of hidden links, revealed to the sage the splendour of the divine life itself, although not in its purest form, within the perceptible world. For man to be able to retrace the process of emanation, each degree of being had to suggest its ontological function, its defined nature and a higher reality to which it was bound as to a constitutive structure. The soul made real the link between the perceptible and intelligible worlds by uniting itself with that which represented the highest corporeal level, namely the nature of the heavens. By means of its celestial body the soul could make itself the bond between the two worlds since the *spiritus* omnipresent in the sublunary realm was the instrument of vivification as well as the indispensable medium for its descent into the elementary body. Magic, and the astrological premises that accompanied it, made operational a fully evolved nexus of forms which guaranteed the existence of a sphere in which man's cosmological position took on a new dimension. For if the soul vivified the corporeal world through *spiritus*, and if a *spiritus* of celestial origin was diffused throughout nature, then not only was the soul's process of ascent and descent clarified, but the highest part of the soul was clearly not attached to the corporeal realm. Proof of this was man's ability, under certain conditions, to attain supracosmic levels, to command the elements and to prophesy. The process of ascent was complementary to magic; the two were interwoven and restricted to the initiated. In Ficino's *natura* the soul always preserved a link with its origin. This, in turn, was the foundation for the hypothesis that the soul had a different ontological status and exceptional attributes. Such a hierarchy justified magic and astrology as a reflection of the domination of the body by the soul. In other words, the natural order both revealed a dependence of the corporeal on the spiritual and existed as a potentiality which the soul could activate, correct and modify. Thus, as far as man was concerned, magic and astrology, and the animism they presupposed, referred to the realm of the contingent and the possible, wherein nature was called to behave differently from how it would have behaved if it had been left to itself. This behaviour was not arbitrary because at the operative level magical action was the obverse of the philosopher's awareness, which individuates the laws of the real and pursues them to their source, where it discovers that magical action is not by nature different from the awareness which can be mobilised in us.

There are, however, a number of ambiguities in Ficino's thought. For instance, the circular motion of the *spiritus*, even in the sublunary sphere, entailed an animated, living cosmos, conceived as an organism. This motion could be seen as independent of the Aristotelian laws of rectilinear motion. Another problematic aspect of Ficino's thought was that his attempt to rationalise religious truth – which he only relinquished on the threshold of the Christian mystery – by demonstrating its convergence with the *pia philosophia* involved giving a determining role to certain texts in his reworking of traditional cosmology, elevating them to the status of revelation. This revelation, while dependent on and inferior to its Christian counterpart, threatened to supplant it at the philosophical level. The Hermetic texts were thus placed on the same level as, if not above, Genesis, since they clarified the mysteries of the Scriptures by defining the nature of the soul and the origin of the cosmos in a rigorously philosophical fashion. Above all, Ficino tended to divinise the heavens, especially the sun, which he regarded as the living symbol of the divinity and the heart and source of created life. Thus – in the view of Garin and Yates – he foreshadowed and perhaps determined the fate of Copernicanism and the various natural philosophical responses it generated.[1]

GIOVANNI PICO

Giovanni Pico's writings, before his attack on astrology, attempted to provide a secure basis for human freedom and to reformulate the relationship and contrast between nature and spirit. For Pico magic corresponded exactly, at the operative level, to a mystical and aristocratic conception of the highest form of knowledge. Magic was the activity of an individual who, through a knowledge of the most secret mysteries, could illuminate the divine presence in each and every thing. In this sense magic represented the other aspect of the celestial ladder which leads man to God, and was simultaneously a premise – in so far as it was knowledge – and a consequence – in so far as it was action – of that ladder. Thus natural and demonic magic become two opposing outlets for man's activity, representing his capacity to cooperate with the forces of good or evil. The parallel between the structure of magical action and the modality of the epistemological process thus found its rationale, as in Ficino, in the identity

1. See Yates 1964 and Garin 1975. Garin 1976c is very important for understanding Ficino and Pico in relation to astrology. For a discussion of the Yates thesis, see *Occult and Scientific Mentalities* 1984, and in particular Vickers' introductory essay.

of the ultimate force towards which both moved, the former attempting to
modify natural causality and the latter striving to attain a higher level of
consciousness.

Pico's *Disputationes adversus astrologiam divinatricem*,[2] however, raises
various problems with respect to his earlier work and to the views of Ficino
which, in so far as they relate to the anti-astrological argument, he now
openly attacked. Pico tended to reduce the supralunary–sublunary relationship to that between general and proximate causes and sought thereby to
reassess the extent to which matter determined natural processes. He
stressed that matter was the single cause of disorder, irregularity and
imperfection in the terrestrial sphere and stated emphatically that to regard
the stars as the cause of individual phenomena was to deny their nature and
dignity. The stars only influenced the sublunary sphere as universal agents,
causing regularity and order. The evils which Pico's opponents blamed on
the stars should instead be attributed to matter itself and to the particular
conditions under which the celestial influence – itself unalterable and
unspecifiable – was received. Having restricted the influence of the stars to
the Aristotelian principles of motion, heat and light, Pico divorced
philosophy, understood as the correct attitude towards nature, from
astrology, magic and any other superstitious practices. In particular,
philosophy showed that the putative connection between astral cycles and
the destinies of religions derived from an erroneous application of corporeal
laws to an independent order and thus threatened to include miracles, the
prophets and the unique character of Christianity in a purely naturalistic
perspective. Furthermore, astrology's Egyptian origins, from which it
drew its nobility, betrayed a double inadequacy: its practical and theoretical
shortcomings derived from the Egyptians' imperfect understanding of
astronomy and from their ignorance of natural philosophy. From this shaky
foundation rose causal links between heterogeneous events, which is a precise
definition of the fundamental error of astrology. On the other hand, by
positing matter as that which modifies celestial influences and proximate
causes, that is, by assuming contingency to be intrinsic to nature, Pico
sought to preserve miracles as unpredictable divine interruptions of the
causal chain assumed by astrology. He understood that astrology saw in the
heavens the origin both of that which could be embraced by a rule and of
that which seemingly could not: it recognised disorder neither in
miraculous events nor in events which were simply unusual. Attributing a

2. The *Disputationes* appeared posthumously in 1496, edited by Pico's nephew Gianfrancesco; see
   G. Pico 1946–52.

causal role to the heavens allowed astrology either to assert the natural character of these events or to explain away their rarity. The heavens change from moment to moment and their individual causality only makes sense in so far as it is linked to the web of relationships which define the astral situation at each instant, a web which repeats itself completely or partially only at ever-increasing intervals. Thus it is the rarity of an event which makes it miraculous, not the fact that it belongs to a different order. Here Pico highlights one of the reasons for astrology's success: it offered a rational explanation for something which was inexplicable at the natural and human levels. Because of their ontological superiority, celestial causes were invoked to account for this. So astrology could explain both the existence of occult qualities (which Pico attributed to the properties of light without giving a plausible justification for their variety and diversity) and the fact that at certain moments in history mankind, through courage and self-abnegation, could change its habits and initiate new religious *leges*.

Pico's exceptional success testifies to his acuteness, but resistance to his views should not be underestimated. He accounted comfortably for the differences between the sub- and supralunary spheres, but he had difficulties in explaining the origin of occult effects, even though he attributed them, as Ficino did, to celestial heat. To be consistent with his own logic he had to refer them to the heavens as their natural cause. But was it then possible that the action of the heavens on the elements was not unique and that in certain cases the elements received a specification at source? If, on the other hand, matter and proximate causes are used to explain occult effects, surely Ficino had shown Pico that magical action depended on man's ability to dispose matter to receive celestial influences, that is, it depended on modifying the conditions under which the celestial influences, themselves assumed to be unalterable, were received. Does this not mean that the presuppositions of operative magic could be reconciled with those invoked by Pico to account for celestial action, amounting to a legitimisation of the link between magic and astrology?

The sheer variety of problems which Pico faced suggests that belief in astrology was more than an acceptance of all the specific assumptions which he attacked. That is, astrology offered a relatively straightforward account of a very wide range of natural and human phenomena and seemed especially to explain those phenomena which appeared most mysterious and inexplicable. Therefore, to point out the mathematical shortcomings of the astrologers was merely to point out areas where corrections should be made (as did Cardano in his commentary on Ptolemy's *Tetrabiblos*). The

heterogeneity of the spiritual and the corporeal presupposed the separation
of two levels which astrology, more or less openly, believed that it could
discuss on the basis of experience. The relationship between the conclusions
of the *Disputationes* and the teachings of Ficino was more delicate: the
attempt to reveal the connection between astrology and magic, between
astrology and all the pseudo-sciences, became in Pico an explicit rejection of
that seminal wisdom by means of which Ficino had reconciled Christianity
and the ancient theology.

PIETRO POMPONAZZI

The vitality of astrological beliefs and the difficulty of defining and
delineating the sphere of the occult are important in Pomponazzi's thought,
but they are connected with the problems of establishing the scope of
human knowledge and of answering the teleological questions posed when
man is demoted to mortality. Pomponazzi's *De immortalitate animae* (1516)
combined the hypothesis of the human soul's mortality with that of a drastic
limitation of man's epistemological capacities. The consequences of this
were already evident in his *De incantationibus*,[3] where he defined the causes
of occult phenomena. There, within the framework of a natural determinism embracing all magical phenomena, Pomponazzi developed an ambiguous notion of the miraculous. He denied the reality of miracles in a
theological sense but found a new reality for them elsewhere, claiming that
even Christian miracles could be explained in terms of natural causes. But
before this statement can be understood, it is necessary to clarify his concept
of nature.

In Pomponazzi's view, the heavenly bodies were simply a medium for
the action of the intelligences, so that nature referred to something to
which it was bound and on which it depended but which was beyond it
and transcended it. It was necessary to look both at the particular way in
which the human world, in all its historical and religious complexity, was
part of nature, and at the forms by which the divinity regulated this
complex of phenomena. The notion of nature thus became more
problematic because it had to account for a series of different events,
ranging from the existence of occult qualities to the rise and fall of religions.
Pomponazzi declared that it was necessary to go back to experience, and by

---

3. The *De incantationibus* first appeared in 1556 and was reprinted, together with the *De fato*, at Basle in
1567; both editions were the work of Guglielmo Gratardo. Both works, finished in 1520, were
widely circulated in manuscript.

experience he meant both the observations supplied by astrology and the testimony of reliable historians. In fact, the two factors interwove constantly: astrology showed that the causal nexus between earth and the heavens existed because the astrologers' predictions had been confirmed (which proved the validity of astrology's premises). This was attested by the ancient historians, who taught that all important political and religious changes were preceded or accompanied by exceptional natural events which allowed the changes to be predicted. Christianity, like earlier religions, was subject to this natural causality. Everything had to be explained in relation to a structure which was of necessity always identical to itself; but this raised the problem of the succession of different religions. The doctrine of great astrological cycles allowed Pomponazzi to explain how a religion was born and how it died. The way in which Christianity arose and seemed to be moving towards an end – a prediction made by Cardano and also found prominently in Bruno's *Spaccio* – provided Pomponazzi with a model for the life-cycle of every religion. New celestial influences favoured the emergence and activities of prophets and legislators, allowing them, thanks to miracles, to produce great changes in people's beliefs and to introduce new rites and gods. Diminutions of such influences slowly led to the extinction of these religions. Their succession must therefore be explained with reference to the intervention of intelligences acting through the medium of cosmic cycles. Assigning naturally deter-mined temporal limits to religions assimilated them to the rest of reality, which was subject to generation and corruption. Therefore, all miracles were real, not just Christian ones. But it would never be possible to state with absolute certainty that they were extraneous to the natural order, because their occurrence involved either divine intelligences or celestial bodies with precise, if not entirely understood, modalities of action.

The recourse to experience, even if only within the context of astrology, indicated man's contemplative limit, which was reflected here in the hypothetical or multiple answers given concerning the cause of individual occult phenomena. Such uncertainties demonstrated both how difficult it was to clarify the connection between the earth and the heavens and the extent of the occult sphere, which Pomponazzi could not adequately or unambiguously account for because it lay outside the limited context of active and passive qualities.

The root of this uncertainty was already evident in his *De immortalitate*. Here Averroes' thesis of a unified intellect was presented as both an arbitrary interpretation of Aristotle and a ridiculous opinion *per se*. Man apprehended the universal, but only by abstracting it from the particular because his intellect was connected to his senses. His way of knowing was better defined as *ratio* than as intellect since it proceeded discursively, unlike the intuitions of the intelligences. Reason was thus brought down to the human level, the tool of a limited creature. Only those things which we learnt through reason could shed any light on our condition, which could, however, never be entirely illuminated. The kind of knowledge man achieved located him between animals and the intelligences in the hierarchy of beings. This location guaranteed man's uniqueness with respect to all other earthly creatures but set insuperable limits to his contemplative powers. Thus the difficulty of conceiving immortality within Aristotelianism (because of the impossibility of going beyond the information provided by sense data) coincided with the affirmation of a radical limitation of man's capacities for knowledge – a limitation even more apparent in *De incantationibus* and *De fato*.

In the face of certain traditional objections to the mortality of the soul, Pomponazzi concluded by maintaining that virtue was the specific duty of each human life because man was denied any higher understanding while on earth. Man's epistemological limitation and his self-realisation in his actions also became central themes in Cardano. But it was already clear that the independence of reason had always to come to terms with the uncertain frontiers of that which exceeded our knowledge.

ATTACKS ON ARISTOTLE

Geographical discoveries, emerging experimentalism, technical progress and practical experience all changed the picture of nature. Nature became a more abundant and almost infinite collection of phenomena waiting to be interpreted. The notion that nature offered a collection of discoveries yet to be made was associated with the term *secretum*. The limitations to our knowledge suggested that the decoding of nature could not be the work of a single individual but would eventually be achieved through the collaboration of many researchers, all attentive to the practical aspect of knowledge, a view which Cardano expressed in his *De immortalitate animorum* (1545). This lent weight to criticisms that Aristotelian notions about matter and privation were too abstract. A small number of ordering principles were, of course, necessary, provided that they possessed a physical concreteness. There was a general emphasis on concrete and specific explanation. The appeal to firsthand experience encouraged attentiveness to the particular, always seen as introducing a specific element into the context of general categories. The term *miraculum* therefore meant either the unpredictable variety of natural formations or a general fundamental structure which could be rigorously established. It tended to lose its theological connotation and at times indicated only a phenomenon which, regarded as exceptional if not actually supernatural, was to be rationally reduced to order and regularity through the discovery of its natural causes.

The concept of an independent study of nature, free as far as possible from metaphysical presuppositions, was based on individuating the ever-changing relationship between concrete physical factors. Awareness of man's epistemological limits thus coincided, paradoxically, with confidence in a rationality aware of occult and astrological causality at every level. Magical and astrological survivals in these writers indicated that causal relationships, as they gradually ascended to more complex processes higher in the ontological scale, could only with difficulty exclude specific celestial actions, which were apparently more difficult to individualise. The resultant animist-organic view of nature thus looked to teleology for the ultimate criterion of explanation and intelligibility. Nature appeared as an intelligent activity directed, within the given material conditions, to achieving its own ends and therefore was transparent to man. For other reasons naive forms of anthropomorphism or anthropocentrism were rejected. Mathematics was excluded as unsuitable for defining the intelligible essence of nature, centrality being given instead to the action of celestial warmth and *spiritus* in earthly processes. Reflection on the relationship between rationalism and esotericism was nourished by various factors: the relativity of the independence of the study of nature, the obscurity of the astrological causal nexus, the problematic relationship between the intelligible and the perceptible, and finally the idea that nature was largely unknown although conceivably reducible to ordering physical principles or to purely empirical enquiry. This relationship between rationalism and esotericism, between experience and what governs it, while not entirely intelligible, led some, such as Cardano, Bruno and Campanella, to derive the meaning of their actions from an inspiration higher than nature itself, an inspiration which was, however, always directed to earthly ends even when religious connotations were present.

The Copernican cosmology introduced crucial innovations. It did not, for example, destroy the basis of astrology but raised certain internal problems. Thus, Bruno found it difficult to establish the causality of the fixed stars because in an infinite universe it was only by an optical illusion that they appeared to lie in a single sphere. One decisive factor in particular resulted from the Copernican hypothesis. The character of the 'revelation' which Ficino attributed to sources like the Hermetic texts had led him to reappraise traditional cosmology in relation to the nature of the rational soul and the role of *spiritus* – 'an almost disembodied body', extremely subtle and capable of uniting the perceptible and the intelligible. But Copernican heliocentrism encouraged both a positive reassessment of the Presocratics to the detriment of Aristotle and a sharper look at the way in which the geocentric hypothesis had evolved. Thus, in Bruno's view, Aristotle had confused the appropriate mathematical hypotheses with concrete physical reality, and from this the system of concentric spheres had evolved.[4]

More importantly, the Copernican theory, in so far as it revealed the true structure of the cosmos, was not simply a scientific discovery; it allowed man to look at the plan of creation, to scrutinise God's hidden intentions. Copernican heliocentrism, as Rheticus had already asserted in his *Narratio prima* (1540, 1566), could be regarded on the same level as a genuine revelation. Thinkers like Bruno and Patrizi, who had been deeply influenced by Ficino, began to reverse the relationship between ancient revelation and the structure of the cosmos posited by Ficino. The spiritualisation of the cosmos was no longer dictated by a handful of esoteric texts. Instead, it was the new image of the cosmos which guided a re-reading of the ancient texts, which then provided indirect confirmation of the correctness of the new cosmology. The new book of nature now had the deciding vote in the interpretation of revelation. For various reasons, Bruno moved from the Copernican hypothesis to postulating an infinite universe. The views of Nicholas of Cusa on the infinity of the universe certainly played a role in this, but there seem to have been two decisive reasons for Bruno's belief.[5] One was the sheer immensity of the Copernican universe:[6] in order to account for the absence of stellar parallax, it was necessary to postulate an enormous distance between the sphere of Saturn and the sphere

---

4. See Bruno 1879–91, I, 2, pp. 171–2 (*De immenso*, VI.2). Reassessment of the Presocratics – either wilfully misrepresented by Aristotle or taken out of context – is found, with differing emphases, in Bruno, Cardano, Campanella, Patrizi and Telesio. In Cardano it is associated with the espousal of Hippocrates against Galen. There is no specific study of the relationship between the reassessment of Presocratic natural philosophy and the return to the ancient theology.

5. Koyré 1957 is still useful for Nicholas of Cusa's conception of an infinite cosmos. It is hardly necessary to stress the influence of Nicholas' 'coincidence of opposites' on Bruno's philosophy at the moral, physical and metaphysical levels.

6. Copernicus had already discussed *immensitas* and the *immensum caelum comparatione terrae* in his *De revolutionibus orbium caelestium* (I.6). The *Narratio prima*, which Bruno probably knew from the 1566 reissue with the *De revolutionibus*, deals with the same topic.

of the stars. The other was that once the earth had been promoted to the rank of the other planets the totality of the processes of generation and corruption produced on the earth could be explained only by reference to the sun's heat and the earth's motion and position with respect to the sun. All the functions of the celestial spheres, especially those of the sphere of the fixed stars with respect to the sublunary sphere, seemed to vanish together with the explanations that depended on them and with the finite character of the cosmos.

GIROLAMO CARDANO

Cardano's *De subtilitate* (1550) seems to mark the beginning of a new phase in European culture, characterised by ideas and influences which did not come solely from Italy or from a pure interest in studying nature as a homogeneous unity in isolation from metaphysical or social considerations. By this time, Cardano already had a lengthy career as a physician and a philosopher behind him, not to mention the great mathematical achievement of his *Ars magna* (1545). This experience enabled him to focus on some of the central issues in the philosophy of nature.

The influence of Erasmus, representing the finest fruits of European humanism, met and was united in Cardano's thought with the influence of Pomponazzi, representing the zenith of sixteenth-century Aristotelianism.[7] In different ways Erasmus and Pomponazzi gave directions for man to fulfil his moral and practical duty while heeding the intrinsic restrictions on man's metaphysical power. Erasmus, in particular, had worked out in his *Enchiridion* an ethic which recognised the ineluctable requirements of human nature, and his articulation of the relationship between reason and the passions was no longer expressed in terms of diametric opposition. At the same time he was moving towards a recognition of the unspoken rationality of the Christian message, and this reconciled him to the share of the rational that, like a divine signature, was found in man. The Christian message thus encountered in man an inner consent which arose from the very nature of those to whom it was addressed. Nature and reason – albeit in the theological and ethical terrain – therefore tended to be united in Erasmus, while the notion of reason on its own became so problematic, in the *Encomium moriae* for example, as to invite repeated accusations of scepticism.[8]

7. See Nardi 1958 and Schmitt 1983a for the problems of Renaissance Aristotelianism.
8. In his *De servo arbitrio* (1525) Luther frequently accuses Erasmus of scepticism. See O'Rourke Boyle 1983, who characterises their respective positions in the debate about free will as sceptic and Stoic.

Pomponazzi connected human mortality both with an epistemological limitation which threatened to undermine his own philosophical conclusions and with a purely animal destiny that seemed to arise from the determinism of his *De fato*. In his *De incantationibus* the quantity of natural phenomena which could not be referred to active and passive qualities indicated how vast was the domain of the occult, which in turn lay beyond epistemological certitude. Thus, it was necessary to invoke the heavens to account for decisive human actions in history and religion. Astrology certainly seemed to be empirically guaranteed, but it introduced causes external to the physical world and emphasised the uncertainty of any conclusions that might be formulated by a finite being. Above all, the plausibility and coherence of Aristotelianism seemed to entail premises which, since they were not self-evident *per se*, threatened to undermine the integrity of Aristotle's philosophy, itself reduced to being just one of several possible ways of discussing reality.

From Pomponazzi and Erasmus Cardano inherited an interest in the forms in which knowledge was expressed. This culminated in his formulation of the contrast between 'human knowledge' and 'natural knowledge' in his *De sapientia* (1544). This contrast was a first, embryonic distinction between a rhetorical-moral type of knowledge, used for dominating and deceiving others, and a knowledge, directed primarily but not exclusively at nature, constructed from facts and capable of expansion in time. From Erasmus and Pomponazzi Cardano also inherited the link between man's metaphysical limitations and his practical and moral purpose. This legacy constantly conditioned Cardano's studies of nature to the point where they were seen as the rational discovery of the structure of reality. The idea of man committing his practical capacities to his moral purpose became a programme to improve the conditions of human life by transforming nature (the category of *utilitas* was already central in Erasmus). Alongside this aspect of Cardano's thought and whenever he moved from the specific to the general causes of phenomena, or where ignorance of such causes led him to metaphysics proper, there was constant reference to a superior and anxiety-provoking realm inaccessible to reason alone. From this arose his attempt to produce a complete systematisation of astrology, equally rigorous in its mathematics and in its account of all celestial change since the ancients had founded the discipline. At the same time, Cardano, like others mentioned here, tackled the difficult relationship between rationalism and esotericism, between faith in reason, fully aware of its tools and called upon to develop a programme of unheard-of novelty and scope, and the awareness of reason's limitations. Nature's independence, often defended against anthropomorphic or anthropocentric explanations and against religious explanations of phenomena that could be accounted for in physical terms, therefore left considerable space open for astrology; at the same time, it also implied the *sui generis* independence of the human world, regulated by natural laws no less rigid than those of physics. These laws arose from the immutable psychology of the individual and were therefore invariable in time, constituting the structure of the human world. Based on dominion and deception, they condemned him to failure and therefore to unhappiness in his relations with others. These notions formed the background to the *ars vivendi* constructed by Cardano on a foundation of cynicism, which claimed not only its own morality but also a higher one. This cynicism, furthermore, underlay his interpretation of history as the history of the violence undergone by the humble and the oppressed, as described in his *Proxeneta* (posthumously published in 1627) and *Encomium Neronis* (1562).

The *De subtilitate* may be described as an encyclopaedia of nature in the sense that it deals with each of the levels according to which nature is structured, ranging from the elements to man and beyond to the obscure area of demonic influence. Despite almost discounting the *Physics* and *De caelo*, Cardano, like many of the thinkers discussed here, made much use of Aristotle's works of natural history. He focused on the relationship between teleology and material necessity, and on two issues in particular.

The first was his concern for man's capacity to transform nature for his own ends. (In his autobiography, Cardano claimed to be the first to move in this direction.) This capacity appeared to vary inversely with the increasing complexity and superior organisation of the products of nature, but seemed to be extensive and effective at the elemental level. Cardano had clearly learnt this from experience and from techniques acquired in the most disparate fields of knowledge, as well as from his work with the machines that were becoming increasingly important in his day.

The second was the opening up of a historical dimension to knowledge. Though this dimension relied on the accumulation of experiences in time, Cardano did not hesitate to see his own function as decisive in identifying the methods to be followed. He placed his own speculations on the same timeless level as the perception of intelligible truths contemplated by the *sapiens*.

None of this came to grips with society seen in terms of the laws of nature which regulated it – even less did it touch the civil role of religion within society. Religion was, of course, destined to change, but according to rhythms not determined by man. There was also the problem of the immortality of the soul and of free will, the latter thrown into disarray by the very astrology Cardano had, in his commentary on Ptolemy's *Tetrabiblos* (1554), set himself to restore. The appeal to astrology underlines another salient feature of Cardano's philosophy. He was no longer willing to accept the authority of Aristotle and Galen in physics and medicine, and was a champion of the indispensable role of experience, even if always subject to rational verification; his view of nature oscillated between the extreme simplicity of the principles needed to account for all living processes – basically, warmth and moisture – and the immense variety of phenomena which had to be explained in terms of these principles. He stressed the determinant importance of celestial warmth as the agent in every process of generation, sufficient even to account for the spontaneous generation of man, if not for his highest intellectual processes. This led him into cosmological problems. Almost sarcastically hostile to Copernicanism, he tended not only to emphasise the decisive role of celestial heat but also to question the Aristotelian notions about matter and movement that enforced the rigid separation of celestial and sublunary events.

Cardano, too, sought in the heavens the explanatory key for religious and historical changes in the human world. He saw himself as the learned man destined to perfect, or at least to advance, many branches of knowledge by raising them to a higher level beyond rational explanation. When he encountered the metaphysical restrictions mentioned above, he did not hesitate to invoke a higher inspiration which guided him into the realm of mysticism and which was mysterious and enigmatic, even to those whom it guided.

BERNARDINO TELESIO

Telesio was less wide-ranging than Cardano and more closely involved with anti-Aristotelian criticism. The first version, in two books, of his *De rerum natura iuxta propria principia* appeared in 1565. It is livelier but less organised and effective than the definitive 1586 version in nine books.[9] It begins with the works of Aristotle, criticising Peripatetic cosmology precisely at the moment when the senses (and therefore direct experience) were being claimed as the principal criterion for our evaluation of reality.

9. Sertorio Quattromani produced a synthesis of Telesio's philosophy in Italian, first published in Naples in 1589; see Quattromani 1914.

This position, sometimes considered simplistic and metaphysically naive,[10] is important for two reasons. One is the postulation of an insuperable limit to our knowledge, demonstrated by our inability to decide definitively on the constitution of the heavens because of the limitations of our observational instruments. The second factor is an emphatic denunciation of the arbitrary superimposition of abstractly rational schemata on to concrete physical processes which should instead be investigated *iuxta propria principia* (according to their own principles). Telesio's position drew strength from its analytical rigour. It is evident that his position presupposed a substantial identity of the principles that act at the cosmic level and those basic to our knowledge, otherwise the two factors (epistemological limitations and the validity of the senses) would be irremediably opposed.

Telesio thus found in the concreteness of the two principles of heat and cold (which are both incorporeal and perennially opposed, as well as acting on matter within a space entirely without qualitative determinations) the causes of all terrestrial physical processes. He based the relative cosmic locations of the sun and the earth on the attributes of heat and coldness, and on their opposition. The sun was impelled to perpetual motion by the nature of fire and heat; the earth was destined by its own weight to immobility. This arrangement balanced the conflicting tendencies which made life possible. The sun was the unique natural fire and the basis for a cosmology to which all physical processes and their equilibrium were referred. Telesio could thus eliminate the complex physical and metaphysical paraphernalia necessitated by the Aristotelian relationship of earth and heavens. He required only the wise intervention of an ordering mind at the beginning of creation and the constant physical interaction of the two principles of heat and cold. In Telesio's universe everything was sentient and aware of being sentient. Otherwise it would not have been possible to carry out a project which relied only on natural principles. Here the distinctive feature of Telesio's thought is to be found. By confining metaphysics to a level different from the physical, he emphasised that not only man's awareness but also his moral life and even his physical constitution would have to be investigated from the moment when the basic cosmic process became specifically manifest in man.

It is not surprising, therefore, that Telesio chose the *spiritus* of the human organism – the specific form in which fire and celestial warmth appropriate

10. See Gentile 1911 in particular.

earthly matter and turn it into a living organism – as the ultimate criterion
to explain all epistemological processes from memory to intellect. He had to
admit that the *spiritus* at the root of the human organism was itself a sense
since everything in nature which is capable of conserving itself can do so
only because it possesses in some degree a comprehension of reality
allowing it to distinguish between that which threatens and that which
favours its survival. His treatment of human awareness thus culminated
with the recognition of the superiority of sensation to all other levels of
awareness because it was presented passively, as a real physical modification,
but also as capable of initiating a form of discourse (possibly too swift for
conscious awareness) which allowed all the other forms of knowledge.
From these premises evolved the thesis of the character of the natural
realities, within us, of vice and virtue. These realities were changeable in the
individual but could be misunderstood if attention was not paid to their
dependence on an essential function of the *spiritus*, namely its self-
preservation and its inevitable connection with the different temperaments.

   Telesio's critique touched every aspect of Aristotelian philosophy, from
physics to cosmology, from epistemology to ethics. The quality of his
textual analysis and his intellectual rigour in clarifying physical problems
influenced Bruno and, especially, Campanella, and ultimately found an
echo in Bacon. The strength of his position was that it could be applied to
situations beyond those he himself had foreseen. His ambiguity resided in his
conception of the study of nature; his attempt to limit it within precise
boundaries encountered insuperable obstacles. On the one hand, he
postulated the existence of a human soul of divine origin, superior to the
spiritus, thus introducing a level of discourse higher than that of his original
enquiry. On the other hand, his positing of a divinity that had decided the
rationality of everything from the beginning had to come to terms with the
joint collapse of the Aristotelian relationship between the sublunary sphere
and the heavens and between the heavens and the realm of the intelligible.
Above all, the notion of *spiritus*, which was central to the magical and the
medical traditions, made it possible to reintroduce a vision of nature that
more strongly emphasised the living character of everything and the
consequent connection between man and cosmos. Thus, Telesio was able to
reopen both the metaphysical problem and the problem of how magic
worked. This was to exercise many of his followers, starting with
Campanella. These problems also help to explain the difficulties Telesio had
with ecclesiastical censorship.

THE STRUGGLE WITH AUTHORITY

Cardano was arrested and tried between 1570 and 1571. Bruno was in prison from 1592 until 1600, when he was burnt at the stake. In 1593 Telesio's works were condemned. In 1594 Patrizi's *Nova de universis philosophia* was condemned. Campanella was a prisoner of the Inquisition from 1594 to 1597 and again from 1599 to 1628. A number of factors have to be considered before the full complexity of this dissidence can be understood. Censorship was tighter in Italy than elsewhere; and also these writers were prolonging, in a different form, a tradition which felt itself to be outside the knowledge premised on orthodox religious belief. Equally, Platonism posed the censors with a number of dilemmas that some of these writers attempted to use as levers in order to impose, if only in embryonic form, their own programmes.[11] Admittedly, Telesio and Cardano both bowed to ecclesiastical authority, though in the latter's case he saw it almost as the wise man's duty, given the futility of opposing something like religion which enjoyed a higher necessity. Some were entirely sincere in their views. Consider, for instance, the extended and unresolved debate about the genuineness of the conversion of Campanella, whom some historians regard as the emblematic figure of the Counter-Reformation.[12] Beyond all this, however, there are underlying factors which explain, for example, how Patrizi could propose his philosophical synthesis as the new ideology of the Catholic Church. Clearly it was the unstable situation which encouraged Bruno to return to Italy where, in the wake of Patrizi's views and their short-lived success, he might be able to adapt the extremism of his anti-Christian views to the complexities of the situation. As Mocenigo, Bruno's first accuser at his trial, put it: 'When Patrizi went to Rome, Bruno said this pope is an honest man because he favours philosophers, and I too may hope to be given preference; and I know that Patrizi is a philosopher and that he does not believe in anything.'[13]

These words tell us much about Patrizi and Bruno, as well as other nature philosophers. The issues are subtle, but two factors stand out. First, the anti-Aristotelianism of both took a radical form which undermined the entire spectrum of philosophical certainties. This paralleled the ferment of new religious beliefs, some of which claimed a prophetic legitimisation, thus emphasising the delicacy of the church's situation. Second, the scientific

11. See Rotondò 1982.   12. See Di Napoli 1947.   13. A. Mercati 1942, pp. 56–7.

revolution held out the promise of a Christian apologetic different from the polemical opposition of these writers. To be sure, the new science would have been unthinkable without their decisive contribution to the cosmological renewal, but their analysis of man and of the human world proceeded with an extreme open-mindedness and freedom.

GIORDANO BRUNO

The new philosophy did not immediately welcome the revolution in astronomy. Cardano was hostile towards heliocentrism; he saw it as proof of how even the most ridiculous products of the human intellect occasionally found a practical justification. Telesio would have nothing to do with the notion that the earth moved and refuted it for reasons which were central to his philosophy. Bruno, however, found in Copernicus the means of demolishing Aristotelian physics and cosmology and of revealing the interrelation between the finiteness of the cosmos, traditional metaphysics and the Christian religion.

Bruno regarded Copernicus as the *matematico* who had succeeded in renovating and correctly describing the movements of the heavens. But his description, while adequate for practical purposes, was not a sufficient foundation for a new natural philosophy. Copernicus' assumptions about physical nature – the mobility of the earth, the centrality of the sun – were merely the starting-point for Bruno's philosophy, as can be seen in his *Cena de le Ceneri* (1584). By developing some of the ideas found in Nicholas of Cusa, above all the coincidence of opposites, and by carrying to its extreme consequences the fact that it was technical factors which had induced Copernicus to posit a universe which was so very much larger (a point already stressed by Rheticus in his *Narratio prima*), Bruno set himself up as a metaphysician, postulating the coincidence of matter and divinity. In his *De la causa, principio et uno* (1584), he deduced the infinity of the universe from the infinity of God's omnipotence. The cosmos appeared to be made up of innumerable solar systems similar to our own, so it made no sense to talk about celestial spheres and differences between the supra- and sublunary realms when elemental processes were everywhere identical. Stellar movements were not characterised by mathematical perfection. But rather, according to a unifying hypothesis which extended the laws of becoming to everything and which favoured an organic type of explanatory model, they were seen as moving in response to a purpose which presided over the life of the cosmos and made it intelligible. The junction of the physical and the metaphysical in Bruno's thought was not entirely without problems. The celestial world was still privileged at the expense of our own; he was ambiguous towards astrology because of the new way he approached eschatological questions; and it was still difficult to distinguish *spiritus*, diffused throughout infinite space and animating the stars, from divinity. Indeed, in some of Bruno's writings this *spiritus* appeared to be the divine body, where the coincidence of matter and divinity posited not only an indissoluble link between the two but also the irreducibility of the divine to the cosmic, even when the latter was thought of as infinite. He regarded this as legitimating his claim to be able to look at physical problems from various points of view: atomist, Paracelsian and so on.

Bruno still considered his metaphysical reform to be as much prophetic as philosophical in its attack on the origins and foundation of Christianity, and he also regarded it as an attempt to regenerate social harmony. The Reformation marked the end of one cycle and the beginning of a new one, for which Bruno saw himself as the standard-bearer. Just as Rheticus regarded Copernicus' discoveries as a revelation of God's creation, so too did Bruno, who was much more aware of the implications of heliocentrism than Copernicus had been. If the intelligible world was not in fact something which could put itself beyond the finite world, Christ's Incarnation – which lay at the heart of the theological controversy about transubstantiation which was poisoning Europe – became meaningless. Indeed, it became possible to restore Ficino's ancient Hermetic magical religion of nature, of which Christianity was a misunderstanding because it had comprehended the letter but had not grasped the inner allegorical and ethical significance of the myths and the cult of nature that they indicated.

The insuperable gulf between human and divine – which was the correct way to express the relationship between the two terms, in contrast to the Reformation's notion of the absolute relevance of man's interior world to his salvation – led Bruno to posit a relative autonomy of the human world that derived its legitimacy from that gulf. It also led him to maintain the necessity of describing an intermediate, allegorical-symbolical sphere as the single point of encounter at which the divine disclosed itself to man. From this there arose a naturalistic ethic in which human rationality, supplying the needs of civic life, could not but be in harmony with the laws given to man by God. Seen from the other side of the insuperable gulf, such laws could not aim at the greater glory of the divine – a goal by definition denied to man. Instead their goal was to increase the well-being and civic splendour of man. In his *Spaccio de la bestia trionfante* (1584), Bruno turned the formula *soli Deo gloria* upside down into *soli homini gloria*. The content of human reason therefore agreed with God's laws, according to a new and different conjuncture between reason and esotericism, no longer linked to a traditional cosmological structure. This conjuncture was valid at both the social level and at the higher level of the sage, who in this way re-established communication between the human and the divine, thus setting himself up as an alternative to Christ. According to Bruno, there were two different religious planes in civic life. The higher one, a combination of the political and the religious, agreed with reason and human nature, and also with the goals that the divinity required man to reach. The lower plane, characterised by a purely interior religiosity, was reached by those who could not raise themselves above the phantasms of their own imaginations. They might, indeed they had, to continue to nourish themselves on those illusory 'mystical foods', those myths of otherworldly salvation by which the impostor Christ bound men to himself by playing on their fear of death. Faced by the danger Christ posed to society, the political authorities had reduced him to a purely interior factor, the source of the masses' fear of death, and thus useful in governing them.

Christ had played on the fear of death, promising man an illusory metamorphosis (through the Eucharist) which would bring eternal life. Jesus had therefore broken the law of nature, setting himself up as the unique and irreplaceable intermediary between man and God. In his *Spaccio* Bruno taught the opposite, namely that the metamorphosis of man into divinity only occurred at an intermediate level between the two terms, a level which defined the natural character of civic laws and of religion. In his *Eroici furori* (1585), he tried to realise this encounter at the highest possible level. The intellect and love of the *furioso* coincided with the divinity, in a manner reminiscent of Nicholas of Cusa, reaching ever-higher levels but never attaining perfect coincidence. This limit could, however, be seen as a positive factor in that there was no ultimate level which could not be transcended. The medium called upon to operate this coincidence had to be none other than nature, which was itself a divinity and the authentic and indispensable mediator between the human and the divine. It was apparently only from the height of this last, supreme level that Bruno could address the human world on the civic and religious planes.

FRANCESCO PATRIZI DA CHERSO

Patrizi's *Nova de universis philosophia* (1591) outlined his proposals for a new ideology for the Catholic Church. Based on the authority of an ancient theology in the Platonic mould, it would replace the scholastic Aristotelianism which had dominated the church for four centuries and would reunite Christianity. Patrizi defended his orthodoxy by appealing to the Fathers and by deploying the force – the only kind which Patrizi regarded as persuasive – of *rationes* and demonstrations. This was the programme which he attempted to initiate when teaching in Rome (Clement VIII had called him to teach at the Sapienza in 1592). Patrizi's work reopens the problem of the significance and religious implications of the esoteric conceptions inspired by Florentine Platonism. This revival was linked in Patrizi's thought, as in Bruno's, with a cosmological renewal that had important metaphysical consequences. Patrizi's claim to have recovered the meaning of the divine and its relationship with the world challenged all of Aristotelian physics and raised new metaphysical problems about the intelligible world. His metaphysics was founded on an incorporeal element, similar to light, which connected the ineffable supreme unity to creation at every level. Like his predecessors, he began with the senses, but then developed a metaphysics of light that questioned the link between Aristotelian cosmology and the intelligible world. He tried to show how an infinite space filled with the emanations (*lumen*) of light (*lux*) could explain the processes of life in the material world, the structure of the heavens, the heavenly bodies and their movements, as well as the nature of an extra-corporeal region in which eternal beings resided. The relationship between the different worlds thus implied a distinction and a subordination, but the constant and decisive action of an incorporeal element at every level allowed the immediacy of divine action, whose presence in this relationship he stressed. Patrizi's attitude to the astronomical revolution (he favoured a moving earth and a reconsideration of its position in the cosmos) testifies to the primacy of the physical deductions drawn from his metaphysical principles. As in Ficino, however, the assumption that Christianity's importance was entirely in a speculative and atemporal realm threatened to deprive it of its historical dimension.[14]

TOMMASO CAMPANELLA

Bruno often referred to the astronomical/astrological debate inspired by the nova of 1572, the comet of 1577 and the great conjunction of 1583 that was

---

14. The recent renewal of interest in Patrizi has led to a deeper appreciation of his *Nova de universis philosophia* and *Discussiones peripateticae*, which he published at Basle in 1581. With considerable historical erudition, he accused Aristotle of having attacked those predecessors from whom he took his philosophy. See Muccillo 1981; Vasoli 1983b, pp. 559–83; and Wilmott 1984, 1985.

deemed to denote religious changes. This conjunction, from which
Cardano anticipated the emergence of a new and entirely exceptional *lex*,
was no doubt the origin of the religious reform which Bruno proposed in
his *Spaccio*. Regarding the first two celestial phenomena, Bruno complained
that events which jeopardised the Aristotelian cosmology by casting doubt
on the immutability of the heavens were misunderstood and regarded as
miracles, thus nourishing a climate of apocalyptic expectation. He also
mocked the belief that the great conjunction portended a universal
conflagration.

Campanella, in particular in his *Articuli prophetales* (1609), took a
considerable interest in this astronomical/astrological situation and related
subsequent astrological events to it in an attempt to reveal its hidden
meaning.[15] At the philosophical level, Campanella was interested in
Ficino's Neoplatonism, in the natural history studies of Giambattista Della
Porta and in the thought of Telesio, which he saw as a means of liberation
from Aristotelianism, as is evident in, for instance, his *Del senso delle cose e
della magia* (first written in Latin in 1590). Campanella's magical-operative
concerns in the *Del senso* relied on Telesio's ideas as the foundation for the
thesis of a universal animation and as a means of explaining a broad range of
experiences. Thus, the superiority of the senses to other modes of knowing –
which seemed to depend on the senses even in the most complex operations
and might even be thought of as 'weakened sensation' – allowed
Campanella to refute Aristotelian epistemology. At the same time, the
centrality of the senses provided a sound operative base, thanks to that
universal *consensus* which united all things, including man. Campanella's
dependence on Telesio is evident at the cosmological level as well, but he
developed his views to the point where the key to the understanding of all
physical processes opened the way to magical operative models involving
man–nature and man–man relationships. In the *Del senso*, on the other hand,
magic was presented as a tool for utilising natural processes by reproducing
them; it imitated nature by imitating the mechanisms of nature itself. The
magus continually extended his field of activities, referring them not so
much to the creation of an artificial world as to the actualisation of an ever-
present potentiality which tended to coincide with the concept of nature.
All these elements never entirely disappeared from Campanella's work;

15. Campanella 1977, p. 251: 'Credo igitur sextum sigillum incepisse in anno 1583, postquam lamina
    illa apparuit et postubi coniunctiones magnae, transactis omnibus triangulis signorum coelestium,
    ad primum revertuntur, ut mox dicemus. Unde Cardanus a 1583 expectat rerum mutationem
    ingentem; nova quoque stella in anno 1572 hanc aetatem intimasse potest.' There are several other
    passages in a similar vein.

after his conversion they became part of a general epistemological system which, while evolved for apologetic motives, never lost sight of the need for radical reform. Campanella did not reject any of the secular fields of enquiry – from medicine through astrology to magic – because he believed that it would be possible to integrate them into an orthodox system. Through the metaphysical concept of *primalitates* (each creature, like the divinity, was in its own fashion power, wisdom and love) and in full awareness of the fact that in front of the highest mysteries of theology reason was reduced to stammering, this synthesis reached the highest level, represented by the certainty of prophecy, which was seen as an uninterrupted chain of revelation from the biblical prophets to contemporary mystics. Campanella could therefore present his philosophy as orthodox and capable of confronting the two principal enemies of the faith: Aristotelianism and Machiavellianism.[16] It was also able to deal comprehensively with the individual sciences, eliminating what was dangerous to religion.

Beneath its professions of extreme naturalism, his philosophy presents certain ambiguities. For example, the natural foundation of his epistemology had to legitimise a higher level from which, in turn, he had to draw the conditions of its intelligibility. Thus, in his *Città del Sole* (1602) he declared that Christianity had only added the sacraments to natural law, where it was destined by its higher rationality to impose itself. So the superiority of the senses to the intellect was valid both at an inferior level – that of the perception of perceptible reality – and also at the higher level of the perception of future events by superior inspiration, a perception which was called upon to constitute the level of revelation. Prophecy, thus promoted to the rank of *scientia experimentalis*, could therefore be considered as the highest form of *gratia gratis data*, by which the divinity guided and provided for man, and also as the highest form of magic, namely divine magic.[17]

Cardano died in 1576 and Telesio in 1588; Bruno was burnt in Rome in 1600. So Campanella was now working in a very different climate. From his various prisons, he had to stay in touch with a world whose scientific and religious coordinates were changing rapidly.

Under such circumstances his attitude towards Copernicanism is

---

16. Campanella 1977, pp. 214–15, attacks 'Aristotelismum, negantem mundi a Deo creationem, et providentiam, et amicitiam cum hominibus, et animarum singularum immortalitatem, et religionem a Deo datam, et paradisum, et purgatorium, et infernum a Platone et Stoicis asserta, dicentem esse fabulas, et includentem Deum primo orbi, ut moveat . . . et negantem daemones et angelos, et somnia ab eis, et apparitiones . . . Machiavellismus [est] tyrannorum officina, detestans religionem et omnia ad regnandum temporaliter humana studia impellens. Apprime concors Aristotelismo, quia aliud saeculum melius non agnoscit.'

17. Campanella 1949–, v (*De gratia gratis data*).

particularly important because it clarifies some decisive steps in his thought. His retention, despite numerous doubts, of Telesio's cosmology with its immobile earth as one of his axioms put him in an awkward situation with regard to developments in the astronomical revolution. He argued that such developments seemed to vindicate not only Copernicus and Galileo, but also those who spoke of an infinite cosmos and an infinity of solar systems, such as Bruno, whom he often mentioned in his *Apologia pro Galileo* (1616) and his *Metaphysica* (1638). These arguments also surface in his *Theologia* where, amid numerous oscillations, Campanella's fundamental position can be traced to Telesio, though developed in a theological direction. In the wake of Galileo's astronomical discoveries, Campanella declared that it was a time of great uncertainty as far as the most important issues were concerned.[18] Nonetheless, he seemed convinced of the validity of the most diverse routes to understanding the structure of the cosmos. Like the reality of creation, this structure seemed to be an object which could be investigated but not entirely apprehended by reason. This attitude clearly reveals how difficult it was to unite nature and the Bible, the two books of creation, when their contents were understood as both an explanation and a sign of God's will in two different but converging realms. Moreover, it was essential to bear in mind that both books had a temporal dimension and development. The problem of God's double revelation, which also exercised Bruno and Galileo, became particularly dramatic when scientific discovery became the integrating element of an historical development whose significance was not only scientific but also religious.

Campanella's position on this issue leads to two central points in his thought. First, the difficulty of knowing the structure of the heavens was the difficulty of grasping a sphere of being which was, in his opinion, still linked with the destiny of the soul and the life of the divinity. The investigation of natural phenomena was always threatening to spill over into theology, where it was impossible to attain definitive results. Second, Campanella rejected the mathematical interpretations which astronomers, beginning with Copernicus, had given for recently discovered celestial phenomena, reaffirming that such phenomena were genuine novelties introduced by God into an apparently atemporal cosmic order.[19] He thus

18. Campanella 1927, p. 176 (A Galileo, 8 marzo 1614): 'Tutti filosofi del mondo pendeno ogge dalla penna di Vostra Signoria, perch' in vero non si può filosofare senza uno vero accertato sistema della costruzione de' mondi, quale da lei aspettiamo; e già tutte le cose son poste in dubbio, tanto che non sapemo s'il parlare è parlare.'
19. Campanella 1977, p. 118: 'Dicam tamen hoc unum, mundum videlicet esse in manu Dei quasi horologium, et secundum placitum illius motus et agendi patiendique mensuras sortiri.'

identified such phenomena as signs of the imminent apocalypse. It is worth mentioning here the thesis that the sun was gradually approaching the earth. In the context of Telesio's cosmology, based on an opposition of heat and cold, this process signified the progressive extinction of one of the two agent causes and the victory of the other. From Campanella's millenarian point of view, it converted the subordination of Christianity to philosophy predicted by Bruno into a programme for the religious unification of all mankind under a single Pastor, presaging the golden age and the return of man and nature to a primordial condition where error and sin no longer existed. Campanella's prophetic and reforming vocation are thus expressed in works whose utopian character does not conceal the re-emergence of the attempt to demonstrate the highest things on rational grounds. In this Campanella resembles the other thinkers who have already been considered. Amidst the uncertainties of physics and cosmology, on the one hand, and the inaccessible *arcana* of theology, on the other, Campanella too sought a common ground for faith and reason, for rationalism and esotericism, on which to construct his practical and reforming activity.

TOWARDS MODERN SCIENCE AND PHILOSOPHY

In his *Spaccio*, Bruno praises both the intellect and the hand, emphasising the necessity for their joint action in order to modify the 'orders' of nature. Francis Bacon's *Novum organum* opens by indicating that enquiry into nature would only be fruitful if it started from an awareness of the intrinsic limitations of knowledge, whether considered as pure contemplation or as practical operation devoid of theory. As with Cardano, man's epistemological limitation is converted into a practical programme for the general transformation of nature for purposes useful to man. The temporal dimension which Cardano also had posited as a consequence of this limitation gave rise to the idea of progress as a result of collaboration and of the accumulation of knowledge in the most rigorous and systematic fashion. Bacon's belief that the discovery of natural laws and the dominion over nature would complete the work of the creation – understood as something unfinished, left to man to complete and perfect – was also an echo of the religious inspiration that in different guises ran throughout the new philosophy of nature. Bacon's debt to this line of thought indirectly emphasises, however, the problematic relationship between it and the scientific revolution.[20] According to what Kepler told Galileo, it was these

20. See *Spiritus* 1984, pp. 265–81 (Rees); the remainder of the volume is also relevant to this topic.

thinkers, and Bruno in particular, who had opened up the new vistas in cosmology.[21] Galileo, however, often suppressed their names and in any case had been educated in a different tradition. Moreover, he displayed a lively awareness of purpose and method which cannot be reconciled with any legacy to him from, for instance, Campanella.[22] But Galileo's distinction between the written book of God and the book of nature resembles a similar distinction in Bruno's thought, and the similarity is not diminished by the different emphasis that both gave to mathematics. For Galileo as well, to establish the mathematical laws of the cosmos using a yardstick that was adequate to what had been God's procedure and also such that our awareness was on the same qualitative, if not quantitative, plane as divine awareness, meant to possess a key capable of unlocking God's *modus operandi* and the secret intentions of his legislative will in nature. In other words, his discoveries also coincided with the emergence of a revelation.

Galileo's relationship with the philosophy of nature shows equally clearly its limits within the scientific revolution. By rejecting, as Aristotle had done, the possibility of a mathematical account of physical phenomena which was not merely a matter of practical approximations but which might reveal their deepest structures – that is, by favouring the notion of a ceaseless coming-into-being which could not be understood in terms of an intelligible structure – the philosophy of nature was in opposition to both Galileo and Descartes. It was not by chance that Descartes noted the efficacy of the work of the *novatores* more in the context of the criticism of Aristotelian philosophy than in the construction of a new philosophy.[23] The methodological characteristics of the philosophy of nature appeared to be inadequate in the face of new scientific developments, especially those in physics. Certainly, the programme outlined in the *Discours de la méthode* developed at its highest level as a realisation of a scientific morality and as a reform of the human world, moving from the individual plane to that of the dominion of the human race over nature and the transformation of man's intentions towards it. But the Cartesian dream of a *mathesis universalis* had already allied itself with the attempt to construct a new metaphysical foundation for the new learning.[24]

Other factors, however, worked to prolong the influence of the philosophy of nature. The initially limited achievements of mathematical

21. See Kepler 1610.
22. Galilei 1890–1909, IV, p. 738: 'Io stimo più il trovar un vero, benchè di cosa leggiera, che 'l disputar lungamente delle massime questioni senza verità nissuna.'
23. See, e.g., Descartes 1897–1910, I, pp. 156–70 (letter to Isaac Beeckman, 17 October 1630).
24. See Gilson 1951.

physics (consider, for instance, how long it took for dynamics to acquire a mathematical expression), the different times at which the individual disciplines acquired scientific status, religious interference in speculations of the most diverse kinds – these are just some of the reasons why it continued to retain some of its authority. Animistic concepts like *spiritus*, occult speculation and the old hypothetical accounts of the structure of matter persisted, drawing strength from the difficulty of explaining the phenomena of life by mathematical coordinates. In areas of speculation which overlapped with ethics and religion, the continuing vitality of the philosophers of nature was guaranteed by the audacity and novelty of their teaching, which had influence throughout Europe. In ethics, Cardano formulated a view of history and of the human world which was open-minded to the point of cynicism; and he came to be regarded as one of the masters of irreligion and *libertinage*. In the more narrowly religious field, Bruno's anti-Christian polemics enjoyed an underground success, inspiring thinkers like John Toland. Bruno's views were destined to flourish anew in the eighteenth century, no longer for their explicit paganism but as a reappraisal of the relationship between politics and religion in the past and as an example of the possibility of reconciling them by means of a tolerance unknown in modern times.

10

ASTROLOGY AND MAGIC

A SCEPTIC'S DEFINITION OF MAGIC

When Henricus Cornelius Agrippa published an enlarged edition of his *De occulta philosophia* in Cologne in 1533, seven years after he had written his invective *De incertitudine et vanitate scientiarum atque artium* (1526), he appended to it a *Censura sive retractio* in which he reprinted the chapters on magic from *De incertitudine*. Since in these chapters Agrippa's ardour for occult wisdom had somewhat abated, we may take their definition of natural magic to be the tempered judgement of a man who was, in any event, sincere in his Christian piety and skilled as a vulgariser of other people's ideas. 'That magic is natural', he explained,

which, having observed the forces of all things natural and celestial and having examined by painstaking investigation the sympathy among those things, brings into the open powers hidden and stored away in nature; thus, magic links lower things (as if they were magical enticements) to the gifts of higher things . . . so that astonishing miracles thereby occur, not so much by art as by nature to which – as nature works these wonders – this art of magic offers herself as handmaid.

Agrippa recognised that magic was an art, a practical technique, but he also insisted on a theoretical content in magic, an analytic basis in the study of nature. Learned men had called magic 'the highest point of natural philosophy' because they saw in it speculative as well as pragmatic responses to the cosmos.[1] The obverse of this learned *natural magic*, was sinful *demonic*

---

1. Agrippa 1533, pp. CCCLII–III: 'Naturalem magiam non aliud putant quam naturalium scientiarum summam potestatem, quam idcirco summum philosophiae naturalis apicem eiusque absolutissimam consummationem vocant . . . Magia itaque naturalis ea est, quae rerum omnium naturalium atque coelestium vires contemplata, earundemque sympathiam curiosa indagine scrutata, reconditas ac latentes in natura potestates ita in apertum producit: inferiora superiorum dotibus, tanquam quasdam illecebras, sic copulans . . . ut exinde stupenda saepe consurgant miracula, non tam arte quam natura cui se ars ista ministram exhibet haec operanti'; see nn. 11, 22 below; *Umanesimo e esoterismo* 1960, pp. 144–5 (Zambelli); Nauert 1965, pp. 32–3, 98, 106, 111–13, 192–3; Müller-Jahncke 1973. On Agrippa, as on Renaissance magic in general, the many articles of Paola Zambelli are fundamental; for Agrippa, see Zambelli 1960, 1965, 1966, 1969, 1973b, 1976, 1985 and also her editions of Agrippa: *Testi umanistici su l'ermetismo* 1955, pp. 105–62 and Agrippa 1958.

magic. Warning that 'natural magic has sometimes relapsed into sorcery and theurgy (most often through strategems of evil demons)', Agrippa raised the spectre of demonology that haunted the Renaissance revival of ancient magic as it animated the concurrent witchcraft craze.[2] When Agrippa described magic as a linking of inferior to superior entities, he alluded also to astrology as an ingredient of the magical worldview: 'magic is so connected and conjoined with astrology that anyone who professes magic without astrology accomplishes nothing'. But the *magus* who understands the powers of the stars can tap forces 'hidden and stored away in nature', secret or occult powers that produce the characteristically 'astonishing' effects of magic, the same powers that lent their name to Agrippa's most famous book, *De occulta philosophia*.[3]

Although one may speak retrospectively of an 'occultist tradition' in European culture, Renaissance philosophers would have found the term 'occultism' as strange as 'humanism'; both words have their uses, nonetheless, as historical categories. European occultism includes the concepts of magic, astrology, demonology and occult natural power to which Agrippa referred in the definition above; it also embraces the related notions of divination, illusion, witchcraft, numerology, cabala and theurgy that he treated elsewhere.[4] Despite its having been obscured by polemics that began with the Greek philosophers and the Church Fathers and reverberate in the debates of modern anthropologists and students of religion, this complex of ideas constitutes a coherent tradition in western intellectual history. Variations in the tradition, such as the rise of witchcraft beliefs in the Middle Ages, left intact the kinship among these concepts, whose collective development saw its two strongest moments in late antiquity, in the centuries of Plotinus, Porphyry and Proclus, and again in the Renaissance, in the age of Agrippa, Ficino and Pico.[5]

In his *Censura sive retractio*, Agrippa named the inventors of magic and blamed them for their impious legacy. Some, like Zoroaster, Hermes Trismegistus and Kirannides, were mythical or semi-mythical progenitors

2 Agrippa 1533, p. CCCLV: 'Hinc patet hanc naturalem magiam nonnunquam in goëtiam et theurgiam reclinantem, saepissime malorum daemonum vaframentis erroribusque obretiri'; Nauert 1965, pp. 245–8; cf. Zambelli 1985, pp. 76–7.

3 Agrippa 1533, p. CCCLII: 'Magia . . . cum astrologia sic coniuncta atque cognata est ut qui magiam sine astrologia profiteatur is nihil agat sed tota aberret via'; see n. 1 above.

4 Agrippa 1533, pp. CCCLIV–LXII; Copenhaver 1978a, pp. 31–42, 97–171; the eight volumes of Thorndike 1923–58 contain the most detailed description of occult beliefs from late antiquity to the seventeenth century.

5. Parinetto 1974, pp. 121–31, 165–76; Douglas 1975, pp. 29–40, 73–89, 105–13; Sharpe 1975, pp. 72–96, 149–51, 190–4; Evans-Pritchard 1965, pp. 26–47, 56–7, 78–9; Hull 1974, pp. 5–9; M. Smith 1978, pp. 1–7; Aune 1980, pp. 1507–16, 1536, 1557; Cohn 1975.

of a *prisca sapientia*; their chief service to the occultist tradition was to make it venerable by locating it in a distant and sacred past. Others were historical figures, and some of these were important in the history of philosophy: the Neoplatonists Iamblichus, Proclus and Synesius; the Arab sage Alkindi; and such heroes of medieval Christendom as Albertus Magnus, Roger Bacon and Ramon Lull.[6]

Some of the medieval works in which Agrippa sought his arcane wisdom had marginal, even scandalous reputations in the Renaissance. The most notorious was 'the book published under the name of *Picatrix*', the Latin title for the Arabic *grimoire* only recently confirmed as a source for Marsilio Ficino's refined theorising on magic as well as Agrippa's more sensational compendium on the occult.[7] Certain other medieval texts, like the *Liber aggregationis* or the *Speculum astronomiae* attributed to Albertus Magnus, have scarcely mattered to the history of philosophy because uncertain authorship or the certainty of false ascription protected the philosopher's good name by detaching it from books of such ill-repute. This apologetic strategy finally fails in the face of undoubtedly genuine works – the *De mineralibus* of Albertus, the *De occultis operibus naturae* of Thomas Aquinas, the *De universo* of William of Auvergne – in which prominent philosophers acknowledged and defended principles of occultism. As long as medieval thinkers shared the metaphysical, physical and cosmological premises of ancient philosophy, some concessions to magic were inevitable since the elements of the magical worldview were common ideas well respected by ancient philosophers. The revival of ancient learning in the Renaissance could only deepen the conviction – already familiar in the Middle Ages – that the *magus* and the philosopher used much the same conceptual lexicon. 'Natural magic they consider nothing less than the chief authority among the natural forms of knowledge', wrote Agrippa of his fifteenth-century predecessors, '[and] on that account . . . they call [it] the most perfect achievement of natural philosophy.'[8]

6 Agrippa 1533, pp. CCCLII–LV; 1958, pp. 41–8, 51–5; Walker 1972, pp. 1–21, 29, 33–5, 59; Zambelli 1965, 1969; *Magia, astrologia e religione* 1974, pp. 48–82 (Zambelli); Copenhaver forthcoming a, b and c; D'Alverny and Hudry 1974, pp. 139–41, 149–67; Wellmann 1928; Röhr 1923; Hopfner 1974; Thorndike 1923–58, I, pp. 641–9, II, pp. 517–92, 616–91, 862–73; Yates 1982–4, I, pp. 9–125.
7 Agrippa 1533, p. CCCLIII: 'Ex recentioribus vero scripserunt in naturali magia . . . Albertus, Arnoldus de villa nova, Raimundus Lullius, Bachon, et Apponus, et autor libri ad Alfonsum sub Picatricis nomine editus, qui tamen una cum naturali magia plurimum superstitionis admiscet, quod quidem fecerunt et alii'; Garin 1969, pp. 389–419; 1976a, pp. 245–6; 1976c, ch. 2; Perrone Compagni 1975, pp. 237–47; Delcorno Branca 1976, pp. 470–1.
8 Introduction to Albertus Magnus, Pseudo- 1973, pp. xi–xvii, xxx–xlviii; Albertus Magnus 1977; Introduction to Albertus Magnus 1967, pp. xxix–xli; McAllister 1939, pp. 1–9; Thorndike 1923–58, II, pp. 338–71, 593–615, 692–745; see n. 1 above.

GIOVANNI PICO AND THE SECULAR ARISTOTELIANS

Given his own dispositions and those of his age, it is not surprising that Jacob Burckhardt saw the question of occultism differently. He relegated magic and astrology to the last pages of *Die Cultur der Renaissance in Italien*, where, in his final chapter on morality and religion, he claimed that the revival of antiquity affected Renaissance belief 'most powerfully . . . not through any doctrines or philosophical system but through a general tendency' to admire classical culture above all others. Among the weapons of the 'army of superstition' against which 'the clear Italian spirit' fought the good fight of reason were magic, astrology and other delusions which, according to Burckhardt, appealed to the uncultured popular mind but also found support in the seductive dogmas of antiquity. Even Ficino, the 'distinguished' Platonist, fell prey to these errors. By contrast, Giovanni Pico's attack on astrological determinism 'made an epoch in the subject', and Burckhardt believed that its 'first result . . . was that the astrologers ceased to publish their doctrines'. This gross underestimate of the volume of astrological publication in early modern Italy can be attributed partially to the state of historical scholarship in 1860 and partially to Burckhardt's mentality, which permitted him to fit the evidence to his hermeneutic strategies. Admiring the catholic syncretism of Giovanni Pico, 'the only man who . . . defended the truth . . . of all ages against the one-sided worship of classical antiquity', Burckhardt reported the celebration of human freedom and dignity in Pico's *Oratio* without mentioning that for the young Count of Mirandola the supremely free man was the *magus*.[9]

Even if Burckhardt had given more weight to ancient philosophy as the vehicle of magical belief – or as its antidote – he might well have discounted the role of technical philosophical analysis in the aphoristic and rhetorical enthusiasms of Pico's early work. The *Oratio* and *Conclusiones* of 1486 present a manifesto for magic, but they do not provide a theory of magic; even the more discursive but hastily written *Apologia* of 1487 falls short of the extensive and coherent theoretical statement that finally emerged in 1489 with the third book of Marsilio Ficino's *De vita libri tres*, titled *De vita coelitus comparanda*. Although the Pico of the *Oratio* and *Conclusiones* knew the Platonic, Neoplatonic and Hermetic sources revealed by Ficino since 1463, he had no occasion to apply his philosophical learning systematically

---

9 Burckhardt 1860, pp. 197, 354, 512–24; *Damned Art* 1977, pp. 32–3 (Burke); Thorndike 1923–58, V, pp. 42, 104–11, 161–71, 182–8, 193–201, 204–6, 228–74, 571–3, VI, pp. 99–101, 124–33, 137–40.

to a specifically occultist problem before he began the *Disputationes adversus astrologiam divinatricem* in 1493.[10]

Pico knew that pagan and Christian philosophers had conceded the efficacy and legitimacy of a natural magic distinct from the demonic magic 'in use among the moderns, which the church rightly banishes . . . because it comes from the hand of the enemies of primal truth'. This licit *magia naturalis* is the 'practical part of natural knowledge' and 'nothing other than . . . the most perfect achievement of natural philosophy'. Its method of operation is to join powers naturally disjoined in the cosmos: 'the wonders of the art of magic do not exist except by unifying and activating those things sown and separated in nature'. Thus, the manipulation of natural, material objects becomes a magical technique, but on the basis of 'a more secret philosophy' Pico was forced to admit that certain artificial objects, 'characters and figures, have more power in an act of magic than any material quality'. Pico wished to enhance natural powers not only through human artifice but also through the verbal and angelic magic that he discovered in cabala. He asserted, in fact, that 'there can be no magical activity of any efficacy unless . . . it includes an act of cabala'. And since Pico understood cabala to be 'an exact metaphysics of intelligibles and angelic forms' as well as 'a very solid philosophy of natural things', it seems clear that his audacious programme for natural magic had celestial ambitions. The *Oratio* that introduced the *Conclusiones* launched this bold project in the full flush of humanist oratory, with all its erudite apparatus amplified by a syncretism that reached beyond Greek and Latin learning to the wisdom of the Arabs, Hebrews and Chaldaeans.[11]

So young, so learned, so sure of his powers – no wonder Pico represented even for Burckhardt 'the lofty flight which Italian philosophy would have

---

10. G. Pico 1942, pp. 18–27; 1946–52, I, p. 3; 1973, pp. 4–8, 13–16; Garin 1976c, pp. 87–8; see n. 22 below.
11. G. Pico 1973, pp. 10–20, 78–80: '*Conclusiones Magice numero XXVI secundum opinionem propriam.* 1. Tota Magia, que in usu est apud modernos, et quem merito exterminat ecclesia, nullam habet firmitatem . . . quia pendet ex manu hostium prime veritatis . . . 3. Magia est pars practica sciencie naturalis . . . 11. Mirabilia artis magice non sunt nisi per unionem et actuacionem eorum que seminaliter et separate sunt in natura . . . 15. Nulla potest esse operatio magica alicuius efficacie nisi annexu habeat opus cabale explicatum vel implicitum . . . 24. Ex secretioris philosophie principiis necesse est confiteri plus posse caracteres et figuras in opere magico quam possit quecunque qualitas materialis'; 1942, p. 148: 'Proposuimus et magica theoremata in quibus duplicem esse magiam significavimus, quarum altera daemonum tota opere . . . constat . . . Altera nihil est aliud . . . quam naturalis philosophiae absoluta consummatio'; *ibid.*, p. 158: 'Hi sunt libri scientiae Cabalae, in his libris merito Esdras . . . sapientiae fontem, idest de intelligibilibus angelicisque formis exactam metaphysicam, et scientiae flumen, idest de rebus naturalibus firmissimam philosophiam esse, clara in primis voce pronuntiavit'; Garin 1937a, pp. 90–105; Secret 1964, pp. 24–41; Scholem 1974, pp. 196–201; Yates 1964, pp. 87–91; *L'opera e il pensiero* 1965, I, pp. 160–7, 172–3, 183–4 (Yates).

taken had not the Counter-Reformation annihilated the higher spiritual life of the people'. Burckhardt knew that Pico's conception of human freedom in the cosmos empowered man 'to have what he chooses, to be what he wants', but he seems not to have realised that one dimension of this freedom was magical. Licit magic makes man 'prince and master' of creation, even of the wicked spirits who tempt him to forbidden demonic magic.[12] Man is a 'lesser world': the structure of his being mirrors the greater world of the cosmos, and his understanding gives him access to the 'occult alliances and affinities of all of nature'. Many of the occult bonds that tie the human microcosm to the macrocosm of nature lie within the domain of astrology. Pico's astrology did not diminish man by determining his fate; it gave cosmic dimensions to human freedom by showing man 'the links of concord [by which] all these worlds bestow their natures . . . on one another in mutual liberality'.

God the craftsman blended our souls in the same mixing bowl with the celestial souls and of the same elements; let us see that we do not wish to be the slaves of those whom nature wished us to have as brothers . . . We must beware . . . of yielding more to heaven . . . than is necessary . . . The Chaldaeans warn about this, saying, 'Do not aggravate fate.' . . Let us not form images of the stars in metal but . . . an image of the word of God in our souls.

These lines from the *Heptaplus* of 1489, in which Pico preserved the cosmological fundamentals of his natural magic, also foreshadow his forceful and detailed attack on astrological determinism in the *Disputationes*.[13]

This anti-determinist current was evident in Pico's thought from the beginning. And even at the end of his career, the enlargement of this polemic in the *Disputationes* entailed neither a complete disavowal of astrology nor a repudiation of natural magic. Admitting a general celestial

---

12. G. Pico 1942, p. 106: 'O summam Dei patris liberalitatem, summam et admirandam hominis felicitatem! cui datum id habere quod optat, id esse quod velit'; *ibid.*, p. 152: 'Ut enim illa [magia mala] obnoxium mancipatumque improbis potestatibus hominem reddit, ita haec [magia bona] illarum principem et dominum'; Burckhardt 1860, pp. 197, 354.
13. G. Pico 1942, p. 192: 'Quoniam scilicet astricti vinculis concordiae uti naturas iam etiam appellationes hi omnes mundi mutua sibi liberalitate condonant . . . Nec potuerunt antiqui patres aliis alia figuris decenter repraesentare nisi occultas, ut ita dixerim, totius naturae et amicitias et affinitates edocti . . . Tritum in scholis verbum est, esse hominem minorem mundum . . .'; *ibid.*, pp. 242–4: 'temperatos animos nostros ab opifice Deo in eodem cratere ex iisdem elementis cum caelestibus animis, videamus ne nos illorum servos velimus quos nos fratres esse natura voluit . . . Cavendum igitur ne . . . plus caelo dantes, plus tribuentes quam sit necesse, . . . voluntati opificis et ordini universi repugnemus . . . Hos admonent Chaldaei dicentes: "Ne augeas fatum." . . . Quare neque stellarum imagines in metallis sed illius, idest Verbi Dei, imaginem in nostris animis reformemus'; Garin 1937a, pp. 169, 178; 1976c, pp. 87–91; Cassirer 1927, p. 88.

influence on terrestrial phenomena, Pico denied that it could be resolved into discernible relations between particular heavenly causes and corresponding earthly effects; no one could know enough to cast a horoscope or tie a man's fate inexorably to one star or another. Pico limited astrological influence to material objects, which included man's body but not his mind or will; he also restricted the forms of celestial power to heat, light and motion. The rigour of this latter restriction weakened, however, in his description of *calor* and *lux*, which resemble Ficino's magical *spiritus* more than the heat or light of modern physics. If Pico's effort to reform astrology by naturalising it was incomplete, the strength and scope of his reasoning were sufficient to establish the framework of the debate on astrology through Kepler's time.[14]

Pico's warning in the *Heptaplus* against making 'images of the stars in metal' runs contrary to advice on characters and figures that he had given three years earlier in the *Conclusiones*. Innocent VIII's condemnation of his theses in 1487 had taught Pico prudence by 1489. The most notorious thesis claimed that 'there is no department of knowledge (*scientia*) that gives us more certainty of Christ's divinity than magic and cabala'. Since Pico denied in another thesis 'that Christ's deeds could have been done either by the method of magic or by the method of cabala', it seems likely that his intention was pious: to use his understanding of the merely natural powers of magic to illuminate the genuinely miraculous acts that testify to true divinity. To the church, however, Pico's brash thesis can only have seemed an affront to orthodox theology, as Pedro García's *Determinationes magistrales* of 1489 made quite clear. Since Pico was never closer to Savonarola than when he began the *Disputationes* in 1493, it may be that the friar provoked him to the fuller expressions of piety that characterise this last, monumental work of his – which was only part of a larger project left unfinished at his death in 1494.[15]

Although Pico's learning was subtle and broad, the most consistent and most original element in his approach to magic and astrology was his abiding ethical interest: magic enlarges man's powers; astrology cannot limit man's freedom. A greater emphasis on natural philosophy in the

14. Garin 1937a, pp. 170–1, 175–80; 1976c, pp. 91–8; G. Pico 1942, pp. 270–2; 1946–52, I, pp. 202–8, 216–18; Cassirer 1927, pp. 122–3; *L'opera e il pensiero* 1965, II, pp. 322–5 (P. Rossi); Walker 1958, pp. 54–6; 1985, § X, pp. 125–6.
15. G. Pico 1973, pp. 5–8, 79: '7. Non potuerunt opera Cristi vel per viam magie vel per viam Cabale fieri . . . 9. Nulla est sciencia que nos magis certificet de divinitate Cristi quam magia et cabala'; García 1489, sigs. h iiii–o iii; Garin 1937a, pp. 30–6, 42–8; Yates 1964, pp. 105–6; Weinstein 1970, pp. 185–91, 212–16; Crouzel 1977, pp. 30–4; Zika 1976, pp. 107, 116–17, 124–7, 131, 135–8.

analysis of magic and astrology characterised a number of his contemporaries and near-contemporaries associated with the University of Padua and other *studia* of northern Italy. By the early fifteenth century, a tradition of secular Aristotelianism stimulated more by medicine than theology had established in these universities a pattern of education in which astrology was a prominent ingredient in an arts curriculum strongly inclined towards natural philosophy. Graduates of these schools looked to the stars and planets as indices of regularity in physical causation. Their discussions of immutable astrological influence opened some of the same questions that were to be asked in Pico's *Disputationes*: How is human freedom preserved in a universe of natural causes? How does myth or revelation count as evidence bearing on astrological theory? Despite the subsidiary role of theology at Padua, the characteristic *aporia* in these fifteenth-century debates – as later in Pomponazzi's day – was a theological question motivated (paradoxically) by the desire to read Aristotle's science without extraneous theological commitments. Aristotelian cosmology allowed for intelligences guiding the stellar and planetary spheres, and to this extent a mitigated Christian demonology might be reconciled with Peripatetic natural philosophy. But a fully developed demonology, such as had become normal in orthodox Christianity, offended the naturalist sentiments of important Italian Aristotelians. Yet in other ways, especially in their attitudes toward astrology, Aristotelian thinkers who wished to rout the demons from philosophical discourse contributed to the growth of occultist belief in the Renaissance.[16]

In 1503, Alessandro Achillini prepared a *Quaestio de subiecto physionomiae et chiromantiae* whose publishing history suggests that it was the most popular of his works. Achillini's *Quaestio* was a methodological introduction to the more practical *Chyromantiae et physionomiae anastasis* (1504) of Bartolomeo Della Rocca or Cocles, a vagrant seer whose risky speciality was predicting misfortune for minor Italian princes by reading their faces or their palms. Until a client's relative had him murdered in 1504, Cocles enjoyed Achillini's encouragement. The philosopher took the soothsayer seriously, establishing in Aristotelian terms that palmistry and physiognomy were valid forms of knowledge (*scientiae speculativae*) based, like medicine or astronomy, on principles of natural philosophy. The attribution to Aristotle of nearly twenty treatises on chiromancy and physiognomy

---

16. Garin 1937a, pp. 177–8; 1976c, pp. 87–8; G. Pico 1942, pp. 3–5; Cassirer 1927, pp. 123–5; Walker 1958, p. 54; Schmitt 1983a, p. 100; Kristeller 1964a, p. 75; *Scienza e filosofia* 1983, pp. 345–72 (Zanier); Siraisi 1981, p. 179.

(one of them published by Achillini in his *Opus septisegmentatum* of
1501) doubtless encouraged a Peripatetic analysis of divination. Achillini
found a place for fortune-telling in his hierarchy of sciences, but he balked at
demonology. He could not reconcile Aristotelian and Averroist conceptions of form and matter, soul and body with Christian ideas about demons.
Although faith required him to accept that demons existed, Achillini could
not justify his assent in rational terms, and on this point he admitted a
conflict between philosophy and theology. Having excluded demons as
causes of events unexplainable in ordinary natural terms, he attributed them
either to trickery or to poorly understood natural agencies such as
imagination.[17] This latter strategy gave ample room for occult explanation,
i.e., the appeal to extraordinary phenomena (imagination, *spiritus*, various
occult virtues and powers) that might be natural and non-demonic but were
'hidden' because they were less evident than the four elements and four
qualities. A magic based on such natural effects and directed towards health
or some other legitimate goal might be unobjectionable, but there is
evidence that members of the north Italian universities also used riskier
magical means for more questionable ends. In 1503, Agostino Nifo wrote
that he had 'seen an infinity of books about images, and they all claim that
this art is inherently true though difficult to discover, and no doubt they
practise it to carry women away and to do many other things . . .
Moreover, this is a subject of study in many universities; frightening things
happen there, and it is hard to save such phenomena on Peripatetic
principles.' Having witnessed the popularity of occultism in the universities
and having weighed his own considerable experience with astrology and
the other secret arts, Nifo was less inclined than Achillini to dismiss much of
the problem as trickery, and, since he had more reason to worry about
ecclesiastical opposition, his conviction that demons were superfluous in
Aristotle's universe did not prevent him from resorting to the Platonic and
Neoplatonic demonology that Ficino had made available. Nifo's sincerity is
hard to evaluate. Although he eventually denounced the argument that
demons were invented to terrify the simple-minded, he had been educated
in the naturalist tradition that bred such cynicism. Shifts and inconsistencies
in his works make it difficult to distinguish opportunist evasion from
genuine compromise or to isolate his personal views.[18]

17. Zambelli 1978, pp. 59–86; Zanier 1975b, pp. 32–3; Schmitt and Knox 1985, pp. 21–4, 45–50;
    Thorndike 1923–58, v, pp. 39–47.
18. Nifo's commentary on the *Destructio destructionum* of Averroes, cited in Zambelli 1975, p. 142: 'Vidi
    tot libros de imaginibus quot sunt infiniti, et omnes testantur istam artem esse veram in se, licet
    difficilis inventionis, et sine dubi[o] faciunt rapere mulieres et multa . . . Praeterea in multis

Much clearer was Pietro Pomponazzi's position in his treatise *De naturalium effectuum causis sive de incantationibus* (1520), the culmination of the secular Aristotelian debate on occult phenomena. Pomponazzi felt that the philosopher must give a rational account of the many reports of extraordinary effects that cannot be attributed to fraud; because demons are excluded from such explanations on epistemological (demons cannot know singulars) and physical (demons are incapable of contact action) grounds, only astrological influences or other natural forms of occult causation remain. The *De incantationibus*, along with the *De fato*, also written around 1520, shows how Pomponazzi's desire to reduce all human experience to strictly natural causes gave enormous scope to astrology. Going beyond the condemned propositions of Siger of Brabant, Pomponazzi argued that the stars rule not only nature but also history, even sacred history; a horoscope can account for the rise of Christianity, as of any religion. In the third book of *De fato*, Pomponazzi presented alternatives to the rigid determinism that governed man as a merely natural being, but in the larger context of his work these attempts to repair the damage to free will ring hollow.[19]

If Pico's efforts to naturalise astrology had tended to limit the astrologer's pretensions, Pomponazzi's programme of naturalisation had the opposite effect. All terrestrial events had celestial causes; even God's effects on earthly affairs were mediated astrologically; consequent constraints on human freedom were no great concern.[20] Tiberio Russiliano Sesto, a student of Nifo's who heard Pomponazzi lecture in Bologna in 1518, echoed these extreme positions in his *Apologeticus* of 1519. Like Pomponazzi, he criticised Pico's *Disputationes*, but in four hundred theses he tried to emulate the younger Pico of the *Conclusiones*. Tiberio's alteration of Pico's condemned thesis on magic, cabala and divinity shows how the secular Aristotelian embrace of a naturalised occultism could accommodate and transform other occultist traditions: 'Through no department of knowledge will we be able to gain more certainty of *the coming* of Christ than through magic, *by which all things sublunar are recognised*.' By retaining *magia* – defined as a means of distinguishing the sublunary from the celestial – but omitting cabala, Tiberio proclaimed his naturalism, and by specifying Christ's *adventus* rather than his *divinitas*, he alluded to that feature of a determinist

universitatibus legitur et ibidem apparent res terribiles, et difficile est salvare talia per fundamenta peripatetica'; *ibid.*, pp. 129–71; *Scienze, credenze* 1982, pp. 300–5, 313–17, 352–68 (Zambelli); Zanier 1975b, pp. 31–2; Thorndike 1923–58, v, pp. 75–84, 162–4, 182–8.

19. Zanier 1975b, pp. 1–16; Pine 1973, pp. 4–6, 12, 33; Graiff 1976, pp. 331–2, 335, 344–50, 356; Garin 1976c, pp. 116–17; Thorndike 1923–58, v, p. 97; Shumaker 1982, pp. 59–63.
20. Garin 1976c, pp. 109–11; Cassirer 1927, pp. 85–7, 110–12.

naturalism that Pico most detested, the referring of the central events of sacred history to the agency of the stars. Since the *uniqueness* of Christianity could never be proved by horoscopic techniques that applied equally to other religions, astrological explanations of the *facts* of Christian history were cold comfort for the orthodox: no wonder that critics of Pomponazzi and his followers preferred the demons to the stars.[21]

FICINO'S PHILOSOPHICAL THEORY OF MAGIC

To supplement their thorough knowledge of Peripatetic doctrine, Nifo, Pomponazzi, Russiliano and other Aristotelian philosophers could look not only to the later Neoplatonic sources which Ficino had translated and published in 1497 but also to Ficino's elaboration in 1489 of a comprehensive and philosophically grounded theory of magic in *De vita coelitus comparanda*. This work is the fullest Renaissance exposition of a theory of magic and the most influential such statement written in post-classical times. In its final chapter, Ficino explained how

nature is a magician, as Plotinus and Synesius say, everywhere baiting traps with particular foods for particular objects . . . The farmer prepares his field and seeds for gifts from heaven and uses various grafts to prolong life in his plant and change it to a new and better species. The physician, the scientist and the surgeon bring about similar effects in our bodies . . . The philosopher, who is learned in natural science and astronomy and whom we are wont rightly to call a magician, likewise implants heavenly things in earthly objects by means of certain alluring charms used at the right moment.[22]

Ficino took natural magic to be as much the province of the natural philosopher as cosmology, astronomy or matter-theory. The wisdom of the *magus* and the learning of the *philosophus* were distinguishable but interdependent parts of the same enterprise whose magical and philosophical content Ficino derived from the same sources in his *prisca sapientia* – including Plato himself, as comparison of the passage above with the

21. Tiberio's *Apologeticus*, cited in Zambelli 1977, p. 13: 'Per nullam scientiam de adventu Christi magis certificari poterimus quam per magiam, per quam omnia sublunaria cognoscuntur'; *ibid.*, pp. 9–21, 24–9, 48; Zanier 1975b, pp. 33–7, 42–3, 48–9, 80–4; 1979, pp. 211–25; see also n. 15 above.
22. Ficino 1576, I, p. 570: 'Ubique igitur natura maga est, ut inquit Plotinus atque Synesius, videlicet certa quaedam pabulis ubique certis inescans . . . agricultura praeparat agrum seminaque ad coelestia dona et insitionibus quibusdam vitam plantae propagat et ad speciem alteram melioremque perducit. Similia quaedam efficit et medicus, physicus et chirurgus in corpore nostro . . . Idem quoque philosophus, naturalium rerum astrorumque peritus, quem proprie magum appellare solemus, certis quibusdam illecebris coelestia terrenis opportune quidem, nec aliter inserens quam . . . agricola'; Plotinus, *Enneads* IV.4.40, 43–4; Synesius, *De insomniis* 132D; a fuller bibliography for this section on Ficino may be seen in Copenhaver 1984, 1986, forthcoming a and b.

following text from his commentary on the *Symposium* will reveal. 'Why', asks Ficino,

do we think that Love is a magician? Because all the power of magic consists in love. An act of magic is the attraction of one thing by another in accordance with a certain natural kinship. The parts of this world, . . . the organs of this enormous living being . . . borrow and loan each other's natures. Common love grows out of common kinship, and common attraction is born of love. This is true magic . . . Acts of magic, therefore, are acts of nature, and art is her handmaid . . . Out of natural love all nature gets the name magician.

Although the idea of erotic magic as a cosmic force was already explicit in Diotima's conversation with Socrates, Ficino's analysis of the *Symposium* strengthened and extended it under the influence of Plotinus, Synesius and other Neoplatonists, whose contributions to Ficino's theory of magic are fundamental.[23]

De vita coelitus comparanda is an excursus from Ficino's commentary on Plotinus; he attached it as book III to a medical treatise whose first two sections were devoted to health and longevity. In the first chapter of *De vita* III, which deals with celestial means for improving human life, Ficino wished to establish the basis of astrological causation – and thence of all natural magical action – in intermediation among terrestrial, celestial and supercelestial entities. His starting-point was *Enneads* IV.3.11, in which Plotinus had briefly mentioned the magical animation of cult-statues as a specific instance of soul's ability to affect body, the latter issue being Plotinus' subject in the ten preceding chapters of *Enneads* IV.3.[24] Ficino, who misdated the *Hermetica* and considered Hermes Trismegistus the primeval source of Platonism, surely recalled the god-making passages of the Hermetic *Asclepius* when he read what Plotinus said about the statues. No doubt he realised that an ensouled statue posed threats and promised powers much as an astrological talisman, which for philosophical as well as religious reasons was a crux in Ficino's argument, a limiting case of natural magic. Whatever his interest in the statues when he encountered them in Plotinus, Ficino delayed mentioning their Hermetic avatars until the

23. Ficino 1956, pp. 220–1 (VI.10): 'Sed cur magum putamus amorem? Quia tota vis magice in amore consistit. Magice opus est attractio rei unius ab alia ex quadam cognatione nature. Mundi autem huius partes, . . . ingentis huius animalis membra . . . mutuant invicem naturas et mutuantur. Ex communi cognatione communis innascitur amor, ex amore communis attractio. Hec autem vera magica est . . . Magice igitur opera nature opera sunt; ars vero ministra . . . Et natura omnis ex amore mutuo maga cognominatur'; Plato, *Symposium* 202E–203D; Zambelli 1973a, pp. 128–30; *Magia, astrologia e religione* 1974, pp. 60–1, 70 (Zambelli).
24. Ficino 1576, I, pp. 529–33, 573; Plotinus, *Enneads* IV.3.1–11; Ficino 1937, I, pp. xii, lxxxiv; *Umanesimo e esoterismo* 1960, p. 18 (Garin); Walker 1958, p. 3, n. 2; see n. 36 below.

midpoint of *De vita* III.[25] In the beginning of this book, he concentrated instead on the metaphysics and psychology of Plotinus, particularly his notion of λόγοι σπερματικοί.

Plotinus claimed that these seminal reasons, associated with Soul as intermediary between Mind and Body, linked species or forms in matter with ideas in Mind. Seminal reasons were the dynamic terms in a system of causation and communication joining material objects to immaterial ideas through the medium of Soul. 'The soul of the world', explained Ficino, 'possesses at least as many seminal reasons of things as there are ideas in the divine mind, and with these reasons [Soul] makes the same number of species in matter. Thus, each and every species corresponds through its own seminal reason to an idea, and often through this reason it can easily receive something of value from on high.' Equipped with this metaphysical information, the philosopher-magician had reason to manipulate species of material objects to attract the higher immaterial powers with which they are joined through Soul and its λόγοι.[26] But because the Peripatetic concept of substantial form was the key to his theory of magic, it was also important to Ficino that the magical junction between matter and Mind should reach the form of things as well as their species; it was convenient, then, that the same word, εἶδος, served Plotinus for both 'form' and 'species'. Ficino believed with Thomas Aquinas that the substantial form of a material object – the principle that makes the object what it is, a member of its species – is educed from the potency of its matter by the power of the heavenly bodies. Although the first eleven chapters of *Enneads* IV.3 established a connection between lower forms in matter and higher immaterial forms, Ficino also needed Neoplatonic support for his claim that these higher forms included *figurae* in the heavens, i.e., the zodiac, the decans, the planetary conjunctions and oppositions.[27]

Ficino found the necessary evidence in the last third of *Enneads* IV.4. In order to acquit the gods of complicity in the base affairs of mortals, Plotinus argued in these chapters (which contain a coherent theory of magic) that the efficacy of prayer and magic does not prove that the gods intend the effects

25. Ficino 1576, I, pp. 548, 561, 571; *Asclepius* 23–4, 37–8; Plotinus, *Enneads* IV.3.11.1–6; Walker 1958, p. 41, n. 2; 1972, pp. 1–2, 10–14, 18, 20–1.
26. Ficino 1576, I, p. 531: 'anima mundi totidem saltem rationes rerum seminales divinitus habet quot ideae sunt in mente divina, quibus ipsa rationibus totidem fabricat species in materia. Unde unaquaeque species per propriam rationem seminalem propriae respondet ideae, facileque potest per hanc saepe aliquid illinc accipere'; *ibid.*, pp. 571–2; *Umanesimo e esoterismo* 1960, pp. 19–23 (Garin).
27. Ficino 1576, I, pp. 531–2, II, pp. 1737, 1746; Plotinus, *Enneads* IV.4.35.67.9; Thomas Aquinas, *Summa theologiae* 1.65.4 resp.; 91.2 *ad* 3; 115.3 *ad* 2; II–II.96.2 *ad* 2; *De occultis operibus naturae* 9–11; Sleeman and Pollet 1980, cols. 290–300; Copenhaver 1984, pp. 535–8, 541–6.

of these human acts. The response to a magical charm comes not intentionally from heavenly will but spontaneously from the organic sympathies that bind the living cosmos together. Of the metaphors illustrating Plotinus' reasoning, the most intricate compares the cosmos to a dancer; changes in the cosmos to changes in a dancer's body; and configurations (σχηματισμοί) of parts of the cosmos (stars and planets) to a dancer's gestures. The stars in a celestial figure no more cause the events signified by the figure than the dancer's gesturing limb causes what the dancer's whole body communicates. The dancer and the cosmos are the true causes of meanings communicated and events signified, but as the dancer thinks beyond particular gestures to the whole performance, so the cosmos has no intention of forming the physical figures made up of stars, much less the terrestrial events influenced by the figures. Weaving an elaborate fabric of puns, Plotinus applied the word σχῆμα not only to the dancer's gestures but also to the stellar and planetary figures; more broadly, his σχῆμα referred to any figure, shape or form.[28]

Thus, the celestial σχήματα of Plotinus are also εἴδη or forms; they participate as λόγοι of soul in the system of psychic intermediation set forth in the first part of *Enneads* IV.3. Since lower forms celestially educed in matter also qualify as λόγοι, the Plotinian apparatus of form, figure, λόγος and species satisfied certain requirements that Ficino had established for a naturally efficacious talisman: 'A talisman (*imago*) will be more effective if the elementary power in its matter is well adapted to the specific power naturally implanted in the same matter and if this also adapts to the other specific power to be received through a figure from the action of the heavens.' A gem carved with a zodiacal figure meets the requirement for cosmic conformity if its substantial or specific form adapts, as a member of the same species, to a figure or form in the heavens. In Plotinian terms, the λόγος that is the εἴδος of the gem is in the same order with the λόγος that is a σχῆμα made of stars.[29] Ficino's other requirements, however, were for ontological conformity between the specific form educed in the gem and the elementary material constituents of the gem; and for taxonomic conformity between the *figura* carved on the gem and a celestial figure of the same species.

The abject status of matter in the metaphysics of Plotinus ruled out a

28. Ficino 1576, II, pp. 1745–6; Plotinus, *Enneads* IV.4.31–7; Sleeman and Pollet 1980, cols. 983–6; *Umanesimo e esoterismo* 1960, p. 29 (Garin); Walker 1958, p. 3, n. 2; Copenhaver 1986.
29. Ficino 1576, I, p. 554: 'Praeterea imaginem efficaciorem fore si virtus in materia eius elementaris conveniat cum speciali eiusdem virtute naturaliter insita, atque haec insuper cum virtute altera speciali per figuram coelitus capienda'; *ibid.*, pp. 531–2, 542, 552, 558, II, p. 1746; Plotinus, *Enneads* IV.4.34.9–11, 33–8; 35.4–8, 12–22, 65–70; 40.14–19.

strong, active relationship between material qualities and substantial form, so Ficino had to seek his ontological conformity elsewhere, in the Peripatetic and scholastic conception of hylemorphic composition. And to give fuller meaning to the notion of taxonomic kinship between artificial and celestial figures of the same kind, he turned to Thomas Aquinas as well as Proclus, both of whom treated various aspects of this question in more detail than Plotinus.[30] Before seeing how Proclus and Thomas Aquinas contributed to Ficino's magic, it will be useful first to examine the uses of Iamblichus, Synesius and the *Chaldaean Oracles* in *De vita* III, for these later Neoplatonic texts also led Ficino in directions not set by the *Enneads*.

All magic for Plotinus was natural magic, nothing more nor less than the realisation of cosmic sympathies. Plotinus never mentioned theurgy, a magical approach to divinity introduced by Porphyry, so he had no reason to sort out good religious magic from bad demonic magic. Although magic is not a fit occupation for the sage because its concerns are merely material, it is not bad as such; any evil that comes of magic is human evil. In the first part of his treatise *De insomniis* (which Ficino translated and whose pneumatology he exploited), Synesius recapitulated the magic-theory of *Enneads* IV.4 but emphasised its moral dangers. He distinguished a good magic that freed man from matter from a bad magic that trapped him in it.[31] Similarly, in *De mysteriis* (which Ficino also translated) Iamblichus described a lower theurgy and a higher theurgy. The mechanisms and objects of lower theurgy are material, while the higher theurgy to which it leads seeks to transcend matter. While acknowledging the continuity of the two theurgies, Iamblichus preferred the higher to the lower. Moreover, he distinguished theurgy, which aims at contemplating the true forms (εἴδη) of the gods, from thaumaturgy, which merely handles their images (εἴδωλα), and his leading example of false thaumaturgy is εἰδωλοποιία, or statue-making. Ficino knew that Iamblichus shunned statue-magic as dangerous demonolatry and that in condemning this form of thaumaturgy he had in mind the bad Egyptian magic of the *Hermetica*, as opposed to a more refined Chaldaean magic. Ficino cited the *Chaldaean Oracles* together with Synesius for their doctrine of ἴυγγες or *illices*, immaterial magical baits that paralleled the function of the Plotinian λόγοι in bringing higher powers earthward.[32]

---

30. Deck 1967, pp. 74–7; *Cambridge History* 1970, p. 256 (A. H. Armstrong); see n. 27 above; nn. 34–5, 39–42 below.
31. Ficino 1576, I, pp. 549, 570–1, II, p. 1969; Plotinus, *Enneads* IV.4.40.1–12, 42.14–17, 43.12–19; Synesius, *De insomniis* 131A 7–9, 132C 3–5, 132D 10–13, 133B 14–C 2; A. Smith 1974, pp. 92–4, 122–7, 147; A. H. Armstrong 1955–6, p. 77; Dodds 1968, pp. 285, 291–5; Walker 1958, p. 39, n. 1.
32. Ficino 1576, I, pp. 530–1, 551, 558, 571, 573, II, pp. 1890–2; Synesius, *De insomniis* 132C 3–4; Iamblichus, *De mysteriis* 91.9–15, 130.3–6, 167.9–176.2, 190.8–12, 246.16–248.2; *Chaldaean Oracles*

Ficino also called attention to Iamblichus' repudiation of the deceitful and demon-ridden Egyptians in the concluding chapter of *De vita* III, but in the same place he associated the same Hermetic statue-magic with the Plotinian metaphysics that he so much admired. On the specific topic of the Hermetic statues as on the broader question of talismanic magic, Ficino ended his treatise ambiguously, and his ambiguity was probably a product of his having been the first Latin philosopher since antiquity to have read in Greek not just Plotinus but most of the surviving texts of Neoplatonism. Had a lesser erudition permitted him to base his theory of magic only on Plotinus, he might have avoided the temptation implicit in the higher theurgy of Iamblichus. This religiously motivated magic, which aimed loftily at contemplation and union with the divine, could only have been seductive for the Platonist in Ficino, but the Christian in him must have trembled to approach heaven on paths not blessed by the church. And as a reader of Iamblichus, Ficino must also have known that later Neoplatonism compromised the very idea of a natural magic immune to demonic influence. For Iamblichus natural objects have magical power precisely because they are tokens (συνθήματα) or signs (σύμβολα) of demonic and divine presence whose activation is automatic, unconstrained by the magician's intentions.[33] If all magic was natural magic for Plotinus, for his successors there could be no purely natural magic – a problem that Ficino must have understood better than any of his contemporaries.

Another Neoplatonist who treated natural objects as magical tokens of the divine was Proclus, whose Περὶ τῆς καθ' ''Ελληνας ἱερατικῆς τέχνης Ficino translated under the title *De sacrificio*, imbedding it into his theory of magic in *De vita* III. Proclus' point in *De sacrificio* was that magic had a metaphysical and cosmological basis in various interactions between heavenly and earthly entities. In the *Platonic Theology*, the *Elements of Theology* and other works known to Ficino, Proclus set forth more extensively the philosophical principles outlined in the brief *De sacrificio*.[34] What Proclus wrote about σειραί (chains) or τάξεις (orders) was particularly useful to Ficino in filling out what Plotinus taught about communication between various entities (e.g., the animal lion, a lion carved on a gem,

frgs. 77, 150, 206; Psellus, *Commentarius in Oracula Chaldaica* 1133ᵃ3–ᵇ4, 1149ᵃ10–ᵇ11; G. Pico 1942, p. 152; A. Smith 1974, pp. 90–9, 105–7, 110, 149; Walker 1958, p. 42, n. 3.

33. Ficino 1576, I, pp. 571, II, pp. 1882, 1898–9; Iamblichus, *De mysteriis* 96.11–97.19, 232.5–234.4; Copenhaver forthcoming b; see n. 25 above.

34. Ficino 1576, I, pp. 549–52, 570, II, pp. 1928–9; *Catalogue des manuscrits* 1924–32, VI, pp. 139–51 (Proclus, *De sacrificio*); Proclus, *Elements of Theology* 28–9, 32, 103, 105 in 1963, pp. ix–xi, xx, xxii, 216–19, 222–3, 254; Zintzen 1965, pp. 77–9, 84, 91, 94–6; Rosán 1949, pp. 73, 104–5, 213, 245–54; Copenhaver forthcoming a.

the constellation Leo) within the same species or kind. In *De sacrificio* Proclus described a hierarchical taxonomy of things that make up the universe and a set of rules governing relations among them. The lion and the cock, for example, are in the same solar order whose chief or *henad* is Apollo. The cock crows at sunrise; Leo is a solar constellation. But the cock stands higher than the lion in the solar series because he is a creature of the air, nearer to the sun and clearly receptive to it in his waking behaviour. To ward off the lion-faced Apollonian demon who haunts the noon hour, it will therefore be effective to carve a cock on sunstone. Ficino described this and other instances of Proclus' chains or orders:

> From each and every star . . . there depends a series of things proper to it, even to the very lowest. Under the heart of Scorpio, after its demons and its men and the animal scorpion, we can also locate the plant aster . . . Under Sirius, the solar star, come first the Sun, then Phoebean demons as well, which sometimes appeared to men in the form of lions or cocks, as Proclus testifies . . . And there is no reason why the lion fears the cock except that in the Phoebean order the cock is higher than the lion. For the same reason, says Proclus, the Apollonian demon, who sometimes appeared in the shape of a lion, immediately disappeared when a cock was displayed.[35]

Ficino's magic, which may seem bizarre and idiosyncratic, is actually based on his original and subtle analysis of important philosophical positions from respected and authoritative thinkers such as Proclus and Plotinus.

Contrary to common opinion, however, Ficino's theory of magic in *De vita* III cannot reasonably be called Hermetic any more than it can be called Galenic or Thomist, even though (as we shall see) these latter adjectives are less misplaced than the former. Although he had translated fourteen of the Hermetic discourses into Latin early in his career, his intimate knowledge of the Greek *Hermetica* led Ficino to cite them nowhere in his treatise on magic, where he seldom mentions the name of Hermes Trismegistus. None of the three passages (only two actually mention Hermes) that refer to the god-making texts of the Latin *Asclepius* is unambiguously favourable to the thrice-great Mercurius – and no wonder, since Ficino had doubts about

---

35. Ficino 1576, I, pp. 549–50: 'desuper ab unaquaque stella . . . seriem rerum illi propriam usque ad extrema pendere. Sub ipso Scorpionis corde post eiusmodi daemonas atque homines scorpiumque animal, collocare possumus etiam herbam asterion . . . Sub stella solari, id est Syrio, solem primo, deinde daemonas quoque Phoebeos, quos aliquando sub leonum vel gallorum forma hominibus occurrisse, testis est Proclus . . . Nec alia ratione leo veretur gallum nisi quoniam in ordine Phoebeo gallus est leone superior. Eadem ratione, inquit Proclus, Apollineum daemonem, qui nonnunquam apparuit sub figura leonis, statim obiecto gallo disparuisse'; *Catalogue des manuscrits* 1924–32, VI, p. 150 (Proclus, *De sacrificio*); Proclus, *Elements of Theology* 140–5 in 1963, pp. xvii, 129, 208–9, 257–60, 267, 273; Rosán 1949, pp. 67, 85–7, 104; Walker 1958, pp. 49–50.

talismans operating naturally, let alone idols working demonically.[36] As for the other Greek treatises, anyone who reads them will understand why Ficino failed to cite them in a philosophical work devoted to the theory of magic. Ficino's *Hermetica* are not about magic, and what philosophy they contain is of small interest; they are banal expressions of a spirituality whose main concerns were theology, cosmogony, cosmology, anthropogony, anthropology, psychology, ethics, soteriology and eschatology. Although some of the treatises allude to ingredients of the magical worldview that was a given in the Hellenistic culture that produced them, these few astrological and magical commonplaces could be of little theoretical value to Ficino, especially when compared to the riches he found in Proclus or Plotinus. From a philosophical point of view, even the non-magical piety of the *Hermetica* is eclectic and incoherent: unlike the Neoplatonic systems with which it is often confused, the *corpus Hermeticum* has little to offer anyone who requires a consistent conceptual and terminological framework for analysis of the problems it presents. As far as Renaissance magic was concerned, the chief task of Hermes Trismegistus was genealogical or doxographic. Along with Zoroaster (to whom Ficino usually gives priority as an inventor of magic), Orpheus, Plato and other *prisci sapientes*, Hermes could lend eponymous authority to the practice of magic even if his contributions to its theory were slight.[37]

More significant were the two god-making passages that Ficino (like Augustine) found in the Latin *Asclepius* and described in the culminating chapter of *De vita* III. His ambivalence about the Hermetic statues was ethical and religious, not physical or metaphysical; he doubted their legitimacy, but he did not seriously question their efficacy. To them as to astrological talismans he granted the power to attract celestial gifts. But because the statues were pagan idols inhabited by demons and constructed

36. Ficino 1576, I, pp. 548, 561, 571–2, II, pp. 1836–71; Marcel 1958, pp. 255–8, 487–96, 747–9; Ficino 1937, I, pp. cxxix–cxxxi; cf. Yates 1964, pp. 28–35; see also Kristeller 1956a, pp. 223–4, 233; 1960, pp. 3–10; *Catalogus translationum* 1960–, I, pp. 137–56; Walker 1972, pp. 13–21; Lefèvre d'Étaples 1972, pp. 134–7; Purnell 1976, pp. 155–8; Grafton 1983, pp. 88–92; see nn. 31–3 above; nn. 39–42 below.

37. Ficino 1576, I, pp. 25, 156, 268, 386, 673, 854, 871–2, II, pp. 1537, 1836; Festugière 1944–54, II, pp. 5, 7, 10, 44–7, IV, pp. 54–78; 1967, pp. 34–40, 53–5, 66–7; Copenhaver forthcoming a and c. Other references in *De vita coelitus comparanda* (pp. 540–1, 550) are not to the Greek treatises that Ficino translated or to the Latin *Asclepius* but to works classified among the 'popular' – as opposed to 'philosophical' – *Hermetica* by Festugière 1944–54, II, p. 1; 1967, pp. 30–2. Claims (to my mind dubious) for a stronger relation than Festugière would allow between the popular and the philosophical treatises have been made by Yates 1964, p. 44, n. 2, and Garin 1977, pp. 342–4. For the debate on Hermeticism, see also Garin 1976b, pp. 462–6; 1976c, pp. 44, 52, 73–4, 81; Westman and McGuire 1977; Schmitt 1981, §IV; Copenhaver 1978b; Vickers 1979; *Occult and Scientific Mentalities* 1984, pp. 1–6 (Vickers).

as part of a religious fraud, it was difficult not to put them beyond the line that divides unarguably sinful demonic magic from conceivably licit natural magic. Talismans, if cleared of demonic influence, are the limiting case of natural magic that falls on the safer side of the line: to certify their legitimacy and his orthodoxy, Ficino called on Thomas Aquinas.[38]

Unlike Augustine, who objected even to undecorated amulets, Thomas in the *Summa contra gentiles* grudgingly and briefly admitted that certain decorated talismans might be permissible to Christians if they were not addressed to demons. If the marks on a talisman are signs – words, for example – that can only be directed to another personal intelligence, then the being addressed must be an evil spirit. But if the marks are pictures – zodiacal *figurae*, for instance – their activity need not involve persons. The figure of a lion cut into a stone awakens the powers of the celestial Leo (another *figura* or σχῆμα in Plotinian terms) because the carving of the lion on the stone places the talisman in the same species with the heavenly lion. Ficino explains Thomas' position in this way: he thinks that a talisman gains celestial power through its figure

not so much because such a figure is in this matter as because such a composite object has now been situated in some particular species of the artificial such that it conforms to the heavens. [Thomas] says this in book III of the *Contra gentiles*, where he ridicules characters and letters added to figures, but figures not so much unless in place of certain signs they are directed to demons.[39]

The 'composite object' of which Ficino writes is a substance, the hylemorphic union of matter and form. To say that substantial form makes the composite what it is, is, from another point of view, to say that this object belongs to a species of like objects; 'substantial form' and 'specific form' are names for different aspects of the same principle. But Thomas taught that figure is an accident, not a substance at all, yet it is *like* a substance because it locates the figured artificial composite in a species and because the figure (or shape) of a natural composite gives most information about its

---

38. Ficino 1576, I, pp. 548, 561, 571; *Asclepius* 23–4, 37–8; Augustine, *De civitate Dei* VIII.24; see nn. 32–3 above.
39. Ficino 1576, I, p. 558: 'Thomas . . . minus tribuit imaginibus. Tantum namque virtutis duntaxat per figuras coelitus putat acquirere quantum conducat ad illos effectus [naturales] . . . Non tam quia [figura talis] sit in ea materia quam quoniam compositum tale iam positum est in certa quadam artificii specie qualis cum coelo consentiat. Haec ait in libro Contra gentiles tertio, ubi characteres et literas figuris additas ridet, figuras vero non adeo nisi pro signis quibusdam ad daemones adiunguntur'; Thomas Aquinas, *Summa contra gentiles* III.104–5; *Summa theologiae* II–II.96.2 resp., ad 1–2; *De occultis operibus naturae* 14, 17–20; Augustine, *De doctrina Christiana* II.23.36, 29.45; Walker 1958, pp. 42–4; Copenhaver 1984, pp. 528, 531–3 and especially 537, n. 39, where the first eight words of the passage translated are a mistaken interpolation.

species. As Ficino put it, *figura* is *quasi-substantialis*. Thus, in addition to the well-known Thomist doctrine of celestially educed substantial forms, which reinforced the Plotinian principle of cosmic conformity between the εἶδος of the talisman and the σχῆμα in the heavens, Ficino also found in Thomas taxonomic and ontological conformities missing or indefinite in Plotinus. The engraving of the figure put the talisman in the species (the τάξις of Proclus) of its heavenly analogue, thus assuring their taxonomic kinship. And the truly expert *magus*, who had read his Aquinas, would also stimulate an ontological connection by matching a material quality of the talisman, such as its colour, taste or texture, to the series of forms, earthly and heavenly, with which the talisman was meant to communicate. Thomist hylemorphism encouraged the stronger interactivity between matter and form that was impeded by the poverty of matter in the metaphysics of Plotinus.[40]

Other properties of matter indispensable to the *magus* were called *qualitates occultae* or 'hidden qualities' to distinguish them from the 'manifest' features of matter perceptible through the primary (hot, cold, dry, moist) or secondary (soft, hard, sweet, sour, etc.) qualities arising from the four elements and their combinations. Ficino had read the work, *De occultis operibus naturae*, in which Thomas certified the existence and efficacy of occult qualities and associated them with the substantial forms educed in matter by stellar and planetary power. As a physician writing a book on astrological medicine, Ficino also knew that the topic of substantial forms and occult qualities was a favourite in medieval medical literature, where Taddeo Alderotti, Arnald of Villanova, Jacopo da Forlì and many other eminent physicians debated the issue.[41] Occult qualities had entered the medical tradition secondarily from Avicenna's *Canon* but originally from Galen, who called them ἰδιότητες ἄρρητοι or 'undescribable properties'.

40. Ficino 1576, I, p. 555: 'Sed ne figuris nimium forte diffidas, meminisse iubebunt, in regione hac sub luna elementari, elementarem quoque qualitatem posse quam plurimum in transmutatione videlicet ad aliquid elementare tendente, calorem scilicet et frigus et humorem atque siccitatem. Qualitas autem quae minus elementares materialesve sunt, scilicet lumina, id est colores, numeros quoque similiter et figuras, ad talia forsitan minus posse, sed ad coelestia munera, ut putant, valere permultum. Nam et in coelo lumina et numeri et figurae sunt ferme omnium potentissima . . . Sic enim figurae, numeri, radii, quum non alia sustineantur ibi materia, qua[s]i substantiales esse videntur'; Thomas Aquinas, *Summa contra gentiles* II.58.92; III.104; *Summa theologiae* I.3.7 resp.; 7.1 ad 2; 50.2 ad 1–2; 65.4 resp.; 76.3, resp.; 85.5 ad 3; 118.2 ad 2; *Commentarium in Physica*, lib. 7, lect. 5; *Commentarium in Metaphysica*, lib. 7, lect. 2; *De occultis operibus naturae* 7, 9, 11, 14; Copenhaver 1984, pp. 539–46; see nn. 27, 29, 30 above.
41. Ficino 1576, I, pp. 558, 562, 573; Thomas Aquinas, *Summa theologiae* I.45.8 resp.; 65.4 resp.; 115.3 ad 2; *Commentarium in De generatione*, lib. 1, lect. 8; *Commentarium in De anima*, lib. 2, lect. 14; Siraisi 1981, pp. 64–6, 141–2, 146, 150–61, 179, 258; Zanier 1977, pp. 21, 23, 47; Hutchison 1982, pp. 233–53; Copenhaver 1984, pp. 539, 542–9.

Galen believed that he could explain many medical phenomena by reducing them to the elements and manifest qualities of post-Aristotelian matter-theory. But because certain problems – various drugs, foods, poisons, antidotes and amulets, for example – resisted this reductive strategy, Galen reluctantly referred them to qualities that he could not describe, and he connected such qualities with action καθ' ὅλην τὴν οὐσίαν, 'from the whole substance'. The great Moslem physicians eventually (and reasonably) identified Galen's whole substance with Aristotle's substantial or specific form, thus opening another channel of magical activity for Ficino's astral medicine.[42] Given the well-established medical teaching on occult qualities and substantial forms, which was respectable enough to convince even St Thomas, Ficino could confidently forge another link in his magical chain of causation binding earthly to heavenly objects.

To complete this review of magical principles that Ficino found in authoritative philosophical and medical texts, we may end with the topics of πνεῦμα or *spiritus* and imagination. The basic function of *spiritus*, conceived as tenuous matter or crass spirit or something in between, was to bridge the gap between man's material and immaterial components. Since Galen's time, the concept of medical spirits, based on Peripatetic and Stoic sources, had accounted for various physiological and psychological processes without obligatory reference to magical action, but Galen also knew that Plato's description of the ὄχημα or vehicle of the soul implied an astrological context for spirits. Since the Stoic πνεῦμα operated as a principle of coherence both in the cosmos and in the human microcosm, it was natural for the Neoplatonists to expand Plato's idea into the fully developed doctrine of the astral body of the soul, an aetheric or spiritual garment accreted by the soul as it descends through the stars and planets into an earthly body. The astral origins of this spiritual vehicle enhance magical capacities implicit even in the innocent medical spirits, which, because they unite things held separate under normal requirements for contact action, helped explain phenomena otherwise unexplainable. Thus, Ficino used medical *spiritus* to account naturalistically for *fascinatio* or the evil eye, but he also employed the magical consonance between cosmic and human spirits to show how music of proper astrological proportions acting through the medium of *spiritus* could awaken a beneficent resonance between a man and

---

42. Galen 1821, VIII, pp. 339–40 (*De locis affectis* v.6), XII, pp. 192, 356 (*De simplicium medicamentorum temperamentis* IX.1.4, XI.1.34), XIX, pp. 677–8 (*De renum affectibus*); Avicenna 1507, f. 33; Röhr 1923, pp. 95, 99, 108–13; Copenhaver 1984, pp. 525–6, 540–1.

a planet, which always emits a music of its own.[43] If *spiritus* is the basic medium for Ficino's magic, man's chief magical faculty is the imagination, which as the Peripatetic common sense or as fantasy links corporeal objects to the incorporeal subject, soul or mind. Since imagination, a faculty of the lower soul, transmits sense data from material objects to the immaterial mind, it is closer to matter than the higher faculties of will and intellect and hence more sensitive to astral influences that act directly on matter but not on soul. Thus, when Ficino read in Avicenna that imagination could act outside the body of the subject and in Synesius that an imaginative πνεῦμα constitutes the soul's astral body, he had important confirmations for his theory of astrological magic.[44]

PHILOSOPHY AND OCCULTISM IN THE LATER RENAISSANCE

Given the propensity of Renaissance thinkers to infer the value of an idea from its age (a habit of mind whose strongest expression was the *prisca sapientia* that Ficino helped make famous), it is difficult to exaggerate the influence of the revival of ancient learning on the renaissance of occultism – in particular, the realisation that Greek and Latin philosophers gave serious consideration to magic, astrology and demonology and often admitted their reality. Although Ficino called on various scholastic and Moslem authorities – Thomas Aquinas, Albertus Magnus, Alkindi, the *Picatrix* – in composing *De vita* III, for a man of his humanist commitments the absence of classical testimony would have made a philosophical theory of magic unthinkable. The newest and most prominent witnesses were the Neoplatonists whom Ficino introduced to the Latin West, but the humanist impulse to return to the sources also stimulated a closer scrutiny of other texts, including some familiar to the Middle Ages, that nourished the debate on occultism. Through the medical writers and the Neoplatonists, fragmentary evidence of Stoic views on πνεῦμα influenced Ficino's magical *spiritus*, and Pomponazzi cited 'the opinion that the Stoics held . . . that all

---

43. Ficino 1576, I, pp. 178, 555, 562–3, 612, II, pp. 1357–8, 1453, 1885; Walker 1958, pp. 3–18, 38–40; 1985, § x, pp. 120–3; *Spiritus* 1984, pp. 223–6 (Walker); Culianu 1981, pp. 369–72, 389–94; see n. 14 above; see also M. J. B. Allen 1984a, pp. 25–7 for the special connection between music and demons in Ficino.
44. Ficino 1576, I, pp. 562, 609, 651; Thomas Aquinas, *Summa theologiae* I.111.3–4; 114.4; Avicenna 1507, f. 33ᵛ; Kristeller 1953a, pp. 250, 392; Klein 1970, pp. 65–72; Walker 1958, pp. 38–40, 76–80; E. R. Harvey 1975, pp. 49–50.

things are subject to fate such that all are foreseen and preordained by God'.
Telesio and his follower (see below) took inspiration from the Presocratics
for a matter-theory which, by challenging Peripatetic hylemorphism,
weakened one of the traditional foundations of magic but also engendered
new reasons for belief in magical vitalism. Newly translated pseudo-
Pythagorean texts like the *De mundi anima* attributed to Timaeus of Locri
and the *De universi natura* assigned to Ocellus of Lucania, as well as the
biographies of Pythagoras by Porphyry and Iamblichus, lent philosophical
authority to geomancy, numerology, cabala and other occult sciences
associated especially with Pythagoras. Astrology, by contrast, stood
threatened when Giovanni Pico's nephew, Gianfrancesco, became the first
Latin writer to take full advantage of the sceptical attack on astrology in the
Adversus mathematicos of Sextus Empiricus. Although medieval scholars
knew the philosophical medicine of Galen, the Renaissance knew more of it
and knew it better in the original Greek. Medical and philosophical
philology bore magical fruit in the work of Jean Fernel, whose *De abditis
rerum causis* (1548) is an apotheosis of occult qualities based on a close analysis
of such key terms as ἰδιότητες ἄρρητοι and καθ᾽ ὅλην τὴν οὐσίαν in Galen and
Pseudo-Alexander of Aphrodisias.[45]

But for Fernel, as for most proponents or opponents of magic, the most
authoritative (if not the most abundant) texts were to be found in Aristotle
or Plato. Fernel took a whole chapter of *De abditis* to argue 'out of Aristotle
that the forms and first substances of all things are drawn from heaven'.
Fernel's opponent, Thomas Erastus, who understood the importance to his
rival of Aristotle's doctrine of forms, remarked that 'Aristotle would have
left us a better philosophy if he had understood the true origin of forms . . .
[which is] not from the heavens by the cycles of the stars . . . [but from]
God's command.' While Erastus chose to refute the authorities with whom
he disagreed – Aristotle, Plato, Galen, Avicenna, Thomas Aquinas –
another tactic was to assert that occultism was simply beneath the
philosopher's dignity.[46] Giovanni Pico, who knew better, used this
rhetorical ploy in the *Disputationes*, claiming that 'Plato and Aristotle . . .

45. Pomponazzi 1957, p. 190: 'Superest igitur . . . pertractare opinionem quam Stoici tenuerunt . . .
    quod omnia subsunt fato sic quod omnia sunt praevisa et a Deo praeordinata'; Walker 1958, pp. 12,
    38; 1985, § x, pp. 123–6; Verbeke 1945, pp. 37, 172–3, 219; Sambursky 1959, pp. 2, 5, 27, 66; n. 56
    below; Heninger 1974, pp. 46–9, 59–61, 234–5; Copenhaver 1977; Schmitt 1967, pp. 49–54; Popkin
    1979, pp. 18–23; Long 1982, pp. 185–6; Fernel 1550, pp. 155–6, 195, 219, 281; Bianchi 1982, pp. 187,
    196–8, exaggerates the differences between Fernel and Galen on occult qualities.
46. Fernel 1550, pp. 101–8 (cap. 8): 'Rerum omnium formas primasque substantias de coelo duci ex
    Aristotele'; Erastus 1574, pp. 31–6, 87–8: 'Si Aristoteles veram formarum originem ita, ut nos
    novimus, percepisset, philosophiam nobis . . . meliorem . . . reliquisset . . . Haec [forma] non ex

thought it unbecoming ever to say a word about [astrology] in all their philosophy, damning it more by their silence than anyone else by speaking or writing.' Modern critics, lacking Pico's intimacy with the texts, have made similar if artless remarks, which are especially misleading in Aristotle's case. Certain methods or traits in Aristotle, particularly his empiricism, and some of his theories, such as the role of contact action in physics, seem to have convinced modern readers that Peripatetic philosophy and occultism are incompatible in principle, but this judgement can only rest on modern notions of magic and astrology that have little to do with the views of Thomas Aquinas, Pomponazzi or Fernel. These thinkers and many others knew the Aristotelian texts that were *loci classici* for the magical worldview of the Renaissance. Besides providing the basic physics and metaphysics for the key doctrines of occult quality and substantial form, Aristotle contributed to belief in astrological influence on earth and man, the life and divinity of the heavenly bodies, the relationship of microcosm to macrocosm, *spiritus*, imagination and the astral body, and the alchemical theory of transmutation. Quoting from the *Meteorology* and *De generatione et corruptione*, John Dee explained how

> the most auncient and wise Philosophers . . . [have] left unto us sufficient proufe and witnesse . . . that mans body, and all other Elementall bodies, are altered, disposed, ordred, pleasured and displeasured by the Influentiall working of the Sunne, Mone and the other Starres and Planets . . . [Aristotle's] *Meteorologicall* bookes are full of . . . demonstrations of the vertue, operation and power of the heavenly bodies.

Aristotle, of course, could also be cited in opposition to occultism, as could Plato, who had combatted the sophists by comparing their deceits to magical tricks. Modern historiography, inspired by Anglo-American empiricism, has generally had less trouble associating the 'idealist' Plato with magic than admitting similar connections for the hard-headed Stagirite. It was clear to Ficino and his Renaissance readers, in any event, that Plato's *eros* was a powerful magic force.[47]

coelo astrorum conversionibus rebus singulis acquiritur . . . sed iussus Dei est ab initio rebus singulis inditus'; Aristotle, *Meteorology* I.2 (339^{a}11–32); *De generatione animalium* III.11 (762^{a}18–20); *Problems* x.15 and 64; *De caelo* I.9 (278^{b}10–17); *Metaphysics* XII.6–8 (1071^{b}2–74^b); Walker 1958, pp. 156–7, 162; Thorndike 1923–58, v, pp. 653–63.

47. G. Pico 1946–52, I, p. 48: 'Plato et Aristoteles . . . indignam putaverunt de qua verbum aliquando facerent tota sua philosophia, plus eam silendo quam quisque voce scriptisve condemnantes'; Dee 1570, sig. b iii^v; Aristotle, *Physics* II.2 and VIII.2 (194^{b}13–14 and 252^{b}25–30); *De caelo* I.3 (270^{b}1–12); *Meteorology* I.4 and II.4 (341^{b}6–25 and 359^{b}28–360^{a}17); Rattansi 1966, pp. 128, 131; cf. Zambelli 1972, p. 280; 1973a, pp. 121–3, 128–30, 135–6; Thorndike 1923–58, I, pp. 24–7, II, 249–54; see nn. 16–21, 23, 46 above; on John Dee, see Clulee 1977 and *Occult and Scientific Mentalities* 1984, pp. 57–71 (Clulee).

If theoreticians of magic and their opponents found support in the philosophical remains of antiquity, the profession of philosophy in the Renaissance also organised its studies along lines that continued to stimulate interest in occultism. Topics well established in most of the standard divisions of philosophy encouraged speculation relevant to occultism. Metaphysicians and natural philosophers studied problems of cosmology, matter-theory, causality, substance, form and quality whose development and resolution shaped the discussion of such central occultist doctrines as astrological influence and occult properties. The freedom of man's will was as contentious for moral philosophy as for astrology. The antithesis between demonology and astrology asserted by Pomponazzi raised grave questions for the theologians. In psychology and philosophical medicine the imaginative faculty of the soul and its spiritual junction with the body were topics of long-standing importance.[48] Gianfrancesco Pico published a treatise *De imaginatione* in 1501 along traditional philosophical lines. Although Gianfrancesco admitted that the fantasy was a target of demonic meddling, for the most part he passed over the magical imagination exploited by Ficino and limited himself to ethical analysis. Around the time when he published *De imaginatione*, Gianfrancesco was writing a more ambitious book that helps explain his reticence on magical imagination. The purpose of the *Examen vanitatis doctrinae gentium*, unpublished until 1520, was to protect Christian faith by destroying pagan philosophy. Continuing in the *Examen* and in *De rerum praenotione* (1506–7) the campaign motivated by Savonarola but interrupted by his uncle's death, Gianfrancesco saw astrology and natural magic as special threats to religion, yet his sceptical fideism did not produce a wholesale denial of occultism. In 1523 he published *Strix sive de ludificatione daemonum*, a dialogue that attributed all magic to demonic deceits and put full credence in witchcraft.[49]

Thus, while Gianfrancesco's scepticism eroded the philosophical grounds for certain occultist beliefs, it posed little threat to occultism as such. In fact, his polemics foreshadowed a new period in the development of the occultist tradition. After (if not because of) the publication of the *Examen*, one sees less reliance on the usual philosophical arguments for magic and astrology, less confidence in their certainty, but more willingness to find new bases for occultist beliefs than to reject them. As in Gianfrancesco's case, disavowals

---

48. See nn. 12–14, 16–21, 27, 30, 40–2, 44 above.
49. G. F. Pico 1984, pp. 8, 11–14, 33–4, 38, 74–5; Schmitt 1967, pp. 191–3; Walker 1958, pp. 147–9; *Damned Art* 1977, pp. 36–40 (Burke).

of occultism in the later Renaissance were almost always partial; even Reginald Scot, who followed Pomponazzi in rejecting demons and then outdid him by dispensing with determinist astrology, repeated a litany on natural magic that can be traced back to Giovanni Pico.[50] In *De incertitudine et vanitate scientiarum* (1526), Agrippa retracted the demonic magic of his earlier *De occulta philosophia* (1510), but in 1533 he published an expanded version of the same work, including the recanted demonology. Agrippa's scepticism about astrology, which predated the original *De occulta philosophia*, was epistemological uncertainty rather than thorough physical and metaphysical criticism. He always doubted astrology but never abandoned it, and his confidence in natural magic remained intact even in *De incertitudine*. A letter written around 1526 reveals the fideism and quietism that motivated *De incertitudine*, whose relation to the younger Pico's similar work remains unclear. 'If the life and fortune of mankind comes from the stars', asked Agrippa, 'why should we worry? Why should we not leave these things to God and the heavens, since they can neither err nor do evil? . . . Let us consign hours and times to God the Father, who established them by his power.' This damping of curiosity about messages from the stars offered no challenge to the theoretical basis of their influence.[51]

It has been argued that Agrippa's scepticism was of a piece with his occultism in that both were anti-rational and merely empirical. Although the latter charge has a basis in anti-magical polemic reaching back to Galen, the former misses a crucial point: that even Agrippa tried to provide a rational theoretical foundation for his magic, chiefly in the first book of *De occulta philosophia*, where most of the philosophical content is lifted from the eminently rational writings of Ficino and the Neoplatonists. Agrippa's demonic magic outreached its Renaissance predecessors in its boldness, but in philosophising about natural magic he merely copied ideas from Ficino and others without developing them. Furthermore, he overwhelmed his blatantly derivative theory with a tonnage of recipes and anecdotes that leave the impression of chaotic wonder-mongering, more in the spirit of Pliny than Plotinus.[52] Paracelsus, whose death in 1541 preceded by a decade *Paracelsus*

50. Scot 1886, pp. 169–73, 236–7; see n. 11 above; *Damned Art* 1977, p. 109–11, 126–9, 132–5 (Anglo).
51. From a *Prognosticon* of Agrippa's published in *Umanesimo e esoterismo* 1960, p. 168 (Zambelli): 'Si ab astris est hominum vita atque fortuna, quid sollicitamur? Quin deo hec et celis (qui nec errare, nec malum agere possunt) relinquimus? . . . linquamus horas et momenta deo patri, qui ea posuit in sua potestate'; *ibid.*, pp. 144–52, 155–6; Nauert 1965, pp. 154, 199, 204–13, 268; Walker 1958, p. 90; see n. 1 above.
52. Garin 1950b, pp. 661–2; Zambelli 1960, pp. 171–2; *Umanesimo e esoterismo* 1960, p. 144 (Zambelli); Nauert 1965, pp. 122–4, 134, 148–9, 200–2, 237–9, 245–8, 261.

the full burgeoning of his fame, followed and surpassed Agrippa in his admiration for German mysticism, his assimilation of Ficinian and Neoplatonic magic and, above all, his forsaking the logic and book learning of Plato, Aristotle and Galen for the sake of observation, experience and the mechanical arts. Paracelsus found the Greek and Latin classics remote in time and space from his own eschatological circumstances. As a German who witnessed the first decades of the Reformation, he wondered how the old books of the pagan South could speak to the New Hebron, the imminent golden age before the end of time in which the adept in medicine, magic and natural philosophy would follow the light of nature towards the perfection of the arts and sciences. When Paracelsus proclaimed that he had more to learn from travelling to observe (*erfahren*) nature and technique in action than from any library, he echoed the devaluation of traditional learning in Agrippa and Gianfrancesco Pico, but he also joined Agrippa in preserving certain elements of the occultist tradition, especially natural magic. From *experientia*, from reading the book of nature in preference to human books, comes *scientia*, a knowledge which is more than the subjective contents of the knower's mind. *Scientia* exists autonomously in the object of experience; much like the substantial form of Avicenna or Thomas Aquinas, it emanates from the stars and defines the object as one of its kind. The identification and manipulation of such terrestrial products of the heavens is natural magic. Just as the models for Paracelsus' *magus* were more scriptural (Moses, Solomon, the μάγοι of Matthew's gospel) than classical, so the epistemology behind his magic had its roots more in the German mysticism of Sebastian Franck than in the pagan mysticism of Plotinus. By emphasising the immediacy of a *scientia* which is as real in the known object as in the knower, Paracelsus transferred to the plane of natural philosophy or natural magic the mystic's direct, inward vision of God's word. Likewise, faith more than learning became the basis of the Paracelsian magician's operation, as of the Christian mystic's union with God. In a later debate between Johannes Kepler and Robert Fludd, this Agrippan-Paracelsian-Teutonic anti-philosophy of magic, mediated by the alchemical spiritualism of Valentin Weigel and Jacob Boehme, earned the new title 'theosophy', a term which describes some of the features of Agrippa's occultism better than the word he chose, *philosophia*.[53] The divergent attitudes of Agrippa, Gianfrancesco Pico and Paracelsus towards

53. Koyré 1971, pp. 133–4, 156–7, 166, 177; R. M. Jones 1959, pp. 133, 141, 148–50, 154, 173, 180; Pagel 1958a, pp. 40–4, 54–65, 80–1, 207–9, 218–27, 284–9, 295–301, 336; Webster 1982, pp. 4–5, 17–23, 48–57, 61, 80–4.

the legitimacy and efficacy of magic converged in a common distrust of traditional philosophical analysis that coloured subsequent explorations of occultism.

In his autobiography, *De vita propria* (1575–6), Girolamo Cardano complained that 'by means of these [philosophical] doctrines . . . men strive . . . to discern the incorporeal form and separate. . . . the souls of things from the physical structure; putting thereby experiments in casuistry . . . before true scientific knowledge, so that out of a limited field of experience they come to far-reaching conclusions'. A few pages later, the author of the encyclopaedic *De subtilitate* (1550) and *De rerum varietate* (1557), reckoning the tally of his life's work, revealed the nature of his 'true scientific knowledge' when he calculated that 'of problems solved or investigated I shall leave something like forty thousand, and of minutiae two hundred thousand'.[54] An equal hunger for the minute, the particular and the manifold filled the twenty chapters of Giambattista Della Porta's *Magia naturalis* (1558, 1589) with 'experiences' and 'experiments' but left little room for theory. In the English translation of 1658, Della Porta's recapitulation of Ficinian and Neoplatonic philosophy occupies only about sixteen of 409 pages. In addition to the famous chapter on optics, Della Porta gave directions for 'experiments' (a physical demonstration of magnetic polarity, a technique for assaying by displacement of water) that sometimes approach the modern sense of the word, but these appeared alongside recipes for preserving cherries and blanching lettuce leaves or advice on

how to procure a shag-hair'd Dog. In sawting time . . . strew their kennels . . . where they lie and couple . . . with the fleeces and hides of beasts; and so, while they continually look upon those sights, they will beget shag whelps like Lions.

Of Della Porta, the organiser of scientific academies and the rival of Galileo, Cassirer wrote that such 'empiricism leads not to the refutation but the codification of magic'.[55]

Della Porta, Cardano, Paracelsus, Fracastoro and other contributors to the sixteenth-century debate on occultism are often counted among the school of Renaissance nature philosophers. The most independent thinker of this group, Bernardino Telesio, taught that observation and sense perception are the only true foundations of philosophy, but his book *De rerum natura iuxta propria principia* (1565, 1586) is the work of a

---

54. Cardano 1962, pp. 215, 219; *Occult and Scientific Mentalities* 1984, pp. 231–3, 242 (Maclean); Thorndike 1923–58, v, pp. 563–79.
55. Della Porta 1658, pp. 1–16, 53, 93, 130, 193, 355–81, 384; Cassirer 1927, pp. 160–1.

metaphysician, not an observer of Della Porta's type. Expertly trained in the Aristotelianism of Padua, Telesio became disenchanted with the Peripatetic style as *a priori* verbalising, and he attempted to replace Aristotle with his own remarkably original system. Some of Telesio's novelties helped discredit ideas that had long been fundamental ingredients of magical thought; others worked to prolong the career of the occultist tradition by opening new explanatory options. Both these consequences of Telesio's revisionism, which was not primarily concerned with occultist issues, were more important for the future of the theory of magic than any of his specific views on astrology or occult qualities. Setting aside the whole armoury of Aristotle's metaphysics as unrelated to sensation, Telesio reduced the principles of his own system to two sensible, active forces, heat and cold, along with matter, a passive substrate. As opposites, heat and cold struggle perpetually for the sole possession of matter; each is equipped for this contest with a *sense* of self-preservation describable mechanically as an intrinsic impulse for existence and expansion (pleasure) and against contraction and annihilation (pain). *Spiritus*, the most powerful combination of heat and matter, became for Telesio a material soul that performs all man's necessary psychological functions. Since this soul is nothing but hot matter, it cannot have the formal, autonomous properties of the Aristotelian-scholastic soul.

Telesio's radical new philosophy encouraged magical thinking not so much because he, like many others, found a place in his system for the ubiquitous *spiritus* as because he provided a new theoretical basis (with precedents in Presocratic and Stoic thought) for the cosmic vitalism that had always been prominent in the occultist worldview. When Telesio said that matter was percipient and supported his claim in mechanical terms of expansion and contraction, his arguments were more like rational analysis than enthusiastic assertion, more like science than poetry. He thus established credible philosophical foundations for the magical 'pansensism' whose fullest expression was Tommaso Campanella's *De sensu rerum et magia* (1620). On the other hand, Telesio's critique of Peripatetic hylemorphism – a common exercise among the nature philosophers – nullified the doctrine of substantial forms and hence diminished the prospects for a coherent theory of occult qualities. Francesco Patrizi aimed another blow at Aristotle's doctrine of forms in his *Discussiones peripateticae* (1581), but the main motive for his anti-Aristotelianism was admiration for Platonism. Patrizi translated Proclus, Hermes Trismegistus and the

Chaldaean Oracles and developed a cosmic psychology reminiscent of the teachings on *anima mundi* to be found in those writings.[56]

Although Giordano Bruno echoed his Italian contemporaries in criticising Peripatetic hylemorphism and revived earlier arguments of Giovanni Pico in sometimes objecting to astrology, the general tenor of his work was strongly sympathetic to occultism, whether in later writings specifically addressed to magic (*De magia; Theses de magia; De vinculis in genere*, 1590–1) or in earlier books (*De umbris idearum*, 1582; *Lo spaccio de la bestia trionfante*, 1584; *Lampas triginta statuarum*, 1586–8) of broader content. In a decade of prolific writing, Bruno's ideas changed and sometimes conflicted as intellectual passions drove him from enthusiasm to enthusiasm. Inconsistency of thought and idiosyncrasy of form will make any catalogue of Bruno's mind disorderly. He preserved Aristotle's terminology of matter and form, for example, even though he gave matter a privileged, divinised status alien to Aristotelian philosophy. Bruno saw matter as a real substantial principle – stable, persistent, capable of receiving all forms and therefore nobler and more durable than any limited form that must eventually disappear. Disregarding individual species and genus as illusions of merely logical diversity, he concluded that the forms indicated by these notional distinctions lacked substantiality. From such a critique of substantial form to Molière's jokes about dormitive virtue it was a small step but a perilous one for the theory of magic.[57] Yet Bruno's anti-Aristotelianism opened no breach with occultism.

On the contrary, his disenchantment with Aristotle made him receptive to Neoplatonic and Hermetic authorities even friendlier to a magical worldview. Thus, the same Bruno who discarded substantial form as an inefficacious accident of matter accepted Ficino's position on seminal reasons as the basis of occult virtues. The whole Ficinian theory reappeared in Bruno, who added his own touches (Lullism, the art of memory, a more extravagant Hermetism) and ignored the constraints of orthodoxy. He placed Ficino's seminal reasons among the links (*vincula*) that bind man not only to the stars but also to astral demons attracted into the Hermetic statues standing in the temple of memory. Bruno's conception of memory and

56. Van Deusen 1932, pp. 20–2, 25–45, 53, 68–70, 79–80, 92; Kristeller 1964a, pp. 95–103; Walker 1958, pp. 189–91; Thorndike 1923–58, VI, pp. 370–71; Brickman 1941, pp. 13–14, 18, 31–6, 42–4, 59–60; see nn. 59–60 below.
57. Bruno 1879–91, III, pp. 1–258, 397–491, 637–700, especially pp. 695–6; 1958, pp. 178–82, 245–9, 264–73, 547–829; Yates 1964, pp. 192–9, 211–16, 231–2, 262–7, 307–11; Védrine 1967, pp. 262, 269–82, 352; Michel 1962, pp. 36, 42, 133–8; Ingegno 1978, pp. 212–13, 215–16.

imagination, like the theurgy of Iamblichus, turned magic inwards toward the operator's soul and upwards to the One; the interiority of this contemplative impulse lends credence to the view that Bruno's magic underlay a larger project of cultural and religious reform. On the other hand, since *spiritus* can carry an astral image outside the operator and seal it in another's soul, the powers of Bruno's imagination are also external and practical.[58]

When he wrote in *De magia* that '*magus* means a wise man who has the power to act', Bruno emphasised the operative character of magic, its motivation in man's will and its expression in concrete human action. Campanella, who became an advocate of the new Galilean science, also valued magic for its utility, although neither his theoretical nor his pragmatic interest in magic ripened until after he met Della Porta (1589) and read Cardano. The young author of *Philosophia sensibus demonstrata* (1591), a Telesian apology, was a critic of astrology, but by 1626 he and Pope Urban VIII were practising a medical astrology defensible as natural magic yet vulnerable to the demonic dangers of Ficino's planetary music. The unauthorised publication in *De fato siderali vitando* (1626) of these papal adventures complicated Campanella's already troubled career. His most extensive treatment of magic, *De sensu rerum et magia*, was another product of his youth that appeared only in 1620.[59] It brought Telesio's theory of sensate matter to one of its possible conclusions, 'that the world is a feeling animal . . . [whose] parts partake in one and the same kind of life'. Like any higher organism, the living cosmos possesses a 'spirit . . . both active and passive in nature . . . capable of suffering everything and of acting with everything. The soul in things both suffers and enjoys with the things themselves.' Imagination, a faculty of the soul, acts 'when the spirit takes in something and thinks of it'. The operations of soul, spirit and imagination in the cosmos account for its wonders:

What marvel is there in the fact that the rooster is feared by the lion? . . . The lion is a heavy-spirited beast . . .; the rooster is of subtle and sharp spirits; and when these rooster-spirits pass through the air, they penetrate those of the lion and render them fearful.

Although this passage recalls similar remarks on the cock and the lion in Proclus and Ficino, Campanella has removed the alleged fact of the cock's

58. Yates 1964, pp. 192–9, 211–16, 231–2, 262–7, 270, 307–11, 322–35; 1966, pp. 199–236, 243–59; cf. Ingegno 1978, pp. xii, 143; see n. 32 above.
59. Bruno 1879–91, III, p. 400: 'A philosophis ut sumitur inter philosophos, tunc magus significat hominem sapientem cum virtute agendi'; Garin 1950b, pp. 657–8; Védrine 1967, p. 354; Di Napoli 1947, pp. 338, 356, 359, 361; Walker 1958, pp. 203, 207–17.

superiority from the theoretical context in which Ficino and Proclus had explained it, i.e., a metaphysical context. Campanella's analysis of the cock's dominance is wrong and perhaps arbitrary, but it is nonetheless physical, which accounts for the popularity of this and similar appeals to fluids, vapours, effluences and other progeny of *spiritus* long after the scientific revolution and the rise of the mechanical philosophy.[60]

Campanella's wish to reduce occult phenomena to mechanical contact, material force or physical structure emerged again in the fourteenth book of his monumental *Theologia* (begun in 1613), where he discussed the passage from Thomas Aquinas on which Ficino had based his claim that an astrological *figura* is like a substantial form. 'Images and characters are controversial', wrote Campanella:

> St Thomas . . . seems to attribute to them, from the influence of the heavens, some virtue . . . so that if one makes a lion in gold under the sign of Leo, it acquires a power . . . leonine in nature . . . beyond what virtue the gold possesses . . . These [zodiacal] images do not actually exist in heaven, but heat sent from the constellation Leo to a climate and region of our Earth is or becomes similar . . . to leonine heat . . . Wherefore, although the image and the figure as such . . . are not active, yet inasmuch as the figure is placed in an artificial species connected with a natural species produced by the heavens, St Thomas said that it can receive influence . . . Although the figure is artificial, a work of design, its execution in a physical body comes under the heavens, as do other motions . . . Clearly, no action comes from an artificial or a natural body unless the figure suits that action . . . [And] local motion [is necessary] in an astrological figure if it is to receive influence and to act . . . This action occurs through a quality of sympathy, like that between iron and a magnet, whose mode of action they avow to be occult.

In this remarkable passage, the Dominican Campanella preserves the Thomist approval of figurate talismans, but he does not depend on the metaphysical basis of that approval, the doctrine of substantial forms. In place of Peripatetic hylemorphism, against which he had raised objections like Telesio's and Bruno's as early as the *Philosophia sensibus demonstrata*, Campanella proposed notions of structural resonance and physical force that were only distantly related to Ficino's metaphysical *figurae* yet served as well as them to uphold a theory of magic.[61]

---

60. Campanella's *De sensu rerum et magia*, translated in *Renaissance Philosophy* 1967, pp. 360–1 (1.8), 362 (1.9), 375 (v.5); Di Napoli 1947, pp. 350–7; see nn. 35, 43, 56 above.

61. Campanella 1949–, XIV, pp. 192–4: 'De imaginibus autem et caracteribus siderum controvertitur. Etenim Divus Thomas, 3 contra Gentiles c. 105, videtur eis tribuere ex coelesti influxu aliquid virtutis . . . uti si fiat leo in auro sub Leonis signo, sortiatur, ultra id quod aurum habet virtutis, etiam vim roborandi et strenuitatem conciliandi, his praesertim qui natura leonini sunt . . . In coelo quidem imagines istae non sunt, sed calor qui ex asterismo Leonis ad Telluris nostrae clima et regionem demittitur, similis est vel fit . . . leonino calori . . . Quapropter licet imago et figura in

FRANCIS BACON: THE REFORM OF MAGIC IN THE ABANDONMENT OF TRADITIONAL PHILOSOPHY

Francis Bacon knew the Renaissance philosophers who had nourished Campanella's magic – Ficino, Cardano, Della Porta, Telesio – and he also understood the anti-philosophical and occultist impulses expressed by Agrippa and Paracelsus. At times he had harsh words for all of them as complicit in the moral and intellectual scandal begun by the Greek philosophers, continued by the scholastics and to be ended by himself. But Bacon's vision of the history of philosophy as a chronicle of degeneracy left him in many respects an heir of that history, and nowhere more than in his attitudes towards occultism.[62] In *De augmentis*, for example, he described an *astrologia sana* similar in many ways to the iatromathematics of Ficino's *De vita* III. Though he denied the existence of a *spiritus mundi*, he conceded the influence of the heavens on human spirits and he granted that the imagination could affect the transmission of spirits, even their communication to other persons, as in *fascinatio*. He worried that 'the inquiry how to raise and fortify the imagination' might constitute 'a palliation and defence of a great part of ceremonial magic' if it convinced people that natural rather than demonic powers were at work in 'ceremonies, characters, charms, gesticulations [and] amulets'. Indeed, this was his own conviction; he affirmed 'that imagination has power, . . . that ceremonies . . . strengthen that power, and that they be used sincerely and intentionally for that purpose, and as a physical remedy, without any the least thought of inviting thereby the aid of [demonic] spirits'. The admission that 'many things . . . work upon the spirits of man by secret sympathy and antipathy . . . [as in] the virtues of precious stones . . . [that] have in them fine spirits' takes on new meaning in light of a recent discovery: that, in addition to his methodological reforms, Bacon also intended to formulate a substantive natural philosophy, a physical system one of whose chief ingredients was a

---

quantum figura non habeat activitatem, tamen prout reponitur in specie artificiali per ordinem ad naturalem, quae a coelo fit, dixit Divus Thomas quod potest recipere influxum . . . Et quidem licet sit opus arbitrarium figuratio et artificiosa, eius tamen exequutio in corpore physico subiicitur coelo, sicut ceteri motus . . . Palam enim est quod neque artificialia neque naturalia corpora, quibus actio aliqua fit, absque figura commoda illi actioni non sunt . . . [Et] motus localis in figura astrologica [necessarius est] ut influxum recipiat et agat . . .; actio enim ista fit per qualitatem sympathiae, sicut magnetis in ferrum, cuius agendi modum profitentur occultum'; Di Napoli 1947, pp. 331–40; see nn. 39–40 above.

62. P. Rossi 1974, pp. 3–129; Anderson 1948, p. 136; Walker 1958, pp. 189–91, 199; 1985, § x, p. 121; Rees 1975, pp. 81–92, 101; unless otherwise indicated, translations from Bacon's Latin works are those in F. Bacon 1857–74, IV and V.

pneumatic (spiritual) theory of matter expressed in the context of a 'semi-Paracelsian' cosmology.[63]

Despite his belief in the astrological and magical efficacy of *spiritus* and imagination, Bacon concluded that ceremonies invoking these natural powers are unlawful because they enable man to achieve his material ends without labour. Bacon's strongest objections to magic were ethical; in this respect, they reflected his views on the failings of philosophy, which in the past had seduced man from truly useful learning. Plato had tempted philosophy to its original sin of abstract, sterile contemplation, and then he compounded the error by confusing philosophy with religion. Aristotle, whose faults were fewer, turned philosophy toward verbalism, dogmatism and sophistry. 'Plato made over the world to thoughts', wrote Bacon, 'and Aristotle made over thoughts to words.' As mere speculation detracts from the crucial work of observation, so magic aims 'by a few easy and slothful observances' to pluck the fruit that God commanded man to seek in the sweat of his brow. Bacon preferred the mechanical arts to the magical because they were collective, collaborative and institutional, whereas magic isolated the individual in selfish quests that 'aim rather at admiration . . . than at utility'.[64] Joined to this moral indictment were certain physical and metaphysical departures from the post-Ficinian theory of magic, derived for the most part from Paracelsus, Telesio and the other nature philosophers. Most important was Bacon's rejection of metaphysical hylemorphism and his reformulation on physical grounds of a magical theory of forms and occult qualities.

Bacon conceived of magical phenomena as those 'wherein the . . . cause is . . . small as compared with the . . . effect'. From this disproportion of cause and effect follow amazement and difficulty of explanation.

Those arts . . . that take more from fancy and faith than from reason and demonstrations are three in particular: astrology, natural magic and alchemy, whose ends, however, are not ignoble . . . Magic proposes to recall natural philosophy from a miscellany of speculations to a magnitude of works . . . But the methods thought to lead to these ends are full of errors and nonsense, both in theory . . . and in practice.

---

63. F. Bacon 1857–74, II, pp. 656–7, 660; IV, pp. 347–54, 400–1 (for Latin text, see I, pp. 553–9, 608–9); P. Rossi 1974, pp. 18–20, 25; Walker 1958, pp. 199–200; 1985, § X, pp. 122, 127–8; Rees 1975, pp. 81, 85–6; 1977, pp. 110–13; 1980, pp. 552–3.
64. F. Bacon 1857–74, II, p. 86; IV, pp. 84, 401 (for Latin text, see I, pp. 192–3, 609); P. Rossi 1974, pp. 14–15, 34, 40–1, 48, 52–3, 92–100; Walker 1958, pp. 201–2; 1985, § X, p. 127; Anderson 1948, pp. 107, 207.

Because the utilitarian promise of the magical arts could rescue philosophy from its moral doldrums, Bacon said he 'would rather have [them] . . . purified than altogether rejected', and he suggested programmes for the reform of natural magic and astrology. Even 'superstitious narratives of sorceries, witchcrafts [and] charms' became legitimate objects of enquiry. Bacon urged that the word 'magic', 'which has long been used in a bad sense, be again restored to its ancient and honorable meaning . . . I . . . understand it as the science which applies the knowledge of hidden forms (*formae abditae*) to the production of wonderful operations; and by uniting . . . actives with passives, displays the wonderful works of nature.' In the absence of this reform, a 'popular and degenerate natural magic . . . lays the understanding asleep by singing of specific properties and hidden virtues, sent as from heaven and . . . learned from the whispers of tradition'. This is the otiose magic that 'makes man no longer alive and awake for the pursuit and enquiry of real causes'.[65]

The new magic that Bacon advocated was the operative manifestation of his metaphysics, as mechanics was the practical expression of his physics. Metaphysics for Bacon was 'the investigation of forms', but the forms he had in mind were not the 'toys of logic' that he and the nature philosophers scorned in Aristotle. 'Of a given nature to discover the form or true specific difference or nature-engendering nature or source of emanation', Bacon explained,

is the work and aim of human knowledge . . . In nature nothing really exists beyond individual bodies performing pure individual acts according to a fixed law . . . And it is this law . . . that I mean when I speak of forms . . . The form of a nature is such that given the form the nature infallibly follows . . . [Form] deduces the given nature from some source of being which is inherent in more natures . . . He who knows the forms of yellow, weight, ductility, fixity, fluidity . . . and so on and the methods for superinducing them . . . in some body . . . [may achieve] the transformation of that body into gold.

Obviously, the Baconian form is not the Peripatetic abstraction, but its exact contours are obscure – a generative force, a defining essence, a taxonomic distinction, a natural law, a material quality, an alchemical

65. F. Bacon 1857–74, I, pp. 456–7: 'Artes ipsae, quae plus habent ex phantasia et fide quam ex ratione et demonstrationibus, sunt praecipue tres; *Astrologia, Naturalis Magia*, et *Alchymia*; quarum tamen fines non sunt ignobiles . . . Magia sibi proponit naturalem philosophiam a varietate speculationum ad magnitudinem operum revocare . . . Sed viae atque rationes quae ducere putantur ad hos fines, tam in theoria illarum artium quam in praxi, erroris et nugarum plenae sunt'; IV, pp. 245, 296, 349, 355, 366–7, 425 (for Latin text, see I, pp. 362–3, 498, 554, 559, 573–4); *Occult and Scientific Mentalities* 1984, p. 355 (Clark); Capp 1979, pp. 180–90; K. Thomas 1971, pp. 350–2, 661–3.

additive, any of these will answer to Bacon's description which, however, seems most akin to the fixed and distinguishing material properties of an object.[66] This becomes clearer as one leafs through Bacon's illustration of his method for the investigation of forms, a long list of 'instances' that gradually isolate the nature of heat, the particular material quality that Bacon chose as the first exemplary object of his technique. To organise his inductive method, Bacon outlined twenty-seven categories of 'prerogative instances', the last of which are 'instances of magic' marked by that imbalance of cause and effect that makes them 'seem like miracles'.[67]

Bacon regarded this feeling of mystery as an obstacle to learning. He condemned 'the easy passing over of the causes of things by ascribing them to secret and hidden virtues and properties (for this hath arrested . . . inquiry)'. He did not deny the existence of occult virtues and sympathies, but he traced them to imperceptible physical structures in bodies called 'latent configurations' (*latentes schematismi*).

What are called occult and specific properties or sympathies and antipathies are in great part corruptions of philosophy . . . Inner consents and aversions (*consensus et fugae*) or friendships and enmities (for I am . . . weary of the words sympathy and antipathy . . . [because of the] superstitions and vanities associated with them) are either falsely ascribed or mixed with fables or from want of observation very rarely met with . . . [Genuine] consents . . . are found in greatest abundance . . . in certain medicines, which by their occult . . . and specific properties have relation . . . to limbs or humours or diseases.

Having thus confirmed a tradition of pharmaceutical magic reaching back two millennia and more, Bacon explained that the genuine but occult phenomenon of consent 'is nothing else than the adaptation of forms and configurations (*symmetria formarum et schematismorum*) to each other'. In adopting the term *schematismus*, Bacon may not have known the kindred language in Plotinus, and in listing a series of consents in 'sulphur, oil . . . greasy exhalation, flame, and perhaps the body of a star' he may not have had in mind the τάξις of Proclus that it resembles.[68] He had, however, read Ficino's *De vita* III, the Renaissance treatise on magic that first fully exploited the philosophies of Proclus and Plotinus, and in any event, whatever the manner of their mediation, the resemblance of Bacon's magical ideas to

---

66. F. Bacon 1857–74, IV, pp. 119–22, 126, 146, 366–7, 398 (for Latin text, see I, pp. 227–31, 234, 257–8, 573–4, 606); Anderson 1948, pp. 154–62, 207.
67. F. Bacon 1857–74, IV, pp. 127–55, 245 (for Latin text, see I, pp. 236–68, 362–3); Anderson 1948, pp. 207, 219.
68. F. Bacon 1857–74, II, pp. 671–2; IV, pp. 124–5, 233, 242–4, 366–7 (for Latin text, see I, 233–4, 349–50, 359–61, 573–4); Rees 1975, pp. 91, 97–8; see nn. 28, 35 above.

their Neoplatonic ancestors is apparent – as are the differences. In the case of occult phenomena, Bacon's investigation of forms ended in the discovery of forms, configurations and symmetries more physical than their Greek analogues but still more magical than the quantitative conceptions of force and structure that were to emerge in the new science and philosophy of which Bacon is considered a prophet.

VII

MORAL PHILOSOPHY

II

MORAL PHILOSOPHY

THE TRIPARTITE DIVISION OF MORAL PHILOSOPHY

In the Renaissance moral philosophy was divided into three parts: ethics, oeconomics and politics. This division corresponded to Aristotle's *Nicomachean Ethics* and *Politics* and the pseudo-Aristotelian *Oeconomics*, the basic texts used in university teaching of moral philosophy. Aristotle referred in passing to this type of tripartite division,[1] which was later codified and adopted by his Greek commentators as the standard Peripatetic classification of practical philosophy.[2] This tradition, transmitted to medieval Latin philosophy by Boethius and Cassiodorus, is reflected in the classification of sciences presented by Hugh of St Victor and other twelfth-century authors, even though they lacked the Aristotelian texts on which it was based.[3] Dominicus Gundissalinus, for example, in his *De divisione philosophiae*, written around 1150 and based on both Arabic and Latin sources, divides practical philosophy into the science of governing a state, ruling one's own family and controlling oneself.[4] With the rise of the universities in the thirteenth century and the availability in Latin of the Aristotelian *Ethics*, *Oeconomics* and *Politics*, the triad of ethics, oeconomics and politics became the normal structure for the moral philosophy curriculum.[5]

Renaissance authors continued to follow the tripartite division which they inherited from their medieval predecessors. The traditional scholastic organisation of moral philosophy was used by humanists and philosophers, Aristotelians and Platonists alike.[6] It continued to be a standard feature of

---

1. *Eudemian Ethics* 1.8 (1218^{b}13–14).
2. See, e.g., Simplicius 1907, p. 4.26–8.   3. See Weisheipl 1965.
4. Dominicus Gundissalinus 1903, pp. 134–40 identifies the three parts of practical philosophy as *scientia gubernandi civitatem, scientia regendi familiam propriam* and *gubernacio sui ipsius*.
5. For the University of Leipzig see Ehrle 1925, p. 206 n. 6; for Oxford see *Statuta Antiqua* 1931, p. 235 and Weisheipl 1964, p. 175; for the University of Greifswald see *Cambridge History* 1982, p. 19 (Kenny and Pinborg); see also Overfield 1984, p. 41.
6. Bruni 1506, f. 126^v; *Reden und Briefe* 1970, p. 12 (Argyropulos); Landino 1974, I, p. 10; Acciaiuoli 1535, sig. ★ iv^{r-v}; Zini 1547, f. 11^r; Lambin 1565, sig. A 3^r; Vieri 1577, p. 9. Some Renaissance authors noted that the tripartite division derived from Simplicius: see R. Maffei 1506, f. 496^r; Béraud 1515, sig. a iii^v.

moral philosophy treatises and textbooks in the sixteenth and well into the seventeenth century.[7]

In his commentary on book 1 of the *Nicomachean Ethics*, the Byzantine philosopher and theologian Eustratius of Nicaea (*c.* 1050-*c.* 1120) explained the tripartite division in terms of subject-matter: the individual man was the subject of ethics; the home and its inhabitants were the subject of oeconomics; and the state was the subject of politics.[8] Eustratius' work was part of a corpus of Greek commentaries translated into Latin along with the *Nicomachean Ethics* by Robert Grosseteste in the 1240s.[9] Albertus Magnus, who used this corpus a few years later in the lectures which he gave on the *Ethics*, explained that according to the 'Commentator Graecus' each of the three disciplines of moral philosophy dealt with man's behaviour. They differed, however, because man could be considered in relation to himself or to others; and the others could be further divided into two categories: his family and his fellow-citizens.[10] Albertus' student, Thomas Aquinas, developed this argument along similar lines in his commentary on the *Nicomachean Ethics*. Since man was by nature a social animal, he was dependent on others, who could be divided into two groups: one domestic, the other civil. It was on this basis that moral philosophy was divided into three parts: *monastica*, which concerned the actions of the individual; *oeconomica*, the actions of the domestic unit; and *politica*, the actions of civil society.[11]

Although some Renaissance philosophers drew directly on Eustratius for their explanations of the tripartite division of moral philosophy, most adopted his scheme as expounded and elaborated by Thomas Aquinas.[12] Thomas himself was only rarely cited, but his arguments and terminology frequently appear in Renaissance discussions of the subject.[13] Each author

7. R. Maffei 1506 (lib. 26); Javelli 1651; Nores 1578; Brisanius 1588; Golius 1606, 1622 and 1634; Keckermann 1607a, 1607b and 1607c; Timpler 1612; Burgersdijk 1629 and 1644.
8. Eustratius, Michael of Ephesus and Anonymous 1892, pp. 1–2.
9. Eustratius, Michael of Ephesus and Anonymous 1973–, I, pp. 38*–45*; see also McEvoy 1982, pp. 471–7.
10. Albertus Magnus 1951–, xiv, 1, p. 3: 'homo dupliciter potest considerari: vel secundum se vel in comparatione ad alterum, et in comparatione ad alterum dupliciter: vel ad domesticos coniunctos vel ad omnes communiter qui sunt sub eadem civitate'.
11. Thomas Aquinas 1934, p. 4: 'moralis philosophia in tres partes dividitur. Quarum prima considerat operationes unius hominis ordinatas ad finem, quae vocatur monastica. Secunda autem considerat operationes multitudinis domesticae, quae vocatur oeconomica. Tertia autem considerat operationes multitudinis civilis, quae vocatur politica.'
12. Figliucci 1551, p. 1 cites Eustratius; F. Piccolomini 1594b, p. 7 refers to Thomas, whose exposition 'Latinorum multi sequuntur.'
13. Javelli 1651, p. 5: 'adverte quod homo . . . dupliciter considerari potest: primo secundum se . . .; secundo, ut est pars multitudinis . . . Multitudo autem cuius homo est pars, duplex est, scilicet

tended to adapt and embellish the basic formula, but most accepted the principle that ethics dealt with the individual, oeconomics with the family and politics with the state.[14] As a variation on this theme, some suggested that ethics trained the good man, oeconomics the good head of household and politics the good citizen and magistrate.[15]

In the sixteenth and early seventeenth centuries another explanation of the difference between the three parts of moral philosophy gained currency. According to this view, ethics was concerned with general principles, whereas oeconomics and politics dealt with the specific application of these principles to the home and state.[16] On these grounds, some authors argued that moral philosophy should be divided into two parts: one theoretical and general, consisting of ethics; the other practical and specific, consisting of oeconomics and politics.[17]

There was no consensus about the relative importance of the three disciplines. Some authors maintained that politics was far superior to ethics and oeconomics because it concerned the good of the state, which was a higher and more perfect good than that of the individual or the family.[18] Others gave pride of place to ethics as the most fundamental and comprehensive of the disciplines.[19] There was, however, general agreement that the study of moral philosophy should begin with ethics, proceed to oeconomics and conclude with politics.[20]

The term 'ethics' derives from the Greek word ἦθος, meaning disposition

familia sive domus, et civitas'; see also Vermigli 1582, p. 3; Giffen 1608, p. 2; *Collegium Conimbricense* 1612, sig. aaa 2[r]. Thomas' term *monastica* was sometimes adopted as a synonym for ethics; see Fox-Morcillo 1566, p. 121, and Valerius 1566, p. 5.

14. Landino 1974, I, p. 10: 'In eo . . . quod tibi ipsi moderaris, ethica, in eo quod familiam privatamque domum administras, oeconomica, in eo denique quod rem publicam geris et cum civibus versaris, politica traduntur'; see also La Torre 1855, p. 383; Nifo 1645, pp. 17–18; R. Maffei 1542, f. 2[r]; Toletus 1600, f. 2[r].

15. Golius 1634, p. 1: 'Philosophia practica in tres partes distribuitur. Quarum una . . . ἠθικὴ appellatur, qua ostenditur, quodnam sit officium viri boni. Altera vocatur οἰκονομικὴ, qua ostenditur, quod sit officium boni patrisfamilias. Tertia nominatur πολιτικὴ, qua traditur officium boni civis et boni magistratus'; Florimonte 1554, p. 18: 'Filosofia morale . . . insegna a far l'huomo buono, et mostra a i principi o a i maestrati come possono fare il regno o la città loro felice; et al padre di famiglia come habbia a governare casa sua'; see also Heiland 1581, pp. 1–2; Magirus 1601, p. 7.

16. Burgersdijk 1629, p. 9: 'Ethica . . . tradit generalia principia, ex quibus vitae practicae mores formandi sunt . . . tum in familia, quod fit in Oeconomica; tum in civitate, quod fit in Politica'; see also Zwinger 1586, VI, p. 1558; Donaldson 1620, p. 3.

17. F. Piccolomini 1594b, pp. 7–10; Waele 1620, pp. 7–8; Burgersdijk 1629, p. 9.

18. Clichtove justifies this position on the basis of *Politics* I.1 (1252[a]1–6) in Lefèvre d'Étaples 1972, p. 367. See also Lambin's preface to his edition of Nepos 1569, sig. aaa 1[v].

19. Fox-Morcillo 1566, p. 221; Camerarius in his edition of Aristotle and Xenophon 1564, p. 44.

20. Acciaiuoli 1535, sig. ★ V[r]; A. Piccolomini 1542, f. 52[r]; Figliucci 1551, p. 1; Vermigli 1582, pp. 4–6; see, however, Piccart 1605, pp. 120–4, who argues that politics should precede oeconomics.

or character. Ethics concerned the formation of man's moral character or, in the Latin terminology, his *mores*.[21] But before philosophers could even begin considering how to train man's character, they first had to understand his nature.

RENAISSANCE CONCEPTS OF MAN

There was nothing particularly new or original about Renaissance views of man. The various themes and motifs which were used to deplore the misery of the human condition or to exalt the dignity of man were for the most part borrowed from classical, biblical, patristic and medieval sources.[22] The Renaissance was, however, characterised by an increased and intensified interest in the exploration of man's nature.[23]

In the *De remediis utriusque fortunae* Petrarch claimed (without justification) that he was the first to write about the dignity of man. Others, he said, had attempted to discuss the topic, but had given up because it was easier to write about human misery.[24] Petrarch probably had Pope Innocent III in mind, for in the prologue to his *De miseria humane conditionis*, he had announced his intention to write about the dignity of human nature as well, but had failed to do so.[25] In fact, Petrarch was specifically asked by the Grand Prior of the Carthusians to fulfil Innocent's promise by writing a treatise on the dignity of man.[26] The fifteenth-century humanist Bartolomeo Facio, in his *De excellentia ac praestantia hominis*, also took up the challenge to complete the task which Innocent, preoccupied with pressing papal business, had left unfinished.[27] Spurred on by Facio's treatise, Giannozzo Manetti wrote his *De dignitate et excellentia hominis*, in which he intended not so much to complete Innocent's work by presenting the other

---

21. Heiland 1581, p. 2: 'Circa quid versatur haec scientia? Circa mores hominum, unde et nomen habet: ἦθος enim, ingenium hominis, indolem et mores significat'; R. Maffei 1542, f. 3ʳ: 'Ethica: ἦθος est animi seu habitus seu compositio seu conformatio, unde mores nascuntur.'
22. Gentile 1925, pp. 35–96; Garin 1938; Trinkaus 1940, pp. 64–79, 1970 and 1983, pp. 343–63; Baker 1947; Kristeller 1956a, pp. 279–86; Buck 1960; Rice 1969, pp. 176–7; Sozzi 1982; Melammed 1982; Giustiniani 1985, p. 187.
23. For Renaissance concepts of women see Maclean 1980.
24. Petrarch 1577, p. 732 (II.93): 'Et si de hoc nemo hactenus, nisi fallor, scripserit, aggressique aliqui destiterint, quod . . . humana miseria nimis multa prorsus evidenter emineat, foelicitas parva et latens stilo altius fodienda sit'; see also Raimondi 1947.
25. Innocent III 1955, p. 3: 'dignitatem humane nature Christo favente describam'.
26. Petrarch 1581, pp. 961–3 (*Epistolae seniles* XVI.9); see also Trinkaus 1970, I, pp. 179–99.
27. Facio 1611, p. 149: 'De hominis excellentia scribere nuper aggressus sum . . . de qua quidem re acceperam Innocentium . . . in eo libro, in quo humanas miserias complexus est, pollicitum esse sese scripturum, sed . . . pontificatus negotiis impeditum, quod promiserat, non praestitisse.' Facio's treatise (1448) was a reworking of *De dignitate hominis et excellentia humane vite* by the Olivetan monk Antonio da Barga; see Trinkaus 1970, I, p. 209 and 1983, p. 356.

side of the story as to challenge it by refuting the view that man's condition was one of unrelieved misery.[28]

Yet there were also those who agreed with the pessimistic assessment of man presented in the long tradition of Christian *contemptus mundi* literature.[29] Poggio Bracciolini's *De miseria humanae conditionis*, written in 1455, not only borrowed Innocent's title but also elaborated many of the themes he had discussed. For example, Innocent had outlined the miseries peculiar to each of the ages of man. Poggio took up this motif, using his rhetorical skills to paint an even more depressing picture of man's progress from the depravity of infancy to the decrepitude of old age.[30] An equally bleak view of the ages of man was presented about fifteen years later by Giovanni Garzoni in his *De miseria humana*. As a doctor, he was inclined to dwell on the physical aspects of human suffering, which he described in gruesome detail: 'Some people's eyes grow weak; others have their noses amputated; some are tortured by toothache; others have their tongues cut out.'[31] The same topos was used by Erasmus in his *Moriae encomium*; but he gave it an ironic twist by attributing the lament to Folly.[32]

Some discussions of man were set out as dialogues, in which the first interlocutor catalogues the afflictions which make life wretched. His arguments are then refuted by the second interlocutor, who describes the happiness of man's existence. For example, Aurelio Brandolini's *De humanae vitae conditione* begins with King Matthias Corvinus of Hungary deploring man's physical suffering and spiritual anxiety. However, Petrus Lucerinus, Bishop of Novara, proves to him that life on earth must be pleasant and agreeable since no one willingly departs from it. Moreover, man's terrestrial happiness is increased by anticipation of the future beatitude which his soul will enjoy eternally in heaven.[33] A similar debate

28. Manetti 1975, p. 2 refers to Facio's 'opusculum quoddam precipuum et egregium'; on p. 100 (lib. IV), he argues against those who have written 'vel de laudatione et bono mortis, vel de miseria humane vite', such as Innocent III (p. 111).
29. Bultot 1963-4.
30. Innocent III 1955, pp. 12-16; Poggio Bracciolini 1964-9, I, p. 104: 'Infantia, pueritia, pubertas, adolescentia, nonne cum stulticia, lascivia, impudentia, incontinentia redundent, sunt miseria plenae? Quid harum aetatum vita differt a beluis? . . . vita [decrepitorum] . . . infinitis pene confecta molestiis, . . . ut solum doloris et laboris particeps esse videatur.'
31. Garzoni 1505, sig. A vii^v: 'Quidam oculis debiles fiunt; quibusdam nares abscinduntur; quidam dolore dentium torquentur; quibusdam lingua exciditur.'
32. Erasmus 1969-, IV,3, p. 108: 'quot calamitatibus hominum vita sit obnoxia, quam misera, quam sordida nativitas, quam laboriosa educatio, quot iniuriis exposita pueritia, quot sudoribus adacta iuventus, quam gravis senectus'.
33. Brandolini 1543, p. 80: 'Potest haec misera aut molesta vita appellari, in qua tantae opes, tam multae voluptates ac suavitates sint, ut . . . nemo . . . ab ea nisi invitus discedat?'; p. 105: 'animus . . . perfruitur . . . spe atque expectatione futurae illius beatitudinis'.

occurs in Fernán Pérez de Oliva's *Diálogo de la dignidad del hombre*. The opening speaker, Aurelio, attempts to prove that man is a worthless and miserable creature. His arguments are then systematically rebutted by Antonio, who defends the dignity both of man's soul and his body.[34]

One of the ways in which man was defined was in relation to the lower animals. Drawing on Pliny the Elder and Lactantius, some Renaissance authors described man as a stepchild of nature, for he alone among animals comes into the world naked and defenceless. Man lacks the fur, feathers, scales, shells, spines and horns which protect other animals; he is less strong than the bull, less swift than the tiger and less cunning than the lion; he can neither fight effectively nor flee quickly.[35] But man receives one gift which compensates for all his natural disadvantages: reason. Indeed, man is born naked and defenceless precisely because he can use his intellect to clothe and arm himself.[36] According to Marsilio Ficino, man's reason gave him godlike powers. For while animals were dependent on the particular bodily gifts provided by nature, man's intellect gave him an unlimited capacity to provide for himself.[37] It was also argued that man's reason allowed him to dominate animals who were physically superior to him. He might lack the ox's strength, but the ox ploughed the field for him. Man, moreover, made his clothing from the skins of animals and dined on their flesh.[38] Those who complain about our weakness in comparison to animals should seriously consider, suggested Benedetto Varchi, whether they would prefer to swim like a fish or run like a deer rather than to walk and talk like a man.[39]

Anselm Turmeda's *Disputa de l'ase* consists of a debate between the author and an ass about whether men or animals were more noble. Turmeda, a Franciscan friar from Majorca who converted to Islam, adapted the work from one of the *Epistles of the Brethren of Purity*, a tenth-century Arabic encyclopaedia.[40] Anselm argues that men are superior to animals because they build houses, towers and palaces. The ass, however, points to the intricate edifices made by bees, spiders and birds. Anselm then argues

34. Pérez de Oliva 1982, p. 78: '(Antonio) Sobre el hombre es nuestra contienda: que Aurelio dize ser cosa vana y miserable; y yo soy venido a defenderlo'; see also Solana 1941, II, pp. 46–61.
35. Pliny, *Naturalis Historia* VII.1–5; Lactantius, *De opificio Dei*, capp. 2–3; Pérez de Oliva 1982, pp. 81–2; Boaistuau 1982, pp. 77–8; Campanella 1620, p. 150 (II.25).
36. A character in the dialogue *Della condizione de l'uomo* (Brucioli 1982, p. 19) claims that man was born 'ignudo e inerme perché d'ingegno si poteva armare e vestire di ragione'; Boaistuau 1982, p. 79: 'il est pour son grand profit et advantage armé d'entendement, et vestu de raison'; see also Magirus 1603, p. 3.   37. Ficino 1964–70, II, p. 224 (XIII.3).
38. Petrarch 1577, p. 739 (II.93): 'Non est tibi bovis robur, at tibi bos arat'; Campanella 1620, p. 150 (II.25): 'homo superat animalia, vestitur ipsorum pellibus, carnibus vescitur ipsorum'.
39. Varchi 1858–9, II, p. 612 (*Sopra la pittura e scultura*): 'Eleggeremo più volentieri il nuotare che l'andare? . . . ci piacerà più il correre, che il discorrere?'.
40. *La disputa de los animales* 1984; see also Rico 1970, pp. 90–6.

that men eat the flesh of animals. But the ass replies that worms eat men's flesh, as do lions and vultures. None of the traditional arguments which Anselm puts forward for man's superiority are accepted by the ass, until he produces his final proof: God incarnated himself as a man. With this *deus ex machina*, Anselm wins the debate: the animals concede that man is more noble and humbly agree to serve him.[41]

Turmeda's *Disputa* was unquestionably an eccentric work, but his use of the Incarnation as the central argument for the dignity of man was not unusual. The fact that God chose to become a man rather than an angel or any other animal had always been used by Christian philosophers as an important proof of human excellence. This argument lost none of its potency in the Renaissance.[42] Indeed, Manetti went so far as to claim that even if the fall had not occurred, Christ would still have descended to earth in order to glorify man by taking on human flesh.[43]

God had not only become man, he had also made man Godlike: 'Let us make man in our image, after our likeness' (Genesis 1:26). This biblical text was a popular topic for patristic exegesis and was widely influential among medieval Christian authors.[44] It continued to be cited or alluded to in the Renaissance as a powerful argument in defence of man's dignity.[45] Most authors believed that it was man's immortal soul and his intellect which resembled God.[46] Many also repeated the scholastic argument that the soul conformed to the image of the trinity, for according to Augustine, it was divided into three parts: memory, intellect and will.[47] Pushing the resemblance between God and man even further, Nicholas of Cusa, in his

---

41. Turmeda 1984, pp. 80–2; p. 139: 'je vous accorde que les filz d'Adam sont de plus grand noblesse et dignité que nous aultres animaulx, et que Dieu tout puissant nous a créez pour vostre service'. The *Disputa* was written in Catalan in 1417–18, but only the 1544 French translation survives.

42. Nemesius of Emesa, *De natura hominis*, cap. 1; Honorius of Autun, *Liber XII quaestionum*, cap. 7; Boaistuau 1982, p. 43: 'Mais quel tesmoignage de la dignité de l'homme! lequel son createur a tant prisé que de son eternité est devallé et descendu au monde, et a prins le vestement de la chair, et s'est faict homme.' See also Petrarch 1577, p. 734 (II.93); Facio 1611, p. 158; G. Pico 1942, p. 266 (*Heptaplus*); Pérez de Oliva 1982, p. 96.

43. Manetti 1975, p. 98: 'si primi nostri parentes nequaquam peccassent, Christus nihilominus e celis in terras descendisset . . . ut hominem per hanc humilem humane carnis susceptionem mirabiliter et incredibiliter honoraret glorificaretque'.

44. Garin 1938; on Gregory of Nyssa, see Muckle 1945; on Lactantius, see Perrin 1981, pp. 419–29; on S. Pier Damiani, see Bultot 1973; see also Eustratius, Michael of Ephesus and Anonymous 1892, p. 6; Hermes Trismegistus, Pseudo- 1945–54, I, p. 10 (I.12).

45. Petrarch 1577, pp. 732–3 (II.93); Bosso 1493, sig. a v^r; Zwingli 1905–83, VI, 3, pp. 116–17 (*Sermonis de providentia dei anamnema*); Carbone de Costacciaro 1585, ff. 17^v–19^r; see also Trinkaus 1970.

46. Nanni Mirabelli 1503, f. 150^r: 'Anima facta est similis deo, quia immortalem et indissolubilem fecit eam deus'; Fox-Morcillo 1566, p. 133: 'in homine animus praestantissima est pars, eaque Dei similitudinem habet'; see also Brandolini 1543, p. 56; Sensi 1577, f. 112^r; Camerarius 1578, p. 14; Daneau 1588, f. 36^r.

47. Augustine, *De trinitate* X.11; Pérez de Oliva 1982, pp. 94–5; Benivieni 1984, pp. 175–6; see also Trinkaus 1970.

De coniecturis, likened the human mind's creation of its own mental or conjectural world to the divine mind's creation of the real world. It was as the creator and ruler of his own mental universe that man resembled God.[48]

Man was not merely the image of God but was himself a second god, a terrestrial and mortal divinity, ruler of the earth and king of all God's creations.[49] Although this anthropocentric view is found in classical philosophy, especially in Stoicism, the most influential source for patristic, medieval and Renaissance authors was Genesis 1:26–8, in which God gives man dominion over the earth and everything that moves upon it.[50] Renaissance man lived in a world which had been specially built for him and over which he was lord and master. Fields and mountains, animals and plants, even metals and stones were put on earth solely for his convenience and use.[51]

Another of God's gifts to man was a body which surpassed all other created beings in beauty and symmetry because it reflected the divine image on which it was modelled.[52] According to Henricus Cornelius Agrippa, man's body was so perfectly designed that he was in the literal sense the measure of all things: temples, houses, theatres, ships, even Noah's ark, had all been designed according to the proportions of the human body.[53] Using Cicero and Lactantius as their models, many Renaissance authors wrote elaborate catalogues of the parts of the human body, describing the particular beauty and utility of each limb and organ, from head to toe and from brain to intestines.[54] Of all man's bodily attributes, the one which

---

48. Nicholas of Cusa 1932–, III; see also Watts 1982, pp. 27–8 and 110.
49. Bruni 1741, II, p. 138: 'Homo . . . est quasi mortalis quidam Deus'; Giorgi 1525, sig. Q iii^r: 'audendum est dicere hominem quidem terrenum Deum esse mortalem'; Bovelles 1982, p. 148 (cap. 19): 'Sapiens est . . . terrenus quidam mortalisque Deus'; Du Bartas 1935–40, II, pp. 393–4 (*La Première Sepmaine*): 'un second Dieu . . . chef de l'univers . . . roy des animaux'; Boaistuau 1982, p. 38: 'Roy et Empereur de tout ce qui estoit contenu en cest univers'.
50. On the Stoics, see Pohlenz 1970, I, pp. 99–101; on the Church Fathers, see Spanneut 1969, pp. 380–4; see also Cicero, *De natura deorum* II.62–3; Philoponus, *De opificio mundi* v.1.
51. Manetti 1975, pp. 80–1: 'Nostre sunt terre, nostri agri, nostri campi, nostri montes . . . nostri boves, nostri tauri, nostri cameli . . . nostra maria, nostri omnes pisces . . .'; Buonamici 1591, p. 1001: 'Homini elementa serviunt . . . multis etiam plantis lapidibusque atque metallis medicae vires datae sunt ad unam eius salutem'; see also M. Fox 1983, for the use of this theme by the sixteenth-century Jewish philosopher MaHaRaL.
52. See Giorgi 1525, sig. Q iiii^r. Manetti 1975, p. 30 notes that in some churches God is painted 'instar hominis'. The ass in Turmeda 1984, pp. 88–91 counters this type of argument by pointing out that men use a lamb to depict Christ and a cow, eagle and lion to depict three of the Evangelists; Matthew, who is usually depicted as a man, is conveniently omitted by the ass.
53. Agrippa 1533, p. 160; see also Magirus 1603, p. 3. On the human proportions of Noah's ark, see Ambrose, *De Noe*, cap. 7, and Augustine, *De civitate Dei* xv.26.
54. Cicero, *De natura deorum* II.54–9; Lactantius, *De opificio Dei*, capp. 7–15; Manetti 1975, pp. 5ff.; Brandolini 1543, pp. 49ff.; Pérez de Oliva 1982, pp. 98ff.; Boaistuau 1982, pp. 49ff.; Du Bartas 1935–40, II, pp. 394ff. (*La Première Sepmaine*).

most distinguished him from other animals was his upright posture. For while all other animals were face down with their gaze fixed on the earth, man alone stood erect with his face and eyes turned towards the heavens. This immensely popular topos, found in classical, patristic and medieval sources,[55] was used by Renaissance philosophers, humanists, theologians and poets as proof that man was destined to contemplate the spiritual and heavenly realm, which was his true home.[56]

Man's body, however perfectly formed, still connected him to the temporal and mortal world of animals. His soul, however, united him with the eternity and immortality of God. It was thus man's most noble possession and his greatest source of dignity.[57] His true distinction, moreover, resided in the highest part of his soul, the rational faculty, since according to the generally accepted Aristotelian psychology the vegetative and sensitive souls were shared by plants and animals, but the rational soul was peculiar to man. So while the highest faculty in animals was sense-perception, in man it was cognition.[58] Renaissance authors took great delight in praising man's intellect and in cataloguing the marvels it had accomplished, among which they listed the construction of Brunelleschi's cupola for the Florentine cathedral and the invention of printing.[59]

Because man consisted not only of an immortal soul but also of a mortal body, he united within himself the temporal and the eternal, the earthly and the divine. The ancient Neoplatonists therefore described man as the ontological link between the material and intelligible worlds. This notion of man as the *vinculum mundi* who ties together the universe influenced a number of Church Fathers and medieval authors.[60] It is found in the works

55. Plato, *Cratylus* 399C; Aristotle, *De partibus animalium* IV.10 (686ᵃ27–8); Cicero, *De natura deorum* II.56; Ovid, *Metamorphoses* I.84–6; Silius Italicus, *Punica* XV.84–7; Manilius, *Astronomica* IV.905–8; Lactantius, *Divinae Institutiones* II.1; Gregory of Nyssa, *De hominis opificio* cap. 8; Boethius, *De consolatione philosophiae* V.m.5; Peter Lombard, *Sententiae* II.16.
56. Petrarch 1577, p. 734 (II.93); Facio 1611, p. 156; Manetti 1975, p. 5; Brandolini 1543, pp. 53–4; Mair 1530, f. 164ᵛ; Ricchieri 1542, p. 84 (III.11); Pérez de Oliva 1982, p. 98; Zwingli 1905–83, VI, 3, p. 120 (*Sermonis de providentia dei anamnema*); Du Bellay 1966, p. 121 (*Les Regrets* 53); see also Patrides 1982; Sozzi 1982, pp. 12–20.
57. Erasmus 1969–, V, 1, p. 74 (*De contemptu mundi*): 'Corpore quidem, excepta figura, nihil a brutis absumus, anima vero non parum ad divinam illam atque aeternam naturam accedimus'; Ricchieri 1542, p. 59 (II.22): 'Omnis nostra dignitas ab anima est, quae vehiculum est ad deum . . .'; see also Paleario 1696, p. 168 (*De felicitate*); Florimonte 1554, p. 14; Fox-Morcillo 1566, p. 133.
58. Aristotle, *Nicomachean Ethics* I.7; Bruni 1741, II, pp. 138–9; Florimonte 1554, pp. 34–5; Nores 1578, f. 5ᵛ; Heiland 1581, p. 183; Piccart 1605, p. 4.
59. For Brunelleschi, see Manetti 1975, p. 59; for printing, see Boaistuau 1982, p. 61.
60. Nemesius of Emesa, *De natura hominis*, cap. 1; Gregory of Nyssa, *De hominis opificio*, cap. 2; Augustine, *De civitate Dei* IX.13; *Asclepius*, cap. 6; John Scotus Eriugena, *De divisione naturae* IV.10; Hugh of St Victor, *De sacramentis* II.1.

of a variety of Renaissance authors,[61] but it played a particularly important role in the philosophical system of Ficino. Soul, the category to which man belonged, was according to him the lowest being in the intellectual world and the highest in the corporeal world.[62] It, therefore, held the central place in the scheme of five ontological hypostases adapted by Ficino from the *Enneads* of Plotinus and also from Proclus' commentary on the *Parmenides*: God, Angel, Soul, Quality and Body.[63] Ficino's disciple Francesco da Diacceto described how soul united the intelligible and corporeal realms in such a way that it neither lost its connection with the divine nor became corrupted by matter, so that it was 'truly the bond and knot of the universe'.[64]

Man's soul not only tied together the categories of being, it also in some sense contained them all within itself. This was the reason, according to Ficino, why God had incarnated himself as a man. By uniting himself with human nature, he was united with all creation.[65] The theory that man was composed of all the elements in the universe and was therefore a small world or microcosm was essentially a Platonic doctrine, found above all in the *Timaeus*. But from antiquity onwards it had influenced thinkers of all philosophical persuasions.[66] It was used extensively by philosophers with a Platonic bent of mind, such as Nicholas of Cusa, Marsilio Ficino and Francesco Giorgi, but also appealed to a wide range of writers.[67] It was

61. Acciaiuoli 1535, f. 195ᵛ: 'homo autem videtur esse medium inter alia animalia et essentias separatas'; Pomponazzi 1954, p. 38: 'bene enuntiaverunt antiqui cum ipsum [sc. hominem] inter aeterna et temporalia statuerunt, ob eam causam, quod neque pure aeternus neque pure temporalis sit, cum de utraque natura participet'; Zwinger 1566, p. 6: 'Homo ... mundi vinculum'; Rhenanus 1969, p. 43 describes man as 'utriusque mundi copula'.
62. Ficino 1964–70, III, p. 113 (XVI.1): 'in eo gradu locata est hominis anima, ut sicut succedit proxime mentibus, ita proxime terrena praecedat corpora'; see also G. Pico 1942, p. 266 (*Heptaplus*).
63. Ficino 1964–70, I, p. 137 (III.2): 'in quinque gradus... omnia colligamus, Deum et angelum in arce naturae ponentes, corpus et qualitatem in infimo; animam vero inter illa summa et haec infima mediam'; see also Kristeller 1953a, pp. 435–7; M. J. B. Allen 1982, who points out that Ficino used tetradic and hexadic, as well as pentadic, schemes.
64. Diacceto 1563, p. 109 (*De amore libri tres* II.2): 'nec adeo degenerat a mundo intelligibili, ut divinae conditionis expers sit; nec adeo vergit in corpus, ut materiae sordibus participet... Ex quo universi nodus ac vinculum iure dicta est'.
65. Ficino 1576, I, p. 21 (*De Christiana religione*): 'naturae ... humanae Deus uniatur oportet, in qua sunt omnia'.
66. Conger 1922; Allers 1944; Olerud 1951; Festugière 1944–54, I, pp. 92–4; Spanneut 1969; Rico 1970; D'Alverny 1976; Bertola 1984. The expression μικρὸς κόσμος was coined by Aristotle in *Physics* VIII.2 (252ᵇ26).
67. Nicholas of Cusa 1932–, I, pp. 126–7 (*De docta ignorantia* III.3): 'Humana vero natura ... intellectualem et sensibilem naturam complicans ac universa intra se constringens, ut microcosmos aut parvus mundus a veteribus rationabiliter vocitetur'; see also III, p. 143 (*De coniecturis* II.14); Vives 1782–90, III, pp. 334–5 (*De anima et vita*): 'Nec immerito illud fere placuit, hominem parvum quendam mundum appellari, quod vim naturamque rerum omnium sit complexus'; Agrippa 1533, p. 160; Ficino 1981, pp. 121–2; Giorgi 1525, sig. Q iiᵛ; Castiglione 1947, pp. 482–3; Ricchieri 1542, p. 56 (II.18); Varchi 1858–9, II, p. 625; Sensi 1577, f. 3ʳ; Magirus 1603, pp. 1–2.

often stated that man was a microcosm because he was composed of the same four elements as the cosmos: fire, air, water and earth.[68] For Paracelsus the four elements were combined in man into a fifth essence or quintessence, in which the celestial and elemental worlds were united.[69]

In the view of Giovanni Pico della Mirandola man was a microcosm in which all forms of life were contained. Men therefore had the potential to become whatever type of being they chose. Although there were many discussions of man's protean nature in patristic and medieval literature, Pico gave this traditional idea a striking new formulation.[70] In his famous 1486 *Oratio*, God tells Adam that he has been given no fixed place in the universe. He is therefore free to fashion himself into whatever form of life he selects: he can sink to the level of an animal or rise to the heights of a god.[71] Pico thus removed man from the centre of the Neoplatonic hierarchy of being and allotted him instead an indeterminate ontological status.

Pico's *Oratio* became a popular and influential work, often quoted and imitated.[72] More importantly, many of his ideas filtered into the thought of sixteenth-century thinkers, who developed and adapted them according to their own perspectives. Filippo Beroaldo in his commentary on Apuleius' *Golden Ass* elaborated Pico's notion of man's metamorphic capacity.[73] And Francesco Piccolomini's account of man as the creator of his own perfection clearly drew on Pico's assertion of man's freedom to fashion himself.[74] Juan Luis Vives used the *Oratio* as the basis for his *Fabula de homine* (1518), in which man is allegorised as an actor who plays every role in the universe from the lowliest plant to the highest divinity.[75] The notion that man has no fixed place in the universal hierarchy was developed by Charles de Bovelles

68. Du Bartas 1935–40, II, p. 391 (*La Première Sepmaine*): 'En nous se void le feu, l'air, et la terre, l'onde|Et brief, l'homme n'est rien qu'un abregé du monde'; see also Vives 1782–90, V, p. 156 (*Vigilia in Somnium Scipionis*).

69. Paracelsus 1922–33, Abt. I, XII, pp. 36–9 (*Astronomia magna*): '[Got] hat ausgezogen das wesen von den vier elementen zusamen in ein stück . . . Also ist der mensch die kleine welt, das ist, alle eigenschaft der welt der mensch in ime . . . Also ist der mensch das fünfte wesen und ist microcosmus'; Abt. I, IX, p. 220 (*Opus Paramirum*): 'nichts ist im himel noch auf erden das nicht sei im menschen'.

70. Lubac 1974, pp. 184–204.

71. G. Pico 1942, pp. 104–6 (*Oratio*); see also p. 192 (*Heptaplus*): 'Tritum in scholis verbum est, esse hominem minorem mundum, in quo mixtum ex elementis corpus et caelestis spiritus et plantarum anima vegetalis et brutorum sensus et ratio et angelica mens et Dei similitudo conspicitur.'

72. Pérez de Oliva 1982, pp. 93, 96; see also the writings of Hieronymus Pico published in Schmitt 1984, § V, pp. 70–3.

73. Beroaldo 1500, f. 266ʳ: 'Sic homines transfigurantur in lupos fiuntque versipelles, quando induunt lupinam voracitatem; sic mox ex lupis in pristinam faciem revertuntur pristinamque vestem resumunt, quando exutis improbis moribus et lupina deposita natura ad humanos mores et humanam rationem . . . regrediuntur'; see also Krautter 1971, pp. 65–71.

74. F. Piccolomini 1594b, p. 2: 'summopere gloriari vales, si tuo labore, studio, cura et diligentia perficeris . . . cum sis tuae integritatis, tuaeque perfectionis faber'.

75. Vives 1782–90, IV, pp. 3–8; see also Colish 1962; Rico 1970, pp. 117–28.

in his *Liber de sapiente* (1509). Man, according to Bovelles, is a mirror who stands outside and opposite the rest of creation in order to observe and reflect the world. He is thus the focal point of the universe in which all degrees of reality converge.[76]

Luther's concept of man was in sharp contrast to this exalted picture of human potentiality, for he centred his view on the fall. Christians who lamented man's misery had always pointed to the evil consequences of the fall; and even those who praised his dignity did not entirely ignore it.[77] But Luther, in order to stress man's total dependence on redemption through Christ, insisted that human nature was wholly corrupted by original sin.[78] Man was therefore unable to make any contribution to his own salvation. Instead of the autonomous self-creator described by Pico, Luther saw fallen man merely as raw material which received its ultimate form from God.[79] Erasmus rejected this view of man as a lump of clay which God moulded like a potter.[80] In Protestant thought, however, the spiritual impotence and depravity of post-lapsarian man became a central doctrine. Man's high opinion of himself, according to Calvin, had to be deflated, and he had to be convinced of his own corruption and debility. For only then would man realise that he was lost and hopeless without divine grace.[81]

Like the Reformers, the Catholic sceptic Michel de Montaigne was concerned to destroy man's presumption and lower his excessive estimate of his own worth. Unlike them, however, he did not focus his attention on man's salvation. Instead he turned his critical gaze on many of the standard Renaissance views of man and gradually undermined the foundations on which they stood. He questioned, for instance, the belief that men were

76. Bovelles 1982, p. 176 (cap. 26): 'Homo nichil est omnium et a Natura extra omnia factus et creatus est: ut multividus fiat sitque omnium expressio et naturale speculum, abiunctum et separatum ab universorum ordine, eminus et e regione omnium collocatum, ut omnium centrum'; see also *Charles de Bovelles* 1982, pp. 101–8 (Magnard).

77. Salutati 1957, p. 77 (cap. 33): 'Pone tibi ante oculos, miser homo, statum tue miserabilis voluntatis . . . Transgressione quidem primorum parentum hac pena tenetur cuncta posteritas, ut . . . nunc non peccare penitus nequeamus'; Petrarch 1577, p. 733 (II.93): 'Nisi . . . peccati iugum sponte subiissetis, omnium quae sub coelo sunt dominium haberetis.'

78. Luther 1883–, XVIII, p. 786 (*De servo arbitrio*): 'Si credimus Christum redemisse homines per sanguinem suum, totum hominem fateri cogimur fuisse perditum.'

79. *Ibid.*, XXXIX, 1, p. 177 (*De homine*): 'tota creatura, nunc subiecta vanitati, materia Deo est ad gloriosam futuram suam formam'; see also Mostert 1983.

80. Erasmus 1703–6, IX, col. 1248 (*De libero arbitrio diatribe*): 'ad quid valet totus homo, si sic in illo agit Deus, quemadmodum figulus agit in luto?'; cf. Rom. 9:21.

81. Calvin 1863–1900, II, cols. 209–24 (*Institutio religionis Christianae* II.3: 'Ex corrupta hominis natura nihil nisi damnabile prodire'); see also Battenhouse 1949; Trinkaus 1983, pp. 317–39; F. Wilson 1751, p. 265: 'quocunque te vertas, intelligis te nihil esse, nisi sordes, vitium, infirmitatem, scelus, adeoque omni odio dignum; omne auxilium, omnem salutem atque dignitatem a Deo exspectandam'; see also Baker-Smith 1984.

(margin note: Montaigne's attack on man's superiority)

superior to animals. Man's upright posture, which supposedly distinguished him from the animals, was in fact surpassed by camels and ostriches, whose necks were set even higher and more erect than man's.[82] Nor was Montaigne sympathetic to the complaint that nature had treated animals better than man by giving them more adequate covering. Man's skin was just as protective as that of animals, as could be seen from the example of the ancient Gauls and the Irish who managed without wearing any clothes at all.[83] Indeed, man was let down not by nature but by his own reason, of which he was so inordinately proud. It was pure presumption on man's part which led him to rate the uncertain knowledge he acquired through reason more highly than the infallible dictates of nature. Man's knowledge did little or nothing to improve the quality of his life, whereas natural instinct, which guided animals, provided them with peace, tranquillity, security, innocence and health.[84] Pierre Charron, who developed many of Montaigne's ideas in his *De la sagesse* (1601), concluded that man's superior intellect cost him more than it was worth. For it was the source of his greatest woes: vice, passion, irresolution, despair. By contrast, animals, who simply lived according to nature, were more secure, happy and content than men.[85]

Man's belief in the anthropocentric teleology of creation was, for Montaigne, another proof of human vanity and self-aggrandisement: 'Who persuaded him that this wonderful motion of the vault of heaven, the eternal light of these torches that roll so proudly above his head, the terrifying movements of this infinite sea, have been established and have lasted so many centuries for his convenience and use?'[86] But perhaps the most revolutionary aspect of his concept of man was Montaigne's conviction that he could learn about human nature by studying one individual man: himself. Since the time of Petrarch, there had been a personal and subjective quality in some Renaissance ethical thought. But

(margin note: Renaissance subjectivity)

82. Montaigne 1965, p. 484 (II.12): 'l'ancoleure des chameaux et des austruches, je la trouve encore plus relevée et que droite la nostre'; see also Tahureau 1981, p. 164, who points out the dangers of man's erect posture. 83. *Ibid.*, pp. 456–7 (II.12).
84. *Ibid.*, p. 460 (II.12): 'La vanité de nostre presomption faict que nous aymons mieux devoir à nos forces qu'à sa [i.e. la nature] liberalité nostre suffisance'; p. 487: 'De quel fruit pouvons nous estimer avoir esté à Varro et Aristote cette intelligence de tant de choses? Les a elle exemptez des incommoditez humaines?'; p. 485: 'à eux [i.e. les animaux] nous laissons . . . la paix, le repos, la securité, l'innocence et la santé'; see also A. C. Keller 1957; *Montaigne* 1982, pp. 77–100 (McFarlane); on Montaigne's scepticism, see Popkin in this volume, pp. 682–4 below.
85. Charron 1824, I, pp. 203–23.
86. Montaigne 1965, p. 450 (II.12): 'Qui luy a persuadé que ce branle admirable de la voute celeste, la lumiere eternelle de ces flambeaux roulans si fierement sur sa teste, les mouvemens espouvantables de cette mer infinie, soyent establis et se continuent tant de siecles pour sa commodité et pour son service?'

Montaigne was the first to assert that each man bore the entire form of the human condition and therefore to see himself in all his individuality as the central subject of moral philosophy.[87]

THE SUPREME GOOD

In *Nicomachean Ethics* 1.2 (1094ª18–26), Aristotle described the final goal of mans's life as the attainment of the supreme good (τὸ ἄριστον). This he defined as that end which is desired only for its own sake, while other things are desired for the sake of it. From antiquity to the Renaissance, the enquiry into man's supreme good or *summum bonum*, that is, the attempt to determine the ultimate purpose for which he was born, was generally accepted as the defining characteristic of ethics.[88]

The supreme good, according to Aristotle, was happiness (εὐδαιμονία), since other things, such as wealth, honour and pleasure, were sought in order to achieve happiness, but it was desired solely for its own sake.[89] His view was so thoroughly adopted by scholastic philosophers that the term happiness (*felicitas* or *beatitudo*) became synonymous with the *summum bonum*.[90] As to what constituted this happiness or supreme good, there had always been considerable disagreement among philosophers. Renaissance discussions of the subject often began by referring to the fact that, according to Augustine, Varro had postulated the existence of 288 possible philosophical sects, each with a different position on the *summum bonum*.[91] Bruni

---

87. *Ibid.*, p. 805 (III.2): 'On attache aussi bien toute la philosophie morale à une vie populaire et privée que à une vie de plus riche estoffe: chaque homme porte la forme entiere de l'humaine condition'; p. 622 (II.16): 'Puis que la philosophie n'a sçeu trouver aucune voye pour la tranquillité, qui fust bonne en commun, que chacun la cherche en son particulier!'; see also Kristeller 1965a, pp. 66–7; Screech 1983, p. 6.

88. Augustine, *De civitate Dei* VIII.8: 'moralis . . . [est pars philosophiae] ubi quaeritur de summo bono'; Landino 1980, p. 119: 'In ea [parte philosophiae, quam Graeci ethicen, nos de vita et de moribus nominamus] . . . nos nihil aliud quaerimus nisi primum bonorum malorumque fines'; Javelli 1651, p. 633: 'Omnes qui de moralibus scripserunt, et antiqui philosophi et sacri theologi, intentionem suam compleverunt in investigatione summi boni et ultimi finis ad quem natus est homo'; Lambin 1565, sig. A 3ʳ⁻ᵛ: 'In exquirendo . . . summo hominis bono philosophiam moralem esse occupatam . . . perspicuum est'; F. Piccolomini 1594b, p. 9: 'in libris de moribus . . . praesertim consideratur summum bonum'.

89. Aristotle, *Nicomachean Ethics* 1.7 (1097ª34–1097ᵇ6).

90. *Cambridge History* 1982, pp. 673–86 (Wieland).

91. Augustine, *De civitate Dei* XIX.1; Fox-Morcillo 1566, p. 124: 'Siquidem in extremi boni adeptione sitam esse foelicitatem, nemo est philosophorum omnium qui ignoret; sed quid sit illud ultimum bonum, minime adhuc inter ipsos constat, planeque omnes hac in re dissentiunt usque adeo, ut ducentas et eo amplius philosophorum sententias de summo bono a Varrone commemoratas, divus Augustinus affirmet'; see also Petrarch 1958, p. 91; Giorgi 1525, sig. D vʳ; Zwinger 1586, VI, p. 1561; Talon 1583, p. 1020; Keckermann 1607a, p. 9. Cf. the remarks of Scala discussed by Grafton in this volume, pp. 772–3 below.

attempted to reconcile the views of the major philosophical schools by arguing that their disagreements over man's supreme good were merely verbal and that in reality their positions were quite similar.[92] But most Renaissance authors recognised that there was a bewildering diversity of conflicting and contradictory opinions about the source of man's happiness.[93] Some, wrote Montaigne, placed it in virtue, others in pleasure; still others thought it lay in following nature, or in knowledge, or in having no pain, or in not being deceived by appearances.[94]

While pagan philosophers disagreed about the *summum bonum*, Christians were in fundamental agreement that God was the source of man's ultimate happiness. This belief was held by Renaissance philosophers no less than their medieval predecessors.[95] They universally accepted the fundamental Christian doctrine that man would only attain his supreme good after death, when his immortal soul would enjoy the perpetual vision, contemplation and fruition of God.[96] The meagre and ephemeral felicity available to man on earth hardly deserved the name of happiness, according to Hieronymus Wolf, and could more aptly be termed a diminution of misery.[97] In the opinion of Facio, man could never find happiness on earth because he was by nature dissatisfied with whatever he had and always desired more. This Faustian discontent would not be allayed until he attained perfect and eternal beatitude in heaven.[98] Alfonso de La Torre claimed that the prophets had experienced a complete vision of God in their

---

92. Bruni 1928, p. 27 (*Isagogicon*): 'etsi verbis pugnent, re tamen et effectu proximae sunt'.
93. Beroaldo 1513, f. 112ʳ (*Oratio de foelicitate*): 'de hac foelicitate . . dissentiunt; nec vulgus sapientesque concordant; immo nec ipsi philosophi inter se conveniunt'; Carbone de Costacciaro 1585, f. 201ʳ: 'Maxima semper inter eos, qui de moribus scripserunt, de humana felicitate extitit concertatio'; *Collegium Conimbricense* 1612, col. 15: 'De nulla . . . re apud philosophos tanta dogmatum varietas . . . fuit, ut de hominis felicitate.'
94. Montaigne 1965, p. 578 (II.12): 'Les uns disent nostre bien estre loger en la vertu, d'autres en la volupté, d'autres au consentir à nature; qui, en la science; qui, à n'avoir point de douleur; qui, à ne se laisser emporter aux apparences.'
95. Reisch 1504, sig. qq iiiᵛ: '[Deus] est finis ultimus et beatitudo seu foelicitas perfecta ad quam homo creatus est'; F. Zabarella 1655, p. 101: 'tribus his, Deo intelligendo, tenendo, fruendo, beatorum constat vera, certa consummataque felicitas'; Filelfo 1552, p. 19: 'si totius . . . hominis bonum, felicitatem esse volumus, hanc vero aliud nihil esse quam Deum'; Landino 1980, p. 76: 'Christianorum . . . una sententia est . . . ultimum atque extremum omnium bonorum deum esse.'
96. Bosso 1493, sig. b viiᵛ: 'Pulcherrimo . . . et gloriosissimo illo fruemur divinitatis spectaculo, in quo et tota et consummata beatitudo consistit'; Fox-Morcillo 1566, p. 134: 'Summum . . . hominis bonum . . . est perpetua quaedam et constans cernendi Dei fruendique voluptas'; Du Vair 1945, p. 57: 'cette dernière et plus parfaite félicité consiste au regard de la face du Père des lumières'.
97. See Wolf's commentary in Cicero 1569, col. 6: 'Quae profecto non tam felicitas est, quam diminutio quaedam miseriarum'.
98. Facio 1611, pp. 108–9: 'Guarinus: . . . sentio neminem in hac vita beatum esse posse . . . Est enim insitus natura mortalibus inexplebilis quidam appetitus, ut quo maiora quis adeptus sit, eo plura desideret.'

own lifetime and that wise men through their intellect and erudition were able to understand something of the divine essence. But the majority of men, who were neither wise nor prophetic, had to wait until the next life to be united with God and thus attain the supreme good.[99]

Scholastic philosophers had worked out a compromise solution to the conflict between the Christian and Aristotelian views of happiness. They argued that although perfect and complete happiness was only attainable in heaven, there was nonetheless an imperfect and inferior happiness which was available to man while on earth.[100] This formula continued to be widely used in the Renaissance. Johannes Versor, for instance, explained that in the *Nicomachean Ethics* Aristotle was not discussing perfect happiness, which could only be attained in the afterlife, but rather human and mortal happiness, which could be experienced in this life.[101] Another late scholastic philosopher, Petrus Tartaretus, defined God as man's ultimate good in an absolute sense and Aristotelian happiness as the best of merely human goods.[102] The humanist Agostino Dati also asserted that happiness was two-fold: the true happiness to be enjoyed in heaven, which was never mentioned by Aristotle; and the incomplete, flawed happiness man achieves by his own powers, which Aristotle discussed thoroughly.[103] In his commentary on Boethius' *De consolatione philosophiae*, the Flemish theologian Dionysius Carthusianus claimed that the terrestrial happiness described by Aristotle was relative, not absolute. In the present life, since we can only see God through a glass darkly, we are unable to experience true, divine happiness. But we can achieve a limited felicity, the first stage of that perfect beatitude which will be our reward in the future life.[104] For the Spanish Jesuit Francisco Suárez, the natural happiness of this life, although not perfect and real in comparison with the supernatural happiness of the

---

99. La Torre 1855, pp. 400–1; see also Delfino 1556, pp. 254–62, a plagiarised Italian version of La Torre's work.   100. *Cambridge History* 1982, pp. 657–72 (Wieland).

101. Versor 1491, f. 118ᵛ: 'in hac vita [Philosophus] non ponit perfectam felicitatem, sed talem qualis potest competere humane et mortali vite . . . perfecta et vera felicitas non potest haberi in hac vita'.

102. Tartaretus 1514, f. 3ᵛ: 'ipsa [felicitas] est ultimus finis; quod non est intelligendum simpliciter, quia deus est ultimus finis, sed debet intelligi inter bona humana'.

103. Dati 1503, f. 164ʳ (*Epistolae* II): 'Duplex . . . illa [felicitas] a doctis viris traditur. Una, quae vera beatitudo est . . ., qua in coelesti patria fruendum sit, quam nunquam Philosophus disserit . . . Altera, quae ex solis naturalibus parari consuevit, nequaquam perfecta, sed manca quaedam atque inchoata . . . Hanc vero . . . copiose et graviter Aristoteles disserit.'

104. Dionysius Carthusianus 1532–40, XIII, f. 10ʳ: 'Est . . . duplex beatitudo. Una viae, alia patriae. Beatitudo viae est . . . inchoatio quaedam felicitatis futurae, quae est praemium beatitudinis viae . . . [Philosophus] asserit hominem hic posse esse felicem, secundum quid, non simpliciter . . . in vita praesenti non cognoscimus deum nisi per speculum in aenigmate [I Cor. 13:12].'

next, was nonetheless the highest and ultimate good attainable within the limited framework of the human condition here on earth.[105]

CLASSICAL ETHICS AND CHRISTIANITY

Not all religions are bound up with a system of ethics. Worship of the Greek gods, for instance, by no means entailed imitation of their behaviour, which could hardly be described as morally instructive. But Christ's actions, as reported in the gospels, have always been regarded by his followers as an ideal and model. The moral values preached in the Sermon on the Mount were very different from those declaimed in the Agora and Forum. Nonetheless, Christianity never entirely rejected the ethical philosophy of pagan antiquity. Instead it attempted to appropriate the useful aspects of classical ethics, while abandoning or avoiding any doctrines which overtly contradicted Christian dogma. Opinions varied among Church Fathers as to the relative proportion of wheat to chaff in classical ethics; and some philosophical schools, such as Platonism and Stoicism, fared better in patristic literature than others, such as Aristotelianism and Epicureanism. Attitudes toward pagan ethics were continually revised and challenged, especially in the thirteenth and fourteenth centuries, when scholastic philosophers, following the lead of Thomas Aquinas, devised elaborate strategies to make Peripatetic ethical doctrines compatible with Christian dogma. The increased interest in classical philosophy which arose during the Renaissance did not bring with it any diminution in the tension between Christian and pagan ethics. Renaissance authors drew heavily on ancient philosophical sources in their effort to establish a system of ethics which was appropriate for laymen living in the secular world of the present life. But they never forgot that these laymen were Christians, whose immortal souls were destined for a far higher goal in the next life.

One solution to this perennial problem was the eclectic approach recommended by St Basil. He suggested that Christians reading the works of pagan authors should imitate bees, who select only certain flowers and take only what is useful from them, leaving the rest behind.[106] Citing Basil as his authority, Bartolomeo Scala claimed that the ethical doctrines of

---

105. Suárez 1856–78, IV, p. 45 (*De fine hominis* IV.3): 'necesse est . . . ut pro tempore huius vitae aliquid sit optimum . . . illud ergo habebit rationem beatitudinis huius vitae, quae licet comparata ad illam, quam speramus, sit imperfecta et revera non sit beatitudo'.
106. St Basil, *De utilitate studii in libros gentilium*, cap. 4. This work was translated into Latin by Bruni and enjoyed considerable popularity in the fifteenth century; for his preface, see Bruni 1928, pp. 99–100; see also Schucan 1973.

ancient philosophers were not to be entirely neglected, but rather followed selectively and cautiously, so that one took in what was profitable while avoiding what was erroneous.[107] Theodor Zwinger wanted Christians to reap the harvest ploughed by Plato and sown by Aristotle, but with a pious and judicious selectivity, assenting to whatever agreed with faith, but rejecting anything which disagreed.[108] Erasmus also subscribed to this view. Although he warned against adopting the moral habits of the pagans when studying their literature, he nevertheless admitted that their works contained much that was conducive to upright living. And good advice, even if it came from a pagan, was not to be spurned.[109]

Indeed, pagan authors like Cicero had often presented such good advice that Erasmus felt they put Christians to shame. Although Christians claimed to follow the divinely inspired morality of the gospels, for the most part they did not even live up to the moral standards set by mere pagans relying solely on natural reason.[110] In a similar vein, Vives complained that the pagan Seneca taught Christians what he by right should have learnt from them.[111] Philippe Le Plessis thought his slothful and morally lax contemporaries could learn a good deal from the pagan Aristotle, who spoke with such divine inspiration about virtue, despite the fact that in place of Christ's preaching he had heard only Plato's.[112] According to Francisco Thamara, in the preface to his Spanish translation of Xenophon's *Oeconomicus*, God had permitted the works of many ancient authors to survive precisely in order that they might serve as a reproach to Christians, who despite their illumination by the light of true faith were more blind and obtuse than these virtuous pagans.[113]

107. Scala, *Epistola de nobilioribus philosophorum sectis*, published in Stein 1888, p. 551: 'Neque . . . is sum qui antiquiorum scripta philosophorum negligenda putem. Sed imitandae mihi videntur apes, ut ait Basilius, quae in adeundis floribus . . . ex singulis id assumunt quod melli faciundo aptum vident.'

108. Zwinger 1566, p. 16: 'Plato arat; Aristoteles serit; nos cum iudicio et pietate fruges demetamus . . . ut in quibus cum sacrosancta fide nostra consentiunt, iis assentiamur; in quibus ab eadem discrepant, antiquior apud nos sit dominae scripturae quam pedissequae philosophiae auctoritas.'

109. Erasmus 1703–6, v, col. 7 (*Enchiridion militis Christiani*): 'nolim te cum Gentilium litteris, Gentilium et mores haurire. Alioqui permulta reperies et illic ad recte vivendum conducibilia; neque adspernandum, quod etiam Ethnicus auctor bene monet.'

110. Erasmus 1906–58, IV, p. 67 (preface to his 1520 edition of Cicero's *De officiis*): 'quam turpe sit non id perspicere pectus Evangelica luce illustratum, quod perspectum est iis quibus sola nature scintilla praelucebat'.

111. Vives 1973, p. 27: 'Audi Senecam, hominem gentilem, Christianos edocentem quae illum conveniebat potius a Christianis discere.'

112. See his preface to Aristotle 1553b, sig. aa iii^r: 'Cest Ethnique, qui . . . n'ouist iamais pour Christ preschant que Platon, parle si divinement de la vertu.'

113. Xenophon 1546, p. 205: 'permitio Dios que [las escripturas] permanesciessen por tantos tiempos . . . para castigo y reprehension de nosotros los Cristianos, que siendo alumbrados por aquella luz

The basic premise underlying all these views was that classical morality, although vastly inferior to Christian, was not in fundamental conflict with it. Ancient ethics had thus mapped out a path which led in the direction of the true Christian homeland, but which stopped short at the boundaries of the temporal world. Although, according to Petrarch, virtue was not man's final goal, as pagan philosophers had thought, nonetheless the right road to that goal (which was, of course, God) passed through the virtues.[114] A similar view was expressed by Poggio Bracciolini, who claimed that the ancients had taught essentially the same moral precepts as Christians. But while pagan philosophers had regarded these doctrines solely in the context of this life, Christians saw them as a preparation for the next.[115] Andrea Camuzio, challenging those philosophers and professors of Scripture who claimed that the study of philosophy, especially Aristotelian, was at variance with Christianity, maintained that so far from conflicting with the dogmas of sacred theology, the doctrines of Aristotle and Plato were in complete agreement with them.[116] For Crisostomo Javelli Christian moral philosophy transcended that of Plato and Aristotle as much as the unfailing brilliance of the sun outshone the lustre of the stars and moon.[117] Nevertheless, Javelli did not deny the validity or utility of Peripatetic and Platonic ethical doctrines, which he in fact discussed in great detail. He merely pointed out their limitations in comparison with the infallibility and perfection of Christian dogma.

There was, of course, considerable sensitivity to the differences between classical and Christian concepts of morality. Salutati, for example, stressed the fact that while pagan philosophers had dealt primarily with external actions as judged by others, Christians were far more concerned with the internal quality of their behaviour as evaluated by their own consciences.[118]

verdadera de nuestra fe . . . estamos porventura mas ciegos y torpes y mas descuyadeos que estos varones excelentes'.

114. Petrarch 1955, p. 746 (*De sui ipsius et multorum ignorantia*): 'Etsi . . . non sit in virtute finis noster, ubi eum philosophi posuere, est tamen per virtutes iter rectum eo ubi finis est noster'; see also Foster 1984, p. 168.

115. Poggio Bracciolini 1984–, II, p. 40: 'quod gentilium habet philosophantium doctrina, id totum fere respicit presentem vitam; quod vero nostri tradunt, id ita presentis vite rationem haberi concedit, ut sit tanquam viaticum future'.

116. Camuzio 1541, p. 18: 'ego sum huius sententiae, ut existimem sacrosanctae theologiae praecepta Aristotelis atque Platonis placitis nulla ex parte reluctari, quinetiam conspirare in omnibus'; see also Schmitt 1982.

117. Javelli 1651, p. 378: '[Christianae moralis philosophiae] dignitas et celsitudo supra Peripateticam et Academicam tanta utique erit, quanta est solaris claritas indeficiens supra astrorum lunarisque globi refulgentiam eclipsabilem.'

118. Salutati 1891–1911, II, p. 184: 'virtutes . . . non ex operibus acquiruntur, sicut philosophi tradunt, sed sunt bona mentis qualitas . . . quam solus Deus in nobis operatur'; 1947, p. 334: 'Timeamus . . . conscientie nostre secretum et illam quasi testem cunctis que facimus adhibeamus'; see also Garin 1943–6; Witt 1983, pp. 416–29.

Clichtove, in his commentary on Aristotle's *Magna moralia*, described the virtues produced by reason and recommended by philosophers as mere shadows of those inspired by Christ. For while in human virtues it was man who acted, in divine ones it was the Holy Spirit which acted through man, using him as an instrument.[119] Yet despite their awareness of such important distinctions between classical and Christian morals, most Renaissance philosophers regarded the two ethical systems as basically compatible.

Most, but not all. The Florentine canon Matteo Bosso, whose eloquent erudition was admired by Angelo Poliziano and Giovanni Pico, rejected the notion that philosophers could make any contribution to man's happiness. For lacking the spiritual light of true wisdom which only Christ could fully and perfectly provide, they wandered in the dark and committed childish errors.[120] Such opinions were by no means limited to the priestly caste. In his *De transitu Hellenismi ad Christianismum* (1535), the humanist Guillaume Budé wrote: 'The happy life should not be discussed in the Stoa, or in the Academy, or in the clever debates of the Peripatetics, but rather we should philosophise in the school of the gospel, the Olympus of theory, the paradise, so to speak, of theosophical contemplation.'[121]

In the mid fifteenth century Lorenzo Valla mounted a thoroughgoing attack on those who attempted to assimilate classical ethics to Christian doctrine, for he believed that ancient morality had been totally superseded by the teachings of faith.[122] Vives, who shared this point of view, complained that his contemporaries neglected the infallible guidance provided by sacred doctrine, preferring to put their faith in dim-sighted and half-blind philosophers. Why, he asked, do we base our doctrines about virtues and vices on the dreams of pagans instead of the divine philosophy of Christianity which God has provided for us?[123]

119. Clichtove 1537, f. 3ʳ: 'virtutes quas parit ratio, quasque praedicant philosophi, umbrae earum sunt quas spiritus CHRISTI in membris suo insertis corpori operatur . . . In illis agit homo; in his agitur potius, ac organum est.'

120. Bosso 1495, sig. D vᵛ: '[Vera sapientia] lux animi est, sine qua tamquam caligine offusa omnis est vita. Et . . . hanc perfectam et plenam intulit Christus. Unde philosophi, quibus Christiana non illuxit foelicitas, sunt vagati per tenebras erroresque pueriliter'; for Poliziano and Pico, see Bosso 1492, sig. a iiʳ⁻ᵛ; see also Soranzo 1965.

121. Budé 1557, I, p. 227 (III): 'Non in Porticu, non in Academia, non in ambulatione arguta, de vita beata disputandum est; sed in schola Evangelii, in Olympo theoriae, et velut in qua paradiso theosophicae contemplationis philosophandum'; see also Penham 1954; De la Garanderie 1976, pp. 209–60.

122. L. Valla 1970a, p. 2: 'ego . . . planum faciam . . . nihil cum virtute gentilitatem, nihil recte fecisse'; see also Gray 1965, p. 46.

123. Vives 1782–90, VI, p. 210 (*De causis corruptarum artium* VI.1): 'nos illis [philosophis] credimus lusciosis et lippis, doctrinam aperte coelestem negligimus . . . Quod si, ut par est, pluris facimus divinam nostram philosophiam, quam esse a Deo nobis collatam pro certo habemus, quorsum attinet de virtutibus et vitiis ex illorum hallucinationibus statuere?'

The validity of classical ethics was also challenged by Protestants, such as Lambert Daneau. As a rigorous Calvinist, Daneau saw the fall as the key factor in understanding human behaviour. Since ancient philosophers had not taken original sin into account, none of their moral precepts was in his view of any use to post-lapsarian man.[124] Moreover, their opinions were vain and invalid because they were based solely on corrupt human reason. On these grounds, Daneau rejected the whole tradition of classical moral philosophy and presented instead a complete ethical system based on the law and word of God as revealed to Moses in the Ten Commandments.[125]

For Philipp Melanchthon, the fall was also the central issue in ethics. He believed, however, that although man's spiritual understanding of God's law was totally vitiated by original sin, his rational knowledge of the law of nature, which was part of divine law, remained intact. So man was still able to judge whether external actions were right or wrong.[126] Moral philosophy, according to Melanchthon, was the explication of the law of nature by the use of reason for the purpose of establishing rules to govern behaviour.[127] It was perfectly acceptable, indeed desirable, for Christians to use classical philosophy in the exegesis of the law of God as found in nature, provided they kept it strictly separate from the law of God as revealed in the gospels. For ethics had nothing to do with the will of God or the remission of sins; it was exclusively concerned with rules governing external action and civil society. Conversely, theology had nothing to do with these ethical rules: 'For Christ did not come to earth in order to teach moral precepts which were already known by reason, but rather to remit our sins and deliver the Holy Spirit to those who believed in him.'[128]

By delineating these two different spheres of influence, Melanchthon was in effect applying Luther's doctrine of the two kingdoms to ethics. In his treatise *Von weltlicher Obrigkeit* (1523), Luther distinguished between the sacred kingdom, in which true Christians are ruled by Christ through the Holy Spirit, and the secular kingdom, in which non-Christians are ruled by

124. Daneau 1588, f. 110ᵛ: 'quum philosophi ipsam naturae nostrae vitiositatem minime agnoscant (quae est omnium in nobis peccatorum fons), ii quoque vitio et fonti non medentur'.

125. Daneau 1577 (lib. II); see also Fatio 1976.

126. Melanchthon 1834–60, XVI, col. 23 (*Philosophiae moralis epitome*): 'manet iudicium de honestis actionibus exterioribus, . . . quod ipsum tamen est lex naturae et pars legis divinae'.

127. *Ibid.*, col. 167 (*Ethicae doctrinae elementa*): '[Philosophia moralis] est explicatio legis naturae, demonstrationes ordine in artibus usitato colligens, quantum ratio iudicare potest, quarum conclusiones sunt . . . praecepta de regenda disciplina in omnibus hominibus'; see also Hartfelder 1889, pp. 231–8.

128. *Ibid.*, col. 281 (*Enarrationes aliquot librorum Ethicorum Aristotelis*): 'Non enim venit Christus in mundum, ut praecepta de moribus doceret, quae iam ante norat ratio, sed ut remitteret peccata, ut credentibus in ipsum donaret Spiritum sanctum.'

political authorities through laws and coercion. Since the secular kingdom is also established by God and is necessary in order to preserve society, Christians must obey its authority, provided it does not impinge on their higher loyalty to God by interfering in matters of faith.[129] For Melanchthon the ethical precepts established by ancient philosophers performed the same function as the laws of the state: they governed the external actions of those who had not yet been enlightened by the Holy Spirit and helped to preserve the peace and order of civil society. Just as it was right for Christians to obey the laws of the state, so it was also incumbent on them to follow the precepts of moral philosophy.[130] Indeed, the innate knowledge of right and wrong, on which these precepts were based, was one of God's greatest gifts to man and should by no means be ignored. By strictly separating ethics and theology, Melanchthon was able to delimit an area, governed by natural law and coterminous with civil society, in which it was legitimate and beneficial for Christians to use pagan moral doctrines.[131]

Among Protestants, Melanchthon's arguments were extremely influential, for they made possible a strong defence of classical ethics against those who wanted to restrict Christian moral education to the Bible. Joachim Camerarius justified his commentary on Aristotle's *Ethics*, and Hieronymus Wolf his edition of Epictetus' *Enchiridion*, on the grounds that the study of moral philosophy was not to be rejected but rather embraced by Christians, as part of God's bounty to man.[132] Bartholomaeus Keckermann declared that although ethics differed from theology, it by no means conflicted with it. For if it did, it would mean that good morals were contrary to piety, while barbarous and scandalous behaviour, which disrupted society, was conducive to it.[133] According to Keckermann, pagan ethical doctrines

---

129. Luther 1883–, XI, pp. 267: 'Lieber herr, ich bynn euch schuldig zü gehorchen mit leyb unnd gütt, gepietet myr nach ewr gewalt mass auff erden, so will ich folgen. Heysst yhr aber mich glewben . . . so will ich nicht gehorchen'; see also *Reich Gottes* 1969.
130. Melanchthon 1834–60, XVI, col. 281 (*Enarrationes*): 'ut legibus publicis obtemperare rectum est, ita rectum est et philosophicis praeceptis parere'.
131. *Ibid.*, col. 23 (*Epitome*): 'Nec habet humana natura ullam dotem praestantiorem hac notitia, hoc est, discrimine honestorum et turpium'; col. 168 (*Elementa*): 'Philosophia moralis nequaquam est Evangelii promissio, sed pars est legis, sicut lex naturae, quae de disciplina concionatur . . .: ita veram philosophiam amplecti et probare et ea uti recte potest [Christianus].'
132. Camerarius 1578, p. 15: '[non] studium sapientiae et prudentiae abiiciendum aut negligendum est; sed potius hoc tanquam maximum bonum a Deo collatum hominibus et gratissimo animo amplecti et accurate custodire debemus'; Epictetus 1561, p. 13: 'Non . . . reliquiae divinae lucis in natura humana contemnendae sunt, sed magnificendae et studiose excolendae.'
133. Keckermann 1607a, p. 5: 'qui opinantur ethicam repugnare s[acrae] theologiae, quid aliud aiunt, quam bonos mores esse adversos pietati? Quod si boni mores repugnent pietati, necesse est . . . barbariem, imo omne genus flagitiorum, quo turbatur haec humana societas, amicum esse pietati'; see also Muller 1984.

were not to be damned, as some critics had claimed, but rather carefully separated from theology and restricted to civil morality.[134]

The attempt to establish the proper relation between Christian and classical moral doctrines and the effort to determine the supreme good of man were two of the most important issues in Renaissance ethics. The analysis and resolution of these problems varied considerably, however, depending on which of the ancient philosophical sects was being discussed. Aristotelian, Platonic, Stoic and Epicurean ethics each gave different answers to the question of the *summum bonum*, and each had different areas of conflict and agreement with Christianity.

ARISTOTELIAN ETHICS

Throughout the Renaissance, ethics as a professional and university discipline was Aristotelian. The evidence of statutes and inaugural lectures proves that in all major European universities, whether ethics was taught by scholastic philosophers or humanists, in the Protestant stronghold of the University of Wittenberg or the Jesuit Collegio Romano, Peripatetic texts and doctrines formed the basis of instruction.[135]

The Leiden theologian Antonius de Waele noted that although some thought Plato's ethics surpassed Aristotle's as much as Aristotle's physics surpassed Plato's, Aristotelian rather than Platonic writings had nonetheless been used over the past several centuries for the teaching of ethics.[136] One of the main reasons for Aristotle's continuing predominance was that his well-organised and methodical treatises were far more useful from the teaching point of view than Plato's highly rhetorical and unsystematic dialogues.[137] Melanchthon chose Peripatetic rather than Platonic ethics as the foundation

134. *Ibid.*, pp. 7–8.
135. For Florence, see *Reden und Briefe* 1970, pp. 3–30 (Argyropulos) and pp. 158–60 (Filelfo); for Pisa, see Kristeller 1956a, p. 298; for Padua, see *Platon et Aristote* 1976, pp. 105–46 (Poppi); for Rome, see Muret 1789, I, pp. 59–75; for Spanish universities, see Robles 1979, pp. 45–69; for Salamanca, see Pagden 1975, pp. 308–11; for Coimbra, see *Estatutos* 1963, pp. 317 and 329; for Paris, see Grabmann 1926–56, III, pp. 128–41, *University Records* 1944, p. 247 and Lambin 1565; for Leiden, see Dibon 1954–, I, pp. 59–61; for Cambridge, see Hackett 1970, pp. 277 and 299; for Oxford, see *Statuta Antiqua* 1931, p. 235 and Weisheipl 1964, p. 175; for Freiburg im Breisgau, see Ott and Fletcher 1964, p. 117; for Greifswald, see *Cambridge History* 1982, p. 19 (Kenny and Pinborg); for Wittenberg, see Petersen 1921, p. 170; for the Jesuits, see *Monumenta paedagogica Societatis Iesu* 1965–, II, p. 180 and the 1599 *Ratio studiorum* in Farrell 1970, p. 45.
136. Waele 1620, sig. † 3^{r-v}: 'licet sint, qui existiment Platonem in doctrina morum tanto esse superiorem Aristotele, quantum in rebus physicis Aristoteles Platonem antecellit, obtinuit tamen iam aliquot seculis inter Christianos, ut Aristotelica scripta in scholis atque academiis . . . Platonis commentationibus praeferrentur'; on Waele see Lohr 1982, p. 228.
137. Kristeller 1956a, p. 288; *Platon et Aristote* 1976, p. 136 (Poppi).

of Protestant education partly because Plato's doctrines, although often full
of wisdom, were ambiguously expressed and frequently couched in irony,
thus making them less suitable than Aristotle's treatises for pedagogic
purposes.[138] Zwinger, who had a Ramist obsession with method,
appreciated Aristotle's systematic treatment of ethical doctrines. He
declared that although Aristotle might not be equal to his teacher Plato in
devising arguments, he was not far inferior, while in method he was
superior.[139] Jason de Nores, a Cypriot noble who taught moral philosophy
at the University of Padua in the late sixteenth century, found Aristotle's
Ethics well ordered and organised, but lacking in the stirring rhetoric and
inspiring examples necessary to arouse virtuous behaviour. Plato, on the
other hand, was eloquent and stimulating but deficient in organisation and
order. In the opinion of Nores, it was only Cicero who managed to
combine rhetorical elegance with methodical treatment, thus producing
the most effective ethical treatises.[140] Yet Aristotle so dominated the field
that Nores felt obliged to defend Cicero's moral works by demonstrating
that they covered the same territory as the *Nicomachean Ethics*. He therefore
argued that *De finibus* corresponded to book I, *De officiis* to books II–VI, the
Tusculan Disputations to book VII, and *De amicitia* to books VIII and IX. For
book X, however, he offered no Ciceronian equivalent.[141]

   Although the *Magna moralia* and *De virtutibus et vitiis*, which were both
thought to be genuine Aristotelian works, received some attention during
the Renaissance, the *Nicomachean Ethics* remained the most important text
for the study of Aristotelian ethical doctrine, and the commentary remained
the predominant method of exegesis.[142] Moreover, commentaries written
in the thirteenth and fourteenth centuries continued to be influential, as can
be seen by the number of printed editions of these works, especially in the
period up to about 1520.[143] The medieval commentator who exerted the

138. Melanchthon 1834–60, XI, col. 348 (*De Aristotele* <1537>): 'male intellectae Platonis ironiae, ineptum hominem prorsus infatuarunt. Aristoteles contra discentium utilitati consulere, et scholas iuvare voluit'; col. 655 (*De Aristotele* <1547>): 'Nec ego nego plurima apud Platonem Ethica reperiri sapientissime cogitata. Sed sermones sunt ambigui multi diversis locis sparsi'; XVI, col. 280 (*Enarrationes*): 'Aristoteles, cum sit amans methodi, pleraque rectius dicit quam caeteri philosophi'.
139. Zwinger 1586, VI, p. 1558: 'Aristoteles inventione praeceptori suo Platoni si non par, non multo tamen inferior, methodo etiam superior.'
140. Nores 1597, p. 157: 'In M. Tullio nec ordo, nec methodus, nec perspicuitas, nec exempla, nec eloquentiae vis, nec concitatio animorum ad honestas actiones desideratur'; on Nores see Lohr 1979, pp. 541–2.
141. *Ibid.*, p. 51: 'Libri De finibus respondent primo Ethicorum. Libri Officiorum respondent secundo, tertio, quarto, quinto, sexto Ethicorum. Libri Tusculanarum respondet septimo Ethicorum . . . Dialogus de amicitia respondet octavo et nono Ethicorum.'
142. Aristotle 1970, I, 1, pp. 91–240. For commentaries on the *Magna moralia*, see Clichtove 1537 and Case 1596b. On the *De virtutibus*, see *Ethik im Humanismus* 1979, pp. 87–112 (Schmitt); Kraye 1981.
143. Printed editions of medieval commentaries are listed by Lohr 1967 to 1974a; see also Cranz and Schmitt 1984.

widest ranging and longest lasting influence on the interpretation of
Aristotle's *Ethics* was Thomas Aquinas, known by his followers as 'the
Expositor'. His *Expositio* continued to be printed well into the seventeenth
century and was studied by humanists as well as scholastics, Protestants as
well as Catholics.[144] Agostino Nifo praised Thomas' interpretation of the
Ethics for its lucidity, while both John Case and Theodor Zwinger argued
that Thomas often provided more help in understanding Aristotle's
meaning than recent commentators who were more learned and could read
the text in Greek.[145] Many humanists did of course find Thomas' style and
terminology repellent. Denys Lambin, for example, even when citing
Thomas with approval, translated his scholastic Latin into more palatable
Ciceronian vocabulary.[146] But even those who criticised his interpretations
had clearly read his commentary with considerable care and still thought it
worthwhile to argue against him.[147]

Scholastic commentaries on the *Nicomachean Ethics* continued to be
written as well as read during the Renaissance. In 1509 two philosophers
teaching at the University of Paris, Nicolas Dupuy and Gilbert Crab,
published Jean Buridan's commentary on books I–VI along with their own
quaestiones on books VII–X.[148] Johannes Versor, Petrus Tartaretus and John
Mair in their commentaries on the *Ethics* all adopted the typical scholastic
format of *quaestiones, dubitationes, responsiones* and *conclusiones*, while
Antonius Silvester broke Aristotle's arguments down into syllogisms,
enthymemata and corollaries. The *Cursus Conimbricensis* on the *Ethics*, first
published in 1593, still retained many scholastic features, such as the use of
quaestiones and the division of the *disputationes* into numbered *articuli* and
conclusiones.[149]

144. Cranz 1978; Pagden 1975, p. 309. On Thomas' interpretation of Aristotle's *Ethics*, see Papadis 1980 and Elders 1984. For Thomas' influence in the Renaissance, see Poggio Bracciolini 1984–, I, p. 16: 'Expositorem [Aristotelis] habeo Thomam de Aquino, virum egregium et facundum prout patitur pondus rerum'; Francesco Maturanzio's *Oratio in laudem Divi Thomae Aquinatis* in Zappacosta 1984, pp. 112–25; see also Gray 1965; Kristeller 1967a; J. W. O'Malley. 1974.

145. Nifo 1645, p. 49 (*De vera vivendi libertate*): 'Thomas dilucidus eius [sc. Aristotelis] interpres'; Case 1596a, p. 533: 'Multi hodie cum audiunt nomen Thomae, supercilia statim contrahunt . . .; sed si isti serio unam vel alteram quaestionem in illo sine praeiudicata sententia legerint . . . aurum splendidissimum forsan se invenisse dixerint'; Zwinger 1566, p. 23: '[Thomas Aquinas] coniectando multa assecutus est, quae caeteri, quantumvis lingua graeca probe instructi, aut ignorarunt, aut tanquam manifesta neglexerunt.'

146. Lambin 1558, p. 377 ad VI.12 (1144ᵃ29–30): 'D. Thomas . . . hunc locum explicat: "in hoc animi aspectu atque oculo, id est in solertia ingenerari prudentiam non sine virtute"'; cf. Thomas Aquinas 1934, p. 418 (VI.10.1273): 'in anima, "huic visui" idest huic cognoscitivo principio scilicet dinoticae, habitus prudentiae non fit sine virtute morali'.

147. For Ermolao Barbaro's critiques, see Kristeller 1956a, p. 349; see also Muret 1789, III, pp. 176 and 195.

148. Aristotle 1509; on Dupuy and Crab see Lohr 1974b, p. 271 and 1975, pp. 725–6.

149. Versor 1491; Tartaretus 1514; Mair 1530; A. Silvester 1517; *Collegium Conimbricense* 1612.

Humanists like Donato Acciaiuoli and Raffaele Maffei, while not entirely shunning scholastic argumentation and terminology, attempted to produce a clear exposition of Aristotle's text written in an elegant Latin style, concentrating more on philological than logical analysis and citing classical rather than medieval authorities.[150] Jacques Lefèvre d'Étaples, one of the most important proponents of the new style of commentary, criticised the scholastic method of dreaming up *quaestiones* and intricately subtle arguments, which he claimed interfered with the understanding of the text. His own commentary, entitled *Moralis in ethicen introductio* (which in turn was commented upon by his student Clichtove), provided simple but eloquent explanations of Aristotle's meaning, illustrated by historical, literary and biblical exempla, designed to stimulate the reader to practise the ethical rules he was studying.[151] Pier Vettori also criticised scholastic *quaestiones*, which he found more harmful than helpful, noting that this method of exposition was not employed by the wisest and most learned of medieval commentators, Thomas Aquinas.[152]

Beyond this basic distinction between scholastic and humanist styles of exegesis, Renaissance commentaries on the *Nicomachean Ethics* also came in a variety of shapes and sizes, designed to suit a wide range of interests and tastes. Melanchthon, Vermigli and Javelli all focused on the similarities and differences between Christian and Aristotelian ethical doctrines, while Lambin, Muret and van Giffen gave more attention to philological issues.[153] Some commentaries were written in the vernacular, such as those of Felice Figliucci, Galeazzo Florimonte and Giulio Landi. The last two were composed in dialogue form: Florimonte claimed to report a discussion in which Nifo instructed the Prince of Salerno on Aristotle's *Ethics*, while Landi attempted (without notable success) to transform the Latin commentary of Lefèvre and Clichtove into conversational Italian.[154] There were also commentaries, intended for use in schools and universities, which employed the question-and-answer format, a didactic method popular

---

150. Acciaiuoli 1535 is based on the lectures given by the Greek émigré Johannes Argyropulos at the Florentine *Studio*; R. Maffei 1542; E. Barbaro 1544 is apparently a collection of lecture notes for the course he taught at Padua in 1474–5 and shows little humanist influence; see also E. Barbaro 1943, I, p. 92 and Kristeller 1956a, pp. 337–53.

151. Lefèvre d'Étaples 1533; see also 1972, p. 42: 'Quaestionum et argumentationum . . . viam non tenui, quod mores non longa verborum disceptatione, sed sana intelligentia et recta educatione . . . parentur, et quod plerumque contra agendorum propositiones ac regulas contentiosos excogitare nodos plus obesse quam prodesse soleat auditoribus.'

152. Vettori 1584, p. 7: 'D. Thomas sapientissimus vir nullas aut paucas admodum [quaestiones] huiuscemodi in suas doctissimas elucubrationes in hos libros inseruit.'

153. Melanchthon 1834–60, XVI, cols. 277–416; Vermigli 1582; Javelli 1651; Lambin 1558; Muret 1789, III, pp. 135–466; Giffen 1608.   154. Figliucci 1551; Florimonte 1554; Landi 1564–75.

since the Middle Ages.[155] Another type of commentary consisted of brief book-by-book or chapter-by-chapter summaries. The briefest were those of Johannes Herbetius, who not only managed to epitomise each book of the *Ethics* in two or three sentences but also reduced the argument of the entire work to one pithy paragraph.[156] Zwinger, on the other hand, turned the entire work into a series of dichotomous synoptic tables, in the manner of his teacher Ramus.[157]

Alongside the commentaries, and gradually replacing them, were a large number of ethical treatises and textbooks primarily, although not always exclusively, based on Aristotle. Francesco Filelfo, for example, claimed to follow an eclectic approach in his *De morali disciplina*, but in fact drew mostly on Peripatetic moral doctrines.[158] Giovanni Nesi added a good deal of Platonic and Christian material to his dialogue *De moribus*, but it nonetheless remained deeply indebted to the *Ethics* commentary written by the principal interlocutor, Donato Acciaiuoli.[159] Francesco Piccolomini and Bartholomaeus Keckermann both produced large-scale works which attempted to provide a comprehensive treatment of the major issues in the field of ethics. Yet although they discussed the topics in a framework and order which differed from Aristotle's, he was still their primary source.[160] Individual chapters or sections of the *Ethics* were sometimes used as the source for treatises on particular moral issues. For example, Giovanni Pontano's *De liberalitate* was based on IV.1, *De magnificentia* on IV.2 and *De magnanimitate* on IV.3. The first of these works, along with the corresponding Aristotelian text, was heavily drawn upon by Antonio Brucioli in his *Dialogo della liberalità*.[161] The *Nicomachean Ethics* was even transformed into an allegorical epic poem entitled *Civitas veri sive morum*. Composed by Bartolomeo Delbene and explicated by Theodore Marcile, it describes the month-long spiritual odyssey of the poem's dedicatee, Marguerite, Duchess of Savoy, who travels through the City of Truth in order to reach the Temple of Wisdom, where she ultimately meets and converses with the *magister sapientiae*, Aristotle.[162]

155. Heiland 1581 was written for the University of Heidelberg; Case 1596a for Oxford; Golius 1634 for the Strasburg Academy.
156. Herbetius 1579; see also R. Maffei 1506, ff. 496^r–502^r; Tunstall 1554.
157. Zwinger 1566, p. 23 explained why he did not share his mentor's dislike of Aristotle; see also Höltgen 1965 and Gilly 1977–9.
158. Filelfo 1552, p. 2 describes himself as 'nulli philosophorum scholae ita addictum quo minus per omnia eorum praecepta vagari liceat'.
159. Nesi s. xv; see also Bonfanti 1971; K. M. Shaw 1972.
160. F. Piccolomini 1594b; Riccoboni 1610 is explicitly based on Piccolomini's treatise; Keckermann 1607a; see also A. Piccolomini 1542, a vernacular work which attempts the same broad coverage.
161. Pontano 1965, 1969; Brucioli 1982, pp. 419–31. 162. Delbene 1609.

ARISTOTELIAN ETHICS: THE SUPREME GOOD

In *Nicomachean Ethics* 1.7 (1097ᵇ23–1098ᵃ20), Aristotle attempted to define the characteristics of happiness, which according to him was man's supreme good. It was first of all necessary, he argued, to establish man's particular function. This could not be nutrition and growth, which man shared with plants, nor sensation, which he shared with animals. It must therefore be rational behaviour, of which he alone was capable. Happiness thus consisted in the good and proper exercise of man's rational faculty or, as Aristotle put it, the activity (ἐνέργεια) of man's soul in accordance with virtue (ἀρετή), and if there were a number of virtues, in accordance with the best and most perfect of these. To this definition he added two corollaries: first, that the activity must last throughout a complete lifetime, for just as one swallow did not make a summer, one virtuous action did not constitute a happy life; and second, that the complete realisation of happiness also required a modicum of bodily and external goods, such as health and wealth. Aristotle insisted on the point that happiness was not achieved by the mere possession of virtue but rather by the active exercise of it. For it was possible to have a virtuous disposition without producing any good result, as in the case of a person who spent his whole life asleep, living a merely vegetative existence, or who was impeded from action by some disastrous misfortune. We would not consider such a person happy. A virtuous activity, however, by definition entailed acting and acting well, and this, for Aristotle, was the essence of happiness.[163]

The Aristotelian formula for happiness, as recounted by Renaissance authors, was thus a life-long activity in accordance with virtue supplemented by sufficient bodily and external goods.[164] In his *Oratio de foelicitate*, Filippo Beroaldo encapsulated this doctrine for his listeners in an easily remembered if uninspired distich:

> Foelix cui constant bona corporis et bona mentis
> Necnon fortunae munera parta deae.

> Happy is he who goods of body and soul attains
> And also the gifts of the Goddess Fortune gains.[165]

---

163. 1.5 (1095ᵇ32–1096ᵃ2); 1.8 (1098ᵇ29–1099ᵃ7); x.6 (1176ᵃ33–1176ᵇ6).
164. Bruni 1928, p. 26 (*Isagogicon*): 'Felicitatem in bonis animi [Peripatetici] reponunt, quae sunt maxima et praecipua bona. Corporis autem et externa adesse homini oportere aiunt'; Nesi s. xv, f. 26ᵛ: 'Diximus foelicitatem esse optimam actionem ab animo profluentem in vita perfecta cum corporis et fortune bonis coniunctam'; Ficino 1937, II, p. 8 (*De quatuor sectis philosophorum*): 'Summum bonum volunt Peripatetici in perfecta virtutis actione consistere. Etenim cum absque corporis fortuneque commodis perfecte agere nemo possit, homini tot ac tanta utriusque bona adesse putant oportere, ut modeste simul et liberaliter possit degere.'
165. Beroaldo 1513, f. 122ᵛ (*Oratio de foelicitate*).

Renaissance interpreters of Aristotle's thought always emphasised the secondary status of bodily and external goods compared with those of the soul. Landino pointed out that while these goods made the happy life happier, their absence did not take away the primary source of happiness: virtue.[166] Case used a dichotomous Ramist diagram to illustrate the distinction between the essence of happiness, which required only goods of the soul, and the existence and embellishment of it, which required goods of the body and of fortune:

Distinctio bonorum

Bona respiciunt foelicitatem, aut quoad
{ essentiam et sic solum bona animi requiruntur

existentiam et ornatum, et sic bona corporis et fortunae requiruntur.[167]

Keckermann made a similar distinction between the completeness of happiness, which was affected by external goods, and its essence, which was not, in the same manner that having five fingers on each hand affects a man's completeness but not his essence.[168]

The main function of external goods in procuring happiness was their role as instruments by means of which virtuous actions could be performed. Discussions of this issue tended to focus on the need for money in order to practise many of the moral virtues.[169] This was brought home with melodramatic effectiveness by Galeazzo Florimonte when he asked: 'What kind of happiness would it be for a man to see his father dying of hunger and not have the means to help him?'[170] There were of course moral attitudes which even paupers could possess, such as patience and contempt for worldly goods.[171] But for the more positive and showy virtues like liberality, money was a necessity.[172] Although Aristotle stressed that happiness could be achieved with only moderate means, he also gave scope to the wealthy man through the virtue of magnificence ($\mu\epsilon\gamma\alpha\lambda o\pi\rho\acute{\epsilon}\pi\epsilon\iota\alpha$),

---

166. Landino 1980, p. 63.   167. Case 1596a, p. 44; see also 1596b, p. 148.
168. Keckermann 1607a, p. 15.
169. Nifo 1645, p. 99 (*De divitiis*): 'felix per divitias exercere potest plurima virtutum opera, ut magnificentiae, liberalitatis, fortitudinis, iustitiae, temperantiae, et caeterarum id genus'; Tartaretus 1509, f. 8ᵛ: 'difficile est magnanimum [hominem] exercere ardua sine divitiis'.
170. Florimonte 1554, p. 43: 'che felicità saria quella d'un huomo, che veggendo morire suo padre di fame, non lo potesse aiutare?'
171. Lefèvre d'Étaples 1533, f. 52ᵛ: 'pauperes multis virtutibus clarescere possunt, ut patientia, rerum contemptu, et reliquis'.
172. Pontano 1965, pp. 7–8; F. Barbaro 1915, p. 49; Sensi 1577, f. 123ʳ.

which entailed the appropriate expenditure of large sums of money for public buildings, religious offices and the like.[173] This virtue enjoyed a considerable vogue in the Renaissance, to some extent because it could be used as a suitably classical compliment when praising wealthy patrons such as Cosimo de' Medici.[174]

Aristotle's belief in the moral utility of external goods did not escape criticism or qualification. Poggio Bracciolini, for instance, made one of the interlocutors in his dialogue *De avaritia* accuse Aristotle of including goods of fortune among the components of a happy life just so that he could justify asking Alexander the Great for funds.[175] While few secular authors went so far as Antonio da Romagna in praising Franciscan poverty as a virtue, many were uneasy about wealth and felt its ethical status was at best ambiguous.[176] Salutati, while admitting that riches could be used for the good, nonetheless asked: 'Who when receiving a large sum of money does not also acquire pride and avarice, the source and root of all sins?'[177] Alessandro Piccolomini argued, somewhat tautologically, that riches were used virtuously in virtuous hands but sinfully in sinful hands.[178] Florimonte was more pessimistic. He maintained that men were so inclined to pursue pleasure that it was practically impossible for them to use wealth well because they were unable to resist the many opportunities for dissolute living which it offered them.[179] The Calvinist Florens Wilson, who had an even lower opinion of human nature, thought it was very rare indeed for a wealthy man to avoid the besetting sin of pride.[180]

While Aristotle assigns an important but ancillary role to goods of the body and of fortune, he maintains that happiness itself is an activity in conformity with the best and most perfect of the virtues. It was therefore necessary to examine the different types of virtue in order to determine

---

173. *Nicomachean Ethics* x.8 ($1178^b33-1179^a9$); IV.2 ($1122^a18-1123^a33$).
174. T. Maffei s. xv; see also Fraser Jenkins 1970, pp. 165–6, who demonstrates that Thomas Aquinas' interpretation of magnificence influenced Maffei; Pontano 1965, p. 101 (*De magnificentia*): 'Aetate nostra Cosmus Florentinus imitatus est priscam magnificentiam tum in condendis templis ac villis, tum in bybliothecis faciendis'; see also Florimonte 1554, p. 101, who translates this passage and repeats it verbatim.
175. Poggio Bracciolini 1964–9, I, p. 19: 'Scio . . . aliquos credidisse, adiunxisse illum [sc. Aristotelem] ad vitam beatam bona fortunae, ne si in sola virtute animi felicitatem posuisset . . . adimeretur sibi facultas petendi illa ab Alexandro a quo multa suscepit.'
176. Antonio da Romagno 1980, pp. 77–8; see also Baron 1938b, p. 13.
177. Salutati 1957, pp. 123–4: 'Quis . . . cum accepit magnam pecuniam, non simul accepit et superbiam, caput, et avariciam, radicem omnium peccatorum?'
178. A. Piccolomini 1542, f. 150ᵛ: 'si come le richezze in man del virtuoso sono instrumento di molto bene, così per contrario in man di chi non le merita, . . . venenose si trovano'.
179. Florimonte 1554, p. 25: 'per la somma inclinatione dell'animo nostro alle delitie, et per la gran comodità che la ricchezza ne porge à vivere dissolutamente, è quasi impossibile all'huomo usarla bene'.
180. F. Wilson 1751, p. 116: 'magna est . . . hominum raritas, qui rerum abundantia non insolescant'.

which was best. In *Nicomachean Ethics* I.13 he divides the virtues into two categories: intellectual (διανοητική) and moral (ἠθική). This classification corresponds to his division of the soul into a rational and irrational part, the latter of which is subdivided into a vegetative faculty, completely devoid of reason, and an appetitive faculty, which participates in reason through obedience to the rational soul. The five intellectual virtues (science, art, practical wisdom or prudence, intelligence and theoretical wisdom), which Aristotle discusses in book VI, belong to the rational soul, while the twelve moral virtues (courage, temperance, liberality, magnificence, magnanimity, appropriate ambition, gentleness, affability, truthfulness, wittiness, modesty and justice), which he discusses in books II–V, belong to the appetitive part of the irrational soul.

Aristotle's account of the psychological foundation for his division of the virtues was for the most part accepted without challenge.[181] Javelli and Vettori both noted, however, that the division of the soul in the *Ethics* differed from that put forward in *De anima*. Javelli explained this discrepancy by arguing that Aristotle's division of the soul into five faculties in *De anima* was a general classification, whereas the division into rational and irrational parts was appropriate only to the specific issues discussed in the *Ethics*.[182] Vettori came to the similar conclusion that although Aristotle had rejected the bipartite division in *De anima*, he used it in the *Ethics* because it was particularly suited to his doctrine of the virtues.[183]

Another issue discussed in relation to the Aristotelian system of moral and intellectual virtues was that it departed from the Platonic-Stoic-Christian scheme of the four cardinal virtues: prudence, justice, courage and temperance.[184] Johannes Caesarius explained the difference in a positive light, claiming that Aristotle had wanted to give a more precise account of happiness than other philosophers had done and, therefore, not content with only four virtues, had sought out the twelve sources from which they originated.[185] Others, such as Suárez, found no real incompatibility between the two arrangements since the four cardinal virtues were also

181. A. Silvester 1517, ff. 26ᵛ–8ʳ; *Reden und Briefe* 1970, p. 26 (Argyropulos); Estrebay 1549, ff. 57ᵛ–8ʳ; Nores 1578, f. 6ᵛ; Heiland 1581, pp. 18–19; Magirus 1601, pp. 109–11.
182. Javelli 1651, p. 21: 'haec divisio sola opportuna est praesenti proposito . . . Relicta igitur illa universali divisione in quinque genera potentiarum, quoniam de ea . . . sufficienter actum est in libris De anima, utendum est nunc divisione, qua dividuntur partes animae per rationalem et irrationalem.'
183. Vettori 1584, p. 65: 'Videtur . . . Aristoteles divisionem hanc minime probare in III libro de animo, quae tamen ab ipso nunc recipitur, ut accommodata huic doctrinae de moribus tradendae'; on the difference between the psychology of the *Ethics* and *De anima*, see Nuyens 1948, pp. 190–3.
184. On the cardinal virtues see Mähl 1969.
185. Caesarius in Lefèvre d'Étaples 1972, p. 104: '[Aristoteles] exactius humanam felicitatem describere voluit, non his quattuor [virtutibus] contentus ex duodecim fontibus eas emanare deprehendit.'

included in Aristotle's scheme.[186] But there was still a discrepancy, since Aristotle had classified prudence or practical wisdom (φρόνησις) as an intellectual virtue, while placing justice, courage and temperance in the category of moral virtues. Reisch, who attempted to combine the two schemes, resolved this problem by claiming that practical wisdom was both an intellectual and a moral virtue: intellectual in terms of its essence, moral in terms of its matter.[187] Henri Estienne, however, came to the conclusion that by excluding practical wisdom from the moral virtues, Aristotle had disagreed with the view consistently held by poets, historians and the vast majority of philosophers, who had all accepted the scheme of four cardinal virtues.[188] Fox-Morcillo, on the other hand, agreed with Aristotle that practical wisdom was an intellectual virtue, but rejected the four other virtues in that category. He argued that science, art, intelligence and theoretical wisdom were only virtues to the extent that they obeyed practical wisdom and were concerned with the investigation and judgement of the good. But when they were involved solely in contemplation, without any moral end in sight, they could not be considered virtues. Why, he asked, should intelligence be considered an intellectual virtue and not reason, the will and other faculties of the soul? And if art, science and theoretical wisdom were virtues, why not also mathematics, the liberal arts, natural philosophy and, for that matter, whatever else could be known?[189]

In *Nicomachean Ethics* x.7–8, Aristotle gave his definitive answer to the question of which was the best and most perfect virtue and therefore the foundation of human happiness. Since according to him the most excellent part of man was his rational soul, it necessarily followed that the most perfect virtue was intellectual rather than moral and also that it was related to the highest part of the intellect. This virtue was theoretical wisdom (σοφία), and the activity in accordance with it was the contemplation of the most exalted objects, which for Aristotle were celestial and divine. He argued that the contemplative life was superior to the moral or active life because it was more continuous, more pleasurable, more leisured and loved

186. Suárez 1856–78, IV, p. 487 (*De actibus qui vocantur passiones* III.5.1).

187. Reisch 1504, sig. OO IVᵛ: 'Prudentia secundum essentiam intellectualis habitus est; secundum materiam vero moralis.' Aristotle states at x.7 (1178ᵃ16–19) that practical wisdom is intimately connected to the moral virtues.

188. Estienne 1590, p. 442 (*De Aristotelicae ethices differentia ab historica et poetica*): 'De numero . . . virtutum quae . . . cardinales vulgo appellantur, cum historicis consentire poetae videntur. Atque ut inter se consentiunt, ita et philosophis omnibus assentiuntur, paucis exceptis: ex quibus est Aristoteles, PRUDENTIAM in earum numero non ponens.'

189. Fox-Morcillo 1566, p. 235: 'si intelligentia virtus dicenda est, eaque intelligibilis, cur non etiam eodem modo sit ratio, voluntas, caeteraeque animi facultates . . .? Porro si ars, scientia, sapientia, virtutes esse deberent, quidni sint quoque mathematicae disciplinae, liberales artes, physica, prima philosophia, ac demum quidquid sciri possit?'

more for its own sake. The moral virtues were less self-sufficient because they required a certain amount of external goods for their operation. They were also connected to the emotions and hence man's lower nature. Contemplation, in contrast, required no external goods and was connected to the divine element in man, his intellect. Moreover, since the contemplative man imitated the sole activity of the gods, he was most beloved by them. So by living in accordance with the moral virtues, a man would achieve a certain level of happiness; but by devoting himself to contemplation, he would be the happiest of men.[190]

Aristotle's belief that the contemplative life constituted man's happiness and therefore his supreme good was universally accepted by commentators on the *Nicomachean Ethics*, who could hardly disagree with such a fundamental principle in the work. It was also one of Aristotle's most influential ethical doctrines, taken up by a wide variety of philosophers, humanists and vernacular authors.[191] But various criticisms were made: Figliucci, for instance, agreed that the contemplative life was superior to the active but thought it was unhealthy and particularly bad for the digestion.[192] Lorenzo Valla objected to Aristotle's argument that contemplation was the sole activity of the gods. For according to Valla, contemplation was a learning process and therefore an inappropriate activity for the gods, who already knew everything. It was, furthermore, inconsistent for Aristotle to claim that man was a political animal and then to exhort him to imitate gods who did nothing but contemplate and therefore had no social relations whatsoever.[193] For the Neoplatonist Pletho, Aristotle's description of contemplation as the most pleasurable activity was proof that his views differed little from those of Epicurus, who also placed the supreme good in pleasures of the soul.[194] Salutati maintained in his treatise *De nobilitate* that Aristotle was mistaken in describing the contemplative search for truth as man's supreme good, for man's desire to know the truth could never be fulfilled. An infinite number of truths would always remain hidden from him, and he would not be able to attain the perfect knowledge of spiritual matters which was the goal of speculative

---

190. Aristotle also argued that the contemplative life was superior to the active in *Politics* VII.13 (1333^a 16–1333^{b}3).
191. E.g., Buonamici 1591, pp. 52–3; Barnaba Senese 1979, p. 39; E. Barbaro 1969, pp. 61–8 and 135; Castiglione 1947, p. 437; Brucioli 1982, p. 483; Della Barba 1554, pp. 95–7; for the political implications of this issue, see Skinner in this volume, pp. 420–30 below.
192. Figliucci 1551, p. 337: 'la contemplazione si potrebbe dire cosa trista, essendo nociva al corpo e impedendo la digestione'.
193. L. Valla 1970a, pp. 77–8; see also *Arbeit, Musse, Meditation* 1985, pp. 181–223 (Panizza).
194. Pletho 1866, col. 905: '[Ἀριστοτέλης] οὐ πολύ τι διάφορον λέγων τοῦ Ἐπικούρου'.

happiness.[195] Salutati in this work opposed the Peripatetic view on the grounds that man's supreme good lay in his will, not in his intellect, and in the enjoyment of God, not in the knowledge of him. Fox-Morcillo also thought that Aristotelian contemplation inevitably resulted in frustration. But for him its futility lay in the fact that it was not possible to understand the ultimate causes of things while still in the present life. When contemplative activity was limited to this life, it did not make men supremely happy but rather vexed and tormented them, like the vulture which daily devoured the liver of Prometheus.[196]

It was sometimes argued that contemplative happiness, as described by Aristotle, was only accessible to an elite minority, whereas moral and active happiness was more suited to the majority of men. Salutati (whose position on this as on other issues tended to waver considerably) cited Aristotle's dictum in *Topics* III.2 (118^a11-13) that it was better to be a philosopher than to make money, but not for the man who lacks the necessities of life. Therefore, Salutati maintained, while the contemplative life was better, it should not always be chosen by everyone. And although the active life was inferior, it was often to be preferred.[197] It was Bruni's opinion that both the active and contemplative lives had certain things to recommend them. For while the latter was more divine and exquisite, the former contributed more to the common good.[198] But when a fellow humanist wrote to him asserting that the *summum bonum* resided in action rather than contemplation, Bruni leapt to Aristotle's defence. He admitted that only a few men had actually achieved contemplative happiness but argued, with the proverb, that all truly excellent things were rare. Bruni also claimed that many more would be capable of attaining this exalted happiness if they earnestly and sedulously applied themselves.[199] This issue was also dealt with by Pomponazzi, who argued in his *Tractatus de immortalitate animae*

---

195. Salutati 1947, p. 164: 'licet Philosophus disputet finem hominis esse speculationem veritatis, non potest hoc dictum veritatem habere, quoniam hoc desiderium non potest impleri, cum infinite lateant veritates, nec possibile sit unum aliquem scire que cuncti sciunt, nec in noticia creaturarum spiritualium et perfectam earum rationem, ubi speculatio desinat, pervenire, circa quas felicitatem humanam speculando vult esse'; see also *Arbeit, Musse, Meditation* 1985, pp. 153–79 (Kahn).
196. Fox-Morcillo 1566, p. 145: 'cur non . . . [contemplatio] infoelix potius censebitur, quando id quod assequi non potest, magno investigationis labore exquirit; et ut Promethei iecur vultur ille . . . ita nos levis haec contemplatio solicitet et angat'.
197. Salutati 1891–1911, III, p. 305: 'Melior est contemplativa, fateor; non tamen semper nec omnibus eligibilior. Inferior est activa, sed eligendo multotiens preferanda.'
198. Bruni 1928, p. 39 (*Isagogicon*): 'Contemplativa quidem divinior plane atque rarior, activa vero in communi utilitate praestantior.'
199. Bruni 1741, II, p. 137. He was replying to a letter, now lost, by Lauro Quirini; see also Segarizzi 1904, p. 7.

that only a part of mankind was capable of achieving perfect happiness through the productive and speculative intellects. But while not everyone could make things like a craftsman or contemplate like a philosopher, everyone could be a good and virtuous person and thereby reach perfect active or moral happiness by means of the practical intellect.[200]

Although Aristotle admitted that even the contemplative man to some extent lived in society and therefore had to act in accordance with the moral virtues, he never specified how the active and contemplative components of life were to be combined.[201] Many interpreters of the *Ethics* assumed that the attainment of moral virtues was an essential preliminary or adjunct to the achievement of contemplative happiness, although Aristotle himself did not say so. Figliucci described the morally virtuous life as a ladder, a door and a means of reaching contemplative beatitude.[202] According to Nifo, the moral virtues calmed the emotional disturbances within the soul and thus freed it to be lifted up into the contemplation of divine objects.[203] Nores believed that it might be possible for someone to raise himself to the level of speculation without having gone through the preparatory stages of acquiring practical wisdom and becoming a good person. But although such a man would be rightly considered learned and intelligent, he could not be called happy, since happiness could never be secured without the moral virtues.[204] Javelli also held that contemplative happiness must be combined with morally virtuous behaviour. For Aristotle had described the happy man as beloved by God, and surely it was absurd to assume that God could love someone who was wicked. Aristotle had clearly indicated, in Javelli's view, that happiness consisted in speculation combined with piety and moral goodness. Therefore since those men who are called wise and learned are only rarely pious and virtuous, only rarely can they be called happy.[205] Ciriaco Strozzi, on the other hand, maintained that Aristotle dealt with two separate and distinct types of happiness in the *Nicomachean*

200. Pomponazzi 1954, p. 191: 'universalis finis generis humani est secundum quid de speculativo et factivo [intellectu] participare, perfecte autem de practico'.
201. x.8 (1178[b]5–7). For modern discussions of this issue, see *Essays on Aristotle's Ethics* 1980, pp. 7–34 (Ackrill), 341–57 (Wilkes), 361–76 (McDowell), 377–94 (Rorty).
202. Figliucci 1551, sig. * iii[v]: 'La felicità humana . . . che consiste ne l'operare virtuosamente, è scala, porta e mezo per condurne a l'altra felicità e beatitudine contemplativa.'
203. Nifo 1645, p. 38 (*De vera vivendi libertate*): 'sedatis . . . perturbationibus . . . propter virtutum moralium exercitationem, animus afficitur ut libere attolli possit in . . . divinarum rerum contemplationem'; see also Burgersdijk 1629, p. 37: 'virtus moralis animum hominis ad divinam hanc sapientiam praeparat'.
204. Nores 1578, f. 16[r]: 'non trovandosi giamai felicità senza le virtù morali'.
205. Javelli 1651, p. 141: 'quoniam viri docti ac sapientes dicti rari sunt pii erga Deum et boni moraliter, ideo rari possunt dici beati'.

Ethics: in book I he discussed the kind which was acquired through practical wisdom, while in book X he treated the perfect happiness which was achieved through theoretical wisdom.[206]

One of the reasons Aristotle adduced for the superiority of contemplative over active happiness was that it was more self-sufficient. While it was possible to contemplate in solitude without any external equipment, the exercise of moral virtues such as liberality required both goods of fortune, to be liberal with, and other people, to be liberal to. Of course even the philosopher required food, drink and so on to survive. But anything more than the basic necessities of life might prove a hindrance to contemplation.[207]

Some commentators in interpreting these passages emphasised the point that external goods tended to impede speculation. Javelli, for example, maintained that concern for such things distracted and disturbed the soul. Figliucci, citing the example of Job, claimed that contemplative happiness was perfected by adversity. And Leone Ebreo argued that poverty, according to the Peripatetics, was actually necessary in order to achieve the deepest contemplation.[208] In Mair's view the wise man was content with only a few books. Indeed, the wiser he was the fewer books he needed, since the truly learned man carried his library around in the bookshelves of his mind.[209]

Not surprisingly, many scholars disagreed with these views. Valla claimed that he needed money and rather a lot of it in order to buy the many books which were necessary for him to pursue his studies.[210] By way of illustrating the fact that men of learning also needed adequate clothing, Vettori cited Petrarch's bequest of a warm gown to the poverty-stricken Boccaccio in order to protect him from the cold.[211] Muret had no sympathy with those philosophers who argued that it was impossible to contemplate while encumbered with worldly goods. They seemed to him

206. Strozzi 1599, sig. D iii^r: 'Agit . . . hic [i.e., lib. X] philosophus de felicitate ea, quae sapientia comparatur, cum in primo egerit de ea quae prudentiae officiis nobis conciliatur.'
207. *Nicomachean Ethics* X.7 (1177^a27–1177^b1); X.8 (1178^a23–1178^b7 and 1178^b33–1179^b9).
208. Javelli 1651, p. 144; Figliucci 1551, p. 341; Leone Ebreo 1929, p. 24.
209. Mair 1530, f. 163^r: 'Paucis libris vir sapiens contentus est, et quanto sapientior, tanto pauciorum codicum est indigus. Egregie autem eruditus in scrinio pectoris librariam circunfert'; see *Nicomachean Ethics* X.7 (1177^a32–4).
210. L. Valla 1962, II, p. 312 (*De professione religiosorum*): 'Mihi vero codices necessarii sunt et pecuniae eaeque non paucae, unde codices plurimos . . . coemam.'
211. Vettori 1584, p. 599: 'fertur Franciscum Petrarcham Ioanni Boccaccio, pauperi homini, dilargitum fuisse pelliceam vestem, qua posset frigus a se depellere; illa [bona] autem vix videntur carere posse studiosi litterarum artiumque liberalium'; for the bequest, see Petrarch 1957, p. 82; for his own views on this issue, see Petrarch 1933–42, II, p. 159 (VIII.3).

to protest too much, thereby revealing their excessive attachment to these goods. Nor could he see why poverty was any less of a hindrance to studies than wealth.[212]

ARISTOTELIAN ETHICS: MORAL VIRTUE AS A MEAN

In *Nicomachean Ethics* II.6 Aristotle defined a moral virtue as a disposition to observe the mean in relation to both actions and emotions. Surrounding each moral virtue were two vices, one characterised by excess, the other by deficiency. The virtue of liberality was thus the mean between the vices of prodigality and miserliness in relation to giving money. Similarly, courage was the mean between rashness and cowardice in relation to fear. The mean was not the mathematical midpoint but rather the amount appropriate to the specific circumstances, while the two extremes consisted in doing or feeling too much or too little in a particular situation. This was one of the most popular Aristotelian ethical doctrines, discussed not only in commentaries but also in moral philosophy textbooks and treatises, both scholastic and humanistic, as well as a wide variety of vernacular literature.[213] But, like other influential aspects of Aristotelian ethics, it also provoked considerable controversy.

Around 1441 Lauro Quirini wrote to Leonardo Bruni criticising Aristotle's notion of virtue as a mean. He claimed that practical wisdom, temperance and justice were in fact extremes rather than means. In reply Bruni first pointed out that Aristotle had formulated this doctrine only in relation to moral virtues and, therefore, it was not applicable to intellectual virtues such as practical wisdom. He then went on to demonstrate that since the two extremes of temperance were totally dissolute behaviour and complete insensibility, it must itself be a mean between these two vices. Justice, moreover, was concerned with equity, and that which was equitable was by definition equidistant between too much and too little. Quirini also argued that since Aristotle considered moderation to be the hallmark of virtue, it necessarily followed that it was more praiseworthy to be moderately temperate or just than to be extremely so. Bruni disagreed, explaining that the temperate man was not moderately but entirely

212. Muret 1789, I, p. 63 (*De moralis philosophiae laudibus*): 'Neque vero video, qui minus impedimento sit egestas studiis quam divitiae.'
213. Reisch 1504, sig. NN IV^v; Tartaretus 1509, f. 4^r; Almain 1526, f. 48^r; A. Piccolomini 1542, f. 81^v; Valerius 1566, p. 93; Salutati 1891–1911, II, p. 184; 1947, pp. 136–8; Pontano 1965, pp. 6–7; 1969, p. 8; Leone Ebreo 1929, p. 23; Alberti 1969a, p. 200; Rucellai 1960–81, I, p. 15; Brucioli 1982, pp. 281–4; Montaigne 1965, p. 364 (II.4).

temperate, his moderation being in relation to corporeal pleasure, not to temperance itself.[214]

The Platonist Pletho objected to the Peripatetic doctrine of the mean because he believed that it was measured in terms of quantity rather than quality. He claimed that Aristotle determined which things were appropriate to fear on the basis of how great or small they were. Platonists, on the other hand, used quality as their sole criterion: whatever was dishonourable was to be feared, no matter how great or small it was; similarly, whatever was not dishonourable was not to be feared, regardless of size or quantity.[215] According to Fox-Morcillo, however, there was no significant disagreement between Platonists and Peripatetics on this issue. For although Plato himself never mentioned this doctrine, both Apuleius and Albinus confirmed that he, like Aristotle, had thought that virtue was situated in the middle of two vices.[216] Fox-Morcillo himself was only in partial agreement with this view. He thought there were three different types of emotions: those which were by nature good, such as benevolence and pity; those which were always bad, such as hatred and envy; and those which were neutral, such as joy or fear. The mean did not apply to emotions in the first category, which retained their goodness whether they were excessive or deficient; nor to the second, which even when restrained were wicked; but only to the third, which when moderate were virtues but when extreme were vices.[217] Theophilus Golius made a similar distinction, which he applied to actions as well as emotions. The doctrine of the mean was not relevant to those actions which were *per se* good, such as worshipping God or honouring one's parents, nor to those which were *per se* bad, such as stealing, harming others or consorting with prostitutes, but only to those which were indifferent, such as eating, drinking, sleeping, acquiring wealth or seeking honours.[218]

The most outspoken critic of Aristotle's treatment of virtue was Lorenzo Valla. In his dialogue *De vero falsoque bono* Valla, speaking through the interlocutor Antonio da Rho, argued that there were not two vices opposed to each virtue, as Aristotle had maintained, but rather for each virtue there was only one contrasting vice. In relation to fear, Aristotle had delineated one virtue, courage, and two vices, cowardice and rashness. Valla, however, claimed that Aristotle had conflated two separate and distinct virtues under

214. Bruni 1741, II, pp. 140–2; see also Segarizzi 1904, p. 7.
215. Pletho 1866, col. 904: 'τὸ μὲν αἰσχρὸν πᾶν δεινόν, ἄν τε μέγα, ἄν τε μικρὸν ᾖ, τὸ δ᾽οὐκ αἰσχρὸν θαρραλέον πᾶν ἀξιοῦντες εἶναι.'
216. Fox-Morcillo 1566, p. 223: 'Plato vero, quanquam nullam eius mediocritatis, quod ego viderim, fecerit mentionem, tamen Apuleius in libro de illius philosophia [sc. *De Platone et eius dogmate* II.5], Alcinousque [sc. Albinus, *Didaskalikos* cap. 30.4] virtutes in meditullio vitiorum positas ab illo esse ipsumque idem cum Aristotele sensisse, confirmant.'   217. *Ibid.*, p. 224.
218. Golius 1634, pp. 55–6.

one name: courage, which means fighting bravely, and caution, which entails retreating wisely. So, according to Valla, there were not one virtue and two vices related to fear but rather two virtues and two vices: as regards fighting, the virtue was courage and the contrasting vice rashness; while as regards not fighting, the virtue was caution and the opposing vice cowardice. Likewise, in abstaining from pleasures, the virtue was temperance and the vice insensibility; while in enjoying pleasures, the virtue was cheerfulness and the vice licentiousness. In giving money, the virtue was liberality and the vice prodigality; while in not giving money, the virtue was thrift and the vice miserliness.[219]

Valla also objected to Aristotle's assumption that the middle course was always good, while the extremes were necessarily excessive or deficient. Valla, who was not known for his moderation, thought that the extremes were sometimes preferable to the mean. For example, it was better to be exceedingly beautiful or wise than moderately so, and also better to be minimally, rather than moderately, malformed or foolish.[220] In his *Dialecticae disputationes*, Valla even suggested that the mean itself was a vice, adducing the example of God rebuking the Angel of Laodicea in Revelation 3:16: 'Because thou art lukewarm, and neither hot nor cold, I will spew thee out of my mouth.'[221] His position was defended on aesthetic grounds, too, since he found the fair-skinned Germans and black Ethiopians more attractive than the dusky Egyptians and dark Indians. Finally, he repeated the argument that it was clearly preferable to attain a superlative degree of qualities such as beauty, learning and virtue than just a fair to middling one.[222]

Valla's censure of Aristotle was applauded by Vives in his *De causis corruptarum artium*. He summarised Valla's arguments, adding a few of his own, and supported his view that each virtue was opposed by only one vice. His only disagreement with Valla was that, with stereotypical Spanish seriousness, Vives refused to regard cheerfulness as a virtue, although he did consider it to be the opposite of licentiousness.[223]

Francisco Sanchez no doubt knew Valla's views on this subject, either

219. L. Valla 1970a, pp. 95–7.
220. *Ibid.*, p. 100: 'Extrema . . . pulchritudo, extrema sapientia melior est quam mediocris. Rursus minima deformitas, minima stultitia melior est quam mediocris'; for a similar argument see Aulus Gellius, *Noctes Atticae* IV.9.14.   221. L. Valla 1982, I, p. 80.
222. *Ibid.*, p. 81: 'Quid, nonne summe formosus atque omnium formosissimus, summe doctus, summa virtute preditus preponendus mediocriter formoso, mediocriter docto, mediocri virtute predito?'
223. Vives 1782–90, VI, p. 214 (VI.2): '[Aristoteles] merito est reprehensus a Laurentio Valla in tertio volumine de Voluptate'; p. 215: 'qui fruitur licitis [voluptatibus], vel *humanus* est, vel (ut Valla dicit) *hilaris*; tametsi haec virtus non est, contra quam Valla sentit'. Vives' arguments in support of Valla were criticised by Keckermann 1607a, p. 74.

directly or through the summary given by Vives. For although phrased in different terms, his attack on Aristotle's definition of virtue as a mean was based on the same premises. Sanchez, like Valla, claimed that there was only one vice in opposition to each virtue, but he argued this point in terms of logic, asserting that each thing had only one contrary. In support of this position, he not only cited the Bible (Ecclesiasticus 33:15: 'there are two and two, one against another') and Plato (*Protagoras* 332C-D and the spurious *Second Alcibiades* 139B), but also Aristotle himself, who asserted in *Metaphysics* x.4 (1055ᵃ19-21) that one thing cannot have more than one contrary. Indeed, because the doctrine of virtue as a mean was inconsistent with this position, Sanchez believed that the *Metaphysics* and *Ethics* were not written by the same author.[224] He also argued that the contrary vice of each virtue was in fact closely related to it. So, like Valla, he held that the contrary of liberality was the kindred vice of prodigality, while miserliness was the opposite of thrift, which it resembled. Similarly, rashness was the contrary of courage, while cowardice was opposed to caution. Adding a further example of his own, perhaps inspired by his continual troubles with the Inquisition, Sanchez claimed that the true contrary of the religious man was not the heretic but the hypocrite.[225]

Although Aristotle's definition of moral virtue as a mean attracted a fair amount of criticism, it should be kept in mind that virtually all commentators on the *Ethics* accepted and expounded his view, forming the basis for its wide diffusion in both philosophical and popular literature. Moreover, it was precisely because this doctrine was so influential that it became a particular target for attack by those who wanted, for whatever motive, to challenge the primacy of Aristotelian ethics.

ARISTOTELIAN ETHICS AND CHRISTIANITY

Renaissance Aristotelians inherited from their medieval predecessors the formula of two-fold happiness, which enabled them to see this-worldly, imperfect Aristotelian felicity as compatible with other-worldly, perfect Christian beatitude.[226] One of the premises on which this theory was based

---

224. Sanchez 1766, III, p. 505 (*Doctrina del estoico filosofo Epicteto*): 'tengo por cierto, que el autor de la *Metafísica*, no es el que hizo las *Ethicas*'.
225. *Ibid.*, p. 506: 'Los proprios y verdaderos contrarios de las virtudes son aquellos que tienen gran semejanza y parantesco con la misma virtud . . . como liberalitas, profusio; fortitudo, audacia; parcitas, avaritia; cautus, timidus. Ansi que el contrario de religioso es el hypocrita, no el hereje'; see also Breva-Claramonte 1983, pp. 7–13.
226. Versor 1491, f. 10ᵛ; Tartaretus 1509, f. 9ᵛ; 1514, f. 3ᵛ; Acciaiuoli 1535, ff. 2ᵛ, 11ᵛ, 184ʳ; Riccoboni 1610, p. 678.

was that Aristotelian happiness pertained only to man's earthly existence, not the afterlife.[227] But as Javelli pointed out, Aristotle had neither affirmed nor denied the possibility of happiness in the future life.[228] Zwinger interpreted the fact that Aristotle had not explicitly rejected the notion of eternal beatitude as evidence of his tacit acceptance of the idea.[229] Similarly, Nifo explained Aristotle's silence on this issue as a result not of his disbelief in celestial happiness but rather of his unwillingness to investigate any matters which transcended human understanding. Nifo maintained, however, that even though Aristotle had not expressly affirmed the existence of happiness in the future life, there were various hints in his works that he had some notion of it. For example, in *Nicomachean Ethics* I.11 Aristotle stated that the dead receive some benefit from the good actions of their friends. How could this be, asked Nifo, if there were no happiness after death? Also, in *Oeconomics* III.1 Aristotle described the immortal glory bestowed by the gods on Alcestis and Penelope for their faithfulness. According to Nifo, who accepted this spurious work as genuine, Aristotle seemed to be asserting that the happiness which comes to us after death is a reward from the gods for our virtuous behaviour.[230] Case supported his claim that Aristotle believed in the immortality of the soul and thus the eternity of speculative happiness by citing *Ethics* x.7–8, where the divine nature of both the intellect and the contemplative life is described.[231]

Ranged against this school of thought were those who emphatically rejected Aristotle's moral doctrines as irreconcilable with the dogmas of religion. In 1517 Luther wrote theses not only against the Catholic Church but also against scholastic theology. Amongst the latter was a denunciation of Aristotle's *Ethics* (on which he himself had lectured some eight years earlier at the University of Wittenberg) as the worst enemy of grace.[232] Luther's main quarrel was not so much with Aristotle himself as with those scholastics who he felt had replaced the invaluable teachings of Christ with

227. Estrebay 1549, f. 2ᵛ: 'Aristoteles . . . de quaerendo summo deo et expetenda post mortem foelicitate non agebat'; F. Piccolomini 1594b, p. 457: 'finis [ultimus] a Peripatetico non in futura, sed in hac vita constituitur'.
228. Javelli 1651, p. 20: 'De felicitate alterius vitae [Aristoteles] non loquitur affirmative, nec negative.'
229. Zwinger 1566, p. 15: 'cum aeternam illam beatitudinem [Aristoteles] non neget, neque impugnet, eam profecto tacite videtur admittere'.
230. Nifo 1645, p. 49 (*De vera vivendi libertate*): 'In quibus verbis . . . videtur [Aristoteles asserere] . . . felicitatem, quae post mortem nobis advenit, conferri a diis, ut virtutum praemium iis, qui secundum virtutes . . . vixerunt.'
231. Case 1596a, pp. 514–15: 'Quis haec legit et non fatetur Aristotelem animi immortalitatem sapuisse? Sic enim loquitur, ut ergo divinum quiddam mens est, sic vita ei congruens divina est. Omnes ergo debemus quoad poterimus niti ad immortalem gloriam.'
232. Luther 1883–, I, p. 226: 'Tota fere Aristotelis Ethica pessima est gratiae inimica.'

the worthless precepts of the Philosopher.[233] It was only with Melanchthon's strict demarcation between ethics and theology that this problem was resolved, making it possible for Aristotelian moral philosophy to become an integral part of Protestant education.[234]

Attacks on Peripatetic ethics also came from the Catholic camp. Vives pointed his finger at Aristotle and those who followed him as the principal causes of the corruption of ethics. It was bad enough, he argued, that the revealed truths of Christianity were neglected in favour of the flimsy conjectures of pagan philosophers. But it added insult to injury that it was Aristotelian ethics which dominated contemporary philosophy since, unlike Platonism and Stoicism, it was completely incompatible with Christian morality: first, because Aristotle limited happiness to the present life; and second, because the earthly felicity which he described not only differed from but actually conflicted with the beatitudes of this life recounted by Christ in the Sermon on the Mount.[235] So, for example, Aristotle defined magnanimity as the desire for great honours. But anyone at all could seek honours: the most morally depraved of men or the most foolish of women. On the other hand, for Plato, Cicero, and Seneca, this virtue consisted less in seeking honours than in treating them as of little or no importance, an attitude which in Vives' view accorded far better with Christianity.[236]

Like Luther, Omer Talon objected more to Aristotelians than to Aristotle himself. Indeed, he claimed that if Aristotle were raised from the dead and instructed in Christianity, he would burn his own books and damn those very doctrines which certain foolish Christians stupidly approved and stubbornly followed.[237] The foolish Christians he had in mind were the scholastic philosophers of the University of Paris, whose views he attacked in his 1550 lectures on the first book of the *Nicomachean Ethics*. He was especially critical of their attempts to reconcile the human felicity described by Aristotle with the divine beatitude promised in the Bible. Had God, he

233. *Ibid.*, v, p. 645 (*Operationes in Psalmos*): 'Qua impietate nobis vestem hanc abstulerunt et laceraverunt et loco eius "telas araneorum" (ut Isaias 59.[6] vocat) idest . . . scelerati nebulonis Aristotelis Ethica, nobis pro Christi vestimentis aptaverunt.' Zacharias Palthenius, in his preface to Magirus 1601, sig.):(4^r, explained that Luther's attack on Aristotle's *Ethics* 'ad retundendam scholasticorum doctorum inscitiam pertinet, qui philosophiam Aristotelis imperite cum doctrina ecclesiae confuderunt'; see also Nitzsch 1883; Eckermann 1978; Junghans 1985, pp. 153–62.
234. See pp. 323–6 above.
235. Vives 1782–90, VI, p. 211 (*De causis corruptarum artium* VI.2): 'Aristoteles in vita hac quaerit beatitudinem, alteri nihil relinquit'; p. 213: 'Dominus noster octo beatitudines vitae huius recenset [Mt. 5:3–11], multum ab Aristotelicis diversas, immo adversas'; see also Kater 1908, pp. 18–23.
236. Vives 1782–90, VI, p. 216; on magnanimity in pagan and Christian ethics, see R. A. Gauthier 1951.
237. Talon 1583, p. 1009: 'si Aristoteles hoc tempore a mortuis excitaretur, eaque opinione, quam de Deo et Christo habemus, imbueretur, confestim decreta sua tolleret, penitusque damnaret, quae inepti quidam Christiani stultissime probant et pertinacissime sequuntur'; see also p. 1091.

asked, said anything about two types of happiness, one human, the other divine? On the contrary, he had not held out the prospect of any happiness here on earth for man, but rather had exhorted him to seek eternal life in heaven.[238]

Like Vives, Talon thought that the Peripatetic notion of earthly happiness was totally opposed to Christian morality. By giving an essential role to corporeal and external goods, Aristotle had denied the supreme good to those who were physically misshapen, of low birth, childless or poor. But in this way he had in fact deprived himself of happiness, for according to Diogenes Laertius v.1 Aristotle wore rings and extravagant clothing in order to distract attention from his own disfigurement.[239] Christ, however, promised a completely different sort of beatitude from which the lame, the blind, the hunchbacked and the deformed were not excluded. Talon also claimed that while Christ had said that it was more difficult for a rich man to enter heaven than for a camel to go through the eye of a needle, Aristotle had said that only a rich man, indeed a very rich one, could attain happiness.[240] This is a considerably distorted account of Aristotle's views, for although he acknowledged that certain moral virtues, such as magnificence, required great resources, he nonetheless insisted that happiness, particularly contemplative happiness, could be achieved with very little wealth.[241] Talon, as Zwinger rightly pointed out, showed more harshness in ridiculing Aristotle than sound judgement in explicating him.[242] Talon's commentary on the *Ethics* was also criticised by Nicolas Boucher, the future Bishop of Verdun, who argued that he had confused moral philosophy with theology. Boucher, apparently influenced by Melanchthon, maintained that the law of nature, on which ethics was based, was in agreement, not conflict, with the law of God and that therefore Aristotelian ethical doctrines were not at variance with the morality of the gospels, as Talon had said.[243]

In order to establish the precise relationship between Aristotelian and biblical morality, some authors made detailed comparisons of Peripatetic

238. *Ibid.*, p. 1089: 'Quid . . . Deus de hominis felicitate? Duplicemne statuit, unam humanam, alteram divinam? In humana mundanaque vita felicitas nulla a Deo proponitur. Tota cohortatio eius est ad caelestam illam aeternamque vitam.'   239. *Ibid.*, p. 1068.
240. *Ibid.*, p. 1090: 'Aristoteles ait neminem nisi divitem et quidem maximis divitiis affluentem esse beatum . . . Deus ait diviti introitum difficiliorem esse in caelum, quam camelo in foramen acus [Mt. 19:24].'   241. *Nicomachean Ethics* x.8 (1178^b33–1179^a9).
242. Zwinger 1566, p. 23: 'cum ad interpretationem Aristotelis . . . accessisset, plus in traducendo acerbitatis, quam in declarando iudicii, vir pius alioqui et eruditus adhibuit'.
243. Boucher 1562, p. 140: 'Lex naturae legi divinae non repugnat, sed consentit . . . Aristotelis igitur doctrina de moribus Evangelio non repugnat, sed consentit'; on Boucher, see Aristotle 1970 I, 1, pp. 172–3; on Melanchthon, see pp. 323–4 above.

ethical doctrines with those of the Bible. The Siennese philosopher and
theologian Pietro Rossi wrote a *Concordantia Veteris Testamenti et Aristotelis*,
in which he claimed that the Solomonic books prefigured Aristotle's
writings, so that Proverbs corresponded to the *Magna moralia*, Ecclesiastes
to books I–IX of the *Nicomachean Ethics*, and the Song of Songs, which dealt
with the union of the soul with God, to book x, in which Aristotle discussed
contemplative happiness.[244] The interests of the Italian Protestant Pietro
Martire Vermigli centred rather on defining the areas of agreement and
disagreement between the *Ethics* and the gospels. He noted that the two
ethical systems concurred in their insistence that virtuous habits must be
translated into actions in order to produce happiness. They differed,
however, in their notions of virtue. For Aristotelian moral virtues were
acquired through habit, while Christian virtues such as faith, hope and
charity were inspired by the Holy Spirit.[245] Vermigli's purpose in making
such comparisons was not merely academic: he wanted to use them in order
to demonstrate the superiority of Christian to pagan morality.[246] And by
Christian Vermigli meant Protestant, for many of his arguments relied
heavily on Calvinist theology. He argued, for example, that Christian
happiness was far more stable and secure than Aristotelian because it was
based on divine predestination and justification by faith rather than mere
human works.[247]

In his *Compendium ethicae Aristotelis ad normam veritatis Christianae
revocatum*, Waele attempted to steer between what he saw as the two
prevalent dangers in contemporary treatises on ethics: the Scylla of the
scholastics, who made theology conform to Aristotelianism rather than vice
versa; and the Charybdis of authors like Melanchthon and Daneau, who
concentrated so much on theology that their works were of little use in
understanding Aristotle and other pagan philosophers. Waele's solution
was to base his treatise solidly on the *Nicomachean Ethics* but to note
whatever errors appeared and correct them according to the truths of
Christianity.[248] He rejected Daneau's method of organising the virtues

244. Fioravanti 1981, pp. 89–92.
245. Vermigli 1582, pp. 116, 320; for other comparisons between the Aristotelian and theological
     virtues see Almain 1526, ff. 48^v–9^r; Reisch 1504, sig. NN v^r.
246. Vermigli 1582, p. 9: 'vehemens accenditur Christianismi cultus ex Ethnicorum ethicis. Nam per
     collationem intelligimus quam philosophicis praestant quae in divinis literis traduntur.'
247. *Ibid.*, p. 234: 'ex fide ac gratia nos voluit Deus iustificari, non ex operibus, ut firma sit promissio
     [Rom. 4:16], et ne in illa titubemus ad nostram respiciendo infirmitatem'.
248. Waele 1620, sig. † 7^r: 'Nos . . . conati sumus . . . materias ab Aristotele in Ethicis ad Nicomachum
     praecipue tractatas . . . eodem fere ordine compendiose proponere, et errores in eis observatos ad
     veritatis Christianae normam corrigere.'

according to the second table of the Decalogue and adopted instead Aristotle's scheme of moral and intellectual virtues. But he made certain to explain why Christian therapy for overcoming vices, such as intemperance, was so much more effective than the merely human remedies offered by pagan philosophy.[249] He also pointed out that while Aristotle defined moral virtue as a fixed disposition to observe the mean, according to Christianity it consisted in the harmony and agreement of one's actions and habits with the law of God. Since, however, the law of God consisted of general precepts which did not, on the whole, refer to specific actions, it was necessary to supplement it with examples of praiseworthy conduct taken from the Bible. Exempla and precepts from pagan sources were not to be rejected out of hand, provided they did not conflict with those taken from Scripture.[250]

Conversely, exempla and precepts from Scripture were used by many Renaissance commentators in order to illustrate and supplement the pagan morality of Aristotle's *Ethics*. This tradition dates back to the medieval Greek commentary by Eustratius of Nicaea, who made frequent references to the Old and New Testaments.[251] Biblical and Christian material was often used to give striking examples of particular virtues: the courage, for instance, of the Apostles and martyrs.[252] This often happened in the case of superhuman virtue, which Aristotle described in *Ethics* VII.1 as heroic or divine in scale. Thus, for Lefèvre d'Étaples, the virginity of Mary and the abstinence of John the Baptist illustrated the most exalted level of temperance; for Mair, St Laurence exemplified superhuman courage, while Job was the model of heroic patience; and for Herbetius, this divine degree of virtue was to be found in those praised in Psalm 82:6: 'I have said, Ye are gods.'[253] Some authors, such as Zwinger, identified heroic virtue with the specifically Christian virtues of faith, hope and charity: a view dismissed by Francesco Piccolomini as appropriate for theologians but not for those interested in interpreting Aristotle.[254]

Christian doctrines were also cited for purposes of contrast as well as

---

249. *Ibid.*, pp. 147–50 and 165–6; on Daneau, see p. 323 above.
250. Waele 1620, pp. 92–3: 'Exempla vero laudata quae apud ethnicos occurrunt, aut praecepta quae de virtutibus reliquerunt, a nobis non sunt plane reiicienda, modo cum praeceptis et exemplis sacris non pugnent.'
251. See Eustratius, Michael of Ephesus and Anonymous 1892, p. 4 for references to Abraham, Isaac, Jacob, Moses and Jesus.
252. Filelfo 1552, p. 75: 'Quod nobilissimae fortitudinis genus in sanctissimis Christi Apostolis, caeterisque martyribus non reperias?'; see also Reisch 1504, sig. PP ii^v.
253. Lefèvre d'Étaples 1533, f. 42^v; Mair 1530, f. 106^{r-v}; Herbetius 1579, f. 81^v.
254. Zwinger 1566, p. 6: 'Christiana . . . pietas ternario numero heroicas hasce virtutes (quas vulgo theologicas vocant) complectitur'; also F. Piccolomini 1594b, pp. 282–3.

confirmation. Hubert van Giffen, for instance, pointed out that although the Aristotelian gods did not practise moral virtues (*Ethics* x.8), the Christian God did.[255] Similarly, after discussing Aristotle's somewhat ambiguous position on the extent to which the dead are affected by the fortunes of the living (*Ethics* 1.9), Muret noted that Christians had no doubts on this issue, for they knew that their good actions and prayers were received with joy by the dead.[256] Vettori and Riccoboni, commenting on Aristotle's claim that the gods were not to be praised but rather honoured (*Ethics* 1.12), both informed their readers that the Christian custom was instead to praise God as well as to honour him.[257]

The authors who made the most extensive use of the Bible in their commentaries on the *Ethics* were those, like Lefèvre d'Étaples and his student Clichtove, who regarded Aristotelian precepts as rungs on a ladder leading towards the higher morality of the gospels.[258] The assumption underlying this view, explicitly expressed by Lefèvre, was the basic agreement and affinity between Aristotelianism and Christianity.[259] Landi captured this spirit in his dialogue *Le attioni morali*, where the interlocutor 'Jacopo Fabro' states that Aristotelian ethics conform so closely to the doctrines of the gospels that one might almost say that the Christian life is nothing other than moral philosophy, although of course it has a more exalted foundation, superior means and a more noble end.[260] Mair held a similar view, claiming that in the *Ethics* Aristotle spoke about moral virtues with godlike inspiration, disagreeing in no way with Christian orthodoxy.[261] Even the Platonist Diacceto wrote that in the *Ethics* Aristotle had in great detail and with consummate care paved the way which led up to heaven.[262] Burgersdijk took a more cautious approach, merely claiming that very little in the *Ethics* departed from Christian truth and was therefore to be avoided.[263]

---

255. Giffen 1608, p. 822: 'Nos Christiani aliter didicimus, qui omnium etiam moralium virtutum actiones Deo tribuendas censeamus.'
256. Muret 1789, III, pp. 230–4.   257. Vettori 1584, p. 60; Riccoboni 1610, p. 495.
258. Clichtove 1537, f. 42ʳ describes Christ as 'virtutum omnium exemplum absolutissimum'; Lefèvre d'Étaples 1533, f. 42ᵛ states that the highest level of virtue 'in domino nostro, domino virtutum . . . cumulatissime est inveniri'.
259. Lefèvre d'Étaples 1972, p. 21 refers to the Aristotelians 'quorum theologia Christianae sapientiae magna concordia affinitateque consentit atque coniuncta est'.   260. Landi 1564–75, I, p. 25.
261. Mair 1530, f. 8ʳ: 'In his . . . libris Ethicorum divinitus de moralibus virtutibus [Aristoteles] loquitur, consone ad orthodoxam fidem, nullo modo ab ea discrepat.'
262. Diacceto 1563, p. 323 (*Praefatio in libros Aristotelis de moribus*): '[Aristoteles] locupletissime exquisitissimeque sternit munitque viam, qua nobis ad superos gradiendum est.'
263. Burgersdijk 1629, sig. ★ 5ᵛ: 'in paucissimis ab Aristotelis sententia recederem, ubi id Christiana veritas omnino postulat'.

PLATONIC ETHICS: THE SUPREME GOOD

The humanists who produced translations of Plato's works concentrated on those dialogues which were particularly concerned with ethical issues.[264] But the few professional philosophers who lectured on Plato were usually more interested in metaphysics and cosmology than in ethics.[265] Platonism did nonetheless make an impact on the ethical thought of a small number of Renaissance thinkers and through them exerted an important influence on the literary culture of the era.[266]

The central issue in Platonic, as in Peripatetic, ethics was the nature of the supreme good. Renaissance Platonists, like Aristotelians, saw contemplation as man's highest goal. Ficino, the founder of Florentine Neoplatonism, wrote in his *Argumentum de summo bono* that the supreme good consisted in the contemplation not of any created good but of the highest good, that is, God. The knowledge of God was therefore the soul's *summum bonum*.[267] In an earlier work Ficino had stated that according to Plato the supreme good was to become like God.[268] The connection between these two positions is made clear in his *Theologia platonica*, where he explained that the intellect, when it understands objects, transforms itself into their image and becomes like them. So when our intellect understands God through contemplation, we become Godlike.[269]

According to Landino, a close associate of Ficino's in the Florentine Academy, Plato had taught that the supreme good consisted in the contemplation of divine things.[270] Nesi, another Florentine in contact with this circle, asserted – citing Ficino as his authority – that Plato had placed the *summum bonum* in God, the archetype of all the forms.[271] This interpretation continued to be expounded in the sixteenth century. Pompeo della Barba and Francesco de' Vieri both identified the form of the Good with God and described the Platonic supreme good in terms of divine

---

264. *Medioevo e Rinascimento* 1955, I, pp. 339–74 (Garin).
265. One exception is Agrippa, who apparently lectured on the *Symposium*: see his 'Oratio in praelectionem Convivii Platonis' in Agrippa *c.* 1630, II, pp. 1062–73.
266. Kristeller 1956a, pp. 287–9; 1961a, pp. 34–5; *Platon et Aristote* 1976, pp. 93–104 (Schmitt).
267. Ficino 1937, II, p. 96: 'summum anime bonum in eo bono quod est in bonorum genere summum, id est Deus. Quapropter in ipsa Dei cognitione summum est anime bonum.'
268. Ficino 1937, II, p. 8 (*De quatuor sectis philosophorum*): '[Plato censet] . . . summum . . . bonum Deo similem fieri.'
269. Ficino 1964–70, II, p. 250 (XIV.2): 'Non possumus . . . Deo per intellectum similes effici, nisi Deum intelligendo, quippe cum quibuslibet aliis rebus intellectus tunc fiat similis, quando eas intelligendo se in earum imagines transfigurat.'   270. Landino 1980, p. 119.
271. Nesi s. XV, f. 11ʳ: 'Platonem . . . in solo sempiterno immensoque Deo, idearum omnium archetypo, summum bonum posuisse et nos saepe legimus et Marsilius Ficinus . . . in sua theologia apertissime obtestatur.'

contemplation.[272] Javelli claimed that in the *Theages* Plato had referred to man's highest good as the speculation about divine beings, thus including the intelligences as well as God; but in the *Symposium* he had specified that our happiness consisted primarily in the contemplation of God.[273] In the view of Fox-Morcillo, Plato's belief that the contemplation of God was man's supreme good was not only apparent in his own works, above all the *Philebus* and *Republic*, but was also confirmed in the writings of Apuleius, Albinus, Plotinus, Iamblichus, Proclus, Porphyry and all the rest of the Platonists.[274]

It was a fundamental tenet of Platonic philosophy that this contemplation of God could not be perfectly achieved until the soul had freed itself from its connection with the body. Many Renaissance Platonists interpreted this to mean that the supreme good could only be attained after death, when the soul permanently escaped from its corporeal prison. As Lorenzo de' Medici wrote, our soul would never find pure truth while it was weighed down by the terrestrial burden of the body.[275] Plato, according to Landino, had denied that we could attain happiness until we were liberated from our earthly chains and restored to our true nature.[276] Leone Ebreo described how the soul, when released from its bodily prison, became united to God and shared the eternal joy experienced by angels and other immaterial beings.[277] A number of Platonic dialogues were adduced as evidence in support of this view: the *Phaedo, Symposium, Republic* and above all the *Epinomis*, now considered to be of doubtful authenticity.[278]

Ficino also held that the soul could not attain knowledge of God and thereby become Godlike until it had separated itself from the body.[279] He

272. Della Barba 1554, p. 98: 'la felicità nostra consiste nel vedere Dio'; Vieri 1577, sig. b 8ᵛ: 'il sommo bene dell'anima è cercare Dio . . . così dice . . . Platone nel Fedone'.
273. Javelli 1651, p. 325: 'Licet . . . Plato in divinorum entium speculatione nostram beatitudinem locaverit, primo tamen in Dei Maximi speculatione; . . . et quidem quod in huius divinissima speculatione nostram reposuerit felicitatem patet in *Symposio* [210E–212B].'
274. Fox-Morcillo 1566, p. 126: 'In . . . Dei contemplatione constitui foelicitatem [Plato] existimavit; atque hanc etiam esse ipsius sententiam, non modo ex eius scriptis constat, sed omnes Academici uno ore confirmant. Id enim Apuleius Alcinousque de illo testatur; idem fatetur Plotinus . . ., Iamblichus, Proclus, Porphyrius ac reliqui omnes.'
275. Medici 1914, II, p. 51 (*Altercazione*): 'mai non trova la nostr'alma | la pura verità formosa e bianca, | mentre l'aggrava este terrestre salma'.
276. Landino 1980, p. 71: 'negat Plato beatos nos esse posse, nisi postquam a terrenis vinculis soluti in naturam nostram liberi redierimus'.
277. Leone Ebreo 1929, pp. 46–7.
278. Vieri 1577, p. 158: 'Platone ci dimostra, che la beatitudine non s'ha in questo mondo ma nell'altro, e nel principio dell'Epinomide [973C], un'altro [luogo] simile nell' Assiocco [370 B–D], molti altri ancora ne sono nel Fedone, nelle Leggi, nella Republica, et nelle lettere'; Talon 1583, p. 1079. After citing *Republic* 608C and *Phaedo* 67A, wrote: 'Idemque Plato scribit in Epinomide et in Convivio'; Zwinger 1566, p. 15: 'Neminem . . . in hac vita beatum fieri posse, sed post mortem tantum, Plato diserte in Epinomide testatur.'
279. Ficino 1937, II, pp. 96–7; 1964–70, II, p. 249 (XIV.1): 'anima ab huius corporis vinculis exempta puraque decedens, certa quadam ratione fit deus'.

believed, on the other hand, that a very small number of people could reach this state during the present life, albeit imperfectly and for brief periods of time. Plato, Xenocrates and Plotinus had managed to abstract themselves temporarily from their bodies through the intensity of their contemplative meditation, while St Paul in II Corinthians 12 had described his soul's ascent to the third heaven in a divine rapture.[280] Using this same text, Giovanni Pico claimed that a few people could achieve a state so remote from corporeal concerns that, like St Paul, they could say that they did not know whether they were in the body or out of it. This ecstatic trance could, however, only be maintained for a very short period of time.[281] Benedetto Varchi took the view that man as a species had the potentiality to ascend to heaven while still living and to become not merely an angel but a quasi-divinity, though this apotheosis was achieved by very few.[282] Francesco Piccolomini, citing *Epinomis* 973C, maintained that the souls of a small number of men could, while still conjoined to the body in mortal life, become united in a temporary and limited manner to the Good Itself and the One. It was thus possible to attain the supreme good in the present life, but only imperfectly; the soul's perfect union with the *summum bonum* could not occur until the next life.[283] Javelli noted that although in *Epinomis* 973C and 992B Plato asserted that a few men could achieve happiness in this life, he seemed to deny this in *Phaedo* 66D–E, where he stated that the true philosopher could only hope to attain pure wisdom after death. This apparent contradiction was resolved, according to Javelli, if one recognised that the happy few referred to in the *Epinomis* got merely a slight taste of the supreme good in the present life. So while these men were happy in comparison with those who did not possess moral virtues and speculative habits, they had not achieved the perfect beatitude of those whose souls were permanently freed from their bodies and could therefore enjoy unimpeded contemplation of God.[284]

Whether this perfect beatitude consisted more in the contemplation or in the enjoyment of God, that is, whether the supreme good was attained primarily through an act of the intellect or of the will, was a matter of

280. Ficino 1964–70, II, pp. 201–2, 204 (XIII.2); see also Kristeller 1953a, pp. 323–5; 1956a, p. 282.
281. G. Pico 1942, p. 530 (*Commento sopra una canzona de amore*): 'sono pochi, che in tutto remossi sono dalla cura del corpo e possono con Paulo dire di non sapere se siano o nel corpo o fuori del corpo, al quale stato qualche volta perviene un uomo ma stavvi poco'.
282. Varchi 1858–9, II, p. 612 (*Sopra la pittura e scultura*): '[l'uomo] può, ancora vivendo e colle terrene membre, volare al Cielo e divenire non pure Angelo, ma quasi Dio'; p. 626: 'quelli pochi . . . che fatti più che uomini, anzi divenuti dii, non invidiano a Giove nè il nettare, nè l'ambrosia'.
283. F. Piccolomini 1594b, p. 425; see also A. Piccolomini 1542, f. 23ʳ; Waele 1620, p. 19.
284. Javelli 1651, p. 323: 'Cum . . . in Epinomi[de] aliquos perpaucos felicitari pro hac vita concedere videtur, intelligendum arbitror per quandam levem degustationem, et in respectu, ita quod respectu aliorum qui morales virtutes et speculativos habitus non possident, vel non adeo perfecte, beati nuncupari possunt.'

controversy among Renaissance Platonists. Ficino, in his commentary on
the *Philebus*, the first version of which was written between 1464 and 1469,
argued strongly in favour of the supremacy of contemplation over
enjoyment in the attainment of happiness on the ground that the intellect
was a higher power than the will.[285] Ficino's intellectualist position is also
portrayed in Landino's *Disputationes Camaldulenses*. In this dialogue,
written about 1472, the interlocutor Marsilius maintains that the *summum
bonum* is located in our reason, in which we are very similar to angels, rather
than our appetite or will, in which we are indistinguishable from cattle.[286]

But when Ficino discussed this question with Lorenzo de' Medici at the
Villa Careggi, probably in 1473, they both came to the conclusion that the
will rather than the intellect contributed more to man's happiness.[287] This
occasion was commemorated by Lorenzo in his poem *Altercazione* and later
by Ficino in his *Epistola de felicitate*. In their accounts of this discussion, they
both used the image, taken from Plato's *Phaedrus* 246–7, of the intellect and
will as twin wings, which allow the soul to ascend to heaven; and they both
interpreted the celestial ambrosia and nectar which the soul consumes at the
divine table as, respectively, the vision of God achieved by the intellect and
the joy derived from that experience by the will.[288] Finally, both affirmed
that the nectar of the will's joy was superior to the ambrosia of the intellect's
vision, primarily because the intellect's knowledge of God was less perfect
and fulfilling than the will's love.[289] This voluntarist view was also adopted
by Nesi, who exhorted philosophers to enter the sacred temple of the
divinity not through the door of the intellect but rather through that of the
will.[290] And Vieri maintained that although happiness could be attained
either by the intellect through cognition or by the will through love, it was
love which had the greater power.[291]

285. Ficino 1975, pp. 369–71 (cap. 37: 'Felicitas pertinere videtur ad sapientiam potius quam ad
     voluptatem et intellectu magis accipi quam voluntate'): 'supremum bonum in potentia capitur
     superiori potius quam inferiori. Intellectus autem praestantior est quam voluntas.'
286. Landino 1980, p. 73: 'ratio nos angelis simillimos reddit, appetitu autem nihilo a pecude differimus.
     Non erit igitur in voluntate, sed in ratione summum bonum collocandum.'
287. For the dating of this discussion, see Medici 1977–, I, p. 497.
288. Medici 1914, II, pp. 55–6; Ficino 1576, I, p. 663. Similar uses of this image are found in Ficino 1956,
     pp. 259–60 (VII.14); 1975, pp. 352–5 (cap. 34); and 1981, pp. 77–9 (cap. 2); see also M. J. B. Allen
     1984a; for somewhat different interpretations of this passage see Poliziano 1553, p. 407;
     F. Piccolomini 1594b, p. 424.
289. Ficino 1576, I, p. 663: 'Gaudium in ea felicitate est praestantius visione. Quia quanto magis est apud
     Deum in hac vita meremur amando, quam inquirendo, tanto maius in illa vita praemium amori,
     quam inquisitioni tribuitur'; Medici 1914, II, p. 56: 'sì poca è nostra mortal vista | che vera
     cognizion di Dio non dona | . . . Ma quello ha volontà perfetta e buona | e Dio veramente ama.'
290. Nesi, *Oratio de charitate* in Vasoli 1972, pp. 158–9.
291. Vieri 1577, p. 176: 'ma con più forza fa questo l'amore'.

Some of Ficino's contemporaries noted the apparent discrepancy between the intellectualism of his *Philebus* commentary and the voluntarism of his *Epistola de felicitate*. In an attempt to defend the consistency of his position, Ficino wrote to Paolo Orlandini in 1496 maintaining that in the commentary on the *Philebus* he was discussing a natural process, in which the intellect guides and satisfies the will. In the letter on happiness, however, he was describing a supernatural or ecstatic experience, in which the will, inspired by divine love, draws the intellect into God.[292] Whether or not this explanation satisfied Orlandini, others remained troubled by Ficino's position on this issue. Francesco Piccolomini, for one, could not understand why a scholar as well versed in Plato as Ficino had contradicted, in his letter on happiness, the view expressed in the *Philebus* that the supreme good consisted primarily in the soul's contemplative, rather than its appetitive, faculty.[293] Leone Ebreo, on the other hand, attempted to synthesise the intellectualist and voluntarist positions by integrating cognition and enjoyment into a single act: the intellectual love of God. According to Filone, one of the speakers in his *Dialoghi d'amore*, there are those who believe that the supreme good consists in the soul's understanding of God, since this is its most noble and spiritual act; while for others the *summum bonum* is the soul's love of God, since this act occurs after, and as a direct result of, the intellect's knowledge. Filone, however, argues that these are both preliminary and imperfect stages of happiness when compared with the soul's ultimate act of union with God, in which perfect cognition and love are combined.[294]

THE PLATONIC THEORY OF LOVE

The theory that the supreme good could be attained by means of love was one of the most influential doctrines of Renaissance Neoplatonism.[295] Plato's most elaborate discussion of his theory of love occurs in the *Symposium*, particularly in Socrates' account of the discourse delivered by

---

292. Ficino 1975, pp. 487–9; see also Kristeller 1953a, pp. 274–310.
293. F. Piccolomini 1594b, p. 425: 'Plato in Philebo primas tribuit summi boni partes [facultati contemplandi]; secundo autem loco ad facultatem appetendi . . . Propterea miror de Marsilio Ficino in Platone satis versato, quod in epistolis suis oppositum asseruerit ac confirmaverit.'
294. Leone Ebreo 1929, p. 46: 'la felicità non consiste in quello atto conoscitivo di Dio il quale conduce l'amore, né consiste ne l'amore che a tal cognizione succede; ma sol consiste ne l'atto coppulativo de l'intima e unita cognizione divina . . . E quello è l'ultimo atto e beato fine'; see also *Platon et Aristote* 1976, pp. 293–306 (Melczer); Soria Olmedo 1984, pp. 102–46.
295. Festugière 1941; Nelson 1958.

Diotima (201D–212A).[296] This priestess-like figure explains that the initiate into the mysteries of love-matters (τὰ ἐρωτικά) should progress methodically, ascending step by step, beginning with the love of one particular beautiful body and moving upwards to the love of the beauty manifested in all beautiful bodies. The next stage is the recognition that the beauty of souls is superior to that of bodies. Then comes the contemplation of the beauty of ways of life and laws; after that, the beauty of branches of knowledge. Finally, the initiate reaches his goal by attaining a wondrous vision of the wholly incorporeal, imperishable, transcendent and universal form of the beautiful, in which all particular beautiful things participate.

It was primarily through Ficino's widely read *Commentarium in Convivium Platonis, De amore* that the Platonic love-theory expounded in the *Symposium* came to have such an important impact on Renaissance thought. Ficino defined love as the desire for beauty and described beauty as a ray which emanated from God and progressively penetrated the created world, moving downwards from the angelic mind to the material substance of bodies. All beauty in the universe was therefore the radiance of the divine countenance.[297] Paralleling the graduated descent of beauty from God to the lower hypostases, love ascended step-by-step up the ladder which Diotima described to Socrates: from the beauty of the body to that of the soul, from the soul's beauty to that of the angelic mind, and from there finally to God.[298] Ficino stressed that although God was reached by means of his creations, we were not to love them for themselves but rather to love God in them: 'In bodies, we shall love the shadow of God; in souls, the likeness of God; in angels, the image of God. Thus, in the present life we shall love God in everything so that in the next we might love everything in God.'[299]

---

296. The *Phaedrus* was also interpreted by some as a dialogue concerning love: see Figliucci's preface addressed 'alle donne veramente nobili et virtuose' in Plato 1544, sig. A ii[r]: 'il gran Platone . . . ci insegnò qual fusse un vero, buono, et santo amore, et quale un finto, tristo et lascivo'.
297. Ficino 1956, p. 142 (1.4): 'Cum amorem dicimus, pulchritudinis desiderium intelligite'; p. 184 (v.4): 'Pulchritudo est splendor divini vultus'; see also Diacceto 1563, p. 115 (*De amore* II.6): 'declaratum est . . . amorem . . . perfruendae et effingendae pulchritudinis desiderium'; 1983, p. 15 (1.2): 'amorem esse necesse est, quando pulchri desiderium est'; Figliucci 1564, f. 48[r]: 'amore non è altro che desiderio di bello . . . e la bellezza che quaggiù vediamo non è altro che un raggio di quella divina'; Agrippa *c.* 1630, II, pp. 1063–4 (*Oratio*): 'Omnes . . . conveniunt in hac summa, non aliud esse amorem quam desiderium pulchritudinis . . . Pulchritudo autem omnis, sive incorporea sive corporea, nihil aliud est quam divini vultus splendor in rebus creatis relucens.'
298. Ficino 1956, p. 230 (VI.15): 'A corpore in animam, ab anima in angelum, ab angelo [Diotima Socratem] reducit in deum.'
299. *Ibid.*, p. 239 (VI.19): 'In corporibus quidem [diligemus] dei umbram; in animis dei similitudinem; in angelis, eiusdem imaginem. Ita deum ad presens in omnibus diligemus ut in deo tandem omnia diligamus'; see also Agrippa *c.* 1630, II, p. 1072 (*Oratio*).

The Platonic love-theory expounded in Ficino's commentary on the *Symposium* was summarised and put into poetic language by Girolamo Benivieni in his canzone 'Amor dalle cui', modelled on the late thirteenth-century Aristotelian canzone of Guido Cavalcanti 'Donna me prega.'[300] In 1486 Giovanni Pico wrote a *Commento* on Benivieni's poem, intending it as an introduction to a commentary on the *Symposium* which he planned to write but never completed.[301] Discussing Benivieni's poetic account of the soul's ascent to God through love, Pico elaborates on the theme of Diotima's ladder, distinguishing six stages by which we ascend from the desire to unite corporeally with sensual beauty to the desire to unite spiritually with intelligible beauty. The sequence begins with the visual perception of the corporeal beauty of a particular individual and ends with the soul's union with the universal and first mind. Pico believed that while the human soul was still attached to the body it could not attain the seventh and ultimate stage of celestial love. So instead of uniting with the first Father, the source of all beauty, the soul must rest contentedly at his side.[302]

The step-by-step ascent of the lover's desire from the merely physical beauty of an individual body to the purely intellectual and divine beauty of God became a standard feature in Renaissance discussions of Platonic love.[303] This theme, often mingled with Petrarchan motifs, is also found in literary works, such as *Gli Asolani* of Pietro Bembo. In book III of this dialogue, first published in 1505, the speaker Lavinello recounts his conversation with an old hermit, modelled on Socrates' Diotima, who tells him that our souls can never be satisfied by earthly beauty, for being themselves immortal they cannot be content with a mortal thing. We are therefore continually desirous of true, divine and eternal beauty, to which the false and transient beauties of this life can nonetheless elevate us, provided we do not linger with them but recognise them for the vain and deceitful shadows they are.[304]

Twenty-three years later Bembo himself appeared as an interlocutor in Castiglione's *Il libro del cortegiano*, where he gives an account of Platonic

300. Cavalcanti's canzone is mentioned by Ficino 1956, p. 240 (VII.1) and also served as the inspiration for the *Lezzioni d'amore*, a sixteenth-century treatise on Platonic love by Vieri 1973, p. 77: 'nella quale si tratta d'Amore et insieme si espone la Canzone di Guido Cavalcanti'.

301. G. Pico 1984, p. 58, n. 15: 'Omnia praeludium est commentariorum quae in Platonis Symposium meditamur.'

302. G. Pico 1942, pp. 566–9. He believed, however, that the soul could achieve temporary separation from the body in an ecstatic trance: see above, p. 351.

303. See, e.g., Diacceto 1563, pp. 136–7 (*Panegyricus in amorem*); Vieri 1577, pp. 10–11; Varchi 1858–9, II, p. 626; Javelli 1651, p. 325.   304. Bembo 1960, pp. 491–3.

love to the noble men and women at the court of Urbino: 'By the ladder whose lowest rung bears the image of sensual beauty, let us ascend to the sublime abode where heavenly, gracious and true beauty dwells, hidden in the secret recesses of God so that profane eyes may not see it.'[305] Bembo's address concludes with the hymn 'O Amor santissimo', in which love's role in conducting the soul to the perfect felicity of union with God is asserted in language redolent of the New Testament.[306] This solemn and religious tone is somewhat undercut, however, when Lady Emilia tugs at the hem of Bembo's robe and warns him to take care that his high-flown thoughts do not cause his soul to depart from his body. 'That would not be the first miracle', replies Bembo, 'which love has worked in me.'[307]

PLATONIC ETHICS AND CHRISTIANITY

Most Renaissance philosophers held the view that Plato's ethical doctrines were far closer to Christianity than those of other pagan philosophers, in particular Aristotle. According to Nesi, Aristotle was by natural inclination an earth-bound scientist and therefore, unlike Plato, could not ascend to the third heaven to which St Paul had been lifted.[308] Zwinger thought that the ancients had been right to call Plato *divinus* and Aristotle δαιμόνιος since the former knew about heavenly things, the latter, about earthly.[309] Luther declared, in his Heidelberg disputation of 1518, that Platonic philosophy was better than Aristotelian precisely because Plato directed his efforts towards that which was divine and immortal, separate and eternal, imperceptible and intelligible; Aristotle, on the contrary, dealt only with that which was sensible and singular, entirely human and natural.[310] Plato's method of philosophising, stressed Nifo, derived from the faith of his ancestors; Aristotle's was essentially empirical, based on memory, sense impressions and experience.[311]

The consequence was that Plato's moral doctrines could be more easily

---

305. Castiglione 1947, pp. 496–7: 'per la scala che nell'infimo grado tiene l'ombra di bellezza sensuale ascendiamo alla sublime stanzia ove abita la celeste, amabile e vera bellezza, che nei secreti penetrali di Dio sta nascosta, acciò che gli occhi profani veder non la possano'.
306. *Ibid.*, pp. 497–8; see also J. R. Woodhouse 1978, pp. 179–80.
307. Castiglione 1947, p. 498: ' "Guardate . . . che con questi pensieri a voi ancora non si separi l'anima dal corpo." "Signora . . . non saría questo il primo miraculo, che amor abbia in me operato." '
308. Nesi s. xv, f. 144[r–v].
309. Zwinger 1566, p. 15: 'recte veteres Platonem divinum, Aristotelem δαιμόνιον vocavere, quod alter sublimia sapiat, alter terrena'.
310. Luther 1883–, LIX, p. 424; see also Junghans 1985, pp. 167–71.
311. Nifo 1645, p. 48 (*De vera vivendi libertate*): 'Plato ex fide maiorum philosophatur; Aristoteles autem ex memoriis, sensibus atque experientiis.'

integrated than Aristotle's with Christianity. Tommaso Contarini, Archbishop of Candia, pointed out that while for Plato the highest human virtues were religion, piety towards God and sanctity, Aristotle had not included any of these in his own list of virtues.[312] Fox-Morcillo found Aristotle's insistence on the necessity of external goods for the attainment of happiness incompatible with the Christian belief that perfect felicity consisted solely in a direct and immediate vision of God. Plato, on the other hand, along with Plotinus, Iamblichus, Proclus and the entire school of Platonists were, in his view, virtual Christians because they placed man's highest good in the contemplation and enjoyment of God.[313]

Fox-Morcillo also maintained that Plato's belief that happiness was only attainable in the future life was far closer to Christian doctrine than was Aristotle's claim that it could be achieved during this life.[314] Ficino had made the same point, disputing Aristotle's opinion that true happiness could be obtained while the soul was still connected to the body, and endorsing Plato's insistence that the soul could only reach the blissful state it desired when separated from its corporeal bonds.[315] Since in Ficino's eyes Platonic philosophy was part of a long tradition of 'ancient theology' which had been originally inspired by Moses and looked forward to Christianity, he naturally emphasised those elements in Platonism which he believed prefigured Christianity.[316] Most later thinkers were introduced to Platonism in the highly Christianised interpretation presented by Ficino, whose influence extended from the idiosyncratic Franciscan Giorgi to the evangelical humanist Rabelais.[317] Vieri carried Ficino's programme even further in his *Compendio della dottrina di Platone in quello, che ella è conforme con la fede nostra*. He too stressed that one of the fundamental bases of agreement between Platonic philosophy and Christianity was the doctrine that happiness was only to be achieved in the next life.[318] Not only Platonists but also Aristotelians, such as Francesco Piccolomini, admitted that Plato was much closer than Aristotle to Christian theologians in placing the *summum bonum*

312. T. Contarini 1572, f. 29ʳ.
313. Fox-Morcillo 1566, pp. 136–7: 'Christianus . . . Plato, qui foelicitatem in Dei contemplatione posuit. Christianus Plotinus, qui hominem Deo frui verum esse summum bonum affirmat. Christianus Iamblichus, Proclus, ac tota Platonicorum schola, quae religioni nostrae hac in re videtur consentire.'   314. *Ibid.*, p. 128.
315. Ficino 1576, I, pp. 662–3 (*Epistola de felicitate*).
316. Ficino's 1489 letter to Martin Prenninger in Klibansky 1981, p. 45: 'Plato noster una cum rationibus Pythagoricis atque Socraticis legem sectatur Mosaycam auguraturque Christianam'; see also Gandillac 1982, pp. 157–68; on the 'ancient theology', see Walker 1972.
317. Giorgi 1525, sigs. i iiiʳ–i iiiiʳ; Rabelais 1970, esp. pp. 280–314; see also Screech 1979, pp. 187–94; Levi 1984.   318. Vieri 1577, p. 158; see also 1590, p. 12.

in the future life.[319] Furthermore, according to Piccolomini's follower Riccoboni, while for Aristotle the greatest happiness was contemplation in itself, for Plato as well as for Christian theologians it was contemplation of the supreme good, that is, God.[320]

But Plato's very proximity to Christianity was sometimes perceived as a danger. Cardinal Bessarion in his *In calumniatorem Platonis* warned against abusing the similarity between Platonism and Christianity by accommodating Christ's words to Platonic doctrine rather than vice versa.[321] Scala pointed out that despite the fact that there was much in Platonism which agreed with Christianity, there were also doctrines which blatantly contradicted the Bible and therefore had to be rejected. The Platonists believed, for example, that although man's soul was created by God, his body was formed by the secondary gods.[322] Landino noted another discrepancy: whereas Platonists thought that the soul was created before the body, Christians rightly believed that God gave being to the soul and placed it in the body at one and the same time. Therefore since Christian dogma regarded the soul as having no existence before that of the body, it was at odds with the Platonic doctrine that the soul entered the lower world in order to purge itself of the faults which it had committed before its union with the body.[323]

The spiritual difficulties which wholehearted allegiance to Platonic philosophy could entail are well illustrated by the case of Benivieni, whose youthful Platonic canzone 'Amor dalle cui' was inspired by Ficino's commentary on the *Symposium* and was itself commented upon by Giovanni Pico.[324] Some twenty years later, however, when the poem was published, Benivieni – who had become a follower of Savonarola – claimed that both he and Pico had come to have doubts about the propriety of discussing love in Platonic rather than Christian terms.[325] These doubts led him to compose a counter-poem, a Christian canzone entitled 'Amor sotto

---

319. F. Piccolomini 1594b, p. 282: 'Cum nostris theologis eatenus consentiunt Platonici, quatenus ipsi quoque futuram vitam . . . inspexerunt.'
320. Riccoboni 1610, p. 808.   321. Bessarion 1927, p. 102.
322. Scala, *Epistola de nobilioribus philosophorum sectis*, published in Stein 1888, p. 551: 'Aberrant . . . cum animam ab summo deo, corpus autem a diis, quos Plato appellat secundos, factum profitentur [*Timaeus* 42E]. Scriptum est enim: fecit hominem ad imaginem et similitudinem suam [Gen. 1:26], neque homo sine corpore, cum ex animo constet et corpore, a deo creatus est.'
323. Landino 1980, p. 217: 'Nostri . . ., qui ita a deo animas creari rectissime sentiunt, ut eodem momento et creentur et suis corporibus infundantur, non eas in hoc inferiori mundo versari volunt, ut conmissa purgarent.'   324. See above p. 355.
325. G. Pico 1942, p. 447 (*Commento*): 'nacque nelli animi nostri qualche ombra di dubitazione, se era conveniente a uno professore della legge di Cristo, volendo lui trattare di Amore . . . trattarne come platonico e non come cristiano'.

cui', in which he presented a parallel version of the Platonic love-theory in complete conformity with orthodox Christian dogma. In the eighth stanza of the new poem, the ascent of love is made not by means of Diotima's ladder but rather by eight steps based on Augustine's *De doctrina Christiana* II.7: fear, compunction, renunciation of the flesh, humility, extirpation of vice, virtue, purity and charity.[326]

An ambivalent attitude to Platonic ethics can be seen in the writings of Calvin. On the one hand, he approved of Plato as the only ancient philosopher who had recognised that man's supreme good was his union with God.[327] But on the other hand, Calvin's belief that human depravity was the result of original sin led him to reproach Plato for his conviction that all vice was caused merely by ignorance.[328] No such equivocations are found in Melanchthon's account of Platonic ethics. He considered the Platonist's doctrine of purifying virtues to be an invention of the devil, who had deliberately imitated Christian dogma in order to obscure and undermine it by convincing those who did not know any better that philosophy in no way differed from Christianity and that man could live well by the strength of reason alone.[329] Melanchthon objected so strongly to this blurring of the distinction between Platonic and Christian ethics because in his view, as we have seen, it was of primary importance to recognise the essential difference between faith and reason and to respect the boundary lines which separated moral philosophy from Christianity.[330] The issues raised by Melanchthon influenced later Protestant philosophers even when they were more sympathetic to Platonism. Waele, for instance, was willing to compare Plato's purifying virtues to those mentioned by Christ in the Beatitudes. But he nonetheless concluded that Plato's views were wrong because he did not understand that our minds and souls were only truly purified by grace and the Holy Spirit.[331]

---

326. Benivieni 1984, esp. pp. 159 and 176–8.
327. Calvin 1863–1900, II, col. 729 (*Institutio religionis Christianae* III.25.2): 'De summo fine bonorum anxie disputarunt olim philosophi . . .; nemo tamen, excepto Platone, agnovit summum hominis bonum esse eius coniunctionem cum Deo'; see also *Platon et Aristote* 1976, pp. 391–402 (Malet-Yvonnet).
328. Calvin 1863–1900, II, col. 206 (*Institutio religionis Christianae* II.2.25): 'merito reprehensus est Plato quod omnia peccata ignorantiae imputarit'; see, e.g, Plato, *Meno* 77D–E; *Protagoras* 345B.
329. Melanchthon 1834–60, XVI, col. 282 (*Enarrationes*): 'Platonici imitatione Christianae doctrinae finxerunt virtutes καθαρτικὰς, quibus animi purgentur, sed illas nugas commentus est Diabolus, ut obscuraret doctrinam Christianam, et opinionem faceret imperitis doctrinam Christianam nihil differre a philosophia, et rationis vires ad recte vivendum . . . satis esse.' For the Platonic doctrine of *virtutes purgatoriae* see Macrobius, *Commentarium in Somnium Scipionis* I.8.
330. See above, pp. 323–4. 331. Waele 1620, pp. 48–9.

STOIC ETHICS: THE SUPREME GOOD

Stoic ethical doctrines were well known during the Middle Ages. They had been transmitted directly through the works of classical Latin writers, above all Seneca and Cicero, and indirectly through the works of Christian Latin authors, many of whom had found Stoic beliefs compatible with their own religious dogmas. Even when Aristotelianism became the centre of the university moral philosophy curriculum in the thirteenth century, Stoicism continued to have an important and wide-ranging influence on medieval ethical thought.[332] Although a few Greek texts presenting new information on Stoicism, such as the seventh book of Diogenes Laertius' *Lives of the Philosophers* and the *Enchiridion* of Epictetus, became available in the fifteenth century, Renaissance philosophers relied for the most part on the same Latin works as their medieval predecessors. The moral essays and letters of Seneca, which had inspired many authors in the Middle Ages, also found a receptive audience in a variety of Renaissance writers.[333] And humanists, like their medieval predecessors, used Cicero's *De finibus* and *De officiis* as major sources of information on Stoic ethical philosophy.[334]

The supreme good according to the Stoics was virtue. Indeed, it was the only good, and vice was the only evil. Everything else, including so-called bodily and external goods, such as health and affluence, they regarded as morally indifferent.[335] The Stoics reckoned that the truly wise man would not allow such random factors to affect his happiness, but would base it rather on his own subjective state of mind, the only element in his life completely under his conscious control.[336] The attainment of the supreme good could not therefore be hindered by the vicissitudes of fortune; on the contrary, external adversity provided an ideal opportunity for developing and displaying the internal virtue which alone determined human happiness.[337] Virtue, for the Stoics, consisted in following nature, which they regarded as the immanent manifestation of divine reason. To behave virtuously was thus to live in harmony with nature and thereby obey the laws of universal reason.[338] Virtue for the Stoics was not a path to reach some higher goal but rather was itself the sole and self-sufficient aim of man's existence.

332. Colish 1985; Verbeke 1983; Spanneut 1969.
333. Manetti 1979; Brucioli 1982, pp. 445–51 (*Della povertà*); see also Panizza 1984.
334. See the commentaries in Cicero 1537, 1560 and 1569.
335. The Stoics did, however, allow that some indifferent things (ἀδιάφορα) were to be preferred (προηγμένα), while others were to be rejected (ἀποπροηγμένα); see Cicero, *De finibus* III.16.52–3.
336. Epictetus, *Enchiridion*, cap. I.   337. Seneca, *Epistulae* LXXI, XCVIII.
338. Diogenes Laertius, VII.87.

The rigorous and strict morality of Stoicism appealed to certain Renaissance scholars such as Niccolò Niccoli, who was portrayed by his friend Poggio Bracciolini as a proponent of the Stoic doctrine that virtue alone was sufficient to live the good life.[339] Although Poggio himself at times affected a Stoic disdain for wealth and its benefits, he usually took the more moderate view that material goods were acceptable, provided they were used wisely and well.[340] This ambivalent attitude had characterised the humanist movement since the time of Petrarch, who had admired the moral perfection of Stoic ethics but felt its demands were unrealistic and inhuman.[341] Similarly, Salutati, who had given the highest praise to the Stoics in his *De laboribus Herculis*, later in his life began to question their doctrines. He admitted that virtue and vice were the only moral goods and evils but insisted that the various fortunes and misfortunes which befell men were natural, if secondary, goods and evils, and therefore could not be dismissed with Stoic indifference.[342] In Alberti's dialogue *Della famiglia*, the character Lionardo refuses to admit that being poor is a bad thing, claiming that virtue alone is sufficient to produce happiness. But these noble sentiments are challenged by the more realistic Adovardo, who tells him not to be such a 'Stoic' and to admit that poverty is a very miserable state for everyone.[343] It was, in fact, difficult to give wholehearted support to Stoic moral precepts, because the standards of behaviour demanded were so unrelentingly high. Even the Stoics themselves had admitted that only an ideal wise man could consistently live up to them. So, whether they approved or disapproved of Stoic morality, most Renaissance authors concurred in the view, commonly held since antiquity, that it was stern, rigid, harsh and severe.[344]

Even in the Middle Ages Stoic moral doctrines had seemed unreasonable to many philosophers. Thomas Aquinas, for example, had stressed that man was composed of a body as well as a soul and therefore needed certain material goods merely to keep alive.[345] The Epicurean humanist Cosma

339. Poggio Bracciolini 1964–9, I, p. 83 (*De nobilitate*): 'Non eget alterius ope aut fortunae adminiculis virtus . . . cum in ea satis sit praesidii ad bene beateque vivendum.'
340. Poggio Bracciolini 1984–, II, p. 43: 'si opes, divitie, dignitates . . . offerantur honeste, non arbitror ullo modo esse reiciendas'.
341. Petrarch 1955, pp. 22–215 (*Secretum*); see also Foster 1984, pp. 163–73.
342. Salutati 1951, I, p. 311: '[Stoici] super alios ad vere virtutis essentiam . . . accedebant'; 1891–1911, III, p. 417: 'Nichil malum, nisi turpe moraliter fateor. Naturaliter autem et secundum fortunam multa mala sunt'; see also Witt 1983, pp. 358–67.   343. Alberti 1969a, pp. 96–7.
344. Salutati 1891–1911, II, p. 292; Barnaba Senese 1979, p. 39: Bruni 1928, p. 26 (*Isagogicon*); Poggio Bracciolini 1984–, II, p. 17; Giorgi 1525, sig. D v^r; Vettori 1584, p. 582; Montaigne 1965, p. 218 (1.33).
345. *Summa theologica* I–II.59.3 and II–II.125.4; see also Baron 1938b, p. 3.

Raimondi made the same point in a letter written about 1429. If we were composed only of a soul, he wrote, then the Stoics would be right. Since, however, we consist of both body and soul, why do they look after the latter but neglect the former, which is the domicile of the soul and the other part of man?[346] Nores, following Cicero's *De finibus*, argued that the Epicureans went to the opposite extreme by attributing the supreme good entirely to the body, just as the Stoics had to the soul, while the middle position was taken by the Peripatetics, who assigned it partly to the soul and partly to the body.[347] Montaigne, never one to endorse extreme views, favoured Aristotelian moderation, noting that neither pure virtue nor pure sensual pleasure would be serviceable to us without some admixture.[348] Those who place all good in virtue, claimed Aonio Paleario, do not appear to realise that we are living beings and as such require food and drink, sleep and relaxation, clothes and shelter.[349]

Others, such as Versor, rejected the Stoic view of the *summum bonum* because it so plainly contradicted the generally accepted belief that misfortune was inimical to happiness.[350] The notion that someone could be happy while suffering imprisonment, torment, poverty, torture or the murder of his sons seemed inhuman to Bruni, who considered such hardness more appropriate to a rock than to a man.[351] Figliucci also attacked this Stoic doctrine on the Aristotelian grounds that someone who was in the midst of torment and calamity would not be able to act virtuously and therefore would not be happy.[352] Virtue, according to Beroaldo, was the most important constituent of happiness, but by no means the only one: corporeal and external goods were also necessary.[353] In the preface to his 1561 edition of Epictetus, Hieronymus Wolf related another criticism which had been levelled against Stoic philosophers. They admitted that they themselves had not attained the exalted status of wise men, which made them either the most foolish or the most arrogant of men: most foolish, if they thought that the perfection which they could not find in

---

346. Published in Zenzo 1978, p. 59: 'cur animum curant, corpus negligunt, animi domicilium ipsiusque hominis partem alteram?'
347. Nores 1597, p. 168: 'Epicurei . . . totum pene summum bonum attribuebant corpori, Stoici totum animo, Peripatetici partem animo, partem corpori.'
348. Montaigne 1965, p. 673 (II.20).   349. Paleario 1696, p. 168 (*De felicitate*).
350. Versor 1491, f. 113^r: 'hoc est contra communem opinionem hominum: quia estimant infortunium repugnare felicitati'.
351. Bruni 1741, II, p. 12; see also *Humanismus und Ökonomie* 1983, pp. 94–5 (Trusen).
352. Figliucci 1551, p. 341: 'uno, che in tormenti et in calamità è posto, è impedito da l'operare, onde non è felice'.
353. Beroaldo 1513, f. 119^v (*Oratio de foelicitate*): 'decernimus in virtute esse quidem plurima ad faciendam foelicitatem, sed haud quaquam omnia'.

themselves was to be found in human nature; most arrogant, if they were trying to persuade others to live up to standards which they themselves could not maintain.[354]

The Stoic assumption that virtue is its own reward was ridiculed by Lorenzo Valla in his dialogue *De vero falsoque bono*. Using his characteristic linguistic and rhetorical approach to philosophy, Valla had his speaker point out that the Stoic argument was circular and meaningless. For according to their theory, I act courageously for the sake of virtue. But what is virtue? Acting courageously. This was not an ethical principle, in Valla's view, but mere word play: I am to act courageously in order to act courageously.[355] Not only was the Stoic *summum bonum* based on empty rhetoric, it also rested on a fundamental misunderstanding of human nature. Valla did not believe that men ever committed virtuous deeds selflessly, as the Stoics claimed. He insisted instead that they were always motivated, whether or not they admitted it, by the desire to secure their own fame, glory or some other personal advantage.[356]

Some philosophers agreed with the view expressed by Cicero in *De finibus* v.8.22 that the Stoics had taken over Peripatetic ethics wholesale, merely adopting different names for the same concepts.[357] Others recognised and tried to explain the differences between the two systems. Francesco Piccolomini, for example, argued that Stoic morality was primarily directed towards private, and Peripatetic towards public, life. Moreover, although both schools placed the supreme good primarily in virtue, the Aristotelian doctrine that happiness depended on goods of the body as well as those of the soul was closer to the way people actually spoke and felt than the Stoic belief that the *summum bonum* was comprised of virtue alone.[358] Waele maintained that it was possible to reconcile the Stoic view that the supreme good consisted of virtuous habits with the Peripatetic view that it consisted of virtuous actions. The Stoics, he said, did not claim that virtuous habits should not be transformed into actions but merely that even if a man's internal virtue could not be exercised externally, he would nonetheless remain happy. The Peripatetics, on the other hand, did not

354. Epictetus 1561, pp. 14–15.
355. L. Valla 1970a, p. 47: 'Fortiter faciam. Cur? Propter honestatem. Quid est honestas? Fortiter facere. Ludus videtur hic esse non preceptum . . . Fortiter faciam ut fortiter faciam.'
356. *Ibid.*, p. 62: 'est . . . ostendendum eos . . . nullam honestatis, omnem utilitatis habuisse rationem, ad quam omnia referenda sunt'.
357. Vettori 1553, p. 96; Keckermann 1607a, pp. 10–11; Burgersdijk 1629, pp. 69–71.
358. F. Piccolomini 1594b, p. 412: 'Stoici summum bonum considerarunt in vita privata, . . . Aristoteles vero in vita civili'; p. 413: 'Constat . . . sententiam Peripateticorum magis esse consimilem communi usui loquendi sensibusque ac experientiae magis respondere.'

regard any actions as virtuous unless they derived from virtuous habits. Furthermore, when they spoke of virtuous actions, they meant above all internal ones, such as contemplation, which could not be impeded by external circumstances.[359]

THE STOIC THEORY OF THE EMOTIONS

The Stoics conceived of virtue as conformity with the rational law of nature; vice, on the other hand, consisted in following the irrational impulses of the emotions. The condition of immunity from suffering (ἀπάθεια) appropriate for the wise man did not, however, mean total impassivity and emotionlessness, since the Stoics believed that certain emotions were rational and therefore good (εὐπαθείαι): joy, precaution and wishfulness.[360] But all others, which they categorised under the four general headings of pleasure, distress, fear and desire, were designated as passions (πάθη) and were by definition wrong and vicious. These impulses had to be totally eradicated if the wise man was to achieve the desired state of virtue and happiness.[361]

This Stoic tenet was the inspiration for Petrarch's *De remediis utriusque fortunae*, his stated purpose in writing it being to restrain or, if possible, to extirpate the passions of the soul both from himself and from his readers.[362] Petrarch's work and the Stoic doctrines which underlay it found a large and receptive audience among Renaissance readers. But not everyone was convinced of the psychological validity of the Stoic position. Did it not require superhuman powers, asked Scala, for a man to overcome his emotions entirely and to use his reason to repress, as Epictetus had recommended in the third chapter of the *Enchiridion*, his natural impulse to feel grief when his wife or child died? Such things were certainly not easy, replied Poliziano, but they were not beyond man's capacities.[363] The essence of Epictetus' moral philosophy could be summed up, he said, in two simple words of advice: bear and forbear, a phrase reported by Aulus Gellius which gained currency in the sixteenth and seventeenth centuries as the motto for one of Andrea Alciato's emblems.[364]

359. Waele 1620, pp. 28–34.   360. Diogenes Laertius, VII.116.
361. Cicero, *De finibus* III.10.35; *Tusculan Disputations* III.17.37; V.15.43.
362. Petrarch 1581, p. 963 (*Epistolae seniles* XVI.9): 'Est mihi liber in manibus, De remediis ad utranque fortunam, in quo . . . nitor et meas et legentium passiones animi mollire, vel si datum fuerit extirpare.'
363. Poliziano 1553, p. 407 (*Epistola pro Epicteto stoico*): 'Non sunt quidem haec factu facilia; non supra hominis tamen sunt vires.'
364. *Ibid.*, p. 393: 'Sustine et abstine'; see Aulus Gellius, *Noctes Atticae* XVII.19.6: 'Verba haec duo dicebat [Epictetus]: ἀνέχου et ἀπέχου'; see also Alciato 1985, Emblem 34.

Some Renaissance philosophers, such as Camerarius and Burgersdijk, were careful to point out that the Stoics did not demand the eradication of all emotions but rather the repression of the impulsive and reckless ones, which they regarded as diseases of the soul; their goal was peace of mind, not total passivity.[365] Most authors, however, tended to give a somewhat oversimplified account of the Stoic position, maintaining that they wanted all emotions to be uprooted. This extreme doctrine was then contrasted, often unfavourably, with the more moderate Peripatetic view that the emotions should merely be controlled. Aristotle had applied his doctrine of moral virtue as a mean between two extremes to emotions as well as to actions. So in his view a deficiency of emotions was just as wrong as an excess, since virtue entailed feeling the right emotion towards the right object at the right time and to the right extent.[366] Far from seeing the emotions as obstacles to the attainment of the supreme good, as the Stoics did, Aristotle regarded them as, at least potentially, incentives and aids to virtuous behaviour: anger, for instance, could in certain circumstances spur men on to courageous actions.[367]

Salutati's increasing disillusionment with Stoic ethics in the 1390s derived principally from his realisation that it was beyond his powers, and presumably those of most other men, to feel no emotion whatsoever in the face of personal misfortune. Aristotle's view that emotions should be moderated but not eliminated seemed to him to provide a psychologically more realistic basis for morality than the Stoics' impossible demand that death and calamity should be neither feared nor lamented.[368] Like Salutati, Tartaretus believed that the repression of emotion required by the Stoics exceeded man's capacities. He too supported the Aristotelian position that virtue consisted not in getting rid of emotions but rather in controlling them and preventing them from going against right reason.[369] This Peripatetic moderation also struck Wilson as far more reasonable and humane than the Stoic demand for the radical removal of emotions.[370] In his commentary on Aristotle's *Ethics* Figliucci argued that by

365. Camerarius 1578, p. 31; Burgersdijk 1629, pp. 70–1.
366. *Nicomachean Ethics* ii.6; see also p. 339 above.
367. *Ibid.*, iii.8 ($1116^b23-1117^a9$). For a similar view, see Plutarch, *De virtute morali* 451D–E.
368. Salutati 1891–1911, iii, p. 463: 'Maior est auctoritas Aristotelica Peripateticorumque moderatio quam illa severitas, imo duricies et inaccessibilis ratio Stoicorum. Malum est equidem sine dubio mors timendaque prius quam veniat; horrenda cum venit et postquam venerit non irrationabiliter lacrimanda'; see also Witt 1983, pp. 355–67.
369. Tartaretus 1509, f. 29ᵛ: 'non est de ratione virtutis facere hominem sine passione, quia istud excedit communem facultatem hominum. Sed de ratione virtutis est passionem moderari et impedire ne insurgat contra rectam rationem.'
370. F. Wilson 1751, p. 49: 'Multo . . . aequior atque humanior est Aristoteles noster, qui . . . [non] στέρησιν, hoc est, privationem, sed μετριότητα, hoc est, mediocritatem retinendam praecipit.'

eliminating all feelings from the soul, the Stoics would also eliminate moral virtue. For it was moderate feelings which moved the soul to act according to the mean and thereby acquire virtuous habits.[371] The Stoics were wrong to demand that the emotions should be rooted out, wrote Lambin, for they had been given to us by nature for our benefit: anger to incite us to courage; love and desire to inspire us to support virtue and defend justice; hatred to make us flee from and detest injustice and depravity. Moreover, the emotions were so intimately connected to the body that it would be just as difficult to eliminate them from man as to remove his blood, nerves or *spiritus*.[372] Arguing along similar lines, Burgersdijk maintained that if we were not willing to believe that nature had given man his appetitive faculty, from which the emotions proceeded, in vain or even in error, then we had to accept that not all emotions were evil.[373]

Certain emotions, claimed Waele, were judged good by all men; for example, pity towards the unfortunate and the natural affection between parents and children.[374] Admittedly, wrote Nifo, women and effeminate men, as well as uncivilised and unlearned people, feel more pain and pity than they should. But only those who are hardened and lack either sense or sensibility feel no pain or pity at all.[375] Calvin, in his commentary on Seneca's *De clementia*, took exception to the statement that pity was a mental defect (II.4). Against Seneca, he cited Pliny the Younger, Cicero, Vergil, Horace, Juvenal and St Augustine, all of whom expressed strong approval of this emotion. Calvin himself regarded pity not merely as a virtue but as an essential quality in the character of a good man.[376]

One of the most persuasive Renaissance opponents of the Stoic theory of the emotions was Montaigne. Like many other critics, he rejected the notion that pity was a vice and also regarded the noble impassivity to which the Stoics aspired as, for most men at any rate, unattainable.[377] He leaned instead towards the Aristotelian view that one should attempt to moderate emotions rather than rid oneself of them entirely.[378] And he was in

371. Figliucci 1551, pp. 145–6: 'togliendo gli Stoici tutti gl'affetti . . . togliono insieme la virtù morale'; see also Lenzi 1979, p. 163.   372. Lambin 1565, sigs. C 2ᵛ–3ᵛ.   373. Burgersdijk 1629, p. 69.
374. Waele 1620, p. 65: 'quidam affectus ab omnibus hominibus judicantur boni, ut misericordia erga miseros, *storgae* naturales inter parentes et liberos, etc.'
375. Nifo 1645, p. 203 (*De misericordia*): 'Molles . . . ac mulieres, barbari, atque indoctae gentes plus dolent atque miserentur quam oportet; duri vero et qui sensu aut mente carent, nec miserentur, nec dolent.'
376. Calvin 1969, p. 358: 'Illud sane nobis persuasum esse debet, et virtutem esse misericordiam, nec bonum hominem esse posse, qui non sit misericors.'
377. Montaigne 1965, pp. 8 (I.1), 1019–20 (III.10).
378. *Ibid.*, p. 47 (I.12): 'Le sage Peripateticien ne s'exempte pas des perturbations, mais il les modere'; see also *Montaigne* 1982, p. 79 (McFarlane); Screech 1983, p. 124.

agreement with the Peripatetic claim that most virtuous actions received necessary stimulus from the emotions; bravery, for instance, could not be perfected without the aid of anger.[379] Most importantly, however, Montaigne felt that the Stoics' demand for superhuman moral virtue was yet another example of the most characteristic of human vices: vanity and presumption. Try as he might to repress his emotions, even the wise man could not control his natural inclination to pale with fear and blush with shame. By these small signs nature indicated her authority, which neither reason nor Stoic virtue could overthrow, and taught man his own mortality and fragility. 'It is enough for the wise man to restrain and moderate his inclinations', wrote Montaigne, 'for to do away with them is not in his power.'[380]

STOIC ETHICS AND CHRISTIANITY

Like Platonism, Stoicism had been perceived from the patristic era onwards as fundamentally compatible with Christianity and had never incurred the condemnation of the church, as Aristotelianism periodically had done.[381] Indeed, many Stoic ethical doctrines were adopted by Christian writers: most notably, the notion of the four cardinal virtues, which St Ambrose took over from Cicero and assimilated into the Christian tradition.[382] One factor which helped to foster this positive attitude to Stoicism was a collection of forged letters attributed to Seneca and St Paul. In this correspondence, accepted as genuine from the time of St Jerome to the mid fifteenth century, the Stoic philosopher expressed sympathetic interest in the message preached by the Apostle to the Gentiles, thus contributing to the view that Stoic and Christian morality were in basic agreement.[383]

Yet certain aspects of Stoic ethics did trouble some of the Church Fathers. Lactantius, for instance, rejected both the Stoic insistence that the emotions should be eradicated and the Peripatetic view that they need only be moderated, preferring instead the Christian belief that they should be redirected down the true path. Fear was transformed from a vice into the greatest of virtues when directed towards God.[384] Augustine took a similar

---

379. Montaigne 1965, p. 567 (II.12): 'il est connu que la pluspart des plus belles actions de l'ame procedent et ont besoin de cette impulsion des passions. La vaillance . . . ne se peut parfaire sans l'assistance de la cholere.'
380. *Ibid.*, p. 346 (II.2): 'Luy suffise de brider et moderer ses inclinations, car, de les emporter, il n'est pas en luy.' 381. Stelzenberger 1933; Spanneut 1969; Verbeke 1983.
382. Mähl 1969. 383. Bocciolini Palagi 1978; A. Momigliano 1950b; Panizza 1976.
384. Lactantius, *Divinae institutiones* VI.17.

position: in Christianity it was not whether a pious man was angry which mattered, but why he was angry; not whether he was afraid, but what he feared. He further chastised the Stoics for condemning pity as a vice and rejected their concept of passionless virtue as inappropriate for Christians.[385] These views prompted at least some medieval authors to question whether Seneca's views were as close to Christianity as they might seem.[386] Another stumbling-block to the acceptance of Stoicism by Christians was its determinism, which led John of Salisbury to conclude in his *Entheticus* that although in many things the Stoic agreed with the law of God, he also taught much that opposed it.[387]

Although Renaissance authors were well aware of the important distinctions between Stoicism and Christianity, many of them managed to combine the two ethical systems by focusing on areas of agreement and avoiding issues where conflict was inevitable. Using this method, Petrarch mingled Stoic and Augustinian ideas in his *Secretum*, carefully omitting any doctrines which were incompatible with faith.[388] Rabelais likewise achieved a sophisticated fusion of Stoic and evangelical morality in his *Gargantua*, as well as in the *Tiers* and *Quart Livres*, without in any way compromising his Christian commitment.[389] Although such writers readily combined philosophical and religious themes, they always maintained a strict sense of priorities, remaining firm in the conviction, as Petrarch put it, that in philosophy as in all other disciplines, 'we must first and foremost be Christians'.[390]

Others, however, were less willing to side-step the conflicts which inevitably arose between Christian and Stoic ethics. Salutati at first questioned whether any man, except Christ, could achieve the emotionless virtue demanded by the Stoics.[391] Later he concluded that not even Christ had attained this state, for he had wept and bellowed at the death of Lazarus.[392] So, in Salutati's view, the Stoic doctrine of apathy was in conflict not only with nature but also with the example set by Christ himself.[393] Christ's anger at the scribes and Pharisees was used in similar fashion against the Stoics by Clichtove, who corroborated the point by citing Augustine's view that those emotions which followed right reason

385. Augustine, *De civitate Dei* IX.5; XIV.6.   386. Panizza 1984, pp. 72–3.
387. John of Salisbury 1975, p. 152: 'In multis igitur legi consentit et idem | Adversus legem multa docere solet.'   388. Petrarch 1955, pp. 22–215.   389. Screech 1956.
390. Petrarch 1933–42, II, pp. 55–6 (VI.2): 'Sic simus omnia, quod ante omnia cristiani simus.'
391. Salutati 1891–1911, II, p. 310: 'Que quidem perfectio nescio si potuit alicui mortali homini, preter Salvatorem nostrum, aliquando contingere.'
392. *Ibid.*, III, p. 413: 'Christus super Lazarum infremuisse legitur et flevisse.'
393. *Ibid.*, p. 465: 'Stabit contra te natura, stabit et Christi, si cetera deficere videantur, exemplum.'

were neither diseased nor vicious.[394] Calvin rejected the views of those contemporary followers of Stoicism who considered not only weeping and moaning but even feeling sadness and concern to be vices. Christ had wept and moaned at his own misfortunes and those of others; and he had taught his disciples to do likewise.[395] Vermigli thought that the Aristotelian acceptance of the emotions was closer to Christianity than the Stoic repudiation of them: 'Christ wept; the prophets and saints wept. And we are told to feel compassion for the suffering.' [396] Melanchthon complained that the Stoics wanted to eradicate all emotions, good and bad alike; whereas the good ones, such as fear of God, trust and love for one's wife and children, were actually required by divine law.[397].

Another issue which troubled many Christians was the Stoic doctrine that virtue was the supreme good and was therefore to be sought for its own sake. Although this view was clearly admirable, it betokened, as Facio pointed out, an ignorance of God, who was the true supreme good and for whose sake all virtue should be sought.[398] The characters in Platina's *Dialogus de falso et vero bono* come to a similar conclusion, deciding that virtue is a *bonum* but not the *summum bonum*, which resides in God alone.[399] Christian virtue, according to Valla, was not pursued for its own sake, as something hard, severe and arduous, or for the sake of worldly profit. It was instead a step towards the perfect happiness of the next life.[400] Or, as Bosso put it, virtue was not itself the supreme good but rather the only means by which it could be attained.[401]

By making virtue its own reward, wrote Erasmus in the preface to his edition of Seneca, the Stoics had made man responsible for his own happiness. Piety, however, taught us that man owed his highest felicity not to himself but to divine munificence.[402] In Calvin's opinion, those philosophers who considered that virtue should be sought for its own sake, rather than for the glory of God, were so inflated with arrogance that they

394. Clichtove 1537, f. 42^r; see Augustine, *De civitate Dei* xiv.9.
395. Calvin 1863–1900, ii, col. 521 (*Institutio religionis Christianae* iii.8.9): 'Nam et suis et aliorum malis ingemuit et illacrymavit [Dominus], nec aliter discipulos suos instituit.'
396. Vermigli 1582, p. 234: 'flevit Christus, fleverunt prophetae ac sancti. Et iubemur condolere dolentibus'; see also Waele 1620, p. 66: 'Christus tristatus fuit ob mortem Lazari . . . Laetatus fuit ob successum praedicationis Evangelii . . . Misertus fuit turbae cum inedia premeretur.'
397. Melanchthon 1834–60, xvi, col. 54 (*Philosophiae moralis epitome*): 'Stoici volunt evelli omnes affectus, bonos et malos. Lex Dei econtra flagitat bonos affectus, timorem Dei, fiduciam, dilectionem, amorem coniugis, liberorum, et alios pios motus.'
398. Facio 1611, pp. 134–6. 399. Platina 1518, ff. clxxx^r–iv^v. 400. L. Valla 1970a, p. 110.
401. Bosso 1492, sig. g. iii^v: 'summum in se bonum virtus nequaquam habet; sed vehiculum magis dicenda est sine quo ad illud perveniri non potest'.
402. Seneca 1529, sig. a 3^v: 'At pietas nobis persuasit . . . hominem nihil habere ex sese boni, sed summam suae felicitatis debere munificentiae numinis.'

appeared to seek virtue solely so that they could boast of it.[403] For Montaigne as well, it was pride and the desire for self-aggrandisement which were at the root of the Stoic belief in man's ability to achieve his own happiness through virtue. If, however, man was truly to achieve the divine state he desired, it would not be by means of 'his Stoic virtue' but rather through 'our Christian faith'.[404]

NEOSTOICISM

The attempt to demonstrate that such conflicts between Stoic virtue and Christian faith were more apparent than real was one of the primary aims of Neostoicism. This movement arose as a direct response to the bloody religious and civil wars which tore Northern Europe apart in the second half of the sixteenth century. In an era of political anarchy and moral chaos, the severe and rigorous ethical philosophy of the Stoics no longer appeared quite so excessive and extreme. Indeed, it seemed to many that the only way to control those inflamed passions which were ravaging society was to eliminate them completely, as the Stoics had recommended. But an equally important factor in this revival of Stoicism was the deliberate attempt on the part of its promoters to stress the fundamental compatibility of Stoic tenets with Christian moral teachings.[405]

The first and greatest promoter of Neostoicism was the Flemish scholar Justus Lipsius, who initiated the movement in 1584 with his *De constantia in publicis malis*. This dialogue, set during the revolt of the Low Countries against Spain, begins with Lipsius expressing his desire to escape from the turbulence and civil strife of his native land. His wise friend, however, counsels him that it is not his country which he should flee but his emotions.[406] For all emotions are harmful and should be extirpated because they disturb the equilibrium of the soul.[407] This is of course a standard Stoic doctrine. But instead of equating virtue with mere apathy, Lipsius gives his philosophy a more forceful and positive quality by concentrating on steadfastness (*constantia*), which he defines as 'an upright and immovable mental strength, which is neither lifted up nor depressed by external or

---

403. Calvin 1863–1900, II, col. 507 (*Institutio religionis Christianae* III.7.2).
404. Montaigne 1965, p. 604 (II.12): 'C'est à nostre foy Chrestienne, non à sa vertu Stoique, de pretendre à cette divine et miraculeuse metamorphose.'
405. Zanta 1914; Abel 1978; Oestreich 1982.
406. Lipsius 1675, IV, p. 527 (I.1): 'non patria fugienda, Lipsi: sed adfectus'.
407. *Ibid.*, p. 535 (I.7): 'Laedunt omnes [adfectus] turbantque animum.'

accidental circumstances'.[408] So not only the war and its destruction, but everything which happens outside the soul, whether it be involved with money, politics or health, is to be disregarded; and all our energies are to be directed towards the cultivation of that steadfastness which alone will bring us the peace and tranquillity which we desire.

It was Muret who had introduced Lipsius to the serious study of Seneca. Muret was interested in Seneca as a stylistic counter-weight to the Ciceronianism prevalent in his day. But in his 1585 edition of Seneca's works, his admiration was restrained by a contempt for certain Stoic doctrines, which he derided as foolish and fatuous.[409] Lipsius, by contrast, was as interested in Seneca's philosophy as in his terse and pointed style. Above all, he found in the strong religious strain of this ancient pagan an attitude towards virtue which made him seem 'almost Christian'.[410] In his *Manuductio ad Stoicam philosophiam*, published in 1604, Lipsius went out of his way to demonstrate that Stoic moral doctrines, especially as expounded by Seneca and Epictetus, could be reconciled with Christian dogma. After adducing the authority of the many Church Fathers who had written favourably about Stoic ethics, he cited passages from these two authors in which their contempt for worldly goods and love of things divine indicated a spirit which was not only compatible with but indeed conducive to Christian piety.[411]

The Neostoicism which Lipsius developed as a response to the traumatic upheavals which were disrupting life in the Low Countries was soon adapted by Guillaume Du Vair to serve the needs of Frenchmen suffering through the evil days of the Wars of Religion. Du Vair, a man of action (and later a bishop) rather than a systematic philosopher, wrote in the vernacular and addressed a wide popular audience, who he hoped would derive comfort and consolation from the combination of pagan Stoic doctrine and Christian teaching which he presented in his *Philosophie morale des Stoïques*. This work first appeared as a preface to the 1594 edition of his French

408. *Ibid.*, pp. 530–1 (I.4): 'Constantiam hic appello, rectum et immotum animi robur, non elati externis aut fortuitis, non depressi.'
409. See his comments on *Epistula* CVI in Seneca 1585, p. 214: 'Stoicorum multae graves sententiae erant; multae etiam insigniter fatuae.'
410. See the dedicatory letter to Pope Paul V in his edition of Seneca 1605, sig. ★ 3ᵛ: 'En, Annaeum Senecam, laudatissimum inter omnes veteres scriptorem et virtutis studio paene Christianum . . . deponimus ad sacros tuos pedes'; see also Grafton 1985, pp. 639–41.
411. Lipsius 1675, IV, p. 675 (I.17), after citing Jerome (*In Isaiam* IV.11): 'Stoici nostro dogmati in plerisque concordant', writes: 'Concordant? Ita; et . . . . occulte ad nostrum dogma et ad pietatem ducunt'; see also Saunders 1955.

translation of Epictetus and was indeed primarily based on the *Enchiridion*, which he claimed merely to have rearranged and supplemented with precepts and examples taken from other Stoic authors as well as observations based on his own experience.[412] Du Vair believed, as did Lipsius, that it was imperative to gain complete control of one's emotions, for they were the winds which stirred up storms within the soul. These tempests could only be calmed by a correct disposition of the will, which would bring about a peace of mind as steadfast and immovable as a rock amid turbulent waves.[413] The way to achieve this enviable state was to disregard everything which it was not in the power of the will to control: health, wealth, reputation and the like. For none of these things in any way impinged on the true and only good, which for Du Vair, as for all Stoics ancient and modern, was virtue.[414]

Neostoicism also migrated to Spain, where a long tradition of interest in Seneca, a Spaniard by birth, ensured a favourable reception. Epictetus was an equally important figure in the late Renaissance revival of Stoicism, and it was in Francisco Sanchez' preface to his translation of the *Enchiridion* that the characteristic themes of Neostoicism were introduced into Spain. Sanchez, who was probably from a family which had only recently converted to Christianity and was under constant suspicion of heresy and unorthodoxy from the Inquisition,[415] went out of his way to show the degree to which Epictetus' writings conformed with the Bible. He even maintained that if only the Stoic philosopher had not spoken of the gods in the plural, the *Enchiridion* would be similar to Ecclesiastes and the Epistles of St Paul.[416] Sanchez concluded his preface by citing Psalm 119:1: 'Blessed are the undefiled in the way, who walk in the law of the Lord', which he claimed was the very goal of Epictetus' philosophy.[417]

The most noteworthy exponent of Spanish Neostoicism was Francisco de Quevedo, who composed a verse translation of Epictetus' *Enchiridion* and also wrote the *Nombre, origen, intento, recomendación y decencia de la doctrina*

412. Du Vair 1945, p. 61.
413. *Ibid.*, p. 72: 'Voilà . . . les vents d'où naissent les tempêtes de nôtre âme . . . le bien de l'homme et la perfection de sa nature consiste en une droite disposition de sa volonté . . . [avec laquelle il] s'établira un repos d'entendement ferme et immobile comme un rocher parmi les flots.'
414. *Ibid.*, p. 65: 'la vertu, que nous avons montré être le vrai bien, est de telle nature qu'elle se sert indifféremment de choses contraires'.   415. Breva-Claramonte 1983, pp. 7–13.
416. Sanchez 1766, III, p. 506 (*Doctrina del estoico filosofo Epicteto*): 'Nuestro Epicteto . . . conforma mucho con las sagradas letras; y tanto, que si de su doctrina solo se quitasse el hablar de los Dioses en plural, se parece al Eclesiastes de Salomon, y a las Epistolas de S. Pablo.'
417. *Ibid.*, p. 507: 'A èste fin apunta Epicteto.'

estoica, first published in 1635 and heavily influenced by Lipsius' *Manuductio*.[418] Like Sanchez, Quevedo made strenuous efforts to relate Stoicism to the Bible and in particular attempted to demonstrate that the doctrines expounded by Epictetus derived ultimately from the Book of Job. Building on Lipsius' suggestion that the founder of Stoicism, Zeno of Citium, and his followers might have had contact with natives of Judaea, Quevedo firmly asserted that the biblical account of Job's patient endurance in the face of terrible adversity was in fact the original source of the Stoic philosophy of resignation.[419] He even went so far as to claim that Epictetus' statement in chapter 53 of the *Enchiridion*: 'If it is pleasing to the Gods, so let it be' was a literal translation of Job 1:21: 'Nothing has happened but what has pleased the Lord.'[420]

The English version of Neostoicism, like its continental counterparts, had a strong Christian component. In the preface to his 1598 English translation of Du Vair's treatise, Thomas James stated that no one should find it surprising that 'Christians may profit by the Stoicks' since 'no kinde of philosophie is more profitable and neerer approching Christianitie.'[421] This view was also held by the Anglican bishop Joseph Hall, whose prominent role in promoting Stoic moral philosophy led him to be nicknamed 'our English Seneca'. But Hall made it absolutely clear that although in his attempt 'to teach men how to be happy in this life' he had followed Seneca as a philosopher, he had nonetheless 'gone beyond him as a Christian and a divine'.[422] Indeed Hall, unlike other Neostoics, saw the demand for complete emotionlessness as incompatible with Christianity: 'I would not be a Stoic, to have no passions; for that were to overthrow this inward government God hath erected in me; but a Christian, to order those I have.'[423] In an essay entitled *Christian Moderation*, he took an Aristotelian rather than a Stoic position on anger, not only citing St Paul's injunction: 'Be angry, and sin not' (Ephesians 4:26), but also warning that in certain circumstances a deficiency of this emotion might be regarded as a sin: 'If a man can be so cool, as, without any inward commotion, to suffer God's

418. Quevedo 1945–60, II, pp. 788–814 (*Doctrina de Epicteto*); I, pp. 872–9 (*Doctrina estoica*); see also Castellanos 1947; Ettinghausen 1972.
419. Quevedo 1945–60, I, p. 875: 'no sólo es posible, sino fácil, antes forzoso el haber . . . los estoicos visto los libros sagrados, siendo mezclados por la habitación con los hebreos'; cf. Lipsius 1675, IV, pp. 650–1 (*Manuductio* I.10).
420. *Ibid.*, p. 874. The passage from Job appears in the Vulgate ('Sicut Domino placuit, ita factum est') and the Septuagint but not in the Hebrew text of the Bible.
421. Du Vair 1951, p. 45.   422. J. Hall 1863, VI, p. 1 (*Heaven upon Earth*); see also Chew 1950.
423. *Ibid.*, VII, p. 457 (*Meditations*).

honour to be trod in the dust, he shall find God justly angry with him for his want of anger.'[424]

Pierre Charron, whose commitment to Neostoicism was combined with and tempered by his interest in philosophical scepticism, had learnt from the bloody conflicts between Catholics and Protestants that dogmatic religious commitment was no guarantee of virtuous conduct. He therefore concluded that piety was completely distinct from probity, although both were necessary for the good life.[425] Since in his view moral virtue had nothing to do with merit or grace, he was able to present the tenets of pagan philosophers such as Seneca and Epictetus alongside the teachings of Christianity without adapting one to the other. By treating morality and religion as two separate and autonomous spheres, Charron distinguished himself from other Neostoic philosophers and took a stance which would increasingly characterise the study of ethics.

EPICUREAN ETHICS: THE SUPREME GOOD

For most medieval and Renaissance moral philosophers, Epicureanism was the unacceptable face of classical ethics. Of the four major ancient philosophical schools, Epicureanism had the worst reputation and the least influence.[426] The Epicurean doctrine which aroused the most hostility was the belief that pleasure was the supreme good. Because Epicurus regarded the attainment of pleasure ($\dot{\eta}\delta o\nu\dot{\eta}$) as the ultimate goal of life, he was frequently vilified as a sensual hedonist. But although he did not deny the importance of gratifying the senses, he in fact identified the highest pleasure with the complete absence of bodily pain and mental affliction.[427] He furthermore regarded the pains and pleasures of the mind as greater than those of the body.[428] For Epicurus the highest pleasure, and thus the supreme good, was an absolute tranquillity and peace of mind ($\dot{a}\tau a\rho a\xi i a$), which when attained by the wise man would continue to make him happy even while his body was being tortured.[429] Epicurus also held that although in general pleasure was to be sought and pain avoided, those pleasures which brought with them greater pains were to be avoided, while those pains which resulted in greater pleasures were to be sought.[430] Since it was

---

424. *Ibid.*, VI, p. 437 (ch. 15). For Aristotle's position on anger, see *Nicomachean Ethics* III.8 (1116[b]23– 1117[a]9) and p. 365 above.

425. Charron 1824, II, p. 148 (II.5): 'ce sont deux choses bien distinctes, et qui ont leurs resorts divers, que la piété et probité, la religion et la preud'hommie, la devotion et la conscience'; see also Kogel 1972, pp. 50–76.

426. Radetti 1889; D. C. Allen 1944; Kristeller 1965a, p. 36; Garin 1959; Pagnoni 1974.

427. Vatican Saying 33; Cicero, *De finibus* 1.37–8.   428. Diogenes Laertius, X.137.

429. *Ibid.*, X.118; Cicero, *Tusculan Disputations* II.7–17.   430. Diogenes Laertius, X.129.

precisely the sensual pleasures of the body which were most likely to result in pain, the Epicurean wise man, far from indulging in hedonistic excesses of eating, drinking and sex, was cautious and moderate in his pursuit of corporeal pleasures.

One of the most sympathetic portrayals of Epicurus and his philosophy was presented by Seneca. He not only praised Epicurus personally for his moderation, sobriety and virtuousness, but also cited a number of his sayings, which he regarded as fundamentally compatible with his own rigorous and austere Stoicism.[431] Seneca had recognised that the Epicurean doctrine of pleasure was not designed to stimulate the appetite to desire more but rather to train it to be satisfied with less. The paradoxical combination of hedonism and asceticism at the core of Epicurean ethics was well illustrated by Seneca's description of the garden of Epicurus, where the motto was: 'Here our supreme good is pleasure'; but the meagre fare provided for guests consisted only of bread and water.[432] There was, however, one major tenet of Epicureanism which Seneca could not accept. Epicurus maintained that virtue was not pursued for its own sake, as the Stoics believed, but rather on account of the pleasure which invariably accompanied it. While Seneca endorsed the Epicurean view that the virtuous person was happy, he rejected the notion that it was the pleasure which resulted from the virtue, and not the virtue itself, which constituted the happiness.[433]

For many medieval authors Epicurus and his sect were nothing more than shameless voluptuaries.[434] But even in the Middle Ages this popular and caricatured view of Epicureanism was counterbalanced by more subtle and informed accounts. One of the most influential of these was St Jerome's description, drawn primarily from Seneca, of Epicurus as a champion of pleasure who nonetheless believed that one should live on humble fruits and vegetables since finely prepared foods were more likely to produce indigestion than delectation.[435] Epicurean ethical doctrines were treated with considerable sophistication by Peter Abelard, who suggested that their

---

431. Seneca, *Epistulae* II.5–6; VIII.8; XXVIII.9; *De vita beata* XII.4–XIII.2.
432. Seneca, *Epistulae* XXI.10.   433. Diogenes Laertius, X.138; Seneca, *Epistulae* LXXXV.18–19.
434. Martianus Capella, *De nuptiis Philologiae et Mercurii* II.213: 'Epicurus . . . mixtas violis rosas et totas apportabat illecebras voluptatum'; Isidore of Seville, *Etymologiae* VIII.6.15: 'Epicurei dicti ab Epicuro quodam philosopho amatore vanitatis . . . quasi volutans in caeno carnali, voluptatem corporis summum bonum adserens'; John of Salisbury 1975, p. 154: 'Nil Epicurus amat, nisi quod ventri Venerique | Immolat'; see also Radetti 1889; Pagnoni 1974, pp. 1445–57.
435. Jerome, *Adversus Jovinianum* II.11; for the later influence of Jerome's account, see John of Salisbury 1909, II, pp. 275–6 (VIII.8); Burley 1886, pp. 272–3 (cap. 64); Ricchieri 1542, p. 495 (XIII.25); Alessandro 1551, p. 133 (III.11).

concept of pleasure was not based on sensuality but on that inner tranquillity of the soul which resulted from a good conscience.[436] Thomas Aquinas was aware that the Epicureans, even though they placed the supreme good in pleasure, scrupulously cultivated the virtues in order that the opposite vices would not impede their pleasures.[437] And in the *Convivio* Dante presented a brief summary, based on Cicero's *De finibus*, of the Epicurean doctrine of pleasure, noting that it was nothing other than the absence of pain.[438]

Renaissance authors continued to rely on Cicero and Seneca for information about Epicureanism. But in addition to these traditional sources, two new texts became available in the early fifteenth century. By far the more important of these was Diogenes Laertius' *Lives of the Philosophers*, book x of which contains three letters by Epicurus and a list of his principal doctrines, introduced by a detailed account of his life and philosophy. This work, which became available in Latin translation in the late 1420s, made it possible to gain extensive firsthand knowledge of Epicurus' writings, which before had been known only in the snippets cited by Seneca. Diogenes Laertius soon became essential reading for any serious attempt to understand Epicurean doctrines.[439]

The other newly recovered text was Lucretius' *De rerum natura*. Virtually unknown since the ninth century, this poetic exposition of Epicurean philosophy was discovered in 1417 and gradually entered the repertoire of classical authors cited and studied by humanists.[440] Although admired for the artistry of his poetry, Lucretius never attained the popularity and canonical status of Horace, Vergil and Ovid, precisely because of his commitment to unacceptable Epicurean doctrines, such as the denial of the immortality of the soul (III.417–1094) and the assertion that pleasure was the guide of life (II.172). Aldus Manutius, in the preface to his 1500 edition of *De rerum natura*, recommended the poem not because its content was true or worthy of belief – since much of it disagreed with Platonic and Peripatetic doctrines, not to mention Christian theology – but because Lucretius, following the example of the Greeks, had put philosophical doctrines into

---

436. Abelard 1970, pp. 99–103.
437. Thomas Aquinas 1934, p. 21 (I.5.57): 'Epicurei, qui voluptatem summum bonum existimabant, diligenter colebant virtutes. Sed tamen propter voluptatem, ne scilicet per contraria vitia eorum voluptas impediretur.'
438. Dante, *Convivio* IV.6.12: '[Epicuro] dicea che "voluptade" non era altro che "non dolore", sì come pare Tullio recitare nel primo di Fine di Beni.'
439. See, e.g., Ficino 1576, I, pp. 1011–2 (*Liber de voluptate*); Bosso 1492, sigs. a vii^v, b ii^r; see also Pagnoni 1974, pp. 1457–60.   440. *Catalogus translationum* 1960–, II, pp. 349–65.

elegant and learned verse.[441] Scholars frequently gave high praise to Lucretius' Latin style while denouncing his philosophical views or passing over them in silence.[442]

The *De rerum natura* posed particularly difficult problems for its Renaissance commentators. The youthful enthusiasm for Lucretius which led Ficino to compose a commentary on the poem was replaced by the mature judgement that the results of his profane studies must not be publicised but rather consigned to the flames.[443] Nonetheless, he cited the poem frequently not only in his *Liber de voluptate* but also in his discussion of love in the commentary on the *Symposium*.[444] Giovan Battista Pio, in his commentary on Lucretius (1511), attempted to mitigate the hostility directed against the Epicurean doctrine of pleasure by stressing that it consisted in a tranquil state of the soul, achieved by investigating the secrets of nature. According to Pio's interpretation of Epicurus and Lucretius, the pleasure derived from this scientific speculation not only surpassed all others but also had the effect of deterring us from our desire for corporeal and sensual pleasures.[445] Lambin defended his 1563 Lucretius edition and commentary by arguing that there was much in the poem which was in agreement with the views of other philosophers and much which was impressive and almost divine. As for those elements which were false, absurd or in conflict with Christianity: 'let us reject, spurn and repudiate them'.[446] Hubert van Giffen made the same point in his 1566 edition and commentary, asserting that not everything in the work was impious or inept; indeed much of it was distinguished and worthy of note: Lucretius' condemnation of ambition, cruelty and avarice, for instance, as well as his saintly teachings about frugality and moderation.[447]

Renaissance authors agreed that according to Epicurean ethics the

---

441. Manutius 1975, I, p. 34: 'non quod vera scripserit et credenda nobis – nam ab academicis etiam et peripateticis, nedum a theologis nostris multum dissentit – , sed quia Epicureae sectae dogmata eleganter et docte mandavit carminibus, imitatus Empedoclem'.

442. Isaac Casaubon praised Lucretius as 'Latinitatis auctor optimus' but denounced his view of the soul as 'stultissimus': see *Catalogus translationum* 1960–, II, pp. 352–3; see also Grafton 1983, p. 81; for Joseph Scaliger's view of Lucretius, see G. W. Robinson 1918, p. 158; see also *Épicurisme* 1969, pp. 696–8 (Jehasse).   443. Ficino 1576, I, p. 933 (*Epistulae* XI).

444. *Ibid.*, pp. 1009–12 (capp. 17–18); 1956, pp. 249–51 (VII.5–6), 256 (VII.11); see also Nifo 1645, p. 289 (*De amore*); Varchi 1858–9, II, pp. 625–6 (*Sopra la pittura e scultura*).

445. Pio 1514, sig. B 2^v: 'scrutatio secretorum naturae, ex cuius contemplatione voluptas oritur omnem voluptatem excedens'; f. 7^r ad 1.55ff.: 'studium philosophiae facile nos a corporis voluptatibus deterrebit'; see also Raimondi 1974; Del Nero 1983.

446. Lucretius 1563, sig. a 3^v: 'Illa quae sunt commentitia, quae absurda, quae cum religione Christiana pugnantia, reiiciamus, aspernemur, improbemus'; see also his use of Lucretius, 'poeta gravis idemque philosophus', in his oration in praise of moral philosophy: Lambin 1565, sigs. B 3^r, C 1^v–2^r.

447. Lucretius 1566, sigs. ⋆ 4^v–⋆ 5^r.

supreme good was pleasure.[448] They disagreed, however, about the nature of that pleasure. Some merely grouped Epicureans together with the followers of Aristippus and Eudoxus as voluptuaries single-mindedly devoted to sensuality.[449] Many used the ancient topos which compared Epicureans to pigs or cattle on the ground that by making pleasure the supreme good they put man on a level with the lower animals.[450] Petrarch, for instance, wrote: 'Not only is Epicurean happiness, which consists in pleasure, no happiness at all, it is extreme misery. For what is more miserable for a man than to subordinate human good to that of cattle, that is, to subordinate reason to the senses?'[451] Petrarch knew from his reading of Seneca and Cicero that Epicurus himself had led a virtuous life. No one, he wrote, would deny that he was a good man. But equally no one would claim that he was a good philosopher. Although he had said much that was wise and admirable, it was all directed toward the most indecent of ends: pleasure.[452] Many others also felt that to make pleasure the *summum bonum* was to equate men with cattle or to reduce human life to that of plants and animals, which was a virtual death.[453]

A number of other issues were raised by Renaissance critics of Epicurean ethics. Bruni, for instance, attacked Epicurus because, unlike Plato and Aristotle, he had not included wealth among the goods. Epicurus took this unorthodox position, according to Bruni, because he believed that profligates who squandered their patrimony on indecent pleasures were happy.[454] In Nifo's opinion, the corruption of Epicurus lay in his attempt to make his doctrine of pleasure acceptable to all men by appealing to their individual vices. Epicurus thus offered something for everyone: he prohibited the indolent from participating in politics, the slothful from

448. Alonso de Cartagena's treatise against Leonardo Bruni published in Birkenmajer 1922, p. 180; George of Trebizond 1984, p. 106; G. Valla 1501, sig. LL ii^r; Fox-Morcillo 1566, p. 124; Nores 1597, p. 168.

449. Salutati 1891–1911, IV, p. 118; 1951, II, pp. 488–9, 493; Beroaldo 1513, f. 112^v (*Oratio de foelicitate*); Giorgi 1525, sig. D v^r; Lefèvre d'Étaples 1530, f. 13^v; Mair 1530, f. v^r; Heiland 1581, p. 171.

450. Cicero, *In Pisonem* 37; *De finibus* II.33.109; Horace, *Epistulae* I.4.15–16; Plutarch, *Non posse suaviter vivi secundum Epicurum* 1091C; Augustine, *Enarrationes in Psalmos* LXXIII.25: '[Epicurum] ipsi etiam philosophi porcum nominaverunt.'

451. Petrarch 1933–42, I, p. 115 (III.6): 'illa [felicitas] Epycuri, in voluptate consistens, non solum nulla felicitas, sed extrema miseria est; quid enim homini miserius quam humanum bonum bono pecudis, hoc est rationem sensibus, substravisse?'   452. Petrarch 1943, p. 169 (III.77).

453. Zwinger 1566, p. 5: '[vita] stirpium aut brutorum (quae vita Epicurea est, mortique simillima)'; see also Facio 1611, p. 131; Brandolini 1543, p. 88; Scala, *Epistula de nobilioribus philosophorum sectis*, published in Stein 1888, p. 547; Lambin 1565, sig. A 4^v.

454. Bruni 1741, II, p. 11: 'si divitias in bonis [Epicurus] non putat, ob id movetur, credo, quia prodigos et asotos, id est pro obscoenis voluptatibus patrimonia devorantes sua beatos censet'; cf. 1928, p. 28 (*Isagogicon*), where Bruni is more positive towards Epicureanism.

exercising and the cowardly from fighting; the irreligious were told that
there was no divine providence; and the miserly were taught that they could
live on bread and water.[455] Nifo also presented a novel attack on the
Epicurean belief that we act virtuously on account of the pleasure it gives us.
If that were the case, he argued, since some shameful actions bring us greater
pleasure than virtuous ones, we should be much more inclined to perform
them: a doctrine which no one of sound mind would accept.[456]

Epicureanism continued to be attacked throughout the Renaissance even
though ancient sources embodying a more sympathetic and accurate view
of Epicurus and his philosophy were readily available. As one of the
characters in Giordano Bruno's dialogue *De gli eroici furori* remarks, people
continue to believe the traditional view of Epicurus as a sensualist 'because
they do not read his books or those which give an unprejudiced account of
his views'.[457] As late as 1615 Giulio Cesare Vanini could still assert that the
only pleasures recognised by Epicurus were palatal or venereal and that the
Epicurean supreme good consisted in food, drink and sexual pleasure.[458]
Others took a more cautious line. Both Keckermann and Waele held that if
the conventional view of the Epicurean supreme good as corporeal pleasure
was correct, then the doctrine was to be condemned outright. If, on the
other hand, this pleasure consisted in mental joy, as many ancient and
modern authors had maintained, then the doctrine was misguided but could
nonetheless be corrected. Neither Keckermann nor Waele, however, was
willing to say which of these contradictory interpretations was valid.[459]

But others did assert categorically that the pleasure which the Epicureans
regarded as the supreme good consisted in tranquillity of the soul rather
than stimulation of the body.[460] Jean Gerson considered this to be the view
of the Epicurus described in Seneca's letters. But he thought that there was
another philosopher of the same name who, like Aristippus, Sardanapalus
and Muhammed, had placed human happiness in the pleasures of the
body.[461] Sanchez maintained that Epicurus himself had placed happiness in

455. Nifo 1645, p. 324 (*De amore*): 'ignavum [Epicurus] prohibet accedere ad rem publicam, pigrum
exercere, timidum militare; irreligiosus [audit] Deos nihil curare; . . . qui nimium parcus est discit
aqua et polenta vitam posse tolerari'.
456. *Ibid.*, p. 38 (*De vera vivendi libertate*): 'si propter voluptatem honesta ageremus, cum maior voluptas
sit in aliquibus turpibus, longe maius illa essent agenda: quod nemo sanae mentis probaret'.
457. Bruno 1958, p. 1053: 'Perché non leggono gli suoi libri, né quelli che senza invidia apportano le sue
sentenze'.
458. Vanini 1615, p. 150 (xxvi): 'Epicurus non alias agnoscebat voluptates quam palati titillationem et
Veneris'; p. 156 (xxvii): 'erat fundamentum [Epicureorum], summum bonum consistere in cibo,
potione, et obscoena voluptate'.   459. Keckermann 1607a, p. 10; Waele 1620, pp. 23–4.
460. Pletho 1866, col. 905; Ficino 1937, II, pp. 82–3; Brucioli 1982, p. 476 (*Della felicità umana*); Estrebay
1549, f. 13ᵛ.   461. Gerson 1960–73, V, pp. 93–4 (*Beati qui lugent*); Pagnoni 1974, pp. 1454–5.

the pleasures of the soul but that his followers had perverted and misunderstood his doctrine by interpreting it in the corporeal sense.[462] The Coimbra
commentators asserted that Epicurean pleasure was both spiritual and
corporeal and that it resided above all in freedom from physical pain and
mental stress.[463]

But the relationship between the pleasures of the body and those of the
soul was still problematic. How, for example, could Epicurus assert that all
happiness derived from the pleasures of the senses while at the same time
maintaining that manifestly non-sensual pleasures, such as virtue, frugality
and modesty, also brought happiness? One answer, suggested by Francesco
Zabarella, was that Epicurus may have subscribed to the epistemological
dictum that there was nothing in the intellect which was not previously in
the senses. He would therefore have believed that all our mental notions
were preceded by and based upon physical sensations; and just as without
these sensations, we should understand nothing, neither could we feel any
sadness, joy or happiness. All happiness, therefore, would be derived from
the senses.[464] Vermigli pointed out that Epicurus' claim that the wise man
was mentally happy even while suffering physical torture was completely at
odds with his belief that the absence of pain was the supreme good. Vermigli
did not find this self-contradiction surprising since Epicurus regarded
dialectic, which was the science of correct reasoning, with contempt.[465]

The apparent discrepancy between the virtue and frugality of Epicurus'
life and the hedonism of his philosophy was also noted. Poggio Bracciolini
jokingly invited a friend to a pleasure garden jointly presided over by the
Epicurus who lived on bread and water and the Epicurus who thought
happiness derived from titillation of the senses.[466] Others condemned the
doctrine of pleasure which Epicurus advocated but praised the virtuous life
which he led.[467] Landino confessed that he simply did not know what to
think of Epicurus. When one examined his life, there was no one more just,
brave or temperate. But when one read his books, there was nothing softer

462. Sanchez 1766, III, p. 504 (*Doctrina del estoico filosofo Epicteto*): 'el deleyte del animo es el que dà la
     bienaventuranza. Esta opinione de Epicuro vinò a ser tan abominable, por ser mal entendida de sus
     sequaces, y tomada corporalmente.'   463. *Collegium Conimbricense* 1612, col. 19.
464. F. Zabarella 1655, p. 29 (I.8): 'notionem omnem intellectivam praecedit aliqua sensatio; qua
     sensatione sublata nihil est quod intelligamus, ita et nihil quo tristemur, nihil etiam quo
     gaudeamus, nihil ergo quo feliciores simus, et ita sensus ope gignitur felicitas'.
465. Vermigli 1582, p. 115: 'non tamen hoc mirum, quia dialecticam, quae est recta disputandi ratio,
     [Epicurus] contempsit'; see Diogenes Laertius, X.31.
466. Poggio Bracciolini 1984–, II, p. 18.
467. Nesi s. XV, f. 10ᵛ: 'Eius . . . inconstantissima oratio voluptate, constantissima autem vita honestate
     beatorum finem terminasse videtur'; see also Brandolini 1543, p. 87.

or more effeminate.[468] One of the interlocutors in Landino's *Disputationes Camaldulenses* remarks that most people even when they live a dissipated existence speak as if they were models of restraint and self-discipline. Epicurus, on the other hand, although he speaks as if he were a shameless profligate, rivals even Socrates in the virtuousness of his life.[469] Muret made the same point, noting that while some moral philosophers did not practise the virtue which they preached, the Epicureans did not preach the virtue which they practised.[470]

For Quevedo, however, there was no conflict between Epicurus' life and his teachings. Seeing Epicurus entirely through the eyes of Seneca, Quevedo found the abstemiousness and piety of his life to be complemented and paralleled by the moral rigour of his teachings. Epicurus, he wrote, had placed happiness in pleasure and pleasure in virtue: a doctrine which was Stoic in all but name.[471] Further proof, in Quevedo's view, that Epicurus was effectively a Stoic was the fact that he appears more frequently in Seneca's works than Socrates, Plato, Aristotle or even Zeno, the founder of the sect.[472] Charron, like Quevedo, regarded Epicurean and Stoic ethics as fundamentally compatible and called on Epicurus, as presented by Seneca, to testify in favour of Stoic doctrines.[473] Montaigne had held a similar view of Epicurean moral doctrines, claiming that 'in the firmness and rigour of their opinions and precepts, the Epicurean sect is in no way inferior to the Stoic'.[474]

While Epicurus the Stoic manqué found several adherents and advocates, almost no one was willing to speak in defence of Epicurus the Epicurean. A striking exception is Cosma Raimondi, a humanist from Cremona who wrote a letter around 1429 in which he described himself as a devoted follower of Epicurus. Raimondi enthusiastically endorsed the view that the supreme good consisted in pleasure both of the mind and of the body. For not only, he claimed, do we have an innate desire in our minds to seek out and seize pleasure, nature has also given us a variety of sense organs precisely

468. See Landino's 1460 letter published in Lentzen 1971, p. 228.
469. Landino 1980, p. 58: 'Plerique . . . mortalium etiam cum turpissime vivant, vultu tamen ac verbis summam prae se continentiam ac severitatem [ferunt] . . . Hic autem cum ea dicat, quae ne asotae quidem sine rubore proferunt, in vita tamen et moribus ne Socrati quidem concedit.'
470. Muret 1789, I, p. 72 (*De moralis philosophiae necessitate*).
471. Quevedo 1986, p. 5: 'Epicuro puso la felicidad en el deleite, y el deleite en la virtud, doctrina tan estoica, que el carecer de este nombre no la desconoce.' The differences between Seneca and Epicurus on this issue (see p. 375 above) are ignored by Quevedo.
472. *Ibid.*, p. 18: 'Más frecuente es Epicuro en las obras de Séneca que Sócrates y Platón y Aristóteles y Zenón.'   473. Charron 1824, II, p. 279 (II.12).
474. Montaigne 1965, p. 422 (II.11): 'en fermeté et rigueur d'opinions et de preceptes, la secte Epicurienne ne cede aucunement à la Stoique'.

so that we will be able to enjoy pleasure in all of its forms.[475] Filelfo also praised Epicurus, although less wholeheartedly than Raimondi, for recognising that even though corporeal pleasures were inferior to mental ones, they were not to be entirely neglected. Because Epicurus was concerned with the total man, body and soul, rather than just one part of him, Filelfo felt that his views were preferable to those of philosophers such as Pythagoras and Socrates, who concentrated on the soul to the exclusion of the body. Filelfo could not see how it was possible to ignore the body if one wanted to know oneself or to do anything aright.[476] Further proof of the importance of corporeal pleasure was the fact that the immense joy which the soul would attain when it saw and contemplated God would become even more delightful and abundant when the body was restored to the soul.[477] Filelfo's use of the belief in the resurrection of the body as an argument in support of the doctrine of pleasure demonstrates how Epicureanism and Christianity, strange bedfellows on the face of it, were occasionally brought into conjunction by Renaissance philosophers.

EPICUREAN ETHICS AND CHRISTIANITY

Patristic opinion was generally, although not universally, hostile to Epicureanism.[478] For although Epicurus believed in the gods, he maintained that these divine beings were entirely indifferent to human affairs. This doctrine led to the widespread and persistent conviction that he and his disciples were atheists. Dante placed the Epicureans in the sixth circle of Hell along with the heretics, and well into the sixteenth century dictionaries continued to cite Epicurus and Lucretius as classic examples of atheism.[479] Even those who understood that Epicureans denied the providence rather than the existence of the gods found the doctrine as absurd as it was pernicious.[480] And equally damaging in Christian eyes was the Epicurean denial of the immortality of the soul.[481]

Such doctrines presented serious difficulties to philosophers like

---

475. Published in Zenzo 1978, p. 62: 'Est . . . in mentibus nostris naturalis quidam sensus capiundae et prosequendae voluptatis'; p. 61: 'Sensus ei [i.e. homini] plures [natura] dedit quam varios, quam distinctos, quam necessarios, ut cum voluptatum genera essent plura, nullum relinqueretur cuius ille particeps non foret.'

476. Filelfo 1502, f. 54ʳ: 'quomodo corporis oblivisci queat, non intelligo, qui vel seipsum nosse, vel aliquid recte agere instituerit'.

477. *Ibid.*, f. 54ʳ: 'omne gaudium nonne vel iucundius fiat, vel cumulatius, cum animo corpus fuerit restitutum?'

478. See, e.g., Lactantius, *Divinae Institutiones* III.17; Augustine, *Confessiones* VI.16; see also *Reallexikon* 1950–, V, cols. 774–819 ('Epikur und die Christen'); Jungkuntz 1962.

479. Dante, *Inferno* X.13–16; Bianca 1980b, p. 84.

480. Vanini 1615, p. 152 (XXVII): 'quid est dicere Deum esse, et non cunctis maxime hominibus providere, nisi ignem esse, et non calefacere?'

481. See, e.g., E. S. Piccolomini 1984, I, p. 37; Pomponazzi 1954, pp. 176–8.

Quevedo who admired many aspects of Epicureanism and wanted to break down Christian hostility towards it. He admitted that Epicurus had held erroneous beliefs but argued that he and all other pagan philosophers should not be attacked for those things which they had failed to see because they were deprived of the light of faith vouchsafed to Christians. They should instead be valued for those things which they were able to see.[482] Because of the heretical ideas expressed in Lucretius' *De rerum natura*, editors and commentators whose interest in the text was primarily literary still felt obliged to protect themselves by explicitly condemning its philosophical content.[483] Paleario even composed an anti-Lucretian poem, significantly entitled *De animorum immortalitate*, in which he imitated the Roman poet's style while vehemently attacking his doctrines from a Christian point of view.[484]

Despite the manifest and irreconcilable disagreements between Epicureanism and Christianity, a few medieval philosophers had noticed a certain similarity between the earthly pleasure which Epicurus described as the supreme good in this life and the heavenly pleasure which Christ promised as the soul's reward in the next. The Philosopher in Peter Abelard's *Dialogus* tells the Christian that the tranquillity of the soul and complete absence of suffering taught by Epicurus differed in name only from the kingdom of heaven preached by Christ.[485] John of Salisbury, Abelard's student, described the path taken by the Epicureans as an obstacle course, full of dangers, errors and vanities, leading ultimately to disappointment and frustration since the happiness and peace of mind they wanted could never be attained by means of the false pleasures of this life. But the very goals which Epicurus had sought in vain could be secured in the next life if one followed instead the true road of virtue, faith and reverence for God.[486]

This analogy between Epicurean and Christian pleasure became a much more prominent theme during the Renaissance. Valla used it as the central idea in his dialogue *De vero falsoque bono*, in which an Epicurean defeats a Stoic by proving that men, even when they appear to be acting for the highest of motives, are nonetheless following a natural instinct to pursue pleasure.[487] The dialogue is concluded, however, by a Christian, who

---

482. Quevedo 1986, p. 35: 'estimemos lo que vieron y no les acusemos lo que dejaron de ver'.
483. Lambin's preface to Lucretius 1570, sig. e 1ʳ: 'vehementer quidem errat Epicurus et nos Christiani valde ab eo dissentimus'.
484. Paleario 1536, p. 10: 'cum quidam . . . Deos nullos omnino esse crederent, atque ex ea re animorum mortalitatem firmissime asseverarent, adversus hos . . . consistendum fuit'.
485. Abelard 1970, p. 106: 'Quam . . . beatitudinem Epicurus voluptatem, Christus vester regnum celorum nominat.'   486. John of Salisbury 1909, II, p. 423 (VIII.25).
487. L. Valla 1970a, p. 41: 'Omnia . . . voluptate determinant nec soli qui agros . . . sed qui urbem colunt, magni, parvi, greci, barbari . . . ipsa natura magistra et duce.'

begins by reproaching both sides for following the doctrines of philosophers rather than those of God. But in the end he decides in favour of the Epicurean because his view of man as a pleasure-seeking being is not only more realistic and honest than that of the Stoic but also much closer to Christianity. For Christ did not teach that virtue was its own reward but rather offered man the perfect happiness and eternal pleasure of heaven as the ultimate reward for his virtue.[488] By pointing out the Epicurean aspects of Christianity, Valla demonstrated that the idealised view of man presented by the supposedly more acceptable sects of classical philosophy was inadequate and hypocritical. He further showed that only when pagan ethical doctrines were completely turned on their head, replacing earthly by heavenly values, could they have any relevance for Christians.

In the opinion of Paolo Giustiniani, it was not even necessary for the Christian to defer gratification until he reached heaven, for the greatest pleasure imaginable in this life was to love God with all one's heart.[489] For Erasmus, in his early treatise *De contemptu mundi*, the most likely source of Epicurean pleasure here on earth was, ironically, the monastic life. Had not Epicurus himself said that those pleasures which bring with them greater discomfort should be avoided? And did not monks avoid promiscuity, adultery and insobriety? Had not Epicurus also taught that we should sometimes suffer lesser pains in order to avoid greater ones? And did not monks endure vigils, fasts, solitude, silence and such inconveniences so that they would not have to suffer worse torments?[490] Towards the end of his life Erasmus returned to the same theme in the colloquy entitled 'Epicureus'. Here, however, he attributed the Epicurean life to virtuous lay Christians rather than cloistered monks.[491] But the basic point was the same: true pleasure, the only sort worth having, did not come from sensual delights, which were invariably accompanied by more pain than pleasure, but from living a pious life, which alone reconciled man to God, the source of his supreme good.[492] The interlocutor Hedonius even goes so far as to say that no one better deserves the name of Epicurean than Christ, 'for he alone reveals the life which is sweetest and most full of true pleasure'.[493]

488. *Ibid.*, pp. 109–10; see also Gabotto 1889; Timmermans 1938; Delcourt and Derwa 1968, pp. 120–3; Pagnoni 1974, pp. 1461–71; Fubini 1975.
489. Giustiniani 1967–, II, p. 154 (*Cogitationes quotidiane de amore Dei LXI*): 'Si voluptas, que animo percipitur, summum et extremum est hominis (in hac vita loquor) bonum, quid aliud querimus quam Deum toto corde amare?'; Pagnoni 1974, pp. 1474–7.
490. Erasmus 1969–, V, 1, p. 74: 'tota vitae nostrae ratio Epicurea est!'; see also Bultot 1969.
491. *Ibid.*, I, 3, p. 721: 'nulli magis sunt Epicurei quam Christiani pie viventes'; see also Timmermans 1938; Delcourt and Derwa 1968, pp. 129–33.
492. *Ibid.*, p. 725: 'sola . . . pietas reddit hominem beatum, quae Deum summi boni fontem homini sola conciliat'.
493. *Ibid.*, p. 732: 'is unus ostendit vitam omnium suavissimam veraeque voluptatis plenissimam . . .'.

The Utopians in Thomas More's mythical land are not formally Christians and have not received a heaven-sent revelation. Nevertheless many – although by no means all – of their attitudes and actions reflect the true spirit of Christ's teachings. The ethical principles of the Utopians, for example, although Epicurean in placing the highest good in pleasure, were coupled with a belief in the immortality of the soul and in an afterlife where virtue would be rewarded and vice punished.[494] They were therefore willing to forgo the meagre and evanescent pleasures of this life in favour of the immense and eternal joy with which God would repay their pursuit of virtue.[495] Like Valla and Erasmus, More believed that all pagan moral philosophy had been superseded by Christianity. But when the doctrines of classical antiquity had been transformed and transvalued by the higher morality of the gospels, it was possible to incorporate them into a Christian system of ethics.

This Christian transformation and transvaluation of pagan ethics was not acceptable to Melanchthon. He rejected the Epicurean view that man was naturally inclined towards pleasure and that therefore it was his supreme good. It was not man's essential nature which made him a pleasure-seeker, argued Melanchthon, but rather his depravity. It was one of the evil consequences of the fall that man disobeyed his reason, which would have led him to seek virtue, and followed instead his corrupt desire to pursue pleasure.[496] Melanchthon, who was always concerned to keep moral philosophy completely separate from religion, objected even more strongly to the view that Christianity was based on the Epicurean premise that men should behave virtuously in order to gain the reward of heavenly pleasure. Although we were offered rewards and punishments in the Bible, these were secondary and unimportant compared to our supreme good, which was to know God and obey him, not for the sake of our pleasure but on account of his will.[497]

During the Renaissance Epicurean ethics never managed to break free from the Christian interpretations imposed on it by its opponents and

494. More 1963–, IV, pp. 160–2: 'Animam esse immortalem, ac dei beneficentia ad felicitatem natam, virtutibus ac bene factis nostris praemia post hanc vitam, flagitijs destinata supplicia'; see also Skinner 1967, pp. 157–60.
495. More 1963–, IV, p. 166: 'brevis et exiguae voluptatis vicem, ingenti ac nunquam interituro gaudio rependit deus'.
496. Melanchthon 1834–60, XVI, col. 32 (*Philosophiae moralis epitome*): 'si esset integra natura, . . . tota natura raperetur ad virtutem'; see also Waele 1620, p. 27: 'quod homo ad corporis voluptates sua natura proclivis est, illud non habet ex prima sui creatione . . . sed ex corruptione et peccato'.
497. Melanchthon 1834–60, XVI, col. 35: 'Naturale . . . iudicium est mentis humanae . . . quod Deo debeatur obedientia propter ipsius voluntatem, etiamsi non sequerentur poenae aut praemia: ergo voluptas non est finis, sed agnoscere Deum et Deo obedire'; see also cols. 175–6 (*Ethicae doctrinae elementa*).

proponents alike. It was not until the mid seventeenth century with Pierre Gassendi's work on the life and philosophy of Epicurus that scholars began to take a more secularised and dispassionate view of Epicureanism, judging it on its own merits rather than with reference to Christianity.[498]

498. Gassendi 1658, III, pp. 1–94 (*Philosophiae Epicuri syntagma*); v, pp. 167–236 (*De vita et moribus Epicuri*); see also *Épicurisme* 1969, pp. 707–15.

VIII

POLITICAL PHILOSOPHY

12

POLITICAL PHILOSOPHY

THE MEDIEVAL INHERITANCE

'It has been the achievement of the Italians', wrote Poggio Bracciolini in his *De nobilitate*, 'to spread to all other nations a proper understanding of *humanitas, virtus* and the whole art and science of living a communal life'.[1] There is much truth in Poggio's seemingly extravagant boast. If we wish to understand the origins and development of Renaissance political thought, we must certainly focus our main attention on the city-states of the *Regnum Italicum* and the forms of political literature to which they gave rise.[2]

The revival of Roman law

By the time Poggio was writing in the 1440s, the Italian city-states had already enjoyed a long and distinguished history. They first began to establish themselves as independent communes around the year 1100, and by the end of the twelfth century most of them had adopted an elective system of government centred on an official known as the *podestà*, so-called because he was invested with supreme power or *potestas* in the administration of the community's affairs.[3] At the same time they began to evolve a new and distinctive form of political literature, a literature of advice-books devoted to explaining the duties of a *podestà* and how best to discharge them. The earliest known example is the anonymous *Oculus pastoralis* of 1242, the doctrines of which were later expanded by Giovanni da Viterbo in his *De*

---

1. Poggio Bracciolini 1964–9, 1, p. 67: 'ab Italis . . . humanitas, virtus ac omnis vivendi ratio et disciplina ad reliquas nationes defluxit'.
2. A word of explanation, however, needs to be inserted at the outset if this claim itself is not to seem exaggerated. If we use the term 'Renaissance' simply to refer to the general cultural development of Western Europe between the early fourteenth and early seventeenth centuries, it is obvious that such a focus will be far too narrow. For on that account Hooker no less than Machiavelli will have to be accounted a Renaissance political theorist. The present chapter seeks to suggest, however, that there are good reasons – at least in the case of social and political philosophy – for applying the term mainly in a more restricted way to denote a particular scale of values and style of thought that flourished within that general period. On this issue see also the introduction to the present volume, esp. p. 5.   3. Waley 1978. pp. 25–36.

regimine civitatum and Brunetto Latini in his *Livres dou trésor*, an encyclopaedic work of the 1260s which ends with a discussion of 'The government
of cities'.[4]

For all their independence and self-confidence, however, the city-states
remained an anomaly within the legal structures of thirteenth-century
Europe. Technically they were mere vassals of the empire, which
vigorously pursued its claims over northern Italy throughout the late
twelfth and early thirteenth centuries. By this time, moreover, the
emperors were able to support their traditional demands by invoking the
authority of Roman civil law, the study of which had become a major
academic discipline in the course of the twelfth century under the
inspiration of Irnerius and his followers at the University of Bologna. To
these early Glossators it seemed incontestable that the *Codex* of Justinian
viewed the *Imperator* as sole *princeps* and 'lord of the whole world'. Equating
this figure with the Holy Roman Emperor, they concluded that, despite the
de facto independence of the Italian city-states, they must be altogether
subject *de iure* to the imperial power. As the Bolognese Glossator Lothair
explained in a famous judgement solicited by the emperor himself at the end
of the twelfth century, if the *Imperator* is the sole *dominus mundi*, he must at
the same time be the sole bearer of *imperium*, the one authority capable of
making laws and commanding obedience.[5]

Even more anomalous than the *de facto* independence of the city-states
was their republicanism, the fact that they placed their highest executive
and judicial functions in the hands of a salaried official elected for a strictly
limited period of time. The basic assumption of most writers on statecraft at
this period was that all government must rather be seen as a God-given form
of lordship. As John of Salisbury put it in his *Policraticus* of 1159, all rulers
constitute 'a kind of image on earth of the divine majesty'; they not only
stand above the laws but 'can be said to partake in a large measure of divine
virtue themselves'.[6] From this it was widely agreed to follow that
hereditary monarchy must be not merely the best but the only conceivable
form of legitimate rule. This is taken for granted by John of Salisbury and
such imitators as Helinandus of Froidmont,[7] while Gerald of Wales in his

---

4. For the dating of the *Oculus* see Sorbelli 1944, p. 74. For Latini's discussion see Latini 1948, part III,
   chs. 63–105 (pp. 391–422). Sorbelli dates the completion of Giovanni's treatise to 1263 (p. 96) and
   Latini's to 1266 (p. 99), in part correcting Hertter 1910, pp. 51–3.
5. Gilmore 1941, pp. 15–19.
6. John of Salisbury 1909, I, p. 236: 'in terris quaedam divinae maiestatis imago . . . magnum quid
   divinae virtutis declaratur inesse principibus'. For the date of the *Policraticus* see Berges 1938, p. 291.
7. Helinandus' treatise *De bono regimine principis* of *c*. 1200 largely follows John of Salisbury, almost
   word for word.

De principis instructione of *c.*1217 positively insists that 'the establishment of a princely form of power is actually a matter of necessity among men, no less than it is among the birds, the bees and the rest of brute creation'.[8] Finally, it was universally accepted – in line with the inescapable authority of St Augustine – that God's purpose in ordaining such princely powers must have been, as John of Salisbury adds, 'to repress the wicked, to reward the good' and to uphold the law of God on earth.[9]

While the city-states were anomalous, however, they were also powerful, rich and determined. So we find that, while a succession of emperors throughout the later Middle Ages strove to impose their wills on these recalcitrant fiefs, the cities strove with even greater energy to vindicate both their independence and their traditions of self-government. This struggle was of course waged primarily on the battlefield, but at the same time the cities built up an armoury of ideological weapons designed to combat imperial claims to suzerainty over them. The authority they chiefly invoked in this initial attempt to develop a civic ideology was – as with their opponents – that of Roman civil law. By the end of the twelfth century, a number of Glossators were beginning to reinterpret the *Codex* in a new and influential way, using it to support instead of question both the autonomy of the cities and their republican way of life.[10]

The earliest of the leading Glossators to expound the *Codex* in this fashion was Lothair's great opponent Azo, a native of Bologna and a celebrated teacher of civil law at the university there. Glossing the concepts of *iurisdictio* and *merum imperium* in his *Summa super codicem*, Azo wrote in such a way as to vindicate the sovereignty of all communities possessing *de facto* independence. 'We must begin', he announces in his section *De iurisdictione*, 'by considering the meaning of the term *iurisdictio* itself.' 'It is a power', he goes on, 'publicly established as a matter of necessity, of stating that which is lawful and right and establishing that which is equitable.'[11] So far this was of course orthodox doctrine. But as soon as Azo turns to ask who can lawfully possess such power, and hence exercise *merum imperium*, he announces a radical new departure. 'I admit', he says, 'that the very highest

8. Gerald of Wales 1891, p. 8: 'nec solum in apibus, avibus et brutis animalibus, verum in hominibus . . . principalis potestas est necessaria.' For the date of composition of this treatise see Berges 1938, p. 294.
9. John of Salisbury 1909, I, pp. 236–7: 'instituta est ad vindictam malefactorum, laudem vero bonorum'.
10. An analogous reinterpretation of the Decretals can be found among canonists of the same period. See Mochi Onory 1951.
11. Azo 1966a, p. 67 (III.13): 'videamus ergo in primis quid sit iurisdictio . . . [est] potestas de publico introducta cum necessitate iuris dicendi et aequitatis statuendae.'

iurisdictio rests with the *princeps* alone.'[12] However, it cannot be doubted 'that any magistrate in a city has the power to establish new law'.[13] 'So my position is', he concludes – in a direct allusion to his debate with Lothair – 'that it must be lawful for *merum imperium* to be wielded by these other higher powers as well.'[14]

If we turn to Azo's *Quaestiones*, moreover, we find him defending the sovereignty of independent kingdoms in precisely the same terms. Commenting on the dispute between John of England and Philip Augustus of France, in the course of which the latter had been criticised for ceding certain rights of vassalage, Azo remarks that the first point to be made on the king's behalf is that 'because it is evident nowadays that every ruler possesses the same power within his own territory as the emperor, it follows that it must have been for the king to act in this matter just as he pleased'.[15] A proposition of the most momentous consequence for the defence of national autonomy against the legal pretensions of the Holy Roman Empire is thus announced as if it were already accepted in practice as the merest commonplace.

From the point of view of the city-states, however, Azo's greatest contribution was that he also defended a doctrine of popular sovereignty. For this aspect of his argument he relied on a distinctive analysis of the term *universitas*, the central concept in the Roman law theory of corporations. The earliest Glossators had originally invoked this theory to furnish an account of the place within cities or kingdoms of such lesser corporations as guilds, monasteries and the new phenomenon of universities. But by the end of the twelfth century – especially in the writings of Azo's teacher Bassianus – they had also begun to use the term to denote any collectivity possessing its own juridical standing.[16] As a result they came to speak of entire bodies of citizens as instances of *universitates*, as bodies politic capable of speaking with a single voice and acting with a unified will in the disposition of their affairs. It was this application of the term that Azo went on to put to such revolutionary use.

First he argued that the consent of the whole people considered as a *universitas* is always needed if the highest powers of *iurisdictio* are to be

12. *Ibid.*, p. 68: 'plenissimam iurisdictionem soli principi competere dico.'
13. *Ibid.*, p. 68: 'quilibet magistratus in sua civitate ius novum statuere potest.'
14. *Ibid.*, p. 69: 'sed merum imperium etiam aliis sublimioribus potestatibus competere dico.' For the significance of this contention see Calasso 1957, pp. 83–123.
15. Azo 1888, pp. 86–7: 'quilibet hodie videtur eandem potestatem habere in sua terra, quam imperator, ergo potuit facere quod sibi placet.'
16. See Michaud Quantin 1970b, p. 28, and cf. Black 1984, pp. 44–53.

lawfully instituted. He derived this conclusion from his interpretation of the *Lex regia*, the law whereby the people of Rome were alleged to have made the original grant of *iurisdictio* to the emperor at the inception of the principate. Glossing this enactment in his *Lectura super codicem*, Azo concluded that 'the power of the emperor to make law' arose lawfully because 'it was assigned to him by the people' in whose hands it must originally have reposed.[17] So far this too was orthodox teaching among the Glossators, who must unquestionably be regarded as the source of the doctrine – later so central to scholastic and contractarian political thought – that all legitimate political authority must derive from an act of consent.[18] Azo parts company with his teachers, however, when he goes on to argue that, even after the establishment of a prince with full *iurisdictio*, 'the power to make laws, if it was a power the people possessed before that time, is one they will continue to possess afterwards'.[19] As Azo himself observes, the accepted interpretation of the *Lex regia* had always been that 'even though the Roman people at one time possessed the power to make laws, they no longer possess it, having transferred all their authority to the emperor by means of the *Lex regia* itself'.[20] This had been Irnerius' view, subsequently endorsed by such distinguished Bolognese Glossators as Rogerius and Placentinus. But Azo denies it outright. 'We should rather say', he insists, 'that the people never transferred this power except in such a way that they were at the same time able to retain it themselves.'[21] We can see how this is possible, he adds, once we introduce the idea of the *populus* considered as a *universitas*. 'For it is not the people who are excluded by the *Lex regia* from the power to make laws, but merely the individuals who make up the body of the people. They are indeed excluded, but not the people considered as a *universitas*.'[22]

If the people transfer and yet retain the power to make laws, who is the true possessor of that power in the last resort? Azo is fully aware of the question, and answers it later in his *Lectura* by introducing a distinction between a ruler's relationship to his subjects *ut singulis* and *ut universis*, a distinction destined to be endlessly cited in the later literature on the concept of *merum imperium*. He presents his solution in the course of glossing the title

17. Azo 1966b, p. 44 (1.14.11): 'potestas [imperatoris] legis condendae . . . in eum transtulit populus'.
18. See Tierney 1982, pp. 29–53.
19. Azo 1966b, p. 44 (1.14.11): 'potestas legis condendae . . . si populus ante habebat, et adhunc habebit.'
20. *Ibid.*, p. 44: 'populus Romanus non habet potestatem legis condendae, quod olim habebat: sed lege regia in eum transtulit populus omne ius quod habebat.'
21. *Ibid.*, p. 44: 'vel dic quod non transtulit ita quin sibi retineret'.
22. *Ibid.*, p. 44: 'hic non excluditur populus, sed singuli de populo . . . ideo singuli excluduntur, non universitas sive populus'.

concerned with *Longa consuetudo*. Here he begins by considering the standard objection to the suggestion that, in the exemplary instance of the Roman people, the right to make laws was never given up. Even if they initially retained it, the objection runs, 'it must by now have lapsed through loss of use, with the result that today it is lodged entirely in the emperor's hands'.[23] Azo first counters by repeating his earlier contention that the people 'never transferred this power at all except in such a way that they were able at the same time to retain it'.[24] But he now adds the crucial corollary that, 'from this it follows that, although the emperor is of greater power than any individual member of the populace, he is not of greater power than the populace as a whole'.[25] The emperor's unquestionable authority to legislate is thus rendered compatible with an unqualified defence of the *populus sive universitas* as the ultimate bearer of sovereignty.

As Azo recognises, this doctrine carries with it two further and even more radical implications, both of which he underlines in glossing the title *De legibus* in his *Summa super codicem*. Although we habitually speak of rulers as the bearers of *iurisdictio*, strictly speaking 'we should speak of the right to exercise that power being transferred to them only in the sense of being conceded, because the people will not in the least have abdicated the power themselves'.[26] The true status of a ruler is in short merely that of a *rector*, an official whose authority is assigned to him simply as a matter of administrative convenience. The other implication is that the people must retain the capacity to depose their ruler and resume the exercise of their own sovereignty should their ruler at any time fail to discharge his duties satisfactorily. This in fact happened, as Azo remarks, at one famous moment in the history of the Roman people, 'for even after they had transferred their power to make laws, they were nevertheless able to revoke that transfer at a later point'.[27]

Azo's way of defending the people's authority to set up and set down their own chosen forms of government remained an important element in the ideology of the Italian city-states throughout the later Middle Ages and the Renaissance. During the thirteenth century, Hugolinus and his pupils at Bologna continued to develop the details of Azo's case, while a number of

---

23. *Ibid.*, p. 671 (VIII.53.2): 'abrogandae per desuetudinem, hodie est omnis potestas et omne ius in imperatorem.'
24. *Ibid.*, p. 671: 'sed nec est ita translata quin sibi retinuerit'.
25. *Ibid.*, p. 671: 'unde non est maior potestatis imperator quam totus populus, sed quam quilibet de populo.'
26. Azo 1966a, p. 9 (I.14): 'potestas . . . dicitur enim translata id est concessa, non quod populus omnino a se abdicaverit.'
27. *Ibid.*, p. 9: 'nam et olim transtulerat, sed tamen postea revocavit.'

canonists followed Huguccio of Pisa's lead in deploying a parallel argument to elucidate the relationship between the pope and the *universitas* of the church.[28] In the fourteenth century, the first and most eminent of the Post-Glossators, Bartolus of Sassoferrato, defended a very similar theory of inalienable popular sovereignty in his *Tractatus de regimine civitatum*.[29] Finally, one of the most influential of the humanist commentators on the *Codex*, Mario Salamonio, restated essentially the same populist interpretation of the *Lex regia* in his *De principatu* of *c*.1514, thereby bequeathing the argument to the age of the Reformation and beyond.[30]

The rediscovery of Aristotle

A generation after Azo's death in 1230, a new intellectual movement arose that proved to be of even greater significance for the defence of the Italian city-states and their distinctive way of life. It originated with the rediscovery of Aristotle's *Politics*, the full text of which was made available in Latin for the first time with William of Moerbeke's translation of 1260. Although the *Politics* was first seriously studied at the University of Paris, it soon became obvious that Aristotle's central doctrines were of special relevance to the *Regnum Italicum*, particularly his emphasis on city-states as the appropriate units of political analysis in I.1 (1253[a]) and his enthusiasm for elective systems of ruling and being ruled in III.1 (1275[a]). So it is not surprising to find that, in the half-century after Moerbeke's translation began to be widely used, almost all the most original and influential adaptations of Aristotle's ideas came from Italian writers on the newly named subject of 'political science'.[31]

The first and greatest of these scholastic commentators was St Thomas Aquinas, scion of a noble Neapolitan family,[32] who composed his unfinished *De regno*[33] as well as beginning his *Summa theologiae* in the course of the 1260s. He in turn exercised a direct influence over a number of other Italian members of the Dominican Order, many of whom attended his lectures on Aristotle at Paris as well as studying his commentaries. These included Remigio de' Girolami, a native of Florence and the author of a Thomist tract *De bono pacis*; Ptolemy of Lucca, whose *De regimine principum*

28. Tierney 1955, pp. 132–53.   29. Skinner 1978, I, pp. 53–65.   30. *Ibid*., I, pp. 148–52.
31. The scholastic background to Renaissance political thought is especially well discussed in *The Renaissance* 1982, pp. 153–200 (Rubinstein).
32. For the significance of Thomas Aquinas' Italian background see Catto 1976.
33. Note that, although I am using Spiazzi's edition of this work, in which it is printed, together with Ptolemy of Lucca's continuation *De regimine principum*, in the form of a single text under Ptolemy's title, I prefer (to avoid confusion with Ptolemy's work) to cite Thomas Aquinas' treatise under its alternative title, *De regno*.

was long assumed to be the work of Thomas Aquinas himself; and Henry of
Rimini, the author of a major treatise of moral and political theory, largely
Thomist in inspiration, entitled *Tractatus de quatuor virtutibus cardinalibus*. By
the end of the century the same path from Italy to Paris and back again was
being travelled by philosophers and theologians of all persuasions,
including the two most famous writers on politics of early fourteenth-
century Italy: Giles (or Aegidius) of Rome, whose *De regimine principum*
remained one of the most widely-cited contributions to its genre
throughout the Renaissance; and Marsilius of Padua, the author of the
greatest work of political Aristotelianism, the *Defensor pacis* of 1324.

Aristotle gave these writers a new confidence as well as a new armoury of
concepts with which to challenge the orthodox Augustinian assumption
that all governments are imposed by God's ordinance as a mere remedy for
human sinfulness. Generally they begin by affirming that 'to live a social
and political life together', as Thomas Aquinas puts it, 'is altogether natural
to mankind',[34] and that 'living in a city is living in a perfect community,
one that is capable of supplying all the necessities of life'.[35] To turn to
consider the purposes served by such *communicationes politicae*, they offer a
purely Aristotelian – and hence a strongly positive – account of the values
such communities are able to promote. 'First among these', in Thomas'
words, 'is the preservation of the unity of peace',[36] a sentiment strongly
echoed by Remigio and Marsilius in the titles of their treatises.[37] As well as
maintaining peace on earth, however, there is an even greater blessing that
well-ordered political societies are said to bring. By preventing strife, they
are able to supply us with a framework of security within which we can
hope to pursue our own chosen ends and thereby attain happiness. As
Marsilius explains – quoting directly from the *Politics* – the highest goal of
any political community is 'that of enabling us not merely to live together,
but to live the good life in the manner most appropriate to mankind'.[38]

---

34. Thomas Aquinas 1973, p. 257 (I.1): 'naturale autem est homini ut sit animal sociale et politicum, in
    multitudine vivens'.
35. *Ibid.*, p. 259 (I.2): 'in civitate vero, quae est perfecta communitas, quantum ad omnia necessaria
    vitae'.
36. *Ibid.*, p. 259 (I.3), Thomas says that the duty 'ut pacem unitatis procuret' is the one 'ad quod
    maxime rector multitudinis intendere debet'. See also Henry of Rimini 1472, [f. 28^r] (II.3): 'finis
    enim qui intenditur in regimine civitatis est pax' and Giles of Rome 1607, p. 456 (III.2.3): 'pax et
    unitas civium debent esse finaliter intenta a legislatore'.
37. Remigio 1959, p. 124 (*De bono pacis*) begins with the claim that 'summum bonum multitudinis et
    finis eius est pax'; Marsilius of Padua 1928, p. 3 (*Defensor pacis*) claims in the opening chapter (I.1.4)
    that 'pacis seu tranquillitatis fructus optimi [sunt] . . . propter quod pacem optare, non habentes
    quaerere'.
38. Marsilius of Padua 1928, p. 12 (I.4.3) says the 'causa finalis civitatis' is that of enabling us 'vivere
    autem ipsum et bene vivere conveniens hominibus'. Cf. also Thomas Aquinas 1973, p. 274 (I.15):
    'ad hoc enim homines congregantur ut simul bene vivant.'

The authority of Aristotle's *Politics* also enabled these writers to challenge the prevailing assumption that all properly constituted political societies must take the form of hereditary and God-given lordships. Aristotle had devoted much of book III of the *Politics* to considering the relationship between different styles of *regimen* and the goals of public life. Far from concluding that monarchical rule is indispensable, he had argued that three different kinds of government are all capable of realising the goal of enabling us 'to live together and to live well'. These he listed as monarchy, aristocracy and what Moerbeke translated as *politia*, 'the case where the body of the people acts in the name of the common good'.³⁹ In book II, moreover, he had even thrown out the further remark – on which he expanded in book IV – that 'there are some experts who maintain that the very best form of polity will be one in which there is a mixture of all of these various different forms of government'.⁴⁰

Confronted with these novel typologies, the schoolmen at first continued to insist that a virtuous monarchy must still be regarded as the best form of rule. This remained Thomas Aquinas' view, both in *De regno* and the *Summa*, and in this judgement he was followed without hesitation by such early disciples as Henry of Rimini and Giles of Rome.⁴¹ Even in these theorists, however, we already find the terms of the debate entirely transformed by the impact of Aristotle's arguments. The reasons now given for preferring a *regimen regni* are no longer connected with the suggestion that God ordains kingly power as a natural form of lordship. Instead the rule of princes is defended on the naturalistic and explicitly Aristotelian grounds that, as Thomas puts it in *De regno*, 'experience shows us that those provinces or cities which live under the rule of a single king are above all able to rejoice in peace, flourish in justice and delight in abundance of wealth'.⁴²

The precise form of monarchical government defended by Thomas Aquinas and his followers is also very far removed from the traditional image of hereditary lordship. Instead they argue for a system of elective monarchy in which there are strong elements of aristocratic and popular control. Thomas presents the classic statement of this commitment in the

---

39. Aristotle 1872, p. 179 (III.4 1279ᵃ): 'quando autem multitudo ad commune conferens vivit'.
40. *Ibid.*, p. 92 (II.3 1265ᵇ): 'quidam quidem igitur dicunt, quod oportet optimam politiam ex omnibus esse civibus mixtam'.
41. Thomas Aquinas 1973, p. 260 (1.4): 'sicut autem regimen regis est optimum'. Cf. 1963c, I, p. 502 (I.II.105.1): 'regnum est optimum regimen'. See also Henry of Rimini 1472, [f. 36ʳ] (II.12): 'regimen regni, in quo unus principatus est cum virtute . . . est optimus inter omnes principandi modos' and Giles of Rome 1607, p. 456 (III.2.3): 'regnum est optimus principatus'.
42. Thomas Aquinas 1973, p. 260 (1.3): 'hoc etiam experimentis apparet. nam provinciae vel civitates quae sunt sub uno rege reguntur, pace gaudent, iustitia florent et affluentia rerum laetantur.' Cf. Giles of Rome 1607, p. 456 (III.2.3): 'hanc autem unitatem et concordiam magis efficere potest . . . si dominetur unus princeps'.

course of his long analysis of the concept of law in the *Summa*. He begins by reiterating that the best form of government is monarchy, the next best, aristocracy. This, he claims, is one of the two major points Aristotle makes about the good ordering of any political society. But Aristotle's other point is that 'the only way to ensure peace among the people is for everyone to play some part in the business of government'.[43] Putting these two contentions together – in a chain of reasoning not to be found in Aristotle – Thomas suddenly draws the conclusion that 'it follows from this that the best form of government, whether of a kingdom or a city-state, must therefore be one in which a single individual is placed in command of everyone else and rules them virtuously, but in which there are others under him who are also capable of governing virtuously, and in which all the citizens are involved in public affairs, not merely as electors of their rulers but as potential members of the government themselves'.[44] The best type of polity, in short, will be a 'well-mixed' or *bene commixta* form of monarchy, one in which the virtues of all the pure types of *regimen* are combined while their shortcomings are balanced out.

Finally, several of these early Thomists display a new and remarkable willingness to criticise the institution of monarchy itself, and to do so from the perspective of the very different arrangements prevailing in the Italian city-states. Thomas Aquinas himself concedes in *De regno* that 'men living under a monarchy are often slower to exert themselves on behalf of the common good', and that 'in consequence of this, as we see from experience, a single city governed by an annually elected *rector* is sometimes capable of achieving more than any king, even if he is ruler of three or four cities'.[45] Henry of Rimini goes even further. Although he begins by defending monarchy as the best form of government, he not only follows Thomas almost word for word in arguing that the best *species regni* is an elective form of mixed monarchy,[46] but also adds the entirely new suggestion that 'if we consider all the polities of Christendom at the present time, the one that appears to approximate most closely to this ideal of a *regimen mixtum* is the

43. Thomas Aquinas 1963c, I, p. 502 (I.II.105.1): 'quorum unum est ut omnes aliquam partem habeant in principatu: per hoc enim conservatur pax populi'.

44. *Ibid.*, I, p. 502: 'unde optima ordinatio principum est in aliqua civitate vel regno, in qua unus praeficitur secundum virtutem qui omnibus praesit; et sub ipso sunt aliqui principantes secundum virtutem; et tamen talis principatus ad omnes pertinet, tum quia ex omnibus eligi possunt, tum quia etiam ab omnibus eliguntur.'

45. Thomas Aquinas 1973, p. 262 (I.5): 'plerumque namque contigit, ut homines sub rege viventes, segnius ad bonum commune nitantur . . . unde experimento videtur quod una civitas per annuos rectores administrata, plus potest interdum quam rex aliquis, si haberet tres vel quattuor civitates.'

46. Henry of Rimini 1472, [f. 37^r] (II.15) thinks that 'principatus mixtus ex tribus est optimus', provided that 'principes eliguntur'.

government of the people of Venice'.[47] The Venetian system is based on a
Dux who is elected for life, supported by 'about four hundred nobles and
gentlemen who take part in public debates', as well as by 'an advisory body
of forty leading citizens known as the *conciliarii*'.[48] The presence of the *Dux*
means that 'this can properly be called a monarchical form of government',
but the *conciliarii* make it resemble a *regimen optimatum*, while the fact that
they are elected 'by the nobles and by many honourable citizens' supplies
'an element of a popular regime' and allows us to conclude that 'all three
forms of government are represented'.[49]

To this analysis Henry adds the further claim – one that was destined to
play a role of increasing importance in later Renaissance thought – that this
unique constitution serves to explain why 'the people of Venice flourish in
so much peace and security'. This is why 'no one oppresses anyone else' and
why 'you seldom if ever hear of murders or even the shedding of human
blood' in Venice.[50] From this moment, indeed, we may date the beginnings
of one of the most potent myths of Renaissance political thought, the myth
of Venice as the *Serenissima*, together with the attribution of this condition
to her special form of government.[51]

Once Aristotle's authority began to be invoked to criticise prevailing
conceptions of monarchy, it proved a short step to the repudiation of the
belief that monarchy in any form deserves to be accounted the best type of
government. The step was duly taken in the next generation, when a
number of Italian schoolmen succeeded in constructing a full-scale civic
ideology, a vision of politics in which the self-governing arrangements of
the city-states figured not merely as legally viable forms of government, but
as nothing less than the best means of bringing about the highest ends of
public life.[52]

47. *Ibid.*, [f. 37ʳ]: 'inter politias nostris temporibus in populo Christiano fuerunt politia gentis Venetorum ad hoc regimen mixtum videtur appropinquare.'
48. *Ibid.*, [f. 37ᵛ] (II.16): 'in ipsa nanque circiter quadrigenti tam ex nobilibus quam etiam ex honorabili populo ad consilia publica admittuntur', with the *Dux* 'praedictus a maioribus quadraginta quos conciliarios vocant'.
49. *Ibid.*, [f. 38ʳ]: (II.16): 'ex tribus regiminibus aliquid participat'. Because of the presence of the *Dux*, 'regimen regni dici potest', because of the *maiores*, 'regimen optimatum', while the fact that 'non solum maiores nobiles sed etiam de populo honorabili' are involved in the election of the *Dux* means there is also 'aliud de politia populi'.
50. *Ibid.*, [f. 38ʳ]: 'venetorum gens tanta pace et securitate fruitur . . . nullius alterius oppressor . . . omnia homicidia vel humani sanguis effusiones aut nunquam aut raro ibi audiuntur.'
51. Fasoli 1958 shows that the celebration of Venice as *Serenissima* was well established by this time. But Robey and Law 1975 point out that Henry of Rimini seems to have been the first writer to attribute this achievement specifically to Venice's political arrangements.
52. For the suggestion that this context best serves to explain Marsilius' preoccupations in the *Defensor pacis*, see Rubinstein 1965.

Ptolemy of Lucca arrives at this conclusion in the final book of *De regimine principum*. He begins by distinguishing the three forms of government Aristotle takes to be based on right reason: monarchy, aristocracy and 'the rule of the many, a form of regime known as a polity (from the Greek word *polis*) because of being especially well suited to cities, as we see above all in various parts of Italy'.[53] Later in his discussion, however, he drastically alters Aristotle's typology, claiming that the fundamental distinction is between 'polities' on the one hand and 'despotic' forms of government on the other, 'monarchy being included under the heading of despotism'.[54] This prepares us for his novel and dramatic conclusion that 'wherever you encounter a people confident of their own intelligence, you will never find them being ruled except by such a "political" form of government'. And this explains, he ingenuously adds, 'why it is that this form of political authority flourishes above all in Italy'.[55]

A similar commitment lies at the heart of Marsilius' *Defensor pacis*. It is true that in chapter 8 he assures us that 'it forms no part of my present purpose to decide which of the well-tempered forms of government is the best'.[56] But it transpires in chapter 12 that this derives from the fact that he makes a categorical distinction between the location of the sovereign power to enact laws and the purely administrative duty of ensuring that such enactments are duly carried out. Marsilius has no doubt that the *pars principans* – the executive and administrative functions of government – can equally well be discharged by a popular or an aristocratic assembly, and even allows in chapter 9 that 'a better method might conceivably be to institute an elective form of monarchy'.[57] But the point he wishes above all to emphasise – 'in line with the truth as well as Aristotle's doctrine in the *Politics*' – is that 'the legislator, that is to say the primary and proper source of the authority to make laws, must be equated with the people, the *universitas* of the citizens as a whole'.[58]

53. Ptolemy of Lucca, *De regimine principum* (IV.1) in Thomas Aquinas 1973, p. 325: '[si autem] per multos . . . tale regimen politiam appellant, a πόλις . . . quia hoc regimen proprie ad civitates pertinet, ut in partibus Italiae maxime videmus'.
54. *Ibid.*, p. 336 (IV.8), Ptolemy discusses the *regimen politicum* and *regimen despoticum*, 'includendo in despotico etiam regale'.
55. *Ibid.*, p. 336: 'qui autem . . . in confidentia suae intelligentiae sunt, tales regi non possunt nisi principatu politico . . . tale autem dominium maxime in Italia viget.' For further discussion see Davis 1974.
56. Marsilius of Padua 1928, p. 29 (I.8.4): 'quis autem bene temperatorum principatuum sit optimus . . . non habet praesentem speculationem'. Note that here and hereafter all chapter references in my text are to dictio i of the *Defensor pacis* unless otherwise specified.
57. *Ibid.*, p. 33 (I.9.5): 'fortasse perfectior est regalis monarchia . . . vel instituitur per electionem'.
58. *Ibid.*, p. 49 (I.12.3): 'nos autem dicamus secundum veritatem atque consilium Aristotelis III *Politicae* capitulo 6°, legislatorem seu causam legis effectivam primam et propriam esse populum seu civium universitatem.'

Marsilius places only one restriction on this otherwise unqualified doctrine of popular sovereignty. The powers of the legislator, he adds, can alternatively be confined to the weightier part (*valentior pars*) of the citizen-body, 'taking into consideration the quality as well as the quantity of the persons involved'.[59] But in essence his conclusion is that, if peace and the means to live the good life are to be preserved, the body of the people must remain sovereign at all times. They must ensure that the *pars principans* is always elected (chapter 9); that he is granted a minimum of discretion to vary the laws (chapter 11); and that he is capable of being removed from office by the electorate at any time (chapter 18).

As we have seen, Ptolemy of Lucca had already arrived at a similar conclusion. But whereas he had merely asserted it, Marsilius offers a careful argument in favour of equating the *legislator humanus* with the *universitas civium*. His strategy is to examine the causes of discord within communities, thereby isolating the main enemies of peace that need to be overcome. One such enemy is faction, the danger that 'if the law is enacted merely by one or a few citizens, they will consult their own good rather than attending to the good of the community as a whole'.[60] But the gravest cause of discord arises when the powers of jurisdiction within a community are in any way divided. This can easily happen if there is no clear judicial hierarchy (as was often the case in the Italian city-states). 'For in such circumstances a citizen may appear before a given judge, ignoring the others, and may be able to obtain an acquittal, only to find himself convicted for contempt by the judges he has ignored.'[61] Even worse, however, are divisions that arise from a source of discord unknown even to Aristotle, a source Marsilius isolates in chapter 19 and discusses with a boldness that won him instant excommunication and lasting notoriety. This source, he declares, is the papacy, 'whose lust for power, based on the so-called *plenitudo potestatis* allegedly handed down by Christ, makes it the leading cause of intranquillity and strife in all cities and kingdoms everywhere'.[62]

It is Marsilius' central contention that, once these enemies of peace are identified, it becomes clear that our only hope of vanquishing them lies in placing all power in the hands of the people. Chapters 12 and 17 argue that,

59. *Ibid.*, p. 49: 'valentiorem inquam partem considerata quantitate personarum et qualitate in communitate'.
60. *Ibid.*, p. 51 (1.12.5): 'si per unum aut paucos quosdam proprium magis quam commune attendentes commodum, lex ipsa feratur.'
61. *Ibid.*, p. 91 (1.17.3): 'quod si tamen appareat coram uno, reliquis spretis, et ab illo fortassis absolvatur a culpa et poena civili, a reliquis tamen damnabitur propter contumaciam.'
62. *Ibid.*, p. 108 (1.19.12): 'affectio principatus, quem sibi deberi asserunt ex eisdem (ut dicunt) per Christum tradita plenitudine potestatis, causa est singularis illa quam intranquillitatis seu discordiae civitatis aut regni factivam diximus.'

if we are to forestall the development of factional or divided jurisdictions, the people must serve as the sole judicial as well as executive authority within their own community. The whole of part II goes on to add that, if the lusts of the papacy are to be bridled, the people must at the same time strip the church of all coercive powers of *iurisdictio*, transferring them to 'the faithful human legislator' within each individual polity. The effect of taking these steps will not only be to restore peace; it will also be to return the church to the condition Christ originally intended, the condition in which the sole function of the priesthood is to preach and practise the Christian faith.

The development of scholasticism

The closing decades of the fourteenth century witnessed the onset of one of the deepest crises in the history of the Catholic Church, the crisis usually known as the Great Schism. It began with the election of two rival popes in 1378, and took an even graver turn with the appearance of a third claimant in 1409. It soon became evident that the only way to heal the Schism would be to remove all three pretenders to St Peter's throne and make a new election altogether. But this required the summoning of a General Council with powers of deposition, and in consequence raised one of the most difficult questions in ecclesiology and political philosophy: on what grounds could the body of the church legitimately claim to depose its own head?

As early as the 1190s, Huguccio of Pisa had already supplied the elements of an answer in the course of his commentary on the Decretals. The church, he had argued, constitutes a *universitas*, and must in consequence embody within it the means to secure its own welfare. It follows that, if a pope persists in notorious crimes that scandalise the faithful, it must be possible for a General Council, acting as a representative body on behalf of the church, to remove him from office for dereliction of his duties.[63]

When the Council of Constance met in 1414, it was essentially this line of reasoning which was successfully revived and put into practice. Cardinal Pierre d'Ailly, one of the leading Ockhamists of the age, argued in very similar terms in his *Tractatus* on the power of the church in 1417. So did his pupil Jean Gerson in his *De potestate ecclesiastica*, the text of which he read to the assembled Council in the same year. So too did Nicholas of Cusa in his *De concordantia catholica*, a more systematic defence of the conciliar thesis which he completed in 1433 and submitted to the Council of Basle in November of that year.[64]

63. Tierney 1955, pp. 75–84, 132–5.   64. See Watanabe 1963, pp. 15, 129 and 152 n. 44.

It is true that these writers at first moved very warily in applying a theory of popular sovereignty to the church. This is particularly true of d'Ailly, who ends his *Tractatus* with a warning that 'properly speaking, the highest power of jurisdiction rests solely with the supreme pontiff as successor to St Peter', and 'is only figuratively and in a certain sense equivocally to be found in the universal church and the General Council representing it'.[65] By the time we come to Gerson's *De potestate ecclesiastica*, however, we find an unambiguous statement of the conciliarist case. The church, Gerson argues, is an example of Aristotle's concept of a *perfecta communitas*, possessed as it is of full autonomy in pursuit of its chosen goals.[66] But if the church is simply a species of the genus of political societies, it follows that the rulers of the church must meet the same criteria of legitimacy as ordinary secular governments. Just as secular rulers are instituted by the consent of a *universitas* on condition that they promote its general welfare, so too the pope must receive his office from the church in the manner of a *rector* and hold it on condition that he aims at the common good in his rule.[67]

This clears the way for the two conclusions in which Gerson is chiefly interested. The first is that, if the pope is simply a *minister*, he cannot possibly be *maior* or greater in authority than the whole *communitas* of the church. Although he holds a *plenitudo potestatis*, this is only conditionally assigned to him; 'the highest ecclesiastical authority remains either in the church itself or else in a General Council sufficiently and legitimately representing it'.[68] His other conclusion is that, if the pope is elected on condition that he promotes the church's welfare, 'it must always be possible for a Council to judge and depose a pope from office' if he fails to do so.[69]

Although d'Ailly, Gerson and their associates were primarily concerned with ecclesiastical issues, they were quite explicit in presenting their conclusions – as their master William of Ockham had done before them – as applicable to all forms of 'perfect' societies. As a result, their distinctive amalgam of Aristotelian and civilian arguments in favour of popular sovereignty came to be highly influential as an analysis of *imperium* within secular states. It was at the University of Paris, especially among Gerson's own pupils, that these arguments took hold above all, rapidly becoming an orthodoxy and reaching a final peak of development in the voluminous

65. Ailly, *Tractatus de ecclesiae autoritate* (III.1) in Gerson 1706, II, p. 950: 'haec plenitudo Jurisdictionis, proprie loquendo, solum residet in Romano, seu Summo Pontifice Petro succedenti . . . tropice & alio modo equivoce est in Universali Ecclesia, & in Concilio Generali ipsam repraesentante.'
66. Gerson 1960–73, VI, 247–8.   67. *Ibid.*, VI, pp. 227–32.
68. *Ibid.*, VI, p. 232: 'potestas ecclesiastica in summa plenitudine est in Ecclesia . . . per seipsam vel per generale concilium eam sufficienter et legitime repraesentans'.
69. *Ibid.*, VI, p. 233: 'papa judicari potest et deponi per concilium'.

writings of John Mair and his numerous followers in the opening decades of the sixteenth century.[70]

Of all Mair's pupils, it was Jacques Almain in his *Questio in vesperiis habita* of 1512 (first published in 1518) who furnished the boldest statement of the claim that the whole body of the church and of the secular state are alike endowed with an inalienable sovereignty. As his point of departure he takes the familiar Aristotelian concept of the *communitas perfecta*, the concept of a fully autonomous body possessing, as a matter of natural necessity, all the means of securing its own welfare and pursuing its chosen goals. To this he adds the legal concept of the *universitas*, arguing that the government of any 'perfect' society, if it is to count as legitimate, must be installed in office by the consent of the members of that society as a whole, in whose hands the power of the sword must originally have reposed.[71]

On these twin foundations Almain erects his central argument: that, even after the ruler of a community has been invested with full *imperium*, the ultimate powers of *iurisdictio* within that community must still be lodged with the body of the people as a whole. He expresses this commitment in the form of two connected claims. One states that a ruler's powers over a community are never 'abdicated' to him; they are only conceded or delegated by the community itself on the understanding that the powers in question will be used for its own benefit.[72] Almain's other claim is that, although a legitimate ruler will obviously be greater in authority than any individual citizen, nevertheless 'the community as a whole retains a power over its prince which can never be renounced'.[73] Rulers are seen, in short, as wielding 'a form of *dominium* which is merely administrative in character'; they are not the owners of their sovereignty, but are merely commissioned to exercise it on behalf of their subjects as a matter of convenience.[74]

Almain's analysis of *imperium* finally enables him to draw a crucial corollary about the limits of political obligation. He has established that, in order to assure the welfare of its members, every body politic must retain an ultimate sovereignty at all times. It follows that, if the *minister* to whom the

70. See Oakley 1965 and Skinner 1978, II, pp. 117–23.
71. Almain 1518, f. LXII[r–v]. See especially f. LXII[v]: 'cum communitas det principi auctoritatem occidendi, sequitur quod est prius in communitate' – the reason being that 'nemo dat quod non habet'. ('Since the community invests its ruler with the power of the sword, it follows that this power must previously have been held by the community, [for] no one can hand over something he does not already possess.') Burns 1983 rightly underlines the fact that the power is a property only of the community, not of its individual members, correcting Skinner 1980.
72. Almain 1518, f. LXIII[r]: 'nulla communitas tota perfecta hanc potestatem [viz. the auctoritas occidendi] a se abdicare potest.' ('No perfect community can abdicate the power of the sword.')
73. *Ibid.*, f. LXIII[r]: 'non potest renunciare communitas potestati quam habet super suum principem.'
74. *Ibid.*, f. LXIII[r]: 'dominium principium iurisdictionis est solum ministeriale.'

citizens have committed their powers with the object of promoting the common good should fail in that task, 'it must be possible, if he rules in such a way as to destroy rather than preserve them, to depose him from office'.[75]

These radical views about *imperium* are obviously far removed from the cautious theory of the mixed constitution originally propagated by St Thomas Aquinas and his disciples. So it is perhaps not surprising to find that a reaction against these essentially Ockhamist and Bartolist doctrines eventually set in, allied with a renewed interest in a purely Thomist approach to the problems of legal and political philosophy. The pivotal figure in this movement was Francisco de Vitoria, a Dominican who began his training at Paris under one of John Mair's pupils, Petrus Crockaert, in the opening years of the sixteenth century.[76] Following Crockaert's lead, Vitoria repudiated Mair's teachings and turned instead to the study of Thomas Aquinas' *Summa*. Returning to his native Spain to become professor of theology at Salamanca in 1526, Vitoria went on to play a leading part in establishing that university as the greatest centre of Thomist philosophy in sixteenth-century Europe.[77] Domingo de Soto, Melchor Cano and Luis de Molina all studied there, as did Francisco Suárez, whose immense corpus of writings may be said to contain a definitive statement of the political doctrines associated with this final flowering of scholastic thought.

Suárez' theory of *merum imperium*, which he chiefly develops in book III of his treatise *De legibus* (1612) includes a number of key doctrines also to be found in the Ockhamist tradition we have just considered. He agrees that the members of any 'perfect' society can be considered together as a legal entity, and that an act of consent on their part is always needed if a legitimate ruler is to be placed in authority over them.[78] He further agrees that the only sufficient reason such a community could have for consenting to exchange its natural liberty for such a degree of subjection to law would be the belief that its welfare would thereby be improved.[79] He is more hesitant about whether this may be said to imply a right of resistance against tyranny, and in book III of *De legibus* he appears to deny the suggestion outright. But by the end of his *Defensio* of 1613 – his polemic against James I of England – he is fully prepared even on this issue to adopt a constitutionalist stance. If the ruler of a community is found not to be acting

---

75. *Ibid.*, f. LXIII^r: 'si non in edificationem sed destructionem regat deponere potest'. Almain cites the *Lex regia* for further corroboration of the point.
76. Renaudet 1953, pp. 593–4 and n. 8.   77. Hamilton 1963, pp. 172–3, 176, 185.
78. Suárez 1971–7, v, pp. 39–40 (III.4.2) and pp. 41–2 (III.4.4).
79. *Ibid.*, v, pp. 11–12 (II.1.5) and pp. 45–6 (III.4.8).

in the name of the common good, but rather to be promoting the works of the devil – as James was certainly doing in denouncing the Catholic faith – then it becomes lawful for the members of that community to forswear their oaths of allegiance and resist.[80]

Suárez remains in explicit disagreement with the Ockhamist and Bartolist traditions, however, in his account of the status enjoyed by legitimate rulers, whether of secular states or of the church.[81] When a *communitas* consents to invest such a ruler with authority, 'it constitutes a false doctrine' to say that this is a mere act of delegation of the people's original sovereignty. 'The transfer of this power is not an act of delegation, but rather a form of alienation', in consequence of which 'it is open to the ruler to make use of this power, either by himself or through his agents, in whatever manner may appear to him most suitable'.[82] This makes it a further falsehood to assert that such a ruler is a mere *minister* who remains *minor universis*, of lesser standing than the body of the people. On the contrary, Suárez insists – drawing on the authority of both Vitoria and De Soto at this point – 'when this power is transferred by a community to a prince', he 'is able to make use of it as its proper owner, holding it by virtue of his own function'.[83] It is, in short, 'completely false to say that, just because a king is granted power by his kingdom, a kingdom is of greater authority than its king'.[84]

This leads Suárez and the other Thomists of the Counter-Reformation to mount a vehement (and, as it proved, a successful) attack on the thesis of conciliarism. The pope, they maintain, is no mere *minister* of the church; he is a true sovereign set in authority over it, with a *plenitudo potestatis* extending to the enjoyment of full control even over the deliberations of General Councils. Finally, the Thomists likewise repudiate any suggestion that the ultimate holder of sovereignty within a secular state is the *universitas* of the citizens acting through a representative assembly. Suárez declares on the contrary that there are many things a lawful ruler can do without ever asking the people's consent, and without thereby giving them any grounds for questioning the legitimacy of his government.[85] The idea that the whole body of the people constitutes the original 'subject' of sovereignty is

---

80. Suárez 1872, pp. 335–6 (VI.12). For other references to the lawfulness of deposition see Sommerville 1982, pp. 530–2, 534 and note.
81. But for a different emphasis see Sommerville 1982.
82. Suárez 1971–7, v, p. 49 (III.4.11): 'translatio huius potestatis a republica in principem non est delegatio sed quasi alienatio . . . ut per se vel per alios utatur eo modo quo illi magis videbitur expedire'.
83. *Ibid.*, v, p. 46 (III.4.9): 'haec potestas . . . ab illa [communitate] transfertur in principem ut tanquam proprius dominus illa utatur et ut habens illam ex vi proprii muneris.'
84. *Ibid.*, v, p. 42 (III.4.5): 'regnum esse supra regem, quia illi dedit potestatem . . . omnino falsum est'.
85. *Ibid.*, v, pp. 217–20 (III.15.3–4).

thus rendered compatible with the rising absolutism of early seventeenth-century Europe.

Conservative though the Spanish theologians may have been in their theory of *imperium*, there was one topic on which they adopted a remarkably radical stance, while managing at the same time to extend the traditional subject-matter of political philosophy. This was in relation to the conduct of their fellow-countrymen as colonists in the New World. To many contemporary observers, Spain's policy of annexation and enslavement appeared to pose no special problems of political morality. The earliest political Aristotelians had generally taken it for granted that, in the words of Giles of Rome, Aristotle had 'proved' that 'some people are slaves by nature, and that it is appropriate for such people to be placed in subjection to others'.[86] Licensed by such high authority, the category of 'slaves by nature' came to be widely used in the course of the sixteenth century to justify the behaviour of the Spanish imperialists. At a special conference on the issue convened by the emperor at Valladolid in 1550, Juan Ginés de Sepúlveda argued that, since the Indians possessed no knowledge of the Christian faith, they deserved to be categorised as 'slaves by nature' whose way of life was one of 'natural rudeness and inferiority'. The Spanish conquests, he concluded, ought in consequence to be viewed as a just war against infidels, while the policy of enslaving the local inhabitants ought to be recognised as a helpful means of converting them.[87] Half a century later this remained the view of such theocratic writers as Campanella, whose *Monarchia messiae* includes a further defence of the Spanish conquests on the grounds of their contribution to the spread of Christianity.[88]

To the Thomist theologians, however, and above all to Vitoria, such arguments seemed to overlook an even more crucial Aristotelian category: that of the 'perfect society', with its own chosen form of *dominium*, which it is open to any group of people to establish, without benefit of revelation, simply on the basis of their natural understanding of the rules of justice. Armed with this concept, Vitoria proceeds to develop a courageous and thoroughgoing defence of the Indians in a long essay entitled *De Indis recenter inventis*. The crucial question, he begins by affirming, is 'whether these barbarians were true lords in relation to private and public affairs before the coming of the Spanish'.[89] His answer is that 'without doubt these barbarians were true rulers, both in public and private affairs, no less than if

---

86. Giles of Rome 1607, p. 380 (II.3.13): 'quod aliqui sunt naturaliter servi, et quod expedit aliquibus aliis esse subiectos'.
87. Hanke 1959, p. 44. But for a different (not wholly convincing) interpretation of *servus* see Fernandez-Santamaria 1977, pp. 209–14.   88. Campanella 1960, pp. 74–5 (cap. 15).
89. Vitoria 1933–6, II, p. 292 (I.4): 'utrum barbari isti essent veri domini ante adventum Hispanorum et privatim et publice'.

they had been Christians'. So he insists without qualification that, heathen though they be, 'there is no justification whatever for despoiling either their princes or subjects of their property on the grounds that they were not true owners of it'.[90]

These scholastic debates about the nature of *iurisdictio* and *imperium* were not of course without their parallels in Renaissance Italy. At the time of the Great Schism, one of the leading advocates of the conciliar thesis was an Italian, Cardinal Francisco Zabarella, whose treatise *De schismate* appeared as early as 1408.[91] Even at the end of the fifteenth century, it is not uncommon to find the republicanism of the Italian city-states being defended in a purely scholastic style. The best-known instance is that of Girolamo Savonarola, whose *Trattato* on the government of Florence, published just before his fall in 1498, argued for a broadly based form of republican government in precisely the terms already used by his fellow-Dominican Ptolemy of Lucca almost two centuries before.[92]

Generally speaking, however, the themes and idioms of Italian political literature began to diverge sharply from those characteristic of scholasticism by the middle years of the fourteenth century. With Marsilius' great treatise of 1324, we not only reach the culmination of the scholastic defence of the Italian city-states; we also come to the end of the period in which the political theorists of the *Regnum Italicum* made their most creative contribution to the development of scholastic political thought. Thereafter we find them asking new questions, citing new authorities, proclaiming new values, all in a style usually felt to be far more typical of the Renaissance than anything so far discussed. It is with these contrasting developments in Italy, accordingly, and with their eventual impact on the rest of Western Europe, that the rest of this chapter will be principally concerned.

POLITICAL THOUGHT IN RENAISSANCE ITALY

Some of the new features of Italian political theory in the fourteenth century are best explained as a series of attempts to come to terms with changes in Italian political life. As we have seen, the tradition culminating in

90. *Ibid.*, II, p. 309 (1.23): 'sine dubio barbari erant et publice et privatim ita veri domini sicut Christiani; nec hoc titulo spoliari, aut Principes aut privati rebus suis, quod non essent veri domini.' For a full discussion of the issue of *dominium* see Pagden 1982, pp. 65–80.
91. See Tierney 1955, pp. 220–37.
92. For Savonarola's *Trattato* see Skinner 1978, I, pp. 147–8. For verbal parallels between the discussion of government in Savonarola's *Compendium totius philosophiae* and Ptolemy of Lucca's *De regimine principum* see Weinstein 1970, pp. 292n., 293n.

the work of Marsilius had argued that, to ensure the preservation of peace, the safest plan will always be to vest the ultimate powers of *iurisdictio* in the hands of the people. During the very period when such theories began to be increasingly espoused, however, they began to look increasingly implausible. The close of the thirteenth century witnessed the deepening of factional quarrels in many cities governed by *podestà*, as a result of which there were widespread moves to replace these elective systems of government with the rule of hereditary *signori*, the professed aim being to secure a greater degree of civic unity and peace.[93] Such changes took place in Mantua and Verona in the 1270s, in Treviso, Pisa, Piacenza and Parma by the end of the 1280s and in Ravenna, Rimini and elsewhere before the end of the century.[94] It was thus entirely accurate of Dante to observe in the *Purgatorio*, although his phrasing may have been tendentious, that 'all the cities of Italy' had by that time become 'full of tyrants'.[95]

The acceptance of princely government

One reflection of the above developments was that, even among the protagonists of popular government, a tone of increasing pessimism can be heard about the prospects of combining republicanism with civic peace. Remigio de' Girolami writes with despair about the ruinous effects of faction in his *De bono communi*,[96] as does his fellow-Florentine Dino Compagni in his *Cronica* of the same period.[97] A similar anxiety pervades Albertino Mussato's tragedy *Ecerinis*, in which he vainly sought to warn his fellow-citizens of Padua that their constant feuding would be sure to bring a return of the tyranny they had endured under Ezzelino da Romano half a century before. The Messenger points the grim moral at the moment of announcing Ezzelino's conquest: 'O fearful feuding of the nobles! O fury of the people! The outcome of all your quarrelling is at hand. The tyrant is here, the gift of your own rage.'[98]

But the main effect of civic disorder was to prompt a revival of the suggestion that a strong monarchy should after all be accounted the best

---

93. Ercole 1932, pp. 279–86, 306–11 argued that the *signori* generally assumed power with the consent of the relevant body of citizens. The point is still worth stressing, if only because of the influential contrast developed in Baron 1966 between republican 'liberty' and the 'tyranny' of princely regimes. For a helpful corrective see Robey 1973, pp. 4–10 and references there.
94. Waley 1978, pp. 128–40.
95. Dante, *Purgatorio* VI.124–5: 'Ché le città d'Italia tutte piene|son di tiranni'.
96. See Minio-Paluello 1956, pp. 59–61.
97. Compagni 1939, especially pp. 12–13, 26–31, 40–2.
98. Mussato 1900, p. 32: 'o dira nobilium odia, o populi furor|finis petitus litibus vestris adest|adest tyrannus, vestra quem rabies dedit.'

form of government. Some writers reverted to the age-old claim that the surest means of bringing concord to the *Regnum Italicum* would be to accept the overlordship of the emperor after all. Compagni supports this solution in his *Cronica*,[99] but the most eloquent presentation of the Ghibelline case was undoubtedly Dante's in his *Monarchia*. Dante begins with the familiar Aristotelian assumption that our highest earthly aim should be to live 'in the calm and tranquillity of peace, since universal peace is the finest of all the gifts that have been ordained for our happiness'.[100] He then devotes the whole of his opening book to defending the suggestion that, if the disorders of Italy are ever to be resolved, complete trust must be placed in the emperor as the sole authority capable of ending the prevailing strife.

A yet more backward-looking defence of universal monarchy was also revived at this time. Pope Boniface VIII, in a series of pronouncements culminating in the Bull *Unam sanctam* of 1302, restated with unparalleled ambitiousness the papacy's traditional 'hierocratic' claim to bind and loose in all temporal as well as spiritual affairs. The argument was widely repudiated even by the theologians, who generally concentrated on vindicating the more moderate thesis of 'indirect' temporal control later defended by such Counter-Reformation papalists as Bellarmine. Yet it survived for an astonishingly long time, surfacing in the writings of such unrepentant theocrats as Tommaso Campanella as late as the start of the seventeenth century. In Campanella's utopian dialogue of 1603, *La Città del Sole*, the ruler is a priest 'who is head of all spiritual and temporal affairs'.[101] And in his *Monarchia messiae* of 1605, the argument culminates in the claim that 'since the incarnation, the apostolic power of the papacy has been placed in authority over every kingdom in the world'.[102]

Among Italian writers of the fourteenth century, however, the most usual proposal was that the numerous local *signori* who had come to power ought simply to be accepted with gratitude as bringers of a stabler form of government. Padua became a leading centre of such writings in favour of princely rule, just as it had earlier provided the context for Marsilius' great statement of the opposing case. Ferreto de' Ferreti, a member of Mussato's humanist circle at Padua, composed a verse panegyric *De Scaligorum origine*

99. Compagni 1939, especially p. 210.
100. Dante 1965, p. 143 (1.4.2): 'in quiete sive tranquillitate pacis . . . quod pax universalis est optimum eorum que ad nostram beatitudinem ordinantur'.
101. Campanella 1962, p. 5: 'È un Principe Sacerdote tra loro . . . questo è capo di tutti in spirituale e temporale.'
102. Campanella 1960, p. 65: 'post incarnationem Pontificiam potestatem Apostolicam superpositam super omnia Regna mundi'.

soon after the accession of Cangrande Della Scala as *signore* of Padua in 1328, in which he expressed the hope that Cangrande's descendants 'will continue to hold their sceptres for long years to come'.[103] Pier Paolo Vergerio, who lived in Padua between 1390 and 1405, wrote his *De monarchia* during those years, addressing it to the Carrara lords who were ruling the city by that time.[104] Giovanni da Ravenna, Chancellor of Padua during the 1390s, further celebrated the Carrara family in his *Dragmalogia de eligibili vite genere* of 1404.[105] And Petrarch, who spent the closing years of his life in Padua, wrote his famous account of princely government in the form of a long letter to Francesco da Carrara in 1373.[106]

For all these writers, the highest aim of government is to ensure that, as Petrarch puts it, 'each citizen can live his life in freedom and security, with no innocent blood being spilled'.[107] If this framework for living the good life is to be held in place, he adds, everyone in authority must be concerned above all else with public peace'.[108] But peace can never be secured under any form of communal or republican government. Vergerio treats this as obvious, while Giovanni da Ravenna points to the history of ancient Rome as conclusive evidence of this general truth.[109] The moral is said to be obvious, and all these writers duly point it out: if there is to be any prospect of peace, we must cleave to princely government. As Petrarch triumphantly assures the Carrara family, it is wholly due to their standing as hereditary *signori* that they have 'ruled for so many years over a flourishing community in serene tranquillity and constant peace'.[110]

To these familiar claims a more highflown argument was sometimes added, an argument derived from a fundamentally Augustinian vision of the well-lived life. Such a life, Petrarch affirms, will be one of withdrawal from mundane affairs – *vita solitaria*, as he describes it in the title of one of his most famous books. This alone affords us the leisure or *otium* needed for great literary labours, as well as the tranquillity needed for contemplation and prayer.[111] The same commitment underlies Giovanni da Ravenna's

103. Ferreto 1920, III, p. 100: 'ut longos teneant sceptra per annos'.
104. For the date of composition and biographical details see Robey 1973, pp. 8–9, 20–1.
105. For the date of composition and biographical details see Giovanni da Ravenna 1980, pp. 22–9.
106. For details of this part of Petrarch's life see Wilkins 1959, pp. 141–314. The letter is in the *Epistolae de rebus senilibus* (XIV.1).
107. Petrarch 1554, p. 420: 'ut et cives . . . liberi fuerint ac securi, nec ullius sanguis innoxius fu[n]deretur'.   108. *Ibid.*, p. 420: 'ante alios quietis publicae studiosus'.
109. Giovanni da Ravenna 1980, p. 124: 'per reges Romanum fundatum est et vires cepit imperium. deinde, ubi regi superbo superbi cives parere contempserunt, populariter res acta est . . . quanto fluctu et turbine civitatis.'
110. Petrarch 1554, p. 420: 'per annos florentem patriam, serena tranquillitate et constanti pace tenueris'.   111. See Petrarch 1975, I, pp. 261–565 and cf. pp. 567–809.

Dragmalogia, which culminates in a bitter denunciation of the evils and hypocrisies inevitable in politics and an eloquent defence of the good life as one of rustic retreat. To both writers this suggests a further reason for concluding that, as Giovanni puts it, 'the rule of a single man is always to be preferred, even if the man in question is only of moderate worthiness'.[112] Where one man rules, 'the rest of us are left completely free of public business, and are able to pursue our own affairs'.[113] This is a highly desirable arrangement, indispensable for the completion of any important task, but 'it is one that has rarely existed under a government of the people, though often under the rule of a king'.[114]

The dawn of humanism

As well as the shifts of political allegiance mentioned above, far larger transitions are to be observed in Italian political literature in the course of the fourteenth century. A new set of moral and political values appears, combined with an element of outright hostility – especially evident in Petrarch and his many disciples – to scholastic philosophy. To understand these transformations, we must turn to contemplate the dawn of humanism and the changes it brought to the Italian universities and the conduct of public life.

One of the subjects taught in the Italian universities had always been rhetoric, usually as a preliminary to the study of law. Towards the end of the thirteenth century the subject came to be approached in a new way, evidently under the influence of the methods of instruction prevailing in the French cathedral schools. No longer were the manuals of ancient rhetoric examined simply as sources of practical rules; they were also used as guides to good Latin style. Out of this renewed interest in the language and literature of ancient Rome the first glimmerings of the humanist movement emerged.[115] At Arezzo and especially at Padua in the early fourteenth century, a growing number of *literati* – most of them originally trained as lawyers – began to interest themselves in the full range of the ancient *studia humanitatis*.[116] They immersed themselves in Roman poetry, especially Horace and Vergil; in the Roman historians, especially Livy and Sallust; and in the writings of such moralists as Juvenal, Seneca and above all Cicero,

112. Giovanni da Ravenna 1980, p. 106: 'unius vel mediocriter boni eligibilius esse regimen'.
113. *Ibid.*, p. 132: 'nam ubi unus dominatur, suo quisque negotio prorsus publici securus vacat.'
114. *Ibid.*, p. 118: 'quod monarcha dominante sepe, politia raro, contigisse'.
115. For a classic statement of these themes see Kristeller 1961a. For the French background see Simone 1965. For the indigenous background see G. Billanovich 1981–, Witt 1982 and their many references.
116. For the Paduan background see G. Billanovich 1981–, I, pp. 1–33 and Siraisi 1973, pp. 43–58.

whom they turned into the best-known and most widely quoted author of antiquity.

Once the literature of Rome became a subject of so much fascination, the humanists chiefly busied themselves about the recovery of ancient manuscripts, the editing of texts, the establishment of attributions and so forth. But some of them – above all Petrarch – conceived the wider ambition of restating the themes of ancient poetry, history and moral philosophy, with the hope of bringing about what Leonardo Bruni in his *Dialogi* of 1402 praised Petrarch for having achieved: 'a true restoration of the *studia humanitatis* at a time when such studies had become extinct'.[117] The fruits of these ambitions belong in part to the history of literature, including Petrarch's own revival of the Vergilian epic in his *Africa* and Mussato's pioneering attempt to emulate Senecan verse tragedy in *Ecerinis*. But since the humanists were no less interested in the moralists and historians of ancient Rome, their growing confidence as exponents of the *studia humanitatis* also had an impact of overwhelming importance on the evolution of Renaissance moral and political thought.

The most important new element the humanists introduced was a distinctive vision of the goals of political society, especially the goals appropriate to those entrusted with its leadership. Without ceasing to endorse the assumption that all rulers have a duty to promote peace and security, Petrarch and his disciples added an overriding emphasis on the characteristically Roman ideals of honour, glory and fame. A more complete reversal of the values of scholastic political philosophy would be hard to conceive. Thomas Aquinas and his pupils had of course been aware of this strand of Roman thought, but had always denounced it with vehemence.[118] 'It is altogether inappropriate', Giles of Rome had declared, 'for a holder of kingly power to seek his own fulfilment either in the attainment of glory or even of fame.'[119] Thomas Aquinas in *De regno* had put the point even more forcefully. 'The desire for human glory destroys any magnanimity of character', and 'to hold out such a reward to princes is at the same time very harmful to the people, since the duty of a good man is to show contempt for glory and all such temporal goods'.[120]

117. *Prosatori latini* 1952, p. 94 (*Ad Petrum Paulum Histrum dialogus*): 'hic vir studia humanitatis, quae iam extincta erant, repararit'.
118. Marsilius perhaps constitutes a partial exception. See Marsilius of Padua 1928, p. 81 (1.16.14).
119. Giles of Rome 1607, p. 27 (1.1.9): 'quod non decet regiam maiestatem, suam ponere felicitatem in gloria, vel in fama'.
120. Thomas Aquinas 1973, p. 265 (1.8): 'deinde humanae gloriae cupido animi magnitudinem aufert . . . simul etiam est multitudini nocivum, si tale praemium statuatur principibus: pertinet enim ad boni viri officium ut contemnat gloriam, sicut alia temporalia bona.'

The humanists profoundly disagreed. Petrarch assures Francesco da Carrara that 'true *virtus* never rejects deserved glory', and adds that his whole purpose in offering advice is 'to lead you to present fame and future glory in the best possible way'.[121] He acknowledges that rulers ought to cultivate those qualities 'which serve not merely as a means to glory but as ladders to heaven at the same time'.[122] But this represents his sole concession to the deeply rooted Christian suspicion of *gloria mundi* and those who pursue it. The rest of his letter is filled with exhortations to Francesco 'to undertake such tasks as will bring you a share of glory that your ancestors never attained'[123] and to 'lust after a form of greediness that is generous and beyond reproach: a greediness to obtain the treasure of *virtus* and the outstanding attribute of fame'.[124]

The early humanists also provided a new and characteristic account of how these goals are to be attained. Drawing above all on Cicero, they argued that the key to glory lies in the possession of *virtus generalis*; that 'glory necessarily follows from a love of *virtus*', as Cicero had proclaimed.[125] Petrarch gave influential expression to this belief when he argued that 'true *virtus* brings us glory even when it may not be desired'.[126] By the end of the fourteenth century, this assumption had become firmly entrenched as the leading tenet – almost the defining characteristic – of humanist political thought.

Placing all their emphasis on *virtus* meant that the early humanists found little to say about two issues on which the schoolmen had always supposed it vital to pronounce. The latter had generally recognised that the peace and security of a community will sometimes depend on a ruler's willingness to act with *vis* as well as *virtus*, with military power as well as moral force. As a result, Thomas Aquinas and his pupils had been much preoccupied with the concept of the Just War, seeking to specify the nature of the circumstances in which the waging of warfare can be morally defended.[127] By contrast, the early humanists are apt to stigmatise any appeal to *vis* at the expense of *virtus* as a sign of bestiality, endorsing the Stoic and Ciceronian proposition that

---

121. Petrarch 1554, p. 420: 'vera virtus, dignam gloriam non recuset.' 'rem . . . et famae tuae praesenti, et venturae gloriae saluberrimam feceris'.
122. *Ibid.*, p. 423: 'haec sunt autem non ad gloriam modo, sed ad coelum scalae.'
123. *Ibid.*, p. 426: 'arripe quaeso, et hanc gloriae partem, quam maiores tui omnes . . . non viderunt.'
124. *Ibid.*, p. 428: 'cupiditatem irreprehensibilem generosam, virtutum thesauros, et praeclaram famae supellectilem concupisce.'
125. Cicero, *Tusculan Disputations* 1.38.91: 'cupiditate . . . virtutis, quam necessario gloria . . . consequatur'.
126. See Petrarch 1554, p. 420 for the idea that 'vera virtus' brings glory 'eamque vel invitam'.
127. For the classic defence of the *bellum justum*, see Thomas Aquinas 1963c, II, pp. 222–4 (II.II.40.1).

virtus is the eponymous characteristic of the *vir*, the man of truly manly as opposed to brutish qualities.[128] As a result, they not only place a question mark, if only implicitly, against the doctrine of the Just War; they also exhibit much less interest in arguing systematically about the relations between warfare and government.

The other topic on which their manuals are largely silent concerns the machinery of government. As we have seen, the scholastics had been much preoccupied with ensuring the people a proper share in government, and with confining both secular and ecclesiastical authorities within their proper spheres. By contrast, few of the early humanists have anything of substance to say about these matters at all. Marsilius' hard questions about the relations between spiritual and temporal power largely disappeared from sight until the Reformation revived them with a vengeance. The humanists are generally content to assume that a prince of true *virtus* will of course be a loyal son of the church. Likewise, the careful arrangements devised by scholastic as well as legal theorists to prevent the enemies of peace from seizing control of the apparatus of government are scarcely echoed in early humanist political thought. The basic assumption shared by Petrarch and his successors is that, as long as the ruler himself is a man of *virtus*, the goals of peace and security will be assured.

If *virtus* is such an all-important quality, what does it mean for a prince to possess it? Petrarch's letter to Francesco da Carrara gives a typical and highly influential answer. Such a prince will be distinguished by a number of personal virtues, in particular the avoidance of pride and avarice, the two gravest of the cardinal vices. Above all, however, he will be recognisable by the justice of his rule. Petrarch accordingly devotes his main attention to analysing the concept of justice, in the course of which he discloses, more clearly than at any other point, the overwhelming extent of his debt to Cicero, especially the doctrines of the *De officiis*.

When Cicero discusses justice in book 1 of the *De officiis*, he initially defines it in juristic terms as rendering to each his due (1.5.15). But his main concern is with what it means to speak of receiving one's due, and in answering this question he divides his analysis into two halves. One is taken up with the discussion of generosity (*beneficentia*), a virtue he takes to be inseparably bound up with justice itself. His other contention is that justice is only secured when we avoid *iniuria*, the doing of harm contrary to right (1.13.41). Such harm can arise in one of two ways: either as the product of

128. See especially Cicero, *Tusculan Disputations* II.18.43: 'appellata est enim ex viro virtus'; see also *De officiis* I.9.34 and I.13.41; and cf. Petrarch 1554, p. 433 quoting *De officiis* I.22.74.

fraud, the failure to keep one's word; or else as the product of force, of cruel or brutal treatment (1.13.41). It follows that the indispensable requirements of justice must be *fides*, the willingness to treat one's word as one's bond; and *clementia*, the avoidance of cruelty and violence (1.7.23; 1.11.35). A leader who possesses these attributes will always be loved and admired; and the capacity to inspire love rather than fear is the key to princely glory and fame (II.7.23; II.11.38).

Petrarch and his humanist successors follow this analysis almost word for word. Justice is indeed a matter of rendering to each his due, Petrarch first argues, and this requires not merely the observance of good faith but the exercise of clemency and generosity at all times. If we ask in turn what motives a prince may be said to have for behaving with justice, Petrarch simply refers us directly to the *De officiis*, and especially to the crucial chain of reasoning – endlessly cited by later humanists – to the effect that justice is the sole guarantee of popular affection, while the love of the people is in turn the sole guarantee of governmental security and the prince's own glory and fame.[129]

The theory of republican government

Although the system of government by *signori* had spread through most of the *Regnum Italicum* by the end of the fourteenth century, there were two exceptions to this rule, both of the utmost significance. Florence and Venice each succeeded in fighting off the threat of internal 'tyranny' as well as external conquest, and in the course of doing so became increasingly hostile to the *signori* and their usurpations of traditional liberties. As a result, a new style of political literature began to emerge in both these surviving republics during the early years of the fifteenth century, a literature devoted at once to celebrating their civic greatness and explaining it in terms of their uninterrupted loyalty to their long-established methods of 'free' government.

As we have seen, Henry of Rimini had already sought to explain Venice's achievements by reference to her unique constitution in his treatise of *c*.1300 on the cardinal virtues. His analysis remained well known throughout the fourteenth century,[130] and seems to have exercised a direct influence on Pier Paolo Vergerio, whose *De republica veneta* of *c*.1400 took a further step towards the definitive articulation of the myth of Venice.[131] Vergerio agrees with Henry that the Venetians have proved uniquely successful in

---

129. Petrarch 1554, pp. 421–4.   130. On this point see Robey 1973, pp. 8–9.
131. For the date of composition see Robey and Law 1975, p. 29.

combining civic greatness with the preservation of peace. The explanation, he further agrees, lies in the nature of their constitution. The city 'is ruled by an administration of her optimates, and is thus a form of polity which it is appropriate to call, in Greek terminology, an aristocracy, this being the mean between monarchical and popular forms of rule'.[132] However, her government is far more admirable than a conventional aristocracy, for it contains monarchical and popular elements as well, 'and is thus a mixture of all the praiseworthy forms of polities'.[133] It is because of this mixed constitution, he concludes, and in particular its markedly *stretto* or aristocratic bias, that the Venetians have been able to scale the heights of glory without endangering their free institutions or the cause of civic peace.[134]

By the middle of the fifteenth century, Vergerio's basic insight had been embroidered by a number of other humanists, notably George of Trebizond in the preface to his translation of Plato's *Laws* in the early 1450s. Discussing the constitution of Sparta in books III and IV of the *Laws*, Plato had formulated the earliest theoretical defence of the mixed constitution as the best and stablest form of government. George takes up these remarks and applies them directly to Venice, claiming that the city's aristocratic and 'directed' republicanism constitutes a realisation of Plato's ideal in practice.[135] Dedicating his translation to the Doge, George duly received a handsome remuneration for this flattering explanation of his adopted city's pre-eminence in the arts of government.[136]

By the end of the century, this image of Venice as the *Serenissima* had become definitively fixed. Domenico Morosini drew heavily on it in his *De bene instituta re publica* of *c*.1500, although he conceded that Venice's constitution stood in need of some reformation if the city's admirable peacefulness was to be sustained.[137] Finally, Gasparo Contarini provided a classic summary of the entire argument, together with much empirical detail, in his *De magistratibus venetorum*, a work largely written in the 1520s and posthumously published in 1543. No breath of criticism is allowed to disturb Contarini's analysis. 'There has never been a polity', he insists,

---

132. For the text of Vergerio's *De republica veneta*, see *ibid.*, pp. 36–50, especially pp. 38–9: 'Venetorum respublica optimatum administratione regitur, quod genus civilitatis greco vocabulo aristocratiam licet appellare, que inter regium popularemque principatum media est.'
133. *Ibid.*, p. 39: 'ex omni genere laudabilis politie simul commixta est'.
134. For Vergerio's survey of the three elements in the Venetian constitution see *ibid.*, pp. 39–46. See also F. Gilbert 1977, p. 184.
135. See George of Trebizond 1970.   136. See Monfasani 1976, pp. 102–3, 120–1, 145–6.
137. See Morosini 1969, and for the date of composition see Cozzi 1970, pp. 408–9. Begun in 1497, the work remained uncompleted at Morosini's death in 1509.

'capable of rivalling Venice in the suitability of its constitution and laws for living a good and happy life. The effects of these arrangements are there for all to see in the long continuation of our city in this flourishing state. And when I reflect on this fact, I always find myself amazed at the wisdom of our ancestors, their industriousness, their excellent *virtus* and their incredible love of their country.'[138]

During the first half of the fifteenth century, a no less strident note of patriotism began to resound through the political writings of the Florentine humanists. The tone was set by Leonardo Bruni's *Laudatio florentinae urbis*,[139] a celebration of the city's glory and greatness that took its form from Aristides' oration in praise of Athens, but its main political arguments from the historians and moral philosophers of republican Rome.[140]

Bruni opens with a fulsome description of Florence's civic grandeur: the greatness of her wealth, the splendours of her architecture, the immensity of her power. The rest of the panegyric is given over to explaining how Florence has managed to acquire so many glories. Bruni concentrates on expounding a single and highly influential theme: Florence's greatness is held to be the fruit of her liberty, the outcome of her enjoyment of 'a free way of life'.

When Bruni describes Florence as a free city, what he has in mind is that the community is free in the familiar sense of not being subject to coercion, and in consequence free to act according to its own civic will. His meaning becomes plain as soon as he asks what forces need to be held at bay if liberty is to be preserved. The most obvious is the danger of foreign conquest. To speak of Florence as a free city is thus to say that her citizens have managed to fight off such external threats to their autonomy – especially and most recently the threat posed by Visconti Milan.[141] The other and more insidious danger arises when a powerful individual or faction within a city reduces it to servitude by seizing power and ruling in their selfish interests instead of promoting the common good. To predicate freedom of a city is

---

138. G. Contarini 1571, p. 263: 'nulla tamen fuit, quae institutione ac legibus ad bene beateque vivendum idoneis cum hac nostra conferri possit: quo effectum esse perspicimus, ut neque adeo diuturna ulla unquam perstiterit. quam rem cum mecum ipse considero, magnopere mirari soleo maiorum nostrorum sapientiam, industriam, excellentem animi virtutem atque adeo incredibilem erga patriam charitatem.' For the date of composition of Contarini's treatise, see F. Gilbert 1967, pp. 174–6.
139. For the date of composition see Baron 1968b, pp. 111–23.
140. For Bruni's use of Aristides see *ibid.*, pp. 155–9, 167–9.
141. For the text of Bruni's *Laudatio*, see *ibid.*, pp. 232–63. For this point, see pp. 256–8.

thus to say in addition that its citizens have managed to forestall any such internal threats to their independence of action.[142]

Two institutions above all have enabled the Florentines to maintain their free way of life. To stave off foreign conquest they have evolved a formidable military machine, constantly performing 'outstanding deeds of martial prowess' and 'more than once liberating the whole of Italy from the peril of servitude'.[143] To meet the threat of internal subversion, they have held fast to their mixed republican constitution, thereby protecting the well-being of their community and in consequence the liberty of each individual citizen.

This emphasis on republican liberty represents a new departure in humanist political thought. The previous generation of humanists, including Bruni's own mentor Coluccio Salutati, had already argued that, if freedom is to be preserved, the laws of a community must aim at the common good. But they had generally been content to assume that this ideal can be realised under a prudent and law-abiding *signore* no less than under a republic.[144] By contrast, Bruni and his successors take from the Roman historians – especially Livy and Sallust – a much stricter account of the relations between liberty, the common good and the achievement of civic glory. Sallust had argued in a famous passage of his *Bellum Catilinae* that 'because good men are objects of even greater suspicion to kings than the wicked', the city of Rome 'was only able to rise so suddenly to her incredible level of greatness once she gained her liberty' with the expulsion of her kings.[145] It was this perspective that Bruni and his heirs adopted. They not only argued that, if greatness is to be achieved, liberty must be upheld; they also insisted that, if liberty is to be kept as safe as possible, it is indispensable to maintain a mixed form of republican government.

There is also a contrast to be drawn between Bruni's republicanism and the similar enthusiasm for mixed constitutions displayed by the admirers of Venice. Vergerio and his successors had argued that, to protect civic peace as well as liberty, the government of a republic must always have a *stretto* or aristocratic bias. Bruni by contrast devotes the final section of his *Laudatio* to

---

142. As Bruni explains in section II (*ibid.*, p. 245), this is where Rome eventually failed: the city fell under the yoke of the Caesars, 'pestes atque exitia rei publice, libertatem sustulerant' ('those diseases and destroyers of the republic, who overthrew the people's liberty').
143. *Ibid.*, pp. 254, 256: 'egregia rei militaris facinora . . . non semel ab hac una urbe totam Italiam a servitutis periculo fuisse liberatam'. 144. De Rosa 1980, p. 144.
145. Sallust, *Bellum Catilinae* VII.3: 'nam regibus boni quam mali suspectiores sunt . . . civitas incredibile memoratu est adepta libertate quantum brevi creverit'.

commending a far more *largo* or inclusive mixture. 'It is because Florence
has recognised that what concerns the body of the people ought not to be
decided except by the will of that body itself that liberty flourishes and
justice is conserved in the city in such an exceptionally scrupulous way'.[146]

Although Bruni stresses the importance of military and constitutional
machinery, he only reaches the bedrock of his argument when he asks what
animates these institutions and enables them to flourish. A good Ciceronian,
he answers that the key lies in the possession of *virtus*. By means of this
quality, he asserts at the start of section II, the Romans maintained their
liberty and rose to dominate the world; by means of the same quality, he
adds in a carefully contrived parallel at the start of section III, Florence
promises to attain a comparable greatness.[147]

The previous generation of humanists had of course emphasised the
centrality of *virtus*, but here too Bruni's argument differs in significant
ways. Petrarch and his admirers had still maintained that the best way of life
will always be one of *otium*, of contemplation and withdrawal from public
affairs. Among the humanists of Bruni's generation this commitment is
decisively reversed. Adopting Cicero's slogan that 'what is praiseworthy
about *virtus* is always to be seen in action',[148] they equate *otium* with the
mere dereliction of duty and insist that the life of *negotium*, the *vita activa
civilis*, is always to be preferred. Even before Bruni's commendation of the
Florentines for adopting these values, Vergerio had furnished a classic
statement of the same point of view in his letter to Petrarch in the name of
Cicero, composed in 1394.[149] 'It has always seemed to me', Cicero is made
to say, 'that the man who surpasses all others in his nature and way of life is
he who bestows his efforts on the government of the body politic and in
working for the benefit of all.'[150] This means that 'the most mature and
valuable philosophy must be the one that dwells in cities, shuns solitude and
concerns itself with the good of the community as a whole'.[151]

Discussing the nature of civic *virtus*, Bruni's treatment again differs from
that of Petrarch and his followers. While they had generally confined
themselves to considering the *virtus* of the prince, Bruni and his imitators

146. Baron 1968b, p. 260: 'quod enim ad multos attinet, id non aliter quam multorum sententia decerni
      . . . iudicavit. hoc modo et libertas viget et iustitia sanctissime in civitate servatur.'
147. *Ibid.*, pp. 244, 248.
148. Cicero, *De officiis* 1.6.19: 'virtutis enim laus omnis in actione consistit.'
149. For this dating see Robey 1973, p. 6.
150. Vergerio 1934, pp. 439–40: 'ita semper visum est praestare omnibus vel genere vel vita quisquis ad
      administrandam rempublicam impertiendosque saluti omnium labores se accommodasset.'
151. *Ibid.*, p. 444: 'enim michi matura semper et prestans philosophia visa est, que in urbibus habitat et
      solitudinem fugit, que cum sibi tum communibus studet commodis.'

assume that each and every citizen must cultivate this vital quality if liberty is to be protected and civic greatness attained. A further contrast derives from the fact that the earlier humanists had usually remained faithful to the traditional image of the ruler as a just judge, and had therefore placed all their emphasis on the virtue of justice. By contrast, Bruni develops a more complex and authentically Ciceronian account. He agrees about the centrality of justice, and continues to link it with *beneficentia* and the avoidance of *iniuria*.[152] But he places no less emphasis on the other three 'cardinal' virtues. First he mentions prudence, though only to observe that this is so widely agreed to be a leading attribute of the Florentines as to require no further comment.[153] Next he turns to courage, one of the major themes of the section explaining Florence's military victories.[154] Finally he discusses temperance, the importance of which may be said to underlie the whole of the *Laudatio*'s concluding section on the constitution of Florence. If a city is to remain at liberty, her citizens must avoid all intemperance and disorderliness, so maintaining a 'well-tempered' government. Florence's constitution serves to enthrone precisely this virtue in the hearts of all her citizens, thereby producing 'an unparalleled orderliness, elegance and unity in all her affairs'.[155] On this rousing note Bruni brings his panegyric to a close.

The moral of Bruni's story is that, if the highest goals of our community are to be realised, we must all serve it with the full range of the civic virtues. Implicitly, therefore, Bruni may by said to broach two further themes of classical republicanism: the question of what constitutes the *optimus status* or best state of a commonwealth; and the question of what qualities go to make a truly noble or praiseworthy citizen, a citizen of *vera nobilitas* whose conduct deserves to be honoured and admired. Bruni only mentions these themes in passing, but they form the essence of a closely related literature of Florentine humanism that evolved in the course of the fifteenth century. Buonaccorso da Montemagno was perhaps the first to make these questions central in his *Oratio de vera nobilitate* of 1428. Later the same issues were taken up by Poggio Bracciolini in his *De nobilitate* of *c*.1440, by Platina

---

152. See Baron 1968b, pp. 251–2 for the discussion of *beneficentia* and *liberalitas* and pp. 252–3 for the discussion of *fides*.
153. *Ibid.*, p. 251: 'nam ut prudentiam pretermittam, que omnium iudicio huic uni civitati maxima conceditur'.
154. See *ibid.*, p. 253 on the need for 'magnitudo animorum periculorumque contemptio' ('courage and contempt of dangers') if foreign aggression is to be forestalled.
155. *Ibid.*, p. 258: 'nusquam tantus ordo rerum, nusquam tanta elegantia, nusquam tanta concinnitas'.

(Bartolomeo Sacchi) in his *De vera nobilitate* of *c*.1475 and by many other humanists of similar stamp.

These were not of course the first writers to argue that *virtus vera nobilitas est*. The proposition had been defended by some of the most celebrated Roman poets and moralists – notably Horace, Seneca and Juvenal – and had never been wholly lost to sight. Brunetto Latini revived it in his *Livres dou trésor* in the 1260s, declaring in his analysis of the virtues in book II that '*vertus* alone, as Horace says, is the only true nobility, there being nothing noble at all about those who follow a dishonourable life'.[156] A generation later, the same commitment was magnificently echoed by Dante (Latini's own pupil) in his *Convivio*, the argument of which culminates in the proclamation that 'wherever virtue is to be found, there too one finds nobility'.[157]

With the rise of scholasticism, however, these assumptions were directly challenged. Aristotle had argued in the *Politics* that, because public service requires leisure and the means to sustain it, the most effective and praiseworthy citizens will always be those who are rich as well as virtuous, and owe their wealth to inheritance rather than their own acquisitive skills. As a result, the contention that *vera nobilitas* must be a matter of lineage and wealth together with virtue came to be characteristic of scholastic legal and political thought. Giles of Rome, for example, simply invokes Aristotle's authority in expounding 'the widely accepted view that nobility consists in nothing other than ancient wealth'.[158] Likewise, Bartolus of Sassoferrato offers an extended critique of Dante's arguments in discussing the concept of nobility in his *Commentaria* on the Code.[159]

When the humanists insist, therefore, on the equation between *virtus* and *vera nobilitas*, they are again mounting a direct attack on the values of scholastic philosophy. This can be seen most clearly in Poggio's *De nobilitate*, undoubtedly the most distinguished of the many Florentine contributions to the debate. Poggio's book takes the form of a dialogue between Niccolò Niccoli and the elder Lorenzo de' Medici. Both of them wish to understand the qualities that enable a good citizen to act, as Lorenzo puts it, 'in defence of his country and in support of its communal life'.[160] Lorenzo expounds the orthodox scholastic case, explaining that 'Aristotle, whose genius surpasses that of every philosopher' has 'rightly observed that

---

156. Latini 1948, p. 296 (II.114): 'Mais de la droite nobilité dist Orasces qu' ele est vertus solement . . . Donques n'a en celui nule noblesce ki use vie deshonestes.'
157. Dante, *Convivio* IV.19.4: 'dovunque è vertude, quiv < ?i > è nobilitade'.
158. Giles of Rome 1607, p. 204 (I.4.5): 'nobilitas secundum communem acceptionem hominum nihil est aliud quam antiquatae divitiae'.
159. Bartolus 1588, VI, pp. 114–17 (*In II partem digesti novi commentaria*).

anyone who wishes to attain nobility must possess the virtues in company with wealth'.[161] But Niccolò refuses to be impressed. 'I am well aware', he retorts, 'that Aristotle is held to be the greatest of the philosophers', but the question is not what Aristotle says 'but what appears to be closest to the truth'.[162] If we want the truth, he sweeps on, we must instead turn to Seneca, Juvenal, 'our own Cicero' and above all to the Platonic sources of their thought. We shall then recognise that 'nobility is born of *virtus* alone'.[163] Whether we hope to attain glory for ourselves or for our community, as philosophers or as leaders of civic affairs, the indispensable quality we must cultivate is *virtus*, 'which alone confers nobility on those who possess it, making them worthy of dignity and praise'.[164]

The theory of princely government

Bruni's vision in the *Laudatio* – a vision of the cardinal virtues as the key to republican liberty, of liberty as the key to civic glory – exercised a profound influence over the development of Florentine political theory in the first half of the fifteenth century. Within a decade of the *Laudatio*'s appearance, Cino Rinuccini reiterated essentially the same arguments in his fiercely patriotic *Risponsiva*, addressed to Antonio Loschi.[165] During the 1420s the same scale of values can be found in the writings of Manetti and Acciaiuoli,[166] as well as in Bruni's own *Oratio* of 1428.[167] And in the course of the 1430s the same concern with the role of *virtù* in the maintenance of a *vivere libero* – now expressed in the vernacular – recurs in Alberti's *Della famiglia* and in the resoundingly Ciceronian pages of Matteo Palmieri's *Della vita civile*.[168]

As the century progressed, however, these preoccupations came to seem less and less relevant to the political realities of the *Regnum Italicum* as a whole. Except in Florence and Venice, the *signori* everywhere continued to extend and consolidate their hold, with the result that a majority of humanists came to view their role as political advisers in a rather different light. Increasingly they took their task to be that of furnishing the new princes of Renaissance Italy with manuals of advice on how best to maintain their distinctive forms of personal government.

161. *Ibid.*, pp. 74, 77: 'Aristoteles . . . cuius acumen ingenii omnibus philosophis antecellit . . . recte enim sensit Aristoteles qui virtutes suffultas divitiis voluit nobilitatem praebere.'

162. *Ibid.*, p. 74: 'fateor (Nicolaus inquit) istum principem appellari Philosophorum, sed tamen nulla me cuiusvis impediet autoritas, quin quod mihi simile vero videatur et loquar et sentiam.'

163. *Ibid.*, p. 79: 'nobilitatem ex sola nasci virtute'.

164. *Ibid.*, p. 80: 'eosque solos esse nobiles quibus virtutum officia laudem subministrarunt et dignitatem'. 165. See Witt 1970. 166. See Garin 1954, pp. 211–87.

167. See Skinner 1978, I, pp. 76–7, 79. 168. *Ibid.*, I, pp. 69–84.

Among the earliest recipients of such advice-books were the Visconti
dukes of Milan. Uberto Decembrio addressed his *De republica* to Duke
Filippo Maria in the 1420s,[169] while his son Pier Candido continued in
similar vein with his *De laudibus Mediolanensis urbis panegyricus* of *c*.1435, a
direct reply to Bruni's *Laudatio* and a vehement affirmation of the claim that
the rule of the Visconti is 'admired by other princes, venerated by the
nobility and adored by the people'.[170] Later in the century such advice-
books became legion, with many of the most celebrated humanists of the
age contributing to the debate. Platina, for example, dedicated his *De
principe viro* to the Duke of Mantua's heir in 1471,[171] while Francesco
Patrizi of Sienna addressed his *De regno* to Alfonso of Aragon later in the
1470s.[172] Finally, a group of humanists from the kingdom of Naples issued
similar treatises towards the end of the century, including Giuniano Maio,
Diomede Carafa, Antonio de Ferrariis and Giovanni Pontano, whose *De
principe* is at once a typical and an outstanding example of the genre.[173]

For the most part these mirror-for-princes manuals are simply an
outgrowth of the Ciceronian and Petrarchan traditions we have already
examined. It is true that some new elements are added, largely in
acknowledgement of the increasing stability and self-confidence of princely
forms of government. There is a growing awareness of the need to offer
counsel not merely to rulers but also to their advisers – 'to those who are
nowadays called courtiers', as Pontano remarks.[174] As early as the 1470s
Carafa produced a special advice-book addressed to these new and
important figures in the political landscape, the *Dello optimo cortesano*,[175]
and within a generation this new genre had given rise to a masterpiece,
Baldassare Castiglione's *Il libro del cortegiano*, drafted in the early years of the
new century and first published in 1528.[176]

We also find a much-expanded interest in the more ritualistic aspects of
princely government. Maio's treatise is actually entitled *De maiestate*, and
ends with a chapter on how a ruler should present himself as a suitable figure

169. See Baron 1966, pp. 425–7.
170. Decembrio 1925–58, p. 1013: 'te principes mirantur, nobiles verentur, populi concupiscunt'. For
     the date of composition see Zaccaria 1956, p. 21.
171. For the dedication see Platina 1608, pp. 11–16. On the relations between this treatise and Platina's
     De optimo cive see Rubinstein 1985.
172. For the dedication see F. Patrizi [of Sienna] 1594a, pp. 1–9.
173. Naples as a centre of humanist studies in the fifteenth century deserves more extensive study than it
     has received hitherto. For valuable introductory remarks see *The Renaissance* 1982, p. 174
     (Rubinstein) and on Antonio de Ferrariis, pp. 89–92 (Trinkaus); on Maio see Ricciardi 1968.
174. *Prosatori latini* 1952, p. 1052 (*De principe*): 'quique aulici hodie vocantur'.
175. For the date of composition (1479) see Carafa 1971, p. 64.
176. For the dates of composition and publication see Castiglione 1960, p. xxvii.

of grandeur and awe.[177] The same is true of Pontano's *De principe*, which includes a detailed discussion of the Ciceronian ideal of *decorum*, offering advice on how a prince should dress, speak and generally comport himself in order to proclaim the majesty of his office to the best effect.[178]

For the most part, however, these writers sketch a portrait of the ideal prince which scarcely differs from the one offered by Petrarch and his disciples. Such a ruler must aim, as Pontano puts it, 'to uphold peace among his subjects and a well-balanced government'.[179] He must also aspire to the highest goals of princely leadership, remembering that 'fame and majesty go perfectly together' and in consequence seeking 'to rise to greater glory every day'.[180] Nor do these writers differ from earlier humanists in describing the measures a ruler needs to adopt if he is to succeed in overcoming the malignity of fortune and thereby reach the heights of honour, glory and fame. The only sure method, they agree, is to cultivate *virtus*, the most splendid thing in the world, as Pontano proclaims, 'far more splendid even than the sun', for the blind cannot see the sun, 'whereas even they can recognise *virtus* as plainly as possible'.[181]

Finally, the account of *virtus* to be found in these writers is again a familiar one. The prince must cultivate various personal virtues, in particular those that cluster around the ideal of temperance and include such attributes as moderation, affability and continence.[182] But the most important element of *virtus*, the one that (as Pontano states at the outset) 'makes everyone accept a prince's rule with a glad heart when he possesses it', is justice.[183] This attribute Pontano treats in purely Ciceronian terms. Good princes must always administer something more than strict justice: they must recognise that 'there are two further qualities that ought above all to be cultivated by those who wish to rule, the first being liberality, the other, clemency'.[184] But the central obligation of justice is *fides*: they must keep faith with God, treating justice in that context as equivalent to piety or

---

177. See Maio 1956, esp. ch. 19, pp. 223–31. See also Platina 1608, pp. 68–74 (1.12) on the *maiestas* of the prince.   178. See *Prosatori latini* 1952, pp. 1046–8.

179. *Ibid.*, p. 1046: 'ad quietam populorum et regni moderationem'.

180. *Ibid.*, pp. 1060, 1062: 'cum fama maxime constet maiestas'; 'teque in dies magis ad gloriam excites'.

181. *Ibid.*, p. 1044: 'multo ergo splendidior est virtus [quam solem] . . . quam etiam caeci apertissime videant'.

182. E.g., *ibid.*, pp. 1028–32; Maio 1956, pp. 51–60 (ch. 4); pp. 143–62 (ch. 14) and pp. 163–74 (ch. 15); Platina 1608 (II.11 and II.13).

183. *Prosatori latini* 1952, p. 1024: 'iustitia enim in quo fuerit, eius imperium aequo omnes animo patiuntur'.

184. *Ibid.*, p. 1026: 'qui imperare cupiunt, duo sibi proponere in primis debent: unum, ut liberales sint; alterum, ut clementes.'

righteousness; and they must keep faith with their fellow-men, honouring their word as their bond even when dealing with their enemies.[185]

To summarise it all, Pontano remarks, we may say that the ideal prince must exercise 'justice, piety, liberality and clemency'. This will ensure him the love of his people; and by winning their love rather than making himself an object of fear he will also ensure his own glory and fame.[186] To put the moral the other way round – as Pontano also does – the goal of princely glory must be reached *virtute non vi*: by the *virtus* of the *vir*, the truly manly man, never by means of *vis* or sheer brute force. The ideal prince will be a prince of peace, and Pontano ends by assuring us that 'when he is beloved of all, he will not even need to maintain an army, since everyone will want him to live for ever'.[187]

During the second half of the fifteenth century, something akin to this literature began to burgeon even in the previously inhospitable atmosphere of Florence. With the rise of the Medici to positions of informal but decisive control over the affairs of the republic, a gradual retreat can be observed from the earlier and more stridently republican traditions of Florentine political thought.

This is not to say that the republicans went down without a fight. After Cosimo de' Medici's death in 1464, energetic debates in the *Pratiche* bore witness to the continuing efforts of leading citizens to re-establish a more broadly based form of regime.[188] And as late as 1479 – the year before Lorenzo de' Medici set up his ruling Council of Seventy drawn from the ranks of his own partisans – his increasingly 'tyrannical' policies were violently attacked by his erstwhile supporter Alamanno Rinuccini, whose *De libertate* contains an eloquent restatement of the traditional Florentine ideal of 'free' government.[189]

For the most part, however, the humanists were content to serve the times, and began to explore new lines of argument designed to fortify and celebrate Florence's increasingly oligarchic government. This change of outlook first found expression as a growing enthusiasm for markedly *stretto* as opposed to *largo* forms of republicanism. In particular, the humanists

---

185. *Ibid.*, p. 1026: 'multa consideranda sunt, et illud maxime, quo nihil turpius sit quam fidem non servare; cuius tanta vis est, ut etiam hosti, si data sit, servare tamen eam oporteat.'
186. *Ibid.*, p. 1024.
187. *Ibid.*, p. 1040: 'quem enim quisque amat, eum si fieri possit vivere perpetuo expetit, nullique minus exercitu opus est.'
188. See Pampaloni 1961 and the documents relating to the *Consulte e Pratiche* debates of 1465 published in Pampaloni 1962. For an earlier instance of such opposition see G. Cavalcanti 1973.
189. See Rinuccini's *De libertate* in *Humanism and Liberty* 1978, pp. 193–224 and cf. Varese 1961, pp. 133–48.

began to write in praise of Venice, commending its Dogeship and the aristocratic bias of its constitution, and thereby initiating a powerful movement in favour of reforming Florence's more populist arrangements along Venetian lines.

One of the earliest statements of this point of view can be found in Poggio Bracciolini's *In laudem reipublicae venetorum*. This appeared in 1459, the year after Cosimo de' Medici succeeded in establishing a new and more restricted ruling council in addition to the wider assemblies praised in Bruni's *Laudatio*. The standpoint Poggio adopts is that of an unashamed oligarch. Suppose, he begins, you wish to maintain a polity 'in which the very best men have charge of civic affairs, in which they are in turn controlled by the laws, and are dedicated above all to the promotion of the public interest, with all private concerns being treated as of secondary importance'.[190] In that case it is essential to establish an aristocratic form of government. 'And in my judgement', he adds, 'such a government has never been established in practice in the best possible manner except among the people of Venice.'[191] The key to Venice's achievement is that the city is ruled 'by many ancient and noble families, into whose hands the entire conduct of the government is placed'.[192] 'No role is assigned to the body of the people; the system is one in which all public offices are entrusted exclusively to persons of outstanding capacities within the ranks of the nobility.'[193] This means that 'no internal discord mars the administration of the city's government, no dissension, no quarrels among the citizens'.[194] As a result, they have duly reaped the reward of civic glory. 'Not only have they succeeded in conserving their republic, they have also expanded their power by land and sea, day by day, to the point where their fame and *virtus* have become celebrated throughout the whole world.'[195]

Such expressions of admiration for Venice soon became widespread. Poggio's arguments received strong endorsement, for example, from Francesco Patrizi's *De institutione reipublicae* in the 1460s,[196] as well as from his own son Gianfrancesco's later and very similar eulogy on Venice.[197]

---

190. Poggio Bracciolini 1964–9, II, p. 925: 'apud quos soli optimates civitatem regunt, obtemperantes legibus intentique omnes ad publici status utilitatem, omni rei privatae cura posthabita'.
191. *Ibid.*, II, p. 925: 'talem profecto nunquam nisi apud Venetos fuisse verissime affirmarim'.
192. *Ibid.*, II, p. 929: 'sunt enim familiae perantiquae ac nobiles permultae, in quibus rei publicae gubernatio continetur'.
193. *Ibid.*, II, p. 929: 'nulli plebeo aditus . . . solae nobilitati et ex ea viris praestantioribus publica demandantur officia'.
194. *Ibid.*, II, p. 928: 'nullae inter ipsos administranda re publica discordiae, nulla dissensio, nullae civium contentiones'.
195. *Ibid.*, II, p. 937: 'Veneti eorum rem publicam non conservarunt solum, sed in dies eorum imperium terra marique auxerunt, ut per universum orbem illorum fama virtusque celebretur'.
196. See F. Patrizi [of Sienna] 1594b, pp. 117–19 (III–2).
197. For the younger Poggio's eulogy of Venice, see F. Gilbert 1977, p. 493.

During the last quarter of the century, however, these developments were supplemented and even supplanted by an even more striking shift of political allegiances. After Lorenzo de' Medici's accession to power in 1469 a growing number of humanists responded by offering him their direct support. Turning their backs on the concept of the *vita activa civilis*, they reverted to the contention that monarchy must after all be accounted the best form of government, and that this consideration must be given its due weight even in Florence.

The intellectual resources from which the Florentines gained the confidence to repudiate their republican heritage were largely Platonic in character. One of the ways in which Platonism contributed to the undermining of republican values was by underlining the claim – also suggested in Aristotle's *Nicomachean Ethics* – that the highest and noblest way of life must be one of *otium* or contemplative leisure. Cristoforo Landino's *De vera nobilitate* constitutes one of the most revealing documents in this transformation of Florentine humanism. Composed in the 1480s and dedicated to Lorenzo de' Medici,[198] it is couched in the form of a dialogue between Aretophilus, the lover of virtue, and Philotimus, the admirer of the rich. At first they merely rehearse a familiar set of arguments about true nobility. Philotimus defends the position he describes as 'that of Aristotle, the prince of philosophers, who treats nobility as a matter of *virtus* in conjunction with ancient lineage and wealth'.[199] But Aretophilus retorts that 'the one and only source of true nobility lies in the possession of *virtus*', a quality he equates with the four cardinal virtues.[200] So far there is nothing in the discussion to which Bruni or Poggio could have taken exception. The tone suddenly alters, however, with the introduction of the topic of religious belief. Marsilio Ficino's writings are cited with reverence, and a note of genuine Platonism begins to be audible.[201] The noblest and most praiseworthy way of life, we are now assured, consists in rising above the mundane obligations of the *vita activa* by ascending to the heights of philosophy and finally the realms of beatitude. Both participants endorse this rejection of *negotium* in favour of the pure life of the mind, and Aretophilus summarises their almost mystical conclusion in tones of suitable intensity. 'This, this I say is the only true nobility: it consists solely in

198. Liaci in Landino 1970b, p. 17 shows that it must have been completed after 1485 but before 1487.
199. *Ibid.*, p. 47: 'princeps [philosophorum] Aristoteles in antiquitate generis et opibus virtute partis nobilitatem ponit'.
200. *Ibid.*, pp. 67–8: 'virtus enim . . . quae vera sit, verae nobilitatis sola atque unica datrix est.' *Prudentia* is then discussed at pp. 68–70, *fortitudo* at pp. 70–1, *temperantia* at pp. 71–3, and *iustitia* at pp. 73–4.
201. *Ibid.*, p. 77, Landino cites Ficino 'in suo illo divinissimo *De religione christiana* libro'.

this one excellence of the mind, a form of excellence which is not naturally produced by our own faculties, but is due to the infinite wisdom of God omnipotent himself.'[202]

Landino's treatise gave expression to an outlook shared by growing numbers of humanists in the closing decades of the fifteenth century. The same Platonist elements recur, for example, in Antonio de Ferrariis' *Epistola de nobilitate* in 1488, while in Giovanni Pico della Mirandola's famous *Oratio* of 1486 on the dignity of man we encounter a truly Platonist scorn for 'those whose whole life is dedicated to the pursuit of profit or ambition' in the public realm.[203] Pico's proudest boast is that 'I myself have given up all interest in private as well as public business in order to devote myself entirely to a life of contemplative *otium*', this being an indispensable condition of all the noblest human pursuits, above all the pursuit of truth.[204]

As well as furnishing a defence of the *vita contemplativa*, Plato's authority enabled Lorenzo's humanist supporters to mount a more direct attack on the participative ideals of Florentine republicanism. This they accomplished by invoking the concept of the philosopher-king, a doctrine Landino ingeniously connected with a further defence of *otium* against the demands of active citizenship in book I of his *Disputationes Camaldulenses* in the early 1470s. If the noblest way of life is one of contemplative retreat, as Landino again affirms, 'the best state of a commonwealth' must be one in which the citizens feel confident in placing their affairs in the hands of a wise guardian, thereby freeing themselves to pursue their own higher ends. It follows that monarchy must be the best form of government, a monarchy in which a prudent and philosophical ruler – such as Lorenzo himself – carries the burdens of the *vita activa* on behalf of everyone else.[205]

Finally, if we turn to the treatise *De legibus et iudiciis* composed in 1483 by Lorenzo's own chancellor Bartolomeo Scala, we meet with an even more fulsome defence of the despotism of the wise.[206] Scala's treatise takes the form of a debate between himself and Bernardo Machiavelli, the father of Florence's most celebrated writer on statecraft. Scala contends that the nature of government is such that, 'with so many different problems arising from day to day, it is highly desirable to be able to resolve them with a free

202. *Ibid.*, p. 101: 'haec, haec est, inquam, vera nobilitas, haec unica generositas eius animi, quem non natura ipsa de materiae facultate produxit, sed ipse omnipotens Deus, sapientissimus Deus.'
203. G. Pico 1942, p. 132: 'tota eorum vita sit vel in quaestu, vel in ambitione posita'.
204. *Ibid.*, p. 132: 'relicta omni privatarum et publicarum rerum cura, contemplandi ocio totum me tradiderim'.   205. *Prosatori latini* 1952, pp. 729–31.
206. A. Brown 1979, pp. 295–6, 311–14 valuably emphasises Scala's Platonism.

hand and wide-ranging powers'.[207] The best solution is therefore to recognise that 'it is far better to live under the guidance of a good man and a wise judge than under the kind of dictates that men impose upon themselves'.[208] He ends his speech by coupling his proposal with a dire warning. 'If you fail to put one person in charge of the full range of public affairs, there is nothing in the whole list of things that men have learnt to fear and avoid that you will not have to dread, expect and contemplate.'[209]

Bernardo counters with a traditional defence of the rule of law, a defence later echoed by his famous son in his *Discorsi* on Livy's history of Rome. 'We see all too frequently', Bernardo replies, 'that evil desires are characteristic of those who serve as leaders of men and have control of affairs in their hands.'[210] The only safe course is therefore to place our trust in a structure of laws rather than in the wisdom of a prince, 'this being the only rational way to live our lives'.[211] But Scala repudiates this conclusion outright, thereby turning his back on the most distinctive contribution of Florentine humanism to Renaissance political thought. Instead he holds out the image of the wise guardian, the *pater patriae*, as the perfect ruler of Florence, and offers the figure of Cosimo de' Medici as a complete realisation of this Platonic ideal within the recent history of Florentine public life.[212]

Machiavelli: Il principe *and its context*

By the time of Lorenzo de' Medici's death in 1492, an observer might well have concluded that Florentine republicanism, both in theory and practice, was also about to expire. Within two years, however, the French invasion of Italy changed everything: the Medici were forced into exile, and under the ascendancy of Savonarola the institutions of the republic were restored and augmented. The Medici regained power in 1512, but their position at that stage remained far from secure. In 1527 they were exiled once again, and it was not until the 1530s that they finally succeeded in converting the Republic of Florence into a Medicean principate. During the intervening

207. Scala 1940, p. 269: 'tot sunt que quotidie emergunt earum diversitates, in quibus merito solutiorem facultatem liberiusque iudicium desideres'.
208. *Ibid.*, p. 269: 'vivi potuit melius ad boni viri bonique iudicis arbitrium . . . quam eam sibi imposuisse homines necessitatem'.
209. *Ibid.*, p. 270: 'si ducem rerum omnium actionumque humanarum neglexeris . . . nihil est omnino eorum que timere et fugere merito homines consueverunt non formidandum, non expectandum, non ferendum.'
210. *Ibid.*, p. 277: 'quod tamen quia prevalente cupiditate fieri ab his frequentissime videmus, qui presunt hominibus, et habent rerum gubernacula in manibus.'
211. *Ibid.*, p. 277: 'id est unica recte vivendi ratione'.
212. See especially the invocation at the start of the dialogue of 'Cosimus Medices pater patriae noster sapientissimus civis' and the discussion at p. 273; cf. also A. Brown 1979, pp. 295–6.

period the debate between their supporters and their republican opponents gave rise to a further and extensive literature about the best means of governing Florence. It was one in which the age-old issues of liberty *versus* princely rule were yet again rehearsed, but on this occasion with an unexampled brilliance and depth.

When the Medici were first restored in 1512, a number of writers at once concluded that Florence would be well advised to accept a framework of princely government. One such writer was Paolo Vettori, who addressed some *Ricordi* on the subject to Cardinal de' Medici at the end of 1512.[213] Another was Lodovico Alamanni, whose *Discorso* of 1516 frankly acknowledged the desirability of stabilising the government of Florence under the Medici, and advised them on how to tighten their grip over the city's affairs.[214] But by far the most important observer to adopt this perspective was of course Machiavelli in *Il principe*, the draft of which he completed at the end of 1513.[215]

Machiavelli's masterpiece was thus conceived as a contribution to a familiar and well-worked genre: that of humanist advice-books for princes on the proper ends of government and how best to attain them. If we turn to Machiavelli's specific suggestions, moreover, we find that these too are at first sight almost equally familiar in character. The prince's basic aim, we learn in a phrase that echoes throughout *Il principe*, must be *mantenere lo stato*, to maintain his power and existing frame of government.[216] As well as keeping the peace, however, a true prince must at the same time seek 'to establish such a form of government as will bring honour to himself and benefit the whole body of his subjects'.[217] This explains why Machiavelli admires Ferdinand of Aragon above all other contemporary rulers: his actions have been so great that 'he has become, for fame and glory, the greatest king in all Christendom.'[218] By contrast, this is why he expresses contempt for Agathocles of Sicily, in spite of his astonishing achievements: his methods 'were such as to win him power but not glory', whereas a true prince will always put honour and glory above everything else.[219]

---

213. See Vettori's *Ricordi* in Albertini 1955, pp. 345–7.
214. See Alamanni's *Discorso*, *ibid.*, pp. 362–71.
215. For the date of composition see Machiavelli 1961, pp. 301, 304.
216. For the importance of a contented populace, see especially Machiavelli 1960, pp. 75–6 (ch. 19).
217. See *ibid.*, pp. 101–2 (ch. 26) on the need 'di introdurvi forma che facessi onore a lui e bene alla università delli uomini'.
218. *Ibid.*, p. 89 (ch. 21), Ferdinand's actions are described as 'tutte grandissime', such that 'è diventato per fama et per gloria el primo re de' Christiani'.
219. *Ibid.*, p. 42 (ch. 8), he says of Agathocles' methods that 'possono fare acquistare imperio, ma non gloria'. Cf. also p. 97 (ch. 24).

Turning to the means by which a prince can hope to reach these goals, Machiavelli again discloses his basically humanist allegiances. He places an overwhelming emphasis on the need for rulers to cultivate the quality of *virtù*. The possession of *virtù* is indispensable in the first place if you wish 'to maintain your state'. As chapter 6 declares, 'a new prince will always find it more or less easy to maintain himself in power, depending on whether he possesses the qualities of a *virtuoso* in a greater or lesser degree'.[220] Likewise, it is crucial to the achievement of princely glory. As the concluding exhortation to the Medici insists, it is only by being *prudente e virtuoso* that a new ruler can hope 'to act in such a way as to bring honour to himself' and thereby scale the heights of glory and fame.[221]

There are two points, however, at which Machiavelli startlingly diverges from the normal assumptions of advice-books for princes. As we have seen, the early humanists had often drawn a strong contrast between *virtus* and *vis*, between manly qualities and sheer brute force. By contrast, Machiavelli treats the willingness to exercise force as an absolutely central feature of good princely government.[222] It is entirely due to the neglect of this factor, he insists, that the Italian princes of his own day have found themselves overwhelmed.[223] He even adds, in a moment of dramatic exaggeration, that 'a prince should have no other thought or object, nor should he occupy himself with anything else, than war and its laws and discipline'.[224] His final exhortation repeats the same advice: 'Before all else', he tells the Medici, 'you must raise an army of your own, this being the one foundation for everything else you undertake.'[225]

The other point at which Machiavelli challenges the prevailing assumptions of humanism is in explaining what it means to say that *virtù* is indispensable to a ruler's attainment of his goals. He raises the question immediately after his three central chapters on military power, and opens with a warning that, although many others have discussed how a truly *virtuoso* prince ought to behave, his own analysis 'will depart very radically

220. *Ibid.*, p. 30 (ch. 6): 'un nuovo principe si truova a mantenerli più o meno difficultà, secondo che più o meno è virtuoso'. Cf. also the discussions on p. 34 (ch. 7) and pp. 97–8 (ch. 24).
221. See *ibid.*, p. 101 (ch. 26) on whether the condition of Italy 'dessi occasione a uno prudente e virtuoso di introdurvi forma che facessi onore a lui'.
222. This point is particularly well brought out in F. Gilbert 1965, especially p. 154.
223. See especially the discussion in Machiavelli 1960 (ch. 24) on 'Cur Italiae principes regnum amiserunt' ('Why the rulers of Italy have lost their principalities').
224. *Ibid.*, p. 62 (ch. 14): 'Debbe adunque uno principe non avere altro obietto né altro pensiero, né prendere cosa alcuna per sua arte, fuora della guerra et ordini e disciplina di essa.'
225. *Ibid.*, p. 104 (ch. 26): 'È necessario, innanzi a tutte l'altre cose, come vero fondamento di ogni impresa, provvedersi d'arme proprie.'

from the rules drawn up by those who have already examined these issues'.[226]

His first departure occurs when he mentions those princely virtues and vices which are purely private, as opposed to those which can help or hinder a ruler in discharging his public role. As we have seen, most earlier humanists had addressed themselves rather sternly to this topic, requiring of good princes a particularly high standard of personal morality, sobriety, continence, affability and so forth. For Machiavelli the only question is whether the vice in question 'is one of those that can undermine a prince's government'.[227] If it is not, but is merely a personal weakness of the flesh, a wise prince 'will guard himself against it if he can; but if he finds he cannot, he will continue to indulge it without giving it another thought'.[228]

Far more crucial, however, is Machiavelli's attack on the assumption that had lain at the heart of the whole tradition of advice-books: that the key to maintaining one's state and rising to the heights of princely glory lies in following as strictly as possible the dictates of justice. Machiavelli begins by recalling the standard humanist analysis of justice and its requirements. He considers in turn liberality (chapter 16), clemency (chapter 17), the associated need to be loved rather than feared (chapter 17) and finally the paramount need to keep faith and honour one's word (chapter 18). He acknowledges that 'it would be a most admirable thing if a ruler could display all these qualities'.[229] But he vehemently rejects the fundamental humanist belief that these are the qualities a ruler needs to cultivate if he wishes to attain his highest ends. On the contrary, 'because there is such a great distance between how people live and how they ought to live, anyone who gives up doing what people in general do in favour of doing what they ought to do will find that he ruins rather than preserves himself'.[230]

Machiavelli's main piece of advice to princes is to reconsider the traditional picture of just government in the light of this melancholy but inescapable fact. You will then recognise, he tells them, that you have good

226. *Ibid.*, p. 65 (ch. 15): 'partendomi, massime nel disputare questa materia, dalli ordini delli altri'. For the fullest recent analysis of the resulting theory of princely virtue see Diesner 1985.

227. Machiavelli 1960, p. 66 (ch. 15): 'quelle che li torrebbano lo stato'.

228. *Ibid.*, p. 66: 'guardarsi, si elli e possibile; ma, non possendo, vi si può con meno respetto lasciare andare'.

229. *Ibid.*, p. 65 (ch. 15): 'sarebbe laudabilissima cosa uno principe trovarsi di tutte le soprascritte qualità'.

230. *Ibid.*, p. 65: 'Perché elli è tanto discosto da come si vive a come si doverrebbe vivere, che colui che lascia quello che si fa per quello che si doverebbe fare, impara più tosta la ruina che la preservazione sua: perché uno uomo, che voglia fare in tutte le parte professione di buono, conviene rovini infra tanti che non sono buoni.'

reason to avoid the supposed virtue of liberality;[231] that 'you cannot escape being called cruel';[232] that 'it is much safer for a prince to be feared than loved';[233] and that 'we see from experience in our own times that those princes who have done great things have been those who have set little store by the keeping of faith'.[234] These qualities may indeed be vices; but they are 'the vices by which you are able to rule'.[235]

The truly *virtuoso* prince is characterised, therefore, neither by his willingness to follow the traditional requirements of just government at all times nor by his willingness to discount those requirements altogether.[236] He is characterised by an unerring sense of when to acknowledge the dictates of justice and when to ignore them. He is guided, in short, by necessity rather than justice. 'He never departs from the ways of good government as long as he is able to follow them, but he knows how to enter upon the paths of wrongdoing whenever this is dictated by necessity'.[237]

What is revolutionary about *Il principe* is thus that it offers, in effect, a new analysis of what should count as truly *virtuoso* behaviour. Machiavelli agrees that the term *virtù* denotes those qualities which enable a prince to overcome the vagaries of fortune and rise to honour, glory and fame. But he denies that the qualities in question can in turn be equated with the virtues. A prince of true *virtù* will rather be someone who, in the proverbial phrase, makes a virtue out of necessity; someone who is ready at all times 'to turn and turn about as the winds and the variations of fortune dictate'.[238]

Machiavelli: the Discorsi *and its context*

Although many Florentine political writers felt ready to endorse the rule of the Medici after 1512, the same period also witnessed the last and finest flowering of the city's earlier traditions of republican thought. Among those who continued to urge the republican cause, the overwhelming majority agreed that Florence ought now to settle for an aristocratic or *stretto* form of mixed constitution, the form that Poggio had earlier

231. *Ibid.*, p. 68 (ch. 16).
232. *Ibid.*, p. 69 (ch. 17): 'è impossibile fuggire el nome di crudele'.
233. *Ibid.*, p. 69: 'è molto piu sicuro essere temuto che amato'.
234. *Ibid.*, p. 72 (ch. 18): 'si vede per esperienza, ne nostri tempi, quelli principi avere fatto gran cose che della fede hanno tenuto poco conto'.
235. *Ibid.*, p. 67 (ch. 16): 'vizii che lo fanno regnare'.
236. Which is why Agathocles, who rose to power and sustained himself purely by crime ('per scelera') cannot be accounted a *virtuoso* prince. See *ibid.*, pp. 40–2 (ch. 8).
237. *Ibid.*, p. 74 (ch. 18): 'Non partirsi dal bene, potendo, ma sapere intrare nel male, necessitato.'
238. *Ibid.*, pp. 73–4 (ch. 18): '[E però bisogna che] elli abbi uno animo disposto a volgersi secondo ch' e' venti e le variazioni della fortuna li comandono.'

commended in his panegyric on Venice.[239] The continuation of this strand of thought – now deployed to question rather than support the government of the Medici – can be seen in many treatises of this period, including Antonio Brucioli's *Dialoghi* of 1526 and Pietro Vergerio's *De republica veneta* of the same year.[240] The culmination of this line of argument may be said to come with Donato Giannotti's *Della repubblica di veneziani*, published in 1540, in which the long-standing admiration of Florentine political theorists for Venice as an ideal republic is most fully expressed.[241]

Of all the Florentine theorists who continued to take Venice as their model, by far the most important was Francesco Guicciardini. His numerous political writings between 1512 and 1530 are united by a desire to see a restoration of the Florentine Republic, together with a reformation of its institutions along Venetian lines. The point is first made in his treatise *Del modo di ordinare il governo popolare* of 1512. There Guicciardini argues that the basic weakness of the *largo* constitution established in Florence after the removal of the Medici in 1494 arose from an exaggerated polarity between its monarchical and populist elements. His proposed solution is the introduction of a senate of some two hundred *ottimati*, an institution designed to restore the balance between the two extremes in the most approved Venetian style.[242] The same argument is later developed at greater length in his *Dialogo del reggimento di Firenze* of the early 1520s, in which the constitution of Venice is praised in even more fulsome terms. It is 'the best and most beautiful form of government that has ever been seen, not merely in our own times, but in any city of the ancient world, since the elements of every type of regime – that of the one, the few and the many – are all embodied within it'.[243]

Against this chorus of admiration, however, one powerful and dissentient voice was raised: the voice of Machiavelli in his *Discorsi* on the first ten books of Livy's history of Rome.[244] Turning sharply away from his

---

239. F. Gilbert 1977, pp. 234–6, 495 shows that, during the period of *largo* republican government established in Florence after 1494, the claim that Venice's more *stretto* system offered a superior model was kept alive by a group of disgruntled *ottimati* led by Bernardo Rucellai, whose *De bello italico* includes a eulogy of the Venetian constitution.

240. For a discussion of these and kindred works see *ibid.*, pp. 204–5.

241. For this treatise, drafted in 1526–7, see *ibid.*, pp. 204–11 and Skinner 1978, I, pp. 140–1, 155, 172.

242. See Guicciardini 1932, pp. 218–59 and the discussion in Pocock 1975, pp. 219–71.

243. Guicciardini 1932, pp. 138–9: 'è il più bello ed el migliore governo non solo de' tempi nostri, ma ancora che forse avessi mai a' tempi antichi alcuna città, perche participa di tutte le spezie de' governi, di uno, di pochi e di molti'.

244. See F. Gilbert 1977, p. 203 on the uniqueness of Machiavelli's hostility to Venice and cf. Pocock 1975, p. 186 for the claim that Machiavelli's *Discorsi* 'are best interpreted as a systematic dissent from the Venetian paradigm'.

impulsive endorsement of princely government, Machiavelli devoted the
years between 1515 and 1519[245] to developing a passionate, almost
nostalgic restatement of the political outlook originally associated with
Leonardo Bruni and his followers.[246]

The *Discorsi* are still concerned with the preservation of security and the
attainment of glory and greatness. But the ideal of *grandezza* which
Machiavelli now holds out is no longer a matter of great deeds performed
by individual princes; it is rather a matter of civic glory, a concern in
particular with 'the greatness the city of Rome achieved'.[247] When he
turns, moreover, to ask how this goal of greatness is to be reached, he again
reveals himself a true heir to Bruni and his disciples, as well as the Roman
moralists and historians on whom they had relied. The clearest evidence of
this inspiration occurs in the crucial passage at the start of book II where
Machiavelli considers the root cause of civic glory. His argument takes the
form of a citation (though without acknowledgement) of the famous
passage near the start of Sallust's *Bellum Catilinae* in which, as we have seen,
Rome's greatness had been explained as a fruit of her free way of life.
'Experience shows', as Machiavelli puts it in echoing the argument, 'that
cities have never been able to increase either in power or in wealth except
while they have been able to sustain themselves in a state of liberty'.[248] 'This
makes it easy to understand', he adds with studied understatement, 'how it
comes about that all peoples feel so much affection for living such a free way
of life.'[249]

Explaining what he means by predicating liberty of entire communities,
Machiavelli again discloses the closeness of his links with traditional
Florentine republicanism. As he makes plain in the opening chapters of
book I, he means that the body politic in question enjoys the capacity to act
in pursuit of its own chosen ends, its actions being 'under the control of its
own will' and in consequence directed to seeking the benefit of its members
as a whole.[250]

The next question to ask is obviously what type of regime is best suited to
realising these goals. Machiavelli admits that there is no reason in principle

245. For this dating of the *Discorsi* see Baron 1961.
246. This linkage is luminously suggested in Baron 1966, pp. 428–9.
247. See Machiavelli 1960, p. 280 (II.2) on the desire 'considerare a quanta grandezza venne Roma', and
cf. p. 125 (I.1) and p. 294 (II.6).
248. *Ibid.*, p. 280 (II.2): 'Si vede per esperienza le cittadi non avere mai ampliato né di dominio né di
ricchezza se non mentre sono state in libertà.'
249. *Ibid.*, 'E facil cosa è conoscere donde nasca ne popoli questa affezione del vivere libero.'
250. See especially *ibid.*, p. 129 (I.2) for the distinction between cities living 'in servitù' and those
'governate per loro arbitrio'.

why a good prince should not frame his laws in such a way as to reflect the general will (and so promote the common good) of the body politic as a whole.[251] But 'most of the time, the things that benefit a prince harm his city, while the things that benefit the city harm the prince'.[252] It follows that, to ensure liberty and promote greatness, the wisest course will always be to maintain a republican form of government. 'What brings greatness to cities is not individual benefits but the pursuit of the common good, and there can be no doubt that it is only in republics that this ideal of the common good is properly recognised.'[253]

As we have seen, however, the history of Florentine republicanism had been marked by a deep division of opinion at this point. Bruni's view and that of his followers had been that the ruling councils of such a republic should include both the *grandi* and the *popolo*. But the view prevailing among Machiavelli's contemporaries was that, in order to combine liberty with civic peace, the leading share in government should be confined to the most prominent citizens. Here too Machiavelli reverts to the more traditional standpoint. He cites the fashionable belief that the act of placing any authority 'in the disorderly hands of the common people will always be a cause of infinite dissensions and scandals in a republic'.[254] He describes the *stretto* Venetian system, and mentions the widespread opinion that 'it is because of placing the government in the hands of the nobility' that the ideal of liberty 'has been given a longer life in Venice than it enjoyed in Rome'.[255] Alone among his contemporaries, however, he is adamant in claiming that the Roman system is nevertheless to be preferred in any city aiming at glory and greatness. 'It is always reasonable to expect', he declares, 'that when the common people are set up as guardians of their own liberty, they will take better care of it' than will the nobility.[256]

But what of the long-standing objection that such a *largo* form of republicanism will prove incapable of combining freedom with civic harmony? As we have seen, the earliest defenders of such regimes had sought to deny that they were any less well-ordered than princely

251. See *ibid.*, p. 154 (1.9) for the claim that Romulus' *ordini* had this effect.
252. *Ibid.*, p. 280 (II.2): 'Il più delle volte quello che fa per lui [il principe] offende la città, e quello che fa per la città offende lui.' Cf. also p. 264 (1.58).
253. *Ibid.*, p. 280 (II.2): 'Non il bene particulare ma il bene comune è quello che fa grandi le città. E sanza dubbio questo bene comune non e osservato se non nelle republiche.'
254. *Ibid.*, p. 139 (1.5): 'una qualità di autorità dagli animi inquieti della plebe, che è cagione d'infinite dissensioni e scandoli in una republica'.
255. *Ibid.*, p. 139: '[appresso de' Viniziani], la è stata messa nelle mani de' Nobili', giving 'la libertà di . . . Vinegia più lunga vita che quelle di Roma'.
256. *Ibid.*, p. 139: 'i popolari preposti a guardia d'una libertà, e ragionevole ne abbiano più cura'.

governments – a contention so far from the truth that they soon came to be widely discredited. By contrast, Machiavelli meets the objection with a quite different argument that astonished his contemporaries.[257] He admits that 'if you produce a numerous and well-armed populace in the name of attaining greatness of power, you are sure to find them unmanageable'.[258] But he maintains that, unless you produce such a populace, you have no hope of attaining civic greatness at all.[259] The solution is to accept that a broadly-based republic will lack for serenity, while recognising that this is something to be endured rather than reformed. Rome's domestic unrest was certainly an inconvenience; but 'it was an inconvenience indispensable to the attainment of Roman greatness'.[260]

Finally, Machiavelli once again reveals the closeness of his dependence on classical-republican ideas when he turns to consider how this type of polity is itself to be sustained. What is required is that the citizen-body should possess the quality of *virtù* in a high degree, a quality that Machiavelli takes to embody three leading elements. The citizens must be prudent in all matters of war and peace, knowing how to judge the best courses of action and follow them out.[261] They must be courageous in defence of their liberty, the attribute needed to fight off 'external servitude'.[262] And they must remain 'well-ordered' in civic affairs, ensuring that the business of government is conducted *ordinariamente*, in an orderly and well-tempered style.[263]

For all the closeness of these links, however, between the *Discorsi* and earlier traditions of Florentine republicanism, there can be no doubt that one of Machiavelli's principal aims is to question and subvert these inherited patterns of thought. The first moment at which this becomes evident is – as in *Il principe* – when he considers what should count as truly *virtuoso* behaviour. As we have just observed, he agrees that the term *virtù* names those attributes which enable a citizen to help uphold the liberty and greatness of his native community. He also agrees that the required attributes overlap to a considerable degree with the traditional list of the cardinal virtues, including as they do the need for prudence, courage and

257. For a good example of their reaction see Guicciardini 1965, p. 68.
258. Machiavelli 1960, p. 144 (I.6): 'Pertanto se tu vuoi fare uno populo numeroso ed armato, per poter fare un grande imperio, lo fai di qualità che tu non lo puoi dopo maneggiare a tuo modo.'
259. *Ibid.*, pp. 141–6 (I.6).
260. *Ibid.*, p. 146 (I.6): 'uno inconveniente necessario a pervenire alla romana grandezza'.
261. For the indispensability of prudence in government see *ibid.*, pp. 241–4 (I.49); in warfare see p. 302 (II.10); p. 314 (II.14); p. 362 (II.27).
262. On courage as an attribute of great military commanders see *ibid.*, p. 458 (III.25); on the need for courage in each individual soldier see p. 484 (III.36) and p. 487 (III.37).
263. See esp. *ibid.*, pp. 146–9 (I.7); p. 188 (I.23); p. 191 (I.24); pp. 241–4 (I.49).

temperance. As in *Il principe*, however, he flatly repudiates the further assumption that the most important aspect of civic *virtù* is justice, the virtue that consists in avoiding both cruelty and the ignominy that attends the breaking of faith. On the contrary

the point that deserves to be noted and carried into practice by any citizen who finds himself advising his community is this: whenever what is at issue is the basic security of the community, no consideration should be given to questions of justice or injustice, clemency or cruelty, praiseworthiness or ignominy; rather, setting every other feature of the situation aside, you must be prepared to follow whatever course of action will in fact save the life and preserve the liberty of the community as a whole.[264]

Once again, the touchstone is necessity: it will always prove necessary to be courageous, temperate and prudent; but it will sometimes prove necessary to be unjust.

The other point at which Machiavelli differs profoundly from earlier republican theorists is in considering how the elements of *virtù* are to be enshrined in civic life. Bruni and his followers had tended to be optimistic, even complacent, at this point in the argument. Bruni thought it obvious that the Florentines were by nature prudent, and could be relied upon to display courage in defence of their liberty and a sense of orderliness in the conduct of their affairs. Machiavelli by contrast is deeply pessimistic about human nature. He thinks 'all men are evil, and will always act out the wickedness in their hearts whenever they are given free scope'.[265] He also believes that Christianity has made things worse by encouraging people to behave selfishly, instructing them to concentrate on their own glory hereafter instead of their city's glory here and now, 'an attitude which has weakened the world and left it a prey to wicked men'.[266] To this problem he sees only one solution: if evil and self-interested citizens are to act with *virtù* and serve the common good, they will have to be forced to do so by the coercive powers of the law. 'So we may say that, just as hunger and poverty make men industrious, it is the laws that make them good.'[267]

---

264. *Ibid.*, p. 495 (III.41): 'La quale cosa merita di essere notata ed osservata da qualunque cittadino si truova a consigliare la patria sua: perché dove si delibera al tutto della salute della patria, non vi debbe cadere alcuna considerazione né di giusto né d'ingiusto, né di piatoso né di crudele, né di laudabile né d'ignominioso; anzi, posposto ogni altro rispetto, seguire al tutto quel partito che le salvi la vita e mantenghile la libertà.'
265. According to Machiavelli, *ibid.*, p. 135 (I.3), a lawgiver must 'presupporre tutti gli uomini rei, e che li abbiano sempre a usare la malignità dello animo loro qualunque volta ne abbiano libera occasione'.
266. *Ibid.*, p. 282 (II.2): 'Questo modo di vivere adunque pare che abbi renduto il mondo debole, e datolo un preda agli uomini scelerati.'
267. *Ibid.*, p. 128 (I.1): 'Però si dice che la fama e la povertà fa gli uomini industriosi, e le leggi gli fanno buoni.'

For Machiavelli, accordingly, there remains a further and central question of statecraft, a question to which much of book I is addressed: by means of what specific *leggi e ordini* can we hope to offset our natural corruption and enforce the rule of *virtù* in public life?

First Machiavelli considers the nature of the constitutional laws required to ensure an orderly and well-tempered government. The solution he proposes looks at first glance familiar enough: he places all his faith in a mixed constitution with a bicameral legislature. Because of his pessimistic view of human nature, however, he is led to present this argument in a revolutionary way. His is not the Aristotelian ideal of combining the different social elements together in such a way as to produce the most harmonious mixture. On the contrary, he assumes that 'in every polity there are two opposed outlooks, that of the people and that of the nobility', and that each group will at all times seek to promote its own advantage unless restrained.[268] The course of wisdom is accordingly to take account of these ineradicable hatreds and devise a constitution which turns them to public benefit. This is what the Romans succeeded in doing when they gave the nobles control of the senate while assigning the tribunate to the plebs. Each faction was able to keep watch over the other and prevent it from legislating purely in its own interests. The result was that 'all the laws made in favour of liberty resulted from the discord between them'.[269] Because of the force of law, a community of unsurpassed *virtù* was forged out of a tense equilibrium set up between two basically corrupt groups; and this in turn had the effect of preserving a system of liberty which, in the absence of such *ordini*, the rivals factions would have undermined.

Finally, Machiavelli tackles the even harder question of how to persuade naturally self-interested citizens to act with courage in defence of their communal liberty even at the risk of their lives. The best way to conjure up this further element of *virtù*, he suggests, is to manipulate the *ordini* relating to religion, and above all to insist – as the Romans always did – on the absolute sanctity of oaths. Among the many illustrations Machiavelli offers of how this policy worked, he cites the behaviour of the Roman people after their defeat by Hannibal at Cannae. 'Many citizens gathered together who, despairing of their native land, agreed to abandon Italy and go to Sicily. Hearing of this, Scipio went to find them and, with a drawn sword in his hand, forced them to swear an oath not to abandon their native land'.[270]

---

268. *Ibid.*, p. 137 (I.4): 'sono in ogni republica due umori diversi, quello del popolo e quello de' grandi'.
269. *Ibid.*, p. 137 (I.4): 'tutte le leggi che si fanno in favore della libertà nascono dalla disunione loro'.
270. *Ibid.*, p. 160 (I.11): 'molti cittadini si erano adunati insieme, e sbigottiti della patria si erano convenuti abbandonare la Italia e girsene in Sicilia; il che sentendo Scipione gli andò a trovare, e col ferro ignudo in mano li constrinse a giurare di non abbandonare la patria'.

Taking the oath did not of course remove the people's terror; but it made them more frightened of evading their duties than performing them, since it made them fear above all to break their promise to the gods. The result was that, being forced to act with a courage they could never have commanded of themselves, they stood their ground, eventually defeated Hannibal and thereby secured, by their enforced *virtù*, the liberty they had been ready to give up.

The twilight of humanism

For all its great theoretical distinction, the last phase of Florentine republicanism had no practical effects. After 1530 the Medici went on their travels no more, and by 1569 the Florentine Republic had mutated into the Grand Duchy of Tuscany. This is not to say, however, that the celebration of mixed constitutions came to an end. Venice survived as a republic, and managed to keep alive the theory of republican liberty even in the age of the Counter-Reformation and beyond.[271] Among the many writers who, in the wake of Gasparo Contarini's classic analysis, continued to expatiate on the glories of the *Serenissima*, the most important was Paolo Paruta in his *Discorsi politici* of 1599. Paruta discusses the republic of ancient Rome in the first of his two discourses, that of modern Venice in the second. He traces the process by which the Romans lost their freedom with the coming of the empire, a decline he contrasts in the opening chapter of his second book with the unparalleled success of his own native city in combining greatness with liberty. As with all his predecessors, he finds the key to this achievement 'in the Venetian constitution, all the parts of which are so well disposed' that the common good is invariably served.[272]

By the time Paruta was writing, however, the preoccupations of Italian political theory had largely shifted to accommodate the rise of absolutism, with the result that the printing presses were virtually monopolised by the contrasting genre of advice-books for princes. For the most part these latter-day contributions to an already vast literature content themselves with examining the same range of issues that earlier writers had debated in the heyday of humanism. In some respects, however, they are very much the products of their own age. They make a determined effort to come to terms with Machiavelli's arguments, in strong contrast with the howls of execration that initially greeted the publication of his works in Northern Europe. Guicciardini at once picks up the suggestion that there may be

271. For this theme see Bouwsma 1968.
272. Paruta 1852, II, p. 228: 'in Venezia, la forma e l'ordine del governo civile è in ogni parte ben disposto'.

reasons for political action which form no part of ordinary moral reasoning, and appears to be one of the earliest theorists to speak explicitly of 'reasons of state'.[273] By the end of the century, we find the same phrase being used as the title of dozens of political treatises in which a Machiavellian conception of prudence is elevated to the highest place among the political virtues, the most important being Giovanni Botero's *Ragione di stato* of 1589.[274]

The other distinctive development of the same period is a melancholy one, and serves to mark the end of the active contribution of Italian humanism to the political literature of the Renaissance. It takes the form of an increasing, eventually overwhelming, pessimism about the capacity of even the highest *virtù* to overcome the malignity of fortune. The doubt already surfaces in Machiavelli's *Discorsi*;[275] it is voiced far more strongly in Guicciardini's *Ricordi*;[276] it is used to cast doubt on the possibility of effective citizenship in the writings of such mid-century sceptics as Nicolò Franco and Francesco Doni;[277] and by the time we come to a work like Traiano Boccalini's *Ragguagli di parnaso* in 1613, we encounter a tone of blank despair. The entire age stands condemned as one in which *virtù* can scarcely be recognised, and even when recognised can no longer be pursued.[278]

POLITICAL THOUGHT IN NORTHERN EUROPE

Towards the end of the fifteenth century, the political ideas of the Italian Renaissance at first began to attract the attention and soon to command the allegiance of large numbers of intellectuals throughout Northern Europe.[279] This was of course only one of the many important developments in the history of political theory in Northern Europe during this period. Soon afterwards the Reformation brought with it a new era in political as well as theological debate, in the course of which a number of values central to Renaissance culture were challenged and to some degree superseded. The following discussion, however, will be concerned exclusively with the positive impact of Renaissance culture on Northern Europe,

273. For this claim see R. Maffei 1964, esp. pp. 712–20 and cf. Church 1972, p. 46.
274. For Botero and this literature in general, see Meinecke 1957, pp. 65, 116 and the references in Skinner 1978, I, p. 248 and note.
275. See especially Machiavelli 1960, pp. 322–8 (II.17), the famous chapter on artillery.
276. See Guicciardini 1945, especially p. 15 (no. 30) and p. 61 (no. 189). On the even deeper pessimism of Guicciardini's later *Storia d'Italia* see F. Gilbert 1965, pp. 288, 299.
277. See P. F. Grendler 1969a, especially pp. 75–96.
278. See Boccalini 1948, especially I, pp. 326–8 (LXXXIX) on Machiavelli as a cause of the prevailing corruption of the age. 279. Also, to some degree, in Eastern Europe. See Wyrwa 1978.

and thus with the political theories associated with the so-called Northern Renaissance, a movement of ideas in which the humanism we have so far examined was blended together with a number of indigenous strands of moral and political thought.

The humanist view of princely government

Of the various branches of humanist political literature that came to be studied in Northern Europe in the course of the sixteenth century, by far the most popular proved to be the category of advice-books for princes. Many of the most famous northern humanists of the first half of the century contributed to this well-worked genre. Budé and Clichtove in France, Sturm and Wimpfeling in Germany, Guevara and Osorio in Spain (as well as Ribadeneyra and Mariana later in the century) all published manuals for princes in the time-honoured humanist mould, as did the most celebrated of all the northern humanists, Desiderius Erasmus, whose *Institutio principis Christiani* appeared in 1516.

Distinguished though these writers were, their efforts in this genre were mainly derivative in character, being shaped in large part by the classical authorities and Italian models we have already discussed. They all repeat that, as Budé puts it in *De l'institution du prince*, the aim of a good ruler should be to win 'honour during his lifetime together with good and honourable fame after his death'.[280] They all agree that the key to achieving these goals is (again in Budé's words) to possess 'infinite goodness and marvellous humanity, together with other royal virtues worthy of a king's majesty'.[281] Finally, they all add – more firmly even than their sources – that the only means of acquiring these virtues is to follow the right course of education. So strongly do they emphasise this point that many of their treatises – including those of Sturm, Osorio, Budé and Erasmus – are organised as pedagogic handbooks, specifying the rules and even the details of the curriculum to be drawn up if a young prince is to be placed on the pathway of virtue and in consequence led to glory and fame.

Some of these treatises, however, have more to offer than a mere reiteration of humanist commonplaces. One feature that distinguishes many of them is a new tone of overwhelming hostility to the use of force as an instrument of policy. No longer do they glide urbanely past the problem as we saw both Petrarch and Pontano doing in their manuals for princes.

---

280. Budé 1547, p. 33: 'l'honneur en la vie, et bonne et honorable renommée après la mort'.
281. *Ibid.*, p. 108: 'd'infinie bonté et merveilleuse humanité accompaignée d'aultres vertuz Royales dignes de sa Maiesté'.

Instead they revert to the authentically Stoic doctrine that, if all men are brothers, all warfare must be fratricide.[282] This is partly to be explained – as Erasmus makes plain in his *Querela pacis* – by their desire to undermine the glorification of warfare characteristic of the chivalric code, the values of which were undergoing a nostalgic but destructive revival in Northern Europe at this time.[283] But their attitude also reflects a strong hostility to scholasticism, especially to the Thomist doctrine of the Just War. No war can be just, John Colet boldly replies in his exposition of Romans, for to think otherwise would be to suppose that evil can be crushed with evil, whereas St Paul teaches us that 'there is nothing that conquers evil but good'.[284] Christians often claim, Erasmus adds in the *Querela*, that fighting is inevitable, 'and that war can even be a sacred affair'.[285] 'But if you look into your heart, you will find that it is not necessity that has driven you to fight, but anger, ambition and sheer stupidity'.[286] At this point, as with Colet, Erasmus' contention that 'there is scarcely any peace so unjust that it is not preferable even to the justest war' shades over into a virtually pacifist stance.[287]

Further innovations in the mirror-for-princes literature arose out of the need to come to terms with Machiavelli's arguments. At first the response was one of pure horror, and many treatises were devoted to condemning Machiavelli's theory of princely *virtù* outright. The earliest was Reginald Pole's *Apologia*, addressed to the emperor Charles V in 1539;[288] the most detailed and vituperative were Innocent Gentillet's *Anti-Machiavel* of 1576[289] and Pedro de Ribadeneyra's *Tratado* of 1595, attacking 'the teachings of Machiavelli and the other *politiques* of the present time'.[290] Among Catholic theorists, the same note of unqualified denunciation continued to resound even in the seventeenth century, as the writings of Campanella[291] and Suárez[292] amply attest.

By this time, however, a weary acknowledgement that effective

282. For this theme see Adams 1962, pp. 8, 91–108.
283. See A. B. Ferguson 1960.
284. Colet 1873, p. 194: 'nam nihil est quod vincit malum nisi bonum'.
285. Erasmus 1962, p. 30: 'sanctum etiam bellum est'.
286. *Ibid.*, p. 31: 'tuum ipsius pectus consule, reperies iram, ambitionem, stultitiam huc pertraxisse, non necessitatem'.
287. *Ibid.*, p. 32: 'vix ulla tam iniqua pax, quin bello vel aequissimo sit potior'. Cf. Fernandez-Santamaria 1977, pp. 130–44.
288. For this treatise and its many successors, see Raab 1964, pp. 30–51.
289. See Skinner 1978, I, pp. 250–1, II, pp. 308–9.
290. See the title page of Ribadeneyra 1595, announcing that the work is directed 'contra lo que N. Machiavelo y los politicos deste tiempo enseñan'.
291. See Campanella 1638, p. 349 (v.2.4) on Machiavellian political theory as 'the worst possible'. ('Macchiauelistica politica pessima est'.)   292. Suárez 1971–7, v, p. 161 (III.12.2).

government might have to depend after all on accepting 'reasons of state' was beginning to be widely expressed. As the political fabric of France and then the Netherlands collapsed under the impact of the religious wars, it came to seem less obvious that the maintenance of justice should always be given precedence over preserving the polity itself. Montaigne memorably voices the doubt in his essay *De l'utile et de l'honneste*, in which he explicitly allows for what he calls 'excusable vice' in the conduct of government.[293] Writing at the height of the revolt of the Netherlands in 1589, Justus Lipsius offered an even more forthright statement of the same commitment in his *Politicorum libri sex*. He observes that most moralists 'only approve of the path that leads from virtue to good repute', but complains that 'they seem not to understand this present age or the men who live in it'.[294] They 'vent their rage far too easily on Machiavelli',[295] not recognising that any prince who wishes to survive 'will be skilled in combining what is useful with what is honourable'.[296] Lipsius ends by aligning himself explicitly with Machiavellian reason of state: 'When a prince has to deal with a fox, he will certainly be justified in learning to play the fox himself'.[297]

The theory of the mixed constitution

Although the northern humanists chiefly drew on the literature of advice-books for princes, the contrasting tradition of Italian republicanism also exercised a deep influence in Northern Europe in the sixteenth and seventeenth centuries. The most obvious sign of its impact was that the ideal of the mixed constitution became a crucial topic of debate, especially among political writers in England, the Netherlands and France.

Gasparo Contarini's classic analysis of the Venetian constitution was published at Leiden in 1628,[298] and in the course of the seventeenth century an indigenous tradition of classical republicanism arose in the Netherlands. One of its earliest proponents was Hugo Grotius,[299] some of whose arguments were later echoed by the De la Court brothers and still later by Spinoza.[300] A similar line of development can be traced in English political

293. See Montaigne 1946–8, III, p. 9 (III.1) on how 'les vices . . . deviennent excusables'. Cf. the discussion in Shklar 1984, pp. 10–17, 23–35.
294. Lipsius 1589, p. 201 (IV.13): 'unum illud ad laudem cum virtute directum iter probatur . . . aevum et homines ignorare mihi videntur'.
295. *Ibid.*, p. 205 (IV.13): 'in Machiavellum nimium quidam saeviunt'.
296. *Ibid.*, p. 202 (IV.13): 'eruditum utilia honestis miscere'.
297. *Ibid.*, p. 202 (IV.13): 'cum vulpe iunctum, pariter vulpinarier'.
298. See Haitsma Mulier 1980, p. 218.
299. On Grotius' constitutionalism see C. Edwards 1981.
300. For this theme see Haitsma Mulier 1980, pp. 120–208.

thought. Contarini's treatise was translated in 1599, but long before that a number of Tudor humanists had tried to effect a compromise between the theory of the mixed constitution and the facts of English political life. These had included Thomas Starkey in his *Dialogue* of *c.*1535, which boldly proposed that the English monarchy should become an elective Dogeship;[301] John Ponet in his *Short Treatise of Politike Power* of 1556, which used the theory of the mixed constitution to attack the 'tyranny' of Mary Tudor;[302] and Sir Thomas Smith in his description of the English constitution at the outset of Elizabeth's reign, first published in 1583 under the deliberately ambiguous title *De republica Anglorum*.[303] During the seventeenth century, this tradition also flowered into a native version of classical republicanism, with Machiavelli's *Discorsi* serving as an obvious source of inspiration and James Harrington's *Oceana* of 1656 constituting the most original restatement of the case.[304]

It was in France, however, that the most important debates about the mixed constitution took place. This was partly on account of the early impact of Calvin's *Institutio religionis Christianae*, first published in 1536 and dedicated to Francis I. Calvin's concluding chapter on civil government included a cautious but immensely influential statement of a theory of mixed monarchy, in which he envisaged that 'magistrates of the people appointed to moderate the licence of kings' might be said 'to have a duty to intervene against the ferocious licence of such kings' in the name of the people's liberty.[305] This version of the mixed constitution was taken up above all by the Huguenots after the St Bartholomew's Day Massacre in 1572, and underpins the theory of resistance to tyranny to be found both in Hotman's *Francogallia* of 1573 and the anonymous *Vindiciae contra tyrannos* of 1579.[306]

As soon as the Huguenots renounced their allegiance, however, Jean Bodin came forward in his *Six livres de la république* of 1576 to attack both the theory of the mixed constitution and the revolutionary implications of the suggestion that the powers of the people might legitimately be used to challenge or even to balance the powers of kings.[307] As the title of Bodin's

---

301. Starkey 1948, pp. 104–5. See also pp. 163–4 for an admiring account of 'the most noble city of Venice'. For a discussion of this element in Starkey's thought see Mayer 1985.
302. Ponet 1556, sig. Aᵛʳ–Biiʳ. 303. T. Smith 1982, especially p. 52.
304. See Harrington 1977, especially pp. 161–2 on Machiavelli as 'the only politician of later ages'. For the movement in general see Fink 1962 and Pocock 1975, pp. 361–422.
305. Calvin 1559, p. 561 (IV.20.31): 'populares magistratus ad moderandam Regum libidinem constituti . . . adeo illos ferocienti Regum licentiae pro officio intercedere'.
306. For this movement see Skinner 1978, II, pp. 189–348.
307. For the claim that Bodin's primary concern is to vindicate this absolutist stance, see Franklin 1973 and *Jean Bodin* 1973, pp. 359–78 (Salmon).

great work indicates, his concern is still with the humanist ideal of a *res publica*, a body politic whose actions can claim to reflect the will and promote the good of its members as a whole. But he vehemently rejects the belief that the best means of realising this ideal is to institute a mixed constitution. He explicitly denounces both the Venetians and the Florentines – symbolised by Contarini and Machiavelli respectively – for the absurdity of believing in any such system of divided *imperium*.[308] His own view is that a just and harmonious polity can only be sustained if all powers under the law of nature are assigned to a single ruler who may be said to possess 'sovereignty', a concept Bodin believed himself to have defined clearly for the first time.[309]

Sovereignty need not be embodied in a single person, although Bodin eventually announces a strong preference for hereditary monarchy.[310] But it must never be mixed or divided, for a sovereign must be able to wield 'an absolute and perpetual power over his subjects'.[311] This means that he must be above the laws, capable of enforcing his own edicts even without his subjects' consent, and incapable of being lawfully resisted by any one of his subjects or all of them together.[312]

Of even greater influence than these debates about the mixed constitution was the associated strand of Italian humanism that had taken the concept of *vera nobilitas* as its theme. In France Josse Clichtove discussed this issue in his *De vera nobilitate* of 1512; in Spain, Jeronimo Osorio published a very similar tract entitled *De nobilitate civili et christiana* in 1552; and in England the topic came to prominence even earlier, partly in consequence of the Christian humanist ambition to civilise the feuding magnates who had almost destroyed the body politic in the Wars of the Roses. John Tiptoft, Earl of Worcester, translated Buonaccorso's *Oratio* on true nobility as early as the 1450s,[313] and a similar view of what constitutes *vera nobilitas* recurs in John Heywood's *Gentleness and Nobility* in the 1520s, Sir Thomas Elyot's *Boke Named the Governour* in 1531 and Thomas Starkey's *Dialogue* of *c.*1535, as well as furnishing a central theme of that greatest and strangest work of Tudor humanism, Sir Thomas More's *Utopia* of 1516.[314]

These writers all reiterate the definition of true nobility which we have already encountered in Poggio, Landino and others. They all agree that the

308. Bodin 1583a, p. 253 (II.1).   309. *Ibid.*, pp. 122–61, especially p. 122 (I.8).
310. *Ibid.*, pp. 937–73, especially 961–73 (VI.4).
311. *Ibid.*, p. 122 (I.8): 'La sovveraineté est la puissance absolue & perpetuelle d'une République.'
312. *Ibid.*, pp. 131–5 and pp. 141–4 (I.8); p. 302 (II.5).
313. See Tiptoft's *A Declamation of Nobleness* in Mitchell 1938, pp. 213–41.
314. For More's *Utopia* as a work of essentially Christian humanist allegiances see Hexter 1973, pp. 55–82, and for developments of this theme see Skinner 1978, I, pp. 217–18, 222–4, 255–62 and Logan 1983. But for a very valuable corrective see Bradshaw 1981.

attainment of the highest goal or *optimus status* of a commonwealth depends
on its citizens behaving with the greatest possible degree of *virtus*; they all
conclude that the possession of *virtus* must in consequence be treated as the
sole badge of true nobility. This is Clichtove's view in *De vera nobilitate*,[315]
Starkey's in the *Dialogue*,[316] Elyot's in the *Governour*;[317] most strikingly of
all, it is also the view that underlies the whole argument of More's *Utopia*.

Sir Thomas More: Utopia and its context

The island of Utopia, More informs us in his title, has in fact attained the
optimus status reipublicae. The community lives at peace with its neighbours,
in contrast with the warlike postures adopted by the purportedly Christian
nations of Europe.[318] It also lives in a state of perfect liberty, free from the
threat of internal tyranny as well as external conquest, in consequence of
being governed in the interests of all its citizens and not (as with every other
country in the world) 'as a mere conspiracy of the rich pursuing their own
private interests under the name and title of the commonwealth'.[319]

If we ask how the Utopians have arrived at this happy state, the answer is
that the quality of *virtus* is alone prized and encouraged under their system
of government. Some Utopians even worship ancestors who exhibited this
quality in a high degree,[320] while everyone in Utopia is instructed in the
ways of *virtus*,[321] is incited to behave with *virtus*[322] and learns to take
pleasure in *virtus* alone.[323] The traveller Hythlodaeus points to the effects of
inculcating this scale of values when he first mentions the existence of
Utopia. It is wholly because of the fact that 'matters are so well organised
there that *virtus* has its reward' that the Utopians have attained the best state
of a commonwealth.[324]

With More no less than his humanist contemporaries, these arguments
are deployed in opposition to two earlier theories of citizenship which we
have already examined. One is the scholastic account of the qualities needed
for effective public service.[325] As we have seen, both Aristotle and the

---

315. Clichtove 1512, f. 5ʳ.   316. Starkey 1948, pp. 61–3.
317. Elyot 1962, p. 106.   318. More 1963–, IV, pp. 86–92.
319. *Ibid.*, p. 240: 'nihil . . . aliud quam quaedam conspiratio divitum, de suis commodis reipublicae nomine, tituloque tractantium'.   320. *Ibid.*, p. 216.
321. *Ibid.*, p. 184: 'educatione ad virtutem egregie instructi'. Cf. also p. 228.
322. *Ibid.*, p. 224: 'propositis quoque honoribus ad virtutes invitant'.
323. *Ibid.*, p. 174: 'amplectuntur ergo in primis animi voluptates . . . quarum potissimam partem censent ab exercitio virtutum . . . proficisci'.
324. *Ibid.*, p. 102: 'tam commode res administrantur, ut & virtuti precium sit'. Cf. also pp. 194, 196, 226.
325. It is strange to find Duhamel and others stressing the supposedly scholastic elements in More's *Utopia*. See, for example, *Essential Articles . . . More* 1977, pp. 234–50 (Duhamel). Not only is there incidental satire on scholastic learning in *Utopia* (e.g., p. 158), but More's ideal of *vera nobilitas* directly challenges scholastic political ideas.

schoolmen had argued that the highest goals of a polity can only be reached if enough well-to-do citizens are willing to devote their leisure entirely to its welfare. To this the humanists replied that the possession of inherited wealth can neither be a necessary nor a sufficient condition of serving with distinction in the public sphere. The ideal of acting in a noble or praiseworthy manner can only be 'the commendation and as it were the surname of virtue', as Elyot puts it in summarising the rival humanist conception of good citizenship.[326] More reiterates these arguments with exceptional force. He begins by observing that 'those who applaud and congratulate themselves on their own nobility are simply those who happen to have been born into a family which has been considered rich over a long period of time, for nowadays no one else is considered noble at all'.[327] He then declares that this common understanding of true nobility is not merely detestable but nothing short of insane.[328] It has the effect of enthroning pride at the heart of public life, thereby founding it not on *virtus* – as we must if we are to live happily – but rather on the deadliest of the seven deadly sins, 'the chief and parent of all the evils in the world'.[329] The Aristotelian view of citizenship is thus held to be directly destructive of our hopes of attaining the best state of a commonwealth. It can only give rise to 'an iniquitous and ungrateful form of community in which these so-called nobles are able to enjoy all its gifts'.[330]

The other view of citizenship which More and his contemporaries challenge is the one propagated by Petrarch and his followers and subsequently developed by the Platonists of the fifteenth century. As we have seen, both schools of thought had argued that, while it is of course helpful to place one's talents in the service of one's community, to do so is neither the true end of man nor the means to realise the highest of human purposes. These require that the life of *negotium*, the civic values of the *vita activa*, should be subordinated to the values associated with the *vita contemplativa*, and above all to the quest for religious and philosophical truth.

A favourite literary tactic of the northern humanists is to start by allowing this point of view to be defended with enthusiasm. Starkey's

326. Elyot 1962, p. 102.
327. More 1963–, IV, p. 168: 'ii qui nobilitatis opinione sibi blandiuntur ac plaudunt, quod eiusmodi maioribus nasci contigerit, quorum longa series dives (neque enim nunc aliud est nobilitas) habita sit'.
328. *Ibid.*, p. 156: 'detestantur insaniam qui divitibus illis . . . honores tantum non divinos impendunt'.
329. *Ibid.*, p. 242: 'omnium princeps parensque pestium, superbia'. For the earliest treatments of pride as the deadliest of the sins see Bloomfield 1952, pp. 71–2.
330. More 1963–, IV, p. 240: 'an non haec iniqua & ingrata respublica, quae generosis ut vocant . . . tanta munera prodigit'.

Dialogue, for example, opens with an explicitly Platonist attack on the usefulness of involving oneself in public affairs.[331] Likewise More's *Utopia* begins with Hythlodaeus ridiculing More's earnest plea that one should 'devote one's talents and energy to the public service'.[332] 'Plato has demonstrated', Hythlodaeus retorts, 'why it is absolutely right for men of wisdom to take no part in political life.'[333] With one voice, however, the northern humanists go on to denounce this fashionable repudiation of the *vita activa civilis*, reverting instead to the very different scale of values originally propagated by the moralists of republican Rome. Starkey proclaims that 'to this all men are born and of nature brought forth: to commune such gifts as be to them given, each one to the profit of other, in perfect civility, and not to live to their own pleasure and profit, without regard to the weal of their country'.[334] The figure of More in *Utopia* takes up the same stance. 'If only you could persuade yourself', he tells Hythlodaeus, 'not to avoid the courts of princes, you could do the utmost good in public affairs by dint of your advice, this being the most important duty incumbent on you as a good man.'[335]

As with many other northern humanists, one of More's principal concerns in *Utopia* is thus to restate a central tenet of classical republicanism: that the noblest way of life is one of virtuous public service. He is also concerned, however, to explore the implications of this commitment in a far more radical fashion than any of his contemporaries. The contrast becomes evident as soon as we ask how we can hope to be sure that the rewards of honour are paid to virtue alone, so that the best state of the commonwealth is duly attained. As we have seen, the usual humanist answer was that our rulers and ruling classes must be furnished with the right form of education in the *studia humanitatis*. Hythlodaeus' answer, by contrast, is that this is altogether too superficial a philosophy. If we wish to ensure that virtue alone is honoured, we must first identify and extirpate the causes that currently enable the rewards of honour and civic glory to be paid to those without the least virtue. The root cause, Hythlodaeus claims, has already been identified: the false but prevalent belief that the enjoyment of inherited wealth is indispensable to good citizenship. The remedy is therefore obvious: 'it seems to me certain that there is no possibility of a just

331. Starkey 1948, pp. 22–4.
332. More 1963–, IV, p. 56: 'ingenium tuum atque industram, publicis rebus accommodes'.
333. *Ibid.*, p. 102: 'declarat Plato cur merito sapientes abstineant a capessenda republica'.
334. Starkey 1948, p. 22.
335. More 1963–, IV, p. 86: 'uti ne aulis principum abhorreas, in publicum posse te tuis consiliis plurimum boni conferre. quare nihil magis incumbit tuo, hoc est boni viri, officio.'

or equitable distribution of goods, or of any happiness in mortal affairs, unless the institution of private property is completely abolished'.[336] To corroborate this revolutionary extension of familiar humanist beliefs, Plato's authority is explicitly invoked. 'As that wisest of men readily foresaw, the one and only way to uphold the general welfare is to maintain a complete equality of goods; and I myself do not see how it will ever be possible to attain such an arrangement as long as private property remains in individual hands.'[337]

Hythlodaeus, a true Platonist, rests his case at that point. But it is not clear that the same can be said of More. The figure of More in the dialogue instead brings *Utopia* to a close by raising a further and yet more disconcerting doubt about the conventional values of humanism. We may agree, he concedes, that *virtus* alone deserves honour; we may even think that, if *virtus* is to be honoured, private property will have to be abolished. But 'if such a system were to be instituted, it would at once sweep away all the nobility, magnificence, splendour and majesty which, according to the opinion of most people, represent the true ornaments and marks of distinction in a commonwealth'.[338]

Now, the usual humanist way with such scruples – as we saw, for example, in Poggio's *De nobilitate* – was to insist that the question is not what people in general believe, but what a well-educated humanist can see to be the truth. But More refuses to endorse such easy confidence. He accepts that the scholastic conception of citizenship deserves to be repudiated, and that 'there are many features of the Utopian commonwealth which – though I cannot hope for this – I should like to see established in our own polities'.[339] But he cannot bring himself to accept the full implications of the humanist alternative, especially as it runs counter to so many received beliefs. Perhaps, he concludes, the truth is that the whole question will have to be pondered more deeply.[340]

More's doubts were duly echoed in the subsequent history of early modern political thought. As the contrast between scholastic and humanist principles came to be pondered more deeply in the course of the sixteenth

336. *Ibid.*, p. 104: 'adeo mihi certe persuadeo, res aequabili ac iusta aliqua ratione distribui, aut feliciter agi cum rebus mortalium, nisi sublata prorsus proprietate, non posse.'

337. *Ibid.*, p. 104: 'siquidem facile praevidit homo prudentissimus, unam atque unicam illam esse viam ad salutem publicam, si rerum indicatur aequalitas, quae nescio an unquam possit observari, ubi sua sunt singulorum propria.'

338. *Ibid.*, p. 244: 'qua una re funditus evertitur omnis nobilitas, magnificentia, splendor, maiestas, vera ut publica est opinio decora atque ornamenta reipublicae'.

339. *Ibid.*, p. 246: 'permulta esse in Utopiensium republica, quae in nostris civitatibus optarim verius quam sperarim'.   340. *Ibid.*, p. 244.

century, the humanist ideal of virtuous public service was increasingly challenged and eventually supplanted by a more individualistic and contractarian style of political reasoning, the style perfected by Thomas Hobbes in *Leviathan*. Measuring political liberty by the extent of individual rights, this new tradition found the humanist attempt to connect liberty with virtue and public service at best paradoxical and at worst a sinister misunderstanding of the concepts involved.

Hobbes gives classic expression to these doubts in *Leviathan*, especially in his chapter 'Of the liberty of subjects'. In the course of his analysis he observes that 'there is written on the Turrets of the city of *Luca* in great characters at this day, the word LIBERTAS: yet no man can thence inferre, that a particular man has more Libertie, or Immunitie from the service of the Commonwealth there, than in *Constantinople*'.[341] With this famous sneer, Hobbes decisively repudiated the distinctive ideals of Renaissance political theory, burying them and writing their epitaph in the same breath.[342]

341. Hobbes 1968, p. 266.
342. For reading and commenting on various earlier drafts of this chapter I am deeply indebted to John Dunn, Felix Gilbert, Susan James, Jill Kraye, J. G. A. Pocock, Nicolai Rubinstein, Charles Schmitt and Judith Shklar.

IX

PSYCHOLOGY

13

THE CONCEPT OF PSYCHOLOGY

Philosophers and scientists of the Renaissance did not treat psychology, the philosophical study of the soul, as an independent discipline. Following the medieval tradition, they placed it within the broader context of natural philosophy, and they approached it, like the other sub-divisions of natural philosophy, through the works of Aristotle, notably *De anima* and the *Parva naturalia*. The term *psychologia* itself was coined – apparently by the German humanist Joannes Thomas Freigius in 1575 – to refer to the traditional complex of problems originating from these two works.[1] Thus it is in relation to the Aristotelian tradition, and more specifically to the Aristotelian philosophy of nature, that the meaning and content of psychology in this period must be defined.[2]

Aristotle and his followers defined the soul as the life principle of the individual body – that which differentiated living from non-living things.[3] As such it was the source and formal cause of the specific functions and activities of animate beings, including plants and animals as well as men. Thus before the seventeenth century, when Descartes, Stahl and others moved to divorce the notions of life and soul, there was no clear division between psychology and what we now call biology. Although Renaissance writers emphasised problems of cognition, emotion and volition (the main subjects of *De anima*), the field also included a good deal of plant and animal physiology, based not only on the *Parva naturalia* but also on the 'animal books' of Aristotle and to a lesser extent on the pseudo-Aristotelian *De plantis*.[4] These texts, together with their Greek, Arabic and medieval Latin commentaries, summaries and paraphrases were the main sources used by Renaissance writers on the soul.

1. Lapointe 1972, 1973, referring to the *Catalogus locorum communium* prefixed to Freigius 1575; see also Schüling 1967, p. 7.
2. See the contribution of Wallace to this volume. There are no satisfactory general accounts of psychology between 1350 and 1600. For the sixteenth century, see Schüling 1967 and the sketch in Jansen 1951. 3. Aristotle, *De anima* II.1–2.
4. The 'animal books' included *De generatione animalium*, *Historia animalium*, *De partibus animalium*, *De motu animalium* and *De progressu animalium*; the first three were sometimes known collectively as *De animalibus*. On *De plantis* and its history in the Latin West see Wingate 1931.

The *De anima* was by far the most important of these treatises. Virtually all universities required it to be read for the degree of bachelor of arts, an honour it shared only with the *Physics* among Aristotle's non-logical works.[5] The *Parva naturalia* and animal books gained new importance during the Renaissance, as the object of medical and philosophical study in their own right and as part of the humanist effort to recover and disseminate the entire Aristotelian corpus; by the middle of the sixteenth century some writers even argued that they should precede *De anima* in the order of investigation and teaching.[6] Nonetheless, *De anima* – above all the second and third books – continued to determine the content and order of psychological enquiry. In the sixteenth as in the thirteenth century, students and teachers began by considering the nature and types of soul before moving on to the more specific topics of reproduction, digestion, sensation (including basic optics and acoustics, as well as the higher sensitive functions of memory and imagination), intellection, appetite and will.

If physics was the foundation of Aristotelian natural philosophy, psychology was its culmination, as Aristotle and after him Averroes had noted, since, unlike the other branches of natural philosophy, it treated the principles governing animate rather than inanimate bodies.[7] Because it considered the nature and functions of the specifically human soul and body, among others, psychology overlapped many other areas of enquiry. Philosophers considered psychology relevant to ethics, which required a basic understanding of the soul as the source of man's thoughts and actions and the seat of his ultimate perfection.[8] Because man's intellective soul was regarded as the lowest substance wholly separable from matter, psychology also confronted the problem of immaterial substances, the subject of divine philosophy or metaphysics. Thus Paul of Venice followed the treatise on the soul in his *Summa philosophiae naturalis* by a treatise on metaphysics,[9] and

5. The *Parva naturalia* were often required only for the most advanced licence in arts, while the books on animals and plants usually served only as supplementary texts, as the relatively small number of commentaries devoted to them shows. See, e.g., the degree requirements in *University Records* 1944, pp. 246 (Paris, 1366), 279 (Bologna, 1405), 296–7 (Erfurt, 1420); Ehrle 1925, pp. 205–6n. (Leipzig, 1410); Lhotsky 1965, pp. 236, 243 (Vienna, 1389). Only Oxford and Cambridge seem to have recommended the biological works for a degree: see *Statuta Antiqua* 1931, pp. 234–5 (Oxford, 1431); Hackett 1970, p. 277 (Cambridge, late fourteenth century).

6. E.g., Genua, *De ordine librorum naturalium Aristotelis disputatio* in Aristotle and Averroes 1562–74, suppl. II, ff. 5ʳ–7ᵛ; *De naturalis scientiae constitutione* in J. Zabarella 1607a, pp. 107ff. (cap. 35); F. Piccolomini 1596, f. 6ʳ (*Introductio*, cap. 6).

7. See Aristotle, *De anima*, I.1 (402^{a}4–7); Averroes 1953, I, pp. 4–5 (text 2). For the discussion of the utility of psychology in the Renaissance see the comments on this same passage by Argyropulos in *Reden und Briefe* 1970, pp. 44–6.

8. See, e.g., the sub-title of Francesco Sansovino's Italian translation: *L'Anima d'Aristotile, la cognitione della quale è necessaria molto all'intelligenza dell'etica per esser materia congiunta* (Venice, 1551).

9. Paul of Venice 1503. In the statutes of Bologna *De anima* is followed by readings from the *Metaphysics*; see *University Records* 1944, p. 279.

Agostino Nifo identified the chapters on intellect in *De anima* as part of metaphysics and referred to psychology in general as a 'middle science' (*scientia media*) between that discipline and physics.[10] Finally, *De anima* expounded the principles of intellection and thus contributed to the general theory of knowledge and supplemented logical rules of argument: only when logic was understood not as a science in itself but as instrument of the sciences was the psychological theory of knowledge dissociated from it.[11]

Non-philosophical disciplines, too, relied on the study of psychology: theology, as is obvious in the debate on immortality;[12] rhetoric, which drew its force from the appeal to senses and emotions; and medicine, which also considered the human body. The ties to the last were particularly strong: philosophers writing on the soul incorporated many ideas from Galen, Avicenna and more contemporary medical theorists, while much of the basic physiology contained in *De anima* and the *Parva naturalia* reappeared in courses on medicine and served in the understanding and treatment of mental and physical disease. For this reason the philosophy curriculum at Bologna, intended as propaedeutic to the study of medicine, put special emphasis on *De anima*.[13] In general, therefore, psychology was seen both as the apex of natural philosophy and as a transition to the higher study of medicine.

The many contributions of psychology to other disciplines vindicated the centrality of *De anima* in the university curriculum. At the same time, they opened the discussion of the soul to other intellectual influences. These included humanism, with its emphasis on anthropological and moral questions; Neoplatonism, with its attempt to develop a new cosmology and epistemology; and the religious movements of Reformation and Counter-Reformation. As a result psychology, like ethics, never remained the monopoly of academic specialists; some of the most interesting and original work on the soul took place outside university walls, particularly after 1500, when printing acted dramatically to expand the European intellectual community.

Of all the groups mentioned above, the contribution of the humanists to psychological discussion in the Renaissance was the most far-reaching,

---

10. Nifo 1559 (*In librum collectanearum prooemium*) – a position eliminated in the preface to the later *Commentaria*.
11. See J. Zabarella 1606, pp. 21–2 (I, text 2); F. Piccolomini 1596, f. 7ʳ (*Introductio*, cap. 7).
12. Di Napoli 1963.
13. *University Records* 1944, p. 279. The association was particularly strong in Italy, where medicine and philosophy were taught in the same faculty and often by the same people: Kristeller 1978; Siraisi 1981, pp. 119–39 and ch. 6. On Paris and Northern Europe, see Kibre 1978. Physicians were especially important as commentators on the more physiologically oriented *Parva naturalia* and animal books.

although also the least direct. Most humanists had little interest in technical philosophy, but they called for a general return to the sources of the classical tradition and to the study of Greek. Lamenting in particular the 'corruption' of Aristotle's elegant style by incompetent medieval translators, they embarked on a massive programme of editing and retranslating his works that was to pave the way for a new approach to *De anima* and to Aristotelian philosophy in general.[14] *De anima*, which had previously circulated in the thirteenth-century Latin version of William of Moerbeke, was retranslated twice during the fifteenth century, by the Byzantine émigrés George of Trebizond, who followed the traditional word-for-word method, and Johannes Argyropulos, who was inspired by the humanistic ideal of elegant Latin. It was translated at least five more times into Latin during the sixteenth century and twice into Italian.[15] By the middle of the sixteenth century the *Parva naturalia*, too, had appeared in multiple new translations, together with the Aristotelian books on animals.[16]

Not all these translations had the same influence. Some went through only one edition. Others, notably the elegant Ciceronian versions of Périon and Grouchy, who went so far as to change the title of *De anima* to *De animo*, attracted a wide audience among humanistically educated lay readers. Academic philosophers, however, had different requirements; embedded in a long tradition of Latin discourse, they needed a stable technical vocabulary and favoured those new versions – Argyropulos' *De anima*, for example, and Vatable's *Parva naturalia* – that managed to combine a more up-to-date style with the medieval terminology. Thus although Argyropulos' text became the standard new translation used by academic philosophers, the old version of Moerbeke often accompanied it in *De anima* commentaries from as late as the second half of the sixteenth century.[17]

14. Schmitt 1983a, pp. 64–88; Garin 1951; *Platon et Aristote* 1976, pp. 359–76 (Cranz).
15. The sixteenth century Latin translators included Pietro Alcionio (first edition 1542), Gentian Hervet (1544), Joachim Périon (1549, with Nicolas Grouchy's revisions 1552), Michael Sophianus (1562) and Giulio Pace (1596). The Italian translators were Francesco Sansovino (1551) and Antonio Brucioli (1559). For more information see Minio-Paluello 1972, § 14; *Platon et Aristote* 1976, pp. 360–6 (Cranz); Cranz and Schmitt 1984, pp. 165–7.
16. Translators of the *Parva naturalia* included François Vatable (first edition 1518), Alcionio (1521), Juan Ginés de Sepúlveda (1522), Niccolò Leonico Tomeo (1523), Nifo (1523) and Périon (1550, with Grouchy's revisions 1552). The most important translator of the animal books was the fifteenth-century Greek Theodore Gaza, who worked on *De generatione animalium, Historia animalium* and *De partibus animalium*. For more information see Cranz and Schmitt 1984, pp. 201–12, 167–8, 175–6, 177–8, 201; Schmitt 1983a, p. 85.
17. See *Philosophy and Humanism* 1976, pp. 127–8 (Cranz); *Platon et Aristote* 1976, pp. 362–5 (Cranz); Cranz 1978, pp. 177–8. On the terminological inadequacies of the Périon-Grouchy translation in particular, see Schmitt 1983a, pp. 76–9.

Academic psychology was also influenced by the new availability of the Greek text of Aristotle, first published in the Aldine edition of Aristotle's *Opera omnia* (1495–8). The psychological works were reprinted as part of the *Opera* eight times over the course of the sixteenth century,[18] also appearing frequently in separate editions, with or without Latin translations. During this same period, a number of universities established chairs to teach Aristotle in the original. In this way, we see the gradual emergence during the Renaissance of the historical Aristotle, who called for philological and historical study as well as philosophical analysis. This new approach to Aristotle bore fruit in the writing on *De anima* by Francesco Vimercato and, above all, Giulio Pace.[19]

Even more important for Renaissance psychology was the humanist rediscovery, translation and publication of the Greek commentaries on Aristotle's psychological works. Averroes had cited them often, and Thomas Aquinas had access to some in rare medieval translations, but at the beginning of the fifteenth century they were generally known only by name or indirectly.[20] The first to appear in print, in Ermolao Barbaro's Latin translation, was the paraphrase of *De anima* by Themistius.[21] Fourteen years later, in 1495, Barbaro's compatriot Girolamo Donato published his own translation of Alexander of Aphrodisias' *De anima*.[22] The two other major commentaries on *De anima*, that by Simplicius and that attributed to Philoponus, did not appear in Latin until the 1540s, although they had been used in the Greek several decades earlier by Italian writers such as Giovanni Pico and Agostino Nifo.[23] To these works we should also add Alexander's commentary on *De sensu* and a related work, the *Metaphrasis in Theophrastum De sensibus* of Priscianus Lydus, which became newly and more widely available during the same period. All of these works served as guides to the new Greek Aristotle and represented a significant body of new ideas and interpretations for writers on psychology. Themistius and Alexander, for example, figured prominently in the Renaissance debates on

---

18. Cranz and Schmitt 1984, p. 165.

19. Vimercato 1543; for Pace see Aristotle 1596a and Schmitt 1983a, pp. 37–41.

20. Nardi 1958, pp. 365–420. For the medieval translations see Themistius 1957 and Philoponus 1966. For more details on the transmission and reception of the Greek commentators in the Middle Ages and Renaissance see Cranz 1958; *Catalogus translationum* 1960–, I, pp. 77–135 and II, pp. 411–22 (Alexander of Aphrodisias); III, pp. 75–82 (Priscianus Lydus); Mahoney 1982.

21. Themistius 1481; first Greek edition, Themistius 1534.

22. Alexander of Aphrodisias 1495; another translation of the second book appeared in 1546. The first Greek edition is in Themistius 1534. See Averroes 1953, pp. 393–4.

23. Simplicius 1543, with a second translation, Simplicius 1553; first Greek edition 1527; see, in general, Nardi 1958, pp. 373–442. Philoponus 1544a, 1544b; first Greek edition, Philoponus 1535. The real author of the commentary attributed to Philoponus was apparently Stephanus of Alexandria: Blumenthal 1982.

the unity of the intellect and the immortality of the soul, while Simplicius and Philoponus aided those who wished to reconcile Aristotle to Neoplatonism and Christian dogma respectively.

Most far-reaching of all, however, humanist scholars began to recover and disseminate lost works of classical philosophy from outside the Aristotelian tradition. The most influential such sources for psychology were the dialogues of Plato, especially the *Republic*, *Timaeus* and *Phaedrus*, and a number of Neoplatonic treatises: Plotinus' *Enneads* (above all book IV), Iamblichus' *De mysteriis*, and Synesius' *De insomniis*.[24] These works proposed radically un-Aristotelian models for basic psychological phenomena – vision, for example, and intellection – and injected a new magical and theurgic element into philosophical speculation on the soul. To them we should also add the newly discovered *Enchiridion* of the Greek Stoic Epictetus, which went through countless editions after 1497,[25] and two works from the sceptical tradition: Cicero's *Academica* and the *Outlines of Pyrrhonism* of Sextus Empiricus.[26] The first gave new emphasis to the emotions, which had played a subordinate part in scholastic psychology, while the last two discussed sense deception and cognitive error in a way that challenged fundamental Aristotelian assumptions.

This influx of new material had a dramatic effect on psychology. In the first place, it focused attention on the actual text of Aristotle, as philosophers of the soul from the late fifteenth century onwards struggled to strip away medieval Latin and Arabic accretions in order to recapture the pristine doctrine, to discover what Aristotle actually said and meant. Those most accomplished in Greek engaged in sophisticated exercises of philological reconstruction, as in Giulio Pace's commentary on *De anima* or Simone Simoni's on *De sensu*.[27] And even less historically oriented writers, from Lefèvre d'Étaples to Jacopo Zabarella, produced a purified and simplified reading of Aristotle, rejecting doctrines, such as that of the 'internal senses', that revealed themselves as later interpolations.[28] These efforts at purification were not always successful. Immersed in the earlier interpretations, Renaissance philosophers were unable to reject them entirely. Frequently they even introduced new layers of their own, such as the Neoplatonic veil derived from their reading of Themistius, Simplicius and Priscianus

---

24. Marsilio Ficino's Latin translations of these works were published in the 1490s and reprinted frequently in the sixteenth century.
25. The most influential Latin translation was that of Angelo Poliziano. By 1560 the work had also appeared in German, Italian and French; see the bibliography of editions in Oldfather 1927, 1952.
26. See Schmitt 1983c.   27. *Platon et Aristote* 1976, pp. 364–5 (Cranz); Schmitt 1983a, pp. 81–5.
28. See, e.g., *Humanism in France* 1970, pp. 132–49 (Rice) on Lefèvre d'Étaples.

Lydus.[29] Nonetheless, we can see an increased interest in and sensitivity to the intentions of Aristotle in a wide range of late fifteenth- and sixteenth-century writers on psychology.

In the second place, the new scholarship vastly expanded the range of philosophical reference. Renaissance writers on psychology had access to the works of a wide variety of commentators on Aristotle – commonly divided into the Latins, the Arabs and the Greeks – among whom they could pick and choose according to their own philosophical interests and commitments. Those eager to reconcile Aristotle with Christianity, for example, preferred the authority of the first, while those more influenced by the humanist agenda emphasised the last. Furthermore, sixteenth-century philosophers were no longer confined to the works of Aristotle and his followers, but could confront their doctrines with the radically different views of classical philosophers from other schools. Most academic philosophers ended up by confirming the old doctrines with only minor shifts in emphasis, but others – Ficino among the Neoplatonists, for example, or Montaigne among the sceptics – moved in significantly new directions.

Already in the second half of the fifteenth century we can see signs of these changes outside the universities. From the 1490s onwards the new ideas, sources and approaches appeared with increasing frequency in the work of scholastic writers like Agostino Nifo and Pietro Pomponazzi in Italy, or the circle of Lefèvre d'Étaples in France – writers who in other respects had strong ties to the earlier tradition. The point of real rupture came in the 1520s. Before this time European presses had continued to print the psychological works of fourteenth- and fifteenth-century Latin writers untouched by humanist influences, even as they turned out new translations and editions of classical philosophers. Far from fading, the influence of earlier commentators such as Thomas Aquinas, Albertus Magnus, Duns Scotus and William of Ockham continued to grow throughout the fifteenth century, as self-conscious 'schools' or *viae* of philosophers in the various universities struggled to promote and elaborate their interpretations.[30] About 1525, however, the general interest in high and late medieval

---

29. Mahoney 1982; Nardi 1958.
30. The main self-proclaimed schools in this period included the *via moderna* ('nominalists' and followers of Ockham) and the *via antiqua*, the latter further subdivided into Thomists, Albertists and Scotists; philosophers were also identified as 'Averroists', a term much abused by historians. This situation was most pronounced in northern universities, where the *viae* often had their own colleges, but it prevailed to a lesser extent in Italy as well: see Ritter 1921–2, II; *Antiqui und Moderni* 1974, pp. 439–83 (Gabriel); Meersseman 1933–5; Renaudet 1953, pp. 93–101; and – on Italy – Schmitt 1984, § VIII, pp. 121–6; Kristeller 1974, pp. 45–55; Poppi 1964; Mahoney 1974, 1980; and Matsen 1975.

psychology saw a marked decline. The printing history of Paul of Venice mirrors that of a host of popular fifteenth-century authors: between 1475 and 1525 his commentary on *De anima* was published five times and his *Summa naturalium*, ten; no more editions appeared after 1525.[31] The reasons for this break seem clear. The 'barbarous' Latin prose of the earlier commentators grated on sixteenth-century ears, while their ignorance of the new Greek material rendered them obsolete in tone and content.

We should not overstate the break with the past. Medieval assumptions, problems and terminology continued to permeate sixteenth-century psychology. Indeed, we see a revival of interest in certain aspects of the medieval tradition, as many philosophers reacted against the humanists' historical and philological reading of Aristotle in favour of a more substantive approach.[32] In Italy, on the one hand, this revival gave new prominence to Averroes and extended to his main medieval expositor, the fourteenth-century Jean de Jandun.[33] In Spain and Portugal, on the other, the revival crystallised around the figure of Thomas Aquinas and reflected the rehabilitation of thirteenth-century philosophy under the auspices of the Counter-Reformation. The Jesuits quickly accepted Thomas as the prime interpreter of Aristotle. His writings on psychology, together with those of his late medieval interpreters, were often reprinted after the middle of the century, and their influence spread even more widely through the commentaries put out by the Jesuit College at Coimbra and the College of the Discalced Carmelites at Alcalá.[34] Neither the Italian Averroism nor the Counter-Reformation Thomism of the later sixteenth century should be seen as medieval throwbacks; both incorporated the philological sophistication of the humanists and their appreciation of the powers of printing, as well as a good many of the new Greek sources. In this way, both confirmed the break with the later fourteenth and fifteenth centuries.

It is this abrupt confluence of classical and medieval currents that lends Renaissance psychology its drama and uniqueness. From 1490 on, writers on the soul struggled to accommodate the new materials of the classical

---

31. Lohr 1972a, pp. 317–19. This chronological break appears in all areas of Aristotelian philosophy and in all parts of Europe with the exception of Poland, which remained a pocket of medieval Aristotelianism even after 1525; see Cranz and Schmitt 1984, pp. vii–ix; Schmitt 1983a, pp. 52–3.
32. Schmitt 1984, § VIII, p. 127; 1983a, p. 82.
33. *Philosophy and Humanism* 1976, pp. 116–28 (Cranz); Schmitt 1984, § VIII. On Jandun, see Lohr 1970, pp. 213–14.
34. Cranz 1978. Among the most influential of the earlier Thomists writing on psychology were Dominicus de Flandria, Cardinal Cajetan and Crisostomo Javelli, all active in the decades around 1500. Duns Scotus benefited from the revival of thirteenth-century Latin philosophy and theology, as did, for example, Durandus a S. Porciano, but to a lesser degree than Thomas.

revival and the new religious imperatives of the Protestant and Catholic reformations. The period was a complicated and confused one, and the diversity of the philosophical materials, collected from different schools and traditions, makes it burdensome to exhume the position of a given author. This may have been the reason why psychological discussion declined in manuals and textbooks such as the Coimbra commentaries. It is certainly the reason why philosophers after Descartes attempted to circumvent the whole problem and why modern attempts to reconstruct Renaissance debates remain so tentative, fragmentary and incomplete.

14

THE ORGANIC SOUL

Most modern discussions of Renaissance psychology focus on a single aspect of the subject: the debates over immortality and intellection in late fifteenth- and sixteenth-century Italy. These debates were important and far-reaching (see Kessler in this volume), but to concentrate exclusively on them does not do justice to the much broader set of issues that preoccupied Renaissance writers on philosophical psychology. In particular it slights their real interest in what they sometimes called the 'organic soul' – the principle responsible for those life functions inextricably tied to the bodies of living beings and immediately dependent on their organs. These functions ranged from the vital operations of digestion and reproduction through sensation and emotion to the higher cognitive functions of imagination and memory. They excluded only the two faculties of intellect and will, which according to most philosophers did not require physical organs and could therefore subsist after the body's death; peculiar to man, these latter faculties constituted his immortal soul and differed distinctly from the functions of the organic soul, which humans shared to a greater or lesser degree with plants and animals.

The tendency to concentrate on the intellectual soul and the debates which surround it obscures another, equally important aspect of Renaissance psychology: the existence of a broad consensus concerning the general nature of the organic soul and its functions. As we will see below, many specific issues were disputed even within the Aristotelian tradition; nonetheless, most philosophers, whatever their particular orientation or school, subscribed to a large body of common ideas on the subject. This body of ideas had been codified and elaborated during the thirteenth and early fourteenth centuries by various Latin writers, of whom the most influential for the later period were Albertus Magnus, Thomas Aquinas, Duns Scotus and to a lesser extent Jean de Jandun, William of Ockham and Jean Buridan. Their teachings formed the backbone of philosophical writing on the soul between 1350 and 1600, although, as we will see, they met with increasing criticism after 1500. We find this core of psychological opinion not only in specialised commentaries and monographs but also – and perhaps even more clearly – in the general textbooks used to introduce university students to academic philosophy. Among these the most influential was probably the *Margarita philosophica* (*Philosophic Pearl*), written in the 1490s by the German Carthusian Gregor Reisch.[1] In both sources and their general structure, books x and xi of this work testify to the continuing influence of medieval Latin writers on Renaissance psychology. At the same time they provide an excellent picture of the ideas concerning the soul accepted by most philosophers in the years before 1500, and by many to the end of the sixteenth century.[2]

THE ARISTOTELIAN *KOINE*

Reisch's psychology, like that of the tradition he represented, was a synthesis of ideas from many different sources. Many derived from the works of Aristotle. Some had their roots in other classical traditions, such as Greek Neoplatonism and Galenic medicine, while others grew out of the works of early Christian writers such as St Augustine and Nemesius of Emesa. Still others – and this group was in some respects dominant – were the creation of medieval Arabic writers on Aristotelian philosophy, of whom the most important were Avicenna and Averroes. It is a testimony to the enormous ingenuity of the Latin writers of the thirteenth and early fourteenth centuries that they had managed to weld this collection into a persuasive explanatory system, which for the most part they attributed to Aristotle himself. As inherited by Reisch, this system included a number of elements drawn directly from *De anima* and the *Parva naturalia*, together with many others that Aristotle would not have recognised and probably would have rejected.

Reisch's psychology was above all a faculty psychology. He described the

---

1. Reisch 1517. On this work and its author, see Srbik 1941, Münzel 1937, and Geldsetzer's introduction to the 1973 reprint of Reisch 1517. The *Margarita*, which Reisch expanded and revised in four successive editions between 1503 and 1517, was printed at least ten times in full and several times in part over the course of the sixteenth century. It also appeared in French and Italian translations. Other such textbooks, of widely varying orientations, include Paul of Venice 1503; Hundt 1501; Vives 1538; and Melanchthon 1834–60, XIII, cols. 5–178 (*Liber de anima*). On the use of textbooks as introductions to Aristotelian philosophy, see Grabmann 1939; *Platon et Aristote* 1976, pp. 147–54 (Reulos); and on a slightly later period, Reif 1969; see also Schmitt in this volume.
2. The main exception to this statement regards philosophers with a pronounced nominalist or Ockhamist orientation, who identified themselves with the so-called *via moderna*. As a follower of the *via antiqua*, Reisch differed from the *moderni* on a number of particular issues, including the relation of the soul to its powers, as discussed below. On the distinction between *moderni* and *antiqui* see *Antiqui und Moderni* 1974, esp. pp. 85–125 (N. W. Gilbert), and bibliography therein.

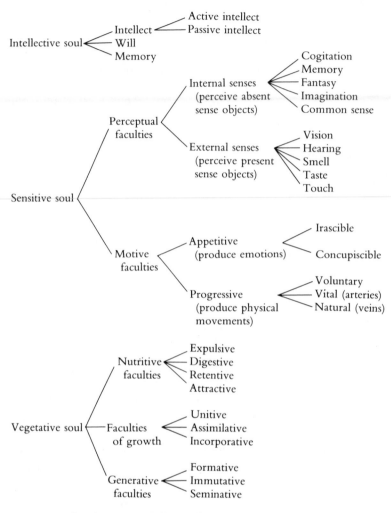

Figure 1 The division of the souls

soul as composed of a large number of separate faculties or powers, each directed towards a different object and responsible for a distinct operation. Like most of his contemporaries, Reisch justified this approach on good Aristotelian grounds. 'All our knowledge is derived from the senses', he wrote. 'But spiritual [i.e., immaterial] substances, including the soul that confers life and motion on living beings, cannot be perceived by the senses. Thus it is difficult to arrive at knowledge of it except through its operations.'[3] Separate but related, the faculties occupied a static hierarchy of dependence and nobility, ranging from the lowest faculty of nutrition to the highest faculty of intellect. As figure 1 shows, they were further grouped into three different kinds of soul.[4] The lowest, called the vegetative soul, included the functions basic to all living things: nutrition, growth and reproduction. The second, the sensitive soul, included all of the powers of the vegetative soul as well as the powers of movement and emotion and the ten internal and external senses. The intellective soul, finally, included not only the vegetative and sensitive powers – the organic faculties – but also the three rational powers of intellect, intellective memory (memory of concepts, as opposed to sense images) and will. All living beings were divided into genera according to the kind of soul they possessed: thus plants were animated by a vegetative soul, 'imperfect' animals (including sponges, worms and bivalves) by a partial sensitive soul, 'perfect' animals (including insects, birds and mammals) by a complete sensitive soul and humans by an intellective soul.[5]

The faculty approach had many advantages. It allowed medieval and Renaissance philosophers to develop a uniform model to explain the enormous variety of activities observed among living beings. At the same time it allowed them to isolate each one of those activities and subject it to independent analysis, rendering the enormous task of understanding the whole more manageable. It also sat well with the analytical methods of scholastic writers, who tended to rely heavily on techniques of logical division and sub-division, as well as with their inclination to see reality as a series of levels defined metaphysically according to their increasing abstraction from matter and theologically according to their increasing closeness to God – a structure sometimes referred to as the 'ladder of nature' or the 'great chain of being'.[6] Like the idea of the great chain, however, this system of faculties was only partly based on Aristotle. Many of the sub-powers, including those serving the three vegetative faculties and certain of the internal senses, corresponded to operations not discussed – or discussed only vaguely – in *De anima*. Furthermore, the notion of faculty itself, although it drew on Aristotle's general account of the soul, was an invention

---

3. Reisch 1517, p. 409 (X.1.1).
4. Although Reisch did not display the faculties in tabular form, this practice was common in fourteenth- and fifteenth-century introductions to psychology. See, for example, Ailly 1494b, facing the first page of cap. 1, and the Oxford student notebook from about 1410, Corpus Christi MS 116, f. 48^{v}.
5. This analysis of faculties and souls is based on Aristotle, *De anima* II.2–3. Imperfect animals were thought to possess only touch and taste among the external senses and to lack the internal senses entirely.   6. See McGinn 1972, pp. 61–102; Lovejoy 1936.

of late classical and Arabic authors. Aristotle had never attributed continuous actuality to the soul's powers (δυνάμεις); he had written of them as potentialities for different kinds of action and had used them primarily as convenient categories for classifying living beings.[7] Thus it was perhaps inevitable that in the later Renaissance, as we will see, many humanistically trained writers on psychology, fortified by a new, philologically informed reading of classical sources, began to reject or revise the notion of faculty which underpinned earlier work on the subject.

Another fundamental aspect of Aristotelian psychology in the fourteenth and fifteenth centuries was the assumption of close ties between body and soul. Aristotle had defined the soul as 'the first actuality of a natural body with organs', a statement which philosophers like Reisch interpreted in the light of their doctrine of substantial form.[8] They did not, however, stop at a consideration of the final and formal causes of psychological phenomena – the soul and its faculties – but concerned themselves as much if not more with efficient and material causes, which they interpreted as the physical processes accounting for these phenomena and the organs in which they took place. Like Aristotle before them, they assumed that each activity of the organic soul could be given parallel psychological and biological accounts. According to Reisch, for example, memory could be described both as the capacity to recall now absent objects and as the retention of past sense images in the form of eddies in the vapours that fill the posterior ventricle of the brain. Thus a man trying to remember something tilts his head back to encourage the flow of spirit towards that organ. Similarly, Reisch interpreted wrath as both the impulse to resist evil and a dilation of the heart, which drives the blood and vapours in veins and arteries towards the extremities. Thus the face of a man prey to anger becomes flushed and swollen.[9] Philosophers agreed that the non-organic or intellective functions were not subject to such analysis; under normal circumstances, however, even they relied on the internal senses to process the sense images from which intellect abstracted its universal notions. Thus even they could be disrupted by physical illness or cerebral indisposition; as Reisch noted, lunatics and idiots possessed a rational soul like other men, but it was prevented from functioning normally by physical abnormalities in the brain which distorted the action of imagination, cogitation or the other internal senses.[10]

7. See Hamlyn 1961, pp. 17–18. The origins of the medieval doctrine of faculty have been traced in Park 1980, pp. 505–8; Michaud-Quantin 1949, 1955; McGinn 1972, pp. 137–44; and Bono 1981, pp. 72–88.   8. Aristotle, *De anima* II.1 (412^{b}5–6). Reisch 1517, pp. 408–9 (X.I.1–2).
9. Reisch 1517, pp. 439–40 (X.2.29–30).   10. *Ibid.*, p. 457 (XI.1.16).

As the preceding examples suggest, this kind of psychology was more than an abstract system; it had in addition a strong observational component. Nonetheless, it remained experiential rather than experimental in character, relying on common experience to suggest and confirm rather than to test proffered explanations. The physical model it assumed was a simple hydraulic one, based on a clear localisation of psychological function by organ or system of organs. The vegetative powers were located in the liver, served by the veins and auxiliary members such as the bladder and genitals. The emotive functions of the sensitive soul resided in the heart, served by the arteries, while its faculties of cognition and voluntary motion had their seat in the brain, served by the nerves, the sense organs, and the muscles. All of these organs relied for their operations on a substance called *spiritus* – a subtle vapour or exhalation produced from blood and disseminated throughout the body by the arteries and nerves, which were assumed to be hollow. The source of all activity in the living body, *spiritus* was often referred to by Renaissance philosophers as the 'first instrument' of the soul.[11]

This physiological orientation allowed Renaissance writers to elaborate a wide variety of practical applications for their psychological theories – applications that figure prominently in both the learned philosophy and the popular self-help literature of the period. Academic philosophers like Agostino Nifo composed treatises on physiognomy and the interpretation of dreams which showed how to deduce psychological states from physical ones and vice versa.[12] Others took up the problem of mental illness, long ascribed to organic causes and classified by medical writers under 'diseases of the head'. Particularly influential in this area was Marsilio Ficino's discussion of melancholy, a condition attributed to an excess of black bile in the brain and elsewhere and marked by symptoms ranging from depression to hallucinations to heightened creativity. Ficino's treatise on the subject inspired a flood of works by sixteenth- and early seventeenth-century authors fascinated by the conjunction of mental pathology and genius.[13] During the same period we also find innumerable works describing ways to strengthen the memory drawn from both the psychological and the biological analysis of that faculty. These ranged from diets and ointments

11. See, in general, Steneck 1976, pp. 123–7, 137–8. The doctrine of *spiritus* was in fact far more complicated than this simple account allows; for an introduction to the various kinds of *spiritus* and their functions, see the accounts in Hundt 1501, cap. 58 and Melanchthon 1834–60, XIII, cols. 88–9 (*Liber de anima*); and the discussions in Putscher 1973, especially pp. 5–69; Bono 1981, ch. 2; Verbeke 1945. 12. Nifo 1523b, ff. 1ʳ–22ᵛ, 110ʳ–121ᵛ. See also Diepgen 1912.
13. Ficino 1978. See, in general, Klibansky, Panofsky and Saxl 1964; Babb 1951.

intended to warm and dry the posterior ventricle of the brain, the organ of memory, to detailed instruction in the 'art of memory', a technique for exploiting the imagistic nature of that faculty by attaching ideas to mental pictures systematically ordered for ease of recall.[14]

As these examples show, Renaissance writers examined a wide variety of phenomena and behaviours, many of which were continuous with modern concerns. Their central interest, however, was in cognition, which for centuries had dominated Latin work on Aristotelian psychology. For this reason they devoted much greater attention to the senses than to any other faculties of the organic soul. (This emphasis appears clearly in the division of Reisch's treatment of the topic: he devoted twenty-nine chapters to sense-perception, while the vital faculties of the vegetative soul merited only three chapters and powers governing motion and emotion were dismissed in two.) As a result, the doctrine concerning sense-perception is in many ways the most complicated and detailed aspect of Renaissance writing on the organic soul. It was also the one most subject to disagreement and debate, and this makes it difficult to summarise in a way that is both uncontroversial in Renaissance terms and comprehensible in ours.

For almost all fourteenth- and fifteenth-century Aristotelians, sensation was the foundation of cognition, a truth which they summarised in the formula: 'There is nothing in the intellect that was not first in the senses.'[15] Reisch defined the sensitive soul in the *Margarita philosophica* as 'that which perceives externally and internally the corporeal forms of corporeal things both present and absent'.[16] The power of sense, in other words, was equipped to receive the sensible forms or images of material objects – to be distinguished from their substantial or specific forms – without the associated matter. It could do so using both organs located on the outside of the body and organs located inside the brain: the former served to sense present objects and corresponded to what were called the five external senses (sight, hearing, smell, taste and touch); the latter dealt with absent, past or non-existent objects and corresponded to the five internal senses.

As Reisch enumerated them – opinions differed on the matter, as we will see – there were five internal senses: common sense and imagination in the

14. Typical discussions in Romberch 1533, ff. 14ᵛ to end; Publicio 1482; Gratarolo 1554 (*De memoria reparanda, augenda, conservandaque, ac de reminiscentia* capp. 1–5). See, in general, P. Rossi 1983; Yates 1966.

15. For the origins of this formula see Cranefield 1970. Among the very few fourteenth- and fifteenth-century Aristotelians to reject this view were a group of Germans who identified themselves as followers of Albertus Magnus; for details see Park 1980, pp. 528–33.

16. Reisch 1517, p. 413 (X.2.1).

anterior cerebral ventricle; fantasy and estimation in the middle ventricle; and memory in the posterior one.[17] Common sense compared the individual data – described as similitudes or images – gathered by the various external senses, and perceived qualities such as size, shape, number and motion that fell under more than one sense. Imagination stored these data before passing them on to fantasy, which acted to combine and divide them, yielding new images, called *phantasmata*, with no counterparts in external reality. Estimation accounted for instinctive reactions of avoidance or trust, while memory, finally, stored not only the images derived from the external sense but also the *phantasmata* and the reactions of estimation; unlike imagination, however, it acted *cum differentia temporis*, recognising its contents as part of past experience. Because the internal senses were less bound to the actual experience, they acted to bridge the gap between external sensation, limited to the knowledge of particulars, and the highest cognitive operation of intellection, which dealt with universals.

As many sixteenth-century writers realised, this account went well beyond the discussion of sensation in *De anima* and the *Parva naturalia*, where Aristotle mentioned the psychological functions of common sense and memory but made no reference to a separate group of internal senses located in the brain. In this matter, as in their development of the doctrine of faculty, Reisch and most of his contemporaries adopted without reservation the various new explanatory entities elaborated by their medieval predecessors concerned to systematise and to fill apparent logical and causal holes in the Aristotelian account of cognition. Another such entity which had become fundamental to their understanding of sensation was the sense image or *species*. Earlier writers had developed this idea to bridge the physical gap between the object and the sense organ and the metaphysical gap between the sense organ and the soul. As Reisch put it, although 'the sense object cannot be received by the sense in its essence on account of its materiality it produces an image which the sense can receive and by which it can be perceived'.[18] This image is the sensible *species*; an immaterial quality impressed on the surrounding medium as a seal on soft wax, it resembles the object as a portrait does the sitter. According to this theory, every sense object constantly emits a multitude of such *species* (visible, auditory, olfactory and so forth) in all directions. Some of these eventually make their

---

17. *Ibid.*, pp. 433–40 (X.2.21–9). On the internal senses in general see E. R. Harvey 1975; Pagel 1958b, pp. 97–103; Clarke and Dewhurst 1972, ch. 3. More detailed studies of particular aspects of the idea are Klubertanz 1952; Bundy 1927, ch. 9; Steneck 1974 (additional bibliography on p. 195).
18. Reisch 1517, p. 414 (X.2.2). On *species* in general see A. Maier 1964–77, II, pp. 419–51; Steneck 1976, p. 132.

way to the appropriate sense organ, where they cause physical changes which in turn change or 'move' the faculty of sense – a motion defined as sensation. Once in the organs of internal sense, the *species* may be impressed on an internal medium, the vaporous *spiritus* filling the sense organs and the nerves. In this form they can travel throughout the body: to the uterus, for example, where they can stamp themselves on the flesh of a developing foetus; to the heart, where they provoke passional reactions; or to the brain, where they are received in turn by the organs of internal sense.

The tradition that Reisch represented aimed to offer a causal analysis of the entire process of sense-perception, to explain it in terms of a complete chain of causes and effects beginning with the object of sense and moving from it to the sensible *species*, the organs of external and internal sense, and ultimately to the sensitive soul itself. Thus the psychology of sense-perception in the Renaissance tended to embrace a much wider variety of problems than the modern field. Renaissance philosophers wanted to understand why a given object emitted only certain types of *species*. What was it about the physical make-up of an apple which made it red to the eye, sweet to the tongue and aromatic to the nose? How did varying the proportions in an object of the prime qualities of hot, cold, wet and dry produce the seven kinds of colour, the ten kinds of odour, or the twelve kinds of taste? They asked why certain media were receptive of some types of *species* and not others, and they examined the rules governing the propagation of each. They discussed the structure and elemental composition of each sense organ to explain why it responded only to a particular type of *species*.[19]

Aristotle had raised and answered most of these questions in *De anima* and *De sensu*, and most authors in this period followed his lead and the lead of the generations of philosophers that had preceded them, although they often disagreed about details. On these as on most other matters, Reisch adopted conciliatory positions which represented a lowest-common-denominator approach to Aristotelian psychology. But even Reisch was not able to avoid controversy altogether: certain issues had polarised the philosophical community enough to make a neutral position untenable. Among these were the related questions of whether sense was active or passive and whether the physical change in the organ provoked by the sensible *species* was adequate to explain the change in the soul known as sensation. In both cases Reisch adopted an Augustinian stance which would have raised the

---

19. Steneck 1976, pp. 133–4. The only modern studies on this vast subject have to do with the sense of sight; see, e.g., Lindberg 1976; Lindberg and Steneck 1972.

hackles of his more strictly Aristotelian colleagues.[20] But in order to understand the issues involved in these and other questions, we must look beyond the bland world of the introductory textbook to the various controversies which informed more advanced levels of Aristotelian writing on the organic soul.

DISPUTED QUESTIONS

The living heart of Aristotelian psychology in the Renaissance lay not in general philosophical textbooks but in a much larger body of literature: commentaries and *quaestiones* on the *De anima* and *Parva naturalia* and treatises on particular topics suggested by them. More technical, more complicated and more detailed than books like Reisch's *Margarita*, these works testify to the great variety of schools and approaches encompassed by the Aristotelian tradition in the fifteenth and sixteenth centuries and to their continuing vitality and evolution. Debate was central to this literature. Renaissance Aristotelians, like their medieval predecessors, were trained in the art of disputation and used to presenting their ideas in the form of 'questions' – discussions of a single problem organised around the refutation of competing opinions using arguments based on authority, reason, faith and experience. Some questions circulated as independent works; more often, however, they appeared as part of a series devoted by an author to a single topic, or were embedded in a commentary on one of the set texts.[21]

To a large extent the questions in the psychological literature of the Renaissance were standardised, although the terms in which they were expressed varied. They also varied in their philosophical interest. Many of them – particularly those associated with the *Parva naturalia* – did not reflect real debates; they were used rather as a pedagogical device to introduce students to ideas, authorities and interpretations basic to the field. When a writer asked 'whether food is the object of the vegetative faculties', for example, or 'whether taste and touch are necessary to all animals', or 'whether some dreams are false', his affirmative answers were foregone conclusions, as were most of his arguments; he presented the negative opinions not as plausible alternatives, but only to motivate the discussion and satisfy the demands of the genre. A significant proportion of questions on the organic soul, however, represented genuine problems for contemporary writers. Such questions raised fundamental issues concerning the

20. Reisch 1517, p. 414 (X.2.1), p. 427 (X.2.14).
21. For a brief introduction to the *questio* genre see Siraisi 1981, pp. 237–48.

nature of sense-perception, the process of generation or the links between body and soul. Their answers reflected real differences of philosophical opinion and allow us to trace real shifts in attitude and interpretation. For this reason it is the disputed questions that allow us to examine most directly the continuing commitments and changing concerns of Aristotelian psychology.

Few (if any) of the questions which most exercised Renaissance writers on the organic soul were original to the period after 1350. Most had first entered the Latin philosophical tradition in the thirteenth and early fourteenth centuries under the auspices of the authors mentioned at the beginning of this section, especially Albertus Magnus, Thomas Aquinas, Duns Scotus, Ockham and Jean de Jandun. These men in turn were building on and responding to the work of two Arabic philosophers, Avicenna and above all Averroes, whose work served as the cornerstone of the later tradition.

Many of the most important disputed questions in Latin psychology in fact had their roots in the parts of Averroes' *Commentarium magnum in Aristotelis De anima libros* where he pointed out issues on which he thought Aristotle had been incomplete or unclear. A typical example was the question 'whether common sensibles [motion, rest, shape, size, number] are sensed in themselves or incidentally', which obsessed Renaissance writers and provoked much of the sixteenth- and early seventeenth-century reflection on primary and secondary qualities.[22] Another was the equally vexed problem 'whether it is necessary for sensation to postulate an agent sense'. Regarding the latter, Averroes noted that Aristotle had never asked whether an extrinsic motor was necessary for sensation as well as for intellection; 'you must consider this problem', he enjoined his readers, 'for it requires investigation' – an invitation to which his Latin audience responded with enthusiasm.[23] Other questions arose out of disagreements between Averroes and Avicenna over how to interpret particular passages in *De anima* or the *Parva naturalia*, particularly those concerning sensation. Are there four internal senses, as Averroes maintained, or five, as claimed by Avicenna?[24] Can sound travel only in air (Averroes), or also in water (Avicenna)? Does odour travel through its medium as *species* (Averroes) or

---

22. Averroes 1953, p. 227 (lib. II ad t. 65); cf. Aristotle, *De anima* II.6 (418[a]7–25). As far as I know, the history of this central question is unexplored. For a brief survey of the range of possible positions, see Suárez 1978–81, I, pp. 454–70 (d. 6, q. 1).

23. Averroes 1953, p. 221 (lib. II ad t. 60). For a survey of medieval and Renaissance responses to this question, see Mahoney 1971a; Pattin 1974–5; and especially L. A. Kennedy 1966.

24. Avicenna 1968–72, II, pp. 5–10 (IV.1); Averroes 1953, pp. 415–16 (lib. III ad t. 6).

as a material vapour (Avicenna)?[25] Albertus Magnus, Thomas Aquinas and other thirteenth-century writers took up these issues, and their conclusions and arguments were repeated and refined by Renaissance writers.

Not all disputed questions, however, were generated within the Aristotelian tradition itself. Several of the most sustained controversies sprang from the collision between the new Aristotelian psychology received through Arabic sources in the twelfth and thirteenth centuries and the older Augustinian tradition – much of it Neoplatonic in thrust – which had previously dominated Latin writing on the soul.[26] Most of these controversies were purely philosophical. Is the soul completely passive in sensation (Averroes on Aristotle), or does it enter actively into sense-perception as well as intellection (Augustine)?[27] Are the faculties of the soul really, i.e., logically and ontologically, distinct from the soul itself (Avicenna and Averroes), or do they merely represent different modalities of the soul's operation?[28] A much smaller number grew out of the conflict between Aristotelian teaching on the soul and Christian theology. The most famous of these had to do with intellection and immortality (see Kessler in this volume), but similar issues also arose concerning the organic soul. Renaissance writers debated whether human beings were informed by sensitive souls in addition to intellective souls – a position that horrified the Jesuit Francisco Suárez as an impossible violation of the church's teaching concerning body and spirit[29] – and they agonised over how to incorporate the divine origin of the human soul into their philosophical account of reproduction.[30]

One final group of questions had its roots in the critique of Latin psychology initiated by William of Ockham in the early fourteenth century and carried through by followers such as Jean Buridan and Johannes de Mirecourt. Using the principle of parsimony and the analytical tools of

25. See Avicenna 1968–72, I, p. 165 (II.5); Averroes 1953, p. 249 (lib. II ad t. 76), p. 277 (lib. II ad t. 97). Surveys in Suárez 1978–81, II, pp. 640–50, 700–4 (d. 7, qq. 6 and 11).

26. See Hamlyn 1961, pp. 43–52, and for general background to twelfth-century writing on the soul McGinn 1972, especially ch. 3; Michaud-Quantin 1949.

27. Hamlyn 1961, pp. 44–5; Augustine, *De musica* VI.5.10; *De trinitate* X.5.7. Cf. Aristotle, *De anima* II.4 (415^b24); II.5 ($416^b33–17^a1$); II.12 (424^a17). See, in general, L. A. Kennedy 1966, p. 469; Pattin 1974–5, p. 102. Renaissance authors often treated this question in conjunction with that concerning the agent sense (see n. 23 above), although, as Kennedy indicates, the issue was separate in its origins and only tangentially related in its implications.

28. See Lottin 1942–59, I, ch. 5; and especially Künzle 1956, pp. 7–170.

29. Suárez 1978–81, I, pp. 318–30 (d. 2, q. 5); on p. 320 Suárez lists several philosophers who argued the opposite position.

30. For the medieval background to this question see Hewson 1975, ch. 4; for the treatment of the same issues in the Renaissance see Deer 1980, part I.

terminist logic, Ockham had attempted to purify Aristotelian philosophy
of what he considered unnecessary distinctions and explanatory entities
introduced by Averroes, Avicenna and their Latin followers. Among the
elements that he singled out for criticism were the real distinction between
the soul and its faculties, and the sensible *species*.[31] In the process he added a
new dimension to the Augustinian question concerning the faculties
mentioned above and generated a new set of questions concerning the role
of *species* in sensation. At the very end of the fifteenth century these and
other questions, which had remained vital among Ockham's followers in
the *via moderna*, gained new prominence in the context of two closely
related developments: the accelerating impulse to read Aristotle in the
context of his late Greek rather than his Arabic and medieval Latin
commentators; and the desire to present a simplified and more accurate
reading of the original Aristotelian text (see chapter 13 in this volume).

In this as in other areas the questions concerning the organic soul that preoccupied Renaissance Aristotelians were continuous with those that
preoccupied their thirteenth- and early fourteenth-century predecessors.
How then, if at all, did fifteenth- and sixteenth-century commentators on
De anima and the *Parva naturalia* transform that tradition? In order to isolate
the special character of Aristotelian psychology in the Renaissance we must
look beyond the disputed questions themselves to the answers given them.
Here also we will find no clear break. In general philosophers of the period
continued to work within the repertory of responses and interpretations
sketched out by the earlier authorities mentioned above. But we can see
beginning in the years around 1500 a marked if gradual shift in emphasis,
which gives Renaissance writing on the organic soul its own flavour and
prepared the way for the developments that were to transform psychology
radically in the seventeenth century.

I cannot trace these changes over the whole range of disputed questions.
The volume of literature to be surveyed far exceeds that available for the
Middle Ages, and secondary studies are almost wholly lacking.[32] The
problem is exacerbated by the sheer diversity of Aristotelian thought in this
period; no linear survey can do justice to the myriad of local and national

31. For the argument concerning *species* see Ockham, I *Sent*. d. 27, q. 3, and II *Sent*. qq. 17–18: Ockham 1494–6, III, sigs. cc 1ᵛ–5ᵛ, F3ᵛ–G4ʳ; and A. Maier 1964–77, II, pp. 433–48. For the argument concerning the soul and its faculties see Ockham, II *Sent*. q. 24: Ockham 1494–6, IV, sig. h 7ʳ⁻ᵛ; and Park 1980, pp. 517–19. On the general nature of Ockham's enterprise, see Moody 1935, pp. 13–30.
32. The main exceptions to this statement are a handful of studies on the agent sense in the Renaissance (references in n. 23 above) and a few discussions of questions concerning generation in the sixteenth century, approached primarily from the viewpoint of the history of biology and medicine (notably Pagel 1967, pp. 237–77; 1969–70; and Deer 1980).

traditions (sometimes quite autonomous), philosophical schools and religious agendas they embraced. In order to give a sense of both the diversity of material and overall patterns of development I will focus instead on a single group of questions concerning the general relation of the organic faculties to the soul on the one hand, and to the body and its organs on the other. The evolving answers to these questions will show the degree to which philosophical psychology was influenced by external concerns ranging from Reformation theology to advances in medical knowledge, and they will illustrate one of the most noticeable tendencies in Renaissance writing on the organic soul: an impulse to favour simpler and more physiological explanations for organic phenomena. The resultant changes in emphasis took Renaissance thinkers further and further from the psychological thought of the thirteenth and fourteenth centuries and moved them in the direction of seventeenth-century writers such as Descartes and Hobbes.

The point of departure for the issue with which we are concerned was the problem mentioned above, 'whether the faculties are really distinct from the soul itself'. Most commentators introduced this question in the context of *De anima* II.2, together with the question 'whether the whole soul is present in the whole body and in each of its parts.'[33] In the case of the organic faculties, the issue could be reduced to a single problem: Does the cause of the differences between the various operations of the soul lie on the level of form or matter? In other words, do those differences arise in the first place from a distinction in the body or from a distinction in the soul?

Through the end of the fifteenth century the majority of Latin philosophers argued that the distinction existed in the soul itself, although they disagreed about its nature. Most – including not only professed Albertists and Thomists but also Italian writers without a rigorous commitment to a particular philosophical school – adopted the position previously worked out by Albertus Magnus and Thomas Aquinas: the distinction between the soul and its faculties was a real one, since the soul belonged to the logical category of substance while the faculties fell under the second species of quality.[34] Those who identified themselves as Scotists,

33. Cf. Aristotle, *De anima* II.2 (413^b11-15), concerning the four principal psychological functions of nutrition, sensation, movement and thought: 'Whether each of these is a soul or part of a soul, and if it is a part, whether it is distinct only conceptually or also spatially – some of these questions are easy to answer, while others present difficulties.'

34. For the positions of Albertus and Thomas see, e.g., Thomas Aquinas, *Summa theologiae* I.77.1, as well as Lottin 1942–59, I, pp. 497–507, and especially Künzle 1956, pp. 144–218. Typical exponents of this line included, at Padua, Paul of Venice (1503, f. 68^{r-v}) and Gaetano da Thiene (1486, sig. c 8^r, and Valsanzibio 1949, pp. 115–17), and at Paris, the Thomist Johannes Versor (1489, sig. a 6^{r-v}).

on the other hand, followed their master in arguing that the distinction, while still located in the soul, was formal only.[35] The only group of writers to take the opposite tack in this period were the so-called 'nominalists', or adherents of the *via moderna*. Drawing on Ockham's principle of parsimony and related arguments sketched out by Buridan in the fourteenth century, they argued that experience, authority and reason all indicated that the distinction of organic operations lay only in the distinction between the various organs responsible for them. The organic soul was located entire in the whole body and in each of its parts (*tota in toto et tota in qualibet parte corporis*, as the formula went), but differences in the shape and composition of the organs allowed only certain operations to be performed in each. Whereas Thomists argued, for example, that the faculty of sight was really different both from the soul as a whole and from its other faculties, and that it had the eye as its particular seat, *moderni* at the University of Paris and elsewhere maintained that the power of sight, as an integral part of the soul, was present in every part of the body. If the eye sees and the foot does not, they claimed, it is because the structure and complexion of the eye is suited to sight while those of the foot are not.[36]

This battery of positions is typical of late fifteenth-century psychological thought, which, like Aristotelian philosophy in general, was increasingly dominated by rival schools self-consciously identified as followers of Thomas, Duns Scotus and Albertus Magnus among the *antiqui*, or of the *via moderna*. [37] But we should not dismiss the debate on the faculties as yet another fruitless manifestation of the backward-looking sterility of late scholastic thought. If the problem became one of the favourite psychological questions used by philosophers to establish their credentials for belonging to a particular school, it also forced them in the process to clarify their ideas on the subject and to argue the old positions in new contexts and new ways. The most obvious beneficiary of this close attention was the 'nominalist' position concerning the faculties. Over the course of the sixteenth century more and more philosophers without any specific commitment to the *via moderna* began to move towards an assertion of the

---

35. Typical examples at the University of Paris included Petrus Tartaretus (1503b, f. 116[r–v]); and Johannes de Magistris (1481, sigs. r 2[r]–3[r]). Cf. Duns Scotus, II *Sent.* d. 16, nn. 17–19 (1891–5, XIII, pp. 43–4).
36. See, e.g., again from Paris, George of Brussels and Bricot 1508, ff. 107[r]–8[v]. Cf. Ockham 1494–6, IV, sig. h 7[r]; Buridan 1518, f. 8[ra]; Ailly 1494b, sig. a 4[v].
37. On this development see the classic study Ritter 1921–2, II, as well as the more recent essays in *Antiqui und Moderni* 1974. The same phenomenon was apparent, although less pronounced, in Italian universities of the same period: Mahoney 1974, 1980; Poppi 1964. On the situation at Paris see Renaudet 1953, chs. 1–3; Élie 1950–1.

identity of the soul and its faculties and a corresponding emphasis on the organs of the body as the key to psychological function below the level of intellection.

To what can we attribute this change? The answer seems to lie in the general convergence around 1500 of the modernist programme and the new Renaissance reading of Aristotle described in chapter 13 of this volume. Drawing on the newly available Greek texts of Aristotle and his late classical commentators, philosophers increasingly sought to excavate the doctrines of the 'real' Aristotle from accretions and interpolations introduced by medieval commentators – of which the elaborate doctrine of the faculties was a signal example. This enterprise preoccupied contemporaries as different from each other as, for example, Josse Clichtove, collaborator of Lefèvre d'Étaples at the University of Paris, and Agostino Nifo at Padua. Working from the Greek tradition, both ended up by questioning the validity of the real distinction between the soul and its faculties – Nifo on technical grounds having to do with the relationship between the subject and its proper passions, and Clichtove on grounds of philology and common sense.[38]

By the middle of the sixteenth century, the doctrine of the faculties had become in some circles an emblem for the tendency of earlier Aristotelian philosophers to lose themselves in meaningless quibbles. In the words of Philipp Melanchthon, the humanist and Lutheran publicist who restructured the philosophy curriculum in the Protestant universities:

there has been a great and foolish battle in the schools about the distinction of the faculties. Concerning the organic powers, it is clear that they are distinguished by their organs; for the soul produces different operations in different organs, just as different sounds are produced in different pipes. Thus if anyone wants to enquire into the faculties and actions of the soul, he must know the organs and parts of the body.[39]

In a typically historicist treatment of the problem, Melanchthon traced the origin of the notion of faculty to the early Christian writer Gregory of Nyssa, who adopted it not for philosophical reasons, but to illuminate 'many matters having to do with the church'.[40] Following Gregory, we may wish from time to time to speak 'as if' the soul had really distinct

38. Nifo 1523a, f. 74^{r-v}; see also Mahoney 1971a, p. 142, 1974, p. 280, Lefèvre d'Étaples and Clichtove 1502, ff. 182^{r-v}, 193^v; see also *Humanism in France* 1970, pp. 132–49 (Rice); Massaut 1968, I, chs. 1–3.
39. Melanchthon 1834–60, XIII, col. 20 (*Liber de anima*). For background to Melanchthon as an Aristotelian writer see Petersen 1921, pp. 38–101.
40. Melanchthon 1834–60, XIII, cols. 6–7 (*Liber de anima*). Melanchthon was probably referring to the *De natura hominis* of Nemesius of Emesa, which circulated during the Middle Ages under the name of Gregory of Nyssa; see *Catalogus translationum* 1960–, VI, pp. 31–68.

faculties, Melanchthon notes, but we should never lose sight of the fact that we are really talking about organs and physiology, and that the whole quarrel about the ontological status of the faculties is in reality a useless debate about words.[41] The Spanish humanist Juan Luis Vives placed it among 'those questions that it is nearly impossible to explain, and that once explained bear no fruit'.[42]

This is not to say that the organic faculties died a swift and silent death over the course of the sixteenth century. As I have already emphasised, the tradition of philosophical psychology was highly pluralistic. Even late in the period we can find statements of the Thomist doctrine in the works of Francisco Suárez and Emmanuel de Goes, author of the Coimbra commentary on *De anima*, both of whom participated in the Counter-Reformation programme to keep alive the doctrines and authority of Thomas Aquinas and other medieval philosophers.[43] In Italy, too, Jacopo Zabarella adopted a characteristically (for him) conservative position in favour of a real distinction between the soul and its faculties. At the same time, however, he noted that 'the majority of recent philosophers follow the [contrary] opinion'.[44] Indeed, by the early seventeenth century most writers on Aristotelian psychology would have agreed with the spirit of Descartes's assessment in the *Meditation sixième*: 'And the faculties of willing, feeling, conceiving, etc. cannot be properly speaking said to be its parts, for it is one and the same mind which employs itself in willing and in feeling and understanding.'[45]

Although Vives and Melanchthon reflect particularly clearly the two main trends in sixteenth-century philosophical discussions of the organic soul, we can see hints of these changes in the works of even philosophical conservatives such as Zabarella. The first such trend was the accelerating tendency to simplify psychological theory by eliminating or reinterpreting traditional explanatory entities and causes introduced into Aristotelian psychology over the course of the late classical period and the Arabic and Latin Middle Ages. In addition to the faculties themselves these included a number of particular psychological operations, most notably the internal senses of cogitation and estimation, which – as many sixteenth-century writers hastened to point out – were nowhere to be found in *De anima*. Even before 1500 there were hints of scepticism concerning the traditional

41. *Ibid.*, cols. 19–20.   42. Vives 1538 (dedicatory epistle); cf., on the faculties, pp. 14, 47.
43. Suárez 1978–81, II, pp. 56–74 (d. 3, q. 1); *Collegium Conimbricense* 1606, pp. 100–4, 175–7 (II, cap. 1, q. 4; II, cap. 3, q. 4).   44. J. Zabarella 1607a, col. 696.   45. Descartes 1897–1910, IX, p. 68.

doctrine of the internal senses at Paris and elsewhere.[46] A hundred years later most philosophers had either conflated them into a single function, usually called imagination, or at least rejected those not attested by Aristotle and his Greek commentators. As Zabarella argued, 'I think in this matter that we should not go back on Aristotle, who set out no other internal faculty of the sensitive soul pertaining to cognition than common sense, fantasy, and memory.'[47]

In the same way – and for many of the same reasons – we witness the gradual disappearance of the sensible *species* from Aristotelian accounts of sensation. Here the process of reformulation was somewhat slower, since earlier philosophers had failed to come up with an adequate substitute,[48] but the tendency was clear. In his commentary on *De sensu* (1566) Simone Simoni noted that the doctrine of *species* had been rejected by some of 'the most illustrious philosophers of [his] time', while Zabarella noted that many recent writers had eliminated them from their discussions of all of the senses except vision.[49] Shortly afterwards, Francesco Piccolomini replaced these travelling images by a sequence of 'motions' or 'spiritual actions' transmitted through the medium – an interpretation that he thought more consonant with the opinion of Aristotle in *De sensu* and that reminds us of Descartes's pressure model in *Le Monde*.[50] By the middle of the seventeenth century, Hobbes was one of many who would have cited the doctrine of *species* as an example of 'insignificant speech'.[51]

The second general change we see over the course of the sixteenth century is the increasing tendency to favour specific physiological over general philosophical explanations for the organic functions – a tendency reflected in the emphasis by Melanchthon and others on the organs rather than the faculties as the principle of differentiation of the organic functions.

---

46. E.g., at Paris, Versor 1489, sig. c 7ʳ, where he doubts the existence of a real distinction between the various internal senses; Tartaretus 1503b, f. 123ʳ, who refers to them as 'whether they are several or only one'; George of Brussels and Bricot 1508, f. 132ᵛ, who tentatively recognise only common sense and imagination; Lefèvre d'Étaples and Clichtove 1502, f. 205ʳ, who argue strongly for a single internal sense.

47. J. Zabarella 1607a, col. 721. See also *Collegium Conimbricense* 1606, pp. 458–63 (III, cap. 3, q. 2, art. 2); F. Piccolomini 1596, ff. 49ᵛ–50ʳ, citing Theophrastus, Alexander of Aphrodisias, Simplicius, Themistius and Philoponus.

48. Ockham's attempt to eliminate the *species* through the doctrine of intuitive cognition found few adherents, even among his followers. See A. Maier 1964–77, II, pp. 433–48; George of Brussels and Bricot 1508, f. 132ʳ. One exception was Johannes de Mirecourt 1958, pp. 415–28 (q. 4).

49. Simoni 1566, p. 90; J. Zabarella 1607a, cols. 831–56 (*De sensu agente*).

50. F. Piccolomini 1596, f. 40ᵛ; Descartes 1897–1910, XI, pp. 97–103; see also T. S. Hall 1970.

51. Hobbes 1946, p. 8 (part 1, ch. 1).

As we have already seen in Reisch's *Margarita philosophica*, there was a strong mechanistic element even in earlier Aristotelian psychology, but it was a kind of macroscopic mechanism based on general intuition and common sense. During the sixteenth century, philosophers began to shy away from the simple older models and to look to classical and contemporary medicine for more precise and convincing substitutes, although most were still content to assimilate the new findings into a streamlined and purified version of the traditional Aristotelian doctrine. In part this change reflected the new interest in Greek sources which permeated philosophical thought; for Melanchthon and his fellow humanists, anatomy ('that ancient medical doctrine', as he called it) was one of the finest products of Greek science and Vesalius the high priest of its restoration.[52] In part it sprang from the highly publicised and intellectually fashionable work of Vesalius himself and his successors at Padua and other Italian medical faculties. In psychology as well as medicine there are signs that anatomy and physiology were beginning to replace demonstrative Aristotelian natural philosophy, at least temporarily, as the prime models of scientific explanation.[53]

In any case, it became commonplace for commentators on *De anima* and other writers in the Aristotelian tradition – even the most conservative – to introduce arguments based on anatomical information into treatments of the organic soul. Some began to approach the vexed problem of the origin of the soul as a problem in embryology rather than in metaphysics or theology; for many sixteenth-century philosophers, unlike their medieval predecessors, the answer lay in the sequential development of the organs rather than in the successive infusion of different levels of soul.[54] Debates concerning the nature and process of sensation were often settled by appeals to the anatomy of the sense organs; for instance Suárez, in his question 'what is the organ of hearing', invoked the dissections of Vesalius and Valverde as well as the doctrines of Aristotle, Simplicius and Thomas Aquinas.[55] Questions concerning the general relation of soul and body could become occasions for detailed exercises in physiology. Consider, for example, Francesco Piccolomini's elaborate discussion of the seat of the soul; in the course of arguing for Aristotle's placement of the soul in the heart he referred to a variety of recent medical experiments including the attempt of Realdo Colombo and Paolo da Urbino to remove the heart from a living

52. Melanchthon 1834–60, XIII, cols. 20, 62 (*Liber de anima*).
53. See *Platon et Aristote* 1976, pp. 217–24, especially 221–3 (Roger).
54. Pagel 1967, pp. 233–47; 1969–70.   55. Suárez 1978–81, II, pp. 684–6 (d. 7, q. 9).

dog.[56] Such arguments did not by any means replace more traditional appeals to authority and *ratio*, but they added a dimension which had been lacking in many of the earlier treatments. In some cases they even prompted dramatic revisions in common doctrine; by the end of the sixteenth century Piccolomini and others were locating the internal senses no longer in the ventricles of the brain, but in its substance and convolutions.[57]

Perhaps the most telling indicator of these changes was the evolving state of the classic question 'whether the sensitive and rational souls are really distinct'. Can we assume, in other words, that each human being has two entirely separate souls – an organic one shared with the higher animals and an intellective one unique to man? The negative position, which held that humans possessed only an immortal and intellective soul, was by far the more common throughout the early Renaissance. The affirmative opinion was identified with Averroes and rejected as both un-Christian and incompatible with the dictates of reason by virtually all writers on *De anima* in the later fourteenth and fifteenth centuries, with the exception of Paul of Venice.[58] From the middle of the sixteenth century on, however, perhaps as a result of the revival of interest in Averroes (see chapter 13 in this volume), we find philosophers more open to this position. Zabarella held it himself and attributed it to 'a number of recent writers, especially Averroists'.[59] It gave a new autonomy and general prominence to the organic soul, together with the physiological forces that governed it, and allowed it to be studied separately, even in man.

But the real significance of this argument appears most clearly in the works of a small but growing number of philosophers who described the organic soul as material – it was already accepted by many to be extended and divisible[60] – and identified it with *spiritus*, the vapour refined from blood that was thought to fill the arteries and the nerves. Melanchthon had tentatively proposed this theory in the 1550s,[61] but it found its most important subscriber in Bernardino Telesio, who despite his deep criticisms of Aristotle stood clearly within the Aristotelian tradition in psychology. In

---

56. F. Piccolomini 1596, f. 8^{r-v}. He received with scepticism their claim that the dog was thereafter seen to walk and bark.
57. *Ibid.*, ff. 12^{r}, 13^{v}; he attributed the emphasis on the ventricles to Avicenna. Other examples in Pagel 1958b, pp. 104–9.
58. Paul of Venice 1503, f. 68^{v}; 1481, sig. d 8^{r-v}. Jean de Jandun held the same position in the early fourteenth century; see McClintock 1956, pp. 58–64 for background and discussion of the issue.
59. J. Zabarella 1607a, col. 707; cf. col. 717. Zabarella argued elsewhere (cols. 399–400) in favour of the plurality of substantial forms.
60. See Suárez 1978–81, II, pp. 10–12 (d. 2, q. 7), for the proponents of this position and their arguments.
61. Melanchthon 1834–60, XIII, cols. 16, 18 (*Liber de anima*).

Telesio's *De rerum natura* (1586) *spiritus* appeared no longer as the instrument of the organic soul, as it had been for Reisch and the rest, but as its very substance – a position he attributed to Aristotle himself.[62] In human beings, according to Telesio, this spirit-soul is supplemented by a separate, incorporeal and individual intellective soul, infused by God; in animals (and plants), however, the incorporeal element is absent, and the entire composite functions, as both Melanchthon and Telesio's follower Campanella put it, like a 'machine' (*machina*).[63]

62. Telesio 1586, p. 223 (v.38), and, in general, pp. 209–12, 216–19 (v.27–8 and 33–4). See also Walker 1958, pp. 190–4; Abbagnano 1941, ch. 6. Francis Bacon was influenced by Telesian teachings on the subject: F. Bacon 1857–74, I, p. 604 (*De augmentis* IV.3); Walker 1985, § X, pp. 124–5.
63. Melanchthon 1834–60, XIII, col. 106 (*Liber de anima*); Campanella 1939, p. 349 (v.6).

15

THE INTELLECTIVE SOUL

Aristotle's teaching on the intellective soul (*De anima* III.4–5) serves as the starting-point for Renaissance discussions and, therefore, predetermines the questions raised and the answers given. In the Averroist tradition, this was treated as the beginning of the entire third book. Chapter 4[1] attempts to define the activity of the intellective soul through analogy to sense-perception and by so doing introduces an interdependence between psychological and epistemological theories. In the fifth chapter,[2] distinguishing between the possible and the agent intellect, Aristotle goes beyond the analogy with sense-perception and alludes to the active role of the soul in the process of knowing. This extremely condensed and enigmatic chapter has provoked many different interpretations, ranging from the outright denial of the agent intellect[3] to the postulation of an agent sense as well,[4] in order to maintain the analogy with sense-perception. For those commentators, however, who kept between these two extremes, III.5 provided both the chance and the need for metaphysical speculation on the ontological status of the intellective soul including its relation to the celestial intelligences and the question of its immortality. It was to this last question that particular attention had to be paid, since on the one hand, Aristotle is not explicit about it, and on the other, Christian doctrine required an affirmation. Thus, for the Middle Ages the question was not whether the human soul was immortal but rather how an immortal soul could fit into the ontological structure of the universe. Consequently, the metaphysical point of view gained prominence, until, in fourteenth-century nominalism, metaphysics lost ground and a new approach was possible from the perspectives of natural philosophy and epistemology.

---

1. Aristotle, *De anima* III.4 (429[a]10–430[a]9) (t. c. 1–16).
2. Aristotle, *De anima* III.5 (430[a]9–25) (t. c. 17–20).
3. Durandus a S. Porciano 1567, ff. 27[a]–8[a] (lib. I, dist. 3, cap. 5); *Cambridge History* 1982, p. 628 (Kuksewicz).   4. McClintock 1956, pp. 10–50; L. A. Kennedy 1966.

THE FIFTEENTH CENTURY: BLASIUS OF PARMA TO NICOLETTO VERNIA

The first period of Renaissance psychology dates from the introduction of this new approach to Italy at the end of the fourteenth century and ends in the last decade of the fifteenth century, when new source materials discovered by the humanists first entered the discussion. The period's main characteristic was the attempt to synthesise 'radical' naturalistic Aristotelianism, based on Averroes and imported from Paris to Padua by Pietro d'Abano,[5] with the Oxford tradition of logical and mathematical analysis developed by Ockham and his followers. This attempt was accompanied by the humanist polemic against both the 'Averroist dogs'[6] and the *barbari Britanni*,[7] and, as time went on, was more and more censured, until finally suppressed by the church.

Blasius of Parma

In some respects, Blasius of Parma may be considered the first Renaissance psychologist.[8] He was the most highly esteemed Italian philosopher at the turn of the century and played a key role in introducing British philosophy to his country.

He was also on good terms with contemporary humanists, such as Coluccio Salutati, thus proving that in spite of outward polemics, an Aristotelian philosopher could be open to new humanist ideas.[9]

Blasius' *Quaestiones de anima* show a naturalistic approach rather close to that of Buridan.[10] Clearly distinguishing between religious belief and philosophical knowledge,[11] he sided with the latter, accepting as true only what is known through experience or reason or inferred from such evidence.[12] Since the essence of the intellect is known neither by itself nor through evident experience,[13] it can only be inferred from the intellectual

---

5. However, as Nardi 1958, pp. 1–74 has proved, Pietro d'Abano was not an Averroist in the sense of Renan 1866, pp. 326–8.
6. Petrarch 1554, f. 812: 'contra canem illum rabidum Averroim'; Renan 1866, pp. 328–38.
7. Garin 1969, pp. 139–66.
8. Lohr 1967, pp. 381–3; *Dictionary of Scientific Biography* 1970–80, II, pp. 192–5; Thorndike 1923–58, IV, pp. 65–79, 657–62; Federici-Vescovini 1979; Blasius 1974.
9. Gherardi 1867, I, 1, p. 136. The extent to which Blasius' meeting Salutati and his circle influenced his thinking is not yet clear. Regarding the role he attributes to fame and glory (Blasius 1974, p. 79: *primum dubium*), he seems not untouched by the humanists' ideas on this subject.
10. Blasius 1974, pp. 25–36, 44–51.
11. *Ibid.*, p. 71: 'Secundum corollarium: . . . ubi tu intendas fidem substentare, cuius est credere, depone tunc habitum philosophicum, cuius est notitiam habere evidentem. Et ubi econverso, te fidem Christi oportet relinquere.'
12. *Ibid.*, p. 74: 'Prima propositio'. 13. *Ibid.*, p. 76: 'Prima et secunda conclusio'.

operations of the soul, which are observable and therefore the phenomena to be saved by the concept of intellect as their supposed cause.[14] Thus the nature of intellect can be determined only through the analysis of intellection. The crucial question of whether the intellect has to be regarded as existing immaterially and independently from the body (being a subject of metaphysics) or as existing only in relation to the body whose form it is (therefore being a genuine subject of natural philosophy) according to Aristotle depends on whether or not there are operations of the soul, independent of the body.[15]

Yet, such operations cannot be observed. If one analyses the process of intellection as analogous to sense-perception, it becomes clear that the soul requires an object, which is simultaneously present and appropriately distanced. Distance, however, implies extension, and extension, matter, so that the object of intellection is necessarially a material one. But since this applies to both external and internal objects, which may be recalled, any concept of intellect has to be represented in matter.[16] Consequently, there is no intellectual operation which is not also a natural process through which matter is formed according to its specific potentiality,[17] the only specificity being that the natural process of intellection is followed by the assent or dissent of the soul, in which truth or error consists.[18] From this materialistic theory of knowledge Blasius infers a necessarily materialistic concept of the soul, according to which the entire soul, including the intellect, is just a particular form, drawn out of the potentiality of matter and passing away with the dissolution of the body.[19]

It is obvious that Blasius' materialism, prefiguring to a certain extent the Alexandrist position of the sixteenth century,[20] fits into neither the medieval philosophical nor religious tradition. He therefore had to justify himself before the Bishop of Pavia in 1396; but the church was satisfied with the declaration that he had never intended to deny Christian belief.[21] In an appendix to his argument Blasius tried to prove philosophically that his

14. *Ibid.*, p. 67: 'nota: . . . Ista conclusio patet, quia omnia possunt salvari.'
15. *Ibid.*, pp. 62–8: 'Secundum articulum'; Aristotle, *De anima* ($403^a8–28$).
16. *Ibid.*, p. 65: 'Quinta conclusio; prima et secunda conclusio'.
17. *Ibid.*, p. 68: 'Tertium dubium: . . . omnis propositio est materialis postquam omnis propositio est subiective in materia et educta de potentia eius'; pp. 74–5: 'Prima propositio: . . . Et sic apparet, quod intellectus est sicut virtus mere naturalis et non voluntaria.'
18. *Ibid.*, pp. 66–7: 'nota: . . . dicamus solummodum quod animam habere scientiam est ipsam assentire'.
19. *Ibid.*, p. 79: 'Ultima conclusio: quod anima intellectiva hominis sit educta de potentia materiae generabilis et corruptibilis, habet quilibet de plano concedere.'
20. *Ibid.*, p. 23; Poppi 1970a, p. 22.
21. Blasius 1974, p. 20: *University Records* 1944, pp. 258f.; A. Maier 1966, pp. 279–99.

concept of the soul permitted moral philosophy, although it lacked a
transcendental principle, and that it could be integrated into metaphysics
based on astrological assumptions.[22]

Paul of Venice

Even if Blasius' radical approach did not have an immediate successor, his
emphasis on the methodological principle of determining the essence of the
soul according to the requirements of the related theory of cognition seems
to have set the tone for future discussion. Paolo Nicoletti da Udine or Paul
of Venice,[23] who had studied at Oxford and introduced Ockhamist logic to
Padua,[24] was notable for two attitudes in natural philosophy. First, he tried
to reconcile Paduan Averroism to the logic of the *moderni*, thereby – at least
as far as the concept of universals was concerned – accommodating the latter
to the needs of the former.[25] Secondly, he endeavoured to elaborate a
genuine philosophy of nature, which for him was identical with Aristotle's
teaching and to a certain extent with that of Averroes, though differing
from the latter on some substantial points.[26]

Paul's psychological teaching can be understood in terms of these
tendencies,[27] at the bottom of which was his theory of universals. While for
Blasius a universal, like any other object of knowledge, was gained by mere
reception of a form by the appropriately disposed matter, for Ockhamists
universals were mere concepts of the mind. Consequently any science, in so
far as it derived from universals, was purely conceptual, lacking the
fundamentum in re.[28] Paul adhered to the Ockhamist principle that the
particular is the starting-point for all knowledge and that the universal is not
merely received in a passive way, but actively produced in the process of
intellection.[29] To maintain a realistic science of nature, however, Paul
argued that this universal stands for something existing outside the mind in
individual things and is gained through abstraction.[30]

22. Blasius 1974, pp. 78f.
23. F. Momigliano 1907; Nardi 1945, pp. 115–32; Perreiah 1967; *Scienza e filosofia* 1983, pp. 85–135
    (Bottin); Lohr 1972a, pp. 314–20.   24. Poppi 1970a, p. 23.
25. *Aristotelismo veneto* 1983, I, pp. 459–68 (Bottin).
26. *Ibid.*, pp. 297–324, 325–47 (Kuksewicz).
27. Paul of Venice 1503, ff. 66rb–92vb; *De anima*, composed in 1408: see *Scienza e filosofia* 1983, p. 93
    (Bottin); Paul of Venice 1481, composed during his later teaching.
28. Ockham 1957, pp. 3–17 (*Expositio super VIII libros Physicorum, prologus*).
29. Paul of Venice 1503, ff. 89vb–90va; 1481, sig. y 4ra (lib. III ad t.c. 11); *Scienza e filosofia* 1983, pp. 109–
    15 (Bottin); *Aristotelismo veneto* 1983, I, pp. 342–5 (Kuksewicz).
30. Paul of Venice 1503, ff. 93vb–4ra: 'Secunda conclusio: universalia habent esse actuale extra animam
    preter operationem intellectus . . . Quarta conclusio: universalia sunt in suis singularibus et
    identificantur cum illis.' *Aristotelismo veneto* 1983, I, pp. 459–68 *passim* (Bottin); *Scienza e filosofia*
    1983, pp. 109–15 (Bottin).

To grasp universals, which are eternal like the species of the particular entities and immaterial in themselves, the possible intellect itself must also be immaterial and eternal.[31] But if such is the case, there must be only one possible intellect for all human beings, since there cannot be a plurality of eternal beings, differing only numerically.[32] Paul's theory of cognition led him to reject the plurality as well as the mortality of the soul and even the doctrine of divine creation; he accepted instead the Averroist theory of the unified intellect. Because of the same theory of cognition, however, Paul disagreed with Averroes regarding the consequences to be drawn from the unity of the intellect.

No doubt, both agreed that instead of the intellect, as Blasius had taught, the *anima cogitativa*, the supreme mode of the sensitive soul and specific to man,[33] served as the inherent form of the human body, being drawn from the potentiality of matter and passing away with the dissolution of the body.[34] Averroes had had the single intellect united to man only in the act of intellection,[35] so that it was the intellect, using man as its instrument, which gained the knowledge, and so that it was one and the same cognition which resulted from different men knowing the same universal. According to Paul, however, the one intellect was the *forma informans* of man, which gave him his essential being and allowed the individual to be the subject of his own knowledge.[36] Thus just as the universality of knowledge was given certitude by the acceptance of eternal and immaterial universals which, according to Averroes, required a single eternal and immaterial intellect, the individuality of knowledge was saved through Paul's theory of the *forma informans*, agreeing with the nominalistically coloured concept of the universals as having actual existence only in the particular.[37]

Finally the problem of how to account for the simultaneous individuality and universality of intellection also dominated his concept of the agent

31. Paul of Venice 1503, f. 88[va–b]: 'Secunda conclusio'.
32. *Ibid.*, f. 88[va]: 'secundo notandum'; f. 88[vb]: 'Quarta conclusio'; 1481, sig. z 7[ra–b] (lib III, ad t. c. 27); *Aristotelismo veneto* 1983, I, pp. 327–30 (Kuksewicz).
33. Paul of Venice 1503, f. 84[ra]; Averroes 1953, pp. 475–6 (lib. III, ad t. c. 33).
34. Paul of Venice 1503, f. 89[ra]: 'Ad primum'; f. 88[ra]: 'Tertia conclusio'.
35. *Ibid.*, f. 88[ra]: 'Secunda conclusio'; Averroes 1953, p. 404 (lib. III ad t. c. 5).
36. Paul of Venice 1503, f. 88[ra]: 'Quarta conclusio: Anima intellectiva unitur homini substantialiter per informationem: ita quod est forma substantialis corporis humani: non solum dans operari, sicut intelligentia orbi, sed etiam esse specificum et essentiale.' According to Nardi 1945, pp. 121–7, Paul was following Siger of Brabant.
37. See n. 30 above. For his concept of individual knowledge, see Paul of Venice 1503, f. 89[ra]: 'Ad tertium . . . diceret Commentator quod in duobus hominibus non potest esse nisi unum intelligere universale, licet plura sint particularia ratione multitudinis fantasmatum. Sed ego pono in eodem intellectu plures intellectiones universales . . . et ita conceditur quod eadem grammatica tua et grammatica mea, sed est alia et alia sicut alia et alia species in intellectu.'

intellect as being the effective principle of the intelligible *species* and of the general process of intellection.[38] In his *Summa* Paul claims that the agent intellect cannot be regarded as a separate substance, but has to be equivalent to the possible intellect, an inherent accident of the intellective soul, for 'if a separate intellect illuminated the *phantasmata* and abstracted the intelligible species, one would not say that the intellective soul was abstracting them'.[39] This means that man would not be actively involved in the act of knowledge. In his later commentary, however, he was preoccupied with the universality rather than with the individuality of intellection, postulating the agent intellect as a separate substance identical with God,[40] thus providing a supernatural and divine guarantee for scientific knowledge.

Here, as throughout his reconstruction of the intellective soul, Paul claims to defend Aristotle's position and consequently that of natural philosophy as such. Yet he does not claim – and in this again he differs from Blasius – that the *ratio naturalis* is identical with evident truth itself and that Christian doctrine, in so far as it teaches the plurality of immortal intellective souls, is subject to mere belief. On the contrary, in his later commentary, after having treated the theory of the unity of the intellect as being the position of natural philosophy, Paul discussed whether this position could be demonstrated through evidence: he denied it, adducing rational arguments for the Christian plurality thesis.[41] Thus, while eager himself not to confuse the argument from natural philosophy with that from Christian doctrine, in his old age – appropriately for the head of the Augustinian Hermits – he readmitted Christian philosophy to the psychological discussion. It was not, it seems, in vain.

Gaetano da Thiene

Paul of Venice's former student and later successor to the chair of natural philosophy, Gaetano da Thiene, not only followed in his master's footsteps, but also tried to develop his ideas further.[42] He followed the Oxford logical tradition, attempting to reconcile the nominalistic to the realistic view of

38. *Ibid.*, f. 90vb: 'Prima conclusio: intellectus agens est principium effectivum speciei intelligibilis et actus intellectionis.'
39. *Ibid.*, f. 89ra: 'Notandum primo . . . Si enim intellectus separatus irridiaret fantasmata et abstraheret species intelligibiles, tunc anima intellectiva non diceretur abstrahere.'
40. Paul of Venice 1481, sig. y 4vb (lib. III ad t. c. 19): 'Nec aliqua intelligentia preter primam, que est Deus, potuit esse intellectus agens.' *Aristotelismo veneto* 1983, I, pp. 338–41 (Kuksewicz); Nardi 1945, pp. 121–7 again relates this position to Siger of Brabant.
41. Paul of Venice 1481, sigs. z 7rb–8ra (lib. III ad t. c. 27): 'Utrum ratione evidenti possit probari unicum esse intellectum omnium hominum'; *Aristotelismo veneto* 1983, I, pp. 327–30 (Kuksewicz).
42. Sartori 1938; Valsanzibio 1949; Wallace 1972–, I, pp. 127–30; *Scienza e filosofia* 1983, pp. 125–34 (Bottin); Lohr 1967, pp. 390–2.

universals. Thus, for Gaetano universals taken as human intentions are posterior to the particular, so that cognition must begin with particulars; yet, taken as universal causes, they must be prior to the particular effect, so that universal knowledge implies knowledge of real causes.[43]

With regard to natural philosophy in general, Gaetano laid the basis for a genuine Aristotelian position in the Averroist tradition, but in psychology his main purpose was to combine the Averroist interpretation with the Latin tradition, especially that of Albertus Magnus.[44] He agreed with Averroes that the soul could not be the substantial form of man, educed from the potentiality of matter, as generally applied to the substantial form of natural beings. This would have resulted in a materialism not only excluding the immortality of the soul, but also removing the distinction between knowledge and sense-perception.[45] On the other hand, he rejected Averroes' solution of the unicity of the intellect – although he mentioned all the arguments in favour of it [46] – since a unified intellect implied that the common intellect, not the human individual, was the subject of intellection and therefore no individual knowledge would have been possible.[47]

Gaetano thus arrives at the alternative, repeated later by Cardinal Bessarion and passing from him to Pomponazzi, that according to Aristotle the intellective soul is either individual or immortal, but cannot be both.[48] Yet, while Bessarion and Pomponazzi use this alternative to counter any attempt at a Thomist interpretation of Aristotle, Gaetano offers the Christian position as a compromise solution to the dilemma. He argues that the intellective soul is multiplied according to the number of bodies, yet not generated from the potentiality of matter, but rather created by God and infused into the predisposed human body. This hypothesis of creation allows for individuality and immortality at the same time. Moreover, it allows the intellective soul to be subject to natural causation as far as

43. *Scienza e filosofia* 1983, pp. 126–9 (Bottin); Gaetano da Thiene 1493, f. 4va (lib. I ad t. c. 8).

44. Besides the commentary on the *De anima* of 1443, there is the earlier *Quaestio utrum intellectus humanus sit perpetuus* from 1436, later included in the editions of the commentary (Gaetano da Thiene 1493, ff. 84va–5rb). See Valsanzibio 1949, pp. 21–7.

45. Gaetano da Thiene 1493, ff. 57va–8ra (lib. III ad t. c. 5): 'Septimo arguitur quod si anima intellectiva esset forma materialis individuata et multiplicata multiplicatione individuorum humanorum, tunc ipsa non reciperet nisi individualiter cum hic et nunc. Consequens est falsum, quia tunc non posset intelligere universaliter.'

46. *Ibid.*, f. 58^{va-b} (lib. III ad t. c. 5: 'Sed si quis Averroi nimis afficeretur').

47. *Ibid.*, ff. 58vb–9ra (lib. III ad t. c. 5: 'Licet ista positio'): 'primo sequitur, quod nullus homo potest intelligere'.

48. Bessarion 1927, p. 375: 'igitur alterum de his duobus dicat necesse est, aut enim unum eundemque intellectum omnibus esse aut una cum corpore animam interire. Quo fit, ut nemo ex Aristotelis opinione possit animam dicere distingui ad corporis distinctionem et eandem post corporis corruptionem permanere.' See Nardi 1965, pp. 23, 138, 197, 270, 373f.

intellection of the particular is concerned and, at the same time, to participate in the process of abstraction and to be exempt from natural causality in volitional acts.[49]

Gaetano's solution, though incompatible with Aristotle's teaching, seems to synthesise various contemporary tendencies. Following Paul of Venice's later approach, he reconciled psychology to Christian dogma, while maintaining the principle of saving the phenomena of intellection. At the same time his position, in so far as it includes free choice, agrees with humanist anthropology[50] and, in so far as it attributes to the intellective soul a supernatural origin and assigns to man an essence intermediate between the two extremes of natural and spiritual,[51] opens the discussion of the soul to approaches from principles beyond pure natural philosophy and to the influences of the rising Neoplatonism. In fact, Gaetano's former student Johannes Argyropulos, lecturing on the *De anima* in Florence in 1460, apparently not only followed the attitude of his Paduan teacher towards Averroes and Christian dogma, but even went further by introducing Plato into the psychological discussion, proving that the Aristotelian concept of agent intellect was compatible with the Platonic theory of reminiscence.[52]

Nicoletto Vernia

Another of Gaetano's former students and his successor for thirty-three years, Nicoletto Vernia,[53] a singularly curious character,[54] was less prepared to accept Gaetano's irenic compromise, at any rate in his youth. Devoted to a rigorous Aristotelian concept of natural science based on a knowledge of real causes and therefore presupposing the existence of *universalia realia*,[55] Vernia's first psychological writing, the *Quaestio de*

49. Gaetano da Thiene 1493, f. 58[ra] (lib. III ad t. c. 5): 'Fuit et tertia positio ceteris tutior et magis credenda: non solum quia fides catholica christianorum eam tenet, sed etiam ex se ipsa. Quia ponit animam humanam non generari ab agente particulari, educente eam de potentia materie, sed ab agente supernaturali, videlicet deo ipso creari ex nihilo, et materie ab agente particulari predisposite infundi et corpori humani uniri secundum esse. Et dicit ulterius, quod ipsa est indivisibilis et multiplicabilis secundum corporum multiplicationem quibus unitur, et est immortalis, et quod ab eius substantia fluunt potentie plures, videlicet intellectus agens, quo active concurrit ad species intelligibiles et intellectiones, et intellectus possibilis, quo ad predicta passive concurrit, et voluntas, qua velle et nolle libere potest.'   50. Trinkaus 1970.

51. Gaetano da Thiene 1493, f. 58[rb–va]: 'Ad septimum dicitur . . . ex quo patet, quod anima intellectiva est medium inter supercelestia et ista inferiora generabilia et corruptibilia per participationem conditionum utriusque extremorum, in quo superiora cum inferioribus coniunguntur . . . quod ipsa est supra naturam et infra intelligentiam'; f. 58[vb] (Ad sextum).

52. V. Brown 1974, pp. 170–2.

53. Ragnisco 1890–1, 1891; Garin 1961, pp. 293–9; Vasoli 1968b, pp. 241–56; Mahoney 1978; *Scienza e filosofia* 1983, pp. 135–73 (Mahoney); Lohr 1972a, pp. 308–9.   54. Nardi 1958, pp. 95–126.

55. *Aristotelismo veneto* 1983, II, pp. 813–42 (Pagallo); Vasoli 1968b, pp. 241–56; *Scienza e filosofia* 1983, pp. 161–3 (Mahoney); Nardi 1958, p. 107.

unitate intellectus,[56] sided with Gaetano in favour of Averroism as being the genuine teaching of Aristotle; and in spite of drawing heavily, as Gaetano had done, on Albertus Magnus, Vernia was eager to reject the creation hypothesis of the Latins on the grounds that it was incompatible with the physical principles of the eternity of the world and the impossibility of creation *ex nihilo*.

Yet, it soon became clear that changing times no longer allowed such a clear-cut Averroism. In 1489 Bishop Barozzi of Padua issued a decree forbidding public discussion of the unity of the intellect and compelled Vernia to recant[57] in a second treatise against Averroes,[58] written in 1492 and approved by the examining bishops in 1499.[59] At first glance it seems to be simply an act of submission to the church. At the outset, Vernia promises to prove that Christian doctrine can be defended against all contradictory philosophical arguments.[60] Later he claims that the Christian hypothesis of a temporal creation of the soul is compatible with Aristotle and provable by natural arguments in accord with the phenomena.[61] Ultimately he admitted that only through revelation and divine illumination can the Christian believer reach this truth, and therefore only *doctores fideles* are qualified to argue the subject. Therefore he submitted his own writing to their critique, recommending the reader to seek further explanations in the treatise of one of his examiners, Antonio Trombetta, professor of metaphysics and theology *in via Scoti* in Padua.[62] And indeed, Trombetta's arguments, though more circumstantial, come rather close to those of Vernia, including the unusual critique of Duns Scotus' remark that Aristotle had not taken a definite position on the immortality question.[63] They differ only in that Trombetta makes great efforts to prove philosophically the temporal creation of the soul, whereas Vernia merely claims that such a proof is possible.

Upon further consideration, however, Vernia's recantation seems to gain

56. Pagallo 1966; *Philosophy and Humanism* 1976, pp. 145–9 (Mahoney). A critical edition by E. P. Mahoney is announced as being 'in press'.   57. Ragnisco 1891.
58. Vernia, *Contra perversam Averrois opinionem de unitate intellectus et de anime felicitate* in Albert of Saxony 1516.   59. Mahoney 1968, p. 27.
60. Vernia in Albert of Saxony 1516, f. 84[ra]: 'Tertio: christiane fidei sincera veritas dilucidabitur solvendo cunctas philosophorum rationes, que huic veritati obviare videntur.'
61. *Ibid.*, f. 89[vb]: 'Unde credo, quod physice etiam loquendo ponendum sit quod ponit fides de ipsa intellectiva anima, propterea quod secundum ipsam apparentia salvantur, secundum alios vero non universaliter . . . Et non tantum credo hec omnia deducta ex fide, sed physice dico omnia possunt probari, et etiam cum Aristotele potest sic dici non dicendo aliquid contra eius principia, ut multi fideles et scientes viri tenent.'
62. *Ibid.*, f. 91[ra]; Trombetta 1498; Poppi 1962, 1964; Lohr 1967, pp. 366–7.
63. Vernia in Albert of Saxony 1516, f. 88[va]; Poppi 1964, pp. 114–17.

in significance. Of course, the central arguments are still epistemological and aimed at explaining the operations of the intellect, both from physical and metaphysical principles, in order to define the ontological status of the soul. Yet, in Vernia's treatise Aristotle is no longer the Philosopher whose teaching is identical with natural philosophy. Instead, philosophical doctrines are collected from all times and schools, including the Presocratics, Plato, the Neoplatonists, the Greek, Arabic and Latin Peripatetics and even Cicero and the Latin poets such as Vergil. Vernia tries to define those points upon which all or the majority of the most famous agree, in order to base his subsequent arguments on their consensus.[64] This approaches the Neoplatonic conception of a common truth underlying all philosophies which Giovanni Pico, in his *Conclusiones*, was attempting to rediscover at the same time.[65] Pico indeed had been a student and friend of Vernia's[66] and they shared the erroneous thesis that Alexander of Aphrodisias in no way denied the immortality of the soul.[67]

The second authority who is weakened or even replaced in Vernia's treatise is Averroes. While intending to reject Averroes' position on the unity of the intellect, Vernia criticised him on this and related points, but he went even further. Using the new Latin translations of Alexander of Aphrodisias, Themistius and a lost translation of Simplicius, Vernia gave them for the first time the highest status as commentators on Aristotle not only on this question, but in general.[68] On Simplicius' authority he accepted the basic concord between Plato and Aristotle,[69] attempting to reconcile their teachings on the eternity of the soul[70] as well as their theory of knowledge, as Argyropulos had done earlier.[71] Thus Vernia's recantation not only provides evidence of the increasing influence of theology on psychological discussions, but also testifies to the impact that humanism and Neoplatonism would have on later Renaissance psychology.

THE PERIOD OF TRANSITION

The period of transition, from about 1490 to 1520, is marked by two tendencies. First, there was the growing pressure from the alliance of

---

64. See, e.g., Vernia in Albert of Saxony 1516, f. 87[ra]: 'Famosiores vero peripatetici . . . voluerunt . . . omnes grecos . . . precipuos Arabes'.   65. G. Pico 1973; Schmitt 1981, § II.
66. Garin 1961, p. 293; Vasoli 1968b, p. 241.
67. Vernia in Albert of Saxony 1516, f. 85[va]; G. Pico 1973, p. 40 (*Conclusiones secundum Alexandrum*, no. 1); Mahoney 1968.   68. *Scienza e filosofia* 1983, p. 135 (Mahoney).
69. Vernia in Albert of Saxony 1516, f. 87[ra] 'ad mentem Aristotelis tum Platonis inter quos, ut Simplicius refert, non est discordia nisi verbalis'.   70. *Ibid.*, f. 87[ra].
71. *Ibid.*, f. 87[ra]; V. Brown 1974, pp. 170–2.

Neoplatonism and the church, which culminated on 19 December 1513 with the Lateran Council's proclamation that individual immortality could be demonstrated philosophically and consequently had to be defended by all philosophers;[72] secondly, the Aristotelians' determined reaction to this pressure led to a reassessment of natural philosophy as a mode of argument in its own right. This development is linked above all with three names: Alessandro Achillini, Agostino Nifo and Pietro Pomponazzi.

Alessandro Achillini

Differing from Nifo and Pomponazzi, who were both former students of Vernia's, Alessandro Achillini was a product of the Bologna medical faculty.[73] At Bologna he was exempt from Barozzi's decree, and his relatively early death prevented him from participating in the prolonged debate following the Fifth Lateran Council. Nevertheless, his *Quolibeta de intelligentiis*,[74] published in 1494, documents an earlier stage in the transition.

At first glance, Achillini, who takes universals to be concepts of the mind and therefore can be regarded as a Renaissance Ockhamist,[75] seems to follow a traditional path in defending the Averroist position to assure the universality of conceptual knowledge.[76] In a seemingly contradictory manner, he maintained that this single intellect was both the assisting form, using man as instrument for its operations as a captain uses a boat, and also the *forma informans* of man, which gave him a specific essence and provided the subject of intellection for the individual being.[77] Here Achillini is still in agreement with Paul of Venice[78] and the medieval tradition stemming from Siger of Brabant, who, in response to Thomas Aquinas, had attempted to adapt Averroes' position to the requirements of individual knowledge.[79]

Having adopted Siger's interpretation, Achillini adhered to it to a degree not required by the Ockhamist argument but seems on the contrary, to overthrow it. Referring to an isolated quotation, he maintained that

72. *Sacrorum conciliorum . . . collectio* 1759–1962, XXXII, p. 842 (*Bulla Apostolici regiminis*); Offelli 1955; Di Napoli 1963, pp. 220–5.
73. Münster 1953; Matsen 1968, 1974; Lohr 1974b, pp. 236–8.
74. Achillini 1494, 1568.   75. Matsen 1974.
76. Achillini 1568, p. 18[a] (quol. 3, dub. 2): 'unus est conceptus essentialis omnium individuorum eiusdem speciei. Ergo unus est intellectus possibilis omnium hominum.'
77. *Ibid.*, p. 23[a] (quol. 3, dub. 4): 'Utrum intellectus possibilis sit forma dans esse hominem. Respondeo quod sic . . . quia homo intelligit.' For the specific structure of this formation, see p. 18[b] (quol. 3, dub. 2): 'Est autem materia informata cogitativa informabile propinquum et ultimate dispositum ad recipiendum intellectum.'   78. See nn. 33–6 above.   79. Nardi 1945, pp. 39–90.

Averroes, following Alexander of Aphrodisias, held that the agent intellect was God,[80] and that God was the best-known principle of knowledge in general,[81] the form of intellection in all intelligences, human as well as celestial,[82] their perfection and happiness.[83] Thus, to reach his end, man must prepare himself through the acquisition of moral virtue and – under the guidance and assistance of the agent intellect – the sciences and the related methodological disciplines, until he becomes capable of intuitive cognition of separate substances and is beatified through union with the agent intellect, God himself. By this process of ascent perfect happiness is gained not only by man, but also by the material world which, transformed into spirituality, returns with the human intellect to its divine origin.[84]

Even if this theory of man's final end as his union with God and the acquisition of knowledge as the path to this ascent is heavily indebted to the Sigerian tradition,[85] its reception through Achillini seems to indicate that Averroist psychology, once adapted to meet the needs of Ockhamist conceptualism, was to make way for the invasion of Neoplatonism into the psychological debate, as a comparison with Pico's *Oratio* clearly shows.[86] At the same time it is clearly a theory which treats philosophy and science not as ends in themselves but merely as a preparation for the final cognition of God, serving to re-establish the superiority of theology over philosophy. Therefore, it may not be fortuitous that when Achillini wrote his *Quolibeta* to be presented to the General Congress of Franciscans at Bologna in 1494[87] he did not even discuss the crucial question of immortality, but left it to the theologians.[88]

Agostino Nifo

While Achillini took the first step in the process of transition, Agostino Nifo, Vernia's former student and later a favourite of Pope Leo X, carried it much further.[89] Eager to collect whatever philosophical material he could, he adopted the humanist programme of returning to ancient sources; he was attracted to Neoplatonic eclecticism and was devoted to the reconciliation

---

80. Achillini 1568, p. 27ª (quol. 4, dub. 1); Averroes 1953, p. 453 (lib. III ad t. 20).
81. Achillini 1568, p. 4ᵇ (quol. 1, dub. 1): 'Deus est simpliciter primo notum. Sed primum principium complexum . . . est notissimum nobis.' 82. *Ibid.*, p. 14ª (quol. 2, dub. 2).
83. *Ibid.*, p. 28ª (quol. 4, dub. 2): 'solum igitur deus est felicitas sibi aut aliis intelligentiis aut homini, quia solum ipse est perfectissimum intelligibile et appetibile propter se.'
84. *Ibid.*, p. 29ᵇ (quol. 4, dub. 3); p. 32ᵇ (quol. 4, dub. 4).
85. Nardi 1945, pp. 77–87; Matsen 1974, p. 26 suggests that Jean de Jandun served as intermediary.
86. G. Pico 1942. 87. Matsen 1974, p. 26.
88. Achillini 1568, p. 28ᵇ (quol. 4, dub. 2): 'Felicitatem autem in alia vita, quam non potuerunt Philosophi naturali ratione inquirere, theologis relinquimus considerandam.'
89. Tuozzi 1903–4; *Dictionary of Scientific Biography* 1970–80, X, pp. 122–4; Lohr 1979, pp. 532–9.

of philosophy with Christian doctrine. Thus he turned out to be more of a scholar than a systematic philosopher, and in spite of a good deal of recent research on the sources of his psychological writings,[90] it remains difficult if not impossible to determine Nifo's definite philosophical position.[91] His works, both in psychology and in other branches of philosophy, were widely discussed throughout the sixteenth century.

Like his teacher Vernia, Nifo started as a good Averroist, not only editing Averroes' commentaries and expounding his *Destructio destructionum*,[92] but also defending the theory of the unified intellect as the original teaching of Aristotle and, in general, Averroes as his true interpreter.[93] Consequently, he held that the philosopher's prime concern was the correct understanding of Aristotle and Averroes.[94] No wonder then that Nifo, along with Vernia, served as one of Trombetta's main targets.[95]

Even so, from the beginning Nifo's Averroism seems to have been coloured with conciliating tendencies from the tradition of Siger of Brabant and Jean de Jandun,[96] in spite of his *De sensu agente*, which was devoted to a refutation of the latter's concept of an agent sense.[97] Nifo, like Achillini, held that the intellect in conjunction with the cogitative soul was the substantial form of man, so that the individual man, not the universal intellect, was the subject of knowledge.[98] He also opened the door to Neoplatonism by considering Simplicius, probably known to him through Giovanni Pico, to be in agreement with Siger and Averroes.[99]

By the time he published the final version of his *De intellectu* (1503), however, and, contrary to his own intentions, the first edition of his commentary on *De anima* had been published,[100] Nifo apparently had abandoned his Averroist orientation and had entered into the vast sea of Neoplatonic syncretism. Here again, he followed Vernia's approach in the recantation of his final years. But thanks to his knowledge of Greek,[101]

---

90. Nardi 1945, pp. 11–45; 1958, pp. 377–83; and Mahoney 1966.
91. Garin 1966, p. 535; Schmitt 1983a, p. 101.
92. Mahoney 1971a, pp. 119f.; Schmitt 1984, § VIII.   93. Mahoney 1970a, pp. 451–4.
94. Nifo 1529, ff. 284–95 (*De sensu agente*); f. 295ʳ: 'Est enim studium philosophorum omnino remotum ab his [sc. passione et ira] . . . sed velint bene inspicere dicta Aristotelis et Averrois.' The treatise was first published in 1497.   95. Mahoney 1976a.
96. Nardi 1945, pp. 11–45; Mahoney 1966.   97. Nifo 1529; Mahoney 1971a.
98. Nifo 1559, col. 720 (lib. III ad t. c. 20): 'Intellectus est forma cogitative, e qua cogitativa constituitur anima rationalis essentialiter et per se, quae anima rationalis habet duas partes, una per quam est educta de potentia materiae, scilicet cogitativam: quae est ultimus gradus partium sensitivarum. Alteram, per quam hoc perficitur et reponitur in specie completa, et est intellectus potentiae, ex quibus tota rationalis anima consurgit, quae est forma substantialis hominis: in eo quod homo.' Nifo 1503, f. 37ᵛᵃ (lib. I, tr. 3, cap. 31); see Nardi 1945, pp. 14–20.
99. Nardi 1958, pp. 377–83.
100. Mahoney 1970a, p. 458.   101. Nardi 1958, p. 382; Mahoney 1970a, p. 458.

Nifo, unlike Vernia, did not depend exclusively on the translations of the Greek commentators by Donato and Barbaro and of Neoplatonic sources like Plotinus and the *corpus Hermeticum* by Ficino, but could draw on the original texts of both Aristotle and the Greek commentary tradition.[102] These, together with the *Latini*, Albertus Magnus and Thomas Aquinas, replaced Averroes as authentic interpreters of Aristotle's teaching.[103]

Fundamental for the change resulting from the new approach was the superimposing of Neoplatonic participation metaphysics on the Aristotelian metaphysics of form and matter. In this context the problem of how the intellective soul can serve as the individual form of man and, at the same time, be the subject of universal knowledge, which in his earlier years had made Nifo adopt Siger's concept of a double soul,[104] is resolved through distinguishing three different kinds of form: one totally separated from matter and universal, like that of the celestial beings; another immersed in matter and therefore individualised, like that of the terrestrial beings; and a third, which is the intermediate between these two extremes, participating in the nature of them both. The third is the human soul, individual with regard to the human body and universal with regard to the spiritual operation of cognition.[105]

In a similar way Nifo resolved the problem of the agent intellect which serves as the active principle enabling man to gain universal knowledge from individual phantasms. With reference to Simplicius Nifo maintained that there are three different agent intellects: the first, the general principle of knowability, identical with God and comparable to the Platonic sun, which illuminates everything; the second, the individual principle of knowledge in the rational soul, which is illuminated by God and illuminates, disposing the intelligible to act upon the possible intellect and the possible intellect to receive the intelligible *species*; and the third, the prime notions or innate propositions through which, as a mere instrument, God illuminates the human soul and the human soul draws its conclusions.[106] Thus, Nifo developed a concept of participation, using the

102. Mahoney 1968, 1982.   103. Mahoney 1976b, 1980.   104. See n. 98 above.
105. Nifo 1503, f. 27^{va-b} (lib. I, tr. 2, cap. 22): 'Dicimus igitur genus formarum tripartitum esse: quedam enim proculdubio forme sunt que et secundum esse et secundum functionem sui officii ac secundum opus se in corpore immergunt . . . sunt et alie porro forme, que et secundum esse et secundum opus corpus ac materiam excedunt . . . Et cum universaliter maxime extremorum communi cursu media cadant, probabile est harum formarum in extremo medias esse, que partim se in materiam immergunt ac partim ab ea solvuntur; cuius quidem generis rationales sunt anime; he quidem in orizonte sunt eternitatis et temporis, ut Plato inquit . . . erit ergo individuus prout forma est quedam hominis, ut vero potestas quedam lucis spiritalis, porro universalis est.'
106. *Ibid.*, f. 41rb (the reference to Simplicius); 1559, col. 710 (lib. III ad t. c. 19); p. 804 (lib. III ad t. c. 36): 'intellectus agens triplex est: quidam, quem Plato soli comparavit et hic Deus est. Qui est intellectus agens universalis omnium intellectorum . . . Alius est, quem Aristoteles lumini comparavit, qui est

Platonic notion of innate ideas as the intermediate between the universal divine and the individual human agent intellect. In Themistius, the first and third agent intellects are said to be unified, while the second is multiplied,[107] but all three are considered to be unified in the act of cognition.[108] Using this concept Nifo succeeded in reconciling Averroes' theory with the claim for individuality of the human intellectual soul found in the Latin tradition and in making both compatible with Alexander's agent intellect as God.

As is obvious from such a solution, Nifo's reasoning was less concerned with the natural philosopher's saving the phenomena than with the constitution of a set of metaphysical principles unspecific enough to allow for an integration of as many concepts of the phenomena as possible. Indeed, when a concept resisted such an integration, as with Averroes' denial of an individual intellect or with Jandun's assumption of an agent sense, the decisive argument for Nifo does not seem to have been an insufficient explanation of the phenomena, but the supposition of a starting-point based on the wrong general principles.[109]

The same attitude towards philosophical argument allowed Nifo to maintain that the immortality of the individual human soul was true not only in terms of Christian revelation, but also on the grounds of philosophical demonstration.[110] Of course, Nifo did not conceal that some of the most celebrated Latin commentators, for instance, Duns Scotus,[111] had regarded the question to be a *problema neutrum* because of Aristotle's contradictory statements and therefore insoluble in terms of natural philosophy.[112] Yet, in order to prove the immortality of the individual soul, he does not rely on a refutation of this position argument by argument, but rather on a collection of statements in favour of immortality drawn from Neoplatonic sources, such as Plato and Plotinus, as well as from Hermes Trismegistus, the son of Prometheus (who is called the first of the Stoics), Cicero, Sallust, Xenophon, Ptolemy and a near infinity of ancient philosophers and different schools.[113] Only then does Nifo add those statements of Aristotle which seem to fit into this general consensus.[114] It is

pars animae rationalis . . . Tertius est intellectus agens, ut instrumentum immediatum omnium intellectorum speculativorum; et hic sunt propositiones primae, nobis per naturam insitae.' Mahoney 1970b. For the concept of the agent intellect as an active disposition, see Nifo 1503, f. 52ra (lib. I, tr. 5, cap. 19); 1559, col. 703 (lib. III ad t. c. 18).

107. Nifo 1503, f. 41rb (lib. I, t. 4, cap. 13).
108. Nifo 1559, col. 804 (lib. III ad t. c. 36); Mahoney 1970b, p. 399.
109. Nifo 1503, f. 58ra (lib. I, tr. 5, cap. 41) (Averroes); 1529, f. 293^r.
110. Nifo 1503, f. 7va (lib. I, tr. 1, cap. 10): 'Ex his perspicuum remanet quanta sit philosophiae utilitas, cum ex ea non tantum rationalis anime immortalitas sciri possit ex verbis Aristotelis, verum et aliorum antiquorum et demonstrationibus apertis.' See Mahoney 1970a, p. 455.
111. Mahoney 1970a, p. 456.   112. Nifo 1503, f. 4va (lib. I, tr. 1, cap. 7).
113. *Ibid.*, f. 5va (lib. I, tr. 1, capp. 8–9).   114. *Ibid.*, f. 6vb (lib. I, tr. 1, cap. 10).

not surprising that when he later goes back to the moral implications of the question, he expressly refers to the principle that what all or most of the wisest men maintain is equivalent to philosophical truth.[115] He concludes by proudly rejoicing in his agreement with Ficino, the founder of Renaissance Platonism.[116]

When in 1513 the Lateran Council decreed the philosophical demonstrability of the immortality of the individual soul, obviously philosophy was conceived in terms of the Neoplatonic syncretism which Nifo introduced into the Aristotelian tradition following the mature Vernia and his friend Pico. The reaction to this decree sprang from a defence of the traditional concept of an autonomous natural philosophy.

Pietro Pomponazzi

The vitality of late fifteenth-century intellectual life at Padua is demonstrated by the fact that the leading figure of this reaction came from the same environment. As a student of and – since 1499 – successor to Vernia, Pietro Pomponazzi was trained in the Averroist interpretation of Aristotle and, at the same time, became well acquainted with Thomism through his teachers Francesco da Nardó and Pietro Trapolin.[117] Even if he did not himself know Greek, he was open to arguments from Neoplatonists like Ficino and Pico, from humanism and also from the recently translated Greek commentators, especially Alexander of Aphrodisias, whose impact on the sixteenth-century debate owes much to Pomponazzi.[118] Thus the torchbearer of Aristotelianism was himself influenced by Neoplatonic syncretism, yet he did not – and this was obviously at the bottom of his acid polemics – submit to the consensus argument, as Nifo had done.[119] Instead he defended reason, experience and the *principia naturalia* as the only criteria of truth for the natural philosopher.[120] In modern times as well as among

115. *Ibid.*, f. 36rb (lib. I, tr. 3, cap. 27): 'famosum est enim per . . . omnes homines cuiusvis secte rationales animas plurificatas esse et quod est famosum omnibus videtur esse consequens naturam; natura enim in hoc ab arte discrepat, quod in omnibus est unimodo, et ars in omnibus vel pluribus . . . Est etiam apud sapientiores hoc maxime approbatum.'

116. *Ibid.*, f. 37ra (lib. I, tr. 3, cap. 28): 'Quo fit ut sermo meus continuus quem auditoribus meis continue predico verificetur, scilicet quod si Averoys positio esset ut dicunt, nullum animal infelicius esset me ac quovis homine. Cum qua sententia Ficinum nostrum inveni nobiscum una concordem.' See Ficino 1964–70, I, p. 38.

117. Nardi 1965, pp. 104–21, 204–30; *Dictionary of Scientific Biography* 1970–80, XI, pp. 71–4; Lohr 1980, pp. 645–65.

118. Kristeller 1956a, pp. 279–86; 1965a, pp. 111–118; *Aristotelismo veneto* 1983, II, pp. 1077–99 (Kristeller); *Enciclopedia cattolica* 1948–54, I, cols. 778–9 ('Alessandrismo').

119. For Nifo, see n. 115 above; for the polemics, see Nardi 1965, p. 279; Poppi 1970b, p. 34.

120. Pomponazzi 1966–70, II, p. 2.8–9: 'tantum enim secundum principia naturalia opinionem istam pertractabo'; p. 9.18: 'hoc videtur esse contra sensum'; p. 11.13: 'tantum enim rationibus innitor'; see also Olivieri 1983.

his contemporaries the most discussed of Pomponazzi's works has been his *De immortalitate animae* (1516).[121] However, as his unpublished lectures prove,[122] this work was the culmination of his life-long endeavour to solve a problem regarding which he had repeatedly affirmed that he would prefer to be taught than to teach.[123]

In his lectures on the soul in 1500 Pomponazzi's only concern seems to have been the exposition of Aristotle according to the commentary of Averroes, whom he believed to be a faithful interpreter, while considering both Aristotle and Averroes to be identical with philosophical truth.[124] From the lectures of 1503/4 onwards, however, he was anxious to explain his own position on the matter, interrupting the running commentary with additional *quaestiones*.

This move was apparently initiated by Pomponazzi's doubts about how the Averroist unicity of the intellect, while being truly Aristotelian, could be brought into line with reason and experience.[125] Whether one argues that the intellect is merely the assisting form of man, like a captain in a boat, as Plato had thought and Pomponazzi initially seems to have believed was the opinion of Averroes, or whether one maintains that the single intellect is the informing form of man, as Achillini and Nifo had done following Siger and which Pomponazzi later regarded as Averroes' true position,[126] there is no way of maintaining man's individual unity as a rational animal, composed of body and soul, and serving as the subject of cognition. He therefore argued that this position of Aristotle and Averroes was both bestial, since it reduced individual man to a mere animal, and fatuous, since it could not be rationally accepted. Therefore, Thomas Aquinas was right in severely attacking it.[127]

For Pomponazzi the Thomist position could not be upheld either. Thomas' teaching that the individual soul was immortal, although in accordance with faith and revelation, was untenable in terms of philosophy, since it was based on the assumption of the divine creation of the human

121. Republished during his lifetime in Pomponazzi 1525, ff. 41ra–51vb; the newest edition is Pomponazzi 1954 (with bibliography of editions, pp. 17–19, and studies, pp. 19–31); for an English translation see *Renaissance Philosophy of Man* 1948, pp. 280–381. See also Yee 1966; Pine 1965; Kristeller 1968.
122. Lohr 1980, pp. 659–63 (nos. 32–9); Ferri 1876; Kristeller 1955; Nardi 1965; Pomponazzi 1966–70, II; Poppi 1970b.
123. Pomponazzi 1966–70, II, p. 9.28–9: 'domini, in ista parte mallem potius esse discipulus quam magister'; Ferri 1876, p. 483; Nardi 1965, p. 187, n. 6.   124. Nardi 1965, pp. 149–52.
125. Pomponazzi 1966–70, II, pp. 63–8; Nardi 1965, p. 166; Poppi 1970b, pp. 41, 90.
126. Pomponazzi 1966–70, II, pp. 27–34; Ferri 1876, pp. 487–9; Nardi 1965, p. 165.
127. Pomponazzi 1966–70, II, p. 8.21–2: 'Videtur enim, quod ista opinio sit fatua et bestialis'; p. 42.7; 1954, pp. 48–68.

soul, which was opposed to the principles of nature.[128] Moreover, philosophically speaking, both Thomas and Averroes (supposing the soul to be an immaterial and incorruptible form acting in a material subject, which, be it the human species or individual man, is a whole composed of parts) had to come to terms with the problem of how the different parts of the body, moved by one and the same soul, act differently; and neither could do so without admitting different material dispositions as additional causes of these actions.[129]

At this point, it was reasonable to ask the philosophical question whether it was necessary to maintain the incorruptibility and immateriality of the soul, or whether it was sufficient to regard those material dispositions as the form and active principle of the human being. Alexander of Aphrodisias had done this in holding the intellective soul to be a form educed from the potentiality of matter. In this way, he accounted both for man's individuality and for the different actions of men and their parts, thereby largely satisfying the requirements of natural philosophy.[130]

As Pomponazzi showed in the beginning of his questions on 'whether the rational soul is immaterial and immortal' of 1504/5, there were two groups of arguments which seemed to call for an immaterial and immortal soul, both originating from its operations. The first concerned intellection, especially with regard to the immateriality of intellectual objects, while the second concerned the volitional operations, especially with regard to the final end of virtue, which seemed to be beyond this life.[131] Concerning the second group, Pomponazzi argued that morality did not necessarily depend on the assumption of a life after death, in which virtue was rewarded and vice punished, but, as Plato and the Stoics had taught, morality was valued most highly when sought as an end in itself, virtue being its own reward and vice its own punishment.[132] The only reason, therefore, why a philosopher should not defend the Alexandrist position remained the *modus intelligendi*, that is, the problem of accounting for intellectual cognition in an individual and material soul.[133]

Pomponazzi's answer to this problem, which was of his own inven-

---

128. Pomponazzi 1966–70, II, pp. 34–41, 68–71, 81–5; Nardi 1965, pp. 238–46 (edition of Pomponazzi's *Quaestio an detur creatio in via Aristotelis et Averrois*); Pomponazzi 1954, pp. 82–102.

129. Pomponazzi 1966–70, II, pp. 71–80.

130. *Ibid.*, p. 93.2–4: 'ideo, ut dixi, stando in puris naturalibus opinio Alexandri multum quadrat'.

131. *Ibid.*, pp. 2–7.

132. *Ibid.*, pp. 21–5; Pomponazzi 1954, pp. 168–230; *Aristotelismo veneto* 1983, II, pp. 1086–7 (Kristeller).

133. Pomponazzi 1966–70, II, pp. 41.29–42.4: 'vidistis opinionem Alexandri et eius substentiationem, et domini, ut dixi, solum argumentum quod est ex parte modi intelligendi inter omnia alia argumenta semper fecit mihi magnam difficultatem, et adhuc non est bene solutum'.

tion,[134] drew on the theory of the soul's intermediate position between the material and immaterial world, as sustained by his Neoplatonic and Neoplatonising contemporaries.[135] Since one and the same human soul acted materially in sense-perception and immaterially in intellection, it must partake of both ontological realms. But where should the soul's essence be placed? The immortalists, Neoplatonists as well as Averroists, had opted for the immaterial world, providing a higher ontological status for man, and had thereby taken on many problems regarding the material being and activity of man which could not be solved according to the principles of nature.[136] Pomponazzi – referring to the principle that the intellectual soul cannot operate without imagination and is therefore dependent on matter *ut obiecto* (as its object) even if it is independent from it *ut subiecto* (as its subject)[137] in terms of natural philosophy – chose the material solution and maintained that the human soul was the highest material form, attaining in its most elevated operations something beyond materiality.[138]

Thus it seemed to him that Alexander's teaching on the individual and mortal soul came closest to what is defensible on rational grounds by the natural philosopher. And indeed up to 1515 he continued to maintain that there was agreement between Aristotle and Averroes, and he referred to Alexander as a reasonable, but at the same time, abominable outsider.[139] In the treatise of 1516, however, he presented Alexander's opinion as the true Aristotelian position, though not mentioning Alexander's name specifically.[140] This does not mean, however, that Pomponazzi identified this position with the truth itself. In all his psychological teaching and writing he emphasised that the full truth in this matter can be gained only through faith and revelation.[141] At the end of his treatise on immortality Pomponazzi – transfering a dictum of Duns Scotus on Aristotle to natural philosophy as such – declared that the question of immortality is a neutral problem

134. *Ibid.*, p. 15.7–12: 'Et domini, ut solvam hoc argumentum faciam, sicut faciebat Mahumetus, qui modo istorum dicta, modo aliorum dicta accipiebat ac aggregabat legesque condebat; sic ego faciam: accipiam dicta aliqua christianorum et aliqua dicta Alexandri, et rationem solvam.'

135. *Ibid.*, pp. 49–50, 59–60; 1954, pp. 38–40; Kristeller 1956a, pp. 283–6; Nardi 1958, pp. 141–3; Poppi 1970b, pp. 61–2; *Scienza e filosofia* 1983, p. 207 (Olivieri).

136. Pomponazzi 1966–70, II, pp. 34–41, 51–60; 1954, pp. 74–102.

137. Pomponazzi 1966–70, II, p. 18; 1954, pp. 104–36.

138. Pomponazzi 1966–70, II, pp. 14–17, 60; 1954, pp. 138–50; Garin 1966, pp. 516–18.

139. Pomponazzi 1966–70, II, p. 46.15–17: 'tamen unum dico, quod credo firmiter et indubitanter quod opinio Commentatoris, Themistii et Theophrasti sit opinio Aristotelis infallanter'; p. 6.22–9: 'stando in puris naturalibus non videtur dissona opinio Alexandri . . . Dico tamen quod opinio ista Alexandri est falsissima'. See also Ferri 1876, p. 486.   140. Poppi 1970b, pp. 39–41.

141. *Ibid.*, p. 10; Ferri 1876, p. 497; Pomponazzi 1954, pp. 232–8.

(*problema neutrum*), incapable of resolution through natural reason.[142] He thereby not only attempted to justify his submission to the church but also qualified his own materialistic position as a reasonable attempt at a philosophically satisfying solution. The question of how the material and the immaterial cooperate in the human soul was, philosophically speaking, still unresolved at best and possibly even beyond the means of philosophical demonstration.

The Pomponazzi affair

In retrospect, Pomponazzi's treatise seems to be a well-balanced rational discourse, whose arguments – *mutatis mutandis* – attract philosophical interest even today. In Pomponazzi's own time, however, the subtlety of his argumentation was overshadowed by his provocation of both ecclesiastical and philosophical authority.[143] In fact, it may well be that such a provocation was intended by the author, who by making a Dominican friar the interlocuter of the initial chapter seems to be hinting at the minister general of the order, Thomas de Vio, later Cardinal Cajetan. Cajetan had maintained in his commentary on *De anima* (1509) that it is impossible to prove the immortality of the soul on philosophical grounds;[144] and he had also been one of the two members of the council who voted against the decree on immortality. At least one of Pomponazzi's opponents, Bartolomeo Spina, himself a Dominican, picked up the hint and consequently attacked both in the same publication.[145]

The first outburst must have been immediate, for as early as February 1518 Pomponazzi published his *Apologia*.[146] The work first quotes and refutes arguments of Gasparo Contarini,[147] his former student, whom he had asked for a critique and who, though not agreeing with his teacher's

---

142. Pomponazzi 1954, p. 232; 1966–70, II, p. 10.
143. See Laurent's introduction to Cajetan 1938, pp. 7.51; Gilson 1961; *Umanesimo europeo* 1964, pp. 31–61, especially the chronological table on pp. 56–9 (Gilson).
144. Congar 1934–5; Giacon 1944–50, I; Lohr 1975, pp. 692–5; Cajetan 1514, f. 49ʳ: 'Ad evidentiam harum difficultatum scito quod non est intentionis mee dicere aut sustinere velle intellectum possibilem esse generabilem et corruptibilem secundum philosophie principia: quoniam hec positio est falsissima, quoniam ex principiis philosophie utpote veris non deducitur recte nisi verum. Hoc autem constat ex fide esse falsum. Igitur non potest ex principiis philosophie sequi. Unde neque ut verum neque ut consonum neque ut probabile philosophie hec scripserim: sed tantum exponens opinionem istius greci, quam conabor ostendere esse falsam secundum philosophie principia.'   145. Spina 1519; Lohr 1982, pp. 171–2.
146. Pomponazzi 1518, republished: 1525, ff. 52–75.
147. Lohr 1975, pp. 721–2; *Aristotelismo padovano* 1960, pp. 109–19 (Giacon). Pomponazzi published Contarini's objections anonymously under the title *Tractatus contradictoris* as an appendix to his *Apologia* in 1518 and 1525. Contarini, having added a second book replying to Pomponazzi's *Apologia*, published his *De immortalitate animae* in 1525; it is also included in G. Contarini 1571, pp. 179–231.

position, retained a degree of reverence and esteem; second, it attacks the philosophical arguments of the Dominican Vincentius de Vicentia and a certain Petrus Manna; and finally, it argues against the theological attacks from the monks, the *cucullati* (hooded ones), as he calls them, who had publicly accused him of heresy and whose arguments he reproaches for going beyond the principles of natural philosophy.[148]

The leading figure was Ambrogio Flandino, an Augustinian Hermit, who besides publishing a treatise himself against Pomponazzi in 1519[149] urged Nifo to write against his former colleague and philosophical opponent.[150] Pomponazzi answered immediately with his *Defensorium*.[151] In this controversy the different attitudes of the two philosophers, which seemed to preclude any possibility of a reasonable discussion, became clear. Nifo admitted that Aristotle had said little or nothing on the status of the soul after death, thereby taking refuge in the teaching of Plato and the other philosophers.[152] Their consensus served as sufficient proof for Nifo, although he relied primarily on the authority of St Thomas, whom he regarded as the most reliable interpreter of Aristotle.[153] Pomponazzi, however, maintained that as a professor at the *Studio* of Bologna he was obliged to explicate Aristotle, and as a philosopher he could not do so without submitting to the conclusiveness of reason.[154] With this statement Pomponazzi ended his part in the affair, refusing to answer any further objection since the foolish prove their stupidity by their own works.[155] He did, however, make a strategic move: he asked his Dominican colleague at Bologna, Crisostomo Javelli, to put forward in an appendix to the

148. Pomponazzi 1518, f. 31[ra]: 'fratrum sive cucullatorum vulgus . . . me omnium litterarum ignarum apertissimumque hereticum esse divulgaverunt'; f. 31[vb]: 'Nulla ratione naturali convinci potest animorum immortalitas, sed animorum immortalitas repugnat naturalibus principiis, ipsaque sola et syncera fide teneri potest.'   149. Lohr 1976a, p. 738; Flandino 1519.
150. Nifo 1518, republished: 1521a. For Flandino's role see the introductory letter to Leo X.
151. Pomponazzi 1519, republished: 1525, ff. 81–108.
152. Nifo 1521a, f. 23[rb]: 'ab Aristotele de statu anime post mortem pauca aut nulla habemus, a Platone vero pluria'.
153. *Ibid.*, f. 16[vb]: 'Thomas vir doctissimus et omnium meo iudicio peripatheticorum princeps'.
154. Pomponazzi 1525, f. 104[ra]: 'quod queritur est quid senserit Aristoteles quidve per rationes naturales de hoc haberi potest . . . Ex mandato enim Leonis decimi et Senatus Bononiensis teneor legere, interpretari et secundum iudicium meum sententiare, quid senserit Aristoteles quid per principia naturalia haberi potest . . . Mandata sequor, iuramentum observo. Non est nostri arbitrii dicere: Aristoteles sic vel non sic tenuit, sed iudicium sumitur ex rationibus et verbis suis . . . Datis enim praemissis, si consequentia conceditur: non est nostrum dissentire conclusioni. Bene est nostrum, non considerare, sed non est nostrum, si concedamus antecedens, ut negemus consequens.' A similar defence was made a hundred years later by Cesare Cremonini; see Renan 1866, p. 479.
155. Pomponazzi 1525, f. 108[rb]: 'Finem itaque huic negotio impono, et quamquam sciam nonnullos alios oblatrasse . . . aliosque oblatraturos adversus nos: minime tamen dignor eis respondere . . . nullo signo alio opus esse fatuis, nam secum signum deferunt; opera enim eorum manifestant eos.'

Defensorium the true Christian teaching on the immortality of the soul in order to prevent the reader from being seduced into error. Javelli not only complied with the request but also, in the introductory letter, justified Pomponazzi's position, stating that the true philosophy was the Christian one based on revelation. With regard to rational philosophy, however, Aristotle was preferable to Plato since the latter, reasoning from the divine, assumed his arguments rather than proving them, while the former, starting from sense-perception, was the true investigator of nature, even if – *pace* St Thomas – his intellect was sometimes clouded when approaching higher questions.[156]

But Pomponazzi's opponents were not yet prepared to give in. Gilson lists five more publications up to 1525 intended to demolish Pomponazzi's arguments and to defend the decision of the Lateran Council.[157] But they drew little attention and were largely an ineffectual rearguard action. The case of Bartolomeo Spina is typical. Well aware of the philosophical alliance between his own former minister general, Cajetan, who had paved the way, and Pomponazzi, who had taken it, Spina in his first treatise reproached his fellow-Dominican for having abandoned Thomas Aquinas' authentic exposition of the philosopher.[158] In the second he accused Pomponazzi of having betrayed the truth, which as a Christian philosopher he was obliged to defend in any case, even if only for the sake of weaker minds.[159] Having

---

156. Lohr 1977, p. 730–3; Javelli in Pomponazzi 1525, f. 108[va]: 'Plato a superis descendit ad sensum, sententias de divinis entibus veluti ab alto demissas magis acceptans quam probans. Qui nempe modus soli theologo innitenti divine revelationi proprie convenit, philosopho autem in humanis versanti fere extraneus. Aristoteles autem veluti callidissimus nature scrutator a sensatis et notioribus paulatim se ad immaterialia elevat . . . Quantum ex sensu elevatus, tantum determinate et constanter philosophari potuit. At quamprimum manuductio ex sensu defecit, caligavit eius intellectus . . . Neque enim philosophia et Aristotelis philosophia convertuntur. Philosophia si quidem in se est scientia mere veritatis, que est divina possessio nobis a patre luminum demissa'.
157. *Umanesimo europeo* 1964, pp. 58–9 (Gilson).
158. Spina 1519, sig. A iv[v] (*Propugnaculum Aristotelis de immortalitate animae contra Thomam Caietanum, epistola*): 'Hoc christiana fides predicat, hoc preclarissimi philosophi demonstrative deducunt edocentque patenter. Mox inter extremos oritur dissidium quidam Aristoteles philosophorum omnium monarcha quantum ex eius dictis elici fas est, in hoc articulo fuerit opinatus. Solatium etenim non mediocre fidelibus affert tam celebrati philosophi testimonium in re tanta: infirmis inter christianos extreme ruine clauditur precipitium . . . Divus Thomas Aristotelis sapientiam efferens illum veritati consensisse declarat. Contra repugnant plurimi. Sed pre ceteris unicus inter Thomistas . . . Caietanus . . . probare sathegit Aristoteli haudquaquam fuisse placitum animam nostram perhennem vivere vitam, immo mortuo corpore illam funditus tolli et interire . . . Et ecce, non multo post quod timebam accidit scandalum in ecclesia dei ut philosophus inter christianos ex falsa illa doctrina (ut is ipse fassus est) fomentum assumens et iam stratam ingressus viam sic animam insequutus sit verborum iniurioso volumine quasi acutissimo mucrone.' On the relationship of Cajetan and Pomponazzi, see also the letter 'Ad lectorem' at the end of the *Flagellum in Apologiam Peretti* in Spina 1519.
159. *Ibid.*, sig. I ii[r] (*Tutela veritatis de immortalitate anime contra Petrum Pomponatium*): 'In toto progressu simpliciter affirmas animam esse absolute mortalem, et in fine concludis esse problema

thus already substituted theological for philosophical argument, the third treatise ended up in mere polemics.[160]

For Pomponazzi's opponents the case was lost. The result of the whole affair, expressed for the first time in Javelli's appendix to the *Defensorium* and reformulated by him in 1536,[161] amounted to a total failure of the 1513 decree. In the future, philosophy would no longer be identical with Aristotle, nor Aristotle with St Thomas and the teaching of the church; a philosopher could be a Thomist, an Aristotelian, a Platonist or anything else, provided that his philosophy was conclusive and coherent.

THE 'SECOND SCHOLASTIC'

Pomponazzi's theoretical success did not mean, however, the end of Christian philosophy. On the contrary, the emphasis on the legitimacy of different ways of philosophising at the same time supported the concept of a philosophy which was based on Christian dogma, as proclaimed by the council. Truth cannot contradict truth, and the truth of philosophy cannot contradict the divine truth of faith.[162] Therefore, as a consequence of the Pomponazzi affair, we can observe not only a divorce of natural philosophy from Christian philosophy, but also a rebirth of Christian philosophy in its own right. The latter was further promoted by the religious quarrels of the Reformation and Counter-Reformation, resulting in two corresponding Christian philosophies.

For the Catholics, this philosophy grew out of the traditional chairs of metaphysics *in via Thomae* and *in via Scoti* and therefore has been called the 'Second Scholastic'.[163] The main promoters of this movement, which went far beyond the chronological limits of the Renaissance, were the Dominicans, the Franciscans and the recently founded Jesuits, with their spiritual centres in Spain and Portugal, which had not been affected as much by the rationalistic tendencies of natural philosophy as Italy had been. In

neutrum secundum philosophiam, et esse animam immortalem secundum fidem. Debueras igitur, si ut philosophus argumentatus fueras, saltem ut theologus respondere, et intellectui pro viribus satisfacere ne videretur fides adeo inrationalia, veluti conaris fieri ut appareant, predicare.'

160. *Ibid.*, sig. I ii^v (*Flagellum in apologiam Peretti*, prohemium): 'Quis nam a fide et ecclesia tam alienus, tam barbarus natione, tam rusticus conditione, tam scelestus moribus pirrata, siccarius vel nemora latro colens, quis inquam, tanto actus furore, tanta agitatus amentia inveniri potuisset, qui contra dei servos . . .'.   161. Javelli 1536.

162. Toletus 1592, f. 8rb: 'Nec enim philosophia vera repugnat veritati divinae . . . que fidei repugnant non esse secundum philosophiam veram. Verum enim non contradicit vero.'

163. Giacon 1944–50; Werner 1881–7, IV; Jansen 1951.

psychology, their basic text remained Aristotle, read in the light of the medieval commentary tradition, especially Thomas Aquinas and Duns Scotus, to whom Cajetan was added, his error in the question of immortality being corrected by Javelli and Franciscus Silvester of Ferrara.[164] Nonetheless, a certain withdrawal from the Aristotelian position was obvious. As Toletus shows very clearly – putting at the beginning of his commentary ten propositions to be held by faith against any argument [165] – the point was not to explain Aristotle but to rationalise Christian doctrine. Consequently not only philosophical but also theological sources, especially Thomas' *Summa contra gentiles*, were taken into account while the literary form of psychological writings tended to change from the commentary to the systematic treatise, which could serve as a textbook and could be inserted into the *cursus completus* of Christian philosophy.

John of St Thomas

Exemplary in this regard is the treatise *De ente mobili animato* by the Spanish Dominican John of St Thomas, first published in 1635 and later integrated into his *Cursus philosophiae Thomisticae*.[166] In this treatise the text of Aristotle's *De anima* is summarised at the beginning of the different sections, which are themselves a sequence of systematically ordered questions. Starting with the metaphysical status of the soul, the questions were intended less to save the phenomena of the cognitive process than the contents of revelation and the rationality of Christian belief, as had already been postulated by Spina.[167] Thus the authority was not Aristotle but Thomas, who was defended not against the natural philosophers and Greek or Arabic commentators but against Duns Scotus and Suárez. Natural philosophy was referred to only in relation to the immortality of the soul, since Cajetan had dared to deny its demonstrability in terms of natural philosophy, thus going against St Thomas.[168]

Considering the process of cognition, John of St Thomas stated that the agent intellect was a part of the soul in real distinction from the possible intellect [169] and that it produced, in cooperation with the imagination as

164. Javelli 1536, ff. 65vb–9vb; Laurent's introduction to Cajetan 1938, p. 49; F. Silvester 1898–1902; Giacon 1944–50, I, pp. 53–9.
165. Toletus 1592, f. 6vb: 'Propositiones aliquot fide tenenda, quibus vera debet esse philosophia consentanea'.
166. John of St Thomas 1937; Di Vona 1968, pp. 195–207; Lohr 1977, pp. 733–6.
167. See n. 159 above; Spina 1519, sig. I ii^r: 'ne videretur fides adeo inrationalia . . . predicare'.
168. John of St Thomas 1937, pp. 278^b–88^b (q. 9, art. 1: 'Quomodo naturaliter constat animam rationalem esse immortalem et per se subsistentem').
169. *Ibid.*, pp. 295^b–304^a (q. 10, art. 1).

instrumental cause, the intelligible *species*.[170] Since the intelligible *species*, which was impressed upon the possible intellect, represented universally, the universal was the first and immediate object of cognition, while the singular could only be recognised by way of reflection.[171] Consequently the intellect could retain the species, but it was unable to record it, because what is recorded is necessarily something singular and therefore must be located in the sensitive soul.[172] On the other hand, the impressed *species* was the object, in relation to which the possible intellect performed the act of intellection, producing the mental concepts: the *species expressa* or *verbum mentis*, that is, the mental word, through which the sensible world is known to man,[173] while what is knowable *per se*, like God, is known immediately, without an intermediary *species*.[174]

As becomes clear from this consideration, John dealt with knowledge not only of the natural but also of the supernatural world, to which the intellective soul belonged and where it would continue to function after death. In addition, John's general tendency was to develop a psychological theory of cognition which followed the metaphysics of Thomas Aquinas, and by denying the immediate cognition of singulars, it destroyed the basis of the nominalistic concept of universals. At the same time, the Dominican was anxious to reject Duns Scotus and the Franciscan Scotist tradition, which had developed a complete course of philosophy of its own.[175]

Bartholomaeus Mastrius and Bonaventura Bellutus

The Scotist philosophy course, which contained a disputation on the soul as well, was the result of the joint endeavours of two Franciscan professors at Padua, Bartholomaeus Mastrius and Bonaventura Bellutus.[176] Although they discussed the positions of the Thomists and of Suárez, as well as those of natural philosophers, such as Francesco Piccolomini and Jacopo Zabarella, the theological orientation of the two Franciscans was obvious. Not only did they add a disputation on the separated soul, not found in Aristotle,[177] but in open contradiction to the title page, they did not even summarise *De anima*. They defended Duns Scotus' position on immortality, in spite of its being entangled in the Pomponazzi affair, and blandly stated that Aristotle was unable to dispel his doubts regarding immortality, the eternity of the

170. *Ibid.*, pp. 304ª–13ᵇ (q. 10, art. 2).   171. *Ibid.*, pp. 322ᵇ–39ª (q. 10, art. 4–5).
172. *Ibid.*, pp. 339ᵇ–44ª (q. 10, art. 6).   173. *Ibid.*, pp. 344ᵇ–56ª (q. 11, art. 1).
174. *Ibid.*, pp. 356ª–66ᵇ (q. 11, art. 2).   175. Giacon 1944–50, II, pp. 203–9.
176. Mastrius and Bellutus 1643, included later in Mastrius and Bellutus 1678; Lohr 1974b, p. 264; 1978, pp. 570–2; Crowley 1948; Jansen 1936.
177. Mastrius and Bellutus 1643, pp. 692–714 (disp. 8).

world, the existence of infinity and temporal creation in a way satisfactory to the Christian believer.[178] Finally, they asserted that in general immortality could not be demonstrated by strictly philosophical means.[179]

With regard to the theory of cognition, these Scotists defended, against Thomas, the immediate intellection of the singular[180] and thus supported the empiricist attitude of the nominalists, even quoting the principle that nothing is in the intellect which has not previously been in the senses.[181] This empiricism was, however, undermined by a voluntaristic relativism which said that the whole dependence of intellection on the imagination was not only confined to the present state of the soul (*pro statu isto*), but was also the unexplainable result of divine omnipotence and therefore neither absolutely necessary nor essential to the nature of the intellect as such.[182]

No wonder, then, that the main concern of the disputation had shifted from the soul 'in this state' to the soul in the 'state beyond'. Thus, the necessity of the intelligible *species* was defended for the sake of intellectual memory, which had to be accepted in order to enable the separated soul to recollect the past;[183] and the concept of intuitive cognition, which requires the immediate presence of its object and is basic for a nominalist theory of cognition,[184] was maintained only for the soul after death.[185] Finally, intellection itself was not understood as a process in time, in the course of which the *verbum mentis* or *species expressa* was produced by the intellect, but was defined as a timeless operation in the sense of the Aristotelian *praxis*,[186] in which the subject of intellection was unified with its object and attained the state of perfection. Considering that a timeless process is the only way to ascribe intellection to God himself,[187] it becomes obvious that these Scotists discussed natural intellection in terms of the supernatural.

178. *Ibid.*, p. 105[b] (disp. 1, q. 10, § 158): 'numquam solvit dubia emergentia ex immortalitate animae, ex mundi aeternitate, ex negatione infiniti et ex negatione creationis temporaneae'.

179. *Ibid.*, p. 94[a] (disp. 1, q. 10, § 133): 'Dicendum est tamen animae rationalis immortalitatem esse de fide et pro statu isto, quamvis efficacissimis rationibus probetur, non tamen vera et rigorosa demonstratione ostendi posse.'

180. *Ibid.*, p. 456[a] (disp. 6, q. 5, § 130): 'bene potest abstrahi a rebus species singularis, immo haec est prima, quae abstrahitur ab intellectu agente'; see also p. 482 (q. 7: 'De cognitione universalis et singularis').

181. *Ibid.*, p. 417[a] (disp. 6, q. 4, § 54): 'in hoc statu nihil est in intellectu quin prius fuerit in sensu'.

182. *Ibid.*, p. 386[a] (disp. 6, q. 1, § 12): 'ordo praefatus inter intellectum et phantasiam non est ex natura rei absolute loquendo, adeo ut talis dependentia intellectus a phantasia referenda sit ad voluntatem divinam sic disponentem sive ex sua libertate et dominio, quod obtinet super omnia, sive ex iustitia punitiva in paenam originalis culpae'.   183. *Ibid.*, p. 419[a] (disp. 6, q. 4, § 67).

184. *Cambridge History* 1982, pp. 460–78 (Boler).

185. Mastrius and Bellutus 1643, p. 430[a] (disp. 6, q. 4, § 87).

186. Aristotle, *Nicomachean Ethics* VI.4 (1140[a]1).

187. Mastrius and Bellutus 1643, pp. 395[b]–406[b] (disp. 6, q. 3), especially p. 400[b] (§ 37): 'in Deo non enim est agere, vel pati, sine istis consistit intelligere divinum, quod univocatur cum nostro in ratione essentiali transcendentali . . . intelligere est vitaliter operari exprimendo obiectum, hoc est,

Franciscus Toletus

The third group engaged in the psychological discussions of the Second Scholastic, the Jesuits, were less limited in their philosophical dimension than the other two, since they were not bound to defend the position of a medieval teacher from their own community. Although Ignatius Loyola, the founder of the Society, had established Aristotle as the basic philosophical authority and Thomas as the guide to philosophy as well as to theology, the Thomism of the Jesuits turned out to be a rather moderate one, which neither closed the doors on differing positions, such as those of the Scotists and the nominalists in psychology, nor prevented its members from developing new positions of their own.[188]

An early example of this attitude was Franciscus Toletus.[189] His commentary on *De anima*, first published at Cologne in 1575, followed the traditional division of Averroes, but also gave the Greek division of the text into chapters and had the third book begin according to the Greek tradition.[190] The authors upon whom Toletus depended were the Latin commentators, especially Thomas, as well as the Greeks and Arabs, with special attention given to Averroes. However rich his commentary, the major philosophical discussion is found in the more than seventy *quaestiones*, which resemble a systematic treatise.

Having already stated that the basic psychological positions of the church were identical with those of the true philosophy,[191] Toletus was less anxious in philosophical argument itself to adhere to the faith and more open to strictly philosophical values. This applied particularly to the problem of immortality. Citing the volitional aspects of the human soul as well as the intellectual ones, he argued that immortality could be demonstrated by natural means,[192] while admitting that Aristotle himself was unclear on the question.[193] He conceded, furthermore, that Pomponazzi might have been right in denying that it was demonstrable in terms of natural philosophy.[194] He concluded with the purely practical argument

attrahere illud ad se intentionaliter eique vitaliter uniri . . . actio significat actionem productivam et elicitivam actus vitalis, operatio autem significat ipsumet actum vitalem, quo ipsum operans perficitur ultimate'.   188. Giacon 1944–50, II, pp. 25–42.
189. Lohr 1982, pp. 199–201; Stegmüller 1935b; Giacon 1944–50, II, pp. 31–66; H. J. Müller 1968.
190. Toletus 1592, f. 115^(ra).   191. See n. 165 above.
192. Toletus 1592, ff. 152^(rb)–9^(vb) (lib. III, q. 16).
193. *Ibid.*, f. 149^(vb) (lib. III, q. 15, concl. 3): 'De statu animae post mortem quaedam habemus ab Aristotele non parvi momenti, sed eiusmodi, ut ex illis multa alia certa liceat demonstratione colligere.'
194. *Ibid.*, f. 152^(va) (lib. III, q. 16): 'Unde erravit Pomponatius dicens animam mortalem secundum philosophiam, et quamvis non esset fortasse error dicere, quod non potest demonstrari naturaliter animae immortalitas, hoc enim dicit Scotus.'

that it was safer to assume the immortality of the soul than to deny it, thus prefiguring Pascal's famous wager.[195]

In his theory of cognition Toletus attempted to find a way through the diversity of positions. He dissented from the Thomists and joined the Scotists and nominalists in maintaining the immediate intellection of the singular[196] and the existence of an intellectual memory.[197] Following Cajetan, he defended the necessity of an agent intellect to illuminate the soul by rendering the *phantasma* into intelligible *species*. But he differed from Cajetan in that he split the illumination process into two phases: the first, an external illumination from which the intelligible species of the singular originated; and the second, an internal illumination of this same species, which produced the universal object of intellection.[198] But he went even further. Denying the necessity of postulating the agent intellect as *realiter* distinct from the possible intellect, as the Thomists had done, he conceded at least the probability of Durandus' position. Durandus had entirely abandoned the distinction between agent and possible intellect and had interpreted intellection as the operation of one and the same intellectual potency in the soul. Toletus, nevertheless, retained the concept of an agent intellect, not because of conclusive arguments, but rather because of common philosophical opinion; the question itself remained open for further investigation.[199]

Commentaria Collegii Conimbricensis: Emmanuel de Goes

A similar attitude is evident in the Portuguese philosopher Emmanuel de Goes, whose exposition of *De anima* constituted one of the Aristotle commentaries from the Jesuit college at Coimbra.[200] Intended to serve as a standard textbook within a *cursus* of Christian philosophy, the commentary itself, while giving the Greek text along with a Latin translation, was

195. *Ibid.*, f. 159[ra] (lib. III, q. 16): 'Tandem melius est et tutius sic opinari . . . Nam aut haec fides et opinio vera est, scilicet animam esse immortalem, et tunc quidem, si quis eam non crediderit, aut credere noluerit, post mortem luet penas . . . Aut non est vera opinio, animam scilicet immortalem, et tunc nihil erit periculi post mortem, sic fuisse opinatos in vita'. See Pascal 1907, no. 233.
196. Toletus 1592, ff. 142[rb]–3[vb] (lib. III, q. 12). 197. *Ibid.*, f. 169[ra] (lib. III. q. 21, concl. 2).
198. *Ibid.*, ff. 144[va]–7[ra] (lib. III, q. 13), especially f. 146[rb] (concl. 5–6); Cajetan 1514, f. 48[r] (lib. III ad t.c. 18).
199. Toletus 1592, f. 146[va] (lib. III, q. 13, concl. 9): 'Puto esse sententiam Durandi probabilem et eorum qui negant intellectum agentem aut saltem sola ponunt ratione distinctum. Neque enim duos habemus intellectus ut videtur, sed unum, sicut nec duas voluntates . . . Et secundo quia ille unus satis esse videtur ad producendum lumen et postea eliciendum species et producendum in se notitiam. Nil enim vetat in seipsum agere actione perfectiva. Et tertio, quia nulla est ratio contra hoc conveniens: tamen quia nec in contrarium rationes habentur convincentes, sequimur communem sententiam.' See Durandus a S. Porciano 1567, ff. 27[r]–8[r] (lib. I, dist. 3, q. 5); Koch 1927. 200. *Collegium Conimbricense* 1609; Lohr 1975, pp. 717–19.

confined to a rather brief explanation, while the philosophical analysis as such was again transferred to the *quaestiones* which followed each chapter and discussed the psychological problems from the Christian point of view.

As a result of this religious preoccupation, at the very beginning of the sections on the human soul the Christian position regarding the ontological status of the soul was firmly stated, i.e., that the human soul was a spiritual substance, self-subsistent, created in time by God, informing the human body and multiplied according to the multiplication of bodies.[201] The way was thus paved for a philosophical demonstration of individual immortality, which was set out in a treatise on the separate soul, added by the editor, Balthasar Alvarez.[202] Alvarez even claimed that immortality could be demonstrated according to Aristotle.[203] Conceding, however, in the end (1) that his arguments were not as conclusive and exact as those in mathematics, but were nevertheless sufficient for the subject-matter[204] and (2) that, in this life, the human intellect might need some special illumination to be able to recognise the truth,[205] Alvarez offered the hand of reconciliation.

The same spirit of reconciliation animated the commentary. The author had access to the whole of the Greek, Arabic and Latin commentary tradition. He did not, however, try to come to terms with it by refuting divergent positions, but rather by making the best of them for his own purposes; and it is obviously not by chance that he repeatedly referred to Agostino Steuco, one of the chief proponents of Neoplatonic syncretism.[206] Consequently, in many questions that were controversial between Thomists and Scotists of the time – e.g., the distinction between the agent and possible intellect,[207] the necessity of the intelligible *species*,[208] the intellection of singulars[209] and the manner in which the intelligible *species* is produced[210] – both positions were considered at least defensible if not equally probable, and no dogmatic decision was arrived at.

201. *Collegium Conimbricense* 1609, cols. 57–112 (lib. II, cap. I, c. 1–7).
202. *Ibid.*, cols. 561–670 (*Tractatus de anima separata*).   203. *Ibid.*, cols. 564–8 (disp. I, art. 2).
204. *Ibid.*, col. 574 (disp. I, art. 3): 'Quod vero proposita argumenta non tam stricte atque evidenter rem conficiant ut illa quae apud Euclidem sunt, non ideo suspiciosa videri debet eorum firmitas et efficacia. In quam sententiam Aristoteles I. Ethicorum, capite tertio [*Nicomachean Ethics* I.3 (1094^b 11)] ita scribit. Dicitur autem satis, si declaretur perinde ac subiecta materia postulat; ipsum enim exactum non est in omnibus simili modo rationibus flagitandum.'
205. *Ibid.*, col. 575 (disp. I, art. 3): 'cum naturali lumine cognitam esse immortalitatem animae asserimus, non excludere nos peculiaria quaedam auxilia et illustrationes mentium, sine quibus fortasse id assequi non potuerunt philosophi post primi parentis lapsum'.
206. Steuco 1591, III (*De perenni philosophia libri XII*); Freudenberger 1935; Schmitt 1981, I.
207. *Collegium Conimbricense* 1609, cols. 415–23 (lib. III, cap. 5, q. 1).
208. *Ibid.*, cols. 428–34 (lib. III, cap. 5, q. 3).   209. *Ibid.*, cols. 434–43 (lib. III, cap. 5, q. 4).
210. *Ibid.*, cols. 443–58 (lib. III, cap. 5, q. 5–6).

Only in regard to the process of intellection itself, where both Thomists and Scotists were rejected, did the author formulate his own position. He considered intellection as mental discourse, through which the *species expressa* or the mental word was produced from the impressed species, but which ceased to exist the moment the process of intellection was completed. That is, knowing and the known were identical in being, but differed formally in so far as the former concerned the fact that the mental word was in the process of coming-to-be (*verbum in fieri*), while the latter signified that the process was terminated at every moment.[211] If one considers that this concept of intellection as mental discourse was also applied to Christ, who was God's mental word,[212] it is obvious that once again human intellection was reconstructed in order to save a theological principle.

Francisco Suárez

The most original Jesuit writer on psychological questions was Francisco Suárez, whose lecture course on the soul was reorganised and published after his death by Alvarez[213] as a supplement to his commentary on Thomas' *Summa theologiae*. Even if Suárez himself had not intended to include his psychological writings among his theological works, as a means of arriving at a better knowledge of God through the knowledge of human nature,[214] the fact that he did not follow the Aristotelian text but instead referred to the *ordo doctrinae* as the guideline of his argument[215] proves that he wanted to write a systematic treatise rather than an exposition of Aristotle. Moreover, his statement that theologians and Christian philosophers, especially St Thomas, were a better source for a philosophy of the intellect than was Aristotle[216] seems to justify the policy of Alvarez.

211. *Ibid.*, cols. 483–94 (lib. III, cap. 8, q. 3–4); col. 493 (lib. III, cap. 8, q. 4, art. 2): 'Secunda conclusio in hac controversia sit verbum non dissidere re ipsa ab intellectione . . . quia utcunque se habeat actio . . . nihil est aliud quam res ipsa in fieri (liceat enim ita loqui) proindeque non distinguitur re a suo termino . . . Sed negandum intellectionem esse causam verbi, non enim est illius causa, sed productio et quasi via, qua intellectus verbum exprimit. Tertia conclusio sit, verbum non esse formaliter intellectionem . . . quia verbum est terminus intellectionis, omnis vero actio distinguitur saltem formaliter a suo termino.'
212. *Ibid.*, col. 486 (lib. III, cap. 8, q. 3, art. 2): 'essentia divina summe praesens est intellectui paterno, et tamen Pater eam intelligendo producit verbum'.
213. Suárez 1856–78, III, pp. 461–816; first edition 1621; edition of the original text: 1978–81, I; Lohr 1982, pp. 180–7; Giacon 1944–50, II, pp. 203–31; Jansen 1951, pp. 349–52.
214. Suárez 1856–78, III, p. 463 ('prooemium'): 'humana mens excellentiam et virtutem suam attentius considerando, et imperfectiones, quas in se conspicit, removendo, ad divinam naturam eiusque perfectiones contemplandas magis provehitur et assurgit'.
215. *Ibid.*, p. 713ᵃ (lib. IV, cap. I, no. I): 'hic tamen praetermitti non potuit propter doctrinae ordinem'.
216. *Ibid.* (lib. IV, prooemium): 'Disputavit Aristoteles de hac materia . . . etsi vero pleraque de intellectu pronuntiet, multo vero plura theologi ac philosophi Christiani, nominatim D. Thomas . . . tradere solent.'

The *ordo doctrinae* of Suárez was determined by the types of questions traditionally discussed by scholastics, and in some cases – e.g., the admission of an immediate knowledge of the singular, which for him was the first known object,[217] or the supposition of an intellectual memory[218] – he felt compelled to join the Scotists instead of Thomas. Yet, Suárez' real philosophical innovation resided in the question of the cooperation of the agent intellect with the *phantasma* in producing the intelligible *species*, which involved the transition from the materiality of the sensible object to the immateriality of the intelligible object as the precondition of knowledge.[219] His predecessors' various attempts to account for this transition were inadequate in the eyes of Suárez, since in principle there seemed to be no way for the material and the immaterial to cooperate, and the only thing imagination and intellect had in common was that both were rooted in one and the same soul and served as its instrument.[220] Suárez' solution, therefore, was to reject any such cooperation and to suppose instead that imagination and intellect acted in perfect harmony and parallelism,[221] so that, whenever the imagination produced a phantasm, the intellect produced an intelligible species and vice versa.[222] To save this parallel operation, however, it was not necessary to postulate an agent intellect as a power of the soul on its own – and, indeed, the agent intellect was not needed in a state of separation, nor was it an article of faith. Suárez, therefore, did not hesitate to concede, as Toletus had done, that the notion of agent intellect was superfluous.[223]

With this theory Suárez came close to the Neoplatonic position of Marcantonio Genua, who, following Simplicius, had taught that the intelligible species, excited by the imagination, flow from the intellect

217. *Ibid.*, pp. 722ª–30ᵇ (lib. IV, cap. 3); Stengren 1965.
218. *Ibid.*, pp. 749ᵇ–52ᵇ (lib. IV, cap. 10).   219. *Ibid.*, pp. 715ᵇ–21ᵇ (lib. IV, cap. 2).
220. *Ibid.*, p. 718ª (lib. IV, cap. 2, no. 7): 'inter phantasma, et intellectum agentem non potest cogitari alia, vel maior unio, quam quod radicentur ambo in eadem anima et supposito, tanquam instrumenta illius'.
221. *Ibid.*, p. 719ᵇ (lib. IV, cap. 2, no. 12): 'est enim notandum phantasma et intellectum hominis radicari in una eademque anima: hinc enim provenit, ut mirum habeant ordinem et consonantiam in operando, unde (quod patebit infra) eo ipso quod intellectus operatur, imaginatio etiam sentit'.
222. *Ibid.*, p. 740ª (lib. IV, cap. 7, no. 4): 'ambae potentiae in eadem anima radicantur, sibique mutuo deserviunt, atque etiam sunt impedimento . . . perfectio quoque imaginationis prodesse potest intellectui, quia quanto melius imaginativa apprehendit, eo meliores species imprimuntur intellectui: sed et intellectus ipse operando movet, ac secum trahit imaginationem. Hinc ergo oritur inter potentias has tam naturalis concomitantia.' See Ludwig 1929; Castellote 1982.
223. *Ibid.*, pp. 740ᵇ–745ª (lib. IV, cap. 8), especially p. 741ᵇ (lib. IV, cap. 8, no. 4): 'quod intellectus agens, aut etiam species intelligibiles dentur, de fide non est'; p. 745ª (lib. IV, cap. 8, no. 13): 'quoniam intellectus agens post hanc vitam semper actione carebit, quod inconveniens censetur, si potentia est distincta realiter, erit ergo virtus eiusdem potentiae . . . quae certe opinio verior apparet, quamvis nihil certum se offerat'.

itself;[224] and Suárez seems to have been well aware of this affinity.[225] He
also came close – although he was not of course aware of it – to the psycho-
physical parallelism which Leibniz taught more than a century later in order
to overcome the problems of Cartesian dualism.[226]

Protestant Aristotelianism: Philipp Melanchthon

While for Catholic Christian psychology the point of reference had been
the decree of the Lateran Council, which resulted from a long debate
between philosophy and theology, and therefore linked Renaissance
philosophy of the soul to the medieval tradition, the Protestant starting-
point was Luther's rejection of the Latin tradition in general. This included
not only medieval theology but scholastic philosophy and Aristotle as well,
who – as Luther stated in accordance with Pomponazzi's position – had
maintained the mortality of the human soul.[227] While this rejection meant
the liberation of theological thought from all kinds of traditional
philosophical limitations, at the same time it resulted in a subjectivism,
which quickly necessitated a theoretical basis for the new religious
orientation.[228] Starting in 1526, Philipp Melanchthon established a
Protestant educational system and composed the required textbooks.[229]
Though free to choose between philosophical schools, Melanchthon opted
for Aristotle as the foundation-stone.[230] Aristotle was thus given the
dominant role in Protestant psychology, though, thanks to Luther's
protests, the attitude towards the philosopher had changed. Above all, the
submission to the doctrines of faith went even further than with the
Catholics. Not only was the study of the soul held to be a means of acquiring
knowledge about God,[231] but Melanchthon adhered so firmly to Christian
doctrine that besides the immortality of the soul he also defended the
resurrection of the body as a psychological fact.[232] Moreover, his definition

---

224. Genua 1576, f. 156[vb] (lib. III ad t. c. 18): 'Dicendum tamen pro declaratione huius quod sicuti
    intellectus progreditur a seipso sic et quae in eo sunt quidditates, ut retro dixit Simplicius. Cum
    vero intellectus videat phantasmata ab illis excitatus et ad se conversus recipit quidditates egressas
    illis correspondentes phantasmatibus, non autem a phantasmatibus.'
225. Suárez 1856–78, III, p. 745[a] (lib. IV, cap. 8, no. 13): 'statim enim ac anima ipsa quippiam cognoscit
    per phantasiam, ab ipso intellectu manat species id repraesentans. Quare efficientia haec
    quodammodo se habet instar emanationis speciei ab intellectu.'
226. Leibniz 1875–90, IV, pp. 477-87 (*Système nouveau de la nature et de la communication des substances*).
227. Luther 1883–, VI, p. 458: 'Leret doch der elend mensch [Aristotle] in seinem besten buch, de Anima,
    das die seel sterblich sey mit dem Corper.' See Petersen 1921; Link 1969.
228. Petersen 1921, p. 40.
229. Melanchthon 1834–60, XI, cols. 106–11 (*In laudem novae scholae*, 1526); Lohr 1978, pp. 576–82;
    Hartfelder 1889; Petersen 1921, pp. 19–108.
230. Melanchthon 1834–60, XI, cols. 278–84 (*De philosophia oratio*, 1536).
231. *Ibid.*, XIII, cols. 5–178 (*Liber de anima*), especially cols. 5–6; Rump 1897.
232. *Ibid.*, cols. 172–8.

of the soul was consciously asserted in opposition to that of natural philosophy.[233] Furthermore, Melanchthon accepted much of the humanists' critique of scholasticism, rejecting the medieval commentaries as mere *cavillationes*,[234] following Cicero in interpreting Aristotle's ἐντελέχεια as ἐνδελέχεια or continuous motion (on account of which he met with severe opposition from his former friend Veit Amerbach)[235] and in emphasising that knowledge in general was acquired for practical ends[236] and psychology in particular should serve the purposes of moral philosophy.[237]

Melanchthon's psychology differs greatly from the usual commentaries on the soul and resembles instead the treatise *De anima et vita* of Juan Luis Vives, with which it was published several times.[238] The order of the various chapters largely follows that of Aristotle, but their content – including both an entire physiology of the human body and the senses, based on Galen, and also a theory of freedom and the passions, usually discussed in the ethics or in rhetoric – makes for a new concept of psychology, which could be called a comprehensive theory of man or anthropology.

Melanchthon was also aware of the traditional psychological questions, but instead of entering into detail he merely stated his own definitive position in the manner of a textbook. Thus he upheld the nominalist distinction between intuitive and abstractive cognition,[239] consequently defending the immediate knowledge of singulars[240] as well as intellectual memory,[241] as the Scotists had done,[242] and generally the empirical basis of human knowledge as a result of original sin.[243] Yet, at the same time, he escaped the epistemological problems of empiricism by accepting innate ideas,[244] which together with universal experience and logical demonstration served as criteria for a certitude guaranteed by the divine will.[245] Finally, he defined the act of knowledge as the formation of the intellectual image and that, in turn, as the act of knowledge itself, thereby – even in the application of this concept to God begetting Christ, his son and image –

233. *Ibid.*, col. 16: 'Anima rationalis est spiritus intelligens, qui est altera pars substantiae hominis, nec extinguitur, cum a corpore discessit, sed immortalis est. Haec definitio non habet physicas rationes.'   234. *Ibid.*, col. 282.

235. *Ibid.*, cols. 13–14; Cicero, *Tusculan Disputations* 1.10.22; Amerbach 1542.

236. Melanchthon 1834–60, XIII, col. 150: 'veras sententias discant, et agnitam veritatem constanter amplectantur et deinde iuxta voluntatem Dei, transferant eam ad usum'.   237. *Ibid.*, col. 6.

238. Vives 1538; Lohr 1982, pp. 224–6; Schüling 1967, pp. 266–9; Sancipriano 1957.

239. Melanchthon 1834–60, XIII, col. 145.   240. *Ibid.*, col. 142.   241. *Ibid.*, col. 145.

242. See nn. 180, 183 above.   243. Melanchthon 1834–60, XIII, col. 143.   244. *Ibid.*, col. 144.

245. *Ibid.*, cols. 149–50: 'Deus vult aliquas esse certas noticias . . . Sunt igitur normae certitudinis iuxta philosophiam tres: Experientia universalis, noticiae principiorum et intellectus ordinis in syllogismo.'

prefiguring the position of the Coimbra commentary.[246] Concerning the problems of a theory of knowledge, Melanchthon's *Liber de anima* could in fact be inserted into the discussion of his Catholic colleagues, testifying to the continuity of the Christian attitude towards psychology, which transcended the religious split of the Reformation.

It was only in the question of how to account for the difference between the possible and the agent intellect that Melanchthon differed conspicuously from the Aristotelians. Instead of following one of the proposed interpretations of Aristotle's text, he introduced a new approach based on the activities of the intellect. He stated that since it was one thing to invent new concepts and another to accept them, the agent intellect was the faculty of invention, while the possible was that of acceptance.[247] At first glance, this seems to be a mere simplification, but it may well be that Melanchthon had in mind the distinction between the inventive and the judicative faculties, defended by both Rudolph Agricola and Melanchthon himself in their works on dialectic,[248] and that he intended it to bridge the gap between psychological epistemology and methodology. In any case, the examples which he adduced to prove that the inventive faculty of the agent intellect was not equally distributed among men prefigured the later development of the concept of genius.

The success of Melanchthon's psychology was unique. Some forty editions and eight commentaries were printed in the sixteenth century.[249] His work had become the psychology textbook for Protestant lands despite its expository shortcomings when compared to the writings of contemporary Catholic authors.

NATURAL PHILOSOPHY

After the Pomponazzi affair Christian philosophers from both confessions aimed at developing a theory of the soul which could save the contents of Christian doctrine. Natural philosophers, on the other hand, generally felt

246. *Ibid.*, col. 145: 'Noticia est mentis actio qua rem adspicit, quasi formans imaginem rei, quam cogitat. Nec aliud sunt imagines illae seu ideae, nisi actus intelligendi . . . Aeternus pater sese intuens gignit filium cogitando, qui est imago aeterni patris'; see nn. 211–12 above.
247. *Ibid.*, cols. 147–8: 'Etsi magnae sunt contentiones de intellectu agente et patiente, tamen si sumimus ab actionibus discrimen, simplex et perspicua est haec explicatio . . . In hac ratiocinatione aliud ex alio invenit. Hic inventor intellectus, et tamquam poëta dicitur agens, seu rectius faciens. Alterum officium est postea inventa intelligere, agnoscere et tamquam dictata accipere. Ab hoc officio nominatur intellectus patiens.'
248. *Ibid.*, cols. 641ff. (*Erotemata dialectices libri IV*); Agricola 1528, p. 141 (lib. II, cap. 1); Vasoli 1968a, pp. 147–82, 278–309.   249. Schüling 1967, pp. 183–6, 288.

free to save the psychic phenomena according to the principles of Aristotelian philosophy, read in the light of various expository traditions, particularly those of the recently discovered and translated Greek commentators. As Bessarion had already stated in the fifteenth century,[250] the natural philosopher, notwithstanding his personal adherence to the Christian belief in individual immortality, had in philosophical terms to choose between the concept of one immortal intellect for all men and that of individual human intellects which died with the body. The first position had been defended by Averroes and his Greek sources Themistius and Simplicius, while the second was the position of Alexander of Aphrodisias: natural philosophers of the sixteenth century were thus divided into two competing schools.[251]

Simone Porzio

There is no doubt that natural philosophers in the strict sense, following Pomponazzi, were of the Alexandrist persuasion, the leading representative of which was Simone Porzio.[252] His *De humana mente disputatio* was even translated into Italian by Giovambattista Gelli, but, apparently through fear of the Inquisition, was never published in that version.[253] Porzio maintained against Philoponus, the autonomy of a natural philosophical approach based on well-defined principles, since when philosophy was mixed with religious elements the result was appropriate neither to physical nature nor to theology.[254] On the other hand, he argued against the followers of Averroes, Simplicius and Themistius, who claimed to interpret Aristotle without being able to find proper evidence in the Aristotelian text.[255] Consequently, Porzio held the true natural theory of the soul to be Aristotle's, but not as interpreted by Averroes, Simplicius and Themistius. He concluded that the soul was the individual and corruptible form of the body, endowed with vegetative, sensitive and intellective powers.[256] All

250. See n. 48 above.
251. Saitta 1961, II, pp. 339–463; Garin 1966, pp. 499–580; *Grande antologia* 1964–, VII, pp. 607–837 ('Aristotelismo'); Kristeller 1965a, pp. 111–18.
252. Fiorentino 1911, pp. 81–153; Lohr 1980, pp. 667–70.   253. Porzio 1551b; Montù 1968.
254. Porzio 1551b, pp. 11–19 (capp. 2–3), especially pp. 12–13 (cap. 3): 'principia ex praescripto scientiae non liceat transilire . . . Nam cum hi Philosophi physica pronuntiata cum sanctissimis et verissimis nostrae religionis decretis confundant: quod inde colligunt, ac concludunt, nec religiosum, nec physicum, minimeque cum rebus ipsis respondens fuerit.'
255. *Ibid.*, p. 3: 'multos quippe audies Averroicos, Simplicianos et Themistianos, qui authoritate magis nomineque philosophi suam sententiam adstruant, quam eam verborum Aristotelis fide confirmare conentur'.
256. *Ibid.*, pp. 17–19 (cap. 3), especially p. 19: 'colligimus rationalem animam, quum sit principium, quo intelligimus, et id quo sentimus, non igitur discretis principiis homo est homo, et animal et vivens, sed una est anima, diversis tamen praedita facultatibus'.

those qualities, such as being separable, impassible and unmixed with body,[257] which were attributed to the intellect by Aristotle and seemingly demonstrated its immortality, referred to its operations rather than to its essence.[258]

Thus Porzio's basic position was identical with that of Pomponazzi, and they differed only in Pomponazzi's more systematic approach. Porzio adhered closely, in a philological way, to the relevant Aristotelian texts. Indeed, his philological analysis of the key term ἐντελέχεια, 'the first actuality of a natural organic body',[259] dominated the entire disputation. Since ἐντελέχεια was understood as meaning 'the perfection and final end reached through a motion'[260] and was identified with the form of a natural being,[261] the soul as the ἐντελέχεια of the human body turned out to be its form as the result of a natural change. Moreover, the possible intellect, not itself being a perfection, but one of the powers of the soul,[262] turned out to be the means by which the soul was moved to its second perfection, that is, knowledge.

The process of intellection, then, had to be reconstructed in terms of a natural motion, through which a form was moved from one subject to the other. The structure of such a motion of formation could easily be observed in sense-perception, where the sense was moved by its object thanks to the activity of a medium like flesh in the case of touch or light in the case of sight. And since it was obvious that in sensation, the higher the sense, the more noble the medium, it seemed only natural that to move the most noble faculty of the intellect a most noble and active medium was required, which might rightly be supposed to be an immaterial substance, such as the one called agent intellect by Aristotle or even, as Alexander argued, God himself.[263]

---

257. Aristotle, *De anima* III.5 (430ᵃ17).

258. Porzio 1551b, pp. 43–4 (cap. 7): pp. 57–8 (cap. 12); p. 61 (cap. 13); p. 74 (cap. 16); p. 93 (cap. 23): 'Aristoteles non tribuit haec tria praedicata intellectui, ut est substantia aut qualitas, sed ut est facultas cognoscendi et hac ratione nulli alii facultati cognoscendi . . . conveniunt.'

259. Aristotle, *De anima* II.1 (412ᵇ5).

260. Porzio 1551b, p. 8 (cap. 1): 'Entelechia peculiari significatione perfectionem et finem postremum per motionem partum significat.'

261. *Ibid.*, p. 9 (cap. 1): 'forma finis habitus per motum appellatur, et hoc pacto dicitur entelechia'.

262. *Ibid.*, p. 10 (cap. 1): 'anima rationalis . . . quando quidem anima, est forma et corporis perfectio: at intellectus est potentia et facultas, qua anima sapit et intelligit'.

263. *Ibid.*, pp. 86–7 (cap. 21): 'Verum cum sensus tactus sit omnium crassissimus, ad usum tangendi sufficiens est qualitas quae tactum afficit et medium, connatum animali, puta caro. Facultas vero videndi, cum sincerissimum constituat organum . . . sincerius quoque medium et actum desiderat ad functiones obeundas. Non enim satis est color: sed lumen necesse est intercedat. Quare quanto sentiendi facultas sincerius habet organum, tanto magis extraneum requirit medium . . . Non est

Thus through his understanding of ἐντελέχεια Porzio reconstructed intellection as an entirely natural process and attributed the immaterial aspects to the intervention of a supernatural agent. In this way he succeeded in reducing psychology to a purely natural discipline. At the same time, the crucial problems of knowledge, which related to the cooperation of material and immaterial aspects of human action, were excluded from psychological consideration and, moreover, man himself was reduced to a natural object deprived of all active powers. Freedom, if there was such a thing, was the proof of man's imperfection rather than of his dignity, since God, the most perfect cause in nature, showed no sign of indeterminacy.[264]

Giulio Castellani

Giulio Castellani,[265] though a nephew of Pier Nicola Castellani, a follower of Nifo,[266] was an open admirer of Alexander, whom he called *deliciae meae* ('my delight');[267] moreover, he regarded Porzio as his forerunner.[268] Concerning the autonomy of natural philosophy,[269] its identification with Aristotle[270] and the endeavour to construct a philologically correct interpretation of the Philosopher,[271] he manifested an attitude similar to Porzio's, excusing himself several times for using scholastic terms.[272] He also discussed the theoretical problems of natural philosophical method as distinct from the universal method of logic,[273] as well as attempting to clarify Aristotle's method in his analysis of the texts.[274] This attempt may have been a consequence of Castellani's general awareness of epistemological problems, which was already evident in his refutation of Ciceronian scepticism,[275] and which emerged anew when he praised

itaque ad sentiendi usum utilis, praeter medium, aliquis sensus agens, sed quia intellectus potentia est longe nobilior omni sentiendi virtute, quam maxime videbatur necessarium . . . vim quandam constituere, qua ipsum intelligere absolveretur. Ad hoc quidem opus . . . operae precium erat absolutiorem substantiam ponere et a rebus materiatis liberam . . . quam quidem virtutem Aristoteles vocavit substantiam separatam et aeternam; Alexander, Deum.'

264. *Ibid.*, p. 96 (cap. 24): 'libertas [sc. arbitrii] cum iudicet potentiam et a privatione proficiscatur, potius mutabilitatem significat . . . In Deo enim . . . non est ista indifferentia, nec opinionum mutatio: sed ut sunt puri actus ita ad unum semper sunt determinatae . . . illa indifferentia et ambiguitas ex naturae nostrae imperfectione et imbecillitate oritur . . . Sed haec explicatius leges in opusculo *An homo volens fiat malus*'; Porzio 1551a, 1551c.

265. G. Castellani 1567; Lohr 1975, p. 704; Garin 1966, pp. 544–8; Saitta 1961, II, pp. 380–6.

266. P. N. Castellani 1525; Mahoney 1970b.   267. G. Castellani 1567, f. 31ʳ (lib. II, cap. 6).

268. *Ibid.*, f. 2ʳ (prooemium).   269. *Ibid.*, f. 3ᵛ (lib. I, cap. 1).   270. *Ibid.*, f. 1ʳ (prooemium).

271. *Ibid.*, f. 2ᵛ (prooemium); ff. 52ʳ–67ʳ (lib. III, capp. 1–11).

272. *Ibid.*, f. 8ᵛ (lib. I, cap. 3): 'quiditates (uti aliquando necesse est, ut supra notavimus, tritis et vulgatis verbis Philosophorum)'; f. 15ʳ ('possibilitas'); f. 25ʳ ('quod quid erat esse'); f. 31ᵛ ('essentia'); ff. 32ᵛ, 44ᵛ ('spiritualis'), etc.   273. *Ibid.*, ff. 19ʳ–24ʳ (lib. II, capp. 1–3).

274. *Ibid.*, ff. 24ʳ–6ʳ (lib. II, cap. 4).   275. G. Castellani 1558; Schmitt 1972, pp. 109–33.

psychology for providing a general basis for the certitude of human knowledge.[276]

In the epistemological discussion of his own treatise on the soul, Castellani followed Porzio only in basic assumptions. He separated the agent from the possible intellect: the first being God, who by illumination frees the *phantasmata* from the shadows of materiality[277] and serves as the general cause of cognition;[278] the latter being part of the form of the human body and in its pure potency comparable to prime matter.[279] On this basis Castellani reconstructed intellection as a temporal and therefore natural process,[280] through which the illuminated *phantasma* draws the intelligible *species*, and consequently intellection, out of the potentiality of the possible intellect, just as the material form is educed out of the potentiality of prime matter.[281] Thus, while in Porzio knowledge was reconstructed as the natural process of the movement of the form from one subject to another, in Castellani it was reconstructed as the natural process of coming-to-be. In both cases, intellection was a necessary process through which man attained knowledge from the outside without taking an active role.

But Castellani was not willing to accept the consequences of his reconstruction according to the principles of nature. Against Averroes he maintained that notwithstanding the identity of the agent intellect with God, or even because of this identity, the principal agent of intellection being always and everywhere present was at man's disposal, so that he could think whenever he wanted to.[282] On the other hand, he not only emphasised that intellection, beyond mere apprehension, meant both the composition of terms in propositions and the connection of propositions to arguments, which were all operations of the soul,[283] but he also ascribed to the possible intellect a specific power to deal actively with the illuminated

276. G. Castellani 1567, f. 21^v (lib. II, cap. 2): 'Ceterum animae disciplina demonstrationis ἀκρίβεια mathematicis scientiis, nedum caeteris cognitionibus longe praestat: propterea quod in ea assignatur causa, qua primis demonstrationum principiis assentimur.'

277. *Ibid.*, ff. 44^a–7^b (lib. II, cap. 12).

278. *Ibid.*, f. 71^b (lib. III, cap. 12): 'intellectus agens non est verum efficiens, sed causa tantum agendique ratio ipsi phantasmati'.

279. *Ibid.*, ff. 26^a–33^a (lib. II, capp. 5–6), especially f. 30^a: 'est actu ens nulla praeditum forma eandem potentiae naturam habens, quam materiae primae tribuimus'.

280. *Ibid.*, ff. 37^b–41^b (lib. II, cap. 9).

281. *Ibid.*, f. 71^b (lib. III, cap. 12): 'phantasma intelligibilem formam non inducit, sed eam sola praesentia ex intellectu possibili educit, in qua inerat potentia: quemadmodum enim naturale agens in materiam primam vere formam non introducit, sed ex illius potestate hanc deducit ad actum, ita prope evenit in intellectu potentia'.

282. *Ibid.*, f. 70^b (lib. III, cap. 12): 'summus et omnia potens Deus cum omni tempore . . . ubicunque adsit . . . nil mirum, si nos cum volumus, illustrare phantasmata haecque actu intelligibilia facere possimus'. 283. *Ibid.*, f. 37^b (lib. II, cap. 9).

phantasma.[284] With these modifications Castellani tried to overcome determinism, the most irritating implication of his approach, even though he failed to formulate a coherent psychology.

Marcantonio Genua

Castellani's deviation from the path of pure natural philosophy did not result, however, merely from a more sophisticated philosophical mind seeing the limitations of Porzio's approach, but rather from the growth of the competing school of Averroists and the followers of Simplicius. Castellani summarised their position and later rigorously destroyed it;[285] nevertheless, traces of his opponents' views remained with him. The crucial point at which Castellani went beyond Porzio – that man knows whenever he wishes to – was also crucial in Genua's commentary, which marks him as the heir to Averroism and the outstanding figure of the Simplician movement.[286]

A tendency to reinterpret the Averroist concept of the unified intellect, after its refutation by Thomas Aquinas, in terms of the Neoplatonic Greek commentary tradition had continued since Siger of Brabant and Jean de Jandun.[287] It was revitalised after the rediscovery of Simplicius and the new Latin translation of Themistius along with the Neoplatonising Averroism of Achillini and Nifo at the turn of the century.[288] It remained attractive, even after Pomponazzi, to all those who, not content with the limited natural approach, searched for a more spiritual nature for man and, adhering to the unicity of the intellect, wished to preserve some form of immortality, if not for the individual man, at least for mankind. This was the case with Francesco Vimercato, whose careful analysis of the Aristotelian text resulted in the statement that even if Aristotle, unlike Themistius, Simplicius and Averroes, never spoke expressly of the unicity of the intellect, nonetheless it was best suited to what he did say and, moreover, it was irrefutable by natural reason.[289] The same was true of Marcantonio Zimara, who because of his *Tabula dilucidationum* to the works of Averroes has traditionally been considered an orthodox Averroist; but recent research has shown that he was also subject to Neoplatonising tendencies.[290]

284. *Ibid.*, f. 45^{r-v} (lib. II, cap. 12): 'phantasma ea quidem ratione, quod ab agente illuminatum est, excitat intellectum nostrum huncque deducit ad actum, qui deinde sic a phantasmate commotus vi et natura propria rem percipit intelligibilem'.
285. *Ibid.*, ff. 5^v–18^v (lib. I, capp. 2–3); Nardi 1958, pp. 383–7.
286. Genua 1576, f. 155ra (lib. III ad t. c. 18).   287. Nardi 1945.   288. Nardi 1958, pp. 365–83.
289. Vimercato 1543, pp. 285–92; Lohr 1982, pp. 217–19; Nardi 1958, pp. 404–11; N. W. Gilbert 1965.
290. Zimara 1537, reprinted in Aristotle and Averroes 1562–74, suppl. III; Lohr 1982, pp. 245–54; Nardi 1958, pp. 321–63; Antonaci 1971–8.

But the real breakthrough of Neoplatonism into Renaissance psychology happened only with Genua.[291] While still claiming to interpret Aristotle in the light of Averroes,[292] he rejected practically all interpretations of *De anima* save that of Simplicius, as was realised by the editors of his commentary[293] and by the Latin translator of Simplicius, Giovanni Faseolo, Genua's former student, who called for the replacement of Averroes by Simplicius.[294]

This substitution of authorities resulted in a concomitant substitution of cosmologies and concepts of nature. While for Aristotle and Averroes nature was governed by the principles of form and matter, time and space, for the Neoplatonists the structure of being was constituted by the principle of participation, through which the One was linked to the many and the lower to the higher. According to Genua, there were two levels of participation, one in the material world, reaching from prime matter to the animals, and the second in the spiritual world, containing God, the celestial intelligences and the rational soul. The link between the two, the material and the immaterial, was man, who, thanks to his cogitative soul, was the supreme animal and at the same time, thanks to his rational soul, was the lowest of the intelligences.[295] To investigate the human soul was therefore of cosmological importance, since it related to the unity of the universe itself. For the same reason, the psychologist or *animasticus*, as Genua called him, was not just a natural philosopher, but had to consider at the same time both the material and the immaterial worlds, physics and metaphysics.[296]

Therefore the human soul as a whole could not possibly be the individual and corruptible form of the body, as the Alexandrists believed, or even the informing form in the sense of Nifo, divided into corruptible, cogitative

---

291. Lohr 1977, pp. 726–30; Nardi 1958, pp. 386–94; *Grande antologia* 1964–, VII, pp. 627–9 ('Aristotelismo').

292. Genua 1576, f. 1va (praefatio): 'in tam vasto difficultatum pelago naturam ipsam, quinimo Deum ipsum ducem, Aristotelem habeamus . . . et omnium princeps Averroes, quem . . . alterum Aristotelem semper habuerimus . . . Io. de Gandavo . . . quandoquidem summus sit Aristotelicus, summus et Averroicus.'

293. *Ibid.* (editors' preface *ad lectorem*): 'Ipse in Aristotele publice explanando, in Averroe interpretando, in Simplicio dilucidando, postremoque in Peripateticorum placitis exponendis eam gloriam quadraginta annorum spatio obtinuit, quae raro admodum et perquam paulis concessa fuit.'

294. Simplicius 1543, f. 35^v (translator's preface to lib. II): 'ita sese res habet, ut quicquid boni, in his praesertim De anima libris Arabs ille dixerit, de hoc [sc. Simplicius] sumpserit . . . huc mentem illam vestram atque ingenii acumen dirigite, alios omnes negligite: Simplicium unum vobis die noctuque versandum proponite'. See Nardi 1958, pp. 394–9.

295. Genua 1576, ff. 125ra–6ra (lib. III, praefatio).

296. *Ibid.*, f. 126ra: 'sic animasticus utriusque induit habitum, et naturalis et divini Philosophi et est artifex medius: nam qua ratione in homine duae illae naturae sic unitae reperiuntur, quo modo dictum est, eadem ratione et scientia haec datur media inter naturalem et divinam'.

and eternal, intellective parts.[297] The rational soul could only assist the human body, which was formed by the cogitative soul, and was linked to it like a captain to his ship or the intelligence to its sphere, through its operations.[298] Since intellection was the operation of the rational soul, it was not just one – albeit the highest – act of man, but rather the dynamic linkage that ensured the unity both of man and of the entire universe.

The structure of this unifying process of intellection had, of course, to be modelled on the structure of the universe itself, that is, participation. And this was the moment when Aristotle entered the picture. His distinction between agent and possible intellect, supplemented by the habitual intellect from the tradition of Simplicius and Averroes, offered the three terms of the model.[299]

The intellect, so long as it remained in itself (then called the *intellectus manens*) was one and eternal; proceeding towards the secondary lives, the *vitae secundae*, of animality, it turned into the rational soul or the *intellectus progressus*. As such, it extended between the eternal and the corruptible and included three aspects: (1) in so far as it still participated in the *intellectus manens*, it was the agent intellect, containing in itself all the intelligible *species* and universal forms; (2) in so far as it proceeded to the human individual, it was the possible intellect, able to receive the intelligible *species* from the agent intellect; and (3) in so far as it had already received some of these *species*, it was the habitual intellect or the perfection of the possible intellect. Once all intelligible *species* had been received, the last of these ceased – along with the possible intellect – to be a distinct part of the rational soul, so that, as a whole, it became identical with the agent intellect, or rather with the *intellectus manens*, which was an eternal intelligence.[300]

Intellection was thus the process through which the *intellectus progressus* returned to the *intellectus manens*. Since with this return the *intellectus progressus* vanished, in the question on the immortality of the soul, which was published separately in 1565, Genua did not hesitate to maintain that the one *intellectus manens* was immortal, while the different aspects of the *intellectus progressus* perished along with the body.[301] The problem which still remained to be solved, however, was how the material and the immaterial cooperated in this intellective process and thereby constituted the unity of the universe. Traditionally – and Genua was well aware of contradicting the common opinion of nearly all the commentators[302] – the

297. *Ibid.*, ff. 36vb–7vb (lib. II ad t. c. 11); Nardi 1958, p. 389.
298. Genua 1576, f. 37rb (lib. II ad t. c. 11); f. 128rb (lib. III ad t. c. 2); f. 185va (lib. III ad t. c. 39).
299. *Ibid.*, f. 152vb (lib. III ad t. c. 17).   300. *Ibid.*, ff. 152vb–4ra (lib. III ad t. c. 17).
301. *Ibid.*, ff. 183rb–9vb (lib. III ad t. c. 39); Genua 1565.
302. Genua 1576, f. 155ra (lib. III ad t. c. 18).

material *phantasma*, illuminated in one way or the other, moved the possible intellect by impressing the intelligible *species* and thereby provided the empirical basis of knowledge. For Genua, such a solution, which allowed the material to move the immaterial, would constitute an offence against the ontological nobility of the intellect. Furthermore, such an impression from the *phantasma* would be superfluous, since the rational soul contained the universal forms in its active part,[303] and therefore was able to produce knowledge by itself.[304] Yet, on the other hand, unless there was some kind of cooperation of the material with the immaterial, the rational soul would have to know constantly[305] and, at the same time, would be unable to serve as the connection between the two worlds. Genua therefore conceded a minimum of cooperation between the *phantasma* and the rational soul in that the material image excited the intellect to operate, or rather, that the presence of the *phantasma* was the occasion for the agent intellect to impress the relevant universal form on to the possible intellect.[306] In the same way, whenever the rational soul speculated on the *species* contained in the habitual intellect, imagination produced the relevant *phantasma*.[307]

Thus, the connection between the material and the immaterial, which was essential for the unity of the universe, turned out to be a kind of *sympathia* or parallelism[308] rather than a real linkage, thus anticipating the psychology of Suárez.[309] While in this parallelism intellection, guided by the inherent forms of the agent intellect, was a necessary process, which could not fail to reach the truth, the role of man as an individual was confined to the non-intellectual, materially determined cogitative soul. Porzio's determinism therefore returned despite the introduction of

---

303. *Ibid.*, f. 153ra (lib. III ad t. c. 17); f. 155rb (lib. III ad t. c. 18).
304. *Ibid.*, f. 155rb (lib. III ad t. c. 18): 'Divine exponens Simplicius notat quod ly potentia capitur ibi pro potentia activa, non autem passiva: quia perfectivus dicitur. Ut sit sensus quod intellectus potentia est materialium potentia intelligibilium [*De anima* III.4 (430^a 7)]: ut ille, qui potentiam illorum ad actum in seipso ducat. Et declarans hoc magis Simplicius inquit: Intelligens materialia circa ipsa operatur; non autem faciens aliquid in eis neque ab illis patiens aliquid; sed per proiectas, quae in eo sunt, causas, cognoscitivum actum illorum proiicit.'
305. *Ibid.*, f. 155rb (lib. III ad t. c. 18): 'quare est, quod semper non intelligimus?'
306. *Ibid.*: 'intellectus agens non est, ut producat species illas in phantasia existentes intelligibiles, sed occasione cuiuscunque phantasmatis, intellectus agens in se ipso possibili producat illius obiecti, uti est, notitiam'.
307. *Ibid.*, f. 184vb (lib. III ad t. c. 39): 'Dicendum igitur . . . quod semper indiget, imo ordine virtutum semper habet, imaginationem, vel praecedentem, vel consequentem'; f. 185rb (lib. III ad t. c. 39): 'Dicendum sicuti iam dictum est, quod intellectus, cum perfectus fuerit, phantasia non erit neque indigebit phantasmate obiective; at ipsum phantasma insequetur et sic poterit verificari quod sine phantasmate et tunc non erit.'
308. *Ibid.*, f. 125vb (lib. III, praefatio): 'sic anima simpathia quadam unitur nobis'.
309. See n. 222 above.

Neoplatonism and its different cosmology. Genua may well have been aware of this similarity, for towards the end of his commentary he maintained that the relation between the cogitative soul and the possible intellect in Averroes was identical with that of the possible to the agent intellect in Alexander.[310] In both cases the crucial problem was how to relate the individual to the universal, the material to the immaterial, so that the individual man was the active subject of knowledge while the universal intellect served to guarantee the truth and universality of the cognition thus attained. Also in both cases, regardless of whether intellection was material or immaterial, the result was a predetermined process, which explained why man arrived at truth, but not why this was not always the case.

Francesco Piccolomini

Although Genua's successor, Francesco Piccolomini,[311] has only a mediocre reputation among historians of philosophy,[312] he was apparently aware of the shortcomings of Genua's position or at least of the critique which, early in his Paduan career, confronted followers of Simplicius in the person of his Alexandrist colleague Federico Pendasio.[313] Piccolomini had answered this critique with an unpublished apology,[314] and apparently with the same intention he published, under the name Petrus Duodus, further discussions on the soul, in which he not only tried to prove that Aristotle defended the immortality of the soul, but also maintained that, since the intellect was supernatural, the investigation of its essence lay beyond the limitations of the natural philosopher.[315]

On the basis of this counter-attack Piccolomini developed his own position in his later treatise on the human mind and in his commentary on *De anima*.[316] On the one hand, he kept distinct the positions of Simplicius, Averroes and Aristotle, as well as those of Plato and Aristotle; but on the other hand, he considered Simplicius' cosmology to be the universal framework, of which Aristotle, the natural philosopher, treated only the

---

310. Genua 1576, f. 185va (lib. III ad t. c. 39): 'eadem fuit Averrois sententia de cogitativa ad intellectum possibilem, quae Alexandri de possibili ad agentem'.

311. Baldini 1980b; Lohr 1980, pp. 626–39.

312. Saitta 1961, II, pp. 423–36; *Grande antologia* 1964–, VII, p. 629 ('Aristotelismo').

313. Nardi 1958, pp. 413–17; Saitta 1961, II, pp. 387–91; Lohr 1979, pp. 556–62.

314. Lohr 1980, p. 636, § 30.

315. F. Piccolomini 1575, p. 173: 'colligimus intellectum humanum esse divinum et immortalem: nam ea forma, quae non est natura, est abiuncta et immortalis; intellectus hominis non est natura, est itaque forma divina et immortalis . . . Nil eorum, quae sunt ex abstractione, est physicae considerationis, intellectus itaque non est physicae considerationis.'

316. F. Piccolomini 1596, pp. 1216–1327 (*De humana mente*); 1602a.

material part and that which pertained to it.[317] As a consequence, Piccolomini mediated between physics and metaphysics, between Aristotle and Neoplatonism, keeping to the former as long as possible but supplementing him with the latter when necessary.

Regarding immortality, for instance, for many years he defended the Averroist position as the closest to that of Aristotle.[318] In the end, however, he reached the view that the one universal mind was supplemented by a finite number of individual human minds, which participated in the unified intellect and were individuated according to the Scotist concept of individuality (*haecceitas*).[319] These minds would be reborn again and again, as Plato had taught, in order to animate different human bodies,[320] not as their material forms, but by assisting them in their operations like a captain in a ship, and thus providing man with his superior ontological status.[321]

The same role of mediator was played by Piccolomini in his theory of knowledge, where he blamed Genua as well as Simplicius for having introduced Platonic innate ideas contrary to the clear intentions of Aristotle,[322] only to introduce himself, in a second phase, innate principles of reasoning and judgement.[323] On the basis of this supposition of innate principles of reasoning, however, he constructed a new concept of the intellective process, which in his view was neither a mere reception of the universal forms emanating from the agent intellect, as in Genua – which would amount to Platonic reminiscence[324] – nor a mere reception of the intelligible *species* impressed by the illuminated *phantasma*, as in Porzio.[325] It consisted rather in a true operation of the soul, through which the intellect produced the content of intellection by reasoning and judging the material image.[326]

---

317. F. Piccolomini 1596, p. 1234 (lib. I, cap. 11); p. 1293 (lib. II, cap. 20); 1602a, p. 883 (lib. III ad t. c. 18); Nardi 1958, pp. 425–6, 439–41.

318. F. Piccolomini 1575, pp. 157, 199; 1596, p. 1293 (lib. II, cap. 20).

319. *Cambridge History* 1982, pp. 463–4 (Boler).

320. F. Piccolomini 1602b, f. 218ᵇ: 'Capita sententiae Simplicii ex commentariis de anima deprompta'. See Nardi 1958, pp. 431–41.

321. *Ibid.*, pp. 1289–91 (lib. II, capp. 17–19); p. 1291: 'Colligo itaque ex sententia Aristotelis mentem non formare corpus, esse tamen formam formarum et maxime dare esse homini, cum constituat supremum hominis gradum et hominem eminentissimum.'

322. *Ibid.*, pp. 1310–15 (lib. III, capp. 9–10); 1602a, p. 881 (lib. III ad t. c. 17).

323. F. Piccolomini 1596, p. 1312 (lib. III, cap. 10): 'Pro resolutione itaque difficultatis dicamus menti humanae rationes competere dupliciter intelligi posse, vel pro facultate et virtute formandi notiones et ratiocinandi vel pro formis in ea insitis, respondentibus ideis. In prima significatione concedi debent, reiici autem in secunda. In prima significatione approbantur ab Aristotele, in secunda vero ab eo reiiciuntur at approbantur ab Academicis.'

324. *Ibid.*, p. 1311 (lib. III, cap. 10): 'ex eo, quod animae huiusmodi rationes per naturam competunt, colligunt Academici, scientiam nostram esse reminiscentiam. Econtrario Aristoteles negat scientiam nostram esse reminiscentiam.'   325. *Ibid.*, pp. 1303–7 (lib. III, capp. 6–7).

326. *Ibid.*, p. 1307 (lib. III, cap. 7): 'conspicue Philosophus affirmat in mente nil recipi, sed solum ex ea prodire iudicium . . . actum intelligendi esse iudicium'; p. 1312 (lib. III, cap. 10): 'munere facultatis ratiocinantis, ex effectis elevamur in causas et ex propriis accidentibus elicimus conditionem et

As a consequence of this interpretation of intellection, the Aristotelian distinction between the possible and the agent intellect also gained new meaning. According to Piccolomini, they were neither two different substances, as in Alexander, nor different parts or powers of the soul, one working on the other, as in most of the commentators. Instead they were terms denoting that in the act of knowledge, as in sense-perception, the soul was passive in so far as it was stirred into operation by the *phantasma* and converted into the known object, while it was active in so far as it produced the known object by judging the *phantasma*.[327] Since the agent intellect had been reduced to the power of judging, and the intellection was regarded as identical with judgement, cognition had regained the character of a creative human activity, no longer determined by necessary processes, but rather, in terms of truth and error, dependent on whether the judgement was correctly or incorrectly pronounced.[328] Piccolomini therefore devoted book III, chapters 1–5 to the formal analysis of the method of composing terms to phrases and phrases to syllogisms, since what was usually done by nature was perfected through the application of art.[329]

Piccolomini thus introduced into psychology the theory of method and judgement, which until then had been discussed only in logic.[330] This unusual turn – Piccolomini's concept of human intellection as judgement – would seem arbitrary if he had not revealed, in his praise of rationality as the specific faculty of man in comparison with the divine intelligences as well as with brute animals,[331] the Neoplatonic basis of his interpretation of

essentiam formae rerum'; 1602a, p. 881 (lib. III ad t. c. 17): 'Mens vero agit per facultatem eminenter intelligibilia includentem, et ideo agit iuxta formam ei oblatam, sine propria ei insita ratione et forma.'

327. F. Piccolomini 1596, p. 1235 (lib. III, cap. 12): 'Dum enim haec mentis essentia primo consideratur ut nudata, ut apta indui et ut a phantasmate excitatur, dicitur mens potestate. Eadem, ut abstrahit, iudicat, componit, ratiocinatur, dicitur agens . . . Colligamus itaque mentem hominis esse particulam humanae animae, et esse essentiam unam, cui distincta ratione, duae differentiae competunt, agendi et patiendi, invicem non pugnantes'; p. 1307 (lib. III, cap. 8); 1602a, p. 880 (lib. III ad t. c. 17): 'Hae differentiae tanquam modi, ratione distincti, et sunt differentiae, per quas constituitur integra particula animae et integrum principium intelligendi . . . Hae differentiae etiam in sensu reperiuntur, nam in sensu quoque locum habent facere et fieri'; p. 884 (lib. III ad t. c. 18): 'In horum progressio antecedit passio illa, per quam excitatur ab obiecto, mediat actio, quae est iudicium, sequitur passio, per quam fit omnia, nam fit intelligibile et redditur locus eius, quia iudicat, quae passio et actio cum in mente, tum in sensu locum habent.'

328. F. Piccolomini 1596, p. 1300 (lib. III, cap. 4): 'ex recta compositione simplicium a mente facta, consurgit veritas enunciationis, ex perversa, mendacium, et hoc est id verum et falsum, quod in compositione et divisione dicitur locum habere. Veritas dicitur ens, quia rerum conditioni respondet, mendacium non ens, quia a rerum conditione recedit.'

329. *Ibid.*, pp. 1295–1303 (lib. III, capp. 1–5); p. 1302 (lib. III, cap. 5): 'Haec ratiocinatio fieri potest et natura tantum et arte naturae adhibita, et dum fit arte, perfectius fit, quam dum fit sola natura.'

330. See N. Jardine in this volume.

331. F. Piccolomini 1596, p. 1303 (lib. III, cap. 5): 'Hoc tertium humanae mentis officium maxime proprium hominis est et cum eo reciprocatur, nam solus homo est animal rationale, caetera enim vel sunt supra rationem, ut seperatae mentes, vel infra ut iumenta et ferae: Solus homo est particeps officii ratiocinandi.'

Aristotle's psychology,[332] although it differed substantially from that of Genua. Looking back on the field of psychology from Piccolomini, one might say that his way of combining Aristotle with Neoplatonism had been latent since Melanchthon admitted innate principles of reasoning into the context of Aristotelian teaching.[333] Looking forward, Piccolomini could be regarded as anticipating the transcendental approach of Kant, except for the Neoplatonic cosmology, which disappeared in the course of the centuries.

Jacopo Zabarella

The most gifted of Piccolomini's opponents and the one who was probably responsible for his unfavourable reputation was Jacopo Zabarella, who disagreed with Piccolomini on the theory of method and differed from him no less on the theory of the soul.[334] While Piccolomini always remained faithful to Simplicius' framework as propounded by Genua, Zabarella – in spite of being a former student and nephew of the latter and the dedicatee of his commentary on *De anima*[335] – clearly followed a natural philosophical approach.[336] Thus, he opposed the definition of psychology as a middle discipline between physics and metaphysics,[337] rejected Neoplatonic tendencies in interpreting Aristotle,[338] and left the question of immortality to the theologians, since Aristotle, as a natural philosopher, had not been explicit about it.[339]

According to Zabarella, the subject-matter of psychology was the animate body or, more precisely, the soul as the form and essence of the animate body.[340] An adherent of the Alexandrist tradition, including the philological endeavours of its representatives,[341] he also admired Averroes and maintained a strongly naturalistic bent.[342] Therefore Zabarella reconstructed the process of intellection on the lines of sense-perception, following what he – and Genua before him[343] – took to be the common

---

332. Ficino 1964–70, I, pp. 56–8 (lib. I, cap. 4).   333. See n. 245 above.
334. *Dictionary of Scientific Biography* 1970–80, XIV, pp. 580–2; Lohr 1982, pp. 233–42; W. F. Edwards 1960, pp. 1–82; Poppi 1972a; Saitta 1961, II, pp. 385–408; Garin 1966, pp. 548–58; *Grande antologia* 1964–, VII, pp. 632–4 ('Aristotelismo'); Ragnisco 1885–6.
335. Genua 1576 (dedication letter).
336. Dal Pra 1966; Poppi 1972a, pp. 25–33.   337. J. Zabarella 1606, col. 20 (lib. I ad t. c. 2).
338. J. Zabarella 1607a, col. 979 (*Liber de speciebus intelligibilibus*, cap. 1): 'Simplicii et Platonicorum sententiam tanquam Aristoteli manifeste adversantem reiicimus et ab hac nostra disputatione penitus excludimus.'
339. J. Zabarella 1606, col. 906 (lib. II ad t. c. 2); 1607a, col. 1004 (*Liber de speciebus intelligibilibus*, cap. 8).
340. J. Zabarella 1606, col. 20 (lib. I ad t. c. 2): 'subiectum enim statuimus corpus animatum, ita ut de anima agatur ut de eius principio'.   341. *Ibid.*, cols. 873, 879, 893, 901, etc.
342. *Aristotelismo padovano* 1960, pp. 91–107 (W. F. Edwards).   343. See n. 302 above.

tradition of Greeks, Arabs and Latins, that is, that the intelligible *species*, produced concurrently by the *phantasma* and the illuminating agent intellect, moved the possible intellect to cognition.[344] At the same time, he was aware of the innovations resulting from the contribution of the followers of Simplicius, who, to avoid the sort of epistemological determinism found in Porzio, had denied the merely passive character of intellection and emphasised instead its productive elements. This can be seen in Castellani's position[345] and, with the utmost clarity, in Piccolomini's definition of intellection as *iudicatio*.[346]

As a result, Zabarella modified the traditional notion of the object of knowledge, which was no longer the intelligible *species* as such, but the intelligible *species* that had been judged, the *species intelligibilis iudicata*.[347] To be known, the *phantasma*, which was gained by sense-perception, therefore had to undergo a double process. Itself material and consequently containing the universal structure only in a confused and unintelligible way, it had to be illuminated by the agent intellect, so that the universal in the individual was rendered distinct and intelligible.[348] Since this illumination was generally required for any act of knowledge in the same way, its agent did not have to be an individual operating individually in the different acts of intellection, but rather could be a universal one, which rendered reality in general intelligible, thus serving as an all-embracing guarantee of intelligibility. The agent intellect could therefore be identified in the Alexandrist manner with God himself as the principle of intelligibility.[349]

With the metaphysical requirements of intellection taken for granted, the main epistemological problem shifted to the manner in which the intelligible *species* was turned into a *species iudicata* or known object. Piccolomini, who regarded the agent intellect as part of the rational soul, had attributed the function of judgement to this active aspect of the human mind, which was equipped with innate principles of judgement and consequently of intellection.[350] Zabarella, considering the agent intellect as

344. J. Zabarella 1607a, cols. 979–1006 (*Liber de speciebus intelligibilibus*); Poppi 1970a, pp. 182–94.
345. See n. 283 above. 346. See n. 326 above.
347. J. Zabarella 1607a, col. 999 (*Liber de speciebus intelligibilibus*): 'Ad hoc dicimus speciem intelligibilem non dici intellectionem quatenus solum recipitur, sed simul etiam quatenus iudicatur, adeo ut species recepta et iudicata idem sit quod intellectio.'
348. J. Zabarella 1606, col. 882 (lib. III ad t. c. 18); cols. 916–21 (*Liber de mente agente*, capp. 4–5).
349. *Ibid.*, col. 936 (*Liber de mente agente*, cap. 13): 'non potest intellectus agens esse aliud quam illud solum, quod primum intelligibile et maxime omnium intelligibile est; ab hoc enim et a nullo alio possunt alia reddi intelligibilia; maxime autem omnium intelligibilis Deus est; et est primum in genere intelligibilium; ergo nihil aliud statui potest intellectus agens nisi solus Deus'. See Poppi 1972b. 350. See nn. 323, 327 above.

the divine cause of general intelligibility, could renounce innate principles and retain the Aristotelian teaching of the inductive acquisition of the first principles themselves.[351] But he had instead the problem of restoring to the human mind an active faculty which would account for the act of judgement. Therefore he redefined – following a suggestion from Genua[352] – the possible intellect as an active faculty as well.[353] This equally active and passive human intellect, which Zabarella called *patibilis* instead of *possibilis*,[354] considered all that was offered to it by the illuminated *phantasma*, contemplated whatever it wanted to, and in doing so selected and abstracted those structures it wished to know and through judging, understood them and became itself the object of knowledge.[355] Intellection therefore was not a process automatically determined whenever an exterior impulse was given, but rather depended essentially on human will and intention.

Zabarella divided the problem of knowledge into three distinct aspects, the first of which was the general intelligibility of reality. Since this problem was a metaphysical one, it lay beyond the consideration of psychology and could be solved only through the supposition of the existence of a universal principle of intellection, which for the Alexandrists was identified with the agent intellect or God.[356] The second aspect lay in the question of the powers which the human soul must have in order to gain knowledge. This was the proper subject-matter of psychology, and it was resolved by expanding the possible intellect into an active as well as a passive power, since every act of human knowledge was receptive as well as productive. The third aspect was the question of how to make the best use of this power. This again was not the concern of the natural philosopher, who dealt with necessary being and determined processes. Since it depended on human

351. J. Zabarella 1606, col. 956 (*Liber de ordine intelligendi*, cap. 5).
352. See n. 304 above.
353. J. Zabarella 1606, col. 923 (*Liber de mente agente*, cap. 7): 'patibilis intellectus speciem quidem recipiendo patitur, sed eam iudicando agit . . . quo fit ut intellectio dicatur actio immanens, quia fit ab ipso patibili intellectu et in ipsomet recipitur'.
354. See n. 353 above.
355. J. Zabarella 1606, col. 922 (*Liber de mente agente*, cap. 6): 'haec enim omnia in eo phantasmate confusa et indistincta erant, sed ab agente illustrata offeruntur patibili intellectui clara atque distincta, ut ipse ea omnia intuens possit contemplari id, quod vult, tam totum confusum quam singulam quidditatem in eo emicantem et eam omissis aliis intelligere'.
356. *Ibid.*, col. 933 (*Liber de mente agente*, cap. 12): 'Quoniam igitur intellectus agens est substantia separata, certum est declarationem essentiae ipsius non ad naturalem pertinere, sed ad metaphysicum. Naturalis enim considerare ipsum non potest nisi prout est agens respectu humani intellectus.'

volition, it pertained to a kind of practical philosophy, comparable to ethics, that is, to logic and methodology, conceived as instrumental disciplines.[357]

This three-fold division, together with the attribution of the different aspects to the relevant disciplines, allows for a more general definition of Zabarella's place in the history of psychology. Traditionally, Renaissance psychology was primarily concerned with the theory of knowledge for anthropological or cosmological reasons, since the essence of man – defined as *anima rationalis* in the Aristotelian or as *nexus mundi* in the Neoplatonic tradition – had to be described in terms of the physical or metaphysical assumptions necessary to save the phenomena of the highest human activity. Therefore, the antagonisms between the material and the immaterial, between the individual and the universal, between the mortal and the immortal, attracted particular attention. As a consequence, at the turn of the sixteenth century the church felt that it was necessary to enter into this debate in order to defend its own metaphysical interest. The result, however, was that natural philosophy proclaimed its declaration of independence and propagated a deterministic concept of intellection on the basis of pure natural philosophy. The attempt to destroy this naturalistic determinism in the middle of the sixteenth century was accompanied by the reactivation of Neoplatonic metaphysics. Nevertheless, at the same time, there was a shift of emphasis from the ontological to the operational aspects of intellection, which was related to the methodological debate going on at the same time.[358]

This shift of emphasis is evident in Piccolomini, who not only defined intellection as judgement, but also tried to integrate methodology into psychology, thereby subordinating method to innate principles of reasoning, which were possessed through participation and made room for a science which reproduced the ontological structure of nature. Piccolomini's integration of methodology into psychology thus meant the submission of method to metaphysics.

Zabarella also contributed to this shift of emphasis. But just as in logic he had defended the autonomy of method as a means of arriving at knowledge

357. *Ibid.*, col. 947 (*Liber de ordine intelligendi*, cap. 1): 'quum enim habitus non sint menti nostrae naturales, sed ex nostro arbitrio pendeant et ex arbitrariis actionibus comparentur, solae autem facultates, quibus eos acquirere apti sumus, naturales dici possint, de solis facultatibus agere debuit philosophus naturalis, de habitibus vero non ipse, sed alius, ut moralis, sic doctrinae ordo arbitrarius est, neque est menti nostrae naturalis, sola autem facultas procedendi ab hoc ad illud naturalis est, ideo de facultate disserit philosophus naturalis, de ipso autem ordine loquitur logicus, a quo de eo tanquam de re arbitraria regulae et praecepta traduntur'.
358. N. W. Gilbert 1960; Vasoli 1968a.

against Piccolomini's ontologically based order of nature,[359] in psychology he was also anxious to preserve disciplinary autonomy. While psychology provided the anthropological basis for knowledge by considering the necessary psychological prerequisites of knowledge, it did not, as it did in Piccolomini, also provide the principles of the methodological procedure for employing them. Zabarella's shift of emphasis from the determined to the volitional aspects of intellection therefore did not result in an attempt to integrate methodology into psychology, but rather to direct the epistemological interest from psychology to methodology. For psychology was concerned with what was necessary and therefore always equally present in any human mind, even if unconsciously. Methodology, on the other hand, was concerned with the use man made of these natural faculties. Since this use could be true or false, better or worse, truth and error depended entirely on whether or not man used the correct method.

When one reads the first pages of Descartes's *Discours de la méthode*, it becomes obvious that Zabarella's was the position of the future. But with Zabarella Aristotelian psychology ceased to play the prominent role which it had occupied in philosophical and especially epistemological discussions throughout the Renaissance. Nonetheless, it is evident that the psychological discussions of the Renaissance contributed substantially to the development of philosophy from the Middle Ages to modern times.

359. Ragnisco 1885–6; Poppi 1972a; W. F. Edwards 1960.

X
METAPHYSICS

16
METAPHYSICS

The subject-matter of metaphysics has been debated since the time when Aristotle first conceived the idea of the science. He himself speaks of 'the science we are seeking' and describes it differently in different places. In *Metaphysics* IV.1 (1003ᵃ21–6) he speaks of a science which studies being as being and contrasts this science with the special sciences, like the mathematical disciplines, which investigate the attributes of a part of being. Two chapters later, IV.3 (1005ᵇ2), Aristotle speaks of a science which he calls 'first philosophy' because it grounds the first principles or axioms of the special sciences. But in book VI.1 (1026ᵃ18–19) he distinguishes three types of speculative science, physics, mathematics and 'divine science', so that one must ask how he understood the relationship between the general science of being, first philosophy and divine science. It is clear that divine science studies objects that are separate from matter and not subject to change. But Aristotle seems to have wanted to identify this science both with the investigation of being and with the science of the principles of the sciences, on the ground that divine science concerns itself with the highest principle of being in general and can for this reason preside over the special sciences. At the same time, each of these definitions of metaphysics must be understood in accordance with Aristotle's own idea of what science is. In his conception, scientific knowledge is attained by way of the definition of the essential natures of things and the demonstration of the attributes which necessarily belong to them. Basically, Aristotle understood reality as an ordered structure. Even where his definitions are definitions of events, these are understood not in their variability as a process, but rather as reified. His science of metaphysics deals therefore with all reality according to its fixed essences and their necessary attributes and has consequently a static character, like the ancient society which it reflected.

In the course of history it was Aristotle's conception of metaphysics as divine science that gave rise to the most difficulties. The encounter of his idea of God as first substance with divergent religious traditions often forced later thinkers to modify the conception of metaphysics as the science of being. In late antiquity those philosophers who came to the defence of the pagan gods tended to interpret metaphysics as the science of intelligible reality, arranged in hierarchical degrees, separate from matter, but mediating between the divine and the material worlds. In Islam the doctrine of God's oneness compelled philosophers and theologians to emphasise the great gulf which separates the necessary being of the creator from the radically contingent being of the created world. Medieval Latin Christianity learnt of both of these approaches through Avicenna and Pseudo-Dionysius. The notions of a necessary first substance and a hierarchy of intelligences readily found a place in the contemplative and ordered society of the Middle Ages. The Christian notion of a God active in himself as triune and active in the world as incarnate as the fundamental articles of a faith thought to be even more certain than scientific knowledge would seem to have demanded a new definition of science and a new definition of the reality which metaphysics studies. But, paradoxically, it was only with the revolutionary social changes that marked the period under consideration in this volume – a period in which the medieval faith was breaking down – that a vision of reality as dynamic process and a new understanding of science emerged.

   This new conception of reality appeared in various guises, as a new mathematics, as the idea of a magical control over nature, as a conflict between Plato and Aristotle, or in connection with the doctrine of God. It was resisted by scholastic authors, who sought for apologetical reasons to maintain Aristotle's static notion of being. But as more and more new sciences – sciences connected with this new vision of reality and often undreamt of in antiquity – came to maturity, even thinkers in the Aristotelian tradition were forced to reopen the question of the definition of metaphysics and its relationship to the individual sciences. Since each of these problems – the problem of God and the problem of the science of being – had its own history, I shall treat them separately.

METAPHYSICS AS THE SCIENCE OF GOD

It was in the territories bordering on Islam – in Catalonia and in the kingdoms of Toledo and Sicily – that a conception of knowledge and reality belonging specifically to the Renaissance appeared. The commerce and trade which flourished in the Mediterranean basin formed its material basis; the spirit which animated it was the rare spirit of openness and tolerance which was born of the contact between the three great civilisations of Islam,

Judaism and Christianity. In Toledo Christians and Jews laboured together to make available to the Latin West the Greek philosophy and science which had been transmitted in Arabic. Frederick II of Sicily corresponded with Moslem philosophers in the search for solutions to problems arising out of the confrontation between pagan science and the Christian tradition. In the territory of Barcelona and on the Catalan coast of southern France Jewish scholars expelled from Moslem Spain by the intolerance of the Almohade monarchs translated Arabic works into Hebrew, Hebrew and Arabic works into Latin, and even Latin works into Hebrew.

One of the most remarkable figures in this interchange was that of the Majorcan Ramon Lull.[1] The island of Majorca was not only a centre of commercial intercourse in the Mediterranean world, but also a point where Islam, Judaism and Christianity met. Even after the *reconquista*, Moslems made up half of the population of the island. Lull was born in 1232, some years after James the Conqueror retook Majorca from the Saracens. He died in 1316 on a ship which was bringing him home from his last voyage to North Africa, after he had – according to the local tradition – been stoned almost to death while preaching the Christian faith. This *vir phantasticus*, who clothed himself as a pilgrim and probably spoke Arabic better than Latin, sought tirelessly in Europe, North Africa and the Near East to win over the powerful of his time to the cause of understanding and concord between peoples. Conscious of the fact that he stood at the frontier between the three great religions, he sought – as an *arabicus christianus* – to use methods proper to the Arabic tradition to convince Moslems and Jews of the truth of Christianity.

In the pursuit of this goal, Lull's life became one of incredible literary production. In spite of his preaching, teaching and restless travel, Lull wrote some 280 works, many of them very extensive. In accordance with his purpose, these works were composed not only in Latin, but also in Catalan and Arabic. Although the ideas in them show a rapid development, his goal remained always the same. He wanted to write a book which would make the Christian doctrines of the Trinity and Incarnation intelligible to Moslems and Jews. He called his book the *Ars inveniendi veritatem*, *The Art of Finding the Truth*, and, regarding it as a task imposed by God himself, worked unflaggingly on the composition of this art for more than thirty years. His energy was not limited, however, to composing works directly concerned with his art. He wrote in Latin on philosophy and theology, on

1. Concerning Lull see Carreras y Artau 1939–43, I, pp. 231–640; Colomer 1961; Pring-Mill 1961; Platzeck 1962–4; Hillgarth 1971.

logic and natural science, and composed in Catalan a great many popular, didactic works in all sorts of literary forms. As *procurator infidelium* he directed petitions to popes and cardinals and sketched in several tracts a plan for the crusade. In his efforts to bring Moslems, Jews and Christians together, Lull was not only active as an author. He also struggled for the establishment of a new type of educational institution, different from the Latin universities of Paris and Oxford, in which a true dialogue between the three great Mediterranean civilisations might be possible. In repeated petitions to popes and kings he pleaded for the foundation of colleges in which clerics prepared to die for their faith might learn the languages and doctrine necessary for preaching to Saracens and Jews.

Although he was and remained a layman, Lull decided to dedicate his life to a missionary apostolate. To this end he planned at first to go to Paris to learn Latin and scholastic theology. He was advised, however, by Ramon de Penyafort – the same superior of the Dominican Order whose inspiration stood behind the *Contra gentiles* of Thomas Aquinas – to return to his native Majorca, where he could learn not only Latin but also Arabic and something of Moslem thought. Lull not only mastered the Arabic language but also conceived, on the basis of Arabic models, the idea of a new science which would serve his missionary purpose. Because this science was addressed to peoples of all faiths, it should not be specifically theological, but rather a general science which could be applied to all the particular sciences of his time. He changed, therefore, the name of his *Ars inveniendi veritatem* to *Ars generalis* and submitted the work to constant revision throughout his life.

Behind this general science there lay, however, the fundamental vision of a natural theology which should approach the true God through a method of contemplation on the divine names. Lull called these names 'dignities' or 'axioms' and listed in the final form of the art nine of them: goodness, greatness, eternity; power, wisdom, love; virtue, truth and glory.[2] His idea seems to have been based on an Islamic method of contemplation which attempted to ascend by way of created reflections of the divine perfections to the infinite perfection which is God himself. He thought that through contemplation on combinations of these names, which are common to all religions, agreement could be reached between Moslems and Jews, Greek and Latin Christians. One recognises the Neoplatonic *Bonum est diffusivum sui* behind goodness as the first of the dignities, the twelfth-century triad of

2. Lull 1959–, XIV, pp. 21–2 (*Ars generalis ultima* III).

potestas, sapientia, benignitas behind the second group of three divine names and, most importantly, Anselm of Canterbury's *maximum* behind the inclusion of greatness.

But Lull's inspiration for the way in which these names are to be understood seems to have been taken from Islamic mystical writers. He composed a *Liber de centum nominibus Dei* in which he tells us that the Moslems believe that God has placed even more power in his names than in animals, plants and precious stones.[3] His method of contemplation can, therefore, only be understood correctly if we take the dignities to stand for active powers. He insisted that we must refer all the powers which they designate to the supreme power of God, who created all things. Accordingly, Lull developed his method of contemplation not only by spelling out – horizontally, so to speak – nine different names of God, but also by making explicit – vertically – three degrees of the powers of the names. He conceived his art as a means of ascent which proceeds by way of two stages, a transcending of sense-knowledge by an ascent from the positive to the comparative degree of the dignities (*bonum→melius*) and a transcending of rational knowledge by an ascent from the comparative to the superlative degree (*melius→optimum*). Lull argued that sensation cannot form a valid basis for truth; it remains on the positive level of sensible objects. Reason can, however, rise to the comparative level in that it attains rational knowledge of these objects; Aristotle and Averroes attained this level. But this level is still not the level of true science. If the objects of the sense world are good and great, the objects of the rational world are better and greater. But God is with respect to all creatures the best and greatest – *optimum et maximum*. Only through a second ascent, therefore, can the intellect attain the level of eternal truth. On this superlative level the differences we had encountered on the first two levels disappear. Because God is the best in the superlative degree, it is no longer possible to distinguish him as such from the greatest or the most powerful. At the superlative degree of reality the mystic discovers the supreme being in whom all the divine names coincide or fall together.

In his works Lull sought above all to render intelligible the Christian doctrine on which all missionary intent had foundered, the doctrine of the Trinity. For this purpose he had recourse to an analysis of what it means when we say that the powers of the divine names are active. He held that we cannot truly call something good which does not produce a good. Because

3. Lull 1905–50, XIX, pp. 79–81 (*De centum nominibus Dei*, praef.).

action presupposes a principle or source, that which is produced, and a bond between them, he spoke not only of dignities but also of their acts and the 'correlatives' of action. To designate these correlatives, he formed new words which appear strange in Latin and were probably formed on the analogy of the forms of the Arabic verb. In a sermon given in Tunis he explained: 'Actus . . . bonitatis dico bonificativum, bonificabile, bonificare; actus etiam magnitudinis sunt magnificativum, magnificabile, magnificare; et sic de aliis omnibus divinis dignitatibus.'[4] Lull generalised this idea to the extent that he could speak even of the abstract moments of activity as *-tivum*, *-bile*, and *-are*. He defined these moments as substantial and intrinsic principles of action which are valid for all reality. In this way he was able to recognise images of the triune God in all aspects of the created world, in the form, matter and conjunction which make up corporeal things, in the form, subject and property which constitute the nature of the angels and even in the three dimensions of bodies and the two premises and one conclusion of the syllogism. Lull was aided in his apologetic purpose by the analysis of the knowledge of the illuminated mystic current among some Moslem thinkers. Certain Christian controversialists writing in Arabic had taken up as an analogy for the Trinity Aristotle's description of God as νόησις νοήσεως as it had been expanded in Neoplatonism from two to three terms. Some Moslem writers accepted this idea for mystical knowledge of God in which the knower, the object known and the act of knowing itself are one. Lull was able to join this analogy with Augustine's famous comparison of the Trinity with human love. In a little book called *De amic e amat* he maintained that true, active love presupposes a lover, the beloved, and the love itself which unites them.[5]

Because the correlative principles are intrinsic to all activity, it follows that not only being and activity but also being and relatedness are identical. Accordingly, Lull added, in the later forms of the art, nine relative dignities to the absolute ones: difference, contrariety, concordance; greaterness, lesserness, equality; beginning, middle and end.[6] Contrariety and lesserness are encountered in the created world, but on the superlative level of the divine activity there remain only equality and concordance. The divine *optimans* can only produce a divine *optimatum* which is its equal; the difference between them must be transcended in the concordance which is a divine *optimare*, the three forming the beginning, middle and end of all things. In the sermon quoted above Lull concluded: 'per praedictarum . . .

---

4. Lull 1959–, VIII, pp. 289–91 (*Vita coaetanea* 26).   5. Lull 1905–50, IX, pp. 379–431.
6. Lull 1721–42, V, pp. 6–12 (*Ars inventiva veritatis* I, fig. 2); 1959–, XIV, p. 22 (*Ars generalis ultima* III).

dignitatum . . . substantiales actus intrinsecos et aeternos, aequaliter et concordanter acceptos . . . probant evidenter Christiani in una simplicissima divina essentia et natura esse trinitatem personarum, scilicet Patris et Filii et Spiritus sancti'.[7] Thus for Lull the correlative unfolding of all things became an absolute ontological principle. Even the divine unity known through faith must be structured; as an active unity it must have a moment which is to be united. If God is truly one in an active sense of the word, he must be triune, even though on the superlative level of the divine activity the manner in which God is triune eludes man's understanding.

Having thus discovered the Christian Trinity in the mediated unity of the most simple divine essence, Lull also sought, by means of the dynamic principles of his art, to make intelligible the doctrine, known to Christians by faith, of the Incarnation of Christ. To this purpose he distinguished between the necessary activity of the principles *ad intra* and their contingent activity *ad extra*. Fire, for example, must necessarily burn, but whether it heats water or earth is contingent. In the same way, whereas the divine activity *ad intra* is necessary, the creation of the world is dependent on the divine will. But given creation, the infinite first cause can only achieve concord with its effect 'in Filii Dei incarnatione, per participationem scilicet unionis creatoris et creaturae in una persona Christi'.[8]

Ramon Lull was a man born long before his time. In the Europe of the later Middle Ages his ideas could find but little influence. His vision of a Mediterranean civilisation embracing Christianity, Judaism and Islam ran counter to the growing independence and self-sufficiency of the Latin peoples. His methods of proving the doctrines of the faith had to be rejected by contemporary scholastic theologians concerned with protecting the role of the clergy in the interpretation of Christian revelation. His dynamic understanding of reality could, in his own time, only be regarded as a threat to the hierarchical structure of feudal society. Although he sought tirelessly and with great ingenuity to propagate his ideas, the lack of an institutional basis made Lull appear as an eccentric outsider in the closed world of the medieval universities. In the early fourteenth century we know only of several manuscript collections of his works, a few disciples in Paris and a small school in Majorca, whose traces soon disappear.

By the end of the century, however, he seems to have found some followers in parts of France and Spain. His teachings were condemned by Jean Gerson in Paris and the Dominican Inquisitor in Aragon. His doctrine

7. Lull 1959–, VIII, pp. 289–91 (*Vita coaetanea* 26).   8. *Ibid.*, VIII, p. 291 (*Vita coaetanea* 27).

offered, in fact, an alternative not only to the voluntarism of nominalist teachers in the theological faculties but also to the separation of theology from philosophy defended both by Thomist theologians and by Averroist professors in the arts faculties of the universities. It was not the complicated procedures and combinatoric method of the art that appealed to thinkers of this period, but rather Lull's dynamic understanding of the divine nature, his doctrine of man and his confidence in the infallible certitude which is within the grasp of man's intellect. At the beginning of the fifteenth century Ramon Sibiuda, professor of philosophy, theology and medicine at the University of Toulouse († 1436),[9] connected Lull's doctrine with that of Anselm of Canterbury. The fundamental rule on which he constructed his *Liber creaturarum* was Anselm's definition of God as *id quo nihil maius cogitari potest*.[10] Sibiuda made the claim that this rule, which is rooted in man's nature, provides the basis not only for a complete treatment of the doctrine of God, but also for a general science – like the Lullian art – which should ground the statements of all the other sciences. His work is a natural theology in the sense that it uses only rational arguments and makes no appeal to Scripture, but it extends beyond the doctrine of God to cover the doctrine of the Trinity, creation, man, his fall and redemption and the ultimate ordering of his actions. Because Sibiuda's purpose was to strengthen the faith of Christians in the face of conflicting interpretations of the Bible, he contrasted the book of creation, which was the first book given by God to man, with the book of Scripture, which was given to man because he had become blind and could no longer read the first book. Both books contain all the doctrines necessary for salvation. Because God is the author of both, there is a profound agreement or concord between them. But whereas the book of Scripture can properly be interpreted only by clerics, the book of creation was given to all men and cannot be falsified. Creation is a book in which clerics and laymen alike can read. Just as Lull had tried through the general science of his art to convince Moslems and Jews that the articles of the Christian faith agree with truths accessible to man's understanding, so also Sibiuda sought to show the agreement between the book of Scripture and the book of creation. Creation is a ladder by which all men can ascend to the knowledge of God himself. In the dynamic activity of created reality the life of the Trinity itself is reflected. The knowledge contained in the book of creation is the *radix omnium scientiarum*, the foundation of the traditional arts of the *trivium* and *quadrivium* as well as of

---

9. Concerning Sibiuda see Carreras y Artau 1939–43, II, pp. 101–75.
10. Sibiuda 1966, pp. 81–3 (*Liber creaturarum*, tit. 63).

physics and metaphysics. In the infallible arguments it provides, the intellect experiences itself as the interpretation of truth in that it recognises the impossibility of a contradictory view.[11] Sibiuda's *Liber creaturarum*, which is preserved in many manuscripts and printed editions of the fifteenth and sixteenth centuries, is an important witness to the diffusion of Lull's teaching in France.

It was, however, in Italy – at Padua in the early fifteenth century – that the first signs of a permanent Lullism appear. Italy offered a fertile soil for the formation of a school whose device was that of universality and tolerance. Whereas instruction in philosophy in French and English schools was subservient to theological interests, medicine and law were the goal of the arts course in Italian universities. At Padua the new humanism had been accepted quite early and even made inroads in the university. When the city came into the Venetian orbit, humanistic ideals increasingly became a challenge to the rigid Aristotelian tradition in the arts faculty. In this context, Lull's ideas seem to have appealed to some thinkers who were in search of a new conception of man and his dignity. Indeed, the role of the Venetian Republic as mediator between East and West created an intellectual atmosphere in the Veneto which was, in many respects, similar to that which had reigned in Majorca in Lull's own time. Her commerce and trade extended beyond the confines of Latin Europe to Turkish merchants in the mountains of Anatolia, Moslem tradesmen on the steppes of northern Syria and Mongol princes along the Black Sea coast. The trading agreements which the city concluded with the Ottoman rulers – in spite of clerical strictures against dealing with the infidel – contributed to a new, enlightened spirit of understanding and respect towards men of different traditions. Her internal stability and orderly system of government – sustained by a sound constitution and a patrician élite – provided the conditions necessary for the development of a vision of man in which both inner nobility and outward elegance and decorum were essential elements.

The belief in the harmony between philosophical speculation and a resolute religious stance, between intellectual and moral gifts, was the foundation on which Venetian humanism was based. The new culture which appeared in Venice and the Veneto in the late fourteenth century was diametrically opposed to the abstract conception of science which had been dominant among both scholastic theologians and the secular Aristotelians of the medieval arts faculties. Petrarch, who lived in Venice from 1362 to

11. *Ibid.*, pp. 25*–52* (*Liber creaturarum*, prologus).

1367 in a house on the Riva degli Schiavoni, had to defend the new culture against Averroist attacks. In his *De ignorantia* he maintained that knowledge of nature is useless unless man knows his own nature, the end for which he is born, whence he comes and where he is going.[12] At the same time, Venetian humanism was the response to a challenge. Through her possessions in the Aegean and Ionian islands and along the Dalmatian coast, the republic was confronted by a civilisation which was differently structured from and culturally superior to anything in the West. The earliest efforts to meet the Byzantine challenge concerned the Greek language and were made outside the universities. Guarino da Verona, who had studied Greek in Constantinople, taught the language and its literature at Venice from 1414 to 1419, before taking up residence at the court of Ferrara. But Greek influence also made itself felt in the established schools. Vittorino da Feltre, who studied and taught privately at Padua from about 1400 to 1423, formed a school at the court of Mantua which was later recognised as a university. In accordance with the new trends Vittorino assigned a significant place in the school's curriculum to the tradition of ancient Greek mathematics. His successor as head of the school translated Archimedes, the most important of the Greek mathematicians and an author highly esteemed by Petrarch himself.

In these circles there appeared a new understanding of human knowledge, an understanding that rendered obsolete the medieval encyclopaedia of the sciences which was based on Aristotelian theories. The difference was made not simply by the mass of new material which these scholars and their associates brought together in newly founded private libraries and made available in new translations. Through the contact with Greek culture, the Veneto learned of a world in which philosophy and a long literary tradition were unified in a way which set Byzantium clearly apart from the West, where science was done in Latin and literature in various vernaculars. With the growing acquaintance with Greek literature the need for a new encyclopaedia became more and more apparent, an encyclopaedia which would include not only practical wisdom, natural philosophy and the new mathematics, but poetical truth as well. At the very beginning of the fifteenth century Pier Paolo Vergerio composed at Padua one of the most influential educational treatises of the Italian Renaissance, *De ingenuis moribus et liberalibus studiis*. The passages in this work dealing with the *quadrivium* suggest that Vergerio saw mathematical method as an alterna-

12. Petrarch 1906, pp. 24f. (*De ignorantia sui ipsius et multorum aliorum* 2).

tive to Aristotle's analytics. Even more significant was the fact that he abandoned the Aristotelian division of the sciences to return to the traditional scheme of the liberal arts.[13] The fact that this ancient scheme was drawn on to organise the new material and the new interests reflects a fundamental shift – one which was taking place during this period – in the western understanding not only of human knowledge but also of man's own nature. Out of the need to formulate a conception of knowledge which transcended the differences between Greek, Latin and the vernaculars, between East and West, was born a new vision of man himself. Whereas medieval scholastics had constructed their theological syntheses in accordance with the Aristotelian theory of science but on the principle that man's intellect was darkened and his nature corrupted by Adam's fall, thinkers in Venice and the Veneto at the beginning of the fifteenth century returned to the scheme of the liberal arts to express their renewed consciousness of his moral integrity, his aesthetic sensibility and the creative vigour of his spirit.

It was in this context that the Catalan Ramon Lull made his appearance in the Veneto. His ideas seem to have been introduced at Padua about the time of Venice's decisive victory over Genoa at Chioggia in 1381. It was at this time that Padua and its university came into the Venetian orbit. As a Mediterranean power, Venice had many points of contact with Catalonia, Aragon and Majorca. Her prosperity was based in large measure on the maritime trade in salt, a commodity which originated not only in the Levant but also in the Balearic Islands. Sicily had been under Aragonese domination since the end of the thirteenth century. In 1409 Martin of Aragon united the two kingdoms and shortly thereafter Alfonso V of Aragon united those of Sicily and Naples. Both the Venetians and the Catalans had extensive interests within the Byzantine Empire, Venice through her island possessions, Catalonia through the duchies of Athens and Neopatras. Catalonian humanism – like that in Venice – had its origin in these contacts. As Catalan writers first turned their attention to classical literature, they manifested – just as did their Venetian counterparts – more interest in Greek than in Latin authors. From the middle of the fourteenth century, cultural exchange between Italy and Catalonia was very active. Catalan translations were made not only of classical and patristic authors but also of writers like Brunetto Latini, Dante, Boccaccio and Marco Polo. At the same time, Italian translations were made of Catalan works. The interest

---

13. Vergerio 1972–3.

in the works of Ramon Lull seems to have arisen quite early. In accordance with the new encyclopaedic tendency in Italian humanism, his *Libre de meravelles* was translated into Italian in the Veneto in the late fourteenth century. At the beginning of the fifteenth we encounter the names of various Catalan scholars at Naples, Venice and Padua who commented on Lull's art and tried to disseminate his views.

It seems that it was at Padua, while pursuing studies in canon law at the university, that Nicholas of Cusa first became acquainted with Lull's ideas. During the six years he spent in the city (1417–23) the receptive young Nicholas discovered Byzantine culture, the new mathematics and all the new sources which Venetian humanism had made available. He soon brought these discoveries into a system. The framework into which he fitted them was not, however, that of the scholastic philosophy he had studied at Heidelberg, but rather that supplied by the dynamic understanding of reality proposed by Ramon Lull. The combination of the Venetian vision of man's dignity and Lull's metaphysics worked a revolution in the history of philosophy.

In the earliest of his works – a Christmas sermon preached at Coblenz in 1430 – Nicholas brought together the most diverse types of material, authorities typical of the scholastic period as well as sources which presage the beginning of a new epoch: the Bible and the Talmud, the *Sibylline Oracles* and *Hermetica*, Greek and Latin Church Fathers and scholastic doctors. To structure the sermon, which had as its theme the biblical text 'In the beginning was the word', Nicholas drew on the Lullian triad *principium, medium, finis*, arranging his material under three headings: the names of God, who is the principle and origin of all things; the eternal generation of the word and the temporal creation of the world in God's likeness; the Incarnation of the word, which is necessary after Adam's fall so that God's work may attain its end. Thus, at the very beginning of his career, Nicholas proposed a comprehensive vision of all reality, God, the world and man. The sermon takes as its point of departure Lull's philosophy of action. In the first part Nicholas offers a proof for the Christian doctrine of the Trinity. He maintains – in typically Lullian fashion – that we must attribute the highest activity to the divine essence, because otherwise God would be otiose, which is impossible. He concludes by way of Lull's doctrine of the 'correlatives' of action to the three divine persons: 'In omni autem actione perfecta tria correlativa necessario reperiuntur, quoniam nihil in se ipsum agit, sed in agibile distinctum ab eo, et tertium surgit ex agente et agibili, quod est agere. Erunt haec correlativa in essentia divina tres personae, quare

Deum trinum vocamus.'[14] Nicholas continues by distinguishing clearly between the necessary action of God *ad intra* and his contingent activity *ad extra*. God the Father is the principle of the necessary production of the word, who is the middle term in the inner-trinitarian relations. The triune God is the principle of the contingent creation of the world, which is in turn the middle term in a movement that tends to an end that is God himself. His argument is reminiscent of Lull's pleas for religious dialogue and foreshadows his own *De pace fidei* of 1453. He holds that the names with which Jews, Greeks, Latins, Germans, Turks, Slavs, Saracens and Ethiopians described God are all in basic agreement; they fall together in the one name which God himself has revealed, the Tetragrammaton. But whereas the names used by the various nations are derived from God's contingent, extrinsic activity, the Tetragrammaton alone describes God according to his necessary, intrinsic dynamism. He goes on, in the second part of his sermon, to explain that because the divine goodness has willed its own creative diffusion in time, all things in the diffused goodness which is the universe we know are made in the dynamic likeness of the triune God, unfolding their goodness in their innate 'correlatives', the abstract moments of activity which Lull designated in his late works as *-tivum*, *-bile*, and *-are*: 'Sicut enim divina bonitas est ex bonificante Patre, bonificabili Filio et bonificare Spiritu sancto, ita bonitas effluxa hoc vestigium trinitatis intra se gerit, ut nulla bonitas creata esse possit sine bonificante, bonificabili et bonificare. Ita quidem de amore, esse, veritate et ceteris omnibus a Deo effluxis.'[15]

In this early sermon, however, Nicholas was not prepared to go as far as Lull had gone with regard to the Incarnation of Christ. Lull had maintained that the Incarnation was absolutely necessary – that, given the decree of creation, God must will the union of the divine and human natures in the person of Christ, because it is only in this way that the creator can achieve concord with his creation. This view implied a break with the medieval concept of man. According to the scholastic theologians human nature was damaged by original sin. Man's intellect was impaired by the fall of Adam, so that revelation was made necessary even for truths accessible to man's natural faculties. In the third part of the sermon we have been considering Nicholas retained the medieval idea. Creation is ordered to God through man, but the Incarnation is necessary after the fall because man's sin has rendered it impossible for creation to reach its end. A decade later he modified this view, however. In his *De docta ignorantia* – the

14. Nicholas of Cusa 1932–, XVI, p. 7 (*Sermo* I.6).   15. *Ibid.*, XVI, p. 12 (*Sermo* I.14).

structure of which is adumbrated in the early sermon – Christ is presented as the necessary bond of union (book III) between an infinite God (book I) and his infinite creation (book II).[16]

This change was the consequence both of Nicholas' ever-deepening commitment to the Venetian idea of man's dignity and of the ever-increasing range of sources on which he drew. During the period of his engagement at the Council of Basle (1432–7), he had broadened immensely his knowledge of the philosophical traditions of late antiquity and the early Middle Ages. He learnt the differences between the Platonic tradition and the 'Aristotelian sect' which was entrenched in many universities. Whereas in his earliest sermons he had drawn on Macrobius for Platonic opinions, he now began to make use of Plato himself – especially the *Timaeus* – of Philo, Proclus, Pseudo-Dionysius and John Scotus Eriugena. Most important at this stage was the progress he made in understanding twelfth-century speculation. From the time of his earliest sermons Nicholas had made use of Anselm of Canterbury, Bernard of Clairvaux, Peter Abelard and the Victorines. But during the period at Basle and just preceding the *De docta ignorantia* of 1440 he seems to have paid particular attention to the works of Anselm and to authors like Thierry of Chartres, Clarembald of Arras and Alain of Lille, writers associated with the School of Chartres.

In his *De docta ignorantia* Anselm's *maximum*, the *id quo maius cogitari nequit*, and the Chartrain triad, *unitas, aequalitas, connexio*, play a fundamental role. Book I treats of God as the infinite source of all things and analyses the necessary processions within this *maximum* in terms of the Father's original unity, the Son's generated equality and the union of both in the Spirit – in accordance with the original intention of the triad. But books II and III go further, applying the triad to the contingent creation of the universe. The conclusions are epoch-making. Since the primal unity which is at the origin of all things has been identified with Anselm's *maximum*, it follows that the universe which emanates from it must be its equal, that is, also a *maximum* or infinite. The Incarnation of Christ provides the connection or bond of unity between the absolute infinity of the first cause and the 'contracted' infinity of its effect.

Despite his long and profound meditation on the speculation of the twelfth century, Nicholas did not forget the original inspiration that he had found in the works of Ramon Lull. A note made in preparation for one of the sermons dating from this period shows that he understood the Chartrain

16. *Ibid.*, 1.

triad dynamically, in the sense of Lull's correlatives of action: 'In essentia igitur virtutis absolutae est vis unitiva, quae est vis virtuificans, quae est Pater; est vis aequalificabilis seu virtuificabilis, Filius; et [vis] connexionis sive virtuificare, quae est Spiritus sancti.'[17] Anselm's *maximum* was also understood dynamically – as it applied both to God and the universe. The absolute *maximum* which is God generates out of a unitary, eternal -*tivum* an equal, eternal -*bile*, and from both proceeds a unifying, eternal -*are*. In the same way, the contracted *maximum* which is the universe unfolds in three correlatives, out of 'the possibility of matter' into 'the soul of the world' and 'the spirit of all things', tending to its own perfection.[18]

Whereas the Absolute is in eternal possession of its own intensive perfection, the universe is a *maximum* – that is, infinite – in the sense that it is the limit of the perfection to which created reality can approach, but never attain. Nicholas used a word borrowed from Lull to distinguish God's absolute infinity from the contracted, asymptotic infinity of the universe. Like Lull, he not only distinguished between God's necessary activity *ad intra* and his contingent activity *ad extra*, but also applied this distinction to the activity of creatures. To explain how the distinction applies to creaturely activity, Lull had employed the example of an accidental quality in a subject. The form of whiteness is active within itself, but when it contingently whitens (*albificat*) this or that body, it is 'contracted' in the body.[19] Nicholas understood this idea as applying to God's contingent activity of creation, but emphasised its dynamic character even more than Lull had done. Just as whiteness can seek to increment its contracted perfection by whitening more and more individual bodies, so also the creator can so create the world that it tends to increase its perfection by numerical multiplication. This was one of the reasons why Nicholas spoke of creation as an 'explication'. Not only does God's activity of creation not cease with the bestowal of being on the world, but the world which God has created is itself active, tending to a perfection which it cannot reach within a finite time. Although the particular, individual things of which the world is made up all tend to their own perfection, no individual thing can attain the full perfection of its species. The species is the limit to which the perfection of the individual approaches, the genus that of the species, the contracted *maximum* which is the universe that of the genera.[20]

These ideas had far-reaching consequences. Nicholas insisted repeatedly

17. *Ibid.*, XVII, p. 96 (*Sermo* XXXVIIA.6). 18. *Ibid.*, I, pp. 81–99 (*De docta ignorantia* II.7–10).
19. Lull 1959–, XV, typescript (*De ente reali et rationis* II.1).
20. Nicholas of Cusa 1932–, I, pp. 119–23 (*De docta ignorantia* III.1).

that there is no proportion – no analogy – between the infinite and the finite. The absolute *maximum* cannot be thought of as admitting degrees of 'more' and 'less'. It is from the outset removed from all idea of measurement. To avoid the notion that the Absolute can be understood as the superlative of a comparison, he maintained that in the first principle opposites – *maximum* and *minimum*, infinite and infinitesimal – fall together or coincide. From the absolute *maximum* everything else is infinitely far removed. This first consequence of Nicholas' Lullian understanding of Anselm's *maximum* implied the rejection of the hierarchical conception of reality which medieval thinkers had borrowed from Neoplatonic sources to support their view of society. If the distance between God and created things is infinite, then each individual thing in the world will be at an infinite distance from him and no creature, as such, more perfect than another. Further consequences demanded radical changes in the medieval view of the world. God's contingent activity is the origin of the universe, his perfection its unattainable goal. Having recourse to a paradoxical image used by the ancients, Nicholas described God as an infinite sphere whose centre is everywhere and circumference nowhere. The universe is, accordingly, bounded by God, not by a motionless sphere. The elements have, within the universe, no natural places and motion is relative. The earth is not the lowest degree of being at the centre of the universe, but rather a star as noble as all the others.[21]

The distinction between necessary and contingent activity was also crucial for Nicholas' idea of man. Bringing together the Lullian conception of Christ's mediate place between the first cause and its effect and the Venetian vision of human dignity, he defined man by way of his relationship to God and the world. In the third book of *De docta ignorantia* he maintained that in the person of Christ, absolute infinity and contract infinity fall together.[22] Christ is the link – the dynamic -*are* – joining the -*tivum* which is God and the -*bile* which is the universe, because as man he is the supreme limit of the active tendency of the universe to its perfection. With respect to creation, Nicholas held that man is a 'human world' or a microcosm.[23] Although he was referring to the traditional motif which saw man as a world in miniature, he modified the medieval understanding of this idea radically. Man is a microcosm not because he comprises in himself all the different degrees of reality and thus is subject to all its conflicting forces, but rather because – situated at the centre of creation, at the horizon

---

21. *Ibid.*, I, pp. 99–110 (*De docta ignorantia* II.11–12).
22. *Ibid.*, I, pp. 119–32 (*De docta ignorantia* III.1–4).   23. *Ibid.*, III, p. 143 (*De coniecturis* II.14).

of time and eternity – he unites in himself the lowest level of intellectual reality and the highest reach of sensible nature and is thus a bond which holds creation together.[24]

With respect to the creator, man is a 'human god' or a 'second god',[25] because of the creative power of his mind. Just as God is active *ad extra*, creating real things and natural forms, so also man can bring forth rational things and artificial forms – mathematical ideas, instruments and tools and works of art. The mathematical sciences have their origin in man's mind, just as real beings have theirs in the divine intellect. In producing tools and works of art, man uses materials he finds in nature, but the forms he gives them are not mere imitations of natural things. They are true productions of his own mind. Man's creative power thus approaches that of God, but whereas God brings forth what he understands, man is able only to understand what God has brought forth. His mind does not – like that of God – produce real beings, but can only represent them and appropriate them to itself.[26]

The metaphysical distinction between necessary activity *ad intra* and contingent activity *ad extra* was important for Nicholas' understanding of man's dignity because it enabled him to analyse more profoundly the nature of human knowledge. Lull had maintained that things like fire and whiteness have their own necessary, proper and intrinsic correlatives of action, whereas their objects *ad extra* (earth or water, this or that body) are contingent and appropriated to them. Nicholas drew the consequences of this idea for human knowledge. The sensible things which the mind encounters in the world are not necessary objects of knowledge. Even the things which the mind itself produces – a geometrical theorem or the form of a spoon – are objects appropriated by the mind to itself. The proper object of the mind must be an interior reality. Just as the proper object of fire is not earth or water but rather fire itself as ignitable, so also the proper object of the mind can only be the mind itself as knowable. To discover its true self, the mind must withdraw from the otherness which is involved in sense-perception and rational knowledge and turn inward. It must turn away from its contingent activity *ad extra* and ascend to its own necessary, intrinsic dynamism. The condition of the mind's return to itself is a deliberate, prior choice. Man's ultimate autonomy is grounded not only in his faculties of knowledge, but also in his ability freely to choose. Through his faculties of knowledge man can comprehend all things; through his

24. *Ibid.*, XII, p. 91 (*De venatione sapientiae* 32). 25. *Ibid.*, III, p. 143 (*De coniecturis* II.14).
26. *Ibid.*, III, pp. 126–9 (*De coniecturis* II.12); *ibid.*, V (1983 edn), pp. 92–112 (*Idiota de mente* 2–3).

freedom he can become all things, a human god, angel or beast. He has the ability to choose to belong to himself, to free himself from the world and realise all the interior potentialities of his nature.[27]

In thus reflecting on himself, man becomes a proper object of knowledge for himself. Since the knowledge of an object presupposes a disposition in the object enabling it to be known, man thus discovers himself as knowable. To explain the necessary process of human knowledge *ad intra*, Nicholas drew, accordingly, on Lull's theory of the correlatives of action: the knower (*intelligens*) knows himself as knowable object (*intelligible*) in the activity of knowing (*intelligere*). This triadic structure does not imply a splitting up of man into three separate entities. Man knows himself as knowable, but relates this knowable object to himself. At the same time, he becomes conscious of his own finitude. His knowledge is limited not only because it has to have recourse to sensible images. In order to understand the things which the mind discovers in the world – things which are in constant process, tending to their own perfection – it must reduce them to the static categories of discursive reason. Its knowledge of things can, therefore, only be approximate and never precise. Even its knowledge of those things brought forth by its own creativity is restricted, because its ideas can only be realised in an alien matter. Above all, however, it is in his effort to discover himself that man is confronted with the limitations of his nature. Although he must free himself from exterior things to find himself, the nature of his mind compels him to go out to things before he can begin to return to himself.[28]

In his reflection on himself, man thus achieves a new modesty, a modesty which gives birth to the realisation that there must exist – beyond his own contracted, asymptotic infinity – an absolute, transfinite *maximum* which is not only the origin and source but also the end and perfection of all things. There is no proportion, no analogy, between the absolute infinity of God and the contracted infinity of created reality. But because God himself is the condition of the encounter between himself and man, his transcendence is not infringed upon by being taken up in the process of human knowledge. The triadic structure of the necessary, intrinsic mode of understanding permits union without identification. God is knowable not as are the exterior things which are the contingent objects of human knowledge, but as the complementary part of the process of knowledge which takes place in the meeting of two subjects, each of whom experiences himself as knower

---

27. *Ibid.*, III, pp. 138–46 (*De coniecturis* II.14); *ibid.*, V (1983 edn), pp. 92–120 (*Idiota de mente* 2–4).
28. *Ibid.*, III, pp. 126–83 (*De coniecturis* II.12–17); *ibid.*, V (1983 edn), pp. 92–105 (*Idiota de mente* 2).

and known, while both are united in the activity of knowing. In *De visione Dei* Nicholas exclaimed: Because you are *intellectus intelligens* and *intellectus intelligibilis* and *utriusque nexus*, the created intellect can attain in you – its knowable God – union with you and beatitude. He described this union as a vision. God sees each individual unceasingly, giving him his being. The condition of man's seeing God is that he be in complete possession of himself. He must freely respond to God's glance with his own. Through his free choice of himself, man is able – beyond rational concepts and the coincidence of opposites – to see God directly.[29]

Man realises himself, all the interior potentialities of his nature, as an individual, eye-to-eye with God. The triadic structure of his knowledge makes him an image of the divine knowing. In his encounter with the exemplar – a transcendent exemplar which is his truth, the beginning, middle and end of his striving – man arrives at the dynamic repose which is the activity of knowing. The measure of his own truth is the degree of intensity with which he reflects the divine exemplar. He is a living image because the intensity of his perfection is subject to continuous variability as it approaches the perfection of the exemplar, a limit which is unattainable because of the lack of proportion between the infinite and the finite. The gulf which separates exemplar and image, God and man, could only be bridged if God himself assumed human nature and elevated it to a maximum perfection.[30]

Nicholas's conception of Christ as the God-man is the culmination of his understanding of man and his interior dignity. The created universe must be infinite, because otherwise the creator would not be effective to the maximum degree. But the infinity of the universe is only a contracted infinity, an unendlessness which ever approaches, but can never attain, absolute perfection. The fulfilment of the perfection of the universe demands the union of creator and creature. This does not imply that Christ is a mediate nature between divinity and humanity, but rather that in his person the *maximum absolutum* and the *maximum contractum*, the divine nature and the created nature of the universe, are brought together. Christ is the *medium connexionis* between God and the world because as an individual he is the fulfilment of all the interior potentialities of the species and through him the human species is the fulfilment of the universe. He is a perfect

29. Nicholas of Cusa 1485, I, f. 109ʳ (*De visione Dei* 18); cf. *ibid.*, ff. 101ᵛ–102ʳ (cap. 7), ff. 113ᵛ–14ʳ (cap. 25).
30. Nicholas of Cusa 1932–, V (1983 edn), pp. 3–57 (*Idiota de sapientia* I); *ibid.*, V, pp. 105–31 (*Idiota de mente* 3–5).

microcosm because he is the bond holding creation together. He is a human god because he is the perfect image of the divine exemplar. In his human nature he is the supreme limit of the active tendency of the species to its perfection and in his divine nature he is the perfect image of the Father.[31]

Nicholas' metaphysics is an achievement of great originality. His synthesis represents a high-water mark in the evolution of the new understanding of reality which had appeared in Western Europe about the beginning of the twelfth-century Renaissance. He brought together Anselm's ontological approach to the problem of the knowledge of God, the Chartrain dialectic of unity, equality and connection, Lull's dynamic conception of being, the Renaissance vision of man's dignity and – as we shall see – the late medieval theories of degrees of perfection which were developed at Paris, Oxford and Padua. This new tradition, although forced for a time underground by medieval Aristotelianism and the concomitant necessity of defining the relation between the new science and the Catholic faith, found representatives throughout the thirteenth and fourteenth centuries in German universities, particularly in the School of Albertus Magnus.

It was in this context that Nicholas originally encountered the Platonic tradition proper. He had, very early in his career, gone beyond the medieval Augustinians, beyond the *Liber de causis*, John Scotus Eriugena and the cosmological theories of the *Timaeus*. By the fourth decade of the fifteenth century, he was able to recognise not only the distinction between Platonic doctrine and that of the 'Aristotelian sect' which was entrenched in many universities, but also the connection between the negative theology of Pseudo-Dionysius and the Platonic theory of a transcendent One which is beyond language and knowledge, as propounded by Proclus and the Neoplatonists. In his youth he had studied the medieval translation of the first part of Plato's *Parmenides*. His discovery of Albertist scholasticism at Cologne and Paris encouraged him to deepen his knowledge of Proclus' version of Plato's teaching through two works which had been made available by William of Moerbeke in the thirteenth century, the commentary on the *Parmenides* and *The Elements of Theology*, upon which the pseudo-Aristotelian *Liber de causis* was based.

Nicholas' contact with the School of Albertus Magnus profoundly affected his approach to the thought of Ramon Lull. At Cologne, he made the acquaintance of Heimeric de Campo, who represented the Albertist

---

31. *Ibid.*, I, pp. 119–32 (*De docta ignorantia* III.1–4).

tradition in the arts faculty of the university from about 1422.[32] Both men were active at the Council of Basle and both proposed metaphysical solutions to the conciliar problem, Heimeric in various works which blend Albertist scholasticism with Lullian methodology, Nicholas in the great tract whose very title betrays its Lullian inspiration, *De concordantia catholica*. At Padua Nicholas had encountered a Lull who offered a new vision of human dignity. In Germany he was constrained to develop, out of Lull's chaotic literary production, a consistent metaphysics – to bring together Lull's dynamic understanding of reality and the Neoplatonic One which is beyond being. The notion of concordance provided the link between the two approaches. Whereas Proclus had proclaimed: 'in omni oppositione necessarium est unum exaltatum esse ab ambobus oppositis',[33] Nicholas drew on the Lullian idea to give a new, active turn to the Neoplatonic conception of the One and thus opened the way from the dialectical constructions of ancient metaphysics to the dynamic systems of modern times.

Through his relentless effort to go back to the sources of medieval thought, Nicholas of Cusa was able to make a decisive contribution to the revival of Platonism in fifteenth-century Italy. The early humanists who turned away from the abstract intellectualism of the schools in the search for a literary and aesthetic approach to philosophical and theological questions had from the first been impressed by the unified way in which language and literature, ancient philosophy and Christian teaching were transmitted in the Byzantine tradition. In Cicero and Augustine they discovered a Plato in whom philosophical penetration, moral concern and literary elegance were combined. Petrarch, in particular, was convinced that the true aim of philosophy was to show the way to salvation. In Plato he found a pagan philosopher who came very close to revelation. Following the lead of the author of the *Confessiones* and the *Soliloquia*, he read the *Timaeus* as an account of the origin of things which seemed to anticipate almost everything that John's gospel had said about the word of God. At the same time, his colleagues were at work uncovering an Aristotle who was quite different from the Aristotle represented in the universities. In one prophetic night Petrarch formulated a programme against the 'sophistry of the moderns'. In his *De ignorantia* he bequeathed this programme to the Renaissance under three headings: the necessity of studying Plato and Aristotle directly rather than as distorted by the medieval commentators,

32. Concerning Heimeric see Meersseman 1933–5; Colomer 1961; Lohr 1968, pp. 213–14; Kałuża 1970.   33. Proclus 1864, pp. 1123–4 (*In Parmeniden* VI, 137D).

the value of eloquence and poetry as supreme forms of human expression and the conviction that the Christian message completes and triumphs over that of antiquity.[34]

Petrarch's enthusiasm gave the stimulus to the study of the Greek language, to the zealous search for Greek manuscripts and to the translation of a good part of the vast corpus of literature handed down by the Byzantines. In the period between Manuel Chrysoloras' teaching of Greek at Florence (1397–1400) and the arrival of the Greek prelates at the Council of Florence (1438) the more prominent of the humanists were attracted as much by Greek patristic writers as by the classical authors. Niccolò Niccoli's famous library contained a rich collection of the works of the Greek Fathers – Athanasius, Basil, the two Gregorys, John Chrysostom. Ambrogio Traversari turned to these works for the light they could throw on the beliefs and practices of Christianity at the time when the Eastern and Western Churches were one. About 1410 Leonardo Bruni translated Basil's famous *Discourse to Christian Youth on Studying the Classics*, a work which vindicated classical learning by showing its utility for the believer and the agreement which reigned between Christian and classical moral precepts.

Moreover, the early fifteenth-century humanists discovered, under the influence of the Byzantines, a tradition in which Plato and Aristotle were not in conflict but complemented one another. In Byzantium both thinkers had been studied as integral parts of an ancient literary heritage. Philosophers and theologians alike often combined Aristotle's logic and natural philosophy with a Neoplatonic metaphysics which sought to harmonise the thought of both men. It was in accordance with this tradition that Bruni translated not only various Platonic dialogues but also Aristotle's works on moral philosophy. The humanists of this early period knew nothing of the metaphysical Plato of the *Parmenides* and nothing of the apocryphal literature associated with his name. The discovery that the Platonic tradition in Byzantium preserved not only the dialogues but also Neoplatonic writings like those of Plotinus and Proclus, along with works ascribed to enigmatic figures like Hermes Trismegistus, Orpheus, Pythagoras and Zoroaster, was reserved for the next generation.

The new period began with the arrival of the Greeks at the Council of Florence. Among the members of the Greek delegation was the aged philosopher Georgius Gemistus, who took the surname of Pletho because of its similarity to that of the founder of the Academy. Pletho – layman,

---

34. Petrarch 1906, pp. 37–83 (*De ignorantia sui ipsius et multorum aliorum* 4).

adviser to the emperor and resolute opponent of the union of the Greek and Latin churches – revered not only Plato but also the Neoplatonic philosophers, and appealed frequently to works like the *Orphic Hymns* and the *Chaldaean Oracles*. In accord with Proclus, he interpreted the higher gods of ancient Greece as metaphysical principles and the lesser deities as stellar or planetary powers. In accord with the *Orphic Hymns*, he maintained the efficacy of the ancient religious rites – not for their objective effect on the deity addressed, but rather for the subjective transformation of the adept. Although accused, late in life, of wanting to return to ancient paganism, he seems, in reality, to have seen in Platonism the ideological basis for the restoration of the fortunes of the Byzantine Empire.

It was from Morea, where he had spent most of the years of his long life teaching, that Pletho thought the reform of the empire should emanate. Whereas at Constantinople the territory of the Palaeologi was, at this period, reduced to little more than the city itself, their Peloponnesian despotate – in spite of conflicts with both the Turks to the east and the Latin states to the west – enjoyed a brief period of economic and cultural prosperity. In his school at Mistra, the capital, and on various diplomatic missions, Pletho sought the restoration of ancient Greek values and a political reform inspired by ancient Hellenic models. The Platonic philosophy was to supply the foundation for an appeal to the continuity of the entire Hellenic tradition.

Byzantium stood before the deadly threat of the Ottomans to the east, but Pletho and many other members of the Greek delegation to the Council of Florence saw union with the Latin Church as an even greater danger to the Hellenic tradition than the struggle with the Turks. From the very beginning of the Council their fears were confirmed. Whereas the Greeks argued on the basis of the simple and unadorned words of the holy Fathers, the Latins sought to convince by the syllogism and by logical demonstrations. Even some of the men of the Eastern Church well disposed to union regarded the dialectical procedures which the Latins applied to the texts of the Fathers and the claim of the Roman pontiff to be the final arbiter in case of disagreement as aggravating, rather than alleviating, the schism. Although men like Bessarion and Mark of Ephesus were perfectly capable of using all the resources of rational argumentation, they were scandalised by the conception of theology that the Latins seemed to them to advocate, a theology abstract, intellectualistic and speculative rather than practical, and without relevance for salvation, a theology which presented Christian doctrine deductively after the manner of Euclid's *Elements*.

The convocation of the Council of Florence coincided with the victory of the papacy over conciliarism and the establishment of Thomism as the dominant theological school in the West. It was, above all, the Aristotelianism of the Latin theologians that the Byzantines found objectionable – not only the use of the vocabulary of Aristotelian metaphysics in the discussion of the inner-trinitarian processions, but also the insertion by Albertus Magnus and Thomas Aquinas of Aristotle's natural philosophy into their presentations of theological doctrine. The Greek theologians were acquainted with Thomism through the efforts of Dominican missionaries in the East; some of their own number had even espoused Thomistic teaching. They knew that Thomas' inclusion of Aristotelian theses in his *Summa* of theological doctrine was part of an effort to show the agreement between teachings, like those of the Trinity and Incarnation, which are accessible to man only through faith, and teachings, like those of the existence of God, his providence and man's immortality, which can be proven by natural reason. But they also knew that his interpretation of Aristotle's thought did not always agree with that of the Hellenic tradition.

The Byzantine theologians, speaking generally, regarded Latin Aristotelianism as the unwarranted intrusion of cosmic, that is, worldly, knowledge into the science of God and the saints. Pletho, for his part, charged the Latins not only with being unacquainted with Platonic philosophy but also with misunderstanding Aristotle's teaching, having been misled by Averroes, the Arabic Peripatetic, to believe that the Philosopher's works contained the sum total of human wisdom. In the famous treatise Περὶ ὧν 'Αριστοτέλης πρὸς Πλάτωνα διαφέρεται, which he composed during his brief sojourn at Florence 'for the benefit of the Platonists' in Italy, Pletho opposed the Latin view that Aristotle taught that God is the creator of all things, that he has direct providence over the world and that the human soul is immortal. Aristotle was wrong in holding that the heavens are composed of a fifth element, that beatitude is to be found in contemplation, that virtue is a mean between two opposed vices, that first substance, the sensibly perceived individual thing, is prior to second substance, the universal. Because he rejected Plato's theory of ideas, Aristotle remained only at the level of physics, concerned not with being, but only with change. His God is not the creator of all things, but only the first principle of motion in a world which is itself eternal.[35]

---

35. Pletho 1866.

Pletho's treatise opened the celebrated controversy concerning the relative superiority of Plato and Aristotle, a controversy which was continued for several decades by Byzantine scholars both in Greece and in Italy, and then until well into the sixteenth century in Latin countries. The first attack against Pletho's work was composed by Georgius Scholarius, who, though at the time a layman like Pletho, had also taken part in the Council of Florence.[36] Scholarius – at the Council a supporter of the union of the two churches – was strongly influenced by Latin scholasticism and seems to have known Thomas Aquinas even better than he knew the Greek tradition. His work, which was written some five years after Pletho's, is a defence of the agreement between Aristotle and Christian theology. In it Scholarius tries to show that it is possible to defend Aristotle's doctrine of the eternity of the world and still hold the biblical doctrine of God's efficient causality in creation. He rebukes Pletho for using Proclus' interpretation of Plato without acknowledgement and speaks deprecatively of his Italian friends who admire Plato's literary gifts, but are unable to appreciate the philosophical depth of Aristotle. Some five years later, Pletho replied to Scholarius' attack, adding an important new element to the debate. He maintained that Plato continued the *prisca theologia* of Zoroaster, Hermes Trismegistus, and Pythagoras and is, for this reason, nearer than Aristotle to Christian teaching, except perhaps that of the Arians. Shortly after Pletho's death in 1454, Scholarius – having become a monk, Patriarch of Constantinople, and a resolute anti-unionist – answered Pletho's reply by having his chief work burnt because of its paganising tendencies.

The controversy was brought to Italy during the fifties by a third Byzantine in whose works the ideological background of the dispute came clearly to the surface. George of Trebizond was one of the Greek scholars enlisted by Pope Nicholas V for the ambitious project of making available in Latin the Greek classical and patristic heritage. Nicholas had made Rome a major humanistic centre and under his patronage George produced translations of many Greek Fathers, along with Plato's *Laws* and the *Epinomis*, Aristotle's principal treatises on natural philosophy and some works of Demosthenes and Ptolemy. George's entrance into the controversy regarding Plato and Aristotle reveals the fact that, at least at this stage, the dispute concerned less the respective merits of the two classical philosophers than it did the role of philosophy in theology. His intervention – which can be regarded as a consequence of the victory of the papacy at

---

36. On Scholarius see *Dictionnaire de théologie catholique* 1923–72, XIV, cols. 1521–70; Turner 1969; Tavardon 1977.

Basle – was aimed at defending the clerical programme of a Christian Aristotelianism supporting revealed theology.

George's reservations with regard to the idea of a *prisca theologia* from which Plato's doctrine derived are patent in his translation of the *De preparatione evangelica* of Eusebius of Caesarea (1448). Eusebius had sought to show that the 'philosophy of the Hebrews' was superior to pagan cosmogonies. George, on the ground that the pope had commanded him to remove harmful passages, abbreviated the sections in which Eusebius claimed that Plato had used the Old Testament as a source.[37] Then, in the original prefaces to his translation of the *Laws* (*c.* 1450) and in the accompanying outline of the contents of the work made for Nicholas, he denounced the social and moral poisons which the work contained (although he was able at the same time, when seeking patronage in Venice, to praise the Venetians for having taken the inspiration for their mixed constitution from Plato's work).[38] Some years later, in his polemic against Theodore Gaza's new translation of Aristotle's *Problems* (1456), George accused Gaza of deliberately falsifying Aristotle's meaning with the intention of overthrowing the Christian Aristotelianism of the great scholastic doctors, Thomas Aquinas, Albertus Magnus, Duns Scotus and Giles of Rome.[39]

George's polemic against Gaza was the prelude to his violent *Comparatio philosophorum Aristotelis et Platonis* (1458), which maintained the superiority of Aristotle to Plato in every respect. The treatise is divided into three books. The first compares the learning of the two philosophers to Aristotle's advantage. George does not deny Plato's formal elegance, but condemns it rather, as being without philosophical value and serving only to seduce the ignorant. The second book extends the comparison to the question of their respective agreement with Christian doctrine. Plato only seems to agree with Christianity; in fact, he retained Greek polytheism and taught a doctrine of creation from unformed matter as well as the pre-existence of souls. Aristotle, on the other hand, taught monotheism, creation *ex nihilo*, and the immortality of the human soul. The third book denounces Plato's immorality and pernicious influence in political life. He concluded by revealing the genealogy behind Pletho's philosophy. Plato's idealism led to Epicurus' materialism, Platonic eros led to Epicurean hedonism and Muhammad's union of both led to Pletho's paganism.[40]

37. See Mras' introduction to Eusebius 1902–, VIII, I, pp. xxviii–xxxii.
38. See Monfasani 1976, pp. 102–3, 161–2. 39. George of Trebizond 1942.
40. George of Trebizond 1523.

There is a strong apocalyptic element in George's thought. He saw Islam and the Ottomans as threatening to overwhelm western civilisation and Platonism as a part of this threat. What he regarded as Gaza's perversion of Aristotle's *Problems* convinced him of the existence at Rome of a Platonic conspiracy to undermine Christian theology. The *Comparatio* traced this conspiracy back to its origins. It saw Pletho as the prophet of a new, universal, Platonic religion meant to supersede both Christianity and Islam. Pletho's rationalism implied the end of revealed religion and the irrelevance of attempts, like that of Thomas Aquinas, to develop a Christian Aristotelianism which would buttress it.

This was the juncture at which Nicholas of Cusa was able to make a very profound contribution to the controversy. Having been named cardinal by Nicholas V in 1448, Nicholas became a member of the Roman Curia in 1458. In spite of the heavy obligations of his office as Bishop of Brixen (1450–8), he had made every effort to keep abreast of the growth of Platonism in Italy. He was well known to the humanists gathered in Rome, especially to Cardinal Bessarion. His library provides eloquent testimony to his interest in the latest philosophical literature. He was in possession of the most important of the new Latin translations: those of the Greek Fathers by Traversari and George of Trebizond, of Plato's dialogues by Bruni and Decembrio, of Aristotle's moral philosophy by Bruni, of Eusebius' *De preparatione evangelica* by George of Trebizond. He had a copy of Petrarch's programmatic *De ignorantia*. About the time of his appointment to the Roman Curia he seems to have found new interest in the Plato of the *Parmenides*. During the years 1458–9 he returned to and annotated Proclus' commentary on the work. In 1459 he composed his *De principio*, in which the influence of Proclus' interpretation is particularly evident. In the same year George of Trebizond translated, at the cardinal's request, the complete *Parmenides*. Although George – reluctant to admit that anything of philosophical value could be found in Plato – attributed to Nicholas a purely historical interest in the work, the latter had requested this new translation because of the incomplete character of the medieval version.

Nicholas was also the moving force behind the Latin translation of Proclus' *Platonic Theology* by Pietro Balbo of Pisa and the edition of Apuleius by Giovanni Andrea de' Bussi, both undertaken about this time. We encounter these two old friends of Nicholas – the former was a fellow-student at Padua, the latter, his long-time secretary – in the dialogue *De non aliud* of 1461. In the first part of this work Nicholas instructs his personal physician, the Portuguese Ferdinand Matim, in the meaning of his new definition of the first principle of all things as *non aliud*, the Not-Other. The second part discusses the contributions made to this idea by Aristotle, represented by Ferdinand, Proclus, represented by Pietro, and Plato himself, represented by Giovanni Andrea.

Nicholas' account of Aristotle's contribution amounted to a very severe criticism of the Philosopher's metaphysics, but one much more profound than those we have encountered thus far. In the *De non aliud* he concerns himself less with questions like the eternity of the world and the immortality of the soul than with the roots of Aristotle's errors. Although Nicholas had, in fact, taken over from Aristotle theories such as those of universal ideas, matter and form and substance and accident, he rejects Aristotelian metaphysics. Like many of the Byzantines, he limits Aristotle's merits to the areas of natural and moral philosophy. Aristotle failed in first or 'mental' philosophy, because he was never able to define clearly the subject of the science, the 'being' or 'substance' which is the same – Not-Other – in different things. The deepest reason for his failure is to be found in the fact that he never ascended beyond sense and reason to the certitude of intellectual vision. Reason is able only to approach certitude; it can never attain it. The way to the absolute vision of the intellect is opened only by the realisation that the Not-Other and the Other are beyond contradiction.[41]

Nicholas did not, however, limit his criticism to Aristotle's philosophy. He also regarded the Platonic definition of the first principle of things as inadequate and deficient. In the *De non aliud* he rejects the idea of calling the One of the *Parmenides* the first principle of things because the first principle cannot be other than the things which derive from it.[42] Whereas Plato had spoken of the One and the Indefinite Dyad as first principles, the Neoplatonists preferred the expression 'the Other' to 'the Indefinite Dyad', and thought of unity as original and otherness as somehow derived from it. Christian readers of these authors identified, accordingly, God with the One and creation with the Other or Not-One. It was in this context that Nicholas came to his definition of the first principle as the Not-Other. Because the first principle cannot be opposed to anything, he proposed the substitution of the name 'Not-Other' for the 'One'.

The question was not simply one of extrinsic denomination. Nicholas makes it clear that his Not-Other should not be understood as the first principle itself, but rather as the concept of the first principle. In contradistinction to the notion of the One, to which in Proclus even

41. Nicholas of Cusa 1932–, XIII, pp. 44–7 (*De non aliud* 18–19).
42. *Ibid.*, XIII, pp. 52–4 (*De non aliud* 22).

thought is foreign, the notion 'Not-Other' reveals itself as active and dynamic, in that it is self-defining. Not-Other has no need of an Other to define itself. Nicholas explains: '"Non aliud" est non aliud quam non aliud.'[43] Not-Other defines itself in the three-fold repetition of the name, unfolding in the dissoluble unity of the first principle's nature at once its trinitarian structure *ad intra* and its creational and conservational efficacy *ad extra*.[44]

With the notion 'Not-Other' Nicholas intended not only to go beyond Plato and Aristotle, but also to propose an alternative to the Christian Aristotelianism of the scholastics. The Thomistic approach to the problem of God was meant to underline the necessity of revelation. In Thomas' view, reason is capable of demonstrating the fact of the existence of God as the ground of all being, but can say nothing of his essence or nature. The idea of a triune God is beyond philosophical speculation and can only come from revelation. Nicholas did not separate philosophy and theology in this way. He did not seek an abstract knowledge of God's existence, but rather a knowledge of the nature and activity of God which can lead to salvation. In the spirit of Anselm of Canterbury, his concern was to understand the things which the believer knows of God through revelation. Anselm's *unum argumentum* is not an argument for the existence of God; it attempts rather to fill out more clearly the believer's concept of God, by proving that the being he worships possesses its existence with the inner necessity of its nature. In the same way, Ramon Lull could take God's existence for granted and concentrate on the effort to show that his creative activity, which is known through revelation, implies his triune nature before creation.

It was not as a Platonist but rather in accord with this latter tradition that Nicholas entered the debate concerning the relative superiority of Plato and Aristotle. Although the *De non aliud* employed modified Platonic terminology, the other works of this later period echo now familiar ideas. In the *De venatione sapientiae* of 1462, Nicholas gives a summary account of his life-long pursuit of wisdom, how he set out from the idea of a *docta ignorantia* to return by way of *non aliud* and the Chartrain triad of *unitas*, *aequalitas* and *connexio* to a doctrine clearly based on Lull's correlatives of action. According to his own account the name Not-Other represented logically an early stage in his effort to solve the problem of a trinitarian concept of God.[45] But in the *De non aliud* the metaphysical aspect of the *Parmenides* is no longer central. At this late stage of his career, Nicholas was much more

---

43. *Ibid.*, XIII, p. 4 (*De non aliud* 1).   44. *Ibid.*, XIII, pp. 47–58 (*De non aliud* 20–4).
45. *Ibid.*, XII, pp. 38–41 (*De venatione sapientiae* 14).

interested in Plato's description of the process of thought by which the mind approaches its highest object. Not-Other cannot be approached by seeking to penetrate directly into the mysteries of the divine nature. In accordance with the Anselmian programme of *fides quaerens intellectum*, Nicholas seeks with the name a negative sort of understanding. If God were not Not-Other, there would be otherness in his nature and his creative activity would not be one with the world, which is impossible. In accordance with Lull's dynamic understanding of reality, the name is meant to designate both the active God in whom there is no otherness and the creative God who is not other than the world because he is the active principle of its being and activity. In accordance with Ramon Sibiuda – whose *Liber creaturarum* formed a part of Nicholas' library – this type of understanding is open to all believers and is not the privilege of clerical interpreters of the tradition.

Nicholas' emphasis on the epistemological aspect of the *Parmenides'* teaching represented an important step forward in the Renaissance understanding of the Platonic tradition. But his approach to Plato's thought was still dominated by the dialogues with which the Middle Ages had already been acquainted. At the very time, however, when he was engaged in writing his *De non aliud*, scholars in Italy were beginning to put the knowledge of Plato on a new basis. Although the leading figures in this development were no longer limited to Byzantine refugees, men like Bessarion, who had made Italy his home after the conclusion of the Council of Florence, still played an important role. Having been named cardinal in 1439, Bessarion was an energetic defender of the union of the Eastern and Western Churches and became one of the leading figures in the circle of humanists which Nicholas V gathered around himself. Immediately after the publication of George of Trebizond's *Comparatio*, he took up the defence of Plato in his *In calumniatorem Platonis*, a tract which was written at first in Greek and several times revised before appearing in Latin in 1469. In this work Bessarion refutes George's charges point by point. The first book answers the claim that Plato's learning was deficient. Not only did Plato agree with Aristotle in natural philosophy, but he also made important contributions to other parts of the encyclopaedia of the liberal arts which were neglected by Aristotle, above all mathematics. Of divine things no one spoke more sublimely than the founder of the Academy. The charge that Plato was a teacher of immorality is refuted by Bessarion in the fourth and final book of his work.

The second and third books of the *In calumniatorem* form the part of the treatise which was, in the context of the debate, the most significant. These books deal with the question of the agreement of the two classical philosophers with Christian doctrine. With a sure sense for the historical context in which Plato and Aristotle wrote, Bessarion maintained that the teaching of neither the one nor the other could have agreed with Christian doctrine. Since both lived before Christianity, it would be anachronistic to expect them to be orthodox Christians. Both accepted ancient polytheism and believed in demons and the pre-existence of souls. Aristotle had, contrary to George of Trebizond's claim, no knowledge of the Christian Trinity. Not only is it false that he taught that the world was created by God freely and *ex nihilo* and that God's providence extends to *inferiora*, but it is also impossible, on Aristotelian principles, to prove that the human soul is immortal. Throughout the work Bessarion treats Aristotle's thought with great respect, but holds, nevertheless, that Plato came much nearer than he did to Christian doctrine. Plato did not deny divine providence. His account of the production of the world approached the revealed doctrine of creation. Pseudo-Dionysius borrowed much from the *Parmenides*, especially in his *De divinis nominibus*. What Plato says about the One agrees with the doctrine of the *supersubstantialis Dei divinitas* taught by the supposed disciple of St Paul. God is not a being among beings, but rather the principle of all beings, himself beyond being. In the *Republic*, Plato seems even to have had a presentiment of the Christian notion of the word of God. The teaching of his disciple, Plotinus – whose work could, in the generally accepted view of the period, have been influenced by Pseudo-Dionysius – resembled very nearly the doctrine of the trinity of persons in God.[46]

Bessarion's tract offered, for the first time in the West, an ample and balanced account of Platonic doctrine, based on a profound knowledge not only of all of Plato's works but also of his ancient commentators. At the same time, the *In calumniatorem*, in accordance with the Byzantine scholarly tradition, insisted on the fundamental agreement between Plato and Aristotle. Without denying the great gulf between paganism and Christianity, Bessarion also emphasised the continuity between classical and patristic thought. His famous library, which included about twice as many Greek as Latin titles, not only contained Plato and Aristotle, along with their commentators, and Neoplatonic writers like Plotinus, Iamblichus and Proclus, but was also especially strong in the works of the Greek Church Fathers. Similarly, Johannes Argyropulos, another Greek theologian who had remained in Italy after having attended the Council of Florence, began

46. Bessarion 1927.

his teaching in the *Studio* of Florence in 1457 by seeking, in a course on Aristotle's *Ethics*, to reconcile Plato and Aristotle. Both he and Bessarion produced new Latin translations of Aristotle's *Metaphysics*, works which enjoyed a wide diffusion in early printed editions.

It is, therefore, all the more remarkable that the first translation of the entire corpus of Plato's writings was made in conscious opposition to the Aristotelianism of the schools and without explicit reference to Greek ecclesiastical writers. Marsilio Ficino's translations and systematic treatises are, *ex professo*, Platonic works. The project of translating Plato's dialogues was begun in the same year that Nicholas of Cusa composed his *De venatione sapientiae*. But whereas for Nicholas Platonism was but one part of philosophical culture and for Bessarion the agreement between Plato, Neoplatonism and revelation was of primary importance, Ficino seemed almost to place Platonism before even the Christ of the gospels. He saw Plato and Platonic writers as part of an ancient theological tradition antedating even Moses himself. His translations – which were undertaken at the command of Cosimo de' Medici – were part of an effort to recover this tradition. Cosimo's commission to translate Plato's dialogues was accompanied by the command to put into Latin the works of Hermes Trismegistus, the mythical Egyptian sage who was believed to have been, along with Orpheus, Zoroaster and Pythagoras, the remote source of Plato's teaching. The translation of the *Hermetica* was completed in 1463, that of Plato's works by 1469. In the course of his life Ficino commented on the most important of the dialogues: *Timaeus*, *Symposium*, *Philebus*, *Parmenides* and *Phaedrus*. He translated and commented on Plotinus, making this writer available to the western world for the first time. He supplemented the medieval versions of Neoplatonic works by translating works of Porphyry, Iamblichus and Proclus. Of Byzantine writers he translated Psellus' *De demonibus* and copied out with his own hand the Greek text of several works of Pletho.

Ficino's translations of Plato opened a third period in the history of Florentine Platonism. Whereas in the period before the Council of Florence both Plato and Aristotle were read, above all as works of Greek literature, the Council had turned attention to the speculative side of Greek thought. In the second period which thus began, not only the Greek controversy about the relative superiority of Plato and Aristotle but also the exclusive Aristotelianism of the Averroists in the arts faculties and the Thomists among the theologians gave rise to the notion that the philosophical approaches of the two thinkers were fundamentally opposed – an attitude which neither the ancients nor the Byzantines would have understood. In the period immediately after the Council many humanists at Florence showed a distinct inclination towards the Platonic approach. Conducive to this was certainly the flourishing cultural life at Florence. Brunelleschi's cupola had been completed just before the Council, and under Cosimo de' Medici the construction of new palaces was transforming the city. But there was a darker side to the exclusiveness of the turn to Plato which marked the beginning of the third period.

The fall of Constantinople in 1453, the financial crisis of 1464–5, the death of Francesco Sforza in 1466 along with the collapse of the alliances dependent upon him, the assassination of Galeazzo Maria in 1476, the Pazzi conspiracy of 1478: all contributed to the pessimism which pervades the work of Ficino and his contemporaries. The withdrawal of wealthy families from civic life – expressed both in the spaciousness of the inner courtyards of the new palaces and in the flight from the city to extravagant villas in the countryside – presaged the approaching end of an age and a change in humanism itself. About the time that Florence shifted her allegiances from Venice to Milan, reflection among humanists shifted from the virtues of civic responsibility to literature and artistic creativity. Speculation on the divine meaning behind mythological tales, on the nature of beauty, on true nobility, on the purpose of friendship, on the precedence of the contemplative over the active life, on man as creative and perfectible, characterised the new era. The discussion of man's dignity shifted from his place in the state to his place in the hierarchy of being. Humanists were no longer active politicians, like Leonardo Bruni, interested in moral philosophy and the models they could find in Plutarch's *Lives*. Rather they were teachers and professional philosophers, dedicated to a life of reflection far removed from political activity. They were, moreover, courtiers, dependent on the benevolence of a prince. Although Cosimo actually belonged to the older generation which sought guidance in the moral philosophy of both Plato and Aristotle, Ficino often made appeal to his Platonism and to his association with Pletho, in an effort to establish a connection between Mistra and the Platonic Academy in Florence. In reality, his appeals were concealed admonitions to Lorenzo de' Medici. Whereas earlier generations had praised Cosimo as *pater patriae*, and then as the Maecenas who made the scholarly life possible, for Ficino he was an Augustus who had presided over a now lost golden age.

The Platonism of Marsilio Ficino defined man by his aspirations, by his yearning for a better world. The significance of his great undertaking was not limited to making available for the first time in Latin the works of Plato and the Platonists. Of even greater importance was the fact that in Plato he found the key to the most important knowledge for man – the knowledge of the divine and immortal principle within himself. His own Platonic tracts inaugurated a metaphysical tradition in the Italian Renaissance, a metaphysical tradition different from any that had gone before. Earlier humanists – even in writing on the theme of man's dignity – manifested a great diffidence in confronting metaphysical questions. But their influence set Ficino's Platonic metaphysics apart from that of a Bessarion, in whose thought man's place in the universe, his experience of the contemplative life and the theory of love had little importance. Humanist concerns also distinguished his metaphysics from the optimistic speculations of a Nicholas of Cusa, for whom the idea of man's mortality did not constitute the point of departure for philosophy.

The turn to metaphysics thus made Florentine Platonism a phenomenon unique in the history of philosophy. Of the factors which led to this development, the weightiest was perhaps the need to formulate a religious creed which was broader than that of medieval Latin Christianity. This need was felt at Florence in a special way. From the time of Cosimo de' Medici the horizons of the city were no longer limited to the Italian peninsula. Her growing fleet and profitable Turkish trade made her increasingly a challenge to the interests of Venice in the Levant. The Council of Florence had made the city the meeting-place of eastern and western religious convictions – as Cosimo had foreseen when he brought the Council to the city. The sight – in the streets and squares of the city – of richly attired eastern dignitaries and bearded Byzantine prelates attended by Moslem and Moorish servants gave the question of the agreement between philosophy and religion a new urgency.

The traditional scholastic metaphysics of being, which had experienced a rebirth as a result of the outcome of the Council of Basle, was incapable of meeting this challenge. The victory of the papacy over conciliarism was accompanied by a narrowing of the Catholic vision and a return to an official metaphysics meant to supply a guarantee for the Latin clergy's view of itself as the unique interpreter of revelation. On the other hand, the nominalism which flourished in northern universities, by denying the possibility of man's knowledge of universal concepts, rendered any sort of philosophical justification of revealed doctrines – doctrines like that of the immortality of the human soul – impossible. At the same time, the Averroist Aristotelianism which had grown up in Italy had a secular character and tended to disregard the religious dimension in philosophical problems. Although the professors in the arts faculties had come increasingly to concern themselves with questions like that of man's immortality, the orientation of their teaching was towards the study of medicine and paid little attention to ecclesiastical concerns. Furthermore, their treatment of the problem of the soul was not able to meet the exalted demands of the Renaissance idea of man's transcendent dignity since the doctrine of the soul belonged, in accordance with the Aristotelian classification of the sciences, not to the science of immaterial reality but to physics.

An approach was needed which avoided the fideism of the nominalists, the secularism of the Averroists and the clericalism behind the Christian Aristotelianism of the Thomists. As a consequence of the notion that the philosophies of Plato and Aristotle were opposed, Ficino sought an alternative to these Aristotelianisms in Platonic metaphysics. He proposed a very subtle reading of Plato, a reading that not only insisted – as Pletho and Bessarion had done – on the basic agreement between Christian theology and the philosophical tradition to which Plato belonged, but also stressed – in accord with the *Hermetica* – the harmony of cosmic processes and the animate nature of the universe. For Ficino God is the One beyond being. He is the perfect Truth who collects into the ineffable simplicity of his own nature the endless multiplicity of the ideal archetypes of things. He is the infinite Good who diffuses himself in all things and remains present, more interior to them than they are to themselves. The universe which emanates from God constitutes a hierarchy in which each being has its place according to its degree of perfection, a hierarchy descending through the orders of angelic minds and rational souls to corporeal forms and unformed matter. God pours the ideas of all things into the angelic mind. Mind generates the reasons for governing things in soul. Soul generates forms in matter. The entire cosmos is an active, living being. Its Soul possesses as many seminal reasons as there are ideas in Mind. By way of these reasons Soul generates the forms of material things. The world-soul is united to the body of the world by spirit, a fifth, ethereal essence, containing all the qualities of the four elements. Through spirit the divine power passes from the celestial spheres to the sublunar world. The human soul, thus situated between time and eternity, participates in the nature of the universal soul. Like the world-soul, it is joined to a corruptible body by the unifying power of spirit, the soul's ethereal vehicle and immortal garment, the seat of imagination and the instrument of perception and bodily movement. Man is a microcosm, imitating God with unity, the angels with mind, soul with reason, brute animals with sensation, plants with nutrition and inanimate things with simple being. He is the true bond of all things, the knot tying the world together, who can ascend in thought from the forms evident to the senses to the world-soul, from the seminal reasons in Soul to Mind and from the ideas in Mind to the Good itself.[47]

The Neoplatonic inspiration of this world-view is evident. Following Plotinus' division of reality into a hierarchical series of realms or spheres of being emanating from a transcendent One, Ficino proposed a set of five ontological hypostases: the One, Mind, Soul, Quality (forms in matter) and Body.[48] As in Plotinus, Ficino's metaphysics centred on the relationship of man to the divine, that is, of Soul to the One, a relationship mediated by the intelligible-intellectual world of the ideal archetypes of things, that is, by Mind. Nevertheless, Ficino made profound changes in this Platonic theology. His God is not the absolutely impersonal One, who, blessed in his solitude, cares not for the world which proceeds from him. Ficino's God is a personal God who knows himself and all things in himself as their first cause. Although he saw an anticipation of the Christian doctrine of the Trinity in Plato's triad of unity, truth and goodness in the act of creation, Ficino rejected any attempt to assimilate Plotinus' first three hypostases to the Father, Son and Spirit of Christian theology. Because Mind, which is the corner-stone of Plotinus' metaphysics, is not of the same substance as the One, but rather subordinate to it – as is also Soul to Mind – Ficino broke with the Plotinian concept, assigning some of Mind's attributes to God, others to the angels. In his view, the status of Mind as supreme thinker and supreme thought and as creator of the universe belongs to the One. Moreover, Ficino does not devaluate finite being as Neoplatonic metaphysics does. Although he speaks of things as emanating from God, he thinks of emanation as an act which has its roots in God's free goodness. God has created the world not by necessity of nature, but in accordance with a certain purpose of his will. God's relationship to things is not subject to the determinism implied by emanation, but is contingent on his love of the world. Love not only ascends from man to God, but also descends from on high. God loves the world as his creature and, as such, the world is worthy of love. Ficino's hierarchy of being is, accordingly, not static in the sense that an ontological gulf separates its spheres. For the philosopher of the Florentine Academy, all things are interrelated. The universe has a dynamic unity and its various degrees and parts are bound together by active affinities.[49]

47. Ficino 1964–70, I, pp. 73–173 (II–IV).
48. *Ibid.*, I, pp. 39, 128 (I.1; III.1).   49. *Ibid.*, I, pp. 73–127 (II).

The specifically humanistic character of Ficino's approach – setting it off from that of the ancient Neoplatonists – appears most clearly in his doctrine of Soul. Whereas in Plotinus the world-soul is simply the prime individual instance in the generic category of soul, Ficino identified Soul with the world-soul and maintained that individual human souls participated in its nature. As the universal bond of things, Soul has the role of mediating between the ideal and material worlds. The world-soul impresses the seminal reasons which it possesses as forms on the corporeal world. The forms are conveyed from the celestial spheres to the sublunar world by the spirit of the world. The seminal reasons in things are conceived as active powers, as individual spirits or deities ruling the celestial signs. The signs are the reservoirs in which these powers are stored.[50] Man's task – the task of the human soul – is to perfect himself and the world in which he lives. To this purpose he can make use of the seminal powers in things. The arts he has invented are founded on the universal harmony which exists in the world. They seek to exploit the natural affinities and occult qualities in things. The physician, for example, seeks to bring together celestial influences in the medicines he prescribes in order to effect favourable physical dispositions in the human body. The influences transmitted by the signs and planets can also work on man's imagination and enable him to produce poetry, music and works of art. The arts thus give man magical power over nature. They have been bestowed on him by the spirits ruling the heavens. By listening to God's voice in the seminal powers of things, man is able to transform the world. This type of magic works through the spirit of the world and is good. There is another magic which is illicit, because it seeks to operate through the soul of the world and involves demons. But natural magic ministers to the powers of nature and wants to assist the world in its tendency to perfection. It is, therefore, the most sublime part of natural philosophy.[51]

Ficino's conception of the power of Soul over nature enabled him to give a systematic place to the Renaissance theme of man's dignity. Like that of Nicholas of Cusa, his praise of man is founded on human creativity. But whereas Nicholas stressed man's intellectual inventiveness, Ficino appealed to the miracles man has worked in the arts and in government. Man does not only use nature, but adorns, beautifies and transforms it. The great cities, the wonders of sculpture, painting and architecture, the endless tools and instruments that man has brought forth prove that he is not the subject of

50. *Ibid.*, I, pp. 128–43 (III).   51. Ficino 1576, I, pp. 531–72 (*De vita* III).

nature, but rather its master. Man is not like the animals dominated by the one element in which they live; he uses all the things of the world, as lord of all. He is able to unfold his potentialities in all the spheres that make up reality. He lives the life of plants by cultivating his body, that of animals by sharpening his senses, that of man by living in accord with reason, that of the angels by his penetration into the divine mysteries.[52] Referring to the planetarium of Archimedes, Ficino exclaimed that man's genius approaches that of the creator of the heavens because, having observed the regularity and order reigning in the spheres, he could, given the necessary materials, bring them forth himself.[53] Man's creativity situates him at the centre of the universe, between spiritual and sensible reality. In spite of his corporeality, his mind is divine. It is because – as a god on earth – he cares for all things that he is the knot holding the parts of the world together.[54]

Ficino thus anticipated a concept – that of genius – which would gain increasing importance in the late sixteenth century. But this positive vision of man was, at the same time, tempered by an opposed concept which he could have found in Augustine and the medieval mystics – that of alienation. For Ficino, there is a latent absurdity in man's condition. Immutable like higher things, but subject to change like inferior ones, he is at once the most and least perfect of creatures. Through his intelligence, he is able to dominate temporal things and is open to eternal realities. Not satisfied by dominion over the world, he seeks restlessly the reasons for things. Compelled ceaselessly to pursue potentialities, he is the most wanting and the most unhappy of creatures. His constant struggle to transcend himself situates him on the horizon between eternity and time and makes his nature a historical one, always projected into the future. In this *inquietudo animi* Ficino finds the proof of the divinity of man's soul. It is because he possesses the divine fire that man is – like Prometheus – unable to find repose. His longing to be united with all reality can be stilled only by God's own infinity. But if man is destined for the infinite, his desire can only find definitive fulfilment beyond death. If man were not immortal, he would be an incomplete nature – which would be contrary to God's wisdom and goodness and to the place he has assigned to man at the centre of creation.[55]

The human soul is an immaterial reality, using a body. As such, it is not confined to a determined sphere of being. Man has no fixed essence, but can descend to the level of the beasts or ascend in thought to the sphere of the

---

52. Ficino 1964–70, II, pp. 196–296 (XIII–XIV).   53. *Ibid.*, II, pp. 223–9 (XIII.3).
54. *Ibid.*, I, pp. 137–43 (III.2).   55. *Ibid.*, I, pp. 38–9 (I.1); II, pp. 269–73 (XIV.7).

angels or even to that of God himself. Ficino used Neoplatonic terminology, but gave it a dynamic turn by emphasising the circularity in Plotinus' scheme. The One goes out to Mind and Soul, but Soul returns to Mind and Mind to the One. Soul seeks to become the plenitude of all the species, by turning back to the one act of mind. Mind seeks to become all things in act, to comprehend the highest One in all the species, by turning back to their one act.[56] In speaking of ascending in thought to the One, Ficino distinguished – in a way similar to that of Lull and Nicholas of Cusa – between logical understanding and dialectical contemplation. The thought by which the human soul is able to transcend itself is not the process of discursive reasoning based on the abstraction of universal ideas, but rather an intuitive vision of intelligible reality which ascends in stages from forms in things and innate ideas to the eternal ideas and ultimately to the idea of the Good itself. Ficino regarded the contemplation of immaterial things to be the proper task of the metaphysician. The soul is led to this science by ascending from moral to natural philosophy and thence to mathematics before arriving at this supreme form of contemplation.

The dignity of man is founded on his innate desire for this highest degree of contemplation. This desire is not purely intellectual, but has also a voluntary component. Turning to Augustine and the Christian tradition, Ficino went beyond the Platonic notion of *eros*. Just as the act of creation requires the union of the divine intellect with the divine liberality, so also man's innate desire to comprehend the One forms one act with his free choice of the One. The contemplation to which Ficino refers involves not only the thought which actively constitutes its objects, but also the love which actively binds them together. The innate attraction and occult qualities which were encountered on the level of natural philosophy become, in metaphysics, the desire for transcendence, the intellectual love of God. In the highest act of contemplation the knowledge of the divine truth coincides with the enjoyment of the divine goodness. In one of his last works, Ficino interpreted the myth of the *Phaedrus* in accordance with this vision. Plato's charioteer is the youth at the foot of Diotima's ladder, intent on leading the individual soul by divine inspirations to the notion of Soul's immortality, so that Jove, the celestial world-soul, might conduct it thence together with all human souls as a company of gods beyond the intellectual heaven, to the gates of the transcendent One, to God himself.[57]

In spite – or perhaps because – of the originality of his project, Ficino

---

56. Ficino 1975, pp. 306–9 (I.31).   57. Ficino 1981, pp. 82–129 (*In Phaedrum comm.* 4–11).

seems to have been very hesitant about the reception his ideas would find. Not only did he take a great deal of time to complete his translations and commentaries, but the publication of his works was often long delayed after their completion. He seems especially to have wanted to have his project seen not as something new, but rather as continuing a long tradition of Platonism. Towards the end of his life, in a letter to a friend who had requested instruction about Platonic philosophy, he sought to relate his writings to a distinguished line of Latin Platonists: Augustine, Boethius, Chalcidius and Macrobius in the patristic period; Henry of Ghent and Duns Scotus among the medievals. He presented his versions of Plato and Platonist authors as supplementing the medieval translations of Pseudo-Dionysius, the *Liber de causis*, Avicebron and Avicenna, as well as the translations of Proclus made by Moerbeke in the thirteenth century. In his list of Platonic works he included both Bessarion's *In calumniatorem* and 'quaedam speculationes' of Nicholas of Cusa, wanting apparently to have these two cardinals appear as underwriting the orthodoxy of his own approach. The omissions he makes in the letter lead to the same conclusion. No mention is made of Origen or Pletho, of Lull or the writers of the School of Chartres, no doubt because of scholastic reservations about their teaching.[58]

It was certainly for a different reason that Ficino made no reference to Thomas Aquinas in this history. In his *Theologia platonica* he had used Thomas' *Contra gentiles* extensively and extended, as Thomas had done, the Aristotelian notions of act and potency to explain the finitude of participated being. Both he and Thomas wanted to show the fundamental agreement between philosophy and Christian doctrine, but their approaches differed radically. Although Thomas had made much use of Neoplatonic sources, he tended increasingly to distance himself from the *platonici* as the incompatibility between Platonic philosophy and the apologetics he had based on Aristotle became clear to him. He had sought to show that revelation was necessary because, although philosophy could demonstrate the existence of God and man's immortality, knowledge of God's essence and man's true destiny was beyond its comprehension and belonged to the realm of supernatural theology. It was this separation of philosophy from theology that had made scholasticism abstract and intellectualistic and led to the introduction – so repugnant to the Byzantines at the Council of Florence – of 'cosmic' or worldly questions into the salvific science of theology.

Ficino's intention was to substitute 'Platonic theology' for this 'Christian philosophy'. Against the Thomists of the period following the Council of Basle, whose Aristotelianism was aimed at supplying reasons for submission to papal authority, he sought to provide 'Platonic reasons' supporting Christianity, for those – not only Latin and Byzantine Christians, but also Turkish Moslems – who could not accept a religion on authority alone.[59] He saw the Platonic theology he proposed as a pre-Christian adumbration of supernatural revelation. Just as God had granted to the Hebrews the wisdom which Moses brought down from Sinai, so also he raised up among the pagans philosophers like Hermes Trismegistus, Orpheus, Zoroaster and Pythagoras who had anticipated – however partially – the truths of the Christian faith. Plato was the Attic Moses who inherited this pristine theology. Far from separating philosophy and religion, Plato brought together in his own person both the philosopher and the priest. Although he remained on the level of the Mosaic law, his teaching foreshadowed Christian revelation. He was able, moreover, to support his teaching with Pythagorean and Socratic reasons accessible to all men.[60] The Platonic theology was therefore a religious doctrine inherent in man's nature. Although it had – like Judaism – been irrevocably superseded by Christianity, it offered the best introduction to the religion which had been supernaturally revealed to man in Christ. Its true heirs were John the Evangelist, Dionysius the Areopagite and Augustine. The later *platonici* – Plotinus in a pre-eminent way – had penetrated into many of the secrets of Plato's text, but, in the final analysis, they represented a heretical current in Platonism which left the main stream after it had become Christian. Because they did not recognise the equality of the word with God, they were unable to understand the myth of the *Phaedrus*. Behind Plato's charioteer was Christ himself, leading angels and men to God. Christ is the world-soul in whom all individual human souls participate. It is his Incarnation that makes man the knot, the link, holding the world together. Ficino concluded with a new dynamic understanding of the idea that man is the *imago Dei*: God became man so that man might become God.[61]

Ficino's attempt to formulate a Platonic metaphysics which would

59. Ficino 1964–70, I, pp. 35–7 (prooem.).
60. Letter to Prenninger in Klibansky 1981, pp. 45–7.
61. Ficino 1576, I, pp. 20–2 (*De Christiana religione* 16–18).

support the Christian doctrine of God ran counter to the Thomistic apologetics which the papacy had made its own after the Council of Basle. Ficino's diffidence saved him from condemnation; the same was not true of the youthful Giovanni Pico della Mirandola. The stages in the struggle between the two approaches are clearly reflected in the history of Pico's career. Pico was born in the year that Ficino began his Platonic studies. After studies in philosophy at Ferrara and Padua, he arrived in Florence in 1484, just as Ficino's translation of Plato was coming off the press. In the course of his university studies he had been reared in the Aristotelian tradition of the schools. The period at Padua influenced his intellectual development in a special way. He gained there a thorough acquaintance with the teachings of the scholastics, the Latin Averroists and Averroes himself. Even after he came to live in Florence, 'to explore the camp of the Platonists', he continued to invoke the authority of the great scholastic masters, Albertus Magnus, Thomas Aquinas, Henry of Ghent, Giles of Rome and Duns Scotus. Where many of the Florentines had turned, with Ficino, exclusively to Plato, Pico regarded all the various philosophies as but different expressions of the one truth.

In his earlier attempts to establish the harmony between all these philosophies, Pico also sought to show the fundamental agreement of philosophy with Christian doctrine. This effort was made, however, not in the spirit of the Thomistic idea of a Christian Aristotelianism, but rather through Proclus and the *prisci theologi* whom Ficino had made available. It was Pico himself who, inspired by the departed soul of Cosimo de' Medici, incited Ficino to translate and comment on Plotinus. His discovery, among cabalistic doctrines, of proofs for the Trinity and for the divinity of Christ could only confirm to this newcomer to the Florentine Academy the basic viability of Ficino's approach to the problem of the relationship between philosophy and religion. The famous 900 *Conclusiones* which he planned to dispute at Rome in 1486 provide an idea of the synthesis in which he planned to bring all this material together.

But the condemnation of his theses by Pope Innocent VIII in 1487 wrought a profound change in Pico. After the charge – made by the papal commission – that some of the theses were heretical because they effectively reduced faith to rational knowledge, Pico came progressively to abandon the *prisci theologi* and cabala. His ultimate submission to the Thomistic programme can, no doubt, be ascribed in part to the powerful influence of Girolamo Savonarola, himself author of Thomistic textbooks. It brought, in any event, the third period in the history of Florentine Platonism to a close.

At first Pico had tried, in his own way, to continue along the path Ficino had indicated. In his celebrated *Oratio de dignitate hominis* he outlined a metaphysical view of man's place in nature quite similar to that of the Florentine master. Man has a privileged place in the universe because of a decision of the creator himself. When the creation of the whole universe had been completed, God decided to add a being capable of admiring the greatness of the world and loving its beauty. Thus he undertook the creation of man. Since all the creator's gifts had by then been distributed among the other creatures, God decided that man should have a share of all the gifts that had been given to the others. For this reason, man has no fixed essence or nature. He is neither celestial nor earthly, neither mortal nor immortal. Possessing within himself the possibility of being all things, he is outside the hierarchy of beings. He may descend to become a plant or an animal; he may rise to become a celestial being or an angel, or he may even be united with God himself.[62] Several years later in the *Heptaplus*, a commentary on the opening verses of Genesis, Pico again stressed the idea that man is outside the hierarchy of beings and has no fixed essence. His exposition begins by distinguishing three different worlds – the elemental, the celestial and the supercelestial which make up the universe. After discussing this hierarchy, Pico introduces man as a new creation whose task it is to unite the other three worlds which God has made.[63]

Pico expressed these ideas with great originality. But his understanding of them placed him clearly in the tradition we have been tracing in this section. His notion of man as the bond and juncture of three worlds echoes the theme of man as microcosm that we have encountered in Nicholas of Cusa and Ficino. The notion of man as an incomplete nature brings to mind the idea of a *latitudo formarum* which was applied, as we shall see, by certain fourteenth-century scholastics even to the substantial forms of created things. Even where he is most original, Pico does not deny his indebtedness to the tradition. Whereas the *Oratio* stressed the notion that it is through his freedom that man has to perfect his nature, the *Heptaplus* recalled that man is an intellectual being, the unique nature who is able to know the whole of creation and in it its creator. Above all, Pico situated himself firmly in the theological tradition which sought to give reasons for Christian doctrines.

62. G. Pico 1942, pp. 102–6 (*Oratio*).   63. *Ibid.*, pp. 266–70, 300–4 (*Heptaplus* IV, prooem.; v.6).

As in Lull, Nicholas of Cusa and Ficino, the principal themes of his early thought come together in the person of Christ. For Pico, man is the consummation of all inferior natures, and in the same way Christ is the consummation of all men. Because man as the image of God is the bond which holds creation together, it was fitting that he should be joined in an ineffable union with Christ, who is the image of the invisible God, the first-born of all creation.[64]

The third period in the history of Florentine Platonism was characterised by a search for new sources, for sources which could give expression, within a metaphysical framework, to the new dynamic understanding of reality which distinguished the Renaissance period and show the fundamental agreement between true philosophy and the totality of Christian doctrine. Ficino drew on the pristine tradition found in the works of Hermes Trismegistus, Orpheus, Zoroaster and Pythagoras for this purpose. Pico cast his net even more widely, seeking to decode the pre-Christian revelation which he thought had been made by God in the cabala. His famous *Conclusiones* of 1486 contain statements taken not only from the scholastics, from Arabic, Hebrew and Greek commentators on Plato and Aristotle and from the *prisci theologi*, but also from the Jewish cabalists.

Cabala, the techniques of which Pico learnt from Spanish Jews who had been forced to seek a new home in Italy even before the catastrophe of 1492, was essentially a method of contemplation on Gods's attributes. Man can know nothing of God's hidden, inner nature. Only through his attributes can man know something of the divine life. The attributes describe God's inner life and are not – like the Neoplatonic emanations – outside of him. They name the stages in which the divine life pulsates. Cabala used, as did Ramon Lull, the image of the tree to describe the way in which creation reflects this divine life. God's inner nature is the hidden root of the tree, while the attributes are represented by its branches. The tree forms the skeleton of the universe, spreading its branches throughout the whole of creation to form the primordial man, Adam. Like the *Ars lulliana*, cabala used techniques for manipulating the letters of the Hebrew alphabet in order to discover such hidden meanings behind the text of the Bible. It was believed that when God gave the law to Moses, he also revealed to the chosen its secret meaning. This cabalistic tradition was said to have been passed down orally through the ages.

Pico recognised not only the similarity of the cabalistic techniques to

---

64. *Ibid.*, pp. 220, 308 (*Heptaplus* 1.7; v.7).

those of Lull's *Art*, but also similarity of the teachings of cabala to the philosophical ideas of Pythagoras and Plato which Ficino had found to be so close to Christianity. In the *Oratio* Pico tells us that when he had procured the books of the science of cabala, he found in them a religion which was not so much Mosaic as it was Christian: the mystery of the Trinity, the Incarnation of the word, the divinity of the Messiah, the same things about original sin, its expiation by Christ and the end of the world that we read in Paul and Dionysius the Areopagite, in Jerome and Augustine.[65] Similarly, in the *Heptaplus* Pico maintained that Moses hid, behind the account of creation, not only all the secrets of philosophy, but also foreshadowings of the coming of Christ. The mutual correspondences found in creation betwen the angelic, celestial and elemental worlds lead by way of the microcosm – which is man – to Christ, through whom alone creation can return to the creator.[66]

But the papal condemnation of the thesis that no science proves the divinity of Christ better than magic and cabala came slowly to work a change in Pico's attitude. The thesis was thought heretical because it seemed to make the assent of faith dependent on rational arguments. One of the members of the commission, in his refutation, charged Pico with seeking certitude of evidence rather than the firm adherence of faith.[67] In his *Oratio* Pico had, in fact, made extravagant claims for philosophy. Through it, he asserted, the soul can ascend to God himself. The knowledge of divine things is not qualitatively different from that of the other parts of philosophy. From the purification worked by dialectic and moral philosophy man may ascend by way of the illumination effected by natural philosophy to the perfection of theological knowledge.[68] In his *Conclusiones* Pico had maintained that on the principles of cabalistic science it is impossible to deny the Christian doctrine of the Trinity. The combinations of the letters of the name 'Jesus' prove that that he is God and the Son of God.[69] Already in the *Heptaplus*, however, Pico became more cautious. In this work he tell us that grace is necessary for knowledge of the doctrines of faith. Religion builds on philosophy, but only in the way in which grace builds on nature. Philosophy can take man no further than natural happiness. The wise men of this world know nothing of the true wisdom which theology is.[70]

65. *Ibid.*, p. 160 (*Oratio*). 66. *Ibid.*, pp. 168–98 (*Heptaplus*, prooem.; prooem. aliud).
67. See Carreras y Artau 1939–43, ii, pp. 560–3. 68. G. Pico 1942, pp. 120 (*Oratio*).
69. G. Pico 1973, pp. 83–4 (*Conclusiones cabalisticae secundum opinionem propriam*, concl. 5–8).
70. G. Pico 1942, pp. 324–38 (*Heptaplus* vii, prooem.).

The recognition of a type of knowledge accessible only through faith led Pico to modify his early conviction that all philosophies were but different expressions of the one truth. In the tract *De ente et uno* – composed some two years after the *Heptaplus* – he no longer speaks of proofs for the doctrines of the Trinity and Incarnation, but stresses instead that God dwells in darkness. In a long chapter which recalls in part Thomas Aquinas' questions on the same subject, he attempts to remove the imperfections in the names we apply to God, imperfections which derive from the created things they signify. In order to ascend to the dark cloud in which God dwells, man must enter into the *lux ignorantiae*. With a long citation from Pseudo-Dionysius, Pico concludes that all affirmations and all negations about God are equally impossible.[71]

Along with the claim for a philosophical knowledge of God's essence, all references to the *prisci theologi* and cabala have disappeared from the *De ente et uno*. Pici cites 'the Egyptians', Iamblichus, and Olympiodorus only to reject them. He maintains that the 'Platonists' of the Academy, in their opposition to Aristotle, have falsified the true teaching of Plato and exaggerated the differences between the founders of the two great schools. In the theses of 1486 Pico had made the fundamental harmony between Plato and Aristotle the first of his *Conclusiones paradoxae*. In the *Apologia* which he published a year later, he defended the notion that the principles of the two philosophies are in basic agreement. Pico intended to demonstrate in detail the *Concordia Platonis Aristotelisque* in a work which occupied his last years. But because this work was and remained unfinished, he undertook – at the request of Angelo Poliziano, who had given him an account of a dispute between himself and Lorenzo de' Medici concerning being and the One – to clarify in a separate monograph the relationship not between the later members of the schools, but between the two great philosophers themselves.

The main obstacle to this concordance was the Platonists' claim to possess a mystery unknown to Aristotle, the One beyond being, identified by them with the God of Christianity. This doctrine they opposed to the famous Aristotelian dictum *Ens et unum convertuntur*. The cornerstone in Pico's argument had necessarily to be an examination of the *Parmenides*, the Platonists' chief witness for their esoteric doctrine. He started by firmly denying the validity of the dialogue as evidence in a metaphysical discussion, maintaining that it cannot be considered a dogmatic tract, but only an exercise in dialectic. The idea of an unbridgeable gulf between the teaching of Plato and Aristotle has arisen not only from a misunderstanding

71. *Ibid.*, pp. 406–22 (*De ente et uno* 5).

of Plato, but also from an insufficient knowledge of Aristotle. Even granting that the first hypothesis of the *Parmenides* proclaims the 'One beyond being', it would still not follow that Plato had found a purer philosophical formula for God than Aristotle. For, according to Pico's interpretation, Aristotle also taught a transcendent God, who is the Good itself and the One beyond the being known to us, and he did so even more clearly than Plato had done. With the help of the distinction made by Thomas Aquinas between being itself and participated being, Pico maintains that God – the One – is identical with being itself, but above being in the second sense.[72]

In the *De ente et uno*, Pico was mounting a frontal assault on Ficino's account of Platonic metaphysics. The weapons he used were Thomistic distinctions. Not only the distinction of being itself and participated being, but also the scholastic doctrine of the transcendentals were taken over by him in their entirety.[73] The *De ente et uno* represents the abandonment of the long tradition which ran from Anselm and Lull to Nicholas of Cusa and Ficino in favour of the Christian Aristotelianism proposed by Thomas Aquinas. The rejection of the idea of a higher type of intellectual knowledge, through which the dynamic implications of the Christian dogmas of the Trinity and Incarnation could be harnessed for a new metaphysics, involved a radical change in the Renaissance view of man. Although Pico makes an appeal for the unity of mankind based on oneness, truth and goodness, his idea of man, which had in his earlier works been grounded in the concrete person of Christ, has become an abstract idea. Pico's language reflects that of Paul's Letter to the Colossians, but he avoids any reference to the Resurrection.[74] The distinction between natural and supernatural, which was meant to protect the clergy's role in the interpretation of revelation, has put an end to the idea of a cosmic Christ in philosophy. Similarly, Pico's espousal of Thomas Aquinas' account of the Aristotelian ontology meant the outright rejection of Ficino's reinterpretation of Platonic metaphysics. To argue as Pico does in the *De ente et uno* is in effect to do away with Ficino's attempt to introduce a dynamic moment into the divine unity by transferring a number of the attributes of the Plotinian mind to the One. To establish the agreement of Plato and Aristotle on Thomistic terms he was compelled to abandon the active conception of reality which had, up to his time, been the foremost characteristic of Renaissance philosophy.

72. *Ibid.*, pp. 388–406 (*De ente et uno* 1–4).   73. *Ibid.*, pp. 426–38 (*De ente et uno* 8–9).
74. *Ibid.*, pp. 438–40 (*De ente et uno* 10).

Pico's *De ente et uno* – along with the death of Savonarola and the fall of the Medici – marked a turning-point in the history of metaphysics as the science of divine things. It also marked the end of the third period of Florentine Platonism. Platonism continued to play an important role both in philosophy and in the arts and sciences. But the continuity of the tradition which understood reality dynamically – a tradition respected by Ficino's interpretation of Plato – was broken or became at least irrelevant for metaphysics as the science of God. After Pico, the history of metaphysics shifted from the problem of God to the problem of being. It is no accident that the Fifth Lateran Council determined not only the supremacy of the pope to the councils, but also the metaphysical demonstrability of man's immortality.

The tradition of a dynamic understanding of reality which had been represented by Lull, Nicholas of Cusa and Ficino became associated with Renaissance magic and occultism. The idea of man's creativity was paralleled by the notion of a magical control over nature and by the vision of a new technology. These ideas led, in turn, to the demand for a new system of the sciences and to the works of men like Henricus Cornelius Agrippa and Giordano Bruno. At the same time, the Renaissance was characterised by a great explosion of knowledge. The immense amount of traditional knowledge which classical scholars made available rendered the Aristotelian encyclopaedia of the sciences less and less tenable. Juan Luis Vives and Petrus Ramus made great efforts to develop ways of presenting this great body of knowledge in a methodical fashion for the purpose of instruction. Both of these strains came together around the end of the sixteenth century, but they do not belong to the history of metaphysics. They are treated in other parts of this volume.

METAPHYSICS AS THE SCIENCE OF BEING

The authors we have considered up to this point developed the doctrine of God independently of and often in avowed opposition to the Aristotelian metaphysics. Their ideas can, however, be described as metaphysical to the extent that they involve reality not accessible to the senses. The difference concerned less the subject-matter than the method. Aristotle's approach to reality comprised two steps: an inductive one, which attempts to discover the universal principles of the world by analysing its appearances, and a deductive one, which tries to reconstruct the world from the principles which have been discovered. On the basis of repeated sense experiences, reason first uncovers the identity which underlies the perceived mutability, the universal form or essence. Ascending thus from the concrete, sensible thing to the general concept, from the particular to the universal judgement, reason arrives ultimately at the common, first principles of all reality and all science, such as the law of contradiction, which Aristotle discusses in the fourth book of the *Metaphysics* (IV.3–5). In a second step the philosopher then descends from these principles by way of syllogistic demonstration to the individual phenomena with which he began. Aristotle found the model for this deductive step in contemporary geometry: a systematic presentation of laboriously won knowledge as conclusions from principles which are true, evident and indemonstrable. But he brought this method into the context of his own thought by requiring that the syllogistic conclusions be linked by the fixed essences discovered in the inductive first step. Aristotle thus does not distinguish, as we do, between science and philosophy. For him the particular speculative sciences, like physics and mathematics, are philosophical, but they are distinguished from metaphysics because they deal with a portion of reality and its proximate principles, whereas metaphysics enquires into all reality and its ultimate principles. But Aristotle does not decide whether this science is to be 'wisdom' in the sense of dealing with all reality, 'first philosophy' in the sense of investigating the first principles of all science or 'divine science' as the science of a supra-sensible, first reality.

The Renaissance authors we have been considering found little they could use in Aristotle's approach. Their goal was a higher type of knowledge, an intellectual vision which transcended not only sense-perception but also reason itself. Nicholas of Cusa went furthest in this regard. In his view the upward path to the One is not the ascent from one type of being to another. Rather each individual being is the manifestation of the unfolding dynamism of the infinite and each manifestation images in itself the whole of reality. Instead of a hierarchical chain of being Nicholas stressed the interrelatedness of things as the proper object of knowledge. These dynamic relationships are the symbols of God, not the static essences of things. The intellect encounters the infinite beyond reason in the coincidence of opposites. Man's intellectual vision is a *docta ignorantia*, an 'ignorance' because it is cut off from a knowledge of the essences of things, but 'learned' because it attains certain knowledge by way of conjecture.

When he writes that we know truth in the otherness of conjecture[75]

75. Nicholas of Cusa 1932–, III, p. 58 (*De coniecturis* I.11).

Nicholas alludes to Ramon Lull's approach to the question of the knowledge of supra-sensible reality. Wanting to demonstrate with necessary reasons the Christian doctrines of the Trinity and Incarnation to non-believers, Lull rejected the Aristotelian syllogism which proceeds by way of essences in favour of a higher form of proof resembling Plato's dialectical method of accepting a statement provisionally in order to discover whether or not it implies a contradiction. His approach regards beliefs and opinions as conjectures or hypotheses and attempts to supply a sufficient reason for assent through a negative type of understanding. The question which is implicit in every belief or opinion is first expressed in the form of two contradictory hypotheses. Then in accordance with the principle that a proposition is necessary when its contradictory implies a contradiction, the argument concludes to the truth of one of the hypotheses by drawing out the consequences of the other and showing that they are impossible. Lull's method wants to ascend from belief to a higher type of understanding in which the intellect experiences itself as the interpretation of truth, recognising that it cannot assent to the opposite conclusion. His method is clearly related to the *fides quaerens intellectum* of Anselm of Canterbury and the notion of necessary reasons for the faith which were sought by Anselm, Richard of St Victor and others in the twelfth century. For the history of metaphysics the distinction between Lull's approach and that of Aristotle is important because it provides the reason for the scholastic conception of the science of supra-sensible reality as the science of being rather than as a doctrine of God.

Around the turn of the thirteenth century – in a step which marks the beginning of scholasticism in the strict sense of the term – the masters in the newly established Latin universities consciously rejected Anselm's programme. Traditionally the task of the theologians had been the presentation of the teaching of the Bible and the Church Fathers. But as a result of the twelfth-century translations from Greek and Arabic, a vast amount of new scientific material complicated their task immensely. Their answer to this challenge was the idea of a scientific presentation of theological doctrine, an idea which in turn forced them to try to locate their teaching within the Aristotelian classification of the sciences as it was known through the works of Boethius and various Arabic treatises. Some of the theologians maintained in accordance with theology's salvific purpose that their science was to be related to Aristotle's practical sciences; others emphasised the speculative aspect of the doctrine of God and thus were confronted with the problem of the relationship between Christian theology and Aristotle's metaphysics.

All of these authors, however, agreed that their explanation of traditional doctrine had to be in accord with Aristotle's conception of deductive science. Aristotle's conception lent itself to their enterprise not only because the articles of faith could be taken as the axioms or indemonstrable principles for a deductive presentation of biblical and patristic teaching. It also provided a systematic place for the apologetic side of the theologian's task. With the expansion of Europe in the territories around the Mediterranean basin and the increasing missionary activity of the newly founded mendicant orders, the faith had to be presented not only to believers but also to Saracens, Jews and the pagan Tartars who had recently invaded the Near East. While Christian doctrines could not be proved, it was thought that their acceptance could be shown to be at least reasonable because they were congruent with fundamental philosophical doctrines like the existence of God and the immortality of the human soul. For this reason revealed theology and metaphysics were brought together in terms of Aristotle's theory of science. According to the Philosopher the particular sciences have their own proper principles but there are common or general principles for all the sciences. The scholastics proposed therefore employing the articles of faith as the proper principles of theological science and using Aristotelian metaphysics for the common principles of basic philosophical doctrines.[76]

It was, however, not only Aristotle's methodology that led the theologians to opt for his programme as opposed to that of Anselm. Aristotle's ideas provided an ontological foundation for traditional theological concepts, such as 'essence', 'nature', 'person' and 'subsistence' in trinitarian theory, and 'substance' and 'accident' in the theory of grace and transubstantiation. His fixed essences and static conception of reality matched, moreover, their own hierarchical view of the world. Most importantly, his conception of metaphysics as the science of being enabled them to maintain the necessity of revelation for knowledge of God's nature. The question of the proper subject-matter of metaphysics was, no doubt, occasioned by the ambiguities in Aristotle's presentation and by the divergencies among his Greek and Arabic interpreters, but it had its theological aspect as well. Medieval commentators on the *Metaphysics* were forced to take up the question whether Aristotle thought of his science as first philosophy, divine science or the science of being. All the earlier commentators, however, saw this question against the background of the scientific character of revealed theology.

76. See Lang 1964; Lohr 1985.

Thomas Aquinas, for example, clearly went beyond the literal interpretation of Aristotle's text when he held that the relationship of being in
general – the subject of metaphysics as the science of being – to the first substance – the subject of divine science – was one of causality. With one eye on
the theological doctrine of creation, Thomas explained that the subject-
matter of metaphysics is *ens in communi*, that is, all the things that fall under
the notion of 'being in general', and that the doctrine of God was included
in this framework as the doctrine of the principle or cause of being. His
position served several purposes. First, it made it possible for him to
maintain the unity of metaphysics as a science, since according to Aristotle a
science treats not only the subjects belonging to its genus, but also their
essential properties and principles. Secondly, it enabled him to exclude the
possibility of an independent natural theology. For Thomas God is not one
of the subjects metaphysics deals with, but their cause. Thirdly, Thomas'
position on the subject of metaphysics provided an argument for the
necessity of revealed doctrine. Although the theologian as apologist can
demonstrate God's existence on the principle of causality, God's nature
remains beyond human understanding since our knowledge takes its
departure from sense experience. In Thomas' succinct formulation, we can
know *that* God is, but not *what* he is.[77] Metaphysical investigation aims at
the knowledge of God, but for the scholastic theologian this knowledge is
accessible only to the believer.

Decisive for the conception of metaphysics which was dominant among
scholastic thinkers during the period covered in this volume was the analysis
made by Duns Scotus, a thinker for whom the connection between
revelation and metaphysics as the science of being is even closer than it is for
Thomas Aquinas. Scotus begins with an examination of traditional
metaphysics which amounts to a critique of natural reason. Aristotle's
metaphysics, he maintains, does not get beyond physical reality. Because
he was compelled – not having access to revelation – to take sense
knowledge as his point of departure, Aristotle could discover principles and
draw conclusions, but apply them only in the physical order. His
metaphysics is consequently mixed with error and unable to answer
questions of God's nature and man's destiny. But the revelation of the
existence of spiritual reality has opened a new horizon for metaphysics.
Since the mind is able to comprehend immaterial reality from the moment
that it attains access to it, Scotus concluded that the first object of the

77. Thomas Aquinas 1963c, I, p. 13 (1.3, div.).

intellect is not the *ratio quidditatis sensibilis*, as Aristotle and Thomas had maintained, but rather *ens sub ratione entis* – a concept which is so broad that it includes everything whose existence is not contradictory, which is transcendent because it is anterior to all modes and determinations and which must be univocal because it applies to all things in the same way.

Duns Scotus pleaded accordingly for the elaboration of a new, autonomous metaphysics, independent of the physical sciences. In view of revelation it is possible to conceive a pure metaphysics, not limited by human faculties of knowledge. This new science of being would be open to all reality, pure knowing of pure knowability. The subject of this science is not, however, God as the personal, triune God known through revelation. Such knowledge is beyond science, which can deal only with universal concepts. Metaphysics can grasp the divinity only as infinite being. In order to be able to make certain assertions about immaterial reality Scotus introduced, in addition to the simple properties of being like unity, truth and goodness, disjunctive transcendentals like act and potency, identity and otherness, necessity and contingency, infinity and finitude. Whereas Averroes maintained that only physics, by beginning with motion, can prove the existence of God as prime mover, Avicenna made much use of the dialectics of necessity and contingency in order to find a metaphysical proof. For Scotus the most fundmental disjunction is that of infinity and finitude. Since the members of the disjunction imply one another, the metaphysician can conclude from limited being, known *a posteriori*, to the existence of the other pole, unlimited being.

These conclusions involve some basic changes in the conception of metaphysics in its relation not only to revealed theology, but also to the speculative science of physics, which Aristotle regarded as 'second philosophy' in opposition to metaphysics as 'first philosophy'. When the metaphysician arrives at the knowledge of infinite being, he has the same unclear and confused notion of God that one would have of man when he knew only what the notion 'animal' means. Revealed theology as the knowledge of a triune God is, therefore, still necessary, but metaphysics with its analysis of the notion of being supplies the basis for its scientific development. Moreover, since metaphysics as the science of being as being excludes a natural knowledge of God as God, one might envisage the possibility of a natural theology which had as its subject God as prime mover, using physical proofs like those of Averroes. In fact, one of Scotus' pupils, Nicholas Bonet, followed this course, distinguishing for the first time clearly between *Metaphysica* and *Theologia naturalis* in the titles of the

corresponding books of his philosophical *Summa*. Foreshadowing some of
the systematic works of the sixteenth century, his *Metaphysica* deals with the
nature and subject of the science and the properties and categories of
being.[78] Finally, the notion of finite being, opposed to infinite being, but
including both immaterial and material reality, involves a category of being
unknown to Aristotle and makes possible the idea of a science which studies
corporeal reality in a metaphysical way, as *ens mobile*, in contradistinction to
the Aristotelian physics, whose subject is *corpus mobile* – a cosmology
distinct from natural science.

   In spite of these efforts to establish an agreement between revelation and
the science of being, philosophy and theology in the course of the
fourteenth century drifted farther and farther apart. From the beginning of
the thirteenth century, when the schoolmen first turned their attention to
Aristotle and the great scientific works of antiquity, an enormous amount
of progress had been made in natural philosophy. By about the year 1300
the West had caught up with Islamic lands in the natural sciences and
surpassed them in technological innovation. These advances gained for the
university faculties of arts a new autonomy. Freed from its traditional role as
the handmaid of theology, the arts faculty became an institution equal to the
faculties of medicine, law and theology. The breach became permanent in
the year 1277 through the condemnation by the Bishop of Paris of 40
theological and 179 philosophical propositions. Since the philosophical
propositions were condemned on the ground that they entailed consequences contrary to revealed teachings, the theologians were forced to turn
their attention from the composition of systematic summaries of Christian
doctrine to the positive task of finding the sources of the propositions they
had regarded as axiomatic. At the same time the condemnation constrained
the philosophers to attempt to free natural science from the tyranny of
Aristotle's worldview. The fact that many of Aristotle's doctrines – his
determinism, his notion of the eternity of the world, his denial of God's
power to create an extramundane void or a plurality of worlds – were in
conflict with Christian teachings made it impossible to maintain that he had
spoken the whole truth. A good part of the progress which was made in
fourteenth-century science was rendered possible only by a rejection of the
metaphysical assumptions which lay behind Aristotle's astronomy and
theory of local motion or his neglect of certain areas in mathematics like the
theory of proportions and infinite series.

---

78. Concerning Bonet see Lohr 1972a, pp. 284–6.

Throughout the fourteenth century the interest of the masters of arts centred on natural philosophy and the linguistic speculation which accompanied it. Although the progress which was made in these fields demanded a general reassessment of Aristotle's theory of science, metaphysical speculation on the part of scholastic authors during this period seems to have dried up. Comparatively few commentaries on Aristotle's *Metaphysics* were written, and among those that were one notes a shift in attention from the earlier attempt to forge a link between theology and metaphysics to an effort to clarify the relationship between metaphysics and physics. Jean Buridan, for example, who himself contributed much to the fourteenth-century progress in logic and natural philosophy,[79] held that metaphysics is the most excellent of the speculative sciences because it is prior to all the others. He paid deference, of course, to the idea that revealed theology is the most perfect science, but noted that it is a science *sui generis* because it is founded on the articles of faith. Metaphysics is prior to mathematics and physics because it is the most universal science, its subject-matter – the concept of being – including not only material things, but also immaterial reality like God and the intelligences. Metaphysics is also the most certain of the sciences since it grounds the principles of all the particular sciences, while its own principles are evident and universally valid. But although Buridan thus emphasised the role of metaphysics as first philosophy, he questioned Aristotle's division of the speculative sciences according to degrees of abstraction from matter. He maintained that metaphysics and physics both deal with the same subjects: things mutable and immutable, their causes, the prime mover. They differ, however, because physics considers the principles of things to the extent that they are principles of change, whereas metaphysics considers them as the principles of being. The task of demonstrating the existence of God belongs therefore only to metaphysics. Physics cannot ascend beyond an immaterial prime mover or prove that the prime mover it discovers is identical with God.

The field in which the greatest advances in natural philosophy were made was that known as the *latitudo formarum* or the mathematical theory of the intensity of qualities. This theory was related to metaphysical notions which were revolutionary and which, had they been exploited, would have meant the end of the static, Aristotelian conception of reality. The theory of the *latitudo formarum* had its origin in one of those strange combinations of the theological with the philosophical which characterised scholasticism. For

79. Concerning Buridan see Lohr 1970, pp. 161–83; A. Ghisalberti 1975.

the schoolmen, following Aristotle, virtues like charity and qualities like heat were accidental forms. In order to deal with such problems as the way in which a person grows in charity or a body grows hotter, Duns Scotus suggested a quantitative treatment of increases or decreases in a quality (heat) by way of the addition or subtraction of degrees of intensity (temperature). By a quantitative treatment Scotus meant not simply an extrinsic assimilation of quality to quantity. His suggestion is rather connected with the idea of degrees of perfection which is implicit in his dialectical approach to reality. Since the terms 'infinity' and 'finitude' originally refer to quantity, they cannot be transferred without qualification to perfections which have no dimensions. He distinguished therefore between a *quantitas virtutis*, referring to the intensity of a perfection and admitting an actual infinity, and a *quantitas extensa*, characterised by three dimensions and admitting only a potential or indefinite infinity. It was in the former sense that the late fourteenth-century scholastics understood the measure of the intensity of a quality (temperature, for example) and not as the extension of a quality in a subject (the quantity of heat).

In accordance with the general tendency in Renaissance thought to emphasise the dynamic aspect of reality, the masters in the faculties of arts concentrated on the problem of variations in intensity, especially in connection with local motion. At Oxford methods were developed to express the amounts by which a quality (the local motion, say, of a free-falling body) increases or decreases in intensity (velocity) as a function of its extension (time). On the basis of this work a radically new conception of geometry made its appearance at Paris. Nicole Oresme advanced the idea of representing the rate of change of an intensity graphically by plotting intensity as a latitude (ordinate) against extension as a longitude (abscissa). The notion of expressing continuous variability in terms of coordinates marks a break with the static geometry of pure form which the West had inherited from antiquity in favour of a geometry of motion in which figures are generated by the movements of points and lines. The difference of approach may be illustrated by two possible ways of formulating definitions in geometry. The circumference of a circle can be defined statically as the locus of all points in a plane at a given distance from a centre or dynamically as the curve generated by a point moving in a plane at a constant distance from a centre.

The metaphysical significance of these developments lies not only in the fact that we encounter in them the same dynamic view of reality that we have found in writers like Ramon Lull. They are also important because they led some scholastic theologians to attempt to generalise the ideas of the masters of arts. Jean de Ripa, a Franciscan theologian who read the *Sententiae* at Paris at about the same time that Oresme's work was published, took the decisive step. Whereas the work of the artists concerned accidental forms, Ripa introduced the notion of variability into substantial forms. In connection with the fourteenth-century debates about the beatific vision, he sought to define the conditions under which a union of creature and creator is possible. For this purpose he had recourse to the Scotist dialectic of infinity and finitude. But whereas Scotus emphasised the contingency and the structural not-being which finite reality includes, Ripa attempted to define the upper limits of the activity of finite reality. For him forms are accordingly not static, immutable essences, but include an ontological intensity which can be measured as a distance between the relative nothingness of finite reality and a supreme terminus to which it tends as to its own unattainable perfection.[80] Both forms of the *latitudo formarum* then found their place in the metaphysics of Paul of Venice. Paul, who brought these doctrines from Oxford and Paris to Padua about the beginning of the fifteenth century, not only included the *latitudo formarum* under the categories quality and habitus, but also recognised a *latitudo perfectionalis entium*, or grades of ontological perfection measured according to their distance from a zero degree. It was probably in this form that Nicholas of Cusa became acquainted with the doctrine during the period of his studies in the University of Padua.

Nicholas knew the works of Archimedes and the discussion of Zeno's paradoxes in the *Parmenides* (128ff.) of Plato, but when he sought mathematical symbols to illustrate his conception of metaphysics he turned not to the classical geometry of form, but to Oresme's new geometry of motion. Nicholas approached the problem in terms of knowledge rather than of being. He sought to aid the mind in its ascent to the absolutely infinite by way of three steps.[81] The first was the consideration of finite mathematical figures, figures which are generated by the motion of points, lines and planes. Just as for Oresme a line was generated by the motion of a point, so also Nicholas defined the line as the unfolding or explication of a point. From the new geometry's concern with the problem of continuous variation, he concluded that knowledge consists in the determination of proportions or ratios and that perfect exactitude in measurement is consequently unattainable. In a second step the mind ascends by transferring

80. Concerning Jean de Ripa see Combes 1956; Vignaux 1959.
81. Nicholas of Cusa 1932–, I, pp. 24–5 (*De docta ignorantia* I.12).

these considerations to infinite figures. From the method of definition of, say, a point along a line in terms of its movement from a minimum to a maximum value, Nicholas learnt the correct method of dealing with the infinite and the infinitesimal not merely as potentialities, but as the actualities which are the upper and lower limits of the activity of finite reality. Wanting to illustrate his idea that for the understanding of dynamic reality a *transcensus* from rational to intellectual knowledge is necessary, he took the example of a polygon as a variable magnitude inscribed in a circle. For rational knowledge the polygon and the circle are fixed essences which exclude one another, because according to the principle of contradiction an attribute cannot at the same time belong and not belong to a subject. But if we, by conjecture, imagine a polygon the number of sides of which increases to infinity, we can see, by the vision of the intellect, that the polygon with a maximum number of sides will coincide with the circle. This is a conclusion which is not bound by the limitations of empirical observation and to which the intellect cannot withhold its assent. In a third and final step the mind then extends these conclusions to the absolutely infinite God. Oresme had remarked that for a form which was represented graphically by a semi-circle the rate of change reaches a minimum at the point of maximum intensity. Similarly, Nicholas maintained that in the absolutely infinite One, to whom no finite thing can be set in proportion, maximum and minimum coincide.

The fourteenth-century achievements in natural philosophy were not limited to physics and geometry. Important advances were also made in chemistry, geology and biology – sciences to which Albertus Magnus had given the impetus a hundred years earlier. Among the works which formed his Aristotelian encyclopaedia of the sciences, the commentaries *De meteoris*, *De mineralibus* and *De animalibus* enjoyed a vast manuscript diffusion in the fourteenth and fifteenth centuries. Problems like the pre-existence of forms in matter, the persistence of elemental forms in compounds and the way that the soul informs the embryo were discussed at Paris in terms of his synthesis. But because Aristotle's encyclopaedia was understood as a system of the sciences, some Parisian masters of arts at the beginning of the fifteenth century also turned their attention to Albertus' *Metaphysica* and *Liber de causis et processu universitatis* for the philosophical foundations for the solution of such problems. In these authors we encounter a view of reality not unlike that which we have discovered in Lull, Nicholas of Cusa and Jean de Ripa. In dealing, for example, with the traditional question of the distinction between essence and existence, Johannes de Nova Domo, who taught in the arts faculty at Paris until about 1420,[82] employed the dynamic image of a river flowing from its source and maintained that the essence of a thing is that from which its existence proceeds. For the intrinsic term of such activity he spoke of an *esse essentiae*, and for the extrinsic term, of an *esse existentiae*. Since the distinction between essence and existence is thus not a real one, Johannes rejected the opinion – proposed by Thomas Aquinas – that spiritual beings each form a distinct species and held that they are numerically distinct, the principle of individuation among them being their *quod est*.

The significance of the authors like Johannes de Nova Domo who turned to Albertus' metaphysical works lay not only in the fact that they sought to transform the traditional scholastic encyclopaedia of the sciences by integrating into it the active conception of reality which had been developed by some of the masters of arts. They also attempted explicitly to incorporate the earlier writers we have considered in the first section of this chapter into their synthesis. They seem to have known Ramon Lull through the works which he left to the Carthusian monastery of Vauvert near Paris. Heimeric de Campo, who taught in the arts faculty at the University of Cologne from about 1425, seems also to have learnt of the speculative side of Lull's thought through Nicholas of Cusa. He had studied at Paris under Johannes de Nova Domo and met Nicholas at Cologne when the latter arrived there from Padua. Heimeric took up Lull's understanding of reality as a triadic structure, but he attempted to bring it into accord with scholasticism by expressing it in terms of Johannes' distinction of essence, existence and *quod est*.

Heimeric was aware that Lull's view of reality implied an understanding of the relationship between faith and reason radically different from that which the scholastics had worked out in the thirteenth century. In the scholastic understanding the task of the theologian was to present Christian doctrine systematically. Reason had the function of ordering the data; faith provided the principles for the presentation. In Heimeric's understanding, as in that of Lull, faith provided a conjecture or hypothesis which the intellect sought to understand by eliminating other possibilities. This was not simply a theoretical question; it concerned the structure of medieval society itself. Specific to scholasticism was the notion that the presentation of Christian doctrine should be in accordance with Aristotle's theory of science. The scholastics took the articles of faith as the indemonstrable

---

82. Concerning Johannes de Nova Domo see Meersseman 1933–5, *passim*; Lohr 1971, p. 264.

axioms for the presentation because thereby the clergy's understanding of itself as the interpreter of the tradition was assured. The fourteenth-century progress in natural philosophy implied a different understanding of Aristotle's theory – science as research rather than as deductive presentation – and a different conception of the scientist: as a seeker after truth rather than as a member of a privileged class in possession of it. But up to Heimeric's time the masters of arts seem to have taken the institutional structure of the university as given and concerned themselves rather with the solution of individual problems in natural philosophy than with the theory of science which their work implied.

The inner crisis which thus affected scholasticism at the beginning of the fifteenth century was also concealed by the understanding of metaphysics as the science of being. As divine science metaphysics clearly belonged to the theological faculty's domain, but as first philosophy it was the concern of the masters of arts. Metaphysics was understood as the science of being in order to bridge this gap, but the Albertist attempt to understand essence and existence in a new way brought the crisis to the surface. We do not know how Heimeric would have solved the problem of clerical and lay participation in science, but his approach can perhaps be divined by his position in the conciliar debate. Employing the distinction between essence, existence and *quod est*, he understood the church as composed of an apostolic shepherd who governs and a catholic flock which gives its consent, both brought together in a conciliar fold. His Lullian interpretation of the Albertist distinction thus enabled him to assert to the full two rival concepts of ecclesiastical authority, the hierarchical and the popular. But this solution could only serve to make more critical the situation of metaphysics as the science of being between a clerical theology founded on revelation and a secular science based solely on human reason.

The new science was a source of concern to many who saw the tradition of evangelical faith endangered by rationalism and extreme realism. Jean Gerson, Chancellor of the University of Paris and a leading figure at the Council of Constance,[83] maintained that revelation is the foundation of all the sciences because metaphysics (as first philosophy) grounds the particular philosophical disciplines and for metaphysics revelation is necessary. Because the sciences can only comprehend the essences of things through concepts, they deal with an intra-mental world. The function of metaphysics is to establish contact with extra-mental reality through the concept of

---

83. Concerning Gerson see Bauer 1973.

being. But it is impossible for the natural powers of reason to comprehend reality in its entirety. Although God is being in the supreme degree, man is not able to understand his nature as creator. The *conceptus divinus* which the *conceptus entis* must include is therefore beyond human reason. Only on the intellectual level of faith and mystical theology can man approach a knowledge of God which would ground the possibility of knowledge and truth and make metaphysics possible.

Gerson knew that he was writing in a time of profound crisis, a time in which the medieval conception of the church and the scholastic conception of metaphysics with which it was so closely connected were threatened at their foundations. He objected to the extreme realism with which Wyclif had tried to give his ideas of religious reform an ontological foundation because he thought that the supposition of necessary essences in God would limit God's supreme freedom. On the same ground he opposed Ripa's Scotist transpositions of abstractions into reality. He was also acquainted with the Parisian Lullism of the early fifteenth century and wrote repeatedly against Lull's notion of necessary reasons for the articles of the faith. Although Gerson, along with many of his contemporaries, accepted Anselm's ontological conception of God, he argued against natural theologies which would confuse the Christian God with the Good. Were God a nature which must diffuse itself, it would be possible to deduce the properties of his nature – a conclusion which is contrary to God's absolute freedom. There is a profound unity behind the positions with which Gerson confronted the errors of his day. Appealing to Scripture, he pleaded for the notion of God as creator and supremely free. But because of the divine liberty, man can know of God only those things he has revealed. Because revelation is necessary, theology cannot be equated with the secular sciences which are accessible to the layman. Gerson rejected Lull's theory of necessary reasons because it implied a conception of theology, the church and scientific endeavour itself which is not conformable to this clerical understanding.

The adoption of Lull's ideas by Nicholas of Cusa called forth a somewhat different reaction on the part of the Heidelberg professor Johannes Wenck. Wenck had been an adherent of the Council of Basle and stood at first on the side of the Albertists. But when confronted with Nicholas' *De docta ignorantia*, he rejected the notion of a higher, innate type of understanding and returned to Thomas Aquinas' emphasis on the origin of all human knowledge in sense-perception. Thomas' epistemology also found supporters at Cologne. Gerard de Monte opposed Heimeric's interpretation of

Albertus and tried to show the concordance of Albertus and Thomas. In Paris the secular master of arts Johannes Versor gave both form and substance to this budding renaissance of Thomistic doctrine. Versor composed commentaries in the form of questions on almost all of the texts in the university corpus of Aristotle's works. His questions on the *Metaphysics* are based on Thomas' doctrine with some important precisions reflecting the Scotist teachings we have seen above. Metaphysics is a universal science comprehending all types of created reality. The *ens in quantum ens* which metaphysics studies is not to be undersood as the being common to God and creatures, but rather the being which is common to created things, whether material or immaterial. Metaphysics deals therefore with being as it is divided into substance and accidents. God is treated in metaphysics only as the cause of being. The concept of being is analogous with respect to its inferiors, but not with respect to God. There is no particular science of the intelligences; they are treated in the universal science of metaphysics as created immaterial being. Corporeal things are treated in metaphysics *sub ratione entis*, and in the particular science of physics as *corpus mobile*.

Whereas the fourteenth century was quite limited in the production of works on metaphysics but very rich in new approaches to metaphysical problems, in the following century we find the situation reversed. From the time of the Council of Constance to that of Luther almost as many commentaries on Aristotle's *Metaphysics* were composed as in the preceding two centuries taken together. In the universities the courses on physics and mathematics lost the popularity they had enjoyed; the courses on metaphysics and ethics became the most esteemed – and the most expensive. But at the same time an increasing tendency to return to the classical teachers – Thomas, Albertus, Duns Scotus – manifested itself. Many of the commentaries written in this period were super-commentaries on Buridan and Versor. In spite of humanistic ideas of interpretation, scholastic commentaries of the fifteenth century were not exegetical, but strictly philosophical in character. They covered only the first twelve books of Aristotle's work, generally omitting book xi and occasionally book iii or even i–iii. Most of the commentaries were written in the form of questions, allowing an increasing independence of Aristotle's text. Fourteenth-century problems in the theory of science notwithstanding, the commentators neglected the question of metaphysics as first philosophy. Those authors who took the subject-matter of metaphysics to be being as it is divided into substance and accidents tended to comment on Aristotle's work in conjunction with his *Categories,* whereas those who thought of metaphysics primarily as the doctrine of God tended to treat the *Metaphysics* in conjunction with the *Physics* and *De anima* foreshadowing the later enumeration of metaphysical realities: God, the world and the human soul. A corresponding tendency to neglect Aristotle's *De caelo, De generatione et corruptione* and *Meteorology* can be observed; the biological works and the works of moral philosophy were taken up by a completely new type of philosopher.

The termination of the Council of Basle marked a turning-point in the history of metaphysics as the science of being. The victory of the papacy put an end to attempts like those of Heimeric de Campo and the young Nicholas of Cusa to use the ideas of Ramon Lull to support the theory of the supremacy of the Council. The distinctive interpretation of the philosophy of Albertus Magnus which was developed by Heimeric and Johannes de Nova Domo disappeared from Paris after the Anglo-Burgundian alliance and was able to maintain itself for a brief time only in the universities, like Cologne and Cracow, which adhered to the Council. The victory of the papacy was accompanied by a return to the ideas of Thomas Aquinas. This was due not only to Thomas' ecclesiology, but also to his position on the relationship between philosophy and revealed doctrine and, more fundamentally, to the conception of clerical and lay participation in science which could be derived from it. Thomas had distinguished between truths which can be proved by reason, like the existence of God and the immortality of the human soul, and truths which are accessible only to faith, like the doctrines of the Trinity and the Incarnation. For the latter type of supernatural truths revelation is absolutely necessary, but because of the human inclination to error, revelation can support reason even for some doctrines which can be demonstrated rationally. Philosophy is autonomous in its own realm, but philosophical doctrines which entail consequences contrary to revealed doctrine must be rejected.

Whereas Scotism and Buridanism had been represented more or less continuously in Paris, Thomism came to the fore only about the time when the university was reorganised after the Council and the end of the Hundred Years War. Significantly, it was not the Dominicans, but rather secular masters of arts like Johannes Versor who first espoused Thomas' doctrine. The liberty which the Thomist position allowed in the resolution of philosophical questions had to appeal to teachers concerned to preserve the independence of the arts faculty and sustain the progress which had been made in natural philosophy during the preceding century. At the same time, the theological faculty found Thomas' doctrine acceptable because his conception of reality matched their own hierarchical view of the world and because his doctrine of creation avoided any emanationist understanding of the relationship between God and the world. Above all, Thomas' epistemology offered a qualified guarantee for clerical authority. His teaching that all human knowledge has its origin in sense experience enabled the theologians to maintain that revelation is both necessary and reasonable, necessary because God's essence must remain beyond man's natural understanding, reasonable because revelation agrees with and supplements basic philosophical conclusions. Thomas' rejection of the view that revealed doctrines are accessible to the layman through a type of intellectual knowledge higher than reason made it possible for the clergy to maintain its view of itself as the unique interpreter of the tradition.

Basically, the idea of a Christian Aristotelianism which fifteenth-century masters of arts at Paris found adumbrated in Thomas Aquinas, the idea of a philosophy autonomous in its own realm, but guided both positively and negatively by revelation, represented a kind of pragmatic sanction, defining the powers of the clergy in its relation to science. The idea was closely connected with the situation after the Council of Basle. Just as the papacy had to recognise the authority of secular rulers in the temporal sphere, so also the clergy – whose function had traditionally been that of teaching – had to admit the self-sufficiency of the secular sciences and to concede the limitation of its role in this sphere to that of surveillance. An important role in formulating the idea of such an Aristotelianism was played by the Thomist conception of metaphysics as the science of being. On the one hand, Thomas' view enabled the theologians to recognise the autonomy of the philosophical sciences, while continuing to maintain the scientific character of their own discipline. Whereas the particular sciences, including theology, have their own proper principles and methods, metaphysics was, in the Thomistic view, a general science of all reality and supplied the common principles for all the sciences. On the other hand, the fundamental law both of Aristotle's logic and of his metaphysics understood as the science of being, the law of contradiction, provided the theoretical grounding for the theologians' negative control over science, the condemnation of doctrines which entailed consequences contrary to revelation. It was, in fact, in this way that the thirteenth and fourteenth centuries had eliminated many of the foreign elements – doctrines like that of the unicity of the human intellect – in the Aristotelianism which the West had inherited from Arabic thinkers. The fifteenth century continued this process. Just at the time when in Italy many were proclaiming that Platonic philosophy was more in accord with Christianity than Aristotelian, the scholastics in Paris were excluding the extreme realism of Wyclif, the emanationism of the Albertists and the idea of an intellectual type of knowledge higher than reason on the ground that these doctrines conflicted with the divine freedom or the notion of a gratuitous revelation.

This scholastic Aristotelianism developed primarily in the universities of Northern Europe. Whereas the secular masters by whom the idea was first propounded wanted above all to assert the autonomy of the philosophical sciences, for the members of the mendicant orders, who subsequently espoused it as a part of their own efforts at reform, the principal concern was to preserve the traditional conception of revelation and the hierarchical view of society so closely connected with it. Through the friars the scholastic idea was brought to Italy around the middle of the fifteenth century. Here it encountered a radically different form of Aristotelianism. The Italian faculties of arts were oriented less towards theology than to medicine, and the Aristotelianism they taught was concerned less with the hereafter than with the concerns of men in this world. In the University of Padua there was no proper theological faculty until the middle of the fourteenth century, and then it was formed not by the secular clergy, but by aggregating to the university the existing theological schools of the mendicant orders. It was only about the middle of the fifteenth century that the Dominican and Franciscan friars succeeded in having chairs erected in the arts faculty for Thomist and Scotist metaphysics.

The conflict between the two Aristotelianisms broke out almost immediately. It concerned Aristotle's teaching with regard to the immortality of the soul and, more fundamentally, his conception of metaphysics. Scholastic Aristotelianism had in fact included in its metaphysics of being several key elements which were not strictly Aristotelian. By defining the subject-matter of metaphysics as being as it is divided into finite and infinite being or into created and uncreated being, or even as the being common to God and creatures, the scholastics had quietly introduced the scriptural notions of God's infinity and the world's creation into Aristotle's science. These definitions of metaphysics implied the possibility of considering the world and the human soul not simply physically – as *corpus mobile* and *corpus animatum* – as in Aristotle, but also as metaphysical objects – *sub ratione entis*. The proofs both of God's existence and of the soul's immortality had from the very beginning formed an essential part of scholastic apologetics. These definitions made it possible to give metaphysical, rather than simply physical, proofs of both. Even more importantly, these definitions understood reality as graded hierarchically in a chain of being ascending from matter to God (or, after the introduction of the theory of the *latitudo formarum*, from nothingness to God). The schemes of participation or ontological composition which the scholastics employed in order to account for the various degrees of perfection in the chain served as a metaphysical basis for the defence of the traditional grades in society which were being increasingly called in question at the time.

The definition of metaphysics as the science of created and uncreated being thus betrayed the clerical interests which lay behind the notion of a Christian philosophy. It was this conception of metaphysics which called forth the violent reaction of the Italian Aristotelians. Most of these authors rejected the scholastic metaphysics of degrees of perfection. Even those who accepted the doctrine of the *latitudo formarum* denied that it could be applied to a metaphysical hierarchy of perfection, refusing to admit the possibility of measuring perfection according as to how nearly individual things approach the infinite perfection of God. Their position amounted to a rejection of the hierarchical principle in general. A standard objection ran thus: if the distance between God and created things is infinite, then each individual thing outside of God will be at an infinite distance from him and thus no creature more perfect than another.

Although the debate was between two divergent conceptions of reality and, on a deeper level, between two divergent conceptions of society, it was carried on in terms of the correct understanding of Aristotle's doctrine. Whereas the scholastics had introduced the notions of infinity and creation into their Aristotelianism, the secular Aristotelians maintained that according to Aristotle God is finite and the world eternal. The conflict came to a head in the celebrated controversy concerning the immortality of the soul which surrounded Pietro Pomponazzi, professor of philosophy in the Universities of Padua and Bologna at the beginning of the sixteenth century. In the year 1513 the Fifth Lateran Council condemned certain philosophers who taught that at least according to philosophy it is true that the human soul is mortal.[84] Pomponazzi had dealt with this subject repeatedly in the course of his university lectures on Aristotle's *De anima*, but the actual controversy began only in 1516, with the publication of his *Tractatus de immortalitate animae*. Pomponazzi maintained that according to Aristotle the doctrine of the soul belongs to physics as a part of the doctrine

---

84. *Sacrorum conciliorum . . . collectio* 1759–1962, XXXII, pp. 842–3.

dealing with *corpus animatum*. Accordingly, if one begins with Aristotle's principles, it is impossible to prove the immortality of the soul. All material forms are generated from the potency of matter and therefore corruptible. But the soul is a material form. None of its operations are carried out without a corporeal organ. Knowledge begins in sensation and understanding itself depends on sensible images. Were it possible to supply a metaphysical proof based on the idea that the soul is not educed from the potency of matter, but rather directly created by God, one could possibly hold that the soul is both a spiritual substance and the form of the body. But Aristotle knew nothing of creation. For him the presence of immaterial operations in a material form is a contradiction, and the notion of a spiritual substance which is also the form of the body is impossible.

The difficulty with Pomponazzi's position was not simply that it denied the possibility of giving an Aristotelian proof of immortality. First of all, his argument upset the theologians' naive conception of a fundamental agreement between Aristotelian philosophy and Christian faith. They had rejected contemporary attempts to enlist the Platonic conception of man in the service of Christianity because the idea of the body as the instrument of the soul and at the same time the source of the evil inclinations in man conflicted, in their eyes, with the Christian doctrines of the Incarnation and the necessity of grace for salvation. In Aristotle's view of man as a substantial unity, they had found a natural basis for the doctrine that original sin affects the whole man. Pomponazzi's position brought out the problems in this view. Moreover, his claim that the soul's operations do not transcend their corporeal origins jeopardised the Thomist thesis that revelation is necessary because human knowledge has its origin in sense experience. Most seriously, Pomponazzi's position endangered the principle which provided the warrant for clerical surveillance over doctrinal questions. Were he right in maintaining that according to Aristotle the soul is mortal, then Aristotle's psychology ought to have been condemned in accordance with Aristotle's own metaphysical principle of contradiction, on the ground that it entailed a conclusion contrary to revealed doctrine. Pomponazzi's assertion that, as a Christian, he believed that the soul is immortal, while denying the possibility of a rational demonstration, only served to increase the theologians' apprehension. The formulation of the Lateran Council's condemnation shows that the Fathers were less concerned about the question of immortality than they were about the view that a doctrine could be true in philosophy, but contradict a truth in theology. In fact, they made it an obligation of the professors to justify by reason the assent to all those Christian doctrines which are accessible to man's natural powers.[85]

It was especially the traditional proponents of the notion of a Christian philosophy, the theologians of the Dominican Order, who took up the challenge. Although some of them continued to hold that the abandonment of the Christian interpretation of Aristotle would endanger the faith, two of the most important Dominican writers were prepared to make some concessions to Pomponazzi. Cardinal Cajetan, who as General of the Order was present at the Lateran Council, had been one of Pomponazzi's colleagues at the University of Padua. Confronted with the latter's naturalistic interpretation of Aristotle, he saw himself forced to defend the basic principle that a doctrine cannot be true in philosophy and false in theology. Accordingly, he distinguished between Aristotle and the true principles of philosophy. Aristotle's position cannot result from the principles of philosophy because nothing can be concluded from true principles which is not true, and it is known by faith that Aristotle's position – at least in Pomponazzi's interpretation – is false. Crisostomo Javelli, regent in the Studium of the Order at Bologna during the time when Pomponazzi was professor in the university there, took the discussion a step further. In a move decisive for the sixteenth-century history of the science of being, he argued that, whatever Aristotle's opinion might be, the immortality of the soul is a position rationally demonstrable – not in physics, but rather in metaphysics. Bringing the idea of creation back into the science of being and with it Thomas Aquinas' related notion of a real composition of essence and existence in created reality – a notion which had been neglected in the Thomist School because of the increasing separation of philosophy from theology – Javelli maintained that the soul is not generated from the potency of matter. Its existence comes to it from outside, through creation. The soul is the substantial form of the body it animates, but because it is composed of essence and existence, it is a spiritual substance and consequently immortal.

The Pomponazzi affair thus had far-reaching consequences both for the conception of metaphysics as the science of being and for the complex interrelationships between philosophy, theology and natural science in the sixteenth century. Its development had been foreshadowed by the establishment of chairs for metaphysics in the Paduan arts faculty, by the increasing tendency of scholastic commentators on Aristotle to concentrate on the *Metaphysics*, *Physics* and *De anima*, by the growing number of

85. *Ibid.*

commentaries composed on Thomas' tract *De ente et essentia* and by the increasing stress on the common heritage in Albertism, Thomism and Scotism. Nevertheless, the controversy concerning the immortality of the soul marks a turning-point in the history of metaphysics. By making the human soul a metaphysical object as *ens immateriale*, the scholastic philosophers brought to full term the evolution which had begun by the inclusion of corporeal things in metaphysics *sub ratione entis*. By assimilating Duns Scotus' fundamental disjunction between infinite and finite being to the distinction between uncreated and created being, they could present a united front behind a science of being, independent of that of Aristotle, which by the light of natural reason studies God as *ens increatum*, the world as *ens creatum materiale*, and the human soul as *ens creatum immateriale*.

Philosophy thus became metaphysics, while the subject-matter which had belonged to the Aristotelian physics was free to become natural science. The abandonment of Aristotle by the theologians played an important part in the emancipation of the natural sciences from Aristotelian philosophy. Whereas in the fourteenth century scientific developments had usually been fitted into Aristotle's encyclopaedia, in the fifteenth century the traditional framework was made less and less tenable by new approaches and new materials, by new sciences and a new technology. But up until Pomponazzi's time the Aristotelian framework had been retained because of the apologetic purposes of the theologians. The formulation of an independent philosophy dealing with God, the world and man *sub ratione entis* relieved the scientists of the obligation to relate their conclusions to Aristotelian principles. It was for this reason that the professors in the arts faculties of the Italian universities in the late sixteenth century were reduced to offering simply an exegesis of the Philosopher's text and that – long before Galileo – natural philosophy was free to go its own way.

These developments forced scholastic authors to rethink the question of the subject-matter of metaphysics. The difficulties due to the new relationship between metaphysics and natural philosophy were compounded by the necessity of explaining Aristotle's own hesitation about the nature of metaphysics, especially about the role which metaphysics should play as first philosophy. One of Pomponazzi's opponents, Antonio Bernardi of Mirandola,[86] maintained that there is one universal science (distinct from natural science) which deals with all reality. The subject-matter of this science is *ens inquantum ens*, and it includes in itself all things as

---

86. Concerning Bernardi see Lohr 1974b, pp. 268–9.

passions or modes or species of being. The particular sciences of physics, mathematics and metaphysics are not independent sciences, but only parts of this universal science, in the same way that zoology and biology are parts of natural science.

Another opponent of the secular Aristotelianism in Italian universities, the Jesuit Benito Pereira, was willing to concede some of Pomponazzi's points. He was ready to admit that Aristotle had not proved the immortality of the soul and that elements of the doctrine of the soul had to be taken from physics and revelation. Nevertheless, he held that the doctrine of the soul also belonged – along with the doctrine of God and the intelligences – to metaphysics. But because this science, in accordance with the Thomist understanding, could treat these types of reality only as principles or causes, he maintained that another science was needed which could deal with them *per se*. Pereira therefore proposed a division of traditional metaphysics into two specifically distinct sciences: one which would deal with the most universal predicates of things and another which would deal with immaterial reality. The first science, which he called 'first philosophy' or 'universal science' – it will later also be called 'ontology' – would treat *ens inquantum ens* (as containing in itself all things), the transcendentals (one, true and good, act and potency, whole and part and the like) and being as it is divided into the ten categories (substance and accidents). The second science, which he called 'divine science', 'theology', 'wisdom' or 'metaphysics in the proper sense of the word', would deal with immaterial reality – God, the intelligences and the human soul – not as principles of being, but rather as species of reality. Material reality would be studied in first philosophy as one of the grades of being and in physics as *corpus naturale*. Because the principles dealt with in first philosophy are also encountered in material things, Pereira rejected the traditional division of the speculative sciences according to degrees of abstraction. In his conception only divine science deals with reality separate from matter; first philosophy deals with the ultimate principles of all reality, both material and immaterial. The former is a particular science, the latter, a universal one.

Pereira was one of the leading professors in the Collegio Romano of the newly founded Jesuit Order when the work *De communibus omnium rerum naturalium principiis et affectionibus* – in which this revolutionary division of metaphysics into two distinct sciences was first proposed – appeared at Rome in 1576. His colleagues had included the celebrated Juan Maldonado, who later lectured on metaphysics, the *De anima* and theology in the

Collège de Clermont, Paris, and Cardinal Franciscus Toletus, who was just completing his very successful commentaries on Aristotle's logic and natural philosophy when the *De principiis* was published. Pedro da Fonseca published his famous *Commentarii in libros Metaphysicorum* at Rome one year after Pereira's work was printed and had already conceived the idea of the *Cursus Collegii Conimbricensis*. The understanding of the philosophical enterprise which these men shared was, of course, that their work should serve the cause of Catholic theology. Ignatius Loyola had prescribed that the professors of the order should follow Aristotle in philosophy and Thomas Aquinas in theology, but they enjoyed considerable liberty in developing their idea of a Christian philosophy. Pereira and his colleagues were at ease with the mathematics and natural science which had developed especially in Italy during the sixteenth century and perfectly acquainted with the philological progress which humanism had made in the study of Aristotle's text. They knew not only Albertus Magnus, Thomas Aquinas and Duns Scotus, but also Averroes and the newly translated Greek commentaries on Aristotle, including the commentaries on the *Metaphysics* by Alexander of Aphrodisias and Syrianus. Pereira's demand for a science which dealt with God, the intelligences and the human soul *per se* was a part of the response of the professors of the Collegio Romano not only to Pomponazzi's fideism, but also to contemporary theological questions, to the new approaches to the problem of God proposed by Lull, Nicholas of Cusa and Ficino, to the philosophical interpretations of classical mythology which had such a vogue in the Renaissance and to the efforts of the missionaries of the Jesuit Order in lands as far away from Christianity as India and Japan.[87]

Pereira's demand for a distinct science of being which would treat the principles and transcendental properties of reality was, on the other hand, directly related to the problem posed by secular Aristotelianism in Italy. Loyola's prescription that Jesuit philosophers should follow Aristotle was part of his concern for sound, Catholic doctrine in the schools of the order. At first the professors of philosophy in the Collegio Romano seem – like many of their contemporaries – to have thought that they could simply identify the doctrine of Aristotle with that of the Catholic Church. In planning the philosophy courses in the Collegio the first problem encountered was not that of defending Aristotle's orthodoxy, but rather that of excluding those sections of his works which were not relevant for

87. On Jesuit Aristotelianism and sixteenth-century metaphysics see Lohr 1976b.

theology. But the threat posed by the new Aristotelianism demanded a more precise definition of the way in which the notion of sound doctrine was to be applied to the interpretation of Aristotle's text. Some of the professors of the Order held that the soul is immortal not only according to true philosophy, but also according to the mind of Aristotle himself. Others were willing to admit that Aristotle had not proved immortality and understood Loyola's prescription in the sense that Aristotle is to be followed except where his teaching is contrary to faith or the common doctrine of the scholastic doctors. Pereira belonged to the second group. As the result of a long controversy concerning the teaching of philosophy in the Collegio Romano in the course of which Pereira was repeatedly accused of adhering to Averroistic ideas, the Jesuit Order formulated principles for the choice of philosophical opinions by its professors. Because Aristotle's principles cannot – as Cajetan had pointed out some years earlier – have been true principles of philosophy if they led to false conclusions, the Collegio drew the attention of its teachers to the necessity of the search for and preservation of the common axioms of philosophy and theology.

Its approach amounted to an exegetical programme. Aristotle himself had regarded the opinions of his predecessors as stuttering attempts to express his own ideas and sought by the use of dialectics to discover among their theories the true principles of a question under discussion. In the same way the professors of the Collegio Romano were to seek the true principles of Aristotelian philosophy, not only the first principles of being, but also the axioms on which Aristotle's conception of science was founded. With these epistemological first principles in hand Aristotle could be reinterpreted or even rewritten to agree with the true principles of philosophy, that is, those which lead to Catholic doctrine. It was in accordance with this hermeneutic that Pereira defined 'first philosophy' not only as the science of being, but also as the science of science itself. Conscious of the fact that the basic problem with which scholasticism was confronted was that of maintaining the fundamental principles of its worldview, he held that metaphysics as first philosophy also had the task of expounding and defending its *principia generalia naturali lumine manifesta* in the face of the doubts and uncertainty which secular Aristotelianism had called forth.

The project of rewriting Aristotle in accordance with the true principles of philosophy had also been taken up in Iberian universities, at first at Valencia – where Pereira had begun his studies – and then at Alcalá and Salamanca. In Spain the project developed within a different context, but the understanding of metaphysics that it involved agreed with Pereira's conception of first philosophy as the science of the common principles of all the sciences. For Spanish scholastics of the second half of the sixteenth century the threat to the Christian interpretation of Aristotle came not from secular Aristotelianism, but rather from what they had come to regard as an excessive concentration on logic and natural philosophy in the arts faculties of their universities. Since for them metaphysics had the apologetic function of establishing the principles for showing the fundamental agreement between Christian doctrine and Aristotelian philosophy, it had to be part of a philosophy completely independent of revealed theology. But in Iberian universities metaphysics was taught not as the culmination of the arts course, but in theology. Consequently, the effort to restore to metaphysics its proper place in the course of studies implied the reformation of the entire philosophical curriculum. The reform movement began at Valencia when the university took various institutional measures similar to those taken by the Jesuit Order in Rome. In 1540 new statutes for the arts faculty were promulgated according to which metaphysics was to be read after logic and natural philosophy as the third part of a three-year cycle. In 1548 a statute decreed that Aristotle was to be interpreted according to the mind of Thomas Aquinas. In 1587 a chair for metaphysics was established in the arts faculty.[88]

It was as a part of this reform movement that the great systematic works of the Spanish scholastics on metaphysics were composed. Medieval works on the *Metaphysics* had been either literal commentaries on the text or written in the form of questions closely following Aristotle's order. The systematic treatises of the late sixteenth century – which received the name of *disputationes* – represented a literary form which was new. They abandoned Aristotle's aporetic arrangement and attempted to present metaphysics *per methodum doctrinae*, that is, as an organic whole derived from the first principles of philosophy. In the formation of these works the decisions made at Valencia regarding the teaching of metaphysics played an important role. The basic structure of the new *disputationes metaphysicae* was determined by the statute of the university that the following books of Aristotle's work were to be read: I (the nature of metaphysics), V (its terminology), VII (the doctrine of substance) and XII (its divisions). One of the professors in the arts faculty at Valencia, Bartolomé José Pascual, in his inaugural lecture of 1565, *De optimo modo explanandi Aristotelem*, also made some suggestions for the presentation of Aristotle's doctrine which

88. See Gallego Salvadores 1972.

influenced the structure of the new treatises. He maintained that in explaining Aristotle's works one should rearrange the material in its logical order, add what is lacking, omit what is superfluous or has been added by others and clarify ambiguous and obscure passages. In dealing with possible additions he suggested a comparison between Aristotle's rules for scientific demonstration based on first principles with Euclid's geometrical method. In treating possible omissions he noted that the discussion of motion which is found both in the *Physics* and the *Metaphysics* need be dealt with only in explaining *Physics* I and that the discussion of the causes which is also found in both works could be taken up as a part of the explanation of philosophical terminology in *Metaphysics* V.

Two other authors who made proposals for the reform of the arts curriculum at Valencia emphasised the importance of finding the true principles of Aristotelian science. Juan Bautista Monllor, in his paraphrase of the *Prior Analytics* (1569), explained that Aristotle's own works on the syllogism and the theory of proof were composed according to the analytic or resolutive method; they show how one should establish and arrange first principles for the demonstration of theorems in a scientific discipline. Pedro Juan Núñez, in his *De recta ratione conficiendi curriculi philosophiae* (published in 1594, but probably written somewhat earlier), divided the study of metaphysics into two parts, in a way which was similar to the division of the science proposed by Pereira. The major part of metaphysics deals with the principles of things and comprises the last three books of the *Metaphysics*; the other part concerns the principles of the sciences and is contained in the earlier books of Aristotle's work. The study of speculative philosophy should begin with this second part, then take up natural philosophy and conclude with the books on the principles of things. Aristotle treated the two parts of metaphysics in one work because the first principles of the sciences correspond to the first principles of things.

The endeavour to reform the arts course by restoring to metaphysics its role as rector of all the sciences – as first philosophy in Aristotle's sense – characterised the scholastic treatises of the *Siglo de oro* on this science. The earliest printed systematic treatise on metaphysics was published at Valencia under the title *Disputatio metaphysica de ente et eius proprietatibus*, in the same year that the chair of metaphysics was established in the arts faculty. Whereas the author – Diego Mas, a Dominican friar and one of the leading professors in the faculty[89] – composed works on logic and natural

---

89. Concerning Mas see Lohr 1978, pp. 569–70.

philosophy in the form of commentaries on Aristotle's treatises, his *Disputatio metaphysica* is an independent tract which seeks to set limits to the particular sciences and present metaphysics, the science of the first principles of all reality, as the foundation for the reform of the philosophical curriculum. The *Disputatio* is made up of a discussion of the concept of being and the scholastic doctrine of the transcendentals. In accordance with the teaching of Thomas Aquinas, God is dealt with only as the cause of being. To avoid duplication, Mas relegated the discussion of the Aristotelian causes to physics.

A second treatise on metaphysics arranged *secundum ordinem doctrinae* was published ten years later at Toledo by the Augustinian friar Diego de Zúñiga.[90] This author's treatise is found in his *Philosophiae prima pars, qua metaphysica, dialectica, rhetorica et physica declarantur*, a work which forms part of a comprehensive plan for reforming the university curriculum in philosophy. Zúñiga's teaching seems to have been at least in part a response to attacks by contemporary sceptics against Aristotelianism; he is concerned throughout the work to demonstrate the scientific character of the entire Peripatetic philosophy. At the same time the structure of his treatise is clearly dependent on university practice: it is divided into an introduction on the concept of being, the predicables and philosophical terminology (corresponding to books I and V of Aristotle's *Metaphysics*) and a treatment of the categories of substance and accident (corresponding to books VII and XII). Like Pereira, Zúñiga regarded the doctrine of God as a particular science, distinct from metaphysics.

The same basic structure may be observed in the celebrated *Disputationes metaphysicae* of Francisco Suárez, a work which appeared in the same year as Zúñiga's treatise. It seems, in fact, that the idea of rewriting Aristotle on metaphysics in the form of systematically arranged disputations originated with the famous Jesuit theologian. Before he dedicated himself exclusively to the teaching of theology as professor, first in the Collegio Romano of the Order (where he was a colleague of Benito Pereira) and then in the Universities of Alcalá and Salamanca, Suárez had taught both philosophy and theology in various smaller Jesuit colleges in Spain. In the prooemium to the *Disputationes metaphysicae*, which were published during his incumbency at Salamanca, he tells us that in composing the work he made use of his lecture-course on metaphysics from this earlier period. A reflection of these original *Disputationes* can be found in the *Expositio in*

90. Concerning Zúñiga see Lohr 1982, pp. 178–9.

Table 1. *Organisation of treatises on metaphysics*

ARISTOTLE	COBOS (1583)	MAS (1587)	ZÚÑIGA (1597)	SUÁREZ (1597)
I Subject-matter and dignity of metaphysics			I.1–2 De philosophia	I De natura metaphysicae
	I De ente in communi	I De ente; 2 De essentia et existentia	I.3 De eo quod est	2 De conceptu entis
	2–5 De passionibus entis	De proprietatibus entis; 3 De uno; 4 De veritate; 5 De bonitate	I.4 De re, aliquo, uno, vero, bono; 5–6 De vero contra academicos et alios	3–11 De passionibus entis: De unitate, veritate, bonitate
V Philosophical lexicon: 1–2 Principle; 3 Element; 4 Nature; 5 Necessary; 6 One, Many; 7 Being; 8 Substance; 9 Same, Other; 10 Contrary; 25–6 Part, Whole; 30 Accident	6–7 De ente in actu et potentia, necessario et contingenti		II.1–9 De rebus singulis et universis (praedicabilibus) II.10 De toto et partibus; 11 De causis; 12 De principio et elemento; 13 De natura; 14 De necessario. III.1–4 De eo quod est per accidens; 5–11 De vi et actione; 12 De eodem et diverso; 13–14 De contrariis	12–27 De causis
VII Substance and its principles XII Types of substance	8–10 De substantia 11–12 De accidentibus		IV.1 De rerum generibus IV.2 De substantia IV.3–8 De accidentibus	28 De divisione entis in infinitum et finitum; 29–30 De primo et increato ente; 31 De essentia et esse entis finiti 32 De divisione entis creati in substantiam et accidens 33–4 De substantia creata 35 De immateriali substantia 36 De substantia materiali 37–53 De accidentibus 54 De ente rationis

libros Metaphysicae of one of Suárez' pupils from this period, the Jesuit Cristóbal de los Cobos. This work, which was composed about five years earlier than the *Disputatio metaphysica* of Diego Mas, first treats the concept of being and its properties, then discusses the terms, 'act' and 'potency', 'necessity' and 'contingency', and concludes with an account of the categories of substance and accident. In his mature *Disputationes* Suárez followed this structure, but substituted a long treatise *De causis* for the discussion of the terminology and expanded considerably the final section on the divisions of substance and accident by including a treatment of the doctrine of metaphysical entities which had developed during the Middle Ages: *ens increatum, ens creatum immateriale* and *materiale.*

All of these treatises formed part of a collective attempt to rewrite Aristotle's metaphysics in accordance with the true principles of philosophy. Their authors followed the suggestions of their colleagues in Rome and Valencia concerning the proper, philosophical interpretation of Aristotle. They found the fundamental structure of their works in those books of Aristotle's *Metaphysics* which were prescribed for the lectures in philosophy. They omitted the lists of metaphysical problems in books III and XI and the matter which properly belongs to physics in books VIII and XI. They rearranged the material, bringing together Aristotle's remarks on the nature, dignity and subject-matter of metaphysics from books I–IV and VI to form an introduction on the relationship between metaphysics and philosophy and on the concept of being, while combining the Philosopher's scattered notes on unity and truth from books IV–V and X with the scholastic treatise on the transcendentals to make up a tract on the properties of being. They completed these *praeambula* to metaphysics by adding to Aristotle's philosophical lexicon (book V) material from books VII–IX and the *Physics* to form a tract on the causes. Understanding metaphysics to be the science of substance and its various divisions, they brought together the teaching of books VII and XII with some material from the *Physics* to form a final tract on metaphysics proper (see table 1).

One feature set Suárez' mature *Disputationes metaphysicae* apart from the treatises of his colleagues: his use of the now familiar distinction of reality into three fundamental types: infinite, finite immaterial and finite material. Suárez employed this distinction not only in structuring his tract on the divisions of substance and accident (disp. XXVIII–LIII), but also in formulating his definition of the subject-matter of metaphysics as the real being which includes God, the intelligences, material substances and real accidents (disp. I.I). As we have seen, the scriptural doctrine of creation lies behind this distinction; Suárez' use of it justified his description of his own philosophy as Christian. Whereas the secular Aristotelians of the Italian universities had maintained that for Aristotle himself the world was eternal, Suárez made the relationship of finite reality to the infinite, creative power of God the very foundation of his Christian reinterpretation of the Philosopher's thought. It was his reflection on this relationship that led him to define the subject-matter of metaphysics as real being. Finite being is that which can be constituted in actual existence by God's absolute power. Consequently, real being cannot simply be identified with actual being; it must include possible being, not only that which exists, but also that which can be thought of as possibly existing. Suárez attempted to clarify this concept of real being as that which can be thought of as possibly existing by distinguishing it from *entia rationis*, like figments and chimeras. Although both real beings and beings of reason can have being in the intellect, the former differ from the latter in that they are able through God's creative power to achieve an existence which is actual and objective outside the intellect. Pure beings of reason are incapable of actual existence because such concepts involve a contradiction. The concept of the real being which is the subject of metaphysics is therefore objective in the sense that real being can be thought of as possible, because its essence contains no contradictory notes.

This understanding of the subject-matter of metaphysics served two purposes. On the one hand, it guaranteed the role of metaphysics as first philosophy and thus supplied a philosophical basis for the attempt of the Spanish scholastics to reform the curriculum in arts. On the other, it restored to metaphysics the unity which was threatened by Pereira's proposal to distinguish the science of being from the science of God. Metaphysics is first philosophy for Suárez because it explains and confirms the axioms which are common to philosophy and theology. It shows that metaphysical statements are possible as scientific statements of universal validity because in them the individual, finite things we know are perceived as bearers of something absolute – the absolute necessity of non-contradiction which penetrates all reality. On the basis of the ultimate, most certain axiom of the Aristotelian philosophy, Suárez proposed a reinterpretation of Aristotle's metaphysics which would not only avoid the errors which led to conclusions at variance with Christian doctrine, but also make possible a systematic, deductive presentation of Christian philosophy and a solid reformation of the arts curriculum. But metaphysics is, for Suárez, also the science of being itself, the science which deals with the nature, properties and divisions of all reality. As such, it shows that the necessity of all finite reality is grounded in the fact that finite reality is a possible object of God's infinite, creative power. At the same time, metaphysics is theology because God is the necessary being whose absolute power can bring into actual existence those things which contain no contradictory notes. Metaphysics as divine science is for this reason the condition of the possibility of metaphysics both as the science of being as such and as first philosophy. Metaphysics is one science and not three because it studies all these objects under the one aspect under which they all agree. Because all real things can be thought of under the aspect that they involve no contradiction, the objective concept of being – beyond the divisions of infinite and finite, immaterial and material, substantial and accidental – is the *a priori* principle of all reality and all knowledge.

Suárez' *Disputationes metaphysicae* fixed the method of instruction in metaphysics for centuries, not only in Catholic schools, but also in Protestant academies and universities. The clarity, comprehensiveness, systematic character and originality of the work have often been praised. At the same time, it must be recognised that Suárez stood not so much at the beginning as at the end of a long tradition. If his work was original, its originality consisted above all in the way in which it articulated the tradition to respond to the sixteenth-century situation. First of all, Suárez wrote on metaphysics not as a philosopher, but as a Catholic theologian writing shortly after the close of the Council of Trent and under the watchful eye of the Spanish Inquisition. In the prooemium to the *Disputationes* he emphasised that philosophy should be Christian and the servant of revealed theology. Because in his theological teaching he had to make use of the metaphysical principles which are presupposed in scholastic theology, he decided – at the time of his return from Rome to Spain – to interrupt his commentary on the third part of Aquinas' *Summa* (which deals with the Incarnation of Christ) in order to compose a systematic treatise on metaphysics on the basis of his earlier lecture-course. The way in which Suárez' metaphysics was conditioned by theological concerns may be observed in the disputations which he added in the crucial, central section of his work: disp. xxxi on the essence and existence of finite being and disp. xxxiv on the distinction between supposite and nature. These disputations were meant to form the philosophical basis of his treatment of the Incarnation.

But Suárez wrote on metaphysics not only because of its relevance for the solution of specifically theological problems. The *Disputationes* also represent a theologian's reply to the philosophical challenges of the sixteenth century. In reaction to the growing scepticism which marked the latter part of the century, Suárez stressed the scientific character of first philosophy. His attempt to ground all knowledge in the law of non-contradiction is no doubt to be seen in connection with the attacks of contemporary sceptics – like Francisco Sanches, who was acquainted with the Jesuits of the Collegio Romano – against the Aristotelian encyclopaedia of the sciences. His colleague, Diego de Zúñiga, answered the sceptics explicitly in his *Metaphysica* as a part of his treatment of the doctrine of truth as a transcendental property of being. Moreover, in response to new approaches to the doctrine of God and to the needs of Christian missionaries, Suárez stressed the natural knowledge of God which metaphysics provides. In doing so, he sought a middle way between Ramon Lull's trinitarian approach to the problem of God and Benito Pereira's proposed division of metaphysics into a science of being and a science of God. He wrote against Lull's trinitarian theory and attacked specifically the supra-rational methodology which underlay it.[91] Although he rejected Pereira's proposal, natural theology forms the centre about which the *Disputationes* revolve (disp. XXVIII–XXX). For Suárez the God known through natural reason is the principle of a system which begins with the primal division of reality into creator and created and proceeds through the divisions contained in finite being to reach all types and grades of reality.

Finally, Suárez' metaphysics was meant as a response to what many of his colleagues regarded as an over-emphasis on logic and natural philosophy in the Spanish universities of the early sixteenth century. Suárez agreed that the arts curriculum was in need of reform, but in his view reform could not consist simply in establishing a place for metaphysics in the philosophy course. True reform involved the transformation by the science of being of the entire encyclopaedia of the philosophical sciences. This final and most important aspect of Suárez' reaction as a theologian to contemporary philosophical challenges was as much a reply to Pomponazzi's fideism as it was a consequence of the Spanish situation. The secular Aristotelianism of the Italian universities which had so divided the professors of the Jesuit Collegio Romano endangered the very specific view of the relationship between Christian doctrine and the Aristotelian philosophy which characterised scholasticism. Because the fundamental doctrines of the faith – the doctrines of the Trinity and the Incarnation, for example – were thought to transcend man's natural powers, the scholastics maintained that

91. Suárez 1856–78, I, pp. 560–73 (*De Deo uno et trino* III.1.9–12).

revelation is absolutely necessary; reason can at best discover natural analogies to the supernatural mysteries – like the philosophical distinction of supposite and nature as applied to the Incarnation. Because, however, certain doctrines of the faith – the existence of God and the immortality of the human soul – were, as Aristotelian philosophy had showed, accessible to man's unaided reason, the scholastics argued that the assent to the articles of the faith was not unreasonable. Pomponazzi's position seriously undermined this method of apologetics. If Aristotle's actual teaching conflicted with the Christian doctrines of creation and immortality, the scholastic approach to the act of faith through Aristotle's philosophy was impossible. Indeed, the very conception of scholasticism, based on the role of the clergy as the privileged interpreters of the *depositum fidei*, was called into question. Were Pomponazzi's interpretation of Aristotle's philosophy correct, then both the scholastic understanding of nature with its static, hierarchically ordered essences and the scholastic understanding of theology as a scientific presentation of Christian doctrine with the articles of faith as its axiomatic first principles would be without foundation.

Suárez' reinterpretation of Aristotle's metaphysics was meant to meet this challenge. He was ready to admit that the Aristotelian, physical argument for God's existence, which began from motion, was not able to reach an uncreated, immaterial substance. But he maintained that it was possible to employ Aristotelian philosophical principles to prove the existence of God and the immortality of the soul – not in physics, but rather in metaphysics. By way of the metaphysical argument from efficient causality one can arrive at an infinite, first being. From man's intellectual activity it is possible to argue metaphysically to the spirituality of the human soul which is, as an immaterial substance, immortal. It was for this reason that Suárez had recourse to the distinction of reality into *ens infinitum, ens creatum immateriale* and *ens creatum materiale*. He was fully aware of the fact that the use of this distinction implied the division of metaphysics into the parts which would later be called natural theology, rational psychology and cosmology. But the distinction met the increasing need for an independent treatment of the problem of God, rendered the growing crisis of the Aristotelian physics as the science of *corpus mobile* irrelevant to scholastics and provided the basis for a defence of the scholastic understanding of the world. It also supplied the foundation of the reform of the arts curriculum in post-Tridentine Catholic schools with metaphysics as the science of being explaining and confirming the natural principles of all things and all knowledge in the service of revealed theology.

These schools were the seminaries decreed by the Council. In this completely new type of institution the Christian Aristotelianism which had grown up in the University of Paris and received its most mature formulation in Rome and Salamanca moved out of the main stream of European intellectual history. Much as the contemporary chroniclers of the Catholic religious orders collected the historical monuments of their past, the men who taught in these schools sought to bring together in a systematic way the speculation of what they subconsciously recognised as a closing age. Their teaching gave rise to a new literary form, the *cursus philosophicus* or summary of scholastic teaching in philosophy. The *cursus* was generally written in the form of disputations on the works of Aristotle, but two features set it off from the earlier commentaries and disputations. First, although the order of Aristotle's books on speculative philosophy was generally followed, the majority of the authors of these compendia abandoned the Philosopher's conception of physics. Since the purpose of the *cursus* was to provide the basic philosophical knowledge necessary for the study of revealed theology, they reinterpreted the parts of Aristotle's natural philosophy as metaphysics. The understanding of the science of being which had been developed by Christian Aristotelians since the time of Javelli provided the foundation for their interpretation of the individual tracts. Anticipating the later cosmology, they grouped the *Physics*, *De caelo*, *De generatione et corruptione* and *Meteorology* together as parts of the science which deals not with *corpus mobile*, but rather with *ens mobile*. In order to be able to maintain that the *De anima* provides the principles for the demonstration of the immortality of the soul, they took the subject-matter of the book to be *ens mobile animatum*, thus founding the science which would later be called rational psychology. Although the authors of these textbooks often disagreed on the question whether the *Metaphysics* deals properly with the general science of ontology or the particular science of natural theology, they were practically unanimous in the view that Aristotle's book supplied the principles for the various parts of the science of being. They broke, therefore, at this point with the traditional order of Aristotle's works and generally treated the *Metaphysics* before, not after, the works on physics.

The *cursus philosophicus*, thus constituted, was meant to be an answer to the syncretism, scepticism and new encyclopaedism which threatened the scholastic view of the world. By anchoring all the parts of the philosophy curriculum in the science of being, the authors of these works hoped to save the static, hierarchical understanding of reality which medieval thinkers had based on Aristotle's philosophy and on which the clergy had founded its conception of its role in society. But amidst the social upheavals of the period, this end could only be attained by a deliberate restriction of the authors' philosophical horizons. An increasing narrowness was consequently a second characteristic of the *cursus*. Whereas writers like Pereira and Suárez had still attempted to master the entire tradition, the philosophy professors of the post-Tridentine Catholic schools had less and less direct knowledge of the Greek and Arabic sources and even a very limited acquaintance with their own medieval Latin authorities. Because their teaching was directed in each case to the members of a specific religious community, they stressed the importance of its uniformity. Disturbed by the doctrinal confusion which marked the Renaissance period, they tended increasingly to return to the teaching of one of the great thirteenth-century doctors, the Dominicans, Carmelites and Benedictines turning to Thomas Aquinas, the Franciscans to Duns Scotus, the Capuchins to Bonaventure, the Augustinians to Giles of Rome and the Servites to Henry of Ghent. Shortly after the close of the Council, for example, the Carmelite Order founded a college for philosophical studies in the University of Alcalá. In order to assure the preservation of safe, approved, and uniform teaching in the order, the master general imposed on the lectors of the college the task of writing a *cursus artium* in the form of disputations on the works of Aristotle and in agreement with the teaching of Thomas Aquinas. It is true that the more recently founded orders – the Jesuits, in particular – enjoyed more freedom in the choice of opinions, but their flexibility was generally stigmatised as eclecticism by the members of the older orders, and even in these later foundations authors of the *cursus* found their principal inspiration in the thirteenth century.

The approach adopted by both differed, however, radically from that of their models. Whereas their medieval counterparts had written for the most part as theologians, trying to show the fundamental harmony between Christian revelation and the newly recovered Greek science, the scholastics of the baroque period abandoned this effort, recognised the autonomy of the natural sciences and were content to leave the development of them to laymen (except where scientific conclusions conflicted with Christian doctrine). They intended to write as philosophers and sought to fill in with the *cursus* a gap which had been left by the medievals. Nevertheless, their philosophy was meant to serve an apologetic purpose. In the *cursus* natural philosophy became metaphysics as part of an effort to defend a worldview in which revelation appeared necessary, its acceptance reasonable and the clergy's role as its interpreter guaranteed. This approach carried the day in the schools of the Counter-Reformation. Summaries of scholastic philosophy were composed in Spain by the Jesuits Pedro Hurtado de Mendoza and Francisco de Oviedo, the Dominican John of St Thomas and the Carmelite college of Alcalá; in France by the Cistercian Eustachius a S. Paulo (who is said to have had an influence on Descartes); in Italy by the Jesuit Cosma Alamanni and the Franciscans Bartholomaeus Mastrius and Bonaventura Bellutus; and for use in Germany and Eastern Europe by the Jesuit Roderigo de Arriaga.

In Protestant Germany the Aristotelian philosophy underwent an evolution which paralleled, in many ways, that in Catholicism. But there are many paradoxes in the German development. As is well known, Luther rejected Aristotle and the scholastic mixture of philosophy and theology. But within a hundred years of the Reformer's disputation of 1517 *Contra scholasticam theologiam*, metaphysics – either as the science of being or as natural theology – had come to occupy a central place in Protestant universities, whether they leaned to Calvinism as in Heidelberg and Marburg, to a strict Lutheranism as in Wittenberg and Jena or took a more moderate stand as in Altdorf and Helmstedt. Protestant theologians of the latter part of the sixteenth century found in Aristotle an instrument with which they could meet the challenges which arose after the prophetic spirit of the early Reformation had cooled. Disputes within Lutheranism and between Lutherans and Calvinists about the nature of Christ and the doctrine of justification made precise definitions of terms like 'substance' and 'accident', 'nature' and 'person' absolutely imperative. Challenges from Catholicism, Socinianism and what was regarded as a new atheism forced theologians to seek a common ground for discussion. The institutional structure of the new university system forced them to maintain the scientific character of their discipline.

Nevertheless, it was not in the theological faculty that metaphysics made its first appearance. There the prejudice against the scholastic μιξοφιλοσοφοθεολογία was too strong. The acceptance of Aristotle's science of being seems rather to have been a logical consequence of the prior acceptance of his natural philosophy and general conception of what science is. The Reformation had for a time cut Germany off from the progress in the natural sciences which was made in Italy in the fifteenth and sixteenth centuries. When German thinkers turned to the new science, they were also confronted by the secular Aristotelianism of the Italian universities and the same problem that Catholic authors had had to face – the problem of the double truth. The paradox is that they found answers to the problem in the works of Iberian Jesuits. By the end of the century, Fonseca, Pereira and Suárez were standard references in the newly founded Protestant universities. Paradoxical also is the fact that in Germany Aristotle's natural philosophy had, before the close of the sixteenth century, been dethroned by a strange mixture of Aristotelianism and biblical ideas meant to account for Christian doctrines like that of the glorified bodies of Christ and the redeemed after the Resurrection. As the new experimental science then gained adherents, the theologians simply dropped Aristotle's physics and turned their attention almost exclusively to his metaphysics and natural theology.

Aristotelian natural philosophy entered the German university through the medical faculty. It was Melanchthon himself who opened the door. Although he seems at first to have thought that he could content himself with collecting scriptural commonplaces and limit his philosophical efforts to the production of humanistic compendia for rhetoric, dialectics and moral philosophy, the university curriculum soon forced him to turn his attention to the other parts of philosophy. From about 1530 Melanchthon began to compose textbooks on physics and psychology and to edit various classical works on arithmetic, geometry and astronomy for use in the schools. By 1550 his university discourses had turned to subjects like anatomy, the motion of the heart and the dignity of medical science. In the 1540s Jacob Schegk of Tübingen not only wrote commentaries on Aristotle's logic and natural philosophy, but also translated the *De mixtione* of Alexander of Aphrodisias and the commentary of Georgius Pachymeres on the *De lineis indivisibilibus* and edited Aristotle's *De anima* with excerpts from Simplicius' commentary.

From the late 1550s on increasing numbers of Germans went to Italy to study. One of the first was Bruno Seidel of Erfurt, who studied medicine at the University of Padua from 1557 to 1560. In the 1560s Johannes Caselius, a pupil of Melanchthon and later the leading humanist in the newly founded University of Helmstedt, made two extended visits to Italy, studying under Pier Vettori and Carlo Sigonio. In the 1570s Philipp Scherb, the founder of the School of Altdorf, visited Rome and Bologna and studied metaphysics in Padua under the Dominican Tommaso Pellegrini, before receiving his doctorate in medicine at the University of Basle. At the same time, many Italians fled, because of their religious convictions, to the North. Although many of them took refuge in Geneva, Paris and England, a good number also found a home in the Calvinist cities of Germany. In the 1550s Girolamo Zanchi became professor of physics at Strasburg and published there in 1554 a new edition of Aristotle's *Physics*. Simone Simoni, who had studied in Padua, became, after short sojourns in Geneva, Paris and Heidelberg, professor of philosophy and medicine at the University of Leipzig; he remained there until 1581, when he was dismissed by the Elector of Saxony because he refused to sign the *Formula concordiae*. Giulio Pace, who had also studied in Padua, taught law in Geneva from 1575 to 1585, publishing his influential edition of Aristotle's *Organon* there, before becoming professor of law at the University of Heidelberg. A new epoch for German philosophy began in 1594 with the publication in Basle of Jacopo Zabarella's *Opera logica* by Johann Ludwig Hawenreuter, doctor of medicine and professor of logic, physics and metaphysics at the University of Strasburg.

But the professors of medicine were forced by the long-standing prejudice against Aristotle in Reformation Germany to justify the study of natural philosophy. It was in this context that metaphysics made its appearance in the schools. In 1564 Wolfgang Meurer, professor of logic and medicine at Leipzig, pleaded, in a preface to a new edition of Aristotle's *De anima*, that the use of philosophy was both necessary and legitimate. In 1573 Nicolaus Taurellus, professor of medicine at Basle,[92] published his *Philosophiae triumphus*, a work in which he justified the use of philosophy on the ground that it not only does not conflict with revealed truth, but can also supply the very foundations for belief. Taurellus wanted to develop a Christian philosophy which would harmonise the Aristotelian worldview with the data of biblical revelation. This effort was to be truly philosophical and provide reliable rational proofs, certain conclusions derived by strict deduction from the innate first principles of science. For the theory of proof Taurellus was able to use the work of Jacob Schegk, under whom he had studied at Tübingen. For the theory of knowledge he took up the teaching of Melanchthon. The *praeceptor Germaniae* had recognised the task which fell to philosophy of expressing the knowledge of reality which can be gained by reason, independent of revelation. Combining Stoic and Ciceronian ideas, he set down, in one of his later works, three norms – in addition to revelation – for the certitude of doctrine: the universal experience of men, the innate knowledge of first principles and the syllogistic presentation of conclusions. He held that the knowledge of God's existence, eternity and creation of the world are such innate principles. He distinguished between truths which are known only through revelation and

92. Concerning Taurellus see Lohr 1982, pp. 190–1.

truths accessible to reason which are confirmed by revelation. As an example of the latter, he appealed to the fact that the universal experience of men that the earth is stationary, while the sun moves, is confirmed by Scripture.[93]

Although this theory of knowledge effectively served to open the door to philosophy in Protestantism, Taurellus recognised that its conception of the relationship between faith and reason was simplistic. Christian philosophy, he maintained, has the task not only of refuting the objections of unbelievers, but also that of leading them to the faith. The relationship between faith and reason is not a theological, but rather a philosophical problem. In his approach to this problem, Taurellus made use of Melanchthon's revisions of some fundmental Lutheran positions. Man's nature was not substantially, but only accidentally affected by the fall of Adam. He is free, but limited; grace perfects his freedom. His unaided reason can know the essences of things, but revelation is necessary to know God's salvific will. Taurellus concluded that the experience of human finitude is the end of philosophy and the beginning of faith. Using the word in a Protestant work for the first time, he described this method of philosophising as 'metaphysical'.

The problem of the relationship between faith and reason was, however, not to be solved so easily. Among the ideas which German students brought back from Italy was the interpretation of Aristotle developed by Andrea Cesalpino at Pisa. According to this celebrated botanist and professor of medicine, Aristotle knew nothing of creation. God is, for him, not the efficient, but rather the constituent cause of all things. As intelligence or universal soul, God permeates and organises all reality. In Cesalpino's understanding of Aristotle, all nature is one; the doctrine of matter and form is meant to explain its structure. Intelligences and human souls are parts of God; they are differentiated by a very subtle type of matter. God's activity is the eternal motion of all things. Cesalpino thus confronted Protestant thinkers, who had turned to him because of the needs of medical science, with the same dilemma with which Pomponazzi had confronted Catholic theologians earlier in the century. He explicitly posed the problem of the double truth. Where Aristotle disagrees with revelation, there must be an error in his reasoning. But Cesalpino maintained that his task was simply that of explaining Aristotle's text; the theologians could attend to uncovering its errors.

93. Melanchthon 1834–60, XIII, pp. 149–53 (*De anima: causae certitudinis doctrinarum*).

Taurellus reacted to this challenge in much the same way as the Catholics had done. He admitted that Aristotle had to be corrected or rewritten in accordance with Christian doctrine. He recognised that Aristotle did not treat the question of God's existence and attributes, that he omitted the question of the efficient cause of the world, that he denied God's providence and erred with regard to the eternity of the world, the immortality of the soul and man's future happiness. Against Cesalpino, Taurellus maintained that Aristotle correctly postulated the existence of finite, immaterial substances, although incorrectly accepting the power of demons. He held that Aristotle's God was not merely the *Deus rotator* of Cesalpino, but rather the *actus purus* which agreed with Christian teaching. He concluded that Aristotle's works could be useful in the schools, but only to the extent that they confirm revealed truths. Accordingly, he published at Hanau in 1596 his *Synopsis Aristotelis Metaphysices, ad normam Christianae religionis explicatae, emendatae et completae.* This work was the first of a series of textbooks on metaphysics emanating from southern German universities as a result of the tension between Protestant doctrine and the natural philosophy necessary for the study of medicine. Johann Ludwig Hawenreuter had lectured on metaphysics at Strasburg even before the appearance of Taurellus' work, but his commentary on Aristotle's book was first published by his students in 1604. At the newly founded University of Altdorf metaphysics early became an important part of the curriculum. Taurellus had left Basle for the chair of physics and medicine there in 1580. Philipp Scherb was professor of logic, metaphysics and medicine there from 1586 to 1605. Ernst Soner, professor of physics and medicine there from 1605 to 1612, lectured on metaphysics in 1609, but because of suspicions that he inclined to Socinianism, his commentary was not published until after the Thirty Years War.

In these prosperous cities of southern Germany the universities enjoyed a certain autonomy with respect to the political power. The theological faculties found room not only for strict Lutherans, but also for the followers of Melanchthon and Calvin. The study of medicine flourished, and metaphysics, as the link between the two faculties, took its place in the curriculum. In northern German universities metaphysics also made its appearance around the end of the sixteenth century, but with a different function and in a radically different context. The northern German universities and especially their theological faculties were much more closely allied with the political power than those in the southern towns. In the North commerce had, under the strain of foreign competition, declined rapidly in the course of the century. The towns fought a losing battle against the administrative bureaucracy which became the backbone of government in principalities like Saxony, Thuringia, Brunswick and Hesse-Darmstadt. The princes took advantage of the political confusion aroused by the Reformation to subordinate the ecclesiastical institutions within their territories to the secular power. Luther himself, frightened by the social unrest of 1524–5, had placed church authority directly under the influence of the princes by siding with them in the suppression of the peasants. During the uneasy peace which reigned from 1555 to 1618 the princes consolidated their position by making the churches the pillars supporting their sovereignty. The famous principle of the Peace of Augsburg, *cuius regio eius religio*, was used not only to secure religious conformity but also to create an absolutist regime within the individual principalities.

In 1577 the princes took a momentous step in the direction of the discipline and doctrinal uniformity which were necessary for the achievement of their purposes. In that year eighty-six German states and free cities – the majority of them in the North and together making up roughly half of German-speaking Europe – accepted the *Formula concordiae* which defined the Lutheran faith. The *Formula* reasserted Luther's doctrine of free will, sin and grace and his realistic understanding of the sacraments. It also adopted the soteriological doctrine that the work of Christ was of infinite merit because it was the work of a divine person. The *Formula* was directed primarily against the followers of Calvin and Melanchthon, but the princes also took measures to defend the idea that reason and revelation are fundamentally in harmony against certain extremist Lutheran theologians who advanced what was regarded as a new form of the double truth. Going further than the position of the Italian Averroists that philosophy following its own principles often arrives at conclusions in conflict with revealed truth, these thinkers claimed that the doctrines of faith – doctrines like that which proposes that God is one essence in three divine persons – are contrary to reason.

It was in this essentially theological context that metaphysics – understood not as natural theology, but as the abstract science of being – appeared in northern German universities. Whereas the School of Altdorf understood Aristotle's science of *ens inquantum ens* as dealing exclusively with the *ens primum*, professors at the universities of Wittenberg, Jena, Helmstedt and Giessen remained suspicious of the idea of a natural knowledge of God. They looked to metaphysics for precise definitions of the technical terminology needed in controversy with Calvinists and extremist Lutherans. Aristotle's concepts of substance and accident enabled them to give a scientific account of Luther's doctrine of justification and grace. Aristotle's principle *actiones sunt suppositorum* enabled them to explain that the work of Christ was of infinite merit because it was the divine person or supposite, not the divine nature, who performed the salvific act. Aristotle's theory of truth enabled them to defend the basic harmony between reason and revelation; although the doctrine of the Trinity transcends human understanding, they argued that it is not possible to prove that it is in conflict with the principle of non-contradiction. Aristotle's fixed essences and static conception of reality provided them with the foundation for the rigorous orthodoxy necessary in a society in which the churches had the function of preaching the duty of obedience to divinely appointed authority and the universities that of equipping the clergy with the instruments needed for their task.

The principal problem was that of establishing the scientific character of theology. Accordingly, the textbooks on metaphysics which began to appear in northern German universities in the late 1590s – about the same time as those in Strasburg and Altdorf – manifest a strong interest in Aristotle's theory of science. David Chytraeus, the founder of the University of Helmstedt, defended the turn to metaphysics by appealing to the fact that Melanchthon had recognised the value not only of the philosophical lexicon in book v of Aristotle's work, but also of the theory of truth elaborated in book IV.[94] This preoccupation rendered their understanding of the *Metaphysics* somewhat different from that of the Spaniards we have studied above. The Spanish authors were, for the most part, members of theological faculties and concerned to work the scholastic doctrine of the transcendentals into Aristotle's doctrine of being and substance; they could exclude parts of the *Metaphysics* as belonging properly to physics and therefore to the domain of their colleagues in the arts faculties. The Germans, on the other hand, as members of faculties of philosophy, sought to overcome the repetitions, inconsistencies and discrepancies between the various parts of Aristotle's work by interpreting it in terms of the theory of science developed in the *Posterior Analytics*. Since a science, for Aristotle, treats not only the subjects belonging to its genus but also their essential properties and principles, they tended to take books I–VI as preliminary, books VII–VIII as dealing with the principles of substance, books IX–X with its properties and book XII with its species.

The earliest German textbook on metaphysics was published by the

94. According to Thomasius 1705, pp. 75–6.

Wittenberg professor Daniel Cramer[95] in 1594, two years before Taurellus' *Synopsis*. Cramer's *Isagoge in Metaphysicam* is a very modest attempt to present the contents of Aristotle's *Metaphysics*, but the work is important because its basic structure was retained in other early German textbooks. After a preface on the subject-matter of metaphysics, he reversed the order of the two central sections of Aristotle's work, dealing in his book I with the properties of being (act and potency, *ens per se* and *ens per accidens*, the transcendentals), in his book II with its principles (the categories and the principles of natural substance) and finally in his book III with its species (the intelligences). Cramer's work was not strictly a commentary on the *Metaphysics*, but rather a textbook written in the form of questions and answers on points of metaphysical doctrine. The treatises of his successors were also independent of Aristotle's text and sought to apply and develop his thought. In so doing, the German school-metaphysicians were willing to draw on Catholic scholastics and Italian naturalists for their material, as it fitted their purposes. In 1596 the questions of Johannes Versor on the *Metaphysics* were published at Wittenberg with a preface emphasising the importance of metaphysical terminology for theological controversy with the Calvinists. Cramer, like Versor, regarded the doctrine of God and the intelligences not as a particular science, but as an integral part of metaphysics. The influence of Duns Scotus' approach to Aristotle's science of being may be observed in the introduction of disjunctive transcendentals among the properties of being in two of the most important treatises on metaphysics composed in Germany in the seventeenth century, the *Exercitationes metaphysicae* (1603–4) of the Wittenberg professor Jakob Martini[96] and *Metaphysica commentatio* (1605) of Cornelius Martini of Helmstedt.[97] Scotus, it will be recalled, denied the possibility of a natural knowledge of God, but added disjunctive properties like act and potency, necessity and contingency, infinity and finitude to the simple transcendentals of the earlier scholastics in order to make possible assertions about immaterial reality.

Decisive for the development of German metaphysics as the science of being was the publication of Suárez' *Disputationes metaphysicae* at Mainz in 1605, eight years after its first publication at Salamanca. Suárez' work was well suited to the purposes of the Lutheran thinkers. He understood metaphysics as a general science of being and rejected the idea of an independent natural theology. He provided the philosophical basis for the

95. Concerning Cramer see Lohr 1975, p. 726.
96. Concerning Jakob Martini see Lohr 1978, pp. 568–9.
97. Concerning Cornelius Martini see Lohr 1978, pp. 567–8.

Table 2. *Organisation of metaphysics in German textbooks*

ARISTOTLE	CRAMER (1594)	J. MARTINI (1603–4)	C. MARTINI (1605)	SCHEIBLER (1618)
I–VI Introductory	Philosophiae partes De subiecto metaphysicae	I.1 De natura et divisione philosophiae; I.2 Definitio metaphysicae; I.3 De ente	Subiectum Argumenta librorum Explicatio transcendentis primi entis	De philosophia I.1 De natura metaphysicae I.2 *Pars Generalis* De subiecto metaphysicae; De ente et essentia I.3 De affectionibus
IX–X Properties of substance: act and potency, unum, verum	I. De affectionibus entis; De divisione entis in ens per se et ens per accidens; actus et potentia; verum, bonum, unum	I.4 De causis et causatis; 5 De necessario et contingenti; 6–10 De uno; 11 De finito et infinito; 12 De perfecto et imperfecto; 13 De priori et posteriori; 14 De eodem et diverso; 15 De aequali et simili; 16 De veritate	De potentia et actu; De causis; De necessitate et contingentia; De finito et infinito; De imperfectione et perfectione; De priori et posteriori; De vero; De bono; Res; Aliquid	entis in genere; I.4–10 De uno, vero, bono I.11–23 De ente perfecto; *De completo et incompleto*; De infinito et finito; De actu et potentia; De necessitate et contingentia; De permanente et successivo; De absoluto et respectivo I.24 De ente rationis *Pars Specialis*
VII–VIII Principles of substance: substance and accident; material substance XII Types of substance	II. De summis entibus et praedicamentis; De principiis substantiae naturalis III. De intelligentiis et substantiis divinis	II.1 De divisione entis II.2–6 De substantia corporea; De intelligentiis; De Deo; De creatione et conservatione; De cultu divino II.7–11 De accidente	De substantia De intelligentiis De primo ente	II.1 De substantia in genere II.2–4 De Deo; De angelis; De anima separata II.5–10 De accidente

treatment of the Incarnation. Most importantly, he provided a foundation for a refutation of the theory of double truth proposed by some extremist theologians. Suárez' *Disputationes* describe a confessionally neutral, possible world to which all those who accepted the doctrine of creation could subscribe. In an effort to avoid the errors which led to conclusions at variance with Christian doctrine, Suárez offered a reinterpretation of Aristotle's doctrine in accordance with its most fundamental axiom, the principle of non-contradiction. Armed with the concept of being which Suárez propounded on the basis of this principle, Lutheran theologians were able to respond to the threat to orthodoxy which came from the extremists. Distinguishing clearly between that which belongs to reason and that which belongs to revelation, they maintained that reason in its own sphere cannot contradict revelation. But the philosophical idea of God which man is able to attain is not such that we can say that it conflicts with the revealed idea. The influence of Suárez' approach may be observed as early as the works of Cornelius and Jakob Martini and most clearly in the *Opus metaphysicum* (1617) and *Epitome metaphysica* (1618) of Christoph Scheibler, professor of logic and metaphysics at Giessen[98] (see table 2).

In spite of such efforts to maintain the integral character of metaphysics, Lutheran writers came increasingly to regard an independent natural theology as a necessity. They distinguished between traditional metaphysics, as a discipline which had the task of explaining certain generally valid terms and principles, and a discipline which was often called *pneumatologia* because it dealt with the nature, properties and activities of spiritual being. Although this development took place in the period after the Thirty Years War, its roots may be found in the period under consideration in this volume. Scheibler himself contributed to the distinction of the two subjects by publishing a separate textbook on *Theologia naturalis* (1621). In the preface to this work he gave a practical reason for treating the subject separately – to limit the extent of his general treatment of metaphysics – but the division was in fact a natural consequence of his own distinction between a *metaphysica generalis* and a *metaphysica specialis*. Also contributory to the separation of the two sciences was the publication at Cologne in 1595 of the *De communibus omnium rerum naturalium principiis* of the Jesuit Benito Pereira. The Wittenberg professor Johannes Scharf[99] referred in the preface to his *Pneumatica* (1629) to Pereira's distinction between first philosophy as

98. Concerning Scheibler see *Allgemeine Deutsche Biographie* 1875–1912, xxx, pp. 700–2; Petersen 1921, pp. 306–8 and *passim*; Wundt 1939, pp. 119–23 and *passim*.
99. Concerning Scharf see Lohr 1980, pp. 717–18.

the science of being and metaphysics as the science of God, and maintained that it was well founded.

The distinction between the science of being and natural theology was also occasioned by a new understanding in Lutheran orthodoxy of the nature and method of revealed theology. On the one hand, a Protestant apologetics appeared about the beginning of the seventeenth century, called forth by the necessity of defending not only the use of philosophy in theology against the agnosticism of the followers of Fausto Sozzini, but also the biblical doctrine of creation against the increasing influence of Stoicism and Epicureanism and the fundamental significance of the faith against a growing spirit of indifference in religious matters. On the other hand, the need was increasingly felt to make the presentation of revealed theology more scientific. Lutheran orthodoxy was opposed to the private interpretation of Scripture and put forward a new understanding of the *analogia fidei* according to which individual biblical texts should be interpreted within the system of the articles of faith. Melanchthon's topical method was therefore succeeded by efforts to present an ὑποτύπωσις of Christian doctrine, such as Paul himself had provided in Romans, or a *corpus doctrinae integrum*, showing the logical interconnections between individual teachings. A similar evolution had taken place in early scholasticism, but whereas thirteenth-century writers generally understood revealed theology as a theoretical science in Aristotle's sense, Lutheran authors of the late sixteenth century tended to regard it as a practical one.

The publication at Basle in 1594 of Jacopo Zabarella's *Opera logica* played an important role in this development. Whereas the theoretical sciences employ a synthetic method in the presentation of doctrine, drawing conclusions from first principles, the practical sciences make use of an analytic method – described by Zabarella – which takes as its point of departure the end or purpose of an action and seeks to discover the means and principles by which this end might be attained. Applied to theology, this method would present eternal beatitude, for example, as the end to be achieved, soteriology as the means to the end, Christology as its principle and the doctrine of man and creation as concerning the subject by whom the end is to be attained. The analytic method became the standard approach in Lutheran dogmatics with the publication in 1619 of Georg Calixt's *Epitome theologiae*. Calixt was a pupil of Cornelius Martini and professor of theology at Helmstedt, but the method was adopted at Jena and Wittenberg as well. At the same time, Calixt regarded philosophy as the condition for the scientific development of revealed theology. In accordance with the apologetic tendency which had appeared in seventeenth-century Lutheranism, he sought to develop rational proofs for the truth of the Christian religion, assigning to philosophy the task of proving not only the existence and attributes of God and the immortality of the soul, but also the necessity of revelation on the basis of God's providential care for men. This understanding of the relationship between philosophy and theology opened the way for the free development in Lutheranism of natural theology as a theoretical science, distinct from the practical science of revealed theology.

The analytic method had little success in those German territories – like the Palatinate, Nassau, Hesse-Kassel and several smaller principalities bordering on the Netherlands – which leaned towards Calvinism and rejected the *Formula concordiae*. In accordance with the architectonic spirit of Calvinist scholasticism, Reformed theologians at the universities of Heidelberg and Marburg and later at Herborn and Burgsteinfurt regarded their science as essentially speculative and followed the synthetic method in the presentation of doctrine. Rejecting the Lutheran transposition of the tracts on salvation and soteriology in systematic works on theology, they took the glory of God and predestination as their point of departure. Reformed dogmatics began with God as the first cause and final goal of all things, and treated his eternal decrees of providence and predestination before taking up his government of the world in time. In this conception natural theology formed an integral part of the *cognitio Dei perfecta* at which theology aimed. Consequently, whereas Lutheran writers on metaphysics sought to maintain the unity of Aristotle's science and only reluctantly admitted the necessity of an independent natural theology, Calvinist authors tended to distinguish clearly between two sciences, a science of God to the extent that he is accessible to human reason and a science of being understood as a universal science which supplies the principles for all the particular sciences.

For the formulation of the distinction they turned to the Jesuit Benito Pereira. In the preface to his *Isagoge in primam philosophiam* (1598) the Marburg professor Rudolphus Goclenius spoke of two separate sciences, a universal science called 'first philosophy' and a particular science called 'metaphysics'. First philosophy deals with being, its properties and its principles; metaphysics studies the various types of immaterial being: God, the intelligences and the human soul. Goclenius composed no treatise on metaphysics as the science of God, but his *Isagoge* is an introduction to first philosophy as the science of being. The work has two parts, the second of which deals with individual questions in the form of disputations. The first part, entitled *Praecepta metaphysica*, contains his complete treatment of the science. The first chapter deals with the definition of first philosophy and the notion of being, chapters 2–15 take up the simple and conjunct properties of being and the last three chapters treat substance and accident as its principles. Goclenius seems to have been aware of the difficulties involved in restricting the term 'metaphysics' to the science of God while speaking of the science of being as 'first philosophy'. In his *Lexicon philosophicum* (1613) he made a new and important addition to philosophical terminology. In the article on abstraction he divided the speculative sciences according to the types of abstraction from matter that characterise them; that employed in physics he described as 'physical', that made use of in the science of God and the intelligences as 'transnatural' and that used in the science of being and the transcendentals as 'ontological'.[100] The term occurs here in its adjectival form, but it soon appeared as a noun. The term 'ontology' made it possible to recognise the claim of the science of being to be metaphysics just as much as the science of God. It was in this way that the term 'metaphysics' came to designate both the universal science of 'first philosophy' or 'ontology' and the particular or special science of 'natural theology'.

The significance of the Calvinist approach to metaphysics was not limited, however, to terminological innovation. In the works of authors like Clemens Timpler of Heidelberg and Steinfurt, Bartholomaeus Keckermann of Heidelberg and Danzig and Johann Heinrich Alsted of Herborn there appeared a new, unified vision of the encyclopaedia of the scientific disciplines in which ontology had the role of assigning to each of the particular sciences its proper domain. This new vision was grounded in a conception of the scientific enterprise which was specifically a product of the Renaissance, a conception which set it apart from the Aristotelianism of both Catholic scholasticism and Lutheran orthodoxy. According to the traditional Aristotelian understanding, scientific knowledge was made up of conclusions which are not only true but also certain, because they are the result of a demonstration based on an evident principle or cause. Science was the habit or faculty by which the mind is disposed to assent to such conclusions. The habit of science was thought of as being acquired by an act of demonstration and increasing as more and more conclusions were drawn from principles. Writers of the Reformed Confession broke with this conception. In their approach science was understood not as a habit but as a body of knowledge, systematically ordered so as to make it possible for a learned man to impart the habit of scientific knowledge to others by correct

100. Goclenius 1613, pp. 13–19.

explanation. Their notion of a *corpus doctrinae* differed from the Lutheran idea in a way which betrayed the influence of humanism. Whereas Lutheran writers concerned themselves exclusively with theological doctrines and sought simply to show the logical connections between individual theological teachings, the Calvinists saw theological doctrine as part of the sum total of the knowledge which has been gained by man in the course of history and transmitted to the present generation by written and oral tradition. The task of the scientist was to systematise the teachings of each of the disciplines – including theology – and to relate them to one another in a new encyclopaedia of knowledge.

At the same time, men like Keckermann departed in another way from the traditional definition of scientific knowledge. According to Aristotle, only necessary, universal statements can be scientific; there can be no demonstration of contingent, singular facts and no science of changeable things as such. But because Reformed theologians wanted to assure the scientific character of theological conclusions, they extended the range of scientific validity beyond the universal conclusions which natural theology can derive from the properties of things to the singular, historical facts, dependent on God's providential care, which revealed theology holds, on the testimony of Scripture, to be principles of knowledge. In his *Praecognita philosophica*[101] Keckermann presented a general theory of science in which he appealed to the norms of certitude which had, as we have seen, been proposed by Melanchthon: revelation, the universal sense experience of men, common innate notions and the orderly presentation of syllogistic conclusions. Keckermann went beyond Melanchthon, however, by defining the *intellectus ordinis in syllogismo* as a *facultas artificialis acquisita per certam disciplinam*. By 'faculty' he meant an internal source of certitude which is a habit or disposition – in accordance with the Aristotelian conception. By the 'discipline' through which the habit is acquired he meant the external body of doctrine which the learned man must master. The most significant word in Keckermann's definition is the word 'artificial'. He described the habit acquired by the learned man not as 'scientific' but as 'artificial', because it concerns conclusions which belong to all the liberal arts and includes both universal conclusions drawn from the nature of things and singular, contingent conclusions based on testimony, for the reason that knowledge of both types of conclusion can be gained by the systematic application of methodical principles.[102]

101. Keckermann 1607d, I, pp. 118–24.   102. See Ritschl 1906.

The emphasis in this new theory of science was thus placed, above all, on the orderly, systematic presentation of doctrine. A discipline in the liberal arts is a system of precepts and rules, methodically ordered, through which one can – with the requisite natural ability and corresponding practice – gain the habit of knowledge in the liberal arts. Around the beginning of the last quarter of the sixteenth century the term 'system' began to be used by Reformed theologians for ordered compilations of Christian teachings. The term acquired its technical sense of a body of knowledge unified by a single idea or principle in writers like Keckermann. These thinkers understood each of the liberal arts as a system of precepts and rules according to which a given subject-matter is arranged for correct explanation. The precepts (*praecepta*) are made up of definitions and distributions. The rules (*regulae*) are made up of conclusions; they are called 'theorems' in the speculative disciplines and 'canons' in the practical ones. The principle or idea according to which the precepts and rules are ordered is not merely an external principle, so that the elements are simply parts of a whole, but one which grounds the knowledge of the elements and coordinates their real functions. Theological rules are derived, by the analytical method, from revelation; philosophical rules, by the synthetic method, from *ipsa rerum naturalium natura* or *notitiae nobiscum natae*. Revealed theology is a discipline consisting of rules (*loci communes*), disposed systematically for the understanding of the book of Scripture. Natural theology is that part of the discipline of pneumatics which consists of rules concerning God's existence, essence, eternal decrees and temporal government of the created world, as they can be read in the book of nature. The other two parts of pneumatics are angelography and psychology.

The idea of each of the liberal arts as a system found its logical counterpart in the idea of the encyclopaedia of the arts. It was at this point that the new conception of scientific knowledge espoused by Reformed thinkers affected the traditional role of metaphysics as the queen of the sciences. Keckermann and Timpler composed systems of logic, rhetoric, physics, mathematics, optics, astronomy, geography and the various parts of practical philosophy. Keckermann and Alsted also drew up systems of theology. All of these systems taken together were regarded as forming a unified whole. Alsted[103] published a complete edition of Keckermann's works in 1613 under the title *Systema systematum*. His own *Cursus philosophici encyclopaedia* appeared in

103. Concerning Alsted see *Dictionnaire d'histoire et géographie ecclésiastiques* 1912–, II, cols. 773–5; Petersen 1921, p. 311; Wundt 1939, pp. 80–3, 236–9 and *passim*; *Lexikon für Theologie* 1957–67, I, col. 368.

1620 and ten years later his complete *Encyclopaedia* for all four university faculties. For each of these authors the system of metaphysics (see table 3) had the task of assigning to each of the disciplines its proper domain and place in the encyclopaedia of the arts. Pneumatics was to deal with spiritual reality, physics with corporeal reality as corporeal, mathematics with quantity, practical philosophy with human actions as moral, law with human actions as political, medicine with the human body as to be cured. Accordingly, the metaphysics which – as first philosophy – formed the foundation of this encyclopaedia was no longer understood as a science in the Aristotelian sense, but rather as one of the liberal arts. Metaphysics thus became closely connected with the theory of the arts, which these authors, employing the Greek word, entitled 'technologia'. Timpler[104] prefaced the second edition of his *Metaphysicae systema methodicum* of 1606 with a *Technologia seu tractatus generalis de natura et differentiis artium liberalium*. Alsted opened his *Encyclopaedia* with a general account of the new theory of scientific knowledge. Under the title *Praecognita philosophica*, he treated the theory of the principles of knowledge, the theory of the habit of knowledge, the theory of the arts and didactics. For the third section of this introduction he also used the neologism 'technologia'.

Clemens Timpler was the thinker who followed out most consistently the consequences of the understanding of metaphysics as one of the liberal arts. Because the individual systems which make up the encyclopaedia of the liberal arts are bodies of doctrine, the discipline which coordinates them must itself be less a theory of being than a theory of knowledge. Although, *ordine inventionis*, this discipline follows the other disciplines, it must, *ordine doctrinae*, precede all of them. Consequently, Timpler proposed that the subject-matter of metaphysics is not being, but rather the intelligible, πᾶν νοητόν. Metaphysics is distinct from logic which also deals with the same subject because it is a speculative discipline, whereas logic is a practical one. In a definition which is only comprehensible against the background of the Reformed theory of knowledge, Timpler defined metaphysics as the 'ars contemplativa quae tractat de omni intelligibili quatenus ab homine naturali rationis lumine sine ullo materiae conceptu est intelligibile'.[105] The designation *res* applies to everything concerning which it is possible to form an intelligible proposition. It includes, therefore, not only being, but also privations of being and not-being itself. Not-being must be considered by metaphysics because it is intelligible, at least *per accidens*; without the notion of not-being it would be impossible to defend the rule of non-contradiction

104. Concerning Timpler see Lohr 1982, pp. 194–6.   105. Timpler 1606, p. 1 (1.1).

Table 3. *The systems of metaphysics*

GOCLENIUS (1598)	TIMPLER (1606)	KECKERMANN (1609–13)	ALSTED (1611)
1.1 De definitione primae philosophiae / De subiecto	1.1 De natura metaphysicae / 2 De nihilo et essentiae / 3 De ente et eius distributionibus	1 *De ente primario sive de substantia* / 1 De metaphysica; 2 De ente improprie dicto; 3 De imagine entis; 4 De opposito entis seu de negatione et non-ente; 5 De ente proprie dicto; 6 De substantia	De natura metaphysicae / 1 *De transcendentibus* / 1 De ente; 2 Aliquid et Res
1.2 *De entis affectionibus*	1 *De attributis simplicibus entium* / 4 De existentia; 5 De duratione	7 *De principiis substantiae*: De dependentia a Deo; 8 De compositione seu concretione; 9 De principiis internis: De essentia substantiae; 10 De existentia substantiae	[*Principia:*] 3 De essentia; 4 De existentia; 5 De duratione
3 De uno et multis; 4 De eodem et diverso; 5 De vero et falso; 6 De bono et malo	II *De attributis coniunctis et absolutis* / 1 De perfectione et imperfectione; 2 De simplicitate et compositione; 3 De unitate et multiplicitate; 4 De infinitate et finitate; 5 De illocalitate et localitate; 6 De necessitate et contingentia; 7 De possibilitate et impossibilitate; 8 De veritate et falsitate; 9 De bonitate et malitia	11 *Modi entis in genere* / 12 *Modi instar qualitatum primi*; 13 Unitas; 14 Veritas; 15 Bonitas; 16 Perfectio et plenitudo; 17 Pulchritudo; 18 Finitudo seu determinatio essentiae et existentiae	[*Modus primus:*] 6 De unitate; 7 De veritate; 8 De bonitate; [*Modus ortus unitus:*] 9 De ordine; 10 De numero; 11 De perfectione; 12 De pulchritudine

which is the most fundamental law of thought. The subject-matter of metaphysics is, therefore, divided into an *intelligibile negativum* and an *intelligibile positivum*, into *nihil* and *aliquid*. The latter is divided into *essentia*, that through which a being is that which it is, and *ens*, which is in turn divided into *ens reale* and *ens rationis*. In Timpler's derivation of the attributes of being there appears clearly the Calvinist emphasis on the gulf which separates the infinite from the finite. Only existence and duration apply to all reality. Not-being enters into all other attributes. Timpler even subsumed the traditional transcendentals under the conjunct attributes, allowing them no absolute validity. Because they are attributes of finite being only, they admit of contrariety: unity and multiplicity, truth and falsity, goodness and malice. Timpler's system of metaphysics thus explains the immanent distinctions of the intelligible, then derives the simple and conjunct attributes of reality and finally concludes by presenting its ultimate divisions into *substantia increata, substantia creata immaterialis* and *substantia creata materialis*.

In these Reformed treatises no attention is paid to the question whether anything outside the mind corresponds to such systems. They are purely rational constructions; the burden of verification is placed on the discipline of revealed theology. In this regard they recall the dilemma with which the history of medieval metaphysics closed. Shortly before the Council of Basle Jean Gerson had maintained that metaphysics can only establish contact between the intra-mental world of the sciences and extra-mental reality through the concept of being, but at the same time that an adequate concept of being is only possible with the concept of God, for which revelation is necessary. Timpler and his colleagues also stood at the end of an epoch. In the first years of the Thirty Years War Heidelberg and Marburg were lost to the Reformed Confession; the former university became Catholic, the latter, Lutheran. Steinfurt and Herborn suffered disastrous losses and were unable to maintain their position. After the war Calvinist philosophy disappeared from the German territories, while the problem of grounding metaphysics without revelation became more and more acute.

XI

PROBLEMS OF KNOWLEDGE AND ACTION

17

FATE, FORTUNE, PROVIDENCE AND
HUMAN FREEDOM

These concepts constitute one of the fundamental philosophical problems about human destiny in general and about human actions in particular. Is the individual a rigidly defined link in a universal chain of being in which birth, life and death have been entirely preordained by physical cosmic forces? Or can the individual control his life and, by means of more or less independent decisions, direct it to some consciously chosen goal? Such questions are as old as humanity itself. Sometimes they are coloured by religious beliefs or magical and astrological superstitions and scarcely emerge into popular awareness. At other times they stimulate the philosophical reflections which are humanity's first steps away from a dark and fearful fate towards a rational understanding of natural and historical events.

THE PROBLEM IN ANTIQUITY AND THE MIDDLE AGES

In antiquity philosophy could not entirely disburden itself of εἱμαρμένη, the mysterious fate which ruled men and gods, impervious to protests and invocations. Except for thinkers like Plato, Aristotle and Plotinus, who achieved a profound and rigorous grasp of the first principle, the bulk of Greek, Hellenistic and Roman thought tended to be drawn by its monistic and materialist metaphysics into a kind of cosmic necessity which denied human freedom and excluded providence (πρόνοια) and the contingency of events (τύχη). The first centuries of the Christian era teemed with tracts about fate. One current was represented by Alexander of Aphrodisias, who, following Aristotle, asserted the possibility of contingency, that is, ἐνδεχόμενον. By contrast, evolving Neoplatonism petrified the causal links between the degrees of being, thus unleashing a frenzy of magical-mystical practices which profoundly affected the purity of man's religious relationship with the divine. The Church Fathers, steadfast in their biblical conception of a personal deity who created the world out of love and whose intelligence guides each single being according to its own nature towards its own good, reacted against fatalistic theories that subjugated human life to the stars. According to the Fathers, fate was an empty word, a diabolical deceit designed to strip man of any awareness of personal responsibility for his actions. Augustine, who had run the gauntlet of such theories, hated the word 'fate' itself: 'abhorremus praecipue propter vocabulum, quod non in re vera consuevit intelligi.'[1] Against Epicurean atheism and Stoic immanentism, he asserted free will, the efficacy of prayer and the dominion of providence in the world and in human affairs.

Boethius somewhat softened the psychological, not to mention theoretical, aversion of earlier Christian thinkers towards fate. He regarded it as nothing more than the movement and disposition imprinted by the divine mind onto created beings situated in a providential scheme directed to a particular end.[2] In *De consolatione philosophiae*, the masterpiece he composed in prison, Boethius drew heavily on classical sources to produce a rational and Christian synthesis of the topics associated with fate, namely fortune and chance, divine foreknowledge and providence and freedom of the will. Boethius' eirenic approach and solutions were an influential legacy to the Middle Ages and Renaissance.

Scholasticism, which had begun to tackle more strictly theological problems like predestination as early as the ninth century with Gottschalk (d. *c.* 870) and Anselm,[3] aimed to systematise the whole field. According to Thomas Aquinas, with whom this process culminated, nothing here below is determined by fate, either in the pagan mythological sense or because subject to astral bodies. No events, even so-called chance occurrences, can escape God's intelligence and loving attention to the secondary causes of nature and to human will. Even if astral and demonic forces occasionally affect and change our understanding (whose functioning is structurally linked to our sensations), any such influence is indirect and is, in any case, entirely blocked by the interior decisions taken by free will.[4] Into the general scheme of a providence which maintains the particular mode of action of the individual natural, necessary or free causes, Thomas also reintroduces the predestination of the elect to paradise and of the sinners to damnation. This provoked much later confusion and, as we shall see, an indignant refutation by Pomponazzi in his *De fato*.[5] Apart from these theological complications, two further positions trace their philosophical roots in Christian thought to a belief in God's absolute transcendence and

1. Augustine, *De civitate Dei* v.9.
3. See Gottschalk 1945. For Anselm, see *De libertate arbitrii* (*c.* 1080–5); *De concordia praescientiae et praedestinationis et gratiae Dei cum libero arbitrio* (1107–8).
4. Thomas Aquinas, *Summa theologiae* I, q. 115, aa. 3–6; q. 116, aa. 1–4. For a comparison with Boethius see Mauro 1981.   5. Thomas Aquinas, *Summa theologiae* I, q. 22, a. 4; q. 23, a. 5.

his loving freedom in creating the universe out of nothing: the liberation of human freedom from cosmic influences and from 'secondary deities', and the declaration that eternal divine foreknowledge can coexist with the free positing of future contingents by human judgement. The consequence of this radical metaphysical conception is two-fold: God is not bound by physical laws and may freely intervene wherever and whenever he chooses, and man is not the passive victim of irrational forces extraneous to laws divinely incorporated into the universal order of being. No one realised more clearly than Duns Scotus just how innovative this was for Christian thought.[6] He discerned the unfolding of a supreme freedom and assigned primacy in man's psychological make-up to the spontaneous volitional tension of love rather than to the cogent objectivity of intellective judgements.

HUMANIST DISCUSSIONS

In some respects the fragmentation of scholasticism was well under way by the second half of the thirteenth century. More than anything else, Latin Averroism helped to reactivate a number of ancient and deterministic ideas. Several propositions censored by Étienne Tempier at Paris in 1277[7] indicate a revival of astrology and a denial of personal responsibility and freedom of choice at all social levels. Fourteenth-century Dominican and Franciscan theologians stopped building on tradition and fell into sterile controversy about the priority of the intellect and the will.[8] At the same time Ockhamist nominalism was undermining the possibility of a metaphysical account of being, tending instead to concentrate on the immediate perception of phenomena in their ceaseless becoming. This signalled an interest in scientific knowledge for its own sake, though that knowledge took hybrid and simplistic forms. In the astrology of the period, for instance, it is not easy to distinguish the fruits of observation and mathematical calculation from information derived from the traditional judicial astrology of horoscopes and elections.

Notwithstanding the methodological rigour of individuals like Pietro d'Abano and the analyses made by Nicole Oresme, works such as those of Guido Bonatti, Cecco d'Ascoli and Ristoro d'Arezzo, as well as the teaching of Blasius of Parma in various north Italian universities,[9] were profoundly

---

6. See Gilson 1952, pp. 316ff.; Poppi 1966, pp. 67–92; *Regnum hominis* 1978, I, pp. 277–302 (Poppi).
7. See *Chartularium* 1889–97, I, pp. 543ff.   8. See *Cambridge History* 1982, pp. 629–41 (Korolec).
9. See Federici Vescovini 1979, 1983, especially chs. 7 and 8.

equivocal about astrological determinism and the possibility for man and society to choose their own destinies. Only later, with Galileo, Kepler and Newton, when the heavenly bodies were finally reduced to matter sustained by the universal laws of gravitation did people begin to lose their belief in astrology.[10]

The fourteenth century marks a sharp break with the past and points unmistakably to the modern era. The entire continent of Europe was convulsed by immense social, political, economic and religious changes as well as natural calamities like the Black Death. Every corner of society was infiltrated by new anxieties: people wondered whether they still had any freedom or whether they had fallen under the tyranny of occult, stellar and irrational forces. In this situation individuals like Dante, Petrarch and Salutati were the effective defenders of man's dignity and freedom from the newly translated Greek and Moslem astrology and from the determinism of the Averroist physicians and physicists. Precisely these problems are the subject of Salutati's lengthy *De fato, fortuna et casu*.

In the *Divina commedia* Dante personifies fortune mythologically as an intelligence which, in accordance with God's instructions, moves the celestial sphere that brings blessings and other 'worldly splendours'.[11] In the sixteenth canto of *Purgatorio*, while refuting the false insinuations of Guido del Duca, Marco Lombardo expatiates on the causes of the universal corruption of society in his day. The malice of men cannot be ascribed to stellar influences, or to some fatal necessity which compels them to evil, because God has endowed each man with the intelligence and the will to perceive the good ('light is given to you for good and for ill') and to follow it in his actions. Virtue thus conquers even those inclinations to evil which are subject to some degree of stellar influence.[12]

Petrarch is already marked as a 'new man' by his discerning choice of classical sources and of teachers such as Cicero, Seneca, Vergil and Plato. His letters and other writings reveal an innate distaste for the philosophical views of his contemporaries – English terminist logic, Arab medicine, the empty abstractions of the Aristotelians, fatalism and that naturalistic rigidity which suffocates human freedom and immobilises history by denying the inexhaustible creativity of the spirit.

In a celebrated letter to Boccaccio he accuses astrologers of brazen ignorance and foolish profanity. In another letter, addressed to Francesco Bruni in plague-ridden Venice in 1362, he notes that fate does not consist in

---

10. See A. Maier 1966, pp. 219–50.
11. Dante, *Inferno* VII.67–96.   12. Dante, *Purgatorio* XVI.64–81.

the motions of the stars but in divine decrees and natural causes. 'What', he asks, 'is the use of the soothsayers? What is the point of the astrologers? Why do the *mathematici* waste their time in useless speculations?' To be sure, they can predict eclipses, rainfall and the direction of the wind, but only God knows what will be our freely willed decisions. Mockingly he bids the fools to pay no attention to the circlings of the stars. The stars have no power, or at least, no power that we clearly understand. It is pure chance if the mendacity of the astrologers produces some small morsels of truth. Let them therefore leave us alone and stop trying to trap people in the abyss of ignorance.[13]

Petrarch's position in respect to fortune – a notion which pervades his writings – is less clear. He explores a wealth of classical imagery, but his conception of fortune shifts uneasily between the philosophical notion of an orderly, causal necessity and the popular idea of a blind, irrational and instinctive force.[14] In his *De remediis utriusque fortunae*, however, he builds on Boethius to develop a greater awareness of how human virtue and reason can withstand fortune's relentless claims. This humanist approach was to enjoy a remarkable ascendancy over thinkers and *literati* from Boccaccio (for example, in the second day of the *Decameron*) down to the Renaissance.[15]

Patristic and scholastic doctrines and the new insights from classical antiquity find a more mature synthesis in the work and indeed in the life of Coluccio Salutati, Chancellor of Florence. Like his venerated master Petrarch, he makes a cult of human freedom and activity. These are articulated through the acquisition of a *sapientia* closely linked to *eloquentia*, because beyond individual moral growth and the contemplative ideal, each man is a citizen who must work for the common good of his city or state. Though full of admiration for the moral heroism of the Stoics, Salutati is mindful that we are neither ruled by fate nor blindly led by natural forces. It is through our commitment to overcoming the adversities of fortune and historical circumstances that we become virtuous: 'virtuosi non natura sed operibus efficimur'.[16] The myth of Hercules – the central theme of Salutati's *De laboribus Herculis* – recurs in humanist celebrations of man's constructive capacities and of the dignity which raises him to the level of the stars, that is, to the level of a divinity.

13. Petrarch, *Epistolae seniles* III.1 (to Boccaccio, 1363); I.7 (to Bruni, 1362).
14. See Heitmann 1958, especially p. 43 and the general bibliography on p. 25, n. 2.
15. For the development of the literary theme of fortune and its various symbols (wheel, storm, sail, etc.) from antiquity to the end of the Renaissance throughout Europe, see Doren 1922–3.
16. Salutati 1891–1911, II, p. 106.

Despite having praised the astrologer who had calculated the horoscope for the victory at Cascina in 1365, Salutati soon became harshly critical of astrology. In a treatise composed between 1396 and 1399 he addressed the question – put to him by the Cistercian prior Felice Agnobelli – whether the violent rivalries which were tearing apart the city of Perugia should be ascribed to human will or to a fatal conjunction of other, external causes. Although not particularly original, this work is coherent and draws upon an astonishing range of sources, summarising Christian views on the theme *De fato, fortuna et casu* in a cogent and discriminating fashion.[17] Granted that the hierarchy of beings is irradiated by a fundamental divine causality, fate is merely the organisation and interrelationship of secondary causes as these are thought and willed by divine providence. Fate, therefore, does not change the essential nature or the specific causality of beings, but coexists in a necessary fashion with agent beings and in a contingent fashion with operative beings. Salutati thus defends personal human responsibility theologically and metaphysically. Astrology and other occult divinatory arts, he shows, should not have any credibility because of the enormous complexity and variety of astral interrelationships, because of the extreme unreliability of our observational instruments and finally because of the impossibility of calculating the reactions of individual people (books I and II).

Like his treatment of fate, Salutati's treatment of fortune and chance reveals an erudite philological sensitivity to classical usage. However, he restricts fortune and chance to natural situations and choices. Though unforeseeable and beyond the scope of our choices, such circumstances are still contained within the providential plan governing our lives (books III and IV). In conclusion, Salutati firmly underlines human freedom and responsibility, saying to the Perugians at one point: 'The cause of your ills is neither fate nor the stars above, but is in your own sinfulness. People of Perugia, the cause is in yourselves.'[18]

By the first half of the fifteenth century the energetic quest for classical sources and the thirst for new, or more faithful, translations from the Greek had given scholars a direct and almost complete knowledge of classical

17. Salutati 1985. See also Gasperetti 1941; Rüegg 1954. A similar treatise, *De fato*, attacking poetic myths and astrological misconceptions, had been written a few years earlier (between 1381 and 1385) by Francesco de Caronellis, a Franciscan in the convent of S. Antonio at Padua. The work is dedicated to Antonio della Scala, the ruler of Verona, and makes abundant reference to classical writers and medieval theologians; see Griffante 1983, p. 15.
18. Salutati 1985, p. 216: 'Non est . . . constellatio celi vel fatum vobis imminens tot malorum causa, sed vestra vitia, Perusini! In vobis causa est . . .'

thought. In addition to modernised versions of Aristotle and of much of the *corpus Platonicum*, the recently recovered Stoic and Epicurean texts widened intellectual horizons even further.

As a rule, the Stoic doctrine of moral virtue was greatly esteemed, even though humanists tended to reject most of the monistic-materialist metaphysics and the notion of fate which supported it. Following the Fathers, humanists preferred to approach pagan concepts of God and providence from a Christian point of view. However, with the Epicurean proposition that *voluptas* is the ultimate goal of life, we find a radical break from the patristic view. While Christian thinkers had habitually vilified this proposition, some humanists tried to harmonise Epicurean with Christian doctrine. They found in Epicurus' morality of pleasure a fuller and more human account of the tendency towards goodness and happiness which is imprinted on human nature. They rejected, of course, the elements of atheism and rigid determinism which they found in the Epicurean theology and physics.[19]

Underlying the philological expertise and elegance of humanist writing we can see a new conception of life and a fresh concern for political and historical events. Belief in divine providence where worldly matters were concerned was somewhat enfeebled. Man must now struggle alone against adversities seemingly sent by a blind fortune. Some humanists, like Poggio Bracciolini in his *De miseria humanae conditionis* and his *De varietate fortunae*, passionately champion a rational virtue which can overcome ill fortune. Others, like Leon Battista Alberti, dwell rather on the wretchedness of the human condition as a plaything of mysterious powers outside our control. In his *Della famiglia* (1433–4) Alberti visualises a situation where virtue prevails over fortune, but when he discusses *fatum et fortuna* (in one of his *Intercoenales*, *c.* 1439) human destiny is ineluctably at the mercy of fate. He admits, however, that prudence and steadfastness can greatly assist man as he is tossed to and fro in the chaos of existence: 'plurimum tamen in rebus humanis prudentiam et industriam valere non ignorabimus'.[20] In the letter *Somnium de fortuna* (June 1444) written from Vienna to Procopius of Rabenstein, Enea Silvio Piccolomini, the future Pius II, imagines travelling

19. This view of Epicureanism was anticipated in Bruni's *Isagogicon moralis disciplinae* (*c.* 1425) and vigorously defended in Cosma Raimondi's *Defensio Epicuri contra stoicos et peripateticos* (*c.* 1430); it was taken up again by Filelfo around the middle of the century, by Ficino in his *De quattuor sectis philosophorum* (1457) and by Bartolomeo Scala in his *Epistola de nobilioribus philosophorum sectis et de eorum inter se differentia* (formerly attributed to Giovan Battista Boninsegni); see Garin 1961, pp. 72–92.

20. See Garin 1975, pp. 131–96; the lengthy bibliography in *Dizionario biografico degli Italiani* 1960–, I, pp. 702–19. Doren 1922–3, pp. 132–3 looks at the motif of fortune in Alberti; see also Sasso 1953.

to the kingdom of *Fortuna*. His description resembles Alberti's and the closely argued dialogue makes it very clear that as far as Piccolomini is concerned only the wise and virtuous man can challenge fortune and escape.[21]

Despite the contradictory voices, such as that of Alberti, it seems fair to conclude that humanists generally countered the irrationality of life and destiny with constructive optimism. In his old age Poggio Bracciolini put this sentiment explicitly: 'The strength of fortune is never so great that it will not be overcome by men who are steadfast and resolute.'[22] Fortune *per se* is either nothing, or it is simply the encounter between vigilant human reason and the forces – equally rational – which God has embedded in nature.

One of the most unsettling thinkers of the period is Lorenzo Valla, whose philological acumen and rhetorical logic permitted new and deeper insights into the mysteries of the Christian faith itself and kindled a fierce polemic with scholastic philosophy and theology. In 1439 he composed his *De libero arbitrio*, a dialogue with the twin goals of discovering 'whether divine foreknowledge precludes free will, and whether the views of Boethius on this matter were correct'.[23]

Cassirer, surprisingly, said of this work that it was the first time since antiquity that the question of freedom had been considered from a purely secular point of view, before the tribunal of natural reason. In fact, there is little new in the first of Valla's questions – except the exemplum of a pagan parable – though his theological conclusions are clearly fideistic. Unlike Salutati's treatise, which was soon forgotten, Valla's remained influential until Leibniz and was invoked – with differing motives and interpretations – by both Erasmus and Luther. As in the *De voluptate*, Valla attacks Boethius' *De consolatione philosophiae*, for discussing the problems of free will and foreknowledge in a pagan fashion, for not mentioning Christ and for failing to reach any real conclusions because his excessive zeal for philosophy drew him to Aristotle instead of St Paul ('nimis philosophiae amator fuit'). The theologians who followed this *nova via* went so far as to make philosophy the mistress of theology, compelling her to follow philosophy's methods to the letter. Valla, by contrast, hopes that Christians and especially theologians 'would not yield so much to philosophy and waste so much labour on it'.

---

21. See E. S. Piccolomini 1551, pp. 611–16 (*Epistola* CVIII).
22. Poggio Bracciolini 1964–9, I, p. 131 (*De miseria conditionis humanae*).
23. L. Valla 1934, p. 17. Regarding this work see also the introduction and Italian translation in L. Valla 1953, pp. xxv–xxvii, 251–82.

Valla's point of departure was not so much anti-scholastic as anti-rational. All the same, the dialogue presents fully the dilemma of how to reconcile human self-determinism with God's foreknowledge and provi-dence. If man enjoys free will, one cannot hold that God has known the result from the beginning, because in that case each individual would have to do exactly what God had foreseen and foreknown. On the other hand, if man is not free, any striving for morality and the common good is futile, and any reward would be just as unfair as the punishments meted out to sinners. Clearly, if God had foreseen Judas' betrayal, Judas could not have acted in any other way than that divinely foreseen for him. A dilemma like this is an invitation to religious doubt, but Valla calmly states that there is no connection between the simple foreknowledge of future events and the will's determination to bring them about. The former is an act of divine intelligence, the latter an independent decision of the human will: 'The fact that God knows beforehand what a man will do results in no necessity that he should do it, because man acts according to his own will: that which is voluntary cannot be necessary.' Just as our knowledge of past and present events does not necessitate their happening, so it is with God's knowledge of future events. Knowing our will better than we do, God always knows what actions will arise from it, but this in no way affects the freedom of our decisions. 'So foreknowledge is merely knowing and the rest is free will.' The example chosen – Apollo predicting the miserable destiny of Sextus Tarquinius, who was to be exiled for his crimes – emphasises the fact that this is merely the prediction of a destiny over which Apollo has no power: 'I know destiny; I do not decide it. I can complain about fortune, but I cannot change it. What I have is merely the ability to foreknow and predict.' The unfortunate king then blames Jupiter for having wanted human beings to be the way they are, some mild and good, others inclined to evil.

As Valla notes, the force of this example consists in its sharp division between foreknowledge and divine will. This merely restates but does not solve the fundamental problem. God's will is an unfathomable mystery, as Paul noted in the Epistle to the Romans, when discussing the selection of Jacob instead of Esau; the motives for this choice are hidden even from the angels. These motives are utterly beyond human comprehension and justification, but man knows with the certainty of faith that such choices are dictated by a completely wise and pure will. What does it matter that reason is an inadequate tool? Faith is a more certain foundation than philosophy: 'We do not know the cause of a thing; what does it matter? We stand by our faith, not by the demonstrability of reason.' Boethius' attempt to overturn

Paul's views, by attributing to human efforts what is, in fact, purely the effect of God's mercifulness, constitutes in Valla's opinion the high cost of theology's acquiescence to philosophy. This kind of rationalism leads, Valla says, away from God and truth: 'In my opinion no one who likes philosophy so much can be pleasing to God.' Luther later adopted these observations in his denunciation of Erasmus' Pelagianism.

Valla's undeniable fideism and his passionate condemnation of philosophical rationalism in theological debate account for the slenderness of his contribution to the controversy about freedom.[24] This controversy was to be reactivated in a much more vigorous manner by Pomponazzi nearly a century later.

THE ASTROLOGICAL IMPLICATIONS

In the second half of the fifteenth century the problem of determinism versus freedom was closely linked with renewed attacks against astrology and magic which culminate in Giovanni Pico della Mirandola's *Disputationes adversus astrologiam divinatricem* (1494) and the reactions to it – favourable and unfavourable – over the following decades. The arrival of Greek scholars in Italy with the Council of Florence and after the fall of Constantinople kindled a bitter debate amongst Italian intellectuals about the importance of Platonism and its relationship with Aristotelianism. Georgius Gemistus Pletho's version of Plato, for instance, contained elements of Neoplatonic and Christian theology and was strongly coloured by esoteric doctrines from the East.[25] In it, man was reduced to a subordinate position in a hierarchy of cosmic forces. Theodore Gaza reacted against this view in a treatise on fate that was inspired by an Aristotelian belief in the rationality of natural laws.[26]

Marsilio Ficino was wary about Pletho's approach and tried independently to find a place for genuine Platonic thought within the edifice of Christian philosophy and theology. To this end he dedicated his life, his philological skills and his incomparable aesthetic sensibility. To understand *his* Plato (*Plato noster*) fully he plunged into a programme of reading and translating that embraced the entire spectrum of antique magical-mystical literature, from the *Chaldaean Oracles* and the *corpus Hermeticum* to the

24. L. Valla 1934, pp. 7–10, 19, 29, 33, 50, 48. See also Cassirer 1927, ch. 3; Di Napoli 1971, pp. 163–76.
25. See *Nicolò Cusano* 1970, pp. 175–93, especially p. 181 (Kristeller): 'The treatise contains a short and tight statement of strict determinism and does not reveal much else of Pletho's thought, let alone of his Platonism.' See Pletho 1858, pp. 64–78 (II.6).
26. See Taylor 1925a; F. Masai 1956; Garin 1958a, pp. 153–219.

followers of Neoplatonism. From this material Ficino derived his conception of the human spirit as independent of, and superior to, celestial forces. He vigorously championed this independence in a number of important works, including his *Theologia platonica* (1469–74) and his *Disputatio contra iudicium astrologorum* (1475–7); but he became immersed in magical and astrological beliefs in the *De vita coelitus comparanda* (1489), which even includes a horoscope for Christ, and in the *De sole et lumine* (1493). The famous letter to Poliziano (20 August 1494), responding to the news that Pico's *Disputationes* were being criticised for their ambiguity towards magic and the *prisca theologia*, reads like an attempt to pre-empt similar criticisms of his own work. It is significant that the long list of late fifteenth-century Florentine astrologers given by Luca Gaurico in his address at Ferrara – the *De inventoribus et laudibus astronomiae* (1507) – is headed by 'Marsilius Ficinus florentinus'.[27]

At the Aragonese court in Naples, Giovanni Pontano was thinking along similar lines to Ficino. In the brief poem *Urania* (1476–80) and in the *De rebus coelestibus* (1494) he recognised a powerful, irrational and capricious astral influence on human behaviour and destiny, though he exempted from it the most personal and spiritual of freely chosen decisions.[28] He reiterated this view in his *De fortuna* (1500): 'Where reason has greatest sway, fortune is most ineffectual.' It is not entirely clear how Pontano reconciles human life to the shadowy imperatives of a fate which orchestrates the stars to affect human activities and possessions adversely.[29]

Despite his rigorously Aristotelian training, even Giovanni Pico fell under the spell of Ficino's fascination with the *pia philosophia* that would reconcile and unite heaven and earth. This is evident in the section on *Conclusiones magicae et orphicae* for the 1486 disputation in Rome. By contrast, the famous *Oratio*, which precedes it, contains a splendid celebration of human freedom. God has placed man at the midpoint between the superior, divine realm and the inferior, animal world, and has made him entirely independent of rigid stellar and natural laws; thus man, uniquely endowed with reason and judgement (*ratione consilioque*), may

---

27. See *L'opera e il pensiero* 1965, II, p. 243 (Zambelli); Walker 1958, pp. 3–59.
28. See Tateo 1960a; De Nichilo 1975.
29. See Pontano 1518, f. 284^r; see also f. 308^v: 'Nec temere igitur nec praeter rerum naturam ac rationem dictum est a nobis, fortunam tum fati ministram esse illique et obsequi et famulari, tum executricem eorum omnium, quae a stellis portendantur ac coelo, vel suum ipsius coeli potius ac stellarum effectum . . . Et vero quamquam nonnumquam vis maxima est coeli eaque fortasse insuperabilis, iuverit tamen, quod prudentis est officium hominis illud graviter praestitisse ne ignaviter superemur.' See the full analysis of these three books of Pontano on fortune in Doren 1922–3, pp. 121–8.

choose his own destiny and achieve divine immortality.[30] In the *Disputationes*, his last work, Pico further stresses this independence from astral and demonic influences, from physical and instinctual determinism, so as to highlight man's self-fashioning capacities. Man, unique among earthly creatures, can freely and consciously fashion himself as he wishes through his own activity: 'The condition of our birth is that we should become what we want to be.'[31] All nature unfolds according to the causality of the laws which God has set in the secondary causes. From the rational and Christian points of view, fate is merely that necessity which God has written into nature itself and which is obedient to him. This is his providence in the world. Fortune is not a divinity, as the pagans believed; nor is it some mythological entity which participates in human affairs, whatever impression to the contrary might be created by chance encounters with causes beyond our control.[32]

Nature thus rationally structured presents itself to the calm scrutiny of human reason and observation (*ratio et experimentum*). It is necessary, however, to eliminate the fantasies of astrology, of the occult sciences which use astral symbols, of the mantic arts and of cabala, all of which corrupt natural knowledge and encourage idolatry. Pico gives a ferociously radical condemnation of magic – 'an amalgam of idolatry, astrology and superstitious medicine'.[33] While astronomy is the entirely praiseworthy and serious mathematical study of celestial dynamics, astrology is a degeneration, void of sense, certainty and truth, and no more than superstitious rigmarole which steals man's liberty and replaces it with anxiety.[34]

It has been suggested that Pico's assault on astrology was too rhetorical and abstract, and that if the human mind was to be opened to a mathematical and mechanical conception of the universe an entirely

30. G. Pico 1942, p. 106: 'Tu, nullis angustiis coërcitus pro tuo arbitrio, in cuius manu te posui, tibi illam praefinies [naturam]. Medium te mundi posui ut circumspiceres inde commodius quicquid est in mundo. Nec te caelestem neque terrenum, neque mortalem neque immortalem fecimus, ut tui ipsius quasi arbitrarius honorariusque plastes et fictor, in quam malueris tute formam effingas. Poteris in inferiora quae sunt bruta degenerare; poteris in superiora quae sunt divina ex tui animi sententia regenerari.'   31. *Ibid.*, pp. 108–10.
32. G. Pico 1946–52, I, p. 430 (IV.3): 'Fortuita fieri dicimus quae praeter intentionem operantis eveniunt; quare tantum in rebus humanis fortuna dicitur, ut quae solae consilio rationeque fiunt . . . Fortunam vero non intelligimus aut numen, aut naturam, aut rem omnino aliquam causam talis eventus, sed potius excludimus, tantum fortuna factum dicentes ac si dicamus "ita evenit forte, non ex aliqua causa".'
33. *Ibid.*, II, p. 524 (XII.6). Di Napoli 1965, p. 277 notes that this work marks 'il rifiuto della magia, la svalutazione della *prisca theologia*, l'abbandono della cabbala come dottrina ermeneutica e come metodo alfabetario'. For a penetrating analysis of the conceptual structure and the meaning of Pico's *Disputationes* see Zanier 1981, pp. 54–86.   34. G. Pico 1946–52, I, pp. 36–46 (prooemium).

different approach was called for.[35] Others, however, have regarded Pico's ethical *pathos* as compensating for his logical and epistemological weaknesses and as prefiguring the new natural science of Kepler. His indestructible belief in man's self-determination, freedom and spiritual dignity demands that man cast off the shackles of cosmic determinism and astral forces. In Cassirer's words: 'This faith in man's creativity, and in the autonomy of that creativity, is the genuinely humanistic conviction with which Pico overwhelmed astrology.'[36] Pico's relentless refusal to entertain the slightest stellar influence or physical causality in human self-determination marks the zenith of faith in humanity. After the ferment of the fourteenth and fifteenth centuries Petrarch's legacy bears its finest fruit. Apart from unravelling the untenable hybrids of pagan and Christian doctrine which were so dear to Ficino's Florentine circle, Pico's compellingly rational arguments lent clarity to an incipient scientific approach, allowing it to analyse natural causality without the distraction of mythical, irrational and occult forces.[37]

PIETRO POMPONAZZI

Pomponazzi played a key role in the sixteenth-century controversy about astrology. Two works, both finished in 1520, deal with the topic. The first, *De naturalium effectuum causis sive de incantationibus*, does so systematically; the second, *De fato, de libero arbitrio et de praedestinatione*, refers frequently and favourably to astrological predictions.

In the *De incantationibus* Pomponazzi asserts that Pico understood nothing of astrology, adding that: 'apart from arrogance, petulance and superficial glitter, the *Disputationes* contain nothing of value'. Spitefully, he insinuates that the book was not even Pico's own work and that he merely provided stylistic embellishments.[38]

---

35. See Thorndike 1923–58, IV, pp. 529–32; *L'opera e il pensiero* 1965, II, pp. 315–31 (P. Rossi).
36. Cassirer 1927, p. 125.
37. The contrasting responses of Pico's contemporaries confirm the fact that the *Disputationes* divided scholars into proponents and adversaries of astrology for more than a century. On the one hand, there were Giovanni Abioso's *Dialogus in astrologiae defensionem* (1494), Lucio Bellanti's *Liber de astrologica veritate et in Disputationes Ioannis Pici* (1498) and Pontano's *De rebus caelestibus* (1494); on the other hand, there were Savonarola's *Trattato contro gli astrologi* (1495), Thomas Murner's *Invectiva* (1499) and Gianfrancesco Pico's *De rerum praenotione* (1507). The intricate controversy soon crossed the Alps and added to the new religious controversies. Francesco Giuntini published his *Defensio bonorum astrologorum. De astrologia judiciaria adversus calumniatores* late in the sixteenth century while Jean Bodin's *Démonomanie des sorciers* and Johan Wier's *De praestigiis* discussed the social and legal implications of witchcraft and the witch-trials. For further discussion of the whole issue see *L'opera e il pensiero* 1965, II, pp. 239ff. (Zambelli), pp. 333–56 (Mesnard); Garin 1969, pp. 421–48; Perrone Compagni 1975; Zanier 1977; *Scienza e filosofia* 1983, pp. 345–72 (Zanier); *Grande antologia* 1964–, XI, pp. 388–9; Zambelli 1973b.
38. Pomponazzi 1556, p. 286 (cap. 12).

Despite an almost puerile credulity about reported marvels, whether ancient or recent, Pomponazzi sharply separates the religious and scientific sides of astrology. He regards an astrological account of even the most shattering events – such as the end of a civilisation or the birth of a great religion, even Christianity – as being rationally possible and acceptable. The true cause must be identified, however, and contrary to popular opinion, it does not lie in a miraculous intervention by God or demons. Instead, it is the eternal, unalterable causality, immanent in cosmic laws, which reveals itself in the motions and interrelationships of the stars. Upon these phenomena all sublunary events – physical or human – necessarily depend.[39]

Some thinkers, such as Symphorien Champier, Johannes Reuchlin and Philipp Melanchthon, countered Pico's radicalism by granting magic and astrology a degree of influence, though always subject to God and freedom, and only after carefully distinguishing between the natural and demonic varieties. Pomponazzi seems instead to have had the single aim of eliminating any supernaturalism whatsoever, so as to be able to ascribe everything to natural forces. Cassirer sees this respect for the regularity and sovereignty of natural laws as a step forward in the search for scientific explanations: 'astrological causality becomes a condition for the conceivability of nature'.[40] The rigour of scientific knowledge thus replaces the arbitrary and miraculous interventions of faith.

The second of Pomponazzi's books mentioned above was completed at Bologna on 25 November 1520, and it is the most important Renaissance work on the problems of freedom. Ambrogio Flandino, a noted opponent of Pomponazzi on the question of the soul's mortality, even accused him of collusion with the Lutherans in order to destroy the Christian Church.[41] Despite this charge, we find no explicit reverberations of the theological earthquake initiated by Luther's recent exegesis of the Epistle to the Romans and his 1520 series of meditations on Christian liberty. In fact, the immediate motive for Pomponazzi's treatise was his reading of Alexander of Aphrodisias' work on fate, published by Hieronymus Bagolinus at Verona in 1516, which he had only very recently (*nuperrime*) acquired. Beyond this external circumstance, however, lay a deep hunger which no amount of searching through the 'infinitorum paene auctorum scripta' had ever assuaged.[42]

39. *Ibid.* (capp. 10–12); and for the similar views expressed by Pomponazzi in academic lessons at Bologna in the same period, see Graiff 1976. An opposing view is expressed by Nifo in his *De daemonibus* and subsequent works: see Zambelli 1975.
40. Cassirer 1927, p. 110.
41. *Philosophy and Humanism* 1976, pp. 70–99 (Lemay).   42. Pomponazzi 1957, pp. 2–3.

Pomponazzi disregards flowery humanist treatises and concentrates on Alexander, Aristotle, Boethius, Averroes, Thomas Aquinas, Duns Scotus and William of Ockham. The five sections of the work are devoted respectively to: confuting Alexander; listing and evaluating other theories about fate; an analysis of the volitional act; providence; and predestination. He develops his arguments systematically, concisely and idiosyncratically, using a relentless series of syllogisms in scholastic fashion. The two themes are entirely consonant with his mature philosophical programme, which is to discredit Christian doctrine at the philosophical level in favour of a mechanistic and Stoic metaphysics and ethics.

Alexander of Aphrodisias objected to the Stoic notion of fate as a necessary natural causality on the grounds that such a notion eliminates chance, precludes contingency and, above all, obliterates man's freedom to make his own choices. Pomponazzi, *substinendo stoicos*, counters by stating that from the point of view of an indeterminate agent the necessity of an event is compatible with its fortuitousness – as, for instance, when a stone, following its own laws of falling, encounters the head of an unwitting bystander (1.6). He roundly condemns the idea that contingency should be understood *ad utrumlibet* as ontological indifference, that is, as the possibility for an effect to be or not to be. Contingency refers, Pomponazzi says, only to things which sometimes happen and sometimes do not, such as whether or not it will rain next month. If it does rain, that happens necessarily: 'And this is the true meaning of contingency. Any other meaning of the word is an illusion and a deception, at least where natural things are concerned' (1.7.2.23).

When considering Alexander's view of free will as self-determination between two contradictory choices, Pomponazzi drily notes that such a position goes against a fundamental Aristotelian principle, namely that movement cannot be self-initiating, but must be caused from without; otherwise this would permit the absurdity of something being created out of nothing. If it is true that 'no secondary cause can move if not itself moved', man's will, in deciding to choose one option instead of another, would have to be determined by some higher and external cause. According to the Stoics, this motive cause is providence, or the stars, which not only incline but also compel the will with the same necessity as an agent acts upon its material instrument (1.9.2). To be sure, man does not act entirely instinctively and blindly, as an animal does, because man has the capacity to think. But, since man is unaware of the true, higher, external factors which condition any given choice, he has the illusion of interior freedom and of making his own decisions. This illusion is the fruit of man's ignorance: 'It is held without qualification that this is within the power of the will which it in no way is. In fact, numerous factors are concealed from us, which we would not divulge if we saw them' (1.9.3.3).

Despite having inserted human will into the universal hierarchy of natural causes, Pomponazzi is at pains to show that Stoic determinism is compatible with moral responsibility because everyone does good or evil *scienter et voluntarie* according to their inner nature and uncompelled by external pressures. For Pomponazzi, the existence of good and evil, and the concomitant praising of the virtuous and rebuking of sinners, is part of the *ordo universi*. Just as in the natural realm we praise a fine wine and crush a noxious insect, so too in the field of morality. However, since virtue already contains its highest reward, we should not look forward to another reward in the afterlife because the afterlife cannot be philosophically demonstrated, and the soul's immortality is believed in only because it is a revealed truth. Everything is therefore subject to the providential order of fate. Nothing escapes God's knowledge, for as the cause of everything, he permits no contingency, whether in physical nature or in human affairs. This Stoic account seems to Pomponazzi to be the most rational because if we allowed freedom, bearing in mind both the extreme difficulty of finding a truly virtuous man and the ocean of iniquity which is human history, we would have to conclude that God, or his providence, could not or did not know how better to nourish our freedom (1.11–15).

The starting-point of the second book is the paradoxical claim that fate or providence can coexist with freedom. In making this claim Christian doctrine – even if, in the light of faith, it is the only true doctrine – presents the rational point of view with a number of insoluble problems. A review of previous opinions on the subject shows that all thinkers had to reject either providence or freedom; the Epicureans, for instance, rejected the former and the Stoics the latter. There is no point in bothering with the intermediate positions, developed from Aristotle by Chalcidius, Alexander and Themistius, which propose, absurdly, to limit providential necessity to the heavens, or at most extend it only to the species of the sublunary world, excluding individual beings. Against the atheist *sectae*, Pomponazzi argues that denying providence is the same as denying the existence of God. As for Aristotle, we must not shrink from noticing the obvious contradictions between his general principles about the necessity of motion as laid out in the *Physics* and the statements about contingency and freedom in the

Ethics.[43] Pomponazzi notes how strange it is that no theologian had yet noticed these contradictions in Aristotle's thought. The debate between the *opinio christiana* and the Stoic view is therefore still open.

Christians declare that providence embraces everything which exists, including individuals, and infallibly knows the future decisions of the human will, which nevertheless retains its own freedom to make unpredetermined choices. So, Pomponazzi continues, we must choose one of two propositions: if, on the one hand, God knows our future decisions, we are no longer able to do otherwise; on the other hand, if we claim to make our own choices, then they do not fall within divine causality. Consequently, God would not infallibly know all reality because in the case of human choices he 'moveretur a rebus', that is, his knowledge would be determined by things. In other words, to assign the initiative to human will is to deny God's omniscience and causality in the universe.

In this dilemma Pomponazzi would prefer, he says, to be a slave of fate rather than a servile denier of divine providence: 'malo enim esse servus quam sacrilegus' (II.3.19). So he opts for the Stoic belief which denies human freedom in order to affirm divine providence: 'they preferred to be servants and followers than to be impious and blasphemous'. Since God operates from necessity, they concluded logically that everything must happen with ineluctable necessity, even in human affairs: 'they believed that everything was fated and arranged according to providence and that there is nothing in us which is not done by providence' (II.1.77).

Thus human will depends on God as a saw depends on the hand of a carpenter. We as individuals do not play the role of an active principle but merely that of a subject in which the will resides and which it uses to carry out the dispositions of the unique, universal and divine efficient cause expressed in natural and cosmic laws. In this way we can explain how astrology can predict the destinies of individuals and of entire civilisations. Equally, we may say that all good and evil in the world come from providence, which has arranged things so as best to display the virtuous and to enrich nature with variety. Just as we are not surprised when wolves devour sheep, so we should not be astonished when the wealthy and the powerful exploit the poor. 'It is necessary that there should be sin;

---

43. *Ibid.*, pp. 182–3 (II.5.59): 'Mihi autem videtur quod Aristoteles sibi contradixit et quod aperte negat fatum, ut manifestum est in fine I libri *De interpretatione* 6, et IX *Metaphysicae*, et per omnes *Libros morales*; ex suis tamen principiis videtur sequi quod omnia fato proveniant, veluti deductum est. Quare sibi ipsi contrarius videtur.'

providence intends there to be sins and is itself author of sins' (II.7.1.34).[44] Pomponazzi concludes that this Stoic view, while contrary to Christian faith, is the best answer to the arguments of those who deny free will. Furthermore, it conforms entirely to Aristotle's principles for the natural laws of motion, even if Aristotle himself had to repudiate those principles in order to salvage human freedom.

In the third book Pomponazzi goes deeper into the nature of the will and its relationship with the intellect. He begins by restating the incompatibility of the Christian theory of free will with Aristotle's position. Aristotle asserts that God operates in the world necessarily and states that, other things being equal, opposed or merely differing effects could no more proceed from the same cause than a will could freely choose two contrary options. Since reason is incapable of certitude, it is better to rely on God's wisdom.

Anticipating a doctrine that was to be demonstrated by Spinoza and adopted by transcendental idealism, Pomponazzi declares that the will is the same as the intellective faculty or, if we prefer to speak in terms of two separate powers, the freely willed act is the proper and efficient mode of the intellect, granted that the will complies passively with the free act. To avoid certain scholastic errors which Pomponazzi had already refuted, we should choose one of two cases:

Either the intellect and the will are one and the same power or, if they are different, the intellect is the power wherein the act of free will is properly found since it is there constitutively, whereas it is in the will improperly and in a secondary way since it merely concurs passively in these acts. Freedom, however, consists more in activity than in passivity. (III.4.1)

Therefore, the active cause of the act which is willed or not willed resides in the intellect. The will passively accommodates in itself the image of the object and the suggested intellective thought. Immediately after, however, when it concerns the executive or elective power of one of the alternatives, the will reassumes its pre-eminence in relation to both object and intellect: 'In this choice, the will is the prime mover' (III.6.8).[45]

44. *Ibid.*, p. 204 (II.7.1.39): 'Neque ex hoc quod pauperes conculcentur a divitibus arguit defectum vel crudelitatem in Deo, sicuti quod ovis devoretur a lupo, et lupus lanietur a canibus, et canes a leonibus. Nam licet considerando in particulari hoc videatur iniustum et impium, in ordine tamen ad universum non videtur tale . . . neque mundus esset perfectus nisi talia in ipso reperirentur.' Bearing in mind that the Stoics also held the human soul to be mortal, man's condition is compared with that of cattle and chickens, *ibid.*, p. 205: 'Nam ita erit de hominibus respectu deorum quale est de nostris bobus et nostris gallinis, in quibus nulla videtur esse crudelitas vel iniustitia.' His comments on Aristotle in his lectures reveal an identical position: Graiff 1976, pp. 340–1.
45. It is worth looking at Pomponazzi's own account of the various phases into which the act of choice falls, *ibid.*, p. 252 (III.6.8): 'Erit igitur iste ordo in electione actus voluntatis: Nam primo intellectus

This is a crucial statement. It allows the will to become the principle of independent initiative. Indeed, as a result of the genuine identification of the two faculties, the will must necessarily follow the intellect's moral judgement about an object. Pomponazzi goes on to recognise that the will possesses an ultimate refuge in which to exercise its freedom. This refuge consists of a suspension of the act of volition or choice in the face of intellective deliberation, even when the individual's greatest good and happiness are at stake. This is not, however, a positive act of commission, but a purely privative act of omission: 'It is nevertheless in the power of the will to will and to suspend an act – thus freedom is preserved' (III.8.10).

By permitting the suspension of the will, the act of withdrawal from the universal necessity of reality as presented to the intellect, Pomponazzi contradicts what he had repeatedly stated in his first two books about man's complete dependence on the order of being. This contradiction reveals the pull of a more orthodox Christian view of liberty. It hints perhaps at an unresolved interior struggle between Pomponazzi's naturalistic Stoic vision and a sincere yearning for a greater human dignity, where man's virtue is the fruit of his freely willed choice for the good.[46] A probable explanation is that Pomponazzi did not concede a negative initiative to the will out of philosophical conviction 'by extending the notion of choice to include suspension of the act' (III.10.16), but rather that he suggests it as a possible line of defence for the *opinio christiana*, taking as a spring-board the veracity of faith instead of mere natural reason. It is therefore purely a dialectical exercise, in keeping with his assertion of the primacy of faith and his repeated wish to cling to it, even at the cost of sacrificing the intellect.

This interpretation is confirmed by Pomponazzi's conclusion. Concerning the Stoic view he is emphatic that 'while staying purely in the natural realm – in so far as it is accessible to human reason – none of these opinions is less likely to be contradicted'. Having summarised the counter-arguments and their responses, he concludes: 'I do not see any natural reason which contradicts this view' (epilogus sive peroratio, 7).

In the fourth book he considers the coexistence of human freedom, which is essentially variable and indeterminate, with divine providence,

practicus consultat de agendo et demonstrat voluntati quid sit agendum; et secundum hoc intellectus concurrit active, et voluntas passive non quidem quoniam tunc velit, sed intelligendo quid sit agendum et consilium recipiendo. Deinde hoc habito, voluntas habet potestatem exequendi et non exequendi quod sibi consultum fuerit, et ex sui potestate, exempli gratia, eligit partem affirmativam contradictionis. In hac electione voluntas est primum movens, obiectum est secundum movens motum a voluntate et per se specificans actum; consilium autem et obiectum sumptum in ratione praesentantis concurrunt ad istam electionem non primo et per se, sed in ratione adiuvantis et causae sine qua non.'   46. Pine 1973.

which is immutable and eternal. He takes issue with Boethius and Thomas Aquinas and proposes a solution to the problem posed by the assertion that acts are determined in knowledge because they are determined in being. Consequently, while future acts are still contingent and have the possibility of occurring or not, divine knowledge is also indeterminate. In other words, God would only know that a particular individual might, or might not, sin at some future date. If, on the other hand, he sees our acts as already produced by the will and activated in time, then his knowledge is utterly certain and determined because all reality is present to his intellect for all eternity. And knowledge, as Aristotle said, is always knowledge of something which is (IV.2–3).[47]

In the fifth book Pomponazzi denounces the Thomist account of predestination and discloses his own preference for that of the Stoics. Though fully aware that this is an entirely theological thesis, Pomponazzi subjects everything to the pure elective will of God which has established a degree of order between the parts of the whole independently of any human achievements. Pomponazzi thus falls back on a solution analogous to that of Thomas Aquinas (V.7).[48]

Pomponazzi's subjection of human freedom to natural and astral laws drops a curtain on the rhetorical and lyrical humanist celebration of man's exaltation above the material universe by virtue of his divinely endowed free spirit. Machiavelli too, in the famous chapter 25 of *Il principe* (1513), after dispassionately surveying the cruelty of politicians and of politics in his day, set pessimistic limits to human initiative by assigning half of what happens to the hostile domain of *fortuna*.

Opponents and proponents of freedom were soon divided along the lines drawn by Pico and Pomponazzi. There was little noteworthy elaboration of these positions, though Simone Porzio did develop the naturalistic background of Pomponazzi's *De fato* by suggesting a more precise and materialist conceptualisation of God as the prime mover of the universe. The disenchantment of the world seemed complete. Concepts like freedom, fortune, fate and providence were entirely explained away as the expression and activity of natural laws. Already in the sixteenth century the Copernican revolution was beginning to elbow man aside from the centre of the stage of nature and history. The situation clearly prefigures the modern materialistic-mechanistic conception of reality where man's place is peripheral.[49]

47. *Philosophy and Humanism* 1976, pp. 100–15 (Pine).
48. Di Napoli 1970, especially p. 200 (also in 1973, pp. 85–159).
49. The sixteenth century's attention to the notion of fortune was encouraged by (often dramatic) military and political events, as narrated in Machiavelli's *Il principe*, as well as by the sudden reversals

THE THEOLOGICAL CONTROVERSY

After 1520 the controversy about freedom became markedly theological, and the motives which fuelled it were by no means exclusively philosophical. Protestant theology proposed variations of a 'theological fatalism' – that is, the total dependence of human freedom on the efficacy of grace. The Catholics defended a degree of human initiative and interaction with the necessary divine motion. Precisely how man's will and divine grace cooperate was debated but not entirely resolved by the various currents of post-Tridentine theology. Here we can only survey the main points made by the most important contributors to the debate, beginning with Erasmus and his *De libero arbitrio diatribe sive collatio* (1524). The theological context in which this work was composed means that it cannot be regarded as a product of the previous homocentric phase of the debate, which was now superseded.

Despite urgent imperial and papal pressure that he commit himself against Luther, Erasmus hesitated. A humanist of vast classical learning, his ideas about the moral and theological reform of the church favoured concord between the factions, and involved the cultural and philological re-education of courtiers and churchmen. Erasmus was temperamentally averse to hand-to-hand combat; his inclination was away from fanaticism and towards a noncommittal attitude wherever it was not expressly forbidden by faith. Unlike so many scholastics and humanists, he was not concerned with the nature and existence of freedom, but instead with the possibility of cooperation between human will and supernatural salvation. In other words, is man merely passive, as Luther, following Wyclif, asserted, or can he, under the influence of grace, actively do good and evil?

After defining the kernel of the Protestant position according to the radical formulation of Luther's *Assertio omnium articulorum per Bullam*

---

and successes experienced by the great mercantile dynasties which ruled much of Italy. See Procacci 1951, who considers a number of late fifteenth-century and early sixteenth-century European writers, including Machiavelli and Guicciardini. Doren 1922–3 is useful for the new literary and figurative approaches to fortune. F. Piccolomini 1583 devotes useful chapters to fate, providence, astronomy and fortune; he moves from an analysis of the various obstacles to human freedom to a serenely rational interpretation of natural causality, disagreeing with the *doctissimus Pomponatius*, who 'rationem satis levem insolubilem censuit' about the question of fate (p. 128). For a preliminary analysis of Porzio 1551a and 1553, see Saitta 1961, II, pp. 367–80. Regarding his unpublished writings, see Garin 1966, II, pp. 541, 576. In the bibliography at p. 569 Garin also lists the unpublished *Questiones de casu* [or *de fato?*] *fortuna et casu* by Antonio Fracanziano; see also Sireni 1563, 1580. The disconcerting works of Girolamo Cardano would need a separate discussion. Though on the threshold of a mathematical approach to science his ideas were still heavily involved with magical-astrological notions of a Neoplatonic provenance: see Corsano 1961b.

Leonis X novissimam damnatorum (1520)[50], Erasmus tried to diminish the
exaggerated importance of the controversy by setting it in the broader
context of the salvation which Christian revelation promises. He stressed
the inappropriateness of debating moral issues before the great mass of
believers who are unqualified to evaluate the arguments. He proposed to
disregard the immense legacy – bequeathed by the Fathers, martyrs, saints,
theologians, councils and so on – of statements favouring the belief that
man's freedom can contribute to his salvation. Instead he considered only
what the Bible had to say on the subject, because he knew that Luther
admitted no other authority than the Bible as interpreted by himself.[51]

Accordingly, Erasmus defined freedom as 'a power of the human will, by
virtue of which man can devote himself to everything which leads him
towards or away from salvation'.[52] Then he notes that even after the fall,
human intelligence and will, though wounded, nevertheless retained some
residue of their previous ability to discern the truth and strive after the good
– otherwise no sin could be imputed to man. Thus, the Scriptures, which
continually appeal to man's will to cooperate with God, are contradicted by
both Pelagius and Luther. The first attributes too much to human will, and
the second, regarding man as totally corrupt, demands a wholesale
cleansing of man by grace that acts through us on our entirely passive will.
Undoubtedly the divine initiative in the process of salvation must have
priority because the first impulse and the continued support for the sinner to
return to God comes from his mercifulness. Temperately, but very emphatically, Erasmus stressed that there must be some minimum of
cooperation and personal responsibility in man's answer to God, otherwise
there would be no sense in salvation and damnation and in the praise and
blame which the Bible directs at man. Indeed, there would be no way of
comprehending God's motives for rewarding some people and punishing
others if both had lived their lives out of pure necessity, dragged along
willy-nilly by some heavenly force.

50. Erasmus 1703–6, IX, cols. 1215–48. At col. 1229, there is a quotation from Luther's *Assertio*: 'Unde,
inquit, et hunc articulum necesse est revocare. Male enim dixi, quod liberum arbitrium ante gratiam
sit res de solo titulo, sed simpliciter debui dicere, liberum arbitrium est figmentum in rebus, seu
titulus sine re, quia nulli est in manu quippiam cogitare mali aut boni, sed omnia, ut Wyclevi
articulus Constantiae condemnatus recte docet, de necessitate absolute eveniunt.'
51. *Ibid.*, cols. 1215–20. Juan Ginés de Sepúlveda is incorrect, therefore, when he accuses Erasmus of
having underrated the weight of nature and the demonstrative force of human reason, and of
having allowed himself to be drawn on to his adversary's chosen ground, namely the Bible; see
Ginés de Sepúlveda 1526.
52. Erasmus 1703–6, IX, cols. 1220–1: 'Porro liberum arbitrium hoc loco sentimus vim humanae
voluntatis, qua se possit homo applicare ad ea quae perducunt ad aeternam salutem, aut ab iisdem
avertere.'

Against both positions Erasmus stresses that even the Bible must be understood with moderation. Luther's obsessive exaltation of God's works and his reduction of man to a mere instrument of grace, capable of no action except faith, lead ultimately to the idea that God's discrimination between the saved and the damned is incomprehensible: 'While we are fully occupied singing the praises of faith, we must be careful not to destroy freedom, because if we do, I cannot see how we could resolve the problems of justice and divine mercy.'[53]

The biblical passages which sanction – or proscribe – man's voluntary collaboration with God can easily be reconciled. We must acknowledge the primacy of grace, though with the proviso that it has to be willingly accepted and not merely imposed on its recipients. Against the aggressive dogmatism of the factions which were lacerating the social fabric, Erasmus concluded, in the best humanist tradition, by adopting the middle way: 'Some good, however imperfect, might come from this moderation; but man will not be able to claim any credit for it.'[54]

In the *Loci communes rerum theologicarum* of 1521, the first compendium of Lutheran theology, Melanchthon had stated that 'nulla est voluntatis nostrae libertas'. But the modesty and courtesy of Erasmus' *Diatribe* won him over, and he moved towards the position, balanced like that of Erasmus between grace and freedom, which he was to expound in subsequent editions of the *Loci communes*. Melanchthon certainly could not endorse Luther's fulminating riposte, the *De servo arbitrio* (1525). This work, always one of Luther's favourites, was widely read, and it has been described as 'undeniably one of the most important books of the century'.[55] In it Luther's new theology and his philosophical view of man reach their mature phase. The inscrutable majesty of God is supremely exalted, and man in his vanity and self-importance is consigned to the nethermost depths. Luther grants human will and reason no credit at all in distinguishing good from evil on the way to salvation. As Pierre Mesnard has correctly

53. *Ibid.*, col. 1243: 'Caeterum hic cavendum erat, ne dum toti sumus in amplificandis fidei laudibus, subvertamus libertatem arbitrii, qua sublata, non video quo pacto possit explicari quaestio de iustitia, deque misericordia Dei.'
54. *Ibid.*, col. 1247. The term *moderatio* frequently recurs in the defence against Luther. *Hyperaspistes diatribae adversus servum arbitrium Martini Lutheri: ibid.*, x, cols. 1249–1536, followed by *Adversus calumniosissimam epistolam Martini Lutheri*, cols. 1537–58. See the posthumous collection of essays in Cantimori 1975, especially pp. 40–59, 60–87, 142–57; and see the introduction by Mesnard to *De libero arbitrio* in Erasmus 1970, pp. 177–201. A useful background to the cultural, political and ecclesiastical events in Europe of the time may be found in *Storia della Chiesa* 1975, especially pp. 172–84 (the bibliography concerning the Luther–Erasmus polemic is updated from the original edition published in 1967). 55. See Boisset 1962, p. 28.

pointed out, *De servo arbitrio* marks Luther's final break with the Christian focus on man and the evangelical liberalism of the Renaissance.[56]

At the end of the book Luther does admit that Erasmus alone had managed to identify and analyse the crux of the problem. But this does not prevent Luther from launching a vicious personal attack on him. What can a man like Erasmus, he wonders, possibly achieve in theology and scriptural exegesis? He is a sceptic, a pettifogging quibbler in the worst traditions of medieval scholasticism. He prizes peace and quiet even above truth and the commands of Christ, whom he hardly mentions in his writings. He is pliant and evasive. He will do anything to avoid a confrontation. In short, he has too much human wisdom and no evangelical understanding at all. His treatise is dreary and ineffectual, and, adds Luther, 'I have never seen a book on free will that was so feeble – except in its stylistic elegance.'[57]

It is not true that the Bible is obscure, Luther continues, and it is quite wrong to suppose, as Erasmus does, that where the authentic Christian life is concerned, it is not important to sort out the problem of free will. Erasmus begins by saying that we can do nothing without grace, but he goes on to endow the human will with enough power to fulfil its own commands and even to earn eternal life. These contradictions necessarily arise when we claim to use our reason to investigate the enigma of God's will and to criticise God himself for not acting as we think he should: 'The flesh does not think God worthy to be called good and just, if he says or does anything which goes beyond the legal definitions in the *Codex Justinianus* and book v of Aristotle's *Ethics*.'[58] Instead of criticising God's words through syllogism and grammar in order to make room for our own struggle for goodness, we should humbly understand that biblical imperatives are not evidence of human moral potential but rather reveal our impotence and our dependence on God's will and actions if we are to attain salvation. Freedom can achieve nothing where goodness and eternal life are concerned. This is clear from the Scriptures, and it is useless, indeed dishonest, to slide into metaphorical or figurative interpretations which, following certain of the worst ancient commentators, lead the believer towards heresy. Erasmus recognised in certain pagans morally exemplary actions which are outside the sphere of grace. Instead of demonstrating the natural benevolence of

56. See Mesnard in Erasmus 1970, p. 200.
57. Luther 1883–, XVIII, p. 615 (*De servo arbitrio*): 'ut ineptiorem librum de libero arbitrio non viderim, excepta orationis elegantia'.
58. *Ibid.*, p. 729: 'non dignatur Deum caro gloria tanta, ut credat iustum esse et bonum, dum supra et ultra dicit et facit, quam definivit Codex Iustiniani, vel quintus liber Ethicorum Aristotelis.'

freedom, these actions constitute a theft of divine glory because such people acted as they did out of self-interest and vanity.[59]

The Christian must understand that he is not guided by his own good will, but exclusively by the Spirit of God. Whatever he does, he does necessarily: he may do good if God permits him to be dominated by faith, or do evil if God lets him fall under the sway of Satan. Man's coming into being and the maintenance of his existence owe everything to God – likewise, everything pertaining to salvation proceeds from divine providence.[60]

As Paul never tired of saying in his Epistle to the Romans, our justice is not a function of works in accord with the law but is due entirely to the free gift of grace. Man's task is not to understand rationally but simply to adore the supreme mystery of salvation which God performs regardless of human merits. Erasmus' openly Pelagian attempt to reserve a corner for free will in this exclusively divine action had already been radically refuted by St Paul; he condemned the self-justificatory efforts of pagans and believers alike when he attacked 'both the Pelagians with their notion of total merit and the sophists with their notion of man's minuscule merit'.[61] Luther concluded that freedom is a prerogative of God alone because he is an absolute and utterly perfect being. The entire contingent universe is subject to his eternal consciousness and control, and therefore we must admit – and this is also a rational conclusion – that 'there can be no free will in man, in the angels or in any other creature'.[62]

As has already been mentioned, Melanchthon initially followed Luther on the question of freedom, but after reflecting on the theological and legal consequences of a doctrine which blamed God for our sins, gradually modified his position. In the 1548 edition of the *Loci communes*, free will is 'a faculty for devoting the self to grace'. In his *Initia doctrinae physicae* (1549) and *Ethicae doctrinae elementa* (1550), he reviews the Aristotelian and medieval idea of freedom of choice and argues in its favour against Stoic determinism, which confuses the laws of nature with the operations of the human will. Fausto Sozzini reacted in a similar way against the dark fatalism

59. *Ibid.*, pp. 742–3. 60. *Ibid.*, p. 754.
61. *Ibid.*, p. 771: 'conteritque [Paulus] uno fulminis huius ictu tam Pelagianos cum suo toto merito, quam sophistas cum suo pusillo merito'.
62. *Ibid.*, p. 786: 'nullum potest esse liberum arbitrium in homine vel angelo aut ulla creatura'. Regarding the new anthropology demanded by Luther's revolutionary theology, see Gherardini 1982, especially pp. 48–82, which has an extensive bibliography; see also Cantimori 1975, pp. 88–111.

of Calvin in his *Praelectiones theologicae* and especially in the letter *Ad philosophum B.*[63] Indeed, in his desire to defend human freedom he goes so far as to question God's foreknowledge and predestination. By contrast, the Lutheran denial of freedom was taken even further by Zwingli and Calvin. In his *De vera et falsa religione commentarius* (1525) and his more philosophical *De providentia Dei sermo* (1530), Zwingli maintained that God was the sole cause of the universal activity of beings, which were merely the instruments of his will. In the absence of secondary causes, it must be admitted that evil was also to be ascribed to providence, but with tenuous logic he tried to exonerate God from human sinfulness on the basis of his holiness and sublime goodness.

Calvin's *Institutiones Christianae religionis* (1536) and *De servitute et liberatione humani arbitrii* (1543) similarly regarded man as nothing more than the instrument of a divine sovereignty which despotically imposes its eternal decrees even to the extent of willing human sinfulness. Calvin was vigilantly intolerant of any independent initiative by man where God is concerned. Thus, he asserted that man's will is compelled by a necessity which urges it to evil, even when it goes against his better judgement and against reason itself. Even when man is a victim of these irresistible and irrational forces, he is still responsible for his sins. Calvin gloried in the direct and inscrutable intervention of providence in the physical and human sphere and deplored the revival of Stoic and Epicurean theories about God's absence from his creation – an absence too often filled with pagan beliefs about fate and fortune.

In the Reformation debate, therefore, Pomponazzi's philosophical fatalism was infiltrated by a fideistic fatalism of the opposite kind. The latter is equally destructive of man's reality; in the first case because he is the victim of material cosmic forces, and in the second because he is the victim of a predestined will. Man's highest faculties are systematically demoted and denied; his works are entirely disregarded, and his moral commitments discarded as illusory. Whether by fate or predestination, man is a slave without the dignity of choosing his own destiny. The reaction to this prostration of the human soul before an inscrutable God – according to the celebrated thesis of Max Weber's *Die protestantische Ethik und der 'Geist' des Kapitalismus* (1904–5) – was an explosion of secular commerce leading to the early forms of capitalism.

---

63. See *Bibliotheca fratrum polonorum* 1656, I, pp. 368ff., 542ff. (The addressee of the anonymous letter may be the philosopher Nicolas Bernaud.) With reference to discussions about freedom and the determinism of grace, see Zambruno 1983, especially pp. 55–64.

The Catholic position, adopted by the Council of Trent, defended the church's traditional doctrine of human freedom which had been forged in the great theological schools of Louvain, Paris, Coimbra and Salamanca. The problems of predestination and foreknowledge, of providence and grace and of where freedom stands in relation to salvation were fiercely debated throughout the latter half of the sixteenth century. After the condemnation of the Belgian theologian Michel de Bay, the main confrontation was between the Dominicans, led by Domingo Bañez, and the Jesuits. The latter's standard-bearer was Luis de Molina, whose famous tract *Concordia liberi arbitrii cum gratiae donis, divina praescientia, providentia, praedestinatione et reprobatione* (Lisbon, 1588) by adopting the notion of a *scientia media* attempted to reconcile the infallibility of grace and God's will with the human will's freely given consent.[64]

The paradox by which two propositions as apparently contradictory as freedom and predestination were both considered correct generated an insoluble controversy in which the participants accused one another of Calvinism and Pelagianism. Eventually in 1596 Clement VIII issued his *Congregatio de auxiliis divinae gratiae*, which reasserted freedom of discussion and forbade the theologians from issuing reciprocal excommunications.

The impossibility of a satisfactory theological solution demonstrated quite clearly the complexity and theoretical difficulty posed by the problems of freedom and fate, providence and fortune. Indeed, when translated into the contemporary terms of a secular society and a rationalist mentality, these problems still trouble us today. Despite the removal of strictly theological concepts and of astrology – vanquished by a fuller scientific understanding – genuine anguish about personal destiny is by no means absent at the popular level, where there still is a lively interest in magic and horoscopes. At a more self-reflective level, there is deep concern for the defence of human liberty from the new mechanistic conceptions of reality. The battle for man's freedom and self-determination seems never to be entirely lost. Nor, on the other hand, is it ever entirely won, and each generation must fight over the same ground anew.

64. See *Dictionnaire de théologie catholique* 1923–72, XII, 2, cols. 2959–89 ('Predestination'); Rahner 1975.

18

THEORIES OF KNOWLEDGE

INTRODUCTION

The theory of knowledge, as *a* or *the* central branch of philosophy, is a post-Renaissance phenomenon that develops from certain critical movements in Renaissance thought. If epistemology deals with the three basic questions set forth in John Locke's *Essay Concerning Human Understanding*: What is the origin, the extent and the certainty of human knowledge?, these were not the central issues for most Renaissance thinkers. Most accepted Aristotle's explanation in *De anima* of how we gain information and form concepts, and Aristotle's account in the *Prior* and *Posterior Analytics* of how the concepts abstracted from sense experience are connected by logical inferences to provide knowledge.

Certain problems were raised in the Renaissance about whether the Aristotelian account could lead to 'higher' or 'the highest' knowledge, or whether it was adequate to account for religious knowledge. Various critics of Aristotelian thought challenged each element of Aristotle's account, his empiricism, his theory of concept abstraction and his theory of logical connections of concepts. In addition, radically different proposals were offered about how knowledge is acquired and what it is about, ranging from various Platonic views, to various claims about how to acquire esoteric knowledge, to doubts about whether any genuine knowledge could be acquired.

Although Renaissance philosophical interests dealt mainly with metaphysical and ethical issues, and with problems in logic and natural science, nonetheless some of the epistemological issues that were raised in discussing these matters led to the central problems of knowledge that philosophers have been struggling with from the time of Francis Bacon and René Descartes up to the present.

I will deal first with problems about knowledge raised within the world of Aristotelian philosophers and their critics, then with the alternative epistemologies offered by the nature philosophers, Platonists, Neoplatonists, Hermeticists and cabalists, epistemologies that range from exoteric to esoteric theories, and finally to critical and sceptical views, leading to the modern problems of knowledge.

ARISTOTELIANISM

The main stream of academic philosophy up to the end of the sixteenth century was, of course, scholastic Aristotelianism, accepting pretty much without question Aristotle's explanation of how knowledge is attained through sensory activity, when the sense organ is functioning properly, in its proper medium, for its proper objects. Then, the form of the object known is abstracted by the intellect, and is known conceptually. This explanation applied to natural objects, and from the time Aristotelianism became the basic structure of thought among Islamic, Jewish and Christian thinkers in the Middle Ages, was supplemented with accounts usually incorporating Platonic or Neoplatonic elements of how religious knowledge is gained. Among Renaissance Aristotelians the discussion of whether God's existence and nature can be known by natural means and through natural evidence continued.[1] Francisco Suárez insisted that evidence from nature, or physics, was inadequate to establish the necessity of God's existence. He devoted a good deal of effort to advancing a metaphysical *a priori* proof of God's existence and to showing how human knowledge of God's nature is gained by analogy.[2] The type of analysis offered by Suárez is an extension of the discussion of religious knowledge offered in the earlier tradition by Maimonides, Thomas Aquinas, Duns Scotus and hosts of other medieval thinkers. Suárez' formulation may be the last significant one in this tradition.

However, also within the world of Aristotelian-oriented thinkers, a more troublesome problem about spiritual knowledge was raised by the so-called Latin Averroists, especially some of those connected with the University of Padua in the fifteenth and sixteenth centuries. These philosophers were not unaware of various humanistic attacks on the merits of Aristotle's philosophy. Their Aristotelianism was not just a sterile repetition of medieval arguments and theories. Rather, it gained new vigour and strength from the recovery and study of the Greek texts of Aristotle. It also was infused with the knowledge and perspective of some of the Greek commentators on Aristotle, such as Alexander of Aphrodisias.

1. Kristeller 1979, pp. 32–50.   2. Mourant 1967.

Perhaps the most famous student of Paduan Aristotelianism was Pietro Pomponazzi.[3] His *De immortalitate animae* (1516) is primarily on a metaphysical issue, the nature of the human soul; but it does raise a most serious epistemological issue about the relationship of natural and religious knowledge. The human intellect depends upon the body in order to gain any sense information, the source of any knowledge. The most carefully argued sections of his work tried to answer all objections to the contention that the Aristotelian view is that of human mortality. Then in the concluding chapter Pomponazzi said that we must keep 'the saner view', namely that the question of the immortality of the soul is a neutral problem like that of the eternity of the world, which cannot be settled by natural reasoning. Since the experts disagree, we can only gain certain knowledge through God. That the soul is immortal is an article of faith, and should be accepted on the basis of revelation and Scripture. 'Wherefore we must assert that beyond doubt the soul is immortal'[4] on the basis of faith and revelation, and not follow the wanderings of wise men, who have become fools when they try to work this out by natural reason and examination of the arguments of the great philosophers.

Pomponazzi was far from being the first to take note of the fact that rational conclusions drawn from Aristotelian premises conflict with basic claims of Judaism, Christianity and Islam. Medieval thinkers such as Averroes, Maimonides and Thomas Aquinas brought out conflicts between philosophical truth (in Aristotle's system) and religious truth based on Scripture or the Koran. For example, they discussed at length the fact that Aristotle's premises would lead a philosopher to conclude that the world was eternal, which contradicted the facts about the world presented at the beginning of Genesis. All three thinkers, Averroes, Maimonides and St Thomas, were accused of holding a theory that something could be true in philosophy and false in religion, or vice versa, that is, that there could be two kinds of truths, which contradict each other. The condemnation in 1277 of the teaching of some of Aristotle's views at the University of Paris reflects the concern to stamp out this potentially heretical view. Various thinkers from then on in both the Christian and Jewish worlds were accused of propounding the doctrine of double truth, and each denied it. Pomponazzi came after a long debate going back into the Islamic Spain of Averroes' and Maimonides' time over whether philosophical and religious truths are compatible.

---

3. Kristeller 1979, pp. 192–5; *Renaissance Philosophy of Man* 1948, pp. 257–79 (Randall's introduction to Pomponazzi).
4. *Renaissance Philosophy of Man* 1948, p. 380 (Pomponazzi, *De immortalitate animae*).

Eighteenth- and nineteenth-century interpreters saw Pomponazzi's effort as a statement of secret atheism based on the theory of the double truth. (1) A proposition, that the soul is mortal, is the rational outcome of (Aristotelian) philosophy. (2) The proposition that the soul is immortal is an article of faith. Therefore (1) can be true in philosophy and (2) in theology. And, since Pomponazzi devoted fourteen densely argued chapters to establishing (1), and a brief conclusion to stating (2), these interpreters assumed that he really believed the philosophical denial of the immortality of the soul. If Pomponazzi or his successors, Jacopo Zabarella and Cesare Cremonini, held the theory of the double truth, this would be a significant epistemological position with far-reaching implications for philosophy and religion, depending upon which kind of truth one took as more veridical or credible. Interpreters from at least as far back as Pierre Bayle at the end of the seventeenth century to Paul Oskar Kristeller in our time have claimed that Pomponazzi was probably quite sincere, and was showing the limits of human rational knowledge when applied to theological and religious issues, an epistemological view that has been asserted in the Judaeo-Christian tradition as far back as biblical times.[5] Kristeller pointed out that Pomponazzi continued to teach in a university under church control, and died peacefully without ever being arrested or charged with heresy.[6] Pomponazzi did show very forcefully and at length that the best philosophical explanation was that the human soul was mortal. This may well have been intended, as some of Bayle's later analyses appear to have been, to expose the weakness and limits of reason and to prepare the reader to accept some kind of fideism. Pomponazzi represents a striking indication of the possible inadequacy of Aristotelian theory to deal with fundamental Judaeo-Christian theological beliefs. As such it posed an epistemological limit for Aristotelian philosophy, by someone working within the prevailing Aristotelian tradition.

A small but influential minority posed other limitations on the value of Aristotle's method and theory for gaining knowledge, some from the perspective of humanist studies, some from some sort of Platonic or esoteric perspective, and some finally from a sceptical perspective.

THE HUMANIST CRITIQUE OF ARISTOTELIANISM

With the recovery of so much more classical learning during the Renaissance, some realised that Aristotle, rather than being 'the Master of

5. Bayle 1740, III, pp. 777–83 ('Pomponace, Pierre'); see also Kristeller 1979, pp. 199–200; 1974, pp. 53–5; *Renaissance Philosophy of Man* 1948, pp. 274–5 (Randall's introduction to Pomponazzi).
6. Kristeller 1967b.

them that know', was just one of many ancient thinkers, and that his accomplishments might actually be far less than had been claimed by his ardent scholastic followers. The humanist critique of scholasticism beginning with Petrarch in Southern Europe in the mid fourteenth century and Erasmus in Northern Europe a century or so later was at first not really a philosophical critique, in the form of organised arguments. It was a pointing to other sorts of knowledge to be found in the classical world, in writers like Cicero and other Latin sages and in Greek philosophers and moralists. It was also, as Petrarch said at length in his *De sui ipsius ignorantia*, a pointing to many empirical facts and practical considerations, with moral applications that indicated the inadequacy of scholasticism for understanding man and the world. The humanist criticism also took the form, especially in Erasmus, of satire of the activities of the scholastic professors and trivialising the vaunted knowledge they claimed to produce. The early humanists indicated the sterility and uselessness of the knowledge and method of knowing being put forth at the universities. Instead Petrarch, Erasmus and others insisted that what was most important was the *philosophia Christi*. 'To be a true philosopher is nothing but to be a true Christian', Erasmus said. Worthwhile knowledge would be gained by returning to pure religious activities, and not by revelling in the subtleties of scholastic disputation.[7]

Petrarch, Erasmus and others like them may have done more to undermine confidence in both the methods of knowing and the purported knowledge emanating from the university centres of learning than more technical philosophical critics, as far as the general intellectual public was concerned. However, the technical analyses of the Aristotelian method of gaining knowledge set forth by such figures as Lorenzo Valla, Rudolph Agricola, Juan Luis Vives and Petrus Ramus attempted to show that Aristotelian logic was just an abstruse, artificial and abstract way of manipulating ideas and symbols that led to neither concrete nor genuine knowledge. The vaunted Aristotelian logic machinery was in fact really a form of sophistry. Valla, Agricola, Vives and Ramus were not just insulting the logicians, or pointing out their ignorance of classical literature or the barbarousness of their Latin expression. Much more they were offering a technical analysis of what is involved in scholastic reasoning, why it is not a method of discovering new knowledge and what should replace it. Scholastic logical training concentrated on establishing the validity of

---

7. *Renaissance Philosophy of Man* 1948, pp. 47–133 (Petrarch, *De sui ipsius et multorum ignorantia*); Erasmus 1979.

syllogistic reasoning. But, the humanist critics pointed out, this did not aid in the pursuit of truth. Utilising some of the sceptical material in Cicero's writings, they contended that there were great difficulties in discovering truth, and that the best that men could do was work out methods of discovery, arts of reasoning, which would lead to the most probable or most useful knowledge rather than to valid but vacuous syllogistic conclusions.

Hammering at the artificial character of Aristotelian-scholastic logic, the humanists insisted it was bound to lead to results of no value to human beings. Instead what was needed was a natural logic that conformed to the way people think. This would be a logic of discovery that presumably would lead to actual knowledge. The great work of Ramus, when he was professor in Paris, was to work out the details of such a natural logic. His scheme, widely followed in the Protestant world, even in New England, like that of Valla and Agricola, did not really establish a certain method of arriving at truth, but rather a series of procedures for dealing with intellectual problems without artificially reducing them to syllogistic form to be examined without regard to their content.[8]

We will see later on that building on some of these humanist criticisms, a full-scale epistemological dissection of Aristotle's theory of knowledge was developed by the sceptic Francisco Sanches.

NEOPLATONISM

A different kind of criticism came from those concerned with Platonic thought. Prior to the emergence of Renaissance Platonism in the views of Ficino and Pico, an application of a medieval strain of Neoplatonism led to a scepticism about the possibility of knowledge acquired by natural sensory means, while insisting on another approach in the quest for truth. This appears in the writings of Nicholas of Cusa. His most famous work, *De docta ignorantia* of 1440, begins by pointing out why all human natural knowledge is uncertain. It goes on to argue that 'Nothing could be more beneficial for even the most zealous searcher for knowledge than his being in fact most learned in that very ignorance which is peculiarly his own; and the better a man will have known his own ignorance, the greater his learning will be.'[9] Our finitude and the limitations of our faculties make us realise our ignorance about what is divine and infinite. By the senses we just perceive and can only affirm what we perceive. By discursive reason, we

8. Kristeller 1979, p. 127; Ong 1958a; N. W. Gilbert 1960; Risse 1964; L. Jardine 1983.
9. Nicholas of Cusa 1954, pp. 8–9.

‌‍‍

‍‍

can only arrive at approximate knowledge. Full knowledge involves knowledge of God, which is beyond us because it transcends our finitude. Hence, we can only know by the *via negativa*, negative theology, finding out what God is not. Nicholas of Cusa combined the negative theology of Pseudo-Dionysius the Areopagite and John Scotus Eriugena with his own analysis of the nature of the infinite. In terms of his examination of the process of human knowing and the ultimate object of human knowledge, he indicated that enlightened ignorance would be a far better state than irremediable ignorance. This enlightened ignorance would involve endless approximation of knowledge of God through knowing what God is not and cannot be.[10]

A quite different form of Platonism, also including a good deal of Neoplatonism, was presented by Marsilio Ficino, who inaugurated the movement of Renaissance Platonism. One of his major undertakings was the *Theologia platonica* (1474). In this and in his many commentaries on Platonic and Neoplatonic works, he tried to show that by contemplation we can reach illumination from Platonic ideas, thereby approaching ultimate knowledge, which is knowledge of God. Platonism, in Ficino's broad sense of it – encompassing a wide variety of ancient theories from Platonic and Plotinian to Hermetic ones – would lead people to a true understanding of Christianity. There is, for Ficino, a harmony between Platonism and the Christian faith, and Platonism is part of the divine revelation. Although most of his writing is on the cosmology of the divine world, there is an epistemological part to his philosophy, namely how human beings become able to know the world as it really is. We have to seek knowledge by reason. Our souls have two tendencies, one towards the corporeal world and the senses, and the other towards God. The second represents the rational part of the soul. The mind seeks to go beyond temporal change and tries to find its end and good in eternity. Knowing God would involve knowing infinite truth and goodness. By use of the intellect we can rise towards this end, which we could not do by use of our senses. But as long as we have our bodily existence, we are limited in our ability to know. When the soul can rise above this, it can attain eternal life 'and the brightest light of knowledge, rest without change, a positive condition free from privation, tranquil and secure possession of all good and everywhere perfect joy'.[11] The Platonic process of knowing by turning the soul towards ideas rather than sensory matters begins a process of knowing

10. These points are made in his *De docta ignorantia*.
11. *Renaissance Philosophy of Man* 1948, p. 212 (Ficino, *Five Questions Concerning the Mind*).

that can only be completed when we can transcend our present physical existence. The mind through contemplation withdraws from the body and from its concerns. It withdraws into itself. Gradually it comes to know its own nature, to know the intelligible world of Platonic ideas and to know God himself. Direct knowledge of God is, at best, only briefly obtainable by the wisest of mortals during their lifetimes. Such knowledge is the highest goal of all mankind and can be attained by most people in the eternal world after bodily death. Ficino used the contention that direct knowledge of God was man's highest goal as evidence of the immortality of the soul, since such knowledge could only be gained by most people after this corporeal life. Ficino's picture of ultimate knowledge is a combination of Platonism, Neoplatonism and a somewhat mystical Christianity.[12]

Ficino's work influenced many others to turn to Platonism as a source of knowledge and understanding of the world. One of those whom he greatly influenced was Giovanni Pico della Mirandola. Pico brought with him a knowledge not only of Greek sources, but also of Jewish and Arabic thought. He wanted to harmonise all ancient wisdom, including Plato, Aristotle, Neoplatonism, Hermeticism and Jewish cabalism. Pico, along with Ficino, believed there was a *prisca theologia*, an ancient philosophy and theology that was to be found in the pagan writings of Hermes Trismegistus, Zoroaster, Orpheus, Pythagoras; in the religious writings of Moses and the cabala; in Chaldaic, Egyptian and Arabic sources. All of this could be harmonised, bringing together the ancient pagan and Judaeo-Christian wisdom, and the derivative wisdom of Plato, Aristotle and the Neoplatonists. In the vast variety of human theories and beliefs he sought to find some common truth, some perennial philosophy that had come down through the ages. In this venture, Pico urged the study of all kinds of philosophy, of various esoteric approaches to knowledge, such as cabalism. There are, he believed, universal truths, which appear in all philosophical traditions. We must try to separate out these truths, as best we can, through considering all kinds of philosophical views from ancient to modern ones. This would not lead us to ultimate understanding, but would lead us as far as philosophy can. God is darkness. We can learn something through Pico's vast syncretist approach. But finally some religion is needed to guide us. Religion became for Pico the fulfilment of philosophy. Philosophy is only a preparatory effort in this direction.[13]

---

12. Kristeller 1953a, pp. 213–437.
13. G. Pico 1942, pp. 101–65 (*Oratio de hominis dignitate*); see also Kristeller 1956a, pp. 279–86; *Renaissance Philosophy of Man* 1948, pp. 215–22 (Kristeller's introduction to G. Pico).

Pico's concern for cabalistic studies brought an esoteric element into Renaissance theories of knowledge. The cabala, a series of Jewish treatises written around AD 1200 but purporting to contain an ancient wisdom known to one of the mystical rabbis of antiquity, Simeon bar Yochai, represented a radically different and non-philosophical way of seeking knowledge and understanding the world. This body of Jewish literature was just becoming known in Europe in the last decades of the fifteenth century, carried out of Spain when the Jews were exiled from there in 1492. Johannes Reuchlin, one of the first to promote Hebrew studies in Europe, was concerned to find ultimate religious knowledge through cabalistic study. This esoteric search for knowledge continued to take place in the seventeenth century and is found surfacing amongst such diverse groups as the Cambridge Platonists and the early Rosicrucians, as well as in the philosophy of Leibniz.[14]

Another Platonic element in the quest for knowledge was developed by Leone Ebreo, who was apparently connected with the Florentine Platonic Academy. His *Dialoghi d'amore* became an important statement of the dynamic element, love, in Plato's theory of knowledge, which is supposed to lead to higher and higher levels of knowledge. Leone's dialogues, reprinted often in the Renaissance in various languages, provided an explanation of how humans move from love in the ordinary sense to a higher love that leads to genuine knowledge.[15]

NATURE PHILOSOPHERS

The opening up of studies of a wide range of pagan and Judaeo-Christian philosophies and of non-rational means of understanding the world, through magic, cabalistic theories and the like led to the presentation of many novel theories about the nature of the world. A group of such theories, breaking with Aristotelian and Neoplatonic physics and cosmology, offered what are called 'nature philosophies'. The examination of these views belongs mainly to the study of metaphysics and science in the Renaissance. However, an aspect of these theories is relevant here, namely the kind of knowledge adherents of these views thought was possible.

Some thinkers – including Girolamo Fracastoro, Bernardino Telesio, Theophrastus Paracelsus and Giordano Bruno – rejected aspects of the Aristotelian theory of knowledge, insisting on more careful empirical

14. Blau 1944; Secret 1958a.   15. Leone Ebreo 1929.

investigation. For some, the aim was to get a clearer image or picture of the external object, rather than an abstraction of its form. Elements of Democritean-Epicurean theories of sense-perception were revived to buttress this appeal to a more incisive empiricism than that involved in the Aristotelian theory of knowledge. (And some of this was adopted in Francis Bacon's proposals for a *Novum Organum*.)

These nature philosophers held, in quite different ways, that beyond gaining an accurate account of nature, one had to develop a special power of experiencing or apprehending the real natures of things and their interrelationships. The theories of how this is to be done range over alchemical, magical, cabalistic and Neoplatonic views. So, their empiricism was accompanied by supra-rational or extra-rational ways of obtaining basic truths. Bruno, for instance, held that human ideas are just the shadows or reflections of divine ideas. Nature can be understood in so far as it expresses these divine ideas. Human beings start their quest for knowledge from the objects of sense-perception and are able to move upwards to divine ideas, though not to ultimate understanding of divine and original unity. Part of nature is intelligible, though nature as a whole, like God, is infinite and beyond our intellectual faculties.[16]

One great expositor of occult philosophy in the Renaissance, Henricus Cornelius Agrippa, portrayed human beings as belonging to three worlds, the terrestrial world of elements, the world of heavenly bodies and the world of spirit. Man as a microcosm is the ontological link between these worlds and is thus able to know each of them. So, for Agrippa, human knowledge depends upon man's ontological nature. Man contains the harmonious unity of the three worlds, and is thereby a microcosm that reflects the harmonious unity of the world in the macrocosm. Man's soul is able to know the effluences of the world-soul and to know in the sympathies and antipathies of things the latent powers in things that can be used by magical power. Thus, for Agrippa (at least when he was expounding occult philosophy) nature's secrets, her hidden powers and forces, can be known by occult means, by magic, and this is the most important knowledge. (We will see shortly that at one phase in his career, Agrippa rejected all forms of knowledge, occult or otherwise, and produced an important work in the history of scepticism.) Agrippa also believed that cabalistic research into the characters and secret meanings of Hebrew letters and words would lead man to the highest possible knowledge, namely knowledge of God.[17]

---

16. Yates 1964; Walker 1958.   17. Yates 1964, pp. 130–43; Nauert 1965; Prost 1881–2.

Paracelsus emphasised the importance of a genuine empirical method, but insisted that the data of experience have to be systematised through relating them to the terrestrial, sidereal and spiritual worlds. Man is a microcosm of the world and through alchemical, astrological and other means can learn the secrets of the macrocosm. The theory of man as the microcosm of the world played an important role in explaining, for the occultists, how we could pass from knowledge of ourselves to knowledge of the macrocosm, the universe. This Neoplatonic view allowed thinkers like Agrippa and Paracelsus to try to transform their data about man into data about the entire universe.[18]

SCEPTICISM

During the sixteenth century various naturalistic theories of the world were put forward, combining empirical and speculative elements offering a wide range of theories about man, his place in nature and his relation to God. Some of these theories had germs of metaphysical views that were to be developed into new systems of the world in the succeeding centuries. The confusion of the competing theories of the world, of man, of nature and of God led in part to the development of a new sceptical critique of Renaissance philosophy and science.

On the one hand, the humanist challenge to traditional scholastic ideas, the rediscovery of so many ancient outlooks, the discovery of so many new facts about the world, geographical, astronomical, anatomical, and the monumental upheaval in religious thought involved in both the Reformation and the Counter-Reformation all posed sceptical questions about accepted ideas. In a whole range of areas of intellectual concern, people were questioning accepted views. Sometimes this questioning led to asking if there could be any certain, unassailable knowledge about the natural or human worlds. In addition, some theologians and philosophers from the fourteenth century onwards, especially in the Ockhamist tradition, began to question whether, if God was totally omnipotent, we could be sure of anything. Can we be certain of any so-called necessary truths, if God is really all-powerful and can negate them? Can we be sure of any fact, if God has the power to change the past? The sceptical implications of the exploration of what is involved in the notion of an omnipotent God, acting only according to his will, were set forth by the fourteenth-century thinker Gregory of Rimini. His ideas played a role in seventeenth-century

18. Pagel 1958a; Webster 1982.

scepticism, as evidenced by considerations of problems raised by him by Descartes and Bayle.[19] All of this, coupled with the revival of Academic and Pyrrhonian sceptical arguments, developed into a fully-fledged sceptical challenge to all claims to knowledge, a challenge that was to play a vital role in the attempts by Descartes, Bacon and others to find an unshakeable basis for the new knowledge emerging from the new science.

The investigation of how and when ancient scepticism was rediscovered indicates that the major ancient texts stating the sceptical arguments, Sextus Empiricus' *Outlines of Pyrrhonism* and *Against the Dogmatists*, Cicero's *Academica* and Diogenes Laertius' *Life of Pyrrho*, were hardly known in the Middle Ages. There are three medieval Latin manuscript translations of Sextus' *Outlines of Pyrrhonism*, but no indication that anyone read them or commented on them. Cicero's account of Academic scepticism was slightly known – a few manuscripts existed – but the work was very little studied before the fourteenth century. And the section of Diogenes about Pyrrho and Pyrrhonism was not known at all. It is in the fifteenth and sixteenth centuries that these three basic sources of information about ancient scepticism were discovered and were actively studied and applied to the issues of the time.

Cicero's *Academica* was known to Petrarch, Valla and others. It was printed in 1471 with Cicero's other philosophical works. But it is only from the 1530s onwards that it gets taken seriously and is commented on, that it is used positively and that refutations are offered.[20]

Diogenes' *Life of Pyrrho* was translated into Latin in the 1430s and was printed several times before 1500. Charles Schmitt claims that the original Latin translation is the source of the use of the word *scepticus* in the Latin vocabulary.[21] The word appears in the medieval Latin translations of Sextus, but was not adopted by anyone. Sextus' works or his ideas were probably known by Byzantine writers; they are first mentioned in western literature in the early fifteenth century, while the texts began to be studied for philosophical purposes in the early sixteenth century by Gianfrancesco Pico. Sextus' writings were published in Latin translations in 1562 and 1569, and may have been published in English in Elizabethan times. The Greek text, however, was not published until 1621. Philosophers from Montaigne onwards studied this treasury of ancient scepticism and employed its arguments in formulating modern scepticism.[22]

---

19. Funkenstein 1986; Bayle 1740, IV, pp. 56–8 ('Rimini, Gregoire de').
20. Schmitt 1972, 1983c.   21. Schmitt 1983c, p. 233.
22. Schmitt 1967, 1983c; Popkin 1979, pp. 18–41.

Scepticism is a challenge to any claims to knowledge. The formulations in Cicero, Diogenes and Sextus provided well-organised groups of arguments to challenge claims to knowledge in various areas of human concern – philosophy, science, ethics and so on. The central thrust of some of these arguments was to show that any conflict of views could only be judged if one had an adequate standard or criterion. But any criterion could be challenged, and this dispute would require another criterion, and so on. The issue involved fitted only too well into the religious controversies of the time. Erasmus took a sceptical stance in his dispute with Luther and tried to suspend judgement, as the ancient sceptics did, on whether man had free will. Luther fought back saying that the Holy Spirit is not a sceptic, and judgement day is coming. The problem of the criterion by which one recognises or measures the true faith came up over and over again, and sceptical arguments were used by Protestants and Catholics to undermine the others' dogmatism. Sebastian Castellio opposed Calvin's assurance in his dispute with Servetus by challenging Calvin's claims to certainty and suggesting a reasonable scepticism instead. Catholic polemicists, from Gentian Hervet, the translator of Sextus, to St François de Sales, to Juan Maldonado and his disciple, François Veron, all challenged the Reformers to justify their claims to knowledge, and Protestant defenders tried to reverse the question and throw it back against the Catholics.[23]

Interest in scepticism as more than a weapon in the religious controversies first appears in Gianfrancesco Pico's work *Examen vanitatis doctrinae gentium*, written during the decade 1510–20. The younger Pico was disturbed by the humanist thought being offered around him that was based on pagan ideas and by the strong reliance of contemporary theologians on Aristotle's views. Pico was attracted to Savonarola's ideas and to some of the anti-intellectual tendencies of his movement. So, he decided to discredit the entire philosophical tradition of antiquity. His book surveys ancient philosophy and then in the second part turns to the problem of attaining certainty. Sextus is discussed at length, and his arguments are used to demolish any rational philosophy, including, of course, Aristotle's. This would liberate men from vainly accepting pagan theories. Pico's conclusion was not to convince people that all was in doubt, but rather that one should turn from philosophy as a source of knowledge to Christian revelation instead.[24]

The occult philosopher Agrippa published a strange work in 1526, *De*

---

23. Popkin 1979, pp. 1–17.   24. Schmitt 1967; Popkin 1979, pp. 20–3.

incertitudine et vanitate scientiarum declamatio, which has led him to be listed as one of the early sceptics of the Renaissance. His book is a diatribe against every kind of intellectual activity. He said he was doing this to humble human pride and lead people to true religion. Very little actual sceptical argument occurs, though sceptical sources are used.[25]

In less bombastic fashion various theologians, Catholic and Protestant, used sceptical arguments to indicate that human reason is incapable of leading men to knowledge of divine matters and of metaphysics, and so they should turn to faith. Cardinal Jacopo Sadoleto felt he had to oppose this growing scepticism about whether anything could be known by rational means, and defend the classical philosophical tradition.[26]

In the circle around Petrus Ramus, there was serious discussion of the import of scepticism. One of Ramus' friends, Omer Talon, wrote a work in 1548 entitled *Academica*, presenting Cicero's account of Academic scepticism. Talon saw scepticism as a justification of Ramus' attacks on Aristotle and Aristotelianism and as a means of liberating human thought. Then Talon added the usual Renaissance sceptical statement of fideism: 'What then is to be done? Must we believe nothing without a decisive argument, must we abstain from approving anything without an evident reason? On the contrary; in religious matters a sure and solid faith will have more weight than all of the demonstrations of all of the philosophers.'[27] (A somewhat similar view appears in another work, *Academica*, published by Pedro de Valencia in 1596.)[28]

Talon's efforts led to Ramus being attacked as a new sceptic, and his movement being seen as dangerous to both philosophy and religion, since it would undermine any basis for any beliefs. One member of Ramus' circle, Guy de Brués, wrote a critique of this new scepticism in 1557 in the form of a dialogue amongst members of the Pléiade, in which some of them argue for scepticism and others answer the arguments. The work is not very exciting philosophically, but indicates how important discussion about scepticism and how to refute it had become by the middle of the sixteenth century.[29] One could cite other indications in many other writers. The really important philosophical presentations of scepticism appear almost simultaneously from two distantly related authors in France, Francisco Sanches, professor at Toulouse, and his cousin, Michel de Montaigne.

Sanches in his *Quod nihil scitur*, written in 1576 and published in 1581, presents a very acute scepticism in the form of an intellectual critique of

25. Popkin 1979, pp. 23–6.   26. *Ibid.*, pp. 26–7.   27. Cited *ibid.*, p. 29.
28. *Ibid.*, p. 36.   29. *Ibid.*, pp. 30–1.

Aristotelianism. Analysing the Aristotelian theory of knowledge, Sanches first attacked the Aristotelian conception of definitions. He insisted that all definitions are arbitrary and have no necessary relation to what is named. Names keep changing, so that by combining names and definitions, we do not thereby know anything about objects. Sanches then attacked Aristotle's theory of science as acquiring knowledge through demonstrations. First, how do we know the concepts employed? Only through particulars, which is what Aristotle was trying to explain. In a demonstration, the syllogism is supposed to produce scientific knowledge. But can it? We can only be sure the premises are true if we know the conclusion is, and not vice versa. How can we tell if 'all men are mortal' is true, if we do not know that the conclusion 'Socrates is a man' is true? Also, we can prove anything syllogistically by just starting with the right premises. So, Aristotle's logical system is useless in acquiring knowledge. We cannot gain certitude by finding true definitions; we cannot find the real causes of things, for we would have to find the causes of the causes and so on.

Instead, what we should seek is perfect knowledge of a thing by immediate intuitive apprehension. This can be done for one particular at a time. Any generalisations beyond this will lead to dubious abstractions and chimeras. The certain knowledge of particulars becomes dubious when we realise the frailty and unreliability of human senses, and our inability to know objects individually because they are related. Hence genuine scientific knowledge is unattainable. All we can accomplish is to attain a limited, imperfect knowledge of some things present in experience. Sanches was a professor of medicine, and wrote extensively on medical matters, setting forth the limited information that he had gathered. He presented the most precise and organised case for scepticism during the Renaissance and for the negative claim of the Academics, *nihil scitur*. He probably influenced later thinkers such as Pierre Gassendi, and initiated a 'scientific method' (a term he seems to have introduced) for achieving some kind of organised empirical information even if all is ultimately in doubt.[30]

His cousin, Michel de Montaigne, was the most significant and influential figure in the development of Renaissance scepticism. A thoroughgoing humanist, Montaigne read the classics, including the newly translated sceptical ones. A child of religious wars, the son of a Catholic father and a Jewess turned Protestant mother, he knew the sceptical arguments of the Reformers and Counter-Reformers. He personally knew many of the protagonists of the contending groups of his day and became an adviser to

---

30. For detailed discussion and bibliography, see *ibid.*, pp. 36–41.

the leader of the Protestant cause, Henri de Navarre, as well as being Mayor of Bordeaux.

Montaigne's presentation of his sceptical viewpoint occurs most completely in the longest and most philosophical of his essays, *Apologie de Raimond Sebond*, which was apparently written at the period when he was most affected by his reading of Sextus. He carved phrases and slogans from Sextus into the rafter-beams of his study. The *Apologie* was written after Montaigne had translated the *Theologia naturalis* of Sebond (Sibiuda), a forceful rationalist theologian of the fifteenth century. Some readers were not convinced of the reasoning and asked Montaigne for further explanation. In his rambling style Montaigne 'defended' Sebond by showing the inadequacy of reason in all areas. Therefore Sebond's use of it in theology was no worse than anyone else's rational efforts. In the course of developing this explanation, Montaigne presented various layers of doubt drawn from Sextus and Cicero. He showed the unreliability of human senses and of human reason. He showed the conflict of human opinions on almost any subject whatsoever and the inability of people to justify their views in science, philosophy or theology. 'The participation that we have in the knowledge of truth, whatever it may be, has not been acquired by our own powers.' It is only based on faith.[31]

As Montaigne intensified the sceptics' case, he returned over and over again to the fideistic motif as the only solution. We lack reliable criteria for judging our senses or our reason. The more we try to justify our views, the more dubious they become. So, 'there cannot be first principles for men unless the divinity has revealed them; all the rest – beginning , middle and end – is nothing but dreams and smoke'.[32] Montaigne wove Sextus' series of tropes and his evidence that all reasoning is circular or leads to an infinite regress through a vast variety of human knowledge. The ancient philosophers and scientists and the new ones like Copernicus and Paracelsus are challenged. The varieties of human behaviour, as revealed in classical literature and in the accounts of the explorers, indicate we can have no assurance about how to behave. As one wallows in these many sceptical currents, Montaigne pointed out that trying to know reality is like trying to clutch water. So, we should rest content in our world of appearances, accepting the customs, mores and religion of our society until and unless God chooses to enlighten us.

Montaigne showed his contemporaries that sceptical difficulties would prevent them from justifying any particular rule of faith, any particular set

31. Montaigne 1922–3, II, p. 230 (II.12); see also Popkin 1979, pp. 42–65.
32. Montaigne 1922–3, II, p. 285 (II.12).

of human opinions and any alleged claims of scientific knowledge. He offered them only reliance on faith as a solution, and many had doubts about his sincerity. His *Essais* were extremely popular, and, at least in the *Apologie*, posed the modern problem of knowledge. How do we know anything? What can we know? How certain can we be? He was read by Bacon, Descartes, Pascal and very many others. His views were presented didactically by Pierre Charron in *De la sagesse* (1601), which went through numerous editions. This *nouveau pyrrhonisme* of Montaigne became the challenge that now had to be met if a new foundation for human knowledge was to be found. Thus, through scepticism, the theory of knowledge became the central focus of modern thought. The epistemologies of Aristotle, Plato, the Neoplatonists, the nature philosophers, the mystics, the cabalists and the rest no longer seemed adequate to meet the challenge raised by the revival and revitalisation of the arguments of the Greek sceptics. Although Aristotle's answer tended to be what was still taught in the seventeenth-century schools, the modern philosophers sought other ways of dealing with the sceptical crisis. So, the scepticism which slowly developed in the Renaissance in the shadow of official Aristotelianism, forms of Platonism and Neoplatonism and various bizarre views of nature gradually became central, and posed problems that were to be critical in philosophy from then on. And as the proposed fideism of the Renaissance sceptics lost its lustre or conviction, the revived scepticism was to become one of the main forces undermining belief in traditional Judaism and Christianity.[33]

Thus, a revived and revitalised scepticism, which grew out of many of the currents of Renaissance thought, made the problem of knowledge crucial for later philosophy. In questioning all of the theories in philosophy, science and theology of the time, the sceptics made it crucial for thinkers to find a satisfactory justification for their knowledge claims. Hence, the questions: Where does our knowledge come from, what can we know and how certain is our knowledge? became central. New theories of knowledge had to be offered to deal with the epistemological crisis brought on by the growth and spread of scepticism at the end of the Renaissance. The older theories of Aristotle and the scholastics seemed to have been overthrown, and the new knowledge being developed by the new scientists seemed to require another kind of foundation. Hence, in the post-Renaissance philosophical world the theory of knowledge became a central part of philosophical discussions.

33. Popkin 1979, pp. 66ff.; Penelhum 1983.

19

EPISTEMOLOGY OF THE SCIENCES

The range of Renaissance discussions of cognitive status and means of acquiring knowledge in the various *scientiae* is extensive. Certain difficulties attendant on the attempt to survey this field deserve mention at the outset. To start with it should be noted that only a small part of the field has been subject to scholarly attention. Further, much of the recent literature is primarily concerned with the issue of continuity between Renaissance epistemology and the epistemologies associated with the 'new' science of the seventeenth century, sometimes with scant regard to intellectual, disciplinary and generic contexts. Epistemology of the sciences is not, it should go without saying, a Renaissance notion: no Renaissance category even remotely corresponds to 'the sciences' or 'the natural sciences' in our senses of the terms; and current conceptions of epistemology are at best dimly foreshadowed in Renaissance logic and psychology. In imposing an artificial unity on discussions of method and status in the *scientiae* we run obvious risks of anachronism in selection and interpretation of material.

In the following account attention is confined to topics in the epistemology of disciplines that were, from the curricular point of view, orthodox – natural philosophy, medicine and mathematics. This is a drastic restriction, for much of the most innovative debate of the period on questions of attainment of knowledge concerns disciplines whose credentials as *scientiae* were perceived as questionable: the 'unorthodox' sciences, astrology, alchemy, natural magic and so on; and the practical and operative disciplines, architecture, cartography, military engineering and the like. The survey opens with accounts of three sixteenth-century debates concerned, respectively, with: the status of 'demonstrative regress', a means whereby it was widely supposed that the proximate causes of natural phenomena could be established; the grounds of certainty in mathematics; and the status of hypotheses in astronomy. In the next section other major debating points are touched on in an attempt to convey the extent and diversity of Renaissance treatments of method and status in the *scientiae*. Two of the topics considered in the opening sections figure centrally in modern theses about continuity in the epistemology of the sciences. Demonstrative regress has been claimed as a link in a tradition of scientific methodology stretching from Aristotle to Galileo; and sixteenth-century controversy about the status of astronomical hypotheses has been presented as a confrontation between 'realist' and 'fictionalist' views of mathematical hypotheses that can be traced from Greek antiquity to the present day. The final section ventures some reflections on the vexed question of continuity in the epistemology of the sciences.

DEMONSTRATIVE REGRESS

Demonstrative regress (*regressus demonstrativus*) is a procedure which combines an inference from an observed effect to its proximate cause with an inference from the proximate cause to the observed effect. This composite process plays a central role in many sixteenth-century accounts of method of discovery in natural philosophy.[1]

A crucial source for the doctrine of *regressus* is *Posterior Analytics* I.13, in which Aristotle contrasts two sorts of syllogisms, ἀπόδειξις τοῦ διότι, 'demonstration of the reasoned fact', and ἀπόδειξις τοῦ ὅτι, 'demonstration of the fact'.[2] One of his examples of the former is (slightly expanded): heavenly bodies which are near the earth do not twinkle; the planets are near the earth; hence the planets do not twinkle. This syllogism demonstrates the presence of an observed effect, *not twinkling*, in a subject, *the planets*; and it does so by means of a middle term, *being near the earth*, which constitutes the proximate cause of that effect. By rearrangement of terms a 'demonstration of the fact' is obtained in which the middle term specifies the effect rather than the cause. Thus we have: heavenly bodies which do not twinkle are near the earth; the planets do not twinkle; hence the planets are near the earth. Part of Aristotle's intention in this passage is, it seems, to distinguish demonstrative syllogisms from related syllogisms whose premises, whilst true, fail to explain their conclusions.[3] Nevertheless, by the sixteenth century the question of the way in which the two alleged species of demonstration may be combined to yield knowledge of the causes of natural phenomena had come to be widely regarded as crucial for the interpretation of the *Posterior Analytics* and for the understanding of Aristotle's own procedure in natural philosophy.

---

1. Sixteenth-century treatments of *regressus* are surveyed in Risse 1964; *Aristotelismo veneto* 1983, I, pp. 221–77 (Papuli). See also Randall 1961; W. F. Edwards 1960; Kosman 1964; Papuli 1965, 1967; Poppi 1969, 1972a; Wallace 1972–, I, 1984, ch. 3; Bottin 1972; N. Jardine 1976.
2. These are G. R. G. Mure's renderings in Aristotle 1910–52, I.
3. Cf. Aristotle 1975, pp. 149–50; Patzig 1981, pp. 145–50.

The connections of *regressus* with earlier discussions of the nature of scientific demonstrations are little understood, and the following remarks are tentative.[4] Latin commentary on the *Posterior Analytics* tended from the outset to see it as largely concerned with proximate causes of natural phenomena, showing little appreciation of what many present-day commentators regard as Aristotle's attempt to model on geometry a conception of a science as a deductive hierarchy and to show how diverse phenomena may be understood in the light of general principles.[5] Given this view of the work, it is hardly surprising that a passage that gives explicit examples of syllogisms dealing with proximate causes should have become a major focus of interest.

More specific fuel for the elaboration of *regressus* was provided by passages in which Aristotle contrasts 'absolute' (ἁπλῶς) and 'accidental' (κατὰ συμβεβηκός) knowledge and by those in which he distinguishes things 'better known to us' (ἡμῖν γνωριμώτερον) from things 'better known in nature' (τῇ φύσει γνωριμώτερον).[6] To obtain absolute knowledge of an effect we cannot, the *regressus* theorists argued, proceed directly to the demonstration of that effect through its proximate cause; for though causes are better known in the natural order, effects are better known to us, because evident to our senses. Rather, the two types of demonstration, demonstration of the fact, which proceeds from effect to proximate cause, and demonstration of the reasoned fact, which proceeds from proximate cause to effect, must be combined. The precise mode of combination of the two types of demonstration needed to bring about the absolute demonstration (*demonstratio potissima*) of the effect which is productive of absolute knowledge was widely debated. The following scheme is, however, found in a considerable number of accounts. (1) By observation we obtain accidental or 'confused' knowledge of an effect. (2) By induction combined with demonstration of the fact we obtain accidental knowledge of its cause. (3) Through a noetic process of *negotiatio* (*meditatio, consideratio*) we obtain absolute or distinct knowledge of the proximate cause, grasping the necessity of the link between it and its effect. (4) By demonstration of the reasoned fact we obtain absolute knowledge of the effect, knowledge of it through the cause which necessitates it.

A further important factor in the development of *regressus* was the conflation of species of demonstration of the *Posterior Analytics* with other methods and procedures. For example, in *Physics* I.1 Aristotle mentions two

4. On the sources of *regressus* see Randall 1961; Crombie 1953; Bottin 1972; *Cambridge History* 1982, pp. 496–517 (Serene).   5. Cf. Kosman 1964, chs. 1, 2.

6. For example, *Posterior Analytics* I.2 (71^{b}9–12); *Prior Analytics* II.23 (68^{b}35 ff.); *Physics* I.1 (184^{a}10 ff.).

procedures, one going from the universal to the particular, the other from the particular to the universal. In Latin commentary these were widely identified (often on the authority of Themistius and Averroes) with demonstration of the reasoned fact and demonstration of the fact respectively.[7] Further conflations arose in commentary and exegesis of Galen's *Ars medica*, the analytic and synthetic procedures mentioned at the beginning of the treatise being identified with the two supposed species of demonstration.[8] It seems that it was partly as a result of these conflations that the nature and validity of *regressus* came to be regarded as a key to an understanding of the way in which the masters of antiquity had attained their knowledge in natural philosophy.

By way of example, let us consider the account of *regressus* offered by Agostino Nifo in his *Physics* commentary of 1506. He first raises a basic difficulty which faces those who regard *regressus* as productive of knowledge, its apparent circularity.

But on this issue I customarily raise the question whether there are two procedures in natural [sciences], one from an effect to the discovery of the cause, the other from the cause discovered to the effect. It seems not, because then there would be a circle in demonstrations . . .[9]

Nifo goes on to retail a defence of *regressus* against the objection:

Recent authors are of the opinion that four types of knowledge occur. The first is [knowledge] of the effect through sense or observation. The second is the discovery of the cause through the effect, which is obtained by *demonstratio signi*.[10] The third is the *negotiatio* of that same cause by the intellect, by which, together with the first, knowledge of the cause is so much increased that it is worthy to be made the middle term of a *demonstratio simpliciter*. The last is knowledge of the reason for the same effect through a cause so established that it may be the middle term.[11]

Later Nifo modified his views on *regressus*. Where in his *De anima* commentary of 1498 he had given an account close to that just outlined, in the 1520 edition he denies that a process of *negotiatio* is always involved;[12]

7. Themistius 1900, p. 1; Aristotle and Averroes 1550–2, IV, f. 4[va].   8. See below p. 704.
9. Nifo 1552, f. 5[v]: 'Sed circa haec dubitare solitus sum, utrum in naturalibus sint duo processus, unus ab effectu ad causae inventionem, alter a causa inventa ad effectum. Videtur quod non, quia tunc esset circulus in demonstrationibus . . .'
10. Nifo's terminology reflects the widespread identification of the 'demonstration of the fact' of *Posterior Analytics* I.13 with the syllogism 'from probabilities or signs' (ἐξ εἰκότων ἢ σημείων) of *Prior Analytics* II.27.
11. Nifo 1552, f. 8[r]: 'recentiores volunt esse quatuor notitias. Prima est effectus per sensum, aut observationem. Secunda est inventio causae per effectum, quae quidem demonstratione signi habetur. Tertia est eiusdem causae per intellectus negotiationem, ex qua cum prima crescit notitia causae in tantum, ut digna sit effici medium demonstrationis simpliciter. Ultima est eiusdem effectus notitia propter quid per talem causam sic certam, ut sit medium.' Cf. Randall 1961, pp. 42–3.   12. See Poppi 1969.

and in the posthumous 1540 edition of his *Physics* commentary there is added the following much-quoted *recognitio*:

But when I more carefully ponder the words of Aristotle and the commentaries of Alexander, Philoponus and Simplicius, it appears to me that in the regress which occurs in the demonstrations of natural sciences, the first process, by which the discovery of the cause is syllogised, is a mere syllogism, because merely conjectural,[13] since through it the discovery of the cause is syllogised only conjecturally. The second process, moreover, by which the reason for the effect is syllogised through the cause, is *demonstratio propter quid*, not that which makes us know absolutely, but rather *ex conditione*, given that that is the cause, or given that the propositions which exhibit the cause are true and that there can be no other cause . . . But you will object, because then science concerning nature would not be science. It should be said that science concerning nature is not science absolutely as is mathematical science; but it is science *propter quid*, because the discovery of the cause, which is obtained through conjectural syllogism, constitutes the reason for the effect.[14]

It is unclear whether Nifo's reservations about our ability to apprehend with certainty the causes of observed effects are general or apply only to certain difficult questions in natural philosophy. There are, however, other signs of a moderate scepticism in his later commentaries. Thus he argues against the view that the definitions on which demonstrations are based are self-evident, claiming that they are *nota per se* only in the sense that they are not demonstrable from something else.[15] And he is ready to admit that the non-demonstrative methods of Aristotle's *Topics* have a place in enquiry in natural philosophy.[16] However, a caveat is in order: though Nifo is a shrewd and scholarly interpreter, it is hard to detect a systematic body of philosophical doctrine in his eclectic and often eccentric pronouncements.[17]

When we turn to the account of *regressus* offered by Jacopo Zabarella in

13. 'Conjectural' is potentially misleading here. Elsewhere Nifo characterises 'demonstration of the fact' as *coniectura necessaria*: Nifo 1553b (1st edn, 1523), f. 13ʳ. In the passage of Philoponus to which Nifo is probably referring, the term τεκμηριώδης is applied to such demonstrations, and the term is rendered by *coniecturalis* in the only Latin translation then published of Philoponus' commentary, that of Theodosius: Philoponus 1559 (1st edn, 1539), p. 44ᵇ. 'By a reliable criterion' is perhaps an appropriate gloss.

14. Nifo 1552, f. 6ᵛ: 'Sed cum Aristotelis verba et Alexandri, ac Themistii, Philoponi, ac Simplicii commentaria diligentius revolverim, videtur mihi in regressu, qui fit in naturalibus demonstrationibus, primum processum, quo syllogizatur causae inventio, esse syllogismum tantum, quoniam coniecturalis tantum, cum per ipsum solum coniecturabiliter syllogizetur causae inventio: secundum vero, quo syllogizatur per inventionem causae propter quid effectus, esse demonstrationem propter quid, non qui faciat scire simpliciter, sed ex conditione, dato quod illa causa sit, vel dato quod propositiones verae sint, quae represent causam et nulla alia causa esse possit . . . Sed occurres, quia tunc scientia de natura non esset scientia. Dicendum, scientiam de natura non esse scientiam simpliciter, qualis est scientia mathematica, est tamen scientia propter quid: quia inventio causae, quae habetur per syllogismum coniecturalem, est propter quid effectus.' Cf. Randall 1961, pp. 43–5. 15. Nifo 1553b, f. 33ʳ.

16. Nifo 1540 (1st edn, 1535), ff. 9ʳ–10ʳ. 17. Cf. Vasoli 1974, p. 437.

his influential *Opera logica* of 1578, we find ourselves in very different territory. Here *regressus* is at the heart of an elaborate and systematic account of the processes of cognition and the functions of logic, an account that shows no trace of scepticism about our ability to attain knowledge of causes through demonstrative methods.[18]

The work opens with a treatise on the nature of logic in which Zabarella argues that it is to be considered not as a practical art or theoretical science in its own right, but rather as a midwife to the arts and sciences, being the source of the 'instruments, by which truth in every matter is known and discerned from falsity'.[19] In the four books *De methodis* he distinguishes *ordines*, procedures for communicating existing knowledge, from methods *sensu stricto*, procedures for the acquisition of new knowledge.[20]

Zabarella claims that 'demonstration of the reasoned fact' (*demonstratio propter quid* or *methodus compositiva*) and 'demonstration of the fact' (*demonstratio quod* or *methodus resolutiva*) are the sole methods in this strict sense. He goes to great lengths to show that other procedures, for example, the 'Platonic' composition and division used in the hunt for definitions and the *resolutio* (ἀνάλυσις) whereby mathematicians work back from theorems to principles, are not genuinely productive of knowledge.[21] He goes on to argue that the two demonstrative methods provide all that is needed to attain the goal of natural philosophy. That goal is knowledge of the definitions of *affectiones* – observable states of bodies, such as being eclipsed, not twinkling and thundering. Such a definition must specify the genus, subject and proximate cause of the state in question: thus thunder is defined as a noise produced in a cloud by the extinction of fire. The genera and subjects of *affectiones* are *praecognita*, 'things known in advance', and the two demonstrative methods provide all that is needed, Zabarella claims, to achieve distinct knowledge of proximate causes.[22]

This last claim is apparently open to the Aristotelian objection that it overlooks the process of induction, described in the last chapter of the *Posterior Analytics*, which leads from individual sense experiences to the grasp of universals. It turns out that Zabarella, whilst fully acknowledging

---

18. On Zabarella's account of the nature and functions of logic see W. F. Edwards 1960; Corsano 1958–63, 41: 507–17; Poppi 1972a; *Aristotelismo veneto* 1983, I, pp. 155–72 (Risse). On Girolamo Balduino's account, to which Zabarella is much indebted, see Papuli 1967, pp. 125–200. On the *fortuna* of Zabarella's logical doctrines see, for example, Petersen 1921; J. Zabarella 1578, pp. xi–xxviii (Vasoli's introduction to the 1985 reprint).

19. J. Zabarella 1607b, cols. 51–2: 'instrumenta quibus in omni re verum cognoscatur, et a falso discernatur'.   20. *Ibid.*, cols. 138–9.   21. *Ibid.*, cols. 231ff., 266–7.

22. *Ibid.*, cols. 264–6, 294–318. Zabarella's argument depends on his interpretation of Aristotle's obscure treatment in *Posterior Analytics* II of the relations between definition and demonstration.

the role in the acquisition of *scientia* of this type of induction, does not consider it as an independent form of inference. With respect to its role in the discovery of causes it can, he suggests, be regarded as an inferior form of demonstration of the fact, inferior because whereas demonstrations of the fact can reveal to us recondite causes inaccessible to the senses, for example, the prime mover as the cause of the diurnal rotation of the heavens, induction can make known only causes accessible to the senses, for example, fire as the cause of smoke.[23]

Induction is not, Zabarella claims, strictly speaking a form of inference.[24] To understand this assertion we have to turn to the theory of cognition expounded in his *De rebus naturalibus* of 1590 and in his massive uncompleted *De anima* commentary, published posthumously in 1605. There Zabarella claims that our knowledge of universals is not acquired by inference from observations. Rather sense experiences give rise to images which render the 'possible intellect' (*intellectus possibilis*) or rational soul receptive to representations of the universals present in the mind of God. The vehicle of this inspiration is the 'active intellect' (*intellectus agens*). Induction is not therefore a form of inference, but should rather be considered a process 'from the same to the same', from the representations of universals that constitute the individuals of the external world to representations of those same universals inspired into the human mind by the transcendent active intellect. Perhaps it is his confidence in divine revelation of universals, triggered by the images whose formation in the imagination follows sense experience, that makes Zabarella so confident of the ability of the natural philosopher to apprehend the premises on which demonstrative syllogisms depend.[25]

To see this confidence in action let us turn to the most elaborate of his examples of the application of *regressus*.[26] The effect to be explained is the generation and corruption of substances, the observed fact that physical objects of each natural kind come into existence and ultimately cease to be.

Let us take as an example the demonstration of Aristotle in book I of the *Physics*, by which from the generation of substances he shows that prime matter occurs: from a known effect an unknown cause. For generation is known to us by sense but the underlying matter is in the highest degree unknown. So after the proper subject, that is a perishable natural body, in which each is originally present, has been considered, it is demonstrated that there is present in it a cause, on account of which the effect is present in the same, and it is *demonstratio quod* which is thus formed: where there is generation there is underlying matter; but in a natural body there is

23. *Ibid.*, cols. 268–71.   24. *Ibid.*, cols. 270, 1277.   25. Cf. Skulsky, 1968, p. 356.
26. J. Zabarella 1607b, cols. 484–9; cf. also 1607a, cols. 137–42.

generation; so in a natural body there is matter. In this demonstration the minor premise is known to us confusedly, because we do in fact observe that natural bodies are generated and perish, but we do not know the cause. The major premise, although it is not known by sense, easily becomes known when some mental consideration has been applied.[27]

Now that we have completed the first phase of the *regressus*, we have discovered that prime matter is present in all natural bodies: we have 'confused' knowledge of the cause of generation and corruption. But we do not yet, Zabarella claims, have 'distinct' knowledge of the cause, for we do not yet know that it is the proximate cause of generation and corruption rather than a mere constant concomitant. To discover this we must undertake a *consideratio* or *negotiatio* about the essential nature of prime matter. Zabarella gives as the *negotiatio* an exposition of Aristotle's theory of prime matter.

Matter therefore having been discovered through generation is not yet known to be the cause of generation, because it is not yet known what that matter is. For this reason Aristotle, who wished to teach us a distinct, not merely a confused, knowledge of principles, as much as a natural philosopher can have, began to investigate the nature and conditions of the matter which he has discovered . . . He taught us first of all how it differs from privation. For the function of matter is to underlie contraries and to receive them. The function of contraries, moreover, is for each to drive the other out of the same matter. Hence matter persists under each contrary and never perishes . . . Therefore in its own nature matter must lack all forms and have the potentiality to receive all. This is without doubt the nature of matter, that it is nothing in actuality but everything in potentiality.[28]

27. J. Zabarella 1607a, col. 485: 'sumamus demonstrationem Aristotelis in libro I Physicorum, qua ex generatione, quae substantiarum est, ostendit materiam primam dari ex effectu noto causam ignotam: generatio enim sensu nobis cognita est, subiecta vero materia maxime incognita. Accepto igitur subiecto proprio, scilicet corpore naturali caduco, cui primo utraque inest, in eo demonstratur causam inesse, propterea quod in eodem inest effectus, et est demonstratio quod, quae ita formatur: ubi est generatio, ibi est subiecta materia: at in corpore naturali est generatio, ergo in corpore naturali est materia: in hac demonstratione minor propositio est nobis nota confuse: quoniam generari quidem, et interire naturalia corpora cernimus, sed causam ignoramus: maior vero propositio quanquam sensu non cognoscitur, aliqua tamen adhibita mentali consideratione facile innotescit.'

28. *Ibid.*, col. 488: 'Materia igitur per generationem inventa, nondum cognoscitur esse causa generationis: quia quid sit ipsa materia, adhuc ignoratur: propterea Aristoteles, qui principiorum cognitionem nobis tradere voluit non modum confusam, verum etiam distinctam, quantam naturalis philosophus habere potest, coepit materiae inventae conditiones, et naturam investigare . . . Docuit in primis quomodo a privatione differat: materiae namque officium est substare contrariis, et ea recipere: contrariorum vero officium est se ab eadem materia mutuo pellere: ideo materia manet sub utroque contrario, et nunquam interit . . . debet igitur materia secundum suam naturam carere omnibus formis, et omnium recipiendarum potestatem habere: haec absque dubio est natura materiae ut nihil sit actu, sed potestate omnia.' The qualification 'quantam naturalis philosophus habere potest' may well imply a contrast with the knowledge of first principles, which is the province of the metaphysician: cf. *ibid.*, cols. 529, 780, 1267.

As a result of this *negotiatio*:

It readily becomes apparent to us that such matter is the cause of generation. For because it has the capacity to receive all forms and prescribes for itself no particular form, but is equally suited to receive a form and its privation, it comes about accordingly that nothing possessing matter can be eternal, but of necessity it eventually perishes, and from it something else is generated.[29]

Zabarella concludes that now that we have distinct knowledge of the cause we are in a position to set out a demonstration of the reasoned fact: wherever prime matter occurs there is generation; but prime matter occurs in a natural body; so generation occurs in a natural body. We have achieved the desired distinct knowledge of the generation and corruption of substances, for we now have certain knowledge of it through the cause which necessitates it.[30]

THE CERTAINTY OF MATHEMATICS

As we have seen, in the Aristotelian tradition achievement of 'absolute demonstration' (ἀπόδειξις ἁπλῶς, usually rendered as *demonstratio potissima* or *simpliciter*), was generally regarded as problematic in natural philosophy, because of the lack of evidence to us of the hidden causes on which such demonstrations often depend. In mathematics, however, it was widely held that the two types of priority, priority 'for us' and priority 'for nature', coincide.[31] So no process of working back from what is evident to our senses to what is naturally prior but hidden from us is required; rather the necessary principles on which *demonstratio potissima* depends are immediately evident to us.

In his *Commentarium de certitudine mathematicarum* of 1547 the Siennese philosopher Alessandro Piccolomini challenges the view that mathematics owes its certainty to the status of its demonstrations as *demonstrationes potissimae*.

First we intend to show both by reasons and by testimonies that mathematical demonstrations are not those *demonstrationes potissimae* that Aristotle devises in

---

29. *Ibid.*, col. 488: 'facile nobis innotescit, talem materiam generationis causam esse: quoniam enim potestatem habet recipiendi omnes formas, et nullam certam formam sibi praescribit, sed aeque apta est recipere formam, et eius privationem: ideo facit ut nullum materiam habens possit esse perpetuum, sed ex necessitate aliquando intereat, et ex eo aliud generetur'.
30. *Ibid.*, col. 489.
31. Averroes was often cited in support of this view: see, e.g., Aristotle and Averroes 1550–2, I, f. 374^r; IV, f. 6^v.

Posterior Analytics. In the second place . . . it is our intention to set out the reason for which mathematical disciplines can be said to be in the first grade of certainty.[32]

In the opening chapters he offers an account of the nature of logic and of the demonstrative methods it provides.[33] The conditions for *demonstratio potissima* are, on this account, stringent. The premises must be necessary, the major premise having the form of a definition, and the middle term must specify the immediate cause of the effect demonstrated.[34] There follow chapters on the aims, objects and methods of mathematics, the latter including a discussion of the resolutive method of the classical geometers.[35] The crux of the argument comes in chapter 11, in which Piccolomini sets out a series of ways in which mathematical demonstrations fail to satisfy the conditions for *demonstratio potissima*: they do not specify causes in any of the four genera of causes; the middle term is not always immediate, since there may be many mathematical demonstrations of the same property of a subject through different middle terms; and the major premise does not always have the form of a definition.[36]

Piccolomini rests his case for the certainty of mathematics on an account of the objects of mathematical knowledge that he attributes to Proclus:

So Proclus derives from Plato the view that the mathematical things themselves, about which demonstrations are made, are neither sensible things altogether in a subject, nor entirely freed from it, but that these mathematical figures are formed in the imagination, the occasion being afforded by quantities found in sensible matter. Moreover, the intellect derives those universal principles from these quantities that are in the imagination.[37]

Separation of the objects of mathematics from sensible matter is a standard ground for the certainty of mathematics in the period, but Piccolomini's position is less usual in relating the certainty of mathematics to the constructive role of the imagination.

The issues raised by Piccolomini attracted considerable attention in the

32. A. Piccolomini 1565, f. 69ᵛ: 'Primum et rationibus et authoritatibus, demonstrare intendimus mathematicas demonstrationes non esse illas potissimas, quas in [Posterioribus Analyticis] construit Aristoteles. Secundo vero loco . . . causam assignare est animus, qua mathematicae disciplinae in primo esse gradu certitudinis dici possunt.' For a detailed exegesis of this work see Giacobbe 1972a; see also Schüling 1969, pp. 45ff.
34. *Ibid.*, ff. 88ᵛ–94ʳ.   35. *Ibid.*, ff. 94ᵛ–100ʳ.   36. *Ibid.*, ff. 100ʳ–5ᵛ.
37. *Ibid.*, f. 95ʳ: 'Concludit ergo Proclus ex Platone, quod res ipsae mathematicae, de quibus fiunt demonstrationes, nec omnino in subiecto, sensibiles sunt, nec penitus ab ipso liberatae, sed in ipsa phantasia reperiuntur figurae illae mathematicae, habita tamen occasione a quantitatibus in materia sensibili repertis. Intellectus autem, ex iis, quae in phantasia sunt in quantitatibus, rationes illas universales colligit.'

following decades. Pietro Catena, Francesco Barozzi and Giuseppe Moletti, all teachers of mathematics at Padua, concerned themselves with the nature of mathematical demonstrations and the sources of certainty in mathematics, as did the logician Bernardino Tomitano, and the Jesuit theologian and natural philosopher Benito Pereira.[38] Let us consider briefly the responses of Francesco Barozzi, who sets out to refute Piccolomini, and of Pietro Catena, whose position is closer to Piccolomini's.

Barozzi's *Quaestio de certitudine mathematicarum* of 1560 challenges Piccolomini's distinctions between mathematical demonstration and *demonstratio potissima*. To Piccolomini's claim that mathematical demonstrations never appeal to causes, Barozzi responds by insisting that in dealing with *materia intelligibilis* they specify both formal and material causes.[39] However, in trying to counter others of the distinctions alleged by Piccolomini, Barozzi makes substantial concessions, allowing that not all mathematical demonstrations are *demonstrationes potissimae*.[40] He then turns to the issue of certainty. From Aristotle he extracts three criteria for the relative certainty of sciences: a science which demonstrates both a fact (*quia*) and its reason (*proper quid*) is more certain than one that demonstrates only the fact; a science that deals with immaterial objects is more certain than one that deals with material objects; and one that deals with simple objects is more certain than one that deals with what is complex.[41] Since *demonstrationes potissimae* reveal both facts and their reasons, mathematics possesses the first grade of certainty by the first criterion. By the second criterion it has a degree of certainty intermediate between those of *scientia divina* and *scientia naturalis*, given that its objects are quantities partly conjoined with material bodies and partly separate from them.[42] Barozzi concludes: 'It is abundantly clear that [mathematics] is to be put in the first grade of certainty not only because of the matter subject to it (as a most erudite modern author held), but also on account of its *potissimae demonstrationes*.'[43]

38. On Catena see Giacobbe 1973, 1981; Crapulli 1969, pp. 45–55. On Barozzi see Giacobbe 1972b; Schüling 1969, pp. 52–3; Rose 1977. On Moletti see *Aristotelismo veneto* 1983, I, pp. 509–17 (Carugo); on Tomitano, *Aristotelismo veneto*, II, pp. 607–21 (Davi Daniele). On Pereira see Giacobbe 1977; Crapulli 1969, pp. 93–9; Schüling 1969, pp. 47–9.
39. Barozzi 1560, ff. 21rff. A detailed exegesis is given by Giacobbe 1972b.
40. Proof by *reductio ad absurdum*, for example, is not *demonstratio potissima*: ibid., 27r–v.
41. Ibid., ff. 32v–3r.   42. Ibid., f. 33r.
43. Ibid., f. 33v: 'non solum propter subiectam sibi materiam (ut voluit eruditissimus recentior) verum etiam propter suas potissimas demonstrationes in primo certitudinis ordine ponendam esse, abunde patet'.

In his treatises of 1556 and 1561 on mathematical passages in Aristotle, Pietro Catena emphasises the autonomy of the methods of mathematics.[44] He follows Piccolomini in denying the occurrence of *demonstratio potissima*: 'no mathematical demonstration is *potissima*, and because of that mathematical disciplines are not sciences, if Aristotle's teaching is adhered to'.[45]

Catena's brief *Oratio pro idea methodi* of 1563 presents a case for the certainty of mathematics that represents a substantial elaboration of Piccolomini's claims. He first considers the certainty that accrues to mathematics from its objects. There are, he maintains, three kinds of things with which our speculations may be concerned.

For some things that are bound up in matter come under consideration together with it; while others that are joined to matter are conceived without it by the mind. A third kind of things, however, is remote from all matter and is completely known in every respect without it. The first are most obscure, because not only are they in matter, but they are not even separated from it by our thought. For this reason they are never represented by our intellect genuinely and faithfully. Those things which lack all matter . . . are surely the ones most evident and perspicuous by nature to the eyes of the mind; but since we are left to the help of the senses, from which all our knowledge originates so long as we are confined in this body [lit. pleasant prison], it comes about that things in themselves most clear are, on account of the feebleness of our mind, quite hidden in Cimmerian darkness. There remains the third kind of things, which inhere in the material thing itself, but are separated from it by our thought; and these are the only things that are known to us exactly and do not by their obscurity engulf the eye of the mind in darkness or injure it with too much light and brilliance. So wherever we are we see the triangle, the rectangle and other things of this kind without any coverings, because they are the sort of things that are grasped by the senses and because we contemplate the form itself apart from matter and do not consider wood, iron or anything of that kind. And this evidence and certainty of the mathematical disciplines is evident from [their] subjects and the things themselves.[46]

44. Catena 1556, 1561. The former work is striking in its recognition of the centrality of geometrical science in Aristotle's *Organon*. (Catena assumes Aristotle's familiarity with Euclid's *Elements*. As was usual in the period he indentifies the geometer with Socrates' disciple Euclid of Megara: see Giacobbe 1981, pp. 48–9.) See Giacobbe 1981 for editions of these works and of Catena 1563.
45. Catena 1556, p. 90: 'Dico secundo . . . quod nulla demonstratio mathematica est potissima, et ob id mathematicae nullae sunt scientiae si stetur in doctrina Aristotelis.'
46. Catena 1563, f. 4^{r-v}: 'Quaedam nam materiae implicitae, cum ea pariter in considerationem veniunt. Aliae autem materiae adiunctae, absque ea mente concipiuntur. Tertium vero genus rerum semotum est ab omni materia, et absque ipsa omnifariam intellectu pernoscitur. Primae sunt obscurissimae, quia non solum sunt in materia, sed ne cogitatione quidem nostra ab illa seiungantur: et ob id intellectui nostro, neque pure, neque sincere unquam representantur. Quae vero carent omni materia, . . . sunt quidem illae, mentis oculis natura illustrissimae, atque evidentissimae. Verum cum in illarum speculatione destituamur auxilio sensuum, a quibus proficiscitur omnis nostra cognitio, quandiu in hoc laeto carcere detinemur, fit, ut res per se lucidissimae, propter imbecillitatem mentis nostrae, cymeriis reddantur tenebris obscuriores.

Next Catena considers the principles on which all mathematical demonstrations depend. These he divides into 'common notions' (*communes conceptiones*) and definitions of mathematical entities. Both sorts are, he claims, of the utmost evidence, the former because they are preconditions for all reasoning, the latter because they deal with the perspicuous objects of mathematics.[47]

The final source of certainty of mathematics considered by Catena is that which accrues from its method:

> In the third place we said that the certainty of any discipline is principally made known on the basis of method and from the series of demonstrations that are included in it. For whatever things are arranged so that they are interconnected in a certain close order and so that prior things confer solidity and strength on posterior ones, posterior things depend on preceding ones and nothing altogether self-contained and separate from the others is found – such things deserve confident trust according to all sound judgements.[48]

He goes on to assert that the excellence of this mathematical method is attested by its serving as an ideal, though a scarcely attainable one, for all other disciplines.[49] He concludes by claiming for mathematics, in addition to practical utility and nobility of subject-matter, the highest grade of certainty by virtue of the nature of its objects, the clarity of its principles and the sequential nature of its demonstrations.[50]

THE STATUS OF ASTRONOMICAL HYPOTHESES

In medieval and Renaissance classifications of knowledge 'mathematical' and 'physical' study of the heavens are sharply separated. Mathematical astronomy forms one of the four mathematical arts of the *quadrivium*, whereas physical study of the heavens forms a specialised branch of natural philosophy. This gulf is reflected in sixteenth-century teaching careers and

Reliquum est tertium genus rerum, quae re quidem ipsa materiae inhaerent, sed cogitatione nostra ab ea seiunguntur: atque hae solae sunt, quae nobis adamussim cognoscuntur, nec mentis aciem sua obscuritate tenebris involvunt, neque nimia luce et fulgore, eam perstringunt. Itaque trigonum, tetragonum, et alia huiusmodi, quia talia sunt, qualia sensibus usurpantur, et quia formam ipsam absque materia contemplamur, neque lignum, ferrum, vel quippiam huiusmodi consideramus, ea sine ullis involucris, ubicunque sumus intuemur. Atque haec quidem mathematicarum disciplinarum, ex rebus ipsis et subiectis evidentia, atque certitudo apparet.' 47. *Ibid.*, f. 5^r.
48. *Ibid.*, f. 6^r: 'Tertio loco, certitudinem alicuius disciplinae praecipue declarari dicebamus ex methodi ratione, atque ex serie demonstrationum, quae in illa continentur: quaecunque nam sic explicantur ut denso quodam ordine inter se connectantur, utque priora robur ac firmitatem posterioribus largiantur, posteriora pendeant a praecedentibus, nihilque prorsus, vel absolutum, vel separatum ab aliis reperiatur, certam sibi fidem, apud omnia solida iudicia promerentur.'
49. *Ibid.*, f. 6^{r-v}. 50. *Ibid.*, ff. 7^v–8^v.

university curricula.[51] It is reflected also in the genres of literature of the
period concerned with celestial matters. Physical astronomy is primarily
represented in commentary on *De caelo* and *Metaphysics Λ*, and in
specialised treatises on the substance and nature of the heavens. The primary
texts of mathematical astronomy, Sacrobosco's *De sphaera* and Peurbach's
Theoricae novae planetarum, are silent on natural philosophical issues.
However, the isolation of the two disciplines should not be exaggerated.
Following Thomas Aquinas, astronomy was often recognised as a *scientia
media*, a branch of mathematics having special affinities with natural
philosophy. In judicial astrology, widely taught alongside mathematical
astronomy throughout the period, the two disciplines mingle freely.
Further, though the primary textbooks of mathematical astronomy are
devoid of natural philosophy, a considerable number of fifteenth- and early
sixteenth-century commentaries on them discuss the substance and sources
of motion of the celestial orbs. In these commentaries we find discussion of
the potential conflict between mathematical astronomy and natural
philosophy, a potential conflict that arises from the postulation by
astronomers of epicycles and eccentrics, orbs whose centres of motion do
not coincide with the centre of place in the universe, that is, the earth's
centre.[52]

Two medieval reactions to this perceived tension between astronomy
and natural philosophy deserve mention. In the later medieval period there
was widely adopted a most ingenious compromise between the Aristotelian
cosmology of substantial concentric spheres and the Ptolemaic planetary
models with their epicycles and eccentrics. Though there was considerable
variation on points of detail, the basic strategy was to realise Ptolemaic
epicycles and eccentrics by substantial spheres and spherical shells, the so-
called 'partial orbs' (*orbes partiales* or *particulares*). The partial orbs of each
planetary model were embedded in a substantial 'total orb' (*orbis totus*), a
spherical shell centred on the earth. The total orbs were supposed to form a
plenum and were identified with the Aristotelian concentric orbs.[53] This
compromise proved resilient, providing as it did the framework for the
planetary models of Peurbach's *Theoricae novae planetarum*, the main
textbook of 'advanced' mathematical astronomy in the Renaissance period.
In marked contrast is the uncompromising stance of Averroes and certain of
his followers.[54] Here, whilst it is conceded that planetary models which

---

51. See, for example, Westman 1980; Schmitt 1984, § XIV, and forthcoming a.
52. See N. Jardine 1982.   53. This compromise is described in E. Grant 1981b, § II.
54. See Carmody 1952; *Dictionary of Scientific Biography* 1970–80, XII, pp. 1–9 ('Ibn Rushd').

invoke centres of motion away from the centre of the universe constitute the only known predictively adequate astronomy, the reality of such planetary models is denied outright on the grounds that Aristotle's natural philosophy of the heavens, as set out in *De caelo* and *Metaphysics* Λ, allows only orbs centred on the earth. Averroes had expressed the hope that someone might succeed where he had failed in providing a predictively adequate astronomy properly founded in celestial physics and metaphysics, and a serious attempt to construct a purely concentric astronomy was made by his near contemporary Alpetragius (al-Bitruji).[55] In the period with which we are concerned Averroes' hope was echoed by Alessandro Achillini and Agostino Nifo,[56] and Alpetragius' attempt was emulated in the concentric systems of Girolamo Fracastoro and Giovanni Amici.[57]

In the later Renaissance we find a proliferation of noncommittal and sceptical attitudes, involving doubt or denial of the reality of epicycles and eccentrics, but unlike Averroist concentrism making no recommendation of an alternative type of arrangement as the basis for a sound astronomy. One such moderately sceptical position is that of Wojciech (Adalbertus) de Brudzewo, who taught mathematics at the University of Cracow from 1474 to his death in 1495. His commentary on Peurbach's *Theoricae novae planetarum* is thought to have been a prescribed text at the time of Copernicus' studies there. In the course of his commentary on Peurbach's model (*theorica*) for the sun, Wojciech makes the following declaration:

Whether these eccentrics really exist in the spheres of the planets no mortal knows, unless we are to declare them, and likewise epicycles, to have been disclosed by some revelation of spirits (as some claim). If not, then they have been formed from the imagination of mathematicians alone, as Albeon [Richard of Wallingford] testifies in the first part of his [work] in chapter 10, saying: 'Not that there are amongst the heavenly bodies eccentrics or epicycles of this sort, as the mathematical imagination contrives for itself, a thing which no educated man could suppose to be plausible. It is rather that without mathematical imaginings of this sort there cannot be set out the art concerning the regular motions of the stars which is so to establish their places at any given time that they may not conflict with the ways in which they appear to us.'[58]

55. *Dictionary of Scientific Biography* 1970–80, xv, pp. 33–6 ('Al-Bitruji').
56. Achillini 1498; Nifo 1514.   57. Amici 1536; Fracastoro 1538.
58. Wojciech de Brudzewo 1900, pp. 26–7: 'Qui quidem ecentrici an veraciter existant in sphaeris planetarum, nemo mortalium novit, nisi fateamur illos (ut nonnulli aiunt), similiter et epicyclos, revelatione spirituum propalatos, si non extunc sola imaginatione mathematicorum effictos, sicut testatur Albeon, in prima sui capitulo decimo, dicens: "Non quod in coelestibus sunt huiusmodi ecentrici aut epicycli, sicut imaginatio mathematica sibi fingit, quod nullus disciplinatus potuit verisimiliter putare, sed quia sine huiusmodi imaginationibus mathematicis, de stellarum motibus regularis ars tradi non potest, quae sic earum loca ad quodvis momentum certificet, quod a nostris aspectibus non discordent."' Cf. Richard of Wallingford 1976, I, pp. 278–9 (*Tractatus Albionis* 1.10).

Elsewhere in the work Wojciech sharply distinguishes between the concerns of astronomers and those of philosophers who study the heavens. Though both are concerned with celestial motions, the philosopher is concerned only with the nature and motion of the total orbs. The astronomer, on the other hand, is concerned to offer an account of the apparent celestial motions, for which purpose he has to consider in addition the motions of partial orbs, that is epicycles and eccentrics.[59] Wojciech's doubts about the existence of partial orbs do not extend to the Aristotelian total orbs. Indeed, he himself ventures into what is, by his criteria, philosophical territory, discussing at some length the nature of the total orbs, the causes of their motions and the order in which they are arranged.[60]

This combination of attitudes – sharp separation of mathematical astronomy from natural philosophy, acceptance of the Aristotelian concentric spheres and licensing of mathematical astronomy to employ for the purpose of saving the celestial phenomena models that are, taken at face value, doubtful if not false – becomes widely prevalent in the course of the sixteenth century, being promoted by such influential authors as Erasmus Reinhold and Benito Pereira.[61] It is evidently a compromising stance designed to stave off conflict and, in didactic contexts, to forestall the asking of awkward questions. There is evidence of a connection between its spread and awareness of Copernicus' work,[62] a plausible supposition given that with the advent of the Copernican system the area of potential conflict between mathematical astronomy and orthodox natural philosophy was greatly expanded, and expanded moreover into theologically sensitive areas.

There are a number of sixteenth-century writers, however, whose scepticism about astronomy goes far beyond that associated with this cautious compromise. For example, in a work of 1586, the humanist poet, wit and polemicist Nicodemus Frischlin claims that the true nature of the heavenly bodies is incomprehensible to us by virtue of their perfection, simplicity and great speed of motion; and he goes on to make the following assertion:

God the creator of things placed these bodies so far away from our senses that we are unable to produce principles of demonstration for them (as we can in the sciences of other things) or to discover what is natural and familiar, by means of which we may afterwards set out the causes of particular appearances. That is why we have recourse to aids from elsewhere and seek hypotheses from arithmetic and

59. *Ibid.*, pp. 17–18.   60. For example, *ibid.*, pp. 11–13.
61. On the prevalence of this attitude see Duhem 1908; Blake 1966; Westman 1975; Aiton 1981; N. Jardine 1984, ch. 7.   62. Cf. Westman 1975.

geometry. Hence we construct so many lines, we fashion so many circles, we imagine so many points, we devise so many eccentric and epicyclic orbs, and even little epicycles as well.[63]

Frischlin is not content merely to deny the physical reality of astronomers' planetary models. Such hypotheses are, he maintains, actively misleading if used for purposes other than the calendrical and chronometric uses licensed by the Scriptures, for they encourage astrologers and they foster the erroneous view that the celestial motions really are irregular.[64]

In his *Prooemium mathematicum* of 1567 Petrus Ramus gives a mocking history of astronomy in which he denounces it for its unnecessary use of fictitious hypotheses; and he pleads for the restoration of the pristine 'astronomy without hypotheses' possessed by the Babylonians, Egyptians and Greeks before Eudoxus.[65] It seems that this is a plea for a calculus of apparent celestial coordinates, a plea apparently premised on a radical scepticism about our capacity to acquire knowledge of the true dispositions and motions of heavenly bodies.[66]

Neither Frischlin nor Ramus offers sustained arguments for the unattainability of knowledge of the heavens. In Nicolaus Ursus' (Baer) scurrilous treatise of 1597, written to rebut the charge of plagiarism of Tycho Brahe's world-system, we find a more systematically defended sceptical position.[67] Firstly, Ursus cites the crass absurdity of all past hypotheses in support of his assertion that it is scarcely possible in astronomy to arrive at true hypotheses.[68] The history of hypotheses which follows, a history partly derived from Ramus, in which he mocks all the various world-systems that have been proposed, is evidently supposed to substantiate the premise of this induction on the history of science.[69] Secondly, there is what may, with a degree of anachronism, be called an argument from observational equivalence. Ursus draws attention to the existence of very different hypotheses: those of Ptolemy, those of Copernicus, those of Tycho and those of his own variant of the Tychonic system, all equally

---

63. Frischlin 1586, p. 41: 'Cum enim Deus Opifex rerum, illa corpora tam procul a sensibus nostris removerit: ut (quod in aliarum rerum scientiis facere possumus) principia demonstrationum non queamus ex ipsis gignere, et *oikeia* ac vernacula invenire: quibus postea singularum apparentiarum causas reddamus: ideo nos ad aliena confugimus praesidia, petimusque nobis hypotheses, ex arithmetica et geometria. Nam hinc tot lineas extruimus, tot circulos fingimus, tot puncta imaginamur, tot orbes eccentricos et epicyclos, imo etiam epicycliscos comminiscimur.'
64. *Ibid.*, pp. 258–60.   65. Ramus 1567, pp. 211–17.
66. Ramus' plea for an astronomy without hypotheses has been variously interpreted: see, for example, Hooykaas 1958, ch. 9; Aiton 1975; *Dictionary of Scientific Biography* 1970–80, XI, pp. 286–90 ('Peter Ramus').   67. Ursus 1597; partial translation in N. Jardine 1984.
68. Ursus 1597, sigs. A iv^r, B iv^v.   69. *Ibid.*, sigs. C ii^r–D ii^v.

adequate for predictive purposes. He even suggests that the contrivance of predictively adequate hypotheses is an easy business.[70] Given Ursus' tacit assumption that predictive adequacy provides the sole warrant for astronomical hypotheses, the existence of observationally equivalent planetary models and world-systems clearly supports his sceptical position.

The negative and sceptical attitudes to astronomy that became so widespread in the latter part of the sixteenth century provoked interesting defences of the discipline at the hands of Christophorus Clavius, Michael Maestlin and Maestlin's student, Johannes Kepler. Clavius and Maestlin are both primarily concerned with the question of the existence of epicycles and eccentrics. Both are cautious in their claims. Thus Maestlin does not try to defend the literal truth of a particular set of planetary models, but maintains only that with the help of geometry we can infer *a posteriori* from the celestial phenomena that some one of the various possible predictively adequate arguments of orbs exists 'in nature' (κατὰ φύσιν).[71] Similarly, Clavius asserts only that the existence of epicycles and eccentrics is *credibilis*, given that they have the capacity to predict the celestial phenomena and that they are not (despite the objections of the *Averroisti*) at odds with the principles of natural philosophy.[72] Kepler's far more detailed and ambitious defence of astronomy addresses the epistemological problems raised by the conflict of the Ptolemaic, Copernican and Tychonic world-systems, promotes the unification of mathematical and physical astronomy and defends a view of the history of astronomy as evincing an accumulation of truths about the form of the cosmos.[73]

THE RANGE OF EPISTEMOLOGY OF THE SCIENCES

The three epistemological debates reviewed above concern orthodox sciences. It should be emphasised again that much of the most lively and original Renaissance debate on questions of cognitive status and method concerns disciplines whose credentials as *scientiae* were perceived as questionable: the unorthodox sciences and the mechanical and practical disciplines.[74] In confining our attention to orthodox sciences we pass over,

70. *Ibid.*, sig. A iv^r.   71. Maestlin 1597 (1st edn, 1582), pp. 28–9.
72. Clavius 1581, pp. 434 ff. On Clavius' 'moderate realism' see Blake 1966; Wallace 1981a, pp. 129–59; N. Jardine 1979.
73. Kepler, *Apologia pro Tychone contra Ursum*, composed 1600–1, first published in 1858, text and translation in N. Jardine 1984.
74. On epistemological aspects of unorthodox disciplines see, for example, Pagel 1958a; Yates 1964; Nauert 1965; Walker 1958; Debus 1968; Vasoli 1974, pp. 407–75; Copenhaver in this volume, pp. 264–300. On the epistemological aspects of practical and operative disciplines see especially P. Rossi 1962; Crombie forthcoming, part 4.

for example, a whole complex of epistemological doctrines concerning microcosm and macrocosm, signs and signatures and the 'lights' of grace and nature, doctrines that have sometimes been taken to constitute the conceptual framework for the most creative thought of the period.[75]

The range of debating points in the epistemology of natural philosophy is a wide one.[76] Major topics include: the distinction between the mode of consideration of natural things appropriate to natural philosophy and the modes appropriate to other disciplines; the two types of priority operative in natural philosophy, priority 'for us' and priority 'for nature';[77] the natures and sources of knowledge of the different kinds of principles of demonstration (*dignitates, suppositiones, definitiones*, etc.); and the nature and grounds of the necessity that is required of the premises of demonstrations. There is extensive discussion too of the types of causation, their relative importance and their relations to demonstration and to the definition of substances and properties. In this context the Aristotelian tradition shows considerable powers of innovation. For example, in Zabarella and others efficient causation comes to be assigned a dominant role in natural operations, the agency of material, final and formal causes being mediated by external or 'internal' efficient causes;[78] and in Andrea Cesalpino's works a distinction between entities and processes that exist *ex necessitate* and those which come about 'for the sake of something else' (*alicuius gratia*) is applied in novel ways in his discussions of transmutation and mixture of bodies and of the structure and organisation of plants and animals.[79]

In the realms of methodology of natural philosophy *regressus* is but one of a considerable range of topics. It has, for example, been maintained that there was an Aristotelian tradition of treatments of inference *ex suppositione* or *conditione*, a form of *a posteriori* inference that reveals *verae causae* and has a special role in the subalternate sciences: those that depend upon a higher science for their principles.[80] Further, there was a fair amount of discussion of the various types of *inductio* (ἐπαγωγή) that figure in Aristotle, discussion that generally distinguished sharply between the 'demonstrative' induction which leads from individual sense experiences to apprehension of universals and other forms of induction, including induction by enumeration. There is also considerable discussion of the status of the argument 'from probabilities

---

75. See, for example, Foucault 1966, ch. 2; Yates 1979, part 1.
76. See Wallace in this volume.   77. See Kosman 1964, chs. 1–5, for a detailed treatment.
78. J. Zabarella 1607a, cols. 590ff. On later developments of these doctrines see Reif 1962, ch. 5.
79. Cesalpino 1571 (lib. I, q. vii); 1583, p. 23. On Cesalpino's teleology see *Aristotelismo veneto* 1983, I, pp. 477–507 (Capecci).
80. See Wallace 1981a, pp. 129–59; 1981b; *Aristotelismo veneto* 1983, I, pp. 349–78 (Wallace). Reservations are expressed by McMullin 1983, Wisan 1984.

or signs' which figures in the *Prior Analytics*, identified by some commentators with the demonstration of the fact of the *Posterior Analytics*.[81] The relation of these discussions to the extensive treatment of signs and signatures that occurs in magical, alchemical and medical contexts would repay study.[82] These and other debates on the nature of method in natural philosophy take place against a background of extensive discussion of the role of logic as a source of methods in the arts and sciences, and of the roles of demonstrative and dialectical methods on the one hand and metaphysical insight on the other in the pursuit of natural philosophy.[83]

It is potentially misleading to describe *regressus* and the methodological discussions which surround it as 'Aristotelian', for throughout the period they draw on and interact with other traditions. For example, at the beginning of his *Ars medica* Galen mentions three ways of ordering material: analysis, synthesis and 'division' ($\delta\iota\acute{\alpha}\lambda\upsilon\sigma\iota\varsigma$).[84] This cryptic passage greatly exercised the commentators. In 'Ali Ibn Ridwan's exposition, which became available in Latin around 1300, Galen's analytic and synthetic methods are identified with Aristotle's $\dot{\alpha}\pi\acute{o}\delta\epsilon\iota\xi\iota\varsigma$ $\tau o\hat{\upsilon}$ $\ddot{o}\tau\iota$ and $\dot{\alpha}\pi\acute{o}\delta\epsilon\iota\xi\iota\varsigma$ $\tau o\hat{\upsilon}$ $\delta\iota\acute{o}\tau\iota$, respectively; and the analytic method is further identified with the method of analysis practised by geometers.[85] Pietro d'Abano, in his immensely influential *Conciliator differentiarum philosophorum*, composed around 1310, further conflated these methods with the two procedures mentioned by Aristotle at the beginning of the *Physics*, the one proceeding from particular to universal, the other from universal to particular.[86] This collage of methods was elaborated and modified at the hands of a series of medical writers, including Torrigiano dei Torrigiani (the *Plusquam Commentator*), Gentile da Foligno, Jacopo da Forlì and Ugo Benzi, all much concerned to establish the credentials of medicine as *scientia*.[87]

In a brief but masterly work of 1508 the humanist scholar and physician Niccolò Leoniceno brought philological expertise and knowledge of the classical commentators to bear on the issue of the number and nature of the methods of medicine and natural philosophy.[88] Leoniceno distinguishes sharply between ways of ordering the contents of an entire discipline for

81. *Prior Analytics* II.27. This identification derives from the classical commentators: see references in Bottin 1972; N. Jardine 1976.
82. On signs in these contexts see, for example, Arber 1938, ch. 8; Pagel 1958a; Hacking 1975, ch. 5.
83. Risse 1964, pp. 201–439. See also Corsano 1958–63, 41: 507–17; Papuli 1967; Poppi 1972a.
84. Galen 1821, I, p. 305.   85. 'Ali Ibn Ridwan 1487, f. 151ʳ⁻ᵛ.   86. Abano 1504, ff. 9ᵛ⁻12ᵛ.
87. See, for example, Randall 1961; *Philosophy and Humanism* 1976, pp. 283–305 (W. F. Edwards); Siraisi 1981, ch. 5; *Scienza e filosofia* 1983, pp. 375–94 (Movia); French 1985.
88. Leoniceno 1532 (*De tribus doctrinis ordinatis secundum Galeni sententiam liber*; 1st edn, 1508). On this work see *Philosophy and Humanism* 1976, pp. 283–305 (W. F. Edwards); Mugnai Carrara 1983.

teaching purposes (*ordines docendi*) and procedures for investigating particular questions (*modi doctrinae*).[89] To the first category he assigns the three procedures of Galen's *Ars medica*. In the latter category he recognises syllogistic demonstration together with three 'Platonic' methods for hunting down definitions, *resolutio* (which he is at pains to distinguish from other resolutive procedures, including the resolutive or analytic method of the geometers[90]), *divisio* and *definitio*. Much of the extensive sixteenth-century Italian writing on medical method follows Leoniceno in this classification.[91] The Paduan physician and Galen editor Giovanni Battista da Monte makes interesting use in his account of therapeutic method of the investigative procedures recognised by Leoniceno together with inference *a signo* which, he claims, is needed to relate the general conclusions of medical science to particular patients.[92] It has been shown that da Monte's account forms a part of his programme for a reform of the teaching of therapeutic medicine designed to bring it more into line with the doctrine of Galen's *Methodus medendi*.[93]

Where there is a substantial secondary literature on Italian debates in the epistemology of natural philosophy, there is a dearth of recent studies of 'northern' developments. For example, the epistemology of Philipp Melanchthon and its influence have received little recent attention, despite the great intrinsic interest of his *De anima* and the likely historical importance of the views of the *Praeceptor Germaniae*.[94] Similarly, although the methodological innovations of Petrus Ramus have been the focus of considerable scholarly attention,[95] the works of his French and German Aristotelian opponents have been little studied.[96]

When we turn to the epistemology of mathematical science we find again a considerable diversity of topics. Catena's *Oratio pro idea methodi* is but one of a number of works of the latter part of the sixteenth century which set up the deductive hierarchy of geometry as a model of perspicuous organisation for other disciplines.[97] Further, there is an interesting body of late sixteenth-century speculations on the nature of 'universal mathematics' (*mathesis universalis*), speculations inspired by reflection on book v of

89. Leoniceno 1532, p. 69.   90. *Ibid.*, pp. 62ff.
91. On sixteenth-century treatments of medical method see N. W. Gilbert 1960, pp. 102–5; Wightman 1964, 1973; Wear 1973; Bates 1977.
92. Da Monte 1558, pp. 83ff., 112ff. (*Methodus medicinae universalis*). For a detailed account of Da Monte's methodology see Bylebyl forthcoming.   93. Bylebyl forthcoming.
94. See, however, Sartorius von Waltershausen 1927; Maurer 1962; Kessler in this volume, pp. 516–18.   95. See especially Ong 1958a; Vasoli 1968a, pp. 333–601.
96. In particular Jacob Schegk's massive *De demonstratione* would repay further study: see Risse 1964, pp. 256–9; Schüling 1969, p. 44.   97. Schüling 1969; see also De Angelis 1964.

Euclid's *Elements* and passages from Proclus' *Commentary on the First Book of Euclid's Elements* which suggested the existence of a mathematical master science prior to arithmetic and geometry and concerned with order and proportion.[98] Proclus' commentary on Euclid plays a major role too, both as source and as foil, in Ramus' radical but often obscure pronouncements on the status of mathematics, pronouncements which range from 'Platonist' claims about the certainty, intuitive evidence and edifying power of mathematics to remarks which imply that he viewed mathematical propositions as precepts derived from observation for practical purposes of measurement, calculation and prediction. Both the content and fortunes of Ramus' epistemology of mathematics deserve further study.[99] Yet another Proclean topic with an interesting *fortuna* is geometrical analysis. Considerable attention was paid to the cryptic passages in Aristotle, Pappus and Proclus, which describe geometrical analysis as if it were a method for working back from problems or theorems to the principles by which they may be solved or proved.[100]

I have already mentioned the importance of psychology, and in particular the *De anima* commentary, as a context for questions about the means of attaining scientific knowledge.[101] Certain other issues in Renaissance intellectual history deserve mention as contexts for the epistemology of the sciences. The period is one in which substantial changes occurred in classification and subordination of the arts and sciences both as expressed in encyclopaedias and compendia and as embodied in university curricula. The large literature on classification, subordination and precedence in nobility and certitude of the sciences provides a major context for the epistemology of the sciences.[102] A second important context for epistemology is that provided by Renaissance discussions of ordering and disposition of material within particular disciplines.[103] It would be anachronistic to regard this literature as merely concerned with teaching,

98. Crapulli 1969.
99. On Ramus' views on method in mathematics see Verdonk 1966, ch. 6; 1968; Schüling 1969, pp. 103ff. On the didactic context see Margolin 1976.
100. On the classical sources see Hintikka and Remes 1974.
101. On Renaissance *De anima* commentary see *Platon et Aristote* 1976, pp. 359–76 (Cranz); Kessler in this volume.
102. On the connections between epistemology and classifications of the arts and sciences in the sixteenth and early seventeenth centuries see the major study by Schmidt-Biggemann 1983. Wallace 1984, pp. 126–48, considers some late sixteenth-century Jesuit discussions of classification and subordination of the sciences. The importance of the literature on precedence as a context for epistemology is noted by Vasoli 1974, p. 425.
103. This literature is surveyed by N. W. Gilbert 1960; Vasoli 1968a.

rather than with discovery and investigation; for the goal common to many of these treatises, that of showing how to knit facts and principles together into a body of rational science, is one that cuts across the discovery/communication distinction. The sixteenth-century literature on ordering and disposition of the sciences is vast. Discussion of axiomatic methods has already been touched on. Ramist didactic method and the furious polemics which surrounded it appear to have had substantial impact in the epistemology of the sciences.[104] A further sixteenth-century development with important, but as yet little explored, epistemological implications is that of humanist promotion of the use of 'dialectical' methods of presentation and persuasion that concentrate on probable argument – argument by analogy, citation of *exempla* and so on – rather than demonstration in the strict Aristotelian sense.[105]

The historiography of the sciences undergoes great changes in the course of the sixteenth century. To start with there is a move away from a conception of the arts and sciences as having emerged fully fledged at the hands of the sages of antiquity towards a view of them as gradual products of prolonged endeavour.[106] Related to this is a development of awareness of the importance of social and cultural factors in the growth of knowledge, the basic traditional historiographic motifs of *successio* and *translatio studii* being augmented by speculations about the roles of, for example, education, printing and the amassment of observations on the growth of knowledge.[107] Further, by the end of the century there is a measure of awareness of progress in the mathematical sciences as constituted not merely by the development of new artifacts and better methods of calculation and prediction but also by improvement at the theoretical level.[108] These historiographical developments are, I suggest, of paramount importance for the epistemology of the sciences; for their outcome is the emergence in the seventeenth century of notions of linked practical and theoretical progress through systematic and collaborative endeavour, notions that are presupposed by the major seventeenth-century programmes for the advancement of the sciences.

104. See, for example, Hoppe 1976, pp. 25–32, on its influence on methods of classification of organisms; Hannaway 1975 on its role in the constitution of chemistry as a discipline.
105. On humanist promotion of probable argument and its links with development of discourse *in utramque partem* as a didactic vehicle see Vasoli 1968a; C. J. R. Armstrong 1976; L. Jardine 1977 and in this volume; Schiffman 1984. On the possible importance of this for the epistemology of the sciences see Vasoli 1974, pp. 637–8; N. Jardine 1979; Dear 1984.
106. See, for example, P. Rossi 1962; Maravall 1966; A. Keller 1972.
107. N. Jardine 1984, ch. 8.   108. *Ibid.*

THE PROBLEM OF CONTINUITY

The sixteenth-century epistemological topics outlined above have played a considerable role in the controversy about the question of continuity between the 'new' sciences and epistemologies of the seventeenth century and earlier developments. In its earlier phases this controversy was tied up with large questions about the relative contributions of 'humanism' and 'scholasticism' to 'the scientific revolution'. Latterly it has involved also the issue of the relative importance for the development of science of orthodox and university-centred learning on the one hand and unorthodox and extra-curricular learning on the other. A number of recent authors have expressed reservations about the terms of these debates, both on the grounds that they are often premised on highly questionable assumptions about the link between scientific progress and conformity to a 'scientific method' and on the grounds that they tend to overlook the great diversity of late Renaissance programmes for the reorganisation and reform of learning and the constitution of new sciences.[109] The following observations on the epistemological topics discussed above are concerned only with the more specific question of continuity within the domain of epistemology of the sciences.

Regressus, and the tradition of discussion of the nature, form and limits of scientific demonstration of which it forms a part, has occasioned the liveliest controversy. Randall, Crombie and others discerned in this tradition the progressive elaboration of an experimentally oriented hypothetico-deductive methodology, claiming substantial anticipations of the methodology of the 'new science' as typified by Galileo.[110] Randall, indeed, went so far as to assert on the strength of these parallels that 'the "father" of modern science, in fact, turns out to be none other than the Master of them that know', to which Olschki memorably replied that 'some fossil material collected from the last ramifications of scholasticism will never restore to Aristotle the paternity of modern science'.[111] Such extreme positions are less in evidence today. The claim that experimental and hypothetico-deductive orientations arose in the tradition of Aristotelian discussions of demonstrative method has been subjected to serious criticism. In particular, it now seems clear that the sixteenth-century Aristotelian emphasis on the

---

109. Cf. P. Rossi 1982; Schmitt 1984, § 1.
110. Randall 1961; Crombie 1953. (The suggestion that *regressus* as articulated by Zabarella anticipates aspects of Galileo's methodology is to be found in Cassirer 1911.) For a balanced account of the controversy sparked off by Randall's claims see *Aristotelismo veneto* 1983, I, pp. 435–57 (Berti).
111. Randall 1940, p. 203; 1961, p. 63; Olschki 1943, p. 355.

central roles of demonstrative induction and other *a posteriori* forms of inference cannot be interpreted as showing a concern with experiment in science.[112] Further, it has been shown that the scattered references to resolutive and compositive methods in Galileo's mature works are more closely affiliated to classical and Renaissance accounts of resolution and composition in geometry than to the demonstrative syllogisms of *regressus*.[113] On the other hand few would now contest the claim that Galileo's conception of science shares with the Aristotelian conception of a demonstrative science the ideals of certainty and demonstration from evident principles.[114]

The sources and fortunes of the sixteenth-century Italian discussions of the status of mathematical demonstrations and the grounds of certainty in mathematics have been little studied. These debates are, however, reflected in the treatments of the status of mathematics by Christophorus Clavius, Giuseppe Biancani and Galileo's friend and mentor Jacopo Mazzoni, treatments which interestingly combine insistence on the certainty and excellence of mathematics and mathematical demonstration with emphasis on the substantial role of mathematics in the study of nature.[115]

The issue of the status of astronomical hypotheses provides the context for perhaps the most striking of epistemological continuity theses. Pierre Duhem maintained that it is possible to trace from classical antiquity to the physics of his day two epistemological traditions in mathematical science, a realist (and in his view misguided) tradition in which the aim of mathematical science is taken to be that of uncovering the real causes which underlie the phenomena and a 'fictionalist' (and in his view fruitful) tradition in which the aim is taken to be that of economically classifying and predicting the phenomena.[116] Duhem's thesis is questionable on several scores. In particular, there is, at least for the sixteenth century, little evidence of views on the status of hypotheses in other mathematical sciences – optics,

112. See especially Skulsky 1968; Schmitt 1981, § VIII.

113. N. W. Gilbert 1963. See also *Aristotelismo veneto* 1983, I, pp. 435–57 (Berti); Wallace 1984, pp. 146, 302.

114. However, there remain important questions about the date, intention and relation to his mature works of the treatises in Galileo's hand, *De praecognitionibus et praecognitis in particulari* and *De demonstratione*: see Carugo and Crombie 1983; *Aristotelismo veneto* 1983, I, pp. 349–78 (Wallace); Wallace 1984. The treatises, which deal with questions arising from Aristotle's *Posterior Analytics*, contain material probably derived from lectures delivered by Paolo Valla at the Collegio Romano in 1588. The *De demonstratione* includes the *quaestio: An detur regressus demonstrativus?* On the sources and contents of these logical treatises see Wallace, 1984, ch. 1.

115. On Clavius see Galluzzi 1973; Homann 1983; Wallace 1984, pp. 136–40. On Mazzoni see Purnell 1971, 1972; Galluzzi 1973. On Biancani see Schüling 1969, pp. 53–5; Giacobbe 1976; Wallace 1984, pp. 141–7.   116. Duhem 1908; 1913–59, IV, 2, chs. 8–9, VI, 1, chs. 10–11.

music, mechanics and the like – comparable to those which were prevalent in astronomy; thus Duhem's interpretation of attitudes to astronomical hypotheses as representative of general epistemological attitudes to mathematical science is called in question. Further, there can be little doubt that Duhem's partition of views into 'realist' and 'fictionalist' fails to do justice to the range of views in the period.[117] We have seen that two of these sixteenth-century attitudes to astronomical hypotheses, the Averroist treatment of the hypotheses of orthodox astronomy as straightforwardly false on natural philosophical grounds and the 'realist' view that Ptolemaic planetary models are realised in a plenum of substantial orbs, have medieval origins. The question of medieval antecedents to the various sceptical attitudes to astronomy that proliferate in the later Renaissance is more problematic. Some of the arguments used in the sixteenth century for holding all astronomical hypotheses to be doubtful appear to derive from medieval Averroist arguments for the falsity of Ptolemaic hypotheses despite their capacity to save the phenomena. But it remains unclear whether there is any substance to Duhem's linking of 'fictionalism' in late medieval astronomy with allegedly sceptical tendencies in nominalist epistemology.[118] If in fact the spread of sceptical attitudes to astronomy in the sixteenth century has little or no medieval precedent, the question arises of the extent to which it can be related to the sixteenth-century revival of interest in forms of classical scepticism.[119] This question requires further study, as does the question of the import of the sixteenth-century debates on the status of astronomical hypotheses for seventeenth-century epistemology of the sciences.

In conclusion a couple of reflections on the question of epistemological continuity are in order. First, the evidence strongly suggests that no general answer to the question is to be had. Where, for instance, the case for a substantial Aristotelian component in the scattered methodological comments of Galileo's mature works is a questionable one, the case is solid for substantial (though very different) Aristotelian components in the methodologies of Francis Bacon and William Harvey. Similarly, where sixteenth-century debates on the status of astronomical hypotheses provide a context for Kepler's epistemology, it seems unlikely that any comparably specific context can be established for Descartes's epistemology of science. Secondly, it seems that in the study of Renaissance epistemology of the sciences concentration on questions of continuity and impact on 'the new

---

117. *Copernican Achievement* 1975, pp. 244–75 (Donahue); N. Jardine 1984, ch. 7.
118. Duhem 1913–59, VI, pp. 616–18.   119. See N. Jardine 1987.

science' is not only apt to lead to retrospective bias in selection of material and anachronism of interpretation, but is also premature. Only a small part of this vast field is even touched on by recent scholarship, and there are but a handful of studies that examine epistemological writings of the period in detail in terms of their genres, their disciplinary and intellectual contexts and the concerns and projects of their authors.

XII
PHILOSOPHY AND HUMANISTIC DISCIPLINES

20

RHETORIC AND POETICS

THE SCOPE OF RHETORIC AND POETICS

The modern reader approaching Renaissance texts in the expectation of finding a clear-cut distinction between rhetoric and poetics will soon be disappointed. Their isolation as critical terms is a product of post-Romantic literary theory, deriving from a period in which traditional rhetoric had been banished from education. To approach a rhetorical culture like the Renaissance with post- or even anti-rhetorical expectations is obviously anachronistic, and can only produce complaints about the 'confusion' of rhetoric with poetics. To us the two disciplines seem to be directed to different goals: poetics, deriving from *poiesis*, is the art of making a poem or work of literature, whereas rhetoric is concerned with constructing effective, that is, persuasive discourse. A pure poetics would consider the artwork on its own, while rhetoric would see it in terms of its effect on an audience. But in the Renaissance, as in other periods, poetry used techniques of proof and persuasion, addressed itself to the practical intellect and existed as a force for good or evil in the world. Renaissance readers did not regard literary works as autotelic; indeed, the concept that any work of art could be self-ended, without a function in human life, would have been foreign. In that period classical rhetoric, enthusiastically revived, provided a comprehensive system both for creating and for evaluating works of literature, by which they meant not just poetry, drama and fiction, but also letters, history and philosophical treatises. While rhetoric and poetics were notionally separate disciplines from philosophy, given a distinct and subordinate place in the university arts curriculum, in practice during the Renaissance both became attached to ethics. Indeed, the main justification for their existence was often said to be their ability to convey the teachings of moral philosophy with more powerful effect.

Rhetoric distinguished five stages of composition: *inventio*, the discovering of material; *dispositio*, its structuring and arrangement; *elocutio*, its formulation in language; *memoria* and *pronuntiatio*, its memorising and

715

appropriate delivery (the last two stages were originally developed for speeches delivered in a forum or law-court, but came to have other practical applications in the Renaissance). Rhetoric also distinguished three kinds of oration (and, by extension, any literary work): the judicial or forensic type, concerned with proof and disproof, as in a court of law; the deliberative type, involving persuasion and dissuasion, as in politics; and the demonstrative or epideictic type, devoted to praise and blame. Each type of speech had a style appropriate to itself, as did the various literary genres, the choice of which was governed by the principle of decorum. Writers and readers were trained to observe the constituent parts of an oration, in one popular version *exordium, narratio, divisio, confirmatio, confutatio, conclusio.* Rhetoric also had a detailed lore of linguistic devices, the tropes and figures of speech that made language more effective in its appeal to the mind and the emotions. The history of rhetoric shows these doctrines appearing afresh in every generation. The complete scheme of rhetoric appears throughout Renaissance literature.

Poetics, as understood in the Renaissance, was a more limited art. While rhetoric governed the whole art of language, an *ars poetica* was either a treatise on literary composition as such – in which case, as in Horace's *Epistula ad Pisones* (the *Ars poetica*), it was a verse rhetoric addressed to the poetic genres of tragedy, comedy and epic – or it was a manual for the specific techniques of verse composition, metre, stanza form and diction. Since most of these *artes poeticae* also included discussion of the figures and tropes, the distinction between rhetoric and poetics collapses again. The sense of *poetica* as that branch of literary criticism treating of poetry begins to emerge in late sixteenth-century commentaries on Aristotle's *Poetics*, but these are themselves often deeply rhetorical, conflating Aristotle with Cicero or Horace, whose *Ars poetica* shows many debts to classical rhetoric. Any attempt to define a poetics uninfluenced by rhetoric in this period would be futile. Indeed, it is significant that recent literary theory has recognised that all forms of communication imply some kind of rhetoric, and that the literary work only comes into existence through the collaborative activity of the reader.

Expectations of a clear-cut distinction will be defeated again when we look at the types of literature in which discussions of rhetoric and poetics are found. Since both are language arts, and since language was so important to Renaissance humanism, material is widely scattered. Grammar, the first stage of the *trivium*, taught the ability to read and write Latin. But from the time of Quintilian the grammar teacher had also taught authors, so that the grammar curriculum included literary criticism, metrics and expositions of rhetoric: more than thirty Renaissance grammarians also wrote works on rhetoric. Niccolò Perotti's *Rudimenta grammatices* (1468) included a manual of epistolary style, as did that of another influential grammarian, Giulio Sulpizio Verulano, while the vast *Commentarii grammatici* of Johannes Despauterius (1510–20) includes treatises on poetic genres, epistolary composition and an extensive *Ars versificatoria*. Conversely, the *Novum epistolarium* (1484) of Giammario Filelfo and Sulpizio's *De componendis et ornandis epistolis* (1489) define the divisions of the oration, the *genera dicendi* and the *colores rhetorici*,[1] a practice which survived at least until 1586, in the *English Secretorie; or Plaine and Direct Method of Enditing of all Manner of Epistles or Letters . . . also tropes, figures . . .* by Angel Day.

The new importance given to language in Renaissance humanism meant that rhetoric was seen as a vital accomplishment in the *vita activa*. Any work on man in his social relationships, whether as a ruler over subordinates or at court *inter pares*, is liable to include a section in praise of the utility of eloquence. This is true from Castiglione, *Il libro del cortegiano* (1528) and Matteo Palmieri, *Libro della vita civile* (1529) to Stefano Guazzo, *La civile conversatione* (1574); and from Sir Thomas Elyot, *The Governour* (1531) to the works of Peacham and Puttenham in the 1580s and 1590s. The growing nationalism in sixteenth-century literature, the claim that each of the vernaculars was just as capable of eloquence as Greek or Latin, naturally absorbed rhetoric into what might today be classified as linguistics. The *Questione della lingua*[2] produced works which proclaimed their native tongue to be supremely suited to rhetoric and poetry. So Joachim Du Bellay devotes the first book of his *Deffence et illustration de la langue françoyse* (1549) to this topic, then discusses a series of issues in poetics and rhetoric: versification, neologism, rhythm, rhyme and the figures of rhetoric.

More extended discussions are found in the rhetorics and poetics proper, whether commentaries on classical works or new creations. Between the early humanist notes on the *Ars poetica* by Cristoforo Landino (1482) and Iodocus Badius Ascensius (1500) and the *De poetica Aristotelis cum Horatio collatus* (1599) of Antonio Riccoboni, no less than twenty commentaries on Horace appeared in Italy alone. From the mid-century these were influenced by the growing interest in Aristotle's *Poetics*, the two texts being fused into one essentially rhetorical construct. The resulting hybrid, which totally evades the modern distinction between poetics as a discipline

---

1. On the overlap between grammar and rhetoric see Padley 1976; *Renaissance Eloquence* 1983, pp. 303–30 (Percival), 331–55 (Henderson).   2. R. A. Hall 1942; Vitale 1960; R. F. Jones 1953.

concerned with internal structure and rhetoric as an art directed towards the audience, results, according to Weinberg 'in hopeless deformation of the texts involved', revealing 'the philosophical naïveté' of its practitioners.[3] But what he calls 'confusion' – as if those writers were in possession of that distinction and had ignored it – might better be seen as eclecticism, or that familiar Renaissance ability to reconcile differing traditions. At all events, these works of synthesis include an enormous range of topics: the function of literature to give pleasure and instruction ('aut prodesse volunt aut delectare poetae': Horace, *Ars poetica* 333f.), the role of poetry to teach, to delight and to move (taken over from rhetoric, as in Cicero, *Brutus* 185; *De oratore* II.27.15), the pre-eminence of *elocutio*, which virtually comes to be equated with poetry, the classifying of literature into the deliberative, judicial, and demonstrative modes, and the system of rhetorical figures. These commentators grasped the rhetorical implications of Horace's work and made them more explicit. From Landino on it was assumed that his work offered a systematic treatment of the rhetorical sequence *inventio, dispositio* and *elocutio*, and Horace's text was divided in various ways to show its coherence with Cicero or Quintilian. The result amply demonstrates the extent to which rhetoric has absorbed poetics.

When Aristotle's *Poetics* was disseminated and commented on, it too was absorbed by a rhetorical culture and reinterpreted to fit. Giorgio Valla's Latin translation appeared in 1498 and the Greek text in 1508, but the work attracted little attention before Alessandro de' Pazzi's edition of the Greek with a Latin translation (which was to become standard) in 1536. Even then, the Averroes paraphrase, in Alemannus' translation, was published at Venice in 1481 and 1515, while new translations of Averroes based on the fourteenth-century Hebrew version appeared from Abraham de Balmes (1523; 1560) and Jacob Mantino (1550; 1562).[4] Averroes had reinterpreted the *Poetics* as a treatise on epideictic rhetoric, and Francesco Robortello, in the first of the great commentaries (1548), repeats this emphasis while assimilating the *Poetics* to his own rhetorical system. Modern expectations that Renaissance commentators would faithfully reproduce Aristotle's concern with the autotelic work of art are frustrated by their subordination of the *Poetics* to an aesthetic in which poetry and drama were thought of as intended to be addressed to the audience, and designed to improve them morally through the use of rhetorical devices and by purging them of the

---

3. Weinberg 1961, I, pp. 53–6.
4. For details of the publishing history and interpretation of the *Poetics* see Weinberg 1961, I, pp. 349–634, II, pp. 635–715, with some corrections by Tigerstedt 1968.

debilitating passions of pity and fear. The controversy about whether Aristotle intended to relate *catharsis* to the audience and their emotions or to the events within the play may never be settled. But the moralising interpretation can be justified and makes sense within this view of literature. As has been rightly said, Giorgio Valla, 'like other Renaissance critics, . . . is not aware of any opposition between Aristotelian autotelism and Horatian didacticism', for the 'all-pervading rhetorical tradition in education and literature' assimilated both to itself.[5] However reluctant scholars may be to accept the fact, the major commentaries on the *Poetics* in the Italian sixteenth century are all basically rhetorical.[6] Yet Weinberg's antithesis between Horace and Aristotle is too extreme. Aristotle's *Poetics* complements his *Rhetoric* and takes over some categories from it, not neglecting the relation artwork–audience, while Horace gives much space to the perfecting of the work of art. If it is true that recent 'studies of Renaissance poetic criticism have tended to be too negative toward the value of the Horatian . . . influence and correspondingly oversanguine about the good influence of Aristotle's *Poetics*',[7] that is symptomatic of the continuing modern suspicion of rhetoric.

Many of the commentaries concern themselves with the major issues in Aristotle's work, but do so within a Horatian or a rhetorical frame. Thus Robortello in 1548 relates Horace's demand that the poet please and instruct to Aristotle's concept of imitation, making pleasure gained by the process of imitation subordinate to profit gained by its content, the praise of virtue exciting us to emulation, the dispraise of vice deterring us from it. These neo-Aristotelians are in fact applying to *mimesis* the basic principle of the epideictic or demonstrative genre.[8] The dichotomy *aut prodesse aut delectare* could be resolved on the side of instruction, the result being to align poetry with moral philosophy, or on that of pleasure; either way the stress shifts from the work of literature to the audience. Castelvetro's radical reinterpretation defines pleasure as that which the unlearned part of the audience receives, the better educated ones deriving instruction (an unfortunate dichotomy). Imitation, that key issue in the dispute between Platonists and Aristotelians, could be taken as *mimesis* of life, with the proviso that the poet must be knowledgeable in ethics or politics, or it could have the rhetorical sense of *imitatio* of other writers. It came to mean for

5. Tigerstedt 1968, pp. 19, 23.
6. Weinberg 1961, I, pp. 56, 64, 65, 398, 428–9, 444, 463, 476, 511, 563, II, pp. 642ff., 712, 790, 801.
7. Trinkaus 1966, pp. 80–3.
8. For other instances of epideictic rhetoric applied to the *Poetics* see Weinberg 1961, I, pp. 375, 380, 385, 389, 429, 441, 447, 458, 470, 489, 536, 544, 546, 565, 582, 586, II, pp. 643, 653, etc.

some theorists 'a kind of heightened and vivid portrayal which appeals to the senses rather than to the intellect', an idea that derives from the rhetorical concept of ἐνάργεια (Aristotle, *Rhetoric* III.11).[9] Rhetoric is clearly the source of the terminology in many treatises, such as Pier Vettori's account (*Commentarii in primum librum Aristotelis de arte poetarum*, 1560) of how tragedy works to *arouse* fear or *move* the audience to pity.[10] Many writers include accounts of *elocutio* and the rhetorical figures, continuing this unification of poetics and rhetoric.

Great though the number of commentaries on Horace and Aristotle is, even more numerous are the editions and commentaries on the classic rhetoric texts. The humblest of these were the *progymnasmata* or preliminary exercises of Aphthonius, Theon and Hermogenes, dating from the second to the fifth centuries. In the late 1470s Rudolph Agricola's Latin translation of Aphthonius answered a real need for elementary composition models (χρεία or the ethical issue; maxim; encomium; ἠθοποιία; ἔκφρασις), and it became a popular school text for two hundred years, being absorbed in turn by the new rhetorics of the Renaissance, such as Richard Rainolde's *A Booke Called the Foundacion of Rhetorike* (1563).

Slightly higher up the scale were those eminently practical handbooks to style and composition, Cicero's *De inventione* and the pseudo-Ciceronian *Rhetorica ad Herennium*, which had been the main surviving texts after the fall of Rome, with well over 1,000 extant manuscripts making them 'the major works of Latin antiquity for the Middle Ages'.[11] In the Renaissance they continued to flourish, the *Ad Herennium* acquiring some 140 editions with notes and commentaries and *De inventione* almost as many. As for Cicero's mature rhetorical works, some 255 commentaries have been identified in the period between 1477 and 1600, the *Topica* being most popular (77 commentaries), followed by *De partitione oratoria* (71) and *De oratore* (56). The most surprising result of this enquiry undertaken by John O. Ward concerns the popularity of Cicero's speeches, which produced nearly 500 commentaries.[12] Taken in conjunction with the humanists' interest in translating Greek orations and with the many contexts in which orations were delivered, this helps to underline the importance of spoken oratory in the Renaissance,[13] after its total neglect in the Middle Ages.

9. *Ibid.*, 1, p. 633. On ἐνάργεια and its cognates see J. Martin 1974, pp. 252, 288–9.
10. Weinberg 1961, 1, p. 464: 'ad timorem *iniiciendum*, et ad misericordiam *movendam* accommodatos', 'ad metum *iniiciendum*, et ad misericordiam in animis spectatorum *excitandam*'.
11. *Medieval Eloquence* 1978, p. 54 n. 74 (Ward).
12. *Renaissance Eloquence* 1983, pp. 126–73 (Ward).
13. *Reden und Briefe* 1970; *Renaissance Eloquence* 1983, pp. 1–19 (Kristeller); J. W. O'Malley 1979; Trinkaus 1966.

If Cicero dominates both as theorist and practitioner, the other classical authorities enjoyed their popularity too. Aristotle's *Rhetoric* has yet to receive the scholarly attention given the *Poetics*, but the fact that seven new versions appeared in the sixteenth century, compared to two in the fifteenth[14] – the commentators including George of Trebizond, Ermolao Barbaro, Antonio Riccoboni, Marcantonio Maioragio, Marc-Antoine Muret, Alessandro Piccolomini and Johannes Sturm – shows that the sister art was not neglected. Second only to Cicero in influence was Quintilian, whose *Institutio oratoria* had 18 editions by 1500, a further 130 by 1600.[15] If other, less famous but also influential, Greek and Roman rhetorics were added to this list – Hermogenes, Demetrius, Longinus, Menander, Rutilius Lupus and so on – we would begin to grasp the range of the Renaissance revival of classical rhetoric.

The influence of a text can be charted in part through its printing history. But with a subject like rhetoric the influence of classical antiquity is all-pervasive, since the new rhetorics produced from the 1430s on are all more or less digests of classical rhetoric, whether printed in Latin or in the vernaculars. Rhetoric had reached such a stage of elaboration by Hellenistic times that there was in any case little room for further development. The course of Renaissance rhetoric is essentially one of synthesis, of varying degrees of completeness, addressed to differing contexts or goals. Just as the *Poetics* of Aristotle could be adapted to such new genres as romance, the pastoral or even the madrigal,[16] so rhetoric could find some new forms to deal with. But for the most part it was a question of selecting and rearranging from a common stock, the superiority of one author over another emerging in the overall arrangement, scope, or use of telling quotations. 'Collector, non author, ego sum', says Susenbrotus modestly at the outset of his rhetoric book,[17] and he might have been speaking for all his fellows. George of Trebizond, in his epoch-making *Rhetoricorum libri V* (1433–4; ten editions by 1547), denigrated all previous rhetoric but incorporated *De inventione* 'almost totally', drew heavily on *Ad Herennium* and Quintilian (despite criticising him), and above all synthesised the Latin rhetorical tradition with Hermogenes.[18] His work was typical of many, as the sixteenth century was to show in ever-larger compilations, such as Bartolomeo Cavalcanti's *Rhetorica* (1559; ten editions by 1585)[19] or Antonius Lullius' *De oratione libri vii* (1558). The prize perhaps goes to the

14. Monfasani 1976, p. 332; Cranz and Schmitt 1984, pp. 220–1; Erickson 1975.
15. Murphy 1981.   16. Weinberg 1961, I, p. 560.
17. Susenbrotus 1953. This work, first published in Zurich *c.* 1541, went through twenty-three editions by 1600.
18. Monfasani 1976, pp. 248–89.   19. *Renaissance Eloquence* 1983, pp. 47–50 (La Russo).

Thesaurus rhetoricae of Giovanni Battista Bernardi (1599), which indexes no less than 5,000 rhetorical terms and cites thirty-nine authorities.

The fusion of rhetoric and poetics can be seen in the very structure of these works. The *De arte poetica* of Girolamo Vida (1527), a verse treatise in the manner of Horace, consists of three books, the first devoted to the training of the poet and the defence of poetry, the second to *inventio* and *dispositio*, the third to *elocutio*. In the parts, as in the whole, it is a typically rhetorical treatise. The six dialogues of Antonio Minturno's *De poeta* (1559), running to nearly six hundred pages, discuss poetry, the poetic, tragedy, comedy, lyric and style in a totally eclectic way, fusing Horace, Plato, Aristotle, Cicero and Quintilian into a fundamentally rhetorical work. Minturno is able to assimilate so many different sources because he can superimpose them all on to the complete system of rhetoric. The ultimate fusion of all forms of knowledge about literature was performed by Julius Caesar Scaliger in his *Poetices libri VII* (1561), a work of 310 chapters and nearly 1,000 pages. The seven books discuss genres, verse forms, the *genera dicendi*, poetic forms, style (with an influential regrouping of the rhetorical figures), ancient and modern poets and much else. Scaliger differs from other Renaissance treatise-writers in degree only; but he resembles them in another way, that is, in the mingling of critical discourses, prescriptive, descriptive, legislative and apologetic. The legislative approach lays down what is a poem, poetry or poet; what defines and differentiates the genres. The prescriptive work gives the would-be writer specific instructions on how to compose, according to rhetoric and poetics. The descriptive mode analyses writers or works, often with a polemical intent, praising some and denigrating others; while the apologetic mode defends poetry or literature in general against its enemies. Whereas modern criticism tends to separate each kind of discourse, Renaissance works can happily blend two, or all four, and then add, as Scaliger does, extensive historical and autobiographical sections, including printing his own Latin verse. Before such eclecticism tidy modern categories seem inappropriate.

A special place in the history of Renaissance rhetoric must be given to its use by the church. The great model for sacred rhetoric was St Augustine's *De doctrina Christiana*, which answered the early church's distrust of pagan culture by urging the need to arm truth with eloquence. The Ciceronian tradition, with its celebration of the orator's power over man's feelings, is to be used to defend religion from its enemies, and also to expound Christian belief in sermons that may freely use rhetorical devices, as sanctioned by their frequent application in the Bible. The great inheritor of Augustine's legacy was Erasmus, whose *Ecclesiastes, sive concionator evangelicus* (1535) has been called 'the single most important treatise on the theory of sacred oratory' since Augustine.[20] Yet Erasmus tried to change the emphasis in preaching rhetoric, substituting the *genus deliberativum*, which stresses persuasion by argument, for the *genus demonstrativum*, which uses the techniques of praise and blame, *laus* and *vituperatio*. The history of preaching practice and theory from the late fourteenth to the seventeenth centuries shows the influence of classical rhetoric on many elements of content and form, improving both the didactic and the expressive function of sermons and homilies. The leaders of the Reformation soon grasped the importance of rhetoric, Luther reiterating time and again 'Dialectica docet, rhetorica movet', insisting that the preacher be 'a rhetorician and a dialectician, that is, he must teach and exhort', express himself clearly, illustrate his discourse with biblical examples and be 'capable of admonishing the evil-hearted, the unruly and the indolent'.[21] Luther's stress on the sermon as the main means of propagating the new doctrine meant that special care had to be given to the education of preachers, and 'training in rhetoric became for the very first time in history a basic requirement in the training for the priesthood'.[22] The pedagogue who translated Reformation ideas into textbook form was Melanchthon, in *De officiis concionatoris* (1529), which determined the course of Lutheran preaching for several generations. Among the many Catholic preaching-manuals one of the more interesting is the *Rhetorica christiana* of the Franciscan Diego Valades (1579), who drew on his nineteen years as a missionary among Mexican Indians to extol the value of rhetoric in winning souls.

The church also had an interest in rhetoric books proper. Melanchthon, professor of Greek and rhetoric at Wittenberg (where he delivered 180 academic orations), produced a *De rhetorica* in 1519, revised it in 1521 as *Institutiones rhetoricae*, and again in 1531, when it appeared as *Elementorum rhetorices libri duo*, with a further revision in 1542.[23] The basic sources are Cicero and Quintilian, but rhetoric is applied to theological ends, with an important development of the topics. His book was widely used, imitated and even pirated; the unauthorised version *De rhetorica libri tres* (1521) became the main source of the first rhetoric in English, Leonard Cox's *The*

20. *Renaissance Eloquence* 1983, p. 243 (J. W. O'Malley).
21. Cited by Stolt 1974, p. 52: 'Ein Prediger muss ein Dialektiker und Rhetoriker sein, das heisst, er muss lehren und ermahnen. Wenn er etwas lehren will, muss er zunächst genau bezeichnen, danach definieren; . . . fünftens diese seine Worte mit Gleichnissen weiter ausschmücken; sechstens die Schlechten, Widerspenstigen und Faulen tadeln.'
22. *Renaissance Eloquence* 1983, p. 224 (Dyck).   23. Melanchthon 1968, pp. 36–7, 39–42.

Arte or Crafte of Rhetoryke (c. 1530). The leading Catholic rhetoric book of this and the following century was *De arte rhetorica* (1562) of Cyprian Soarez, S. J. The title page announces its authorities, Aristotle, Cicero and Quintilian. Like Vida, it adopts the following sequence of composition: book I on *inventio*, book II on *dispositio*, book III on the three remaining parts. Soarez' work is well organised, concise and thorough, and no doubt deserved to become the main rhetoric-text for the Jesuit Order in the 1599 *Ratio studiorum*. It enjoyed at least 134 printings in forty-five different European cities over a period of 173 years, appearing both in enlarged and abbreviated editions. One of the peculiarities of the rhetoric book in all periods is that it has no inherent shape or size: being a handbook with a practical end, outside itself, it can be larger or smaller as the occasion, and publishing context, demands. The trend towards inclusiveness, especially in the Jesuit colleges, produced in the next century vast tomes of a thousand pages or more. When one considers the number of editions of each book, and the fact that school texts might be reused for several generations, the probable total of titles on rhetoric that appeared between the invention of printing and 1600 might be perhaps five thousand, while the total number of users would be in the hundreds of thousands. In every sense, then, it is right to link Renaissance humanism with 'the rhetorical tradition in western culture',[24] and to observe that we are as yet far from appreciating the extent of rhetoric's domain.

THE MEDIEVAL INHERITANCE

Renaissance writers on rhetoric and poetics claimed that they owed their knowledge and inspiration not to the Middle Ages but to classical antiquity. Although some assertions of independence from medieval traditions need to be viewed with caution, this claim seems largely justified. The appreciation of rhetoric and poetics during the Middle Ages suffered from various vicissitudes, beginning with the loss or misinterpretation of many of the major texts. Aristotle's *Poetics* was translated but had little diffusion and influence; the paraphrase of it by Averroes, assimilating it to epideictic rhetoric, was widely circulated and influential. If not assimilated to rhetoric, the *Poetics* was taught as a logical work. Aristotle's *Rhetoric* survives, in William of Moerbeke's Latin translation, in more than a hundred manuscripts, but the kind of commentary that it received related it, too, to dialectics, ethics or psychology.[25] Medieval knowledge of Ciceronian

24. Kristeller 1979, pp. 23–4.   25. Boggess 1970; Murphy 1966, 1969.

rhetoric was based on the early *De inventione* and the spurious *Ad Herennium*; the *De oratore* was known of, and alluded to superficially, but hardly used, while the *Orator* and *Brutus* had disappeared altogether. As for the great compendium of Quintilian, the *Institutio oratoria* survived in two badly mutilated versions lacking half the text, including many of the most important passages for a wider concept of rhetoric.[26] Even the texts that survived were known through abridgements or through the schematic and derivative accounts in the encyclopaedias which, with all their deficiencies, often formed the only channel of information extant.

Not only had the texts been lost: so had their contexts. The Middle Ages knew little about the democracy of Greece and of Rome before the emperors, with the vital role played by rhetoric in politics and law. When it lost these social functions in antiquity, rhetoric had been transplanted to education, literature and philosophy. As the knowledge of these disciplines survived the Dark Ages only intermittently, so an awareness of the meaning or purpose of rhetorical devices declined. The role of rhetoric in democratic politics or law-cases had little relevance for much medieval culture, and the functional nature of the figures and tropes of rhetoric in appealing to the will and influencing judgement – the whole psychology of persuasion – was forgotten.

In the revival of school and university education in the eleventh to thirteenth centuries, rhetoric occupied its place in the *trivium* alongside grammar and logic, but with a much reduced importance. Dialectic appropriated the commonplaces, definition and proof, while moral and political questions were transferred to theology. Logic became the most important university subject, as seen by the Paris curriculum of 1215, where even the set text for rhetoric, book IV of Boethius' *De differentiis topicis*, subordinates rhetorical argumentation to dialectical theory. The subordination of rhetoric to dialectic was increased by the fact that the basic textbook of Latin rhetoric until *c.* 1150, the *De inventione*, failed to deal with three of the five divisions of rhetoric, *elocutio, pronuntiatio* and *memoria*.[27] Limited to *inventio* and status-theory, rhetoric was seen as an inferior branch of logic, concerned with particular rather than general issues.

At the same time that rhetoric lost standing in the universities it found a niche at a lower intellectual level in the specialised arts of discourse, the arts of poetry, letter-writing, preaching and – to a more limited extent – speechwriting (the *ars arengandi*). Each *ars* was developed to meet the needs of a different social group, which was unlikely to study or practise one of the

26. Lehmann 1959; Winterbottom 1967.   27. *Medieval Eloquence* 1978, pp. 42–3 (Ward).

others. The *artes poetriae* were composed by professional teachers of *ars grammatica*, but limited themselves to the techniques of Latin verse composition for younger schoolboys. The *Ars versificatoria* of Matthew of Vendôme (*c.* 1175) is typical in its concern with composition in the narrowest sense, the choice and arrangement of words in a line, rather than composition as plot or structure.[28] The development of formal techniques at the expense of wider creative issues is marked in the *ars dictaminis*, whose manuals taught highly formalised techniques of assembling letters out of stereotyped phrases, and whose authors turned their back on larger cultural perspectives.[29] *Dictamen* was used for practical correspondence in law and diplomacy, but retained little trace of rhetoric's original social role. The arts of preaching, which occasionally stress the need for moving the congregation's feelings, bear more relation to classical rhetoric and its teachings on persuasion, but still prefer to concentrate on form.[30]

In all three *artes* we note a split between theory and practice, as ever greater concentration on practical precepts goes along with a loss of awareness of function or purpose. Questions of content are discussed in terms of form only, or fragments of classical rhetoric are applied to wholly inappropriate goals. The 'principle of disjunction' between form and content which Erwin Panofsky diagnosed in medieval art applies to much of medieval rhetoric.[31]

THE RENAISSANCE REDISCOVERY OF RHETORIC

A knowledge of the state of rhetoric during the Middle Ages helps us understand the major shift of interest that occurred in the Renaissance. Rhetoric now became a key subject in humanist education, as classical ideas on language as the mark of human civilisation were eagerly appropriated to a contemporary context. The praise of language in Isocrates' *Antidosis*, *Nicocles* and introduction to *Helen* as the instrument given man for politics and the *vita activa*, the means of doing good in society, were taken over by Cicero in formulations that were to be echoed innumerable times in the Renaissance. Every student in this period would have been familiar since childhood with the praise of *ratio* and *oratio* in De officiis (1.16.50) as the gifts that define humanity and bond society, or the related passages in De

28. Kelly 1966, pp. 263–4.   29. Wieruszowski 1971, pp. 373–7, 424–7.
30. McKeon 1952, pp. 290–1; *Medieval Eloquence* 1978, pp. 113, 116 (Jennings).
31. Panofsky 1960, pp. 83–4, 104, 107; Vickers 1987 ('The medieval fragmentation of rhetoric').

inventione (1.1–5) and *De oratore* (1.8.30ff.) celebrating oratory as the power to influence men, defend liberty and guarantee human civilisation. The Ciceronian image of the orator as culture-hero, whose power was exercised in defence of justice and ethics, had an enormous influence on the Renaissance. This Isocratean-Ciceronian tradition of properly developed language as at once a proof of humanity and a condition of social health can be found in the earliest stages of the revival of rhetoric, in the late fourteenth century. The statutes of the University of Florence in 1397, concerning the public reading and teaching of rhetoric, are a digest of these Ciceronian texts:

The priors with the colleges, considering that the art of rhetoric is not only the instrument of persuasion for all the sciences, but also the greatest ornament of public life, and since this faculty embraces the precepts for advocating or opposing anything we wish, and concerns itself with the sure methods of the notarial offices: lest so appropriate a pursuit for the Florentine Studium decay [a new professor is to be appointed].[32]

The propagator, if not the founder of the new humanist attitudes to rhetoric and philosophy was Petrarch, for whom language had all the Ciceronian connotations of social bonding, humanity and altruism. In a letter to Tommaso da Messina 'on the study of eloquence', which dates from the 1350s, he defined eloquence as the counterpart to philosophy, arguing that we should 'correct not only our life and conduct, which is the primary concern of virtue, but our language usage as well. This we will do by the cultivation of eloquence.' Language is the tool by which the mind can display its good traits, and convert others to doing good through conversation or writing. Eloquence is a vital aid to practical ethics, rousing the self and others to a life of virtue.[33] The Spanish humanist Vives put it

---

32. Cited by Struever 1970, p. 105: 'Domini cum collegiis, considerantes quod ars rhetorica non solum omnium scientiarum persuasorium instrumentum est, sed rerum publicarum maximum ornamentum, quoniam hec facultas suadendi dissuadendique cuncta que volumus precepta complectitur, et circa dictandi ministerium certis rationibus occupatur; ne tantum decus in Studio florentino deficiat, sed continuo reflorescat . . .'.

33. Petrarch 1975–85, I, pp. 47–50. For the Latin text see Petrarch 1933–42, I, pp. 45–7 (I.9): 'exhortor ac moneo ut non vitam tantum et mores, quod primum virtutis est opus, sed sermonis etiam nostri consuetudinem corrigamus, quod artificiose nobis eloquentie cura prestabit . . . Que [sc. eloquentia] si nobis necessaria non foret et mens, suis viribus nisa bonaque sua in silentio explicans, verborum suffragiis non egeret, ad ceterorum saltem utilitatem, quibuscum vivimus, laborandum erat; quorum animos nostris collocutionibus plurimum adiuvari posse non ambigitur. . . . Veruntamen quantum quoque ad informationem humane vite possit eloquentia, et apud multos auctores lectum et quotidiana experientia monstrante compertum est. . . . Postremo, si ceterorum hominum caritas nulla nos cogeret, optimum tamen et nobis ipsis fructuosissimum arbitrarer eloquentie studium non in ultimis habere.'

concisely: 'Your tongue is the one instrument nature gave to you for doing good.'[34]

In fifteenth-century Italy two centres above all, Florence and Padua, had a formative influence on the rediscovery of rhetoric. In Florence the impact of the humanist chancellors – Coluccio Salutati, Leonardo Bruni, Poggio Bracciolini – associated rhetoric with the *vita activa* and with the struggle for liberty.[35] Although not free from Florentine self-glorification, their letters, orations and historical works did prove the effectiveness of rhetoric in politics. These chancellors were also scholars: Salutati had a famous library and was one of the first serious humanist textual critics, and his invitation of Chrysoloras to Florence was crucial in establishing the study of Greek. For the influence of rhetoric on education we must turn to northern Italy, where a remarkable succession of teachers revolutionised the subject. Pier Paolo Vergerio, professor of logic at the University of Padua, published in 1392 his *De ingenuis moribus*, the first treatise to claim a knowledge of Latin letters as basic to higher learning. Giovanni da Ravenna was the 'artis rhetoricae professor' at Padua from 1382 to 1405 and was succeeded in 1407 by one of the greatest Latin scholars of the time, Gasparino Barzizza, who lectured annually on the *De oratore* and Aristotle's *Rhetoric*. Barzizza also took students as boarders, among them Vittorino da Feltre, Francesco Filelfo and George of Trebizond, who all became leading teachers and scholars of rhetoric. The great humanists of this generation, hired by rival *condottieri* anxious to increase their prestige, were in the forefront of the reshaping of rhetoric in education. Guarino at Ferrara and Vittorino at Mantua established school curricula dominated by rhetoric and grammar, which implied the intensive study of Greek and Latin literature, history and philosophy, with a reading list of classical authors far ahead of most universities. The greatest scholars of the time, Guarino, Poggio and Filelfo, sent their sons to Mantua; other pupils included Lorenzo Valla, Niccolò Perotti and Theodore Gaza.

The importance of the history of education in this story is that it shows how rhetoric was not just rediscovered but read and taught in a different way. While medieval readers approached an already fragmented rhetorical tradition (as they did classical antiquity as a whole) as a storehouse of verbal devices from which items could be removed at will, to be applied to other

34. Vives 1555, I, p. 154 (*De ratione dicendi* lib. III, cap. 12): 'Quid enim refert impetas quempiam ferro, an lingua? nisi quod grauius sermone laedere, quo instrumenti natura magis ferebat, ut eo prodesses.'
35. See Garin 1961, pp. 3–37; Ullman 1963; Witt 1983; Cantimori 1937; Herde 1965; and Baron 1966, subject to the caveats expressed by Ullman 1963, pp. 33, 47–8 and Seigel 1966.

purposes, in the new schools of the early fifteenth century we find for the first time a concept of the study of literature as a separate discipline which could lead to moral and social improvement. Rhetoric, as the established authority on the study of language, genre and literary form, became a key tool in the rediscovery of the past. This new sense of a coherent purpose led to a reunification of rhetoric. George of Trebizond, who had studied with and later worked as a teacher for Vittorino, completed in 1433–4 his *Rhetoricorum libri V*, one of the most important texts in Renaissance rhetoric. Where, in the Middle Ages, rhetoric had become limited to *inventio* and status-theory in one tradition, with *elocutio* studied separately, and applied to several other practical disciplines regardless of its function in a whole scheme, George decided to treat all five of the orator's duties, thus reuniting 'the parts of classical rhetoric which the various medieval *Artes* had separated or suppressed'.[36] He also reclaimed for rhetoric the topics, which the medieval logicians had appropriated, and synthesised Byzantine and Latin traditions to produce the most systematic treatise on rhetoric yet. George was prophetic of many Renaissance rhetoric books in his conscious formulation of rhetoric as the central discipline for civic life. In an *Oratio de laudibus eloquentie*, delivered at Venice in the early 1430s, he echoed Cicero in stating that human nature consists in reason (*ratio*), yet reason cannot do men any good unless bodied forth in speech (*oratio*). Language is equated with doing good, and since rhetoric enters every aspect of public and private life 'most rightly do the ancients seem to name it the art of humanity, "the most important part of the civil science which is the mistress and lord of all human affairs . . . the most noble instrument of politics" ', an essential training for public life and civil leadership.[37] As he put it in his rhetoric book, it is enough for a man to study the 'causes of things . . . if he seeks nothing else but to know; but if he hungers for the glory of ruling the republic, let him devote himself to rhetoric'.[38]

36. Monfasani 1976, p. 269. Another early Renaissance text to reunite the five parts of rhetoric independently of George of Trebizond (its main source being the *Ad Herennium*) was the Hebrew rhetoric of Judah Messer Leon, *Sēpher Nōpheth Sūphīm* (Mantua, *c.* 1475): see Judah Messer Leon 1983.
37. Monfasani 1976, pp. 259–60: 'Quare mihi rectissime humanitatis hanc artem maiores nominasse videntur. Aristoteles vero, quem in rhetoricis Cicero sequitur, civilis scientie, que rerum humanarum omnium magistra et domina est, maximam ac nobilissimam esse partem iudicavit'; pp. 366–7: 'Nec tamen mihi diutius hec cogitanti aut genus politice aut idem omnino ei oratoria facultas videtur, verum ita unicum, singulare, et nobilissimum instrumentum eius ut vel singulis ipsius partibus non deserviat, sed imperet.'
38. Monfasani 1976, pp. 295–6: 'Quamobrem nobis placet si quis propter etatem utrumque habiturum non sperat si nil aliud nisi ut sciat querit causis rerum verisque scientiis ei potius elaborandum; sin reipublice gloriam appetit, rhetorice incumbendum est.'

The importance of rhetoric to the civil life lay in its ability to translate ideas into action, through the means of persuasion. All Renaissance rhetoric, and much of its poetics, is premised on the superiority of action over contemplation, and of the necessity of communicating. Petrarch draws on Ciceronian tradition in declaring thought and language to be mutually dependent, and anticipates many later writers in denouncing silence or withdrawal from society. Man's duty was to take part in social life, to make virtue a practical, not a theoretical attribute. Salutati was not alone in equating the study of literature with virtue and *humanitas*. Since, as Cicero had said, 'the whole praise of virtue consists in action', then the end of learning must be virtue, not mere erudition, and 'eloquence is essential to the *studia humanitatis* because of the necessity of moving the will to action'.[39] Reason, virtue and the social order all depend on the right use of language. *Elocutio*, far from being a mere ornament, was the faculty to which Cicero had devoted the greatest care, rightly so, according to Quintilian, 'for the verb *eloqui* means the production and communication to the audience of all that the speaker has conceived in his mind, and without this power all the preliminary accomplishments of oratory are as useless as a sword that is kept permanently concealed within its sheath'.[40] The corollary of such a belief, repeatedly echoed in Renaissance texts, is that the study of eloquence was to be pursued for utility, not ornament, and for the frequently asserted – though seldom properly defined – motive of the common good. Poliziano eulogised rhetoric for its political utility: 'there is nothing more fertile and useful than to persuade one's fellow-citizens by means of words, so that they perform actions advantageous to the state and refrain from those that are damaging'.[41] Such formulations, with their implicit assumption of a one-party state, or a unanimity of political or ethical attitudes, were naive, but nonetheless the praise of eloquence in these terms did much to increase its status.

39. Struever 1970, p. 59, citing Salutati 1891–1911, IV, p. 223: 'sed iam satis de logica dictum sit . . . et ad rethoricam, que cum voluntate congreditur, veniamus. Ambe quidem, licet diverso tramite, finem unum intendunt, quamvis una dilucidet intellectum ut animo sciat, altera disponat ut velit, et alia ratione illa probet ut doceat, hec vero persuadeat ut inclinet.' See also Cicero, *De officiis* I.6.19.
40. Quintilian, *Institutio oratoria* VIII. pr. 14–17: 'Eloqui enim est omnia, quae mente conceperis promere atque ad audientes perferre, sine quo supervacua sunt priora et similia gladio condito atque intra vaginam suam haerenti.'
41. Cited by Garin 1958b, pp. 83–4 (*Oratio super Fabio Quintiliano et Statii Sylvis*): 'Quid autem tam utile tamque fructuosum est quam quae tuae Reipublicae carissimisque tibi hominibus utilia conducibiliaque inveneris posse illa dicendo persuadere, eosque ipsos a malis inutilibusque rationibus absterrere?' Cf. Cicero, *De oratore* I.8.30–3.

RHETORIC AND PHILOSOPHY

Although rhetoric was often linked with philosophy in the Renaissance, it is
not easy for us to estimate their true relationship, which was neither stable
nor always clearly formulated. Since the humanists were in a sense
grammarians, philologists and rhetoricians, one modern reaction is to
question whether they were philosophers at all. Certainly some rhetoricians
claimed that they were doing philosophy, and the more aggressive among
them believed they could do it better than the philosophers. To evaluate
their work, paradoxical though it may seem at first, it is better to be a
rhetorician than a philosopher. The charge so often brought against
Renaissance philosophy, that it merely synthesised already existing schools
of thought without producing a system of its own – unlike the ages
immediately before and after it – undoubtedly applies to rhetorical
philosophy, which is largely based on Stoicism, with an opportunistic use of
Plato and Aristotle. To approach it, then, in the expectation of systematic
thought is to arrive at the position of J. E. Seigel, who amasses evidence of
'contradictions' in Petrarch and Salutati on such issues as the excellence of
the active or contemplative lives.[42] Yet these were topics on which it was
possible to be of two minds, the determining factor being the context.
Rhetoric taught that discourse was to be adapted to the situation and
audience (Aristotle, *Rhetoric* II.13, 1390^{a}25ff.). The question of whether to
choose the monastic life should be evaluated according to the age, education
and expectations of the person making that choice. It was a relative, not an
absolute issue.

The relativity of rhetorical discourse, the fact that its whole activity,
forensic, deliberative or demonstrative, concerns the field of human action
and human choice, made it suspicious to those philosophers with an
absolute concept of truth or justice. The conflict between philosophy and
rhetoric, a running battle from Plato to Kant and Croce, has usually derived
from a philosopher's dissatisfaction with rhetoric. The charges made by
Plato in the *Gorgias*, that rhetoric deals with the arts of appearance, has no
real knowledge (ἐπιστήμη) but merely opinions (δόξαι), no inherent
subject-matter and no access to the truth (*Gorgias*, 452–66), were certainly
known to some Renaissance rhetoricians, for the dialogue had been
translated by Leonardo Bruni. In answering them they could draw on the

42. Seigel 1968, pp. 49–52, 70–4.

reasoned defence made by Aristotle at the opening of his *Rhetoric*: that rhetoric is the counterpart of dialectic, sharing its universality of range; that it is essential to human society, from law and politics to everyday life, especially useful in self-defence (since 'the use of rational speech is more distinctive of a human being than the use of his limbs'); that if it can be abused so can 'all good things except virtue', particularly those that are most useful; that it is an art or τέχνη whose use needs to be understood and improved (1354ᵃ–1355ᵇ). Renaissance defenders of rhetoric could also draw on the more aggressive counters of the Roman rhetoricians, such as Cicero's assertion that 'to us orators belong the broad estates of wisdom and learning, which have been allowed to lapse and become derelict through our absorption in affairs, have been invaded by persons too generously supplied with leisure, persons who actually . . . banter and ridicule the orator after the manner of Socrates in Plato's *Gorgias* . . .'.[43] Quintilian devotes less space to philosophy, but in equally aggressive vein proclaims that under his leadership rhetoric will approach the philosophers who 'usurped the better part of the art of oratory', that is, 'the principles of upright and honourable living', and 'demand back what is ours by right'.[44]

One way of handling Plato's attack on rhetoric was to turn it around against him, as Cicero did with the comment that 'it was when making fun of orators that he himself seemed to be the consummate orator'.[45] So Theodore Gaza, in the recently discovered lectures he gave on taking up the chair of Greek and eloquence at Ferrara in 1446, said that although the *Gorgias* was intended to dissuade students from the rhetoric of the sophists, 'in eloquently arguing his case, Plato proves the great power and worth of rhetoric'.[46] Such a light, ironic tone was seldom used in Renaissance disputes between rhetoric and philosophy. More characteristic is the attack made by Lorenzo Valla in *De voluptate* (1431; revised 1433), based on Quintilian but exceeding him in violence.

Valla's dialogue is notoriously difficult to interpret, and since some of the opinions are uttered by *personae* for the two main philosophical schools,

43. *De oratore* III.31.122: 'nostra est, inquam, omnis ista prudentiae doctrinaeque possessio, in quam homines quasi caducam atque vacuam abundantes otio nobis occupatis involaverunt, atque etiam . . . irridentes oratorem ut ille in Gorgia Socrates cavillantur . . .'
44. Quintilian, *Institutio oratoria* I, pr. 10: 'Neque enim hoc concesserim, rationem rectae honestaeque vitae (ut quidam putaverunt) ad philosophos relegandam'; *ibid.*, 17: 'Nunc necesse est ad eos aliquando auctores recurrere, qui desertam, ut dixi, partem oratoriae artis, meliorem praesertim, occupaverunt, et velut nostrum reposcere.'
45. *De oratore* I.11.47: 'quo in libro [sc. *Gorgias*] in hoc maxime admirabar Platonem, quod mihi in oratoribus irridendis ipse esse orator summus videbatur'.
46. *Renaissance Eloquence* 1983, p. 180 (Monfasani).

Stoics and Epicureans, who are demolished in turn in favour of Christianity, perhaps Valla may not be identified with them. However, in this exposure of the deficiencies of ancient philosophy there does seem to be a consistent thread asserting the superiority of rhetoric. In the *prooemium* Valla announces that he intends to use 'the sword that is the word of God', and by drawing on faith and God's word 'destroy our enemies – that is, the philosophers – partly with their own swords, partly by inciting them to civil war and mutual destruction'.[47] In book I Vegio, the exponent of Epicureanism, dismisses philosophy as 'a soldier or lower officer at the orders of Oratory, his commander and (as a great writer of tragedies calls her) his queen'.[48] He laments that Cicero had not exercised his right to reclaim from philosophers the parts of rhetoric they had stolen, and wishes he had 'raised against those sneak thieves of philosophers the sword he had received from Eloquence, queen of all, and to punish them as criminals. Truly how much more clearly, solemnly, and magnificently the same subjects are dealt with by the orators than by the obscure, squalid and anaemic philosophers!' Vegio announces that he will dispute on this topic violently, according to the usage of the orators, who have always addressed the most important topics while philosophers chattered in their nooks and crannies. Orators are the true leaders of men.[49] In book III, Antonio, defender of Christianity, rebukes Boethius for being more friendly to the dialecticians than the rhetoricians: 'How much better it would have been for him to speak oratorically rather than dialectically! What is more absurd than the procedure of the philosophers? If one word goes wrong, the whole argument is imperilled', whereas the orator has many resources.[50] What was a vice of rhetoric for Plato becomes in Valla's hands a virtue.

Modern commentators on Valla agree that he wished to subordinate philosophy to rhetoric, and thus 'accomplish that revenge on behalf of oratory' which he criticised Cicero for not having carried far enough.[51] One can doubt whether 'revenge' is the proper spirit in which to pursue this

---

47. L. Valla 1977, p. 50: 'gladio, quod est verbum Dei . . . ita nos bene speremus putemusque fore ut allophilos, id est philosophos, partim suo mucrone iugulemus, partim in domesticum bellum ac mutuam perniciem concitemus'.

48. *Ibid.*, p. 74: 'Siquidem philosophia velut miles est aut tribunus sub imperatrice oratione et ut magnus quidam tragicus appellat regina.' Cf. Euripides, *Hecuba* 816–18.

49. *Ibid.*, pp. 74–6: 'Sed tamen mallem ut . . . si qui repugnassent, gladium illum quem a regina rerum eloquentia acceperat in latrunculos philosophos strinxisset et male meritos male mulctasset. Quanto enim evidentius, gravius, magnificentius ab oratoribus illa disseruntur quam a philosophis obscuris, squalidis, et exanguibus disputantur.'

50. *Ibid.*, p. 272: 'At quanto satius erat oratorie quam dialectice loqui! Quid enim ineptius philosophorum more ut si uno verbo sit erratum tota causa periclitemur?'

51. Seigel 1968, pp. 137–69; Gerl 1974; Vickers 1986.

discussion. Valla's extremism may in the end rebound on him. Mario Nizolio was just as extreme, wanting to 'throw out all dialecticians and rhetoricians', rejecting the logical works of Aristotle as 'vicious'. In their place rhetoric would become the truly universal art, its subject being everything in human knowledge.[52] Rather like Valla's *Totalitätsanspruch*,[53] this position comes dangerously close to the megalomaniac claim that Plato maliciously put into the mouth of Gorgias, that rhetoric 'includes practically all other faculties under her control' (456B).

Disputes such as these generate much heat but little light. A sounder idea of the relation between rhetoric and philosophy in the Renaissance can be gained from other passages in Cicero and Quintilian, such as the distinction in *De oratore* that of the three divisions of philosophy, physics, dialectic and ethics, the orator's province is the third, the moral science of human nature, *vita et mores* (1.15.66–9). In the *Institutio* Quintilian agreed that orators must concern themselves with the actual practice and experience of life (XII.2.6–20). This large area, including ethics and psychology – dealt with in inter-related terms by Aristotle in his *Ethics* and *Rhetoric* – became the focus for much Renaissance rhetoric. Moral philosophy provided the materials or subject-matter for rhetoric, but was also its goal.

Rhetoric drew on the philosophers for its definition of the virtues and vices (Soarez even went back to Cicero: *De arte rhetorica* 1.43–8), without making any original contribution to ethics in theory or terminology. But Renaissance writers were eager to claim that the practical application of ethics was made by poetry and rhetoric. In 1562 Antonio Posio pronounced rhetoric 'the instrument of the moral philosopher', being applied to law, politics and affairs of state, while 'to it indeed is added poetics, which must not be rejected from a perfect state'.[54] Annotating the *Poetics* in 1575, Alessandro Piccolomini related poetry to 'the practical intellect', that is, to the 'architectonic' science of civil prudence or politics, an identification made frequently in the later years of the century, most notably in Sidney's *Apology for Poetry*.[55]

52. Breen 1968; McKeon 1972, pp. 217–19.   53. Gerl 1974, p. 78.
54. Posio 1562, sig★ 5ᵛ: 'Rhetorica enim est instrumentum moralis philosophi, quo bonae proponuntur leges . . . Accedit vero Poetica, quae ab optima Repub[lica] non est abiicenda.' Cited by Weinberg 1961, I, p. 17; see also pp. 26–7, 486.
55. A. Piccolomini 1575, sig. †† 6ᵛ states that all arts aim at 'qualche honesto giouamento, et commodo dell'humana vita . . . essendo la poesia anch'ella un'habito dell'intelletto prattico intorno à cose fattibili; et per conseguente potendosi chiamar'arte; et essendo trà tutti gli altri così fatti habiti honoratissima, et in nobilità alla civil prudentia, architetonica di tutte l'arti, vicinissima'. Cited by Weinberg 1961, I, pp. 10–11: see index, *s.v. Poetics*, II, p. 1160, for other linkings of poetry with the 'architectonic' science; also Sidney 1965, pp. 104, 167–8.

The main claim made for the twin arts of rhetoric and poetry was that they could instil virtue in our breasts and remove vice, or alternatively make us follow the one and flee the other. In the first formulation Scipione Ammirato wrote in 1560 that 'the end of poetics is to introduce virtue into the soul by driving vice out of it'.[56] In the second version, the flee/follow opposition, which derives from classical rhetoric and philosophy, Giacopo Grifoli declared that whoever reads the poets 'will not only know with the greatest clarity what things are to be done and what ones avoided', but will also be filled with pleasure.[57] This whole ethical tradition clearly derives from epideictic rhetoric, where the incentive to virtue and deterrent from vice are achieved by praise or blame. As Piccolomini put it in his vernacular commentary on the *Poetics*, 'through the imitation of virtuous men and the expression of their praise, we come to be aroused and excited to virtue . . . On the other hand, if we hear vices and wicked actions expressed through poetic imitation and, as they are expressed, reviled and vituperated we immediately begin to dispose ourselves to flee and to hate vicious actions . . .'[58] In this mode, perhaps the most popular of all the links between rhetoric, poetics and moral philosophy in the Renaissance, writers could cite the authority of Aristotle, who had linked praise with the celebration of a man's good qualities, blame with the response to vice (*Rhetoric* I.9; cf. *Nicomachean Ethics* I.12, II.3, III.1). Aristotle was also cited in the Averroes version of the *Poetics*, which begins: 'Every poem and all poetic discourse is blame or praise.' Poems 'concern matters of will – the honourable or the base', and poets 'impel' men to virtue and 'repel' them from vice.[59] The moral-rhetorical basis of such a conception of poetry was wholly acceptable to the Renaissance, as we can see from Salutati's definition of the poet – fusing Quintilian with Averroes – as 'a perfect man skilled in praise and blame'.[60]

56. Ammirato 1642, III, p. 386 (*Il dedalione overo del poeta dialogo*): 'il fine della poetica è indur nell'anima la virtù discacciandone il vizio'. Cited by Weinberg 1961, I, p. 280; see also pp. 136, 143, 315, 320.
57. Grifoli 1557, pp. 62–3 (*Oratio de laudibus poetarum*): 'non modo quae sequenda, quaeque fugienda sint appertissime cognoscat, sed iucundissima quoque voluptate capiatur'. Cited by Weinberg 1961, I, p. 277.
58. A. Piccolomini 1575, sig. ††7ʳ: 'con l'imitation degli huomini virtuosi; et con la spressione delle lodi loro, veniamo ad infiammarci, et ad escitarci alla virtù . . . se i vitij, et le scelleratezze dall'altra banda sentiamo con poetica imitation' esprimere et esprimendo vilipendere, et vituperare; subito cominciamo a disporsi alla fuga, et all'odio delle vitiose attioni . . .'. Cited by Weinberg 1961, I, pp. 544–5; see also pp. 9, 90, 191, 212, 268–9, 277, 317, 429, 536, II, pp. 653, 748, 753, 792, 902–3, 1046.
59. Hardison 1962, p. 35.
60. Salutati 1951, I, p. 68 (1.13): 'vir optimus . . . laudandi vituperandique peritus'; cited by Hardison 1962, p. 36; see also Ullman 1963, pp. 25, 95. For the survival of Averroes' definition up to the 1580s see Weinberg 1961, I, p. 209, II, pp. 751, 764–5.

In this ethical role of poetry two other rhetorical concepts were important, *flectere* and *movere*, both of which derive from Cicero's definition of the role of the orator (*Orator* 21.69; *Brutus* 185). The persuasive powers of rhetoric were endlessly celebrated in the Renaissance, and given iconographical expression in the 'Hercules gallicus', who is shown leading men around by chains which emerge from his mouth to their ears. The crucial intermediary between hearing and doing is willing, and it is no accident that a new stress on the will and voluntaristic psychology accompanied the revival of rhetoric.[61] As Francis Bacon put it in 1605: 'The duty and office of Rhetoric is to apply Reason to Imagination for the better moving of the will.'[62] Any power ascribed to rhetoric was automatically transferred to poetry, whose excellence for many Renaissance theorists lay precisely in its power to arouse the passions and to move its audience to virtue. So Pontano, in his dialogue *Actius de numeris poeticis et lege historiae* (dating from the 1490s) wrote that 'the end of both orator and poet is to move and carry away the listener'.[63] For Scaliger all human communication in language has one end only, whether in philosophy, rhetoric or literature, namely persuasion. The 'soul of persuasion is truth, truth either fixed and absolute, or susceptible of question. Its end is to convince, or to secure the doing of something.'[64] The goal of oratory is not elegant speaking but persuasion to action. It was the promise of power over men's minds and deeds that gave persuasion such a remarkably high status in Renaissance rhetoric. Poets not only teach things, as the philosophers do, but do so more powerfully, Bartolomeo Maranta wrote, because 'they move the passions and display the habits' so vividly that their discourse becomes living, not abstract.[65] This concept of poetry as a super-rhetorical force was memorably expressed by Sir Philip Sidney, celebrating the poet's

61. Garin 1958b, pp. 34–8; Struever 1970, pp. 58–9, 74.
62. F. Bacon 1857–74, III, p. 409 (*The Advancement of Learning* II).
63. Cited by Weinberg 1961, I, pp. 87–8, from Pontano 1943, p. 233: 'Utriusque etiam, oratoris ac poetae officium est movere et flectere auditorem'.
64. J. C. Scaliger 1561, p. 2 (lib. I, cap. 1): 'An vero omnibus his, Philosophicae, Civili, Theatrali, unus . . . finis propositus sit? ita sane est. Unus enim idemque omnium finis, persuasio. . . . Forma persuasionis, veritas: sive certa, sive ambigua. Finis, opus vel intellectionis, vel actionis.' There seems little substance to the claims that in the Renaissance 'the emphasis in rhetoric had shifted from persuasion to style and imitation', so that rhetoric and poetics declined to the cultivation of fine language with no ethical or political import: Kristeller 1979, p. 251. Weinberg's survey of sixteenth-century poetics abounds with statements on the function of rhetoric and poetics in persuading to virtue, and he discovers, as the century progresses, an increasing emphasis on politics: Weinberg 1961, I, p. 346.
65. Maranta 1561, f. 126ᵛ: 'cum non solum res doceant ut illi sed exemplis corroborent. Melius etiam quia significantius cum in movendis affectibus explicandisque habitibus poetae res ipsas ita ob oculos ponant ut intueri ac tractare illas videamur'; cited by Weinberg 1961, I, p. 487. For similar statements, none of them, however, making this connection with ἐνάργεια, see Weinberg 1961, I, pp. 213, 544.

ability to tune his feigned matter 'to the highest key of passion' in 'moving' his readers to 'well-doing'. *Movere* is more powerful than *docere*, for it creates the 'desire to be taught', and what greater good can poetry achieve than that 'it moveth one to do that which it doth teach? For, as Aristotle saith, it is not *gnosis* but *praxis* must be the fruit. And . . . *praxis* cannot be, without being moved to practice. . . .'[66]

Sidney's concluding allusion to the *Nicomachean Ethics* exposes an issue that is evident throughout these discussions of the ethical function of rhetoric and poetry, namely that many of their authors were in effect answering Plato. The early humanist defences of poetry, such as Boccaccio's *De genealogia deorum* and Salutati's *De laboribus Herculis*, were addressed more to countering ecclesiastical disapproval of literature in general. After the dissemination of Plato's works in Latin translation the expulsion of the poets from the *Republic* became notorious, and generated both further attacks on poetry in the Platonic mode and abundant defences. The accusations that poets lie, tell false tales about the gods, practise an imitation at three removes from reality and render the soul effeminate and corrupt through the pleasures of verse or song were repeated in severe terms, at times in the language of Catholic theology at its most forbidding.[67] In defence, writers could revive the medieval concept of literature as allegory (a kernel of virtue beneath a pleasing surface), assert that poets do not lie, justify imitation on the grounds of truth to life or moral improvement or even exonerate pleasure. The *delectare* of Cicero and Horace was invoked as the main purpose of literature by some critics; others appealed to the authority of Aristotle's *Poetics*, which says nothing about *docere*, and therefore must imply that pleasure is the sole end of poetry.[68] Another popular argument, as we have seen, was that poetry and rhetoric were the most effective arts in promoting virtue. The negative side of Platonism, then, might be said to have had a positive effect, increasing the ethical status of poetry and rhetoric still further. By analogy with Cato's definition of the orator as a good man skilled in speaking,[69] the theory arose that the poet had first to be a good man, an idea that stretches from Strabo's *Geography* (1.2.5) to Milton. As Aulo Parrasio formulated it in his commentary on Horace's *Ars poetica*, 'it is essential that the poet himself be a wise man, that he understand what things are proper to a good man'.[70]

---

66. Sidney 1965, pp. 110, 112.   67. Weinberg 1961, I, pp. 255–9, 287, 291, 313–14, 346.
68. See Weinberg 1961, I, pp. 25–6, 59, 316, 326, 410, 506, 559, 580, II, pp. 639–40, 665, 933.
69. Quintilian, *Institutio oratoria* XII.1–2: 'vir bonus dicendi peritus'.
70. Parrasio 1531, f. 3ʳ⁻ᵛ: 'Ante omnia oportet ipsum poetam esse sapientem, quae boni uiri sint intelligat. Quod non faciet, nisi ipse sit bonus, nisi omnibus abundet uirtutibus . . .'. Cited by Weinberg 1961, I, p. 97; see also pp. 27, 257, 266; Spingarn 1908, pp. 53–5.

But Platonism had more positive things to offer Renaissance literary theory. One was the concept of 'Ideas', which was turned from that of 'metaphysical substances existing outside the world of sensory appearances as well as outside the human intellect' into 'notions or conceptions residing in the mind of man'.[71] Ironically enough, the conversion of the Platonic idea from its negative role as a judgement on the inferiority of artistic activity to a heightened description of the artist's possession of 'a glorious prototype of beauty' in his own mind, a beauty that cannot be realised in the finished work yet will permeate it with 'a beauty that is more than a mere copy of reality', was the work of a rhetorician, Cicero (*Orator* II.7ff.). The importance that this concept came to have in later sixteenth- and seventeenth-century art and literary theory is due in great part to Florentine Neoplatonism. From this school, too, came the other influential Platonic concept, the *furor poeticus*, as expounded in *Ion* (533–4) and *Phaedrus* (244ff.). In Ficino's reformulation in the *Theologia platonica*, book XIII, poets are second only to philosophers 'among those who separate themselves from the body during life', acting as vehicles for God to speak through, singing in their madness 'many admirable things which afterwards, when their fury has lessened, they do not well understand themselves'.[72] Although Ficino was largely responsible for the dissemination of this idea, another important intermediate was Horace's *Ars poetica*, with its accounts of Orpheus as 'the holy prophet of the gods' and the early poets as inspired teachers of morality: 'honour and fame fell to bards and their songs, as divine'.[73] The problem that this concept poses is its contradiction between a theory of divine inspiration and one of rhetorical invention, with all its stress on planning and craftsmanship. For this reason, while the vatic idea had some influence, as in Girolamo Fraccheta's *Dialogo del furore poetico* (1581), and in Pontus de Tyard's *Solitaire premier, ou, prose des muses, et de la fureur poëtique* (1562), which has the full Neoplatonic theory of divine fury as the means by which the soul can regain its place in heaven, it was also opposed by critics who held to a belief in poetry as an art, with techniques to be mastered, and as a form of knowledge. Ronsard took up the vatic idea in his *Ode à Michel de l'Hospital* in less extreme form, but it had vanished from French poetics by

71. Panofsky 1968, p.6.
72. Ficino 1964–70, II, p. 203 (XIII.3): 'quod multa furentes canunt et illa quidem mirabilia, quae paulo post defervescente furore ipsimet non satis intelligunt, quasi non ipsi pronuntiaverint, sed Deus per eos ceu tubas clamaverit'. See also Kristeller 1953a, pp. 333–4.
73. Horace, *Ars poetica* 391–401: 'Silvestris homines sacer interpresque deorum caedibus et victu foedo deterruit Orpheus . . . sic honor et nomen divinis vatibus atque carminibus venit'. Cf. also Ovid, *Fasti* VI.5–6: 'Est deus in nobis, agitante calescimus illo. Impetus ille sacrae semina mentis habet.'

1610.[74] Significantly, perhaps, his espousal of Platonic theory did not prevent Ronsard from continuing as the most meticulous corrector and reviser of his own poetry.

Although the main classical exemplars for Renaissance poetics and rhetoric were Aristotle, Cicero, Quintilian and Horace, some critics based themselves on Plato. Notable among these is Francesco Patrizi da Cherso, author of a number of original philosophical works. Patrizi was professor of Platonic philosophy at the University of Ferrara, and then at Rome. He published *Discorso della diversità dei furori poetici* (1553); *Parere in difesa dell' Ariosto* (1585), rejecting the Aristotelian criteria of a contemporary attack on Ariosto; *Della historia* and *Della retorica* (1562), consisting of ten dialogues each; and ten dialogues *Della poetica*, of which the first two, *La deca istoriale* and *La deca disputata*, were published in 1586, the others remaining in manuscript until recently. Much of Patrizi's work is polemical, directed especially against Aristotle, whom he wished to have removed from the university curriculum. As he was an ardent Platonist (drawing on Neoplatonic, Neopythagorean and other esoteric sources), it is no surprise that Patrizi attacked rhetoric. But he did so not in terms of the *Gorgias*, but rather because he believed that the search for rhetorical ornament had corrupted the original Adamic language, which had direct access to things. His concept of a 'retorica celeste' is connected to Neoplatonic ideas of a correspondence between the structure of human discourse and that of the cosmos, and it is significant that he aligned himself with the occultist Giulio Camillo, who wished to link rhetoric with alchemy.[75] Other occult ideas in his work include the claim that the poet has the power, through harmony and rhythm, to operate directly on the human soul and to put it in tune with cosmic harmony; the idea that poetic fury reaches men via the planets; and a belief in numerology. This mathematical interest appears in a bizarre way in book VII of *La deca ammirabile*, where he lists five elements of the credible and incredible in literature and states that the poet must draw on both lists, giving twenty-five possible permutations. These, permuted with the three types of subject-matter for poetry (divine, natural, human), give 225 possible combinations, which can be permuted further according to eight traditional logical categories (cause, effect, essence, action, passion, potency, knowledge and will) to give 33,600 forms of poetry.[76] Where other critics of Neoplatonic

---

74. Weinberg 1961, I, pp. 322–3 and index *s.v. furor*; Castor 1964, pp. 26–41; *Renaissance Eloquence* 1983, p. 383 (Gordon).
75. *Testi umanistici sulla retorica* 1953, pp. 32–6; Bolzoni 1974.   76. Bolzoni 1980, pp. 124–6.

cast, such as Giordano Bruno, were rejecting the validity of rules, Patrizi seems to revel in categorisation, classification and permutation.

The main ideas in Patrizi's poetics are anti-Aristotelian. Where Aristotle had defined imitation as the true activity of the poet, Patrizi, defying the linguistic evidence and the laws of argument, claimed that every use of the term *mimesis* in Aristotle has a different meaning, and hence that the concept had no validity. He protests that Aristotle confused the terminology for epic poetry, because his knowledge of Greek was defective; he rejects the need for unity of plot, and indeed the whole concept of plot. This thorough-going negation of the *Poetics* finally gives rise to Patrizi's major positive idea, directed against the concept of poetry as imitating the real and the credible, as expounded by recent Aristotelians like Castelvetro and Mazzoni. Where they state that poets should derive the marvellous from the credible, Patrizi argues that the poet is 'the maker of the marvellous', so that poetry should be based on the incredible, for only this can produce the marvellous.[77] Patrizi elevates the marvellous as an aesthetic category until it becomes both a unifying idea for all levels of poetry and the criterion by which any poem can be evaluated. All poetic genres are subordinated to this goal, the final book of *La deca ammirabile* investigating the ways in which the marvellous can be produced in the reader's mind. While this can be seen as an exercise in psychology, it also seems remarkably like a return to rhetoric in its concern with the effects of the work of art on the audience. As with his retention, despite himself, of the Aristotelian concepts of action, character and passion, the direction and result of Patrizi's polemics were much affected by their targets. His negation of Aristotle drove him into a position determined by Aristotle, in inversion. Whether that was the direction he might have taken on his own may be disputed, as is his status, no Renaissance critic having received such divergent evaluations.[78] Finally, he seems to draw less on Platonism than on his own idiosyncratic amalgam of later traditions.

RHETORIC AND LITERATURE

Despite its amorphous and polysemic nature rhetoric (which here includes poetics) was essentially a practical art, and in one sense can only be fully

---

77. F. Patrizi [da Cherso] 1969–71, II, p. 284, refers to 'il poeta' as 'il facitore del mirabile in verso'; see also p. 307: 'E sia stabilita per ferma conclusione che la poesia habbia per oggetto lo incredibile, perchè questo è il vero fondamento del maraviglioso, che dee essere così principale oggetto d'ogni poesia . . .'.

78. The evaluation of Weinberg 1961, I, pp. 64–5, 600–2, II, pp. 765–86 is scathing; Bolzoni 1980 is uncritical; Hathaway 1962, pp. 9–20, 72–4, 88–91, 413–20, 423–6, 433–4, 455–7 is favourable.

evaluated by its fruits, in written and spoken language. The influence of rhetoric on Renaissance literature is so vast that only a brief outline can be attempted here, beginning with its role in education. The new scheme of the *studia humanitatis*, evolved in the fifteenth century, liberated rhetoric from its connection with dialectic and the *quadrivium*, and gave it much more prominence in university and school curricula. Studies of education throughout Europe all paint the same picture, with local variations: a more intensive study of the classical authorities, from the higher forms at school throughout the university course, with a great stress on practical mastery.[79] Students would be taught the definitions of the main figures of rhetoric, would identify them in the margins of their books or would find them already identified by some helpful editor, such as Angel Day in his *English Secretorie* (1586). They would be taught to compose themes or orations according to the four or six-part models; would be exercised in the three genres; would identify phrases and topoi; would commit all this information to memory, and be ready to apply it in their daily exercises, weekly disputations or annual examinations. Rhetorical processes were absorbed into their intellectual metabolism.

All textbooks were geared to producing proficiency of expression. One of the most popular, with over 200 printings, was Erasmus' *De duplici copia rerum ac verborum commentarii duo*, first published in 1512 with a dedication to John Colet and St Paul's School, and constantly enlarged until 1534. This handbook to acquiring the 'abundant' or copious style discusses, first, abundance of expression, then abundance of subject-matter. Under the first head it itemises how to achieve variety by using the tropes of rhetoric, by varying sentence construction, by manipulating grammar and above all by using synonymous phrases. It is essentially a guide to acquiring a larger vocabulary, an outline of the many different ways in which the same thing can be said, and although devoted to Latin, it left its mark on many writers. It is systematic, but unlike the standard pattern of rhetoric books resembles rather a dictionary or thesaurus. Erasmus also produced two great collections, one of proverbs, the *Adagia* or *Adagiorum chiliades* (1508; enlarged until 1533), one of comparisons or *Parabolae sive similia* (1514; revised until 1522), together with books on letter-writing and preaching, and a polemical work called *Ciceronianus* (1528). This is a contribution to the controversy over Ciceronianism, that fashion for imitating the style of Cicero which led to absurd excesses, such as disciples taking a vow not to read any other writer for five years, or using only words legitimised by

79. Vickers 1981, pp. 116–24; 1982.

Cicero. Erasmus satirises the extremists, especially those who try to write about Christianity while limiting themselves to pagan Latin, but the controversy raised in an acute form an issue that had been troublesome since the beginnings of humanism, imitation. The confusion of imitation in the sense of Aristotelian *mimesis* with this secondary sense of imitating other – especially classical – authors provoked an extensive discussion of such issues as the nature of style, originality and authority, giving rise to the quarrel of the ancients and moderns. Since the rhetorical training recommended by Erasmus and other pedagogues was based on the thorough study and absorption of classical literature and philosophy, the issue was bound to become controversial; yet it tended to revolve always around the same poles. Perhaps the most perceptive comment is that of Vives, who recommends the imitation of models as the best way to develop individuality (*De tradendis disciplinis*, book IV, cap. 4).

When sixteenth-century writers studied the five stages of composition they soon discovered that the one accorded most attention by rhetoric books was *elocutio*. Quintilian's emphasis on this as the most important part of the arts of language was taken to heart by many writers and teachers. Credit for this shift of direction has sometimes been given to Petrus Ramus, who tidied up the twin arts by assigning *inventio* and *dispositio* to logic, leaving rhetoric the three remaining stages. Yet long before Ramus *inventio* was neglected or transferred to dialectic, and *elocutio* came to be seen as the essential domain of rhetoric.[80] In his *Elementorum rhetorices libri duo* (1519; revised until 1542) Melanchthon accepts the distinction that dialectic 'presents the bare matter, while rhetoric adds, so to speak the vesture of words', since 'it shows what is especially proper to rhetoric itself, namely, style, the very word from which rhetoric gets its name'. The true distinction is that 'the end or purpose of dialectic is to teach, but the function of rhetoric is to move and stimulate minds and thus to affect a person'.[81] Melanchthon refers here to the passage in Quintilian, already cited, that was to have the greatest effect on German rhetoric, on the poets of the Pléiade, on French manuals of poetics (which give most space to *elocutio*) and on many Italian critics of the sixteenth century, for whom poetics was essentially equated with *elocutio*. Rhetoricians of all schools declared that *elocutio* was the most

80. H. J. Lange 1974, pp. 35–41.
81. Melanchthon 1968, p. 83: 'Verum hoc interesse dicunt, quod dialectica res nudas proponit. Rhetorica vero addit elocutionem quasi vestitum. Hoc discrimen . . . ego tamen non repudio, quia . . . ostendit, quid rhetorica maxime proprium habeat, videlicet elocutionem, a qua ipsum rhetorices nomen factum est'; p. 85: 'dialecticae finis est docere, rhetoricae autem permovere atque impellere animos, et ad adfectum aliquem traducere'.

important part of rhetoric: George of Trebizond did so;[82] in England
Sherry, Puttenham and Webbe did so; while Soarez in his influential *De arte
rhetorica* gives most space to *elocutio*, his third book being longer than the
others since containing 'rules for expression it is more serviceable'.[83] Vives'
De ratione dicendi (1533) devotes itself entirely to *elocutio*, less to the
prescriptive than to the descriptive side, so becoming a manual on stylistics
for the reader – a shift from orator to reader also made by Melanchthon.

Although often misunderstood and despised by nineteenth-century and
more recent historians, the doctrine of *elocutio* was an integral part of
Renaissance rhetoric because it governed the final stage of composition,
with its crucial power over the will and feelings. As Soarez put it, quoting
Cicero, the orator has three aims: 'proof is a matter of necessity; charm, of
pleasure; and persuasion, the essence of victory'.[84] The two hundred or so
figures and tropes were sometimes described as 'the ornaments of rhetoric',
a term frequently misunderstood in the modern sense of a decoration not
functional to the overall aim. Yet *ornamentum* signified 'equipment or
accoutrements';[85] the ornaments were associated with *amplificatio*, not in
the medieval sense of expanding discourse but in the classical-Renaissance
sense of making it more intense and effective; and the whole system of
ornatus was 'part of the emotional effect to be achieved by words'.[86] Study
of classical and Renaissance rhetoricians will show that they had a coherent
rationale for the figures of speech as being functional, persuasive, not
decorative. So Henry Peacham, in revising his *Garden of Rhetoric* in 1593,
adds many 'cautions' concerning the choice of figures, which should express
important ideas more forcefully, and George Puttenham states the principle
most clearly: 'a figure is ever used to a purpose, either of beautie or of
efficacie'.[87] This awareness of the range of persuasive and mimetic effects
that can be achieved through a knowledge of rhetoric accounts for the great
profusion of figures and tropes in so many of the major poets and
dramatists.

If *elocutio* influenced the detail of language, larger literary forms drew
directly from rhetoric. The structure of Sir Philip Sidney's *Apology for
Poetry* follows the seven parts of a classical oration, as defined by Thomas

82. See Dyck 1969, pp. 66–112; Gordon 1970, pp. 42–4; Weinberg 1961, I, pp. 109, 152, II, pp. 804–5;
    Monfasani 1976, pp. 282, 332; Plett 1975, pp. 77–9, 105.
83. Soarez 1955, p. 266 (lib. III, cap. 1): 'Haec cum ita sint, merito tertius hic liber, qui elocutionis
    precepta continet, ut duobus superioribus utilior est, sic etiam erit aliquanto longior.'
84. *Ibid.*, pp. 265–6: 'Sed probare necessitatis est, delectare suavitatis, flectere vero victoriae.'
85. Ong 1958a, p. 277.   86. *Renaissance Eloquence* 1983, p. 236 (Dyck).
87. Puttenham 1936, p. 202; Vickers 1970, pp. 83–121.

Wilson's *Arte of Rhetorique*. The technique of rhetorical debate, *in utramque partem*, where participants were aligned on opposite sides, was enormously influential on medieval literature and was given a new lease of life by humanist education. Its marks are visible in much Tudor drama, and it is one of the main sources for the mock-encomium, a genre that produced some notable examples in the Renaissance, such as Erasmus' *Moriae encomium* (1511), Agrippa's *De incertitudine et vanitate scientiarum et artium declamatio*[88] and John Jewel's *Oratio contra rhetoricam* (c. 1548). Where the standard interpretation of Giovanni Pico della Mirandola's dispute with Ermolao Barbaro has seen it as a straight attack on rhetoric, it can now be read as a mock one, parodying extremist logicians.[89] As for the genuine encomium, since deliberative and judicial oratory as practised in classical antiquity hardly survived the fall of Rome, epideictic became the most important genre. Most humanist oratory, sacred or secular, is epideictic, and Renaissance rhetoricians tended to see the whole of literature in these terms. In his *Poetices libri VII* Scaliger arranges the literary genres according to the rank of being celebrated, from the most noble – hymns and paeans to the gods (the only form of poetry that Plato allowed in his state) – down through odes, which praise brave men, tragedy, comedy and so on. Similarly Puttenham, in his *Arte of English Poesie* (1589), gives a history and typology of the genres as forms of epideictic oratory.[90] All literary genres were granted this function of praising good and denouncing evil, so important to the Renaissance ethical theory of literature, even lyric. The major genre involved was epic, where the didactic–exemplary role ascribed to the poet resulted in the demand for idealised characters representing extremes of good and evil. In the hands of minor writers this demand produced abstractions that may fit into an ethical scheme but are notably lacking in human interest.

Luckily, the prescriptive bent of literary theory came after the main flowering of Renaissance epic. Ariosto wrote before it, even if his critics managed to force him into this schematic moral frame, and while Tasso may have succeeded in retrospectively interpreting his own work in these terms, as a creative writer he transcended them. The influence of epideictic theory was not always beneficial, for if heroic poetry could be seen as a collection of positive exempla, an incentive to virtue, tragedy could be downgraded to a deterrent exposure of vice. But the focus on praise or blame meant that writers and readers were forced to take up a definite

---

88. Bowen 1972; Korkowski 1976.   89. Breen 1968, pp. 3–28; Panizza forthcoming.
90. J. C. Scaliger 1561, p. 6; Puttenham 1936 (book 1, chs. 10–16, 19, 20, 23–6.)

attitude to human behaviour, so that poetics and rhetoric did justify their claim to answer the question 'how to live'. The pressing task for modern historians is to reconstruct in greater depth the attitudes and mentalities of a culture in which eloquence, conceived as a moral force, was the most important accomplishment of man.

21

THE THEORY OF HISTORY

'What is history?' has been a controversial question from antiquity down to the present, but it was never more vigorously discussed than in the Renaissance ('Che cosa sia storia?' asked Dionigi Atanagi in 1559; eight years later Giovanni Viperano, 'Quid sit historia?' and still a quarter-century after that Tommaso Campanella, 'Quid historia sit?').[1] Then, as before and since, answers ranged widely – from simple happenings (*res gestae*) to God's 'grand design', from a lowly 'art' to an elaborate 'science', from a vague 'sense' to the 'most certain philosophy' (*certissima philosophia*, in the phrase of Andrea Alciato) and indeed to a position, according to Jean Bodin, 'above all sciences'.[2] 'History' could be objective or subjective, could refer to the past or merely to the memory thereof, to ancient testimony or modern reconstruction; but in the fifteenth and sixteenth centuries it rose grandly in the scale of western learning. Through the classical revival it became a liberal art and a literary genre; through the Reformation it became a surrogate for the tradition of 'true religion'; through Counter-Reformation controversy it became a highly organised science. In various ways history became a dominant mode of expression and argument in the later sixteenth century, and its significance for the contacts with philosophy increased accordingly.

HUMANIST THEMES

History in a modern sense was from the beginning bound up with the humanist movement and was indeed a charter member of the *studia humanitatis* (along with grammar, rhetoric, poetry and moral philosophy) from which that movement took its name.[3] Not only was history

---

1. Atanagi 1559, p. 66; Viperano 1567; Campanella 1954 (*Rationalis philosophiae pars quinta, historiographiae liber unus*). The first two are reproduced in *Theoretiker humanistischer Geschichtsschreibung* 1971.
2. Alciato 1953, pp. 220–4 (*Historiae encomium*); Bodin 1951 (1st edn 1566), p. 109.
3. See Kristeller in this volume.

numbered among these 'humanities' but in other senses it had particular relationships with them, beginning most fundamentally with the first two members of the old medieval *trivium*, grammar and rhetoric. According to Quintilian and his humanist followers, the *ars grammatica* was divided into two parts, of which the first was *historia*, that is, the words, the primordial substance of language (*sensus historicus* being equivalent to grammatical or literal interpretation) and the second, 'method' (*methodus*), that is, syntax or form.[4] In this distinction, familiar to most schoolchildren down to the present century, one may see a rudimentary model of scientific method, which Bacon for one defined as the application of reason to experience, which is to say 'history' in a general and 'empirical' sense.[5] The affiliations of history with rhetoric were both formal and epistemological, since it proposed to understand the world in concrete, causal and didactic terms, and moral, since it aimed at right action and perhaps the public good. As 'philosophy teaching by example' (a formula deriving from Dionysius of Halicarnassus), history had an even more direct connection with moral philosophy.[6] As for poetry, although it was usually (that is, Peripatetically) distinguished from history, certain Renaissance authors came to believe that in fact – historically – history had emerged from poetry. In these ways the impetus of 'history' was towards the humanisation of traditional philosophy.

Medieval authors had possessed a 'sense of history' to the extent that they distinguished it formally from annals and substantially from poetry and insisted on its narrative and truthful character, but they showed little awareness of perspective or the scholarly problems of gaining access to 'antiquity'. They were indeed conscious of Christian tradition and various formulae of cultural change – 'reformation' or 'renovation', the conflict of 'ancients' and 'moderns', a 'translation of studies' (*translatio studii* or *sapientiae*, analogous to the *translatio imperii*), ideas of periodisation and even of anachronism – but they lacked the self-conscious, self-confident, self-promoting curiosity of Petrarch and his humanist successors.[7] Petrarch's first motive was a kind of artificial nostalgia. 'Among the many subjects that interested me I dwelt especially upon antiquity,' he wrote, 'for our own age has always repelled me, so that, had it not been for the love of those dear to me, I should have been born in any other period than our own. In order to forget my own time, I have continually striven to place myself in

---

4. Budé 1535, f. xvi^v.   5. See Seifert 1976.
6. Dionysius of Halicarnassus, *De arte rhetorica* XI.2.
7. See especially Schulz 1909; Spörl 1935; Goez 1958; Ladner 1952; Buck 1957, 1958; Renucci 1953.

spirit in other ages.'[8] And so indeed he did in his letters to Cicero, Livy and Homer. Yet Petrarch was also capable of sophisticated historical criticism, perhaps best illustrated in his exposure of a forged Austrian donation, allegedly made by Caesar to the Habsburgs; and he was careful to distinguish his own historical method both from scholasticism and from mere chronicle. 'I am neither the peace-maker among conflicting historians nor the collector of every minute fact', he remarked in the preface to his *De viris illustribus*, 'but rather, I am the copier of those whose verisimilitude or greater authority demands that they be given greater credence.'[9] Whatever their provenance, Petrarch's sentiments and attitudes have been essential for the modern study of history.

At the start humanist ideas of history consisted of hardly more than a litany of classical topoi praising history for its truthfulness (Cicero's *prima lex historiae*) and for its unique combination of pleasure (*voluptas*) and instruction (*utilitas*). Guarino da Verona represented Clio, the muse of history, with a trumpet in one hand and a book in the other, thus symbolising the polarity of history, torn between entertainment and education or between propaganda and erudition.[10] Most famous was the formula of Cicero, that history was 'the witness of time, the life of memory, the mistress of life and the messenger of antiquity'.[11] Such in general was the basis for the praise and conceptual inflation of historical studies carried on by Coluccio Salutati, Leonardo Bruni and other humanists, especially as expressed in letters, prefaces to historical works, educational treatises and finally in a new genre known as the 'art of history' (*ars historica*), on the analogy of the Horatian *ars poetica*.[12] The rising stock of historical studies was reflected in various ways, not only in historiography, including the publication and translation of classical historians, but also in chairs established for the teaching of history from the late fifteenth century and, perhaps most broadly, in certain humanist attempts to revise the traditional classification of the sciences, starting with Polydore Vergil's popular encyclopaedia organised on historical or genetic principles, according to the 'inventors of things' (the inventor of history itself being Moses, though its 'laws' were formulated by Cicero).[13]

8. Petrarch 1955, pp. 2–19 ('Letter to posterity'). See G. Billanovich 1951, 1974; Handschin 1964; Kessler 1978; Mommsen 1959, pp. 106–29. More generally, W. K. Ferguson 1948; Burke 1969.
9. Kohl 1974, p. 139; also Petrarch 1910.
10. Cited by Sabbadini 1922, p. 78.   11. Cicero, *De oratore* ii.2.36.
12. Cotroneo 1971 now replaces E. Maffei 1897. See also Landfester 1972; *Theoretiker humanistischer Geschichtsschreibung* 1971; *Grande antologia* 1964–, x, pp. 1–59 (Vegas); *Late Italian Renaissance* 1970, pp. 91–133 (Spini); Nadal 1965; Reynolds 1953; also n. 39 below.
13. Vergil 1536, p. 49.

It was mainly in the tradition of the *artes historicae* (to which Vergil's chapter on 'who first founded history' indeed belonged) that the Renaissance theory of history was worked out and that history began to declare its conceptual independence. George of Trebizond's treatise on rhetoric (1434), perhaps the first contribution to this genre, defined history not simply as past events (*res gestae*) or even the recollection thereof (*rerum gestarum memoria*) but rather as their accurate description (*rerum gestarum diligens expositio*) according to an order which was topical and chronological (*rerum et temporum ordo*).[14] History was concerned above all with causes, dealing as it did with motives, acts and consequences (*consilia primum, deinde actus, post eventus*). History's interest in vicarious experience (*plena exemplorum*) gave it common ground with oratory, but it was distinct because of its method (*modus historicus*) and its 'verisimilitude'. This line of argument was pursued in a number of later works, including those of Guarino, Lorenzo Valla, Paolo Cortese, Bartolommeo della Fonte, Giorgio Valla, Giovanni Pontano and Polydore Vergil. History was not only separated from rhetoric but also raised above poetry (contradicting Aristotle's dictum that this literary form was more philosophical) because of its explanatory power, practical value and ability, in Guarino's words, 'to gather many ages into one view'.[15] In his oration 'in praise of history' della Fonte went on to provide history with its own pedigree, beginning with Herodotus and Thucydides, while in his *Actius* of 1499 Pontano assembled a sort of *summa* of the humanist conception of history, emphasising its historical relations with poetry but extending its domain over 'places, peoples, nations, tribes, manners, laws, customs' and other aspects of human society.[16]

The largest claims on behalf of history had been made by that archrhetorician Lorenzo Valla in his history of Ferdinand of Spain. 'History is more robust than poetry because it is more truthful', Valla argued. 'It is oriented not towards abstraction but towards truth . . . [and] teaching by example.'[17] It was even superior to philosophy, since 'the discourse of historians exhibits more substance, more practical knowledge, more political wisdom . . ., more customs and more learning of every sort than the precepts of any of the philosophers'. In his *Disputationes dialecticae* Valla provided a theoretical justification for historical studies in the broadest 'philological' sense, while the practical value of historical scholarship he

14. George of Trebizond 1547, pp. 5ff.   15. Guarino da Verona 1915–19, II, p. 458.
16. Cited by Trinkaus 1960; Pontano 1943 (*Actius*).
17. L. Valla 1962, II, pp. 5–6 (*De rebus a Ferdinando Hispaniarum rege . . . gestis*).

demonstrated in a variety of writings, including critical notes on Livy and the New Testament, analyses of the texts of Roman law, translations of Herodotus and Thucydides, his famous 'declamation' on the forged Donation of Constantine and especially his efforts to restore the 'elegance' of the Latin language, which represented the central thrust of his attempts to reconstruct *Romanitas*, ancient civilisation as a whole, illustrating again the Petrarchan combination of aesthetic and historical motives.[18] In these philological enterprises Valla was followed by Erasmus, Guillaume Budé and the great 'critics' of a later generation, including Joseph Justus Scaliger, Isaac Casaubon and Mabillon.

PROTESTANT VARIATIONS

The Protestant Reformation introduced a new, yet also very old, element in the humanist theory and practice of history. It shifted attention again to the problem of tradition, largely religious tradition, but understood in a spiritual as well as an institutional sense; and it restored as well the old Augustinian scheme of history, 'four world monarchies', 'translation of empire' and all.[19] Yet humanist themes were preserved in modified confessional form, most notably in the motto 'back to the sources'. In general Luther celebrated the didactic value of history and on that basis declared that 'historians are the most useful people and the best teachers'.[20] Melanchthon was still more firm in his Ciceronian conviction that 'without history one remains for ever a child', which he tried to put into practice by making the study of history an integral part of his enterprise of 'reforming' the universities of Lutheran Germany by joining humanism and evangelical truth.[21] Calvin was more circumspect, arguing that Scripture and not history was the 'mistress of life'.[22] In general the evangelical Reformers made a fundamental, indeed fundamentalist, distinction between a pure spiritual doctrine, preserved over the centuries by a few scattered 'witnesses to the truth' and 'proto-martyrs', and base 'human traditions', which had produced an accumulation of 'error' (popular topic of historiography) and the corrupt institutions of the modern kingdom of the antichrist.[23] The

18. Kelley 1970a, ch. 1; Gaeta 1955.
19. See Polman 1933; Bertelli 1973; Joachimsen 1910; Bietenholz 1966.
20. Luther 1883–, I, p. 384 (*Vorrede zu Historia Galeatii Capellae*, 1538). Cf. Headley 1963; Lilje 1932.
21. Melanchthon 1834–60, II, col. 862 (*De studiis linguae Graecae*); col. 705 (preface to *Chronicon Carionis*); cf. Brettschneider 1880; Fraenkel 1961.
22. Calvin 1863–1900, II, col. 86 (*Commentarius in Epistolam Pauli ad Romanos*); cf. Berger 1955.
23. Bullinger 1548.

purpose of the 'new learning' was to recover the thought and life of the 'primitive church', especially by applying the techniques of historical criticism to degenerate modern tradition, an effort made by Gallicans like Charles Dumoulin as well as all sorts of evangelical interpreters.

From such perspectives history was once again universal, beginning not merely *ab urbe* but *ab orbe condito*, as Augustine's editor Juan Luis Vives put it, and ending in conjectures about the last judgement.[24] Because of religious controversy the early sixteenth century saw a revival of interest in the speculative philosophy of history. One example was Charles de Bovelles, a student of Lefèvre d'Étaples and admirer of Nicholas of Cusa, who interpreted the process of history as an unfolding (*evolutio*) of God's will and who divided it according to the conventional Augustinian seven ages (from creation to the flood, to Abraham, to David, to the birth of Christ and from Christ to the last times);[25] another was Guillaume Postel, who continued Pico's search for 'concord' with special emphasis on Judaic tradition, prophetic elements and cyclical patterns.[26] This was also the scheme accepted by the magisterial Reformers, including Luther, Melanchthon and Calvin, and by such standard overviews as the influential chronicle of Johann Cario and Nicolas Vignier's *Bibliothèque historiale*. The whole sweep of God's plan was the object of the new science of chronology established by J. J. Scaliger as well as innumerable cosmological, millenarian and prophetic visions which go far beyond the territories of history or of philosophy.

As the official historiographer of the Lutheran party Johann Sleidan was perhaps the most effective promoter of the Reformed vision of history, according to which the culmination of God's plan came with the last of the four great world empires, which reached its political pinnacle with Charles V and its religious perfection simultaneously with Luther.[27] Sleidan's life task was to explain this culminating phase through a pioneering combination of sacred and civil history, Eusebius in a sense joined to Thucydides, the perspective of Luther to the 'political and social sciences' of moderns like Commines and Seyssel. Responding to hostile criticisms, Sleidan issued an 'apology', in which he defended his veracity and non-partisanship in the most conventional Ciceronian terms, while acknowledging also that he had undertaken his work for the glory of God.[28] Sleidan's perspective (as well as

---

24. Vives 1782–90, VI, p. 393 (*De tradendis disciplinis sive de doctrina* V.2).
25. Bovelles 1520. See also Brause 1916; Bouwsma 1957; Patrides 1972.
26. Huppert 1970.
27. Sleidan 1559; see also Kelley 1980. 28. Sleidan 1558 (*Apologia*).

some of his materials) was shared by other Protestant interpreters of Christian tradition, most notably the martyrologists Jean Crespin and John Foxe and the Lutheran ideologist Flacius Illyricus, whose purpose was not only to reconstruct tradition through a revisionist sort of hagiography but also to provide lessons for modern readers.[29]

THE PRACTICE OF HISTORY

In various ways historiographical practice served as an impetus to historical theory in the sixteenth century.[30] Emulation of classical models became more sophisticated, especially with the translation of Greek historians; antiquarian enthusiasm became at once deeper, broader and more critical (resulting in the overthrow of various legends, including those of Roman and Carolingian as well as Trojan origins); the mutual reinforcement between the study of history and the practice of politics increased, especially because of the intrusion of religious controversy; and in general the effort to recapture the letter and spirit of 'antiquity', especially in the form of various national, civic and local traditions, became more intense and more widespread. Nor should one forget the effects of the new typographical art, which not only increased and made permanent the common stock of historical knowledge and interpretation but also shaped attitudes, assumptions and critical standards in more ways than are immediately perceptible. 'The invention of printing', as Guillaume Budé put it, 'is the restitution and restoration of antiquity'.[31]

Humanist historians tried not only to record and to explain but also to give shape to the accessible past on a European as well as a national level. Most influential was the work of Flavio Biondo, who like Petrarch lamented the corruption of the present (*praesens tempus*) but who, unlike him, tried to recapture the contours of the 'Middle Age' in terms of the civilising mission of the Roman Church.[32] Biondo's lead (if not his Romanism) was followed by many national historians writing in the Italian style, most notably Paolo Emilio in France, Polydore Vergil in England and Beatus Rhenanus and others in Germany, all of them marked by critical use of sources as well as conventional rhetorical style. Despite providentialist asides, these authors regarded history in general as a largely human enterprise which concerned the words and deeds of men and the causes and effects thereof (*consilia, causae, dictae, factae, casus et exitus*, in the words of

---

29. Flacius Illyricus 1556; see also Preger 1859–61; Scheible 1966a.
30. This is doubted by Cochrane 1981; the French and German evidence suggests otherwise.
31. Budé 1547, p. 63. 32. Biondo 1483; see also Hay 1959; Cochrane 1981.

Polydore Vergil).[33] This Latinate tradition was followed, often slavishly, by the national historians of the sixteenth and seventeenth centuries, although the best of them – Sigonio, Pasquier, Camden and others – greatly enriched the scholarly base of historical interpretation.[34]

The Florentine tradition of historiography remained the model for political narrative.[35] In his pioneering *Historiarum Florentini populi libri XII* Bruni enquired into social forces as well as individual motives, and in this he was emulated even more acutely by his followers Machiavelli and Guicciardini. Machiavelli shifted emphasis from diplomatic and military to constitutional history and in this connection claimed to find patterns, cyclical as well as dialectical, in the course of the history of his city. In a sense his *Istorie fiorentine* represented a case study in a larger project of political philosophy in which history represented a 'new' humanistic route, while the more general implications of historical analysis Machiavelli presented in his *Discorsi sopra la prima deca di Tito Livio*. Machiavelli applied in particular to Polybius' notion of the repeating historical cycle (ἀνακύκλωσις) to explain the change of constitutions from monarchy (and despotism) to aristocracy (and oligarchy) to democracy (and ochlocracy).[36] Even more pessimistically, Guicciardini followed Machiavelli in this sort of deterministic analysis, arguing that 'past events throw light upon the future, because the world has always been the same as it now is, and all that is now, or shall be hereafter, has been in times past. Things accordingly repeat themselves . . .'[37] This sort of naturalistic historical theory, though not always appropriate or acceptable in an age of religious enthusiasm, held fascination for many later political historians, including those held in the spell of 'Machiavellism' or 'Tacitism' – although the influence of Tacitus was equally important in the encouragement of romantic notions of Germanic origins and national character.[38]

THE THEORY OF HISTORY

The theory of history continued to be pursued most directly in the expanding genre of the *ars historica*, which from the 1540s was increasingly associated with problems of philosophy and method. The Aristotelian view

33. Vergil 1536, p. 49; see also Hay 1952.
34. Besides Cochrane 1981 and Kelley 1970a, see Levy 1967 and A. B. Ferguson 1979 as well as the standard works: Fueter 1936; Thompson 1942, 1.
35. Wilcox 1969; Baron 1966; Ullman 1973, pp. 321–43; Cochrane 1981, *passim*.
36. Machiavelli, *Discorsi* 1.2; cf. *Istorie fiorentine* v.1; see also F. Gilbert 1965; Albertini 1955.
37. Guicciardini 1951, p. 87 (B 114); see also Phillips 1977, 1983; Hassinger 1978.
38. Schellhase 1976; Etter 1966; Buschmann 1930; Tiedemann 1913; Joachimsen 1911; Toffanin 1921; and Borchardt 1971.

that history was inferior to, because less philosophical than, poetry was urged by Sperone Speroni in 1542 and more famously by Francesco Robortello in 1548.[39] Yet Speroni also defended the claims of history to be a species of 'rational philosophy' as well as a true art (as Campanella would do later), while Robortello insisted on the political and moral value of history. The debate over the dignity and purpose of history was carried on repetitiously by a series of authors, including Atanagi, Francesco Patrizi da Cherso, Ventura Cieco, Antonio Possevino, Orazio Toscanella, Antonio Riccoboni, Uberto Foglietta, Alessandro Sardi and non-Italian emulators like Bartholomaeus Keckermann, Reinhard Reineccius, J. J. Beurer and Gerardus Vossius. Perhaps the most penetrating discussion was that of Patrizi, who rejected the Ciceronian-Aristotelian orthodoxy and tried to extricate history from rhetoric by emphasising epistemology – history as 'the memory of human things' grasped according to what Foglietta called the 'Polybian norm' (*norma Polybiana*) of objective truth.[40] If the task of the philosopher was to understand causes, that of the historian was to understand both causes and their effects and so have a better grasp of truth (*cognition del vero*). For Patrizi history was indeed an autonomous, though a very eclectic, science.

The 'universal' character of history, insisted on by all parties in contemporary religious controversies, was urged by other contributors to the 'art of history'. Like Patrizi, the Platonising Spanish scholar Sebastian Fox-Morcillo urged the superiority of history over poetry because of its educational and cultural value, for without history (as Plato had said, and Cicero and Melanchthon after him) men would remain for ever children.[41] The most encyclopaedic celebration of universal history was the treatise of Christophe Milieu published in 1551 and divided into four categories: nature, prudence (the practical and mechanical arts), political organisation (*principatus*) and wisdom (*sapientia*), including literature and history itself besides the other branches of academic learning.[42] In the work of Milieu (as well as that of Polydore Vergil, Louis Le Roy, Henri de la Popelinière and others) we can see the promotion of history to another level, that is, the very

39. Speroni 1542 (*Dialogo della istoria*); Robortello 1548a, repr. in *Theoretiker humanistischer Geschichtsschreibung* 1971, along with the treatises of Atanagi, Patrizi da Cherso, Aconcio, Viperano, Foglietta, Sardi and Speroni, with further bibliography for each. See also n. 12 above.
40. F. Patrizi [da Cherso] 1560, p. 7.
41. Fox-Morcillo, *De historica institutione* in *Artis historicae penus* 1579, including also the treatises of Bodin, Patrizi da Cherso, Pontano, Baudouin, Viperano, Robortello, Milieu, Foglietta, Chytraeus, Secundus, Pezel, Zwinger, Sambucus, Riccoboni and the ancient works of Dionysius of Halicarnassus and Lucian.   42. Milieu 1551.

organising principle of the classification of sciences and a way of looking at particular disciplines, including philosophy and political science.

Religious controversy and the rise of scepticism called the study of history into question, perhaps even a state of crisis, in the middle years of the sixteenth century. In his analysis of the 'corruption of the arts' Vives expressed scepticism about the value of history, while Henricus Cornelius Agrippa, in an even more intemperate assault on the 'vanity of the arts and sciences', denied any fidelity or integrity to the study of history; and such charges were repeated by other critics, for instance Charles de la Ruelle, who refused to believe that history had any moral or political value.[43] Other religious partisans tried to shape history to their own confessional ends. Most famous was the confrontation between the *Ecclesiastica historia* (the so-called Magdeburg 'Centuries'), assembled by Flacius Illyricus and his *équipe* in order to give substance to the Lutheran perspective, and the monumental counter-history constructed by Cardinal Baronius, who accomplished for the Romanist interpretation of the western tradition what Bellarmine and others were attempting to do for theology. A significant by-product of this historical debate was the effort to establish principles of criticism and interpretation. Most wide-ranging on the Catholic side was the work of the Spanish theologian Melchor Cano, whose *Loci theologici* (1563) provided a critique and a rehabilitation of the ideas of tradition and authority.[44] Cano took a very utilitarian attitude towards historical evidence, and in order to make optimum use of it devised a set of rules for historical judgement, authentication, credibility and proof. So, on the Protestant side, did Flacius, who reorganised universal history according to Lutheran 'commonplaces' and formulated the proper 'method of writing history'. In this connection, and even more influentially, Flacius also laid down the rules – indeed founded the modern tradition – of historical hermeneutics, later celebrated and carried on by Schleiermacher, Dilthey and Gadamer.[45]

For history the most fruitful of all interdisciplinary contacts came with the field of law, and indeed this alliance in effect transformed history from a literary 'art' to a social 'science'. The context of this transformation was the massive sixteenth-century search for a proper and effective 'method' not only for particular disciplines but also for knowledge and philosophy in general. The problem of 'method' (*methodus*, but also implied by such terms

43. Vives 1782–90, VI, p. 101 (*De causis corruptarum artium* II.5); Agrippa 1530, cap. 5; La Ruelle 1574.
44. Cano 1776; see also Franklin 1963, pp. 103–15.
45. See Dilthey 1914–36, V, p. 334 (*Die Entstehung der Hermeneutik*).

as *institutio, partitiones, ratio*, etc.) was both pedagogical and 'scientific'; and while the emphasis was usually on mnemonic ordering and utility (after the fashion of Ramus and Melanchthon), some methodologists also considered improving the quality of knowledge and even discovering new knowledge.[46] This was the implication of the approaches of Cano, Flacius and Patrizi, and it would be even more deliberate in the French 'methods' of history in the latter part of the century. In these works attention was very consciously shifted to the reading rather than the writing of history, and so problems of testimony, veracity, authenticity and the criticism of sources became the objects of intense and 'methodical' study. The novelty of the French approach to the theory of history lay in its unique combination of three rather conventional intellectual patterns: the critical techniques of humanist philology, the universal chronological and geographical horizons of Protestant historiography and the sources and to some extent methods of civil law. The result was, both epistemologically and methodologically, to make the study of history more philosophical.

The first of these French 'methods' was François Baudouin's *De institutione historiae universae et eius cum iurisprudentia conjunctione* of 1561, which combined the so-called *mos gallicus* (legal humanism) with the *ars historica*. Like Simon Grynaeus, Baudouin celebrated the position of man in the 'theatre' of the world, which made him not only a protagonist but also an ideally placed observer and judge (*spectator, interpretator* and *iudex* are the key terms).[47] Baudouin had an ideological purpose, which was to preach the ecumenical message of the 'irenic' party in France on the eve of the Wars of Religion and to enquire into problems of Christian tradition; but this detracted in no way from the conceptual value of his attempt to expand and to reform historical studies. 'Historical studies must be placed on a solid foundation of law', he declared, 'and jurisprudence must be joined to history.' Among the reasons for this was that legal sources reflected the very substance of human (social, institutional and political) history, offered means of judging evidence and behaviour and suggested general patterns of historical interpretation. Like jurists, historians had to evaluate testimony, investigate political and social causes and effects, judge human motivation, attend to chronological order, take into account various geographical and anthropological facts and enquire into mythology and the problem of origins. For Baudouin the universalism of the Roman legal tradition was reinforced by the historical perspectives of Eusebius and of Polybius, whose

46. N. W. Gilbert 1960; J. L. Brown 1939.
47. Baudouin 1561; see also Kelley 1970a; Erbe 1978.

conception of history was 'catholic' as well as 'pragmatic' – 'like a body whose members may not be divided', Baudouin quoted. Such was the basis of Baudouin's historical ideal (*historia integra, universa, perpetua* or *perfecta*, as he variously called it).

The most celebrated of all early modern methodisers (next to Ramus and Descartes) was Jean Bodin, whose *Methodus ad facilem historiarum cognitionem* appeared in 1566. Bodin began by asking the standard questions of the *ars historica*, 'What is history and how many are its categories?'[48] Most generally, he answered, it was a 'true narrative', and it could be pursued either on a universal or on a particular level, that is, as a history of nations (*maximae respublicae*) or cities (*minimae respublicae*) or else as biography (*res gestae virorum*). Secondly, it could be viewed as the choice (*delectus*) and classification (*ordo et collectio*) of historical writings, and then as the criticism (*judicium*) of these works in the light of what modern scholarship had to say about the myths of national origins and the old, to Bodin offensively Romanist, theory of the 'four world monarchies', propagated by Sleidan and others and rejected by Bodin. Thirdly, the objective aspect was history as 'action', which is to say the drive of human will successively to sustinence (*necessitas*), comfort (*commoditas*) and finally the amenities of civilisation (*splendor* and *voluptas*). The culmination of these economic, social and cultural phases of history came, of course, in the creation of republics. In this systematic way Bodin set out on the 'new route' mapped out by Machiavelli in his *Discorsi*.

Like Baudouin Bodin wanted to strengthen the alliance between law and history, but he had a more grandiose and philosophical aim than the authors of the 'arts of history'. Like Baudouin, too, he drew upon the legal tradition as well as the art of history and humanist scholarship, but his interests were more eclectic and bound up with French national traditions, with comparative European law and with a system of universal law. According to Bodin, the basic categories of history were identical with those of the law (natural, human or civil, and divine), and its human substance corresponded in general to the 'law of nations' (*jus gentium*) in a modern sense. Bodin's aim was to study this 'world of nations' (as Vico would derivatively call it) through 'universal history' in its broadest sense. 'The best part of universal law resides in history' was his motto (*in historia juris universi pars optima est*).[49] The purpose of his 'method' was to reorganise topically the 'flowers' of history in order to assemble the most relevant materials for political

---

48. Bodin 1951, p. 114; see also Klempt 1960; *Jean Bodin* 1973, with full bibliography.
49. Bodin 1951, p. 108.

thought (*civilis disciplina*). It was in this sense that Bodin proclaimed history to be 'above all sciences' (*super scientias omnes*) and with this in mind that he defined the role of the philosophical historian or philosopher of history (*philosophistoricus*), which was to 'combine the narration of facts with precepts of wisdom'.

Like law itself, the implication was, history was a form of wisdom (*sapientia*), and indeed this was made explicit by another 'method of reading history' published in 1579 by one of Bodin's first disciples. 'Among the aphorisms of the ancients . . .', wrote Pierre Droit de Gaillard, 'the most remarkable was that of Chilon, one of the seven sages: Know thyself. Now this knowledge depends upon history, sacred as well as profane, universal as well as particular.'[50] Gaillard celebrated the alliance (*conference*) of history with other disciplines, indeed with the whole humanist encyclopaedia, and concluded 'in a word, all disciplines take their source and principles wholly from history, as from an overflowing fountain'. For the rest Gaillard's work was a laudatory survey of the contours and glories of French history and the moral and political lessons to be derived from its study.

Building even more comprehensively on Bodin's 'method' was the work of the Huguenot historiographer Henri Lancelot Voisin de la Popelinière, who in 1599 published a pair of works, *Histoire des histoires, avec L'Idée de l'histoire accomplie*, to which was appended 'Le Dessein de l'histoire nouvelle des François'. La Popelinière prided himself on standing 'above passion and party' and, especially in his earlier history of France during the civil wars, on his treatment of the past in terms of cause and effect (*la cause, le progrès, bonne ou mauvaise issue*).[51] For La Popelinière history represented not merely a genre but a mode of thought which affected to interpret the actions of men 'according to the times, the places, their causes, progress and results', and for this reason it was a more useful discipline than either philosophy or political thought. Echoing Bodin, then, La Popelinière concluded that history was above all arts and sciences.

THE PATTERNS OF HISTORY

In his proposal for a 'new history' of France La Popelinière was in fact continuing an old enterprise, which was to find the basic patterns of the national past. The most popular scheme of periodisation, derived from Florus, had been suggested by Claude de Seyssel in his *Histoire singulier du*

50. Gaillard 1579, p. 1; cf. Gaillard 1578. See also Dubois 1977.
51. La Popelinière 1599; see also Kelley 1971.

roy Louis XII and taken up by the royal historiographer Bernard Du Haillan and the regius professor of Greek Louis Le Roy.[52] The conceit of the four ages (applied also to England by Polydore Vergil) included infancy from the beginning to Clovis, youth down to the Merovingians, maturity under the Carolingians and old age under the Capetians. La Popelinière himself proposed a five-stage periodisation – ancient, Roman, Gallic, Frankish and modern French. What was most novel was La Popelinière's aspiration to incorporate into historical narrative an account of the growth of all the arts and sciences. This had also been the intention of Le Roy, whose *De la vicissitude ou varieté des choses en l'univers* (1575) has been called 'the first treatise devoted to the history of civilization'.[53] Le Roy also wrote historical sketches of the history of political thought and of philosophy itself, while La Popelinière (expanding on a conventional theme of the *ars historica*) proposed a most interesting interpretation of the rise and progress of historical consciousness – first a period of 'natural history' (oral tradition and superstition), next 'poetic history' (Homer or Moses, for example), then with the establishment of a rational chronology 'continuous history' expressed in chronicles and annals, fourthly a 'civilised' sort of historical writing coinciding with the emergence of other arts and sciences and finally (so La Popelienière hoped) an age of 'perfect history', which is to say the 'philosophical' kind of history later to be made famous by Voltaire.[54]

By the end of the sixteenth century history had, in the eyes of many observers, attained a position of eminence, sometimes elevated above other disciplines, since it was regarded as the source and even the ordering principle of knowledge. Careful distinctions were maintained between the history of nature and of culture (*res naturales* and *res humanae*, according to Baudouin and Bodin) and between sacred and profane history.[55] Yet in a sense all three of Bodin's varieties of history – natural, civil and divine – found a place in historical thought; for if the Italianate 'art of history' was secular and human, Protestant historiography adopted Eusebian perspectives on divine history, while Bodinian method invoked naturalistic means of explanation, including what Bodin himself called 'geohistory'. In the Renaissance as in the present century a distinction may be made between the analytical and the speculative philosophy of history, the first being represented by discussions of the problems of criticism, explanation and

52. Seyssel 1961; 1981 (Kelley's introduction); see also Le Roy 1570 (*Les Monarchiques*); Du Haillan 1570.
53. Le Roy 1575; see also Gundersheimer 1966.
54. Le Roy 1567, 1553 ('L'origine, progres et perfection de la philosophie'); La Popelinière 1599. See also Baron 1959; Kinser 1971.   55. Baudouin 1561; Bodin 1951.

interpretation in treatises on method, and the second by discussions of universal chronology, periodisation and cultural progress. In that period, too, there were debates between those who regarded history as an autonomous field and those, especially artificial and conservative 'methodisers' like Aconcio and Vossius, who hoped to reduce history to – or perhaps better, to dissolve it in – a logical system.[56] Of course there were also those who denied 'history' in any form and identified the term with the raw material of empirical investigation, according to the style made famous by Francis Bacon.

In the classification of sciences history certainly improved its ranking dramatically, being taught widely in (especially Protestant) universities and gaining parity (for instance in the pedagogical scheme of the Lutheran David Chytraeus)[57] even with medicine, jurisprudence and philosophy. But it was in the company of political philosophy that the study of history rose perhaps highest in the estimation of Renaissance scholars, beginning with Machiavelli's 'new route' and including such later followers as Bodin, whose *Six livres de la République* of 1576 was in effect an expansion of chapter 6 of his *Methodus*. The vogue of Tacitus and the analytical, 'pragmatic' history of Polybius, translated and celebrated by Casaubon in 1609, reinforced the interest in political narrative as practised by Machiavelli, Guicciardini and even Sleidan. 'Political science belongs wholly to history . . .', wrote Casaubon's friend Daniel Heinsius in the early seventeenth century, for 'political science, without history, is tortured and wasted away by tasteless, disgusting and pedantic distinctions and minute divisions of philosophers' – meaning the most superficial of the 'arts of history'.[58] Here sounds again, in the rhetoric of this Dutch scholar, the theme of political humanism: 'If history have no professorship, if all universities be closed', he wrote, 'she will always have an honourable reception in palaces and in the innermost chambers of kings and princes.'

Yet history continued to have a broader philosophical connection. Having reshaped the humanist 'encyclopaedia' by placing it in a long perspective, historical studies in effect subsumed philosophy and created what was already emerging as an academic speciality in the sixteenth century – the history of philosophy. Having become involved in fundamental debates over proper and effective scientific 'method', history raised itself in the eyes of some scholars to the level of an autonomous science and opened the way to the analytical philosophy of history. Having, finally,

56. Vossius 1623. Cf. Cabrera de Cordoba 1611.
57. Klatt 1908, p. 35; see also Scherer 1927.   58. Heinsius 1943, p. 12.

been conscripted into religious controversy by Protestant and Catholic ideologists, history turned to transcendent questions and passed on to an early phase of modern speculative philosophy of history. For Heinsius indeed 'that fretful animal whom we call man' saw a kind of salvation in historical study. 'He would be free from the limits of time and space . . . and would gather into one focus the immeasurably great vastness of generations', Heinsius wrote. 'He would view in a moment an infinite multitude of matters and affairs.'[59] He had become *homo historicus* in a sense which would apply, paradoxically, to Descartes as well as to Descartes's nemesis Vico. And history had become a permanent factor, whether negative or positive, in western philosophy.

59. *Ibid.*, p. 10.

PART 3

SUPPLEMENTARY MATERIAL

XIII

APPENDICES

22

THE AVAILABILITY OF ANCIENT WORKS

INTRODUCTION

How did you study the Presocratics in the Renaissance? This simple question has no simple answer. In 1567 Élie Vinet did so by commenting on a late Latin text, itself adapted from Greek sources: the *De die natali* of Censorinus.[1] In less than a decade Henri Estienne and Joseph Scaliger did so in a far more original and systematic way, by collecting and analysing fragments quoted by Clement of Alexandria, Simplicius and Sextus Empiricus.[2] Ten years after that Isaac Casaubon could go even further, not just assembling *testimonia* and fragments but setting them into a new historical context. In 1584 Scaliger found himself baffled by Diogenes Laertius' statement that Thales had written 'only two works, *On the Solstice* and *On the Equinox*, since he considered other matters capable of being apprehended (κατaληπτά)' (1.23). 'This', Scaliger admitted with unusual humility, 'I do not understand.'[3] But in the same year Casaubon overcame the difficulty with ease. Set the text into its period, he suggested; consider the 'uncultured and primitive' period in which Thales wrote. Surely one should amend the text, economically, by adding an alpha-privative to κατaληπτά. Thales had considered phenomena other than solstices and equinoxes ἀκατάληπτα – 'incapable of being apprehended'.[4] This was a natural attitude, after all, given his position at the very beginnings of Greek thought.[5]

This little story illustrates some of the large problems posed by any discussion of availability of ancient philosophical sources in the Renaissance. It reveals rapid progress in the accumulation of texts, increasing sophistication in their interpretation and the development of a more and more historical perspective towards them on the part of their modern

1. Vinet 1568.
2. Estienne and Scaliger 1573; see Cavini 1977, p. 10. For an earlier publication of the fragments of Pythagoras, see Heninger 1974, p. 66.
3. J. J. Scaliger 1584, p. 180: 'Haec ultima non intelligo.'   4. Diogenes Laertius 1594, ad 1.23.
5. Casaubon may have owed his historical insight to Scaliger; see Grafton 1983–, I, ch. 7.

interpreters.[6] Yet in isolation it could prove deceptive. By no means everyone accepted the evidence and interpretations that these pioneering philologists made available. At the end of the seventeenth century and the beginning of the eighteenth, Isaac Newton and many others still tried aggressively to show that the Presocratics had developed a modern and still valid natural philosophy.[7] New editions and new visions of the texts, however famous the scholars who created them, could not refute well-founded myths about the early history of philosophy. And all generalisations about the state of knowledge of ancient texts in the Renaissance should be made with this substantial reservation well in mind.

Four periods, perhaps, saw the most distinctive developments. From 1390 to 1420, first of all, the range of Latin philosophy, including works little known in the Middle Ages (like Lucretius, *De rerum natura*) and much material familiar then (like the philosophical works of Cicero), was gathered into coherent collections by avid hunters like Poggio Bracciolini under the direction of such obsessive bookhounds as Coluccio Salutati and Niccolò Niccoli.[8] At the same time, the pupils of the émigré Byzantine scholar Manuel Chrysoloras began to retranslate the major ethical and political works of Aristotle and to translate vital new sources like Plato's major dialogues.[9] The work of men like Leonardo Bruni was not always so original as has been argued by believers in the modernity of the Renaissance; some at least of their 'new' translations amounted merely to rewritings of older ones in more classical Latin.[10] Yet the effects of this first burst of interest were profound. The new translations of works of direct political and social bearing, like the pseudo-Aristotelian *Oeconomics*, reached a wide public even outside the university faculties that had traditionally dominated the study of Aristotle.[11] True, the new texts do not yet seem to have infiltrated into formal philosophical teaching; the first professor of Platonic philosophy in an Italian university, Francesco Patrizi da Cherso, assumed his chair late in the sixteenth century.[12] But they had a dramatic impact on the moral and political writings of early fifteenth-century humanists and statesmen.[13]

6. *Storia delle storie* 1981–, I, pp. 138–48, 161–2; Piaia 1983.
7. See in general McGuire and Rattansi 1966; Walker 1972.
8. The standard work remains Sabbadini 1967, now supplemented for Latin authors by *Texts and Transmission* 1983. See also Reynolds and Wilson 1974.
9. See in general Cammelli 1941–54, I.
10. No full study of the humanist translations has been made. See in general the tentative but unsurpassed work of Garin 1951.   11. See, e.g., Soudek 1968.   12. Schmitt 1981, § III.
13. For a case in point see Francesco Barbaro's *De re uxoria* (1415–16) in *Earthly Republic* 1978, pp. 179–228.

In the second period, *c.* 1440–70, great patrons and single-minded 2)
scholars come to the fore. Pope Nicholas V and Cosimo de' Medici paid
stipends to translators like George of Trebizond and Marsilio Ficino, who
were in turn enabled to set about producing full translations of and
commentaries on larger and more technical works of Greek philosophy. If
George's new full translation of and commentary on Ptolemy's *Almagest*
encountered withering criticism from experts in astronomy, his version of
Aristotle's *Rhetoric* exists in twenty-three manuscripts and would eventually be reprinted some twenty-five times, while Ficino's new, complete
Latin Plato, with his commentaries, came to be the distorting window
through which all of educated Europe viewed Plato for centuries.[14] In this
period such late-antique works as the *corpus Hermeticum* received the full
Latin translations that made them the foundation for the natural magic of
the late fifteenth and sixteenth centuries.[15] At the same time, the earliest
printers set to work. At first, to be sure, they concentrated on traditionally
popular texts. Even Galen – whose popularity is usually thought to have
waned in the Renaissance – found only a handful of editions until after 1500
(compared to more than 600 between 1500 and 1600).[16] Yet they did at least
make the standard works – Cicero's *Philosophica*, Pliny's *Naturalis historia* –
accessible not in dozens but in hundreds of copies.[17]

From 1490 to 1530, one great intellectual and publisher dominates the 3)
scene. Aldus Manutius, who settled at Venice in 1494, produced during the
next twenty years a series of *editiones principes* for virtually all the classic
Greek authors. Before 1500, bravely disregarding the technical difficulties
and the limitations of the market, he had printed Aristotle and
Theophrastus. In the 1520s, after Aldus himself was dead, the firm still
managed to bring out Galen and the Greek commentators on Aristotle. By
then a Hellenist could read, in printed form, virtually the whole corpus of
ancient philosophy.[18]

Between 1550 and 1580, finally, the advances of earlier years were 4)
consolidated. In great printing centres like Paris and Basle, bilingual
editions of the Greek texts that Aldus had printed in the original made these
available to the great majority of scholars who could not read Greek

14. George of Trebizond 1984, pp. 322, 671–87, 698–701; Schoell 1926, ch. 1.
15. Yates 1964.   16. Durling 1961.
17. Examination of Flodr 1973 reveals a vast predominance of the Latin Aristotle (11 editions of the
    works, 147 of individual works, 22 of supposititious works, 370 editions of commentaries) and
    Cicero (296 works) before 1500. Yet we should also note that even one edition of a new author (like
    Ficino's Latin Plato) meant a vast increase in accessibility (in the case of the Plato, 1,025 copies were
    made of the 1484 edn. at the cost of a few manuscripts; see Ficino 1937, I, pp. cliv–v).
18. For the range and quality of these enterprises see Sicherl 1976; Lowry 1979.

unaided. Translations could now be compared and evaluated and commentaries assembled, and a lively monographic literature grew up in which controversy raged about the development of ancient thought.[19] The last gaps in the corpus of works in print were plugged by the appearance of Sextus and Stobaeus. And the libraries that were coming to be a regular feature of college and university organisation now made this entire pullulating mass of text and gloss available even for those not rich or dedicated enough to build collections for themselves.

This general survey necessarily glosses over many varieties of individual experience. A great collector and diligent reader like Coluccio Salutati could have direct access to an astounding variety of philosophical sources before the great age of translation (not to mention that of printing) had begun. His library included the Latin standbys like Macrobius on the *Somnium Scipionis*, the *Timaeus* in Chalcidius' translation and the *Phaedo* in Aristippus', Ptolemy's *Almagest* and Apuleius' *Asclepius*, much Aristotle and much Aristotelian commentary.[20] If it did not cover the entire range from Ramon Lull to Cicero's *Laelius*, as Pico's library did a century later, Salutati's collection nonetheless offered a more varied and less exclusively literary selection from the ancient philosophers than one might expect from modern secondary accounts.[21] And finally, we should not forget that the dedicated student could always annex a new text to his collection, at any time, by the simple (if laborious) expedient of making his own copy. To that extent, the increasing availability of texts did not bring about a revolution in the nature of philosophical work, even if it did produce a widening of horizons among philosophers.[22]

More complex than the simple question of availability of texts is the larger one of how – and whether – classical texts took on a new meaning when understood in terms of a different, wider context. Here the evidence seems less ambiguous. An occasional medieval philosopher showed awareness of historical and chronological questions. Nicole Oresme, for example, took pains to point out that the Ptolemy who wrote the *Almagest* in the second century AD could not have been one of the Ptolemies who ruled Egypt before Caesar conquered it.[23] But sensitivity to such issues was uncommon in an intellectual world attuned not to problems of historical context but to nice points of logic and semantics. Medieval philosophers

---

19. See, e.g., Hooykaas 1958.   20. Ullman 1963 reconstructs Coluccio's library.
21. For a reconstruction see Kibre 1936.
22. On the means by which Ficino – using manuscript sources of considerable linguistic difficulty – built up his extraordinary command of the Neoplatonic tradition, see Saffrey 1959; M. J. B. Allen 1984a, ch. 10.   23. Pedersen 1974.

rarely treated the ancients as historical individuals working in a distinct time and place. Instead they treated the wisest ancients, like Plato and Seneca, as impersonal *auctoritates* rather than fallible individuals.[24] Ancients with erroneous views – like Epicurus – they merely abused as believers in the primacy of sensual pleasures, including fornication.[25] And they made little effort to reconstruct the coherent doctrinal schools to which – as well-known texts suggested – the ancient philosophers belonged. Albertus Magnus – for example – called Plato 'princeps Stoicorum' and identified Pythagoreans as well as Platonists as Stoics.[26]

By the fourteenth century, individual humanists had arrived at a more nuanced and historical vision of the ancients. Petrarch, writing *De sui ipsius et multorum ignorantia,* tried to put Cicero in an exact historical position – that of a philosopher whose concentration on moral issues and use of eloquent, persuasive discourse marked him out as the product of the greatest age of Roman culture – and whose polytheism marked him out with equal sharpness as a pagan deprived by the dates of his birth and death of knowledge of the true religion.[27] Cicero, in short, became not *auctoritas* but *auctor* – a human and historical figure whose failings could be explained by reference to his personal failings and the assumptions of his culture.

Soon such views appeared in formal discussions of ancient texts. Pietro da Muglio, commenting on the reference to the death of Socrates in Boethius' *De consolatione philosophiae* I, prose 3, shows us the precise moment at which medieval collections of anecdotes began to be transformed into the beginnings of a critical history of philosophy:

He gives the example of Socrates, who was the teacher of Plato (and Plato was the teacher of Aristotle). And that is an old example, and he says that many felt ill will towards Socrates since the evil always disagree with the good, since good and evil are contraries. And Socrates had many misfortunes in Athens, and was a wise man and suffered many seditions – that is, popular complaints – against himself, especially while the Thirty Tyrants ruled Athens. And those Thirty Tyrants wanted [Socrates] to adore the sun, for they adored the sun, and he refused to do so, and said, 'The sun is a sort of fiery torch.' They, seeing that he refused to believe, at length took him and imprisoned him and condemned him to death. Many – especially Socrates's pupils – took this ill, that he should die, . . . and wanted to break into the prison to rescue him. And he said to them: 'I am unwilling. For I am in my fatherland. If they harm me, what will foreigners do?'[28]

---

24. Even the most learned of the late medieval friars took this view, as is shown by Smalley 1960.
25. So Antoninus of Florence, for whom see Surtz 1957a, pp. 24–5.
26. See in general Stein 1888.
27. *Renaissance Philosophy of Man* 1948, pp. 47–133.   28. Quoted by Garin 1961, pp. 28–9.

By the fifteenth century such interests were finding expression in systematic essays on the lives and views of the ancient philosophers. Leonardo Bruni wrote sharp and coherent lives of Cicero and Aristotle, Sicco Polenton less focused ones of Cicero, Seneca and Pliny; Marsilio Ficino analysed Plato's horoscope as well as his behaviour and his teachings.[29] Bruni also showed that modern scholars could collect δόξαι of the ancient philosophers as Cicero and Varro had done. His *Isagogicon moralis disciplinae*, which now seems a dry and slender treatise based on few and familiar sources, started a fifteenth-century fashion which was ably carried on by Cristoforo Landino, Bartolomeo Scala and Ficino.[30]

The vices of this early literature seem all too apparent to a modern reader. Scala's *Epistola de nobilioribus philosophorum sectis et de eorum inter se differentiis* of April 1458 begins from Varro's idea – reported by St Augustine – that one could distinguish 288 philosophical sects 'non quae iam essent, sed quae esse possent' (*De civitate Dei* XIX.1). In dismissing this classification as over-subtle and reducing the number of real sects to the three that disagreed over the *summum bonum*, Scala merely repeated Varro's own rebuttal of his original hypothesis.[31] In adding to Varro's arguments a long account of the disagreements of the philosophers over the nature of the universe, he merely grafted one piece of tralatician Roman doxography on to another, for his account of the *physici* came almost word for word from Cicero.[32] When he tripped over contradictory evidence in his ancient sources, Scala simply gave all possible interpretations and went off rejoicing, leaving his putative correspondent in the dark:

> On penalties [in the afterlife] the Platonists also go wrong, when they say that all of them are temporary and, so to speak, purgative. For, as the Christians rightly say, many of them are eternal, as St Augustine says in *De civitate Dei* XX. Yet I recall reading in Plato's *Phaedo* that some are hurled down to Tartarus, because of the great sins they committed in their lifetime, so that they may never emerge. And Vergil seems to have drawn from Plato his remark, 'Sedet eternumque sedebit, infelix Theseus' [Unhappy Theseus remains and will remain for ever (*Aeneid* VI.617–18)]. But to judge between these is not for this occasion or this essay; to avoid any error we have stuck to Augustine for now.[33]

And when the evidence was too overwhelming to be cited, Scala simply ignored it – as he did when he pretended that no Christians had accepted Plato's 'ridiculas transmigrationes' of human souls, even though he must have known the texts on transmigration by Origen that had captivated his

---

29. Bruni 1928, pp. 113–20, 41–9.   30. Bruni 1928, pp. 20–41; A. Brown 1979, pp. 263–6.
31. Cf. the text in Stein 1888, p. 541 with Augustine, *De civitate Dei* XIX.1.
32. Cf. the text in Stein 1888, pp. 543–4 with Cicero, *Academica* II.118 and *De natura deorum* I.25–41.
33. Stein 1888, pp. 550–1; for the order of the text see A. Brown 1979, p. 265 n. 30.

contemporary Matteo Palmieri and would form the basis of the *Città di Vita*.[34] Yet even Scala did present, in systematic and accessible form, some generally accurate historical material. And Bruni at least reached a far higher level of learning and acuity. His *Vita Aristotelis*, for all its dwelling on the details of Aristotle's personal appearance, also uses the rhetorical device of σύγκρισις – systematic comparison, a technique practised by Bruni's teacher Chrysoloras[35] – to present genuinely insightful thumbnail sketches of both Aristotle and Plato as philosophers:

> Plato, a remarkable and outstanding man, was endowed with knowledge of many things of all sorts, and so eloquent that his speech seems to surpass human capabilities. But his teachings sometimes seem to fall into the category that rely on the persuasion of a favourably minded audience rather than on rigorous demonstration. For many of his teachings on the nature of the soul and its transmigration and descent into bodies seem to be more pronouncements than proofs . . . Moreover, Plato's doctrines are varied and unclear. For Socrates is brought on in every scene, and races, so to speak, from the starting-block to the finishing-line, and keeps no order in his teachings, but treats now this, now that, arbitrarily, and in argument seems less to say what he thinks than to refute the views of others. But Aristotle was both more cautious in propounding his views – for he sets about nothing that he cannot prove – and more modest in venturing opinions. Indeed, he seems to have striven to be of help in the practical affairs of everyday life rather than to have pondered things alien, disgusting and profitless.[36]

Here Bruni transcended the different stereotypes beloved of humanists and scholastics. He appreciates Plato's eloquence without losing sight of Aristotle's rigour and dedication to the realities of the earthly city. Perhaps, then, it is fair to say that the new philosophical literature of the fifteenth-century humanists at last established that the ancient philosophers had been human as well – and made it possible to see that they were simply different from one another in their aims, methods and styles.

In the course of the fifteenth and sixteenth centuries, the humanists' historical approach to classical philosophy developed in three directions. In the first – and simplest – place, the humanists mastered the language of Greek and Roman philosophy more securely than anyone had since ancient times. Bruni, early in the fifteenth century, stood out from earlier commentators on the pseudo-Aristotelian *Oeconomics* precisely because he knew that in that work 'tragoedia' meant Greek tragedy rather than 'sermo vituperativus'.[37] By the end of the century Angelo Poliziano had produced formidable essays on technical terms like ἐντελέχεια and ἐνθύμημα. Direct study of the Greek text of Aristotle and his commentators repeatedly

34. See, e.g., Walker 1985, § XII.   35. Baxandall 1971, p. 80.   36. Bruni 1928, p. 45.
37. See the elaborate study in *Der Kommentar* 1975, pp. 99–118 (Goldbrunner).

enabled Poliziano to refute both the Byzantine émigrés who had imported
philosophical Greek into Italy and the ignorant Latins 'qui se peripateticos
hodie profitentur'.[38] In the sixteenth century, finally, scholars began to
emend philosophical Greek successfully by conjecture. Michael Sophianus
and Nicasius Ellebodius emended Aristotle's *Poetics* with a better grasp of
his usage and vocabulary than most of their successors in the eighteenth and
nineteenth centuries.[39] And if the new mastery of the terms sometimes led
scholars like Ellebodius and Daniel Heinsius into over-confident efforts to
rearrange the transmitted texts by wholesale transposition,[40] it also laid the
foundation for such solid contributions to historical study as the philosophical lexica of the splendid Rudolphus Goclenius, which set out the key terms
of philosophy systematically, with close attention to individual variations in
context and usage.[41]

Second, and more important, scholars from Valla to Lipsius reassembled
the main tenets of each of the great ancient philosophical schools into
coherent systems clearly different from one another and from Christianity.
In the fourteenth century, for example, Stoicism seemed an ancient
anticipation of Christianity, given its stress on asceticism and self-control,
while Epicureanism seemed a mere code word for antinomianism and
immorality. But the rediscovery of Diogenes Laertius and Lucretius made
clear that Epicurus had been far more than a mere lover of the pleasures of
the flesh. As an individual, he had been a profound student of the fears and
weaknesses of the human spirit and an austere and contemplative sage. As a
thinker, he seemed to have recommended such reasonable positions as the
acceptance of moderate pleasure from the good things of the natural world
or the pursuit of perfect tranquillity of soul.[42] Erasmus and More took
pleasure in showing the high morality of many genuinely Epicurean
beliefs.[43] Meanwhile, closer examination of the tenets of the Stoics showed
that these rested on assumptions about the order of the universe that no true
Christian could accept. By the late sixteenth century no philologist would
commit the solecism of confusing the terms of the ancient philosophical
schools with their Christian homonyms. Isaac Casaubon – who liked to read
Seneca not for information but for consolation in his many troubles –
admitted that the morals he found in the *Epistulae* had not been intended to
be read as he read them. He described his method as one of 'accommodating' sentences that had been false when Seneca framed them to the Christian

38. Poliziano 1489, sigs. b iiii^v–viii^r; 1972, IV, pp. 104–6; cf. Kraye 1983.
39. Kassel 1962; cf. also Wagner 1973.   40. See in general Sellin 1974.
41. Goclenius 1613.   42. Garin 1961, pp. 72–92.   43. Surtz 1957a.

verities that alone could validate them.[44] Still later, Jean Leclerc would use the Christian interpretation of Seneca's *anima* in his manual of hermeneutics as a prime example of misreading the classics.[45]

Third, the late sixteenth and seventeenth centuries saw a vast effort to codify and arrange all of ancient philosophy and modern commentary on it. Polyhistors like Jonsius, Vossius and Fabricius assembled the first systematic biobibliographies of the ancient philosophers. Historians like Hornius and Stanley tried to impose at least a chronological order on the development of the ancient sects. By the middle of the seventeenth century, vast amounts of matter had been collected, to serve as the material for that new and critical study of philosophy that would be created by Bayle and Brucker.[46]

To end as we began, it will not do to exaggerate the prevalence of this historical approach. The humanists rediscovered much that was historically baffling. For example, when they imported Plato from Byzantium, they imported along with him both the pseudepigraphic works of Hermes Trismegistus that were thought to be his sources and the Neoplatonic commentators who had imposed foreign systems on the dialogues. Like most Byzantine scholars, western ones tended to accept the claims of the Neoplatonists, to see them not as appropriating Plato for their own ends but as – in Ficino's words – 'laying bare' the true theology which Plato had veiled 'both by mathematical numbers and figures and by poetic inventions'.[47] The Renaissance thus preserved and passed on to a vast audience many serious errors about the nature and history of Greek philosophy – errors which were, naturally, quite fruitful ones philosophically.

In the second place, the universities and the presses kept producing traditional as well as up-to-date materials. If the publication of medieval Aristotelian commentaries fell off after 1535, it certainly did not cease, and as late as the 1570s the standard large editions of Aristotle normally included the old Latin translations with the commentaries of Averroes.[48] And this traditional form of Aristotelian study experienced, if anything, a renewal at the end of the sixteenth century, when renewed doctrinal controversy impressed the virtues of scholastic theology on Catholics and Protestants alike.

In the third place, and most important, it is not altogether clear that any

44. Casaubon 1850, I, p. 21.   45. Leclerc 1712, I, p. 304.
46. Braun 1973; *Storia delle storie* 1981–.
47. *Prefaces* 1861, p. 601. The Aristotelian corpus also included spurious texts and unhistorical interpretations, of course; see *Platon et Aristote* 1976, pp. 359–76 (Cranz); Schmitt 1984, § IX.
48. Minio-Paluello 1972, pp. 483–500.

Renaissance reader was fully successful in reading his texts historically. After all, Plato and Aristotle worked in contexts that Renaissance scholars could not fully understand, using concepts that generations of commentators had distorted to meet new needs. To that extent, one should not exaggerate the validity of the scholars' new vision of the past of philosophy.[49]

CLASSICAL AUTHORS AND THEIR AVAILABILITY

ALEXANDER of Aphrodisias (*c.* AD 200), a Peripatetic philosopher, wrote on a variety of moral and metaphysical subjects. Some of his works – above all *De fato* and *De intellectu* – circulated in Latin in the Middle Ages and played a prominent role in thirteenth-century controversies over Averroism. These works figured anew in sixteenth-century debates over the freedom of the will and fate, while Alexander's *Opera* reached print in Greek, almost complete, in 1513–16. This renewed interest and wealth of material stimulated retranslations (e.g., *De fato*, 1544) and translations of works previously unavailable (e.g., *Quaestiones naturales et morales*, 1516 (in part), 1541).[50]

APULEIUS (second century AD) was widely known in the Middle Ages as the author of a work on Plato's teachings, an adaptation of the pseudo-Aristotelian *De mundo* and the *Asclepius*, a translation from the Greek *corpus Hermeticum*. His *Metamorphoses* and *Apologia* survived the Middle Ages in one Monte Cassino manuscript and did not circulate until the fourteenth century. These works soon found a receptive audience for their rich information about ancient magic and religion. Giovanni Andrea de' Bussi printed the *Metamorphoses* and other works in 1469, and Filippo Beroaldo equipped it with a rich commentary in 1500. Reassembled and explicated, the Apuleian corpus had considerable impact on Renaissance thought.[51]

ARCHIMEDES (287–212 BC) produced a very large variety of works on mathematics, statics and dynamics. He offered his readers not just a large corpus of demanding mathematical problems and solutions, but an example of science which seemed to lie outside Euclidean norms (in bringing arithmetic and geometry together) and outside Aristotelian prejudices (in treating physical questions quantitatively). Though many of his works circulated in more or less intelligible medieval versions, the Renaissance saw especially intense interest in the Greek texts and their interpretation. Iacobus

49. Cf. *Platon et Aristote* 1976, pp. 359–76 (Cranz).
50. *Catalogus translationum* 1960–, I, pp. 77–131.
51. *Texts and Transmission* 1983, pp. 15–18; Krautter 1971.

Cremonensis translated some of the geometrical texts at the request of Nicholas V. Poliziano and Giorgio Valla both used the Codex A, the now lost source of later manuscripts, and Valla made some of the new material available in his great encyclopaedia *De rebus expetendis et fugiendis* (1501). Regiomontanus and Pirckheimer, among others, used the new material in manuscript. A Greek-Latin edition by Th. Venatorius made both the original texts and Cremonensis' version available in 1544; and for the rest of the sixteenth century such prominent mathematicians as Tartaglia and Commandino occupied themselves with editing and explicating individual parts of the corpus. This new material, and the numerous controversies that attended its publication, form the essential background for the late sixteenth-century transformations of physical science and mathematics.[52]

ARISTOTLE (384–322 BC) left a rich corpus of technical treatises covering both the methods and the substance of most areas of philosophy. These came into wide circulation during the first century BC; in the Middle Ages, Latin versions, made at first from the Arabic and then from the Greek, presented the logical, scientific and metaphysical works to the western public. They provided both the language and the framework for university arts teaching and philosophical discourse for centuries to come. Accordingly, it cannot be said in any simple sense that the Renaissance saw Aristotle's works suddenly made available. True, Renaissance humanists rediscovered, translated (or retranslated) and commented exhaustively on the Aristotelian works that dealt with the literary topics of most interest to them, the *Rhetoric* and the *Poetics*. They used their philological skills to argue about the authenticity of problematic works like the *De mundo* and the *Secretum secretorum*. They retranslated works like the *Oeconomics*, which dealt with the practical problems of ethics that preoccupied humanist moral philosophers; eventually they translated the entire Aristotelian corpus anew from the Greek. And they consistently presented Aristotelian studies as a clear case of the triumph of the new philology over scholastic barbarism – the barbarism seen at its worst in William of Moerbeke's *verbum e verbo* translations. They even mustered the intellectual courage and financial resources to produce four editions of the Greek text of his works (the Aldine *editio princeps* came out in 1495–8) as well as literally innumerable partial ones.

Yet though it is clear that Aristotle reached a large public indeed in the Renaissance, it is not clear that he did so in a radically transformed guise. If

---

52. Archimedes 1880–1, 1 ('Prolegomena' by Heiberg); Clagett 1964–84; Rose 1975.

the earliest printed edition gave Leonardo Bruni's humanist translations of the *Ethics*, *Politics* and *Oeconomics*, the first great edition of the works as a whole was the Venice 1472–4 edition of the old Latin text with the commentaries of Averroes – a form which was repeated much more often for a century to come than Aldus Manutius' brave experiment of printing the Greek alone. Even staunch Hellenists whose first language was Greek, like Argyropulos in the fifteenth century and Sophianus in the sixteenth, respected the Latin philosophical terminology that Moerbeke had helped to create, despite the barbarity of which they constantly complained. Even a humanist like Lefèvre d'Étaples included in his influential editions of the *Ethics* (1st edn, 1497) the medieval vulgate, Bruni and Argyropulos, side by side – thereby showing that he felt as bound by the traditions of university teaching as by the ideals of the humanist programme for renewing Aristotle. And even at the end of the sixteenth century, the great Greek-Latin edition of Casaubon, which presented Aristotle as an ordinary classic author and showed little or no respect for the conventions of modern philosophical discourse, had as a rival the Coimbra commentaries, which offered a far more traditional combination of Latin text and elaborate philosophical commentary – and one that found appreciative readers in English Protestant as well as in Italian and Iberian Catholic universities.

Thanks to printing and the vast expansion in college-level arts teaching, Aristotle had an enormous diffusion in the Renaissance, in the original, in Latin, in the vernacular and in summaries, study guides and manuals of every kind; the most recent list of sixteenth-century Aristotelian printing fills 160 pages. Clearly, too, in the course of the fifteenth and sixteenth centuries the medieval commentaries were less frequently printed (especially after the mid 1530s), and the philosophers as well as the philologists learnt Greek and consulted the original texts; and a basically modern Aristotelian corpus was delimited. But whether the ordinary arts graduate of 1600 knew Aristotle better than he would have in 1300 or 1450 remains to be established.[53]

Anicius Manlius Severinus BOETHIUS (*c.* 480–524) left behind a substantial body of translations from and commentaries on Greek works dealing with dialectic and the *quadrivium*, important works on dialectic and an elaborate dialogue, *De consolatione philosophiae*. His works on music, arithmetic and logic and the *Consolatio* circulated widely in the Middle Ages and soon came into print (1st full edn, 1491–2). And they performed a

---

53. Schmitt 1983a; Cranz and Schmitt 1984; on humanist translations see still Garin 1951.

variety of functions. The *Consolatio*, with the elaborate commentary by Pseudo-Thomas Aquinas, went through some twenty editions before 1500 and served as a basic text in monastic schools and a rich collection of information (much of it wrong or inaccurate) about ancient history and philosophy. Stripped of its medieval gloss, it seemed a vital work of moral philosophy to Thomas More and Justus Lipsius, both of whom drew heavily upon it in their own dialogues on parallel topics; and from the 1560s on the *Consolatio* circulated widely, without explanatory material, as a pocket manual on wise behaviour in dark times. The *Arithmetica* and *Musica* were also treated with respect and used in teaching. Lefèvre d'Étaples, epitomising the former for his students, described it as full of *prisca sapientia*; and his epitome was still serving as the basis of lectures in Tübingen in the 1550s. Boethius evidently hoped to preserve as much as possible of Greek philosophy and science for the Latin world of his own day; he remained a respected source of such knowledge long after the Greek texts came back into print, a thousand years after his death.[54]

CENSORINUS (*c.* AD 238), a Roman grammarian, included rich doxographical information in his strange treatise *De die natali*. Preserved by one eighth-century manuscript and not widely read in the Middle Ages, the text reached print in 1497, and soon became a prime source for the ancients' views on questions as varied as the history of astronomy, the stages of human life and the growth of the human embryo. Writers as diverse as Giraldi, Poliziano and Pomponazzi pillaged it for information even before the edition by L. Carrion (1583) and the study of its contents by J. J. Scaliger (1583) launched systematic study of the work.[55]

CICERO (106–43 BC) provided the Renaissance with its most popular manuals and discussions of rhetoric, its prime models of philosophical dialogue and its fullest knowledge about the ancient philosophical schools. His works circulated widely in the Middle Ages, though not all of them were available and not all that were available were complete. Petrarch could include in his list of favourite books – written while he was still young – *Republic* VI, the *Tusculans*, the *De officiis*, *Academica priora*, *De amicitia*, *De senectute*, *De divinatione*, *De natura deorum*, *Paradoxa*, *De inventione*, *De oratore* (not complete) and speeches rare and common, as well as the (spurious) *Rhetorica ad Herennium*. The chief addition to the texts of philosophical interest were the complete texts of *De oratore*, *Orator* and *Brutus* found at Lodi in 1421 and soon widely available in manuscript.

54. *Boethius* 1981.   55. *Texts and Transmission* 1983, pp. 28–30.

Cicero came into print in the 1470s and flourished at once; his moral
dialogues in particular went through dozens of editions. And in the
sixteenth century some of the most proficient philologists in the world –
Erasmus, Pier Vettori, Denys Lambin and Paulus Manutius – would
undertake complete editions of his works.

Philosophically, Cicero served two rather distinct purposes. On the one
hand, his rhetorical works – and the *De oratore* above all – offered some of
the most powerful alternatives the Renaissance knew to the philosophical
culture of the university arts faculty. In suggesting that the purpose of
intellectual activity lay above all in practical results, in defining and
dramatising the figure of the orator as the true cultural ideal of the ancient
world, and in arguing that eloquence, emotionally effective expression, had
more to offer than ineloquent precision and rigour, he enabled the
humanists not merely to claim an intellectual position alongside that of the
scholastics but even to challenge the scholastics' pre-eminence. To that
extent the newly available *Rhetorica* contributed fundamentally to some of
the most serious philosophical debates of the fifteenth and sixteenth
centuries, as can be seen in such imitations of them as Bruni's *Dialogi* and, in
its own way, Erasmus' *Ciceronianus*. And in the sixteenth century the
Academica, a text widely commented on by humanists trying to reform
dialectic, seemed to offer powerful support for their effort to reform the
schools.

At the same time, though, Cicero's strictly philosophical works – the
moral and religious ones above all – continued to play exactly the role that
had often fallen to them in monastic and cathedral schools. They were ideal
texts for language teaching and informative compendia of the kind of
information literate people needed. Throughout the fifteenth and sixteenth
centuries, then, Cicero's *Somnium* continued to form the most popular
summary of Neoplatonic cosmology; his *De officiis* and *De senectute*
continued to provide most intellectuals' introduction to the ancient schools
of moral philosophy; and all his works served often as *florilegia* of
information and anecdote. It is typical that Copernicus, for all his
concentration on technical astronomy as practised by Ptolemy, found the
inspiration for his work in the account of the ancient heliocentrist Hicetas in
Academica II.123. The Cicero of the Renaissance had a fuller biography, a
purer text and a clearer historical visage than the medieval one; but he was
not wholly the *Cicero novus* that Bruni and others claimed to present.[56]

56. *Texts and Transmission* 1983, pp. 98–142; Nolhac 1907, I, pp. 213–68; Zielinski 1912; Baron 1938a.

DIOGENES LAERTIUS (third century AD) combined earlier doxographic and biographical works into a single history of Greek philosophy.
Though various medieval reworkings of this existed, the availability of the
Greek text in Constantinople and in Italy early in the fifteenth century, and
the provision of a translation into Latin by Ambrogio Traversari, created a
revolution in Renaissance thinkers' view of ancient philosophy. Though the
Greek text did not reach print until 1533, the Latin text went through
seventeen editions between 1472 and 1500 alone; and the outpouring of new
work on the biographies of ancient thinkers that accompanied the recovery
of the text in the early 1400s is sufficient evidence of its impact.

Diogenes was not wholly rewarding. His frivolity irritated even his
editors Froben and Episcopius, who complained that he had not known
how to make the best use of the rich sources at his disposal: 'Quanquam
videtur plus studii adhibuisse in congerendo, quam judicii vel in deligendo
vel digerendo. In dictis philosophorum, in quibus plurimum est acuminis,
concisior est quam optaremus, et interdum, veluti delassatus, fatetur se
multa praetermittere.' Yet his positive characteristics seemed far to
outweigh the negative ones. His model of a collective biography organised
by sects, by rational groups of teachers and disciples, was far more
sophisticated and appealing than the random lives of *Viri illustres* offered by
Jerome and his medieval followers. Accordingly, it remained the formal
model for histories of philosophy until the end of the Renaissance. As late as
1655, Georg Hornius (who would later die a madman) rammed into the
Laertian format the lives of all previous thinkers; his sects included not just
the followers of Thales and Pythagoras but those of Seth, those of Cain and
those of the devil (who appeared as the founder of the sect of the sophists).
And Thomas Stanley, whose *History of Philosophy* appeared in the same
year, paid his homage to Diogenes by winding up his work with Epicurus,
as Diogenes had, though this choice of format was even more illogical in the
seventeenth century than it had been in the third. Meanwhile, Diogenes'
rich quotations from Epicurus made possible the systematic study of
Epicurean natural philosophy which was one of the major achievements of
late sixteenth- and seventeenth-century scholarship, from Lipsius to
Gassendi. And in a sense, even the sparseness of his accounts of the doctrines
of the Ionian and Italian schools had its helpful side; it enabled philosophers
from Bacon to Newton and Vico to find inspiration in what they imagined
to have been the rich, lost philosophies of the Presocratics.[57]

57. Braun 1973; *Storia delle storie* 1981–; quotation from *Prefaces* 1861, p. 380.

EPICTETUS (*fl. c.* AD 100) offered in his *Enchiridion* a handy and reliable manual of Stoic moral philosophy. Translated for the first time into Latin by Niccolò Perotti, it circulated in at least thirteen manuscripts. Translated again, into more classical Latin, by Poliziano, it was printed in 1497. The Greek text became a popular schoolbook during the sixteenth and seventeenth centuries.[58]

EUCLID (*fl. c.* 300 BC) systematised in his *Elements* earlier developments in Greek mathematics, producing a model of rigorous, complex and structurally integrated mathematical argument which remained the standard until the seventeenth century. His work circulated in the Latin Middle Ages in a dizzying variety of full and partial versions. In the sixteenth century printers conflated and scholars updated the main medieval competitors, the Arabic-Latin versions of Gerard of Cremona, Adelard of Bath and Campanus of Novara. Though a Greek text appeared at Basle in 1533 and Commandino produced a very careful translation of the Greek text (and many of the *scholia*) in 1572, little effort was made to imagine what his work had been like before Theon of Alexandria revised it in the fourth century. Still, even if the original Euclid remained submerged for most Renaissance readers under waves of accretions and revisions, the basic structure of his work and the nature of its postulates and proofs was clearly accessible to all who were literate in Latin. As such it could serve – as Grynaeus emphasised in his preface to the *editio princeps* of the Greek – along with dialectic as a model for valid reasoning in any field, 'Ut si quis mentis humanae morem simulacro quodam expressam velit, nullo possit melius quam geometriae.'[59]

GALEN (second century AD), a doctor, philosopher and rhetorician of great skill, learning and loquacity, left behind a vast corpus of works dealing with medicine at every level from the minute details of anatomy and prognosis to the basic principles of natural philosophy and medical ethics. In the Latin Middle Ages his more practical works formed the core of medical research and helped to shape the medical curriculum. But the full richness of his skills and interests became clear only in 1525, when the Aldine edition of his works in Greek revealed that he had been as dedicated to philosophy as to his patients, as interested in textual criticism as in anatomy. By the mid sixteenth century evidence that refuted some of his anatomical and physiological views was already coming to light. But his works remained

58. Epictetus 1954 (introduction by Oliver).
59. *Dictionary of Scientific Biography* 1970–80, IV, pp. 437–59; quotation from *Prefaces* 1861, p. 386.

vastly popular and influential long after individual tenets lost their authority.[60]

HERMES TRISMEGISTUS, a mythical Egyptian sage said to have flourished around the time of Moses, was thought in the Renaissance to have been the author of a corpus of philosophical dialogues written in the second and third centuries. These works offered a rich mixture of Neoplatonic, Gnostic, Jewish and other elements as the consummate revelation of an ancient wisdom, one far older and more powerful than the Greek philosophy which derived from it. Marsilio Ficino considered the Hermetic matter a vital element, perhaps *the* vital element, in the Platonic tradition. He studied the Hermetic *Asclepius* in its ancient Latin version and translated the Greek *Pimander* into Latin early in the 1460s, at the direct request of Cosimo de' Medici, who had Ficino lay aside his work on Plato to tackle Hermes. In his Latin translation Hermes found wide diffusion in manuscript (of which at least forty survive) and print (after 1471). Most Renaissance thinkers believed the corpus genuine, and the larger tradition of a *prisca theologia* which validated it also found only a few critics in the sixteenth century. Accordingly, the work had a deep impact on natural philosophy, learned magic and literature in the Renaissance, though its effect on the scientific revolution – held to be profound by Frances Yates – does not seem to have been important.[61]

HIPPOCRATES (*c.* 460–*c.* 370 BC), traditionally seen as the founder of the Greek medical tradition, was also traditionally taken as the author of a large corpus of medical works ranging in content from laconic records of individual cases through manuals of surgical technique to broad theoretical discussions of the causes of health and disease. Though some of his works passed through Arabic into Latin (along with many pseudepigrapha), and a few became building-blocks in the medieval medical curriculum, it was only in 1526 that the original texts were published in Greek, not to mention Galen's elaborate commentaries on some of them. Medical scholars in sixteenth-century Paris and elsewhere exhaustively explicated the corpus of his works in the light of their practical experience. And his apparent dedication to dispassionate, untheoretical recording of phenomena made him the hero of anti-Galenic thinkers from Paracelsus to J. B. van Helmont. Even Francis Bacon praised 'the ancient and serious diligence of Hippocrates', while reforming doctors in the sixteenth and seventeenth centuries

60. Temkin 1973; Durling 1961.
61. *Catalogus translationum* 1960–, I, pp. 137–50; Yates 1964; Westman and McGuire 1977.

modelled their collections of case histories on the Hippocratean *Epidemics*.[62]
IAMBLICHUS (*c.* 250–325), a Neoplatonist and student of Porphyry, wrote on Egyptian mysteries and Pythagorean tenets. Ficino produced a Latin paraphrase of the *De mysteriis* which he himself described as neither literally accurate nor complete. This found some diffusion in manuscript and considerable popularity in print from 1497 (when Aldus printed it) on; it seems to have been a special favourite of the Lyons printer Tornaesius. It offered important confirmation for the popular belief in an ancient revelation to the wise peoples of the Near East.[63]
ISIDORE of Seville (d. 636) compiled a vast encyclopaedia of the arts and sciences under the title *Etymologiae* – which also suggests something of the way in which he organised the work. He provided not merely trivial linguistic information but an influential model for all later efforts to reveal the content and relations of the liberal arts – as well as many bits of information ultimately drawn from older sources now lost. For all its sketchiness and imperfection in detail, the work remained one of *the* ancient reference books throughout the Middle Ages and the Renaissance; around a thousand full or partial manuscripts survive, and printed texts were widely available after 1470. They give as good an idea as anything can of what the literate man in the street knew of ancient thought.[64]
LONGINUS (first century AD) was thought in the Renaissance to be the author of a treatise *On the Sublime*, perhaps the most original ancient work on style. Published in 1554 by Robortello, the work aroused the interest of philologists rather than that of philosophers. Though the work was soon translated into Latin, it had little impact on literature or on criticism until the seventeenth century.[65]
LUCRETIUS (first century BC) gave in his poem *De rerum natura* the fullest account we have of Epicurean materialism. A long poem designed to free men from fear of the gods hardly fitted medieval needs, and the work found few copyists until Poggio turned up a manuscript in Switzerland in 1417. In fifteenth-century Italy a new classic of Latin poetry could claim a market whatever its theological implications. Poggio's manuscript spawned some fifty others, some of which show signs of intelligent efforts at emendation. Printed editions began in 1473, commentaries (with G. B. Pio's) in 1511. And if few readers understood Lucretius' views fully in the period following his discovery, he still provided a new model for large-scale

62. W. Smith 1979; *Medical Renaissance* 1985.   63. Sicherl 1957.
64. *Texts and Transmission* 1983, pp. 194–6; Saxl 1957, I, pp. 228–41.
65. *Catalogus translationum* 1960–, II, pp. 193–8.

philosophical poems by Michael Marullus and many others. In the sixteenth century, Denys Lambin began the process of uncovering Lucretius' Greek sources that would culminate with the work of Gassendi a century later.[66] MACROBIUS (fifth century AD) left two works, usually transmitted separately until the *editio princeps* of 1472 joined them permanently (as individual Italian scribes had already done in their manuscripts). The commentary on Cicero's *Somnium Scipionis*, preserved in some 230 manuscripts, gave a short and vastly influential account of the basic world picture assumed by Platonic philosophy. The *Saturnalia*, preserved in some 113 manuscripts, was a standard reference book on ancient natural philosophy and much else. Macrobius offered the fullest account in Latin of Neoplatonic allegorical interpretations of classical myth, an account which was exploited eagerly in the twelfth-century School of Chartres and by the humanists.[67]

MARTIANUS CAPELLA (before AD 500) produced in the elaborate form of an allegorical wedding of Mercury and Philology (*De nuptiis Philologiae et Mercurii*), an encyclopaedic account of the liberal arts. Two hundred and forty-one manuscripts attest to his popularity in the Middle Ages; twelve printed editions between 1499 and 1599 show that the work still seemed interesting in the Renaissance. Some printers even separated out those books that dealt with individual disciplines and printed these as formal textbooks. And the book retained its use as a description of the whole range of knowledge throughout the Renaissance.[68]

ORPHEUS was known to the Renaissance as the prototype of the divinely inspired, Egyptian-educated sage. Fragments of verse attributed to him appear in the Neoplatonists and some Fathers; eighty-seven hymns written in Roman times circulated under his name. Ficino translated the hymns in 1462 and incorporated them into his ritual magic. George of Trebizond made many of the fragments available in his Latin version of Eusebius' *Praeparatio evangelica* (printed 1470). The *Orphica* attracted some historical criticism. Bruni knew from Cicero that Aristotle had considered *quae dicuntur Orphei carmina* inauthentic. But on the whole they continued to be taken as authentic relics of an ancient *poesis philosophica*, even by the likes of J. J. Scaliger and Henri Estienne.[69]

John PHILOPONUS (d. after 567), an Alexandrian Christian, wrote

66. Lehnerdt 1904; *Catalogus translationum* 1960–, II, pp. 349–65; Reeve 1980; *Texts and Transmission* 1983, pp. 218–22.   67. *Texts and Transmission* 1983, pp. 222–35.
68. *Catalogus translationum* 1960–, II, pp. 367–81; *Texts and Transmission* 1983, pp. 245–6.
69. Walker 1972, pp. 14–16, 22–41; George of Trebizond 1984, pp. 721–6.

elaborate commentaries and treatises, both explicating the works of Plato and Aristotle and confuting interpretations of them that contradicted basic tenets of Christianity. His commentary on Aristotle, *Physics* I–IV preserves sharp and elaborate ancient criticisms of Aristotle's views on the vacuum and the laws of motion. This work, studied by Gianfrancesco Pico della Mirandola in manuscript, reached print in Greek in 1535 and in Latin in 1539. It was studied by Benedetti and Galileo, among others, and proved to the Renaissance that ancient views on physics had not been monolithically Aristotelian; it may have done more, helping to stimulate Galileo to replace the Aristotelian laws with new ones.[70]

PLATO (427–347 BC) won much admiration but few translations from the ancient Romans. Partial versions of the *Timaeus* by Cicero and Chalcidius gave a tantalising glimpse of Plato's world picture to medieval readers. Versions of the *Meno* and *Phaedo*, completed in the twelfth century, never achieved a wide circulation. In this case above all the Renaissance marked a dramatic change. In the fourteenth century, stimulated by the remarks of Augustine and Cicero, humanists from Petrarch on treated Plato as the master of all philosophers and tried to collect his works in Greek even though they could not read them. From 1397 on the Byzantine émigré Manuel Chrysoloras began reading Plato in Greek with his Florentine pupils. They produced translations, with his help, of the *Republic*, the *Laws*, the *Gorgias* and the *Phaedrus*. Shortly after the mid-century these piecemeal efforts were succeeded by the great enterprise of Marsilio Ficino. With financial support from Cosimo de' Medici, he translated the entire corpus into Latin and fitted it out with commentaries. Though the Greek text was not printed until 1499, Ficino's Latin was an immediate best-seller. The edition of 1484 was printed in the large number of 1,025 copies and nonetheless sold out within six years. And for the next century and more, Ficino's Latin versions and commentary made Plato accessible to European philosophers and poets (whose most eloquent Platonic works are often directly lifted from Ficino's commentary rather than from the original texts).

For all his impact, Plato never achieved the overwhelming diffusion of Cicero or Aristotle. The nature of his works made it impossible for them to serve as a coherent basis for a full university arts course. Moreover, Plato's works were not simply revealed in their purity by the new Greek scholarship of the Renaissance. Ficino inherited from the Byzantines not just

---

70. Schmitt 1981, § XII, forthcoming b.

Plato but the corpus of Neoplatonic interpretations of him, above all those of Plotinus, which he also translated, and those of Proclus. He took these as authoritative expositions, which imparted to the dialogues an orderliness and coherence that they would otherwise have lacked. To be sure, his own interpretations of the dialogues made original use of the elements he found in the tradition; yet without the previous efforts of the Neoplatonists, Ficino would never have been able to bring off his feat of making the *Phaedrus* a formal account of theology. At the same time, Ficino accepted from the Byzantines the notion that Plato himself, for all his literary artistry, occupied only an intermediate position in the chain of philosophers stretching back towards the creation. Where Plato and Hermes Trismegistus agreed, Hermes was to be taken as Plato's source. These assumptions, given currency by the wide circulation of Ficino's Plato, did much to ensure that the Plato of the Renaissance was very far from the original.[71]

PLINY the Elder (first century AD) provided in his *Naturalis historia* an enormous encyclopaedia of ancient science, philosophy and pseudo-science. This circulated (in some 200 manuscripts) throughout the Middle Ages, serving as a standard reference work on ancient science and much else. But with the rise of humanism the text took on a new importance. It began to attract formal commentaries, as it had not in the Middle Ages. The earliest of these, by Giovanni de Matociis early in the fourteenth century, simply sorted out the difference between the Pliny of the *naturalis historia* and the younger Pliny of the *Letters*. But from the later fifteenth century on the *Naturalis historia* attracted a degree of attention rarely equalled. Printed texts multiplied – twenty-two between the *editio princeps* of 1469 and 1489. Philologists attempted to improve the texts, philosophers to reprove Pliny by showing that he had misunderstood either the data or his Greek sources. The Plinian commentary – more than forty appeared – became a characteristic scientific genre of the Renaissance. And the work continued to be a standard reference book and an object of scholarly dissection until well into the seventeenth century. Efforts were even made in Protestant universities to make Pliny take Aristotle's place as the basic text for instruction in natural philosophy. And though these bore little fruit, the text remained basic for anyone interested in the development of ancient natural philosophy.[72]

PLOTINUS (third century AD), the founder of Neoplatonism, gave in his

---

71. Kristeller 1979, pp. 50–65; M. J. B. Allen 1984a.
72. *Catalogus translationum* 1960–, IV, pp. 297–422.

Enneads a systematic but immensely difficult account of the order of the universe and the relations between unity and multiplicity. Argyropulos used him. More influential work was done by Ficino, who mastered his difficult terminology and produced a standard edition and translation. The Latin text reached print in 1492, the Greek in 1580. No work did more to ensure the perpetuation of a Neoplatonic reading of Plato than this powerful and attractive treatise, which appeared with the authoritative recommendation of Ficino as absolutely faithful to the original: 'Principio vos omnes admoneo, qui divinum audituri Plotinum huc acceditis, ut Platonem ipsum sub Plotini persona loquentem vos audituros existimetis.'[73]

PLUTARCH (d. *c.* AD 120) assembled a vast series of essays, known as the *Moralia*, which deal with ethical, religious and pedagogical problems and collect the views of many thinkers (like Posidonius) whose own works do not survive. As early as the fourteenth century, individual works began to be sought out and translated. The entire Greek text was printed by Aldus in 1509, and some of the most influential of the humanists – like Francesco Barbaro in the fifteenth century, and Erasmus in the sixteenth – translated, adapted and plagiarised individual books. In vernacular translation he provided a model of the loose philosophical essay which was imitated by Montaigne and others.[74]

PORPHYRY (third century AD), a vastly productive Neoplatonist, wrote an introduction to Aristotle's *Organon* which was a staple of the medieval arts course (in a Latin version by Boethius). This work and the commentaries on it remained very popular throughout the Renaissance (eighteen editions, and thirty-two commentaries, appeared before 1500). His life of Pythagoras, which would have found a ready market in the Renaissance, in fact did not reach print in Greek or Latin until the seventeenth century.[75]

PROCLUS (fifth century AD) wrote elaborate commentaries on Plato and on Euclid, *Elements* 1. Though his formidably difficult *Platonic Theology* did not reach print in Greek until 1618, Ficino worked through it in manuscript and gave some diffusion to its systematic reordering of Plato's gods in his *Phaedrus* commentary. The Euclid commentary, published in Greek in 1533, and made far more accessible by the careful Latin translation (1560) by F. Barozzi, offered an influential set of arguments about the existence of a single *scientia* which provided the basic theorems and principles of all forms of mathematics, and attractive material about the history of Greek

---

73. Ficino 1937, I, pp. cxxvi–viii; M. J. B. Allen 1984a; quotation from *Prefaces* 1861, p. 603.
74. Hirzel 1912.   75. Flodr 1973 *s.v.* Porphyry.

mathematics as well. This text played a vital role in the widespread late sixteenth-century debates about the nature and foundations of mathematics. Finally, a treatise on the sphere (actually consisting of extracts from Geminus (first century)), was printed in Greek in 1536 and in a Latin translation by Linacre in the same year. This became one of the basic sixteenth-century manuals of elementary astronomy.[76]

Claudius PTOLEMY (second century AD) wrote elaborate manuals of astrology and astronomy. The former, the *Tetrabiblos*, had long been available in the Latin translation of Plato of Tivoli, and reached print in 1484. It found a wide readership throughout the sixteenth century, both within and outside the profession. The latter, the *Almagest*, was perhaps the most imposing single scientific work to survive from antiquity. It offered both a powerful set of arguments in favour of a geocentric world picture and an elaborate and profound mathematical account of the movements of the sun, the moon and the planets from Mercury to Saturn. Gerard of Cremona's translation had long circulated in manuscript and reached print in 1515, while a new translation by George of Trebizond, with commentary, was prepared in 1451 and found ten manuscript copies and four printed editions, the first in 1528. The Greek text was first printed in 1538, with Theon's commentary. But all this activity was in a sense secondary, for neither Latin translation offered a reliable (or even a usable) guide through the formidable technical problems of the text. All Renaissance astronomers approached the *Almagest* through the so-called *Epitome* – in fact a brilliant critical résumé with much supplementary matter – prepared by Peurbach and finished by Regiomontanus in the early 1460s. The inaccurate Venice 1496 edition of this text was Ptolemy's astronomy, for all practical purposes, for the sixteenth century.[77]

PYTHAGORAS (sixth century BC), the founder of an ancient philosophico-religious sect, was all too well known to Renaissance readers through the distorting medium of forged and secondary books: the *Golden Verses* attributed to him, which went through more than 100 editions because they were used in teaching, and won a translation from Ficino and a commentary from the elder Beroaldo; the life of him by Diogenes Laertius; and book xv of Ovid's *Metamorphoses*, another schoolroom standby. He was widely held to have glimpsed some basic Christian truths in advance, and many Renaissance scholars took a hand in the pleasant game of tracing Plato's doctrines back to him.[78]

76. Saffrey 1959; Crapulli 1969.
77. George of Trebizond 1984, pp. 748–50; Swerdlow 1973.   78. Heninger 1974.

SENECA (AD 4–65) provided the Middle Ages and the Renaissance not only with their chief store of tragedies but with a long series of essays on philosophical topics ranging from ethics to natural philosophy. His dialogues survive in more than 100 manuscripts; his letters were a popular source for the precepts of the Stoics in the fourteenth and fifteenth centuries. His works enjoyed a lively printed tradition (six complete editions between 1475 and 1492) and received commentaries and other editorial work from Erasmus and Lipsius. From late in the sixteenth century Seneca became more and more popular as the model of a philosopher living under tyrants and teaching a Stoic morality that would promote survival. Curiously, though, at no point in the Renaissance did the renewed interest in Seneca's work and life or the efforts of the best philologists prevent most readers from thinking him a good Christian.[79]

SEXTUS EMPIRICUS (second century AD) wrote the most systematic treatments of ancient scepticism – and many aspects of ancient logic – to survive. Though a partial translation was made during the Middle Ages and Greek manuscripts circulated in Italy from the early fifteenth century, systematic study of him seems to have begun in the circle of Savonarola, who saw him as a useful tool for confuting the claims to wisdom of the pagans and asked two friends to translate him. Gianfrancesco Pico della Mirandola actually used Sextus heavily in his *Examen vanitatis doctrinae gentium* (1520). But full texts only became available in the wake of the mid-century religious crisis, when many came to see dogmatism as a destructive force in human affairs. Henri Estienne and Gentian Hervet made Sextus available in Latin (*Outlines of Pyrrhonism*, 1562; *Adversus mathematicos*, 1569). And within little more than ten years Montaigne was making brilliant use of this new material in his *Apologie de Raimond Sebond*. Many philosophers followed his lead in the next half-century. The case is a revealing one. Though no Greek text became available until 1621, Pico's summary and the Latin translations provided ample fodder for thought about the sceptical tradition at the time when it was central to European culture.[80]

SIMPLICIUS (sixth century AD) wrote elaborate commentaries on Aristotle's *Physics*, *Categories*, *De anima* and *De caelo*. The Greek text of the *Categories* reached print in 1499, the rest in 1527. The *De anima* commentary, discovered by Giovanni Pico, was used by Nifo even before the text was available in print, and played an important role in the rich sixteenth-century controversies on Averroes' interpretation of Aristotle's

79. Ettinghausen 1972; *Texts and Transmission* 1983, pp. 357–81.
80. Schmitt 1983c; cf. Cavini 1977.

doctrine on the intellect. The *De caelo* commentary played a vital role later in the century, as the richest source available for the history of the homocentric astronomy of Eudoxus and Callippus.[81]

STOBAEUS (fifth century AD) left an anthology of some 500 Greek authors, including many fragments not elsewhere preserved. The Greek text and a translation, edited by Willem Canter, were published by Plantin in 1575. Canter's careful comparison of those sections of Stobaeus' work that derived from the *De placitis philosophorum* ascribed to Plutarch with the original is one of the earliest serious efforts to study the Greek doxographical tradition.[82]

THEMISTIUS (*c.* 317–88) wrote important commentaries on Aristotle. That on the *De anima* in particular proved vital, since Averroes and Thomas Aquinas drew opposed conclusions from it on the vital question of the unity of the intellect. William of Moerbeke had translated it in 1267; Ermolao Barbaro produced a new version in 1481 and L. Nogarola (who complained: 'Hermolai interpretationem, praeter vates et ariolos, intelliget nemo') another in 1559, of book III.[83]

THEOPHRASTUS (372/0–288/6 BC), Aristotle's successor as head of the Peripatetic School, wrote voluminously on many subjects, and some of his work circulated in Latin, under Aristotle's name, during the Middle Ages. But real knowledge of him became possible only in the fifteenth century, after Giovanni Aurispa brought manuscripts of his botanical and other works from Constantinople to Italy. Theodore Gaza translated his works on plants for Nicholas V; these versions, which went through many printings, were themselves fundamental to the sixteenth-century renovation of botany. The first edition of the Greek text of most of his works appeared in 1497, in Aldus' Aristotle. Two great Greek-Latin editions, the latter the work of Daniel Heinsius (1613), added other works, such as the *Characters*.[84]

---

81. Nardi 1958, ch. 13; N. Jardine 1984.   82. *Prefaces* 1861, pp. 584–90.
83. Nardi 1958, ch. 13; quotation at p. 367.   84. *Catalogus translationum* 1960–, II, pp. 239–322.

23

THE RISE OF THE PHILOSOPHICAL TEXTBOOK

THE NATURE OF THE PHILOSOPHICAL TEXTBOOK

We must start by defining what is meant by 'textbook', a modern term more or less equivalent to other formulations such as manual, *cursus*, or *systema*. In the most general way a textbook can be said to be a book specifically designated for classroom use. As the universities developed from the twelfth century onwards, it was the writings of Aristotle which dominated in most scientific and philosophical subjects. In general for the Middle Ages and Renaissance down to the end of the sixteenth century, classroom instruction in philosophy was based upon a direct reading of Aristotle's works in Latin translation, though there were some exceptions. The one branch of philosophy where a manual derived from Aristotle replaced a reading of the master's works quite early was in the field of logic. Thus, Porphyry's *Isagoge* and the *De sex principiis* had both become a part of the Aristotelian logic corpus by the high Middle Ages. In the thirteenth century other manuals came into play, the most famous example being Peter of Spain's *Summule logicales*. Though not entirely absent from the Middle Ages and early Renaissance, textbooks covering other branches of philosophy were not nearly so common.

The philosophical textbook during the period with which we are concerned was nearly always a summary, exposition or expansion based on Aristotle. These often took the form of compendia, i.e., brief, simplified treatments of an Aristotelian text or group of texts. They could also, however, be of a more inclusive nature, expanding upon what was available in the *corpus Aristotelicum*. This form became increasingly popular during the late sixteenth century and dominated for the next hundred years. Such a *cursus* (the term seems to have been used in this sense first at the end of the sixteenth century) filled various gaps in the Aristotelian writings. This is evident, for example, in the textbooks of natural philosophy, where technical astronomy, optics, botany and discussions of metals and stones were added to the traditional subjects contained in the *libri naturales*. These

792

textbooks often incorporated the characteristics of summary and expansion at the same time, by giving either more or less attention to a given topic than was available in the extant works of Aristotle. As time went on and the criticisms of Peripatetic philosophy grew – especially in the course of the seventeenth century – certain manuals came to be quite un-Aristotelian and even anti-Aristotelian.

The need for a synthetic manual to replace the materials contained in the *corpus Aristotelicum* arose where those works came to be considered unsatisfactory in one of several ways, such as (1) a dissatisfaction with the philosophical content of the works; (2) a realisation that Aristotle's mode of exposition was not ideal for pedagogical purposes; and (3) a recognition that, even if Aristotelian philosophy was valid, it did not cover all areas of knowledge it was desirable to include. From these and other considerations, there grew an increasing impetus towards preparing more adequate pedagogical tools.

TEXTBOOKS FROM THE MIDDLE AGES TO THE REFORMATION

The primary function of the textbook is as a teaching tool. This applies to all branches of learning and not merely to philosophy. Some subjects are naturally more suitable to the use of the textbook than others. As medieval university education was organised, instruction was drawn from certain 'set books', if not specifically textbooks in all instances. While philosophy and geometry instruction were largely based on ancient texts, in certain other subjects manuals compiled in the Middle Ages were favoured. Sacrobosco's *Sphaera* in astronomy, Peter Lombard's *Sententiae* in theology and Avicenna's *Canon* in medicine are good examples of 'new' books serving as the instruments of instruction. Many of these books continued to dominate their respective fields until much later: the *Canon*, for example, remained in use until the end of the sixteenth century in spite of many attempts to promote a humanistic reform of medical education.[1]

Philosophy teaching was for the most part based directly on a reading of Aristotle rather than on textbooks. Summarising manuals of one sort or another were, however, used, probably occasionally in the classroom, but more frequently as guides to private study. The best medieval example of such a work is Albert of Orlamunde's *Summa naturalium*, which frequently passed under the name of Albertus Magnus. This thirteenth-century

---

1. Siraisi 1984.

compendium prevailed well into the sixteenth century, especially in Central and Eastern Europe. It survives in some hundred manuscripts and was printed about twenty-five times before 1525 and three times later in the century at Cracow.[2] The tradition of natural philosophy manuals continued into the early fifteenth century with volumes such as Peter of Dresden's *Parvulus philosophiae naturalis*, which frequently circulated with Albert of Orlamunde's work. Peter's compendium is extant in many manuscripts and was printed about twenty-five times between 1495 and 1521.[3] An Italian example of the same genre datable to about 1408 is Paul of Venice's *Summa naturalium*, which contains summaries not only of major natural philosophical works but also of Aristotle's *Metaphysics*. It had a broad manuscript diffusion and was repeatedly printed until about 1525, though its influence did not end there.[4]

Of a different nature were the two compendia from the late fifteenth century prepared by Ermolao Barbaro, a humanist active in the circle of Giovanni Pico and Angelo Poliziano. His *Compendium librorum ethicorum* and *Compendium scientiae naturalis* are very brief outlines of Peripatetic philosophy obviously meant for beginners in these subjects. The former follows the order and arrangement of the first six books of the *Nicomachean Ethics*, while the latter incorporates material from several Aristotelian works. Though they apparently had no significant fifteenth-century manuscript diffusion, both achieved popularity for a generation or so after their first publication by Daniele Barbaro in the 1540s.[5]

About the same time the compendia *ad mentem Scoti* of Nicolaus de Orbellis (d. 1475)[6] enjoyed a certain diffusion from Paris, but they did not gain the same attention as the abbreviations of the central Aristotelian texts made by Thomas Bricot (d. 1516).[7] Both Bricot and Nicolaus, along with innumerable others, were targets of Rabelaisian satire.[8] Bricot's works were not textbooks in the normal sense, but somewhat shortened versions of the set texts. They came just at the time when printing was beginning to matter in the diffusion of philosophical works. Along with the additions made by George of Brussels (d. 1510), they were frequently reprinted between 1486 and 1520.[9] More influential, however, was Petrus Tartaretus, another

2. Lohr 1967, pp. 345–8, who cites the earlier literature. In general see also Grabmann 1939. Another early author of a general philosophical textbook was Nicolaus Bonetus, on whom see Lohr 1972a, pp. 284–6.   3. Lohr 1972a, pp. 352–4.   4. Lohr 1972a, pp. 314–20.
5. Lohr 1968, pp. 236–7.   6. Lohr 1972a, pp. 288–90.   7. Lohr 1973, pp. 173–8.
8. Rabelais 1912–31, III, p. 80 (*Pantagruel*, ch. 7). In the same passage a number of other philosophers are also mentioned, including Petrus Tartaretus and John Mair. See also Erasmus 1906–58, V, p. 102 for criticism of Bricot.   9. Lohr 1968, pp. 155–8.

Scotist active at Paris, whose expositions of Aristotle's logic (and also that of Peter of Spain), natural philosophy, metaphysics and ethics maintained a popularity from the 1490s until well into the seventeenth century.[10] While a part of the same flowering of Scotism at Paris at the turn of the sixteenth century as the works of Bricot and George of Brussels, Tartaretus' expositions gained renewed attention much later through the Venetian editions printed during the half-century around 1600.[11]

Parallel with this development, in which late medieval Scotism and nominalism were being revived in Paris, a new movement was emerging which also produced its own versions of compendious introductions to Aristotle. Humanism came to Paris at the end of the fifteenth century, and the first to champion that approach in Aristotelian studies was Jacques Lefèvre d'Étaples. His *Introductiones* to a large number of required philosophical texts were widely read and deeply influential on various levels of intellectual life, setting the trend for many later developments in Aristotelian studies. Frequently accompanied by one or more Latin versions of the Aristotelian text itself, as well as a commentary, his introductions gave a framework of interpretation which presented for the first time to Northern European audiences the elements of the humanistic Aristotelianism which had developed in Italy during the past half-century and more. Using Platonic and Hermetic themes freely to supplement Aristotle, Lefèvre's introductions were added to by his associate Josse Clichtove and sometimes modified by another colleague, François Vatable. Entitled *paraphrases, introductiones* and *dialogi*, these explanatory works, along with his voluminous commentaries, served to introduce many a reader to a range of Peripatetic philosophical themes. Their printed history spanned about half a century from the 1490s, with several of the works still being printed until the end of the sixteenth century. His *Artificialis introductio in X libros Ethicorum*, for instance, was printed about thirty-five times between 1494 and 1596.[12]

Lefèvre's vast output of Aristotelian works dates from before 1508, though he was active in revising them until much later. A younger contemporary, Frans Titelmans, fused the humanist approach of Erasmus and Lefèvre with a traditional Franciscan religiosity to produce another set of compendia in the 1530s.[13] These appeared on the scene just as the

10. Lohr 1972a, pp. 372–6.
11. For Paris at this period see Renaudet 1953; García Villoslada 1938.
12. Besides Renaudet 1953, see Lohr 1976a, pp. 726–32 and the material collected in Lefèvre d' Étaples 1972.   13. Lohr 1982, pp. 196–8.

Reformation reached a crisis state, but before Jesuit textbook-writing got under way and before there was a concerted effort to revivify Protestant education. Titelmans' works, which all have the title *Compendium*, enjoyed a remarkable *fortuna* into the seventeenth century. In the prefatory epistle to his *Compendium naturalis philosophiae* the author gives us full information on his reasons for writing the book. Besides emphasising its utility for introducing his fellow-Franciscans to natural philosophy, he also stresses the need for something beyond the 'difficult and prolix commentaries' generally available at the time. While there are dialectic books *ad nauseam*, he continues, to the best of his knowledge no one before him had attempted a similar work in physics.[14] Strictly speaking his assertion is not correct, but his effort did mark a new type of compendium which pointed the way to the future.

Very different from the works of either Lefèvre or Titelmans is Gregor Reisch's *Margarita philosophica* (Freiburg, 1503), which both harks back to Albert of Orlamunde and looks forward to the comprehensive manuals of later times. Encyclopaedic in scope but compendious in execution, this work gives a statement of the general level of Northern European learning before the influence of either humanism or religious reform. It covers not only the *trivium* and *quadrivium*, but also the principal branches of philosophy (including moral philosophy). The *Margarita* is unusual for its time in presenting such a wide range of topics in such a brief compass, and it had a deserved success, being reprinted many times, primarily at Strasburg and Basle, and even appearing in an Italian version as late as 1599.[15]

TEXTBOOKS FROM THE REFORMATION TO 1600

The age of the philosophical textbook, in Protestant as well as Catholic Europe, begins with the Reformation. While the roots of such manuals lie in the sort of works we have just discussed, there was a renewed emphasis on providing compendious and up-to-date surveys of the basic fields of

---

14. Titelmans 1542, sig. AA iii^v: 'Sic enim simplicium fratrum conditioni iudicavi utilius, utpote quibus bona diei noctisque pars divinis hymnis declarandis sacris pars agendis mysteriis, et circa proximos exercendis hierarchicis actibus, foret impendenda, ita ut ad philosophiae studia minimum temporis superesset, neque vacaret eorum qui plenius illa tractarunt prolixos et difficilles [*sic*] commentarios evolvere. Ad physicam autem disciplinam in compendium contrahendam meum desiderium peculiariter etiam illud accendit, quod hanc rem a nemine hactenus tentatam conspicerem. Nam in dialecticis vel usque ad nauseam abunde multos invenias, qui totam librorum seriem per ordinem sunt prosequuiti.' Titelmans' *De consideratione dialectica* is mentioned by the early Jesuits for possible use in their schools. See *Monumenta paedagogica Societatis Iesu* 1965-, I, p. 177.
15. Lohr 1980, pp. 685-6.

philosophy within the educational systems on both sides of the religious divide. The Jesuits from the beginning stressed the importance of philosophy – especially Aristotle – in education and ultimately formed the bulwark of a continuing Aristotelianism, even after it had begun to decline elsewhere. Luther's hostility to Aristotle – particularly to the scholastic variety he had known as a university student – is evident everywhere in his writings.[16] There was, in fact, an early attempt, within the Protestant movement, to establish a reformed educational system without Aristotle.[17] This proved to be untenable, however, for the genuine basis of a systematic and comprehensive knowledge still had to derive from Peripatetic learning. Consequently, it was Aristotelianism – in a way only slightly different from the version that continued to flourish in Catholic countries – which became the foundation of the Lutheran educational programme masterminded by Melanchthon and Sturm. It was Melanchthon who set the trend in textbooks and expositions, which were to maintain a remarkable popularity from the time of their first publication mainly in the 1530s and 1540s until the end of the century. Besides several logical compendia, his books include *Philosophiae moralis epitome* (1538), *Initia doctrinae physicae* (1549), *Ethicae doctrinae elementa* (1550) and *Liber de anima* (1553). Inherent in Melanchthon's approach is the assumption that both moral philosophy and natural philosophy are necessary parts of the education of the Christian. Morality, of course, was of the highest priority, but logic and natural philosophy also held a position of respect in Lutheran education. Each of his compendia is brief, simple and to the point.[18]

Melanchthon's approach to physics is solidly based on Aristotle: atomism, Pyrrhonism and the *cavillationes* of late medieval scholasticism are all rejected.[19] The *Doctrinae physicae elementa* is arranged according to the order of exposition of the *Physics*, though a good deal is added on from the other *libri naturales*, and, more importantly, there is a significant section on astronomy. The *Liber de anima* is unusual in several respects. First, the exposition is based primarily on the Greek text, and quotations in the original language abound. Second, there is a very strong emphasis on anatomy and physiology, with recent authorities such as Vesalius and Fuchs being used to supplement traditional knowledge. Third, unlike most expositions of the work – particularly those associated with Italian

16. Nitzsch 1883; Rokita 1971.   17. See Nauert 1979, p. 80.   18. Lohr 1978, pp. 576–82.
19. Melanchthon 1834–60, VII, col. 475 (*Epistolae* lib. XI, no. 4603): 'Non enim a Democrito aut Epicuro, aut aliis, qui usitatam doctrinam corrumpunt, ars petenda est. Eligatur et rerum doctrina, omissis inanibus cavillationibus, quales etiam haec recentior aetas miscuit communi doctrinae non paucas. Studeamus et genere sermonis proprio uti, et non alieno a linguae Latinae consuetudine.'

Aristotelianism – there is little emphasis on the intellectual functions of the soul. Finally, the traditional topic of immortality is given little attention, the discussion being based largely on Scripture rather than the abundant philosophical literature which had grown up in the previous three centuries. The two works on moral philosophy have both Aristotelian and Christian elements, marking out areas of autonomy for each. All of the works are clearly meant to be introductory guides for beginning students, based partially on Aristotle but incorporating many other elements as well. They are all in catechetical form, beginning with the fundamental query in each discipline: 'Quid est physica doctrina?' 'Quid est anima?' 'Quid est philosophia moralis?'

The early post-Reformation Catholic approach is epitomised by the Jesuits. Ignatius Loyola, the founder of the Society, had himself studied at Paris (1528–35), and the experience made a deep and lasting impression on him. This happened just at the time when he was laying the foundation for his new organisation. Theology was the capstone of the new educational system he founded, but a number of other more basic disciplines led up to this, including a broad introduction to systematic philosophy, derived primarily from Aristotle. 'The teaching of Aristotle is to be followed in logic, natural and moral philosophy and metaphysics' is how it is stated in the *Constitutiones* of the Society.[20] Such prescriptions led to the preparation of a series of teaching manuals for the subjects to be taught in the Jesuit colleges, first in the Collegio Romano[21] and then in Jesuit institutions throughout the Old and New World. The pedagogical structure eventually became codified in the *Ratio studiorum* (1585; final version, 1599). The study of Aristotelian philosophy among the Jesuits took various forms – commentaries, expositions, annotated editions of Aristotle and textbooks adapted particularly for classroom use. These books were prepared by men such as Benito Pereira, Franciscus Toletus, Antonio Rubio, Pedro da Fonseca, Francisco Suárez and the Coimbra commentators.

One of the key methods introduced into Jesuit education, based ultimately on Loyola's Paris experience, is the *Modus Parisiensis*, a rigorous, intense and successful mode of educational formation, which provided the pupil with a firm base in the fundamentals necessary for advanced study in any of the current disciplines. It involved several factors including: (1) a close relationship between master and student; (2) the concentration of instruction into small collegial units; and (3) the centrality of the class unit,

20. *Monumenta paedagogica Societatis Jesu* 1965–, I, p. 299. See also Lohr 1976b.
21. García Villoslada 1954.

in which students of the same age and educational accomplishment worked in collaboration with the instructor and progressed to higher levels together.[22] Such a system was ideal for the use of graded textbooks, often written by the teacher himself. Many manuals – not only in philosophy, but also in subjects such as grammar, mathematics or rhetoric – came from this context.

One of the more popular and characteristic textbooks of natural philosophy written by a Jesuit during the second half of the sixteenth century is the *De communibus omnium rerum naturalium principiis et affectionibus libri XV* of Benito Pereira. More substantial than the similar works produced by Melanchthon, it stays fairly close to Aristotle's order of exposition in the *Physics*, but much attention is paid to theological issues (e.g., the eternity of the world), and the approach to Aristotle is given a theological coloration which it does not have in the work of a contemporary such as Jacopo Zabarella. In the preface Pereira clearly states that he is not writing a commentary in the usual sense.[23] However, despite its inclusive title, it does not attempt to provide a general orientation to the increasingly vast range of material which the term *philosophia naturalis* was beginning to encompass.

Besides the Lutherans and Catholics other religious groups had their own systems of education and, consequently, their own approach to the teaching of philosophy. Principal among these were the Calvinists. Though much less favourable to Aristotle and to pagan learning in general than either the Lutherans or the post-Tridentine Catholics, they nonetheless produced impressive systematic expositions of Aristotelian learning, like that by Clemens Timpler at the turn of the seventeenth century. Of a more popular nature and more widely read were the introductions to ethics and natural philosophy prepared by Lambert Daneau. These attempted to avoid the influence of Aristotle and of pagan learning altogether. Daneau's philosophical manuals, part of a massive output covering many subjects, came from Calvinist Geneva and bear titles such as *Physica Christiana* (1576) and *Ethica Christiana* (1577).[24] Representing a tradition which was to have a great influence in the next centuries, he argued that 'profane philosophy' had been responsible for misleading many Christian believers and that new

22. Codina Mir 1968.
23. Pereira 1576, sig. C 4ʳ: 'At licet nobis multas ob causas (quas hoc loco exponere non est necesse) visum non fuerit, commentarios in Aristotelem scribere, quibus eius sententias et verba, sigillatim interpretaremur; sedulo tamen curavimus, ut quicquid Aristoteles iis de rebus, quas hoc opere docemus, usquam sensit, et scriptum reliquit, variis ex libris eius colligentes, suo quoque loco, pertractaremus.'   24. Fatio 1976.

scripturally based versions of the subjects had to be formulated as acceptable substitutes.[25] His aim was precisely that. Cast in the same question and answer form as the manuals of Melanchthon and many others, the *Physica Christiana* begins 'Quid est physica?' But the responses are very different from those usually found in traditional Peripatetic manuals. Daneau's attempt is probably the most concerted effort at an out-and-out rejection of Peripatetic principles on the part of a textbook writer – at least before the crumbling of the system a century later.

Working more to recast the form and method of exposition than the content was Petrus Ramus. He moved to simplify and to make more communicable the whole encyclopaedia of knowledge through a new method based on an organising principle partially founded on visual components. Though generally considered to have been virulently anti-Aristotelian, such was not entirely the case, for Ramus joined a Peripatetic base of knowledge to other sources of enlightenment in an effort to produce an up-to-date and accessible core of information. His real innovation, though not without earlier models,[26] came to the fore in the middle of the sixteenth century and was the introduction of a new way of presenting knowledge. The Ramist impact can be seen in a great number of textbooks on all subjects dating from the second half of the sixteenth century and later. The frequent use of dichotomous tables is one of the elements which characterise his new mode of exposition. Indeed upon occasion entire books, often of great length, were cast in this form, as is the case with several of Theodor Zwinger's expositions of moral philosophy.[27] At the other extreme were brief pamphlets, such as the anonymous one produced at Paris in 1550, which compresses the whole of Aristotle's *Physics* into eight octavo pages of skeletal tables.[28]

Typical of the new approach are the *Quaestiones physicae* (1579) of Ramus' biographer and follower Joannes Thomas Freigius. This massive work of well over 1,000 closely printed pages systematises learning about the natural world, not only from Aristotle but from many other sources as well. Besides the traditional subjects served by the *libri naturales*, we also find among the thirty-six books treatments of sound and music, hydrography, geography, metals, botany, agriculture and much else. This is characteristic of the new type of 'physics' textbook, which is in no way limited to the restricted range of topics contained in the *corpus Aristotelicum*.[29] Freigius also made available a number of similar books in other branches of learning,

25. Daneau 1576, sigs. *ii^v–*iii^r.   26. Höltgen 1965.   27. Zwinger 1565, 1566, 1582.
28. [Anonymous] 1550; see Schmitt 1983a, p. 58 for a sample illustration.   29. Freigius 1579.

creating a sort of encyclopaedia of learned disciplines which foreshadows the great ones of the next century.

By the end of the sixteenth century the textbook mode of exposition had come increasingly into its own. It had begun, if not to replace the direct reading of the Aristotelian text and the perusal of the vast supply of commentaries by then available, at least to provide some competition for the attention of potential readers of philosophical material. This happened primarily in Northern Europe; in Italy in most university contexts the commentary was still the favoured mode of presenting an interpretation. Northern expositors, including John Case in England and Johannes Magirus in Lutheran Germany, provided textbooks largely based on Aristotle and adapted to the pedagogy of the classroom. Neither uses the conventional commentary form, though both frequently follow Aristotelian content quite closely. Besides a textbook on logic, Case wrote volumes on the *Physics*, *Politics*, *Nicomachean Ethics*, and *Magna moralia*, as well as a standard commentary on the *Oeconomics*. Magirus wrote on the *Ethics*, *Physics* and *De anima*. Both gave their works rather elegant titles, which give little hint of the traditional and often pedestrian content. Magirus, for example, wrote a *Corona virtutum moralium* and *Anthropologia*, while Case produced *Lapis philosophicus* (on the *Physics*), *Sphaera civitatis* (on the *Politics*) and *Speculum quaestionum moralium* (on the *Nicomachean Ethics*). In both cases the manuals held their interest well into the next century, still being used at Oxford and Cambridge during the middle years of the seventeenth century.

SEVENTEENTH-CENTURY DEVELOPMENTS

It was during the seventeenth century that the philosophical textbook really began to dominate the teaching of the subject in most formal courses in institutions of higher learning.[30] Not only is this true for the period during which Aristotle continued as the prime authority, that is, until about 1675, but it carries on even up to the present with a changed and changing intellectual content. The later history of the topic is beyond the scope of the present work, but we should give some attention to the developments of the first quarter of the century. One of the evident changes of those years – and one which will continue to be a common practice until much later – is the

---

30. See, in general Thorndike 1923–58, VII, ch. 13; Reif 1962, 1969; Lohr 1976b; Brockliss 1981a, 1981b; *Novità celesti* 1983, pp. 217–28 (Schmitt); Freedman 1984. A useful survey is Fraile 1966, pp. 376-479.

growing tendency for a single author to write *cursus* covering the entire field of philosophy. Sixteenth-century textbook writers had generally written on one or two branches of philosophy or, if they composed manuals on the entire range, these were usually not cast in a unified form and published as a single comprehensive entity.

A good example of the new genre is the *Summa philosophiae quadripartita de rebus dialecticis, moralibus, physicis et metaphysicis* by the Cistercian Eustachius a S. Paulo. This manual, first published in 1609, was widely used throughout Europe.[31] Read in Protestant as well as Catholic countries, with printings at Cambridge, London, Leiden and Geneva, it is typical of the integrated course which was to dominate the seventeenth century. Relatively brief as such works go – after all, eight hundred or a thousand pages is not too much to master in a four-year course of studies – the *Summa* was praised by Descartes,[32] even though his major effort as a philosopher was aimed at undermining the suppositions upon which it is based. Here much of the Aristotelian content remains, though the whole organisation of the individual branches of learning has been recast. The section entitled *Physica*, for example, covers the natural philosophical topics found in the Aristotelian corpus, but also includes subjects such as geography; there is, however, no technical astronomy. In common with many such manuals, the section on animate life (here part 3 of the section on physics entitled 'De corpore animato') has become very physiological with much information drawn from the medical literature grafted on to the Aristotelian core.

A few years later we have one of the first efforts at a vernacular course of the same sort from the pen of Scipion Dupleix, historiographer royal and member of Richelieu's entourage. His *Corps de philosophie contenant la logique, la physique, la métaphysique et l'éthique* (1623) covers more or less the same ground as the Latin manuals like that of Eustachius. Here, however, even the Latin quotations from authors such as Vergil and Seneca are put into French. Much Christian doctrine is incorporated, but no more than is usual in the Latin handbooks, and given its royalist origins, it is not surprising that the writings of Jean Fernel, physician to Henry II, are cited frequently and with approbation.

What was happening by this time – and it became even more prominent in later courses – is that natural philosophy began to outstrip the information available in the other philosophical disciplines in terms of both

31. Lohr 1976a, pp. 725–6.
32. Descartes 1897–1910, III, p. 232, in a letter to Mersenne (11 November 1640), speaks of the *Summa* of Eustachius as 'le meilleur liure qui ait iamais esté fait en cette matiere'. He even had the plan at one stage to annotate the *Summa*; for references to discussions on the point, see *ibid.*, V, p. 601.

length and richness of content. While undoubtedly new and complex things could be said regarding metaphysics and moral philosophy, it was really in the realm of the rising new science that an immense amount of recently discovered information was becoming available and had to be integrated into the *cursus*.[33] In Eustachius' work, for example, logic covers 182 pages; moral philosophy, 130; metaphysics, 84; but natural philosophy requires 308. As time went on the imbalance became even greater, as with Emanuel Maignan's *Cursus philosophicus* (1653). It was from the natural philosophy section of such quadripartite manuals that the textbooks on the subject developed in later years.

Protestant equivalents to these examples are also numerous. The Calvinists Clemens Timpler and Bartholomaeus Keckermann are among the most prominent. Both entitled their works *systema*,[34] and both produced far more comprehensive and detailed expositions than did Eustachius or Dupleix. Their works covered a much wider range of disciplines than was normal, pointing the way to the great encyclopaedias of Johann Heinrich Alsted and Johann Amos Comenius. Keckermann wrote textbooks in the fields of logic, rhetoric, metaphysics, physics, astronomy, geography, theology, ethics, oeconomics and politics. Timpler was scarcely less ambitious, providing *systemata* on logic, rhetoric, metaphysics, physics, optics, physiognomy and practical philosophy (encompassing ethics, oeconomics and politics).

The real age of the textbook, therefore, was only beginning as the conventionally defined period of the Renaissance was ending.

CONCLUSIONS

Although there were medieval and fifteenth-century examples of philosophical textbooks, it was really at the turn of the sixteenth century that the genre came into its own, particularly at Paris. With the coming of the religious split a greater impetus was given to the activity, for such volumes increasingly became features of both Protestant and Catholic education. This tendency became more pronounced in the seventeenth century.

In spite of the rise of the new genre, throughout the Renaissance there continued to be many new commentaries, editions and translations of Aristotle, who remained the central philosophical authority. Aristotelian

---

33. In general see *Novità celesti* 1983, pp. 217–28 (Schmitt).
34. The term *systema* emerges at the turn of the seventeenth century. It may well point in the direction of the new encyclopaedia of the sciences which came increasingly to supplant the textbook based wholly or mainly on Aristotle.

commentaries and editions certainly outnumbered textbooks until the beginning of the seventeenth century. But then the balance changed quite rapidly, so that by about 1620 relatively few new commentaries were prepared (mostly coming from Spain), and the flow of editions and translations ebbed dramatically. The last serious burst of activity in the direction of producing editions with commentary were those initiated by the Coimbra commentators and Giulio Pace, both of which came out in the 1590s. The great bilingual editions of the *Opera* by Isaac Casaubon and Guillaume Duval were completed by 1620, though they continued to be used through the seventeenth century.

It is not always easy to distinguish commentaries from textbooks. Frequently, but not invariably, commentaries have the base text printed along with the comments; however, they always follow the Aristotelian order of exposition. Textbooks sometimes follow the traditional order, but more often rearrange the presentation of subject-matter according to logical or paedagogical criteria. Sometimes the whole order and mode of presentation are changed with much extra material from sources outside the text being introduced. There are also a good number of instances of eclectic type manuals in which Aristotle is only one of a number of authorities, though usually the main one. A good example of this is Magirus' *Physiologia peripatetica*, where the following authorities are cited on the title page as sources for the volume: Plato, Aristotle, Jacopo Zabarella, Arcangelo Mercenario, Thomas Erastus, Jacob Schegk, Julius Caesar Scaliger, Francesco Vimercato, Gasparo Contarini, Ermolao Barbaro and Francesco Patrizi.[35] As the seventeenth century wore on, of course, Aristotle began to lose ground as the main authority, and the more eclectic type of textbook – mainly in natural philosophy – began to predominate.

Finally, it is worth noting that philosophical textbooks in the Renaissance catered for a wide range of levels. Some – for instance, John Case's *ABCedarium moralis philosophiae* (1596) and *Ancilla philosophiae* (1599) – were meant for very young students indeed and covered only the most basic elements in a very unsophisticated way. Others – such as the *systemata* of Keckermann – were much more comprehensive and detailed. More usual was something in between, designed to convey the principles of the subject to a university-aged student, intelligent, but not yet very far advanced in his subject.

---

35. Magirus 1608.

BIOBIBLIOGRAPHIES

This section contains entries on some of the most important Renaissance philosophers. A number of extremely influential men in other fields (e.g., Luther and Calvin, Copernicus and Vesalius) have been omitted even though their influence on philosophical thought was considerable. Moreover, the length of the entries often reflects the relative complexity of an individual's life rather than his significance in the history of philosophy. The bibliography which is appended is not meant to be comprehensive, especially for the best-known and most studied figures. It is divided into two parts. Part I is keyed to a number of standard reference works, cited according to the abbreviations given below. Part II refers to the main bibliography of this volume. A selection of works by the philosophical authors themselves can be found in the bibliography of primary sources.

Abbreviations

ADB Allgemeine Deutsche Biographie, 56 vols., Leipzig, 1875–1912

AK Allgemeines Künstlerlexikon. Die bildenden Künstler aller Zeiten und Völker, Leipzig, 1983–

CHLMP Cambridge History of Later Medieval Philosophy, ed. N. Kretzmann, A. Kenny and J. Pinborg, Cambridge, 1982

CTC Catalogus translationum et commentariorum, ed. P. O. Kristeller and F. E. Cranz, Washington, D.C., 1960–

DBF Dictionnaire de biographie française, Paris, 1933–

DBI Dizionario biografico degli Italiani, Rome, 1960–

DCLI Dizionario critico della letteratura italiana, 3 vols., Turin, 1974

DHE Diccionario de historia de España, ed. G. Bleiberg, 2nd edn, 3 vols., Madrid, 1968–9

DHEE Diccionario de historia eclesiástica de España, 4 vols., Madrid, 1972–5

DHGE Dictionnaire d'histoire et de géographie ecclésiastiques, Paris, 1912–

DL H. Rupprich, *Die deutsche Literatur vom späten Mittelalter bis zum Barock*, 2 vols., Munich, 1970–3

DLM W. Stammler, *Die deutsche Literatur des Mittelalters. Verfasserlexicon*, 2nd edn, Berlin–New York, 1978–

DNB Dictionary of National Biography, 22 vols., Oxford, 1885–1901 (repr. Oxford, 1921–2)

DS Dictionnaire de spiritualité ascétique et mystique, ed. M. Viller, Paris, 1937–

DSB Dictionary of Scientific Biography, 16 vols., New York, 1970–80

DTC Dictionnaire de théologie catholique, 16 vols., Paris, 1923–72

Duhem *SM* P. Duhem, *Le Système du monde*, 10 vols., Paris, 1913–59

Duhem *TB* P. Duhem, 'La Tradition de Buridan et la science italienne au XVIᵉ siècle', *Bulletin italien*, IX (1909), 338–60; X (1910), 24–47, 95–133, 202–31; XI (1911), 1–32

EF Enciclopedia filosofica, 2nd edn, 6 vols., Florence, 1968–9

EI Enciclopedia italiana, 39 vols., Rome, 1929–39

EJ Encyclopaedia Judaica, 16 vols., Jerusalem, 1971–2

Farge J. K. Farge, *Biographical Register of Paris Doctors of Theology 1500–1536*, Toronto, 1980

Garin E. Garin, *Storia della filosofia italiana*, new edn, 3 vols., Turin, 1966

806 _Biobibliographies_

Giacon C. Giacon, _La Seconda Scolastica_, 3 vols., Milan, 1944–50
Lohr C. Lohr, 'Medieval Latin Aristotle commentaries' (1967–73) and 'Renaissance Latin
    Aristotle commentaries' (1974–82). See main bibliography for full references.
NDB Neue deutsche Biographie, Berlin, 1953–
NNBW Nieuw nederlandsch biografisch woordenboek, ed. P. C. Molhuysen and P. J. Blok, 10
    vols., Leiden, 1911–37
Prantl C. Prantl, _Geschichte der Logik im Abendlande_, 4 vols., Leipzig, 1855–70 (repr. Graz,
    1955)
Saitta G. Saitta, _Il pensiero italiano nell'Umanesimo e nel Rinascimento_, 2nd edn, 3 vols.,
    Florence, 1961
Solana M. Solana, _Historia de la filosofía española: época del Renacimiento (siglo XVI)_, 3 vols.,
    Madrid, 1940–1
Thorndike L. Thorndike, _A History of Magic and Experimental Science_, 8 vols., New York,
    1923–58
Totok W. Totok, _Handbuch der Geschichte der Philosophie_, III: _Renaissance_, Frankfurt am Main,
    1980

ACCIAIUOLI, DONATO b. Florence, 1429; d. Milan, 1478. Italian humanist and
philosopher. Educated in Florence; strongly influenced by Johannes Argyropulos.
Florentine statesman and ambassador. Participated in Platonic Academy of Florence. Wrote
commentaries on Aristotle's _Ethics, Politics, Physics_ and _De anima_. Translated Plutarch's lives
of Scipio and Hannibal.
I _DBI_ I, pp. 80–2; Lohr 1967, pp. 400–1.
II Della Torre 1902, pp. 322–425; Garin 1950a, 1954, pp. 210–87; Gatti 1972–3.

ACHILLINI, ALESSANDRO b. Bologna, 1463; d. Bologna, 1512. Italian philosopher.
Graduated doctor of philosophy and medicine at Bologna 1484, where he then taught logic,
natural philosophy and medicine, 1484–1506. Lectured on natural philosophy at Padua,
1506–8. Returned to teach at Bologna, 1508–12. Aristotelian; influenced by William of
Ockham. Also wrote on anatomy, astrology, chiromancy and physiognomy.
I _DBI_ I, pp. 46–7; _DSB_ I, pp. 144–5; _EF_ I, cols. 52–3; Lohr 1974, pp. 236–8.
II Münster 1953; Matsen 1968, 1974, 1975, 1977; _Philosophy and Humanism_ 1976, pp. 518–30
    (Matsen); Zambelli 1978.

AGRICOLA, RUDOLPH (Rudolphus Frisius; Roelof Huysman) b. Baflo near Groningen,
1443/4; d. Heidelberg, 1485. Dutch humanist. Studied at Universities of Erfurt and Louvain,
where he graduated M.A., 1465. Travelled to Italy 1469–79 with interruptions, studying at
Pavia and Ferrara. Returning to Northern Europe 1479, he promoted Italian humanism and
lectured at Heidelberg, 1484–5. Wrote the influential _De inventione dialectica_ (1479), as well as
commentaries (Boethius, Seneca the Elder), humanistic orations, poems, letters and
translations from Greek.
I _DL_ I, pp. 490–4; _DLM_ I, pp. 84–93; _EF_ I, cols. 135–6; _NNBW_ IX, pp. 12–16; Totok, pp.
    280–1.
II Velden 1911; Vasoli 1958a, 1968a, pp. 147–82; Nauwelaerts 1963; Spitz 1963, ch. 2;
    Kessler 1979; J. M. Weiss 1981; Mack 1983a; Cogan 1984.

AGRIPPA, HENRICUS CORNELIUS (Agrippa von Nettesheim) b. near Cologne, 1486;
d. Grenoble, 1535. German philosopher. Studied at University of Cologne. Travelled
widely (France, Spain, England, Germany, Italy, Switzerland) as soldier, physician, teacher.

Served as doctor and astrologer to Queen Mother of France in Lyons, 1524; then as historian and librarian to Margaret of Austria in Antwerp, 1528–30. Returned to Cologne, then to France. Wrote influential treatise on magic, *De occulta philosophia* (1510; enlarged edition 1533); also, *De incertitudine et vanitate scientiarum atque artium declamatio* (1526), rejecting all human knowledge, and advocating instead faith in divine revelation. Influenced by Neoplatonism, Lullism, Hermeticism, cabalism.

I *DSB* I, pp. 79–81; *EF* I, cols. 136–8; *NDB* I, pp. 105–6; Totok, pp. 397–400.

II Prost 1881–2; Nauert 1965; Zambelli 1965, 1966, 1969, 1970, 1976; Bowen 1972; Müller-Jahncke 1973, 1984; Popkin 1979, pp. 23–5; Crahay 1980; Perrone Compagni 1982; Backus 1983.

AILLY, PIERRE D' (Peter of Ailly, Petrus de Alliaco) b. Compiègne, 1350; d. Avignon, 1420/1. French theologian, religious dignitary, Ockhamist philosopher. From 1364 studied at Collège de Navarre, Paris; B.A., 1367; 1368 began study of theology; 1381 *doctor theologiae* and *canonicus* at Noyon. In 1384–9 rector of Collège de Navarre; 1389–95 confessor to Charles VI of France and Chancellor of University of Paris; 1395 Bishop of Le Puy; 1397 Bishop of Cambrai; 1411 cardinal. Defended Immaculate Conception against John of Montson before Clement VII, 1387. From 1396 was active in efforts to end Schism; 1414–17 attended Council of Constance, returning to Avignon 1417. Wrote *Quaestiones super libros Sententiarum; Destructiones modorum significandi; Tractatus exponibilium; Conceptus et insolubilia; Tractatus de anima.*

I *CHLMP*, p. 876; *DSB* I, p. 84; Duhem *SM*, IV, pp. 168–83, IX–X *passim*; *EF* I, cols. 140–1; Lohr 1972, pp. 332–3.

II Salembier 1932; Meller 1954; Oakley 1964; Glorieux 1965; Bernstein 1978.

ALBERTI, LEON BATTISTA b. Genoa, 1404; d. Rome, 1472. Italian humanist, artist, architect. Studied Latin and Greek in Padua *c.* 1416, then obtained doctorate in canon law at Bologna, 1420/1–8. Appointed apostolic secretary to papal Curia in Rome, 1432. Travelled in northern Italy with exiled Pope Eugene IV, 1434–43. After leaving Curia in 1464, worked primarily as architect. Wrote *De pictura/Della pittura* (*c.* 1435); *Della famiglia* (*c.* 1433–41), a dialogue on education, domestic economy, friendship; *De re aedificatoria* (1443–52), a treatise on architecture, engineering, town planning; also, works dealing with moral philosophy, mathematics, physics, ciphers, Roman antiquities, horses, as well as literary compositions in Latin and Italian.

I *AK* I, pp. 828–35; *DBI* I, pp. 702–13; *DSB* I, pp. 96–8; *EF* I, cols. 150–1.

II Michel 1930; Santinello 1962; Gadol 1969; Mancini 1971; *Convegno . . . Alberti* 1974; *Miscellanea di studi albertiani* 1975; Ponte 1981; Mühlmann 1981.

ALMAIN, JACQUES b. Sens, *c.* 1480; d. Paris, 1515. French philosopher and theologian. Studied logic and natural philosophy at Collège de Montaigu under John Mair; M.A. and regent there; 1503–12 regent at Ste Barbe; 1507 rector of university at Ste Barbe. From 1508 studied theology at Collège de Navarre, gaining licentiate 1512; from 1512 professor of theology there. Analysed the status and power of the church and its relations with civil society, with particular reference to the definition and limitations of papal authority in relation to councils, bishops and the secular authorities: *Libellus de auctoritate ecclesiae; Expositio de suprema potestate ecclesiastica et laica, circa quaestionum decisiones Magistri Guillermi de Ockham super potestate summi pontificis; Quaestio resumptiva de domino naturali civili et ecclesiastico.* Favoured retention of wide powers by the king; his *De auctoritate* was very influential within the Gallican party in France. Also wrote *Moralia; Embammata physicalia totius philosophiae naturalis; Commentaria in tertium librum Sententiarum.*

I   *CHLMP*, p. 864; *DTC* I, cols. 895–7; Farge, pp. 15–18; Lohr 1974, p. 242.
II García Villoslada 1938, pp. 165–79 and *passim*; Renaudet 1953 *passim*; Oakley 1965; Muñoz Delgado 1967b; Skinner 1978 *ad indicem*.

ALONSO (GARCIA) DE CARTAGENA (Alphonsus Burgensis; Alphonsus a Sancta Maria) b. Burgos, 1384; d. Villoslada (near Burgos), 1456. Spanish theologian and translator. Son of a converted Jew. Educated at Burgos and Salamanca; master in theology; doctor *in utroque iure*. Dean of Santiago 1417 and Segovia 1420. Councillor to John II of Castille 1420, and tutor to Prince Henry. Attended Council of Basle, 1434–8. Elected Bishop of Burgos 1435, to which he returned, 1439. Controversy with Leonardo Bruni over his translation of *Nicomachean Ethics*. Wrote numerous theological, historical, political and ethical works; sermons; translations from Latin into Spanish (Boccaccio, Cicero, Seneca).
I   *DHGE* I, pp. 702–7; *DHE* I, pp. 740–1; *DHEE* I, pp. 366–7; Lohr 1967, p. 356.
II Birkenmajer 1922, pp. 129–210; Grabmann 1926–56, I, pp. 440–8; Serrano 1942; Fubini 1966, pp. 337–40; Harth 1968; Seigel 1968, pp. 123–33; Pagden 1975, pp. 305–6; Gerl 1981, pp. 24–31.

ARGYROPULOS, JOHANNES (Argyropilo) b. Constantinople, *c.* 1415; d. Rome, 1487. Byzantine philosopher. Attended Council of Ferrara/Florence, 1438–9. Studied arts and medicine at Padua, 1441–4. Taught philosophy at Constantinople, 1448–52. After fall of Constantinople, travelled widely in Europe, 1453–6. Lectured on Greek philosophy, especially Aristotle, in Florence, 1456–71 and 1477–81; and Rome, 1471–7 and 1481–7. Translated several Aristotelian works into Latin: *Nicomachean Ethics*, *De anima*, *Physics*, *De caelo*, *Metaphysics* (Books 1–12 only), *De interpretatione*, *Prior* and *Posterior Analytics*, *Categories*; also translated pseudo-Aristotelian *De mundo* and *Isagoge* of Porphyry.
I   *DBI* IV, pp. 129–31; *DHGE* IV, pp. 91–3; *EF* I, cols. 420–1; Lohr 1970, p. 153.
II Lampros 1910; Cammelli 1941–54, II; Garin 1951, pp. 82–7; Vasoli 1959, 1960; Seigel 1969; *Reden und Briefe* 1970, pp. 1–56; V. Brown 1974; Geanakoplos 1974a; Zippel 1979, pp. 179–97.

BACON, FRANCIS b. London, 1561; d. London, 1626. English lawyer, parliamentarian, scientist, philosopher, essayist, historian. Educated at Trinity College, Cambridge 1573–5, followed by three years in Paris; at Gray's Inn, 1579–82; became a barrister, 1582. Entered parliament in 1584. Solicitor General in 1607; Attorney General in 1612; Lord Keeper in 1617; and Lord Chancellor in 1618. Created Lord Verulam in 1618 and Viscount St Albans in 1621. His political career ended in 1621 when he confessed to bribery. Wrote *Essays* (1597–1625); *The Advancement of Learning* (1605 and a much-expanded Latin version, *De dignitate et augmentis scientiarum* in 1623) attacking scholasticism and putting forward an influential classification of knowledge; *De sapientia veterum* (1609), giving interpretations of ancient myths; *Novum Organum* (1620), presenting an alternative to Aristotelian method; *History of Henry the Seventh* (1622); *New Atlantis* (1624 but published 1627), portraying an ideal society devoted to scientific research; *Sylva sylvarum* (1626), a collection of material concerning natural history.
I   *DNB* I, pp. 800–32; *DSB* I, pp. 372–7; *EF* I, cols. 695–701.
II Dean 1941; Anderson 1948; P. Rossi 1957, 1974; Farrington 1964; *Essential Articles . . . Bacon* 1968; Vickers 1968, 1978; Walton 1971; *Legacy of Francis Bacon* 1971; L. Jardine 1974a; Stephens 1975; Rees 1975, 1977, 1980, 1981; *Francis Bacon: terminologia* 1984; Walker 1985, § x; *Francis Bacon: science* 1985.

BARBARO, ERMOLAO (Almorò; Hermolaus Barbarus) b. Venice, 1454; d. Rome, 1493. Italian humanist, politician, diplomat. Early education in Venice and Rome. Studied at

University of Padua: doctorate in arts 1474 and law 1477. Taught Aristotelian moral philosophy at Padua, 1474–6. Opened private school in Venice, 1484. Active in Venetian political life; several diplomatic missions. Elected Patriarch of Aquileia, 1491. In exile at Rome, 1491–3. Translated Aristotle's *Rhetoric* and Themistius' *Paraphrases Aristotelis*. Translated and commented on Dioscorides. Wrote philological commentaries on Pliny and Pomponius Mela.

I *CTC* IV, pp. 343–4; *DBI* VI, pp. 96–9; *DHGE* VI, pp. 585–6; *EF* I, col. 733; Lohr 1968, pp. 236–7.

II Breen 1968, pp. 2–40; *Medioevo e Rinascimento* 1955, I, pp. 217–53 (Dionisotti); Kristeller 1956a, pp. 337–53; Paschini 1957; *Umanesimo europeo* 1964, pp. 193–212 (Branca); Branca 1973, 1980; Pozzi 1974.

BARBARO, FRANCESCO b. Venice, 1390; d. Venice, 1454. Italian humanist, politician, diplomat. Early education in Venice, then Padua; M.A., 1410 and *doctor artium*, 1412. Returned to Venice; then travelled to Florence, 1415. After entering Venetian senate 1419, pursued active career as politician, administrator and diplomat. Wrote *De re uxoria* (1415/16), a treatise on marriage and domestic duties. Translated Plutarch's lives of Aristides and Cato the Elder.

I *DBI* VI, pp. 101–3; *DHGE* VI, pp. 587–8.

II Sabbadini 1910; Gothein 1932; Kristeller 1956a, pp. 337–53; *Reden und Briefe* 1970, pp. 201–10; M. L. King 1976; *Miscellanea . . . Branca* 1983, III, pp. 133–75 (Griggio).

BESSARION, CARDINAL (Joannes; Basilios) b. Trebizond, *c.* 1403; d. Ravenna, 1472. Byzantine churchman and philosopher. Early education in Constantinople, *c.* 1415–23. Entered Order of St Basil, 1423; ordained priest, 1431. Studied Platonic philosophy at Mistra, *c.* 1433. Became Archbishop of Nicaea, 1437. Attended Council of Ferrara/Florence, 1438–43. Elected cardinal, 1439. Supported union of Greek and Latin churches, 1442. Settled in Rome, 1443. Became influential figure in Curia; various diplomatic missions. Patriarch of Constantinople, 1463. Donated library of Greek manuscripts to Venice, 1468–9. Wrote *In calumniatorem Platonis* (1469) against George of Trebizond, comparing philosophies of Plato and Aristotle. Translated *Metaphysics* of Aristotle and of Theophrastus (1447–50); also translated Xenophon's *Memorabilia* (1444). Wrote many theological tracts.

I *CTC* II, pp. 305–6; *DBI* IX, pp. 686–96; *DHGE* VIII, pp. 1181–99; *EF* I, cols. 884–5.

II Mohler 1923–42; *Aristotelismo padovano* 1960, pp. 173–81 (Mioni); Labowsky 1961–8, 1979; *Centenario . . . Bessarione* 1973; *Miscellanea . . . di studi bessarionei* 1976; Neuhausen and Trapp 1979; Bianca 1980a; Stormon 1980; Monfasani 1981, 1983.

BLASIUS OF PARMA (Biagio Pelacani da Parma) b. Costamezzana (Parma), *c.* 1365; d. Parma, 1416. Italian mathematician, astrologer and Aristotelian philosopher. Studied at Pavia. Taught logic and astrology at Bologna. Frequented cultural circles at Padua and Florence. Wrote commentaries on the *Organon*, *De anima* and *Physics*; also wrote various works on statics and mechanics, reflecting the views of Buridan and the Merton School: *Tractatus de latitudinibus formarum*; *De intentione et remissione formarum*; *De tactu corporum*; *De motu*; *Tractatus de ponderibus*.

I Duhem *SM*, IV, pp. 278–80, 289–90; *DSB* II, pp. 192–5; *EF* I, col. 889; Thorndike IV, ch. 39.

II A. Maier 1951, pp. 270–4, 1966, pp. 279–99; Federici-Vescovini 1979, 1983; Murdoch 1976; *Scienza e filosofia* 1983, pp. 19–69 (Harrison).

BODIN, JEAN b. Angers, 1530; d. Laon, 1596. French political philosopher. His *Les Six Livres de la République* (1576) on the definition and limits of sovereignty exercised wide

influence; opposed both the sovereignty of the people and the doctrine of absolutism attributed to Machiavelli. His *Colloquium Heptaplomeres* (1587) incorporated a plea for natural religion and religious tolerance. Also wrote on historical method: *Methodus ad facilem historiarum cognitionem* (1566); and sorcery: *De la démonomanie des sorciers* (1580).
I *DBF* VI, cols. 758–9; *EF* I, cols. 957–8.
II Chauviré 1914; Moreau-Reibel 1933; Mesnard 1949, 1954; McRae 1955, 1963; Walker 1958, pp. 171–8; Franklin 1963, 1973; *L'opera e il pensiero* 1965, II, pp. 333–56 (Mesnard); Cotroneo 1966; U. Lange 1970; Vasoli 1971; *Jean Bodin* 1973; P. King 1974; *Damned Art* 1977, pp. 76–105 (Baxter); Rose 1980.

BORRO, GIROLAMO b. Arezzo, 1512; d. Perugia, 1592. Italian Peripatetic philosopher. Unsympathetic to humanist, mathematical and Platonic trends in Renaissance philosophy, but emphasised empirical approach to science. Studied theology, philosophy and medicine. Lectured on natural philosophy at Pisa. Wrote *Del flusso e reflusso del mare* (1561); *De motu gravium et levium* (1575), read by Galileo; *De peripatetica docendi atque addiscendi methodo* (1584). In difficulties with the Inquisition, 1567 and 1582–3. Had disputes with Francesco de' Vieri, Francesco Buonamici and Andrea Camuzio, which led to his dismissal from Pisa in 1586. Thought to have returned to Perugia and taught philosophy there until his death.
I *DBI* XIII, pp. 13–17; *DSB* XV, pp. 44–6.
II N. W. Gilbert 1960, pp. 186–92; Wallace 1972–, I, pp. 149–50, 178; Schmitt 1981, §§IX, XI.

BOVELLES, CHARLES DE (Bouelles; Bovillus) b. Saint-Quentin, 1479; d. Ham (near Saint-Quentin), 1567. Studied at Paris, 1495–1503, with Lefèvre d'Étaples. Travelled extensively for some years before settling in Noyon, 1515. Wrote many philosophical and theological works which owe a good deal to the recent Neoplatonism of Ficino and Nicholas of Cusa, though more remote sources such as Pseudo-Dionysius and Ramon Lull are also evident. Among his most characteristic works are *De intellectu*, *De nihilo* and *De sapiente*. Also wrote mathematical works, including the first geometry in French (1511).
I *DSB* II, pp. 360–1; *EF* I, cols. 1041–2.
II Dippel 1865; Brause 1916; Cassirer 1927, pp. 142ff., 154ff.; Groethuysen 1931; Michel 1936; Rice 1958, pp. 106–23 and *passim*; Clagett 1964–84, III, 3, pp. 1180–96; Victor 1978; Joukovsky 1981; *Charles de Bovelles* 1982; Sanders 1984.

BRUNI, LEONARDO (Leonardo Aretino) b. Arezzo, *c.* 1369; d. Florence, 1444. Italian humanist, translator and historian. Secretary to papal Curia, 1405–15. Chancellor of the Florentine Signoria, 1427–44. Translated many Greek authors into Latin (e.g., Aristotle, Plato, Plutarch, Xenophon, Polybius, Procopius); his translations of the *Nicomachean Ethics*, *Politics* and *Oeconomics* were widely diffused in the fifteenth and sixteenth centuries. Wrote life of Aristotle (1429); *Laudatio Florentinae urbis* (*c.* 1401); *Historiarum Florentini populi libri XII* (*c.* 1415–*c.* 1429); a life of Dante; *Isagogicon moralis disciplinae* (*c.* 1425); letters; poems.
I *DBI* XIV, pp. 618–33; *EF* I, cols. 1083–5; Lohr 1971, pp. 316–20.
II Garin 1951, 1974; *Medioevo e Rinascimento* 1955, I, pp. 297–319 (Franceschini); Soudek 1958, 1968; Baron 1966, 1968a, 1968b; Seigel 1966, 1968; Goldbrunner 1968; Harth 1968; Wilcox 1969; *Der Kommentar* 1975, pp. 98–118 (Goldbrunner); *Philosophy and Humanism* 1976, pp. 29–43 (Soudek); Gerl 1981, 1982b.

BRUNO, GIORDANO b. Nola, 1548; d. Rome, 1600. Italian humanist and philosopher. Entered Dominican monastery at Naples, studying theology and classical literature, 1563. In 1576 suspected of heresy; fled to Rome and afterwards other Italian cities. At Geneva 1578, but soon quarrelled with the Calvinists. Visited Toulouse 1579–81 (degree in theology, lectured on Aristotle) and Paris 1581–3, publishing *Ars memoriae, De umbris idearum* and *Candelaio* (all 1582). Settled in England 1583–5, making contact with Sidney and Greville, lecturing on Copernicus and participating in disputations at Oxford; published *La cena de le ceneri, De la causa, principio ed uno, De l'infinito universo e mondi, Lo spaccio de la bestia trionfante* (all 1584) and *De gli eroici furori* (1585). After returning to Paris 1585, he visited Prague and various German cities, including Wittenberg, where he converted to Lutheranism and lectured on Aristotle's logic, and Frankfurt, where he published his Latin poems (1591). Lectured in Zurich, 1591. Same year Giovanni Mocenigo invited him to Venice, but subsequently denounced him to the Inquisition. Conveyed to Rome in 1593 and put on trial over many years, ultimately refusing to recant his philosophical opinions. Executed, 1600.

I   *DBI* xiv, pp. 654–65; *DSB* ii, pp. 539–44; *EF* i, cols. 1088–1100; Lohr 1974, pp. 279–81.
II   Spampanato 1921, 1934; Corsano 1940; A. Mercati 1942; Firpo 1949; Badaloni 1955; Nelson 1958; Vasoli 1958b; Michel 1962; Kristeller 1964a, pp. 127–44; Yates 1964, 1966; Védrine 1967; Papi 1968; Aquilecchia 1971; Ingegno 1978, 1985; Ciliberto 1979; Blum 1980; P. Rossi 1983.

BUDÉ, GUILLAUME (Budaeus) b. Paris, 1467/8; d. Paris, 1540. French humanist and legal writer. Published commentaries on the *Pandects* (1508), which influenced the study of Roman law. Encouraged Francis I to institute royal readers in Hebrew, Greek, Latin and mathematics, forerunners of the Collège de France. First librarian at Fontainebleau. Friend and correspondent of other humanists, including Lefèvre d'Étaples, Erasmus and Rabelais. Wrote *De asse* (1514); *Commentarii linguae Graecae* (1529); *De transitu Hellenismi ad Christianismum* (1534); and *De l'institution du prince* (1547); as well as Greek *editiones principes* (e.g., Eusebius, Dionysius of Halicarnassus, Dio Cassius, Appian) and a Greek New Testament (1550). Also translated various works, including Plutarch and the pseudo-Aristotelian *De mundo*.

I   *CTC* ii, p. 100; *DBF* vii, cols. 611–12.
II   Plattard 1923; Bohatec 1950; Penham 1954; Kelley 1967; Guedet 1969; Rebitté 1969; De la Garanderie 1973, 1976; McNeil 1975.

BUONAMICI, FRANCESCO (Bonamicus) b. Florence (?), c. 1533; d. Orticaia, 1603. Italian Aristotelian philosopher. Professor of logic and natural philosophy at Pisa, 1565–1603, where he taught Galileo. Wrote *De motu* (1591) and commentaries on Aristotelian works; also treatises on literature, including *Discorsi poetici in difesa d'Aristotile* (1597), defending Aristotelian poetics against Castelvetro.

I   Lohr 1974, p. 272.
II   Koyré 1966, pp. 24–47 and *passim*; Helbing 1976, 1982.

BURGERSDIJK, FRANCO (Burgersdicius) b. Lier (near Delft), 1590; d. Leiden, 1635. Dutch theologian and philosopher. From 1604 to 1610 studied classics, rhetoric and dialectic at Amersfort and philosophy at Delft. Matriculated at Leiden and studied philosophy (under Daniel Heinsius), 1610–14; in France and Germany, 1614. Studied theology at Saumur and taught philosophy there, 1616–19. From 1620 to 1635 professor of philosophy at Leiden; from 1620 professor of logic and ethics; from 1628 professor of physics; 1629, 1630, 1634 rector. His textbooks on the main branches of philosophy were widely used throughout Protestant Europe until the end of the seventeenth century.

I   *CHLMP*, p. 860; *DSB* ii, pp. 601–2; Lohr 1974, pp. 287–8; *NNBW* vii, pp. 229–31; Thorndike vii, pp. 402–9.
II   Dibon 1954–, i, pp. 90–126 and *passim*; Thijssen Schoute 1954 *passim*.

CAJETAN, THOMAS DE VIO, O.P. (Cajetanus) b. Gaeta, 1468; d. Rome, 1534. Dominican philosopher and theologian. In 1484 entered order. Studied at Naples, Bologna, Padua, 1484–93; 1494, *magister theologiae*. Professor of metaphysics *in via Thomae* at Padua, 1495–7. Professor of theology at Pavia, 1497–9. *Lector* at Milan, 1499–1501. In 1501–18 held various high positions in Order, also teaching philosophy and Scripture at *Sapienza* in Rome, 1501–8. At Fifth Lateran Council, 1512–17. Raised to cardinalate, 1517. Wrote commentaries on Aristotle and Thomas Aquinas; a Thomist, but incorporated certain of his own ideas (e.g., on the doctrine of analogy). Involved in debate on immortality of soul at Padua, where he had known Pomponazzi.

I DHGE xi, pp. 248–52; DTC ii, cols. 1313–29; EF ii, cols. 403–5; Lohr 1975, pp. 692–5.
II Congar 1934–5; Stegmüller 1935b; Nardi 1945 *passim*; Gilson 1961; Koster 1960; Harrison 1963; Di Napoli 1963, pp. 214–26; *Umanesimo europeo* 1964, pp. 31–63 (Gilson); McCandles 1968; Reilly 1971.

CAMPANELLA, TOMMASO, O.P. b. Stilo di Calabria, 1568; d. Paris, 1639. Italian theologian, philosopher, poet. Joined Dominican Order, 1582. Published *Philosophia sensibus demonstrata* (1591). Twice censured for Telesian views, but disregarded superiors. Tortured by Inquisition 1594, imprisoned at Rome, forced to retract. Arrested in 1599 for conspiring to replace Spanish rule in southern Italy with a utopian republic; wrote *Città del Sole* (*c.* 1602). Imprisoned at Naples, where he wrote: *De sensu rerum et magia*; *Atheismus triumphatus*; *Apologia pro Galileo*; *Theologica*; *Metaphysica*; *Astrologica*; Italian poetry. Freed 1626, but reimprisoned by Holy Office. Eventually released by Urban VIII, for whom he performed protective magical rites. Fled to Paris 1634, obtaining patronage of Richelieu and publishing/republishing several works.

I DBI xvii, pp. 372–401; DSB xv, pp. 68–70; EF i, cols. 1171–80.
II Amabile 1882, 1887; Firpo 1940, 1947; Di Napoli 1947; Walker 1958, pp. 203–36; Corsano 1961a; Yates 1964, pp. 360–97; Badaloni 1965; Femiano 1968; *Tommaso Campanella* 1969; Amerio 1972; Bock 1974; Alunni 1982.

CANO, MELCHOR, O.P. b. Tarançon, 1509; d. Toledo, 1560. Spanish theologian and philosopher. Studied at Salamanca during the post-Tridentine Thomist revival 1527–31, with Francisco de Vitoria. In 1531 joined Dominican Order at College of St Gregory, Valladolid, where he became professor of philosophy and theology. Master of theology at Rome, 1542; 1543 professor of theology at Alcalá and 1546 at Salamanca. Imperial theologian at Trent, 1551. Bishop of Canary Islands, 1552. Archbishop of Toledo and Primate of Spain, 1559. His *De locis theologicis* reveals Vitoria's influence and aims to establish a historical and scientific basis for theology. Also wrote commentaries on *Summa theologiae*.

I DHEE i, pp. 333–4; DTC ii, cols. 1537–40; EF i, cols. 1186–7.
II Caballero 1871; Beltrán de Heredia 1933; Marcotte 1949; Sanz y Sanz 1959; Casado-Barroso 1969; Sanchez-Arjona Halcon 1969, pp. 135–63; Belda Plans 1982.

CARDANO, GIROLAMO b. Pavia, 1501; d. Rome, 1576. Italian polymath, principally mathematics. Studied at Pavia 1520–6, obtaining medical doctorate. Taught mathematics in *piattine* schools of Milan and successfully practised medicine, 1534. Professor of medicine at Pavia, 1543–52 and 1559–60, and at Bologna 1562. In Scotland for most of 1552; his medical skill attracted many English nobles as patients. Accused of heresy (casting Christ's horoscope) 1570, but recanted and went to Rome 1571, obtaining patronage of Pius V. Wrote over 200 works on medicine, mathematics, physics, philosophy, religion and music; among the most influential were: *Ars magna* (1545), presenting the algebraic formula for the solution of third-degree equations; *Quesiti et inventioni diverse* (1546); *De subtilitate* (1550), in reply to which J. C. Scaliger wrote his *Exotericae exercitationes*; *De varietate rerum* (1557); *Opus novum de proportionibus* (1570); and his autobiography, *De propria vita* (1575–6).

I Thorndike v, pp. 563–79; *DBI* xix, pp. 758–63; *DSB* iii, pp. 64–7; *EF* i, cols. 1216–17.
II Morley 1854; Corsano 1961b; Ore 1965; Ongaro 1969; Ockman 1975; Zanier 1975a; Fierz 1977; Ingegno 1980; *Occult and Scientific Mentalities* 1984, pp. 231–52 (Maclean).

CASE, JOHN (Casus) b. Woodstock (near Oxford), *c.* 1540; d. Oxford, 1600. English philosopher. Wrote expositions of Aristotelian logic, physics and moral philosophy; often reprinted in Germany. Studied at Oxford; Fellow of St John's College. Taught logic and philosophy in his own house. *Doctor medicinae* and canon of Sarum, 1589.
I *DNB* iii, pp. 1171–3; *EF* i, col. 1243; Lohr 1975, p. 706.
II Howell 1956, pp. 190–3; N. W. Gilbert 1960, pp. 91, 209–11; Dreitzel 1970, pp. 142ff. and *passim*; Schmitt 1983b.

CESALPINO, ANDREA (Caesalpinus) b. Arezzo, 1524/5; d. Rome, 1603. Italian Aristotelian philosopher, physician, botanist. Studied arts under Simone Porzio and medicine at Pisa, where he became *doctor artium .et medicinae*, 1551; 1556–70 professor of botany; 1570–91 professor of medicine. Professor of medicine in the *Sapienza*, Rome and physician to Clement VIII, 1592–1603. His *Peripateticae quaestiones* (1571) was influential both in Italy and Northern Europe. Also wrote *Demonum investigatio peripatetica* (1580) and *De plantis* (1583).
I *DBI* xxiv, pp. 122–5; *DSB* xv, pp. 80–1; *EF* i, cols. 1351–2; Garin II, pp. 633–9; Lohr 1975, pp. 691–2; Thorndike vi, pp. 324–38.
II Breit 1912; introduction to Cesalpino 1929, pp. 1–93; Viviani 1935.

CHARPENTIER, JACQUES (Jacobus Carpentarius) b. Clermont-en-Beauvais, 1521; d. Paris, 1574. French philosopher and anti-Ramist. Studied at University of Paris; professor of philosophy and *licentiatus medicinae*, Collège de Bourgogne; 1550/1 rector of University; 1566–74 professor of mathematics, Collège Royal. Controversies with d'Ossat and Ramus, 1564–8. Wrote on Peripatetic logic and natural philosophy: *Descriptio universae artis disserendi* (1564); *Descriptio universae naturae* (1560–4). Edited pseudo-Aristotelian *Theology* under the title *Libri XIV de secretiore parte divinae sapientiae* (1572). Wrote a comparison of Plato and Aristotle, more sympathetic to the former: *Platonis cum Aristotele in universa philosophia comparatio* (1573).
I *DBF* viii, cols. 638–9; Lohr 1975, pp. 700–1.
II Waddington 1855, pp. 168–85; Ong 1958a, pp. 220–3 and *passim*, 1958b, pp. 498–504; N. W. Gilbert 1960, pp. 145–52; Vasoli 1968a *ad indicem*; Purnell 1971, pp. 71–3; Kraye 1986.

CHARRON, PIERRE b. Paris, 1541; d. Paris, 1603. French Pyrrhonist philosopher. Studied classics at Sorbonne and jurisprudence at Orléans/Bourges; doctor of law, 1571. Studied theology and ordained, 1576. *Prédicateur ordinaire* to Queen Marguerite; theological canon in several dioceses; vicar-general at Agen and Bordeaux. Began close association with Montaigne, 1589. Wrote *Les Trois Véritez contre les athées, idolâtres, juifs, mahométans, hérétiques et schismatiques* (1593), arguing that the authority of the church provides the sole certainty for man; *De la sagesse* (published 1601, revised edn 1604), emphasising the truth of revelation as the only means of transcending natural law.
I *DBF* viii, cols. 665–6; *EF* i, col. 1361.
II Rice 1958, pp. 178–207; Battista 1966; Gregory 1967; Soman 1970; Horowitz 1971, 1974; D. Bosco 1977; Abel 1978, pp. 153–227; Popkin 1979, pp. 55–62, 114–20 and *passim*.

CHRYSOLORAS, MANUEL b. Constantinople, *c.* 1350; d. Constance, 1414. Byzantine humanist. Emperor Manuel II Palaeologus sent him to raise support among Christian rulers of Western Europe against the Turks. Came to Florence in 1397, where he taught Greek to Leonardo Bruni and other humanists. Travelled in Italy, France, England, Spain on diplomatic missions. An intermediary in attempts to attain Christian unity; helped to fix date and location of Council of Constance, to which he went as papal emissary; but died soon after arrival. Wrote theological treatises; a Greek grammar; letters; a literal Latin translation of Plato's *Republic*, later revised by Uberto and P. C. Decembrio.

I   *DTC* II, cols. 2422–3; *EI* XI, p. 920; Garin I, pp. 286–8.

II Sabbadini 1890; Cammelli 1941–54, I; I. Thomson 1966; Geanakoplos 1976 *passim*.

CLICHTOVE, JOSSE (Jodocus Clichtoveus) b. Nieuport, 1472; d. Chartres, 1543. Flemish humanist and theologian, active in France. Studied at Louvain and Paris (pupil of Lefèvre d'Étaples); 1506 *doctor theologiae*; 1506–12 taught theology at the Sorbonne; 1512–15 at Collège du Cardinal Lemoine; and 1521–6 at Collège de Navarre. Originally associated with French reforming circles of Lefèvre and Briçonnet; but later vigorously opposed heretical trends in the University of Paris. *Canonicus* and *theologicus*, Chartres, 1527–43. In 1528 participated in Council of Sens, Paris. Collaborated with Lefèvre on several influential philosophy textbooks: Aristotelian ethics, politics, logic, natural philosophy, metaphysics; edited patristic authors; from 1517 wrote polemical works, after 1520 especially against Luther.

I   *DTC* III, cols. 236–43; *EF* I, col. 1461; Farge, pp. 90–104; Lohr 1975, pp. 713–14.

II Clerval 1894; Renaudet 1953 *passim*; Massaut 1968, 1974; Chantraine 1971; Kraus 1971; Ashworth 1986.

COLLEGIUM CONIMBRICENSE (*Commentarii conimbricenses*; Coimbra commentaries) A group of texts and commentaries on the major works of Aristotle, prepared by the Jesuits of the University of Coimbra between 1592 and 1598. Initiated by Pedro da Fonseca, who delegated its execution to Emmanuel de Goes. The *cursus* includes expositions of the *Physics* (1592), *De caelo* (1592), *Meteorology* (1592), *Parva naturalia* (1592), *Nicomachean Ethics* (1593), *De generatione et corruptione* (1597) and *De anima* (1598); *In universam dialecticam* (1606) is not of the same exhaustive and rigorous quality as the volumes devoted to the central works of natural philosophy. After the first edition (at Coimbra and Lisbon), the commentaries were frequently reprinted for the next forty years (at Venice, Lyons, Cologne, Mainz) and were widely used throughout Europe during the first half of the seventeenth century.

I   *EF* I, cols. 1590–1; Lohr 1975, pp. 717–19.

II Gilson 1912, 1951; Andrade 1943; Gomes dos Santos 1955; introduction to *Collegium Conimbricense* 1957; Stegmüller 1959; Barcelar e Oliveira 1960; Zilli 1961; Coxito 1966; Schmitt 1983a *ad indicem*.

CONTARINI, GASPARO b. Venice, 1483; d. Bologna, 1542. Italian churchman and Thomist theologian. Studied under Pomponazzi at Padua before embarking on various diplomatic missions, including negotiating the release of Clement VII from Emperor Charles V in 1527. Created cardinal 1535. One of the nine commissioners appointed to consider church reform. Papal legate at Diet of Ratisbon, 1540. Named cardinal-legate to Bologna, but died a few months later. Wrote on various philosophical and theological matters: e.g., *De immortalitate animae, De potestate pontificis, De libero arbitrio*. Critic of Alexandrist Aristotelianism; upheld personal immortality and the autonomy of soul in relation to body.

I   *DTC* III, cols. 1615–16; *EF* II, col. 11; Lohr 1975, p. 721.

II Dittrich 1885; *Aristotelismo padovano* 1960, pp. 109–19 (Giacon); Di Napoli 1963, pp. 277–97; *Umanesimo europeo* 1964, pp. 31–63 (Gilson).

CREMONINI, CESARE (Cremoninius) b. Cento (near Ferrara), 1550; d. Padua, 1631. Italian Aristotelian philosopher. Studied philosophy and law at University of Ferrara, becoming doctor there; 1573–90, professor of philosophy. Ordinary professor of philosophy *secundo loco* at Padua, 1591–1601. Spokesman for the university against the Jesuits, 1591–1606.

Ordinary professor of philosophy *primo loco*, 1601–31. Investigated by Inquisition, 1611–26. Wrote series of commentaries (chiefly on Aristotelian natural philosophy) and several apologetic discourses supporting Aristotelian doctrines (many survive only in manuscript). Colleague of Galileo at Padua.
I *DBI* xxx, pp. 618–22; *EF* II, cols. 148–51; Lohr 1975, pp. 728–39.
II Mabilleau 1881; Del Torre 1968; L. A. Kennedy 1979, 1980; *Aristotelismo veneto* 1983, II, pp. 637–45 (Del Torre) and 647–59 (Drew); Olivieri 1983, pp. 196–203; Schmitt 1984, § XI.

CROCKAERT, PETRUS, O.P. b. Brussels, *c.* 1470; d. Paris(?), 1514. Flemish theologian. Studied under John Mair at Collège de Montaigu, Paris; M.A. and taught philosophy there in nominalist tradition. Became Dominican at convent of S. Jacques and changed philosophically to Thomism, 1503. In 1504 taught *Sententiae*; 1507 taught theology (pupils included Francisco de Vitoria, Domingo de Soto); 1509 *baccalaureus theologiae*; substituted *Summa theologiae* for *Sententiae* as basis of theological instruction. *Licentiatus theologiae*, 1512. Presided over academic disputations in faculty of theology, 1513–14. Edited Thomas Aquinas and commented on *Summule* of Peter of Spain.
I *EF* II, cols. 200–1; Farge, pp. 126–7; Lohr 1975, pp. 739–40.
II García Villoslada 1935, 1938 *passim*; Chenu 1946; Renaudet 1953 *passim*; Wallace 1981a *passim*.

DANEAU, LAMBERT (Danaeus) b. Beaugency, *c.* 1530; d. Castres, 1595. French Calvinist philosopher and theologian. Studied law at Orléans and Bourges; 1557 licentiate; 1559 doctorate. Became advocate at Orléans 1560, but April 1560 moved to Geneva to study theology. Shortly afterwards appointed pastor at Gien. Sought refuge at Orléans, 1563. In 1566 moved to Sancerre; 1572 emigrated to Geneva, where he became a pastor and professor of theology, 1574–81. In 1581–2 professor of theology and pastor of Walloon community at Leiden. Returned to France, 1582. Appointed to Protestant Academy at Orthez, 1584. In 1593–5 professor at Castres. Published polemical works against Génébrard, Osiander, Bellarmine; edited ancient and patristic authors; wrote commentaries on the gospels, Paul, Cyprian, Augustine and Peter Lombard; also, various textbooks attempting to promote a Christianised philosophy divested of pagan elements: *Physica christiana* (1576); *Ethices christianae libri III* (1577); *Christianae isagoges ad Christianorum locos communes libri II* (1583).
I *DBF* x, cols. 88–9.
II Félice 1882; Fatio 1971, 1976.

DECEMBRIO, PIER CANDIDO b. Pavia, *c.* 1392; d. Milan, 1477. Italian humanist. Much of his early life spent in Milan in the service of Filippo Maria Visconti. In 1456–9 in Naples as court secretary to Alfonso, then Ferdinand. Returned to Milan 1459–66, followed by eight years at Este court in Ferrara; then returned again to Milan. Translated works of Appian, Plutarch, Homer, and revised Chrysoloras' translation of Plato's *Republic*, dedicated to Humfrey of Gloucester (*c.* 1440). Also wrote several works on natural philosophy, e.g., *De genitura hominis*.
I *EI* XII, p. 457.
II Borsa 1893, 1904; Ditt 1931; Zaccaria 1952, 1956, 1959; *Medioevo e Rinascimento* 1955, I, pp. 341–74 (Garin); Kristeller 1966b; Sammut 1980; *Vestigia* 1984, I, pp. 75–91 (Bottoni) and 247–96 (Ferrari); Pyle 1984.

DELLA PORTA, GIAMBATTISTA b. Vico Equense, 1535; d. Naples, 1615. Italian philosopher, scientist, dramatist. Interested in natural magic and associated fields of astrology, chiromancy and art of memory. Viewed natural magic as a practical complement to scientific investigation, subject to the boundaries of natural law; attacked demonic magic and theurgic practices. His *Magiae naturalis libri IV* (Naples 1558) went through several editions; it was expanded to twenty books (1589) and later translated into a number of languages. His *De humana physiognomonia* (1586) and *Coelestis physiognomoniae libri sex* (1603) stress the interrelationship between soul and body and incorporate his belief in sympathetic magic and the doctrine of correspondences. Played a major role in founding the Accademia dei Lincei, but his magical interests later led him to establish an independent Accademia dei Segreti. Also wrote several dramatic comedies based on classical models.

I   *DSB* XI, pp. 95–8; *EF* II, cols. 309–10; *EI* XII, pp. 548–9; Garin II, pp. 630–2.

II Fiorentino 1911, pp. 235–340; Gabrieli 1927, 1932; Paparelli 1955, 1956a, 1956b; Corsano 1958–63, 38: 76–97; Badaloni 1959–60, 1961 *passim*; Clubb 1965; Aquilecchia 1976; Muraro 1978.

DIGBY, EVERARD (Digbaeus) b. Rutland *c.* 1550; d. *c.* 1606 (place of death unknown). English anti-Ramist philosopher. St John's, Cambridge, B.A. 1570–1; 1574 M.A.; 1581 B.D.; 1572–3 Lady Margaret fellow; 1585 senior fellow. Taught logic at Cambridge, where Francis Bacon probably attended his lectures. Deprived of his living for misconduct, supporting the (Catholic) idea of voluntary poverty and attacking Calvinists too strongly, 1587. Eclectically combined Neoplatonic, cabalistic and Hermetic material with traditional Thomist and Scotist sources. Wrote *Theorica analytica* (1579), attempting a scientific classification and methodology based on inductive rather than deductive reasoning. Fierce opponent of Ramism; published *De duplici methodo libri duo, unicam P. Rami methodum refutantes* (1580); engaged in polemic with his Ramist ex-student, William Temple.

I   *DNB* V, pp. 955–6; *EF* II, cols. 451–2.

II Freudenthal 1890–1; Sortais 1920, I, pp. 53–6; N. W. Gilbert 1960, pp. 200–8, 231; Vasoli 1968a, pp. 590–601; L. Jardine 1974a, pp. 59–65; Schmitt 1983b, pp. 47–52 and *passim*.

DULLAERT, JOHANNES (Dullardus) b. Werde, *c.* 1470; d. Paris, 1513. French natural philosopher in the Paris tradition of Buridan. Studied under John Mair at Collège de Montaigu, Paris, where he became *magister regens. Magister regens* at Collège de Beauvais, Paris, 1510. Briefly returned to Ghent, but accused of treason against Spain and went back to Paris. Edited works of Paul of Venice and Buridan's *Quaestiones in Physica.*

I   Duhem TB, X, pp. 24–47 and *passim*; Lohr 1976, pp. 720–1; Prantl IV, pp. 256ff.

II García Villoslada 1938 *passim*; Clagett 1959, pp. 638, 653–6; Wallace 1981a, pp. 65–75, 79–84.

DU VAIR, GUILLAUME b. Paris, 1556; d. Tonneins (Lot-et-Garonne), 1621. French statesman and Neostoic philosopher. In 1584 Clerk councillor to Paris Parlement. In 1593 Parisian deputy to États Généraux of the Ligue. In his *Exhortations à la paix* supported Henri de Navarre's claim to the French throne, provided he converted to Catholicism. In 1596 negotiated league against Spain with Elizabeth I; then despatched as Governor to Provence to quell disorder there. First president of Parlement of Aix, 1599. Appointed Bishop of Lisieux, 1617. Guardian of the Royal Seals. Inspired by Epictetus, whom he translated into French *c.* 1585, and by Lipsius; sought to combine Stoicism with Christianity. Wrote *De la sainte philosophie; De la philosophie morale des Stoïques; Traité de la constance et de consolation ès calamités publiques; Traité de l'éloquence française.*

I   *DBF* XII, cols. 950–1.

II Cougny 1857; Radouant 1908; Glaesener 1938; introduction to Du Vair 1951, pp. 1–39; Roques 1957; Julien Eymard 1976; Abel 1978, pp. 114–52.

ECK, JOHANNES (Eckius) b. Egg (near Memmingen), 1486; d. Ingolstadt, 1543. German theologian and philosopher. Studied at Rothenburg, Heidelberg, Tübingen. M.A., 1501. Studied theology at Cologne. In 1502–10 studied theology, mathematics (under Gregor Reisch), geography, law (under Ulrich Zasius) and taught philosophy at University of Freiburg; 1510 *doctor theologiae* there. Professor of theology at University of Ingolstadt, 1510–43. Participated in disputations of Bologna 1515, Vienna 1516 and Leipzig 1519. Participated in Reichstag, Augsburg, 1530. In 1540–1 attended religious conferences at Hagenau, Worms, Regensburg. Prominent Catholic opponent of Luther. Wrote several Aristotelian works.

I   *DHGE* XIV, pp. 1375–9; *DTC* IV, cols. 2056–7; Lohr 1976, pp. 722–3; *NDB* IV, pp. 272–4; Prantl III, pp. 284–90.

II Seifert 1978; Iserloh 1981.

ERASMUS, DESIDERIUS b. Rotterdam, 1466/9; d. Basle, 1536. Dutch humanist and theologian. Educated by Brethren of the Common Life at Deventer. In 1487 became Augustinian canon at Steyn. Ordained priest, 1492. In 1495 studied at Collège de Montaigu, Paris. In Oxford 1499; Louvain 1502–4; Italy 1506–9; England again 1509–14, teaching at Cambridge and establishing contact with More/Colet circle. In Louvain 1517–21; Basle and Freiburg 1529–36. Wrote didactic and satirical works promoting a combination of learning and piety (*philosophia Christi*) and urging church reform: e.g., *Enchiridion militis christiani* (published 1503); *Moriae encomium* (1511); *Colloquia familiaria* (1518–33). Opposed Luther, with whom he debated on freedom of the will. Edited the Greek New Testament with Latin translation, patristic works and classical texts, e.g., Aristotle, Cicero, Seneca. His writings were posthumously placed on the Index.

I   *CTC* IV, pp. 221–2; *DTC* V, cols. 388–97; *EF* II, cols. 913–15; *NDB* IV, pp. 554–60; Totok, pp. 283–314.

II *Bibliotheca Erasmiana* 1893–1908; P. Smith 1923; Bataillon 1937; Renaudet 1954; Margolin 1963, 1977; D. F. S. Thomson and Porter 1963; Kohls 1966; Bené 1969; Halkin 1969; Mesnard 1969; Tracy 1972, 1978; Trinkaus 1976; Stupperich 1977; *Essays . . . Erasmus* 1978; Chantraine 1981; Chomarat 1981; O'Rourke Boyle 1983; Rummel 1985.

FICINO, MARSILIO b. Figline (Valdarno), 1433; d. Careggi (Florence), 1499. Italian Neoplatonic philosopher. Educated in Florence in humanities, philosophy, medicine. Began studying Greek *c.* 1456. Cosimo de' Medici commissioned him to translate *corpus Hermeticum* (completed 1463) and Plato (published 1484). Leading spirit in Florentine Platonic Academy. Ordained priest, 1473. Wrote influential commentary on *Symposium* (1469), explaining Platonic theory of love; *Theologia platonica* (1469–74), on immortality of the soul; *De triplici vita* (1489), touching on magic and astrology; translated and commented on Plotinus (1492). Retired to the country after the Medici were expelled from Florence in 1494.

I   *CTC* I, p. 139; *DTC* V, cols. 2277–91; *EF* II, cols. 1327–31; Lohr 1971, pp. 322–3; Totok, pp. 154–9.

II Festugière 1941; Kristeller 1953a, 1956a *ad indicem*, 1983a; Garin 1954, pp. 288–311; Saitta 1954; Marcel 1958; Walker 1958, pp. 3–59; Tarabochia 1971–2; Zambelli 1973a; Collins 1974; *Platon et Aristote* 1976, pp. 59–77 (Kristeller); Zanier 1977; M. J. B. Allen 1980, 1982, 1984a, 1984b; M. J. B. Allen and White 1981; Copenhaver 1984, 1986 and forthcoming b; *Marsilio Ficino* 1984.

FILELFO, FRANCESCO b. Tolentino, 1398; d. Florence, 1481. Italian humanist. Studied at Padua under Gasparino Barzizza. Taught at Padua, Venice, Vicenza. Secretary of Venetian Republic at Constantinople, 1421–7: studied under Johannes Chrysoloras; collected Greek manuscripts; served on various embassies. Taught at Bologna, 1428. In 1429 called to teach at the Florentine *Studio*, where he quarrelled with many prominent citizens; exiled in 1434 for conspiring against Cosimo de' Medici. In 1434–9 taught at Sienna. In Milan 1439–81, where he served the Visconti and Sforza families; except during 1475–6, when he taught at the Sapienza in Rome. Recalled to Florence in 1481 by Lorenzo but died soon after his arrival. Translated Plutarch, Xenophon, pseudo-Aristotelian *Rhetorica ad Alexandrum*; wrote *De morali disciplina*, a treatise on moral philosophy; also, the dialogues *De exilio* and *Convivium Mediolanense*; Greek and Latin letters and poems.

I   *CTC* I, pp. 214–15, III, p. 445; *EF* II, col. 1341; *EI* XV, p. 281.
II De' Rosmini 1808; *Onoranze . . . Filelfo* 1905; Calderini 1913, 1915; Firpo 1967; Kraye
    1979, 1981; Zippel 1979, pp. 215–53; *Umanesimo e Rinascimento* 1980, pp. 33–44
    (Giustiniani); *Franceso Filelfo* 1986; Adam forthcoming.

FONSECA, PEDRO DA, S.J. b. Cortiçada (now Proença-a-Nova), 1528; d. Lisbon, 1599. Portuguese Jesuit philosopher and theologian. Entered order at Coimbra, 1548. In 1551 joined newly founded University of Évora; 1552–5 studied theology. From 1555 to 1561 professor of philosophy in Colégio das Artes, Coimbra, where he conceived idea for a *Cursus Conimbricensis*, which was delegated to Emmanuel de Goes; main series of commentaries was published in Coimbra 1592–8. Administrative duties in Order, 1561–4. From 1564 to 1566 professor of theology at Évora; 1570 *doctor theologiae* and chancellor of University. Official duties at Rome 1572–82, including contribution to Jesuit *Ratio studiorum*. Visitor of Portuguese province of Jesuits, 1589–92. In 1592 delegate to Jesuit General Congregation, Rome. Wrote *Institutionum dialecticarum libri VIII* (1564); *Isagoge philosophica* (1591); *In universam dialecticam* (published posthumously 1606).

I   *EF* II, cols. 1451–2; Lohr 1976, pp. 739–41; Solana III, pp. 339–66; Totok, pp. 567–9.
II Ceñal 1943; Abranches 1953; Santos Alves 1955; Sousa Alves 1961; introduction to
    Fonseca 1964; Ferreira Gomes 1966; Ashworth 1974a.

FOX-MORCILLO, SEBASTIAN b. Seville, 1526/8; d. at sea, 1560. Spanish philosopher, humanist, political theorist. Early education in Spain; then studied philosophy at Louvain. In 1560 summoned to Spain by Philip II as tutor to Don Carlos, but perished in shipwreck. Wrote *Ethices philosophiae compendium* (1554); *De demonstratione eiusque necessitate ac vi* and *In Platonis Timaeum commentarii* (both 1556); *De naturae philosophia seu de Platonis et Aristotelis consensione* (1560), in which he developed his syncretistic approach to the doctrines of Plato and Aristotle.

I   Lohr 1976, pp. 741–2; Solana I, pp. 573–627.
II U. González de la Calle 1903; Honecker 1914; Lueben 1914; Bernal Zurita 1945; Purnell
    1971, pp. 68–70.

FRACASTORO, GIROLAMO b. Verona, 1470; d. Verona, 1553. Italian physician and natural philosopher. Studied mathematics, medicine (under Leonico Tomeo and Pomponazzi) at Padua; met Copernicus there *c.* 1501; B.A. 1502; then taught logic and medicine. Later practised medicine in Verona. Physician at Council of Trent. Wrote various works on medicine and natural philosophy: e.g., the poem *Syphilis* (1521); *Homocentricorum sive de stellis liber* and *De causis criticorum dierum* (both 1538); *De contagione* (1546), the first work of systematic epidemiology. Contributed to the debate on immortality of the soul; favoured a Democritean corpuscular theory.

I   *DSB* V, pp. 104–7; *EF* II, cols. 1494–5; Saitta I, pp. 177–212.
II G. Rossi 1893; Pellegrini 1948; Di Leo 1953; P. Rossi 1954; Peruzzi 1980.

GAETANO DA THIENE (Caietanus de Thienis) b. Gaeta, 1387; d. Padua, 1465. Italian philosopher and physician. Studied arts and medicine, 1412, Padua; 1417 M.A.; 1418 *doctor artium*; 1429 *doctor artium et medicinae*; 1430–62 taught natural philosophy. *Canonicus*, Padua, 1437. A moderate Averroist in tradition of Paul of Venice; sought to harmonise Averroism and Christian doctrine. Wrote *De intensione et remissione formarum*; commented on William Heytesbury's *Regule* and on several works of Aristotle, e.g., *De caelo* and *Physics*.

I *CHLMP*, p. 860; *EF* II, cols. 1557–9; Lohr 1967, pp. 390–2.

II Sartori 1938; Valsanzibio 1949; Clagett 1959, pp. 651–2; Di Napoli 1963, pp. 97–105; Poppi 1966, pp. 124–9; Wallace 1972–, I, pp. 127–30; *Scienza e filosofia* 1983 *ad indicem*.

GALILEI, GALILEO b. Pisa, 1564; d. Arcetri (near Pisa), 1642. Italian scientist. Studied at Pisa, becoming lecturer in mathematics, 1589. Began work on dynamics, writing *De motu* (1590–2). From 1592 to 1610 lecturer in mathematics at Padua; developed research on motion, made scientific instruments; 1593–1600 still taught Ptolemaic cosmology, but 1597 letter to Kepler evinces preference for Copernicanism. In 1609 improved Dutch-invented telescope; described observations of moon, Jupiter's satellites in *Sidereus nuncius* (1610). Moved to Florence 1610–42 as *primarius philosophus et mathematicus* to Cosimo III. Letter to Castelli (1613) and *Lettera a Madama Cristina di Lorena* (1615; published 1636) confirmed support of Copernican theory and belief that science should be independent from theology. In 1615 denounced by Dominican Niccolò Lorini to Inquisition for Copernicanism. Visited Rome 1615–16 to defend theory; 1616 church condemned Copernicanism and forbade him to propagate it. Expecting greater intellectual freedom under Urban VIII, published *Dialogo sopra i due massimi sistemi del mondo* (1632), favouring Copernican over Ptolemaic cosmology. In 1633 summoned to Rome; forced to retract views and confined for life, first at Rome, then at Florence. In his final work, *Discorsi e dimostrazioni matematiche intorno a due nuove scienze* (1638), applied experimental method to many problems.

I *DSB* V, pp. 237–48; *EF* II, cols. 1564–70; Lohr 1977, pp. 682–9.

II Favaro 1883, 1894–1919; Caverni 1891–1900; Olschki 1919–27; Santillana 1959; Koyré 1966; *Galileo Man of Science* 1967; *Saggio su Galileo Galilei* 1967; Clavelin 1968; Drake 1970, 1973, 1976, 1978; Drake and McLachlan 1975; *New Perspectives* 1978; Galluzzi 1979; Wallace 1981a, 1981b, 1984; *Novità celesti* 1983; Carugo and Crombie 1983; *Aristotelismo veneto* 1983, I, pp. 349–78 (Wallace); *Reinterpreting Galileo* 1986.

GAZA, THEODORE (Theodoros Gazes) b. Salonike, 1400; d. S. Giovanni Piro (Salerno), 1476. Byzantine humanist. Studied at Constantinople. In Italy for Council of Florence (1438), soon settling permanently. In 1442–6 studied under Vittorino da Feltre. Taught at University of Ferrara (first professor of Greek), 1447–9. Later moved to Rome, Naples and Calabria. His patrons included Nicholas V, Alfonso V of Aragon, Cardinal Bessarion. Translated Aristotle's zoological and Theophrastus' botanical works; also compiled Greek grammar.

I *CTC* I, p. 130; *EF* III, cols. 3–4.

II Stein 1889; Gercke 1903; Mohler 1923–42, 1943–9; Monfasani 1976 *passim*; Geanakoplos 1982.

GENUA, MARCANTONIO (Marcus Antonius Januae, Passerus, de Passeriis; Genova de' Passeri) b. Padua, 1490/1; d. Padua, 1563. Italian philosopher and Aristotelian commentator. Studied philosophy and medicine at Padua, becoming *doctor in artibus et medicina*, 1512; 1517 second chair of extraordinary philosophy; 1518 first chair of extraordinary philosophy; 1523 second chair of ordinary philosophy; 1531–63 first chair of ordinary philosophy. Attacked Pomponazzi, accusing him of not understanding either Aristotle or Averroes; also criticised Thomas Aquinas and Duns Scotus. Among his pupils: Sperone Speroni, Jacopo Zabarella.

I *EF* IV, cols. 1382–4; Lohr 1977, pp. 726–30.

II Nardi 1958, pp. 386–94 and *passim*, 1965 *passim*; Di Napoli 1963, pp. 348–50; Poppi 1970a, pp. 35–7.

GEORGE OF BRUSSELS (Georgius Bruxellensis) *fl.* 1495; d. 1510. Taught at Paris arts faculty; did not publish his own lectures, but Thomas Bricot (possibly his pupil) compiled abbreviated texts of Aristotle and published them (sometimes adding *quaestiones* of his own) with George's commentaries or *quaestiones*: e.g., *Quaestiones in totam logicam* (1493).
I Duhem *SM* x, pp. 77–91 and *passim*; Lohr 1968, pp. 155–8; Prantl IV, pp. 199–203.
II Élie 1950–1, pp. 197–200; Clagett 1959, p. 638.

GEORGE OF TREBIZOND (Georgius Trapezuntius) b. Crete, 1395; d. Rome, 1484. Byzantine humanist scholar. Emigrated to Italy, supporting Rome in the debate over reunification of the Greek and Latin churches. In 1416 invited to Venice by Francesco Barbaro. Studied at Padua under Vittorino da Feltre, 1417–18. Taught at Vicenza and Rome. With Vittorino at Mantua, 1430–2. In 1437–43 interpreter with papal Curia at Bologna, Ferrara and Florence. Secretary to Pope Nicholas V 1450, but his faulty translations led to estrangement. Reconciled 1453 with pope. Remainder of his life, apart from 1459–66, spent teaching and writing in Rome. Wrote treatises in Latin and Greek on theology, philosophy and rhetoric; Latin commentary on Ptolemy; translations of Aristotle, Plato, Eusebius and other Christian Fathers. Leading proponent of Aristotle and virulent antagonist of Platonic philosophy; in his *Comparationes* accused Pletho of attempting to subvert Christianity in favour of a revived Neoplatonic, pagan religion; attacked moral probity of Plato; Bessarion replied with his defence of Plato, *In calumniatorem Platonis*.
I *CTC* II, p. 137; *DTC* VI, cols. 1235–7; Lohr 1968, pp. 158–9.
II Mohler 1923–42 *ad indicem*; Cessi 1956, pp. 129–51, 153–81; Vasoli 1968a, pp. 81–99; Monfasani 1976; Lojacono 1985.

GERSON, JEAN b. Gerson (Champagne), 1363; d. Lyons, 1429. French philosopher and churchman. From 1377 studied at Collège de Navarre. *Doctor theologiae*, 1395; succeeded Pierre d'Ailly as Chancellor of University of Paris. Sojourn at Bruges, 1397–1401. In 1401 returned to Paris. Influential in conciliar movement and at Council of Constance 1414–18, defending superiority of conciliar over papal authority. Briefly at Rattenburg, then settled at Lyons. Wrote on logic, metaphysics, epistemology, education; sought to reconcile formalist/Scotist with terminist doctrines; critical of scholasticism, to which he counterposed a mystical philosophy indebted to the earlier Franciscan school of Alexander of Hales and St Bonaventure; developed further Scotus' and Ockham's emphasis on the arbitrariness of the divine will.
I *DS* VI, cols. 314–33; *DTC* VI, cols. 1313–30; *EF* III, cols. 86–8.
II Schwab 1858; Connolly 1928; Morrall 1960; Combes 1963–5, 1973; Posthumous Meyjes 1963; Bauer 1973; Pascoe 1973.

GILES OF VITERBO, O.E.S.A. (Egidio da Viterbo) b. Viterbo, 1465/9; d. Viterbo, 1532. Italian Augustinian Platonist, humanist, prelate. Studied at Padua (under Agostino Nifo); preoccupied with theories of soul; dissatisfaction with Aristotelian views erupted in print later when he attacked impiety and irreligion of Paduan *Studio*; became enthusiastic defender and proponent of Plato and Ficino. In charge of legations to Venice, Naples, Austria, Spain. In 1506 elected Prior General of Augustinian Order. Created cardinal 1517; then Patriarch of Constantinople; Bishop of Viterbo. Wrote treatises (mostly unpublished) on Platonism and cabalism.
I *DTC* VI, cols. 1365–71; *EF* II, col. 755.
II Signorelli 1929; Massa 1949, 1951, 1954; F. X. Martin 1959–60, 1979; Di Napoli 1963 *ad indicem*; Secret 1958b, 1964, pp. 106–20 and *passim*; J. W. O'Malley 1966, 1967, 1968; *Egidio da Viterbo* 1983.

GINÉS DE SEPÚLVEDA, JUAN (Joannes Genesius Sepulveda) b. Pozoblanco (Cordova), 1490; d. Pozoblanco, 1573. Spanish philosopher and jurist. Studied at Alcalá and Sigüenza, 1511–14; and Bologna, 1515–22 (teachers included Pomponazzi), where friendly with Alberto Pio's circle. Commissioned by Giulio de' Medici (Clement VII, 1523–34) to translate Aristotle: *Parva naturalia* (1522); *De generatione et interitu* and *De mundo* (1523); *Meteorology* (1529). By 1523 *doctor artium et theologiae*. At Rome 1522–36, publishing anti-Lutheran *De fato et libero arbitrio* (1526). In 1527 fled to Naples following sack of Rome. In 1529, 1532 member of papal parties visiting Charles V. Professor of moral philosophy, Rome, 1530. Published *Antapologia* (1532) against Erasmus; *Democrates sive de convenientia militaris disciplinae cum Christiana religione* (1535). In 1536 appointed historiographer to Charles V (composed royal chronicles 1536–64), moving to Spain and residing mainly with court until 1550. Completed *Democrates alter sive de iustis belli causis apud Indios* (*c.* 1547), supporting the Spanish conquests in America; it circulated in manuscript in Spain and Italy but remained unpublished due to opposition from Universities of Alcalá and Salamanca. In 1550–1 appeared against Las Casas in the Junta de Valladolid concerning the wars against the Indians.
I *DHEE* iv, pp. 2433–7; Lohr 1977, pp. 694–7; Solana ii, pp. 9–48 and *passim*.
II Andrés Marcos 1947; Losada 1948–9, 1949; Carro 1951, pp. 561–673; Bruton 1953; Giménez Fernández 1962; Hanke 1974 *passim*; Mechoulan 1974; Pagden 1982 *passim*.

GIORGI, FRANCESCO, O.F.M. (Zorzi; Georgius) b. Venice, *c.* 1460/6; d. Asolo, 1540. Italian philosopher. Joined Franciscans before 1482. Perhaps studied at Padua in early years. Critical of Aristotelian-Averroistic doctrines. His *De harmonia mundi* (1525) combines Hermetic, Platonic and cabalistic ideas on astrology, musical theory, psychology and cosmology; depicts universe as a musical harmony governed by numerical laws. Familiar with the works of Ficino and Pico, although carefully avoided Ficino's magical interests. Platonic and Talmudic interests also figure in his *Problemata*, dedicated to Paul III but later censured in parts by the Inquisition.
I Saitta ii, pp. 76–9.
II Secret 1958a, pp. 43–9, 1964, pp. 126–40; Walker 1958, pp. 112–19; Maillard 1971; Vasoli 1974, pp. 131–403; Yates 1979, pp. 29–36, 127–33 and *passim*; Perrone Compagni 1982.

GOCLENIUS, RUDOLPHUS (The Elder; Rudolf Goeckel) b. Corbach, 1547; d. Marburg, 1628. Polymath, active in natural philosophy, grammar, logic, psychology, poetry. Studied at Corbach; 1564 University of Marburg; 1568 University of Wittenberg; *magister* there, 1571. Rector of Stadtschule, Corbach, 1573–5. Rector of Stadtschule, Kassel, 1575–81. Professor of natural philosophy, Marburg 1581; 1589 professor of logic; 1598–1609 also taught mathematics; from 1603 also held chair of ethics; dean many times; rector, 1611. Wrote *Lexicon philosophicum* (1613), which became a standard reference work. Also wrote several commentaries on Aristotle's logical works.
I *ADB* iv, pp. 308–12; *EF* iii, cols. 301–2; Lohr 1977, pp. 701–2.
II Wundt 1939 *ad indicem*.

GREGORY OF RIMINI, O.E.S.A. (Gregorius Tortorici de Arimino) b. Rimini, 1300; d. Vienna, 1358. Italian Ockhamist theologian and philosopher. Joined Augustinians. Studied at Paris, 1322–9, B.A., 1323; and Oxford. Taught at Paris, Bologna, Padua, Perugia. Returned to Paris, 1341–51; read *Sententiae*, 1343–4; *magister theologiae*, 1345. From 1351 to 1356 taught at Rimini. In 1357 general of Augustinian Order. Wrote on the *Sententiae*.
I *DTC* vi, cols. 1852–4; *EF* iii, cols. 370–1; Lohr 1968, p. 171.
II Würsdörfer 1922; Schüler 1934; Trapp 1958, 1962; Leff 1961; García Lescún 1970; *Gregor von Rimini* 1981; Courtenay and Tachau 1982 *passim*.

GROUCHY, NICOLAS DE (Grouchius; Gruchius) b. La Chaussé-sur-Longueville (or Rouen), 1509; d. La Rochelle, 1572. French humanist and translator. Studied philosophy at Collège Ste Barbe, Paris, gaining M.A. In 1534 taught logic at Collège de Guyenne, Bordeaux; and 1547 at Coimbra. In 1550 returned to France, working on translations of Aristotle's works (his *Organon* appeared in Casaubon's 1590 edition) and revisions of Périon's versions. President of Protestant College, La Rochelle, 1572.
I Lohr 1977, p. 707.
II Grouchy and Travers 1878; Leitao Ferreira 1944, pp. 342–73; Schmitt 1983a, pp. 59–61, 76–8.

GUARINO DA VERONA (Guarino Veronese; Guarinus Veronensis) b. Verona, 1374; d. Ferrara, 1460. Italian humanist and educator. Studied at Verona, Padua, Venice and Constantinople. From 1409–1414 in Verona, Bologna and Florence; 1414–19 in Venice. From 1419 to 1429 ran private school, Verona. In Ferrara as tutor to Lionello d'Este, public orator, ambassador, educator, 1429–60; pupils included Ermolao Barbaro the elder, Ludovico Carbone, John Free. Wrote *Regulae grammaticales*, an influential Latin grammar; translated Basil, Lucian (*Calumnia*), Plutarch, Strabo; commented on Cicero, Juvenal, Martial, etc.; wrote lives of Homer and Plato; Latin letters.
I *CHLMP*, p. 862; *CTC* I, p. 207.
II De' Rosmini 1805–6; Sabbadini 1891, 1896, 1922, ch. 5; Woodward 1906, ch. 2; Bertoni 1921; Garin 1961, pp. 402–26; Schweyen 1973; Grafton and L. Jardine 1982.

GUICCIARDINI, FRANCESCO b. Florence, 1483; d. Florence, 1540. Italian historian, political theorist, diplomat. Belonged to a prominent patrician family. After training in law, sent to Spain on a diplomatic mission, 1511–12. Served Medici Popes Leo X and Clement VII in several important governorships (Modena, Reggio, Parma); president of Romagna in 1524; papal representative in Florence in 1530. Later became adviser to Alessandro and then Cosimo I de' Medici but gradually lost political influence in Florence. Wrote political tracts: *Discorso di Logrogno* (1512), recommending a mixed constitution for republics; *Dialogo del reggimento di Firenze* (1521–3), discussing the best form of government for Florence; *Ricordi* (first sketched 1512; completed 1528–30), a series of maxims on men and political affairs; and a critique of Machiavelli entitled *Considerazioni sopra i Discorsi di Machiavelli* (1530). His historical works include: *Storie fiorentine* (1509), covering the period 1378–1509; *Storia d' Italia* (1537–40 but published 1561), a magisterial and widely influential account of the collapse of Italian independence from the French invasion of 1494 to the death of Clement VII in 1534.
I *EI* XVIII, pp. 244–8.
II F. Gilbert 1965; Ridolfi 1978b, 1982; Phillips 1977; Skinner 1978, I *ad indicem*; *Guicciardini* 1984; *Francesco Guicciardini* 1984.

JAVELLI, CRISOSTOMO, O.P. (Chrysostomus Javellus; Chrysostomus Casalensis) b. Canavese, 1470; d. Bologna, 1538. Thomist philosopher and theologian. Taught at Bologna. Wrote commentaries on the main works of Aristotle, e.g., *Compendium logicae isagogicum*. Defended Thomas Aquinas' exposition of Aristotle in several volumes, e.g., *Quaestiones super VIII libros Physices ad mentem D. Thomae*. In ethics favoured Plato over Aristotle as closer to Christian values. Refuted Pomponazzi's *De immortalitate animae* in *Solutiones rationum*, published in conjunction with Pomponazzi's *Defensorium* (1519).
I *DTC* VIII, cols. 535–7; *EF* III, col. 1164; Lohr 1977, pp. 730–3.
II Gilson 1961, pp. 259–77; Di Napoli 1963, pp. 325–35; Kristeller 1967a *ad indicem*.

KECKERMANN, BARTHOLOMAEUS b. Danzig, 1571; d. Danzig, 1609. German philosopher, jurist, theologian. From 1590 studied philosophy at Wittenberg, Leipzig and

Heidelberg; M.A., 1594. Taught in Heidelberg at Studentenburse Paedagogium; from 1597 at Collegium Sapientiae; 1600 professor of Hebrew; 1602 *licentiatus theologiae*. From 1602 to 1609 professor of philosophy and co-rector of Gymnasium at Danzig. Prominent Protestant Aristotelian, particularly concerned with the theoretical elaboration of the concept of *systema*: sets of precepts integral to the formation of various disciplines, e.g., *Systema logicae* (1600); *Systema rhetoricae* (1608); *Systema systematum* (published posthumously 1613). These manuals were widely used throughout Northern Europe in the first half of the seventeenth century. Also wrote *Praecognitorum logicorum tractatus III* (1599), a detailed Aristotelian critique of Ramist method drawing on Jacopo Zabarella.
I   *ADB* xv, p. 518; *EF* iii, col. 1237; Lohr 1977, pp. 738–40.
II   Van Zuylen 1934; Dibon 1954–, i, pp. 89–103; N. W. Gilbert 1960 *ad indicem*; Vasoli 1983a, 1984; Muller 1984.

KEPLER, JOHANNES b. Weil der Stadt, 1571; d. Regensburg, 1630. German astronomer, cosmologist, founder of celestial physics. Studied theology at Tübingen 1589–94, but relinquished a clerical career on being appointed district mathematician and teacher in Graz, 1594–1600. In Prague 1600–12; worked with Tycho Brahe, succeeding him as Imperial Mathematician, 1601–30. His life-long commitments to Neoplatonism, to the reality of the heliocentric cosmos and to explaining planetary motions by physical causes are evident in his first work, *Mysterium cosmographicum* (1596). Later wrote *Astronomia nova* (1609), establishing that the orbit of Mars was an ellipse and extending these results to all planets in *Epitome astronomiae Copernicanae* (1618–21); *Harmonices mundi* (1619), presenting a vision of cosmic harmonies demonstrated through geometry, music, astrology and astronomy; *Tabulae Rudolphinae* (1627), providing perpetual tables for calculating sequential positions of planets for specific days. Also made important contributions to the study of optics, mathematics and philosophy of science.
I   *DSB* vii, pp. 289–312; *EF* iii, cols. 1242–4; *NDB* xi, pp. 494–508.
II   Dreyer 1906; Burtt 1932; Caspar 1948; Dijksterhuis 1950; Koyré 1957, 1961; *Kepler Festschrift* 1971; *Johannes Kepler* 1971; *Internationales Kepler-Symposium* 1973; *Kepler: Four Hundred Years* 1975; Aiton 1975, 1976, 1981; N. Jardine 1984.

LANDINO, CRISTOFORO (Christophorus Landinus) b. Florence, 1424; d. Florence, 1498. Italian humanist and Platonist. Student at Volterra with Angiolo da Todi. From *c*. 1439 at Florence under Medici patronage. From 1458 professor of poetry and oratory at Florentine *Studio*, lecturing on classical poets, Petrarch, Dante. In 1467 Chancellor of *Parte Guelfa*; later secretary of Signoria until retirement. Member of Ficino's circle; cultivated Platonic studies. Wrote commentaries on Dante, Horace, Vergil; Latin poems; translated Pliny into Italian. Also wrote *Disputationes Camaldulenses*, a dialogue comparing the contemplative and active lives, giving higher value to the former.
I   *CTC* i, pp. 209–10, iii, p. 262; Garin, i, pp. 427–32.
II   Di Napoli 1963, pp. 114–20; Fata 1966; Lentzen 1971; Cardini 1973; Field 1980; Rainer Weiss 1981; Kallendorf 1983.

LEFÈVRE D'ÉTAPLES, JACQUES (Jacobus Faber Stapulensis) b. Étaples (Picardy), *c*. 1460; d. Nérac, 1536. French philosopher, theologian, humanist. From *c*. 1475 studied Greek, mathematics, astronomy, music, theology at Paris. Taught philosophy at Collège du Cardinal-Lemoine. Visited Padua, Venice, Rome, Florence, 1491–2. Sought to reform Aristotelianism by humanistic emphasis on accurate texts and by improving traditional logic; Fabrist School later flourished in Protestant universities. Edited Aristotelian, Platonic, mystical works (Pseudo-Dionysius, Lull, Nicholas of Cusa). In 1507 invited to Saint-Germain-des-Prés by former pupil, Briçonnet (later Bishop of Meaux). In 1521 at Meaux, where vicar general 1523. Fled to Strasburg in 1525 when his translation of New Testament was condemned by Sorbonne. In 1526 recalled as tutor to royal family and royal librarian at Blois under protection of Francis I and later Marguerite of Navarre. Published French Bible, 1530.

I   *CTC* I, p. 143; *DTC* IX, cols. 130–59; Lohr 1976, pp. 726–32

II Renaudet 1953 *passim*; Rice 1969, 1971; Vasoli 1968a, pp. 183–214; *Humanism in France* 1970, pp. 132–49 (Rice); introduction to Lefèvre d'Étaples 1972; Bedouelle 1976; *Philosophy and Humanism* 1976, pp. 19–29 (Rice); Copenhaver 1977; Cavazza 1982; Hughes 1984.

LEONE EBREO (Judah Abrabanel; Leo Hebraeus) b. Lisbon, *c.* 1460; d. Naples after 1523. Jewish physician, philosopher, poet. Eldest son of scholar-statesman Isaac Abrabanel, who taught him Jewish-Arabic philosophy; also studied medicine. Left Iberian Peninsula in 1492 at Jewish expulsion. Visited Florence; lived in Genoa, Barletta, Venice; settled in Naples, where physician to Spanish viceroy; 1501 taught medicine and astrology at University of Naples. His *Dialoghi d'amore* (written 1501/2, published Rome, 1535) belong to Ficinian tradition of treatises on Platonic love; syncretises Jewish, Greek, Platonic, Aristotelian, Arabic doctrines; twenty-five editions between 1535–1607; 1551–1660 translated into French, Latin, Spanish, Hebrew.

I   *EF* III, cols. 1472–4; *EJ* II, pp. 109–11; Saitta II, pp. 83–113; Solana I, pp. 465–532.

II Saitta 1928, pp. 85–157; Fontanesi 1934; Dionisotti 1959; Dauriens 1971; Barata-Moura 1972a, 1972b; Carvalho 1978-, I, pp. 149–297; Guanti 1979–80; Soria Olmedo 1984; Ariani 1984.

LEONICO TOMEO, NICCOLÒ (Nicolaus Leonicus Thomaeus) b. Venice, 1456; d. Padua, 1531. Italian philosopher and humanist. Studied at Venice and Padua; 1485 *doctor artium*. Studied Greek in Florence, *c.* 1486. Studied theology for four years at Monte Cassino. From 1497 to *c.* 1509 professor of philosophy at Padua, where he was one of the first to expound Aristotle from Greek text. From 1521 taught privately; Reginald Pole among his students. Translator and commentator of Aristotle and others. Also wrote *Dialogi* (1524); *Opuscula* (1525); *De varia historia libri III* (1531).

I   *EF* v, col. 505; Lohr 1982, pp. 193–4.

II De Bellis 1975, 1979, 1980, 1981.

LE ROY, LOUIS b. Coutances (Normandy), 1510; d. Paris, 1577. French humanist, translator, historico-political theorist. Studied at Paris; 1530 attended lectures in Latin, Greek, jurisprudence at Collège Royal. From 1535 at Toulouse. In 1540 returned to Paris, probably gaining personal secretarial post(s) to nobility. Travelled widely in France, usually following court. Diplomatic mission to England, 1550. In 1572 appointed royal professor of Greek, dividing time between teaching and court obligations. Published *De la vicissitude* (1575), presenting his views on progress, cyclical history, civilisation; reprinted five times by 1584; translated into Italian, English. Translated Plato, Aristotle, Isocrates, Demosthenes into French. Also wrote political/propagandist pamphlets and orations.

II Becker 1896; Weisinger 1954; De Caprariis 1959; Richter 1961; Gundersheimer 1966; Pouilloux 1969; Kelley 1970a *ad indicem*.

LIPSIUS, JUSTUS (Joest Lips) b. Overyssche (Brussels), 1547; d. Louvain, 1606. Flemish humanist, Neostoic philosopher, philologist. Studied with Jesuits at Louvain. Published *Variae lectiones* (1567), dedicated to Cardinal Granvelle, who took him to Rome; engaged in philological study for two years. Travelled widely; teaching at Jena, 1572–4; Leiden, 1579–90; and Louvain, from 1592. Alternated religious adherence according to residence, but

publicly confirmed his Catholicism at Mainz, 1590. Initiated the Neostoic movement with his *De constantia* (1584); later wrote the more substantial *Physiologia Stoicorum* and *Manuductio ad stoicam philosophiam* (both 1604). Also wrote the influential political treatise *Politicorum, sive civilis doctrinae libri sex* (1589); and works on Roman history, e.g., *Admiranda, sive de magnitudine Romana libri IV* (1597). Edited classical texts, especially Seneca and Tacitus.
I   *CTC* II, p. 40; *DTC* IX, cols. 778–83; *EF* IV, cols. 6–7; Totok, pp. 352–5.
II   Faider 1922; Nordman 1932; Glaesener 1938; Ruysschaert 1949; Saunders 1955; Oestreich 1975, 1982; Abel 1978, pp. 67–113.

MACHIAVELLI, NICCOLÒ b. Florence, 1469; d. Florence, 1527. Italian political theorist and historian. Served in the chancellery of Florentine Republic 1498–1512; 1499–1509 diplomatic missions in France, Italy, Germany; advocated militia to defend Florence. When Medici returned to power in 1512, ousted from office. Tortured as suspect in anti-Medici plot 1513, but judged innocent and confined to Villa San Casciano, where composed *Il Principe*. Eventually permitted to re-enter Florence. Participated in meetings of Accademia degli Orti Oricellari, to whom he read his *Discorsi* on Livy (written 1513–19). From 1519 served Medici. When Medici again expelled, and republic re-established in 1527, failed to gain office. Died soon afterwards. Wrote *Arte della guerra* (1521) and *Istorie fiorentine* (1525).
I   *EF* IV, cols. 176–85; *EI* XXI, pp. 778–90; Totok, pp. 122–48.
II   A. H. Gilbert 1939; Sasso 1958; F. Gilbert 1965; Chabod 1965; Procacci 1965; Rubinstein 1966; *Studies on Machiavelli* 1972; *Pensiero politico di Machiavelli* 1972; Hexter 1973; Skinner 1978, I, *ad indicem*, 1981; Ridolfi 1978a; Dionisotti 1980; *Machiavelli attuale* 1982; Münkler 1982.

MAGIRUS, JOHANNES b. Fritzlar, *c.* 1560; d. Marburg(?), 1596. German Lutheran philosopher and physician. Studied philosophy at Padua (under Jacopo Zabarella). Studied medicine at Marburg 1581–5, gaining doctorate 1585. Professor of natural philosophy and physiology at Marburg, 1591. Works include *Anthropologia* (1603); textbooks on Aristotelian natural philosophy and ethics, e.g., *Physiologia peripatetica* (1597) and *Corona virtutum moralium* (1601).
I   Lohr 1978, p. 555.
II   A. R. Hall 1948; Reif 1969, p. 24; Schmitt 1983a *ad indicem*.

MAIR, JOHN (Johannes Maior; Major) b. Gleghornie (near Haddington, Scotland), 1467/9; d. St Andrews, 1550. Scottish Ockhamist philosopher, theologian, political theorist. Studied at Cambridge, 1491/2; Collège Ste Barbe, *c.* 1493; and Collège de Montaigu, Paris; M.A., 1495; taught arts there and, from *c.* 1501, at Collège de Navarre; among his pupils, Jacques Almain, Petrus Crockaert, Johannes Dullaert. *Doctor theologiae*, Montaigu, 1506. From 1518 to 1550 (interrupted by return to Paris, 1525–31) professor of arts and theology at Glasgow and later St Andrews; taught Jean Calvin, John Knox, George Buchanan. Wrote on logic, political theory, ethics; *Historia maioris Britanniae* (1521); commented on *Sententiae*; edited Almain and Duns Scotus.
I   *DNB* XII, pp. 830–2; *DSB* IX, pp. 32–3; *DTC* IX, cols. 1661–2; Farge, pp. 304–11; Lohr 1978, pp. 558–60.
II   García Villoslada 1938, pp. 127–64 and *passim*; Renaudet 1953 *passim*; Burns 1954; Oakley 1962, 1965; Torrance 1969–70; Durkan and Kirk 1977 *ad indicem*; Beuchot 1976; Skinner 1978 *passim*; Wallace 1981a *passim*; Broadie 1985.

MANETTI, GIANNOZZO b. Florence, 1396; d. Naples, 1459. Italian humanist. Studied Latin, Greek, Hebrew in Florence. Served Medici in political and ambassadorial positions. Later secretary to Pope Nicholas V, who commissioned him to translate the Scriptures (only partially completed). Following Nicholas' death, he moved to the court of Alfonso of Aragon, to whom he dedicated his *De dignitate et excellentia hominis*. Also wrote *Dialogus consolatorius*; lives of Seneca and Socrates; many speeches, including oration on the death of Leonardo Bruni.

I   *EF* IV, cols. 261–2; Saitta I, pp. 479–95.

II   Cassuto 1918 *passim*; Garofalo 1946; Garin 1954 *ad indicem*, 1961 *ad indicem*; Badaloni 1963; Wittschier 1968; Trinkaus 1970, I, pp. 230–70; De Petris 1975; Fioravanti 1983.

MARLIANI, GIOVANNI b. Milan, early fifteenth century; d. Milan, 1483. Milanese physician and scholastic philosopher. Studied arts and medicine at University of Pavia. In 1440 elected to College of Physicians, Milan. Probably received doctorate before 1442. Taught natural philosophy and *astrologia* at Pavia, 1441–7. Taught medicine at Milan, 1447–50. In 1450 returned to Pavia, adding medicine to his previous teaching subjects and gaining chair of medical theory, 1469. Appointed court physician to Galeazzo Maria Sforza, probably 1472; retained post under Gian Galeazzo. Giorgio Valla among his students. Wrote *De reactione* (1448), which provoked polemic with Gaetano da Thiene and was later discussed by Pomponazzi; *De caliditate* (1464); *Probatio calculatoris* (1460); *De proportione motuum* (1472).

I   *DSB* IX, pp. 132–4.

II   Clagett 1941, 1959, p. 652.

MARSILIUS OF INGHEN b. near Nijmegen, *c.* 1330; d. Heidelberg, 1396. German nominalist philosopher. Probably studied at University of Paris with Buridan; M.A., 1362; rector 1367, 1371. Visited Rome, 1377–8. Moved to University of Heidelberg 1382, where he was the first rector 1386–92; 1396 *doctor theologiae*. Wrote *Quaestiones* on the *Sententiae* and *Prior Analytics*; commentary on *De generatione*; *Parva logicalia*; *Abbreviationes libri Physicorum*.

I   *CHLMP*, pp. 871–2; *DSB* IX, pp. 136–8; *DTC* X, cols. 151–3; *EF* IV, cols. 319–20; Lohr 1971, pp. 323–34; *NNBW* VIII, pp. 903–4.

II   G. Ritter 1921–2, I; Möhler 1949; Clagett 1959 *passim*.

MELANCHTHON, PHILIPP b. Bretten (Baden), 1497; d. Wittenberg, 1560. German Lutheran humanist and educational reformer. Studied at Heidelberg; B.A., 1511; and at Tübingen, 1512–18; M.A., 1514; lectured on classics. Professor of Greek at Wittenberg, 1518; 1519 *baccalaureus biblicus*; 1519–60 professor of Greek and theology. Friend of Luther. After Reformation, systematised Luther's ideas, publicly defended them and restructured religious education on Lutheran principles. Published editions of, and commentaries on, Thucydides, Aristotle, Cicero, Ovid, Quintilian; wrote Greek and Latin grammars; works on theology, natural and moral philosophy, mathematics, etc. Responsible for the wide use of Aristotle in Lutheran universities.

I   *CHLMP*, p. 878; *CTC* II, pp. 150–1; *DTC* X, cols. 502–13; *EF* IV, cols. 501–6; Lohr 1978, pp. 576–82.

II   Hartfelder 1889; Rump 1897; Petersen 1921, pp. 19–108; Stern 1960; Maurer 1962, 1967–9; Hammer 1967–8; Huschke 1968; Moran 1973; Westman 1975.

MOLINA, LUIS DE, S.J. b. Cuenca, 1535; d. Madrid, 1600. Jesuit philosopher and theologian. Studied law at Salamanca 1551–2 and philosophy at Alcalá 1552–3. Joined Jesuits, 1553. Studied philosophy, 1554–8, and theology, 1558–62, at Coimbra; 1563–7 professor of philosophy. From 1568 to 1583 professor of theology at Évora. *Scriptor* at Évora, 1583–6; and at Cuenca, 1591–1600. Professor of moral theology at Jesuit College, Madrid, 1600. Formulated the doctrine known as Molinism in his *Concordia* (1558), telescoping efficacious and sufficient grace; resulted in controversy with Dominicans; resolved only

when Clement VIII ordered a special Congregation at Rome, 1598–1607. Also wrote *De iustitia et iure* (1593–1600); Aristotelian commentaries.
I   *DTC* x, cols. 2090–2187; *EF* IV, cols. 713–16; Giacon II, pp. 67–168; Lohr 1978, pp. 590–2; Solana III, pp. 401–24; Totok, pp. 542–4.
II   Stegmüller 1935a; Rabeneck 1950; Quaranta 1967; Queralt 1975; Costello 1974.

MONTAIGNE, MICHEL DE b. Montaigne (Périgord), 1533; d. Montaigne, 1592. French essayist. Educated Collège de Guyenne. Studied law at Bordeaux. Purchased judicial office. Became counsellor to Parlement of Bordeaux. Followed court in Paris, Rouen; then abruptly retired to his estates to study and write, 1571. Published *Essais* books I–II (1580). Neutral stance in religious wars, but upheld orthodoxy and authority. From 1576 increasing interest in scepticism. In 1580 travelled through France, Switzerland, Germany and Italy. At Rome *Essais* approved by church with slight alterations. Mayor of Bordeaux, 1581–5. In 1586 retired permanently. Published *Essais* book III (1588). Invented the term *essai* and its form as a distinct literary genre. Early interest in Stoicism and Platonism; but later predominantly influenced by Pyrrhonian scepticism, arguing for a fideistic doctrine of submission to divine revelation as the only means of certainty.
I   *EF* IV, cols. 752–4; Totok, pp. 438–44.
II   Strowski 1906; Villey 1933; Boase 1935; Thibaudet 1963; Frame 1965; Battista 1966; Brush 1966; Friedrich 1967; Sayce 1972; Limbrick 1977; Popkin 1979, pp. 42–65; *Montaigne* 1982; Screech 1983; Schiffman 1984.

MORE, THOMAS b. London, 1478; d. London, 1535. English humanist and lawyer. Chancellor 1529. Executed for denying Henry VIII's headship of English Church. Produced translations from Greek, biographies, poems, political and religious writings. Friend of Erasmus, Colet, Holbein. His *Utopia* (1516), strongly influenced by Plato's *Republic*, gave rise to a literary genre. Also responsible for popularising Giovanni Pico in England.
I   *DNB* XIII, pp. 876–96; *DTC* x, cols. 2472–82; *EF* IV, cols. 810–12.
II   Chambers 1935; Hexter 1952, 1973; Surtz 1957a, 1957b; Marc'hadour 1963; White 1976; *Essential articles . . . More* 1977; De Pina Martins 1979; A. Fox 1982; Marius 1984.

MURET, MARC-ANTOINE (Muretus) b. Muret (near Limoges), 1526; d. Rome, 1585. French humanist. Before 1547 was given professorship at Bordeaux; Montaigne among his pupils. About 1552 began to lecture on philosophy and civil law at Paris, but imprisoned for heresy. After release moved to Toulouse, where lectured on civil law. In 1554 condemned for sodomy and heresy, but escaped to Italy. In 1561 accompanied Ippolito d'Este to France. Returned to Rome 1563, lecturing on Aristotle's *Ethics* until 1567. Wrote *Variae lectiones* (annotations and expositions of many passages from ancient authors); commentaries on Cicero, Catullus, Aristotle's *Ethics* and the pseudo-Aristotelian *Oeconomics*, Plato's *Republic* and Ronsard's *Les Amours*.
II   Dejob 1881; Nolhac 1883; Trinquet 1965, 1966; C. N. Smith 1984.

NICHOLAS OF CUSA (Cusanus; Nikolaus Krebs) b. Cues, 1401; d. Todi, 1464. German philosopher, theologian and churchman. Studied at Heidelberg, 1416; and Padua 1417–23, receiving doctorate in canon law. Studied Germanic law at Cologne. Ordained priest *c.* 1430. In 1432 represented Ulrich von Manderscheid at Council of Basle; wrote *De concordantia catholica* (1433) defending the conciliarist position; but later supported papal party at Council. In 1437 embassy to Constantinople; 1438/9 papal missions to Germany. Began work on *De docta ignorantia* (published 1440), elaborating concepts of *via negativa* and *coincidentia oppositorum*. Cardinal, 1446; 1450 Bishop of Brixen (Bressanone), Legate to

Germany. Fall of Constantinople in 1453 stimulated composition of *De pace fidei*, an appeal for Christian unity. In 1458 at papal court of Pius II. In 1460 returned to Germany, where briefly imprisoned at Bruneck. Returned to Rome, appointed papal representative. Wrote several works on mathematics, theology; sermons influenced by Meister Eckhart.

I   *CHLMP*, pp. 873–4; *DSB* III, pp. 512–16; *DTC* XI, cols. 601–11; *EF* II, cols. 220–6.
II   Vansteenberghe 1920; Gandillac 1942; *Mitteilungen* . . . *Cusanus-Gesellschaft* 1961–; Sigmund 1963; Watanabe 1963; Clagett 1964–84, III, 2, pp. 297–315; Lübke 1968; *Nicolò Cusano* 1970; *Cusanus-Gedächtnisschrift* 1970; Senger 1971; Flasch 1973; *Acta Cusana* 1976–; Hopkins 1978, 1983; Watts 1982; Stadler 1983.

NIFO, AGOSTINO (Suessanus) b. Sessa Aurunca, 1469/70; d. Sessa Aurunca, 1538. Italian philosopher and physician. Studied philosophy under Vernia at Padua, receiving degree *c.* 1490. Later learnt Greek. Taught philosophy at Padua, 1492–9; at Naples and Salerno (also medicine), 1500–13; at Rome, from 1514; at Pisa, 1519–22; at Salerno, 1522–31 and 1532–5; and at Naples (also medicine), 1531–2. In 1520 named Count Palatine. Wrote many Aristotelian commentaries; wrote treatises on Averroes; edited Aristotle and Averroes (1495–6); replaced early Averroism with broader philosophical outlook, incorporating Platonic and Hermetic concepts. Also wrote on astronomy, dialectics, politics, moral philosophy, psychology.

I   *DSB* X, pp. 122–4; Lohr 1979, pp. 532–9; Thorndike V, pp. 69–98 and *passim*.
II   Tuozzi 1903–4; Nardi 1945 *passim*, 1958 *passim*; Valletta 1951; Randall 1961 *ad indicem*; Di Napoli 1963, pp. 203–41 and *passim*; Risse 1964, pp. 218–29; Mahoney 1966, 1968, 1970a, 1970b, 1971a, 1971b, 1976a, 1976b, 1982; Poppi 1966, pp. 222–36, 1970a *passim*; Wallace 1972–, I, pp. 139–53; Zambelli 1975; Ashworth 1976; L. Jardine 1981.

NIZOLIO, MARIO (Nizolius) b. Brescello, 1488; d. Mantua, 1567. Italian humanist. Considered the foremost Ciceronian of his day after publishing *Thesaurus Ciceronianus* (1536; frequently reprinted), a Latin lexicon entirely derived from Cicero. Engaged in polemic with M.A. Maioragio, who wrote *Reprehensionum libri duo* attacking him; to which he replied in *De veris principiis* (1553), which was praised by Leibniz, who reprinted it (1670). Criticised Aristotle, seeking to replace Peripatetic logic and dialectic with Latin grammar and Ciceronian rhetoric.

I   *EF* IV, col. 1040; Garin II, pp. 741–4; Saitta II, pp. 493–509.
II   Pagani 1893; *Testi umanistici sulla retorica* 1953, pp. 99–121 (P. Rossi); Breen 1954, 1955; introduction to Nizolio 1956, I, pp. XV–LXXIV; Corsano 1958–63, 42: 488–94; Crescini 1965, pp. 121–33; Vasoli 1968a, pp. 606–63; Nizzoli 1970; Wesseler 1974.

ORESME, NICOLE b. Bayeux, *c.* 1320; d. Lisieux, 1382. French philosopher, mathematician, translator. In the 1340s studied arts at Paris with Buridan. Studied theology at Collège de Navarre, Paris; by 1349 M.A.; 1355/6 *magister theologiae*; 1356–62 grand master of Collège de Navarre. From *c.* 1360 friend of Dauphin (later Charles V). In 1362 canon at Cathedral of Rouen. In 1363 canon at Sainte-Chapelle; visited papal court at Avignon. Dean at Rouen, 1364; 1377 Bishop of Lisieux (resident from 1380). Translated into French (from Latin) and commented on Aristotelian texts on logic, natural and moral philosophy. Wrote treatises on natural philosophy, theology, and against astrology.

I   *CHLMP*, p. 874; *DSB* X, pp. 223–30; Lohr 1972, pp. 290–8.
II   Curtze 1870; Clagett 1959 *passim*; Grignaschi 1960; Murdoch 1964; Goldbrunner 1968; *Antiqui und Moderni* 1974, pp. 206–20 (Molland); Caroti 1979; Babbitt 1985.

PACE, GIULIO (Julius Pacius) b. Beriga (near Vicenza), 1550; d. Valence, 1635. Italian philosopher and jurist. Studied philosophy at Padua 1565–70; and 1570–4 law (*doctor*

utriusque iuris). Converted to Protestantism. Fled to Geneva, where 1575–85 taught philosophy and law. From 1585 to 1594 professor of law at University of Heidelberg. Taught logic at Sedan, 1595. From 1597 to 1600 professor of philosophy and rector of University of Nîmes. Professor of law 1600–16, Montpellier; 1616–20, Valence; 1620–1, Padua; 1621–35, Valence. Published edition of *Organon* (1584); re-edited Casaubon's *Opera Aristotelis* (1597); wrote *Institutiones logicae* (1595); *Logicae rudimenta* (1598); *Logicae disputationes VIII* (1606); also commentaries on Aristotle's *Physics* and *De anima*.
I Lohr 1979, pp. 546–7.
II Lampertico 1885–6; Vasoli 1974; *Aristotelismo veneto* 1983, II, pp. 1009–34 (Vasoli); Schmitt 1983a *passim*.

PALMIERI, MATTEO b. Florence, 1406; d. Rome(?), 1475. Florentine humanist. Follower of Bruni. At Council of Florence, 1439. Undertook various diplomatic missions for the city. Wrote *Della vita civile*, a dialogue which attempts to integrate active civic virtue and participation with the Platonic ideal of other-worldly contemplation of the good; *La città di vita*; historical and pedagogical works.
I *EF* IV, cols. 1296–7; Garin I, pp. 334–42, 355–6; Lohr 1971, p. 342; Saitta I, pp. 381–90.
II Bassi 1892; Messeri 1894; Boffito 1901; Varese 1961 *passim*; Buck 1968, pp. 253–71; Finzi 1984.

PARACELSUS (Theophrast Bombast von Hohenheim) b. Einsiedln, 1493; d. Salzburg, 1541. Swiss chemist, physician, natural philosopher. Educated in mineralogy, botany and natural philosophy by his physician father; probably also taught by Trithemius. Studied medicine at Ferrara. Served as military surgeon, eventually founding medical practice at Strasburg. Treated Froben and Erasmus at Basle. In 1527 gained appointment as municipal physician and professor of medicine at Basle; but relinquished this in 1528 after litigation with magistrate patient. Became an itinerant physician in Germany, Austria and Switzerland. Scorned organised religion and classical scholarship. Wrote mainly in German. In medicine, rejected authority of Galen and Aristotle, emphasising empirical observation and external aetiology in opposition to humoral concept of disease. His major medical treatise is *Opus paramirum*; also wrote *Archidoxis* (1569, with many reprintings), in which his contributions to inorganic chemistry are summarised. About thirty years after his death, Paracelsian movement developed, including such figures as van Helmont, Boyle, Boerhaave.
I *DSB* x, pp. 304–13; *EF* IV, cols. 1325–6; Totok, pp. 363–72.
II Sudhoff 1894–9, 1936; Darmstaedter 1931; *Nova acta paracelsica* 1944–; Sherlock 1948; Goldammer 1953, 1954, 1971; Pagel 1958a, 1962, 1979; Debus 1965, 1977; *Paracelsus. Werk und Wirkung* 1975; *Paracelsus in der Tradition* 1980; *Kreatur und Kosmos* 1981; Webster 1982.

PATRIZI, FRANCESCO (of Sienna; Bishop of Gaeta) b. Sienna, 1413; d. Gaeta, 1494. Italian humanist and political writer. Actively involved in the political life of Sienna, from which he was eventually exiled and confined to Verona. In 1461 appointed Bishop of Gaeta. Wrote the influential political tracts *De institutione reipublicae* and *De regno et regis institutione*.
I *EF* IV, col. 1403; Saitta I, pp. 370–6.
II Bassi 1893; Chiarelli 1932; Battaglia 1936; Sarri 1938; L. F. Smith 1966–8, 1968, 1974; Schmitt 1972, pp. 49–51, 171–7.

PATRIZI, FRANCESCO DA CHERSO (Franciscus Patritius) b. Cherso, 1529; d. Rome, 1597. Italian Neoplatonic philosopher. Studied at Venice, 1542; at Ingolstadt, 1544–5; at Padua, 1547–54. From 1554 to 1557 served as secretary, administrator to several Venetian noblemen. In 1569–71 and 1574–7 travelled extensively in Mediterranean countries,

including Cyprus, where he perfected his knowledge of Greek. From 1577/8 to 1591/2 first professor of Platonic philosophy at Ferrara. Polemics with T. Angelucci on Aristotle, 1584, and with Jacopo Mazzoni on poetics, 1587. From 1591/2 to 1597 professor of Platonic philosophy at the *Sapienza*, Rome; lectured on *Timaeus*. Wrote *Discussiones peripateticae* (1581), a history and critique of the Aristotelian tradition; *Nova de universis philosophia* (Ferrara, 1591; Venice, 1593), presenting his Neoplatonic theory of light metaphysics; he revised it in an unsuccessful attempt to defuse criticisms by the Inquisition. Also wrote *La città felice* (1553); *L'Eridano* (1557); *Della historia* (1560); treatises on poetics, rhetoric, military history and mathematics. Translated Philoponus, Proclus; produced Latin editions of pseudo-Aristotelian *Theologia, Hermetica, Chaldaean Oracles*.
I *CTC* I, pp. 141–2; *EF* IV, cols. 1403–4; Lohr 1979, pp. 551–3.
II Donazzolo 1912; Arcari 1935; Brickman 1941; Firpo 1950–1; Lamprecht 1950; Menapace Brisca 1952; Kristeller 1964a, pp. 110–26; Zambelli 1967; Muccillo 1975, 1981; Maechling 1977; Henry 1979; Otto 1979; Bolzoni 1980; Vasoli 1983b, pp. 527–83; Wilmott 1984, 1985; Antonaci 1984–; Kraye 1986.

PAUL OF PERGULA (Paulus Pergulensis; Paolo della Pergola) b. Pergula, *c.* 1380; d. Venice, 1455. Venetian theologian and philosopher. Follower of Oxford School of logic, transmitted to Italy by Paul of Venice, with whom he studied at Padua. M.A. *c.* 1420; *doctor theologiae* by 1430. Taught at Venice 1421–54.
I *CHLMP*, p. 875; *EF* IV, cols. 1495–6; Lohr 1972, p. 320; Saitta I, pp. 645–92.
II Segarizzi 1915–16; Boh 1965.

PAUL OF VENICE, O.E.S.A. (Paulus Nicolettus Venetus) b. Udine, 1369/72; d. Padua, 1429. Italian philosopher and theologian. From 1390 studied philosophy, logic and theology at Oxford, where influenced by Averroists, Ockhamists and earlier Augustinians (particularly Gregory of Rimini). Later visited Paris, where probably knew Pierre d'Ailly. In 1395 returned to Italy. By 1408 listed among masters at Padua. Venetian ambassador to Poland, 1413. From 1416 lectured at Padua. In 1420 elected Prior Provincial of Sienna, repelling charges of heresy in same year. In 1424 lectured at Bologna. Visited Rome, 1426. Professor at Sienna, 1427. Returned to Padua, 1428. Expositor of terminist logic; his *Logica* influential in Italy to end of seventeenth century. Also wrote *Summa naturalium*, widely distributed in manuscript and early printed editions; and commentaries on *Posterior Analytics, Physics, De generatione et corruptione* and *De anima*.
I *CHLMP*, p. 875; *DSB* X, pp. 419–21; Duhem *SM* IV, pp. 199–210, X, pp. 377–439; Lohr 1972, pp. 314–20.
II F. Momigliano 1907; Di Napoli 1963 *ad indicem*; Perreiah 1967; Wallace 1972–, I *passim*; Ashworth 1978a; Bottin 1981; *Aristotelismo veneto* 1983, I, pp. 297–324 (Kuksewicz), 459–68 (Bottin), II, pp. 591–606 (Cristiani), 873–86 (Pozzi); *Scienza e filosofia* 1983, pp. 85–124 (Bottin).

PEREIRA, BENITO, S.J. (Benedictus Pererius) b. Ruzafa (near Valencia), by 1535; d. Rome, 1610. Spanish Jesuit philosopher and theologian. Entered Jesuit Order 1552, Valencia. From 1553 to 1556 studied at Collegio Romano, where 1556–8 became professor of *litterae humaniores*; 1558–67 professor of philosophy; 1567–1610 professor of theology. Wrote *Physicorum sive de principiis rerum naturalium libri XV* (1562; reprinted frequently), a natural philosophy textbook; *Adversus fallaces et superstitiosas artes* (1591), rebutting magic and astrology; also, many works on Aristotle, surviving mostly in manuscript.
I *DSB* X, pp. 512–13; *DTC* XII, col. 1217; *EF* IV, cols. 1485–6; Giacon II, pp. 31–66; Lohr 1979, pp. 564–73; Solana III, pp. 373–400.
II García Villoslada 1954 *passim*; Rompe 1967 *passim*; Di Vona 1968 *passim*; Lohr 1976b; Wallace 1981a *ad indicem*.

Périon, Joachim, O.S.B. (Joachimus Perionius) b. Cormery (Touraine), 1498/9; d. Cormery, 1559. French humanist and theologian. Entered Benedictine Order 1517. From 1527 studied philosophy and theology at Paris: 1542 *doctor theologiae*; then professor of theology. Translated most of Aristotle; provoked criticism and revision by J. L. d'Estrebay and N. Grouchy. Wrote *Pro Aristotele in Petrum Ramum orationes II* (1543), in reply to Ramus' *Aristotelicae animadversiones*; and *Pro Ciceronis Oratore contra Petrum Ramum oratio* (1547). Translated part of Plato's *Timaeus* (1540) and several Greek Fathers (1554–9).

I Lohr 1979, pp. 574–76.

II *Périon* 1842; Vasoli 1968a *passim*; *Platon et Aristote* 1976, pp. 377–89 (Stegmann); Schmitt 1983a *passim*.

Petrarch (Francesco Petrarca) b. Arezzo, 1304; d. Arquà (Padua), 1374. Italian humanist and poet. From an exiled Florentine family which later moved to Avignon. Studied law at Montpellier and Bologna. Returned to papal court at Avignon 1326, taking minor orders. Visited Italy for long periods; crowned poet laureate at Rome, 1341. In 1353 moved to Italy; lived in Milan under Visconti patronage, 1353–61; in Venice, 1361–8; in Padua, from 1368. Included in his vast literary output are the Latin treatises *De otio religioso* and *De vita solitaria*; the polemical invective *De sui ipsius et multorum ignorantia*; the Stoic ethical and psychological guide *De remediis*; the dialogue *Secretum*; the Latin epic poem *Africa*; the Italian lyric poetry cycle *Canzoniere*; and Latin letters, which he collected and edited.

I *EF* IV, cols. 1553–7; Totok, pp. 99–100.

II Nolhac 1907; Piur 1925; Gerosa 1927; G. Billanovich 1947–, 1951, 1974, 1981–; *Studi petrarcheschi* 1948–78, 1984–; Wilkins 1955, 1958, 1959, 1961; Heitmann 1958; U. Bosco 1968; Kessler 1978; Trinkaus 1979; *Quaderni petrarcheschi* 1983–; Foster 1984; Mann 1984; Baron 1985.

Piccolomini, Alessandro (Alexander Piccolomineus) b. Sienna, 1508; d. Sienna, 1579. Italian philosopher and humanist. Studied theology and philosophy at Sienna and Padua. Lecturer in moral philosophy at Padua, 1539. In 1540 joined Accademia degli Infiammati. From 1546 to *c.* 1558 in voluntary exile in Rome. Appointed Archbishop of Patras and Coadjutor Archbishop of Sienna, 1574. Wrote influential compendia on natural and moral philosophy, e.g., *Della filosofia naturale* (1551; expanded version, 1565); *Della institutione di tutta la vita dell'huomo nato nobile et in città libera* (1542); Italian translations of Aristotle's *Rhetoric* (1571) and *Poetics* (1572); annotations on the *Poetics* (1575), which provoked considerable controversy; Latin translation of Alexander of Aphrodisias' commentary on the *Meteorology* (1540).

I *CTC* I, pp. 99–100; *EF* IV, col. 1577; Lohr 1980, pp. 624–5.

II Cerreta 1957, 1960; Weinberg 1961 *passim*; Scrivano 1964; Suter 1969; Giacobbe 1972a; Breitenbürger 1975, pp. 137–50 and *passim*; Rose 1975 *ad indicem*; Buck 1983.

Piccolomini, Francesco (Franciscus Carolus Piccolomineus) b. Sienna, 1523; d. Sienna, 1607. Italian philosopher. Studied at Sienna, gaining doctorate in arts and medicine, 1546. Taught there until 1549. Professor of philosophy at Macerata, 1549–50; and at Perugia, 1550–60. From 1560 to 1564 extraordinary professor of natural philosophy at Padua; 1564–5 second ordinary professor of natural philosophy, succeeding M. A. Genua; 1565–98 first professor in same. From 1578 to 1594 controversy with Jacopo Zabarella on philosophical methodology, culminating in publication of *Comes politicus pro recta ordinis ratione propugnator* (1594). Also wrote *Peripateticae de anima disputationes* (1575); many expositions of Aristotelian works and philosophy.

I *EF* IV, cols. 1578–9; Garin II, pp. 656–61, 712; Lohr 1980, pp. 626–39.

II Ragnisco 1885–6; N. W. Gilbert 1960, pp. 173–6; Di Napoli 1963, pp. 379–82; Crescini 1965, pp. 182–8 and *passim*; Baldini 1980a, 1980b.

PICO DELLA MIRANDOLA, GIANFRANCESCO b. Mirandola, 1469; d. Mirandola, 1533. Italian philosopher; Christian sceptic. Received early humanistic education at court of Ferrara; also influenced by Savonarola and uncle Giovanni Pico. From 1499 to 1502 conflict with brothers over title to Mirandola, leading to exile in various Italian cities, 1502–11. Visited Germany 1502, 1505. Briefly recovered Mirandola, 1511; but again exiled, 1511–14. Polemic with Pietro Bembo on imitation of classical authors, 1511–12; published *De imitatione libellus* (1518). In 1514 returned to Mirandola, where assassinated by his nephew, 1533. Wrote on epistemology, psychology, astrology and divine providence: e.g., *De studio divinae et humanae philosophiae*; *De imaginatione*; *De falsitate astrologiae*; *De rerum praenotione*; *De providentia Dei*. His major philosophical work, *Examen vanitatis doctrinae gentium* (1520), contrasts fallible human knowledge with divine revelation through Scriptures.

I   *EF* IV, cols. 1483–4; Garin II, pp. 588–94; Lohr 1980, pp. 641–2.

II Walker 1958, pp. 146–51, 1972, pp. 33–5, 59–62; Schmitt 1967, 1970; Raith 1967; Secret 1976; *The Damned Art* 1977, pp. 32–52 (Burke); Popkin 1979, pp. 20–3 and *passim*; introduction to G. F. Pico 1984.

PICO DELLA MIRANDOLA, GIOVANNI b. Mirandola, 1463; d. Florence, 1494. Italian philosopher and humanist. Studied canon law at Bologna from 1477 and philosophy at Ferrara, 1479 and Padua, 1480–2. Moved to Florence, 1484. In 1485 visited University of Paris, assimilating scholastic ideas. Returned to Florence 1486, afterwards moving to Perugia. Studied Hebrew and Arabic; expanded his knowledge of Averroism; began to study cabala. Wrote *Conclusiones* (1486), intending to dispute them in Rome; certain theses declared heretical or dubious; defended them in *Apologia*, thereby provoking Innocent VIII's condemnation of the whole work. Fled to France, but arrested and imprisoned at Vincennes, 1488. Released through intervention of Lorenzo de' Medici and other Italian princes; allowed to return to Florence. There wrote *Heptaplus* (1489), a mystical interpretation of the Genesis creation myth; *De ente et uno* (1492), attempting to harmonise Platonic and Aristotelian ontological doctrines; *Disputationes adversus astrologiam divinatricem* (published 1496). In final years became a follower of Savonarola. In 1493 Alexander VI lifted censures.

I   *EF* IV, cols. 1580–3; Thorndike IV, pp. 485–511, 529–43 and *passim*; Totok, pp. 159–65.

II Dorez and Thuasne 1897; Kibre 1936; Garin 1937a, 1961, pp. 231–89; G. Mercati 1938; Cassirer 1942; Secret 1964, pp. 24–43 and *passim*; *L'opera e il pensiero* 1965; Di Napoli 1965; Wirszubski 1967, 1969; Walker 1972 *passim*; Lubac 1974; *Miscellanea . . . Branca* 1983, III, I, pp. 327–52 (Perosa).

PLATINA (Bartolomeo Sacchi) b. Piadena, 1421; d. Rome, 1481. Italian humanist and historian. In contact with Ficino and his circle in Florence *c.* 1457. From 1462 lived in Rome. Appointed *abbreviator apostolicus* by Pius II. Joined Accademia Romana. Later fell from favour and imprisoned: first for writing polemics against the pope, then on accusations of impiety and pantheism. Subsequently recovered his position, securing patronage of the new pope, Sixtus IV, who put him in charge of Biblioteca Vaticana, 1475. Wrote a history of the popes: *De vitis omnium summorum pontificum* (1479); also political and ethical treatises, e.g., *De principe*; *De optimo cive*; *De vera nobilitate*; *De falso et vero bono*; biography of Vittorino da Feltre.

I   *EF* V, cols. 40–1; Garin I, pp. 324–7; Saitta I, pp. 390–9.

II Luzio and Renier 1889; Zabughin 1909–12, I, pp. 60–8; introduction to Platina 1913–32; Raybaud 1970; Milham 1972; introduction to Platina 1979; Rubinstein 1985.

PLETHO, GEORGIUS GEMISTUS b. Constantinople (or Mistra), *c.* 1360; d. Mistra, *c.* 1452. Byzantine humanist and philosopher. Established Platonic school, and held high office for several years, at Mistra in Morea; Bessarion among his pupils. From 1438–9 among Byzantine delegation to Council of Ferrara/Florence, giving public lectures and stimulating interest in Platonic and Neoplatonic writings. His major treatise, the *Laws*, is a systematic exposition modelled on Plato's work; survives only in fragments because ecclesiastical authorities ordered all copies to be destroyed as heretical. Also wrote an influential comparison of Platonic and Aristotelian doctrines.

I Garin I, pp. 360–5 and *passim*; Totok, pp. 151–3.

II Gass 1844; Schultze 1874; Taylor 1921; Kieszkowski 1936 *passim*; Zakythinos 1932–53; Anastos 1948; Knös 1950; R. and F. Masai 1954; F. Masai 1956; Garin 1958a, pp. 153–219; Kristeller 1979, pp. 150–68 and *passim*; C. M. Woodhouse 1986.

POGGIO BRACCIOLINI b. Terranova nel Valdarno, 1380; d. Florence, 1459. Italian humanist. Influenced in classical and philological studies by Salutati. At the papal Curia 1404–53, first as scriptor and later papal secretary. While attending Council of Constance discovered many important manuscripts containing lost works by Cicero, Quintilian, Lucretius, etc. Chancellor of Florence, 1453–8. Wrote *De avaritia* (1428–9); *De nobilitate* and *De infelicitate principum* (both 1440); *De varietate fortunae* (1431–48); *Contra hypocritas* (1447–8); *Facetiae* (1438–52); *De miseria humanae conditionis* (1455); and *Epistolae*.

I *DBI* XIII, pp. 640–6; *EF* I, cols. 1048–9.

II Shepherd 1825; Walser 1914; Rubinstein 1958–64; Tateo 1961; Sabbadini 1967 *passim*; Oppel 1977; Goldbrunner 1979; Flores 1980; *Poggio Bracciolini* 1980; *Un toscano del '400* 1980; *Poggio Bracciolini* 1982.

POLIZIANO, ANGELO (Angelus Ambroginus Politianus) b. Montepulciano, 1454; d. Florence, 1494. Italian humanist, philologist, poet. Mainly active in Florence, where protégé of Lorenzo de' Medici and tutor in Medici household until 1480. Taught at the Florentine *Studio* 1480–94; wrote *Lamia* (1492–3), a *praelectio* to his course on Aristotle's *Prior Analytics*; also *Praelectio de dialectica*. Translated into Latin *Enchiridion* of Epictetus and *Problems* attributed to Alexander of Aphrodisias. His philological researches on classical texts and prescriptions for prose style were widely influential. Wrote poetry in Greek, Latin and Italian (*Stanze* and *Orfeo*).

I *CTC* I, pp. 133, 225, IV, p. 272; *DBI* II, pp. 691–702; Lohr 1967, p. 362.

II Micheli 1917; introduction to Epictetus 1954; *Mostra del Poliziano* 1955; *Il Poliziano e il suo tempo* 1957; I. Maïer 1965, 1966; Bigi 1967; Vasoli 1968a, pp. 116–31 and *passim*; Garin 1967, ch. 5; Gardenal 1975; Grafton 1977, 1983–, I, pp. 9–100; Kraye 1983; introduction to Poliziano 1983.

POMPONAZZI, PIETRO (Petrus Pomponatius) b. Mantua, 1462; d. Bologna, 1525. Italian philosopher; strongly influenced by Alexander of Aphrodisias; rejected Averroism, advocating return to Aristotelianism purified of non-Aristotelian accretions. Studied at Padua; M.A., 1487; taught philosophy, 1488–96; *doctor medicinae*, 1496. From 1496 to 1499 taught logic at court of Alberto Pio. Professor of philosophy at Padua, 1499–1509. Briefly taught at Ferrara 1509 before returning to Mantua, 1510–11. Taught philosophy at Bologna, 1511–25. Published *De immortalitate animae* (1516), which provoked counter-attacks from Gasparo Contarini, Agostino Nifo and others; to which he replied in *Apologia* (1518). Also wrote *De naturalium effectuum causis sive de incantationibus* (written 1520; published 1556), attempting a naturalistic explanation of thaumaturgy; *De fato* (published 1567); many expositions of Aristotelian works. Extensive manuscript notes for his lecture courses survive.

I *DSB* XI, pp. 71–4; *EF* IV, cols. 149–54; Garin II, pp. 500–35 and *passim*; Lohr 1980, pp. 645–65.

II Fiorentino 1868; Ferri 1876; Cian 1887; Oliva 1926; Kristeller 1955, 1964a, pp. 72–90; Gilson 1961; Di Napoli 1963, pp. 227–338 and *passim*; *Umanesimo europeo* 1964, pp. 31–63 (Gilson); Nardi 1965; Pine 1965, 1968, 1973, 1986; Zanier 1975b; *Philosophy and Humanism*

1976, pp. 100–15 (Pine); Graiff 1976, 1979; *Aristotelismo veneto* 1983, II, pp. 685–94 (Galimberti), 1077–99 (Kristeller).

PONTANO, GIOVANNI GIOVIANO b. Cerretto (Umbria), 1426/9; d. Naples, 1503. Italian humanist and poet. Studied at Perugia. In 1447 entered service of Aragonese kings of Naples; tutor to the Duke of Calabria; 1486 Chancellor of Kingdom. In 1495 negotiated surrender of Naples to Charles VIII of France after latter's ejection of Ferdinand II. Pardoned when Ferdinand returned, but deprived of office. Wrote prose works on astrology, moral philosophy, political theory, history: e.g., *De rebus coelestibus*; *De prudentia*; *De fortuna*; *De principe liber*; *De bello neapolitano*; also, dialogues, often centring on ethical issues; and poetry, including love lyrics, mythological and didactic verse.
I *EF* v, col. 155; Saitta I, pp. 645–92.
II Tallarigo 1874; Rosselli del Turco 1878; Tanteri 1931; Altamura 1938; Toffanin 1938; Percopo 1938; Tateo 1960a, 1972.

PORZIO, SIMONE (Portius; Porta) b. Naples, 1496; d. Naples, 1554. Italian philosopher. Probably studied philosophy with Achillini and Pomponazzi at Bologna and with Nifo at Pisa (also studying medicine there). Taught logic, then natural philosophy at Pisa, 1520–5. From 1529 to 1545 professor at Naples; and at Pisa, 1547–54. Published works on natural philosophy and psychology. Followed Pomponazzi's doctrine on the soul, most notably in *De humana mente* (1551) and *De rerum naturalium principiis* (1553). Also wrote several commentaries (extant only in manuscript for the most part) on Aristotelian works.
I *CTC* II, p. 320; *EF* v, cols. 165–6; Garin, 540–6; Lohr 1980, pp. 667–70.
II Amenduni 1890; Fiorentino 1911, pp. 83–153; Saitta 1949; Di Napoli 1963 *ad indicem*; De Gaetano 1968; Montù 1968.

QUEVEDO (Y VILLEGAS), FRANCISCO DE b. Madrid, 1580; d. Villanueva de los Infantes, 1645. Spanish literary, philosophical and political writer. Studied theology, law and classics at University of Alcalá. Attended Philip III's court. In 1609 experienced *crise de conscience*, regretting earlier frivolous writings and joining pious Congregación del Oratorio del Olivar. Went to Italy *c*. 1613 as secretary to Duke of Osuna. Later attracted favour of Philip IV and Olivares. Recalled to court and given royal post; but 1639–43 disgraced and imprisoned, probably for satirical allusions to Olivares. Contributed to the diffusion of Christian Neostoic philosophy in Spain. His writings include: *El Busión*, a picaresque novel; *Doctrina moral del conocimiento* (1630); a Spanish translation of Epictetus (1635); *La vida de Marco Bruto* (1644), a Christian Stoic commentary on Plutarch's *Brutus*; and political writings, e.g., *Política de Dios y gobierno de Cristo* (1626) and *La hora de todos y la fortuna con seso* (1635–45).
I *EF* v, col. 483.
II Astrana Marín 1945; Simón Dias 1945; Castellanos 1947; Papell 1947; Chacón y Calvó 1948; Láscaris Comneno 1950, 1955a, 1955b; P. U. González de la Calle 1965; Rothe 1965; Blüher 1969; Ettinghausen 1972.

RAMUS, PETRUS (Pierre de la Ramée) b. Cuth (near Soissons), 1515; d. Paris, 1572. French philosopher and humanist. Studied at Paris from 1527; M.A., 1536. Appointed principal of Collège de Presles, 1546–72. Professor at Collège Royal, 1551. Charpentier's *Animadversiones* (1554) instigated a polemic continuing into 1560s. Conversion to Calvinism 1561 made him vulnerable in increasingly unstable condition of French politics from 1567, so withdrew from Paris. Visited Germany, Strasburg, Basle, 1568–70. Returned to Paris, 1570. Murdered during the St Bartholomew's Day Massacre, 1572. Wrote commentaries on Euclid and several Aristotelian works; favourable to Aristotle in certain spheres, e.g., applied

mathematics; but, after publishing the *Aristotelicae animadversiones* (1543), gained reputation as a virulent anti-Aristotelian polemicist. His reformed system of logic, which despite criticism of traditional forms retained key Peripatetic concepts such as the syllogism, reached definitive form in *Dialectique* (1555). Also wrote grammatical works, e.g., *Scholae grammaticae* (1559); and *De religione Christiana* (published posthumously, 1576).
I *DSB* XI, pp. 286–90; Lohr 1980, pp. 676–82.
II Waddington 1855; Howell 1956, pp. 146–281 and *passim*; Hooykaas 1958; Ong 1958a, 1958b; N. W. Gilbert 1960, pp. 129–44 and *passim*; Yates 1966, pp. 228–38 and *passim*; Verdonk 1966, 1968; Vasoli 1968a, pp. 331–589; Walton 1970, 1971; Schmitt 1972, pp. 78–108; Margolin 1976; Piano Mortari 1978 *passim*; Sellberg 1979; Sharratt 1982; Schmidt-Biggemann 1983; Bruyère 1984; Meerhof 1986; *Pierre de la Ramée* 1986.

REISCH, GREGOR, Ord. Cart. b. Balingen, *c.* 1467; d. Freiburg i. Br., 1525. German Carthusian and encyclopaedist. Matriculated at University of Freiburg, 1487; B.A., 1488; M.A., 1489. Entered Carthusian Order *c.* 1496. Became prior first at Klein-Basle, 1500–2; and then at Freiburg i. Br., 1503–25. Taught Johannes Eck. Correspondent of Erasmus, who claimed that his opinion had the authority of an oracle among Germans. His chief work, *Margarita philosophica* (1503), is an encyclopaedia in catechetical form, widely used as a textbook; it covered, in addition to the subjects of the *trivium* and *quadrivium*, natural philosophy, psychology and ethics.
I Lohr 1980, pp. 685–6; Thorndike V, pp. 139–41.
II Hartfelder 1890; Erasmus 1906–58, II, pp. 29–30, 327; Münzel 1937; Srbik 1941, 1961; introduction to Reisch 1517 (repr. Düsseldorf, 1973).

ROBORTELLO, FRANCESCO (Franciscus Robortellus) b. Udine, 1516; d. Padua, 1567. Italian humanist and philologist. Studied at Bologna. Taught at Lucca, Pisa, Venice, Padua and Bologna. Particularly known for his commentary on Aristotle's *De arte poetica* (1548). Also wrote on Aristotle's *Politics* (1552) and *Topics* (in MS); as well as on philological subjects, e.g., *De arte sive ratione corrigendi antiquorum libros disputatio* (published 1557).
I Garin II, pp. 747–8; Lohr 1980, pp. 693–5.
II Herrick 1946 *passim*; Weinberg 1952, 1961; Carlini 1967; Schmitt 1972 *ad indicem*; Kenney 1974, pp. 29–36; Breitenbürger 1975, pp. 4–28 and *passim*.

SALUTATI, COLUCCIO b. Stignano in Valdinievole, 1331; d. Florence, 1406. Italian humanist. Family exiled to Bologna in his youth. Corresponded with Petrarch, but never met him. Played key role in establishing Florence as the humanistic centre of Italy. Appointed notary in the Florentine chancellery 1374; and chancellor, 1375–1406. Wrote influential political and moral treatises, Latin letters and poetry. Knew little Greek, but encouraged its study and diffusion by bringing Manuel Chrysoloras to teach in Florence.
I *EF* v, cols. 982–3; *EI* xxx, p. 568.
II Novati 1888; Mancini 1920; Garin 1943–6, 1961 *ad indicem*; Iannizzotto 1959; Ullman 1963; Kessler 1968; Witt 1976, 1977, 1983; Lindhardt 1979; De Rosa 1980; Langkabel 1981; introduction to Salutati 1985.

SANCHES, FRANCISCO (Sánchez; Sanctius) b. Tuy or Valença do Minho, 1550/1; d. Toulouse, 1623. Portuguese physician and philosopher. Studied at Collège de Guyenne, Bordeaux, 1562–9. Studied medicine at Rome, 1569–73. *Baccalaureus* of medicine at Montpellier, 1573; 1574 doctor and professor of medicine there. Moved to Toulouse, 1575. Director of Hôtel de Dieu-St Jacques, Toulouse, 1582–1612. From 1585, professor of liberal arts in the university there; and from 1612, professor of medicine. Wrote medical works; commentaries on Aristotle's *De divinatione per somnum*, *De longitudine* and the pseudo-

Aristotelian *Physiognomica*; *Obiectiones et erotemata super geometricas Euclidis demonstrationes* (1575); *Carmen de cometa anni 1577* (1578). His most influential book, *Quod nihil scitur* (1576), attacks scholastic method, asserting that perfect knowledge is unattainable by man, who must be content with the limited information attainable from cautious and rigorous experiment and observation; became a standard work of sceptical philosophy.

I   *DSB* xii, pp. 97–8; *EF* v, cols. 991–2; Lohr 1980, pp. 709–10; Solana i, pp. 377–406.
II Iriarte 1935, 1940; Cruz Costa 1942; Moreira de Sá 1947; *Francisco Sanches* 1951; Crescini 1965, pp. 243–70; Miccolis 1965; Popkin 1979, pp. 36–41; Carvalho 1978–, ii, pp. 505–89.

SCALIGER, JULIUS CAESAR b. Padua, 1484; d. Agen, 1558. Italian-French humanist. Born Giulio Bordon, but later (after moving to France) claimed to descend from the noble Della Scala family. Studied philosophy at Padua 1515–19, where *doctor artium*. Worked on translation of Plutarch in Venice, 1521–4. From 1524 physician to Bishop Antonio Della Rovere at Agen. Upheld Cicero against criticisms of Erasmus, 1528–31. In 1532–3 consul of Agen. Summoned before Inquisition as Huguenot, 1538. Wrote several commentaries on Peripatetic works, including Aristotle's *Historia animalium* and *De plantis* (which he recognised to be spurious), and Theophrastus' *De causis plantarum*. Also wrote *Exotericae exercitationes* (1557) in response to Cardano's *De subtilitate*; *De causis linguae Latinae* (1540); and *Poetices libri VII* (1561).

I   *CTC* ii, pp. 269–71; *DSB* xii, pp. 134–6; *EF* v, cols. 1036–7; Lohr 1980, pp. 714–16.
II Weinberg 1942, 1961 *passim*; V. Hall 1950; M. Billanovich 1968; Ferraro 1971; *Occult and Scientific Mentalities* 1984, pp. 231–52 (Maclean); Jensen 1985.

SCHEGK, JACOB (Jacobus Schegkius; Scheggius; Degen) b. Schorndorf, 1511; d. Tübingen, 1587. German Lutheran philosopher. Early education in Latin, Greek, Hebrew, rhetoric. Studied at Tübingen from 1527 (including theology and medicine); from 1532, professor of logic and held various official positions there; 1553 professor of philosophy and medicine. Retired 1577 because of blindness. Translated Alexander of Aphrodisias' *De mixtione* (1540), Pachymeres' paraphrase of pseudo-Aristotelian *De lineis insecabilibus* (1542); edited Greek version of *De anima* with excerpts from Simplicius' commentary (1544); wrote many commentaries on Aristotelian works or themes. Engaged in polemic with Ramus, *c.* 1570.

I   *CTC* i, p. 113; *DSB* xii, pp. 150–1; Lohr 1980, pp. 718–20.
II Sigwart 1889; Petersen 1921 *passim*; N. W. Gilbert 1960, pp. 158–62; Vasoli 1968a, pp. 527–30, 573–8; Pagel 1969–70.

SOTO, DOMINGO DE, O.P. b. Segovia, 1495; d. Salamanca, 1560. Spanish Dominican philosopher and theologian. Studied at Alcalá *c.* 1512–16. From 1516 studied at Paris under John Mair. Taught philosophy at Alcalá, 1520–4. *Doctor theologiae*, 1525; joined Dominicans at Burgos. Taught philosophy and theology at Salamanca, 1525–49, 1552–60. In 1540–2, 1544–5, 1550–2, 1556–60 Prior of St Esteban. At Council of Trent, 1545–7. Confessor to Charles V in Germany, 1548–50. President of Junta de Valladolid (concerning wars against the Indians), 1550–1. Associated with the sixteenth-century scholastic revival. Wrote commentaries on Aristotle's logical works, *Physics*, *De anima* and on the fourth book of Peter Lombard's *Sententiae*; also wrote *De iustitia et iure libri X* (1553–4).

I   *CHLMP*, p. 859; *DSB* xii, pp. 547–8; *DTC* xiv, cols. 2423–31; Lohr 1982, pp. 167–70; Solana iii, pp. 91–130.
II García Villoslada 1938 *passim*; Brufau Prats 1960; Cura 1960, 1961; Beltrán de Heredia 1960; Hamilton 1963; Muñoz Delgado 1964b; Di Vona 1968 *passim*; Andrés 1976–7, ii, pp. 362–5 and *passim*; Lewis 1980 *passim*; Wallace 1981a *passim*.

STEUCO, AGOSTINO (Steuchus) b. Gubbio, 1497/8; d. Venice, 1548. Italian philosopher, theologian, biblical exegete. In Augustinian convent of Gubbio, 1512/13–1517. In 1518–25 studied at Bologna, learning several oriental languages and Greek. Librarian to Cardinal

Grimani of Venice, 1525–9. Practised religious duties at Reggio 1529–33 and 1533–4 at Gubbio. In 1534 moved to Rome. In 1538 named Bishop of Kisamos, Crete and appointed librarian of Vatican Library. Attended Council of Trent 1546, returning to Bologna 1548. Wrote *Cosmopeia* (1535); *De perenni philosophia* (1540), upholding *prisca theologia* and attempting to combine pagan philosophy with the Christian tradition.

I *EF* vi, col. 173; Saitta ii, pp. 79–82.
II Ebert 1929–30; Freudenberger 1935; *Filosofia e cultura* 1967, pp. 459–89 (Di Napoli), 491–9 (Wiedmann); introduction to Steuco 1540 (repr. New York, 1972); Julien Eymard d'Angers 1976, § iv; Schmitt 1981, §§ i and ii.

SUÁREZ, FRANCISCO, S.J. b. Granada, 1548; d. Lisbon, 1617. Spanish Jesuit philosopher, theologian, jurist. Entered Society of Jesus, 1564. Studied law, philosophy and theology at Salamanca. Taught philosophy at Segovia, 1571–4. Taught theology at Valladolid, 1574–5; at Segovia and Avila, 1575–6; at Valladolid, 1576–80; at Collegio Romano, 1580–5; at Alcalá, 1585–93; at Salamanca, 1593–7; at Coimbra, 1597–1616. Visited Rome, 1604–6. Prominent in the Counter-Reformation revival of scholasticism. Wrote *De legibus* (1612); commentaries and treatises on many works of Aristotle.

I *CHLMP*, p. 859; *DTC* xiv, cols. 2638–728; Lohr 1982, pp. 180–7; Solana iii, pp. 453–513; Totok, pp. 545–62.
II Werner 1889; Lewalter 1935; Masi 1947; Alcorta 1949; Iturrioz 1949; Cronin 1966; Seigfried 1967; Lohr 1976b; Andrés 1976–7 *passim*; *Simposio Francisco Suárez* 1980; Castellote 1982.

TARTARETUS, PETRUS d. Paris, *c.* 1522. French Scotist philosopher and theologian. 1484 M.A. at Paris; 1490 rector; 1496 *licentiatus theologiae*; 1500 *magister theologiae*. Wrote many logical works which stress Scotist realism in opposition to Ockhamist nominalism. Also wrote *Quaestiones* on Aristotle's *Nicomachean Ethics*.

I *DTC* xv, cols. 58–9; Duhem *SM* x, pp. 97–105 and *passim*; *EF* vi, cols. 320–1; Lohr 1972, pp. 372–6; Prantl iv, pp. 204–9.
II García Villoslada 1938 *passim*; Élie 1950–1, pp. 202, 215, 226; Renaudet 1953 *passim*.

TELESIO, BERNARDINO b. Cosenza, 1509; d. Cosenza, 1588. Italian natural philosopher. Studied philosophy and mathematics at Padua, obtaining doctorate 1535. Published three versions of his major work, *De rerum natura* (1565, 1570, and much enlarged in 1586). Later years were mainly – except for long visits to Naples – passed in Cosenza, where he founded *Accademia Cosentina* to promote study of natural philosophy according to his own principles and methods. Rejected Aristotelian doctrines and claimed authority for his own system based on sense experience and nature.

I *DSB* xiii, pp. 277–80; *EF* vi, cols. 363–8; Garin II, pp. 644–56 and *passim*; Saitta iii, pp. 1–79.
II Fiorentino 1872–4; Gentile 1911; Zavattari 1923; Van Deusen 1932; Abbagnano 1941; Soleri 1945; Firpo 1950–1, 42: 30–47; Garin 1961, pp. 432–50; Kristeller 1964a, pp. 91–109; Delcorno 1967; Di Napoli 1973, ch. 7.

TEMPLE, WILLIAM b. Stower (Dorset), 1555; d. Dublin, 1626/7. English Ramist philosopher and divine. Studied at Cambridge. Upheld Ramist logic in polemic with Aristotelian Everard Digby, against whom he wrote *Admonitio de unica P. Rami methodo retinenda* (1580). Secretary to Sir Philip Sidney at Zutphen, 1585. In 1594 secretary of Earl of Essex. Provost of Trinity College, Dublin, 1609. Active in Irish politics, for which he was knighted, 1622.

I *DNB* xix, pp. 520–2; Lohr 1982, pp. 191–2.
II Freudenthal 1890–1; Sortais 1920, i, pp. 53–64; Howell 1956, pp. 194–6, 204–6; Ong 1958a, *passim*; N. W. Gilbert 1960, pp. 202, 206–9; L. Jardine 1974a, pp. 59–69.

TITELMANS, FRANS, O.F.M. Obs. (Franciscus Titelmannus) b. Hasselt, 1502; d. Anticoli di Campagna (Lazio), 1537. Dutch philosopher and theologian. From 1518 studied and taught at 'Het Varken' of the University of Louvain. In 1523 entered the Franciscan Order there, teaching philosophy and theology in its school, 1523–36. In 1527–30 engaged in polemic with Erasmus on Pauline exegesis. Joined O.F.M. Cap. at Rome 1536, where involved in care of sick. In 1537 became provincial of the order's Roman province. Wrote *Compendia* on Aristotelian logic and natural philosophy.
I *DTC* xv, cols. 1144–6; Lohr 1982, pp. 196–8; Thorndike v, pp. 147–52.
II Paquay 1906; Gomes dos Santos 1955; Vosters 1962; Ashworth 1974a *passim*.

TOLETUS, FRANCISCUS, S.J. (Francisco de Toledo) b. Cordoba, 1532; d. Rome, 1596. Spanish Jesuit philosopher and theologian. Studied philosophy at Zaragoza or Valencia and theology at Salamanca while teaching philosophy there. Joined Jesuits, 1558. In 1559–62 professor of philosophy at Collegio Romano; professor of theology, 1562–9. Preached in papal court. Sent on diplomatic missions to various countries from 1571, including that to convert Henri IV of France, 1596. Cardinal, 1593. Wrote influential commentaries on Aristotelian works, including *Physics*, *De anima* and *De generatione et corruptione*; also a commentary on the *Summa theologiae*.
I *DTC* xv, cols. 1223–5; *EF* vi, cols. 497–8; Giacon ii, pp. 25–44, 51–65; Lohr 1982, 199–201; Solana iii, pp. 311–37.
II Stegmüller 1935b; Gómez Hellín 1940; Echarri 1950; García Villoslada 1954 *passim*; Lohr 1976b; Lewis 1980 *ad indicem*.

VALLA, GIORGIO (Georgius Valla) b. Piacenza, 1447; d. Venice, 1500. Italian humanist and translator. Studied at Milan and Pavia. Taught at Milan, possibly 1467–9; at Genoa, 1477–8; and at Pavia, intermittently 1466–84. Went to Venice, 1485. In 1496 imprisoned by the Council of Ten in connection with Milanese intrigues; eventually released after being proved innocent. Wrote commentaries on Greek and Latin authors, e.g., Cicero, Juvenal, Ptolemy. Translated Greek scientific and mathematical works, e.g., Alexander of Aphrodisias, Euclid, Galen, Psellus. Also wrote the encyclopaedic treatise *De expetendis et fugiendis rebus* (published 1501).
I *CTC* i, p. 126.
II Heiberg 1894, 1896; Clagett 1964–84, iii, 3, pp. 461–75; Rose 1975 *passim*; *Giorgio Valla* 1981.

VALLA, LORENZO b. Rome, 1407; d. Rome, 1457. Italian humanist. Studied at Rome. Taught *eloquentia* at Pavia, 1429–33. From 1437 secretary to Alfonso of Aragon. In 1448 returned to Rome, becoming papal secretary and professor at university. Developed a philological approach to classical, literary, scriptural and historical scholarship: e.g., *De falso credita et ementita Constantini donatione declamatio*; *Elegantiae linguae Latinae*; *Collatio Novi Testamenti*. His *Dialecticae disputationes* attacks Aristotelian and scholastic logic and reformulates principles of dialectic on the basis of rhetoric. Also wrote *De libero arbitrio*; and *De voluptate*, later reworked as *De vero bono*, examining Stoic, Epicurean and Christian conceptions of the true good. Translated Herodotus and Thucydides.
I *CHLMP*, p. 871; *EF* vi, cols. 809–11; Garin I, pp. 311–16; Lohr 1971, pp. 315–16; Saitta I, pp. 199–269.
II Mancini 1891; Casacci 1926; Gaeta 1955; Kristeller 1964a, pp. 19–36; Gray 1965; Vasoli 1968a, pp. 37–77 and *passim*; Fois 1969; Trinkaus 1970 *passim*; Di Napoli 1971; Camporeale 1972, 1976; Gravelle 1972; Giannantonio 1972; Gerl 1974; Setz 1975; L. Jardine 1977, 1983; Panizza 1978; Kessler 1980; Vickers 1986.

VALLÉS, FRANCISCO (Franciscus Vallesius) b. Covarrubias, 1524; d. Burgos, 1592. Spanish humanist, philosopher, physician. Studied at Alcalá; 1553 *doctor medicinae*; 1554 professor of medicine. In 1572 appointed physician to Philip II. Wrote *De iis quae scripta sunt physica in libris sacris* (1587), an exegesis of passages from Scripture touching on natural philosophical themes, including astrology, divination, etc. Also wrote commentaries on Aristotle's *Physics* (1562) and *Meteorology* (1558); many works on medical topics.
I *EF* VI, col. 812; Lohr 1982, p. 209; Solana II, pp. 297–347.
II Bullón 1905, pp. 131–51; Ortega and Marcos 1914.

VERGERIO, PIER PAOLO (the Elder) b. Capodistria, 1370; d. Budapest, 1444. Italian humanist. Taught at Florence, 1386; at Bologna, 1388–90; and at Padua, 1390–7. Studied Greek under Manuel Chrysoloras at Florence, 1398–1400. Returned to Padua, 1400–5. In 1405 joined court of Pope Innocent VII, staying with his successor Gregory XII until 1409. Attended Council of Constance, 1414–18. In 1418 accompanied King (later Emperor) Sigismund of Luxemburg to his domains in Bohemia and Hungary, remaining with imperial court until Sigismund's death in 1437. Wrote *De ingenuis moribus* (c. 1401–2), an influential humanist treatise on education; *De republica veneta*; Latin letters.
I *CTC* III, p. 5; *EF* VI, cols. 874–6; Saitta I, pp. 275–81.
II C. Bischoff 1909; Pierantoni 1920; L. Smith 1928; introduction to Vergerio 1934; Robey 1969, 1973, 1980; Robey and Law 1975; *L'umanesimo in Istria* 1983, pp. 7–18 (Robey), 273–356 (Perosa).

VERNIA, NICOLETTO (Nicolettus Vernias Theatinus) b. Chieti, 1420; d. Vicenza, 1499. Italian philosopher. Studied at Pavia. Student of Paul of Pergula in logic at Venice and of Gaetano da Thiene in natural philosophy at Padua. *Doctor artium*, Padua, 1458; 1465–99 succeeded Gaetano as professor of philosophy; 1495 *doctor medicinae*; his pupils included Agostino Nifo and Giovanni Pico. Edited scholastic texts. Most of his earlier works were straightforwardly Averroistic: e.g., *Quaestiones an dentur universalia realia*, which attempts to demonstrate agreement between Averroes and Albertus Magnus on the doctrine of *inchoatio formarum*. Gradually withdrew from extreme Averroism under influence of Ermolao Barbaro and in an effort to reassert his orthodoxy after Pietro Barozzi's *Decretum contra disputantes de unitate intellectus* (1489).
I *EF* VI, col 892; Garin I, pp. 450–4, 535–7; Lohr 1972, pp. 308–11.
II Ragnisco 1890–1, 1891; Nardi 1958, pp. 95–126 and *passim*, 1965 *passim*; Di Napoli 1963 *passim*; Vasoli 1968b, pp. 241–56; Mahoney 1968, 1978; *Philosophy and Humanism* 1976, pp. 144–63 (Mahoney); *Aristotelismo veneto* 1983, II, pp. 813–42 (Pagallo); *Scienza e filosofia* 1983, pp. 135–202 (Mahoney).

VERSOR, JOHANNES, O.P. (Jean Le Tourneur) d. c. 1485. French Thomist philosopher and commentator. By 1435 M.A., Paris; 1458 rector and *magister theologiae*. Proponent of Thomism against Albertism. Wrote commentaries on Aristotle's *Prior* and *Posterior Analytics, Topics, Sophistici elenchi, Metaphysics, Ethics, Politics*, etc. Also commented on the *Summule logicales* of Peter of Spain and *De ente et essentia* of Thomas Aquinas.
I Duhem *SM* X, pp. 111–30; *EF* III, col. 209; Lohr 1971, pp. 290–9.
II Seńko 1958–9; Riesco 1966; Birkenmajer 1970, § 23.

VETTORI, PIER (Petrus Victorius) b. Florence, 1499; d. Florence, 1585. Florentine humanist. In 1522–3 visited Barcelona and Rome. Active in defence of Florence, 1529–30. Private study at San Casciano, 1530–4. In 1534 returned to Florence and worked on edition of Cicero. In 1537 visited Rome. From 1538 professor of Latin at Florentine *Studio*; 1543, of Greek language and literature; 1548, of moral philosophy. Wrote commentaries on

Aristotle's *Nicomachean Ethics* (1584), *Politics* (1576), *Rhetoric* (1548) and *Poetics* (1560).
I   *CTC* II, pp. 35–6; *DCLI* III, pp. 614–16; Lohr 1982, pp. 220–2.
II Rüdiger 1896; Niccolai 1912; Weinberg 1961 *ad indicem*; R. Pfeiffer 1976, pp. 135–6;
    Porro 1983; Grafton 1983–, I, *ad indicem*.

VIMERCATO, FRANCESCO (Franciscus Vicomercatus) b. Milan, *c.* 1512; d. Turin, *c.* 1571.
Italian philosopher. Studied philosophy at Bologna, Pavia, Padua. From *c.* 1540 taught logic
in Collège du Plessis, Paris. First incumbent of chair of Greek and Latin philosophy at
Collège Royal, 1542–61. In 1543–4 supported polemic against Ramus. Professor of
philosophy at University of Mondovi, 1561; councillor to Duke of Savoy; 1567–70 ducal
ambassador to Milan. Wrote commentaries on many Aristotelian works; also, *De anima
rationali peripatetica* (1543); *De principiis rerum naturalium* (posthumously published 1596).
Contributed to Renaissance revival of Plato-Aristotle *comparatio* with his *De placitis
naturalibus Platonis et Aristotelis* (MS, *c.* 1540).
I   *EF* VI, col. 927; Lohr 1982, pp. 217–19.
II Busson 1957, pp. 191–212; Nardi 1958, pp. 404–10; N. W. Gilbert 1965; Schmitt 1983a,
    pp. 78–81 and *passim*.

VITORIA, FRANCISCO DE, O.P. b. Vitoria or Burgos, 1483/92; d. Salamanca, 1546.
Spanish Thomist theologian and jurist. In 1505 joined Dominican Order at Burgos. Studied
Latin and Greek at Paris or Burgos, 1506–9. Studied physics, mathematics and logic, 1509–
10. By 1512 had begun theological studies under Petrus Crockaert, editing Thomas Aquinas'
Secunda secundae. *Doctor theologiae*, 1522. Professor of theology at Dominican *Studium* in
Valladolid, 1523–6. First professor of theology at Salamanca, 1526. In 1527 ordered by
Spanish Inquisition to participate in Valladolid conference examining works and influence in
Spain of Erasmus, whom he criticised for certain unorthodoxies; but continued to support
humanist approach to literary style and classical learning. Contributed to the theory and
practice of war and colonisation (defending the rights of Indians in America). Formulated
concept of international law and government.
I   *DTC* XV, cols. 3117–44; *EF* VI, cols. 992–5; Farge, pp. 424–31; Solana III, pp. 43–89.
II Getino 1930; García Villoslada 1938 *passim*; Beltrán de Heredia 1939; González 1946;
    Hamilton 1963; Noreña 1975, pp. 36–149 and *passim*; Fernandez-Santamaria 1977, pp.
    58–119; Pagden 1982.

VITTORINO DA FELTRE b. Feltre, 1378; d. Mantua, 1446. Italian humanist and educator.
Studied arts at Padua from 1396; afterwards mathematics under Blasius of Parma. Taught
grammar and mathematics at Padua until *c.* 1415. Moved to Venice, studying Greek with
Guarino da Verona. In 1419 returned to teach at Padua. Succeeded Barzizza in chair of
rhetoric, 1421. In 1422 returned to Venice, opening school there in 1423. Later in 1423
accepted invitation by Gianfrancesco Gonzaga of Mantua to become ducal tutor. His school
(the *Giocosa*) in Mantua attracted children of patrician families and of other humanists;
curriculum included Latin and Greek, arithmetic, geometry, natural science, music and
logic; George of Trebizond and Theodore Gaza taught Greek there.
I   *EF* VI, cols. 997–9; *EI* XXXV, p. 505.
II Woodward 1897; *Vittorino da Feltre nel V centenario* 1946; *Vittorino da Feltre: pubblicazione*
    1947; Bosio Boz 1947; *Vittorino da Feltre e la sua scuola* 1981; G. Müller 1984.

VIVES, JUAN LUIS b. Valencia, 1492; d. Bruges, 1540. Spanish humanist, philosopher,
educational and social theorist. Studied at Valencia, 1508; and at Collège de Montaigu, Paris,
1509–12. Tutored and studied privately in Bruges, 1512–16. Taught privately at Louvain,
1517–23. In contact with Erasmus. Published *De initiis, sectis et laudibus philosophiae* and *In*

pseudodialecticos (both 1520) and a commentary on Augustine's *De civitate Dei* (1522). Lectured at Oxford, 1523–5. Attended English court, 1526–8. Returned to tutoring and private study in Bruges 1528–36, publishing *De disciplinis* (1531). Counsellor to Duchess of Nassau, 1537–9. Published *De anima et vita* (1538). Strong opponent of scholastic philosophy, especially logic; influenced by Lorenzo Valla.

I *DSB* XIV, pp. 47–8; *EF* VI, cols. 1000–2; Lohr 1982, pp. 224–6; Solana I, pp. 33–208; Totok, pp. 492–9.
II Kater 1908; F. Pfeiffer 1924; Bonilla y San Martín 1929; Sancipriano 1957; Vasoli 1968a, pp. 214–46; Noreña 1970, 1975, pp. 1–35; *Juan Luis Vives* 1981.

ZABARELLA, JACOPO (Giacomo; Jacobus) b. Padua, 1533; d. Padua, 1589. Paduan Aristotelian philosopher. Studied humanities, logic, natural philosophy and mathematics at Padua; *doctor artium*, 1553; held professorship of logic and natural philosophy. Member of the Accademia degli Stabili. Wrote influential works on logic (in particular on method) and natural philosophy, including *Opera logica* (1578); *Tabulae logicae* (1580); *De naturalis scientiae constitutione* (1586); *De rebus naturalibus* (1590); also, many commentaries on Aristotelian works.

I *DSB* XIV, pp. 580–2; *EF* VI, cols. 1187–9; Garin II, pp. 548–58; Lohr 1982, pp. 233–42.
II W. F. Edwards 1960, 1969; *Aristotelismo padovano* 1960, pp. 91–107 (W. F. Edwards); Randall 1961 *passim*; Di Napoli 1963, pp. 376–9; Risse 1964, pp. 278–90; Poppi 1970a, pp. 37–43, 1972a, 1972b; Bottin 1972; Crescini 1972 *passim*; Schmitt 1981, § VIII; *Aristotelismo veneto* 1983, I, pp. 155–72 (Risse).

ZIMARA, MARCANTONIO b. S. Pietro in Galatina (Lecce), *c.* 1475; d. Padua, 1532. Italian philosopher. From *c.* 1497 studied philosophy at Padua under Nifo and Pomponazzi; 1501–5 taught logic while studying medicine there; 1505–9 professor of natural philosophy. Moved to S. Pietro in Galatina, 1509–18. Professor of natural philosophy and theoretical medicine at Salerno, 1518/19–22. Lectured on metaphysics at Naples, 1522–3. Professor of philosophy at Padua, 1525–8. Edited works by Jean de Jandun, Albertus Magnus and Johannes Baconthorpe. Wrote commentaries and treatises on Aristotelian and Averroistic works and themes. His *Tabula dilucidationum in dictis Aristotelis et Averrois* (1537; reprinted frequently) became standard indices to Aristotle and Averroes.

I *EF* VI, cols. 1212–13; Lohr 1982, pp. 245–54.
II Nardi 1958, pp. 321–63; *Aristotelismo padovano* 1960, pp. 41–51 (Corvino); Poppi 1966, pp. 237–56; Papuli 1967 *ad indicem*; Antonaci 1970, 1971–8; *Aristotelismo veneto* 1983, I, pp. 415–34 (Antonaci); *Scienza e filosofia* 1983, pp. 315–28 (Antonaci).

ZWINGER, THEODOR (the Younger) b. Basle, 1533; d. Basle, 1588. Swiss physician and philosopher. Studied philosophy at Basle. Apprenticed to a Lyons publishing house, 1548–51. Studied languages at Paris, 1551–3, where he made contact with Ramus. Studied medicine at Padua, 1553–9. Professor of Greek language at University of Basle, 1565–71; professor of ethics, 1571–80; professor of theoretical medicine 1580–8. His works include the encyclopaedic *Theatrum vitae humanae* (1565; greatly enlarged in 1586) and commentaries on Aristotle's *Nicomachean Ethics* and *Politics*. Edited works of Francesco da Diacceto (1563).

I Lohr 1982, p. 256.
II Karcher 1956; Portmanns 1969; Gilly 1977–9.

BIBLIOGRAPHY

Note: for purposes of alphabetisation, an umlaut has been treated as an 'e'. Collective volumes are cited under their titles and placed alphabetically according to the first word, excluding articles.

BIBLIOGRAPHY: PRIMARY SOURCES

Abano, Pietro d' (1472). *Conciliator differentiarum philosophorum et precipue medicorum*, Mantua
   (1504). *Conciliator differentiarum philosophorum et precipue medicorum*, Venice
Abelard, Peter (1970). *Dialogus inter philosophum, Iudaeum et Christianum*, ed. R. Thomas, Stuttgart–Bad Cannstatt
Acciaiuoli, Donato (1478). *Expositio super libros Ethicorum Aristotelis*, Florence
   (1504). *Expositio librorum Politicorum Aristotelis*, Venice
   (1535). *Expositio librorum Ethicorum Aristotelis*, Venice
Achillini, Alessandro (1494). *De intelligentiis*, Bologna
   (1498). *Quatuor libri de orbibus*, Bologna
   (1568). *Opera*, Venice
Acta Facultatis Artium Universitatis Sancti Andree, 1413–1588 (1964). Ed. A. I. Dunlop, Edinburgh–London
Acta Facultatis Artium Universitatis Vindobonensis, 1385–1416 (1968). Ed. P. Uiblein, Graz–Vienna–Cologne
Acta Graeca Concilii Florentini cum versione Latina (1953). Ed. J. Gill, 2 parts, Rome
Agricola, Rudolph (1523). *De inventione dialectica libri omnes*, ed. Alardus Amstelredamus, Cologne (repr. Frankfurt, 1967)
   (1528). *De inventione dialectica libri tres*, Cologne
   (1539). *De inventione dialectica*, Cologne (repr. Nieuwkoop, 1967)
   (1703). *Opera*, 2 vols., Leiden
   (1886). 'Unedierte Briefe', ed. K. Hartfelder, in *Festschrift der badischen Gymnasium*, Karlsruhe, pp. 1–36.
Agrippa, Henricus Cornelius (1530). *De incertitudine et vanitate scientiarum atque artium declamatio*, Antwerp
   (1533). *De occulta philosophia libri tres*, [Cologne] (repr. Graz, 1967, ed. K. A. Nowotny)
   (c. 1600). *Opera*, Lyons (repr. New York, 1970, ed. R. H. Popkin)
   (c. 1630). *Opera*, 2 vols., Strasburg
   (1958). '*Dialogus de homine*', ed. P. Zambelli, *Rivista critica di storia della filosofia*, 13: 47–71
Ailly, Pierre d' (1490). *Quaestiones super libros Sententiarum cum quibusdam in fine adiunctis*, Strasburg (repr. Frankfurt, 1968)
   (c. 1490–5). *Destructiones modorum significandi*, Lyons
   (1494a). *Tractatus exponibilium*, Paris
   (1494b). *Tractatus de anima*, Paris
   (c. 1495). *Conceptus et insolubilia*, Paris
   (1980). *Concepts and Insolubles: An Annotated Translation*, ed. P. V. Spade, Dordrecht

Albert of Saxony (1516). *Acutissime questiones super libros De physica auscultatione*, Venice (1522). *Perutilis logica*, Venice (repr. Hildesheim, 1974)

Alberti, Leon Battista (1485). *De re aedificatoria*, Florence (repr. Munich, 1975 in H.-K. Lücke, *Alberti-Index*, IV)
   (1499). *Opera*, Florence
   (1890). *Opera inedita et pauca separatim impressa*, ed. G. Mancini, Florence
   (1942). *Momus o del principe*, ed. G. Martini, Bologna
   (1950). *Della pittura*, ed. L. Mallè, Florence
   (1960–73). *Opere volgari*, ed. C. Grayson, 3 vols., Bari
   (1964). 'Alcune *Intercenali* inedite', ed. E. Garin, *Rinascimento*, ser. ii, 4: 125–258
   (1966a). *On Painting*, trans. J. R. Spencer, rev. edn, New Haven–London
   (1966b). *L'archittetura (De re aedificatoria)*, ed. G. Orlandi and P. Portoghesi, 2 vols., Milan
   (1969a). *I libri della famiglia*, ed. R. Romano and A. Tenenti, Turin
   (1969b). *The Family in Renaissance Florence*, trans. R. Neu Watkins, Columbia, S.C.
   (1976). *De commodis litterarum atque incommodis*, ed. L. Goggi Carotti, Florence
   (1980). *Ludi matematici*, ed. R. Rinaldi, Milan
   (1981). *Il cavallo vivo*, ed. A. Videtta, Naples

Albertus Magnus (1890–9). *Opera omnia*, ed. A. Borgnet, 38 vols., Paris
   (1951–). *Opera omnia*, Münster i. W.
   (1967). *Book of Minerals*, ed. and trans. D. Wyckoff, Oxford
   (1977). *Speculum astronomiae*, ed. S. Caroti *et al.*, Pisa

Albertus Magnus, Pseudo- (1498). *Pulcerrimus tractatus de modo opponendi et respondendi*, Cologne
   (1973). *The Book of Secrets of the Virtues of Herbs, Stones and Certain Beasts*, ed. M. R. Best and F. H. Brightman, Oxford
   (1977). *Quaestiones de modis significandi*, ed. L. G. Kelly, Amsterdam

Alciato, Andrea (1953). *Lettere*, ed. G. L. Barni, Florence
   (1985). *The Latin Emblems. Emblems in Translation*, ed. P. M. Daly, 2 vols., Toronto–Buffalo–London

Alessandro, Alessandro d' (1551). *Genialium dierum libri sex*, Cologne

Alexander of Aphrodisias (1495). *Enarratio de anima ex Aristotelis institutione*, trans. G. Donato, Brescia

'Ali Ibn Ridwan (1487). *Galieni . . . micro Tegni cum commento . . .*, Venice

Almain, Jacques (1505). *Embammata physicalia totius philosophiae naturalis*, Paris
   (1518). *Opuscula*, ed. V. Doesmier, Paris
   (1526). *Moralia*, Paris

Amerbach, Veit (1542). *Quatuor libri de anima*, Strasburg

Amici, Giovanni (1536). *De motibus corporum coelestium*, Venice

Ammirato, Scipione (1642). *Opuscoli*, 3 vols., Florence

Annales de l'imprimerie des Estiennes (1837–8). 2 vols., Paris (repr. New York, 1960)

Annali veneti dall'anno 1457 al 1500 del Senatore Domenico Malpiero (1843–4). *Archivio storico italiano*, 7, 1–2: 1–720

[Anonymous] (1550). *Tabulae in octo libros Aristotelis De auscultatione physica*, Paris

Antonio da Romagna (1980). *Liber de paupertate*, ed. M. C. Ganguzza Billanovich, Florence

Archimedes (1880–1). *Opera omnia*, ed. J. L. Heiberg, 3 vols., Leipzig

Argyropulos, Johannes (1964). 'Compendium de regulis et formis ratiocinandi (Cod. Naz. Firenze, II.II.52)', ed. C. Vasoli, *Rinascimento*, ser. ii, 4: 285–339

Aristotle (1479). *Incipit praefacio Leonardi Arretini in libros Ethicorum*, Oxford
   (1495–6). *Opera . . . cum Averrois commentariis*, ed. A. Nifo, Venice
   (1495–8). *[Opera graeca]*, ed. Aldus Manutius, Venice
   (1496). *Opera nonnulla Latine*, Venice

(1509). *Textus Ethicorum ad Nicomachum*, comment. J. Buridan, N. Dupuy and G. Crab, Paris

(1516–17). *Dialectica cum quinque vocibus Porphyrii*, trans. J. Argyropulos, comment. J. Eck, 2 vols., Augsburg

(1544). *De anima libri tres*, trans. G. Hervet, Lyons

(1549a). *Opera post omnes quae in hunc usque diem prodierunt editiones . . . recognita*, Lyons

(1549b). *De anima libri tres*, trans. J. Périon, Paris

(1551). *L'anima d'Aristotile*, trans. F. Sansovino, Venice

(1553a). *De anima libri tres*, Basle

(1553b). *Les Éthiques à son filz Nicomache*, trans. P. Le Plessis, Paris

(1566). *De moribus ad Nicomachum libri decem*, Basle

(1567). *De moribus ad Nicomachum libri X*, Basle

(1596a). *De anima libri tres*, trans. and comment. G. Pace, Frankfurt

(1596b). *Naturalis auscultationis libri VIII*, ed. and trans. G. Pace, Frankfurt

(1597). *Organum*, ed. and trans. G. Pace, Frankfurt (repr. Hildesheim, 1967)

(1872). *Politicorum libri octo*, trans. William of Moerbeke, ed. F. Susemihl, Leipzig

(1910–52). *The Works*, ed. W. D. Ross, 12 vols., Oxford

(1970). *L'Éthique à Nicomaque*, ed. and trans. R. A. Gauthier and J. Y. Jolif, 2 vols., Louvain–Paris

(1972). *Ethica Nicomachea*, trans. Robert Grosseteste, ed. R. A. Gauthier (Aristoteles Latinus, 26, 1–3), Leiden–Brussels

(1975). *Posterior Analytics*, trans. J. Barnes, Oxford

Aristotle, Pseudo- (1572). *Libri quatuordecim de secretiore parte divinae sapientiae*, trans. and comment. J. Charpentier, Paris

Aristotle and Averroes (1550–2). *Omnia quae extant opera*, 11 vols., Venice

(1562–74). *Omnia opera*, 9 vols., 3 suppl., Venice (repr. Frankfurt, 1962)

Aristotle and Xenophon (1564). *Oeconomica scripta*, trans. and comment. J. Camerarius, Leipzig

Artis historicae penus (1579). Ed. J. Wolf, Basle

Atanagi, Dionigi (1559). *Ragionamento della istoria*, in Paolo Giovio, *La seconda parte dell'istorie del suo tempo*, trans. L. Domenichi, Venice

Augustine (1975). *De dialectica*, ed. J. Pinborg, trans. B. D. Jackson, Dordrecht–Boston

Aurelius, Marcus (1968). *Meditations*, ed. A. S. Farquharson, Oxford

Averroes (1953). *Commentarium magnum in Aristotelis De anima libros*, ed. F. S. Crawford, Cambridge, Mass.

See also Aristotle and Averroes

Avicenna (1507). *Liber Canonis*, Venice

(1968–72). *Liber de anima seu sextus de naturalibus*, ed. S. van Riet, 2 vols., Louvain

Azo (1888). *Quaestiones*, ed. E. Landsberg, Freiburg

(1966a). *Summa super codicem*, ed. M. Viora, Turin

(1966b). *Lectura super codicem*, ed. M. Viora, Turin

Bacon, Francis (1857–74). *Works*, ed. J. Spedding *et al.*, 14 vols., London

(1984). *Francis Bacon's Natural Philosophy: A New Source*, ed. G. Rees, Chalfont St Giles, Bucks.

Bacon, Roger (1983). *Roger Bacon's Philosophy of Nature*, ed. D. C. Lindberg, Oxford

Barbaro, Ermolao (1544). *Compendium ethicorum librorum*, Venice

(1545). *Compendium scientiae naturalis ex Aristotele*, Venice

(1943). *Epistolae, orationes et carmina*, ed. V. Branca, 2 vols., Florence

(1969). *De coelibatu. De officio legati*, ed. V. Branca, Florence

(1973–9). *Castigationes Plinianae et In Pomponium Melam*, ed G. Pozzi, 4 vols., Padua

Barbaro, Francesco (1743). *Francisci Barbari et aliorum ad ipsum epistulae*, Brescia

(1884). *Centotrenta lettere inedite*, ed. R. Sabbadini, Salerno

(1915). *De re uxoria*, ed. A Gnesotto, Padua

Barnaba Senese (1979). *Epistolario*, ed. G Ferraù, Messina

Barozzi, Francesco (1560). *Opusculum in quo una oratio et duae quaestiones: altera de certitudine et altera de medietate mathematicarum continentur*, Padua

Bartolus of Sassoferrato (1588). *Opera omnia*, 12 vols., Basle

Baudouin, François (1561). *De institutione historiae universae et eius cum iurisprudentia coniunctione ΠΡΟΛΕΓΟΜΕΝΩΝ libri II*, Strasburg

Bayle, Pierre (1740). *Dictionnaire historique et critique*, 4 vols., Amsterdam–Leiden–The Hague–Utrecht

Bellutus, Bonaventura: *see* Mastrius, Bartholomaeus and Bellutus, Bonaventura

Bembo, Pietro (1960). *Prose e rime*, ed. C. Dionisotti, Turin

See also Pico della Mirandola, Gianfrancesco and Bembo, Pietro

Benedetti, Giambattista (1585). *Diversarum speculationum mathematicarum et physicarum liber*, Turin

Benivieni, Girolamo (1984). 'Christian Canzone', ed. S. Jayne, *Rinascimento*, ser. ii, 24: 153–79

Béraud, Nicolas (1515). *Metaphrasis in Oeconomicon Aristotelis*, Paris

Beroaldo, Filippo, the Elder (1500). *Commentarii in Asinum aureum Lucii Apuleii*, Bologna

(1513). *Varia opuscula*, Basle

Bessarion, Cardinal (1927). *In calumniatorem Platonis*, in L. Mohler, *Kardinal Bessarion als Theologe, Humanist und Staatsmann*, ii, Paderborn

(1958). *Oratio dogmatica de unione*, ed. E. Candal, Rome

(1961). *De Spiritus Sancti processione*, ed. E. Candal, Rome

Bibliotheca fratrum polonorum quos unitarios vocant (1656). 8 vols., Amsterdam

Billingham, Richard (s. xv). MS Oxford, Bodleian Library, Lat. misc. e. 100

Biondo, Flavio (1483). *Historiarum ab inclinatione Romanorum Imperii decades*, Venice

(1927). *Scritti inediti e rari*, ed. B. Nogara, Rome

Blasius of Parma (1505). *Quaestio de tactu corporum durorum*, Venice

(1909). *Quaestiones de latitudinibus formarum*, ed. F. Amodeo, Naples

(1961a). 'Le questioni di *perspectiva*', ed. G. Federici Vescovini, *Rinascimento*, ser. ii, 1: 163–243

(1961b). '*Questioni inedite di ottica*', ed. F. Alessio, *Rivista critica di storia della filosofia*, 16: 79–110, 188–221

(1974). *Quaestiones de anima*, ed. G. Federici Vescovini, Florence

Boaistuau, Pierre (1982). *Bref discours de l'excellence et dignité de l'homme*, ed. M. Simonin, Geneva

Boccalini, Traiano (1948). *Ragguagli di Parnaso*, ed. L. Firpo, 3 vols., Bari

Bodin, Jean (1577). *Les Six Livres de la république*, Paris

(1583a). *Les Six Livres de la république*, Paris

(1583b). *Apologie de René Hervin*, Lyons

(1596). *Universae naturae theatrum*, Lyons

(1603). *De la démonomanie des sorciers. De magorum daemonomania*, Frankfurt

(1951). *Methodus ad facilem historiarum cognitionem*, ed. P. Mesnard, Paris

(1969). *Methodus ad facilem historiarum cognitionem*, trans. B. Reynolds, New York

(1975). *Colloquium of the Seven About Secrets of the Sublime. . .*, trans. and ed. M. Kuntz, Princeton.

(1980). *Selected Writings on Philosophy, Religion and Politics*, ed. P. L. Rose, Geneva

Boethius (1978). *De topicis differentiis*, ed. and comment. E. Stump, Ithaca
Boethius of Dacia (1969–). *Opera* (Corpus philosophorum Danicorum medii aevi), Copenhagen
Bonaventura, Federicus (1627). *Opuscula*, Urbino
Bono, Pietro (1976). *Preziosa margarita novella*, ed. C. Crisciani, Florence
Borro, Girolamo (1575). *De motu gravium et levium*, Florence
   (1583). *Del flusso e reflusso del mare*, 2nd rev. edn, Florence
   (1584). *De peripatetica docendi atque addiscendi methodo*, Florence
Bosso, Matteo (1492). *De veris ac salutaribus animi gaudiis*, Florence
   (1493). *Recuperationes Fesulanae*, Bologna
   (1495). *De instituendo sapientia animo*, Bologna
Boucher, Nicolas (1562). *Apologia adversus Audomari Talaei explicationem in primum Aristotelis Ethicum librum*, Reims
Bovelles, Charles de (1510). *Liber de intellectu; Liber de sensu; Liber de nichilo*, Paris (repr. Stuttgart–Bad Cannstatt, 1970)
   (1520). *Aetatum mundi septem supputatio*, Paris
   (1982). *Le Livre du sage*, ed. P. Magnard, Paris
   (1983). *De nihilo*, ed. P. Magnard, Paris
Brandolini, Aurelio (1543). *De humanae vitae conditione et toleranda corporis aegritudine . . . dialogus*, Basle
Brerewood, Edward (1619). *Elementa logicae*, London
Breytkopf, Gregorius (1507). *Parvorum logicalium opusculum*, Leipzig
Bricot, Thomas: *see* George of Brussels and Bricot, Thomas
Brisanius, Hieronymus (1588). *Totius philosophiae synopsis*, Lyons
Brito, Guilelmus (1968). *Brito Metricus: A Medieval Verse Treatise of Greek and Hebrew Words*, ed. L. W. Daly, Philadelphia
Brucioli, Antonio (1982). *Dialogi*, ed. A. Landi, Naples
Bruni, Leonardo (1506). *In libros Economicorum*, Paris
   (1741). *Epistolarum libri VIII*, ed. L. Mehus, 2 vols., Florence
   (1928). *Humanistisch-philosophische Schriften*, ed. H. Baron, Leipzig–Berlin (repr. Wiesbaden, 1969)
Bruno, Giordano (1879–91). *Opera latine conscripta*, ed. F. Fiorentino *et al.*, 3 vols. in 8 parts, Naples–Florence
   (1955). *Cena de le ceneri*, ed. G. Aquilecchia, Turin
   (1957). *Due dialoghi sconosciuti e due dialoghi noti*, ed. G. Aquilecchia, Rome
   (1958). *Dialoghi italiani*, ed. G. Gentile and G. Aquilecchia, Florence
   (1964a). *Il Candelaio*, ed. G. Barberi Squarotti, Turin
   (1964b). *'Praelectiones geometricae' e 'Ars deformationum'*, ed. G. Aquilecchia, Rome
   (1973). *De la causa, principio et uno*, ed. G. Aquilecchia, Turin
   (1980). *Opere latine*, ed. C. Monti, Turin
Bruno, Giordano and Campanella, Tommaso (1949). *Scritti scelti*, ed. L. Firpo, Turin
Budé, Guillaume (1532). *De philologia. De studio litterarum*, Paris (repr. Stuttgart–Bad Cannstatt, 1964, ed. A. Buck)
   (1535). *Annotationes. . . in quatuor et viginti Pandectarum libros*, Basle
   (1547). *De l'institution du prince*, Paris (repr. Farnborough, 1966)
   (1557). *Opera omnia*, 4 vols., Basle (repr. Farnborough, 1966)
   (1973). *De transitu Hellenismi ad Christianismum*, ed. M. Lebel, Sherbrooke
   (1977–). *Correspondance*, ed. G. Lavoie, Quebec
Bullinger, Heinrich (1548). *De origine erroris*, Zurich
Buonamici, Francesco (1591). *De motu libri X*, Florence

(1597). *Discorsi poetici in difesa d'Aristotile*, Florence

(1603). *De alimento*, Florence

Burana, Johannes Franciscus (1539). *Aristotelis Priora resolutoria*, Paris

Burgersdijk, Franco (1623). *Idea philosophiae moralis*, Leiden

(1627). *Idea philosophiae naturalis*, Leiden

(1629). *Idea philosophiae moralis*, Leiden

(1637). *Institutionum logicarum libri duo*, Cambridge

(1640). *Institutionum metaphysicarum libri duo*, Leiden

(1644). *Idea oeconomicae et politicae doctrinae*, Leiden

Buridan, Jean (1499). *Compendium totius logicae*, Venice (repr. Frankfurt a. M., 1965)

(1518). *Questiones in libros Aristotelis De anima . . .*, ed. G. Lokert, Paris

(1976). *Tractatus de consequentiis*, ed. H. Hubien, Louvain–Paris

Burley, Walter (1886). *De vita et moribus philosophorum*, ed. H. Knust, Tübingen

Bussi, Giovanni Andrea (1978). *Prefazioni*, ed. M. Miglio, Milan

Cabrera de Cordoba, Luis (1611). *De historia para entenderla y escribirla*, Madrid

Cajetan, Cardinal (1506). *In Porphyrii Praedicabilia et Aristotelis Praedicamenta ac Posteriorum analyticorum libros*, Venice

(1514). *Commentaria in libros Aristotelis De anima*, Venice

(1938). *Commentaria in De anima Aristotelis*, introd. M. H. Laurent, Rome

Calvin, Jean (1559). *Institutio Christianae religionis*, Geneva

(1863–1900). *Opera quae extant omnia*, ed. W. Baum *et al.*, 59 vols., Brunswick–Berlin

(1969). *Commentary on Seneca's 'De clementia'*, ed. F. L. Battles and A. M. Hugo, Leiden

Camerarius, Joachim, the Elder (1578). *Ethicorum Aristotelis Nicomachiorum explicatio*, Frankfurt

Campanella, Tommaso (1620). *De sensu rerum et magia libri quator*, Frankfurt

(1638). *Universalis philosophiae, seu metaphysicarum rerum iuxta propria dogmata partes tres, libri XVIII*, Paris (repr. Turin, 1961, ed. L. Firpo)

(1854). *Opere*, ed. A. d'Ancona, 2 vols., Turin

(1925). *Del senso delle cose e della magia*, ed. A. Bruers, Bari

(1927). *Lettere*, ed. V. Spampanato, Bari

(1939). *Epilogo magno*, ed. C. Ottaviano, Rome

(1939–55). *Quod reminiscentur*, ed. R. Amerio, 2 vols., Padua–Florence

(1941a). *Aforismi politici*, ed. L. Firpo, Turin

(1941b). *La Città del Sole*, ed. N. Bobbio, Turin

(1945a). *Antiveneti*, ed. L. Firpo, Florence

(1945b). *Discorsi ai principi d'Italia*, ed. L. Firpo, Turin

(1949–). *Theologicorum (libri)*, ed. R. Amerio, Florence

(1951). *Opusculi inediti*, ed. L. Firpo, Florence

(1954). *Opere*, ed. L. Firpo, Verona

(1960). *Monarchia messiae*, ed. L. Firpo, Turin

(1962). *La Città del Sole*, ed. A. Seroni, Milan

(1974). *La filosofia che i sensi additano (Philosophia sensibus demonstrata)*, ed. L. De Franco and L. Firpo, Naples

(1975). *Opera Latina Francofurti impressa annis 1617–1630*, ed. L. Firpo, 2 vols., Turin

(1977). *Articuli prophetales*, ed. G. Ernst, Florence

Camuzio, Andrea (1541). *In sacrarum literarum cum Aristotele et Platone concordiam*, Milan

Cano, Melchor (1605). *Opera*, Cologne

(1776). *Opera omnia*, Bassano

Carafa, Diomede (1971). *Dello optimo cortesano*, ed. G. Paparelli, Salerno

Carbone de Costacciaro, Lodovico (1585). *Vir iustus vel de laudibus hominis Christiani centuria*, Venice
Cardano, Girolamo (1663). *Opera omnia*, ed. C. Spon, 10 vols., Lyons (repr. New York–London, 1967)
  (1936). *Ma vie*, ed. and trans. J. Dayre, Paris
  (1962). *The Book of My Life*, trans. J. Stoner, New York
  (1968). *The Great Art*, ed. and trans. T. R. Witner, Cambridge, Mass.
  (1973). *Writings on Music*, ed. C. A. Miller, Rome
Casaubon, Isaac (1850). *Ephemerides*, ed. J. Russell, 2 vols., Oxford
Case, John (1584). *Summa veterum interpretum in universam dialecticam Aristotelis . . .*, London
  (1588). *Sphaera civitatis*, Oxford
  (1596a). *Speculum quaestionum moralium in universam Aristotelis . . . ethicen . . .*, Oxford
  (1596b). *Reflexus speculi moralis qui commentarii vice esse poterit in Magna moralia Aristotelis*, Oxford
  (1597). *Thesaurus oeconomiae . . .*, Oxford
  (1599). *Lapis philosophicus . . .*, Oxford
Castellani, Giulio (1558). *Adversus Marci Tullii Ciceronis Academicas quaestiones disputatio*, Bologna
  (1567). *De humano intellectu disputationes*, Venice
Castellani, Pier Nicola (1525). *Opus de immortalitate animorum secundum Platonem et Aristotelem*, Faenza
Castelvetro, Lodovico (1570). *Poetica d'Aristotile vulgarizzata et sposta*, Vienna
Castiglione, Baldassare (1947). *Il libro del cortegiano*, ed. V. Cian, Florence
  (1960). *Il libro del cortegiano*, ed. G. Preti, Turin
Catena, Pietro (1556). *Universa loca in logica Aristotelis in mathematicas disciplinas*, Venice
  (1561). *Super loca mathematica contenta in Topicis et Elenchis Aristotelis*, Venice
  (1563). *Oratio pro idea methodi*, Padua
Cavalcanti, Bartolommeo (1555). *La rhetorica*, Venice
Cavalcanti, Giovanni (1973). *Trattato politico-morale*, ed. M. T. Grendler, Geneva
Cesalpino, Andrea (1571). *Peripateticarum quaestionum libri V*, Venice (repr. Brussels, 1973)
  (1580). *Daemonum investigatio peripatetica*, Venice
  (1583). *De plantis libri XVI*, Florence
  (1929). *Questions péripatéticiennes*, trans. M. Dorolle, Paris
Charpentier, Jacques (1560–4). *Descriptio universae naturae*, 3 parts, Paris
  (1564). *Descriptio universae artis disserendi*, Paris
  (1567). *Ars disserendi, brevibus scholiis et notis illustrata*, Paris
  (1573). *Platonis cum Aristotele in universa philosophia comparatio*, Paris
Charron, Pierre (1635). *Oeuvres*, 2 vols., Paris (repr. Geneva, 1970)
  (1824). *De la sagesse*, ed. A. Duval, 3 vols., Paris (repr. Geneva, 1968)
Chartularium Universitatis Parisiensis (1889–97). Ed. H. Denifle and A. Chatelain, 4 vols., Paris
Chrysoloras, Manuel (1534). *Graecae grammaticae institutiones*, trans. D. Sylvius, Paris
  (1866). *Epistulae*, in *Patrologia Graeca*, ed. J. P. Migne, CLVI, Paris, cols. 21–60
Cicero (1537). *De finibus bonorum et malorum*, ed. Petrus Joannes Olivarius, Paris
  (1560). *De officiis*, comment. D. Erasmus, S. Birck, V. Amerbach and F. Maturanzio, Paris
  (1569). *Libri tres de officiis*, comment. H. Wolf, Basle
Clavius, Christophorus (1581). *In Sphaeram Ioannis de Sacro Bosco commentarius*, 2nd edn, Rome
Clichtove, Josse (1512). *De vera nobilitate*, Paris
  (1537). *Annotationes in Magna moralia*, Paris
  See also Lefèvre d'Étaples, Jacques and Clichtove, Josse

Colet, John (1873). *Enarratio in Epistolam S. Pauli ad Romanos*, ed. J. Lupton, London
Collegium Conimbricense (1594a). *In octo libros Physicorum*, 2 vols., Lyons
  (1594b). *In libros Meteorum*, Lyons
  (1594c). *In quattuor libros De coelo*, Lyons
  (1594d). *In libros Aristotelis qui Parva naturalia appellantur*, Lyons
  (1598). *In tres libros De anima*, Coimbra
  (1600). *In duos libros De generatione et corruptione*, Lyons
  (1606). *In tres libros De anima*, Venice
  (1607). *In universam dialecticam*, Cologne (repr. Hildesheim, 1976)
  (1609). *In tres libros De anima Aristotelis*, Cologne
  (1612). *In libros Ethicorum Aristotelis ad Nicomachum aliquot . . . disputationes*, Cologne
  (1957). *I. P.ᵉ: Manuel de Góis: moral de Aristóteles*, ed. A. A. de Andrade, Lisbon
[Cologne] (1493). *Copulata super omnes tractatus parvorum logicalium Petri Hispani ac super tres tractatus modernorum*, Cologne
  (1494). *Textus et copulata omnium tractatuum Petri Hyspani etiam parvorum logicalium et tractatus syncathegorematum quem aliqui octavum vocant*, Nuremberg
  (1496). *Copulata commentaria textui omnium tractatuum Petri Hyspani etiam parvorum logicalium et trium modernorum per quam solerter inserta*, Cologne
Compagni, Dino (1939). *La cronica*, ed. I. del Lungo, Florence
Contarini, Gasparo (1525). *De immortalitate animae adversus Petrum Pomponatium*, Bologna
  (1571). *Opera*, Paris (repr. Farnborough, 1968)
Contarini, Tommaso (1572). *De humana tranquillitate*, Venice
Coronel, Antonio (1517). *Tractatus syllogismorum*, [Paris]
Cremonini (1596). *Explanatio prooemi librorum Aristotelis De physico auditu*, Padua
  (1605). *De formis quattuor corporum simplicium quae vocantur elementa disputatio*, Venice
  (1613). *Disputatio de caelo*, Venice
  (1616). *Apologia dictorum Aristotelis de quinta caeli substantia adversus Xenarcum, Joannem Grammaticum et alios*, Venice
Critical Prefaces of the French Renaissance (1950). Ed. B. Weinberg, Evanston
Crockaert, Petrus (1509). *Acutissimae quaestiones et quidem perutiles in singulos Aristotelis logicales libros*, Paris
  (1510). *Quaestiones physicales in VIII libros Physicorum et in III De anima*, Paris

Da Monte, Giambattista (1558). *Opuscula*, Basle
Daneau, Lambert (1576). *Physica Christiana sive de rerum creatarum cognitione*, Lyons
  (1577). *Ethices Christianae libri tres*, Geneva
  (1579). *Methodus tractandae Sacrae Scripturae*, Geneva
  (1588). *Isagoges Christianae pars quinta, quae est de homine*, Geneva
Dante Alighieri (1965). *Monarchia*, ed. P. G. Ricci, Milan
Dati, Agostino (1503). *Opera*, Sienna
Decembrio, Pier Candido (1925–58). *Opuscula historica*, in *Rerum Italicarum scriptores*, ed. L. A. Muratori, xx,1 Bologna
Dee, John (1570). *The Mathematicall Preface to the Elements of Geometrie of Euclid of Megara*, London (repr. New York, 1975, ed. A. G. Debus)
Delbene, Bartolomeo (1609). *Civitas veri sive morum*, comment. T. Marcile, Paris
Delfino, Domenico (1556). *Sommario di tutte le scientie*, Venice
Della Barba, Pompeo (1554). *Spositione d'un sonetto platonico*, Florence
Della Porta, Giambattista (1558). *Magiae naturalis sive de miraculis rerum naturalium libri IV*, Naples
  (1560). *De miraculis rerum naturalium libri IV*, Antwerp
  (1586). *De humana physiognomonia*, Vico Equense

(1589). *Magiae naturalis libri XX*, Naples
(1603). *Coelestis physiognomoniae libri sex*, Naples
(1658). *Natural Magick*, London (repr. New York, 1957)
(1910–11). *Le commedie*, ed. V. Spampanato
(1982). *Criptologia*, ed. G. Belloni, Rome
Descartes, René (1897–1910). *Oeuvres*, ed. C. Adam and P. Tannery, 12 vols., Paris
Diacceto, Francesco da (1563). *Opera omnia*, ed. T. Zwinger, Basle
(1986). *De pulchro libri III*, ed. S. Matton, Pisa
Digby, Everard (1579). *Theoria analytica, viam ad monarchiam scientiarum demonstrans . . . totius philosophiae et reliquarum scientiarum . . . dogmata enucleans*, London
(1580). *De duplici methodo libri duo, unicam P. Rami methodum refutantes . . .*, London
Diogenes Laertius (1594). *De vitis, dogmatis et apophthegmatis clarorum philosophorum libri X*, ed. I. Casaubon, Geneva
Dionysius Carthusianus (1532–40). *Opera*, ed. D. Loer, 13 vols., Cologne
La disputa delle arti nel Quattrocento (1947). Ed. E. Garin, Florence
La disputa de los animales contra el hombre (1984). Ed. E. Tornero Poveda, Madrid
Dolz, Johannes (1511). *Syllogismi*, Paris
Dominici, Giovanni (1940). *Lucula noctis*, ed. E. Hunt, Notre Dame
Dominicus Gundissalinus (1903). *De divisione philosophiae*, ed. L. Baur, Münster
Donaldson, Walter (1620). *Synopsis oeconomica*, Paris
Du Bartas, Guillaume (1935–40). *The Works*, ed. U. T. Holmes *et al.*, 3 vols., Chapel Hill, N. C.
Du Bellay, Joachim (1966). *Les Regrets et autres oeuvres poëtiques*, ed. J. Jolliffe and M. A. Screech, Geneva
Du Haillan, Bernard (1570). *De l'estat et succez des affaires de France*, Paris
Dullaert, Johannes (1506). *Quaestiones super libros Physicorum et super libros De caelo et mundo*, Paris
(1515). *Quaestiones super duos libros Peri hermenias . . .*, Paris
(1520). *Quaestiones in librum Praedicabilium Porphyrii*, Paris
(1523). *Quaestiones in librum Praedicamentorum*, Paris
Duns Scotus, Johannes (1891–5). *Opera omnia*, 26 vols., Paris
Duodus, Petrus: *see* Piccolomini, Francesco (1575)
Dupleix, Scipion (1623). *Corps de philosophie contenant la logique, la physique, la métaphysique, et l'éthique*, Geneva
Durandus a S. Porciano (1567). *In Sententias theologicas Petri Lombardi libri IV*, Antwerp
Du Trieu, Philip (1662). *Manuductio ad logicam*, Oxford
Du Vair, Guillaume (1618). *Les Oeuvres*, Paris
(1624). *De la constance et de consolation ès calamités publiques*, Rouen
(1945). *De la sainte philosophie. Philosophie morale des Stoïques*, ed. G. Michaut, Paris
(1951). *The Moral Philosophie of the Stoicks*, trans. T. James, ed. R. Kirk, New Brunswick

The Earthly Republic (1978). Ed. B. Kohl and R. Witt, Philadelphia
Elyot, Thomas (1962). *The Book Named the Governour*, ed. S. E. Lehmberg, London
Enzinas, Fernando de (1528). *Tractatus de compositione propositionis mentalis*, Lyons
Epictetus (1561). *Enchiridion*, trans. H. Wolf, Basle
(1954). *Enchiridion*, trans. N. Perotti, ed. R. P. Oliver, Urbana
Erasmus, Desiderius (1703–6). *Opera omnia*, ed. J. Leclerc, 10 vols., Leiden (repr. Hildesheim 1961–2)
(1906–58). *Opus epistolarum*, ed. P. S. Allen *et al.*, 12 vols., Oxford
(1962). *Querela pacis*, ed. F. Geldner, Munich
(1965). *Il ciceroniano o dello stile migliore*, ed. A. Gambaro, Brescia

(1969–). *Opera omnia*, Amsterdam

(1970). *La Philosophie chrétienne*, ed. P. Mesnard, Paris

(1974–). *Collected Works*, Toronto

(1979). *In Praise of Folly and Letter to Dorp*, trans. C. H. Miller, Princeton

Erastus, Thomas (1574). *De occultis pharmacorum potestatibus*, Basle

Estatutos da Universidade de Coimbra (1559) (1963). Ed. S. Leite, Coimbra

Estienne, Henri (1590). *Principum monitrix musa*, Basle

Estienne, Henri and Scaliger, Joseph Justus (1573). *Poesis philosophica*, Geneva

Estrebay, Jacques-Louis d' (1549). *In tres priores libros Aristotelis ʾΗθικῶν Νικομαχείων commentaria*, Paris

Eusebius (1902–). *Werke* (Die griechischen christlichen Schriftsteller der ersten Jahrhunderte), Leipzig–Berlin

Eustachius a S. Paulo (1609). *Summa philosophiae quadripartita. De rebus dialecticis, moralibus, physicis, et metaphysicis*, Paris

Eustratius, Michael of Ephesus and Anonymous (1892). *In Ethica Nicomachea commentaria*, ed. G. Heylbut (Commentaria in Aristotelem Graeca, 20), Berlin

(1973–). *The Greek Commentaries on the Nicomachean Ethics*, trans. Robert Grosseteste, ed. H. P. F. Merken (Corpus Latinum Commentariorum in Aristotelem Graecorum, 6), Leiden

Facio, Bartolomeo (1611). *De humanae vitae felicitate. De excellentia ac praestantia hominis*, in F. Sandeus, *De regibus Siciliae et Apuliae*, Hanau

(1978). *Invective in Laurentium Vallam*, ed. E. I. Rao, Naples

Fernel, Jean (1550). *De abditis rerum causis libri duo*, Venice

Ferreto de' Ferreti (1920). *Le opere*, ed. C. Cipolla, 3 vols., Rome

Ficino, Marsilio (1576). *Opera omnia*, 2 vols., Basle (repr. Turin, 1959)

(1937). *Supplementum Ficinianum*, ed. P. O. Kristeller, 2 vols., Florence

(1956). *Commentaire sur le Banquet de Platon*, ed. R. Marcel, Paris

(1964–70). *Théologie platonicienne de l'immortalité des âmes*, trans. and ed. R. Marcel, 3 vols., Paris

(1975). *The Philebus Commentary*, ed. M. J. B. Allen, Berkeley

(1978). *De vita libri tres*, ed. M. Plessner and F. Klein-Franke, Hildesheim

(1981). *Marsilio Ficino and the Phaedran Charioteer*, ed. and trans. M. J. B. Allen, Berkeley–Los Angeles–London

(1985). *Commentary on Plato's 'Symposium' on Love*, trans. S. Jayne, Dallas

Figliucci, Felice (1551). *De la filosofia morale libri dieci. Sopra li dieci libri de l'ethica d'Aristotile*, Rome

(1564). *Dieci paradossi degli Accademici Intronati da Siena*, Milan

Filelfo, Francesco (1502). *Epistolarum familiarium libri XXXVII*, Venice

(1552). *De morali disciplina*, ed. F. Robortello, Venice

(1892). *Cent-dix lettres grecques*, ed. E. Legrand, Paris

Filelfo, Francesco and Landino, Cristoforo (1949). *Testi inediti e rari*, ed. E. Garin, Florence

Flacius Illyricus, Matthias (1556). *Catalogus testium veritatis*, Basle

Flandino, Ambrogio (1519). *De animorum immortalitate liber contra assertorem mortalitatis Petrum Pomponatium*, Mantua

Florimonte, Galeazzo (1554). *I ragionamenti di M. Agostino da Sessa . . . sopra la filosofia morale d'Aristotele*, Venice

Fonseca, Pedro da (1615–29). *Commentarii in libros metaphysicorum*, Cologne (repr. Hildesheim, 1964)

(1964). *Instituições dialécticas (Institutionum dialecticarum libri VIII)*, trans. and ed. J. Ferreira Gomes, 2 vols., Coimbra

(1965). *Isagoge filosófica*, trans. and ed. J. Ferreira Gomes, Coimbra

Fox-Morcillo, Sebastian (1554). *Ethices philosophiae compendium*, Basle

  (1556). *In Platonis Timaeum commentarii*, Basle

  (1560). *De naturae philosophia seu de Platonis et Aristotelis consensione*, Paris

  (1566). *Ethices philosophiae compendium*, Basle

Fracastoro, Girolamo (1538). *Homocentrica sive de stellis*, Venice

  (1555). *Opera omnia*, Venice

  (1955a). *Naugerius*, ed. A. M. Carini, *Studi tassiani*, 5: 107–45

  (1955b). *Scritti inediti*, Verona

  (1984). *Syphilis*, trans. and ed. G. Eatough, Liverpool

Fraunce, Abraham (1588). *The Lawiers Logike*, London

Freigius, Joannes Thomas (1575). *Ciceronianus*, Basle

  (1579). *Quaestiones physicae*, Basle

Frischlin, Nicodemus (1586). *De astronomicae artis cum doctrina coelesti et naturali philosophia congruentia*, Frankfurt.

Gaetano da Thiene (1484). *Expositio in libros De coelo et mundo*, Venice

  (1486). *Expositio super libros De anima*, Vicenza

  (1491). *De intensione et remissione formarum*, Venice

  (1493). *Super libros De anima*, Venice

  (1494). *Declaratio super tractatu Hentisberi Regularum*, Venice

  (1496). *Recollectae super octo libros Physicorum Aristotelis*, Venice

Gaillard, Pierre Droit de (1578). *De utilitate et ordine historiarum praefatio*, in Baptista Fulgosius, *Factorum dictorumque memorabilium libri IX*, Paris

  (1579). *Methode qu'on doit tenir en la lecture de l'histoire*, Paris

Galen (1821). *Opera omnia*, ed. C. G. Kühn, 20 vols., Leipzig (repr. Hildesheim, 1964–5)

Galilei, Galileo (1890–1909). *Le opere*, ed. A. Favaro and I. Del Lungo, 20 vols., Florence (repr. Florence, 1929–39; 1965)

  (1956). *Dialoghi e lettere filosofiche*, ed. C. Rizza, Siracusa

  (1960). *On Motion and on Mechanics*, ed. S. Drake and I. E. Drabkin, Madison

  (1977). *Galileo's Early Notebooks: The Physical Questions*, trans. and ed. W. A. Wallace, Notre Dame

Garcia, Pedro (1489). *Determinationes magistrales . . . contra conclusiones apologeticas Joannis Pici*, Rome

Garzoni, Giovanni (1505). *De miseria humana*, Strasburg

Gassendi, Pierre (1658). *Opera omnia*, 6 vols., Lyons (repr. Stuttgart–Bad Canstatt, 1964)

Gaza, Theodore (1866). *Opera*, in *Patrologia graeca*, ed. J. P. Migne, CLXI, Paris, cols. 985–1014

  (1925). *De fato*, ed. J. W. Taylor, Toronto

  (1975). *Epistole*, trans. and ed. E. Pinto, Naples

Gebwiler, Johannes (1511). *Magistralis totius parvuli artis logices compilatio*, Basle

Genua, Marcantonio (1565). *Disputatio de intellectus humani immortalitate*, Venice

  (1576). *In tres libros Aristotelis De anima exactissimi commentarii*, Venice

George of Brussels (1491a). *Expositio super Summulis magistri Petri Hyspani*, Paris

  (1491b). *Expositio super octo libros Physicorum Aristotelis*, Paris

  (1496). *Cursus quaestionum super philosophiam Aristotelis*, Freiburg i. Br.

  (1504). *Expositio in logicam Aristotelis*, Lyons

George of Brussels and Bricot, Thomas (1486). *Cursus optimarum quaestionum super philosophiam Aristotelis cum interpretatione textus secundum viam modernorum ac secundum cursum magistri Georgii per magistrum Thomam Bricot . . . emendate* [sic] *. . .*, Lyons

  (1508). *Textus abbreviatus Aristotelis super octo libris Phisicorum et tota naturali philosophia*, Lyons

George of Trebizond (c. 1470). *De dialectica ex Aristotele compendium*, Venice

(1522). *De artificio ciceroniane orationis Pro Q. Ligario ad Victorinum Feltrensem*, in Asconius Pedianus, *Expositio in IIII Orationes M. Tulli Ciceronis*, Venice

(1523). *Comparationes phylosophorum Aristotelis et Platonis*, Venice (repr. Frankfurt, 1965)

(1547). *Rhetoricorum libri quinque*, Lyons

(1942). *Adversus Theodorum Gazam in perversionem Problematum Aristotelis*, in L. Mohler, *Kardinal Bessarion als Theologe, Humanist und Staatsmann*, III, Paderborn, pp. 277–342

(1970). *Praefatio in libros Platonis 'De legibus'*, ed. F. Adorno, in *Studi in onore di Antonio Corsano*, Manduria, pp. 13–17

(1984). *Collectanea Trapezuntiana*, ed. J. Monfasani, Binghamton

Gerald of Wales (1891). *De principis instructione liber*, ed. G. F. Warner, London

Gerson, Jean (1706). *Opera omnia*, ed. E. du Pin, 5 vols., Antwerp

(1960–73). *Oeuvres complètes*, ed. P. Glorieux, 10 vols., Paris

Gherardi, Giovanni, da Prato (1867). *Il paradiso degli Alberti. Ritrovi e ragionamenti*, ed. A. Wesselofsky, 3 vols., Bologna

(1975). *Il paradiso degli Alberti*, ed. A. Lanza, Rome

Giffen, Hubert van (1608). *Commentarii in decem libros Ethicorum Aristotelis ad Nicomachum*, Frankfurt

Giles of Rome (1607). *De regimine principum*, ed. H. Samaritani, Rome

Giles of Viterbo (1959). *Scechina e Libellus de litteris hebraicis*, ed. F. Secret, 2 vols., Rome

(1969). *De aurea aetate*, ed. J. W. O'Malley, *Traditio*, 25: 265–338

(1972). *Oratio habita post tertiam sacri Lateranensis concilii sessionem*, ed. and introd. C. O'Reilly, *Augustiniana*, 22: 80–117

(1977). *Oratio prima synodi Lateranensis*, ed. and introd. C. O'Reilly, *Augustiniana*, 27: 166–204

Ginés de Sepúlveda, Juan (1526). *De fato et libero arbitrio libri III*, Rome

(1780). *Opera*, 4 vols., Madrid

(1951). *Demócrates segundo o de las justas causas de la guerra contra los Indios*, ed. and trans. A. Losada, Madrid

(1963). *Tratados politicos*, ed. A. Losada, Madrid

(1968). *Epistolario*, ed. A. Losada, Madrid

Ginés de Sepúlveda, Juan and Las Casas, Bartolomé de (1975). *Apologia*, ed. and trans. A. Losada, Madrid

Giorgi, Francesco (1525). *De harmonia mundi totius cantica tria*, Venice

(1578). *L'Harmonie du monde*, trans. G. Le Fèvre de la Boderie, Paris

Giovanni da Ravenna (1980). *Dragmalogia de eligibili vite genere*, ed. H. L. Eaker and B. G. Kohl, Lewisburg

Giraldi, Lilio (1696). *Opera*, Leiden

Giustiniani, Paolo (1967–). *Trattati, lettere e frammenti*, ed. E. Massa, Rome

Goclenius, Rudolphus (1598). *Isagoge in Organum Aristotelis*, Frankfurt

(1613). *Lexicon philosophicum, quo tanquam clave philosophiae fores aperiuntur . . .*, Frankfurt

(1615). *Lexicon philosophicum Graecum*, Marburg

Golius, Theophilus (1606). *Epitome doctrinae politicae*, Strasburg

(1622). *Epitome doctrinae oeconomicae*, Strasburg

(1634). *Epitome doctrinae moralis*, Cambridge

Gottschalk (1945). *Oeuvres théologiques et grammaticales*, ed. C. Lambot, Louvain

Gouveia, Antonio de (1543). *Pro Aristotele responsio adversus Petri Rami calumnias*, Paris

Grande antologia filosofica (1964–). Ed. M. F. Sciacca, part III:*Il pensiero della Rinascenza e della Riforma*, Milan

Gratarolo, Guglielmo (1554). *Opuscula*, Basle

Gregory of Rimini (1508). *De imprestantiis Venetorum et de usura*, Rimini

(1522). *Super primum et secundum Sententiarum*, Venice (repr. St Bonaventure, N.Y., 1955)

Grifoli, Giacopo (1557). *Orationes*, Venice

Guarino da Verona (1915–19). *Epistolario*, ed. R. Sabbadini, 3 vols., Venice
Guicciardini, Francesco (1561). *Storia d'Italia*, Florence
  (1931). *Storie fiorentine*, ed. R. Palmarocchi, Bari
  (1932). *Dialogo e discorsi del reggimento di Firenze*, ed. R. Palmarocchi, Bari
  (1945). *Ricordi politici e civili*, ed. A. Faggi, Turin
  (1951). *Ricordi*, ed. R. Spongano, Florence
  (1965). *Selected Writings*, ed. C. and M. Grayson, London

Hall, Joseph (1863). *The Works*, ed. P. Wynter, 10 vols., Oxford
Harrington, James (1977). *The Political Works*, ed. J. G. A. Pocock, Cambridge
Harvey, Gabriel (1577). *Ciceronianus*, London
Harvey, William (1628). *Exercitatio anatomica de motu cordis et sanguinis in animalibus*, Frankfurt
Heiland, Samuel (1581). *Aristotelis Ethicorum ad Nicomachum libri decem in . . . usum studiosorum . . . per quaestiones expositi*, London
Heinsius, Daniel (1943). *The Value of History*, trans. G. W. Robinson, Cambridge, Mass.
Henry of Ghent (1520). *Summae quaestionum ordinarium II*, Paris (repr. St Bonaventure, N.Y., 1953)
Henry of Rimini (1472). *Tractatus de quatuor virtutibus cardinalibus*, Strasburg
Herbetius, Johannes (1579). *Argumenta in singulos libros Ethicorum*, Lyons
Hermes Trismegistus, Pseudo- (1945–54). *Corpus Hermeticum*, ed. A. D. Nock and A.-J. Festugière, 4 vols., Paris
Heytesbury, William (1494). *Tractatus de sensu composito et diviso. Regule. . .cum sophismatibus . . .*, Venice
Hobbes, Thomas (1946). *Leviathan*, ed. M. Oakeshott, Oxford
  (1968). *Leviathan*, ed. C. B. Macpherson, Harmondsworth, Middlesex
Humanism and Liberty (1978). Trans. R. Neu Watkins, Columbia, S.C.
Hundt, Magnus (1501). *Antropologium: De hominis dignitate, natura et proprietatibus*, Leipzig
Hunnaeus, Augustinus (1584). *Prodidagmata de dialecticis*, Antwerp

Index de l'Inquisition espagnole: 1551, 1554, 1559 (1984). Ed. J. M. De Bujanda *et al.*, Sherbrooke–Geneva
Index de l'Université de Paris: 1544, 1545, 1547, 1549, 1551, 1556 (1985). Ed. J. M. De Bujanda *et al.*, Sherbrooke–Geneva
Innocent III (1955). *De miseria humane conditionis*, ed. M. Maccarrone, Lugano

Javelli, Crisostomo (1536). *Tractatus de animae humanae indeficientia in quadruplici via scilicet peripatetica, academica, naturali, et Christiana*, Venice
  (1580). *Opera*, Lyons
  (1651). *In universam moralem Aristotelis, Platonis et Christianam philosophiam, epitomes in certas partes distinctae*, Lyons
Johannes de Magistris (1481). *Questiones perutiles super tota philosophia naturali cum explanatione textus Aristotelis secundum mentem Doctoris subtilis Scoti*, Parma
  (1487). *Quaestiones super totum cursum logicae*, Venice
Johannes de Mirecourt (1958). 'Questioni inedite di Giovanni di Mirecourt sulla conoscenza', ed. A. Franzinelli, *Rivista critica di storia della filosofia*, 13: 319–40, 415–49
John of St Thomas (1930). *Cursus philosophicus Thomisticus*, I: *Ars logica*, Turin–Rome
  (1937). *De ente mobili animato*, ed. B. Reiser, Toronto
John of Salisbury (1909). *Policraticus*, ed. C. Webb, 2 vols., Oxford
  (1975). 'The *Entheticus*: A Critical Text', ed. R. E. Pepin, *Traditio*, 31: 127–93
Josse, Johannes (c. 1495). *Expositiones modorum significandi*, Rouen
Judah Messer Leon (1983). *The Book of the Honeycomb's Flow*, trans. I. Rabinowitz, Ithaca

Keckermann, Bartholomaeus (1600). *Systema logicae*, Hanau
(1607a). *Systema ethicae*, London
(1607b). *Systema disciplinae oeconomicae*, Hanau
(1607c). *Systema disciplinae politicae*, Hanau
(1607d). *Praecognita philosophica*, Hanau
(1608). *Systema rhetoricae*, Hanau
(1609). *Scientiae metaphysicae compendiosum systema*, Hanau
(1610). *Systema physicum*, Gdansk
(1617). *Systema compendiosum totius mathematices*, Hanau
Kepler, Johannes (1610). *Dissertatio cum Nuncio Sidereo*, Prague
(1937–). *Gesammelte Werke*, ed. W. von Dyck and M. Caspar, Munich

Lambin, Denys (1558). *In libros De moribus ad Nicomachum annotationes*, Venice
(1565). *Oratio de philosophiae moralis laudibus*, Paris
Landi, Giulio (1564–75). *Le attioni morali*, 2 vols., Ferrara–Piacenza
Landino, Cristoforo (1481). *Commento sopra la Comedia di Danthe*, Florence
(1939). *Carmina omnia*, ed. A. Perosa, Florence
(1970a). *De vera nobilitate*, ed. M. Lentzen, Geneva
(1970b). *De vera nobilitate*, ed. M. T. Liaci, Florence
(1974). *Scritti critici e teorici*, ed. R. Cardini, 2 vols., Rome
(1980). *Disputationes Camaldulenses*, ed. P. Lohe, Florence
See also Filelfo, Francesco and Landino, Cristoforo
La Popelinière, Henri de (1599). *L'Histoire des histoires, avec L'Idée de l'histoire accomplie*, Paris
La Ruelle, Charles de (1574). *Succinctz adversaires . . . contre l'histoire et professeurs d'icelle*, Poitiers
Las Casas, Bartolomé de: *see* Ginés de Sepúlveda, Juan and Las Casas, Bartolomé de
Latini, Brunetto (1948). *Li livres dou trésor*, ed. F. Carmody, Berkeley
La Torre, Alfonso de (1855). *Visión delectable de la filosofía y artes liberales, metafísica y filosofía moral*, Madrid
Leclerc, Jean (1712). *Ars critica*, 4th edn, 2 vols., Amsterdam
Lefèvre d'Étaples, Jacques (1496). *In hoc opusculo he continentur introductiones. In suppositiones. In predicabilia. In divisiones. In predicamenta*, Paris
(1498). *Brevis introductio in libros De anima*, Paris
(1502). *Artificialis introductio . . . in decem libros Ethicorum . . .*, Paris
(1520). *Artificiales nonnulle introductiones*, ed. J. Clichtove, Paris
(1530). *In Aristotelis libros Ethicorum ad Nicomachum commentarius*, Paris
(1533). *Moralis in Ethicen introductio*, comment. J. Clichtove, Paris
(1972). *The Prefatory Epistles*, ed. E. F. Rice, New York
Lefèvre d'Étaples, Jacques and Clichtove, Josse (1492). *Totius philosophiae naturalis paraphrases cum annotationibus*, Paris
(1502). *Totius philosophiae naturalis paraphrases cum annotationibus*, Paris
Leibniz, Gottfried Wilhelm (1875–90). *Die philosophischen Schriften*, ed. C. J. Gerhardt, 7 vols., Berlin (repr. Hildesheim, 1960–1)
Leone Ebreo (1929). *Dialoghi d'amore*, ed. S. Caramella, Bari
(1937). *The Philosophy of Love*, ed. and trans. F. Friedberg-Seeley and J. H. Barnes, London
Leoniceno, Niccolò (1532). *Opuscula*, Basle
Leonico Tomeo, Niccolò (1523). *Parva naturalia explicata*, Venice
(1524). *Dialogi*, Venice
(1525a). *Annotationes in Mechanicas quaestiones*, Venice
(1525b). *Opuscula*, Venice
(1531). *De varia historia libri III*, Venice
(1540). *Explanatio libri I De partibus animalium*, Venice

Le Roy, Louis (1551a). *Trois Livres d'Isocrate*, Paris
  (1551b). *Le Timée de Platon*, Paris
  (1553). *Le Phédon de Platon*, Paris
  (1567). *De l'origine, antiquité, prógres, excellence et utilité de l'art politique*, Paris
  (1570). *Exhortation aux françois pour vivre en concorde*, Paris
  (1575). *De la vicissitude ou varieté des choses en l'univers*, Paris
  (1576). *Les Politiques d'Aristote*, Paris
  (1598). *Discours politiques*, Paris
  (1944). *De la vicissitude ou varieté des choses en l'univers*, ed. B. W. Bates, Princeton
Lipsius, Justus (1589). *Politicorum sive civilis doctrinae libri sex*, Lyons
  (1591). *Epistolarum centuriae duae*, Leiden
  (1675). *Opera omnia*, 4 vols., Basle
  (1939). *Two Bookes of Constancie*, trans. J. Stradling, ed. R. Kirk, New Brunswick
  (1978–). *Epistolae*, ed. A. Gerlo *et al.*, Brussels
Logica Oxoniensis (s. xv) MS Oxford, Bodleian Library, Lat. misc. e. 79
Lucretius (1563). *De rerum natura libri sex*, ed. D. Lambin, Paris
  (1566). *De rerum natura libri sex*, ed. H. van Giffen, Antwerp
  (1570). *De rerum natura libri VI*, ed. D. Lambin, Paris
Lull, Ramon (1721–42). *Opera*, ed. I. Salzinger, 8 vols., Mainz
  (1905–50). *Obres*, 21 vols., Palma de Mallorca
  (1959–). *Opera Latina*, ed. F. Stegmüller *et al.*, Palma de Mallorca–Turnhout
Luther, Martin (1883–). *Werke*, Weimar

Machiavelli, Niccolò (1882). *The Historical, Political and Diplomatic Writings*, ed. C. E. Detmold, 4 vols., Boston
  (1929). *Tutte le opere storiche e letterarie*, ed. G. Mazzoni and M. Casella, Florence
  (1954). *Opere*, ed. M. Bonfantini, Milan
  (1960). *Il principe e Discorsi*, ed. S. Bertelli, Milan
  (1961). *Lettere*, ed. F. Gaeta, Milan
  (1965). *The Chief Works and Others*, 3 vols., Durham, N.C.
Maestlin, Michael (1597). *Epitome astronomiae*, Tübingen
Maffei, Raffaele (1506). *Commentariorum Urbanorum libri octo et triginta*, Rome
  (1542). *Argumenta in libros decem Ethicorum Aristotelis ad Nicomachum*, Venice
Maffei, Timoteo (s. xv). *In magnificentiae Cosmi Medici Florentini detractores*, MS Florence, Biblioteca Medicea-Laurenziana, Plut. xlvii, 17, ff. 78^v–102^v
Magirus, Johannes (1597). *Physiologia peripatetica ex Aristotele eiusque interpretibus collecta . . .*, Frankfurt
  (1601). *Corona virtutum moralium, universam Aristotelis . . . ethicen exacte enucleans*, Frankfurt
  (1603). *Anthropologia, hoc est commentarius eruditissimus in aureum Philippi Melanchthonis libellum de anima*, Frankfurt
  (1608). *Physiologiae peripateticae libri sex cum commentariis*, Frankfurt
  (1614). *Corona virtutum moralium, universam Aristotelis . . . ethicen exacte enucleans*, Frankfurt
Maio, Giuniano (1956). *De maiestate*, ed. F. Gaeta, Bologna
Maiolus, Laurentius (1497). *Epiphyllides in dialecticis*, Venice
Mair, John (1500). *Praedicabilia*, Paris
  (1505). *In Petri Hispani Summulas commentaria*, Lyons
  (1526). *Octo libri Physicorum cum naturali philosophia atque metaphysica . . .*, Paris
  (1528). *Quaestiones logicales cum expositione in veterem Aristotelis dialecticen*, Paris

(1530). *Commentaria in Ethicam Aristotelis*, Paris
(1938). *Le Traité 'De l'infini'*, ed. and trans. H. Élie, Paris
Manetti, Giannozzo (1974). *Vita Socratis*, ed. M. Montuori, Florence
(1975). *De dignitate et excellentia hominis*, ed. E. R. Leonard, Padua
(1979). *Vita Socratis et Senecae*, ed. A. De Petris, Florence
(1981). *Apologeticus*, ed. A. De Petris, Rome
(1983). *Dialogus consolatorius*, ed. A. De Petris, Rome
Manutius, Aldus (1975). *Aldo Manuzio editore*, ed. G. Orlandi, 2 vols., Milan
Maranta, Bartolomeo (1561). *Discorsi*, MS Milan, Biblioteca Ambrosiana, R.118.sup.
Marliani, Giovanni (1482). *Opera*, 2 vols., Pavia
Marsilius of Inghen (1501). *Quaestiones super quattuor libros Sententiarum*, Strasburg (repr. Frankfurt, 1966)
(1516). *Quaestiones super libros Priorum analyticorum*, Venice (repr. Frankfurt, 1968)
(1520). *De generatione et corruptione*, Venice
(1521). *Abbreviationes libri Physicorum*, Venice
(1980). *Treatises on the Properties of Terms*, ed. E. P. Bos, Ph.D. thesis, Univ. of Leiden
Marsilius of Padua (1928). *Defensor pacis*, ed. C. W. Previté-Orton, Cambridge
Marzio, Galeotto (1949). *De doctrina promiscua*, ed. M. Frezzi, Naples
Mas, Diego (1599). *Commentarii in universam philosophiam Aristotelis*, 2 vols., Valencia
Mastrius, Bartholomaeus and Bellutus, Bonaventura (1643). *Disputationes in Aristotelis libros De anima*, Venice
(1678). *Philosophiae ad mentem Scoti cursus integer*, Venice
Mazzoni, Jacopo (1572). *Della difesa della Commedia di Dante*, Bologna
(1576). *De triplici hominum vita . . .*, Cesena
(1597). *In universam Platonis et Aristotelis philosophiam praeludia, sive de comparatione Platonis et Aristotelis*, Venice
Mechanics in Sixteenth-Century Italy (1969). Ed. S. Drake and I. E. Drabkin, Madison
Medici, Lorenzo de' (1914). *Opere*, ed. A. Simioni, 2 vols., Bari
(1977–). *Lettere*, Florence
The Medieval Science of Weights (1952). Ed. and trans. E. A. Moody and M. Clagett, Madison
Mei, Girolamo (1960). *Letters on Ancient and Modern Music to Vincenzo Galilei and Giovanni Bardi*, ed. C. V. Palisca, Dallas
Melanchthon, Philipp (1520). *Compendiaria dialectices ratio*, Wittenberg
(1531). *De dialectica libri quatuor*, Wittenberg
(1537). *Dialectices libri III*, Lyons
(1555). *Erotemata dialectices*, Wittenberg
(1834–60). *Opera quae supersunt omnia*, ed. C. G. Bretschneider and H. E. Bindseil, 28 vols., Halle–Braunschweig
(1910–26). *Supplementa Melanchthoniana*, 5 vols., Leipzig
(1968). *Elementorum rhetorices libri duo*, trans. M. J. La Fontaine, Ph.D. thesis, Univ. of Michigan, Ann Arbor
Micraelius, Johannes (1662). *Lexicon philosophicum terminorum philosophis usitatorum ordine alphabetico . . . digestorum*, Stettin
Mildapettus, Franciscus: *see* Temple, William
Milieu, Christophe (1551). *De scribenda universitate rerum historia*, Basle
Die mittelalterlichen Traktate 'De modo opponendi et respondendi' (1980). Ed. L. M. de Rijk, Münster
Molina, Luis de (1588). *Concordia liberi arbitrii cum gratiae donis, divina praescientia, providentia, praedestinatione et reprobatione*, Lisbon
(1659). *De iustitia et iure libri sex*, 2 vols., Mainz
Montaigne, Michel de (1922–3). *Les Essais*, ed. P. Villey, 3 vols., Alcan

(1946–8). *Les Essais*, ed. J. Plattard, 6 vols., Paris
(1965). *Les Essais*, ed. P. Villey, Paris
(1976). *Oeuvres complètes*, ed. A. Thibaudet and M. Rat, Paris
Monumenta Germaniae paedagogica (1887). Ed. K. Kehrbach, v, Berlin
Monumenta humanistica Lovaniensia (1934). Ed. H. de Vocht, Louvain
Monumenta paedagogica Societatis Iesu (1965–). Rome
More, Thomas (1565). *Omnia opera*, Louvain
    (1947). *The Correspondence*, ed. E. F. Rogers, Princeton
    (1953). *The Latin Epigrams*, trans. and ed. L. Bradner and C. A. Lynch, Chicago
    (1963–). *The Complete Works*, New Haven–London
Morosini, Domenico (1969). *De bene instituta re publica*, ed. C. Finzi, Milan
Muret, Marc-Antoine (1789). *Opera omnia*, ed. D. Ruhnken, 4 vols., Leiden
Mussato, Albertino (1900). *Ecerinis*, ed. L. Padrin, Bologna

Nanni Mirabelli, Domenico (1503). *Polyanthea*, Saona
Nepos, Cornelius (1569). *Liber de vita excellentium imperatorum*, ed. D. Lambin, Paris
Nesi, Giovanni (s. xv). *De moribus*, MS Florence, Biblioteca Medicea-Laurenziana, Plut.
    LXXVII,24
Newton, Isaac (1983). *Certain Philosophical Questions: Newton's Trinity Notebook*, ed.
    J. E. McGuire and M. Tamny, Cambridge
Nicholas of Cusa (1485). *Opera*, 2 vols., Strasburg (repr. Berlin, 1967)
    (1932–). *Opera omnia*, Leipzig–Hamburg
    (1954). *Of Learned Ignorance*, trans. G. Heron, New Haven
    (1981). *On Learned Ignorance: A Translation and Appraisal of the 'De Docta Ignorantia'*, trans.
    J. Hopkins and A. J. Banning, Minneapolis
Nifo, Agostino (1497). *De sensu agente*, Venice
    (1503). *De intellectu*, Venice
    (1514). *Expositio in IV libros De caelo et mundo*, Sessa Aurunca
    (1518). *De immortalitate animae libellum adversus Petrum Pomponatium Mantuanum*, Venice
    (1521a). *De immortalitate animae libellum*, Venice
    (1521b). *Dialectica ludicra*, Venice
    (1523a). *Subtilissima collectanea commentariaque in libros . . . De anima*, Venice
    (1523b). *Parva naturalia*, Venice
    (1529). *In librum Destructio destructionum Averrois commentarii*, Lyons
    (1540). *Aristotelis . . . Topica inventio . . . interpretata atque exposita . . .*, Paris
    (1552). *Expositio super octo Aristotelis libros De physico auditu*, Venice
    (1553a). *Super libros Priorum Aristotelis*, Venice
    (1553b). *In Aristotelis libros Posteriorum analyticorum . . . commentaria*, Venice
    (1559). *Expositio subtilissima necnon collectanea commentariaque in tres libros Aristotelis De
    anima*, Venice
    (1645). *Opuscula moralia et politica*, Paris
Nizolio, Mario (1536). *Observationes in M. T. Ciceronem*, Basle
    (1559). *Thesaurus ciceronianus*, Basle
    (1956). *De veris principiis et vera ratione philosophandi contra pseudophilosophos libri IV*, ed.
    Q. Breen, 2 vols., Rome
Nores, Jason de (1578). *Breve institutione dell'ottima republica*, Venice
    (1597). *In M. T. Ciceronis universam philosophiam de vita et moribus brevis et distincta institutio*,
    Amberg

Ockham, William of (1494–6). *Opera plurima*, 4 vols., Lyons (repr, London, 1962)
    (1957). *Philosophical Writings*, ed. P. Boehner, Edinburgh

Oliver, Thomas (1604). *De sophismatum praestigiis cavendis admonitio*, Cambridge
Oresme, Nicole (1940). *Le Livre d'Éthiques d'Aristote (1370)*, ed. A. D. Menut, New York
  (1943). *Traité de l'espere*, ed. L. M. McCarthy, Ph.D. thesis, Univ. of Toronto
  (1952). *Le Livre de divinacions*, ed. G. W. Coopland, Liverpool
  (1957). *Le Livre de yconomique d'Aristote*, ed. A. D. Menut, Philadelphia
  (1965). *Quaestiones super libros De celo*, ed. C. Kren, Ph.D. thesis, Univ. of Wisconsin, Madison
  (1966). *De proportionibus proportionum* and *Ad pauca respicientes*, ed. E. Grant, Madison
  (1968a). *Le Livre du ciel et du monde*, ed. A. D. Menut and A. J. Denomy, Madison
  (1968b). *Tractatus de configurationibus qualitatum et motuum*, ed. M. Clagett, Madison
  (1970). *Le Livre de Politiques d'Aristote*, ed. A. D. Menut, Philadelphia
  (1971). *Tractatus de commensurabilitate vel incommensurabilitate motuum celi*, ed. and trans. E. Grant, Madison
  (1976). *Quaestio contra divinatores horoscopios*, ed. S. Caroti, *Archives d'histoire doctrinale et littéraire du moyen âge*, 43: 201–310
  (1980). *Quaestiones in libros De anima*, ed. P. Marshall, Ph.D. thesis, Cornell Univ.
  (1985). *De causis mirabilium*, ed. and trans. B. Hansen, Toronto

Pace, Giulio (1595). *Institutiones logicae*, Sedan
  (1605). *In Porphyrii Isagogen et Aristotelis Organum commentarius analyticus*, Geneva
  (1617). *Artis lullianae emendatae libri IV*, Geneva
Paleario, Aonio (1536). *De animorum immortalitate libri III*, Lyons
  (1696). *Opera*, Amsterdam
Palmieri, Matteo (1906–15). *De temporibus*, ed. G. Scaramella, in *Rerum Italicarum scriptores*, ed. L. A. Muratori, XXVI, Città di Castello, pp. 1–127
  (1982). *Vita civile*, ed. G. Belloni, Florence
Paracelsus, Theophrastus (1922–33). *Sämtliche Werke*, 14 vols., Munich
  (1923–73). *Die theologischen und religionswissenschaftlichen Schriften*, ed. K. Sudhoff et al., 8 vols., Munich–Wiesbaden
Parrasio, Aulo Giano (1531). *In Q. Horatii Flacci Artem poeticam commentaria*, Naples
Paruta, Paolo (1852). *Opere politiche*, ed. G. Monzani, 2 vols., Florence
Pascal, Blaise (1907). *Pensées et opuscules*, ed. L. Brunschvicq, Paris
Pasquier, Étienne (1956). *Choix de lettres sur la littérature, la langue et la traduction*, ed. D. Thickett, Geneva
Patrizi, Francesco [da Cherso] (1553). *La città felice . . .*, Venice
  (1557). *L'Eridano*, Ferrara
  (1560). *Della historia dieci dialoghi*, Venice
  (1562). *Della retorica dieci dialoghi*, Venice
  (1581). *Discussionum peripateticarum tomi quattuor*, Basle
  (1591). *Nova de universis philosophia*, Ferrara
  (1963). *L'amorosa filosofia*, ed. J. C. Nelson, Florence
  (1969–71). *Della poetica*, ed. D. Aguzzi Barbagli, 3 vols., Florence
  (1970). *Emendatio in libros suos Novae philosophiae'*, ed. P. O. Kristeller, *Rinascimento*, ser. ii, 10: 215–18
  (1975). *Lettere ed opuscoli inediti*, ed. D. Aguzzi Barbagli, Florence
Patrizi, Francesco [of Sienna] (1518a). *De institutione reipublicae*, Paris
  (1518b). *De regno et regis institutione*, Paris
  (1594a). *De regno et regis institutione*, Strasburg
  (1594b). *De institutione reipublicae*, Strasburg
Paul of Pergula (1961). *Logica* and *Tractatus de sensu composito et diviso*, ed. M. A. Brown, St Bonaventure–Louvain–Paderborn

Paul of Venice (1472). *Logica*, Venice (repr. Hildesheim–New York, 1970)
    (1475). *Logica*, Venice
    (1476). *Summa naturalium Aristotelis*, Venice
    (1481). *Scriptum super libros De anima*, Venice
    (1498). *Expositio super libros De generatione et corruptione*, Venice
    (1499a). *Expositio super octo Phisicorum libros Aristotelis*, Venice
    (1499b). *Logica magna*, Venice
    (1503). *Summa philosophiae naturalis*, Venice (repr. Hildesheim–New York, 1974)
    (1971). *Logica magna (Tractatus de suppositionibus)*, ed. and trans. A. R. Perreiah, St
        Bonaventure, N.Y.
    (1978–). *Logica magna*, ed. N. Kretzmann *et al.*, Oxford
Il pensiero pedagogico dello umanesimo (1958). Ed. E. Garin, Florence
Pereira, Benito (1576). *De communibus omnium rerum naturalium principiis et affectionibus libri
    XV*, Rome
    (1591). *Adversus fallaces et superstitiosas artes, id est, de magia, de observatione somniorum, de
        divinatione astrologica, libri III*, Ingolstadt
Pérez de Oliva, Fernan (1982). *Diálogo de la dignidad del hombre*, ed. M. L. Cerrón Puga,
    Madrid
Périon, Joachim (1540). *In De moribus quae ethica nominantur libros X commentaria*, Paris
    (1541). *In Topicorum libros VIII commentationes*, Paris
    (1543a). *In De republica qui politicorum dicuntur libros VIII observationes*, Paris
    (1543b). *Pro Aristotele in Petrum Ramum orationes II*, Paris
    (1547). *Pro Ciceronis Oratore contra Petrum Ramum oratio*, Paris
    (1548). *Observationes in Porphyrii Institutiones et in universum Aristotelis Organum*, Paris
    (1549). *In De anima libros III observationes*, Paris
    (1554). *Oratio qua Nicolai Grossii calumnias atque iniurias ostendit et repellit*, Paris
Perotti, Niccolò (1517). *Cornucopiae sive linguae latinae commentarii*, Venice
Peter of Spain (1972). *Tractatus Called Afterwards Summule Logicales*, ed. L. M. de Rijk, Assen
Petrarch (1554). *Opera quae extant omnia*, Basle (repr. Ridgewood, 1964)
    (1577). *De remediis utriusque fortunae libri II*, Lyons
    (1581). *Opera*, Basle
    (1869–70). *Lettere senili*, trans. and ed. G. Fracassetti, 2 vols., Florence
    (1898). *The First Modern Scholar and Man of Letters*, trans. J. H. Robinson and W. H. Rolfe,
        New York
    (1906). *Le Traité De sui ipsius et multorum ignorantia*, ed. L. M. Capelli, Paris
    (1910). *Letters to Classical Authors*, trans. M. E. Cosenza, Chicago
    (1933–42). *Le familiari*, ed. V. Rossi and U. Bosco, 4 vols., Florence
    (1943). *Rerum memorandarum libri*, ed. G. Billanovich, Florence
    (1949). *Invectiva contra quendam magni status hominem sed nullius scientie aut virtutis*, ed. P. G.
        Ricci, Florence
    (1950). *Invectivarum contra medicum libri IV*, ed. P. G. Ricci, Florence
    (1955). *Prose*, ed. G. Martellotti *et al.*, Milan–Naples
    (1957). *Testament*, ed. T. E. Mommsen, Ithaca
    (1958). *De otio religioso*, ed. G. Rotondi, Vatican City
    (1975). *Opere latine*, ed. A. Bufano, 2 vols., Turin
    (1975–85). *Rerum familiarium libri I–XXIV*, trans. A. S. Bernardo, 3 vols., Albany
    (1977). *De vita solitaria*, ed. G. Martellotti, Turin
Philoponus, Joannes (1535). *Commentaria in libros De anima Aristotelis*, ed. V. Trincavellus,
    Venice
    (1544a). *In tres libros Aristotelis De anima commentarius*, trans. Matthaeus a Bove, Venice
    (1544b). *In Aristotelis De anima libros commentarius*, trans. G. Hervet, Lyons
    (1544c). *In libros Priorum resolutivorum*, Venice

(1559). *Expositio . . . in libros Analyticos Aristotelis posteriores*, trans. Theodosius, Venice
(1966). *Commentaire sur le De anima d'Aristote*, Louvain
Piccart, Michael (1605). *Isagoge in lectionem Aristotelis*, Nuremberg
Piccolomini, Alessandro (1540a). *De la sfera del mondo libri IV*, Venice
(1540b). *Delle stelle fisse libro I*, Venice
(1542). *De la institutione de la vita de l'huomo nato nobile e in città libera libri X*, Venice
(1551). *Della filosofia naturale*, Rome
(1560). *Della institutione morale*, Venice
(1565). *In Mechanicas quaestiones Aristotelis . . . Commentarium de certitudine mathematicarum disciplinarum. . .*, Venice
(1575). *Annotationi nel libro della Poetica d'Aristotele*, Venice
Piccolomini, Enea Silvio (1551). *Opera*, Basle
(1984). *Commentarii rerum memorabilium que temporibus suis contigerunt*, ed. A. van Heck, 2 vols., Vatican City
Piccolomini, Francesco (1575). *Peripateticae de anima disputationes*, Venice (published under the name Petrus Duodus)
(1576). *Academicae contemplationes*, Venice (published under the name Stefano Tiepolo)
(1583). *Universa philosophia de moribus*, Venice
(1594a). *Comes politicus pro recta ordinis ratione propugnator*, Venice
(1594b). *Universa philosophia de moribus*, Venice
(1596). *Libri ad scientiam de natura attinentes*, Venice
(1602a). *Commentarii duo, prior in libros Aristotelis De ortu et interitu, alter in tres libros eiusdem De anima*, Frankfurt
(1602b). *In tres libros Aristotelis De anima lucidissima expositio*, Venice
(1603). *Discursus ad universam logicam attinens*, Marburg
(1606). *Interpretatio VIII libri Naturalium auscultationum*, Venice
Pico della Mirandola, Gianfrancesco (1573). *Opera omnia*, Basle (repr. Hildesheim, 1969; Turin, 1972)
(1930). *De imaginatione*, ed. and trans. H. Caplan, New Haven
(1973). 'Un inedito di Giovan Francesco Pico della Mirandola: La *Quaestio de falsitate astrologiae*', ed. W. Cavini, *Rinascimento*, ser. ii, 13: 133–71
(1984). *Über die Vorstellung. De imaginatione*, ed. E. Kessler, K. Park and C. B. Schmitt, Munich
Pico della Mirandola, Gianfrancesco and Bembo, Pietro (1954). *Le epistole 'De imitatione'*, ed. G. Santangelo, Florence
Pico della Mirandola, Giovanni (1572). *Opera*, Basle
(1942). *De hominis dignitate, Heptaplus, De ente et uno, e scritti vari*, ed. E. Garin, Florence
(1946–52). *Disputationes adversus astrologiam divinatricem*, ed. E. Garin, 2 vols., Florence
(1973). *Conclusiones*, ed. B. Kieszkowski, Geneva
(1984). *Commentary on a Canzone of Benivieni*, trans. S. Jayne, New York–Bern–Frankfurt a. M.
Pinelli, Gian Vincenzo (1574). [Letter] MS Paris, Bibliothèque nationale, Dupuy 704, f. 28
Pinke, Robert (1680). *Quaestiones selectiores*, Oxford
Pio, Giovanni Battista (1514). *In Carum Lucretium poetam commentarii*, Paris
Platina (1518). [*Opera*], Venice
(1608). *De principe viro*, Frankfurt
(1913–32). *Liber de vita Christi ac omnium pontificum*, ed. G. Gaida, in *Rerum Italicarum scriptores*, ed. L. A. Muratori, III, 1, Città di Castello
(1944). *De optimo cive*, ed. F. Battaglia, Bologna
(1949). *Vita di Vittorino da Feltre*, ed. G. Biasuz, Padua
(1979). *De principe*, ed. G. Ferraù, Messina
Plato (1544). *Il Fedro, ovvero il dialogo del bello*, trans. F. Figliucci, Rome

Pletho, Georgius Gemistus (1858). *Traité des lois*, ed. C. Alexandre, trans. A. Pellissier, Paris (repr. Amsterdam, 1966)
  (1866). Περὶ ὧν Ἀριστοτέλης πρὸς Πλάτωνα διαφέρεται, in *Patrologia graeca*, ed. J. P. Migne, CLX, Paris, cols. 881–932
Poggio Bracciolini (1538). *Opera*, Basle
  (1964–9). *Opera omnia*, ed. R. Fubini, 4 vols., Turin
  (1974). *Two Renaissance Book Hunters*, trans. P. W. G. Gordan, New York
  (1982). 'Poggio Bracciolini as rhetorician and historian: unpublished pieces', ed. M. C. Davies, *Rinascimento*, ser. ii, 22: 153–82
  (1983). *Facetiae*, ed. M. Ciccuto, Milan
  (1984–). *Lettere*, ed. H. Harth, Florence
Poliziano, Angelo (1489). *Miscellaneorum centuria prima*, Florence
  (1553). *Opera*, Basle (repr. Turin, 1971, ed. I. Maïer)
  (1867). *Prose volgari inedite e poesie latine e greche edite e inedite*, ed. I. del Lungo, Florence
  (1954). *Stanze per la giostra, Orfeo, Rime*, ed. V. Pernicone, Turin (repr. Novara, 1968)
  (1972). *Miscellaneorum centuria secunda*, ed. V. Branca and M. Pastore Stocchi, 4 vols., Florence
  (1978). *Commento inedito alle Selve di Stazio*, ed. L. Cesarini Martinelli, Florence
  (1983). *Una ignota 'Expositio Suetoni'*, ed. V. Fera, Messina
Pomponazzi, Pietro (1518). *Apologia*, Bologna
  (1519). *Defensorium sive responsiones ad ea quae Augustinus Niphus Suessanus adversus ipsum scripsit*, Bologna
  (1525). *Tractatus acutissimi, utillimi et mere peripatetici*, Venice
  (1556). *De naturalium effectuum admirandorum causis seu de incantationibus*, Basle
  (1877). *Lettere inedite*, ed. S. Davari, Mantua
  (1954). *Tractatus de immortalitate animae*, ed. G. Morra, Bologna
  (1957). *Libri quinque de fato, de libero arbitrio et de praedestinatione*, ed. R. Lemay, Lugano
  (1966–70). *Corsi inediti dell'insegnamento padovano*, ed. A. Poppi, 2 vols., Padua
Ponet, John (1556). *A Shorte Treatise of Politike Power*, Strasburg [?]
Pontano, Giovanni (1518). *Opera*, Venice
  (1943). *I dialoghi*, ed. C. Privitera, Florence
  (1965). *I trattati delle virtù sociali*, ed. F. Tateo, Rome
  (1969). *De magnanimitate*, ed. F. Tateo, Florence
Porzio, Simone (1543). *De bonitate aquarum epistolae*, Bologna
  (1550). *De coloribus oculorum*, Florence
  (1551a). *An homo bonus vel malus volens fiat*, Florence
  (1551b). *De humana mente disputatio*, Florence
  (1551c). *Se l'uomo diventa buono o cattivo volontariamente*, trans. G. B. Gelli, Florence
  (1553). *De rerum naturalium principiis libri II*, Naples
  (1578). *Opuscula*, Naples
Posio, Antonio (1562). *Thesaurus in omnes Aristotelis et Averrois libros copiosissimus*, Venice
Pratus, Alphonsus (1530). *Quaestiones dialecticae supra libros Peri hermenias*, Alcalá
Prefaces to the First Editions of the Greek and Roman Classics (1861). Ed. B. Botfield, London
Proclus (1864). *Opera inedita*, ed. V. Cousin, Paris
  (1963). *The Elements of Theology*, ed. and trans. E. R. Dodds, 2nd edn, Oxford
  (1982–). *Commentaire sur le Parmenide de Platon*, trans. William of Moerbeke, ed. C. Steel, Louvain
Prosatori latini del Quattrocento (1952). Ed. E. Garin, Milan
Pschlacher, Conradus (1512). *Compendarius parvorum logicalium liber*, Vienna
Publicio, Jacopo (1482). *Oratoriae artis epitomata*, Venice
Puttenham, George (1936). *The Arte of English Poesie*, ed. G. Willcock and A. Walker, Cambridge

Quattromani, Sertorio (1914). *La filosofia di Bernardino Telesio ristretta in brevità et scritta in lingua toscana*, ed. E. Troilo, Bari
Quevedo, Francisco de (1945–60). *Obras completas*, ed. L. Astrana Marín and F. Buendia, 2 vols., Madrid
   (1946). *Epistolario completo*, ed. L. Astrana Marín, Madrid
   (1966). *Política de Dios, govierno de Christo*, ed. J. Crosby, Madrid
   (1986). *Defensa de Epicuro contra la común opinión*, ed. E. Acosta Méndez, Madrid

Rabelais, François (1912–31). *Oeuvres*, ed. A. Lefranc *et al.*, 5 vols., Paris
   (1970). *Gargantua*, ed. R. Calder and M. A. Screech, Geneva
Ramus, Petrus (1543a). *Dialecticae partitiones*, Paris
   (1543b). *Aristotelicae animadversiones*, Paris
   (1543c). *Dialecticae institutiones. Aristotelicae animadversiones*, Paris (repr. Stuttgart–Bad Canstatt, 1964, introd. W. Risse)
   (1548). *Animadversionum Aristotelicarum libri XX, nunc demum ab auctore recogniti et aucti*, Paris
   (1567). *Prooemium mathematicum*, Paris
   (1569). *Scholarum dialecticarum libri XX*, Basle (repr. Hildesheim, 1970)
   (1576). *Commentariorum de religione Christiana libri IV*, Frankfurt
   (1601). *Politica exposita et illustrata*, Frankfurt
   (1964). *Dialectique (1555)*, ed. M. Dassonville, Geneva
Ramus, Petrus and Talon, Omer (1556). *Dialecticae libri duo praelectionibus illustrati*, Paris
Raulin, Johannes (1500). *In logicam Aristotelis*, Paris
Reden und Briefe italienischer Humanisten (1970). Ed. K. Müllner and H. B. Gerl, Munich
Reisch, Gregor (1504). *Margarita philosophica*, Strasburg
   (1517). *Margarita philosophica*, Basle (repr. Düsseldorf, 1973, introd. L. Geldsetzer)
Remigio de' Girolami (1959). *De bono pacis*, ed. C. T. Davis, *Studi danteschi*, 36: 123–36
Renaissance Philosophy, I: The Italian Philosophers (1967). Ed. and trans. A. B. Fallico and H. Shapiro, New York
Renaissance Philosophy: New Translations (1973). Ed. L. A. Kennedy, The Hague
Renaissance Philosophy of Man (1948). Ed. E. Cassirer *et al.*, Chicago
Rhenanus, Beatus (1969). *Briefwechsel*, ed. A. Horawitz and K. Hartfelder, Leipzig
Ribadeneyra, Pedro de (1595). *Tratado de la religión y virtudes*, Madrid
Ricchieri, Lodovico Celio (1542). *Lectionum antiquarum libri triginta*, Basle
Riccoboni, Antonio (1585). *Poetica*, Vicenza
   (1610). *In decem libros Ethicorum Aristotelis ad Nicomachum commentarii*, Hanau
Richard of Wallingford (1976). *An Edition of His Writings*, ed. J. D. North, 3 vols., Oxford
Robortello, Francesco (1548a). *De historia facultate*, Florence
   (1548b). *In librum De arte poetica explicationes*, Florence
   (1552). *In libros Politicos disputatio*, Venice
Romberch, Johann (1533). *Congestorium artificiose memorie*, Venice
Rucellai, Giovanni (1960–81). *Zibaldone*, ed. A. Perosa *et al.*, 2 vols., London
Ruggiero, Ludovico (1590–1) ... *In octo libros Physicorum* ..., MS Bamberg, Staatsbibliothek, Msc. Class., Cod. 62–3
   (1591) ... *In quatuor libros De caelo et mundo* ... *In duos libros Aristotelis De generatione et corruptione* ..., MS Bamberg, Staatsbibliothek, Msc. Class., Cod. 62–4

Sacrorum conciliorum nova et amplissima collectio (1759–1962). Ed. G. D. Mansi *et al.*, 55 vols., Florence–Venice–Paris–Arnhem–Leipzig
Salutati, Coluccio (1891–1911). *Epistolario*, ed. F. Novati, 4 vols., Rome
   (1913). *De tyranno*, ed. A. von Martin, Berlin
   (1947). *De nobilitate legum et medicinae. De verecundia*, ed. E. Garin, Florence

(1951). *De laboribus Herculis*, ed. B. L. Ullman, 2 vols., Zurich
(1957). *De seculo et religione*, ed. B. L. Ullman, Florence
(1985). *De fato et fortuna*, ed. C. Bianca, Florence
Sanches, Francisco (1636). *Opera medica*, Toulouse
(1649). *Tractatus philosophici*, Rotterdam
(1984). *Quod nihil scitur*, ed. and trans. D. S. Rabade *et al.*, Madrid
Sanchez, Francisco (1587). *Minerva*, Salamanca
(1766). *Opera omnia*, ed. G. Mayans, 4 vols., Geneva
Sanderson, Robert (1618). *Logicae artis compendium*, Oxford
Santacroce, Andreas de (1955). *Acta Latina Concilii Florentini*, VI, ed. G. Hofmann, Rome
Sbarroya, Augustinus (1533). *Dialecticae introductiones*, Seville
Scala, Bartolomeo (1940). *De legibus et iudiciis dialogus*, ed. L. Borghi, *La bibliofilia*, 42: 256–82
Scaliger, Joseph Justus (n.d.). Working notes in his copy of Estienne, Henri and Scaliger, Joseph Justus (1573): Oxford, Bodleian Library 8°.c.238.Auct.
(1584). Working notes in his copy of his *De emendatione temporum* (1583): Paris BN, Rés. G.141
Scaliger, Julius Caesar (1540). *De causis linguae latinae*, Lyons
(1556). *In II libros De plantis*, Paris
(1561). *Poetices libri VII*, Geneva–Lyons
(1566). *Animadversiones in VI libros De causis plantarum Theophrasti*, Geneva
(1584a). *Commentaria in De animalibus*, Lyons
(1584b). *Animadversiones in Theophrasti Historias plantarum*, Geneva
Schegk, Jacob (1538). *Philosophiae naturalis . . . disputationes*, Tübingen
(1546). *In VIII Physicorum . . . libros Aristotelis commentaria . . .*, Basle
(1550). *In reliquos naturalium Aristotelis libros commentaria*, Basle
(1556). *Perfecta . . . definiendi ars . . .*, Tübingen
(1564). *De demonstratione libri XV*, Basle
(1570). *Commentaria . . . in hos qui sequuntur Organi Aristotelis libros*, Tübingen
(1584). *Commentaria in VIII libros Topicorum Aristotelis*, Tübingen
Scot, Reginald (1886). *The Discoverie of Witchcraft*, ed. B. Nicholson, London (repr. Totowa, 1973)
Seneca (1529). *Opera*, ed. D. Erasmus, Basle
(1585). *[Opera]*, ed. M.-A. Muret, Rome
(1605). *Opera quae extant omnia*, ed. J. Lipsius, Antwerp
Sensi, Lodovico (1577). *La historia dell'huomo*, Perugia
Servetus, Michael (1553). *Christianismi restitutio*, Vienne (repr. Frankfurt, 1971)
Seton, John (1545). *Dialectica*, London
Seyssel, Claude de (1961). *La Monarchie de France*, ed. J. Poujol, Paris
(1981). *The Monarchy of France*, trans. J. H. Hexter and introd. D. R. Kelley, New Haven
Sibiuda, Ramon (1966). *Theologia naturalis seu liber creaturarum*, ed. F. Stegmüller, Stuttgart–Bad Canstatt
Sidney, Philip (1965). *Apology for Poetry*, ed. G. K. Shepherd, London
Silvester, Antonius (1517). *Expositio in Ethicos libros*, Paris
Silvester, Franciscus (1898–1902). *Commentaria in libros S. Thomae de Aquino Contra gentiles*, ed. G. Sestili, Rome
Simoni, Simone (1566). *In librum . . . De sensuum instrumentis et de his quae sub sensum cadunt commentarius unus . . . In librum Aristotelis . . . De memoria et reminiscentia commentarius alter*, Geneva
Simplicius (1543). *Commentarii in libros De anima Aristotelis*, trans. G. Faseolo, Venice
(1553). *Commentaria in tres libros De anima Aristotelis*, trans. E. Asolano, Venice
(1907). *In Aristotelis Categorias commentarium*, ed. C. Kalbfleisch (Commentaria in Aristotelem Graeca, 8), Berlin

Sireni, Antonio (1563). *De fato libri novem*, Venice
  (1580). *De praedestinatione compendium*, Venice
Sleidan, Johann (1558). *De statu religionis et reipublicae*, Strasburg
  (1559). *De quatuor summis imperiis*, Geneva
Smiglecius, Martinus (1658). *Logica*, Oxford
Smith, Thomas (1982). *De republica Anglorum*, ed. M. Dewar, Cambridge
Soarez, Cyprian (1955). *De arte rhetorica libri III*, ed. L. Flynn, Ph.D thesis, Univ. of Florida
Some Fourteenth-Century Tracts on the Probationes terminorum (1982). Ed. L. M. de Rijk,
  Nijmegen
Soto, Domingo de (1529). *Introductiones dialectice*, Burgos
  (1554). *Summulae*, Salamanca (repr. Hildesheim–New York, 1980)
  (1555). *Super octo libros Physicorum quaestiones*, Salamanca
  (1659–65). '*Cursus philosophicus*', ed. C. de Lerma, 7 vols., Rome
  (1967–8). *De iustitia et iure libri X*, ed. V. D. Carro and M. González Ordóñez, 5 vols.,
  Madrid
Source Book in Medieval Science (1974). Ed. E. Grant, Cambridge, Mass.
Speroni, Sperone (1542). *Dialoghi*, Florence
Spina, Bartolomeo (1519). *Opuscula*, Venice
Starkey, Thomas (1948). *A Dialogue Between Reginald Pole and Thomas Lupset*, ed. K. M.
  Burton, London
Statuta Antiqua Universitatis Oxoniensis (1931). Ed. S? Gibson, Oxford
Statuti delle università e dei collegi dello Studio bolognese (1888). Ed. C. Malagola, Bologna
Steuco, Agostino (1540). *De perenni philosophia*, Lyons (repr. New York, 1972, introd. C. B.
  Schmitt)
  (1591). *Opera omnia . . .*, 3 vols., Venice
Strode, Ralph (1973). *Consequentiae*, ed. and trans. W. K. Seaton. Ph.D thesis, Univ. of
  California, Berkeley
Strozzi, Ciriaco (1599). *Orationes sive introductiones in aliquot Aristotelis De moribus libros*, Paris
Sturm, Johannes (1539). *Partitiones dialecticae*, Paris
Suárez, Francisco (1856–78). *Opera omnia*, ed. M. André and C. Berton, 28 vols., Paris
  (1872). *Defensio fidei catholicae et apostolicae*, Naples
  (1960–6). *Disputationes metafísicas*, ed. S. Rábade Romeo, 7 vols., Madrid
  (1971–7). *De legibus*, ed. L. Pereña *et al.*, 6 vols., Madrid
  (1978–81). *Commentaria una cum quaestionibus in libros Aristotelis De anima*, ed. S. Castellote,
  2 vols., Madrid
Susenbrotus, Joannes (1953). *Epitome troporum ac schematum et grammaticorum et rhetoricorum*,
  ed. and trans. J. Brennan, Ph.D thesis, Univ. of Illinois

Tahureau, Jacques (1981). *Les Dialogues*, ed. M. Gauna, Geneva
Talon, Omer (1583). *Praelectiones in Ciceronem, Porphyrii Isagogen, et Aristotelis primum librum
  Ethicum. . .*, Frankfurt
  See also Ramus, Petrus and Talon, Omer
Tartaretus, Petrus (1503a). *Expositio super textu logices Aristotelis*, Venice
  (1503b). *Clarissima singularisque totius philosophie necnon metaphisice . . . expositio*, Venice
  (1509). *Questiones morales*, Paris
  (1514). *In sex libros Ethicorum questiones*, Basle
  (1583). *Lucidissima commentaria in quatuor libros Sententiarum et quodlibeta Duns Scoti*, 6 vols.,
  Venice
  (1621). *In universam philosophiam opera omnia*, Venice
Telesio, Bernardino (1586). *De rerum natura*, Naples (repr. Hildesheim, 1971)
  (1910–23). *De rerum natura*, ed. V. Spampanato, 3 vols., Modena–Genoa–Rome
  (1965–77). *De rerum natura*, ed. and trans. L. De Franco, 3 vols., Cosenza–Florence

(1978). *Varii de naturalibus rebus libelli*, ed. L. De Franco, Florence
Temple, William (1580). *Admonitio de unica P. Rami methodo reiectis caeteris retinenda*, London
    (published under the name Franciscus Mildapettus)
Testi umanistici sulla retorica (1953). Ed. E. Garin *et al.*, Rome
Testi umanistici sull'ermetismo (1955). Ed. E. Garin, Rome
Themistius (1481). *Paraphrasis in Aristotelis . . . libros De anima*, trans. E. Barbaro, Treviso
    (1534). *Opera omnia*, ed. V. Trincavellus, Venice
    (1559). *In tertium librum De anima paraphrasis*, trans. L. Nogarola, Venice
    (1900). *In Aristotelis Physica paraphrasis*, ed. M. Wallies (Commentaria in Aristotelem
    Graeca, 5, 2), Berlin
    (1957). *Commentaire sur Le Traité de l'âme d'Aristote*, trans. William of Moerbeke, Louvain
Theoretiker humanistischer Geschichtsschreibung (1971). Ed. E. Kessler, Munich
Thomas Aquinas (1934). *In decem libros Ethicorum Aristotelis ad Nicomachum expositio*, ed.
    A. M. Pirotta, Turin
    (1963a). *The Division and Methods of the Sciences*, trans. A. Maurer, 3rd edn, Toronto
    (1963b). *Commentary on the Physics of Aristotle*, trans. R. Blackwell, New Haven
    (1963c). *Summa theologiae*, ed. P. Caramello, 3 vols., Turin
    (1964). *In Aristotelis libros Peri hermenias et Posteriorum analyticorum*, Rome–Turin
    (1973). *De regimine principum*, ed. R. M. Spiazzi, Turin
Thomas of Erfurt (1972). *Grammatica speculativa*, ed. G. L. Bursill-Hall, London
Thomasius, Jacobus (1705). *Erotemata metaphysices*, Leipzig
Tiepolo, Stefano: *see* Piccolomini, Francesco (1576)
Timpler, Clemens (1606). *Metaphysicae systema methodicum*, Hanau
    (1612). *Philosophiae practicae systema methodicum*, Hanau
Titelmans, Frans (1533). *Compendium dialecticae ad libros logicorum Aristotelis . . .*, Antwerp
    (1542). *Compendium naturalis philosophiae*, Paris
Toletus, Franciscus (1587). *Introductio in dialecticam Aristotelis*, Venice
    (1587–8). *Omnia quae hucusque extant opera*, 2 vols., Lyons
    (1592). *Commentaria una cum quaestionibus in tres libros Aristotelis De anima*, Venice
    (1596). *Commentaria una cum quaestionibus in universam Aristotelis logicam*, Cologne
    (1600). *Commentaria una cum quaestionibus in VIII libros De physica auscultatione*, Venice
Tortelli, Giovanni (1501). *Orthographia*, Venice
Trattati di poetica e retorica del Cinquecento (1970–4). Ed. B. Weinberg, 4 vols., Bari
Traversari, Ambrogio (1759). *Latinae epistolae*, ed. L. Mehus, Florence
Trithemius, Johannes (1567). *De septem secundeis*, Frankfurt
    (1973). *De laude scriptorum*, ed. K. Arnold, Würzburg
    (1977). *In Praise of Scribes*, trans. R. Bohrendt, introd. K. Arnold, Lawrence
Trombetta, Antonio (1498). *Quaestio de animarum humanarum pluralitate catholice contra
    Averroym et sequaces in studio patavino determinata*, Venice
Tunstall, Cuthbert (1554). *Compendium et σύνοψις in decem libros Ethicorum Aristotelis*, Paris
Turmeda, Anselm (1984). *Dispute de l'ane*, ed. A. Llinares, Paris

University Records and Life in the Middle Ages (1944). Ed. L. Thorndike, New York
Ursus, Nicolaus (1597). *De hypothesibus astronomicis . . . tractatus*, Prague

Valerius, Cornelius (1566). *Brevis et perspicua totius ethicae seu de moribus philosophiae descriptio*,
    Basle
Valla, Giorgio (1501). *De expetendis et fugiendis rebus*, Venice
Valla, Lorenzo (1471). *Elegantiarum Latinae linguae libri sex*, Rome
    (1922). *The Treatise on the Donation of Constantine*, trans. C. B. Coleman, New Haven
    (1934). *De libero arbitrio*, ed. M. Anfossi, Florence

(1953). *Scritti filosofici e religiosi*, ed. G. Radetti, Florence

(1962). *Opera omnia*, 2 vols., Turin (repr. of Basle 1540 edn, plus other texts)

(1970a). *De vero falsoque bono*, ed. M. Lorch, Bari

(1970b). *Collatio Novi Testamenti*, ed. A. Perosa, Florence

(1977). *De voluptate. On Pleasure*, ed. and trans. A. K. Hieatt and M. Lorch, New Haven

(1982). *Repastinatio dialectice et philosophie*, ed. G. Zippel, 2 vols., Padua

(1983). *Dialogue sur le libre-arbitre*, ed. J. Chomarat, Paris

(1984). *Epistole*, ed. O. Besomi and M. Regoliosi, Padua

Vallés, Francisco (1563). *Controversiarum naturalium ad tyrones pars prima, continens eas quae spectant ad VIII libros Aristotelis De physica doctrina*, Alcalá

(1564). *Controversiarum medicarum et philosophicarum . . . editio secunda*, Alcalá

(1587). *De iis quae scripta sunt physica in libris sacris, sive de sacra philosophia, liber singularis*, Turin

(1588). *Commentaria in IV librum Meteorologicorum Aristotelis*, Turin

Vanini, Giulio Cesare (1615). *Amphitheatrum aeternae providentiae*, Lyons (repr. Galatina, 1979)

Varchi, Benedetto (1858–9). *Opere*, 2 vols., Trieste

Vergerio, Pier Paolo (1924–5). *De principibus carrariensibus et gestis eorum liber*, ed. A. Gnesotto, *Atti e memorie della R. Accademia di scienze, lettere ed arti in Padova*, n.s., 41: 327–475

(1934). *Epistolario*, ed. and introd. L. Smith, Rome

(1966). *Paulus*, ed. F. Semi and S. Cella, *Atti e memorie della Società Istriana di archeologia e storia patria*, n.s., 14: 45–103

(1972–3). *De ingenuis moribus et liberalibus studiis adolescentiae*, ed. C. Miani, *Atti e memorie della Società Istriana di archeologia e storia patria*, n.s., 20–1: 185–251

Vergil, Polydore (1536). *De rerum inventoribus*, Basle

Vermigli, Pietro Martire (1582). *In Aristotelis Ethicorum ad Nicomachum librum primum, secundum ac initium tertii . . . commentarius*, Zurich

Vernia, Nicoletto (1480). *Quaestio an ens mobile sit totius philo[so]phiae naturalis subiectum*, Padua

Versor, Johannes (1489). *In Aristotelis philosophie libros questiones cum dubiis circa easdem occurentibus et textus singulis in locis annotationes*, Lyons

(1491). *Questiones super libros Ethicorum*, Cologne

(c. 1493). *Questiones subtilissime in via sancti Thome super libros De celo et mundo Aristotelis . . .*, Cologne

(1572). *Petri Hispani Summulae logicales cum . . . clarissima expositione*, Venice (repr. Hildesheim–New York, 1981)

Vesalius, Andreas (1543). *De humani corporis fabrica libri septem*, Basle (repr. Brussels, 1964)

(1950). *Illustrations From the Works*, ed. J. Saunders and C. D. O'Malley, Cleveland

Vespasiano da Bisticci (1963). *Renaissance Princes, Popes and Prelates*, trans. W. George and E. Waters, New York

Vettori, Pier (1547). *Commentarii in tres libros Aristotelis De arte dicendi*, Basle

(1553). *Variarum lectionum libri XXV*, Florence

(1560). *Commentarii in primum librum Aristotelis De arte poetarum*, Florence

(1583). *Variarum lectionum libri XXXVIII*, Florence

(1584). *Commentarii in X libros Aristotelis De moribus ad Nicomachum*, Florence

Vieri, Francesco de' (1577). *Compendio della dottrina di Platone in quello, che ella è conforme con la fede nostra*, Florence

(1590). *Vere conclusioni di Platone conformi alla dottrina christiana et a quella d'Aristotile*, Florence

(1973). *Lezzioni d'amore*, ed. J. Colaneri, Munich

Vimercato, Francesco (1543). *Commentarii in III librum Aristotelis De anima*, Paris
   (1550). *In VIII libros Aristotelis De naturali auscultatione commentarii*, Paris
   (1596). *De principiis rerum naturalium*, Venice
Vinet, Élie (1568). *Censorini De die natali liber*, Poitiers
Viperano, Giovanni (1567). *De scribenda historia liber*, Antwerp
   (1985). *On Poetry*, trans. P. Rollinson, Greenwood, S.C.
Vitelleschi, Muzio (1589–90). *Lectiones in octo libros Physicorum et quatuor De caelo*, MS
   Bamberg, Staatsbibliothek, Msc. Class., Cod. 70
Vitoria, Francisco de (1932–52). *Commentarios a la Secunda Secundae de Santo Tomás*, ed.
   V. Beltrán de Heredia, 6 vols., Salamanca
   (1933–6). *Relecciones teológicas*, ed. L. Getino, 3 vols., Madrid
   (1960). *Obras*, ed. T. Urdánoz, Madrid
   (1967). *Relectio de Indis o libertad de los Indios*, ed. L. Pereña and J. M. Pérez Prendes, Madrid
Vittorino da Feltre (1926–7). *Orthographia*, ed. A. Casacci, *Atti della R. Istituto veneto di
   scienze, lettere ed arti*, 86: 911–45
Vives, Juan Luis (1538). *De anima et vita libri tres*, Basle (repr. Turin, 1963)
   (1555). *Opera*, 2 vols., Basle
   (1782–90). *Opera omnia*, ed. G. Mayans, 8 vols., Valencia (repr. Farnborough, 1964)
   (1954). *De anima et vita*, ed. and trans. M. Sancipriano, 2 vols., Florence
   (1973). *De subventione pauperum*, ed. A. Saitta, Florence
   (1979a). *Against the Pseudodialecticians: A Humanist Attack on Medieval Logic*, ed. and trans.
   R. Guerlac, Dordrecht–Boston
   (1979b). *In pseudodialecticos*, ed. C. Fantazzi, Leiden
Vossius, Gerardus Johannes (1623). *Ars historica sive de historiae et historices natura*, Leiden

Waele, Antonius de (1620). *Compendium ethicae Aristotelis ad normam veritatis Christianae
   revocatum*, Leiden
Wilson, Florens (1751). *De animi tranquillitate dialogus*, Edinburgh
Wilson, Thomas (1560). *The Arte of Rhetorique*, London
Wojciech de Brudzewo (1900). *Commentariolum super Theoricas novas planetarum Georgii
   Purbachii . . . A.D. 1482*, ed. L. A. Birkenmajer, Cracow

Xenophon (1546). *Dialogo, el qual trata de la economica*, trans. Francisco Thamara, Antwerp

Zabarella, Francesco (1655). *De felicitate libri tres*, Padua
Zabarella, Jacopo (1578). *De methodis libri quatuor. Liber de regressu*, Venice (repr. Bologna,
   1985, introd. C. Vasoli)
   (1597). *Opera logica*, Cologne (repr. Hildesheim–New York, 1966)
   (1601). *In libris Aristotelis Physicorum commentarii*, Venice
   (1606). *Commentaria in tres libros De anima*, Frankfurt (repr. Frankfurt, 1966)
   (1607a). *De rebus naturalibus libri XXX . . .*, Venice (repr. Frankfurt, 1966)
   (1607b). *Opera logica*, Frankfurt (repr. Frankfurt, 1966)
Zimara, Marcantonio (1508). *Contradictiones et solutiones in dictis Aristotelis et Averrois*, Venice
   (1537). *Tabula dilucidationum in dictis Aristotelis et Averrois*, Venice
Zini, Pietro Francesco (1547). *De philosophiae laudibus oratio*, Venice
Zwinger, Theodor (1565). *Theatrum vitae humanae*, Basle
   (1566). *Aristotelis . . . De moribus ad Nicomachum libri decem tabulis perpetuis . . . explicati et
   illustrati*, Basle
   (1582). *Aristotelis Politicorum libri VIII . . .*, Basle
   (1586). *Theatrum humanae vitae*, 7 vols., Basle
Zwingli, Huldreich (1905–83). *Sämtliche Werke*, 14 vols., Berlin–Leipzig–Zurich

BIBLIOGRAPHY: SECONDARY SOURCES

Aarsleff, H. (1982). *From Locke to Saussure: Essays on the Study of Language and Intellectual History*, Minneapolis

Abbagnano, N. (1941). *Bernardino Telesio e la filosofia del Rinascimento*, Milan

Abel, G. (1978). *Stoizismus und frühe Neuzeit*, Berlin–New York

Abranches, C. (1953). 'Fonseca e a renovação da escolástica', *Revista portuguesa de filosofia*, 9: 354–74

Acta Cusana: Quellen zur Lebensgeschichte des Nikolaus von Kues (1976–). Ed. E. Meuthen and H. Hallauer, Hamburg

Adam, R. G. (forthcoming). *Francesco Filelfo at the Court of Milan*, Rome

Adams, R. (1962). *The Better Part of Valor*, Seattle

Aiton, E. J. (1975). 'Johannes Kepler and astronomy without hypotheses', *Japanese Studies in the History of Science*, 14: 49–71

    (1976). 'Johannes Kepler in the light of recent research', *History of Science*, 14: 77–100

    (1981). 'Celestial spheres and circles', *History of Science*, 19: 75–113

Albertini, R. von (1955). *Das florentinische Staatsbewusstsein im Übergang von der Republik zum Prinzipat*, Bern

Alcorta, J. I. (1949). *La teoría de los modos en Suárez*, Madrid

Allen, D. C. (1944). 'The rehabilitation of Epicurus and his theory of pleasure in the early Renaissance', *Studies in Philology*, 41: 1–15

Allen, M. J. B. (1980). 'The sibyl in Ficino's oaktree', *Modern Language Notes*, 95: 205–10

    (1982). 'Ficino's theory of the five substances and the Neoplatonists' *Parmenides*', *Journal of Medieval and Renaissance Studies*, 12: 19–44

    (1984a). *The Platonism of Marsilio Ficino*, Berkeley

    (1984b). 'Marsilio Ficino on Plato, the Neoplatonists and the Christian doctrine of the trinity', *Renaissance Quarterly*, 37: 555–84

Allen, M. J. B. and White, R. A. (1981). 'Ficino's Hermias translation and a new apologue', *Scriptorium*, 35: 39–47

Allen, P. S. (1914). *The Age of Erasmus*, Oxford

    (1934). *Erasmus: Lectures and Wayfaring Sketches*, Oxford

Allers, R. (1944). 'Microcosmus from Anaximander to Paracelsus', *Traditio*, 2: 319–407

Allgemeine Deutsche Biographie (1875–1912). 56 vols., Leipzig

Altamura, A. (1938). *Giovanni Pontano*, Naples

    (1941). *L'umanesimo nel Mezzogiorno*, Florence

Alunni, C. (1982). '*Codex naturae* et *Libro della natura* chez Campanella et Galilée', *Annali della Scuola normale superiore di Pisa*, ser. iii, 12: 189–239

Amabile, L. (1882). *Fra Tommaso Campanella, la sua congiuria, i suoi processi, la sua pazzia*, 3 vols., Naples

    (1887). *Fra Tommaso Campanella ne' castelli di Napoli, in Roma, in Parigi*, 2 vols., Naples

Amenduni, G. (1890). *Di alcuni particolari della vita letteraria di Simone Porzio incerti o ignoti finora*, Naples

Amerio, R. (1972). *Il sistema teologico di Tommaso Campanella*, Milan–Naples

Amos, F. R. (1920). *Early Theories of Translation*, New York

Anastos, M. (1948). 'Pletho's calendar and liturgy', *Dumbarton Oaks Papers*, 4: 183–305

Anderson, F. H. (1948). *The Philosophy of Francis Bacon*, Chicago

Andrade, A. A. de (1943). 'A Renascença nos *Conimbricenses*', *Brotéria*, 37: 271–84, 480–501

Andrés, M. (1976–7). *La teología española en el siglo XVI*, 2 vols., Madrid

Andrés Marcos, T. (1947). *Los imperialismos de Juan Ginés de Sepúlveda en su Democrates alter*, Madrid

Angelelli, I. (1970). 'The techniques of disputation in the history of logic', *The Journal of Philosophy*, 67: 800–15

Antiqui und Moderni: Traditionsbewusstsein und Fortschrittsbewusstsein im späten Mittelalter (1974). Berlin

Antonaci, A. (1970). 'Il pensiero logico di Marcantonio Zimara (Ricerche sull'aristotelismo del Rinascimento)', in *Studi in onore di Antonio Corsano*, Manduria, pp. 19–70

   (1971–8). *Ricerche sull'aristotelismo del Rinascimento: Marcantonio Zimara*, 2 vols., Lecce–Galatina

   (1984–). *Ricerche sul neoplatonismo del Rinascimento: Francesco Patrizi da Cherso*, Galatina

Apel, K. O. (1963). *Die Idee der Sprache in der Tradition des Humanismus von Dante bis Vico*, Bonn

Aquilecchia, G. (1971). *Giordano Bruno*, Rome

   (1976). 'Giambattista Della Porta e l'Inquisizione', in *Schede di Italianistica*, Turin, pp. 219–54

Arbeit, Musse, Meditation. Betrachtungen zur 'Vita activa' und 'Vita contemplativa' (1985). Ed. B. Vickers, Zurich

Arber, A. (1938). *Herbals: Their Origin and Evolution*, 2nd edn, Cambridge

Arcari, P. M. (1935). *Il pensiero politico di Francesco Patrizi da Cherso*, Rome

Ariani, M. (1984). *Imago fabulosa: Mito e allegoria nei 'Dialoghi d'amore' di Leone Ebreo*, Rome

Aries, P. (1954). *Le Temps d'histoire*, Monaco

Aristotelismo padovano e filosofia aristotelica (1960). *Atti del XII convegno internazionale di filosofia*, IX, Florence

Aristotelismo veneto e scienza moderna (1983). Ed. L. Olivieri, 2 vols., Padua

Aristotle on Dialectic (1968). Ed. G. E. L. Owen, Oxford

Armstrong, A. H. (1955–6). 'Was Plotinus a magician?', *Phronesis*, 1: 73–9

Armstrong, C. J. R. (1976). 'The dialectical road to truth: the dialogue', *French Renaissance Studies, 1540–1570*, ed. P. Sharratt, Edinburgh, pp. 36–51

Art, Science, and History in the Renaissance (1968). Ed. C. Singleton, Baltimore

Ashworth, E. J. (1969). 'The doctrine of supposition in the sixteenth and seventeenth centuries', *Archiv für Geschichte der Philosophie*, 51: 260–85

   (1972). 'The treatment of semantic paradoxes from 1400 to 1700', *Notre Dame Journal of Formal Logic*, 13: 34–52

   (1973a). 'Andreas Kesler and the later theory of consequences', *Notre Dame Journal of Formal Logic*, 14: 205–14

   (1973b). 'The doctrine of exponibilia in the fifteenth and sixteenth centuries', *Vivarium*, 11: 137–67

   (1974a). *Language and Logic in the Post-Medieval Period*, Dordrecht–Boston

   (1974b). '"For riding is required a horse": a problem of meaning and reference in late fifteenth-century logic', *Vivarium*, 12: 146–72

   (1976). 'Agostino Nifo's reinterpretation of medieval logic', *Rivista critica di storia della filosofia*, 31: 355–74

   (1977). 'Thomas Bricot (d. 1516) and the liar paradox', *Journal of the History of Philosophy*, 15: 267–80

   (1978a). 'A note on Paul of Venice and the Oxford *Logica* of 1483', *Medioevo*, 4: 93–9

   (1978b). 'Multiple qualification and the use of special qualifiers in early sixteenth-century logic', *Notre Dame Journal of Formal Logic*, 19: 599–613

   (1978c). 'Theories of proposition: some early sixteenth-century discussions', *Franciscan Studies*, 38: 81–121

   (1978d). *The Tradition of Medieval Logic and Speculative Grammar from Anselm to the End of the Seventeenth Century: A Bibliography from 1836 Onwards*, Toronto

   (1979a). 'The *Libelli sophistarum* and the use of medieval logic texts at Oxford and Cambridge in the early sixteenth century', *Vivarium*, 17: 134–58

(1979b). 'A note on an early printed logic text in Edinburgh University Library', *The Innes Review*, 30: 77–9

(1981a). ' "Do words signify ideas or things?" The scholastic sources of Locke's theory of language', *Journal of the History of Philosophy*, 19: 299–326

(1981b). 'Mental language and the unity of propositions: a semantic problem discussed by early sixteenth-century logicians', *Franciscan Studies*, 41: 61–96

(1982). 'The structure of mental language: some problems discussed by early sixteenth-century logicians', *Vivarium*, 20: 59–83

(1984). 'Locke on language', *Canadian Journal of Philosophy*, 14: 45–73

(1985). 'English *Obligationes* texts after Roger Swyneshed: the tracts beginning "Obligatio est quaedam ars" ', in *The Rise of British Logic*, ed. P. O. Lewry, Toronto, pp. 309–33

(1986). 'Renaissance man as logician: Josse Clichtove (1472–1543) on disputations', *History and Philosophy of Logic*, 7: 15–29

(forthcoming). 'Jacobus Naveros (*fl. c.*1533) on the question: "Do spoken words signify concepts or things" ', in *Logos and Pragma. Studies in the Philosophy of Language. Festschrift for Professor Nuchelmans*, ed. L. M. de Rijk and H. A. G. Braakhuis, Nijmegen.

Astrana Marín, L. (1945). *La vida turbulenta de Quevedo*, Madrid

Atti del Symposium internazionale di storia, metodologia, logica e filosofia della scienza: Galileo nella storia e nella filosofia della scienza (1967). Vinci

Aulotte, R. (1965). *Amyot et Plutarque: La Tradition des Moralia au XVIe siècle*, Geneva

Aune, D. E. (1980). 'Magic in early Christianity', in *Aufstieg und Niedergang der römischen Welt: Principat*, XXIII, 2, Berlin, pp. 1507–57

Babb, L. A. (1951). *The Elizabethan Malady: A Study of Melancholia in English Literature from 1580–1642*, East Lansing

Babbitt, S. K. (1985). *Oresme's 'Livre de politiques' and the France of Charles V*, Philadelphia

Backus, I. (1983). 'Agrippa on "human knowledge of God" and "human knowledge of the external world" ', *Archiv für Geschichte der Philosophie*, 65: 147–59

Badaloni, N. (1955). *La filosofia di Giordano Bruno*, Florence

(1959–60). 'I fratelli Della Porta e la cultura magica e astrologica a Napoli nel'500', *Studi storici*, 1: 677–715

(1961). *Introduzione a G. B. Vico*, Milan

(1963). 'Filosofia della mente e filosofia delle arti in Giannozzo Manetti', *Critica storica*, 2: 395–450

(1965). *Tommaso Campanella*, Milan

Baker, H. (1947). *The Dignity of Man*, Cambridge, Mass.

(1967). *The Race of Time*, Toronto

Baker-Smith, D. (1984). 'Florens Wilson and his circle: émigrés in Lyons, 1539–1543', in *Neo-Latin and the Vernacular in Renaissance France*, ed. G. Castor and T. Cave, Oxford, pp. 83–97

Baldini, A. E. (1980a). 'La politica "etica" di Francesco Piccolomini', *Il pensiero politico*, 13: 161–85

(1980b). 'Per la biografia di Francesco Piccolomini', *Rinascimento*, ser. ii, 20: 389–420

Baldwin, S. (1939). *Renaissance Literary Theory and Practice*, New York

Baldwin, T. W. (1944). *William Shakespeare's Small Latine and Lesse Greeke*, 2 vols., Urbana

Barata-Moura, J. (1972a). 'Amizade humana e amor divino en Leão Hebreu', *Didaskalia*, 2: 155–76

(1972b). 'Leão Hebreu e o sentido do amor universali', *Didaskalia*, 2: 375–403

Barcelar e Oliveira, J. (1960). 'Filosofia escolástica e *Curso Conimbricense*: De una teoria de magisterio a sua sistematização metodologica', *Revista portuguesa de filosofia*, 16: 124–41

Barnes, J. (1982). 'Medicine, experience and logic', in *Science and Speculation: Studies in Hellenistic Theory and Practice*, Cambridge, pp. 24–68

Baron, H. (1932). 'Das Erwachen des historischen Denkens im Humanismus des Quattrocento', *Historische Zeitschrift*, 147: 5–20

  (1938a). 'Cicero and Roman civic spirit in the Middle Ages and early Renaissance', *Bulletin of the John Rylands Library*, 22: 72–97

  (1938b). 'Franciscan poverty and civic wealth as factors in the rise of humanistic thought', *Speculum*, 13: 1–37

  (1959). 'The *Querelle* of the ancients and moderns as a problem for Renaissance scholarship', *Journal of the History of Ideas*, 20: 3–22

  (1961). 'Machiavelli: the republican citizen and author of *The Prince*', *English Historical Review*, 76: 217–53

  (1966). *The Crisis of the Early Italian Renaissance: Civic Humanism and Republican Liberty in an Age of Classicism and Tyranny*, Princeton

  (1968a). *Humanistic and Political Literature in Florence and Venice at the Beginning of the Quattrocento: Studies in Criticism and Chronology*, New York

  (1968b). *From Petrarch to Leonardo Bruni*, Chicago

  (1985). *Petrarch's 'Secretum': Its Making and Its Meaning*, Cambridge, Mass.

Barozzi, L. and Sabbadini, R. (1891). *Studi sul Panormita e sul Valla*, Florence

Bartelink, G. J. M. (1980). *Hieronymus: Liber de optimo genere interpretandi (Epistula 57): Ein Kommentar*, Leiden

Bassi, D. (1892). 'Il primo libro della *Vita civile* di Matteo Palmieri e l'*Institutio oratoria* di Quintiliano', *Giornale storico della letteratura italiana*, 23: 182–207

  (1893). 'L'epitome di Quintiliano di Francesco Patrizi Senese', *Rivista di filologia e d'istruzione classica*, 22: 385–470

Bataillon, M. (1937). *Érasme et l'Espagne*, Paris

Bates, D. G. (1977). 'Sydenham and the medical meaning of "method"', *Bulletin of the History of Medicine*, 51: 324–38

Batkin, L. M. (1979). *Die historische Gesamtheit der italienischen Renaissance*, Dresden

Battaglia, F. (1936). *Enea Silvio Piccolomini e Francesco Patrizi, due politici senesi del Quattrocento*, Florence

Battenhouse, R. W. (1949). 'The doctrine of man in Calvin and in Renaissance Platonism', *Journal of the History of Ideas*, 9: 447–71

Battista, A. M. (1966). *Alle origini del pensiero politico libertino: Montaigne e Charron*, Milan

Baudrier, H. L. (1895–1963). *Bibliographie lyonnaise*, with index by G. Tricot, 15 vols., Lyons–Geneva

Bauer, M. (1973). *Die Erkenntnislehre und der conceptus entis nach vier Spätschriften des Johannes Gerson*, Meisenheim am Glan

Baxandall, M. (1971). *Giotto and the Orators*, Oxford

Beardsley, T. S. (1970). *Hispano-Classical Translations Printed between 1482 and 1699*, Pittsburgh

Becker, A. H. (1896). *Un Humaniste au XVIᵉ siècle: Loys le Roy*, Paris

Bedouelle, G. (1976). *Lefèvre d'Étaples et l'intelligence des Écritures*, Geneva

Belda Plans, J. (1982). *Los Lugares teológicos de Melchor Cano en los commentarios a la suma*, Pamplona

Beltrán de Heredia, V. (1933). 'Melchor Cano en la Universidad de Salamanca', *La ciencia tomista*, 48: 178–208

  (1939). *Francisco de Vitoria*, Barcelona

  (1960). *Domingo de Soto: estudio biográfico documentado*, Madrid

Béné, C. (1969). *Érasme et Saint Augustin*, Geneva

Bennett, A. S. (1969). *English Books and Readers, 1475 to 1557*, Cambridge

Benouis, M. K. (1976). *Le Dialogue philosophique dans la littérature française du seizième siècle*, The Hague

Bentley, J. H. (1983). *Humanists and Holy Writ: New Testament Scholarship in the Renaissance*, Princeton

Berger, H. (1955). *Calvins Geschichtsauffassung*, Zurich

Berges, W. (1938). *Die Fürstenspiegel des hohen und späten Mittelalters*, Leipzig

Bernal Zurita, M. (1945). 'Sebastián Fox Morcillo', *Archivo hispalense*, 4: 201–24

Bernstein, A. E. (1978). *Pierre d'Ailly and the Blanchard Affair*, Leiden

Berschin, W. (1980). *Griechisch-Lateinisches Mittelalter*, Bern

Bertalot, L. (1975). *Studien zum italienischen und deutschen Humanismus*, ed. P. O. Kristeller, 2 vols., Rome

Bertelli, S. (1973). *Ribelli, libertini e ortodossi nella storiografia barocca*, Florence

Bertola, E. (1984). 'La visione del macrocosmo e del microcosmo di Bernardo Silvestre e di Josef ibn Saddiq', *Archivio di filosofia*, 52: 535–90

Bertoni, G. (1921). *Guarino da Verona fra letterati e cortegiani a Ferrara (1429–60)*, Geneva

Beuchot, M. (1976). 'El primer planteamiento teológico-jurídico sobre la conquista de América: John Mair', *La ciencia tomista*, 103: 213–30

Bezold, F. von (1918). *Aus Mittelalter und Renaissance*, Munich

Bianca, C. (1980a). 'La formazione della biblioteca latina del Bessarione', in *Scrittura, biblioteche e stampa a Roma nel Quattrocento*, Vatican City, pp. 103–65

    (1980b). 'Per la storia del termine *atheus* nel Cinquecento: fonti e traduzioni greco-latine', *Studi filosofici*, 3: 71–104

Bianchi, M. L. (1982). 'Occulto e manifesto nella medicina del Rinascimento: Jean Fernel e Pietro Severino', *Atti e memorie dell'Accademia toscana di scienze e lettere 'La Colombaria'*, n.s., 33: 185–248

Bibliografia Galileiana: Primo supplemento, 1896–1940 (1943). Ed. G. Boffito, Rome

Bibliotheca Erasmiana. Répertoire des oeuvres d'Érasme (1893–1908). 7 vols., Ghent

Bietenholz, P. B. (1959). *Der italienische Humanismus und die Blütezeit des Buchdrucks in Basel*, Basle

    (1966). *History and Biography in the Work of Erasmus of Rotterdam*, Geneva

    (1971). *Basle and France in the Sixteenth Century*, Geneva

    (1975). 'Ethics and early printing: Erasmus' rules for the proper conduct of authors', *The Humanities Association Review*, 26: 180–95

Bigi, E. (1967). *La cultura del Poliziano e altri studi umanistici*, Pisa

Billanovich, G. (1947–). *Petrarca letterato*, Roma

    (1951). 'Petrarch and the textual criticism of Livy', *Journal of the Warburg and Courtauld Institutes*, 14: 137–208

    (1953). *I primi umanisti e le tradizioni dei classici latini*, Fribourg

    (1974). 'Il Petrarca e gli storici latini', *Medioevo e umanesimo*, 17–18: 67–145

    (1981–). *La tradizione del testo di Livio e le origini dell' umanesimo*, Padua

Billanovich, M. (1968). 'Benedetto Bordon e Giulio Cesare Scaligero', *Italia medioevale e umanistica*, 11: 187–256

Binnis, J. W. (1978). 'Latin translations from Greek in the English Renaissance', *Humanistica Lovaniensia*, 27: 128–59

Bird, O. (1960). 'The formalizing of topics in medieval logic', *Notre Dame Journal of Formal Logic*, 1: 138–49

    (1962). 'The tradition of logical topics: Aristotle to Ockham', *Journal of the History of Ideas*, 23: 307–23

Birkenmajer, A. (1922). *Vermischte Untersuchungen zur Geschichte der mittelalterlichen Philosophie*, Münster i. W.

    (1970). *Études d'histoire des sciences et de la philosophie du moyen âge*, Wrocław, etc.

Bischoff, B. (1961). 'The study of foreign languages in the Middle Ages', *Speculum*, 36: 209–24

Bischoff, C. (1909). *Studien zu P. P. Vergerio den älteren*, Berlin–Leipzig

Black, A. (1984). *Guilds and Civil Society in European Political Thought from the Twelfth Century to the Present*, London

Blake, R. M. (1966). 'Theory of hypothesis among Renaissance astronomers', in *Theories of Scientific Method*, ed. E. H. Madden, Seattle, pp. 22–49

Blanchet, L. (1920). *Campanella*, Paris

Blau, J. L. (1944). *The Christian Interpretation of the Cabala in the Renaissance*, New York

Bloomfield, M. (1952). *The Seven Deadly Sins*, Ann Arbor

Blüher, K. A. (1969). *Seneca in Spanien*, Munich

Blum, P. R. (1980). *Aristoteles bei Giordano Bruno*, Munich

Blumenthal, H. (1982). 'John Philoponus and Stephanus of Alexandria: Two Neoplatonic Christian commentators on Aristotle?', in *Neoplatonism and Christian Thought*, ed. D. J. O'Meara, Norfolk, Va., pp. 54–63

Boas Hall, M. (1962). *The Scientific Renaissance, 1450–1630*, London

Boase, A. M. (1935). *The Fortunes of Montaigne: A History of the Essays in France, 1580–1669*, London

Bocciolini Palagi, L. (1978). *Il carteggio apocrifo di Seneca e San Paolo*, Florence

Bock, G. (1974). *Tommaso Campanella*, Tübingen

Bodmer, J.-P. (1963). 'Die französische Historiographie des Spätmittelalters und die Franken', *Archiv für Kulturgeschichte*, 45: 91–118

Boethius: His Life, Thought and Influence (1981). Ed. M. Gibson, Oxford

Boffito, G. (1901). 'L'eresia di Matteo Palmieri', *Giornale storico della letteratura italiana*, 37: 1–69

Boggess, W. F. (1970). 'Aristotle's *Poetics* in the fourteenth century', *Studies in Philology*, 67: 278–94

Boh, I. (1965). 'Paul of Pergula on suppositions and consequences', *Franciscan Studies*, 25: 30–89

Bohatec, J. (1950). *Budé und Calvin: Studien zur Gedankenwelt des französischen Frühhumanismus*, Graz

Boisset, J. (1962). *Érasme et Luther: Libre ou serf arbitre?*, Paris

(1967). *Melanchthon, éducateur de l'Allemagne*, Paris

Bolgar, R. R. (1954). *The Classical Tradition and Its Beneficiaries*, Cambridge

Bolzoni, L. (1974). 'Eloquenza e alchimia in un testo inedito di Giulio Camillo', *Rinascimento*, ser. ii, 14: 243–64

(1980). *L'universo dei poemi possibili: Studi su Francesco Patrizi da Cherso*, Rome

Bonfanti, R. (1971). 'Su un dialogo filosofico del tardo '400: Il *De moribus* del fiorentino Giovanni Nesi (1456–1522?)', *Rinascimento*, ser. ii, 11: 203–21

Bonilla y San Martín, A. (1929). *Luís Vives y la filosofía del Renacimiento*, 3 vols., Madrid

Bonner, S. F. (1977). *Education in Ancient Rome*, London

Bono, J. J. (1981). *The Language of Life: Jean Fernel (1497–1556) and 'Spiritus' in Pre-Harveian Bio-Medical Thought*, Ph.D. thesis, Harvard Univ.

Borchardt, F. (1971). *German Antiquity in Renaissance Myth*, Baltimore

Borsa, M. (1893). 'Pier Candido Decembri e l'umanesimo in Lombardia', *Archivio storico lombardo*, 20: 5–74, 358–441

(1904). 'Correspondence of Humphrey, Duke of Gloucester and Pier Candido Decembrio', *English Historical Review*, 19: 509–26

Bosco, D. (1977). 'Charron moralista: Temi e problemi di *La Sagesse*', *Rivista di filosofia neoscolastica*, 69: 247–78

Bosco, U. (1968). *Petrarca*, 4th edn, Bari

Bosio Boz, F. (1947). *Vittorino da Feltre: la vita, le idee, i tempi*, Alba
Bottiglioni, G. (1913). *La lirica latina in Firenze nella seconda metà del secolo XV*, Pisa
Bottin, F. (1972). 'La teoria del *regressus* in Giacomo Zabarella', in *Saggi e ricerche su Aristotele, S. Bernardo, Zabarella . . .*, ed. C. Giacon, Padua, pp. 48–70
(1981). 'Alcune correzioni ed aggiunte al censimento dei codici di Paolo Veneto', *Quaderni per la storia dell' Università di Padova*, 14: 57–60
(1982). *La scienza degli occamisti*, Rimini
Boüard, Michel de (1936). *Une nouvelle encyclopédie médiévale: Le Compendium philosophiae*, Paris
Bouwsma, W. J. (1957). *Concordia mundi: The Career and Thought of Guillaume Postel*, Cambridge, Mass.
(1968). *Venice and the Defense of Republican Liberty*, Berkeley
(1969). 'Three types of historiography in Post-Renaissance Italy', *History and Theory*, 3: 303–14
(1973). *The Culture of Renaissance Humanism*, Washington, D.C.
Bouyer, L. (1955). *Autour d'Érasme: Études sur le Christianisme des humanistes catholiques*, Paris
Bowen, B. C. (1972). 'Cornelius Agrippa's *De vanitate*: Polemic or paradox?', *Bibliothèque d'humanisme et Renaissance*, 34: 249–65
Bradner, L. (1940). *Musae Anglicanae: A History of Anglo-Latin Poetry, 1500–1925*, New York
Bradshaw, B. (1981). 'More on Utopia', *The Historical Journal*, 24: 1–27
Branca, V. (1973). 'Ermolao Barbaro and late Quattrocento Venetian humanism', in *Renaissance Venice*, ed. J. R. Hale, London, pp. 218–43
(1975). *Boccaccio medievale*, 4th edn, Florence
(1980). 'L'umanesimo veneziano alla fine del Quattrocento: Ermolao Barbaro e il suo circolo', in *Storia della cultura veneta*, III, 1, Vicenza, pp. 123–75
Brandão, M. (1948–69). *A Inquisição e os professores de Colégio das Artes*, 2 vols., Coimbra
Braun, L. (1973). *Histoire de l'histoire de la philosophie*, Paris
Brause, K. H. (1916). *Die Geschichtsphilosophie des Carolus Bovillus*, Leipzig
Breen, Q. (1954). 'The *Observationes* in M. T. Ciceronem of Mario Nizolio', *Studies in the Renaissance*, 1: 49–58
(1955). 'Nizolius' *Defensiones . . .*', *Rinascimento*, 6: 195–208
(1968). *Christianity and Humanism*, ed. N. P. Ross, Grand Rapids
Breit, E. (1912). *Die Engel- und Dämonenlehre des Pomponatius und des Cäsalpinus*, Dissertation, Univ. of Bonn.
Breitenbürger, G. (1975). *Metaphora: Die Rezeption des aristotelischen Begriffs in den Poetiken des Cinquecento*, Kronberg/Ts.
Bremme, H. J. (1969). *Buchdrucker und Buchhändler zur Zeit der Glaubenskämpfe: Studien zur Genfer Druckgeschichte, 1565–1580*, Geneva
Brettschneider, H. (1880). *Melanchthon als Historiker*, Insterburg
Breva-Claramonte, M. (1983). *Sanctius' Theory of Language*, Amsterdam
Brickman, B. (1941). *An Introduction to Francesco Patrizi's 'Nova de universis philosophia'*, New York
Broadie, A. (1983). *George Lokert: Late-Scholastic Logician*, Edinburgh
(1985). *The Circle of John Mair*, Oxford
Brockliss, L. W. B. (1981a). 'Philosophical teaching in France, 1600–1740', *History of Universities*, 1: 131–68
(1981b). 'Aristotle, Descartes and the new science: natural philosophy at the University of Paris, 1600–1740', *Annals of Science*, 38: 33–69
Brounts, A. (1970). 'Nouvelles précisions sur la *pecia*: A propos de l'édition léonine du commentaire de Thomas d'Aquin sur l'*Ethique* d'Aristote', *Scriptorium*, 24: 343–59
Brown, A. (1979). *Bartolomeo Scala (1430–1479), Chancellor of Florence*, Princeton

Brown, J. L. (1939). *The 'Methodus ad facilem historiarum cognitionem' of Jean Bodin*, Washington, D.C.

Brown V. (1974). 'Giovanni Argiropulo on the agent intellect: an edition of Ms. Magliabecchi v 42 (ff. 224–228^v)', in *Essays in Honour of Anton Charles Pegis*, ed. J. R. O'Donnell, Toronto, pp. 160–75

Brufau Prats, J. (1960). *El pensamiento político de Domingo de Soto y su concepcíon del poder*, Salamanca

Brush, C. B. (1966). *Montaigne and Bayle: Variations on the Theme of Skepticism*, The Hague

Bruton, O. G. (1953). *The Debate Between Bartolomé de Las Casas and Juan Ginés de Sepúlveda over the Justice of the Spanish Conquest of America: Spain, 1550*, Ph.D. thesis, Princeton Univ.

Bruyère, N. (1984). *Méthode et dialectique dans l'oeuvre de La Ramée*, Paris

Buck, A. (1952). *Italienische Dichtungslehre vom Mittelalter bis zum Ausgang der Renaissance*, Tübingen

(1957). *Das Geschichtsdenken der Renaissance*, Krefeld

(1958). 'Aus der Vorgeschichte der Querelle des anciens et des modernes im Mittelalter und Renaissance', *Bibliothèque d'humanisme et Renaissance*, 20: 527–41

(1960). 'Die Rangstellung des Menschen in der Renaissance: dignitas et miseria hominis', *Archiv für Kulturgeschichte*, 42: 61–75

(1968). *Die humanistische Tradition in der Romania*, Hamburg

(1976). *Die Rezeption der Antike in den romanischen Literaturen der Renaissance*, Berlin

(1983). 'Alessandro Piccolominis moralphilosophische Lehre im Rahmen des Vulgärhumanismus', in *Italien und die Romania in Humanismus und Renaissance: Festschrift für Erich Loos zum 70. Geburtstag*, ed. K. W. Hempfer and E. Straub, Wiesbaden, pp. 1–16

Bühler, C. F. (1960). *The Fifteenth-Century Book*, Philadelphia

(1973). *Early Books and Manuscripts*, New York

Bütler, R. (1948). *Nationales und universales Denken im Werke Etienne Pasquiers*, Basle

Buisson, F. (1886). *Répertoire des ouvrages pédagogiques du XVIe siècle*, Paris

Bullón, E. (1905). *Los precursores españoles de Bacón y Descartes*, Salamanca

Bultot, R. (1963–4). *Christianisme et valeurs humaines. A. La Doctrine du mépris du monde, en Occident, de S. Ambroise à Innocent III*, iv: *Le 11e siècle*, 2 vols., Louvain–Paris

(1969). 'Érasme, Épicure et le "De contemptu mundi"', in *Scrinium Erasmianum*, ed. J. Coppens, ii, Leiden, pp. 205–38

(1973). 'La dignità dell'uomo secondo S. Pier Damiani', in *S. Pier Damiani: Atti del Convegno di studi nel IX centenario della morte*, Faenza, pp. 17–41

Bundy, M. W. (1927). *The Theory of Imagination in Classical and Mediaeval Thought*, Urbana

Burckhardt, J. (1860). *Die Cultur der Renaissance in Italien*, Basle

Burdach, K. (1963). *Reformation, Renaissance, Humanismus*, 3rd edn, Darmstadt

Burke, P. (1966). 'A survey of the popularity of ancient historians, 1450–1700', *History and Theory*, 5: 135–52

(1969). *The Renaissance Sense of the Past*, London

(1972). *Culture and Society in Renaissance Italy, 1420–1540*, New York

Burns, J. H. (1954). 'New light on John Major', *The Innes Review*, 5: 83–100

(1983). '*Jus gladii* and *jurisdictio*: Jacques Almain and John Locke', *The Historical Journal*, 26: 369–74

Burnyeat, M. F. (1982a). 'The origins of non-deductive inference', in *Science and Speculation*, ed. J. Barnes *et al.*, Cambridge, pp. 193–238

(1982b). 'Gods and heaps', in *Language and Logos*, ed. M. Schofield and M. C. Nussbaum, Cambridge, pp. 315–38

(unpublished). 'Enthymeme – logic of persuasion'

Bursill-Hall, G. L. (1975). 'The Middle Ages', in *Current Trends in Linguistics*, ed. T. A. Sebeok, XIII, 1, The Hague, pp. 179–230

Burtt, E. A. (1932). *The Metaphysical Foundations of Modern Physical Science*, London

Buschmann, R. (1930). *Das Bewusstsein der deutschen Geschichte bei den deutschen Humanisten*, Göttingen

Bush, D. (1939). *The Renaissance and English Humanism*, Toronto

  (1952). *Classical Influences in Renaissance Literature*, Cambridge, Mass.

Busson, H. (1957). *Le Rationalisme dans la littérature française de la Renaissance, 1533–1601*, Paris

Bylebyl, J. J. (1979). 'The School of Padua: humanistic medicine in the sixteenth century', in *Health, Medicine and Mortality in the Sixteenth Century*, ed. C. Webster, Cambridge, pp. 335–70

  (forthcoming). 'Teaching *Methodus medendi* in the Renaissance', in *Galens Methode der Therapie*, ed. F. Kudlien and R. J. Durling

Caballero, F. (1871). *Vita del Ill. Melchor Cano*, Madrid

Calasso, F. (1957). *I glossatori e la teoria della sovranità*, Milan

Calderini, A. (1913). 'Ricerche intorno alla biblioteca e alla cultura greca di Francesco Filelfo', *Studi italiani di filologia classica*, 20: 204–425

  (1915). 'I codici milanesi delle opere di Francesco Filelfo', *Archivio storico lombardo*, ser. v, 42: 335–411

Cambridge History of Later Greek and Early Medieval Philosophy (1970). Ed. A. H. Armstrong, Cambridge

Cambridge History of Later Medieval Philosophy (1982). Ed. N. Kretzmann, A. Kenny and J. Pinborg, Cambridge

Cammelli, G. (1941–54). *I dotti bizantini e le origini dell'umanesimo*. I: *Manuele Crisolora*; II: *Giovanni Argiropulo*; III: *Demetrio Calcondila*, Florence

Campana, A. (1946). 'The origin of the word "humanist"', *Journal of the Warburg and Courtauld Institutes*, 9: 60–73

Camporeale, S. (1972). *Lorenzo Valla: Umanesimo e teologia*, Florence

  (1976). 'Lorenzo Valla tra Medioevo e Rinascimento: Encomion s. Thomae, 1457', *Memorie domenicane*, n.s., 7: 3–190

Cantimori, D. (1937). 'Rhetoric and politics in Italian humanism', *Journal of the Warburg and Courtauld Institutes*, 1: 83–162

  (1975). *Umanesimo e religione nel Rinascimento*, Turin

Capp, B. (1979). *Astrology and the Popular Press: English Almanacs 1500–1800*, London–Boston

Cardini, R. (1973). *La critica del Landino*, Florence

Carli, A. and Favaro, A. (1896). *Bibliografia galileiana, 1568–1895*, Rome

Carlini, A. (1967). *L'attività filologica di Francesco Robortello*, Udine

Carmody, F. J. (1952). 'The planetary theory of Ibn Rushd', *Osiris*, 10: 556–86

Caroti, S. (1979). 'La critica contro l'astrologia di Nicole Oresme e la sua influenza nel Medioevo e nel Rinascimento', *Atti della Accademia Nazionale dei Lincei. Memorie. Cl. di scienze morali, storiche e filologiche*, ser. viii, 23: 545–685

Carreras y Artau, T. and J. (1939–43). *Historia de la filosofía española: Filosofía cristiana de los siglos XIII al XV*, 2 vols., Madrid

Carro, V. D. (1951). *La teología y los teologos-juristas españoles ante la conquista de América*, Salamanca

Carugo, A. and Crombie, A. C. (1983). 'The Jesuits and Galileo's ideas of science and of nature', *Annali dell'Istituto e Museo di storia della scienza di Firenze*, 8: 3–68

Carvalho, J. de (1978–). *Obra completa*, Lisbon

Casacci, A. (1926). 'Gli *Elegantiarum libri* di Lorenzo Valla', *Atene e Roma*, n.s., 3: 187–203

Casado-Barroso, F. (1969). *La virtud de la esperanza en Melchor Cano*, Rome

Caspar, M. (1948). *Johannes Kepler*, Stuttgart (Eng. trans. New York, 1959)

Cassirer, E. (1911). *Das Erkenntnisproblem*, I, 2nd edn, Berlin

(1927). *Individuum und Kosmos in der Philosophie der Renaissance*, Berlin–Leipzig

(1942). 'Giovanni Pico della Mirandola', *Journal of the History of Ideas*, 3: 123–44, 319–46

Cassuto, U. (1918). *Gli ebrei a Firenze nell'età del Rinascimento*, Florence (repr. Florence, 1968)

Castellanos, D. (1947). 'Quevedo y su *Epicteto en español*', *Boletín de la Academia Nacional de Letras*, 1: 179–213

Castellote, S. (1982). *Die Anthropologie des Suarez*, 2nd edn, Freiburg i. Br.

Castor, G. (1964). *Pléiade Poetics*, Cambridge

Catalogue des manuscrits alchimiques grecs (1924–32). Ed. J. Bidez *et al.*, 8 vols., Brussels

Catalogus translationum et commentariorum (1960–). Ed. P. O. Kristeller and F. E. Cranz, Washington, D.C.

Catto, J. (1976). 'Ideas and experience in the political thought of Aquinas', *Past and Present*, 71: 3–21

Cavazza, S. (1982). 'Platonismo e riforma religiosa: la *Theologia vivificans* di Jacques Lefèvre d'Étaples', *Rinascimento*, ser. ii, 22: 99–149

Caverni, R. (1891–1900). *Storia del metodo sperimentale in Italia*, 6 vols., Florence (repr. Bologna, 1970)

Cavini, W. (1977). 'Appunti sulla prima diffusione in occidente delle opere di Sesto Empirico', *Medioevo*, 3: 1–20

Ceñal, R. (1943). 'Pedro da Fonseca (1528–1599), su crítica del texto de la metafísica de Aristóteles', *Revista de filosofía* (Madrid), 2: 124–46

(1948). *Filosofía española y portuguesa de 1500–1650: repertorio de fuentes impresas*, Madrid

Centenario del Cardinale Bessarione (1973). *Miscellanea francescana*, 73: 249–386

Cerreta, F. V. (1957). 'Alessandro Piccolomini's commentary on the *Poetics* of Aristotle', *Studies in the Renaissance*, 4: 139–68

(1960). *Alessandro Piccolomini, letterato e filosofo senese del Cinquecento*, Sienna

Cessi, R. (1956). *Saggi romani*, Rome

Chabod, F. (1965). *Machiavelli and the Renaissance*, trans. D. Moore, London

Chacón y Calvó, J.-M. (1948). 'Quevedo y la tradición senequista', *Realidad*, 3: 318–42

Chaix, P. (1954). *Recherches sur l'imprimerie à Genève de 1550 à 1564*, Geneva

Chaix, P., Dufour, A. and Moeckli, G. (1966). *Les Livres imprimés à Genève de 1550 à 1560*, rev. edn, Geneva

Chambers, R. W. (1935). *Thomas More*, London

Chantraine, G. (1971). 'Josse Clichtove: témoin théologien de l'humanisme parisien', *Revue d'histoire ecclésiastique*, 66: 507–28

(1981). *Érasme et Luther: Libre et serf arbitre*, Paris

Charbonnel, R. (1919). *La Pensée italienne au XVIe siècle et le courant libertin*, Paris

Charles de Bovelles en son cinquième centenaire 1479–1979 (1982). Paris

Chastel, A. (1954). *Marsile Ficin et l'art*, Geneva

Chauviré, R. (1914). *Jean Bodin, auteur de la 'République'*, Paris

Chenu, M.-D. (1946). 'L'Humanisme et la réforme au Collège de Saint-Jacques de Paris', *Archives d'histoire dominicaine*, 1: 130–54

Cherniss, H. (1964). *Aristotle's Criticism of Pre-Socratic Philosophy*, New York

Chew, A. (1950). 'Joseph Hall and neo-stoicism', *PMLA*, 55: 1130–45

Chiarelli, G. (1932). 'Il *De regno* di Francesco Patrizi', *Rivista internazionale di filosofia del diritto*, 12: 716–38

Chomarat, J. (1981). *Grammaire et rhétorique chez Érasme*, 2 vols., Paris

Chrisman, M. U. (1982a). *Bibliography of Strasbourg Imprints, 1480–1599*, New Haven–London

(1982b). *Lay Culture, Learned Culture: Books and Social Change in Strasbourg, 1480–1599*, New Haven–London

Christ, K. (1984). *The Handbook of Medieval Library History*, trans. T. M. Otto, Metuchen–London

Church, W. F. (1972). *Richelieu and Reason of State*, Princeton

Cian, V. (1887). *Nuovi documenti su Pietro Pomponazzi*, Venice

Ciliberto, M. (1979). *Lessico di Giordano Bruno*, 2 vols., Rome

Clagett, M. (1941). *Giovanni Marliani and Late Medieval Physics*, New York

(1959). *The Science of Mechanics in the Middle Ages*, Madison

(1964–84). *Archimedes in the Middle Ages*, 5 vols., Madison–Philadelphia

(1979). *Studies in Medieval Physics and Mathematics*, London

Clark, D. L. (1922). *Rhetoric and Poetry in the Renaissance*, New York

(1948). *John Milton at St. Paul's School*, New York

Clarke, E. and Dewhurst, K. (1972). *An Illustrated History of Brain Function*, Oxford

Classical Influences on European Culture, A. D. 500–1500 (1971). Ed. R. R. Bolgar, Cambridge

Classical Influences on European Culture, A. D. 1500–1700 (1976). Ed. R. R. Bolgar, Cambridge

Clavelin, M. (1968). *La Philosophie naturelle de Galilée*, Paris

Clerval, J. A. (1894). *De Judoci Clichtovei Neoportuensis vita et operibus (1472–1543)*, Paris

Clubb, L. G. (1965). *Giambattista Della Porta: Dramatist*, Princeton

Clulee, N. H. (1977). 'Astrology, magic and optics: facets of John Dee's natural philosophy', *Renaissance Quarterly*, 30: 632–80

Cochrane, E. (1981). *Historians and Historiography in the Italian Renaissance*, Chicago

Codina Mir, G. (1968). *Aux sources de la pédagogie des Jésuites: Le 'Modus Parisiensis'*, Rome

Cogan, M. (1984). 'Rodolphus Agricola and the semantic revolutions of the history of invention', *Rhetorica*, 2: 163–94

Cohen, H. J. (1984). *Quantifying Music: The Science of Music at the First Stage of the Scientific Revolution*, Dordrecht–Boston–Lancaster

Cohn, N. (1975). *Europe's Inner Demons*, London

Colish, M. L. (1962). 'The mime of God: Vives on the nature of man', *Journal of the History of Ideas*, 23: 3–20

(1985). *The Stoic Tradition from Antiquity to the Early Middle Ages*, 2 vols., Leiden

Collingwood, R. G. (1946). *The Idea of History*, Oxford

Collins, A. B. (1974). *The Secular is Sacred: Platonism and Thomism in Marsilio Ficino's Platonic Theology*, The Hague

Collison, R. (1966). *Encyclopedias: Their History Throughout the Ages*, New York

Colomer, E. (1961). *Nikolaus von Kues und Ramon Llull*, Berlin

Combes, A. (1956). 'Présentation de Jean de Ripa', *Archives d'histoire doctrinale et littéraire du moyen âge*, 23: 145–242

(1963–5). *La Théologie mystique de Gerson*, 2 vols., Rome–Paris

(1973). *Jean Gerson, commentateur dionysien*, 2nd edn, Paris

Congar, M.-J. (1934–5). 'Bio-bibliographie de Cajétan', *Revue thomiste*, 39: 3–49

Conger, G. P. (1922). *Theories of Macrocosms and Microcosms in the History of Philosophy*, New York

Connolly, J. L. (1928). *Jean Gerson: Reformer and Mystic*, Louvain

Constable, G. (1976). *Letters and Letter-Collections*, Turnhout

Convegno internazionale indetto nel V centenario di Leon Battista Alberti (1974). Rome

Copenhaver, B. P. (1977). 'Lefèvre d'Étaples, Symphorien Champier, and the secret names of God', *Journal of the Warburg and Courtauld Institutes*, 40: 189–211

(1978a). *Symphorien Champier and the Reception of the Occultist Tradition in Renaissance France*, The Hague

(1978b). 'Essay review: *Hermeticism and the Scientific Revolution*', *Annals of Science*, 35: 527–31

(1984). 'Scholastic philosophy and Renaissance magic in the *De vita* of Marsilio Ficino', *Renaissance Quarterly*, 37: 523–54

(1986). 'Renaissance magic and Neoplatonic philosophy: *Ennead* 4.3–5 in Ficino's *De vita coelitus comparanda*', in *Marsilio Ficino e il ritorno di Platone: studi e documenti*, ed. G. Garfagnini, Florence, II, pp. 351–69

(forthcoming a). 'Hermes Trismegistus, Proclus and the question of a theory of magic in the Renaissance', in papers read at the Folger Library conference on Hermes Trismegistus held in March 1982

(forthcoming b). 'Iamblichus, Synesius and the *Chaldaean Oracles* in Marsilio Ficino's *De vita libri tres*: Hermetic magic or Neoplatonic magic?', in *Iter Festivum. A Festschrift for P. O. Kristeller*, ed. J. Hankins *et al.*

(forthcoming c). 'Natural magic, Hermeticism and occultism in early modern science', in *Reappraisals in the Scientific Revolution*, ed. R. S. Westman and D. Lindberg

The Copernican Achievement (1975). Ed. R. S. Westman, Berkeley–Los Angeles

Corbellini, A. (1917). 'Appunti sull'umanesimo in Lombardia', *Bollettino della Società Pavese di storia patria*, 17: 5–51

Cornelius, P. (1965). *Languages in Seventeenth and Early Eighteenth Century Imaginary Voyages*, Geneva

Corsano, A. (1940). *Il pensiero di Giordano Bruno nel suo svolgimento storico*, Florence

(1958–63). 'Per la storia del pensiero del tardo Rinascimento', *Giornale critico della filosofia italiana*, 37: 34–63, 201–44; 38: 76–97, 485–91; 40: 87–91, 175–80, 499–507; 41: 56–64, 507–17; 42: 488–94

(1961a). *Tommaso Campanella*, Bari

(1961b). 'Il *Liber de ludo aleae* di Girolamo Cardano: ragione e fortuna', *Giornale critico della filosofia italiana*, 40: 87–91

Cortesi, M. (1979). 'Il *Vocabularium* greco di Giovanni Tortelli', *Italia medioevale e umanistica*, 22: 449–83

Cosentino, G. (1970). 'Le matematiche nella *Ratio studiorum* della Compagnia di Gesù', *Miscellanea storica ligure*, 2: 171–213

(1971). 'L'insegnamento delle matematiche nei collegi gesuitici nell'Italia settentrionale', *Physis*, 13: 205–17

Cosenza, M. E. (1962–7). *Biographical and Bibliographical Dictionary of Italian Humanists and of the World of Classical Scholarship in Italy*, 6 vols., Boston

Costello, F. B. (1974). *The Political Philosophy of Luis de Molina, S. J. (1535–1600)*, Rome

Cotroneo, G. (1966). *Jean Bodin, teorico della storia*, Naples

(1971). *I trattatisti dell' 'Ars historica'*, Naples

Cougny, E. (1857). *Guillaume du Vair*, Paris

Courtenay, W. J. and Tachau, K. H. (1982). 'Ockham, Ockhamists and the English–German Nation at Paris, 1339–1341', *History of Universities*, 2: 53–96

Coxito, A. A. (1966). 'O problema dos universais no curso filosófico conimbricense', *Revista dos estudos gerais universitários de Moçambique*, ser. v, 3: 5–62

Cozzi, G. (1970). 'Domenico Morosini e il *De bene instituta re publica*', *Studi veneziani*, 12: 405–58

Crahay, R. (1980). 'Un manifeste religieux d'anticulture: le *De incertitudine et vanitate scientiarum et artium* de Corneille Agrippa', in *Acta Conventus Neo-Latini Turonensis. III\<sup\>e\</sup\> Congrès international d'études néo-latines*, ed. J.-C. Margolin, Paris, pp. 889–924

Cranefield, P. (1970). 'On the origins of the phrase *Nihil est in intellectu quod non prius fuerit in sensu*', *Journal of the History of Medicine*, 25: 77–80

Cranz, F. E. (1958). 'The prefaces to the Greek editions and Latin translations of Alexander of Aphrodisias, 1450 to 1575', *Proceedings of the American Philosophical Society*, 102: 510–46

(1978). 'The publishing history of the Aristotle commentaries of Thomas Aquinas', *Traditio*, 34: 157–92

Cranz, F. E. and Schmitt, C. B. (1984). *A Bibliography of Aristotle Editions, 1501–1600*, 2nd edn, Baden-Baden

Crapulli, G. (1969). *Mathesis universalis*, Rome
Crescini, A. (1965). *Le origini del metodo analitico: il Cinquecento*, Udine
  (1972). *Il problema metodologico alle origini della scienza moderna*, Rome
Crisciani, C. (1973). 'The conception of alchemy as expressed in the *Pretiosa margarita novella* of Petrus Bonus of Ferrara', *Ambix*, 20: 165–181
  (1976). 'La *Questio de alchimia* fra '200 e '300', *Medioevo*, 2: 119–68
Crisciani, C. and Gagnon, C. (1980). *Alchémie et philosophie au moyen âge: perspectives et problèmes*, St Denis, Quebec
Critics and Criticism (1952). Ed. R. S. Crane, Chicago
Crombie, A. C. (1952). *Augustine to Galileo: The History of Science, A. D. 400–1650*, London
  (1953). *Robert Grosseteste and the Origins of Experimental Science*, Oxford
  (1977). 'Mathematics and Platonism in sixteenth-century Italian universities and in Jesuit educational policy', in *Prismata: Naturwissenschaftsgeschichtliche Studien. Festschrift für Willy Hartner*, ed. Y. Maeyama and W. G. Saltzer, Wiesbaden, pp. 63–94
  (forthcoming). *Styles of Scientific Thinking in the European Tradition*, Oxford
Cronin, T.-J. (1966). *Objective Being in Descartes and in Suarez*, Rome
Crosby, H. L. (1955). *Thomas of Bradwardine: His 'Tractatus de proportionibus'*, Madison
Crouzel, H. (1977). *Une controverse sur Origène à la Renaissance: Jean Pic de la Mirandole et Pierre Garcia*, Paris
Crowley, B. (1948). 'The life and works of Bartholomew Mastrius', *Franciscan Studies*, 8: 97–152
Cruz Costa, J. (1942). *Ensaio sôbre a vida e a obra do filósofo Francisco Sanches*, São Paulo
Csapodi, C. and K. (1978). *Bibliotheca Corviniana*, 2nd edn, Budapest
Cuendet, G. (1933). 'Cicéron et Saint Jérôme traducteurs', *Revue des études latines*, 11: 380–400
Culianu, I. P. (1981). 'Magia spirituale e magia demoniaca nel Rinascimento', *Rivista di storia e letteratura religiosa*, 17: 360–408
Cultural Aspects of the Italian Renaissance (1976). Ed. C. H. Clough, Manchester
Cura, A. del (1960). 'Domingo de Soto, maestro de filosofia', *Estudios filosóficos*, 9: 391–440
  (1961). 'Domingo de Soto en su ambiente histórico', *Estudios filosóficos*, 10: 119–24
Curtze, M. (1870). *Die mathematischen Schriften des Nicole Oresme (ca. 1320–1382)*, Berlin
Cusanus-Gedächtnisschrift (1970). Ed. N. Grass, Innsbruck–Munich

Dainville, F. de (1940). *La Naissance de l'humanisme moderne*, Paris
Dales, R. C. (1980). 'The de-animation of the heavens in the Middle Ages', *Journal of the History of Ideas*, 41: 431–50
Dal Pra, M. (1966). 'Una *oratio* programmatica di G. Zabarella', *Rivista critica di storia della filosofia*, 21: 286–90
D'Alverny, M.-T. (1976). 'L'Homme comme symbole: le microcosme', in *Simboli e simbologia nell'alto Medioevo*, I, Spoleto, pp. 123–95
D'Alverny, M.-T. and Hudry, F. (1974). 'Al-Kindi *De radiis*', *Archives d'histoire doctrinale et littéraire du moyen âge*, 41: 139–60
The Damned Art: Essays in the Literature of Witchcraft (1977). Ed. S. Anglo, London
Darmstaedter, E. (1931). *Arznei und Alchemie: Paracelsus-Studien*, Leipzig
Dauriens, S. (1971). *Amour et intellect chez Léon l'Hébreu*, Toulouse
Davies, K. (1957). 'Some early drafts of the *De rebus gestis Francorum* of Paulus Emilius', *Medievalia et Humanistica*, 11: 99–110
Davis, C. T. (1974). 'Ptolemy of Lucca and the Roman Republic', *Proceedings of the American Philosophical Society*, 118: 30–50
Dean, L. F. (1941). 'Francis Bacon's theory of civil history writing', *Literary History*, 8: 161–83
  (1947). *Tudor Theories of History Writing*, Ann Arbor

De Angelis, E. (1964). *Il metodo geometrico nella filosofia del Seicento*, Pisa
Dear, P. R. (1984). 'Marin Mersenne and the probabilistic roots of "mitigated scepticism"',
   Journal of the History of Philosophy, 22: 173–205
De Bellis, D. (1975). 'Niccolò Leonico Tomeo, interprete di Aristotele naturalista', *Physis*,
   17: 71–93
   (1979). '*Autokineton* e *entelechia*: Niccolò Leonico Tomeo: l'anima nei dialoghi intitolati al
      Bembo', *Annali dell'Istituto di filosofia, Università di Firenze*, 1: 47–68
   (1980). 'La vita e l'ambiente di Niccolò Leonico Tomeo', *Quaderni per la storia
      dell'Università di Padova*, 13: 37–75
   (1981). 'I veicoli dell'anima nell'analisi di Niccolò Leonico Tomeo', *Annali dell'Istituto di
      filosofia, Università di Firenze*, 3: 1–21
Debus, A. G. (1965). *The English Paracelsians*, London
   (1968). 'Mathematics and nature in the chemical texts of the Renaissance', *Ambix*, 15: 1–28
   (1977). *The Chemical Philosophy: Paracelsian Science and Medicine in the Sixteenth and
      Seventeenth Centuries*, 2 vols., New York
De Caprariis, V. (1959). *Propaganda e pensiero politico in Francia durante le Guerre di Religione
   (1559–1572)*, Naples
Deck, J. N. (1967). *Nature, Contemplation and the One*, Toronto
De Court, M. (1934). *Le Commentaire de Jean Philopon sur le troisième livre du traité de l'âme
   d'Aristote*, Liège
Deer, L. A. (1980). *Academic Theories of Generation in the Renaissance: The Contemporaries and
   Successors of Jean Fernel*, Ph.D. thesis, Univ. of London
De Gaetano, A. L. (1968). 'Gelli's eclecticism on the question of immortality and the Italian
   version of Porzio's *De humana mente*', *Philological Quarterly*, 47: 532–46
Dejob, C. (1881). *Marc-Antoine Muret*, Paris (repr. Geneva, 1970)
De la Garanderie, M. M. (1973). 'Le Style figuré de Guillaume Budé et ses implications
   logiques et théologiques', in *L'Humanisme français au début de la Renaissance: Colloque
   international de Tours*, Paris, pp. 343–59
   (1976). *Christianisme et lettres profanes (1515–1535)*, Thèse, Univ. of Paris IV
De la Mare, A. C. (1965). *Vespasiano da Bisticci, Historian and Bookseller*, 2 vols., Ph.D. thesis,
   Univ. of London
   (1973–). *The Handwriting of the Italian Humanists*, Oxford
Delcorno, C. (1967). 'Il commentario *De fulmine* di Bernardino Telesio', *Aevum*, 41: 474–506
Delcorno Branca, D. (1976). 'Un discepolo del Poliziano: Michele Acciari', *Lettere italiane*,
   28: 464–81
Delcourt, M. and Derwa, M. (1968). 'Trois Aspects humanistes de l'épicurisme chrétien', in
   Colloquium Erasmianum, Mons, pp. 119–33
Della Torre, Arnaldo (1902). *Storia dell'Accademia platonica di Firenze*, Florence
Del Nero, V. (1983). 'La questione dell'anima nel commento di Giovani Battista Pio al *De
   rerum natura* di Lucrezio', *Annali dell'Istituto di filosofia, Università di Firenze*, 5: 29–60
Del Torre, M. A. (1968). *Studi su Cesare Cremonini: cosmologia e logica nel tardo Aristotelismo
   padovano*, Padua
De Nichilo, M. (1975). *I poemi astrologici di Giovanni Pontano*, Bari
Denzer, H. (1972). *Moralphilosophie und Naturrecht bei Samuel Pufendorf*, Munich
De Petris, A. (1975). 'Le teorie umanistiche del tradurre e l'*Apologeticus* di Giannozzo
   Manetti', *Bibliothèque d'humanisme et Renaissance*, 37: 15–32
De Pina Martins, J. V. (1979). *L'Utopie de Thomas More et l'humanisme*, Paris
De Rosa, D. (1980). *Coluccio Salutati*, Florence
De' Rosmini, C. (1805–6). *Vita e disciplina di Guarino Veronese*, 3 vols., Brescia
   (1808). *Vita di Francesco Filelfo*, 3 vols., Milan
Destrez, J. (1935). *La pecia dans les manuscrits universitaires du XIIIe et du XIVe siècle*, Paris

Dewan, L. (1982). 'Obiectum: notes on the invention of a word', *Archives d'histoire doctrinale et littéraire du moyen âge*, 48: 37–96

Dibon, P. (1954–). *La Philosophie néerlandaise au siècle d'or*, Amsterdam

Diccionario de historia eclesiástica de España (1972–5). 4 vols., Madrid

Diccionario de historia de España (1968–9). Ed. G. Bleiberg, 2nd edn, 3 vols., Madrid

Dictionary of National Biography (1885–1901). 22 vols., Oxford (repr. Oxford, 1921–2)

Dictionary of Scientific Biography (1970–80). Ed. C. C. Gillispie, 16 vols., New York

Dictionary of the Middle Ages (1982–). Ed. J. R. Strayer, New York

Dictionnaire de biographie française (1933–). Paris

Dictionnaire de spiritualité ascétique et mystique (1937–). Ed. M. Viller, Paris

Dictionnaire de théologie catholique (1923–72). 16 vols., Paris

Dictionnaire d'histoire et de géographie ecclésiastiques (1912–). Paris

Diepgen, P. (1912). *Traum und Traumdeutung als medizinisch-naturwissenschaftliches Problem im Mittelalter*, Berlin

Diesner, H.-J. (1985). 'Die Virtu der Principi bei Machiavelli', *Zeitschrift für historische Forschung*, 12: 385–428

Dijksterhuis, E. J. (1950). *De mechanisering van het wereldbeeld*, Amsterdam (Eng. trans. Oxford, 1961)

Di Leo, E. (1953). *Scienza e umanesimo in Girolamo Fracastoro*, 2nd edn, 2 vols., Salerno

Dilthey, W. (1914–36). *Gesammelte Schriften*, 12 vols., Leipzig–Berlin

Di Napoli, G. (1947). *Tommaso Campanella, filosofo della restaurazione cattolica*, Padua
  (1963). *L'immortalità dell'anima nel Rinascimento*, Turin
  (1965). *Giovanni Pico della Mirandola e la problematica dottrinale del suo tempo*, Rome
  (1970). 'Libertà e fato in Pietro Pomponazzi', in *Studi in onore di Antonio Corsano*, Manduria, pp. 175–220
  (1971). *Lorenzo Valla: filosofia e religione nell'umanesimo italiano*, Rome
  (1973). *Studi sul Rinascimento*, Naples

Dionisotti, C. (1959). 'Appunti su Leone Ebreo', *Italia medioevale e umanistica*, 2: 409–28
  (1968). *Gli umanisti e il volgare fra Quattro e Cinquecento*, Florence
  (1980). *Machiavellerie*, Turin

Di Ottavio, C. (1976). *El humanismo castellano del siglo XV*, Valencia

Dippel, J. (1865). *Versuch einer systematischen Darstellung der Philosophie des C. Bovillus*, Würzburg

Ditt, E. (1931). *Pier Candido Decembrio: Contributo alla storia dell'umanesimo italiano*, Milan

Dittrich, F. (1885). *Gasparo Contarini (1483–1542)*, Braunsberg

Di Vona, P. (1968). *Studi sulla scolastica della Controriforma*, Florence

Dizionario biografico degli Italiani (1960–). Rome

Dodds, E. R. (1968). *The Greeks and the Irrational*, Berkeley

Donazzolo, P. (1912). 'Francesco Patrizio di Cherso erudito del secolo XVI', *Atti e memorie della Società Istriana di archeologia e storia patria*, 28: 1–147

Donovan, R. B. (1967). 'Salutati's opinion of non-Italian Latin writers of the Middle Ages', *Studies in the Renaissance*, 14: 185–201

Doren, A. (1922–3). 'Fortuna im Mittelalter und in der Renaissance', *Vorträge der Bibliothek Warburg*, 2, 1: 71–144

Dorez, L. and Thuasne, L. (1897). *Pic de la Mirandole en France*, Paris

Douglas, M. (1975). *Purity and Danger*, Harmondsworth, Middlesex

Drake, S. (1970). *Galileo Studies*, Ann Arbor
  (1973). 'Galileo's experimental confirmation of horizontal inertia: unpublished manuscripts', *Isis*, 64: 291–305
  (1976). *Galileo Against the Philosophers*, Los Angeles
  (1978). *Galileo at Work*, Chicago

Drake, S. and MacLachlan, J. (1975). 'Galileo's discovery of the parabolic trajectory', *Scientific American*, 232: 102–10
Dreitzel, H. (1970). *Protestantischer Aristotelismus und absoluter Staat: Die 'Politica' des Henning Arnisaeus (ca. 1575–1636)*, Wiesbaden
Dreyer, J. L. E. (1906). *History of the Planetary Systems from Thales to Kepler*, Cambridge (repr. New York, 1953)
Dubois, C. G. (1977). *La Conception de l'histoire en France au XVIᵉ siècle (1560–1610)*, Paris
Duhem, P. (1906–13). *Études sur Léonard de Vinci*, 3 vols., Paris
    (1908). *ΣΩZEIN TA ΦAINOMENA*, Paris (repr. Paris, 1982; Eng. trans. Chicago, 1969)
    (1909–11). 'La Tradition de Buridan et la science italienne au XVIᵉ siècle', *Bulletin italien*, 9: 338–60; 10: 24–47, 95–133, 202–31; 11: 1–32
    (1913–59). *Le Système du monde*, 10 vols., Paris
Dunbabin, J. (1972). 'Robert Grosseteste as translator, transmitter and commentator: the *Nicomachean Ethics*', *Traditio*, 28: 460–72
Durkan, J. and Kirk, J. (1977). *The University of Glasgow 1451–1577*, Glasgow
Durling, R. (1961). 'A chronological census of Renaissance editions and translations of Galen', *Journal of the Warburg and Courtauld Institutes*, 24: 230–305
Dyck, J. (1969). *Ticht-Kunst: Deutsche Barockrhetorik und rhetorische Tradition*, Bad Homburg

Ebel, J. G. (1969). 'Translation and cultural nationalism in the reign of Elizabeth', *Journal of the History of Ideas*, 30: 593–602
Ebert, H. (1929–30). 'Augustinus Steuchus und seine *Philosophia perennis*: Ein kritischer Beitrag zur Geschichte der Philosophie', *Philosophisches Jahrbuch*, 42: 342–56, 510–26; 43: 92–100
Echarri, J. (1950). 'Un influjo español desconocido en la formación del sistema cartesiano: dos textos paralelos de Toledo y Descartes sobre el espacio', *Pensamiento*, 6: 291–323
Eckermann, W. (1978). 'Die Aristoteleskritik Luthers: Ihre Bedeutung für seine Theologie', *Catholica*, 32: 114–30
Edwards, C. (1981). *Hugo Grotius: The Miracle of Holland*, Chicago
Edwards, W. F. (1960). *The Logic of Jacopo Zabarella (1533–1589)*, Ph.D. thesis, Columbia Univ.
    (1967). 'Randall on the development of scientific method in the School of Padua: a continuing appraisal', in *Naturalism and Human Understanding*, ed. J. P. Anton, Buffalo, pp. 53–68
    (1969). 'Jacopo Zabarella: A Renaissance Aristotelian's view of rhetoric and poetry and their relation to philosophy', in *Arts libéraux et philosophie au moyen âge*, Montreal, pp. 843–54
Égasse du Boulay, C. (1670). *Historia Universitatis Parisiensis*, 6 vols., Paris
Egidio da Viterbo, O.S.A. e il suo tempo (1983). Rome
Ehrle, F. (1925). *Der Sentenzkommentar Peters von Candia*, Münster
Eisenhardt, U. (1970). *Die kaiserliche Aufsicht über Buchdruck, Buchhandel und Presse im Heiligen Römischen Reich Deutscher Nation (1496–1806)*, Karlsruhe
Eisenstein, Elizabeth L. (1979). *The Printing Press as an Agent of Change*, 2 vols., Cambridge
Elders, L. J. (1984). 'St Thomas Aquinas' commentary on the *Nicomachean Ethics*', in *The Ethics of Thomas Aquinas*, ed. L. J. Elders and K. Hedwig, Vatican City, pp. 9–49
Élie, H. (1937). *Le 'Complexe Significabile'*, Paris
    (1950–1). 'Quelques maîtres de l'université de Paris vers l'an 1500', *Archives d'histoire doctrinale et littéraire du moyen âge*, 18: 193–243
Ellinger, Georg (1929–33). *Geschichte der neulateinischen Literatur Deutschlands im 16. Jahrhundert*, 3 vols., Berlin–Leipzig (repr. Berlin, 1969)

Enciclopedia cattolica (1948–54). 12 vols., Vatican City

Enciclopedia filosofica (1968–9). 2nd edn, 6 vols., Florence

Encyclopedia Judaica (1971–2). 10 vols., Jerusalem

English Logic in Italy (1982). Ed. A. Maierù, Naples

Épicurisme au XVIᵉ siècle (1969). *Actes du VIIIᵉ congrès de l'Association Guillaume Budé*, Paris, pp. 639–727

Erasmus, H. J. (1962). *The Origins of Rome in Historiography from Petrarch to Perizonius*, Assen

Erbe, M. (1978). *François Baudouin (1520–1573)*, Gütersloh

Ercole, F. (1932). *Da Bartolo all'Althusio*, Florence

Erickson, K. V. (1975). *Aristotle's Rhetoric: Five Centuries of Philological Research*, Metuchen

Essays on Aristotle's Ethics (1980). Ed. A. O. Rorty, Berkeley

Essays on the Works of Erasmus (1978). Ed. R. DeMolen, New Haven–London

Essential Articles for the Study of Francis Bacon (1968). Ed. B. Vickers, London

Essential Articles for the Study of Thomas More (1977). Ed. R. S. Sylvester and G. P. Marc'hadour, Hamden

Ethik im Humanismus (1979). Ed. W. Rüegg and D. Wuttke, Boppard

Etter, E.-L. (1966). *Tacitus in der Geistesgeschichte des 16. und 17. Jahrhunderts*, Basle

Ettinghausen, H. (1972). *Francisco de Quevedo and the Neostoic Movement*, Oxford

Eucken, Rudolf (1879). *Geschichte der philosophischen Terminologie im Umriss*, Leipzig

Evans, G. R. (1976). 'Inopes verborum sunt Latini: technical language and technical terms in the writings of St Anselm and some commentators of the mid-twelfth century', *Archives d'histoire doctrinale et littéraire du moyen âge*, 43: 113–39

Evans, R. J. W. (1975). *The Wechel Presses: Humanism and Calvinism in Central Europe 1572–1627*, Oxford

Evans-Pritchard, E. E. (1965). *Theories of Primitive Religion*, Oxford

Fabroni, A. (1791–5). *Historia Academiae Pisanae*, 3 vols., Pisa (repr. Bologna, 1971)

Faider, P. (1922). *Juste Lipse*, Mons

Farge, J. K. (1980). *Biographical Register of Paris Doctors of Theology 1500–1536*, Toronto

Farrell, A. P. (1970). *The Jesuit 'Ratio studiorum' of 1599*, Washington, D.C.

Farrington, B. (1964). *The Philosophy of Francis Bacon*, Liverpool

Fasoli, G. (1958). 'Nascita di un mito', in *Studi storici in onore di Gioacchino Volpe*, I, Florence, pp. 445–79

Fata, F. J. (1966). *Landino on Dante*, Ph.D. thesis, Johns Hopkins Univ.

Fatio, O. (1971). *Nihil pulchrius ordine: Contribution à l'étude de l'établissement de la discipline ecclésiastique aux Pays-Bas ou Lambert Daneau aux Pays-Bas*, Leiden

(1976). *Méthode et théologie: Lambert Daneau et les débuts de la scolastique réformée*, Geneva

Favaro, A. (1883). *Galileo e lo studio di Padova*, Florence

(1894–1919). *Amici e corrispondenti di Galileo*, Venice (repr. Florence, 1983, ed. P. Galluzzi, 3 vols.)

Febvre, L. (1947). *Le Problème de l'incroyance au XVIᵉ siècle*, Paris

Febvre, L., Martin, H.-J., et al. (1971). *L'Apparition du livre*, 2nd. rev. edn, Paris (Engl. trans. London, 1976)

Federici Vescovini, G. (1979). *Astrologia e scienza: La crisi dell'aristotelismo sul cadere del Trecento e Biagio Pelacani da Parma*, Florence

(1983). *'Arti' e filosofia nel secolo XIV*, Florence

Félice, P. de (1882). *Lambert Daneau, pasteur et professeur en théologie, 1530–1595*, Paris

Femiano, S. (1968). *La metafisica di Tommaso Campanella*, Milan

Ferguson, A. B. (1960). *The Indian Summer of English Chivalry*, Durham, N.C.

(1979). *Clio Unbound: Perception of the Social and Cultural Past in Renaissance England*, Durham, N.C.

Ferguson, W. K. (1948). *The Renaissance in Historical Thought*, Boston

Fernandez-Santamaria, J. A. (1977). *The State, War and Peace: Spanish Political Thought in the Renaissance*, Cambridge

Ferraro, R. M. (1971). *Giudizi critici e criteri estetici nei Poetices libri VII (1561) de Giulio Cesare Scaligero*, Chapel Hill

Ferreira Gomes, J. (1966). 'Pedro da Fonseca, sixteenth-century Portuguese philosopher', *International Philosophical Quarterly*, 6: 632–44

Ferri, L. (1876). 'Intorno alle dottrine psicologiche di Pietro Pomponazzi', *Atti della R. Accademia dei Lincei*, ser. ii, 3: 333–548

Festugière, A.-J. (1941). *La Philosophie de l'amour de Marsile Ficin et son influence sur la littérature française au XVIe siècle*, 2nd edn, Paris

   (1944–54). *La Revélation d'Hermes Trismegiste*, 4 vols., Paris

   (1967). *Hermétisme et mystique païenne*, Paris

Field, A. (1980). *The Beginning of the Philosophical Renaissance in Florence, 1454–1469*, Ph.D. thesis, Univ. of Michigan, Ann Arbor

Fierz, M. (1977). *Girolamo Cardano*, Basle–Stuttgart

Filosofia e cultura in Umbria tra medioevo e Rinascimento (1967). Ed. F. Ugolini, Gubbio

Fink, Z. (1962). *The Classical Republicans*, Evanston

Fink-Errera, G. (1957). 'Jean Destrez et son oeuvre: la pecia dans les manuscrits du XIIIe et XIVe siècle', *Scriptorium*, 1: 264–80

   (1962). 'Une institution du monde médiéval "la pecia" ', *Revue philosophique de Louvain*, 60: 184–243

Finzi, C. (1984). *Matteo Palmieri: Dalla 'vita civile' alla 'città di vita'*, Perugia

Fioravanti, G. (1981). *Università e città: cultura umanistica e cultura scolastica a Siena nel '400*, Florence

   (1983). 'L'apologetica anti-giudaica di Giannozzo Manetti', *Rinascimento*, ser. ii, 23: 3–32

Fiorentino, F. (1868). *Pietro Pomponazzi: studi storici su la scuola bolognese e padovana del secolo XVI*, Florence

   (1872–4). *Bernardino Telesio ossia studi storici su l'idea di natura nel Risorgimento italiano*, 2 vols., Florence

   (1911). *Studi e ritratti della Rinascenza*, Bari

Firpo, L. (1940). *Bibliografia degli scritti di Tommaso Campanella*, Turin

   (1947). *Ricerche campanelliane*, Florence

   (1949). *Il processo di Giordano Bruno*, Naples

   (1950–1). 'Filosofia italiana e Controriforma', *Rivista di filosofia*, 41: 150–73, 390–401; 42: 30–47

   (1967). *Francesco Filelfo educatore e il 'Codice Sforza' della Biblioteca Reale di Torino*, Turin

Flahiff, J. B. (1942). 'Ecclesiastical censorship of books in the twelfth century', *Mediaeval Studies*, 4: 1–22

Flasch, K. (1973). *Die Metaphysik des Einen bei Nikolaus von Kues*, Leiden

Fletcher, J. M. (1981). 'Change and resistance to change: a consideration of the development of English and German universities during the sixteenth century', *History of Universities*, 1: 1–36

Flint, R. (1894). *History of the Philosophy of History*, New York

Flodr, M. (1973). *Incunabula classicorum*, Amsterdam

Flores, E. (1980). *Le scoperte di Poggio e il testo di Lucrezio*, Naples

Fois, M. (1969). *Il pensiero cristiano di Lorenzo Valla nel quadro storico-culturale del suo ambiente*, Rome

Fontanesi, G. (1934). *Il problema filosofico dell'amore nell'opera di Leone Ebreo*, 2nd edn, Venice

Foster, K. (1984). *Petrarch: Poet and Humanist*, Edinburgh

Foucault, M. (1966). *Les Mots et les choses*, Paris

Fox, A. (1982). *Thomas More: History and Providence*, Oxford

Fox, M. (1983). 'The moral philosophy of MaHaRaL', in *Jewish Thought in the Sixteenth Century*, ed. B. D. Cooperman, Cambridge, Mass., pp. 167–85

Fraenkel, P. (1961). *Testimonia patrum*, Geneva

Fraile, G. (1966). *Historia de la filosofía*, III: *Del humanismo a la Ilustración (siglos XV–XVIII)*, Madrid

Frame, D. M. (1965). *Montaigne: A Biography*, New York–London

Francesco Filelfo nel quinto centenario della morte (1986). *Atti del XVII convegno di studi maceratesi*, Padua

Francesco Guicciardini 1483–1983. Nel V centenario della morte (1984). Florence

Francis Bacon: science et méthode (1985). Ed. M. Malherbe and J.-M. Pousseur, Paris

Francis Bacon: terminologia e fortuna nel XVII secolo (1984). Ed. M. Fattori, Rome

Francisco Sanches no IV centenario de seu nascimento (1951). *Revista portuguesa de filosofia*, 7: 113–240

François, G. (1965). 'Un cours d'explication de Sénèque au XVᵉ siècle', *Scriptorium*, 19: 244–68

Franklin, J. H. (1963). *Jean Bodin and the Sixteenth-Century Revolution in the Methodology of Law and History*, New York

(1973). *Jean Bodin and the Rise of Absolutist Theory*, Cambridge

Fraser Jenkins, A. D. (1970). 'Cosimo de' Medici's patronage of architecture and the theory of magnificence', *Journal of the Warburg and Courtauld Institutes*, 33: 162–70

Freedman, J. S. (1984). *Deutsche Schulphilosophie im Reformationszeitalter (1500–1650)*, Münster

French, R. K. (1985). 'Gentile da Foligno and the *via medicorum*', in *The Light of Nature: Essays in Honour of A. C. Crombie*, ed. J. D. North and J. Roche, The Hague, pp. 21–34

Frenz, T. (1973–4). 'Das Eindringen humanistischer Schriftformen in die Urkunden und Akten der päpstlichen Kurie im 15. Jahrhundert', *Archiv für Diplomatik*, 19: 287–418; 20: 384–506

Freudenberger, T. (1935). *Augustinus Steuchus aus Gubbio*, Münster

Freudenthal, J. (1890–1). 'Beiträge zur Geschichte der englischen Philosophie', *Archiv für Geschichte der Philosophie*, 4: 450–603; 5: 1–41

Friedrich, H. (1967). *Montaigne*, 2nd edn, Bern

Die Frühzeit des Humanismus und der Renaissance in Deutschland (1964). Ed. H. Rupprich, Darmstadt

Fubini, R. (1966). 'Tra umanesimo e concili: Note e giunte a una pubblicazione recente su Francesco Pizolpasso (1370 c.–1443)', *Studi medievali*, ser. iii, 7: 323–70

(1975). 'Note su Valla e la composizione del *De voluptate*', in *I classici nel medioevo e nell'umanesimo*, Genoa, pp. 11–57

Fueter, E. (1936). *Geschichte der neueren Historiographie*, Berlin

Fumaroli, M. (1980). *L'Age de l'éloquence*, Paris

Funkenstein, A. (1986). *Theology and the Scientific Revolution from the Middle Ages to the 17ᵗʰ Century*, Princeton

Fussner, F. S. (1962). *The Historical Revolution*, New York

Gabotto, F. (1889). 'L'epicureismo di Lorenzo Valla', *Rivista di filosofia scientifica*, ser. ii, 8: 651–72

Gabrieli, G. (1927). 'Giovanbattista Della Porta linceo', *Giornale critico di filosofia italiana*, 8: 360–97, 423–31

(1932). 'Giovanbattista Della Porta: Notizie bibliografiche dei suoi manoscritti e libri', *Accademia dei Lincei. Rendiconti. Cl. di scienze morali, storiche e filologiche*, ser. vi, 8: 206–77

Gadol, J. (1969). *Leon Battista Alberti: Universal Man of the Early Renaissance*, Chicago

Gaeta, F. (1955). *Lorenzo Valla*, Naples
Gaetano, A. L. de (1967). 'G. B. Gelli and the rebellion against Latin', *Studies in the Renaissance*, 14: 131–58
Galileo Man of Science (1967). Ed. E. McMullin, New York
Gallego Salvadores, J. (1972). 'La enseñanza de la metafísica en la Universidad de Valencia durante el siglo XVI', *Analecta Sacra Tarraconensia*, 45: 137–72
Galletti, A. (1904–38). *L'eloquenza dalle origini al XVI secolo*, Milan
Galluzzi, P. (1973). 'Il "platonismo" del tardo Cinquecento e la filosofia di Galileo', in *Ricerche sulla cultura dell'Italia moderna*, ed. P. Zambelli, Bari, pp. 39–79
    (1979). *Momento: studi galileiani*, Rome
Gandillac, M. de (1942). *La Philosophie de Nicolas de Cues*, Paris
    (1974). 'Les Secrets d'Agrippa', in *Aspects du libertinisme au XVIe siècle*, Paris, pp. 123–36
    (1982). 'Neoplatonism and Christian thought in the fifteenth century (Nicholas of Cusa and Marsilio Ficino)', in *Neoplatonism and Christian Thought*, ed. D. J. O'Meara, Norfolk, Va., pp. 143–68
Gansiniec, R. (1960). *Metrificale Marka z Opatowca i traktaty gramatyczne XIV i XV wieku*, Wrocław
García Lescún, E. (1970). *La teología trinitaria de Gregorio de Rimini*, Burgos
García Villoslada, R. (1935). 'Pedro Crockaert O. P., maestro de Francisco de Vitoria', *Estudios eclesiásticos*, 19: 174–201
    (1938). *La universidad de Paris durante los estudios de Francisco de Vitoria O. P. (1507–1522)*, Rome
    (1954). *Storia del Collegio Romano*, Rome
Gardenal, G. (1975). *Il Poliziano e Svetonio*, Florence
Garin, E. (1937a). *Giovanni Pico della Mirandola: Vita e dottrina*, Florence
    (1937b). '*'Ενδελέχεια* e *'εντελέχεια* nelle discussioni umanistiche', *Atene e Roma*, ser. iii, 5: 177–87
    (1938). 'La "dignitas hominis" e la letteratura patristica', *Rinascita*, 1: 102–46
    (1943–6). 'I trattati morali di Coluccio Salutati', *Atti dell'Accademia fiorentina di scienze morali 'La Colombaria'*, n.s., 1: 53–88
    (1950a). 'La giovinezza di Donato Acciaiuoli', *Rinascimento*, 1: 43–70
    (1950b). 'Magia ed astrologia nella cultura del Rinascimento', *Belfagor*, 5: 657–67
    (1951). 'Le traduzioni umanistiche di Aristotele nel secolo XV', *Atti dell'Accademia fiorentina di scienze morali 'La Colombaria'*, 16: 55–104
    (1954). *Medioevo e Rinascimento*, Bari
    (1957). *L'educazione in Europa*, Bari
    (1958a). *Studi sul platonismo medievale*, Florence
    (1958b). *L'umanesimo italiano*, 2nd edn, Bari
    (1959). 'Ricerche sull'epicureismo del Quattrocento', in *Epicurea in memoriam Hectoris Bignone*, Genoa, pp. 217–37
    (1961). *La cultura filosofica del Rinascimento italiano*, Florence
    (1965). *Scienza e vita civile nel Rinascimento italiano*, Bari
    (1966). *Storia della filosofia italiana*, new edn, 3 vols., Turin
    (1967). *Ritratti di umanisti*, Florence
    (1969). *L'età nuova*, Naples
    (1970). *Dal Rinascimento all'Illuminismo*, Pisa
    (1974). 'Ritratto di Leonardo Bruni Aretino', *Atti e memorie della Accademia Petrarca di lettere, arti e scienze di Arezzo*, 40: 1–17
    (1975). *Rinascite e rivoluzioni*, Bari
    (1976a). 'Postille sull'ermetismo nel Rinascimento', *Rinascimento*, ser. ii, 16: 245–9
    (1976b). 'Divagazioni ermetiche', *Rivista critica di storia della filosofia*, 31: 462–6
    (1976c). *Lo zodiaco della vita*, Bari (English trans. London, 1983)

(1977). 'Ancora sull'ermetismo', *Rivista critica di storia della filosofia*, 32: 342–7

(1983). *Il ritorno dei filosofi antichi*, Naples

Garofalo, S. (1946). 'Gli umanisti italiani del secolo XV e la Bibbia', *Biblica*, 37: 338–75

Gasperetti, L. (1941). 'Il *De fato, fortuna et casu* di Coluccio Salutati', *Rinascita*, 4: 555–82

Gass, W. (1844). *Gennadius und Pletho: Aristotelismus und Platonismus in der griechischen Kirche*, Breslau

Gatti, D. (1972–3). '*Vita Caroli* di Donato Acciaiuoli', *Bullettino dell'Istituto storico italiano per il medioevo e archivio muratoriano*, 84: 223–74

Gauthier, P. (1980). 'Le *De daemonibus* du Ps. Psellus', *Revue des études byzantines*, 38: 105–94

Gauthier, R. A. (1951). *Magnanimité: L'Idéal de la grandeur dans la philosophie païenne et dans la théologie chrétienne*, Paris

Geanakoplos, D. J. (1962). *Greek Scholars in Venice*, Cambridge, Mass.

(1966). *Byzantine East and Latin West*, Oxford

(1974a). 'The Italian Renaissance and Byzantium: the career of the Greek humanist professor John Argyropoulos in Florence and Rome (1415–1487)', *Conspectus of History*, 1: 12–28

(1974b). 'The discourse of Demetrius Chalcondyles on the inauguration of Greek studies at the University of Padua in 1463', *Studies in the Renaissance*, 21: 118–44

(1976). *Interaction of the 'Sibling' Byzantine and Western Cultures in the Middle Ages and Italian Renaissance (330–1600)*, New Haven

(1982). 'A Byzantine Scholar from Thessalonike, Theodoros Gazes, in the Italian Renaissance', in ʽ*Η Θεσσαλονίκη μεταξὺ ʼΑνατολῆς καὶ Δύσεως*, Thessalonika, pp. 43–58

Geldner, F. (1978). *Inkunabelkunde: Eine Einführung in die Welt des frühesten Buchdrucks*, Wiesbaden

Gentile, G. (1911). *Bernardino Telesio*, Bari

(1925). *Giordano Bruno e il pensiero del Rinascimento*, 2nd edn, Florence

(1940). *Il pensiero italiano del Rinascimento*, Florence

(1968). *Studi su Rinascimento*, 3rd edn, Florence

Gentili, E. (1966). *Bibliografia galileiana fra i due centenari (1942–1964)*, Varese

Gerber, W. (1967). 'Philosophical dictionaries and encyclopedias', in *The Encyclopedia of Philosophy*, ed. P. Edwards, v, New York, pp. 170–99

Gercke, A. (1903). 'Theodoros Gazes', in *Festschrift der Universität Greifswald*, Greifswald

Gerl, H. B. (1974). *Rhetorik als Philosophie: Lorenzo Valla*, Munich

(1981). *Philosophie und Philologie: Leonardo Brunis Übertragung der Nikomachischen Ethik in ihren philosophischen Prämissen*, Munich

(1982a). 'Abstraktion und Gemeinsinn: Zur Frage des Paradigmenwechsels von der Scholastik zum Humanismus in der Argumentationstheorie Lorenzo Vallas', *Tijdschrift voor filosofie*, 44: 677–706

(1982b). 'Humanistische und geometrische Sprachphilosophie: Ein Paradigmenwechsel von Leonardo Bruni zu Francesco Patrizi', *Zeitschrift für philosophische Forschung*, 36: 189–207

Gerosa, P. P. (1927). *L'umanesimo agostiniano del Petrarca*, Turin

Gerulaitis, L. V. (1976). *Printing and Publishing in Fifteenth-Century Venice*, Chicago

Getino, L. G. A. (1930). *El maestro Francisco de Vitoria: su vida, su doctrina e influencia*, Madrid

Gherardini, B. (1982). *La spiritualità protestante*, Rome

Ghisalberti, A. (1975). *Giovanni Buridano: Dalla metafisica alla fisica*, Milan

Ghisalberti, F. (1933). 'Giovanni del Virgilio espositore delle *Metamorfosi*', *Giornale Dantesco*, 34: 1–110

Giacobbe, G. C. (1972a). 'Il *Commentarium de certitudine mathematicarum disciplinarum* di Alessandro Piccolomini', *Physis*, 14: 162–93

(1972b). 'Francesco Barozzi e la *Quaestio de certitudine mathematicarum*', *Physis*, 14: 357–74

(1973). 'La riflessione metamatematica di Pietro Catena', *Physis*, 15: 178–96

(1976). 'Epigoni nel Seicento della *Quaestio de certitudine mathematicarum*: Giuseppe Biancani', *Physis*, 18: 5–40

(1977). 'Un gesuita progressista nella *Quaestio de certitudine mathematicarum* rinascimentale: Benito Pereyra', *Physis*, 19: 51–86

(1981). *Alle radici della rivoluzione scientifica rinascimentale: le opere di Pietro Catena sui rapporti tra matematica e logica*, Pisa

Giacon, C. (1944–50). *La Seconda Scolastica*, 3 vols., Milan

Giannantonio, P. (1972). *Lorenzo Valla, filologo e storiografo dell'umanesimo*, Naples

Giard, L. (1985). 'La production logique de l'Angleterre au XVIe siècle', *Les Études philosophiques*, 3: 303–24

Gilbert, A. H. (1939). *Machiavelli's 'Prince' and its Forerunners*, Durham, N.C.

Gilbert, F. (1965). *Machiavelli and Guicciardini*, Princeton

(1967). 'The date of the composition of Contarini's and Gianotti's books on Venice', *Studies in the Renaissance*, 14: 172–84

(1977). *History: Choice and Commitment*, Cambridge, Mass.

Gilbert, N. W. (1960). *Renaissance Concepts of Method*, New York

(1963). 'Galileo and the School of Padua', *Journal of the History of Philosophy*, 1: 223–31

(1965). 'Francesco Vimercato of Milan: a bio-bibliography', *Studies in the Renaissance*, 12: 188–217

(1971). 'The early Italian humanists and disputation', in *Renaissance Studies in Honor of Hans Baron*, ed. A. Molho and J. Tedeschi, Florence, pp. 201–26

Gilly, C. (1977–9). 'Zwischen Erfahrung und Spekulation: Theodor Zwinger und die religiöse und kulturelle Krise seiner Zeit', *Basler Zeitschrift für Geschichte und Altertumskunde*, 77: 57–137; 79: 125–233

Gilmore, M. P. (1941). *Argument from Roman Law in Political Thought, 1200–1600*, Cambridge, Mass.

(1952). *The World of Humanism, 1453–1517*, New York

(1963). *Humanists and Jurists*, Cambridge, Mass.

Gilson, E. (1912). *Index scolastico-cartésien*, Paris

(1951). *Études sur le rôle de la pensée médiévale dans la formation du système cartésien*, Paris

(1952). *Jean Duns Scot: Introduction à ses positions fondamentales*, Paris

(1961). 'Autour de Pomponazzi: Problèmatique de l'immortalité de l'âme en Italie au début du XVIe siècle', *Archives d'histoire doctrinale et littéraire du moyen âge*, 28: 163–279

Giménez Fernández, M. (1962). *Tratado de Indias y el doctor Sepúlveda*, Caracas

Gingerich, O. (1973). 'A fresh look at Copernicus', in *The Great Ideas Today*, pp. 154–78

(1983). 'Ptolemy, Copernicus, and Kepler', in *The Great Ideas Today*, pp. 137–80

Giorgio Valla tra scienza e sapienza (1981). Florence

Giustiniani, V. R. (1985). 'Homo, humanus, and the meanings of humanism', *Journal of the History of Ideas*, 46: 167–95

Glaesener, H. (1938). 'Juste Lipse et Guillaume du Vair', *Revue belge de philologie et d'histoire*, 17: 27–42

Glorieux, P. (1965). 'L'Oeuvre littéraire de Pierre d'Ailly', *Mélanges de science religieuse*, 22: 61–78

Glucker, J. (1964). 'Casaubon's Aristotle', *Classica et mediaevalia*, 25: 274–96

Gmelin, H. (1932). 'Das Prinzip der *Imitatio* in den Romanischen Literaturen der Renaissance', *Romanische Forschungen*, 46: 83–360

Goez, W. (1958). *Translatio Imperii*, Tübingen

(1974). 'Die Anfänge der historischen Methode: Reflexion in der italienischen Renaissance und ihre Aufnahme in der Geschichtsschreibung der deutschen Humanismus', *Archiv für Kulturgeschichte*, 56: 25–48

Goldammer, K. (1953). *Paracelsus: Natur und Offenbarung*, Hanover
(1954). *Paracelsus-Studien*, Klagenfurt
(1971). 'Bemerkungen zur Struktur des Kosmos und der Materie bei Paracelsus', in *Medizingeschichte in unserer Zeit: Festgabe für Edith Heischkel Artelt und Walter Artelt*, Stuttgart, pp. 121–44
Goldbrunner, H. (1968). 'Durandus de Alvernia, Nicolaus von Oresme und Leonardo Bruni: Zu den Übersetzungen der pseudo-aristotelischen Ökonomik', *Archiv für Kulturgeschichte*, 50: 200–39
(1979). 'Poggios Dialog über die Habsucht: Bemerkungen zu einer neuen Untersuchung', *Quellen und Forschungen aus italienischen Archiven und Bibliotheken*, 59: 436–52
Goldschmidt, E. P. (1943). *Medieval Texts and their First Appearance in Print*, London
Gombrich, E. H. (1972). *Symbolic Images*, London
Gomes dos Santos, M. (1955). 'Francisco Titelmans O. F. M. e as origens do Curso Conimbricense', *Revista portuguesa de filosofia*, 11: 468–78
Gómez Hellín, L. (1940). 'Toledo, lector de filosofía y teología en el Colegio Romano', *Archivo teológico granadino*, 3: 7–18
González, R. C. (1946). *Francisco de Vitoria, estudio bibliografico*, Buenos Aires
González de la Calle, P. U. (1965). *Quevedo y los dos Sénecas*, Mexico
González de la Calle, U. (1903). *Sebastián Fox Morcillo: estudio histórico-crítico de sus doctrinas*, Madrid
Gordon, A. L. (1970). *Ronsard et la rhétorique*, Geneva
Gothein, P. (1932). *Francesco Barbaro. Früh-Humanismus und Staatskunst in Venedig*, Berlin
Grabmann, M. (1926–56). *Mittelalterliches Geistesleben: Abhandlungen zur Geschichte der Scholastik und Mystik*, 3 vols., Munich
(1939). *Methoden und Hilfsmittel des Aristotelesstudiums im Mittelalter*, Munich
Grafton, A. (1977). 'On the scholarship of Politian and its context', *Journal of the Warburg and Courtauld Institutes*, 40: 150–88
(1983). 'Protestant versus prophet: Isaac Casaubon on Hermes Trismegistus', *Journal of the Warburg and Courtauld Institutes*, 46: 78–93
(1983–). *Joseph Scaliger. A Study in the History of Classical Scholarship*, Oxford
(1985). 'Renaissance readers and ancient texts: comments on some commentators', *Renaissance Quarterly*, 38: 615–49
Grafton, A. and Jardine, L. (1982). 'Humanism and the school of Guarino: a problem of evaluation', *Past and Present*, 96: 51–80
(1986). *From Humanism to the Humanities*, London
Graiff, F. (1976). 'I prodigi e l'astrologia nei commenti di Pietro Pomponazzi al *De caelo*, alla *Meteora* e al *De generatione*', *Medioevo*, 2: 331–61
(1979). 'Aspetti del pensiero di Pietro Pomponazzi nelle opere e nei corsi del periodo bolognese', *Annali dell'Istituto di filosofia, Università di Firenze*, 1: 69–130
Grant, E. (1981a). *Much Ado About Nothing: Theories of Space and Vacuum from the Middle Ages to the Scientific Revolution*, Cambridge
(1981b). *Studies in Medieval Science and Natural Philosophy*, London
(1983). 'Celestial matter: a medieval and Galilean cosmological problem', *Journal of Medieval and Renaissance Studies*, 13: 157–86
(1984a). *In Defence of the Earth's Centrality and Immobility: Scholastic Reaction to Copernicanism in the Seventeenth Century*, Philadelphia
(1984b). 'Were there significant differences between medieval and early modern scholastic natural philosophy? The case for cosmology', *Noûs*, 18: 5–14
Grant, W. L. (1965). *Neo-Latin Literature and the Pastoral*, Chapel Hill
Grassi, E. (1980). *Rhetoric as Philosophy*, University Park, Pa.
Gravelle, S. S. (1972). 'Lorenzo Valla's comparison of Latin and Greek and the humanist background', *Bibliothèque d'humanisme et Renaissance*, 44: 269–89

Gray, H. H. (1956). *History and Rhetoric in Quattrocento Humanism*, Ph.D. thesis, Harvard Univ.
  (1963). 'Renaissance Humanism: the pursuit of eloquence', *Journal of the History of Ideas*, 24: 497–514
  (1965). 'Valla's *Encomium* of St Thomas Aquinas' and the humanist conception of Christian antiquity', in *Essays in History and Literature Presented to Stanley Pargellis*, ed. H. Bluhm, Chicago, pp. 37–51
Grayson, C. (1960). *A Renaissance Controversy: Latin or Italian?*, Oxford
Grazia, M. de (1980). 'The secularization of language in the seventeenth century', *Journal of the History of Ideas*, 41: 319–29
Greenfield, C. (1981). *Humanist and Scholastic Poetics*, Lewisburg, Pa.
Gregor von Rimini: Werk und Wirkung bis zur Reformation (1981). Ed. H. A. Oberman, Berlin–New York
Gregorian Reform of the Calendar (1983). Ed. G. V. Coyne *et al.*, Vatican City
Gregory, T. (1953). 'L'*Apologia ad censuram* di Francesco Patrizi', *Rinascimento*, 4: 89–104
  (1955). 'L'*Apologia* e le *Declarationes* di Francesco Patrizi', in *Medioevo e Rinascimento. Studi in onore di Bruno Nardi*, 1, Florence, pp. 385–424
  (1966). 'L'idea di natura nella filosofia medievale prima dell'ingresso della fisica aristotelica: secolo XII' in *La filosofia della natura nel Medioevo*, Milan, pp. 27–65
  (1967). 'La sagezza scettica di Pierre Charron', *De homine*, 21: 163–82
  (1979). *Theophrastus redivivus*, Naples
Grendler, M. T. (1980). 'A Greek collection in Padua: the library of Gian Vincenzo Pinelli (1535–1601)', *Renaissance Quarterly*, 33: 386–416
Grendler, M. T. and P. F. (1976). 'The survival of Erasmus in Italy', *Erasmus in English*, 8: 2–22
Grendler, P. F. (1969a). *Critics of the Italian World, 1530–1560*, Madison
  (1969b). 'Francesco Sansovino and Italian popular history, 1560–1600', *Studies in the Renaissance*, 16: 139–80
  (1977). *The Roman Inquisition and the Venetian Press, 1540–1605*, Princeton
  (1978). 'The destruction of Hebrew books in Venice, 1568', *Proceedings of the American Academy for Jewish Research*, 45: 103–30
  (1982). 'What Zuanne read in school: vernacular texts in sixteenth century Venetian schools', *Sixteenth Century Journal*, 13: 41–53
Griffante, C. (1983). *Il trattato 'De curru carrariensi' di Francesco de Caronellis* (Istituto veneto di scienze, lettere ed arti. Memorie. Classe di scienze morali, lettere ed arti, 39, 2), Venice
Grignaschi, M. (1960). 'Nicolas Oresme et son commentaire à la *Politique* d'Aristote', in *Album Helen Maud Cam*, Louvain–Paris, pp. 95–151
Groethuysen, B. (1931). 'Die kosmische Anthropologie des Bovillus', *Archiv für Geschichte der Philosophie*, 40: 66–89
Grouchy, E. H. de and Travers, E. (1878). *Étude sur Nicolas de Grouchy*, Paris–Caen
Grubmüller, K. (1967). *Vocabularius Ex quo: Untersuchungen zu lateinisch-deutschen Vokabularen des Spätmittelalters*, Munich
Guanti, G. (1979–80). 'Sapienza increata e bellezza nei *Dialoghi d'amore* di Leone Ebreo', *Annali della Facoltà di lettere e filosofia dell'Università di Perugia*, 16–17: 71–103
Guedet, G. (1969). 'État présent des recherches sur Guillaume Budé', *Actes du VIII congrès de l'Association Guillaume Budé*, Paris, pp. 597–628
Guicciardini (1984). *Annali d'Italianistica*, 2: 1–130
Gundersheimer, W. L. (1966). *The Life and Works of Louis Le Roy*, Geneva
Guzzo, A. (1960). *Giordano Bruno*, Turin

Hackett, M. B. (1970). *The Original Statutes of Cambridge University*, Cambridge
Hacking, I. (1975). *The Emergence of Probability*, Cambridge

Haitsma Mulier, E. (1980). *The Myth of Venice and Dutch Republican Thought in the Seventeenth Century*, trans. G. T. Moran, Assen
Halkin, L. E. (1969). *Érasme et l'humanisme chrétien*, Paris
Hall, A. R. (1948). 'Sir Isaac Newton's notebook, 1661–1665', *Cambridge Historical Journal*, 9: 239–50
Hall, R. A. (1942). *The Italian 'Questione della lingua'*, Chapel Hill
Hall, T. S. (1970). 'Descartes' physiological method: principles, positions, examples', *Journal of the History of Biology and Allied Sciences*, 3: 53–79
Hall, V. (1950). 'The life of Julius Caesar Scaliger (1484–1558)', *Transactions of the American Philosophical Society*, 40,2: 85–170
Halleux, R. (1979). *Les Textes alchimiques*, Turnhout
   (1981). 'Les Ouvrages alchimiques de Jean de Rupescissa', in *Histoire littéraire de la France*, XLI, Paris, pp. 241–77
Hamblin, C. L. (1970). *Fallacies*, London
Hamilton, B. (1963). *Political Thought in Sixteenth-Century Spain: A Study of the Political Ideas of Vitoria, De Soto, Suárez and Molina*, Oxford
Hamlyn, D. (1961). *Sensation and Perception*, London
Hammer, W. (1967–8). *Die Melanchthonforschung im Wandel der Jahrhunderte*, 2 vols., Heidelberg
Handschin, W. (1964). *Francesco Petrarca als Gestalt der Historiographie*, Basle
Hanke, L. (1959). *Aristotle and the American Indians*, Bloomington
   (1974). *All Mankind Is One: A Study of the Disputation Between Bartolomé de Las Casas and Juan Ginés de Sepúlveda on the Religious and Intellectual Capacity of the American Indians*, De Kalb, Illinois
Hankins, J. (1983). *Latin Translations of Plato in the Renaissance: A Study in the History of Platonic Scholarship*, Ph.D. thesis, Columbia Univ.
Hannaway, O. (1975). *The Chemists and the Word*, Baltimore
Hardison, O. B. (1962). *The Enduring Monument*, Chapel Hill
Harrison, F. R. (1963). 'The Cajetan tradition of analogy', *Franciscan Studies*, 23: 179–204
Hartfelder, K. (1889). *Philipp Melanchthon als Praeceptor Germaniae*, Berlin
   (1890). 'Der Kartäuserprior Gregor Reisch, Verfasser der Margarita philosophica', *Zeitschrift für Geschichte des Oberrheins*, N. F., 5: 170–200
Harth, H. (1968). 'Leonardo Brunis Selbstverständnis als Übersetzer', *Archiv für Kulturgeschichte*, 50: 41–63
Harvey, E. R. (1975). *The Inward Wits: Psychological Theory in the Middle Ages and Renaissance*, London
Hassinger, E. (1978). *Empirisch-rationaler Historismus*, Bern–Munich
Hathaway, B. (1962). *The Age of Criticism*, Ithaca
Hay, D. (1952). *Polydore Vergil*, Oxford
   (1959). 'Flavio Biondo and the Middle Ages', *Proceedings of the British Academy*, 45: 97–125
   (1961). *The Italian Renaissance in its Historical Background*, Cambridge
   (1977). *Annalists and Historians: Western Historiography from the Eighth to the Eighteenth Century*, London
Headley, J. M. (1963). *Luther's View of Church History*, New Haven
Health, Medicine and Mortality in the Sixteenth Century (1979). Ed. C. Webster, Cambridge
Heath, T. (1971). 'Logical grammar, grammatical logic and humanism in three German universities', *Studies in the Renaissance*, 18: 9–64
Heiberg, J. L. (1894). 'Bidrag til Georg Vallas biographi', *Festskrift til Vilhelm Thomsen*, Copenhagen, pp. 82–9
   (1896). *Beiträge zur Geschichte Georg Valla's und seiner Bibliothek*, Leipzig
Heitmann, K. (1958). *Fortuna und Virtus: Eine Studie zu Petrarcas Lebensweisheit*, Cologne–Graz

Helbing, M. O. (1976). 'Un capitolo del *De motu* di Francesco Buonamici e alcune informazioni sull'autore e sulle opere', *Physis*, 18: 41–63
  (1982). *Ricerche sul 'De motu' di Francesco Buonamici*, 2 vols., Tesi di perfezionamento, Scuola normale superiore, Pisa
Heller, A. (1978). *Renaissance Man*, London
Heninger, S. K. (1974). *Touches of Sweet Harmony*, San Marino
Henry, J. (1979). 'Francesco Patrizi da Cherso's concept of space and its later influence', *Annals of Science*, 36: 549–75
Herde, P. (1965). 'Politik und Rhetorik in Florence am Vorabend der Renaissance', *Archiv für Kulturgeschichte*, 47: 141–220
  (1971). 'Die Schrift der Florentiner Behörden der Frührenaissance', *Archiv für Diplomatik*, 17: 301–35
Herrick, M. T. (1946). *The Fusion of Horatian and Aristotelian Literary Criticism 1531–1555*, Urbana
Hertter, F. (1910). *Die Podestàlitteratur Italiens im 12. und 13. Jahrhundert*, Leipzig
Hewson, M. A. (1975). *Giles of Rome and the Medieval Theory of Conception*, London
Hexter, J. H. (1952). *More's Utopia: The Biography of an Idea*, Princeton
  (1973). *The Vision of Politics on the Eve of the Reformation: More, Machiavelli, and Seyssel*, New York
Higman, F. M. (1979). *Censorship and the Sorbonne: A Bibliographical Study of Books in French Censured by the Faculty of Theology of the University of Paris, 1520–1551*, Geneva
Hilgers, J. (1904). *Der Index der verbotenen Bücher*, Freiburg
Hillgarth, J. N. (1971). *Ramon Lull and Lullism in Fourteenth-Century France*, Oxford
Hintikka, J. and Remes, U. (1974). *The Method of Analysis*, Dordrecht
Hirsch, R. (1955). 'Pre-Reformation censorship of printed books', *Library Chronicle*, 21: 100–5
  (1973). 'Bulla super impressione librorum, 1515', *Gutenberg-Jahrbuch*, 48: 248–51
  (1974). *Printing, Selling and Reading, 1450–1550*, 2nd rev. edn, Wiesbaden
  (1978). *The Printed Word*, London
Hirzel, R. (1912). *Plutarch*, Leipzig
Höltgen, K. J. (1965). 'Synoptische Tabellen in der medizinischen Literatur und die Logik Agricolas und Ramus', *Sudhoffs Archiv*, 49: 371–90
Holmes, G. (1969). *The Florentine Enlightenment*, London
Holzberg, N. (1981). *Willibald Pirckheimer: Griechischer Humanismus in Deutschland*, Munich
Homann, F. A. (1983). 'Christopher Clavius and the Renaissance of Euclidean geometry', *Archivum Historicum Societatis Iesu*, 52: 233–46
Honecker, M. (1914). *Die Staatsphilosophie des Sebastian Fox Morcillo*, Bonn
Hooykaas, R. (1935). 'Die Elementenlehre des Paracelsus', *Janus*, 30: 175–87
  (1958). *Humanisme, science et reforme: Pierre de la Ramée (1515–1572)*, Leiden
Hopfner, T. (1974). *Griechisch-ägyptischer Offenbarungszauber*, Amsterdam
Hopkins, J. (1978). *A Concise Introduction to the Philosophy of Nicholas of Cusa*, Minneapolis
  (1983). *Nicholas of Cusa's Metaphysic of Contraction*, Minneapolis
Hoppe, B. (1976). *Biologie: Wissenschaft von der belebten Materie von der Antike zur Neuzeit*, Wiesbaden
Horowitz, M. C. (1971). 'Pierre Charron's view of the source of wisdom', *Journal of the History of Philosophy*, 9: 443–57
  (1974). 'Natural law as the foundation for an autonomous ethics: Pierre Charron's *De la sagesse*', *Studies in the Renaissance*, 21: 204–27
Howell, W. S. (1956). *Logic and Rhetoric in England, 1500–1700*, Princeton
Hubert, M. (1949). 'Quelques aspects du latin philosophique aux XIIe et XIIIe siècles', *Revue des études latines*, 27: 211–33

Hubien, H. (1975). 'John Buridan on the fourth figure of the syllogism', *Revue internationale de philosophie*, 113: 271–85

Hughes, P. E. (1984). *Lefèvre: Pioneer of Ecclesiastical Renewal in France*, Grand Rapids

Hugonard-Roche, H. (1973). *L'Oeuvre astronomique de Thémon Juif, maître parisien du XIV siècle*, Paris–Geneva

Hull, J. M. (1974). *Hellenistic Magic and the Synoptic Tradition*, Napierville, Ill.

Humanism in France (1970). Ed. A. Levi, Manchester

Humanismus und Naturwissenschaft (1980). Ed. R. Schmitz and F. Krafft, Boppard

Humanismus und Ökonomie (1983). Ed. H. Lutz, Weinheim

Humphrey, K. W. (1964). *The Book Provisions of the Friars, 1215–1400*, Amsterdam

Huppert, G. (1970). *The Idea of Perfect History*, Urbana

Huschke, R. B. (1968). *Melanchthons Lehre vom Ordo politicus*, Gütersloh

Hutchison, K. (1982). 'What happened to occult qualities in the scientific revolution?', *Isis*, 73: 233–53

Hutton, J. (1935). *The Greek Anthology in Italy to the Year 1800*, Ithaca
  (1946). *The Greek Anthology in France and in the Latin Writers of the Netherlands to the Year 1800*, Ithaca

Iannizzotto, M. (1959). *Saggio sulla filosofia di Coluccio Salutati*, Padua

IJsewijn, J. (1971). 'Alexander Hegius (†1498): *Invectiva in modos significandi*', *Forum for Modern Language Studies*, 7: 299–318
  (1977). *Companion to Neo-Latin Studies*, Amsterdam

Ingegno, A. (1978). *Cosmologia e filosofia nel pensiero di Giordano Bruno*, Florence
  (1980). *Saggio sulla filosofia di Cardano*, Florence
  (1985). *La sommersa nave della religione: Studio sulla polemica anticristiana del Bruno*, Naples

Internationales Kepler-Symposium (1973). Ed. F. Krafft et al., Hildesheim

Iriarte, J. (1935). *Kartesischer oder Sanchezischer Zweifel?*, Dissertation, Univ. of Bonn
  (1940). 'Francisco Sánchez el Escéptico disfrazado de Carneades en discusión epistolar con Cristóbal Clavio', *Gregorianum*, 21: 413–51

Iserloh, E. (1981). *Johannes Eck (1486–1543): Scholastiker, Humanist, Kontroverstheologe*, Münster

Italian Renaissance Studies (1960). Ed. E. F. Jacob, London

Itinerarium Italicum (1975). Ed. H. Oberman and T. A. Brady, Leiden

Iturrioz, J. (1949). *Estudios sobre la metafísica de Francisco Suárez*, Madrid

Iverson, E. (1961). *The Myth of Egypt and its Hieroglyphs in European Tradition*, Copenhagen

Jansen, B. (1936). 'Zur Philosophie der Skotisten des 17. Jahrhunderts', *Franziskanische Studien*, 23: 28–58, 150–75
  (1951). 'Die scholastische Psychologie vom 16. bis 18. Jahrhundert', *Scholastik*, 26: 342–63

Jardine, L. (1974a). *Francis Bacon: Discovery and the Art of Discourse*, Cambridge
  (1974b). 'The place of dialectic teaching in sixteenth-century Cambridge', *Studies in the Renaissance*, 21: 31–62
  (1975). 'Humanism and the sixteenth-century Cambridge arts course', *History of Education*, 4: 16–31
  (1977). 'Lorenzo Valla and the intellectual origins of humanist dialectic', *Journal of the History of Philosophy*, 15: 143–64
  (1981). 'Dialectic or dialectical rhetoric? Agostino Nifo's criticism of Lorenzo Valla', *Rivista critica di storia della filosofia*, 36: 253–70
  (1983). 'Lorenzo Valla: Academic skepticism and the new humanist dialectic', in *The Skeptical Tradition*, ed. M. F. Burnyeat, Berkeley, pp. 253–86

Jardine, N. (1976). 'Galileo's road to truth and the demonstrative regress', *Studies in the History and Philosophy of Science*, 7: 277–318

(1979). 'The forging of modern realism: Clavius and Kepler against the sceptics', *Studies in the History and Philosophy of Science*, 10: 141–73

(1982). 'The significance of the Copernican orbs', *Journal for the History of Astronomy*, 13: 168–94

(1984). *The Birth of History and Philosophy of Science*, Cambridge

(1987). 'Scepticism in Renaissance astronomy', in *Scepticism from the Renaissance to the Enlightenment*, ed. R. H. Popkin and C. B. Schmitt, Wolfenbüttel

Jean Bodin: Verhandlungen der internationalen Bodin Tagung in München (1973). Ed. H. Denzer, Munich

Jensen, K. (1985). *Julius Caesar Scaliger's Concept of Language: A Case Study in 16th Century Aristotelianism*, Ph.D thesis, European University Institute, Florence

Joachimsen, P. (1910). *Geschichtsauffassung und Geschichtsschreibung in Deutschland unter dem Einfluss des Humanismus*, Leipzig–Berlin

(1911). 'Tacitus im deutschen Humanismus', *Neue Jahrbücher für das klassische Altertum*, 27: 697–717

Johannes Kepler–Werk und Leistung (1971). Linz

Jones, R. F. (1953). *The Triumph of the English Language*, Stanford

Jones, R. M. (1959). *Spiritual Reformers in the 16th and 17th Centuries*, Boston

Joukovsky, F. (1981). 'Thèmes plotiniens dans le *De sapiente* de Charles Bovelles', *Bibliothèque d'humanisme et Renaissance*, 43: 141–53

Juan Luis Vives (1981). Ed. A. Buck, Wolfenbüttel

Julien Eymard d'Angers (1976). *Recherches sur le stoicisme aux XVIᵉ et XVIIᵉ siècles*, ed. L. Antoine, Hildesheim–New York

Junghans, H. (1985). *Der junge Luther und die Humanisten*, Göttingen

Jungkuntz, R. P. (1962). 'Christian approval of Epicureanism', *Church History*, 31: 279–93

Kallendorf, C. (1983). 'Cristoforo Landino's *Aeneid* and the humanist critical tradition', *Renaissance Quarterly*, 36: 519–46

Kaltenbrunner, F. von (1876). *Die Vorgeschichte der Gregorianischen Kalenderreform*, Vienna

Kałuża, J. (1970). Materiały do katalogu dzieł Heimeryka de Campo', *Studia mediewistyczne*, 12: 3–28

Kalwies, H. (1978). 'The first verse translation of the *Iliad* in Renaissance France', *Bibliothèque d'humanisme et Renaissance*, 40: 597–607

Kapp, F. (1886). *Geschichte des deutschen Buchhandels*, I, Leipzig

Karcher, J. (1956). *Theodor Zwinger und seine Zeitgenossen*, Basle

Kassel, R. (1962). 'Unbeachtete Renaissance-Emendationen zur aristotelischen Poetik', *Rheinisches Museum*, 105: 111–21

Kater, T. (1908). *Johann Ludwig Vives und seine Stellung zu Aristoteles*, Erlangen

Keller, A. (1972). 'Mathematical technology and the growth of the idea of technical progress in the sixteenth century', in *Science, Medicine and Society in the Renaissance*, ed. A. G. Debus, I, London, pp. 11–27

Keller, A. C. (1957). 'Montaigne on the dignity of man', *PMLA*, 72: 43–54

Kelley, D. R. (1967). 'Guillaume Budé and the first historical school of law', *American Historical Review*, 72: 807–34

(1970a). *The Foundations of Modern Historical Scholarship: Language, Law and History in the French Renaissance*, New York

(1970b). 'Philology and the mirror of history', *Journal of Interdisciplinary History*, 1: 125–36

(1971). 'History as a calling: the case of La Popelinière', in *Renaissance Studies in Honor of Hans Baron*, ed. A. Molho and J. Tedeschi, Florence, pp. 771–89

(1975). 'Faces in Clio's mirror: mistress, muse, missionary', *Journal of Modern History*, 47: 679–90

(1980). 'Johann Sleidan and the origin of the profession of history', *Journal of Modern History*, 52: 573–98

Kelly, D. (1966). 'The scope of the treatment of composition in the twelfth- and thirteenth-century arts of poetry', *Speculum*, 41: 261–78

Kennedy, G. A. (1980). *Classical Rhetoric and its Christian and Secular Tradition from Ancient to Modern Times*, Chapel Hill

Kennedy, L. A. (1966). 'Sylvester of Ferrara and the agent sense', *Modern Schoolman*, 40: 464–77

(1979). 'The philosophical manuscripts of Cesare Cremonini', *Manuscripta*, 23: 79–87

(1980). 'Cesare Cremonini and the immortality of the human soul', *Vivarium*, 18: 143–58

Kenney, E. J. (1974). *The Classical Text*, Berkeley–Los Angeles–London

Kepler Festschrift 1971 (1971). Ed. E. Preuss, Regensburg

Kepler: Four Hundred Years (1975). Ed. A. and P. Beer (Vistas in Astronomy, 18), Oxford

Kessler, E. (1968). *Das Problem des frühen Humanismus: Seine philosophische Bedeutung bei Coluccio Salutati*, Munich

(1978). *Petrarca und die Geschichte*, Munich

(1979). 'Humanismus und Naturwissenschaft bei Rudolf Agricola', in *L'Humanisme allemand (1480–1540). 18ᵉ Colloque international de Tours*, Munich–Paris, pp. 141–57

(1980). 'Freiheit des Willens in Vallas *De libero arbitrio*', in *Acta Conventus Neolatini Turonensis*, ed. J.-C. Margolin, Paris, pp. 637–47

Keuck, K. (1934). *Historia: Geschichte des Wortes*, Emsdetten

Kibre, P. (1936). *The Library of Pico della Mirandola*, New York

(1968). 'Giovanni Garzoni of Bologna (1419–1505), professor of medicine and defender of astrology', *Isis*, 58: 504–15

(1978). 'Arts and medicine in the universities of the later Middle Ages', in *Les Universités à la fin du moyen âge*, ed. J. IJsewijn and J. Paquet, Louvain, pp. 213–27

Kieszkowski, B. (1936). *Studi sul platonismo del Rinascimento in Italia*, Florence

King, M. L. (1976). 'Caldiera and the Barbaros on marriage and the family: humanist reflections of Venetian realities', *Journal of Medieval and Renaissance Studies*, 6: 19–50

King, P. (1974). *The Ideology of Order: A Comparative Analysis of Jean Bodin and Thomas Hobbes*, London

Kingdon, R. M. (1964). 'Patronage, piety, and printing in sixteenth-century Europe', in *A Festschrift for Frederick B. Artz*, ed. D. H. Pinkney and T. Ropp, Durham, N.C., pp. 19–36

Kinney, D. R. (1981). 'More's *Letter to Dorp*: remapping the trivium', *Renaissance Quarterly*, 34: 179–210

Kinser, S. (1971). 'Ideas of temporal change and cultural process in France, 1470–1535', in *Renaissance Essays in Honor of Hans Baron*, ed. A. Molho and J. Tedeschi, Florence, pp. 703–55

Kisch, G. (1955). *Humanismus und Jurisprudenz*, Berlin

(1960). *Erasmus und die Jurisprudenz seiner Zeit*, Basle

(1972). *Studien zur humanistischen Jurisprudenz*, Berlin

Klatt, D. (1908). *David Chytraeus als Geschichtslehrer und Geschichtsschreiber*, Rostock

Klein, R. (1970). *La Forme et l'intelligible*, Paris

Klempt, A. (1960). *Die Säkularisierung der universalhistorischen Auffassung*, Göttingen

Klibansky, R. (1981). *The Continuity of the Platonic Tradition during the Middle Ages. Plato's Parmenides in the Middle Ages and the Renaissance*, Munich

Klibansky, R., Panofsky, E. and Saxl, F. (1964). *Saturn and Melancholy*, London

Klippel, M. (1936). *Die Darstellung der fränkischen Trojanersage in Geschichtsschreibung und Dichtung vom Mittelalter bis zur Renaissance in Frankreich*, Marburg

Kloepfer, R. (1967). *Die Theorie der literarischen Übersetzung*, Munich

Klubertanz, G. (1952). *The Discursive Power*, St Louis

Knape, J. (1984). *'Historie' im Mittelalter und früher Neuzeit. Begriffs- und gattungsgeschichtliche Untersuchungen im interdisziplinären Kontext*, Baden-Baden

Kneale, W. and M. (1962). *The Development of Logic*, Oxford

Knös, B. (1950). 'Gémiste Pléthon et son souvenir', *Lettres d'humanité*, 9: 97–184

Knowlson, J. (1975). *Universal Language Schemes in England and France, 1600–1800*, Toronto–Buffalo

Koch, J. (1927). *Durandus de S. Porciano O. P.*, Münster

Koelmel, W. (1981). *Aspekte des Humanismus*, Münster

Kogel, R. (1972). *Pierre Charron*, Geneva

Kohl, B. (1974). 'Petrarch's prefaces to De viris illustribus', *History and Theory*, 13: 132–44

Kohls, E. W. (1966). *Die Theologie des Erasmus*, 2 vols., Basle

Der Kommentar in der Renaissance (1975). Ed. A. Buck and O. Herding, Boppard

Korkowski, E. (1976). 'Agrippa as ironist', *Neophilologus*, 60: 594–607

Korshin, P. J. (1974). 'Johnson and the Renaissance dictionary', *Journal of the History of Ideas*, 35: 300–12

Kosman, L. A. (1964). *The Aristotelian Background of Bacon's Novum Organum*, Ph.D. thesis, Harvard Univ.

Koster, M. D. (1960). 'Zur Metaphysik Cajetans', *Scholastik*, 35: 537–51

Koyré, A. (1957). *From the Closed World to the Infinite Universe*, Baltimore

(1961). *La Révolution astronomique*, Paris (Eng. trans., London, 1973)

(1966). *Études galiléennes*, 2nd edn, Paris

(1971). *Mystiques, spirituels, alchimistes du XVIe siècle allemand*, Paris

Kraus, M. J. (1971). 'Patronage and reform in the France of the Préréforme: the case of Clichtove', *Canadian Journal of History*, 6: 45–68

Krautter, K. (1971). *Philologische Methode und humanistische Existenz*, Munich

Kraye, J. (1979). 'Francesco Filelfo's lost letter De ideis', *Journal of the Warburg and Courtauld Institutes*, 42: 236–49

(1981). 'Francesco Filelfo on emotions, virtues and vices: A re-examination of his sources', *Bibliothèque d'humanisme et Renaissance*, 43: 129–40

(1983). 'Cicero, Stoicism and textual criticism: Poliziano on κατόρθωμα', *Rinascimento*, ser. ii, 23: 79–110

(1986). 'The pseudo-Aristotelian *Theology* in sixteenth- and seventeenth-century Europe', in *Pseudo-Aristotle in the Middle Ages*, ed. J. Kraye et al., London, pp. 265–86

Kreatur und Kosmos: Internationale Beiträge zur Paracelsusforschung (1981). Ed. R. Dilg-Frank, Stuttgart–New York

Kristeller, P. O. (1953a). *Il pensiero filosofico di Marsilio Ficino*, Florence

(1953b). *Die italienischen Universitäten der Renaissance*, Krefeld

(1955). 'Two unpublished questions on the soul of Pietro Pomponazzi', *Medievalia et Humanistica*, 9: 76–101

(1956a). *Studies in Renaissance Thought and Letters*, Rome

(1956b). 'The University of Bologna and the Renaissance', *Studi e memorie per la storia dell'Università di Bologna*, n.s., 1: 313–23

(1960). 'Lodovico Lazzarelli e Giovanni da Correggio, due ermetici del Quattrocento, e il manoscritto II.D.1.4 della Biblioteca comunale degli Ardenti di Viterbo', in *Biblioteca degli Ardenti della città di Viterbo*, Viterbo, pp. 3–25

(1961a). *Renaissance Thought: The Classic, Scholastic and Humanist Strains*, New York

(1961b). 'Un' Ars dictaminis di Giovanni del Virgilio', *Italia medioevale e umanistica*, 4: 181–200

(1964a). *Eight Philosophers of the Italian Renaissance*, Stanford

(1964b). 'An unknown humanist sermon on St Stephen by Guillaume Fichet', in *Mélanges Eugène Tisserant*, VI, Vatican City, pp. 459–97

(1965a). *Renaissance Thought II: Papers on Humanism and the Arts*, New York

(1965b). 'Renaissance Aristotelianism', *Greek, Roman and Byzantine Studies*, 6: 157–74

(1966a). 'Philosophy and humanism in Renaissance perspective', in *The Renaissance Image of Man and the World*, ed. B. O'Kelly, Columbus, pp. 29–51

(1966b). 'Pier Candido Decembrio and his unpublished treatise on the immortality of the soul', in *The Classical Tradition: Literary and Historical Studies in Honor of Harry Caplan*, Ithaca, pp. 536–58

(1967a). *Le Thomisme et la pensée italienne de la Renaissance*, Paris

(1967b). 'Pomponazzi, Pietro', in *Encyclopedia of Philosophy*, VI, New York, pp. 392–6

(1968). 'The myth of Renaissance atheism and the French tradition of free thought', *Journal of the History of Philosophy*, 6: 233–43

(1970). 'La diffusione europea del platonismo fiorentino', in *Il pensiero italiano del Rinascimento*, ed. G. Secchi-Tarugi, Florence, pp. 23–41

(1974). *Medieval Aspects of Renaissance Learning*, Durham, N.C.

(1978). 'Philosophy and medicine in medieval and Renaissance Italy', in *Organism, Medicine and Metaphysics*, Dordrecht, pp. 29–40

(1979). *Renaissance Thought and its Sources*, New York

(1980). *Renaissance Thought and the Arts*, Princeton

(1981). 'Niccolò Perotti ed i suoi contributi alla storia dell'umanesimo', *Res publica litterarum*, 4: 7–25

(1982). *Handschriftenforschung und Geistesgeschichte der italienischen Renaissance*, Mainz

(1983a). 'Marsilio Ficino as a man of letters and the glosses attributed to him in the Caetani Codex of Dante', *Renaissance Quarterly*, 36: 1–47

(1983b). 'Petrarcas Stellung in der Geschichte der Gelehrsamkeit', in *Italien und die Romania in Humanismus und Renaissance*, ed. K. W. Hempfer and E. Staub, Wiesbaden, pp. 102–21

(1984). 'Latein und Vulgärsprache im Italien des 14. und 15. Jahrhunderts', *Deutsches Dante-Jahrbuch*, 59: 7–35

(1985). *Studies in Renaissance Thought and Letters II*, Rome

Künzle, P. (1956). *Das Verhältnis der Seele zu ihren Potenzen*, Freiburg i. Br.

Kuhn, T. S. (1957). *The Copernican Revolution*, Cambridge, Mass.

Kuntz, M. L. (1981). *Guillaume Postel, Prophet of the Restitution of All Things: His Life and Thought*, The Hague

Labowsky, L. (1961–8). 'Bessarion studies. 1–5', *Medieval and Renaissance Studies*, 5: 108–62; 6: 173–205

(1979). *Bessarion's Library and the Biblioteca Marciana*, Rome

La Brosse, O. (1965). *Le Pape et le concile*, Paris

La Calle, U. G. de (1903). *Sebastian Fox Morcillo*, Madrid

Ladner, G. (1952). 'Die mittelalterliche Reform-Idee und ihr Verhältnis zur Idee der Renaissance', *Mitteilungen des Instituts für österreichische Geschichtsforschung*, 60: 41–59

Laird, W. R. (1983). *The Scientiae Mediae in Medieval Commentaries on Aristotle's Posterior Analytics*, Ph.D. thesis, Univ. of Toronto

Lampertico, F. (1885–6). 'Materiali per servire alla vita di Giulio Pace, giureconsulto e filosofo', *Atti del R. Istituto Veneto di scienze, lettere ed arti*, ser. vi, 6: 735–68

Lamprecht, F. (1950). *Zur Theorie der humanistischen Geschichtsschreibung: Mensch und Geschichte bei F. Patrizi*, Winterthur

Lampros, S. P. (1910). 'Ἀργυροπούλεια, Athens

Landfester, R. (1972). *Historia magistra vitae*, Geneva

Lang, A. (1964). *Die theologische Prinzipienlehre der mittelalterlichen Scholastik*, Freiburg i. Br.

Lange, H. J. (1974). *Aemulatio veterum sive de optimo genere dicendi*, Bern–Frankfurt

Lange, U. (1970). *Untersuchungen zu Bodins 'Démonomanie'*, Cologne
Langkabel, H. (1981). *Die Staatsbriefe Coluccio Salutatis*, Cologne
Lapointe, F. H. (1972). 'Who originated the term "psychology"?', *Journal of the History of the Behavioral Sciences*, 8: 328–35
    (1973). 'The origin and evolution of the term "psychology"', *Rivista critica di storia della filosofia*, 28: 138–60
Larkin, M. T. (1971). *Language in the Philosophy of Aristotle*, The Hague
Larwill, Paul H. (1934). *La Théorie de la traduction au début de la Renaissance d'après les traductions imprimées en France entre 1477 et 1527*, Munich
Láscaris Comneno, C. (1950). 'Senequismo y agustinismo en Quevedo', *Revista de filosofía*, 9: 461–85
    (1955a). 'La epistemología en el pensamiento filosófico de Quevedo', *Bolívar*, 45: 911–25
    (1955b). 'La mostración de Dios en el pensamiento de Quevedo', *Crisis*, 2: 427–40
The Late Italian Renaissance (1970). Ed. E. Cochrane, London
Lazzeroni, V. (1940). *La formazione del pensiero cartesiano e la scolastica*, Padua
Leff, G. (1961). *Gregory of Rimini and Innovation in Fourteenth-Century Thought*, Manchester
Legacy of Francis Bacon (1971). *Studies in the Literary Imagination*, 4: 1–226
Le Gentil, J. (1937). 'Nicolas de Grouchy', *Bulletin des études portugaises et de l'Institut Français en Portugal*, 4: 31–46
Lehmann, P. (1959). *Erforschung des Mittelalters*, 2 vols., Stuttgart
Lehnerdt, M. (1904). *Lucretius in der Renaissance*, Königsberg
Leitao Ferreira, F. (1944). *Noticias cronologicas de Universidade de Coimbra*, III, Coimbra
Lenhart, J. M. (1935). *Pre-Reformation Printed Books: A Study in Statistical and Applied Bibliography*, New York
Lennox, J. H. (forthcoming). 'Aristotle, Galileo, and the "mixed sciences"', in *Reinterpreting Galileo*, ed. W. A. Wallace, Washington
Lenoble, R. (1969). *Esquisse d'une histoire de l'idée de nature*, Paris
Lentzen, M. (1971). *Studien zur Dante-Exegese Cristoforo Landinos*, Cologne–Vienna
Lenzi, F. (1979). 'Felice Figliucci, Ficino e l'*Etica Nicomachea* di Aristotele', *Annali dell' Istituto di filosofia, Università di Firenze*, I: 131–64
Levi, A. H. T. (1984). 'Rabelais and Ficino', in *Rabelais in Glasgow*, Glasgow, pp. 71–85
Levy, F. J. (1967). *Tudor Historical Thought*, San Marino, Ca.
Lewalter, E. (1935). *Spanisch-jesuitische und deutsch-lutherische Metaphysik des 17. Jahrhunderts*, Hamburg (repr. Darmstadt, 1967)
Lewis, C. (1980). *The Merton Tradition and Kinematics in Late Sixteenth and Early Seventeenth Century Italy*, Padua
Lexikon für Theologie und Kirche (1957–67). 2nd edn, 11 vols., Freiburg i. Br.
Lhotsky, A. (1965). *Die Wiener Artistenfakultät 1365–1497*, Graz–Vienna–Cologne
Lilje, H. (1932). *Luthers Geschichtsanschauung*, Zurich
Limbrick, E. (1977). 'Was Montaigne really a Pyrrhonian?', *Bibliothèque d'humanisme et Renaissance*, 39: 67–80
Limentani, L. (1924). *La morale di Giordano Bruno*, Florence
Lindberg, D. C. (1976). *Theories of Vision from al-Kindi to Kepler*, Chicago
Lindberg, D. C. and Steneck, N. H. (1972). 'The sense of vision and the origins of modern science', in *Science, Medicine and Society in the Renaissance*, ed. A. Debus, I, New York, pp. 29–45
Lindhardt, R. (1979). *Rhetor, Poeta, Historicus: Studien über rhetorische Erkenntnis und Lebensanschauung im italienischen Renaissancehumanismus*, Leiden
Link, W. (1969). *Das Ringen Luthers um die Freiheit der Theologie von der Philosophie*, Darmstadt
Livesey, S. J. (1982). *Metabasis: The Interrelationship of the Sciences in Antiquity and the Middle Ages*, Ph.D. thesis, Univ. of California, Los Angeles

Loades, D. M. (1974). 'The theory and practice of censorship in sixteenth-century England', *Transactions of the Royal Historical Society*, 5th ser., 24: 141–57

Lockwood, D. P. (1951). *Ugo Benzi: Medieval Philosopher and Physician, 1376–1439*, Chicago

Logan, George M. (1983). *The Meaning of More's Utopia*, Princeton

Lohr, C. H. (1967). 'Medieval Latin Aristotle commentaries: Authors A–F', *Traditio*, 23: 313–413

(1968). 'Authors G–I', *Traditio*, 24: 149–245

(1970). 'Authors: Jacobus–Johannes Juff', *Traditio*, 26: 135–216

(1971). 'Authors: Johannes de Kanthi–Myngodus', *Traditio*, 27: 251–351

(1972a). 'Authors: Narcissus–Richardus', *Traditio*, 28: 281–396

(1972b). 'Addenda et corrigenda', *Bulletin de philosophie médiévale*, 14: 116–26

(1973). 'Authors: Robertus–Wilgelmus', *Traditio*, 29: 93–197

(1974a): 'Supplementary authors', *Traditio*, 30: 119–44

(1974b). 'Renaissance Latin Aristotle commentaries: Authors A–B', *Studies in the Renaissance*, 21: 228–89

(1975). 'Authors C', *Renaissance Quarterly*, 28: 689–741

(1976a). 'Authors D–F', *Renaissance Quarterly*, 29: 714–45

(1976b). 'Jesuit Aristotelianism and sixteenth-century metaphysics', in *Paradosis: Studies in Memory of Edwin A. Quain*, ed. G. Fletcher and M. B. Schuete, New York, pp. 203–20

(1977). 'Authors G–K', *Renaissance Quarterly*, 30: 681–741

(1978). 'Authors L–M', *Renaissance Quarterly*, 31: 532–603

(1979). 'Authors N–Ph', *Renaissance Quarterly*, 32: 529–80

(1980). 'Authors Pi–Sm', *Renaissance Quarterly*, 33: 623–734

(1981). 'Some early Aristotelian bibliographies', *Nouvelles de la république des lettres*, pp. 87–116

(1982). 'Authors So–Z', *Renaissance Quarterly*, 35: 164–256

(1984). 'The Aristotle commentaries of Ludovicus Buccaferrea', *Nouvelles de la république des lettres*, pp. 107–18

(1985). 'Mittelalterliche Theologien', in *Neues Handbuch theologischer Grundbegriffe*, III, Munich, pp. 127–44

Lojacono, E. (1985). 'Giorgio da Trebizonda: la tradizione retorica bizantina e l'idea di metodo', in *Acta Conventus Neo-Latini Bononiensis: Proceedings of the Fourth International Congress of Neo-Latin Studies*, ed. R. Schoeck, Binghamton, pp. 80–100

Long, A. A. (1982). 'Astrology: arguments pro and contra', in *Science and Speculation*, ed. J. Barnes et al., Cambridge, pp. 165–92

Lopez, P. (1972). *Sul libro a stampa e le origini della censura ecclesiastica*, Naples

Losada, A. (1948–9). 'Juan Ginés de Sepúlveda, traductor y comentarista de Aristóteles', *Revista de filosofía*, 7: 499–536; 8: 109–28

(1949). *Juan Ginés de Sepúlveda a través de su 'epistolario' y nuevos documentos*, Madrid (repr. Madrid, 1973)

Lottin, O. (1942–59). *Psychologie et morale au XIIᵉ et XIIIᵉ siècles*, 5 vols., Louvain

Lovejoy, A. O. (1936). *The Great Chain of Being*, Cambridge, Mass.

Lowry, M. (1979). *The World of Aldus Manutius*, Oxford

Lubac, H. de (1974). *Pic de la Mirandole: Études et discussions*, Paris

Luchsinger, F. (1953). *Der Basler Buchdruck als Vermittler italienischen Geistes, 1470–1529*, Basle

Ludwig, J. (1929). *Das akausale Zusammenwirken (Sympathia) der Seelenvermögen in der Erkenntnislehre des Suarez*, Munich

Lueben, R. (1914). *Sebastian Fox Morcillo und seine Naturphilosophie*, Bonn

Lübke, A. (1968). *Nikolaus von Kues*, Munich

Luzio, A. and Renier, R. (1889). 'Il Platina e i Gonzaga', *Giornale storico della letteratura italiana*, 13: 430–40

Mabilleau, L. (1881). *Étude historique sur la philosophie de la Renaissance en Italie: Cesare Cremonini*, Paris

McAllister, J. B. (1939). *The Letter of St Thomas Aquinas 'De occultis operibus naturae ad quemdam militem ultramontanum'*, Washington, D.C.

McCandles, M. (1968). 'Univocalism in Cajetan's doctrine of analogy', *New Scholasticism*, 42: 18–47

McClintock, S. (1956). *Perversity and Error: Studies on the 'Averroist' John of Jandun*, Bloomington

McConica, J. K. (1979). 'Humanism and Aristotle in Tudor Oxford', *English Historical Review*, 94: 291–317

McEvoy, J. (1982). *The Philosophy of Robert Grosseteste*, Oxford

McGinn, B. (1972). *The Golden Chain: A Study in the Theological Anthropology of Isaac Stella*, Washington, D.C.

McGuire, J. E. and Rattansi, P. M. (1966). 'Newton and the "Pipes of Pan"', *Notes and Records of the Royal Society of London*, 21: 108–43

Machiavelli attuale, Machiavel actuel (1982). Ravenna

MacIntyre, A. (1967). 'Ontology', in *The Encyclopedia of Philosophy*, v, New York, pp. 542–3

Mack, P. (1983a). *Rudolph Agricola and Renaissance Dialectic*, Ph.D. thesis, Univ. of London

(1983b). 'Valla's dialectic in the North: A commentary on Peter of Spain by Gerardus Listrius', *Vivarium*, 21:58–72

Mckeon, R. P. (1952). 'Rhetoric in the Middle Ages', in *Critics and Criticism*, pp. 260–96

(1972). 'The transformation of the liberal arts in the Renaissance', in *Developments in the Early Renaissance*, ed. B. S. Levy, Albany, pp. 158–223

Maclean, I. (1980). *The Renaissance Notion of Woman*, Cambridge

McMullin, E. (1983). Review of W. A. Wallace, *Prelude to Galileo*, *Philosophy of Science*, 50: 171–3

McNeil, D. O. (1975). *Guillaume Budé and Humanism in the Reign of Francis I*, Geneva

McRae, K. D. (1955). 'Ramist tendencies in the thought of Jean Bodin', *Journal of the History of Ideas*, 16: 306–23

(1963). 'A postscript on Bodin's connections with Ramism', *Journal of the History of Ideas*, 24: 569–71

Maechling, E. E. (1977). *Light Metaphysics in the Natural Philosophy of Francesco Patrizi da Cherso*, M.Phil. thesis, Univ. of London

Mähl, S. (1969). *Quadriga virtutum: Die Kardinaltugenden in der Geistesgeschichte der Karolingerzeit*, Cologne–Vienna

Maffei, D. (1956). *Gli inizi dell'umanesimo giuridico*, Milan

Maffei, E. (1897). *I trattati dell'arte storica del Rinascimento*, Naples

Maffei, R. de (1964). 'Il problema della "Ragion di Stato" nei suoi primi affioramenti', *Rivista internazionale di filosofia del diritto*, 41: 712–32

Magia, astrologia e religione nel Rinascimento (1974). Wrocław

Mahoney, E. P. (1966). *The Early Psychology of Agostino Nifo*, Ph.D. thesis, Columbia Univ.

(1968). 'Nicoletto Vernia and Agostino Nifo on Alexander of Aphrodisias: an unnoticed dispute', *Rivista critica di storia della filosofia*, 23: 268–96

(1970a). 'Agostino Nifo's early views on immortality', *Journal of the History of Philosophy*, 8: 451–60

(1970b). 'Pier Nicola Castellani and Agostino Nifo on Averroes' doctrine of the agent intellect', *Rivista critica di storia della filosofia*, 25: 387–409

(1971a). 'Agostino Nifo's *De sensu agente*', *Archiv für Geschichte der Philosophie*, 53: 119–42

(1971b). 'A note on Agostino Nifo', *Philological Quarterly*, 50: 125–32

(1974). 'St Thomas and the School of Padua at the end of the fifteenth century', *Proceedings of the American Catholic Philosophical Association*, 48: 277–85

(1976a). 'Antonio Trombetta and Agostino Nifo on Averroes and intelligible species: a philosophical dispute at the University of Padua', in *Storia e cultura al Santo*, ed. A. Poppi, Vicenza, pp. 289–301

(1976b). 'Agostino Nifo and St Thomas Aquinas', *Memorie Dominicane*, n.s., 7: 195–226

(1978). 'Nicoletto Vernia's question on seminal reasons', *Franciscan Studies*, 16: 303–9

(1980). 'Albert the Great and the *Studio patavino* in the late fifteenth and early sixteenth centuries', in *Albertus Magnus and the Sciences*, ed. J. A. Weisheipl, Toronto, pp. 537–63

(1982). 'Neoplatonism, the Greek commentators and Renaissance Aristotelianism', in *Neoplatonism and Christian Thought*, ed. D. J. O'Meara, Norfolk, Va., pp. 169–77, 264–83

Maier, A. (1940). *Die Impetustheorie der Scholastik*, Vienna

(1949). *Die Vorläufer Galileis im 14. Jahrhundert*, Rome

(1951). *Zwei Grundprobleme der scholastischen Naturphilosophie*, 2nd edn, Rome

(1958). *Zwischen Philosophie und Mechanik*, Rome

(1964–77). *Ausgehendes Mittelalter*, 3 vols., Rome

(1966). *Die Vorläufer Galileis im 14. Jahrhundert*, 2nd edn, Rome

Maier, H. (1966). *Ältere deutsche Staatslehre und westliche politische Tradition*, Tübingen

Maïer, I. (1965). *Les Manuscrits d'Ange Politien*, Geneva

(1966). *Ange Politien: la formation d'un poète humaniste (1469–80)*, Geneva

Maierù, A. (1969). 'Lo *Speculum puerorum sive terminus est in quem* di Riccardo Billingham', *Studi medievali*, ser. iii, 10: 297–397

(1972). *Terminologia logica della tarda scolastica*, Rome

Maillard, J. F. (1971). 'Le *De harmonia mundi* de Georges de Venise', *Revue de l'histoire des religions*, 179: 181–203

Mancini, G. (1891). *Vita di Lorenzo Valla*, Florence (repr. Rome, 1971)

(1920). *Sulle traccie del Salutati*, Lucca

(1971). *Vita di Leon Battista Alberti*, 2nd edn, Rome

Mandowsky, E. and Mitchell, C. (1963). *Pirro Ligorio's Roman Antiquities*, London

Manley, L. (1980). *Convention 1500–1750*, Cambridge, Mass.

Mann, N. (1984). *Petrarch*, Oxford

Mann Phillips, M. (1959). *Erasmus and the Northern Renaissance*, London

Manzoni, C. (1974). *Umanesimo ed eresia: M. Serveto*, Naples

Maravall, J. A. (1966). *Antiguos y modernos*, Madrid

Marcel, R. (1958). *Marsile Ficin*, Paris

Marc'hadour, G. (1963). *L'Univers de Thomas More: chronologie critique de More, Erasme et leur époque, 1477–1536*, Paris

(1969). *Thomas More et la Bible*, Paris

Marcotte, E. (1949). *La Nature de la théologie d'après Melchior Cano*, Ottawa

Margolin, J.-C. (1963). *Douze années de la bibliographie érasmienne 1950–61*, Paris

(1976). 'L'Enseignement des mathématiques en France', in *French Renaissance Studies: 1540–1570*, ed. P. Sharratt, Edinburgh, pp. 109–55

(1977). *Neuf années de bibliographie érasmienne 1962–70*. Paris

Marius, R. (1984). *Thomas More: A Biography*, New York

Markowski, M. (1971). *Buridanizm w Polsce w Okresie Przedkopernikanskim*, Wrocław, etc.

Marrou, H.-I. (1958). *Saint Augustin et la fin de la culture antique*, 4th edn, Paris

Marsh, D. (1980). *The Quattrocento Dialogue: Classical Tradition and Humanist Innovation*, Cambridge, Mass.

Marsilio Ficino e il ritorno di Platone (1984). Ed. S. Gentile *et al.*, Florence

Martin, F. X. (1959–60). 'The problem of Giles of Viterbo: A historiographical survey', *Augustiniana*, 9: 357–79; 10: 43–60

(1979). 'The writings of Giles of Viterbo', *Augustiniana*, 29: 141–93

Martin, J. (1974). *Antike Rhetorik*, Munich

Martines, L. (1963). *The Social World of the Florentine Humanists, 1390–1460*, Princeton

Martinich, A. (1981). *Thomas Hobbes: Computatio sive logica*, New York

Marzi, D. (1896). *La questione della riforma del calendario nel 5° Concilio Lateranense (1512–1517)*, Florence

Masai, F. (1956). *Pléthon et le platonisme de Mistra*, Paris

Masai, R. and F. (1954). 'L'Oeuvre de Georges Gémiste Pléthon', *Bulletin de l'Académie royale de Belgique, Classe des lettres*, sér. v, 40: 536–55

Masi, R. (1947). *Il movimento assoluto e la posizione secondo il Suarez*, Rome

Masius, A. (1879). *Flavio Biondo*, Leipzig

Massa, E. (1949). 'Egidio da Viterbo, Machiavelli, Lutero e il pessimismo cristiano', in *Umanesimo e machiavellismo*, Padua, pp. 75–123

(1951). 'L'anima e l'uomo in Egidio da Viterbo e nelle fonti classiche e medievali', in *Testi umanistici inediti sul 'De anima'*, ed. E. Garin et al., Padua, pp. 37–138

(1954). *I fondamenti metafisici della 'dignitas hominis' e testi inediti di Egidio da Viterbo*, Turin

Massaut, J. P. (1968). *Josse Clichtove: l'humanisme et la réforme du clergé*, 2 vols., Paris

(1974). *Critique et tradition à la veille de la réforme en France*, Paris

Matsen, H. S. (1968). 'Alessandro Achillini (1463–1512) as professor of philosophy in the "Studio" of Padua', *Quaderni per la storia dell'Università di Padova*, 1: 91–109

(1974). *Alessandro Achillini (1463–1512) and His Doctrine of 'Universals' and 'Transcendentals'*, Lewisburg

(1975). 'Alessandro Achillini (1463–1512) and "Ockhamism" at Bologna (1490–1500)', *Journal of the History of Philosophy*, 13: 437–51

(1977). 'Students' "arts" disputations at Bologna around 1500, illustrated from the career of Alessandro Achillini', *History of Education*, 6: 169–81

Maurer, W. (1962). 'Melanchthon und die Naturwissenschaft seiner Zeit', *Archiv für Kulturgeschichte*, 44: 199–226

(1967–9). *Der junge Melanchthon zwischen Humanismus und Reformation*, 2 vols., Göttingen

Mauro, L. (1981). 'Il problema del fato in Boezio e Tommaso d'Aquino', in *Atti del congresso internazionale di studi boeziani*, Rome, pp. 355–65

Mayer, T. (1985). 'Faction and ideology: Thomas Starkey's *Dialogue*', *Historical Journal*, 28: 1–25

Mazzacurati, G. C. (1961). *La crisi della retorica umanistica nel Cinquecento (Antonio Riccobono)*, Naples

Mechoulan, H. (1974). *L'Antihumanisme de J. G. de Sepúlveda: Étude critique du 'Democrates primus'*, Paris

The Medical Renaissance of the Sixteenth Century (1985). Ed. A. Wear et al., Cambridge

Medieval Eloquence (1978). Ed J. J. Murphy, Berkeley

Medioevo e Rinascimento: Studi in onore di Bruno Nardi (1955). 2 vols., Florence

Meerhoff, K. (1986). *Rhétorique et poétique au 16ᵉ siècle en France: Du Bellay, Ramus, et les autres*, Leiden

Meersseman, G. G. (1933–5). *Geschichte des Albertismus*, 2 vols., Rome

Meier, M. (1914). *Descartes und die Renaissance*, Münster

Meinecke, F. (1957). *Machiavellism*, trans. D. Scott, London

Melammed, A. (1982). 'The dignity of man in late-medieval and Renaissance Jewish philosophy in Spain and Italy' (in Hebrew), *Italia*, 3: 39–88

Meller, B. (1954). *Studien zur Erkenntnislehre des Petrus von Ailly*, Freiburg i. Br.

Menapace Brisca, L. (1952). 'La retorica di Francesco Patrizio o del platonico antiaristotelismo', *Aevum*, 26: 434–61

Menéndez y Pelayo, M. (1883–4). *Historia de las ideas estéticas en España*, 2 vols., Madrid

(1928). *Historia de los heterodoxos españoles*, Madrid

Menke-Glückert, E. (1912). *Die Geschichtschreibung der Reformation und Gegenreformation*, Leipzig

Mercati, A. (1942). *Il sommario del processo di Giordano Bruno*, Vatican City

Mercati, G. (1925). *Per la cronologia della vita e degli scritti di Niccolò Perotti, arcivescovo di Siponto*, Vatican City

    (1938). *Codici latini Pico-Grimani-Pio*, Vatican City

Mesnard, P. (1949). 'Jean Bodin et la critique de la morale d'Aristote', *Revue thomiste*, 49: 525–62

    (1954). 'Le Platonisme de Jean Bodin', *Bulletin de l'Association Guillaume Budé*, pp. 352–61

    (1969). *Érasme ou le christianisme critique*, Paris

Messeri, A. (1894). 'Matteo Palmieri, cittadino di Firenze del secolo XV', *Archivio storico italiano*, ser. v, 12: 257–340

Metzger, B. M. (1968). *The Text of the New Testament: Its Transmission, Corruption and Restoration*, 2nd rev. edn, Oxford

Miccolis, S. (1965). *Francisco Sánchez*, Bari

Michalski, K. (1969). *La Philosophie au XIVᵉ siècle: six études*, ed. K. Flasch, Frankfurt

Michaud-Quantin, P. (1949). 'La Classification des puissances de l'âme au douzième siècle', *Revue du moyen âge latin*, 5: 15–34

    (1955). 'Albert le Grand et les puissances de l'âme', *Revue du moyen âge latin*, 11: 59–86

    (1969). 'L'Emploi des termes *logica* et *dialectica* au moyen âge', in *Arts libéraux et philosophie au moyen âge*, Montréal, pp. 855–62

    (1970a).*Études sur le vocabulaire philosophique du moyen âge*, Rome

    (1970b). *Universitas: expressions du mouvement communautaire dans le moyen-âge latin*, Paris

Michel, P.-H. (1930). *Un idéal humain au XVᵉ siècle: la pensée de L. B. Alberti (1404–1472)*, Paris

    (1936). 'Un humaniste picard: Charles de Bovelles', *Revue des études italiennes*, 1: 176–87

    (1962). *La Cosmologie de Giordano Bruno*, Paris

Micheli, P. (1917). *La vita e le opere di Angelo Poliziano*, Livorno

Milham, M. E. (1972). 'The manuscripts of Platina's *De honesta voluptate* . . . and its source, Martino', *Scriptorium*, 26: 127–9

Miller, P. (1939–53). *The New England Mind*, 2 vols., Cambridge, Mass.

Minio-Paluello, L. (1956). 'Remigio Girolami's *De bono communi*', *Italian Studies*, 11: 56–71

    (1972). *Opuscula: The Latin Aristotle*, Amsterdam

Miscellanea di studi albertiani (1975). Genoa

Miscellanea di studi in onore di Vittore Branca (1983). 5 vols., Florence

Miscellanea marciana di studi bessarionei (1976). Padua

Mitchell, R. (1938). *John Tiptoft*, London

Mitteilungen und Forschungsbeiträge der Cusanus-Gesellschaft (1961–). Mainz

Mochi Onory, S. (1951). *Fonti canonistiche dell'idea moderna dello stato*, Milan

Möhler, W. (1949). *Die Trinitätslehre des Marsilius von Inghen*, Limburg

Moeller, E. von (1907). *Aymar du Rivail, der erste Rechtshistoriker*, Basle

Mohler, L. (1923–42). *Kardinal Bessarion als Theologe, Humanist und Staatsmann*, 3 vols., Paderborn (repr. Aalen, 1967)

    (1943–9). 'Theodoros Gazes, seine bisher ungedruckten Schriften und Briefe', *Byzantinische Zeitschrift*, 42: 50–75

Molland, A. G. (1974). 'Roger Bacon as magician', *Traditio*, 30: 445–60

    (1982). 'The atomization of motion: a facet of the scientific revolution', *Studies in the History and Philosophy of Science*, 13: 31–54

Momigliano, A. (1950a). 'Ancient history and the antiquarian', *Journal of the Warburg and Courtauld Institutes*, 13: 285–315

    (1950b). 'Note sulla leggenda del cristianesimo di Seneca', *Rivista storica italiana*, 62: 325–44

Momigliano, F. (1907). *Paolo Veneto e le correnti del pensiero religioso e filosofico nel suo tempo*, Turin

Mommsen, T. E. (1959). *Medieval and Renaissance Studies*, ed. E. F. Rice, Ithaca

Monfasani, J. (1976). *George of Trebizond: A Biography and a Study of his Rhetoric and Logic*, Leiden

   (1981). 'Bessarion Latinus', *Rinascimento*, ser. ii, 21: 165–209

   (1983). 'Still more on "Bessarion Latinus"', *Rinascimento*, ser. ii, 23: 217–35

Monnerjahn, E. (1960). *Giovanni Pico della Mirandola*, Wiesbaden

Montaigne:Essays in Memory of Richard Sayce (1982). Ed. I. D. McFarlane and I. Maclean, Oxford

Montù, A. (1968). 'La traduzione del *De mente humana* di Simone Porzio: storia ed esame di un manoscritto inedito', *Filosofia*, 19: 187–94

Moody, E. A. (1935). *The Logic of William of Ockham*, New York

   (1975). *Studies in Medieval Philosophy, Science and Logic*, Berkeley–Los Angeles–London

Moran, B. (1973). 'The universe of Philip Melanchthon: criticism and use of the Copernican theory', *Comitatus*, 4: 1–23

Moreana: Bulletin Thomas More (1963–). Angers

Moreau-Reibel, J. (1933). *Jean Bodin et le droit public comparé dans ses rapports avec la philosophie de l'histoire*, Paris

Moreira de Sá, A. (1947). *Francisco Sanches, filósofo e matemático*, 2 vols., Lisbon

Morley, H. (1854). *The Life of Jerome Cardan of Milan, Physician*, 2 vols., London

Morrall, J. B. (1960). *Gerson and the Great Schism*, Manchester

Mostert, W. (1983). 'Luthers Verhältnis zur theologischen und philosophischen Überlieferung', in *Leben und Werk Martin Luthers von 1526 bis 1546: Festgabe zu seinem 500. Geburtstag*, I, Göttingen, pp. 347–68

Mostra del Poliziano nella Biblioteca Medicea Laurenziana (1955). Ed. A. Perosa, Florence

Mourant, J. A. (1967). 'Suarez, Francisco', in *Encyclopedia of Philosophy*, VIII, New York, pp. 30–3

Muccillo, M. (1975). 'La storia della filosofia presocratica nelle *Discussiones peripateticae* di Francesco Patrizi da Cherso', *La cultura*, 13: 48–105

   (1981). 'La vita e le opere di Aristotele nelle *Discussiones peripateticae* di Francesco Patrizi da Cherso', *Rinascimento*, ser. ii, 21: 53–119

Muckle, J. T. (1942–3). 'Greek works translated directly into Latin before 1350', *Mediaeval Studies*, 4: 33–42; 5: 102–14

   (1945). 'The doctrine of St Gregory of Nyssa on man as the image of God', *Mediaeval Studies*, 7: 55–84

Mühlmann, H. (1981). *Ästhetische Theorie der Renaissance: Leon Battista Alberti*, Bonn

Müller, G. (1969). *Bildung und Erziehung im Humanismus der italienischen Renaissance*, Wiesbaden

   (1984). *Mensch und Bildung im italienischen Renaissance-Humanismus:Vittorino da Feltre und die humanistischen Erziehungsdenker*, Baden-Baden

Müller, H. J. (1968). *Die Lehre vom 'verbum mentis' in der spanischen Scholastik*, Münster

Müller-Jahncke, W.-D. (1973). *Magie als Wissenschaft im frühen 16. Jahrhundert: Die Beziehungen zwischen Magie, Medizin und Pharmazie im Werk des Agrippa von Nettesheim (1486–1535)*, Dissertation, Philipps Universität, Marburg

   (1984). *Astrologisch-magische Theorie und Praxis in der Heilkunde der frühen Neuzeit*, Stuttgart

Münkler, H. (1982). *Machiavelli: Die Begründung des politischen Denkens der Neuzeit aus der Krise der Republik Florenz*, Frankfurt

Münster, L. (1953). 'Alessandro Achillini, anatomico e filosofo, professore dello Studio di Bologna (1463–1512)', *Rivista di storia delle scienze mediche e naturali*, 15: 7–22, 54–77

Münzel, G. (1937). *Der Kartaüserprior Gregor Reisch und die Margarita philosophica*, Freiburg i. Br.

Mugnai Carrara, D. (1983). 'Una polemica umanistico-scolastica circa l'interpretazione delle tre dottrine ordinate di Galeno', *Annali dell'Istituto di Storia della Scienza di Firenze*, 8: 31–57

(1985). 'Nicolò Leoniceno e la fortuna umanistica di Euclide', in *Renaissance Studies in Honor of Craig Hugh Smyth*, 1, Florence, pp. 193–201

Mullally, J. P. (1945). *The Summulae logicales of Peter of Spain*, Notre Dame

Muller, R. A. (1984). '*Vera philosophia cum sacra theologia nusquam pugnat*: Keckermann on philosophy, theology and the problem of the double truth', *Sixteenth Century Journal*, 15: 341–65

Muñoz Delgado, V. (1964a). *La lógica nominalista en la universidad de Salamanca (1510–1530)*, Madrid

(1964b). *Lógica formal y filosofía en Domingo de Soto*, Madrid

(1967a). 'La lógica en Salamanca durante la primera mitad del siglo XVI', *Salmanticensis*, 14: 171–207

(1967b). 'Nota sobre Pedro Cijar, Pedro Aymerich y Jacobo Almain', *Estudios*, 23: 109–16

(1970). 'La obra lógica de los españoles en Paris (1500–1525)', *Estudios*, 26: 209–80

(1972). 'Lógica hispano-portuguesa hasta 1600 (notas bibliográfico-doctrinales)', *Repertorio de historia de las ciencias eclesiásticas en España*, 4: 9–122

(1979). 'Ciencia y filosofía de la naturaleza en el Península Ibérica', *Repertorio de historia de las ciencias eclesiásticas en España*, 7: 67–148

Muraro, L. (1978). *Giambattista Della Porta mago e scienzato*, Milan

Murdoch, J. E. (1964). 'Nicole Oresme's *Quaestiones super geometriam Euclidis*', *Scripta mathematica*, 27: 67–91

(1976). 'Music and natural philosophy: hitherto unnoticed *Questiones* by Blasius of Parma', *Manuscripta*, 20: 119–36

Murphy, J. J. (1966). 'Aristotle's *Rhetoric* in the Middle Ages', *Quarterly Journal of Speech*, 52: 109–15

(1969). 'The scholastic condemnation of rhetoric in the commentary of Giles of Rome on the *Rhetoric* of Aristotle', in *Arts libéraux et philosophie au moyen âge*, Montreal–Paris, pp. 833–41

(1974). *Rhetoric in the Middle Ages*, Berkeley

(1981). *Renaissance Rhetoric: A Short-Title Catalogue of Works on Rhetorical Theory from the Beginning of Printing to A. D. 1700*, New York

Nadal, G. H. (1965). 'The philosophy of history before historicism', in *Studies in the Philosophy of History*, ed. G. Nadal, New York, pp. 49–73

Nardi, B. (1945). *Sigieri di Brabante nel pensiero del Rinascimento italiano*, Rome

(1958). *Saggi sull'aristotelismo padovano dal secolo XIV al XVI*, Florence

(1965). *Studi su Pietro Pomponazzi*, Florence

(1971). *Saggi sulla cultura veneta del Quattro e Cinquecento*, Padua

The Nature of Scientific Discovery (1975). Ed. O. Gingerich, Washington, D.C.

Naudeau, O. (1973). 'La Portée philosophique du vocabulaire de Montaigne', *Bibliothèque d'humanisme et Renaissance*, 35: 187–98

Nauert, C. G. (1965). *Agrippa and the Crisis of Renaissance Thought*, Urbana

(1979). 'Humanists, scientists, and Pliny: changing approaches to a classical author', *American Historical Review*, 84: 72–85

Nauwelaerts, M. A. (1963). *Rodolphus Agricola*, The Hague

Naylor, R. H. (1976). 'Galileo: the search for the parabolic trajectory', *Annals of Science*, 33: 153–72

(1980a). 'Galileo's theory of projectile motion', *Isis*, 71: 550–70

(1980b). 'The role of experiment in Galileo's early work on the law of fall', *Annals of Science*, 37: 363–78

Nebbiai, D. (1978). 'Per una valutazione della produzione manoscritti cinque-seicentesca', in *Alfabetismo e cultura scritta nella storia della società italiana*, Perugia, pp. 235–67

Nel quarto centenario della nascita di Galileo Galilei (1966). Milan

Nelson, J. C. (1958). *Renaissance Theory of Love: The Context of Giordano Bruno's 'Eroici furori'*, New York

Neuhausen, K. A. and Trapp, E. (1979). 'Lateinische Humanistenbriefe zu Bessarions Schrift *In calumniatorem Platonis*', *Jahrbuch der österreichischen Byzantinistik*, 28: 141–65

New Perspectives on Galileo (1978). Ed. R. E. Butts and J. C. Pitt, Dordrecht–Boston

Niccolai, F. (1912). *Pier Vettori (1499–1585)*, Florence

Nicolò Cusano agli inizi del mondo moderno (1970). Ed. G. Santinello, Florence

Nitzsch, F. (1883). *Luther und Aristoteles*, Kiel

Nizzoli, A. (1970). *Mario Nizolio e il rinnovamento scientifico moderno (1488–1566)*, Como

Nolhac, P. de (1883). *La Bibliothèque d'un humaniste au XVIe siècle: Catalogue des livres annotés par Muret*, Rome

(1907). *Pétrarque et l'humanisme*, 2nd edn, 2 vols., Paris (repr. Paris, 1965)

Norden, E. (1923). *Die antike Kunstprosa*, 4th edn, Leipzig

Nordman, V. A. (1932). *Justus Lipsius als Geschichtsforscher und Geschichtslehrer*, Helsinki

Noreña, C. G. (1970). *Juan Luís Vives*, The Hague

(1975). *Studies in Spanish Renaissance Thought*, The Hague

Norpoth, L. (1930). 'Zur Bio–bibliographie und Wissenschaftslehre des Pietro d'Abano', *Kyklos*, 3: 292–353

Nova acta paracelsica (1944–). Basle

Novati, F. (1888). *La giovinezza di Coluccio Salutati (1331–1353)*, Turin

Novità celesti e crisi del sapere (1983). Ed. P. Galluzzi, Florence

Nuchelmans, G. (1980). *Late Scholastic and Humanist Theories of the Proposition*, Amsterdam

Nuyens, F. (1948). *L'Évolution de la psychologie d'Aristote*, Louvain–The Hague–Paris

Oakley, F. (1962). 'On the road from Constance to 1688: the political thought of John Major and George Buchanan', *Journal of British Studies*, 2: 1–31

(1964). *The Political Thought of Pierre d'Ailly: The Voluntarist Tradition*, New Haven

(1965). 'Almain and Major: conciliar theory on the eve of the Reformation', *American Historical Review*, 70: 673–90

Occult and Scientific Mentalities in the Renaissance (1984). Ed. B. Vickers, Cambridge

Ockman, J. (1975). 'Les Horoscopes des religions établis par J. Cardano 1501–76', *Revue de synthèse*, 96: 35–51

Oestreich, G. (1975). 'Justus Lipsius als Universalgelehrter zwischen Renaissance und Barock', in *Leiden University in the 17th Century*, ed. T. H. L. Scheurleer and G. H. M. Posthumus Meyjes, Leiden, pp. 177–201

(1982). *Neostoicism and the Early Modern State*, Cambridge

Offelli, S. (1955). 'Il pensiero del Concilio Lateranense V sulla dimostrabilità dell'immortalità dell'anima', *Studia patavina*, 2: 3–17

Oldfather, W. A. (1927). *Contributions Towards a Bibliography of Epictetus*, Urbana

(1952). *Contributions Towards a Bibliography of Epictetus: A Supplement*, ed. M. Harman, Urbana

Olerud, A. (1951). *L'Idée de macrocosmos et microcosmos dans le Timée de Platon*, Uppsala

Oliva, C. (1926). 'Note sull'insegnamento di Pietro Pomponazzi', *Giornale critico della filosofia italiana*, 7: 83–103, 179–90, 254–75

Oliver, R. P. (1953). 'Giovanni Tortelli', in *Studies Presented to David Moore Robinson*, ed. G. Mylonas and D. Raymond, St Louis, pp. 1257–71

(1958). 'Politian's Translation of the *Enchiridion'*, *Transactions of the American Philological Association*, 89: 185–217

Olivieri, L. (1983). *Certezza e gerarchia del sapere: Crisi dell'idea di scientificità nell'aristotelismo del secolo XVI*, Padua

Olschki, L. (1919–27). *Geschichte der neusprachlichen wissenschaftlichen Literatur*, 3 vols., Leipzig

(1943). 'Galileo's philosophy of science', *Philosophical Review*, 52: 349–65

O'Malley, C. D. (1955). *Jacopo Aconcio*, Rome

O'Malley, J. W. (1966). 'Giles of Viterbo: A sixteenth-century text on doctrinal development', *Traditio*, 22: 445–50

(1967). 'Giles of Viterbo: a reformer's thought on Renaissance Rome', *Renaissance Quarterly*, 20: 1–11

(1968). *Giles of Viterbo on Church and Reform*, Leiden

(1974). 'Some Renaissance panegyrics of Aquinas', *Renaissance Quarterly*, 27: 174–92

(1979). *Praise and Blame in Renaissance Rome*, Durham, N.C.

Ong, W. J. (1958a). *Ramus, Method, and the Decay of Dialogue*, Cambridge, Mass.

(1958b). *Ramus and Talon Inventory*, Cambridge, Mass.

Ongaro, G. (1969). 'Girolamo Cardano e Andrea Vesalio', *Rivista di storia della medicina*, 13: 51–61

Onoranze a Francesco Filelfo nel quinto centenario della sua nascita (1905). Ancona

Onoranze a Francesco Patrizi da Cherso: Catalogo della mostra bibliografica (1957). Trieste

L'opera e il pensiero di Giovanni Pico della Mirandola nella storia dell' umanesimo (1965). 2 vols., Florence

Oppel, J. W. (1977). 'Poggio, S. Bernardino and the dialogue on avarice', *Renaissance Quarterly*, 30: 564–87

Ore, O. (1965). *Cardano the Gambling Scholar*, New York

O'Rourke Boyle, M. (1983). *Rhetoric and Reform: Erasmus' Civil Dispute with Luther*, Cambridge, Mass.

Ortega, E. and Marcos, B. (1914). *Francisco Vallés el divino*, Madrid

Ott, H. and Fletcher, J. M. (1964). *The Medieval Statutes of the Faculty of Arts of the University of Freiburg im Breisgau*, Notre Dame

Otto, S. (1979). 'Die mögliche Wahrheit der Geschichte: Die *Dieci dialoghi della historia* des Francesco Patrizi in ihrer geistesgeschichtlichen Bedeutung', in *Materialien zur Theorie der Geistesgeschichte*, Munich, pp. 134–73

(1984). *Renaissance und frühe Neuzeit*, Stuttgart

Overfield, J. H. (1976). 'Scholastic opposition to humanism in pre-Reformation Germany', *Viator*, 7: 371–420

(1984). *Humanism and Scholasticism in Late Medieval Germany*, Princeton

Owen, G. E. L. (1968). 'Tithenai ta phainomena', in *Aristotle: A Collection of Critical Essays*, ed. J. Moravcsik, London, pp. 167–90

Padley, G. A. (1976). *Grammatical Theory in Western Europe 1500–1700: The Latin Tradition*, Cambridge

Pagallo, G. F. (1966). 'Sull'autore (Nicoletto Vernia?) di un'anonima e inedita *quaestio* sull'anima del secolo XV', in *La filosofia della natura nel medioevo*, Milan, pp. 670–82

Pagani, C. (1893). 'Mario Nizzoli ed il suo lessico ciceroniano'; 'Le polemiche letterarie di Mario Nizzoli'; 'Mario Nizzoli filosofo'; 'Operosità letteraria di Mario Nizzoli'; 'Gli ultimi anni di Mario Nizzoli', *Rendiconti della R. Accademia dei Lincei, Classe di scienze morali, storiche e filologiche*, ser. v, 2: 554–75, 630–60, 716–41, 819–26, 897–922

Pagden, A. R. D. (1975). 'The diffusion of Aristotle's moral philosophy in Spain', *Traditio*, 31: 287–313

(1981). 'The "School of Salamanca" and the affair of the Indies', *History of Universities*, 1: 71–112

(1982). *The Fall of Natural Man*, Cambridge

Pagel, W. (1958a). *Paracelsus: Introduction to the Philosophical Medicine of the Era of the Renaissance*, Basle–New York

(1958b). 'Medieval and Renaissance contributions to the knowledge of the brain and its functions', in *The History and Philosophy of Knowledge of the Brain*, ed. F. N. L. Poynter, Oxford, pp. 95–114

(1962). *Das medizinische Weltbild des Paracelsus*, Wiesbaden

(1967). *William Harvey's Biological Ideas*, Basle

(1969–70). 'William Harvey revisited', *History of Science*, 8: 1–31; 9: 1–41

(1979). 'Paracelsus als Naturmystiker', in *Epochen der Naturmystik*, ed. A. Faivre and R. C. Zimmermann, Berlin, pp. 52–104

Pagnoni, M. R. (1974). 'Prime note sulla tradizione medievale ed umanistica di Epicuro', *Annali della Scuola normale superiore di Pisa, Classe di lettere e filosofia*, ser. iii, 4: 1443–77

Palisca, C. V. (1956). 'Vincenzo Galilei's counterpoint treatise: a code for the *Seconda practica*', *Journal of the American Musicological Society*, 9: 81–96

(1961). 'Scientific empiricism in musical thought', *Seventeenth Century Science and the Arts*, ed. H. H. Rhys, Princeton, pp. 91–137

Pallier, D. (1975). *Recherches sur l'imprimerie à Paris pendant la Ligue (1585–1594)*, Geneva

Pampaloni, G. (1961). 'Fermenti di riforme democratiche nella Firenze medicea del Quattrocento', *Archivio storico italiano*, 119: 11–62

(1962). 'Nuovi tentativi di riforme alla costituzione fiorentina visti attraverso le consulte', *Archivio storico italiano*, 120: 521–81

Panizza, L. A. (1976). *The St Paul Seneca Correspondence: Its Significance for Stoic Thought from Petrarch to Erasmus*, Ph.D. thesis, Univ. of London

(1978). 'Lorenzo Valla's *De vero falsoque bono*, Lactantius and oratorical scepticism', *Journal of the Warburg and Courtauld Institutes*, 41: 76–107

(1984). 'Biography in Italy from the Middle Ages to the Renaissance: Seneca, pagan or Christian?', *Nouvelles de la république des lettres*, pp. 47–98

(forthcoming). 'Pico's 1485 defence of philosophy vs eloquence and Socratic irony'

Panofsky, E. (1939). *Studies in Iconology*, New York

(1955). *Meaning in the Visual Arts*, Garden City

(1960). *Renaissance and Renascences in Western Art*, 2 vols., Stockholm

(1968). *Idea*, Columbia, S.C.

Papadis, D. (1980). *Die Rezeption der Nikomachischen Ethik des Aristoteles bei Thomas von Aquin*, Frankfurt a. M.

Paparelli, G. (1955). 'La *Taumatologia* di Giambattista Della Porta', *Filologia romanza*, 2: 418–29

(1956a). 'Giambattista Della Porta' *Dizionario biografico degli autori*, Milan

(1956b). 'La data di nascita di Giambattista Della Porta', *Filologia romanza*, 3: 87–9

Papell, A. (1947). *Quevedo: su tiempo, su vida, su obra*, Barcelona

Papi, F. (1968). *Antropologia e civiltà nel pensiero di Giordano Bruno*, Florence

Papuli, G. (1965). 'La dimostrazione *potissima* in Girolamo Balduino e nella logica dello Zabarella', *Annali della facoltà di lettere e filosofia dell'Università di Bari*, 10: 283–323

(1967). *Girolamo Balduino. Ricerche sulla logica della Scuola di Padova nel Rinascimento*, Bari

Paquay, A. (1906). *Frans Tittelmans van Hasselt: Opzoekingen over zijn leven, zijne werken en zijne familie*, Hasselt

Paracelsus in der Tradition (1980). Vienna

Paracelsus: Werk und Wirkung. Festgabe für Kurt Goldammer zum 60. Geburtstag (1975). Vienna

Parinetto, L. (1974). *Magia e ragione: una polemica sulle streghe in Italiae intorno al 1750*, Florence

Park, K. (1980). 'Albert's influence on late medieval psychology', in *Albertus Magnus and the Sciences*, ed. J. A. Weisheipl, Toronto, pp. 501–35

Parks, G. B. (1954). *The English Traveler to Italy*, Rome

Paschini, P. (1957). *Tre illustri prelati del Rinascimento: Ermolao Barbaro, Adriano Castellesi, Giovanni Grimani*, Rome

Pascoe, L.-B. (1973). *Jean Gerson: Principles of Church Reform*, Leiden

Patrides, C. A. (1972). *The Grand Design of God*, London

 (1982). *Premises and Motifs*, Princeton

Patterson, A. M. (1970). *Hermogenes and the Renaissance*, Princeton

Pattin, A. (1974–5). 'Pour l'histoire du sens agent au moyen âge', *Bulletin de philosophie médiévale*, 16–17: 100–13

Patzig, G. (1981). 'Erkenntnisgründe, Realgründe und Erklärungen (zu *Anal. post.* A. 13)', in *Aristotle on Science: The Posterior Analytics*, ed. E. Berti, Padua, pp. 141–56

Pedersen, O. (1974). *A Survey of the Almagest*, Odense

Pellegrini, F. (1948). *Fracastoro*, Trieste

Pelzer, A. (1964). *Études d'histoire littéraire sur la scolastique médiévale*, ed. A. Pattin and E. Van De Vyver, Louvain–Paris

Penelhum, T. (1983). 'Skepticism and faith', in *The Skeptical Tradition*, ed. M. F. Burnyeat, Berkeley, pp. 287–318

Penham, D. F. (1954). *De transitu Hellenismi ad Christianismum: A Study of a Little Known Treatise of Guillaume Budé*, Ph.D. thesis, Columbia Univ.

Il Pensiero politico di Machiavelli e la sua fortuna nel mondo (1972). Florence

Percival, W. K. (1975). 'The grammatical tradition and the rise of the vernaculars', in *Current Trends in Linguistics*, XIII, 1, The Hague, pp. 231–75

 (1976). 'Renaissance grammar: rebellion or evolution?' in *Interrogativi dell'umanesimo*, ed. G. Tarugi, II, Florence, pp. 73–89

Percopo, E. (1938). *Vita di Giovanni Pontano*, Naples

Périon (1842). *Allgemeine Encyklopädie der Wissenschaften und Künste*, ed. J. S. Ersch and J. G. Gruber, sect. 3, part 17, Leipzig, pp. 53–9

Perreiah, A. R. (1967). 'A biographical introduction to Paul of Venice', *Augustiniana*, 17, 450–61

 (1982). 'Humanist critiques of scholastic dialectic', *Sixteenth Century Journal*, 13: 3–22

Perrin, M. (1981). *L'Homme antique et chrétien: L'Anthropologie de Lactance 250–325*, Paris

Perrone Compagni, V. (1975). '*Picatrix Latinus*: Concezioni filosofico-religiose e prassi magica', *Medioevo*, 1: 237–337

 (1978). 'La magia cerimoniale del *Picatrix* nel Rinascimento', *Atti dell'Accademia di scienze morali e politiche di Napoli*, 88: 279–330

 (1982). 'Una fonte di Cornelio Agrippa: il *De harmonia mundi* di Francesco Zorzi', *Annali dell'Istituto di filosofia, Università di Firenze*, 4: 45–74

Peruzzi, E. (1980). 'Antioccultismo e filosofia naturale nel *De sympathia et antipathia rerum* di Girolamo Fracastoro', *Atti e memorie dell'Accademia toscana di scienze morali 'La Colombaria'*, 45: 41–131

Petersen, P. (1921). *Geschichte der aristotelischen Philosophie im protestantischen Deutschland*, Leipzig (repr. Stuttgart–Bad Cannstatt, 1964)

Petrucci, A. (1967). *La scrittura di Francesco Petrarca*, Vatican City

Pfeiffer, F. (1924). *Vives und seine Stellung zur Scholastik*, Dissertation, Univ. of Cologne

Pfeiffer, R. (1968). *History of Classical Scholarship from the Beginnings to the End of the Hellenistic Age*, Oxford

 (1976). *History of Classical Scholarship from 1300 to 1850*, Oxford

Phillips, M. (1977). *Francesco Guicciardini: The Historian's Craft*, Manchester
    (1983). 'The disenchanted witness: participation and alienation in Florentine histori-
    ography', *Journal of the History of Ideas*, 44: 191–206
Philosophy and Humanism: Renaissance Essays in Honor of Paul Oskar Kristeller (1976). Ed. E. P.
    Mahoney, Leiden
Piaia, G. (1983). *'Vestigia philosophorum'. Il medioevo e la storiografia filosofica*, Rimini
Piano Mortari, V. (1978). *Diritto, logica, metodo nel secolo XVI*, Naples
Piccolomini, P. (1903). *S. Tizio*, Rome
Pierantoni, A.-C. (1920). *Pier Paolo Vergerio seniore*, Chieti
Pierre de la Ramée (Ramus) (1986). *Revue des sciences philosophiques et théologiques*, 70: 2–100
Pinborg, J. (1967). *Die Entwicklung der Sprachtheorie im Mittelalter*, Münster
Pine, M. (1965). *Pietro Pomponazzi and the Immortality Controversy, 1516–1524*, Ph.D. thesis,
    Columbia Univ.
    (1968). 'Pomponazzi and the problem of "double truth"', *Journal of the History of Ideas*,
    29: 163–76
    (1973). 'Pietro Pomponazzi and the scholastic doctrine of free will', *Rivista critica di storia
    della filosofia*, 28:3–27
    (1986). *Pietro Pomponazzi: Radical philosopher of the Renaissance*, Padua
Pintard, R. (1943). *Le Libertinage érudit dans la première moitié du XVIIᵉ siècle*, Paris (repr.
    Geneva–Paris, 1983)
Pintaudi, R. (1977). *Lessico greco-latino Laur. Ashb. 1439*, Rome
Piur, P. (1925). *Petrarcas 'Buch ohne Namen' und die päpstliche Kurie*, Halle
Platon et Aristote à la Renaissance: XVIᵉ Colloque international de Tours (1976). Paris
Plattard, J. (1923). *Guillaume Budé (1468–1540) et les origines de l'humanisme français*, Paris
Platzeck, E.-W. (1962-4). *Raimund Lull*, 2 vols., Düsseldorf
Plett, H. F. (1975). *Rhetorik der Affekte: Englische Wirkungsästhetik im Zeitalter der Renaissance*,
    Tübingen
Pocock, J. G. A. (1975). *The Machiavellian Moment*, Princeton
Poggio Bracciolini: Mostra di codici e documenti fiorentini (1980). Ed. R. Fubini and S. Caroti,
    Florence
Poggio Bracciolini 1380–1980: Nel 6° centenario della nascita (1982). Florence
Pohlenz, M. (1970). *Die Stoa: Geschichte einer geistigen Bewegung*, 4th edn, 2 vols., Göttingen
Il Poliziano e il suo tempo (1957). Florence
Pollard, G. (1978). 'The pecia system in the medieval universities', in *Medieval Scribes,
    Manuscripts and Libraries*, ed. M. B. Parkes and A. G. Watson, London, pp. 145–62
Polman, P. (1933). *L'Élément historique dans la controverse religieuse du XVIᵉ siècle*, Gembloux
Ponte, G. (1981). *Leon Battista Alberti, umanista e scrittore*, Genoa
Popkin, R. H. (1979). *The History of Scepticism from Erasmus to Spinoza*, rev. edn, Berkeley–
    Los Angeles–London
Poppi, A. (1962). 'Lo scotista patavino Antonio Trombetta (1436–1517)', *Il Santo*, 2: 349–67
    (1964). 'L'antiaverroismo della scolastica padovana alla fine del secolo XV', *Studia
    patavina*, 11: 102–24
    (1966). *Causalità e infinità nella scuola padovana dal 1480 al 1513*, Padua
    (1969). 'Pietro Pomponazzi tra averroismo e galenismo sul problema del *regressus*', *Rivista
    critica di storia della filosofia*, 24: 243–66
    (1970a). *Introduzione all'aristotelismo padovano*, Padua
    (1970b). *Saggi sul pensiero inedito di Pietro Pomponazzi*, Padua
    (1972a). *La dottrina della scienza in Giacomo Zabarella*, Padua
    (1972b). 'L'interpretazione dell'intelletto agente nell'opera di Giacomo Zabarella', in
    Scritti in onore di Carlo Giacon, Padua, pp. 323–38

Porro, A. (1983). 'Pier Vettori editore di testi greci: la *Poetica* di Aristotele', *Italia medioevale e umanistica*, 26: 307–58

Portmanns, L. (1969). 'Theodor Zwingers Briefwechsel mit Johannes Runge: Ein Beitrag zur Geschichte der Alchemie im Basel des 16. Jahrhunderts', *Gesnerus*, 26: 154–63

Posthumus Meyjes, G. (1963). *Jean Gerson, zijn kerkpolitiek en ecclesiologie*, The Hague

Pouilloux, J.-Y. (1969). 'Problèmes de traduction: L. Le Roy et le xe livre de la *République*', *Bibliothèque d'humanisme et Renaissance*, 31: 47–66

Powitz, G. (1979). 'Textus cum commento', *Codices manuscripti*, 5: 80–9

Pozzi, G. (1974). 'Appunti sul "Corollarium" del Barbaro', in *Tra latino e volgare: Per Carlo Dionisotti*, II, Padua, pp. 619–40

Prantl, C. (1855–70). *Geschichte der Logik im Abendlande*, 4 vols., Leipzig (repr. Graz, 1955)

Preger, W. (1859–61). *Matthias Flacius Illyricus und seine Zeit*, Erlangen

Prelog, J. (1983). 'Die Handschriften und Drucke von Walter Burleys *Liber de vita et moribus philosophorum*', *Codices manuscripti*, 9: 1–18

Pring-Mill, R. D. F. (1961). *El microcosmos lul·lia*, Palma de Mallorca

Procacci, G. (1951). 'La *fortuna* nella realtà politica e sociale del primo Cinquecento', *Belfagor*, 6: 407–21

(1965). *Studi sulla fortuna del Machiavelli*, Rome

Prost, A. (1881–2). *Corneille Agrippa: Sa vie et ses oeuvres*, 2 vols., Paris (repr. Nieuwkoop, 1965)

Pruckner, H. (1933). *Studien zu den astrologischen Schriften des Heinrich von Langenstein*, Leipzig–Berlin

Pullapilly, C. K. (1975). *Caesar Baronius, Counter-Reformation Historian*, Notre Dame

Purnell, F. (1971). *Jacopo Mazzoni and His Comparison of Plato and Aristotle*, Ph.D. thesis, Columbia Univ.

(1972). 'Jacopo Mazzoni and Galileo', *Physis*, 14: 273–94

(1976). 'Francesco Patrizi and the critics of Hermes Trismegistus', *Journal of Medieval and Renaissance Studies*, 6: 155–78

Putscher, M. (1973). *Pneuma, Spiritus, Geist: Vorstellung vom Lebensanstrieb in ihren geschichtlichen Wandlungen*, Wiesbaden

Pyle, C. M. (1984). 'Pier Candido Decembrio and Rome', in *Umanesimo a Roma nel Quattrocento*, Rome–New York, pp. 295–307

Quaderni petrarcheschi (1983–). Pisa

Quaranta, C. (1967). *Il potere dell'uomo sui beni corporali nel pensiero di Ludovico Molina S. I.*, Rome

Queralt, A. (1975). 'Libertad humana en Luis de Molina', *Archivo teológico granadino*, 38: 5–156

Quicherat, J. (1860). *Historie de Sainte-Barbe: collège, communauté, institution*, I, Paris

Raab, F. (1964). *The English Face of Machiavelli*, London

Rabeneck, J. (1950). 'De vita et scriptis Ludovici Molina', *Archivum Historicum Societatis Jesu*, 19: 75–145

Radetti, G. (1889). 'L'epicureismo italiano negli ultimi secoli del medioevo', *Rivista di filosofia scientifica*, 8: 552–63

Radouant, R. (1908). *Guillaume du Vair, l'homme et l'oeuvre*, Paris

Ragnisco, P. (1885–6). 'La polemica tra Francesco Piccolomini e Giacomo Zabarella nella Università di Padova', *Atti del R. Istituto Veneto di scienze, lettere ed arti*, ser. vi, 4: 1217–52

(1890–1). 'Nicoletto Vernia, studi storici sulla filosofia padovana nella seconda metà del secolo decimoquinto', *Atti del R. Istituto Veneto di scienze, lettere ed arti*, ser. vii, 2: 241–66, 617–64

(1891). 'Documenti inediti e rari intorno alla vita ed agli scritti di Nicoletto Vernia e di Elia del Medigo', *Atti e memorie della R. Accademia di scienze, lettere ed arti in Padova*, n.s., 7: 275–302

Rahner, K. (1975). 'Grazia e libertà', in *Enciclopedia teologica 'Sacramentum mundi'*, IV, Brescia, pp. 395–402

Raimondi, E. (1947). 'Alcune pagine del Petrarca sulla dignità umana', *Convivium*, n.s., 1: 376–93

(1974). 'Il primo commento umanistico a Lucrezio', in *Tra latino e Volgare: Per Carlo Dionisotti*, II, Padua pp. 641–74

Raith, W. (1967). *Die Macht des Bildes: Ein humanistisches Problem bei Gianfrancesco Pico della Mirandola*, Munich

Randall, J. H. (1940). 'The development of scientific method in the school of Padua', *Journal of the History of Ideas*, 1: 177–206

(1961). *The School of Padua and the Emergence of Modern Science*, Padua

Ranum, O. (1981). *Artisans of Glory*, Chapel Hill

Rattansi, P. M. (1966). 'Alchemy and natural magic in Raleigh's *History of the World*', *Ambix*, 13: 122–38

Raybaud, L.-P. (1970). 'Platina et l'humanisme florentin', in *Mélanges Pierre Tisset*, Montpellier, pp. 389–405

Reallexikon für Antike und Christentum (1950–). Stuttgart

Reason, Experiment, and Mysticism in the Scientific Revolution (1975). Ed. M. L. Righini Bonelli and W. R. Shea, New York

Rebitté, D. (1969). *Guillaume Budé, restaurateur des études grecques en France*, Osnabrück

Redondi, P. (1983). *Galileo eretico*, Turin

Rees, G. (1975). 'Francis Bacon's semi-Paracelsian cosmology', *Ambix*, 22: 81–101

(1977). 'Matter theory: a unifying factor in Bacon's natural philosophy', *Ambix*, 24: 110–25

(1980). 'Atomism and "subtlety" in Francis Bacon's philosophy', *Annals of Science*, 37: 549–71

(1981). 'An unpublished manuscript by Francis Bacon: *Sylva sylvarum* drafts and other working notes', *Annals of Science*, 38: 377–412

Reeve, M. D. (1980). 'The Italian tradition of Lucretius', *Italia medioevale e umanistica*, 23: 27–48

(1983). 'Manuscripts copied from printed books', in *Manuscripts in the Fifty Years after the Invention of Printing*, ed. J. B. Trapp, London, pp. 12–23

Reeves, M. (1969). *The Influence of Prophecy in the Later Middle Ages*, Oxford

Regnum hominis et regnum Dei (1978). Ed. C. Berubé, 2 vols., Rome

Rehm, W. (1930). *Der Untergang Roms im abendländischen Denken*, Leipzig

Reich Gottes und Welt: Die Lehre Luthers von den zwei Reichen (1969). Ed. H.-H. Schrey, Darmstadt

Reif, P. (1962). *Natural Philosophy in Some Early Seventeenth-Century Scholastic Textbooks*, Ph.D. thesis, St Louis Univ.

(1969). 'The textbook tradition in natural philosophy, 1600–1650', *Journal of the History of Ideas*, 30: 17–32

Reilly, J. P. (1971). *Cajetan's Notion of Existence*, The Hague

(1972). 'A preliminary study of a pecia', *Revue d'histoire des textes*, 2: 239–50

Reinterpreting Galileo (1986). Ed. W. A. Wallace, Washington, D.C.

Reiss, E. (1969). 'Conflict and its resolution in medieval dialogues', in *Arts libéraux et philosophie au moyen âge*, Montreal, pp. 863–72

Renaissance Eloquence (1983). Ed. J. J. Murphy, Berkeley

The Renaissance: Essays in Interpretation (1982). London

Renan, E. (1866). *Averroès et l'averroïsme,* 3rd edn, Paris

Renaudet, A. (1953). *Préréforme et humanisme à Paris pendant les premières guerres d'Italie (1494–1517),* 2nd edn, Paris

(1954). *Érasme et l'Italie,* Geneva

Renouard, A. A. (1834). *Annales de l'imprimerie des Alde,* 3rd edn, 3 vols., Paris

Renucci, P. (1953). *L'Aventure de l'humanisme européen au moyen âge,* Paris

Reusch, F. H. (1883–5). *Der Index der verbotenen Bücher: Ein Beitrag zur Kirchen- und Literaturgeschichte,* 2 vols., Bonn (repr. Darmstadt, 1967)

(1886). *Die Indices librorum prohibitorum des sechzenten Jahrhunderts,* Tübingen (repr. Nieuwkoop, 1961)

Reynolds, B. (1953). 'Shifting currents in historical criticism', *Journal of the History of Ideas,* 14: 471–92

(1955). 'Latin historiography, a survey 1400–1600', *Studies in the Renaissance,* 2: 7–66

Reynolds, L. D. and Wilson, N. G. (1974). *Scribes and Scholars: A Guide to the Transmission of Greek and Latin Literature,* 2nd rev. edn, Oxford

Rey Pastor, J. (1926). *Los matemáticos españoles del siglo XVI,* Toledo

Rhetorik: Beiträge zur ihrer Geschichte in Deutschland vom 16.-20. Jahrhundert (1974). Ed. H. Schanze, Frankfurt

Ricciardi, R. (1968). 'Angelo Poliziano, Giuniano Maio, Antonio Calcillo', *Rinascimento,* ser. ii. 8: 277–309

Rice, E. F. (1958). *The Renaissance Idea of Wisdom,* Cambridge, Mass.

(1969). 'The humanist idea of Christian antiquity: Lefèvre d'Étaples and his circle', in *French Humanism,* ed. W. L. Gundersheimer, London, pp. 163–80

(1971). 'Jacques Lefèvre d'Étaples and the medieval Christian mystics', in *Florilegium historiae: Essays Presented to Wallace K. Ferguson,* Toronto, pp. 89–124

Richter, B. L. O. (1961). 'The thought of Louis Le Roy according to his early pamphlets', *Studies in the Renaissance,* 8: 173–96

Rico, F. (1970). *El pequeño mundo del hombre,* Madrid

Ridolfi, R. (1978a). *Vita di Niccolò Machiavelli,* 7th edn, Florence (Eng. trans. London, 1962)

(1978b). *Studi guicciardiniani,* Florence

(1982). *Vita di Francesco Guicciardini,* new edn, Milan

Riesco, J. (1966). 'El ser en la metafísica de Juan Versoris', *Salmanticensis,* 13: 373–84

Rijk, L. M. de (1975). '*Logica Cantabrigiensis:* a fifteenth-century Cambridge manual of logic', *Revue internationale de philosophie,* 29: 297–315

(1977). '*Logica Oxoniensis:* an attempt to reconstruct a fifteenth-century Oxford manual of logic', *Medioevo,* 3: 121–64

Rinaldi, M. D. (1973). 'Fortuna e diffusione del *De orthographia* di Giovanni Tortelli', *Italia medioevale e umanistica,* 16: 227–61

Rinascimento europeo e Rinascimento veneziano (1967). Ed. V. Branca, Florence

Il Rinascimento nelle corti padane (1977). Bari

Risse, W. (1964). *Die Logik der Neuzeit,* 1: *1500–1640,* Stuttgart

(1965). *Bibliographia logica,* 1: *1472–1800,* Hildesheim

Ritschl, O. (1906). *System und systematische Methode in der Geschichte des wissenschaftlichen Sprachgebrauchs und der philosophischen Methodologie,* Bonn

Ritter, G. (1921–2). *Studien zur Spätscholastik,* 2 vols., Heidelberg

Rivolta, A. (1933). *Catalogo dei codici pinelliani dell'Ambrosiana,* Milan

Robey, D. (1969). 'Virgil's statue at Mantua and the defence of poetry: an unpublished letter of 1397', *Rinascimento,* ser. ii, 9: 183–203

(1973). 'P. P. Vergerio the Elder: republicanism and civic values in the work of an early humanist', *Past and Present,* 48: 3–37

(1980). 'Humanism and education in the early Quattrocento: the *De ingenuis moribus* of P. P. Vergerio', *Bibliothèque d'humanisme et Renaissance,* 42: 27–58

Robey, D. and Law, J. (1975). 'The Venetian myth and the *De republica veneta* of Pier Paolo Vergerio', *Rinascimento*, ser. ii, 15: 3–59

Robinson, C. (1979). *Lucian and his Influence in Europe*, Chapel Hill

Robinson, G. W. (1918). 'Joseph Scaliger's estimates of Greek and Latin authors', *Harvard Studies in Classical Philology*, 29: 133–76

Robles, L. (1979) *El estudio de la 'Etica' en España*, Salamanca

Röhr, J. (1923). *Der okkulte Kraftbegriff im Altertum*, Leipzig

Roersch, A. (1910–33). *L'Humanisme belge à l'époque de la Renaissance*, 2 vols., Brussels

Rokita, G. (1971). 'Aristoteles, Aristotelicus, Aristotelicotatus, Aristoteleskunst', *Archiv für Begriffsgeschichte*, 15: 51–93

Rompe, E. M. (1967). *Die Trennung von Ontologie und Metaphysik: Der Ablösungsprozess und seine Motivierung bei Benedictus Pererius und anderen Denkern des 16. und 17. Jahrhunderts*, Dissertation, Univ. Bonn

Roques, P. (1957). 'La *Philosophie morale des Stoïques* de Guillaume du Vair', *Archives de philosophie*, 15: 226–39, 379–91

Rosán, L. J. (1949). *The Philosophy of Proclus*, New York

Rose, P. L. (1975). *The Italian Renaissance of Mathematics*, Geneva

    (1977). 'A Venetian patron and mathematician of the sixteenth century', *Studi veneziani*, 1: 119–78

    (1980). *Bodin and the Great God of Nature: The Moral and Religious Universe of a Judaizer*, Geneva

Rose, P. L. and Drake, S. (1971). 'The pseudo-Aristotelian "Questions of Mechanics" in Renaissance culture', *Studies in the Renaissance*, 18: 65–104

Rosselli del Turco, C. (1878). *Giovanni Gioviano Pontano*, Florence

Rossi, G. (1893). *Girolamo Fracastoro in relazione all'aristotelismo e alle scienze del Rinascimento*, Pisa

Rossi, P. (1954). 'Il metodo induttivo e la polemica antioccultistica in Girolamo Fracastoro', *Rivista critica di storia della filosofia*, 9: 485–99

    (1957). 'Per una bibliografia degli scritti su Francesco Bacone (1800–1956)', *Rivista critica di storia della filosofia*, pp. 75–89

    (1962). *I filosofi e le macchine*, Milan

    (1974). *Francesco Bacone: Dalla magia alla scienza*, new edn, Turin (Eng. trans. London, 1968)

    (1977). 'Sfere celesti e banchi di gru', in *Immagini della scienza*, Rome, pp. 109–47

    (1982). 'The Aristotelians and the "moderns": hypothesis and nature', *Annali dell'Istituto e Museo di storia della scienza di Firenze*, 8: 3–17

    (1983). *Clavis universalis: Arti della memoria e logica combinatoria da Lullo a Leibniz*, 2nd edn, Bologna

Rossi, V. (1956). *Il Quattrocento*, ed. A. Vallone, 6th edn, Milan

Rothe, A. (1965). *Quevedo und Seneca: Untersuchungen zu den Frühschriften Quevedos*, Geneva–Paris

Rotondò, A. (1973). 'La censura ecclesiastica e la cultura', in *Storia d'Italia*, v, Turin, pp. 1397–42

    (1982). 'Cultura umanistica e difficoltà di censori: Censura ecclesiastica e discussioni cinquecentesche sul platonismo', in *Le Pouvoir et la plume*, Paris, pp. 16–50

Rubinstein, N. (1958–64). 'Poggio Bracciolini: cancelliere e storico di Firenze', *Atti e memorie dell'Accademia Petrarca di lettere, arti e scienze di Arezzo*, 37: 215–39

    (1965). 'Marsilius of Padua and Italian political thought of his time', in *Europe in the Late Middle Ages*, ed. J. R. Hale *et al.*, London, pp. 44–75

    (1966). *The Government of Florence Under the Medici (1434–1494)*, Oxford

    (1985). 'The *De optimo cive* and the *De principe* by Bartolomeo Platina', in *Tradizione classica e letteratura umanistica: Per Alessandro Perosa*, i, Rome, pp. 375–89

Rüdiger, W. (1896). *Petrus Victorius aus Florenz*, Halle

Rüegg, W. (1946). *Cicero und der Humanismus*, Zurich

   (1954). 'Entstehung, Quellen und Ziel von Salutatis *De fato et fortuna*', *Rinascimento*, ser. i, 5: 143–90

Rummel, E. (1985). *Erasmus as a Translator of the Classics*, Toronto–Buffalo–London

Rump, J. (1897). *Melanchthons Psychologie in ihrer Abhängigkeit von Aristoteles und Galenos*, Dissertation, Univ. of Jena

Rupprich, H. (1964). *Humanismus und Renaissance in den deutschen Städten und den Universitäten*, Darmstadt

   (1970–3). *Die deutsche Literatur vom späten Mittelalter bis zum Barock*, 2 vols., Munich

Russell, J. L. (1976). 'Action and reaction before Newton', *British Journal for the History of Science*, 9: 25–38

Ruysschaert, J. (1949). *Juste Lipse et les Annales de Tacite*, Turnhout

Ryan, E. A. (1936). *The Historical Scholarship of Saint Bellarmine*, New York

Sabbadini, R. (1885). *Storia del ciceronianismo*, Turin

   (1890). 'L'ultimo ventennio della vita di Manuele Crisolora', *Giornale ligustico*, 17: 321–6

   (1891). 'Vita di Guarino Veronese', *Giornale ligustico*, 18: 4–40, 109–35, 185–206, 261–82, 321–48, 401–32

   (1896). *La scuola e gli studi di Guarino Guarini Veronese*, Catania

   (1910). 'La gita di Francesco Barbaro a Firenze nel 1415', in *Miscellanea di studi in onore di Attilio Hortis*, Trieste, pp. 615–27

   (1922). *Il metodo degli umanisti*, Florence

   (1967). *Le scoperte dei codici latini e greci ne' secoli XIV e XV*, ed. E. Garin, 2 vols., Florence

Sacksteder, W. (1978). 'Hobbes: teaching philosophy to speak English', *Journal of the History of Philosophy*, 16. 33–45

Saffrey, H. (1959). 'Notes platoniciennes de Marsile Ficin dans un manuscrit de Proclus, Cod. Riccardianus 70', *Bibliothèque d'humanisme et Renaissance*, 21: 161–84

Saggio su Galileo Galilei (1967). Ed. C. Maccagni, Florence

Saitta, G. (1928). *Filosofia italiana e umanesimo*, Venice

   (1949). 'L'aristotelico Simone Porzio', *Giornale critico della filosofia italiana*, 28: 279–306

   (1954). *Marsilio Ficino e la filosofia dell'umanesimo*, 3rd edn, Bologna

   (1961). *Il pensiero italiano nell'umanesimo e nel Rinascimento*, 2nd edn, 3 vols., Florence

Salembier, L. (1932). *Le Cardinal Pierre d'Ailly*, Tourcoing

Salvestrini, V. (1958). *Bibliografia di Giordano Bruno*, ed. L. Firpo, 2nd edn, Florence

Sambursky, S. (1959). *Physics of the Stoics*, London

Sammut, A. (1980). *Unfredo Duca di Gloucester e gli umanisti italiani*, Padua

Sanchez-Arjona Halcon, F. (1969). *La certeza de la esperanza cristiana en los teólogos de la Escuela de Salamanca*, Rome

Sancipriano, M. (1957). *Il pensiero psicologico e morale di Giovanni Ludovico Vives*, Florence

Sanders, P. (1984). 'Charles de Bovelles's treatise on the regular polyhedra', *Annals of Science*, 41: 513–66

Sandys, J. E. (1908). *A History of Classical Scholarship*, ii, Cambridge

Santillana, G. de (1959). *The Crime of Galileo*, 2nd edn, Chicago

Santinello, G. (1962). *Leon Battista Alberti*, Florence

Santini, E. (1922). *Firenze e i suoi 'oratori' nel Quattrocento*, Milan

Santoro, M. (1967). *Fortuna, ragione e prudenza nella civiltà letteraria del Cinquecento*, Naples

Santos Alves, M. dos (1955). 'Pedro Fonseca e o *Cursus collegii conimbricensis*', *Revista portuguesa de filosofia*, 11: 479–89

Santschi, C. (1978). *La Censure à Genève au XVIIe siècle*, Geneva

Sanz y Sanz, J. (1959). *Melchor Cano*, Monachil (Granada)

Sapegno, N. (1948). *Il Trecento*, 2nd edn, Milan

Sarri, F. (1938). 'Il pensiero pedagogico ed economico del senese Francesco Patrizi', *Rinascita*, 1: 98–138

Sarton, G. (1927–48). *Introduction to the History of Science*, 3 vols., Baltimore

Sartori, A. D. (1938). 'Gaetano de' Thiene, filosofo averroista nello Studio di Padova (1387–1465)', *Atti della Società italiana per il progresso delle scienze*, 3: 340–70

Sartorius von Waltershausen, B. (1927). 'Melanchthon und das spekulative Denken', *Deutsche Vierteljahrsschrift für Literaturwissenschaft und Geistesgeschichte*, 5: 644–78

Sasso, G. (1953). 'Qualche osservazione sul problema della virtù e della fortuna nell'Alberti', *Il mulino*, 2: 600–18

 (1958). *Niccolò Machiavelli: Storia del suo pensiero politico*, Naples

Saunders, J. L. (1955). *Justus Lipsius: The Philosophy of Renaissance Stoicism*, New York

Saxl, F. (1936). '*Veritas filia temporis*', in *Philosophy and History: Essays Presented to Ernst Cassirer*, ed. R. Klibansky and H. J. Paton, Oxford, pp. 197–222

 (1957). *Lectures*, 2 vols., London

Sayce, R. A. (1972). *The Essays of Montaigne*, Oxford

Scaduto, M. (1964). *Storia della Compagnia di Gesù in Italia*, 2 vols. in 4 parts, Rome

Scaglione, A. (1961). 'The humanist as scholar and Politian's conception of the *grammaticus*', *Studies in the Renaissance*, 8: 49–70

Schalk, F. (1955). *Das Publikum im italienischen Humanismus*, Krefeld

Scheible, H. (1966a). *Die Entstehung der Magdeburger Zenturien*, Gütersloh

 (1966b). *Die Anfänge der reformatorischen Geschichtsschreibung*, Gütersloh

Schellhase, K. C. (1976). *Tacitus in Renaissance Political Thought*, Chicago

Scherer, E. C. (1927). *Geschichte und Kirchengeschichte an den deutschen Universitäten*, Freiburg im Br.

Schiffman, Z. S. (1984). 'Montaigne and the rise of skepticism in early modern Europe: a reappraisal', *Journal of the History of Ideas*, 45: 499–516

Schlobach, J. (1980). *Zyklentheorie und Epochenmetaphorik*, Munich

Schmidt-Biggemann, W. (1983). *Topica universalis*, Hamburg

Schmitt, C. B. (1967). *Gianfrancesco Pico della Mirandola (1469–1533) and His Critique of Aristotle*, The Hague

 (1970). 'Gianfrancesco Pico della Mirandola and the Fifth Lateran Council', *Archiv für Reformationsgeschichte*, 61: 161–78

 (1971). *A Critical Survey and Bibliography of Studies on Renaissance Aristotelianism, 1958–1969*, Padua

 (1972). *Cicero Scepticus: A Study of the Influence of the 'Academica' in the Renaissance*, The Hague

 (1981). *Studies in Renaissance Philosophy and Science*, London

 (1982). 'Andreas Camutius on the concord of Plato and Aristotle with Scripture', in *Neoplatonism and Christian Thought*, ed. D. J. O'Meara, Norfolk, Va., pp. 178–84

 (1983a). *Aristotle and the Renaissance*, Cambridge, Mass.

 (1983b). *John Case and Aristotelianism in Renaissance England*, Kingston–Montreal

 (1983c). 'The rediscovery of ancient skepticism in modern times', in *The Skeptical Tradition*, ed. M. F. Burnyeat, Berkeley–Los Angeles–London, pp. 225–51

 (1983d). 'The *Studio pisano* in the European cultural context of the sixteenth century', in *Firenze e la Toscana dei Medici nell'Europa del'500*, 1, Florence, pp. 19–36

 (1984). The *Aristotelian Tradition and Renaissance Universities*, London

 (1985). *La tradizione aristotelica: fra Italia e Inghilterra*, Naples

 (forthcoming a). 'Astronomy in the universities, 1550–1650', in *General History of Astronomy*, III, ed. M. A. Hoskin, Cambridge

 (forthcoming b). 'Philoponus' commentary on Aristotle's *Physics* in the sixteenth century', in *Philoponus and the Rejection of Aristotelian Science*, ed. R. Sorabji, London

Schmitt, C. B. and Knox, D. (1985). *Pseudo-Aristoteles Latinus*, London
Schnaur, H. (1973). *Modi essendi. Interpretationen zu den Schriften 'De docta ignorantia', 'De coniecturis', und 'De venatione sapientiae' von Nikolaus von Kues*, Aschendorff
Schoell, F. L. (1926). *Études sur l'humanisme continental en Angleterre*, Paris
Scholderer, V. (1935). General introduction to *Catalogue of Books Printed in the Fifteenth Century now in the British Museum*, part VII, London, pp. ix–xxxvii
(1966). *Fifty Essays in Fifteenth- and Sixteenth-Century Bibliography*, ed. D. E. Rhodes, Amsterdam
Scholem, G. (1954). *Major Trends in Jewish Mysticism*, New York
(1974). *Kabbalah*, Jerusalem
Schucan, L. (1973). *Das Nachleben von Basilius Magnus 'ad adolescentes'*, Geneva
Schüler, M. (1934). *Prädestination, Sünde und Freiheit bei Gregor von Rimini*, Stuttgart
Schüling, H. (1963). *Bibliographie der im 17. Jahrhundert in Deutschland erschienenen logischen Schriften*, Giessen
(1967). *Bibliographie der psychologischen Literatur des 16. Jahrhunderts*, Hildesheim
(1969). *Die Geschichte der axiomatischen Methode im 16. und beginnenden 17. Jahrhundert*, Hildesheim
Schultze, F. (1874). *Georgios Gemisthos Plethon und seine reformatorischen Bestrebungen*, Jena
Schulz, M. (1909). *Die Lehre von der historischen Methode bei den Geschichtsschreibern des Mittelalters*, Berlin
Schwab, J-B. (1858). *Johannes Gerson*, Würzburg
Schwarz, W. (1944). 'The meaning of *fidus interpres* in medieval translation', *Journal of Theological Studies*, 45: 73–8
Schweyen, R. (1973). *Guarino Veronese*, Munich
Science and Society: Past, Present and Future (1975). Ann Arbor
La Science au seizième siècle (1960). Paris
Scienza e filosofia all'Università di Padova nel '400 (1983). Ed. A. Poppi, Padua
Scienze, credenze occulte, livelli di cultura (1982). Florence
Scott, I. (1910). *Controversies over the Imitation of Cicero as a Model of Style*, New York
Screech, M. A. (1956). 'Some Stoic elements in Rabelais's religious thought', *Études rabelaisiennes*, 1: 73–97
(1979). *Rabelais*, London
(1983). *Montaigne and Melancholy*, London
Scrivano, R. (1964). 'Alessandro Piccolomini', *La rassegna della letteratura italiana*, 68: 63–84
Secret, F. (1958a). *Le Zohar dans les kabbalistes chrétiens de la Renaissance*, Paris
(1958b). 'Le Symbolisme de la Kabbale chrétienne dans la *Scechina* de Egidio da Viterbo', *Archives de philosophie*, 16: 131–54
(1964). *Les Kabbalistes chrétiens de la Renaissance*, Paris
(1976). 'Gianfrancesco Pico della Mirandola, Lilio Gregorio Giraldi et l'alchimie', *Bibliothèque d'humanisme et Renaissance*, 38: 93–108
Segarizzi, A. (1904). 'Lauro Quirini umanista veneziano del secolo XV', *Memorie della R. Accademia delle scienze di Torino*, ser. ii, 54: 1–28
(1915–16). 'Cenni sulle scuole pubbliche a Venezia nel secolo XV e sul primo maestro di esse', *Atti del R. Istituto Veneto*, 75: 637–67
Seifert, A. (1976). *Cognitio historica: Die Geschichte als Namengeberin der frühneuzeitlichen Empirie*, Berlin
(1978). *Logik zwischen Scholastik und Humanismus: Das Kommentarwerke Johann Ecks*, Munich
Seigel, J. E. (1966). ' "Civic humanism" or Ciceronian rhetoric? The culture of Petrarch and Bruni', *Past and Present*, 34: 3–48
(1968). *Rhetoric and Philosophy in Renaissance Humanism*, Princeton

(1969). 'The teaching of Argyropulos and the rhetoric of the first humanists', in *Action and Conviction in Early Modern Europe: Essays in Memory of E. H. Harbison*, ed. T. K. Rabb and J. E. Seigel, Princeton, pp. 237–60

Seigfried, H. (1967). *Wahrheit und Metaphysik bei Suarez*, Bonn

Sellberg, E. (1979). *Filosofin och nyttan.* 1: *Petrus Ramus och ramismen*, Gothenburg

Sellin, P. (1974). 'From *res* to *pathos*: the Leiden *Ordo Aristotelis* and the origins of the pathetic in interpreting Aristotle', in *Ten Studies in Anglo-Dutch Relations*, ed. J. van Dorsten, Leiden, pp. 72–93

Senger, H. G. (1971). *Die Philosophie des Nikolaus von Kues vor dem Jahr 1440*, Münster

Seńko, W. (1958–9). 'Les Manuscrits des commentaires d'Armand de Bellovisu, de Gérard de Monte et de Jean Versor sur le *De ente et essentia* de St Thomas d'Aquin', *Mediaevalia philosophica Polonorum*, 2: 13–18; 3: 7–16

Serrano, L. (1942). *Los conversos D. Pablo de Santa Maria y D. Alfonso de Cartagena, obispos de Burgos*, Madrid

Setz, W. (1975). *Lorenzo Vallas Schrift gegen die Konstantinische Schenkung*, Tübingen

Shapiro, B. (1983). *Probability and Certainty in Seventeenth-Century England*, Princeton

Sharpe, E. J. (1975). *Comparative Religion: A History*, London

Sharratt, P. (1982). 'Ramus, philosophe indigné', *Bulletin de l'Association Guillaume Budé*, pp. 187–206

Shaw, K. M. (1972). *Giovanni Nesi and the Search for the 'Sommo Bene'*, M.Phil. thesis, University of London

Shaw, P. (1978). 'La versione ficiniana della *Monarchia*', *Studi danteschi*, 51: 298–408

Shea, W. R. (1972). *Galileo's Intellectual Revolution*, London

Shepherd, W. (1825). *Vita di Poggio Bracciolini*, trans. T. Tonelli, 2 vols., Florence

Sherlock, T. P. (1948). 'The chemical work of Paracelsus', *Ambix*, 3: 33–63

Shklar, J. (1984). *Ordinary Vices*, Cambridge, Mass.

Shumaker, W. (1982). *Renaissance Curiosa*, Berkeley

Sicherl, M. (1957). *Die Handschriften, Ausgaben, und Übersetzungen von Iamblichos De mysteriis*, Berlin

(1976). *Handschriftliche Vorlagen der Editio princeps des Aristoteles* (Akademie der Wissenschaften und Literatur: Abhandlungen der geistes- und sozialwissenschaftlichen Klasse, 1976, 8), Mainz

Sigmund, P. E. (1963). *Nicholas of Cusa and Medieval Political Thought*, Cambridge, Mass.

Signorelli, G. (1929). *Il Cardinale Egidio da Viterbo: agostiniano, umanista e riformatore, 1469–1532*, Florence

Sigwart, C. (1889). 'Jacob Schegk, Professor der Philosophie und Medizin', in his *Kleine Schriften*, I, Freiburg im Br., pp. 256–91

Simón Díaz, J. (1945). 'El helenismo de Quevedo y varias cuestiones más', *Revista de Bibliografía Nacional*, 6: 87–118

Simone, F. (1949). *La coscienza della rinascita negli umanisti francesi*, Rome

(1965). *Il Rinascimento francese*, Turin (Eng. trans. London, 1969)

(1966). *Per una storia della storiografia letteraria francese*, Turin

Simposio Francisco Suarez (1980). *Cuadernos salmantinos de filosofía*, 7: 3–394

Singer, D. W. (1950). *Giordano Bruno: His Life and Thought*, London

Siraisi, N. G. (1973). *Arts and Sciences at Padua*, Toronto

(1981). *Taddeo Alderotti and His Pupils*, Princeton

(1984). 'Renaissance commentaries on Avicenna's *Canon*, book I, part I, and the teaching of medical *theoria* in the Italian universities', *History of Universities*, 4: 47–97

Skinner, Q. (1967). 'More's *Utopia*', *Past and Present*, 38: 153–68

(1978). *The Foundations of Modern Political Thought*, 2 vols., Cambridge

(1980). 'The origins of the Calvinist theory of revolution', in *After the Revolution*, ed. B. Malament, Philadelphia, pp. 309–30

(1981). *Machiavelli*, Oxford

Skulsky, H. (1968). 'Paduan epistemology and the doctrine of the one mind', *Journal of the History of Philosophy*, 6: 341–61

Slaughter, M. M. (1982). *Universal Languages and Scientific Taxonomy in the Seventeenth Century*, Cambridge

Sleeman, J. H. and Pollet, G. (1980). *Index Plotinianum*, Leiden

Smalley, B. (1960). *English Friars and Antiquity in the Early XIV Century*, Oxford

Smith, A. (1974). *Porphyry's Place in the Neoplatonic Tradition*, The Hague

Smith, C. N. (1984). 'Muret's *Oratio in funere Caroli IX* and Sorbin's *Oraison funèbre de Charles IX*', in *Neo-Latin and the Vernacular in Renaissance France*, ed. G. Castor and T. Cave, Oxford, pp. 199–215

Smith, L. (1928). 'Note cronologiche vergeriane', *Archivio veneto*, 4: 92–141

Smith, L. F. (1966–8). 'The poems of Franciscus Patricius from Vatican Manuscript Chigi J.VI.233', *Manuscripta*, 10: 94–102, 145–9; 11: 131–43; 12: 10–21

(1968). 'A notice of the *Epigrammata* of Francesco Patrizi, Bishop of Gaeta', *Studies in the Renaissance*, 15: 92–143

(1974). 'Members of Francesco Patrizi's family appearing in his letters and epigrams', *Renaissance Quarterly*, 27: 1–6

Smith, M. (1978). *Jesus the Magician*, New York

Smith, P. (1923). *Erasmus*, New York–London

Smith, W. (1979). *The Hippocratic Tradition*, Ithaca–London

Solana, M. (1941). *Historia de la filosofía española: época del Renacimiento (siglo XVI)*, 3 vols., Madrid

Soleri, G. (1945). *Telesio*, Brescia

Soman, A. (1970). 'Pierre Charron: a revaluation', *Bibliothèque d'humanisme et Renaissance*, 32: 57–79

Sommerville, J. (1982). 'From Suarez to Filmer: a reappraisal', *The Historical Journal*, 25: 525–40

Sonnino, L. A. (1968). *A Handbook of Sixteenth-Century Rhetoric*, London

Soppelsa, M. L. (1974). *Genesi del metodo galileiano e tramonto dell'aristotelismo nella scuola di Padova*, Padua

Soranzo, G. (1965). *L'umanista canonico regolare lateranse Matteo Bosso di Verona (1472–1502)*, Padua

Sorbelli, A. (1944). 'I teorici del reggimento comunale', *Bullettino dell'Istituto storico italiano per il medio evo*, 59: 31–136

Soria Olmedo, A. (1984). *Los 'Dialoghi d'amore' de Leon Hebreo: aspectos literarios y culturales*, Granada

Sortais, G. (1920). *La Philosophie moderne depuis Bacon jusqu'à Leibniz*, 2 vols., Paris

Soudek, J. (1958). 'The genesis and tradition of Leonardo Bruni's annotated Latin version of the (pseudo-) Aristotelian *Economics*', *Scriptorium*, 12: 260–8

(1968). 'Leonardo Bruni and his public: a statistical and interpretative study of his annotated Latin version of the (pseudo-) Aristotelian *Economics*', *Studies in Medieval and Renaissance History*, 5: 51–136

Sousa Alves, V. de (1961). 'O espaço e o tempo imaginários em Pedro da Fonseca', *Studium generale* (Porto), 8: 49–61

Sozzi, L. (1982). *La 'Dignité de l'homme' à la Renaissance*, Turin

Spampanato, V. (1921). *Vita di Giordano Bruno*, 2 vols., Messina

(1934). *Documenti della vita di Giordano Bruno*, Florence

Spanneut, M. (1969). *Le Stoïcisme des Pères de l'Église*, Paris
　(1973). *Permanence du Stoïcisme: De Zénon à Malraux*, Gembloux
Sparn, W. (1976). *Wiederkehr der Metaphysik*, Stuttgart
Specht, R. (1972). 'Über *occasio* und verwandte Begriffe bei Zabarella und Descartes', *Archiv für Begriffsgeschichte*, 16: 1–27
Spingarn, J. E. (1908). *A History of Literary Criticism in the Renaissance*, 2nd edn, New York
Spinosa, G. (1985). 'Alcune versioni greco-latine di Aristotele', *Lexicon philosophicum*, 1: 117–26
Spiritus (1984). Ed. M. Fattori and M. Bianchi, Rome
Spitz, L. W. (1963). *The Religious Renaissance of German Humanists*, Cambridge, Mass.
Spörl, J. (1935). *Grundformen hochmittelalterlichen Geschichtsanschauung*, Munich
Srbik, R. von (1941). 'Die *Margarita philosophica* des Gregor Reisch (†1525): Ein Beitrag zur Geschichte der Naturwissenschaften in Deutschland', *Akademie der Wissenschaften in Wien. Mathematisch-naturwissenschaftliche Klasse. Denkschriften*, 104: 83–205
　(1961). *Maximilian I. und Gregor Reisch*, ed. A. Lhotsky, Vienna
Stadler, M. (1983). *Rekonstruktion einer Philosophie der Ungegenständlichkeit: Zur Struktur des cusanischen Denkens*, Munich
Stäuble, A. (1968). *La commedia umanistica del Quattrocento*, Florence
Starnes, D. T. (1954). *Renaissance Dictionaries, English–Latin and Latin–English*, Austin
　(1955). *Classical Myth and Legend in Renaissance Dictionaries*, Chapel Hill
　(1963). *Robert Estienne's Influence on Lexicography*, Austin
Staudenbaur, C. A. (1968). 'Galileo, Ficino and Henry More's *Psychathanasia*', *Journal of the History of Ideas*, 29: 565–78
Stegmüller, F. (1935a). *Geschichte der Molinismus: Neue Molinaschriften*, Aschendorff
　(1935b). 'Tolet et Cajétan', *Revue Thomiste*, 39: 358–70
　(1959). *Filosofia e teologia nas universidades de Coimbra e Evora no século XVI*, Coimbra
Stein, L. (1888). 'Handschriftenfunde zur Philosophie der Renaissance', *Archiv für Geschichte der Philosophie*, 1: 534–53
　(1889). 'Der Humanist Theodor Gaza als Philosoph', *Archiv für Geschichte der Philosophie*, 2: 426–58
Steiner, G. (1975). *After Babel: Aspects of Language and Translation*, London
Stella, A. (1969). *Anabattismo e antitrinitarismo in Italia nel XVI° secolo*, Padua
Stelzenberger, J. (1933). *Die Beziehungen der frühchristlichen Sittenlehre zur Ethik der Stoa*, Munich
Steneck, N. H. (1974). 'Albert the Great on the classification of internal senses', *Isis*, 65: 193–211
　(1976). *Science and Creation in the Middle Ages: Henry of Langenstein (d. 1397) on Genesis*, Notre Dame
Stengren, G. L. (1965). *Human Intellectual Knowledge of the Material Singular According to Francis Suarez*, New York
Stephens, J. (1975). *Francis Bacon and the Style of Science*, Chicago–London
Stern, L. (1960). *Philipp Melanchthon: Humanist, Reformator, Praeceptor Germaniae*, Halle
Stigall, J. O. (1957). 'The manuscript tradition of the *De vita et moribus philosophorum* of Walter Burley', *Medievalia et Humanistica*, 11: 44–57
Stillwell, M. (1982). *Essays in the Heritage of the Renaissance*, Providence
Stinger, C. L. (1977). *Humanism and the Church Fathers: Ambrogio Traversari (1386–1439) and Christian Antiquity in the Italian Renaissance*, Albany
Stolt, B. (1974). *Wortkampf: Frühneuhochdeutsche Beispiele zur rhetorischen Praxis*, Frankfurt
Storia della Chiesa (1975). VI, ed. E. Iserloh, J. Glazik and H. Jedin, Milan
Storia delle storie generali della filosofia (1981–). Ed. G. Santinello, Brescia
Stormon, E. J. (1980). 'Bessarion before the Council of Florence: a survey of his early writings (1423–1437)', *Byzantina Australiensia*, 1: 128–56

Strowski, F. (1906). *Montaigne*, Paris
Struever, N. S. (1970). *The Language of History in Renaissance*, Princeton
Studi petrarcheschi (1948–78; 1984–). Bologna
Studies on Machiavelli (1972). Ed. M. P. Gilmore, Florence
Stupperich, R. (1977). *Erasmus von Rotterdam und seine Welt*, Berlin
Sudhoff, K. (1894–9). *Versuch einer Kritik der Echtheit der Paracelsischen Schriften*, 2 vols., Berlin
   (1936). *Paracelsus: Ein deutsches Lebensbild aus den Tagen der Renaissance*, Leipzig
Surtz, E. L. (1957a). *The Praise of Pleasure: Philosophy, Education and Communism in More's Utopia*, Cambridge, Mass
   (1957b). *The Praise of Wisdom: A Commentary on the Religious and Moral Problems and Background of St Thomas More's Utopia*, Chicago
Suter, R. (1969). 'The scientific work of Alessandro Piccolomini', *Isis*, 60: 210–22
Swerdlow, N. M. (1973). 'The derivation and first draft of Copernicus's planetary theory: a translation of the *Commentariolus* with commentary', *Proceedings of the American Philosophical Society*, 117: 423–512
Swiezawski, S. (1974–83). *Dzieje Filozofii Europejskiej w XV Wieku*, 6 vols., Warsaw
Szymanski, M. (1982). 'Philosophy and language', *Bibliothèque d'humanisme et Renaissance*, 44: 149–52

Tallarigo, C. M. (1874). *Giovanni Pontano e i suoi tempi*, 2 vols., Naples
Tanteri, V. (1931). *Giovanni Pontano e i suoi dialoghi*, Ferrara
Tarabochia, A. (1971–2). *La presenza di S. Agostino nella 'Theologia platonica' di Marsilio Ficino*, Tesi di laurea, Università Cattolica, Milan
Tateo, F. (1960a). *Astrologia e moralità in Giovanni Pontano*, Bari
   (1960b). '*Retorica' e 'poetica' fra medioevo e Rinascimento*, Bari
   (1961). 'Poggio Bracciolini e la dialogistica del Quattrocento', *Annali della Facoltà di lettere e filosofia, Università di Bari*, pp. 165–204
   (1967). *Tradizione e realtà nell'umanesimo italiano*, Bari
   (1971). *Alberti, Leonardo e la crisi dell'umanesimo*, Bari
   (1972). *Umanesimo etico di Giovanni Pontano*, Lecce
Tavardon, P. (1977). 'Le Conflict de Georges Gémiste Pléthon et de Georges Scholarios au sujet de l'expression d'Aristote τὸ ὂν λέγεται πολλαχῶς', *Byzantion*, 47: 268–78
Taylor, J. W. (1921). *Georgius Gemistus Pletho's Criticism of Plato and Aristotle*, Ph.D. thesis, Univ. of Chicago
   (1925a). *Theodore Gaza's De Fato*, Toronto
   (1925b). 'More light on Theodore Gaza's *De fato*', *Classical Philology*, 21: 233–40
Temkin, O. (1973). *Galenism*, Ithaca
Texts and Transmission (1983). Ed. L. D. Reynolds, Oxford
Thibaudet, A. (1963). *Montaigne*, Paris
Thickett, D. (1979). *Estienne Pasquier (1529–1615)*, London
Thijssen Schoute, C. L. (1954). *Nederlands Cartesianisme*, Amsterdam
Thomas, I. (1964). 'Medieval aftermath: Oxford logic and logicians in the seventeenth century', in *Oxford Studies Presented to Daniel Callus*, Oxford, pp. 297–311
   (1965). 'The written liar and Thomas Oliver', *Notre Dame Journal of Formal Logic*, 6: 201–8
Thomas, K. (1971). *Religion and the Decline of Magic*, London
Thompson, J. W. (1911). *The Frankfurt Book Fair*, Chicago (repr. New York, 1968)
   (1939). *The Medieval Library*, Chicago
   (1942). *The History of Historical Writing*, 2 vols., New York
Thomson, D. F. S. and Porter, H. C. (1963). *Erasmus and Cambridge: The Cambridge Letters*, Toronto

Thomson, I. (1966). 'Manuel Chrysoloras and the early Italian Renaissance', *Greek, Roman and Byzantine Studies*, 7: 63–82

Thorndike, L. (1923–58). *A History of Magic and Experimental Science*, 8 vols., New York
  (1929). *Science and Thought in the Fifteenth Century*, New York

Thyssen, J. (1960). *Geschichte der Geschichtsphilosophie*, Bonn

Tiedemann, H. (1913). *Tacitus und das Nationalbewusstsein der deutschen Humanisten*, Berlin

Tierney, B. (1955). *Foundations of Conciliar Theory*, Cambridge
  (1982). *Religion, Law and the Growth of Constitutional Thought 1150–1650*, Cambridge

Tigerstedt, E. N. (1968). 'Observations on the reception of Aristotelian *Poetics* in the Latin West', *Studies in the Renaissance*, 15: 7–24
  (1974). *The Decline and Fall of the Neoplatonic Interpretation of Plato*, Helsinki

Timmermans, B. J. H. M. (1938). 'Valla et Érasme, défenseurs d'Épicure', *Neophilologus*, 23: 174–9

Tiraboschi, G. (1805–12). *Storia della letteratura italiana*, new edn, 9 vols., Florence

Tocco, F. (1889). *Le opere latine di Giordano Bruno*, Florence
  (1892). *Le fonti più recenti della filosofia del Bruno*, Rome

Toffanin, G. (1921). *Machiavelli e il 'Tacitismo'*, Padua
  (1929). *Che cosa fu l'umanesimo*, Florence
  (1938). *Giovanni Pontano tra l'uomo e la natura*, Bologna
  (1964). *Storia dell'umanesimo*, 2nd edn, 4 vols., Bologna

Tommaso Campanella (1569–1639) (1969). Naples

Torrance, T. F. (1969–70). '1469–1969: La Philosophie et la théologie de Jean Mair ou Major, de Haddington (1469–1550)', *Archives de philosophie*, 32: 531–47; 33: 261–93

Un toscano del '400: Poggio Bracciolini. Catalogo della mostra (1980). Ed. P. Castelli, Terranuova Bracciolini

Totok, W. (1980). *Handbuch der Geschichte der Philosophie*. III: *Renaissance*, Frankfurt am Main

Tracy, J. (1972). *Erasmus: The Growth of a Mind*, Geneva
  (1978). *The Politics of Erasmus*, Toronto

Trapp, D. (1958). 'Gregory of Rimini: manuscripts, editions and additions', *Augustiniana*, 8: 425–43
  (1962). 'New approaches to Gregory of Rimini', *Augustinianum*, 2: 115–30

Trentman, J. A. (1968). 'Extraordinary language and medieval logic', *Dialogue*, 7: 286–91
  (1976). 'The study of logic and language in England in the early 17th century', *Historiographia Linguistica*, 3: 179–201

Trinkaus, C. (1940). *Adversity's Noblemen*, New York
  (1960). 'A humanist's image of humanism: the inaugural orations of Bartolommeo della Fonte', *Studies in the Renaissance*, 7: 90–125
  (1966). 'The unknown Quattrocento poetics of Bartolommeo della Fonte', *Studies in the Renaissance*, 13: 40–122
  (1970). *In Our Image and Likeness: Humanity and Divinity in Italian Humanist Thought*, 2 vols., London
  (1976). 'Erasmus, Augustine and the nominalists', *Archiv für Reformationsgeschichte*, 67: 5–32
  (1979). *The Poet as Philosopher: Petrarch and the Formation of Renaissance Consciousness*, New Haven
  (1983). *The Scope of Renaissance Humanism*, Ann Arbor

Trinquet, R. (1965). 'Recherches chronologiques sur la jeunesse de M.-A. Muret', *Bibliothèque d'humanisme et Renaissance*, 27: 272–85
  (1966). 'Un maître de Montaigne', *Bulletin de la Société des amis de Montaigne*, sér. iv, 7: 3–17

Troilo, S. (1931–2). 'Due traduttori dell'*Etica Nicomachea*: Roberto di Lincoln e Leonardo Bruni', *Atti del R. Istituto veneto di scienze, lettere ed arti*, 91, 2: 275–305

Troje, H. E. (1971). *Graeca leguntur*, Cologne–Vienna
Tschirch, O. (1906). 'Johannes Carion, Kurbrandenburgischer Hofastrolog', *Jahresberichte des historischen Vereins zu Brandenburg*, 36–7: 54–62
Tuozzi, P. (1903–4). 'Agostino Nifo e le sue opere', *Atti e memorie della R. Accademia di scienze, lettere ed arti di Padova*, n.s., 20: 63–86
Turchetti, M. (1984). *Concordia o tolleranza? François Bauduin (1520–1573) e i 'moyenneurs'*, Geneva
Turner, C. J. G. (1969). 'The career of George-Gennadius Scholarius', *Byzantion*, 39: 420–55

Ullman, B. L. (1960). *The Origin and Development of Humanistic Script*, Rome
(1963). *The Humanism of Coluccio Salutati*, Padua
(1973). *Studies in the Italian Renaissance*, 2nd edn, Rome
Ullmann, W. (1977). *Medieval Foundations of Renaissance Humanism*, London
Umanesimo e esoterismo (1960). Padua
Umanesimo e Rinascimento. Studi offerti a Paul Oskar Kristeller (1980). Florence
Umanesimo europeo e umanesimo veneziano (1964). Ed. V. Branca, Florence
L'umanesimo in Istria (1983). Ed. V. Branca and S. Graciotti, Florence

Valletta, G. (1951). 'Il *Principe* di Machiavelli e il *De regnandi peritia* di Agostino Nifo', *Annali della facoltà di lettere e filosofia dell'Università di Napoli*, 1: 137–56
Valsanzibio, S. da (1949). *Vita e dottrina di Gaetano di Thiene, filosofo dello studio di Padova (1387–1465)*, 2nd edn, Padua
Van Deusen, N. C. (1932). *Telesio: The First of the Moderns*, New York
Van Melsen, A. G. (1960). *From Atomos to Atom*, New York
Vansteenberghe, E. (1920). *Le Cardinal Nicolas de Cues (1401–1464)*, Paris
Van Zuylen, W. H. (1934). *Bartholomäus Keckermann: Sein Leben und Wirken*, Leipzig
Varese, C. (1961). *Storia e politica nella prosa del Quattrocento*, Turin
Vasoli, C. (1957). 'Le *Dialecticae disputationes* del Valla e la critica umanistica della logica aristotelica', *Rivista critica di storia della filosofia*, 12: 412–34
(1958a). 'Dialettica e retorica in Rodolfo Agricola', *Atti dell'Accademia toscana di scienze e lettere 'La Colombaria'*, 22: 307–55
(1958b). 'Umanesimo e simbolismo nei primi scritti lulliani e mnemotecnici del Bruno', in *Umanesimo e simbolismo*, Padua, pp. 251–304
(1959). 'Su una *Dialectica* attribuita all'Argiropulo', *Rinascimento*, 10: 157–64
(1960). 'Ricerche sulle "dialettiche" quattrocentesche', *Rivista critica di storia della filosofia*, 15: 265–87
(1968a). *La dialettica e la retorica dell'umanesimo*, Milan
(1968b). *Studi sulla cultura del Rinascimento*, Manduria
(1969). *Umanesimo e Rinascimento*, Palermo
(1970). 'La retorica e la dialettica umanistiche e le origini delle concezioni moderne del "metodo"', *Il Verri*, 35–6: 250–306
(1971). 'Jean Bodin, il problema cinquecentesco della *Methodus* e la sua applicazione alla conoscenza storica', *Filosofia* (Turin), 21: 137–72
(1972). 'Giovanni Nesi tra Donato Acciaiuoli e Girolamo Savonarola', *Memorie domenicane*, n.s., 4: 103–79
(1974). *Profezia e ragione: Studi sulla cultura del Cinquecento e del Seicento*, Naples
(1980). 'Francesco Patrizi e la tradizione ermetica', *Nuova rivista storica*, 64: 25–40
(1983a). 'Logica ed "enciclopedia" nella cultura tedesca del tardo Cinquecento e del primo Seicento: Bartholomaeus Keckermann', in *Atti del Convegno internazionale di storia della logica*, ed. V. M. Abrusci *et al.*, Bologna, pp. 97–116
(1983b). *Immagini umanistiche*, Naples

(1984). 'Bartholomaeus Keckermann e la storia della logica', in *La storia della filosofia come sapere critico: Studi offerti a Mario Dal Pra*, Milan, pp. 240–59

Védrine, H. (1967). *La Conception de la nature chez Giordano Bruno*, Paris

(1971). *Les philosophies de la Renaissance*, Paris

Velden, H. E. J. M. van der (1911). *Rodolphus Agricola*, Leiden

Verbeke, G. (1945). *L'Évolution de la doctrine du pneuma du stoïcisme à S. Augustin*, Paris–Louvain

(1983). *The Presence of Stoicism in Medieval Thought*, Washington, D.C.

Verdonk, J. J. (1966). *Petrus Ramus en de wiskunde*, Assen

(1968). 'Über die Geometrie des Petrus Ramus', *Sudhoffs Archiv*, 52: 371–81

Vestigia: Studi in onore di Giuseppe Billanovich (1984). Ed. R. Avesani *et al.*, 2 vols., Rome

Vicentini, U. (1954). 'Francesco Zorzi O.F.M. teologo cabalista', *Le Venezie francescane*, 21: 121–59

(1957). 'Francesco Zorzi', *Le Venezie francescane*, 24: 25–56

Vickers, B. (1968). *Francis Bacon and Renaissance Prose*, Cambridge

(1970). *Classical Rhetoric in English Poetry*, London

(1978). *Francis Bacon*, Harlow, Essex

(1979). 'Frances Yates and the writing of history', *Journal of Modern History*, 51: 287–316

(1981). 'Rhetorical and anti-rhetorical tropes: on writing the history of *elocutio*', *Comparative Criticism*, 3: 105–32

(1982). 'On the practicalities of Renaissance rhetoric', in *Rhetoric Revalued*, ed. B. Vickers, Binghamton, pp. 133–41

(1986). 'Valla's ambivalent praise of pleasure: rhetoric in the service of Christianity', *Viator*, 17: 271–319

(1987). *In Defence of Rhetoric*, Oxford

Victor, J. M. (1978). *Charles de Bovelles, 1479–1553: An Intellectual Biography*, Geneva

Vignaux, P. (1959). 'Dogme de l'incarnation et métaphysique de la forme chez Jean de Ripa (Sent. prol. q. 1)', in *Mélanges offerts à Étienne Gilson*, Toronto–Paris, pp. 661–72

Villey, P. (1933). *Les Sources et l'évolution des Essais de Montaigne*, 2nd edn, 2 vols., Paris

Vismara, F. (1900). *L'invettiva, arma preferita degli umanisti*, Milan

Vitale, M. (1960). *La questione della lingua*, Palermo

Vittorino da Feltre e la sua scuola: umanesimo, pedagogia, arti (1981). Ed N. Giannetto, Florence

Vittorino da Feltre nel V centenario della morte (1946). Feltre

Vittorino da Feltre: pubblicazione commemorativa nel V centenario della morte (1947). Brescia

Viviani, U. (1935). 'La vita di Andrea Cesalpino', *Atti e memorie della R. Accademia Petrarca di lettere, arti e scienze*, n.s., 18–19: 15–84

Voet, L. (1969–72). *The Golden Compasses: A History and Evaluation of the Printing and Publishing Activities of the Officina Plantiniana at Antwerp*, 2 vols., Amsterdam–London–New York

Voigt, G. (1893). *Die Wiederbelebung des classischen Alterthums*, ed. M. Lehnerdt, 3rd edn, 2 vols., Berlin

Vom Mittelalter zur Reformation (1912–39). Ed. K. Burdach, 14 vols., Berlin

Vosters, S. A. (1962). *Lope de Vega y Titelmans*, Madrid

Waddington, C. (1855). *Ramus (Pierre de la Ramée): Sa vie, ses écrits et ses opinions*, Paris

Wagner, D. (1973). 'Zur Biographie des Nicasius Ellebodius (†1577) und zu seinen 'Notae' zu den aristotelischen Magna Moralia', *Sitzungsberichte der Heidelberger Akademie der Wissenschaften: Philosophisch-historische Klasse*, 1973, 5: 1–42

Waley, D. (1978). *The Italian City-Republics*, 2nd edn., London

Walker, D. P. (1958). *Spiritual and Demonic Magic from Ficino to Campanella*, London

(1972). *The Ancient Theology*, London

(1978). *Studies in Musical Science in the Late Renaissance*, London

(1985). *Music, Spirit and Language in the Renaissance*, ed. P. Gouk, London

Wallace, W. A. (1972–). *Causality and Scientific Explanation*, Ann Arbor

    (1974). 'Three classics of science: Galileo, *Two New Sciences*; Gilbert, *The Loadstone and Magnetic Bodies*; and Harvey, *The Motion of the Heart*', in *The Great Ideas Today*, pp. 211–72

    (1981a). *Prelude to Galileo: Essays on Medieval and Sixteenth-Century Sources of Galileo's Thought*, Dordrecht–Boston

    (1981b). 'Aristotle and Galileo: the uses of ΥΠΟΘΕΣΙΣ *(suppositio)* in scientific reasoning', in *Studies in Aristotle*, ed. D. J. O'Meara, Washington, D.C., pp. 47–77

    (1984). *Galileo and His Sources*, Princeton

Walser, E. (1914). *Poggius Florentinus: Leben und Werke*, Leipzig–Berlin

Walton, C. (1970). 'Ramus and Socrates', *Proceedings of the American Philosophical Society*, 114: 119–39

    (1971). 'Ramus and Bacon on method', *Journal of the History of Philosophy*, 9: 289–302

Warburg, A. (1932). *Gesammelte Schriften*, ed. F. Rougemont and G. Bing, Leipzig–Berlin

Waswo, R. (1979). 'The "ordinary language philosophy" of Lorenzo Valla', *Bibliothèque d'humanisme et Renaissance*, 41: 255–71

    (1980). 'The reaction of Juan Luis Vives to Valla's philosophy of language', *Bibliothèque d'humanisme et Renaissance*, 42: 594–609

Watanabe, M. (1963). *The Political Ideas of Nicholas of Cusa*, Geneva

Watts, P. M. (1982). *Nicolaus Cusanus: A Fifteenth-Century Vision of Man*, Leiden

Wear, A. (1973). *Contingency and Logic in Renaissance Anatomy*, Ph.D. thesis, Univ. of London

Webster, C. (1982). *From Paracelsus to Newton: Magic and the Making of Modern Science*, Cambridge

Wegele, F. X. von (1865). *Geschichte der deutschen Historiographie*, Munich

Weiler, A. G. (1962). *Heinrich von Gorkum (†1431): Seine Stellung in der Philosophie und der Theologie des Spätmittelalters*, Hilversum–Einsiedeln

Weinberg, B. (1942). 'Scaliger versus Aristotle on poetics', *Modern Philology*, 39: 337–60

    (1952). 'Robortello on the *Poetics*', in *Critics and Criticism, Ancient and Modern*, ed. R. S. Crane *et al.*, Chicago, pp. 319–48

    (1961). *A History of Literary Criticism in the Italian Renaissance*, 2 vols., Chicago

Weinstein, D. (1970). *Savonarola and Florence*, Princeton

Weisheipl, J. A. (1964). 'Curriculum of the faculty of arts at Oxford in the early fourteenth century', *Mediaeval Studies*, 26: 143–85

    (1965). 'Classification of the sciences in medieval thought', *Mediaeval Studies*, 27: 54–90

    (1974). 'Motion in a void: Averroes and Aquinas', in *St Thomas Aquinas Commemorative Studies, 1274–1974*, I, Toronto, pp. 467–88

Weisinger, H. (1945). 'Ideas of history during the Renaissance', *Journal of the History of Ideas*, 6: 415–35

    (1954). 'Louis Le Roy on science and progress', *Osiris*, 11: 199–210

Weiss, J. M. (1981). 'The six lives of Rudolph Agricola: Forms and functions of the humanist biography', *Humanistica Lovaniensia*, 30: 19–39

Weiss, Rainer. (1981). *Cristoforo Landino: Das Metaphorische in den "Disputationes Camaldulenses"*, Munich

Weiss, Roberto. (1947). *The Dawn of Humanism in Italy*, London

    (1949). *Il primo secolo dell'umanesimo*, Rome

    (1967). *Humanism in England during the Fifteenth Century*, 3rd edn., Oxford

    (1969). *The Renaissance Discovery of Classical Antiquity*, Oxford

    (1977). *Medieval and Humanist Greek*, Padua

Wellmann, M. (1928). *Die Φύσικα des Bolos Demokritos und der Magier Anaxilaos aus Larissa*, part I (Abhandlungen der Preussischen Akademie der Wissenschaften: Philosophisch-historische Klasse, 1928, 7), Berlin

Welti, M. E. (1964). *Der Basler Buchdruck und Britannien*, Basle
Werner, K. (1881–7). *Die Scholastik des späteren Mittelalters*, 4 vols., Vienna
  (1889). *Franz Suarez und die Scholastik der letzten Jahrhunderte*, 2 vols., Regensburg (repr. New York, 1963)
Wertis, S. K. (1979). 'The commentary of Bartolinus de Benincasa de Canulo on the *Rhetorica ad Herennium*', *Viator*, 10: 283–310
Wesseler, M. (1974). *Die Einheit von Wort und Sache: Der Entwurf einer Rhetor. Philosophie bei Mario Nizolio*, Munich
Westfall, R. S. (1985). 'Scientific patronage: Galileo and the telescope', *Isis*, 76: 11–30
Westman, R. S. (1975). 'The Melanchthon circle, Rheticus and the Wittenberg interpretation of the Copernican theory', *Isis*, 66: 165–93
  (1980). 'The astronomer's role in the sixteenth century: a preliminary study', *History of Science*, 18: 105–47
Westman, R. S. and McGuire, J. E. (1977). *Hermeticism and the Scientific Revolution*, Los Angeles
White, T. I. (1976). 'Aristotle and *Utopia*', *Renaissance Quarterly*, 29: 635–75
Wickersheimer, E. (1936). *Dictionnaire biographique des médecins en France au moyen âge*, 2 vols., Paris
  (1979). *Dictionnaire biographique des médecins en France au moyen âge: Supplément*, ed. D. Jacquart, Geneva
Wieland, G. (1981). *Ethica–scientia practica: Die Anfänge der philosophischen Ethik im 13. Jahrhundert*, Münster i W.
Wieruszowski, H. (1971). *Politics and Culture in Medieval Spain and Italy*, Rome
Wightman, W. P. D. (1964). 'Quid sit methodus? "Method" in sixteenth-century medical teaching and "discovery"', *Journal of the History of Medicine*, 19: 360–76
  (1973). 'Les Problèmes de méthode dans l'enseignement médical à Padoue et à Ferrare', in *Sciences de la Renaissance*, Paris, pp. 187–95
Wilamowitz-Moellendorf, U. von (1982). *History of Classical Scholarship*, trans. A. Harris, ed. H. Lloyd-Jones, London
Wilcox, D. J. (1969). *The Development of Florentine Humanist Historiography in the Fifteenth Century*, Cambridge, Mass.
Wilkins, E. H. (1955). *Studies in the Life and Work of Petrarch*, Cambridge, Mass.
  (1958). *Petrarch's Eight Years in Milan*, Cambridge, Mass.
  (1959). *Petrarch's Later Years*, Cambridge, Mass
  (1961). *Life of Petrarch*, Chicago
Wilmott, M. J. (1984). *Francesco Patrizi da Cherso's Humanist Critique of Aristotle*, Ph.D. thesis, Univ. of London
  (1985). '"Aristoteles exotericus, acroamaticus, mysticus": two interpretations of the typological classification of the *corpus Aristotelicum* by Francesco Patrizi da Cherso', *Nouvelles de la république des lettres*, pp. 67–95
Wilson, C. (1960). *William Heytesbury: Medieval Logic and the Rise of Mathematical Physics*, 2nd printing, Madison
Wind, E. (1967). *Pagan Mysteries of the Renaissance*, rev. edn, New York
Wingate, S. D. (1931). *The Medieval Latin Versions of the Aristotelian Scientific Corpus, with Special Reference to the Biological Works*, London
Winterbottom, M. (1967). 'Fifteenth-century manuscripts of Quintilian', *Classical Quarterly*, n.s., 17: 339–69
Wirszubski, C. (1967). 'Giovanni Pico's companion to Kabbalistic symbolism', in *Studies in Mysticism and Religion*, Jerusalem, pp. 353–62
  (1969). 'Giovanni Pico's Book of Job', *Journal of the Warburg and Courtauld Institutes*, 32: 171–99

Wisan, W. L. (1984). 'On argument *ex suppositione falsa*', *Studies in History and Philosophy of Science*, 15: 1–10

Witt, R. G. (1970). 'Cino Rinuccini's *Risponsiva alla invettiva di Messer Antonio Lusco*', *Renaissance Quarterly*, 23: 133–49

(1976). *Coluccio Salutati and His Public Letters*, Geneva

(1977). 'Salutati and contemporary physics', *Journal of the History of Ideas*, 38: 667–72

(1982). 'Medieval *Ars dictaminis* and the beginnings of humanism: a new construction of the problem', *Renaissance Quarterly*, 35: 1–35

(1983). *Hercules at the Crossroads: The Life and Thought of Coluccio Salutati*, Durham, N.C.

Wittkower, R. (1962). *Architectural Principles in the Age of Humanism*, rev. edn, London

Wittschier, H. W. (1968). *Giannozzo Manetti: Das Corpus der Orationes*, Cologne–Graz

Woodhouse, C. M. (1986). *Gemistos Plethon*, Oxford

Woodhouse, J. R. (1978). *Baldessar Castiglione: A Reassessment of 'The Courtier'*, Edinburgh

Woodward, W. H. (1897). *Vittorino da Feltre and Other Humanist Educators*, Cambridge (repr. New York, 1963)

(1906). *Studies in Education During the Age of the Renaissance*, Cambridge

Worstbrock, F. J. (1976–). *Deutsche Antikerezeption, 1450–1550*, Boppard

Wright, C. (1976). 'Language mastery and the sorites paradox', in *Truth and Meaning: Essays in Semantics*, ed. G. Evans and J. McDowell, Oxford

Würsdörfer, J. (1922). *Erkennen und Wissen nach Gregor von Rimini*, Münster

Wundt, M. (1939). *Die deutsche Schulmetaphysik des 17. Jahrhunderts*, Tübingen

Wyrwa, T. (1978). *La Pensée politique polonaise à l'époque de l'humanisme et de la Renaissance*, Paris

Yates, F. A. (1947). *The French Academies of the Sixteenth Century*, London

(1964). *Giordano Bruno and the Hermetic Tradition*, London

(1966). *The Art of Memory*, London

(1979). *The Occult Philosophy in the Elizabethan Age*, London

(1982–4). *Collected Essays*, 3 vols., London

Yee, R. W. (1966). *The Problem of the Immortality of the Soul in the Works of Pietro Pomponazzi*, Ph.D. thesis, Univ. of Toronto

Zabughin, V. (1909–12). *Giulio Pomponio Leto*, 3 vols., Rome

Zaccaria, V. (1952). 'L'epistolario di Pier Candido Decembrio', *Rinascimento*, 3: 85–118

(1956). 'Sulle opere di Pier Candido Decembrio', *Rinascimento*, 7: 13–74

(1959). 'Pier Candido Decembrio traduttore della *Repubblica* di Platone', *Italia medioevale e umanistica*, 2: 179–206

Zakythinos, D.-A. (1932–53). *Le Despotat grec de Morée*, 2 vols., Paris–Athens

Zambelli, P. (1960). 'A proposito del *De vanitate scientiarum et artium* di Cornelio Agrippa', *Rivista critica di storia della filosofia*, 15: 166–80

(1965). *Di un'opera sconosciuta di Cornelio Agrippa: Il 'Dialogus de vanitate scientiarum et ruina cristianae religionis'*, Castrocaro Terme

(1966). '*Humanae literae, verbum divinum, docta ignorantia* negli ultimi scritti di Enrico Cornelio Agrippa', *Giornale critico della filosofia italiana*, 45: 101–31

(1967). 'Aneddoti patriziani', *Rinascimento*, ser. ii, 7: 309–18

(1969). 'Agrippa von Nettesheim in den neueren kritischen Studien und in den Handschriften', *Archiv für Kulturgeschichte*, 51: 264–95

(1970). 'Cornelio Agrippa, Erasmo e la teologia umanistica', *Rinascimento*, ser. ii, 10: 29–88

(1972). 'Corneille Agrippa, Érasme et la théologie humaniste', in *Colloquia Erasmiana Turonensia*, ed. J.-C. Margolin, II, Paris, pp. 114–59

(1973a). 'Platone, Ficino e la magia', in *Studia humanitatis: Ernesto Grassi zum 70. Geburtstag*, Munich, pp. 121–42

(1973b). 'Il problema della magia naturale nel Rinascimento', *Rivista critica di storia della filosofia*, 28: 271–96

(1975). 'I problemi metodologici del necromante Agostino Nifo', *Medioevo*, 1: 129–71

(1976). 'Magic and radical Reformation in Agrippa of Nettesheim', *Journal of the Warburg and Courtauld Institutes*, 39: 69–103

(1977). *Une réincarnation de Jean Pic à l'époque de Pomponazzi* (Akademie der Wissenschaften und der Literatur: Abhandlungen der geistes- und sozialwissenschaftlichen Klasse, 1977, 10), Mainz

(1978). 'Aut diabolus aut Achillinus: Fisionomia, astrologia e demonologia nel metodo di un aristotelico', *Rinascimento*, ser. ii, 18: 59–86

(1980). 'Scienza, filosofia, religione nella Toscana di Cosimo I', in *Florence and Venice: Comparisons and Relations*, ed. S. Bertelli *et al.*, II, Florence, pp. 3–52

(1985). 'Scholastiker und Humanisten: Agrippa und Trithemius zur Hexerei. Die natürliche Magie und die Entstehung kritischen Denkens', *Archiv für Kulturgeschichte*, 67: 41–79

Zambruno, E. (1983). *Teodoro di Beza di fronte a un 'sicofante'*, Milan

Zanier, G. (1975a). 'Cardano e la critica delle religioni', *Giornale critico della filosofia italiana*, 54: 89–98

(1975b). *Ricerche sulla diffusione e fortuna del 'De incantationibus' di Pomponazzi*, Florence

(1977). *La medicina astrologica e la sua teoria: Marsilio Ficino e i suoi critici contemporanei*, Rome

(1979). 'Noterelle pomponazziane', *Giornale critico della filosofia italiana*, 58: 211–25

(1981). 'Struttura e significato delle *Disputationes* pichiane', *Giornale critico della filosofia italiana*, 40: 54–86

Zanta, L. (1914). *La Renaissance du stoïcisme au XVIe siècle*, Paris

Zappacosta, G. (1984). *Il 'Gymnasium' perugino e altri studi sull'umanesimo umbro*, ed. V. Licitra, Rome

Zavattari, E. (1923). *La visione della vita nel Rinascimento*, Turin

Zenzo, S. F. di (1978). *Un umanista epicureo del sec. XV e il ritrovamento del suo epistolario*, Naples

Zielinski, T. (1912). *Cicero im Wandel der Jahrhunderte*, 3rd edn, Leipzig–Berlin (repr. Darmstadt, 1967)

Zika, C. (1976). 'Reuchlin's *De verbo mirifico* and the magic debate of the late fifteenth century', *Journal of the Warburg and Courtauld Institutes*, 39: 104–38

Zilli, J. B. (1961). *Introducción a la psicología de los Conimbricenses*, Dissertation, Univ. of Bonn

Zintzen, C. (1965). 'Die Wertung von Mystik und Magie in der neuplatonischen Philosophie', *Rheinisches Museum für Philologie*, N.F., 108: 71–100

Zippel, G. (1979). *Storia e cultura del Rinascimento italiano*, ed. G. Zippel, Padua

Zonta, G. (1934). 'Rinascimento, aristotelismo e Barocco', *Giornale storico della letteratura italiana*, 104: 1–63, 185–240

Zoubov, V. (1935–6). 'Une théorie aristotélicienne de la lumière du XVIIe siècle', *Isis*, 24: 343–60

INDEX NOMINUM

Page numbers divided by a dash (e.g., '270–92' or '425–6') indicate either a continuous discussion or at least one occurrence of the name or thing on each of those pages. Many pages referred to contain relevant material in the footnotes as well as in the body of the text, but footnotes are expressly referred to (e.g., '27n' or '349nn') only when relevant material does not also occur in the text. Footnote references give only the number of the page on which the note begins.

This index includes the names of all persons and places mentioned in the twenty-three chapters and the Biobibliographies (persons only). For references to individual works of Aristotle and Plato and to schools and doctrines associated with particular philosophers, see the Index Rerum (e.g., 'Plato: works of'; 'Thomism'). Ancient, medieval and Renaissance authors are cited under the names by which they are generally known. Modern authors are included only when the reference is more than a bibliographical citation. Page references printed in italics are to the individual's entry in the Biobibliographies.

INDEX RERUM

Page numbers divided by a dash (e.g., '270–92' or '425–6') indicate either a continuous discussion or at least one occurrence of the name or thing on each of those pages. Many pages referred to contain relevant material in the footnotes as well as in the body of the text, but footnotes are expressly referred to (e.g., '27n' or '349nn') only when relevant material does not also occur in the text. Footnote references give only the number of the page on which the note begins.

This index contains references to things, concepts and terms mentioned or discussed in the twenty-three chapters but does not cover the Biobibliographies. Page references to chapters or major divisions of chapters devoted to a particular subject are given in italics. For references to individual works by Aristotle and Plato, see under 'Aristotle, works of' and 'Plato, works of'. Anonymous works are entered under their titles. Greek words appear alphabetically according to their transliterated spelling (e.g., '*φρόνησις*' as if it were spelt 'phronesis').

Index rerum 949

animals, study of, *see* zoology
animism, 238, 245, 258, 263
anthropocentrism, 245, 249, 310, 315
anthropogony, 281
anthropology, 281, 492, 517, 533, 756; *see also* man: concepts of
antinomianism, 774
antiqui, see via antiqua
antistrephon, 180
anti-Trinitarian views, 51
ἀπάθεια, 364; *see also* impassivity
apocalyptic thought, 258, 261, 563
ἀπόδειξις, see demonstration (ἁπλῶς, absolute; τοῦ διότι, of the reasoned fact; τοῦ ὅτι, of the fact)
appellation, 149, 167–8
appetite, 456
Arabic: language, 29, 37, 120–1, 539–40, 542; medicine, 60, 231–2; philosophy and science, 60, 145, 201, 230, 268, 285, 465, 468, 475, 538–40, 586, 590, 600, 619, 669, 675; theology, 538, 541–2
archaeology, 131
Archimedean doctrines, 218
architecture, 204, 208, 211, 311, 685
argumentation, 162–3, 169–71, 175–6, 178–82, 188–9, 191, 197, 328, 746; dialectical, 176, 185, 707; mathematical, 782; rhetorical, 725
Arians, 561
aristocracy, 397–8, 400, 417, 419, 427, 753
Aristotelianism, 3, 11, 43, 52, 69–73, 462n, 545–7, 556–7, 568, 570–1, 578, 601, 607–8, 611, 776–8, 791; and astrology, 271–4; and Christianity, 42–3, 226, 237, 319, 321–2, 325, 342–8, 357–8, 367, 460–1, 493, 560–3, 565, 567, 571, 577–8, 583, 590, 595–6, 600–9, 614, 616–26, 658, 670, 786; and cosmology, *see under* cosmology; and epistemology, 668–73, 676–7, 681–2, 684, 686–96, 703–5, 707–10; and ethics, 311, 316–19, 321–2, *325–48*, 362–7, 369, 376, 777; and history, study of, 753–4; and humanism, 132–6, 777–8; and logic, 143–6, 165, 168–70, 174, 178, 182–4, 192, 194–5, 197–8, 600, 607, 672–3, 682, 734, 777; and magic, 271–4, 284, 286–7, 292–3, 295; and metaphysics, 47, 213, 349, 498, 538, 556, 576, 583–8, 591–2, 601–14, 616–18, 620–6, 632, 776–7; and moral philosophy, 303, 360, 564, 599, 776; and natural philosophy, 201, 204, 214, 222–7, 229, 233–4, 560, 564, 566, 590, 596, 605, 607, 617–18, 620–4, 676, 686–93, 698–9, 777, 786; and Neoplatonism, *see under* Neoplatonism; and new philosophy of nature, 244, 247n, 248; and philosophy of language, 103–4; and Platonism, *see under* Platonism; and poetics

and rhetoric, 716–22, 724, 731–2, 734–5, 737, 739–40, 747; and political philosophy, 395–404, 407, 410, 440, 449; and psychology, 311, 333, 455, 458, 460, *464–534*, 567, 603–4, 606, 790–1; and textbooks, *see under* textbooks; anti-, 71–3, 223, 225, 236–7, 244–7, 250–4, 257–9, 262, 292–3, 620, 622, 644, 681–2, 739–40, 793, 800; neo-, 719; post-, 284
Aristotle, works of, 30, 58, 60, 134, 203, 213, 456, 598, 624, 770, 775n, 778, 792–4, 800–4; commentaries, 22, 39, 209, 225–7, 229, 508, 611, 621, 770, 777–8 (Arabic, 145, 455, 460–1, 476, 508, 511, 513, 531, 580, 587, 607, 778; Greek, 20, 70, 78, 120, 135, 145, 194–5, 205, 226, 228, 303, 455, 459, 461, 476, 479, 481, 494, 498, 500, 508, 511, 513, 519, 523, 531, 567, 580, 587, 607, 669, 773, 785–6, 790–1; medieval Latin, 95, 129, 455, 461, 476, 511, 513, 517, 531, 557, 775, 778); editions, 193, 459, 775, 777–8, 791; translations, 20, 95, 203, 458–9, 561, 563, 768, 777; animal books, 455–6 (commentaries, 457n; translations, 458); exoteric works, 94; by title: *Categories*, 143, 193, 213 (commentaries, 599, 790); *De anima*, 202, 211–13, 218, 333, 455–8, 465, 467, 468n, 471–2, 474, 480, 485, 509, 520nn, 602, 606, 618, 621–2, 668 (commentaries, 226–7, 457–60, 462, 473–4, 476–7, 480, 482–3, 485, 488n, 490, 491n, 492, 497, 504, 508, 511–13, 524–7, 529–31, 599, 604, 621, 688, 691, 706, 790–1, 797, 801; translations, 78, 91, 98–9, 458, 512); *De animalibus*, 212, 455n; *De caelo*, 202, 205n, 211–13, 217, 249, 599, 618, 699 (commentaries, 226–7, 229, 698, 790–1); *De generatione animalium*, 455n (translations, 458n); *De generatione et corruptione*, 202, 211–13, 217, 287, 599, 618 (commentaries, 226–9; translations, 84, 105); *De interpretatione*, 143, 157–8, 193; *De motu animalium*, 455; *De partibus animalium*, 455n (translations, 458n); *De progressu animalium*, 455n; *De sensu*, 212, 218, 472 (commentaries, 459–60, 481); *De virtutibus et vitiis*, 326; *Historia animalium*, 455n (translations, 458n); *libri naturales*, 202, 225, 792, 797, 800 (commentaries, 203, 225–6, 228); *Logica nova*, 143–4; *Logica vetus*, 143–4; *Magna moralia*, 326, 346 (commentaries, 322, 801); *Metaphysics*, 19, 147, 213, 342, 537, 585, 587–8, 609–13, 618, 626–7, 699 (commentaries, 213, 587, 590, 598–9, 604, 607, 609, 624, 698; translations, 82–3, 568); *Meteorology*, 202, 211–12, 287, 599, 618 (commentaries, 226; translations, 84);

emotions, 247, 335, 337, 340, 455, 457, 464,
467, 469–70, 517; and rhetoric, 716, 719,
722, 726, 736–7, 743, 780; Aristotelian view
of, 365, 369, 373; Stoic theory of, 364–8,
370, 372–3, 460; *see also individual emotions*
emperor, 392–4, 410; *see also* Holy Roman
Emperor
empiricism, 182, 356, 594; and epistemology,
668, 676–8, 682; and history, study of, 747,
760; and magic, 287, 291; and natural
philosophy, 207–8, 219–25, 229, 233–4; and
new philosophy of nature, 236, 245; and
psychology, 510, 517, 526
ἐνάργεια, 720
encomium, 720, 744; mock-, 744
encyclopaedia of the sciences, *see* classification
of the sciences
encyclopaedias, 635, 706, 725, 748, 777, 784–5,
787, 801, 803
ἐνδεχόμενον, 641; *see also* contingency
engineering, 208; military, 204, 211, 685
ens, see being
ἐντελέχεια, 94, 517, 520–1, 773
enthymeme, 105, 169, 187n, 327, 773
Epicureanism, 61, 64, 80, 120, 136, 183–4, 232,
237, 677; and Christianity, 319, 325, 376–7,
382–6, 630, 642, 647, 733, 774, 784; and
ethics, 319, 325, 362, 374–86; and fate and
free will, 642, 647, 656; and materialism, *see
under* materialism; and natural philosophy,
781
epicycles and eccentrics, 698–702
epigraphy, 131
epistemology, 61, 63, 66, 71–3, 109, 315, 380,
546–7, 653, 668–84, 731, 734, 738; and
history, study of, 747, 754–6; and magic,
271, 273, 289–90, 298; and metaphysics,
537–8, 541, 553–5, 566, 570, 581–3, 585–6,
588–9, 593–4, 597, 600–1, 603, 608, 615–16,
622–3, 632–5; and new philosophy of nature,
239–40, 242–5, 248–52, 258–9, 261; and
psychology, 457, 466, 471, 485, 487–91,
494–8, 509–10, 514–15, 517–18, 520–2,
526–9, 531–4, 603; empirical, *see under*
empiricism; of the sciences, 4, 209–13,
685–711
Epistles of the Brethren of Purity, 308
epistolography, *see* letters
equipollence, 149
eros, see love
eschatology, 237, 255, 281
esotericism, 62, 668–9, 671, 675–6, 739; and
rationalism, 245, 248, 256, 261, 650
essay, 136, 788
essence, 587, 600, 614, 625, 638; and existence,
594–6, 604, 612, 615, 636

Estates General of the Netherlands, 49
estimation, faculty of, 471, 480
eternity of world, *see under* world
ethics, 61, 64, 73, 108, 161, 210, *303–86*, 598,
668, 680, 747, 768, 777, 788; and humanism,
see under humanism; and magic, 270, 281,
297; and new philosophy of nature, 247, 249,
263; and poetics and rhetoric, 715, 719, 724,
727, 730, 734–7, 744–5; and psychology,
456–7, 517, 533; medical, 782; textbooks, *see
under* textbooks; *see also* moral philosophy
Ethiopian studies, 37
Ethiopians, 549
ἠθοποιία, 720
etymology, 107
Eucharist, 256
Euclidean norms, 776
εὐδαιμονία, 316; *see also* happiness
εὐπαθείαι, 364
evil, 360–1, 366, 439, 468, 603; eye, *see
fascinatio*
experience, 220, 290, 356, 469, 473, 478, 486,
500–1, 517, 622–3, 677–8, 682, 747
experimentation, 110, 203, 205, 207–8, 213,
218–25, 234, 244, 290, 469, 708
exponibles, 147n, 148, 151–2, 162–5, 167

faction, 401–2, 409, 418, 440
factive philosophy, 210, 213
faculty psychology, *see under* psychology
faith, 61, 67, 288, 322, 324, 346–7, 368, 383,
501, 503, 507, 511, 516, 538, 543–4, 581–2,
585–6, 591, 596, 604, 608, 616, 623, 630, 656,
670–1, 680–1, 683–4, 733; and reason, *see
under* reason; good, 416, 425–6, 433–4;
justification by, 346, 620, 626; *see also*
fideism
fall of man 314, 323, 385, 544, 547–9, 623
fallacies, 105, 149, 164–5, 168
falling bodies, *see under* motion
fame, 363, 413–14, 416, 425–7, 486n, 738;
princely, 431–2, 434, 443
fantasy, 285, 288, 466, 471, 481
fascinatio, 284, 296
fatalism, *see* determinism
fate, 48, 64, 130, 135, 270, 273, *641–67*, 776
fear, 365, 367–8, 719–20; of God, 369; of the
gods, 441, 784; of ruler by his people, 416,
426, 433–4
felicitas, see happiness
fideism, 288–9, 571, 607, 616, 648, 650, 671,
681, 683–4
fides, see faith
figurae, see figures
figures, 104, 276–7, 282–3, 295; of rhetoric,
716–17, 720, 725, 741, 743, 775

---

republicanism, 389, 390, 395, 399, 408–9, 411, 416–23, 426–31, 434–41, 445–6, 450; *largo*, 426, 437–8; *stretto*, 426–7, 437

res, 66, 91–2; and *verba*, 58

resistance to tyranny, 405–6, 446–7

resolutio, 690, 705; *see also* method: resolutive

Resurrection, 382, 516, 583, 621

revelation, 576–7, 583, 587–90, 596–7, 599, 603, 606, 617, 619, 622–3, 631, 633–4, 638, 670, 674, 680, 691; and reason, *see under* reason

rhetoric, 3, 57–9, 61, 92–4, 103–4, 176–8, 182, 190, 412, 457, 517, 634, 715–45; and history, study of, 746–7, 749, 754; and humanism, *see under* humanism; deliberative, 716, 718, 723, 731, 744; demonstrative or epideictic, 188, 716, 718–19, 723–4, 731, 735, 744; judicial or forensic, 188, 716, 718, 731, 744; textbooks, *see under* textbooks

rights, individual, 452

Roman law, *see under* law

Romanism, 752, 755, 757

Romanitas, 750

Rosicrucians, 676

Sacramentarians, 44

sacraments, 259, 625

St Bartholomew's Day Massacre, 51, 185, 446

St Paul's School, 741

salvation, 255–6, 314, 544, 557, 559, 565, 603, 631

sapiens, see wise man

sapientia, see wisdom

Sapienza, *see* University of: Rome

Saracens, *see* Moslems

Saturn, 246

scepticism, 38–9, 73, 80, 109, 120, 136, 181, 192, 247, 286, 288–9, 460–1, 611, 616, 618, 669, 671, 673, 677–84, 689–90, 699–702, 710, 790; Academic, 136, 183–4, 679, 681–2; Ciceronian, 521, 673, 679; Pyrrhonian, 136, 679, 684; Socratic, 82

scepticus, 679

σχήματα, 277, 282, 283; *see also* figures

σχηματισμοί, 277; *see also* configurations

schematismus, 299; *see also* configurations

scholasticism, 11, 15, 17, 20–2, 50, 57–61, 68, 70, 548, 556–7, 561–2, 578, 580, 586–7, 591, 595, 601, 604, 608, 748, 773, 777, 780; and epistemology, 669, 672–3, 678, 684, 708; and ethics, 316, 318–19, 325, 327–8, 339, 343–4, 346; and fate and free will, 642–3, 645, 648–9, 658; and humanism, 121, 123, 125, 128–9, 132–4, 136; and logic, 157, 173–7, 179, 184, 187, 190, 193, 197, 234, 672–3; and magic, 278, 285, 292, 296; and metaphysics,

538, 565, 570, 579, 583, 586, 588, 591–3, 597–8, 601–5, 608–11, 613–20, 626–7, 630, 632; and moral philosophy, 303; and natural philosophy, 204, 209–10, 216, 225, 229, 231, 590–1, 617, 619; and political philosophy, 393, 395, 397, 399, 402–8, 412–15, 422, 444, 448–9, 451; and psychology, 460–1, 467, 478, 515–17, 521, 601–5; and textbooks, *see under* textbooks; and theology, 540, 543, 545, 547, 549, 576–7, 588, 590–1, 593, 595–6, 630, 775 and translation and terminology, 102, 104–6; Calvinist, 631

School of Albertus Magnus, *see* Albertism

School of Altdorf, *see* University of: Altdorf

School of Chartres, 550–1, 556, 565, 576, 785

schoolmen, *see* scholasticism

schools, *see* education

Schwenkfeldians, 49

science, *see* natural philosophy

science of being, metaphysics as, 537, *584–638*

science of God, metaphysics as, 537, *538–84*, 585, 587, 596, 606, 630, 632; *see also* God: and metaphysics

science of science, metaphysics as, 608–9

scientiae mediae, 204, 214, 457, 698

scientific revolution, 57, 73, 237, 253–4, 261–3, 295, 708, 783

Scotism, 70, 461n, 599, 605; and metaphysics, 507, 593, 597–8, 601; and natural philosophy, 203–4, 213, 227–8, 230; and psychology, 477–8, 493, 509–15, 517, 528; and textbooks, *see under* textbooks

scribes, 13–14, 17–19, 22–4, 26, 28, 36, 117

script: Gothic, 21; humanist cursive, 117; roman, 117

scriptoria, 12, 27

Scriptures, *see* Bible

second philosophy, natural philosophy as, 589

Second Scholastic, 71, 507–18

secrets of nature, *see under* nature

seminal reasons, 276, 278, 293, 571–3

sensation, 456, 464, 470–2, 474–6, 477n, 481–2, 520, 541, 572, 603

sense, 564; agent, 474, 475n, 476n, 485, 497, 499; common, 285, 466, 470–1, 481; deception, 460; experience, 584, 588, 600, 603, 633, 668, 690–1, 703; image, 468, 470–2, 554, 603 (*see also species*: sensible); knowledge, 541, 588, 669–70, 673–4; -perception, 285, 291, 311, 330, 356, 470, 472, 474–5, 485, 487, 491, 503, 506, 520, 529–31, 553, 585, 597, 677

senses, 72, 202, 210, 220, 244, 250–2, 257–9, 374, 378, 380, 457, 466, 470, 517, 572, 574, 673–4, 687–8, 691, 693, 696, 700, 720; external, 466–7, 470–2; internal, 460, 466–8,